SCOTTISH EDUCATION

Edited by T. G. K. Bryce and W. M. Humes

Section editing by
Brian Boyd
Tom Bryce
John Halliday
Colin Holroyd
Walter Humes
Sue Kleinberg
Malcolm L. MacKenzie
Lindsay Paterson
Mary Simpson

Edinburgh University Press

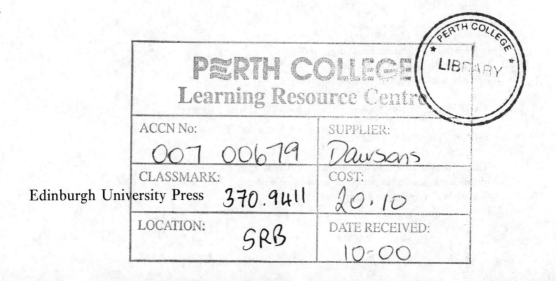

© in this edition Edinburgh University Press, 1999
Copyright in the individual contributions
is retained by the authors

Edinburgh University Press
22 George Square, Edinburgh

Reprinted 2000

Typeset in 10 on 12pt Ehrhardt
by Hewer Text Limited, Edinburgh, and
printed and bound in Great Britain
by Redwood Books, Trowbridge, Wiltshire.

A CIP record for this book is available from the British Library

ISBN 0 7486 0980 6 (paperback)

The right of the contributors to be identified as authors
of this work has been asserted in accordance with the
Copyright, Designs and Patents Act 1988.

Contents

The Contributors

Mr Frank R. Adams is a Senior Lecturer in the Department of Educational Theory and Practice in the Faculty of Education, Moray House Institute of Education, University of Edinburgh.

Professor Robert Anderson is a Professor in the History Department at the University of Edinburgh.

Ms Rowena Arshad is the Director of the Centre for Education for Racial Equality in Scotland and Lecturer in Equity and Rights in the Faculty of Education, Moray House Institute of Education, University of Edinburgh.

Mr Michael Bain is Co-ordinator of the B.Tech.Ed. degree at St Andrew's College, Glasgow.

Mr David Betteridge was formerly Headteacher of Pollokshields Primary School, Glasgow, and a Senior Lecturer in the Faculty of Education at the University of Paisley.

Mr Keir Bloomer is Executive Director of Education and Community Services, Clackmannanshire Council.

Professor Drummond Bone is a Vice Principal at the University of Glasgow.

Dr Brian Boyd is in the Faculty of Education at the University of Strathclyde, Glasgow.

Mr Bob Brewer is a Lecturer in Physical Education in the Faculty of Education, Moray House Institute of Education, University of Edinburgh.

Professor Sally Brown is a Professor in the Department of Education and Deputy Principal at the University of Stirling.

Mr Andrew Bruce is Headteacher of Craigmount High School, Edinburgh.

Professor Tom Bryce is a Professor in the Department of Educational Studies and Vice-Dean (Post-graduate Studies and Research) in the Faculty of Education at the University of Strathclyde, Glasgow.

Dr Douglas Buchanan is a Lecturer in the Department of Curriculum Studies (Science, Technology, Mathematics and Computing) in the Faculty of Education, Moray House Institute of Education, University of Edinburgh.

Ms Alison Cameron is a Policy Adviser in the Department of Education, North Lanarkshire Council.

Mr David Carr is a Reader in Education in the Faculty of Education, Moray House Institute of Education, University of Edinburgh.

Professor Ronnie Carr is the Dean of the School of Education and Languages in the Open University of Hong Kong.

Ms Vivien Casteel is a National Development Officer, Scottish Qualification for Headship, Scottish Office Education and Industry Department, Edinburgh.

Professor Mono Chakrabarti is a Professor in the Department of Social Work in the Faculty of Education at the University of Strathclyde, Glasgow.

Mr Donald Christie is a Senior Lecturer in the Department of Educational Studies in the Faculty of Education at the University of Strathclyde, Glasgow.

Dr Tom Conlon is a Senior Lecturer in the Faculty of Education, Moray House Institute of Education, University of Edinburgh.

Mr Graham Connelly is a Lecturer in the Scottish School of Further Education in the Faculty of Education at the University of Strathclyde, Glasgow.

Mr James C. Conroy is Director of Religious Education and Pastoral Care in St Andrew's College, Glasgow.

Dr Ronald Crawford is Secretary to the Committee of Scottish Higher Education Principals (COSHEP).

Dr John Darling is a Director of the Centre for Educational Research in the University of Aberdeen.

Mr Fernando Almeida Diniz is a Lecturer in the Faculty of Education, Moray House Institute of Education, University of Edinburgh.

Dr Paul Dougall is Head of the Department of Applied Arts in the Faculty of Education at the University of Strathclyde, Glasgow.

Mr David Elliot is Director of Assessment and Quality Assurance in the Scottish Qualifications Authority.

Mrs Sue Ellis is a Senior Lecturer in the Department of Primary Education in the Faculty of Education at the University of Strathclyde, Glasgow.

Mr Barry Finlayson is Head of Business Studies in the Department of Business and Computer Education in the Faculty of Education at the University of Strathclyde, Glasgow.

Dr Gerry P. T. Finn is a Reader in the Department of Educational Studies in the Faculty of Education at the University of Strathclyde, Glasgow.

Dr Tom Fitzpatrick was formerly Vice Principal, Notre Dame College of Education, Glasgow.

Ms Joan Forrest is a Senior Lecturer in Health Education in the Department of Social Studies Education in the Faculty of Education at the University of Strathclyde, Glasgow.

Mrs Gill Friel is Headteacher of Fintry Primary School.

Dr Nisbet Gallacher was formerly Her Majesty's Senior Chief Inspector of Schools.

Mrs Frances Gallagher is an Adviser in Home Economics with Glasgow City Council.

Ms Helen Ganson is a Statistician at the Scottish Qualifications Authority.

Dr Bill Gatherer was formerly Chief Adviser, Lothian Region.

Ms Eleanor Gavienas is a Lecturer in the Department of Primary Education in the Faculty of Education at the University of Strathclyde, Glasgow.

Mr Tony Gavin is Headteacher of St Margaret's Academy, Livingston.

Dr Bob Glaister is Dean of Education at the Open University, Milton Keynes.

Dr Malcolm Green is Convenor of the Education Committee of Glasgow City Council.

Dr Dennis Gunning is Director of Development at the Scottish Qualifications Authority.

Dr John Halliday is a Reader in the Scottish School of Further Education in the Faculty of Education at the University of Strathclyde, Glasgow.

Professor Wynne Harlen is Director of the Scottish Council for Research in Education.

Professor David Hartley is a Professor in Education in the Institute for Education and Lifelong Learning at the University of Dundee.

Ms Louise Hayward is an Assistant Principal at St Andrew's College, Glasgow.

Dr Peter Hillis is a Reader in the Department of Social Studies Education in the Faculty of Education at the University of Strathclyde, Glasgow.

Mr Sandy Hobbs is a Reader in the Department of Applied Social Studies at the University of Paisley.

Mr Colin Holroyd is a Lecturer in the Education Department, and a Consultant in the Teaching and Learning Service, at the University of Glasgow.

Ms Cathy Howieson is a Senior Research Fellow in the Centre for Educational Sociology at the University of Edinburgh.

Mrs Anne Hughes is Head of the Department of Primary Education in the Faculty of Education at the University of Strathclyde, Glasgow.

Dr Walter Humes is Director of Professional Studies at St Andrew's College, Glasgow.

Ms Joyce Johnston is Principal of Fife College of Further and Higher Education, Kirkcaldy.

Professor Richard Johnstone is a Professor and Head of the Education Department at the University of Stirling.

Mr Peter Kimber is Chief Executive of the Scripture Union, Milton Keynes and was formerly Depute Chief Executive at the Scottish Examination Board, Dalkeith.

Professor Gordon Kirk is Dean of the Faculty of Education, Moray House Institute of Education, University of Edinburgh.

Dr Margaret Kirkwood is a Senior Lecturer in the Department of Business and Computer Education in the Faculty of Education at the University of Strathclyde, Glasgow.

Ms Sue Kleinberg is a Senior Lecturer and Programme Co-ordinator (B.Ed Primary) in the Department of Primary Education in the Faculty of Education at the University of Strathclyde, Glasgow.

Professor Michael Leech is Principal of Stevenson College, Edinburgh and a Visiting Professor in the Scottish School of Further Education in the Faculty of Education at the University of Strathclyde, Glasgow.

Mrs Kay Livingston is a Senior Lecturer in the Faculty of Education at the University of Paisley.

Mr George Livingstone was formerly Vice Dean (Undergraduate/Initial Courses) in the Faculty of Education at the University of Strathclyde, Glasgow.

Professor Lindsay Logan is a Professor in the School of Science Education in Northern College, Dundee Campus.

Dr Hamish Long was formerly Chief Executive of the Scottish Examination Board, Dalkeith.

Ms Lesley Low is a Research Fellow in the Institute of Education at the University of Stirling.

Professor John MacBeath is Director of the Quality in Education Centre in the Faculty of Education at the University of Strathclyde, Glasgow.

Professor Tom McCool is a Visiting Professor in the Department of Educational Studies in the Faculty of Education at the University of Strathclyde, Glasgow and was formerly Chief Executive of SCOTVEC.

Mr Drew McCormick is Principal Teacher of Physics in Braidfield Secondary School, Clydebank.

Professor David McCrone is a Professor in the Department of Sociology at the University of Edinburgh.

Mr Donald MacDonald was formerly Head of Geography in the Department of Social Studies Education in the Faculty of Education at the University of Strathclyde, Glasgow.

Mr Stuart MacDonald is Director of the Lighthouse (Festival 1999).

Dr James McGonigal is Head of the Department of Language and Literature at St Andrew's College, Glasgow.

Mr John MacGregor is Head of Chemistry in the Department of Mathematics, Science and Technological Education in the Faculty of Education at the University of Strathclyde, Glasgow.

Dr Gilbert MacKay is a Reader in the Department of Special Educational Needs and Faculty Research Co-ordinator in the Faculty of Education at the University of Strathclyde, Glasgow.

Mr Thomas A. W. N. MacKay is a Consultant Educational Psychologist and an Honorary Lecturer in Psychology at the University of Strathclyde, Glasgow.

Mr Malcolm L. MacKenzie is a Senior Lecturer in Education at the University of Glasgow.

Mr Dugald Mackie is Secretary of the University Court at the University of Glasgow.

Dr David McLaren is a Senior Lecturer in the Department of Educational Studies in the Faculty of Education at the University of Strathclyde, Glasgow.

Mrs Marion McLarty is a Lecturer in the Department of Special Educational Needs in the Faculty of Education at the University of Strathclyde, Glasgow.

Dr Effie Maclellan is a Senior Lecturer in the Department of Educational Studies in the Faculty of Education at the University of Strathclyde, Glasgow.

Mr Henry Maitles is Head of Modern Studies in the Department of Social Studies Education in the Faculty of Education at the University of Strathclyde, Glasgow.

Dr Willis B. Marker was formerly Assistant Principal (In-Service) at Jordanhill College of Education, Glasgow.

Mrs Joan Menmuir is a Senior Lecturer in the Department of Educational Studies in the Faculty of Education at the University of Strathclyde, Glasgow.

Mr Ted Milburn is a Senior Lecturer in the Department of Community Education and Director, Centre for Youth Work Studies in the Faculty of Education at the University of Strathclyde, Glasgow.

Mrs Margaret Mitchell is a Learning Support Co-ordinator in North Ayrshire.

Mr Brian Morris is a Lecturer in the Education Department at Stirling University.

Professor Pamela Munn is Professor of Curriculum Research and Associate Dean (Postgraduate Studies) in the Faculty of Education, Moray House Institute of Education, University of Edinburgh.

Mr Bob Munro is a Senior Lecturer in the Department of Business and Computer Education in the Faculty of Education at the University of Strathclyde, Glasgow.

Mr Cameron Munro is an Education Consultant and was formerly the Parent Officer in Strathclyde Region Education Department.

Mrs Lillian Munro is an Assessment Officer for the 5–14 Assessment Unit in the Scottish Qualifications Authority.

Mrs Angela Napuk is a Researcher in the Institute for the Study of Education and Society at the University of Edinburgh.

Professor John Nisbet was formerly Professor and Head of the Education Department at the University of Aberdeen.

Professor Nigel Paine is Chief Executive of the Scottish Council for Educational Technology, Glasgow.

Professor Lindsay Paterson is Professor of Educational Policy in the Faculty of Education, Moray House Institute of Education, University of Edinburgh.

Mr Keith Pearson was formerly Headmaster, George Heriot's School, Edinburgh.

Dr Willis Pickard is Editor of *The Times Educational Supplement Scotland*, Edinburgh.

Professor David Raffe is Director of the Centre for Educational Sociology at the University of Edinburgh.

Professor Sheila Riddell is Professor of Social Policy (Disability Studies) and Director of the Strathclyde Centre for Disability Research at the University of Glasgow.

Mr Boyd Robertson is Head of Gaelic in the Department of Language Education in the Faculty of Education at the University of Strathclyde, Glasgow.

Mrs Pam Robertson is Depute Course Director for the B.Ed. Honours Music Course and a Senior Lecturer in the School of Humanities at Northern College, Aberdeen Campus.

Dr Isobel J. Robertson is a Lecturer in the Department of Mathematics, Science and Technological Education in the Faculty of Education at the University of Strathclyde, Glasgow.

Mr Alex Rodger was formerly Development Director for Secondary Education and Convenor of the Religious and Moral Education Unit at Northern College.

Ms Angela Roger is a Senior Lecturer in Education in the Institute for Education and Lifelong Learning at the University of Dundee.

Dr Hamish Ross was formerly Depute Director of Education, Grampian Region.

Mrs Sheila Semple is a Lecturer in Careers and Guidance in the Department of Special Educational Needs in the Faculty of Education at the University of Strathclyde, Glasgow.

Dr Bob Sharp is a Senior Lecturer and Course Director for the B.A. Degree Programme in the Scottish School of Sport Studies in the Faculty of Education at the University of Strathclyde, Glasgow.

Professor Richard Shaw is Principal of the University of Paisley.

Mr Mark Sheridan is Head of Music in the Department of Applied Arts in the Faculty of Education at the University of Strathclyde, Glasgow.

Professor Mary Simpson is Professor of Educational Research at Northern College, Aberdeen Campus.

Dr Rebecca Soden is a Senior Lecturer in the Scottish School of Further Education in the Faculty of Education at the University of Strathclyde, Glasgow.

Mr Nicky Souter is a Lecturer in Biology in the Department of Mathematics, Science and Technological Education in the Faculty of Education at the University of Strathclyde, Glasgow.

Dr Paul Standish is a Lecturer in Education in the Institute for Education and Lifelong Learning at the University of Dundee.

Mrs Rae Stark is a Senior Lecturer in the Department of Mathematics, Science and Technological Education and Vice-Dean (Undergraduate/Initial Courses) in the Faculty of Education at the University of Strathclyde, Glasgow.

Mr Alan Starritt is Assistant Director at the Scottish Consultative Council on the

Curriculum and currently on secondment to the Higher Still Development Unit, Dundee.

Dr Ivor Sutherland is Registrar of the General Teaching Council for Scotland.

Professor Sir Stewart Sutherland is Principal of the University of Edinburgh.

Mr Ron Tuck is Chief Executive of the Scottish Qualifications Authority.

Dr Joyce Watt is Reader in the Centre for Educational Research at the University of Aberdeen.

Professor Douglas Weir is a Professor in the Department of Social Studies Education and Dean of the Faculty of Education at the University of Strathclyde, Glasgow.

Mr Graham White is Course Director for PGCE(P) in the Department of Primary Education in the Faculty of Education at the University of Strathclyde, Glasgow.

Mr Tony Williams is a Senior Lecturer and Head of the Language Education Department in the Faculty of Education at the University of Strathclyde, Glasgow.

I

Introduction and Overview

1

An Introduction to Scottish Education

Tom Bryce and Walter Humes

PURPOSE

We have endeavoured in this book to provide a detailed, informed and critical account of Scottish education at the turn of the century. It is timely to attempt such an undertaking not only because of the approach of a new millennium but, more importantly, because of the establishment of a Scottish parliament, for inevitably that will bring change to education. While we would readily admit that the directions of that educational change are not easy to predict, we do believe that some understanding of the present is vital to any sensible evolution of educational practice. Knowing what takes place now in the name of education, and having that knowledge appropriately contextualised and critically understood, is important for the future. An effort has therefore been made in this volume to address each of the sectors in the Scottish educational system and to set out the professional thinking which relates to practice. A comprehensive treatment has been given of pre-school, primary, secondary, further, adult and higher education, together with observations concerning the important contexts – historical, cultural, political, social and economic – within which education is pursued in Scotland. The various chapters have been written by specialists who have drawn upon up-to-date research and contemporary analysis to give fresh insights into educational developments and professional practice throughout the Scottish educational system. Each of the chapters was specially commissioned for this volume.

The text combines material written by educationists with first hand experience of their own organisations and fields of influence (individuals able to give 'insider' perspectives) with commentary and analysis written by academics whose researches enable them to offer illuminating interpretations of how particular aspects of education are conducted in Scotland (individuals able to take 'outsider' perspectives). A deliberate effort has been made to combine concise description with a critical perspective. That is, detailed information is supplemented by an outline of the issues of contention and debate among the professionals concerned with each area. Inevitably the balance of description to critique varies across the chapters, it being more difficult for 'insiders' to be as detached as 'outsiders'. Conversely the knowledge and insight which the 'insiders' have brought to the text is substantial and, in some respects, could not be matched by the 'outsiders'. The book is therefore intended to inform all those who seek to understand educational practice and to know what Scottish educators themselves think about their own educational system; its strengths and achievements, as well as its weaknesses; their pride in it and their concerns for it.

Scottish Education should be of particular use to students and scholars, both native and foreign, as well as to those professionals who are keen to look beyond their own sector or particular specialism. The volume offers an account of how education 'works' in Scotland, according to the one hundred and twenty individuals who have contributed. The wide range of critical reflections presented here set out what matters to educators in Scotland as they look forward to the twenty-first Century.

ORIGINS

The need for a book of this sort has been evident to us for some time, not least in our day to day work in teacher education. Student teachers (and indeed experienced teachers engaged in professional development) must come to terms with complex ideas and practices. Sharing the broad spectrum of thinking which relates to policy and action is an important step in becoming an effective teacher (or in extending one's field of influence and competence). Short, introductory or overview texts about Scottish education are few in number, there being a near-thirty year gap between Leslie Hunter's excellent study *The Scottish Educational System* and Clark and Munn's *Education in Scotland* published in 1997. And although there has been a steady increase in well-researched books concerned with particular aspects of provision, informed accounts spanning the broad front of education are still thin on the ground. Surprisingly, some areas have not been written about at all; where it exists, detail is sometimes difficult to access; where descriptive accounts are available, they are often incomplete; and there are few analytical accounts with a developed perspective.

Furthermore, educational practice has not only become more complex over the decades, differences between Scottish circumstances and related professional thinking and their equivalents elsewhere in the UK and in Europe have themselves become difficult to summarise with ease. Educationists who address audiences outwith Scotland frequently find themselves required to say what is particularly Scottish about Scottish education. How is it distinctive? What do we do that is different from practice elsewhere? The important point is that while Scotland is a part of Europe, it is not a part of England. The conflation of Scotland and England is frequently made by the foreigner when it comes to any consideration of what takes place in schools, colleges and universities in Scotland. It is often a sore point. However, we would be the last to claim that everything about Scottish education is distinctive; rather we have sought to provide a wide range of material in this volume which will allow others to make their own judgements as to what is unique; what is similar but different; and what is indeed comparable to practices elsewhere. In the final analysis, it is left to the reader to weigh things up and to form judgements in the light of the evidence.

THE DESIGN OF THE TEXT

When we began this work, we approached a number of senior and respected members of the educational community and outlined what we sought to do: at that stage we had an outline structure with details of chapter headings and possible authors. Their reactions were largely very favourable; there was a perceived need for a book of this kind and our conception of what it should contain was positively welcomed. This support was echoed by the referees who advised our publishers, Edinburgh University Press, that the venture was desirable and worthwhile, ambitious though it was. Likewise, when The Carnegie Trust agreed to support us with production and editing costs, their own consultants judged the project to be worthy of support. Doubts and apprehensions, and there were a few, were largely concerned with practicalities. Could such a large group of significant individuals be persuaded to write to guidelines and to a manageable schedule? Could the necessary editing be brought about to achieve coherence? Most of all, given how rapidly things change in education, could a volume of such scope and detail be usefully brought about without becoming dated and obsolete upon its production? Our own view, from the outset, was that the experts we had in mind could indeed set down with clarity material of significance and substance which would not date, and which ought to be on record, whether or not some specific detail would be subject to change. With an appropriate formulation, much could and should be written as a substantive and critical record of current activities which would both inform readers and provide a basis upon which subsequent revisions could be made; the volume would provide a reference point for future writers and researchers.

For each of our contributors we drew up a list of content guidelines; a set of headings which specified the subject matter to be addressed in the chapter concerned. Typically, these amounted to ten or twelve points, sometimes expressed in professional 'shorthand', and no doubt something of our own values and orientation was contained in these headings. To take one example, the draft specification for Chapter 43 was as follows:

Section VII Chapter 43.   Guidance and Personal and Social Education in the Secondary School

1. What Guidance is (and is not) and how it operates in the typical school, making brief reference to the key documents in the evolution of guidance practice over (approx) three decades.
2. The role of different staff vis-à-vis duties and specific inputs to Personal and Social Education (PSE) programmes typically provided.
3. Horizontal, vertical (and other) systems of guidance.
4. Conflict for teachers ('wearing two hats') and the considered effect of guidance upon school ethos.
5. Distinctions in practice between guidance and counselling.
6. Links between guidance staff and parents, social work, police, etc.
7. Personal and Social Development (PSD) and PSE; typical programmes available in schools – drugs education, sex education, health education.
8. The continuity of guidance provision from 5–14 to S6.
9. Ever increasing demands (e.g. with Higher Still); changing priorities in vocational and/or curricular and/or personal guidance?
10. Issues of confidentiality, data-protection and legality.
11. Staff development needs and their fulfilment (or not).

We explicitly encouraged each of the contributors to regard such specifications as a guide and to develop their chapter content as they, as experts, saw fit. (The reader might like to match Chapter 43 against the guideline points given above.) They did so, in some cases negotiating shifts of emphasis and content. Only one saw fit to re-write the entire specification to achieve a better conception of the area in question.

The detailed specifications served several purposes. First, in drawing them up we were able to revise our own tentative structure for each of the sections and for the volume as a whole.

When the full set had been completed, we were convinced of the sheer amount which ought to be written to give something of the flavour of Scottish education; and we became painfully aware of those areas where our own knowledge was patchy and uneven. Second, the specifications enabled us, and subsequently contributors, to set boundaries around particular areas, knowing that related topics and complementary treatments would feature elsewhere. We planned to minimise duplication and overlap via the chapter specifications; nevertheless we felt it essential from the outset that, in particular areas, writers coming from quite different perspectives would serve to illuminate the complexity of certain topics. Thus, for example, in the area of local government, quite different emphases are achieved in three chapters, one of which adopts a political perspective, one an operational perspective and one concerned with the difficulties of providing educational development services during periods of considerable political change and serious financial constraint. Third, the full set of chapter specifications enabled us to share with our section editors how we had conceived the sections, the contributory chapters and the work as a whole; as a team, we were able to improve the coherence of the text and to ensure that gaps were filled. The sections were edited as follows:–

SECTION EDITING

Section II	Policy and Provision in Scottish Education	Dr Walter Humes
Section III	The Administration and Control of Scottish Education	Prof. Tom Bryce
Section IV	The Historical, Cultural and Economic Context of Scottish Education	Mr Malcolm MacKenzie
Section V	Pre-school and Primary Education: Organisation and Management	Ms Sue Kleinberg
Section VI	Pre-school and Primary Education: Curriculum	Ms Sue Kleinberg
Section VII	Secondary Education: Organisation and Management	Dr Brian Boyd
Section VIII	Secondary Education: Curriculum	Dr Brian Boyd
Section IX	Further and Higher Education	Dr John Halliday
Section X	Assessment and Certification	Prof. Mary Simpson
Section XI	Scottish Pupils and their Achievements	Prof. Lindsay Paterson
Section XII	Challenges and Responses: Education for All?	Prof. Tom Bryce and Dr Walter Humes
Section XIII	Scottish Teachers, Teacher Education and Professionalism	Mr Colin Holroyd

Some aspects of the structure of the text will be self-evident from the section titles; however certain emphases merit explicit comment at this stage.

SECTION II   POLICY AND PROVISION IN SCOTTISH EDUCATION

This section is intended as an overview of the whole field and contains introductory chapters for each of the four main sectors: Primary, Secondary, Further and Higher Education. The opening chapter contains up-to-date statistics on patterns of provision in

Scottish education, on trends and priorities. It contextualises the provision for education and outlines the key roles of central and local government. Chapter 3 sets out the philosophy and practice of Primary Education and provides a detailed indication of the extent to which Scottish Primary Education is child-centred. The reader who wishes to focus upon Primary schooling should read this chapter prior to those in Sections V and VI. Chapter 4 looks at Scottish Secondary Schools, noting the senses in which they may be said to be 'comprehensive' in character. The reader who is focusing upon Secondary schooling should read this chapter prior to those in Sections VII and VIII. Scotland's Further Education Colleges, which provide post-school education, were until recently the responsibility of local government; now colleges are run independently on the basis of a direct block grant from central government: Chapter 5 provides an introduction to Further Education in the new 'post-incorporation' era. It also outlines the very significant blurring of the Further Education/Higher Education divide.

An introduction to Scottish University Education and something of the character and provision in tertiary education is described in Chapter 6. Very significant changes have taken place in tertiary education in Scotland, as elsewhere, and the overall institutional framework is analysed in this chapter. Following these five chapters are two which contextualise the statutory provision of education in Scotland. Chapter 7 looks critically at the policy process itself, comparing both traditional and alternative interpretations of how change is brought about. Chapter 8 examines the politics of Scottish education, comparing the political parties and their manifestos for the general election in 1997. Scotland has a small but not insignificant private school sector and this, and its influence, is described in Chapter 9. The section ends with our own analysis of the distinctiveness of Scottish education; this chapter endeavours to get behind the myths and traditional claims made about education in Scotland.

SECTION III   THE ADMINISTRATION AND CONTROL OF SCOTTISH EDUCATION

Section III is devoted to an examination of how education is controlled and managed at central and local government levels. It looks also at the key organisations which provide support for teachers at national level. Part of Scotland's unique education system derives from the fact that the Secretary of State for Scotland (who has overall responsibilities for education, amongst other things) is a minister in the UK Government. He (thus far there have been no women holders of this position) sits side by side with the Minister for Education whose duties are confined to England and Wales. The consequences of this are set out in Chapter 11 in addition to the complex of relations between politicians and officials in the Scottish Office responsible for administering the system. Higher Education in the UK is now the responsibility of four separate councils (one each for England, Scotland, Wales and Northern Ireland) and Chapter 12 analyses the detailed operations of the Scottish Higher Education Funding Council (SHEFC) since its inception in 1992. Her Majesty's Inspectorate (HMI) has a reputation for significant influence and central control in Scottish education. Chapter 13 sets out the responsibilities and duties of this small group of people (now numbering less than 100). Scotland's school educational system involves a partnership between central and local administration, as Chapter 14 explains. Chapters 14 and 15 give clear analyses of the details, with Chapter 16 outlining the recent and current provision of local educational development services in Scotland.

Responsibility for advising on the curriculum of Scottish Schools resides technically with the Scottish Consultative Council on the Curriculum (SCCC). Chapter 17 looks closely at the reality of that organisation's work; something of the tensions between HMI and SCCC are evident in this analysis. Responsibility for technology support for the curriculum of Scotland's schools and colleges resides with the Scottish Council for Educational Technology (SCET) which is described in Chapter 18. The section concludes with a look at the roles, responsibilities and actions of Scottish parents; their involvement is greater than that which is now statutorily embraced in the workings of School Boards.

SECTION IV   THE HISTORICAL, CULTURAL AND ECONOMIC CONTEXT OF SCOTTISH EDUCATION

This Section contains several chapters analysing the principal contexts of education in Scotland. Two chapters deal with the historical context, in quite different ways. 1979 saw the election of a Conservative government in the UK (under Margaret Thatcher) and there followed eighteen years of Conservative rule, which brought many challenges to teachers and schools. Chapter 20 charts the history of Scottish education up to 1980, therefore, and Chapter 21 deals with the troubled years which followed. Scottish culture and the growth of nationalism is explored in Chapter 22; it shows how Scottish culture impinges upon education and extends some of the arguments presented in Chapter 10 in Section II. Gaelic education is, of course, significant in Scotland, despite the size of the minority so affected by it. Chapter 23 describes the provision for Gaelic (at primary, secondary, tertiary levels and beyond). Some parts of this chapter could have been included in the Primary and Secondary Curriculum Sections (VI and VIII) but the very nature of the language and the spirited drive to maintain and develop its use are better expressed in a single chapter. Catholic Education also merits a chapter in its own right and the character of denominational schools is given in Chapter 24. (Scotland's state schools are, properly, described as denominational and non-denominational, not Catholic and Protestant as is sometimes crudely stated.) Proportionately more primary and secondary Catholic schools are located in the West of Scotland, in and around Glasgow, for historical reasons. Their distinctive ethos is conveyed in Chapter 24, though reference is made to them in a number of chapters throughout the volume.

In every country, the relationship between education and the economy is complex. Chapter 25 presents a careful analysis of the situation as it pertains in Scotland. In the chapter which follows, the relationship between education 'prior to' work and education 'for' work takes this further. National aspirations, in Scotland as elsewhere, are to widen access and opportunities, particularly to Further and Higher Education and amongst groups traditionally subject to barriers and/or discrimination; Chapter 27 deals with access in the Scottish context. The final chapter in Section IV looks critically at what is fashionably called Values Education, often said to be implicit in teaching methodologies and materials but sometimes given separate curricular treatment.

SECTIONS V TO VIII   PRE-SCHOOL, PRIMARY AND SECONDARY SCHOOL EDUCATION

At the heart of the volume, in Sections V to VIII, are chapters concerned with pre-school, primary and secondary school education. They deal with how schools are organised and managed, and with what is taught in Scottish schools. Children in Scotland go to primary school at age five and authorities are required by statute to provide that primary education; nursery or pre-school provision is not a statutory requirement although it is the intention of the present (Labour) government to make places available for all four year olds. Provision for pre-school age children is made in local authority nursery schools or playgroups, or in some cases private nurseries. Chapter 29 opens Section V with a description of the educational provision for pre-five children, setting it in the context of widely held aspirations to make it available to all. (Political agendas have varied considerably in this respect, particularly during the last decade.) This is followed by chapters concerned with how nursery and primary schools are organised and managed, their ethos and how teachers work with young children. Pupils spend seven years in primary school and at age twelve move from primary to secondary school. The efforts made by teachers to smooth the transition from P7 to S1 (which for some pupils is difficult) are described in Chapter 32: Primary-Secondary Liaison.

The curriculum sections (VI for Primary and VIII for Secondary) do not simply replicate official documentation about what ought to be in the curriculum. They endeavour to describe what is actually taught; the approaches used by teachers; the emphases to be encountered in pupil activity; and the influences of government policy and assessment requirements upon what takes place in Scottish classrooms. While these curriculum chapters are mostly short (approximately 2,000 words) they encapsulate much that is distinctive about Scottish school teaching today. The first chapters in these sections (Chapters 33 and 45), each approximately 5,000 words (as are most others in the volume), give an overview of the curriculum of primary and secondary schools. Thereafter there are chapters for each of the curriculum programmes (or subjects) and these are placed alphabetically within each section. In the Secondary Curriculum Section (VIII), three cross-departmental, or whole-school, curriculum areas are included alongside the traditional subject areas (viz. Careers Education, Information Technology and Health Education).

In Section VII there are chapters concerned with the organisation, management and discipline of secondary schools. Scotland's secondaries incorporate hierarchical management structures and the roles and duties of teachers at the various levels are set out and related to the operation and ethos of the typical school. The pastoral care of pupils is organised by Guidance teachers in Scotland's secondary schools, there being in each school a team of teachers, part of whose remit is to deal specifically with the Personal and Social Education of pupils (Chapter 43). The section concludes with a chapter devoted to the organisation of teaching within classrooms, with a particular focus on what is known as the differentiation of the curriculum (to suit differing abilities, achievements and rates of progress).

SECTION IX   FURTHER AND HIGHER EDUCATION

Children may leave secondary school at sixteen years of age (at the end of S4) though staying-on rates have increased dramatically in recent years. The majority of pupils continue to be educated in secondary schools, in S5 and in smaller numbers in S6, though some will choose to continue their education in a Further Education (FE) College. Since 1985, vocational education programmes have been certificated within a national framework of modular provision. Although this originated in the FE sector, up to a quarter of such national certificates are currently taken in schools, pupils working towards both general and vocational educational qualifications. Inevitably the character of Further Education Colleges is different from that of secondary schools, and the section begins with an outline of the Current Priorities in FE. Something of the diversity and variation in provision in this sector is indicated in Chapter 69. The distinctions between the intentions for liberal and vocational education are carefully set out in Chapter 70. The response of educators to the rapidly changing world of work and the need for tailor-made programmes of study and marketable certificates is conveyed in the chapter which follows; Further Education has been considerably influenced by the needs of industry and commerce in Scotland.

Able pupils in secondary schools will elect to enter Higher Education (HE) from S5 or S6 and, in line with UK government policy, the proportion of the cohort studying at University has risen steadily over the decades, to over 40 per cent. Very significant numbers of young pupils therefore attend Scotland's Universities – both traditional and 'new' (including those which were formerly central institutions or 'polytechnics', to use the more commonly understood English term). There is an increasing blurring between FE and HE and a trend towards co-operation between the two sectors in course provision. Chapter 72 examines how students are taught in both FE and HE.

Higher Education Institutions have become increasingly subject to public scrutiny and audit and Chapters 73–5 view their development in this context, Chapter 73 looking at the curricular structures of Universities. Scotland's Universities have long traditions of service to their communities; the nature of these links and their increasing diversification is described in Chapter 74. Following the publication in 1997 of key government reports on Higher Education (Dearing and Garrick), the priorities for HE continue to be subject to great pressure and Chapter 75 critically assesses the predicament of the University system in Scotland. The section finishes with two chapters concerned with adult and continuing education and the distinctive operation of the Open University in Scotland.

SECTION X   ASSESSMENT AND CERTIFICATION

Assessment and certification probably constitute the greatest sources of influence upon the curriculum and this section is devoted to the very considerable changes which have taken place in recent years in Scotland, not only to the conduct of assessment but to the organisational structures through which formal certification is carried out. The section opens with two chapters which describe the changing patterns in primary and secondary schools. Chapter 78 explains how different assessment is for teachers now compared to a generation ago; innovative grading arrangements and reporting formats have become a source of challenge and demanding workloads. Chapter 79 looks at the progress made to increase the amount of ongoing assessment in classrooms, intended directly to influence learning and teaching (formative assessment).

Scotland has long been used to one single examination body for the certification of general education awards achieved by pupils at the end of secondary school – The Scottish Examination Board (SEB). The certification of vocational awards became the responsibility of a new council in 1985 – The Scottish Vocational Education Council (SCOTVEC). These bodies had quite different origins, character and modus operandi. Concomitant with the bringing together of general and vocational certificate arrangements under Higher Still (to be implemented from 1999 onwards), the two examination bodies were merged into one single authority – the Scottish Qualifications Authority (SQA) – in 1997. Many of the operations of the new SQA derive directly from the practices of SEB and SCOTVEC and these are set out in Chapters 80 and 81, which have been written by the two former Chief Executives in question. Chapter 82 (SQA) has been written by the incoming Chief Executive for the new authority. The section concludes with a discussion of national testing in Scotland, something brought about under Conservative UK legislation but very differently effected in Scotland from England and Wales. The national testing of pupils in primary and secondary schools is not a mandatory requirement in Scotland in the way that it is in England. Schools throughout the country do not conduct tests upon pupils uniformly; teachers choose when to conduct testing and draw from item banks specifically designed for the purpose; their use is therefore 'confirmatory' in character. Chapter 83 provides the detail of how this came about and its present operation (albeit in the climate of a new Labour government still wedded to standards and accountability, as was its predecessor).

SECTION XI   SCOTTISH PUPILS AND THEIR ACHIEVEMENTS

In the section concerned with the Secondary Curriculum (VIII), some of the authors were able to attest to the competence of pupils in their subjects (those few for which there are some firm indicators of achievement). A book concerned with the education of young people ought, however, to say something about those youngsters and about their achievements as demonstrated in national certification results and in the evidence from major research surveys. Section XI does this in several ways. First, Chapter 84 gives something of the character of pupils in Scotland's primary and secondary schools. It draws both upon teachers' views of pupils and pupils' views of themselves, concentrating upon their conceptions of schooling. The chapter draws upon both research evidence and popular images of children and their behaviour.

Chapter 85 describes Scotland's programme of national achievement monitoring, the Scottish Office Assessment of Achievement Programme (AAP), whose annual surveys of what pupils know and can do at three key stages of education (P4, P7 and S2) have been conducted by independent researchers since the early 1980s. The findings in the three surveyed areas, English language, mathematics and science, and the trends emerging from inter-survey comparisons, are analysed (and related to international comparisons in the case of mathematics and science). The two chapters which follow reflect critically upon the national achievements found in SEB and SCOTVEC results over a number of years. The trends concerning pupils' capabilities, evident in the steadily increasing presentations at Standard Grade (S4) and Higher Grade (S5 and S6) and FE/school-based SCOTVEC Certificates, are explored in detail.

The Centre for Educational Sociology at Edinburgh University has conducted a wide range of surveys relating the achievements of young people to a variety of factors including social class, gender and schooling; some of the rich seam of data concerning Scotland's youngsters is set out in Chapter 88. The section finishes with an examination of the research into school effectiveness and school improvement. The Centre for Quality in Education at the University of Strathclyde has, amongst other things, carried out the nationally funded Improving School Effectiveness Project (collaborating with staff from the London Institute for Education) and Chapter 89 relates findings about pupils to various measures of how education is conducted in Scottish primary and secondary schools.

SECTION XII   CHALLENGES AND RESPONSES: EDUCATION FOR ALL?

Educational systems are challenged by the particular difficulties and needs of varied groups of pupils and different systems respond in different ways. Section XII contains a range of professional perspectives in this regard, allowing the reader to see both how we construe the challenges in Scotland and what teachers do in schools, supported by the work of other professional colleagues (in psychological services, in social work, in community education). The first chapter (90) tracks the changing definitions of 'Special Educational Needs' across two decades and examines the current roles of teachers and other agencies in identifying and providing for special needs. Chapter 91 concentrates on the actions of teachers designated currently as 'Learning Support' teachers. Their predecessors a generation ago would have been termed 'Remedial Teachers': the changed discourse indicates that educational practice and its rationale is now quite different. 'Child Guidance' and the work of educational psychologists has also changed in orientation over the years and Chapter 92 analyses the present operations of the Psychological Services; how educational psychologists inter-relate to teachers and their impact upon the educational system.

Both Social Work and Community Education are local authority service provisions quite separate from school education. Social workers do have close links with schools however, largely through their connections with the Guidance system. Where a pupil's difficulties are rooted in problematic family or wider social circumstances, referrals will be made to the local social work department. For some schools, there is necessarily close co-operation between the two professional groups. Chapter 93 describes social work with teachers specifically in mind. Community educators, to some extent because their service constitutes non-statutory provision, operate with a quite different rationale and ethos. On the whole, they try to tailor their work to perceived and expressed community needs. Chapter 94 explains what community education is about and again the details are set out with teachers specifically in mind.

Not all pupils find school satisfactory and Chapter 95 explores the nature and possible origins of disaffection, together with the characteristics of youth culture and anti-school sub-cultures. The final three chapters in Section XII deal with three areas where, in Scotland as elsewhere, challenges derive from prejudice and discrimination, sometimes within the education system itself. One chapter takes up the issue of gender, a second considers racial discrimination, and the third looks at religious prejudice, so-called sectarianism.

SECTION XIII   SCOTTISH TEACHERS, TEACHER EDUCATION AND PROFESSIONALISM

The final section of the book concentrates upon the teaching profession in Scotland; upon Initial Teacher Education (ITE) and subsequent professional development; and with matters concerned with the competence of the workforce. The first chapter is about the Teacher Education Institutions (TEIs) themselves, formerly all distinct (as well as distinctive) Colleges or 'Central Institutions'. The six current TEIs are now parts of the University sector or are presently moving to become so. The largest, formerly known as Jordanhill College, is now the Faculty of Education of the University of Strathclyde (in Glasgow). The chapters which follow deal respectively with the programmes of Professional Studies in ITE and with the varied and changing ways in which post-Initial Teacher Education (in-service staff development) is carried out. The competence of teachers was among the measures of educational accountability made prominent during the Conservative regime and is still on the political agenda. Competences were drawn up for ITE courses and their detail has become the subject of much scrutiny and debate (Chapter 102). The European dimension has been promoted steadily in the past decade, with a number of Scottish schools developing close working links with Europe through projects, exchanges, curricular inserts and permeating devices. There are important implications for teachers in all of this and these are explored in Chapter 103. Issues of interchangeability (concerning work opportunities as well as qualifications) also increasingly affect teachers. The courses which students, of all kinds, are able to pursue in higher education institutions, including TEIs, have in recent years become subject to credit ratings and transferability. Chapter 104 spells out how these operate in Scotland (SCOTCAT Arrangements). The next four chapters in Section XIII are all concerned with research and education, though in different ways. The first looks at the relationship between research and practice and highlights some of the studies designed to explore and improve aspects of schooling in Scotland. Chapter 106 describes the Scottish Educational Research Association (SERA) which has been in existence for twenty-five years; Chapter 107 the Educational Journals which are available in Scotland (including the *Scottish Educational Review* (*SER*) which is the centrepiece of scholarly publication for teachers and lecturers); and Chapter 108 the Scottish Council for Research in Education (SCRE) founded in 1928. The final three chapters focus upon professionalism. The teaching unions are described in Chapter 109. The General Teaching Council (GTC), established in 1965, is responsible for entry to the profession; it accredits ITE courses and formally controls assessment during the two year probationary period (Chapter 110). Chapter 111 rounds off with a view of Scottish Teachers drawing from a wide range of literary, historical and contemporary sources.

SECTION XIV   POSTSCRIPT

In the last chapter (112) entitled 'The Future of Scottish Education' we review the current situation in the light of the evidence and analysis that has been presented in the preceding sections and identify a number of key themes that are likely to remain important in the immediate future. We also reflect on the strengths and limitations of the project as a whole.

REFERENCES, ABBREVIATIONS AND SOME QUALIFICATIONS

The above overview of the chapter contents might be taken to suggest that our conception of the text and what it should contain was easily determined and straightforward. This was not so. There is no self-evidently correct or ideal structure for a book of this scope and scale. Any structure is problematic and the one we have created has probably ensured more coherence in some areas than in others. We hope that it will work well enough for the reader intent upon understanding the range and diversity of education in Scotland.

With regard to coherence in another sense, it should be recognised that with so many contributing authors there are some conflicts and a few tensions evident in the text itself; it would be unreasonable to expect complete consistency of view and interpretation from everyone. In some instances the editors do not share the line taken by the author, nor would we expect to do so. Many issues in education are highly contestable and a healthy system requires vigorous debate. While we drafted all 110 specifications (leaving aside this first and the last chapter) we did encourage the writers to develop them by incorporating their own views. That has happened and we believe the text is much the richer as a result.

Given the general propensities for academics to incorporate as many references in support of their writing as possible, we imposed upon our contributing authors the limit of just six key references per chapter. The six so identified by each writer constitute those texts/articles which it is suggested the reader should consult if keen to pursue the area in question and to develop further understanding. Many of the writers (including ourselves in Chapters 4, 7, 10 and 78) felt it necessary to incorporate additional references and these have been built into the text itself. (The disincentive to clutter the writing as a result was that this counted against the text length which could be submitted!) All educationists share a professional shorthand well known by the profusion of abbreviations and acronyms. We have endeavoured to have these spelled out within each chapter where they are first encountered – for example, the Scottish Office Education and Industry Department (SOEID) – but an additional glossary of terms and abbreviations has been supplied at the end of the volume. This lists all of the items found in the text and it is included in addition to the conventional index.

ACKNOWLEDGEMENTS

At the beginning of this chapter we expressed some of the thinking which lay behind the creation of this text. While we have endeavoured to provide a definitive text on Scottish education, we have done so in the explicit recognition of the very considerable contributions by individuals and groups, by researchers, organisations and institutions throughout Scotland, particularly in the last fifty years. Scholarship concerning Scottish education by Scots men and women has increased steadily over recent years. This volume is intended to complement the endeavour, not only through the inclusion of new contributions by seasoned Scottish writers but also by others who are less well known. We are indebted to them all.

With regard to the editing, from the outset the advice given to us was not to contemplate editing the complete work ourselves but to work with a team. That proved to be valuable and important advice, for the editing turned out to be extremely demanding and time-consuming; the volume would not have seen the light of day had it not been for the good efforts of those friends and colleagues who shared the editing with diligence, patience and care, in some cases taking material from rough first draft, through several revisions, to the final published version contained in the text. To all we express our sincere personal gratitude.

Many others are due our thanks. Secretaries Delsia Maddocks and May Habbick at Jordanhill coped brilliantly with varied manuscripts, multiple disc formats and associated problems; their fortitude and talents over an extended period are much appreciated. John Darling offered useful advice in the early stages of the project but for health reasons had to withdraw from section editing. Donald Gray gave invaluable help in the later stages of the project, including the assembling of the glossary of abbreviations. The Carnegie Trust provided financial support in the form of a grant towards publication costs, for which we are grateful. And we must thank staff at Edinburgh University Press, in particular Nicola Carr. Her reactions during this project ranged from sheer incredulity when we put our proposal forward at the start, to friendship and solid support as we steadily moved to completion. Dr Ian Clark, EUP's copy-editor, negotiated final corrections with wit, courtesy and an unfailing eye for detail. There are others without whose help the book would not have been produced but formal acknowledgement must stop somewhere. Let us therefore conclude by thanking the many pupils, students, teachers and colleagues who have, over the years, taught us about Scottish education and for whom this book might be seen as an expression of gratitude.

II

Policy and Provision in Scottish Education

2

Educational Provision: An Overview

Lindsay Paterson

INTRODUCTION: STRUCTURES AND SECTORS

Scottish educational provision is dominated by four large sectors – primary schooling, secondary schooling, further education colleges, and higher education institutions. Almost everyone progresses from primary at about age 5 to secondary at about age 12, and leaves secondary between the ages of 16 and 18. Most people then move to a college or a university for some post-school education. Alongside these main areas of activity are diverse other sectors – notably, pre-school education, special education, and community education. Nearly all of special education, over 90% of the primary and secondary sectors, about 40% of the pre-school sector, and most of community education are governed by 32 locally elected education authorities. The remainder of these sectors is provided by private and voluntary organisations, most of which charge fees. Three schools are independent but funded by public grants, two of these having become self-governing by the votes of parents under legislation from the Conservative government in 1989. Schools associated with particular religious denominations fully joined the public sector in Scotland in the 1920s, and now are governed and funded in almost exactly the same way as non-denominational schools. The church retains a say in the curriculum and in appointments to senior posts. All the denominational schools in the public secondary sector are Roman Catholic, as are all but two in the public primary sector.

All but two of the forty-five further education colleges are independent incorporated bodies funded by central government via the Scottish Further Education Funding Council, by student fees, and by a variety of private sources (see Chapter 5). These forty-three were removed from the governance of the education authorities in 1993 (but the two small colleges in Orkney and Shetland remained with their education authorities). The higher education institutions are self-governing and subject to the general oversight of the Scottish Higher Education Funding Council, and receive their funds from public grants, student fees, and private sponsorship of research and teaching. The whole Scottish education system costs about £4bn in public expenditure, to which can be added about £500–700m in private expenditure on independent schools and on aspects of higher education – in total about 9% of Scottish gross domestic product.

The main changes in provision in recent decades have concerned post-compulsory education and pre-school education, both having expanded significantly. As far as the broad pattern of provision is concerned, the primary years and the first four years of secondary have not changed nearly so markedly. This contrasts with the 1960s and 1970s when the early years of secondary were transformed by the introduction of comprehensive education, so that selection by measured ability for different types of secondary school was ended in the public sector. Nevertheless, stability of provision has been accompanied by great changes in practice. This chapter is concerned with the statistics of participation in the various sectors of education; it is mostly not concerned with the details of what goes on when students enter. (See Chapters 4 and 5, and Sections V–VIII.)

Statistics quoted are from Scottish Office Statistical Bulletins; the main ones cited are detailed in footnotes to the graphs. Guides to further statistical information can be found in the list of references. Throughout this chapter, the term 'public school' is used with the meaning that it conventionally has in Scotland (as in North America), in other words a school funded by public authorities. Following current Scottish Office practice, the three grant-aided or self-governing schools are included in the public sector. The other types of provision are referred to as independent or voluntary.

PROVISION AND PARTICIPATION

Pre-school

Pre-school education has expanded steadily over the past decade, as Figure 2.1 shows for education authority places. Over one half of 4-year-old children had an education authority nursery place in 1994, as did over one fifth of 3-year-olds. These represent 49,760 places for children aged 3 and 4. The places cost education authorities £57m in recurrent expenditure 1993, about £1,100 per pupil. A further 1.1% of children aged 3 or 4 attended independent nursery schools. These broad national statistics mask large variations by region. Thus, in 1994, 53% of all children aged 3 or 4 had education authority places in Glasgow and Lothian, while only 17.5% did so in Highland and only 3.5% in Argyll and Bute.

Figure 2.1   Pre-school education in education authority nurseries, 1986–94

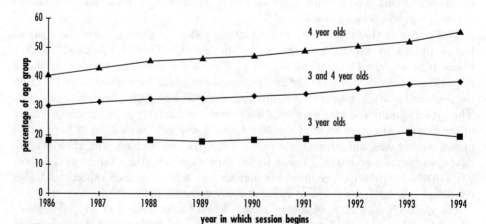

source: SOEID Statistical Bulletin, Edn/A2/1995/16, table 4

Supplementing nursery schools is a variety of day-care arrangements that probably involve some education. In 1994, for example, a total of 80,841 day-care places were available over and above nursery education, this being one quarter of the population aged 0–4, a rise from 54,098 or one-sixth in 1984. Of all the nursery and day-care places, some 40% are provided by education authorities, and the rest by voluntary and private bodies that are registered with the local authority. Not counted here is unregistered care, and, indeed, the dividing line between formal and informal care is vague.

The expansion of nursery education has been encouraged by research evidence that it improves children's educational progression later on – for example, from the Head Start programme in the USA. Developing reading skills at this age has apparently been effective in reducing the educational disadvantage suffered by children in socially deprived areas of the cities. Despite these educational reasons for expanding nursery provision, probably the single biggest influence has been the growth in the proportion of mothers who work outside the home, for whom pre-school education is a form of good-quality childcare.

Primary

Changes in the pattern of primary provision have been largely driven by demographic trends. Numbers of primary pupils reached a peak of half a million in the late 1970s, dipped to about 430,000 in the 1980s, and by 1996 had risen again to 492,888, 98% of whom were attending public schools. In 1996, there were 2,386 primary schools, 97% of them public; this was about 200 fewer than in 1980, closures having been forced by falling rolls and by shifts of population away from rural areas. There were the equivalent of 23,142 full-time primary teachers (97% of them in the public schools). Primary schools cost education authorities £778m in recurrent grants in 1996, or £1,767 per pupil.

Some closures were also caused by the effects of parental choice, the legislation inaugurated in 1980 that allowed parents to choose the school to which their child would go. The incidence of these placing requests has steadily risen since then, as the upper line in Figure 2.2 shows. A school is in danger of closure if a large proportion of its potential pupils have chosen to go elsewhere. Most of the placing requests are for entry to primary one, but in 1995 about 2% of pupils in primaries two to seven had moved directly into one of these years as a result of a placing request. There is a great deal of regional variation in the level of placing requests. It is highest in the urban areas where there is a genuine choice of accessible schools. Thus, in 1995, the incidence in primary one was one quarter or more in Aberdeen, Dundee, East Dunbartonshire, Edinburgh, Glasgow, Inverclyde, and West Dunbartonshire. By contrast, in predominantly rural areas, the rates were low: they were one in ten or fewer in Aberdeenshire, Argyll and Bute, Borders, East Lothian, Highland, Midlothian, Orkney, Shetland, Stirling and Western Isles.

The public schools ranged in size in 1996 from 6% with fewer than twenty pupils to 8% with more than 400. The average size was 191. The small schools are in rural and island areas, and the cost of running them is reflected in the range of average recurrent costs per pupil among the education authorities – in 1996, from £3,126 in Shetland to £1,423 in East Renfrewshire. Many of the small schools have to organise their teaching into composite classes (where children from different year groups are taught together): in 1995, 27% of primary classes were composite, affecting 23% of pupils.

Among the education authority primary schools, 15% are associated with the Roman Catholic Church; they educate 18% of primary pupils. One of the two self-governing schools in Scotland is a primary associated with the Scottish Episcopal Church.

Figure 2.2 Placing requests, 1985–95

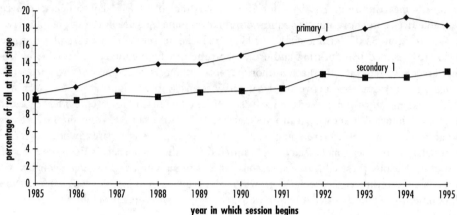

source: SOEID Statistical Bulletin Edn/B6/1997/2; chart 2

Secondary

The size of the secondary sector has been driven by two contradictory trends. The dominant effect has been demographic, as in the primaries; but partly offsetting this has been a sharp rise in the rate of staying on in school beyond age sixteen.

Numbers of pupils in secondary school reached a peak in 1980 at over 400,000, and then fell by over one quarter to under 300,000 by 1990. In 1996, they had recovered again to 334,843 (95% in public schools). In that year, there were 460 secondary schools (88% of them public), with the equivalent of 26,220 full-time teachers (93% in the public schools). About thirty-five schools closed between 1980 and 1996. The recurrent cost of providing the public schools in 1996 was £875m, or £2,760 per pupil.

As with primaries, one of the reasons for school closures was placing requests. The incidence of placing requests is lower than in primary, as Figure 2.2 shows, partly because more communities have just one secondary school and so have no practicable choice on offer. The Figure shows the effects of placing requests as a proportion of the roll in the first year of secondary (S1); a further 1% of pupils in S2–6 entered these years directly as a result of a placing request. The regional pattern was similar to that for primaries.

The public schools ranged in size in 1996 from 1% with fewer than 100 pupils to 11% with rolls greater than 1,000. On the whole, the smaller schools are in rural areas, although size can also reflect an education authority's policies over several decades. Most notably, Fife decided to have large comprehensive schools in an attempt to avoid the concentration of social classes into particular schools. As a result, the average size of their schools in 1996 was 1,216, far above the national average of 786. The same authority has also had a complementary policy of keeping primary schools small, and so its average roll in that sector was just 214, quite close to the average of 191. Small schools cost more to run. Thus, in 1996, the recurrent cost per pupil of secondary education in Fife was £2,465, almost the lowest in Scotland (in East Dunbartonshire it was £2,455 and in East Lothian it was £2,345). In Shetland, by contrast, with an average roll of only 181, the cost per pupil was £4,550.

The only denominational public schools in the secondary sector are Roman Catholic, educating 17% of pupils. There is one grant-aided secondary school which did not transfer to either the education authority sector or the independent sector along with all the other such schools in 1985. There is also one small self-governing school which voted to leave education authority control (although it is negotiating to return).

The main changes in the structure of secondaries have been in the fifth and sixth year, as a result of rising rates of staying on into post-compulsory education. Figure 2.3 shows the trend: not only has the overall rate risen steadily since the mid-1980s, but so has the rate of staying for a whole six years. The proportion entering sixth year in 1995 (44%) was much the same as the proportion voluntarily staying on beyond age sixteen as recently as 1982. Unlike in England, almost all of the staying on beyond age sixteen is in schools: only about 4% of the age group (6% of the people who stay on) enter further education colleges at this stage. The rate of staying on varied regionally. In 1995, it was under 65% in Glasgow, West Lothian and East Lothian, and was over 75% in Argyll and Bute, East Renfrewshire, the Western Isles, Edinburgh, Perth and Kinross and South Ayrshire.

Figure 2.3   Staying-on rates, 1985–95

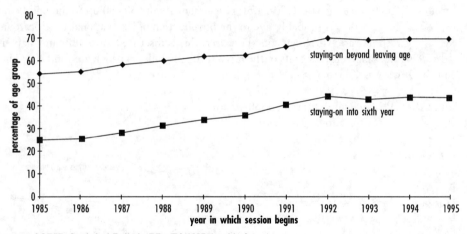

source: SOEID Statistical Bulletin EDn/E2/1997/6, table 2

The immediate cause of rising staying-on rates is improving attainment in the fourth year of secondary school. The Scottish Young People's Survey showed that, in 1991, people who had seven or more Standard Grades at levels 1–3 were almost certain to stay on, whereas two-thirds of people with no Standard Grades at levels 1–3 left. That rising attainment is caused, in turn, by rising levels of parental education, well-educated parents being more likely to encourage their children to succeed at school. It is also shaped by the growing gap between boys' and girls' attainment: in 1995, 74% of girls stayed on, but only 66% of boys. The gender gap is most evident among low-attainers: girls' propensity to stay on is less affected by low attainment than is boys'.

Youth unemployment has only a limited effect on staying-on rates: rates rise when unemployment rises, but do not fall back when unemployment falls. More important than these external influences are the positive attractions of the flexible structures of curriculum and examinations in the fifth and sixth years: when people stay on, they do not feel that they are committing themselves irrevocably to two years of schooling, because there are worthwhile awards to be gained in the meantime. The character of the fifth and sixth year is discussed fully elsewhere in this volume, for example in Chapter 88.

Spanning secondary and primary is special education, for children with severe learning difficulties. In 1995, there were approximately 300 such schools, catering for about 9,000 pupils, and costing £51m in recurrent grants. The size of this sector has remained almost the same since 1980, despite policies of trying to incorporate children with special educational needs into mainstream primary or secondary schools.

Post-school

After leaving school, increasing proportions enter further stages of education, as is shown by the upper line in Figure 2.4. There are two broad sectors which the leavers enter. On the one hand is vocational further education, taking place in forty-five further education colleges. The majority of people in FE colleges are not school leavers, however: in 1995, only 22.6% of students in vocational further education were aged under eighteen. Most students take part-time technician courses while they are working. Indeed, 80% of students at FE colleges attend part-time. The total number of students in FE colleges has been stable at around 220,000 since the late 1980s, after rising from about 150,000 up to the middle of the 1980s. The growth was probably due to the introduction of the National Certificate in 1984, along with its various refinements thereafter: this is discussed more fully in Chapter 87. In 1996, the total recurrent costs of the forty-three FE colleges which are funded by the Scottish Office was £233m.

Figure 2.4   Post-school education, 1980–95

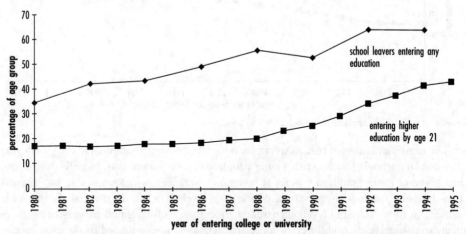

sources: for any education: author's analysis of Scottish School Leavers Survey; for higher education: SOEID Statistical Bulletin Edn/J2/1996/12, table 11 and National Committee of Inquiry into Higher Education, 1997, table 1

The other post-school sector is higher education, which has grown rapidly since the early 1990s. It takes place in both higher education institutions and further education colleges. There are twenty-three higher education institutions, with (in 1994) 17,841 staff. In 1995, higher education institutions cost £850m in recurrent grants from public sources and £375m of private funds.

The lower line in Figure 2.4 shows that, in 1995, 44% of people entered any higher education by the time they were aged twenty-one. The number of students in higher education rose from 109,000 in 1980 to 202,000 in 1994. The proportion of undergraduates who entered part-time courses was 52% in 1980 but only 36% in 1994, because full-time numbers rose more rapidly than part-time ones. But part-time postgraduate study has grown in significance: the proportion of postgraduates who entered part-time courses was 19% in 1980 and 45% in 1994. An increasing proportion of undergraduates were aged over 21 – 23% in 1980, but 37% in 1994.

Rising rates of entry by school leavers have been influenced by rising levels of attainment in the final years of secondary school. But there are other explanations as well. Young women used to be less likely to apply to higher education (despite having good enough school attainment), but this difference has declined. Thus, in 1980, only 43% of under-graduates were female; in 1994, it was 49%. Although social class differences remain in rates of entry, they too have declined. Thus, whereas in 1980 school leavers whose fathers were in professional occupations were six times more likely to enter higher education than leavers whose fathers were in manual occupations, by 1994 that had narrowed to a ratio of 2.5:1. Furthermore, young people from minority ethnic groups in Scotland are more likely to enter higher education than young people who are white.

Rates of entry to higher education by school leavers vary by region. They are highest in the rural areas and in the wealthier areas, and lowest in Glasgow. People are now much less likely than they were even two decades ago to enter their local institution: they travel all over Scotland. But nine out of ten entrants to higher education stay in Scotland. Because Scottish higher education provides 12.5% of higher education places in the UK, while Scotland provides only 9.8% of higher education students, about one in five students at Scottish institutions comes from outside Scotland. In some of the older universities (such as Edinburgh) the proportion from outside is one half.

Scottish higher education differs from that elsewhere in the UK in having a high proportion of students doing higher education courses in further education colleges: the proportion in 1995 was 30% in Scotland, but less than one half of that in England. Among all students in FE colleges, 21% are on higher education courses; but in four colleges, the proportion is over half, and in eight it is under 10%. The type of course in FE colleges is quite different from the courses in universities. Whereas 90% of undergraduates in universities take degree courses, 97% of undergraduates in FE colleges do two-year diplomas. Moreover, 56% of undergraduates in FE colleges study part-time, compared to just 19% in the universities. FE colleges are not only good at offering part-time courses; they also are better than the universities at attracting working-class students, partly because they mainly serve the communities in which they are based.

Community education is a much more diverse sector, and in Scotland has no statutory basis. It is therefore vulnerable to contraction whenever budgets are tight. Nevertheless, it has a significant impact. In 1995, it attracted about half a million participants, about 60% of whom were adults. Most community education takes place in school evening classes or in community centres. But there has also been a slow growth in the number of adults attending secondary-school classes during the day along with teenage children. In 1990, 4.5% of students in secondary schools were adults, but in Lothian this was 7.5% and in Glasgow it was 10%. Further education colleges are in direct competititon with schools for this type of student. The Open University in Scotland meets similar needs at a more advanced level: it has grown at much the same rate as the rest of higher education, from 5,994 students in 1980 to 12,326 in 1993. In the early 1990s, about four-fifths of adult participants in general community education were women, but about 58% of students in the Open University were men. In both community education and the Open University, people who already had a lot of initial education were more likely to take part than people who had left school at the first opportunity.

POLICIES ON PROVISION AND PARTICIPATION

Each sector has been affected by changes in governance and in policy over the last couple of decades, and this is likely to continue. The directions of policy will alter as a consequence of the Labour government elected in 1997, and, over time, will change profoundly after the Scottish parliament is established in 1999.

Although all political parties favour the expansion of nursery education, there have been deep divisions over how best this is to be done. The Conservative government proposed to use a system of vouchers, which parents of children aged four would receive as an entitlement, and which they could then spend in return for a nursery place. Vouchers have long been favoured by the educational right, and this scheme (for the whole of Britain) was believed by some to be a pilot for voucher schemes affecting all education.

The other political parties opposed the vouchers, and the new Labour government moved to abolish them by the session 1998–9. Nevertheless, even some Labour-controlled education authorities used the vouchers to expand nursery provision beyond the level it had been at. Since well under one half of pre-school places are provided by the education authorities, even a non-Conservative government is unlikely to insist on universally public provision. This would fit with the themes of voluntarism in the welfare state which are quite popular in the Labour government, and which the likely dominant political forces in the Scottish parliament would favour.

Both primary and secondary schools have undergone significant changes in govern-ance. These include general supervision by school boards made up of the elected representatives of parents and teachers (with parents in a majority), devolved school management and the Conservative government provisions for public schools to leave the control of education authorities and become self-governing. The election of a Labour government has ended the likelihood of self-government being extended, but the devolution of power to headteachers will continue, if only because the scheme which the Conservatives put in place in Scotland was modelled on one that had earlier been developed by the Labour-controlled Strathclyde Regional Council. The school boards, too, have become widely accepted, and, indeed, became allies of the school professionals in their resistance to certain Conservative government policies in the late 1980s. Devolved management and school boards are likely to make the system less governable than previously. Because they also can be presented as a form of decentralisation, they would be likely to be maintained by the Scottish parliament founded on that same principle.

Some likely future directions of policy have further significant implications for the structure of secondary education. The inspectorate recommended in 1996 that more setting of pupils by ability be adopted in the first two years of secondary. If that recommendation is widely adopted – and the Labour government has not disagreed with it – then the character of the transition from primary to secondary could change substantially. It is also likely to be proposed that pupils should experience fewer discrete subjects in secondary one and some discrete subjects in primary seven, to smooth the present transition from essentially one teacher of all subjects in P7 to as many as fifteen teachers in S1.

None of these changes would exacerbate the differences among secondary schools. But some commentators believe that the Higher Still reforms at the other end of secondary school could reintroduce the distinction between academic and non-academic schools which comprehensive education was supposed to have ended. The fear is that only a few, highly academic schools would teach the proposed Advanced Higher, and that some schools would not be able to teach beyond the Intermediate levels in any but a few subjects. Creating such divisions is not the intention of the policy, but they could emerge by default, partly driven by the effects of parental choice of school, so that academically well-motivated pupils might tend to be concentrated in a minority of schools.

Beyond school, the expansion of higher education is likely to continue following the publication of the report of the National Committee of Inquiry in 1997. Given the importance of the FE colleges in providing higher education in Scotland, and given also their capacity to attract working-class and part-time students, they are likely to be favoured by the Scottish parliament as a main route to expansion, in contrast to England. It is already planned, for example, that a new University of the Highlands and Islands will be based on the network of FE colleges in the area.

The Scottish Office has already followed the recommendation from the National Committee of Inquiry that a funding council for FE colleges be set up, to establish their independence from the Scottish Office. The Scottish Higher Education Funding Council has attracted consensual support since it was established, and is widely seen as a model for guiding all post-school institutions under the parliament. But, because FE remains much closer to the labour market than does higher education, its governance is likely to remain distinct. For example, compared to their reaction to the pre-school voucher scheme, the non-Conservative parties were less hostile to the voucher scheme which the Conservative government introduced for some further education provision (Skillseekers). It is unlikely that it will be abolished, probably because vocational education has always had elements of private provision within it, and has always had to respond to market pressures for skills.

The content of further education itself will be changed by the Higher Still proposals as much as it was by the introduction of the National Certificate in the mid-1980s. Breaking down the barriers between academic and vocational education at this stage might eventually lead to the abolition of the distinction between further and higher education. There would then be a continuum of post-school courses, provided in institutions with a variety of styles and ethos.

Both further and higher education will contribute to the development of lifelong learning, as is currently favoured by all political parties. Lifelong learning is seen not only as a good in itself, but also as a way in which a new democracy could be underpinned by knowledgeable and critical citizens. To harness community education to that purpose, it is likely that the Scottish parliament will want to give it a statutory basis. This would guarantee a relatively secure future for it, but at the expense of tighter control by the inspectorate, and probably also closer association with colleges and universities.

REFERENCES

Munn, P. and M. Clark (eds) (1997) *Education in Scotland: Policy and Practice from Pre-School to Secondary*, London: Routledge.

National Committee of Inquiry into Higher Education (1997) *Higher Education in the Learning Society: Report of the Scottish Committee*, London: HMSO.

SOEID (1997) *Scottish Education Statistics*, Edinburgh: SOEID.

SOEID (1996) *The Scottish School Leavers Survey: the 1994 Leavers*, Edinburgh: SOEID.

SOEID (1996) *Scottish Schools: Costs 1995–97*, Edinburgh: SOEID.

SOEID (1996) *Further Education in Scotland 1996*, Edinburgh: SOEID.

3

Scottish Primary Education: Philosophy and Practice

John Darling

HISTORICAL THEORY

In the middle of this century, to have completed the Froebel course at a training college was to become one of the elite in what is now called 'early stages' teaching. If the course content had rather tenuous links with the philosophy of Friedrich Froebel, it is nonetheless significant that the name of a mid-European theorist should be used to confer status on a professional qualification. Twentieth-century primary education in Scotland has not fought shy of theory.

Froebel developed his ideas from watching Pestalozzi teaching in his innovative school where much of the learning was experiential, a principle which Pestalozzi acquired from reading Rousseau's *Emile*. Another visitor to Pestalozzi's school was Scotland's Andrew Bell who saw no merit in such progressive methods. Bell's own method was monitorialism: one master instructed pupil monitors who then instructed the rest of the children. At best, learning could only have been superficial and mechanical. But if the system was clearly ineffective, it was cheap. By the time Froebel published his *Pedagogics of the Kindergarten* in 1840, monitorial schools had been established in Scotland for some time. According to an inspector's report (in the Committee of Council on Education Minutes 1841–42), one of the better ones seems to have been in Bon Accord parish, Aberdeen:

> On the day of my visit 287 pupils present; and it must be admitted that arrangements enabling a teacher, with only one adult assistant, to conduct with any amount of success the studies of so many, must be characterised by no ordinary degree of skill . . .
> . . . this system, properly understood and efficiently worked, supplies the only means at present within our reach of rendering the schools for the poor in large towns places where instruction can be efficiently given. I am not insensible to its inherent and necessary defects, or to the greater advantages which might be secured by other but more expensive arrangements.

Monitorialism offered a solution to the economic problem of providing schooling in Scotland's burgeoning cities for the labouring classes. For these children, education was seen as being urgently required to combat the three 'I's – ignorance, irreligion and immorality.

Thirty years later, after considerable pressure from the teachers' union, the Educational

Institute of Scotland (EIS), Andrew Bell's money was made available to fund another significant development in Scottish education – the founding at two universities (Edinburgh and St Andrews) of chairs in the 'theory, history and practice of education'. The Bell professors were formally required to include in their lectures the occasional discourse on the merits of monitorialism, but the incumbents seem to have neglected this part of their duties. The foundation of the first university chairs of education speaks volumes for the standing of education in Scotland, and of the school teachers themselves. Again, John Gibson, HMI:

> I have examined 16 parochial schools. The teachers are, generally speaking, highly accomplished men. Eight of them are preachers of the Church of Scotland, five are students of divinity, and the remaining three have gone through a complete course of study at the University of Aberdeen.

The book which set the tone for one important strand in Scotland's educational philosophy was written by an Aberdeen professor of logic. In 1879, Alexander Bain, one of the founding fathers of psychology, published *Education as a Science*. If the religious origins of Scottish schools ensured that combating the three 'I's became a mission to be pursued with zeal, educators themselves seemed to think it prudent to put their faith in the new science of psychology as well as in God. As psychology developed, so did the psychology of education. In people like Godfrey Thomson, Scotland made significant contributions to the study of measurement and the theory and practice of testing; and the importance of these was conveyed to teachers in the course of their training. These preoccupations have often been portrayed as linked to teaching policies which are unenlightened or even oppressive. But in Scotland measurement and testing have often been thought of primarily as tools of diagnostic assessment and aids for pupil guidance. This was perhaps most obvious in the work of William Boyd who taught at Glasgow University from 1907 to 1945 and who pioneered child-guidance clinics. Boyd appeared to see no tension between promoting new techniques of assessment and preaching the ideals of Rousseauesque progressivism. He was a prominent member of the New Education Fellowship, an international organisation formed to promote liberal educational practice. Himself a committed member of the EIS, Boyd encouraged his fellow members to press for and participate in educational research.

The high point of primary education's interest in educational science was its preoccupation in the 1950s and 1960s with the work of Jean Piaget. Seldom read, but endlessly referred to, Piaget's work purported to demonstrate that children went through a stage of 'concrete operations' in which they were unable to think in abstract terms. During this time learning had to be rooted in experience. Not only did the age range identified by Piaget accord with the age of pupils in Scottish primary schools, but the implications to be drawn appeared to match the progressive pedagogical principles in which teachers had already become interested. Primary education had acquired an educational science of its own. The vehicle for transmitting Piaget's teaching was the teachers' training college through which everyone wishing to teach in a primary school had to pass. Reflecting the long-established Scottish interest in educational science, colleges all had psychologists in post. The explication of Piaget became their new calling.

THE MEMORANDUM PHILOSOPHY: SCOTLAND'S *EMILE*?

The critical policy document which was, according to one of its authors, built around Piaget (Farquharson, 1985), was the Primary Memorandum, published in 1965. Officially called *Primary Education in Scotland*, it was written by a committee consisting of three college staff, eight teachers and eight inspectors. The Primary Memorandum constitutes a land-mark which has from the time of publication dominated the developing primary education scene. It was given a notably positive endorsement by the Secretary of State for Scotland whose foreword (after giving the obligatory recognition to Scotland's 'great tradition in education') argues that:

> we owe it to our successors to keep our educational thinking and practice abreast of the needs of our day and to lay foundations on which they can build. In education as well as in industry, science and the arts, progress depends on willingness to push beyond familiar horizons. (SED, 1965, p. iii)

The thinking of the Memorandum has permeated Scottish primary education: its tone still remains a dominant influence, despite some inimical trends in UK politics. Two decades after its publication, a report called *Education 10–14 in Scotland* (Consultative Committee on the Curriculum, 1986) characterised primary education as having been learner-centred ever since the Primary Memorandum. To this day, the primary education experienced by many Scottish children is very much as envisaged in this seminal document.

One attraction of identifying Piaget as the major influence is that this conferred on the committee's thinking the suggestion of principles built upon modern scientific findings; but the truth is that much of the argument sounds more like Rousseau than Piaget. Sig-nificantly, the opening chapter of the Memorandum is called 'The Child'; and it is argued that taking as a starting point what is known about children will lead to certain pedagogical conclusions. In particular, teachers must be sensitive to the way in which children grow and develop: consequently it is the responsibility of the Memorandum to provide an account of this. This is done in a pretty broad way: children are said to develop along similar lines, but at different speeds. The teacher's job is to 'stimulate progress' or to 'supply means of assisting (the pupil's) natural development'. As in Rousseau's *Emile*, it is claimed that 'by satisfying the needs of one stage she (the teacher) provides for development more efficiently than by trying to anticipate or prepare for the next' (SED, 1965, p. 3). And attention is drawn to the fact that

> there are many attainments and skills which children achieve spontaneously, and many things which they discover for themselves at stages in their development when they are ready to do so. (SED, 1965, p. 3)

It is illuminating to note some specific points of indebtedness to the eighteenth-century French philosopher. In, for example, his discussion in *Emile* Book III (Dent/Everyman edition, trans. B. Foxley) of how to teach science, Rousseau counsels the teacher against trying to transmit scientific facts and theories.

> It is not your business to teach him the various sciences, but to give him a taste for them and methods of learning them when this taste is more mature. (Rousseau, 1762, pp. 134–5)

Exactly the same priorities are spelled out in the Memorandum:

> The acquisition of knowledge and skills, once the main aim of education, is no longer as important as it was . . . Much more vital today . . . are the fostering of intellectual curiosity, and the development of the capacity to acquire knowledge independently. (SED, 1965, p. 18)

But for teachers to be successful in fostering enquiry, an appreciation is required of the ways in which children's thinking differs from that of adults. On the importance of avoiding the assumption that children are like adults in their styles of thought, the Memorandum is again *Emile* clearly paraphrased.

> Nature would have them children before they are men . . . Childhood has its own ways of seeing, thinking and feeling; nothing is more foolish than to try and substitute our ways. . . . (Rousseau, 1762, p. 54)

> She (the teacher) must realise that the child is not an adult in miniature: he does not feel, or act or think like an adult. (SED, 1965, p. 3)

In the Memorandum, part, but only part, of this difference is understood in Piagetian terms: where possible, skills and processes should be learned in 'concrete' situations. 'Children should not be expected to achieve symbolic, abstract thinking before they are ready for it' (SED, 1965, p. 13). Again, in stressing the importance of understanding, the Primary Memorandum is following a point insisted upon by Rousseau. In the eighteenth century such an idea was innovative: the fact that in the late twentieth century it is no longer necessary to argue in favour of understanding as an objective is an indication of how influential its proponents have been. And yet it is not so long since mindless monitorialism was in vogue, with rote learning dominating classroom practice long after the demise of Bell's system. The Memorandum insists that children's school work 'should not be for them a mere meaningless manipulation of verbal and other symbols' (SED, 1965, p. 13). Two centuries earlier Rousseau had claimed that this was what learning inevitably became unless the curriculum was based on what was within the child's own experience.

In Rousseau's conceptual framework much is made of the distinction between the artificial/conventional and the natural, indicating that the former category was, if not invariably evil or harmful, at least less desirable: 'natural' was a term of commendation. In the Memorandum there are references to 'natural development' and 'natural curiosity'; and also to 'unnatural silence'! Play is said to be the child's 'natural way of learning'; and it is regretted that this approach is given adequate scope only in the early years. This is explained in a section entitled 'The need for freedom', again echoing an eighteenth-century theme. (Arguably, Rousseau's most famous line is 'Man is born free'.)

The child, according to the Memorandum, should have 'freedom to experiment with language', since, it is claimed, skills of communication and self-expression may be harmed 'by a too early insistence on conventional correctness' (SED, 1965, p. 13). In mathematics there should be 'practical activities' instead of 'lengthy and repetitive mechanical computations'. And the reader of the Memorandum is told – although the underlying reasoning is far from obvious – that if the curriculum is to be meaningful to the child it will have to be 'integrated': 'the curriculum is not to be thought of as a number of discrete subjects, each requiring a specific allocation of time each week or month' (SED, 1965, p. 37).

In the Memorandum mathematics has replaced 'arithmetic'; but perhaps more significantly this is dealt with under the broader heading of 'environmental studies'. In passages like the one above, the term 'subject' is invested with an overtone of the repressive and the out-of-date. It is recommended that subject-centred curricula give way to methods and curricula based on the needs and interests of the child (SED, 1965, p. 60). The Memorandum has sometimes been accused of being vague about what these methods are and how they might be deployed. It does, however, state, 1. that whole class, group, and individual methods all have their place; 2. that there is evidence that while group methods make demands on teachers, the effort required to make the change pays dividends; and 3. that there is no place for seating pupils in formal rows (SED, 1965, pp. 67–68).

Arranging children in rows is often associated with the custom of seating pupils in order of 'merit', a practice which the Memorandum specifically condemns. But the document's strictures on testing go beyond this. Tests, it claims, are accorded too much importance, take up too much time and have a deleterious effect on the curriculum. Poetry, art and music should never be examined, and testing is also inappropriate if history, geography and science are to proceed by way of discovery and enquiry. A distinction is drawn between testing (which is seen as dubious) and assessment (which is not): assessment is primarily to be conducted through the teacher's day-to-day observation. Such assessment is essential for the teacher's purposes, and the need for diagnosis is one factor which may legitimately require recourse to formal testing (SED, 1965, pp. 48–9).

Much of the Memorandum philosophy has come to be accepted to the point where it constitutes a well-established norm. Arguably, it has influenced practice to the point where practitioners now see nothing distinctive in how they teach: it sometimes takes visitors from overseas to register surprise at the absence of the formal traditionalism which many expect to find in Scottish classrooms to remind practitioners that Scottish primary education is indeed child-centred. In the course of their initial teacher education, taken at one of a limited number of training institutions, all primary teachers are socialised into a child-centred approach whether they know it or not. As will be shown later, however, this fundamental philosophy has been subject to qualification in recent years.

THE POLITICS OF PROGRESSIVISM

The Primary Memorandum did not arrive in 1965 as news from nowhere. It has been noted that this kind of thinking had already been in evidence in colleges and universities, and that much of it was anticipated in the writing of Rousseau two hundred years earlier. An explanation has to be found, however, for the child-centred approach being officially sanctioned and endorsed at this time, and for this it is necessary to look beyond schooling to consider some relevant social and political factors.

Acclaim for the Memorandum philosophy required a particular kind of climate. The sixties brought with them a sense of impending change on a radical scale. Everyone was to be liberated from repressive conventions and pointless pressures to conform. The insistence on the right to pursue one's individual lifestyle plus the newly available contraceptive pill led to a reaction against puritanical restrictions in a movement towards what was called 'permissiveness', a term which at that point was used for purposes of approbation. In 'Annus Mirabilis' Philip Larkin famously recorded:

> Sexual intercourse began
> In nineteen sixty-three
> (Which was rather late for me) –
> Between the end of the Chatterley ban
> And the Beatles' first LP

Also in 1963 came the fall of Harold Macmillan, whose slogan 'You've never had it so good' was popularly paraphrased as 'We've never had it so often'. In this context the Conservative Party was beginning to appear woefully out of touch, an impression fatally confirmed by replacing Macmillan with a peer of the realm. Swiftly reduced from the House of Lords to become an elected MP with a Scottish seat, Douglas-Home was asked whether he would be buying a house in his new Perthshire constituency and replied that he owned too many houses already. The Conservatives lost power the following year.

The 'establishment' became a target to be challenged, rejected and mocked. To shock and to scandalise was easy, was fun and, for some, was also profitable. With hindsight, much of this 'radicalism' seems puzzlingly innocuous. Malcolm Muggeridge achieved massive notoriety from some mildly critical observations on the monarchy, remarks which he later claimed were 'sensible' and 'amiable'. And he himself turned censorious when he resigned as rector of Edinburgh University in protest against the new and decadent values of Edinburgh students, their offence being to campaign for the installation of contraceptive dispensers in their union.

Macmillan's legacy was a popular conviction that Britain had a prosperous future. The vaguely egalitarian sentiments of the subsequent Labour government converted this into a belief that some of the nation's apparently plentiful resources should be channelled into sections of society which had not to date received a fair deal. The widely held, if optimistic, belief was that such prioritising in education would unlock the potential not just of countless individuals but of society's future development.

It is not hard to see connections between this social climate and the philosophy being forged in primary education in Scotland. The Primary Memorandum represents a reaction against the old ways. People wanted a better, happier childhood for their offspring, and this included their schooling. The new philosophy appeared to be based on scientific findings about child development; and it took a positive view of the potential of each parent's child. Egalitarianism was also reflected in a major rethinking of a different sector of schooling: secondary schools were to become comprehensive (see Chapter 4). This had an important repercussion for the primary sector since the selectivity exercise involving examinations at the end of the primary years was no longer required. The 'qualifying' examination, like any such examination, dictated the form of the curriculum in the later years. When this straitjacket was removed, a curriculum vacuum was created, and was to be filled by the new primary philosophy.

This, however, is to make change seem easy; in fact there have been significant modifications to the thinking of the sixties, often prompted by concerns about a struggling economy and rising unemployment. Reaction, though certainly evident in Scotland, has been much more strident south of the border where the Plowden Report (1967), which repeated much of the thinking of the Primary Memorandum, came to acquire demonological status in the 1990s.

One factor which helped to bring the new educational thinking under critical scrutiny was the change in atmosphere not in primary schools but in universities. The 1960s was a time of student unrest. Universities were criticised for seeing learning in terms of the expertise and interests of traditional university teachers. There was a demand for a more holistic view of knowledge crediting everyone with insight and understanding. There was a suspicion among British students that continental left-wing theory was not taken adequately into account; nor were Eastern forms of thought. Even rationality itself was viewed as constituting a limiting framework, at least in its most conventional forms. To some professors all this appeared as an appalling challenge, academically, professionally and personally, threatening all that they held dear, including their own positions. And some saw it as the logical extension of the new primary school philosophy with its apparently anti-authoritarian ideas and its rejection of a subject-centred curriculum.

Significant critical volumes appeared in 1969. One was *Perspectives on Plowden* edited by R. S. Peters who held the chair of Philosophy of Education at London University's Institute of Education and who was the most influential educational philosopher in the country. The book offered negative appraisals of some of the key concepts in child-centred thinking – growth, needs and interests. The other major publication in that year was the first of a series of Black Papers published by the Critical Quarterly Society and edited by two English dons, C. B. Cox and A. E. Dyson. This took a much more abrasive and confrontational line. While the first issue was primarily concerned with higher education, the link was already being made with primary education; and in subsequent issues this became a principal focus of concern. The thinking of the Black Papers was so much at odds with mainstream 1960s thinking that it was readily – too readily – ridiculed. What was not then foreseen was that many of its seemingly eccentric ideas would in the 1980s become adopted as policy by a Conservative government.

The Thatcher and Major governments played a role in education which was directive to an extent unimaginable in the period after the war. In England the single most striking development was the imposition of a detailed National Curriculum consisting of ten school subjects. Previously the curriculum had been treated as the preserve of teachers, but under the new arrangements there was said to be a division of spheres of influence: what was to be taught would be laid down, while how it was to be taught would be left to the professional judgement of teachers. In 1991, however, this differentiation seemed to be challenged when the government commissioned a report on English primary teaching from three educationists whose views were already well known. They recommended more whole-class teaching and more subject-based lessons; topic-based enquiry and discovery methods were said to have contributed to underachievement (Alexander et al, 1992). In the eyes of many, the Plowden Report was discredited. In 1992 C. B. Cox wrote in the *Sunday Times* (26 January) that from the very start he had seen it as a 'disaster'. And Rhodes Boyson declared: 'It destroyed the academic opportunities of two, if not three, generations of children'. At the Conservative Party Conference in 1991 John Major intoned: 'The progressive theorists have had their say, and they have had their day'. The *Sunday Times* itself pronounced that the Plowden Report had been 'laid to rest without mourners'.

The extreme, polemical and essentially primitive arguments against progressivism during this period were far from impressive. What was produced by politicians, journalists and academics was less a critique than an assault. If some of this was motivated by a belief that it would gain public support, such judgements seem at best to have been unreliable. In the course of the 1997 general election campaign, John Major declared his enthusiasm for reintroducing selective secondary schooling ('a grammar school in every town'); the Conservative Party was routed by the electorate.

CHANGE AND CONTINUITY

The pattern of the 1997 election results is instructive, with Scotland returning no Conservative members of Parliament. This suggests a significant difference in the climate of ideas north and south of the border. The political situation throughout the Thatcher and Major regimes was that Scotland continued to return a majority of Labour MPs. There was, therefore, a real sense in which Conservative ideas were consistently rejected; and this had an important bearing on educational policy at the primary school stage. One of the most visible consequences of the disharmony between the government and the social culture of

Scotland was the resistance in 1991 to the introduction of standardised testing for all pupils in Primary 4 (eight year olds) and Primary 7 (eleven year olds): the Conservative education minister was forced to withdraw this proposal in the face of determined opposition from teachers and parents alike.

In Scotland, the central feature of the 1990s at the curriculum level has been the development of the 5–14 programme. This envisages a curriculum consisting principally of five broad areas, for each of which there is a set of guidelines intended to represent best practice. This programme evolved through a process of consultation, with Conservative ministers tending to exert pressure along relatively traditionalist lines; for example, one education minister was anxious to see history and geography taught as separate subjects. The programme has been implemented gradually by schools, which have characteristically devoted time set aside for in-service work to consider how the recommendations can best be adapted and fleshed out. The complete programme should be in place by 1999. In each curriculum area it is envisaged that the pupil will progress through five defined 'levels', although it is recognised that pupils will advance at different rates. Externally devised tests are intended to confirm the teacher's judgement about the stage which the pupil has reached, and are used at whatever point the teacher thinks they are appropriate.

The 5–14 programme obviously extends beyond the primary school, and deliberately so, since it is intended to promote continuity between primary and secondary education. But clearly it also has the potential to ensure continuity within the primary school; there is no longer any possibility of individual teachers devising wholly individual or idiosyncratic curricula. Unlike the English National Curriculum, the Scottish programme does not have the force of law: for this to happen would require major change, since the statutory powers of the Secretary of State for Scotland are confined to the issuing of 'guidance' on the curriculum. In practical terms, however, observance of the guidelines is mandatory: they constitute an important part of the framework which the inspectorate uses to judge the work of a school, and no school can today afford to risk an adverse judgement.

The development of national guidelines has not been accompanied by a return to traditional teaching methods. The Inspectorate's recommendation is that there should be variety in teaching methods, with teachers considering which method is most appropriate to each particular piece of learning. Echoing the Memorandum, the Inspectorate publication, *5–14: A Practical Guide* (1994), states: 'Class, group and individual methods all have their place in promoting effective learning and teaching'. Activity methods and enquiry methods are seen as suitable. In the *Guide*, the Inspectorate continues to employ the concept of 'child-centred learning', a phrase which, incidentally, never appears in the Primary Memorandum.

The main change which has taken place in the practice of primary education has been one of curriculum structuring. While this is inevitably designed centrally, there remains scope for decision-making at the level of the school and the individual teacher. It seems reasonable to view this as child-centred education rendered systematic. The philosophy of Scottish primary education, as outlined in the Primary Memorandum, seems not to have been rejected, but continues to be seen as generally acceptable to both teachers and parents; and there is also continued recognition of the value of the Memorandum methods. It is recognised that different children develop at different speeds. And because there has been no adoption of a ten-subject curriculum, Scotland has been able to retain a relatively fluid and flexible curriculum, the interpretation and implementation of which depend heavily on the professional judgement of teachers, either individually or collectively.

If this assessment is correct, it has to be asked why the Scots have largely abstained from the disparagement of educational progressivism and the primary teaching profession which adopted it, which has characterised discussions of child-centred primary education in England. The answer seems to be that in Scotland there is no widespread tension between parents and teachers because in Scottish primary schools, however child-centred, teachers continue to be very much as parents expect them to be. Primary teachers in Scotland have traditionally enjoyed a significant measure of respect, and not without reason. Reflecting the importance attached to education in Scotland, these teachers have themselves been well educated people. From as early as 1926 all male primary teachers were required to hold university degrees, and Scotland's teaching force became all-graduate in advance of teachers in England. From 1966 onwards, with the advent of the General Teaching Council for Scotland, it became impossible to teach without a professional qualification.

It can further be argued that Scottish teachers, perhaps like Scots generally, are rather conservative: deviant thinkers find other occupations to pursue. This is not to say that there is in the profession a hostility to new ideas or an unwillingness to change; but innovations are adopted cautiously and judiciously (see Chapter 10). Child-centred education had to be tried and tested. In England this philosophy was occasionally given a libertarian inter-pretation; and this produced some outlandish school regimes which brought the new approach into disrepute. It is unsurprising that Scotland's primary teachers generated no such fiascos. It is true that the Primary Memorandum modified understanding of educational aims: pupils were to be independent learners, flexible thinkers and well-rounded people. But at the core remained the business of learning; and the child-centred approach was valued as an intelligent and efficient means to this end. In short, child-centred education has tended to be relatively well received in Scotland because it has been practised in a level-headed form. And teachers remained where they had always been – firmly in charge. The relatively high standing of teachers combined with a social culture which is supportive of trade unionism, brought about a powerful profession. One outcome of this is the agreement forced through by the profession on class sizes: no primary class can have more that thirty-three pupils. With such numbers not only are group methods possible, but order tends to prevail.

While the abandoning of classroom authority would be anathema to parents as well as to teachers, at least discipline is now exercised along more humane lines than previously. The eventual abolition of corporal punishment, however, is an achievement for which no-one in Scottish education can be given the credit. Pusillanimously, the educational progressives who wrote the Primary Memorandum refrained from pronouncing on what they described as 'a controversial issue', and contented themselves with recommending that the use of the belt should be reviewed by the profession. Children continued to be belted frequently throughout the 1960s and 1970s. In an enquiry conducted by the Scottish Council for Research in Education (*Pupils' Attitudes to School Rules and Punishments*, 1977) 84 per cent of boys at secondary school reported that they had been belted in primary school, with 34 per cent saying they had been belted 'quite often'. For the girls the corresponding figures were 57 per cent and 13 per cent. In the spring term of 1972 the belt was used four thousand times in Edinburgh's primary schools. The ready application of the belt was constantly glossed over by the profession, with teachers' unions falsely claiming that corporal punishment was used only as 'a last resort'. And if the frequency of belting was seldom reported, what was never remarked on was how hard children were struck. If an errant dog had been dealt such blows, the perpetrator could have been arrested.

Demand for change was confined to a minority amongst both teachers and parents. In the event, abolition was brought about from outside. Two Scottish mothers insisted that their education authority should guarantee that their children would not receive corporal punishment. When their request was refused, a complaint was lodged with the European Commission on Human Rights. In 1982 the European Court ruled that parental objections to corporal punishment had to be respected. Some Scottish authorities began to phase it out, and the House of Commons finally voted for abolition in 1986.

The profession's dragging of heels on this issue shows the conservatism of Scottish education at its worst. But the practice of corporal punishment alongside progressive teaching methods for the best part of two decades does seem to confirm the view that child-centred education was implemented in a way that allowed considerable continuity in the nature of primary schooling: children were to learn and teachers were to remain in authority. It seems likely that its adoption of a non-radical interpretation of child-centred education protected Scottish primary education from the kind of anti-progressive backlash experienced in England. Developments since the late 1980s designed to ensure that the child-centred approach is well structured and managed suggest that primary education will continue in this vein for the foreseeable future.

REFERENCES

Alexander, R., J. Rose and C. Woodhead (1992) *Curriculum Organisation and Classroom Practice in Primary Schools: A Discussion Paper,* London: Department of Education and Science.

Farquharson, E. (1985) The making of the Primary Memorandum, *Scottish Educational Review*, vol. 17, no. 1, pp. 23–32.

McEnroe, F. J. (1983) Freudianism, bureaucracy and Scottish primary education, in W. M. Humes and H. M. Paterson (eds), *Scottish Culture and Scottish Education 1800–1980*, Edinburgh: John Donald, pp. 244–66.

Paterson L. (1996) Liberation or control: what are the Scottish education traditions of the twentieth century?, in T. Devine and R. Finlay (eds) *Scotland in the Twentieth Century*, Edinburgh: Edinburgh University Press, pp. 230–49.

SED (1965) *Primary Education in Scotland*, Edinburgh: HMSO.

SOED (1994) *5–14: A Practical Guide*, Edinburgh: HMSO.

4

Scottish Secondary Education: Philosophy and Practice

Tom Bryce and Walter Humes

PHILOSOPHY AND HISTORY: 'COMPREHENSIVE' EDUCATION?

Some 95 per cent of Scottish pupils receive their secondary education in all-through comprehensive schools catering for the age-range 12–18. This uniformity of provision can be interpreted in several ways. It can be seen as an expression of social unity enabling the vast majority of youngsters to share a broadly similar education prior to entering the adult world in which they will pursue different personal and occupational pathways. It can also be regarded as a manifestation of the democratic will, endorsed at successive general elections in Scotland and surviving even the attacks of the Thatcher years. And it can be viewed as a statement of belief in equality of opportunity whereby all secondary pupils, regardless of class, gender or ethnic background, have a chance to develop knowledge and skills and experience a sense of achievement.

These three principles – social unity, democracy and equality – are sometimes linked to that rather amorphous idea of the Scottish tradition in education (see Chapter 10) which serves an important function in social and political consciousness. Scotland's national identity is defined partly in terms of communal solidarity, a belief in democratic processes and a commitment to social justice. There is, of course, an element of myth in this self-perception but, at the levels at which invocation of the Scottish tradition usually operates – political debate and journalistic rhetoric – strict adherence to reality, past or present, is not necessary. As McPherson and Raab note (in *Governing Education*, Edinburgh University Press, 1988, p. 407) 'myth is simultaneously expressive and explanatory. It is about hearts and minds. It asserts identity, celebrates values, and explains the world through them.' The story (or myth) that Scots tell themselves about the principles underlying secondary education is not to be dismissed as fiction. Rather it is to be understood as one reading – a partial reading – of how the present system has evolved. Partial readings also manifest themselves in operational definitions of what comprehensive schooling means. For some it means non-selection on the basis of ability; for others it relates principally to neighbourhood schooling, and for others again it is most concerned with a common curriculum. Depending on which of these operational definitions is highlighted one will have a different conception of what a comprehensive school is or should be. A particular problem with the internal coherence of the comprehensive philosophy relates to the justification in terms of social unity. Generally, social unity applies in relation to class, gender and ethnic background but in Scotland it does not apply to religion where the principle of divided secondary education has been accepted and endorsed in law since 1918. In West Central Scotland in particular there is widespread provision for children to attend separate Catholic primary and secondary schools. These exist alongside non-denominational schools. Other chapters in this volume provide detail of this significant aspect of Scottish education (see Chapters 24 and 97 in particular).

A brief excursion into the recent history of Scottish secondary education will serve to indicate some of the other elements in the 'comprehensive' story that are often forgotten. It was not until 1936 that the right of all pupils to receive secondary education was officially recognised by the Scottish Education Department. Prior to that, various forms of post-elementary education were available up to the statutory leaving age of 14 (later raised to 15 and then 16) but it was believed that only a minority of pupils could benefit from advanced schooling. George Macdonald, Secretary of the SED from 1922 to 1928, stated confidently that 'the school population falls into two parts – the majority of distinctly limited intelligence, and an extremely able minority drawn from all ranks and classes who are capable of responding to a much more severe call . . . The type [of education] that is best for one is not necessarily the best for the other, and attempts to establish equivalence may result in harm to both' (quoted in Paterson, 'Incubus and Ideology: The Development of Secondary Schooling in Scotland, 1900–1939' in Humes and Paterson, eds *Scottish Culture and Scottish Education, 1800–1980*, John Donald, 1983, pp. 208–209). Macdonald's statement that the able minority is 'drawn from all ranks and classes' can be seen as an attempt to counteract the criticism that SED policy at that time was class-based and elitist. Ability, not social origin, was to be the determining factor, thus enabling that part of the Scottish tradition which emphasises equality of opportunity to be maintained – at least at the level of political discourse. In this, educational administrators were aided by the work of psychologists who developed mental tests which, they claimed, provided reliable measurements of general intelligence of a kind that had predictive value in relation to pupil capability and achievement. Scotland, through the work of Sir Godfrey Thomson and others, was at the forefront of the mental testing movement. Policy makers eagerly embraced the claims of the psychometrists, seeing in them a ready justification for limited (or, later, divided) provision of secondary education. Sir Godfrey Thomson himself was disarmingly frank in his view of schooling:

> [It] acts as a sieve, or a succession of sieves, sorting out pupils into different kinds. In its crude form this idea presents the picture of a ladder of education, up which a competing crowd start, the weaklings to be elbowed off as they endeavour to climb . . . This picture is somewhat repellent . . . Since, however, people clearly differ in their qualities and abilities, it is certain that a period of education will always be a period of sorting. (quoted in Paterson, op. cit. p. 212).

Arguments of this kind continued to operate in the period after the Second World War when the junior/senior secondary system became formalised. Towards the end of their primary schooling, Scottish children were assessed by means of the so-called 'qualifying' examination which was used to determine the type of secondary school to which they would be sent. Junior secondary schools provided three-year courses, largely of a non-academic kind, for pupils who would cease their formal education at fifteen. Senior secondary schools provided five-year courses of academic education leading to Scottish Leaving Certificate examinations (the entry route to higher education). In the 1950s some 35 per cent of the secondary school population in Scotland gained admission to senior secondary schools. In

England during the same period only 20 per cent of pupils gained places at grammar schools (the equivalent of Scottish senior secondary schools). Thus Scotland could claim to be relatively democratic in its provision. Furthermore, in small towns and rural communities, where numbers could not justify the creation of separate schools, 'omnibus' schools catered for the full ability range but with strictly demarcated courses for those who 'passed' and 'failed' the qualifying examination.

Politicians and administrators claimed that junior and senior secondary schools were accorded parity of esteem: they were simply catering for different needs. This was never a convincing argument. Senior secondaries always enjoyed much better provision in terms of buildings, equipment and teaching staff. Other arguments against selection began to emerge. Research evidence cast doubt on the fairness and reliability of the qualifying examination and its English equivalent (the 11-plus). Sociological research concluded that there was indeed a strong social class factor in the allocation of pupils to different types of secondary schooling: working class pupils were disadvantaged in the process of selection. The whole notion of a limited pool of ability was disputed. Instead of early labelling, it was argued, a system which offered opportunity to as many young people as possible would reap benefits not only in terms of individual achievement but also in terms of wider social utility.

The case for fully comprehensive secondary education, admitting all pupils to the same school on a non-selective basis, was made with increasing force. As early as 1947 the Scottish Advisory Council on Education had recommended a comprehensive system together with a common curriculum core and a common examination. This recommendation was ignored by the SED but in the more egalitarian climate following the Second World War it was only a matter of time before the case was won. The process was not painless, however. It is often said that the prior existence of a significant number of omnibus schools north of the border made comprehensivisation much easier than in England, but here too there were bitter arguments about the alleged destruction of schools with fine academic traditions, as John Watt has shown (PhD thesis, University of Glasgow, 1992). And even after the formal decision was taken in 1965 to implement a fully comprehensive system (by which time one-fifth of secondary schools were already comprehensive, admittedly with streamed classes on entry, according to Gray, McPherson and Raffe, 1983) there was much debate about what precisely this should mean and many traditional practices persisted. The development of comprehensive education within secondary schools since then has been rather uneven, certainly during the years of the Conservative government (1979–97) where there were instances of policy change consistent with the concept of social unity (e.g. 'mainstreaming') but rather more where policy change was designed to counter it (e.g. parental choice). To an extent what pupils encounter in secondary schools varies with the relative affluence or poverty of the neighbourhood setting and in the conurbations of the central belt there is probably more variation amongst schools than elsewhere in the country. The parental choice legislation of the 1980s served to manipulate the intake of individual schools, such are the powerful perceptions of the curricula on offer and of the behavioural contagion of the pupils in particular areas. These perceptions have impact upon the philosophy and practice of secondary education.

THE EFFECTS OF PARENTAL CHOICE

The Education (Scotland) Act of 1981 giving parents choice of school, subject to availability of places, has resulted in a substantial minority of pupils (some 10 per cent on average by the late 1990s) attending schools other than their local secondary, that is schools perceived to be desirable, the so-called 'magnet' schools. Inevitably this has altered the range of abilities of pupils attending particular schools and it is sometimes said that schools in certain communities have their tops 'creamed off' as a result. Coupled with legislation concerning standards and accountability, Scotland has had to contend with league tables of its secondary schools, especially those ranked according to academic results – for example, numbers of Standard Grade Credit awards gained by S4 candidates; numbers of Higher Grade C+ passes in S5 – and of course league table positions bolster public perceptions. (Unlike England and Wales, Scottish primary school national test results cannot be assembled for this purpose.) There is widespread belief in the teaching profession that league tables substantially reflect catchment intake rather than school output, and this is especially detrimental in circumstances where home support for scholastic effort by pupils is lacking.

In a pointedly entitled article in the *Times Educational Supplement Scotland* of 10 January 1997, 'How Mean Can An Average Be?', the Headteacher of Bannerman High School in the east end of Glasgow analysed the published figures for his own school by its rather distinctive catchment areas. The overall 'average' performance figures for the school disguise marked correlations between examination results, pupil behaviour and postal code areas. While the directions of the correlations may be unsurprising (the more socially deprived areas having poorer results, lower attendance records and more referrals to the children's panel) their extent is marked. As the Headteacher notes, parents from the more advantaged areas would no doubt be delighted to see the awards for their children appearing in the league tables. The public record for schools deals with such 'averages' and crude judgements are made of schools (and therefore teachers) as a consequence. Perhaps worst of all, league tables mask the determined and often successful efforts which schools now take to counter difficulties – supported study classes, study skill courses, tutoring arrangements during senior school examination preparation. The understandable concerns of the Bannerman Headteacher need to be set alongside the growing body of evidence deriving from school effectiveness and school improvement studies (see Chapter 89) that, even in disadvantaged areas, the efforts of teachers can make a difference.

Following the arrival of the Labour government in 1997 and the antipathy felt by the Scottish Education Minister towards league tables of raw results, versions in 1998 and beyond will carry so-called 'added-value' measures. 'Parent-friendly' details will be provided for each subject department to show what departments add by way of value to pupil achievements as they move from Standard to Higher Grade, together with between-subject differences (within schools) and subject differences between schools across the country. The hard facts are, however, that it is now no longer the case that Scottish secondary schools exclusively serve their local communities; the 'magnets' have become more attractive, while the so-called 'sink' schools fight to stay open, the parental choice policy having coincided with the declining birth rate and falling school rolls. It is difficult to imagine that revised ways of publishing academic results will do much to reverse this trend. Indeed a significant dimension to primary-secondary liaison in some urban schools involves secondary principal teachers unashamedly touting for business during visits to their associated ('feeder') primaries.

In the City of Glasgow, a radical reform of secondary provision is under way which runs counter to the idea of the traditional comprehensive school. This is intended to effect nine school closures and to rationalise the remainder, so saving on an over-supply position of 40 per cent. (In 1997, thirty-eight secondary schools with a capacity for 49,000 places held 29,000 pupils.) The reform plan develops the notion of specialisms for particular schools (dance, music, sport, etc.) and argues for more relevant and flexible curricula. Unashamedly, it runs counter to the concept of the neighbourhood school: 'The proposals [concerning alterations to placement request criteria and to assistance with transport] signify an important departure from territorial planning. The next step would be to abandon catchment areas from all secondary schools' (*Reform of Secondary Education in Glasgow. 'Our Children; our schools; their future'*, Glasgow City Council Consultation Document, November 1997).

From a different perspective, the 1981 Education (Scotland) Act made many secondary schools more comprehensive in pupil character by giving parents whose children would otherwise attend special schools the opportunity to have them taught in mainstream schools. Not only do many comprehensives now take pupils who were formerly educated outwith the mainstream, some have adapted their buildings (e.g. physical access for wheelchair pupils) or their facilities (e.g. specialised equipment for pupils with visual or hearing impairments). Some have completely integrated local special school provision; others have formed particular links with retained special schools, ensuring two-way benefits to pupils and the good use of specialist expertise. The actual pattern of provision varies throughout the country. (See Chapters 90 and 91 for aspects of learning support and specialised provision available in many schools.)

THE SUBJECT-CENTREDNESS OF THE SECONDARY CURRICULUM

It may be an international cliché to say that 'primary teachers teach children and secondary teachers teach subjects' but it is certainly true of Scotland where all-through (six year) comprehensive secondary schools are marked by a subject-centredness of long-standing (and indeed some conservatism). Most of the subjects pre-date comprehensivisation and they were the hallmarks of the senior, but not the junior, secondary schools which preceded them. If the comprehensive ideal in Scotland is characterised by social unity, by equality of access and opportunity and one asks: Access to what?, then one would still have to say to an essentially academic diet driven by subject departments. Even the recent and largely successful moves to give more vocational emphasis to the upper secondary school have been, on the whole, delivered departmentally. Subjects seem to need departments and the working of departments preserves the status quo, resisting that which does not fit. In Scotland's secondary schools it is very evident that the curricular influences are top-down; what goes on in S1 is determined more by what goes on in S5 than by what goes on in P7. When the Munn report addressed the S3–S4 curriculum in the 1970s, the effect was to rationalise and support the existence of subjects (even if the argument was presented in terms of modes, based on Hirst's forms of knowledge). So novel possibilities such as conceptualising the secondary curriculum in different ways, perhaps through issues or school-wide topics, or introducing new subject matter drawing from the social sciences, were not agreed to in Munn and the secondary curriculum has become justified in terms of, and dominated by, its (compulsory) core of traditional subjects.

This core has meant that book-knowledge has tended to be valued at the expense of much else, with the consequence that what is expected for less able pupils working at the Foundation levels of Standard Grade is less demanding but broadly similar in nature (at worst being criticised as merely 'watered-down academic knowledge'). Across the ability range, the innovations of Standard Grade in the 1980s to broaden what should be learned beyond 'knowledge and understanding' were fairly hard fought battles. Practical abilities, investigative skills, problem-solving, oral abilities and so forth got into the secondary curriculum, within subjects, but the strain they create for assessment and certification means they remain somewhat curtailed, indeed are under pressure to be reduced (see Chapter 78 on Assessment), and Higher Still is unlikely to yield further real developments on this front. Given recent challenges to educational thinking to view human potential as multi-dimensional, say from Howard Gardner's 'multiple intelligences' or from Daniel Goleman's 'emotional intelligence', one would have to admit to resistance in Scotland; Scottish educators remain fairly one-dimensional in their outlook (but are probably no different from their English or European counterparts). The emphasis in Scottish secondary education is and always has been upon subject-ability.

EVIDENCE ON THE SUCCESS OF SUBJECTS

Evidence on the success of this orientation is mixed. Benn and Chitty's recent survey of UK schools led them to conclude that Scotland's comprehensives stood out from those in all other areas of the UK. On several indicators, including quality of academic results, staying-on rates and the achievement of vocational qualifications, Scotland is ahead (Benn and Chitty, 1996). This, they argue, is despite Conservative government policies intended to undermine the comprehensive system in Scotland as elsewhere. England may, however, be a poor comparator with which to assess the achievements of Scottish secondary school pupils. Successive reports of the Organisation for Economic Co-operation and Development (OECD) suggest that, on a number of criteria, Scotland compares badly with other developed industrial countries. International studies are notoriously difficult because it is not always possible to obtain data that can be compared directly. Nevertheless, the pattern over a five-year period consistently suggests that the traditional view that Scottish education is among the best in the world is now questionable. Part of the explanation offered by the OECD is under-investment. In terms of the percentage of its gross domestic product devoted to education, the UK as a whole was ranked twenty-third out of twenty-five countries in the most recent survey.

Clearly these judgements about relative success involve many other factors than the structure of the curriculum. What is worth noting, however, is that the curriculum and assessment reforms in Scotland over the last two decades have not challenged subject-centredness in any fundamental way. Even the 5–14 Development Programme, deliberately designed to bring the primary and secondary sectors together, adopted subjects as the basic curriculum unit. The terms used for the curricular areas were certainly primary-friendly (Expressive Arts, Environmental Studies etc.) but their actual content deliberately introduced the detail of secondary subject matter to primary schools.

The Scottish Office Report on *Standards and Quality in Scottish Schools 1992–95* (SOEID, 1996) summarises the strengths and weaknesses detected during that period through the inspections of primary and secondary schools by Her Majesty's Inspectorate (HMI). Breadth of the curriculum is a strength firmly identified in both sectors (and, appropriately, in accord with the first word in the 5–14 Curriculum mantra: 'breadth, balance, continuity, coherence and progression'). For secondary schools, this strength is contrasted with weaknesses in S1 and S2 where insufficient challenge to pupils was detected, and the implementation of 5–14 programmes described as slow, in rather many schools. Later chapters in this volume set out the relatively disappointing pupil achieve-ment data for S1–S2 revealed in a succession of national surveys in English language, in Mathematics and in Science (see Chapter 85). These results accord with the HMI findings and serve to underline the point that Scottish schools do have difficulties at these particular stages. Chapter 78 notes the determined response by SOEID in the case of mathematics teaching. The more general point is that subject specialisation (the main plank of the much vaunted 'breadth') which starts with S1 fails to connect well with pupils and their demonstrated achievements (as shown in Assessment of Achievement Programme surveys) at P7.

It is tempting to deduce that the identity of subjects with departments, and therefore with teachers who work very much independently of teachers in other subjects, is a big part of the problem. Subjects occupy the high ground in secondary education; subject depart-ments are the citadels of power; their structured independence is a serious obstacle in the way of 'continuity, coherence and progression'.

SOEID (1996) records other strengths of secondaries: the good standards in S3–S6 (e.g. the 4 per cent national increase in Standard Grade Credit results over the period 1992–5); learning and teaching at the upper stages (in S5 and S6 described as 'good or very good' in 80 per cent of schools); the positive ethos of schools; their resources; their leadership; and the operations of school development planning. HMI have issued separate reports on almost all of the subjects of the secondary curriculum, in each case drawing upon inspection evidence obtained across lengthy periods (in some cases over ten years). These appear in the series *Effective Learning and Teaching in Scottish Secondary Schools* and are worthy of close reading: publication dates are *Modern Languages* 1990; *History, Modern Studies, English*, all 1992; *Mathematics, Computing*, both in 1993; *Sciences, Religious Education*, both in 1994; *Geography* in 1995; *Home Economics* and *Guidance*, both in 1996; and *Business Education and Economics* in 1997. In all of these, the dedication and commitment of teachers to their subjects is underlined.

THE QUALITY OF LEARNING

The five terms in the 5–14 Curriculum mantra were of course coined to stress the desirably wide range of ideas and skills which pupils should learn as they progress through school. It seems a pity that other equally important terms were not added to 'the five', notably depth and choice. The depth or quality of one's learning, its meaningfulness and significance to the individual, is of vital consequence. As a principle for reflection upon the effectiveness of schooling, 'depth or quality of learning' surely deserves centre stage. Pupils' testimonies as well as research cast some doubts on the true significance of the expanding success rates in secondary certificate numbers at S4–S6. For example, the success of the three science subjects at S5 (they come third, fourth and fifth after the compulsory core subjects English and Mathematics) stands in contrast to the findings from research on adults' grasp of basic science concepts and processes, as revealed in all the 'public understanding of science' literature (see T. G. K. Bryce, 'Towards the Achievement of Scientific Capability', *Scottish Educational Review*, 28.2, pp. 90–9, 1996). In their everyday lives a few years away from school, people show a less than impressive grasp of much of their very specialised learning from the subjects they studied at school. Moreover, anecdotal evidence would suggest that very many pupils indulge in rote learning at the certificate stages, and get away with it. On this, however, Scotland is probably no different from any other country.

In this context the SCCC document *Teaching for Effective Learning* (SCCC, 1996) may be regarded as unusual. Designed to encourage critical reflection by teachers on their teaching strategies, this discussion paper outlines what is known about how people learn and how effective teachers operate. The achievement of meaningful learning where young people are able to reason confidently and use skills and knowledge in real settings are desired targets for education which seem to sit uneasily with the plethora of certificates which mark the end of secondary school. The SCCC document could be said to challenge the celebrated confidence traditionally held for the subject-dominated secondary subject curriculum. It asks teachers to address fundamental questions about their approaches to teaching, including the following:

- How often do I encourage learners to think for themselves and to try out new ideas?
- What techniques do I use to help learners to be more aware of how best they learn and why?
- What assumptions do I make about individual learners when I teach? On what are these assumptions based?
- How would I describe the climate I am seeking to establish in the classroom? What do I say and do to go about establishing this climate? (SCCC, 1996, p. 33).

Encouraging teachers to reflect on these issues as part of the process of professional self-development involves shifting the focus from concerns about curriculum content to questions of pupil engagement and motivation, and pedagogical style. The right conditions for successful learning are thus seen as an essential precursor to the acquisition of subject knowledge.

The thinking behind the SCCC document may serve to challenge the strong degree of intellectual and psychological attachment which most secondary teachers have to their subject. There are other forces at work which may intensify that challenge: the emphasis on cross-curricular 'core skills' in Higher Still; concerns about the negative effects of departmentalism in relation to the S1 and S2 stages of the 5–14 Programme; managerial perceptions that excessive subject-mindedness on the part of teachers can be a barrier to change. The capacity of the teaching force to resist these pressures should not, however, be underestimated. They are likely to have the support not only of the Educational Institute of Scotland (EIS) but also of the General Teaching Council (GTC), whose history is in part a story of careful gatekeeping to ensure that entry to the ranks of secondary teaching is closely linked to formal qualifications in the subject(s) to be taught. This is still regarded as more important than any generic skill in teaching or understanding of the processes of learning.

MIXED-ABILITY TEACHING IN S1 AND S2

Any discussion of teaching for effective learning or of the problems in S1 and S2 is bound to raise the question of how teachers organise their pupils. For several decades the prevailing pattern has been for mixed ability classes to be formed from the intakes from primary school. In official reports, encouragement has been given to teachers to vary their methods and grouping arrangements to suit their particular purposes (therefore sometimes exploiting 'whole class teaching', sometimes using group work, sometimes individualised schemes of instruction). A detailed examination of this matter is given in Chapter 44. It is useful at this juncture to note that secondary subjects vary somewhat in their preferences for mixed ability teaching. It has been common, for example, to find English and Science departments embracing it positively (using group and paired teaching methods not very different from those which most pupils will be comfortable with from their time in primary school) while the Mathematics departments in the same schools are more inclined to set pupils early. The assessment and reporting procedures developed by the 5–14 Development programme are having a significant impact, with P7 achievement grades accompanying pupils as they move into secondary school. Thus having detailed records of who has reached level D, who is only at C, etc. is heightening the debate at S1 as to how pupils should be grouped for teaching purposes. At national level, the Scottish Office took a forthright stance on the matter in *Achievement for All: A report on selection within schools by HM Inspectors of Schools* (SOEID, 1996). Its recommendations favour much greater use of attainment groups and setting as the means of organising pupils; 'direct teaching' is encouraged and said to be more feasible when pupils are set by ability (within subjects). The report was published as a direct follow-on to *Standards and Quality in Scottish Schools 1992–1995* and sets out the official reaction to the disappointments with S1–S2 performance. What is rather surprising is that the 'critical review of the literature pertaining to the ability grouping of classes and within classes' (Harlen and Malcolm, 1997) which the Scottish Office commissioned from the Scottish Council for Research in Education (SCRE) to inform the preparation of *Achievement For All* is not referred to in that publication. Harlen and Malcolm's summary of the somewhat conflicting international research, was that there is no consistent evidence in support of setting. The concerns about S1–S2 raised in SOEID (1996b) are further addressed in *Achieving Success in S1/S2. A Report on the review of provision in S1/S2 by HMI* (SOEID, 1997). The report defines 'direct teaching' in ways which most would describe as 'good teaching' and is notable for its defence of good practice preceding and following S1–S2; HMI want both the breadth advocated by the 5–14 curriculum and the specialisation which follows it, yet have difficulty in solving the problems encountered at the transition. They are forced to assert that the present S1–S2 framework (embraced in 5–14 principles and targets) both prepares pupils to continue with certain subjects and also serves as a satisfactory exit point in relation to the subjects they discontinue. It seems hard to reconcile both arguments. Perhaps the toughest line in the report is the contrast which HMI strike between the quality of the pastoral care which schools effect in the primary/secondary transfer, and the inadequacy of the subject monitoring which they find in so many schools. Thus:

> The monitoring and evaluation of pupils' academic progress in S1/S2 need to be improved in most schools. Although guidance and learning support staff generally deal well with pupils whose performance is causing significant concern to subject teachers, few schools monitor the performance of all pupils sufficiently closely. (*Achieving Success in S1/S2*, SOEID 1997, para. 3.10)

It is thus evident that discussion surrounding the somewhat disappointing achievements of pupils in S1 and S2 in Scotland is vigorous and lively. Teachers, researchers, inspectors and politicians hotly debate possible solutions. Interestingly the debate is now being conducted not in terms of ideological consistency with the comprehensive ideal but more in terms of the practical efficacy of alternative strategies.

There is much less argument about the organisation and arrangements in S3–S6, the Standard Grade programme having evolved three broad curriculum levels for S3 and S4, with the new Higher Still programme soon to put in place (rather more complex) levels for S5 and S6. Chapter 45 provides detail of the practical structures which are found in all schools; the guiding principle is that of differentiated levels with safeguards in favour of pupils when it comes to the national examinations taken at S4 and beyond. By the middle years of secondary there would appear to be widespread acceptance of curricular and assessment patterns which have been designed to encompass the whole range of pupil ability.

SCHOOL AS COMMUNITY

Secondary headteachers, even in schools which are judged successful by conventional indicators (examination success, entry to higher education, low figures for absenteeism, good discipline) would be quick to point out that the life of a secondary school involves much more than the work of subject departments. Schools provide systems of guidance and pastoral care to assist in the personal development of pupils, as well as to offer advice on curricular and vocational choice. Furthermore, they run social education programmes, which cut across subject divisions, and which deal with a wide range of issues of direct interest to young people – health, relationships, sexual behaviour, drugs, the law, personal finance. In most schools, there are well-developed links with the wider community through work experience schemes, environmental projects and charitable activities on behalf of the elderly, the handicapped and the homeless. Schools also offer the opportunity to take part in sports and hobbies, though teacher support for out-of-hours clubs and societies has never fully recovered from a period of industrial action in the 1980s when they withdrew from such activities. Nevertheless, it can reasonably be claimed that there is an 'informal' curriculum which supplements and extends the formal curriculum of subjects and departments.

The aim is to produce a climate which is felt by pupils to be supportive of their overall development. Such a climate is more likely to encourage effort and a positive outlook than one which is seen to be concerned only with academic success. This concern with the values of the school as an institution has always been a prominent feature of the Catholic sector but it is now accorded importance by all schools. There has been much interest in identifying those 'ethos indicators' which are likely to show that the values of community are present in an institution. These include strong leadership, clear goals, open communication, effective links with parents and good teacher-pupil relationships.

All of this is undoubtedly well-intentioned and, where it is successful, it is bound to be of immense benefit to pupils. However, the notion of school as community should not be overstated. Research evidence suggests that guidance provision invariably comes second to subject requirements and that many pupils are sceptical about its effectiveness (see Chapter 43). In some schools, guidance staff devote a disproportionate amount of their time to dealing with 'problem' pupils and so the more positive aspects of their work are under-developed. Again, social education programmes are variable in quality. Pupils sometimes say that they know more about the topics under consideration (e.g. drugs) than the adults leading the discussion. No doubt there is an element of teenage bravado in such responses but they suggest that the self-reporting of schools about the success of these programmes should be treated with caution. As far as extra-curricular activities are concerned, teachers themselves often admit that it is a relatively small proportion of the school population who are actively involved. Many pupils seek, and find, alternatives outside school.

To make these points is not to disparage the genuine efforts of many teachers and schools to make the experience of pupils in their care as worthwhile as possible. It is, however, to suggest two things. The first is that the dominant value system of secondary education continues to derive from the reductionist curriculum structure associated with subject departments and the extent to which academic achievement is evident. The second is that the idea of school as community may be more meaningful to teachers (and perhaps parents) than to a significant proportion of pupils. Professor David Hargreaves has argued that for some pupils schools can be more honestly compared to factories, prisons or asylums. This would involve seeing teachers as production managers, custodians or psychiatric social workers. The images are uncomfortable and no doubt unfair. But they raise disturbing questions about the purposes and effects of a social institution which is routinely assumed to do more good than harm to most of its population.

THE FUTURE OF SECONDARY EDUCATION

It has long been taken for granted in Scotland that the 12–18 all-through comprehensive school is the most rational way of organising post-primary education. The curriculum reform programme, starting with Standard Grade then the 5–14 Programme and finally Higher Still, can be seen as a statement of confidence in existing structures. Scotland has no tertiary or sixth-form colleges of the kind that exist in some parts of England. Demographic factors in many parts of the country provide compelling practical reasons for the comprehensive form of organisation: diverse provision would not be cost effective and would tend to reduce curricular choice within institutions. Furthermore, secondary headteachers argue that mixing older and younger teenagers has benefits for both in relation to progressive maturity, social responsibility and peer support.

There are, however, arguments and pressures (over and above those associated with the proposed rationalisation of provision in Glasgow, previously mentioned) which open up the possibility of alternatives. As the upper secondary school population increases (as a result of staying-on rates) the case for separate provision for post-compulsory students gains in strength. The FE sector will not be slow to see opportunities in offering an alternative to school, particularly as the new Higher Still courses come on stream. For some students the more informal climate of FE colleges will be attractive. This is a trend already in evidence in England. Another alternative has surfaced in the re-opening of the debate about the merits of middle schools catering for the 10–14 or 10–16 age range. Scotland had a brief (and geographically very restricted) flirtation with middle schools in the 1970s but they never enjoyed much support. The current concerns with progression from P6 to S2, described above, have caused some policy makers to think again about the possible attractions of middle schools. At present, however, this option is on the margins of the policy agenda rather than centre-stage.

Under New Labour it has become permissible to 'think the unthinkable' in social policy. Comprehensive education was previously a non-negotiable item in the ideology of the political left. Judging by the changes that have taken place in health and social security, this may no longer be the case. The language of choice, quality, standards and effectiveness is as much part of Labour discourse as it was of the Conservatives. Against this background, it can be expected that the concepts of democracy, equality and social unity, as applied to secondary education, will be subject to further re-definition (perhaps beyond all recognition) in the twenty-first century, just as they were modified in the course of the twentieth century.

REFERENCES

Benn, C. and C. Chitty (1996) *Thirty years on: Is Comprehensive Education Alive and Well or Struggling to Survive?* London: David Fulton Publishers.

Clark, M. M., and P. Munn (eds) (1997) *Education in Scotland. Policy and Practice from Pre-school to Secondary.* London: Routledge. [In particular see Chapter 4 by Brian Boyd, The Statutory Years of Secondary Education: Change and Progress; and Chapter 5 by David Raffe, Upper-Secondary Education].

Gray, J., A. F. McPherson and D. Raffe (1983) *Reconstructions of Secondary Education: Theory, Myth and Practice since the War.* London: Routlege and Kegan Paul.

Harlen, W. and H. Malcolm (1997) *Setting and Streaming: A Research Review,* Edinburgh: Scottish Council for Research in Education.

SCCC (1996) *Teaching for Effective Learning,* Dundee: Scottish Consultative Council on the Curriculum.

SOEID (1996) *Standards and Quality in Scottish Schools 1992–95*: A Report by HM Inspectors of Schools, Edinburgh: SOEID.

5

Further Education in Scotland Post-incorporation

Michael Leech

There are forty-five further education colleges in Scotland, of which forty-three became incorporated bodies on 1 April 1993 under the provisions of the Further and Higher Education (Scotland) Act 1992. This chapter will focus upon the incorporated colleges, which include agricultural colleges, general further education colleges, specialist colleges and one college of technology.

THE RANGE OF WORK IN THE FURTHER EDUCATION (FE) COLLEGE SECTOR

The work covered by colleges is extensive and impressive. The principal activity is vocational education and training. In addition most colleges provide general education courses and access studies leading to higher education, along with adult and community education courses.

Basic education studies covering literacy and numeracy form an important service, sometimes delivered on an outreach basis at community locations in cooperation with local authority community education staff. A wide range of Scottish Qualifications Authority (SQA) National Certificate courses are provided, some in the form of Group Awards. SQA Higher National Certificate courses are delivered on a full-time and part-time basis. Most colleges now provide SQA Higher National Diploma full-time courses. A college of technology is a major provider of degree-level qualifications, and a small number of other colleges are involved in a limited amount of degree provision.

General education usually comes in the form of SQA Higher courses, and some colleges also make such provision at GCSE and GCE A levels. Whilst SQA qualifications predominate, most colleges have courses leading to a wide range of accredited qualifications from other awarding bodies and professional institutions, e.g. The Association of Accounting Technicians, City and Guilds, The Institute of Marketing, The National Examination Board for Supervisory Management and The Royal Society of Arts Examinations Board. The SQA has also developed a useful portfolio of post-qualification courses leading to Professional Development Awards.

Colleges are also widely involved in the provision of underpinning knowledge and workplace assessment for SQA Scottish Vocational Qualifications (SVQs) Levels I to V.

SVQs also form the basis for Skillseeker and Modern Apprenticeship programmes. Non-vocational courses, some of which do not lead to formal qualifications, form the main basis of colleges' contribution to community education in their area. Many school pupils from the age of fourteen undertake vocational studies on school-college partnership programmes.

The 1992 Act required colleges to make provision for special educational needs, and in 1995 the Scottish Office Education and Industry Department (SOEID) issued Circular FE 13/95, which provides guidance on the responsibilities of colleges, including working closely with local authorities, health boards and National Health Service Trusts.

Colleges have considerably expanded their commercial services since 1993, usually through the form of a college company which contracts with other companies and organisations for the delivery of teaching, consultancy and other services, such as employment rehabilitation, job search and advice.

Delivery of courses by flexible and open learning methods, sometimes using video conferencing facilities, has become another key feature of FE college activity. This may involve learning in the workplace, learning at home, evening or weekend study at college or other locations. Colleges are also involved in teaching various courses to international students in Scotland, and in some cases are delivering courses and services in overseas countries. Exchange programmes with European Union institutions are providing study and work experience opportunities abroad and in Scotland.

Lecturing and administration staff from the colleges are contributing to the development of the wider FE system as a whole through service on committees of national bodies, through assessment and verification tasks for awarding bodies, by participation in inspection and other quality assurance activities, and through research and project work, sometimes on a secondment or contract basis.

RECENT HISTORY OF FE COLLEGES: OFFICIAL POLICY AND PRESSURES TO CHANGE

A major policy of the Conservative government through the 1980s was to reduce public expenditure and to devolve power from central and local government to agencies and institutions. In 1988 attention was focused on the education sector by the passing of the Education Reform Act in England, and the Self-Governing Schools (etc.) Act 1989 in Scotland. Whilst colleges continued to be administered by Education Authorities in Scotland, the 1989 Act increased their autonomy and brought about the restructuring of college councils with a large number of employer representatives.

By mid-1991 the Government announced its intention to remove further education colleges from Education Authorities. The White Paper *Access and Opportunity* (Cmnd 1530, Scottish Office 1991) gave details of the wide powers to be granted to colleges; these were enshrined in the Further and Higher Education (Scotland) Act 1992, and the incorporated colleges took up their responsibilities on 1 April 1993 with newly-formed boards of management.

Thus the colleges were made accountable directly to SOEID, which provides annual grant-in-aid on a formula-funding basis. Official policy was indicated in two documents, *Mission and Vision* (Ministerial Speech, Scottish Office, September 1992) and *Quality and Efficiency* (SOED, 1992) and can be summarised thus:

- to improve further education in Scotland
- to develop a more highly trained and qualified workforce
- to raise educational attainment levels of 16–18 year olds
- to contribute towards the expansion of the higher education system
- to improve efficiency and obtain value for money
- to enhance quality.

Each college's starting point upon incorporation was different, depending upon the previous policies of its Education Authority and upon the nature and extent of the land and buildings it took into ownership on 1 April 1993. Such differences have inevitably had a marked effect upon the subsequent financial viability of colleges. The main thrust of government policy has been to achieve efficiency savings across the college sector of about 3.5–4 per cent per annum since incorporation whilst the funding methodology has sought growth in student enrolments. Thus in one sense colleges' behaviour has been characterised by competition, expansion, cost-reduction and vigorous marketing. On the other hand, incorporation has had a liberating effect on colleges as they have strengthened their identity and esteem, and have developed income streams from beyond the public purse. Many colleges have now made capital investment in new or re-modelled accommodation in marked contrast to the utilitarian character of pre-incorporation times. From the earliest days of incorporation, colleges were reminded of the need to cooperate with other colleges and providers, and were therefore faced with the paradox of collaboration and competition.

Another strand of official policy has been to make the incorporated colleges fully accountable as public bodies. Each college is required to submit annually to SOEID a three-year development plan, after consulting the local enterprise company and the Education Authority. It is required to make an annual report available to the public. Its financial operations have to be internally and externally audited and annual accounts presented to the SOEID and again made available to the public. A wide range of performance indicators are used as part of the accountability process. Colleges are also audited by local enterprise companies and by awarding bodies such as the SQA, and several have voluntarily undergone audit processes for other quality awards such as Investors in People and the British Standards Institute. Government policy at incorporation required colleges to invest in computerised management information systems and these are being used for student enrolment and assessment records, for financial management and for reporting on standard performance indicators.

Over and above central government policy for further education, other pressures for change have continued to impact upon colleges since incorporation. Changes in the world of work quickly come through to colleges. These are technological, such as the widespread use of computers including computer-controlled manufacture and assembly. They are economic, such as unemployment and labour market changes, and they are social, such as the far greater public expectation of service and value for money. Such pressures have required changes in curriculum, in teaching and learning approaches (see Chapter 72), in the provision of student services such as financial advice, in up-grading of equipment for learning and in management functions and styles. Further education colleges are now highly funding-sensitive institutions and represent the least stable of all the education sectors in terms of financial operations. Enrolments take place right across an operational year. Typically fewer than half the students in a college study on a full-time basis. Most are aged 18 + ; nearly half aged 25 + .

EFFECTS OF INCORPORATION – PLUSES AND MINUSES

It is important to qualify the following comments on the effects of incorporation with the assertion that, at the time of writing, it is only five years since the change took place, which is a relatively short time given the complex nature of the institutions involved and the wider systems in which they operate. Very different comments might emerge in another five years.

It is necessary to remember that incorporation initially impacted more upon the management and administration functions of colleges than upon the primary function of teaching and learning. Overnight, colleges became employers in their own right, responsible for their own staff, their land and buildings, and for their financial operations. Additional senior administrative staff had to be recruited to manage these functions. Banking, insurance, legal and auditing services had to be purchased through tendering procedures. With no additional funding granted to colleges for operating services, the cost has had to be covered by savings elsewhere in college budgets and/or earning extra income. Some colleges have ameliorated such costs through joint purchasing of such services. The advantage of autonomy over these management functions is the sharpening of account-ability at college level, for example personnel matters can be dealt with on site, and expeditiously, and usually on a face-to-face basis. The responsibility for these and all other matters now rests with the college principal, who is answerable to the college's board of management. The resolution of public complaints, or staff and student grievances, takes place at the level of the college. It has not taken long for the incorporation changes to start to influence the culture of further education colleges and the management styles of senior staff. The drive for efficiency savings and growth in the context of a competitive market place has been a liberating and energising process for some colleges, where the focus has been maintained on the central purpose of teaching and learning, and where senior management has achieved high standards of effectiveness, yet in a businesslike public service ethos. In some situations the new ethos of the market place has encouraged colleges to operate as if they were private companies; excessive managerialism has stifled creativity and dialogue and undermined the professionalism of lecturing staff, which in turn has led to industrial relations problems.

Incorporation has also changed relationships within the wider FE system between colleges. In these early years competition has made some colleges go it alone and be very wary of each other. Some have chosen to collaborate on certain aspects from the inception of incorporation (Finlay et al., 1997, p. 147). Some are starting to do so now, having achieved a certain level of institutional self-confidence and maturity. Yet sudden lurches in funding allocations can change such delicate relationships; so too can the appointment of a new principal or chairman of a board of management. All this has made it problematic at times for some organisations such as schools, local authorities, voluntary organisations, to know how best to build lasting working relationships with colleges. In other cases, such as in Fife, with the development of the FAST-TRAC system, through good quality local leadership, colleges and local agencies have collaborated effectively to raise participation levels of 16–18 year olds in the education system.

One of the more far-reaching effects of incorporation has been upon lecturing and administrative staff in the colleges, as a result of each college becoming an employer. Colleges now have the responsibility for negotiating salaries and conditions of service of all staff. Most have established local recognition and procedure agreements with trade unions. Senior staff and trade union officers have had to develop their negotiating skills in order to bring about effective local agreements. All this has had to be conducted against a background of government policy requiring efficiency savings and greater flexibility from staff. Some colleges have contracted out services, and transferred staff to contracted companies, for services such as cleaning, janitorial, catering, ground maintenance, and more recently temporary lecturing supply.

Ultimately an assessment has to be made upon the extent to which incorporation has brought about an improved college service for students, not least in terms of their individual achievement. A major sample survey was conducted of students and other 'stakeholders' after the Further and Higher Education Charter was introduced in 1994 and this reported favourable perceptions of the further education college sector. The substantial year-on-year growth in enrolments cannot just be put down to better marketing, and the early signs from performance indicator reports on qualification achievements are encouraging. Retention levels on some programmes are giving the new Labour government some cause for concern (SOEID, 1997) but some of this is accounted for by the vigorous efforts to widen participation. Current intentions to link funding to quality must not deter colleges from continuing to widen participation.

It was an aspiration of the Conservative government that mergers of colleges would soon follow incorporation, as part of a drive towards efficiency and rationalisation. At the time of writing there are still forty-three incorporated colleges, with consultations taking place on the merger of just two, in Glasgow. In the prevailing difficult financial climate it is possible that one or two further mergers will take place if a college is pushed to the brink of insolvency. Further education colleges are very much local institutions; they thrive on their localness and their capacity for outreach, and to a certain extent civic pride can be an important ingredient in their survival.

The most significant concern for colleges post-incorporation has been the rapid reduction of public funds available for distribution as grant-in-aid. Even allowing for government efficiency requirements the FE college sector has grown sufficiently to merit better funding from the public purse. What cannot be assessed is whether colleges would have fared better, or have made as much progress, if they had remained under local authority control.

CHANGING RELATIONSHIPS AND THE SOEID

Whilst being part of the local authority system, colleges had relatively little direct contact with the Scottish Office. Ministerial visits were rare, and usually had to be arranged with the full panoply of support from local authority officials and sometimes local councillors. Occasionally a minister might address a conference, but in the main policy was formulated at the local authority level, and local authorities generally took the responsibility of influencing and advocating national policy as far as further education was concerned. The main source of contact at national level was with HM Inspectorate through college inspections and through a wide range of development activities for the sector, for example the Scottish Wider Access Programme. Contact between colleges and civil servants at the Scottish Office was also rare, and it was virtually unknown for civil servants to visit a college.

In the run-up to incorporation the situation changed rapidly and the active involvement of HMI and officials in working groups with the sector was widely welcomed (Howgego, 1993). Likewise ministers began to take opportunities to make policy speeches regarding the future direction of the further education college sector. Subsequently a whole division of officials was created at SOEID for the administration of further education. From there policy guidance and requirements are issued, usually in the form of circulars and letters. Various documents and forms, sometimes using computer technology, have to be completed and sent in at frequent intervals throughout the year. From time-to-time, senior staff have been seconded to SOEID for short periods to bring up-to-date specialist expertise direct from the colleges. Letters of complaint to ministers are taken up directly with colleges now. Ministerial visits to colleges and to sector-specific conferences are regular occurrences. HM Inspectorate are expected to inspect colleges every five years, and are now introducing a self-evaluation model leading to accredited status for colleges. In many ways for colleges, it is like working for a very large local authority, except that the action is much closer to the locus of national policy-making and power. Civil servants have enthusiastically welcomed the opportunity to work closely with colleges, but the funding responsibilities have brought the difficulties some colleges are facing uncomfortably close to the seat of power. The opportunity to second a civil servant into a college has not yet been taken. Another feature of the changing relationships has been the publication by the Secretary of State for Scotland of an annual report to Parliament upon Further Education in Scotland; this provides a good vehicle for promoting the sector as well as recording its achievements.

THE ROLE OF BOARDS OF MANAGEMENT

The 1992 Act provides for the establishment of a board of management for each incorporated college, comprising not less than twelve and up to sixteen members. Not less than one half of the total members of the board are required to be appointed from among persons appearing to have experience of industrial, commercial or employment matters or the practice of any profession. Board membership was initially approved by ministers, but subsequent appointments, including that of the chairman, are now left to the boards themselves. Provision is made for two staff to be elected to the board, and also for a student to be a member. The college principal is a member, with full voting rights. In many ways the role of a college board is similar to the board of a company. It must determine the strategic direction of the college, and it has to adopt policies and strategies for such matters as its property, personnel, and health and safety. It is required to adopt proper financial policies and to ensure the adequacy of accounting systems. It also has to arrange for the internal and external auditing of accounts. The board has responsibility for the appointment of the college principal, who is effectively the chief executive and holds authority for the operation of the college within the policies determined by the board. The SOEID commissioned a study into the operations of college boards; this was published in 1995 (Leishman Management Consulting, 1995). Although this was only two years on from incorporation, board members surveyed believed that incorporation had had a beneficial effect in terms of governance and management of FE Colleges in Scotland. However there were concerns expressed as to how far a board was to be involved in the development of strategy as distinct from reviewing the strategy prepared by college senior management. At the time of the report respondents indicated that the larger colleges had moved furthest in being better able to plan and manage their own affairs.

In 1996 the second report of the Nolan Committee on Standards in Public Life, which covered local spending bodies, gave Scottish college governance a clean bill of health. College boards are now putting into place registers of members' interests and are encouraged to advertise publicly when seeking to fill board vacancies. The National Audit Office is conducting a study of corporate governance in a sample of Scottish further education colleges and its report will be presented to Parliament in due course.

LINKS WITH INDUSTRY AND COMMERCE, COMMUNITY AGENCIES, LOCAL GOVERNMENT

Vocational education and training is at the heart of what each college does, and it follows that strong links with employers in the private, public and voluntary sectors are vital for effective provision by colleges. The links manifest themselves in different ways. The board of management will include at least eight people, often of senior status, from employers in the area. Some course teams will include employer representatives, and advisory committees are used by some departments. The local enterprise company (LEC) forms another key part of the college-employer interface; the LEC has a place on the board of management of each college and in some cases a college principal serves on a LEC board. The LEC may provide useful local labour market information for colleges and is active in business development, some of which will require a training input, as well as in contracting for training.

Colleges typically coordinate much of their activity with employers through the college company, which contracts education and learning provision on a customised basis, and keeps up-to-date records of contacts with employers. Lecturing staff keep in touch with workplace developments through regular contact with employees in day-to-day lectures, through visits to students in work placements and on work experience, through short secondment to employers and through the delivery of education, training and consultancy in the workplace. Many colleges conduct surveys of employers in order to obtain feedback and useful market information. Colleges recognise that there is still room for improvement in such activity. In a recent study (Alex Neil and Roger Mullin Associates, 1996) it was found that companies perceived that private training providers still offer a better service, especially in terms of consultancy, and the ability to communicate and market services. Indications are that much progress is being made, with Scottish colleges recently receiving National Training Awards, Queen's Anniversary prizes and similar recognition for work with industry and commerce.

Colleges have long-established links with voluntary community agencies as part of their on-going commitment to the locality where they are based. Board membership is usually reflective of this type of activity too, and frequently colleges will be working with a local partnership of community agencies for a variety of purposes, including outreach delivery of adult basic education, social care training, adult guidance, and special educational needs. The teaching of English as a second language usually takes place as a community based activity, and can involve home tutoring.

There is often close cooperation between colleges, community agencies and local authorities in the delivery of education and training on a local basis. Many colleges invite councillors to serve on their board of management to help nurture such links. A college is also required to consult with the local authority in the formulation of its development plan. Such links are necessary for the operation of successful school-college partnerships. Colleges will also be aware that the local authority is often one of the larger employers in the locality, from the point of view of education and training services. Likewise local political leadership can still be very influential in terms of involving colleges in economic and business development. Local government in Scotland was re-organised in 1995 and colleges found it necessary to re-forge working relationships with key officials. A small number of new authorities were left with no further education colleges within their boundaries, but each has been involving the college sector in different ways to make up the deficit.

BLURRING OF THE FE/HE DIVIDE

Significant numbers of students are undertaking higher education courses in further education colleges. In 1995–6, over 285,000 students were registered on further education courses in Scottish further education colleges; a further 60,700 were following higher education courses. Between 1994–5 and 1995–6 the number of higher education students in colleges rose by 10 per cent, with a 15 per cent growth in part-time students. At the same time many students are following further education courses in higher education institutions, primarily the new universities. In 1995–6 there were 84,000 such enrolments, mainly on courses of short duration. The Dearing Inquiry into Higher Education (1997) noted these developments and recommended that further education colleges should continue to expand in this type of activity. The Scottish Report of the Inquiry (The Garrick Report 1997) also recommends that a Further Education Funding Council should be created in Scotland, to work alongside the Scottish Higher Education Funding Council, with a joint secretariat. It is foreseen that eventually this could lead to a single Scottish Tertiary Education Funding Council. There is some concern that further education may be subject to mission drift through such arrangements, but others argue that students as a whole will benefit from greater equity of funding across tertiary institutions and from the closer articulation between courses which should ensue from these developments. The recent creation of the University of the Highlands and Islands (UHI) in a partnership involving existing universities and colleges is a further example of the blurring of the FE/HE divide, with funding being drawn from both sectors as well as from other sources. The Labour government's plans for a University for Industry also brings in the prospect of collaboration between colleges and universities with employers to deliver enhanced workplace education and training.

FE INVOLVEMENT IN DEGREE LEVEL WORK

One college of technology in the further education sector is a major provider of degree and degree-equivalent courses. A small number of other colleges are also providing degree courses or parts of degree courses. In most cases the institutional funding comes from the SOEID Further Education Funding Division's grant-in-aid allocation. A limited amount of work is funded through franchise arrangements with a higher education institution. Full-time degree-level students in further education will usually have access to higher education fees and maintenance grants from the Student Awards Agency for Scotland. In all present instances, universities are the degree-awarding institutions. Advantages to students of degree-level work in colleges include proximity to home or work, lower costs, and accessibility to specialist studies in particular localities. Colleges' experience, and capacity to deliver non-full-time flexible courses at times to suit students is of particular relevance. A key challenge for colleges is to bring infrastructure support for degree-level students up to national standards, especially with library services.

FINANCE AND BUDGETARY CONTROL

Under the 1992 Act each college is responsible for its own finances. Income is derived from grant-in-aid on a formula basis from SOEID, with allocations primarily based on the volume of student activity in the previous year, i.e. on a historical basis. Most colleges obtain 70–80 per cent of income in this way. Other income comes from tuition fees, from European Union funds, and from commercial activities, typically through a college company. The principal expenditure item is staffing costs, followed by premises costs and equipment. Colleges are also responsible for the management of any major capital expenditure such as a new or re-modelled building; this will include conducting the tendering process for a design team and contractor and making the various payments through to project completion. Colleges also hold the responsibility for further education bursaries, which can amount to over £1 million for a large institution. They also disburse access funds for students in need of urgent financial support.

End-of-year accounts and balance sheets are subject to external audit and duly published and made available as public documents. The principal is designated the accounting officer, which duties include the signing off of the annual accounts for submission to SOEID. Boards of management appoint an audit committee; a key responsibility is to satisfy itself that value for money criteria are brought to bear on the college's financial transactions. Colleges annually report to SOEID on what capital works are proposed or desired. They have recently been given guidance on drawing up an estate strategy which is now required to be submitted with the development plan. The annual grant-in-aid allocation now forms one total which colleges can draw from in undertaking capital works. Major projects may require extensive borrowing, or use may be made of the Private Finance Initiative. Colleges are also entitled to bid annually to Scottish Enterprise for grants towards new equipment for teaching purposes. These bids are conducted on a competitive basis and support from the local enterprise company is sought.

The FE college sector is the most funding-sensitive of all the sectors of the education service. Students come from so many different routes and through a wide range of attendance modes and length of course, that planning and estimating income is a very sophisticated process, and enrolment volumes throughout an operational year can vary markedly from one year to the next. This is especially true where a college has a majority of non-full-time students. The management of finance and the exercising of budgetary control is probably one of the most significant and challenging tasks for a college, post-incorpora-tion. Current public expenditure policy means that there is less money each year for allocating to colleges through the formula. At the same time colleges are recruiting increasing numbers of students with the effect that they receive less money per unit of resource. Even if a college achieves a very high level of growth it may find that a percentage of such growth is only funded at a marginal rate. Meanwhile colleges performing less well have, controversially, been given a larger grant than enrolments merited – a process called safety netting – in order to maintain stability across the sector. Some colleges which have got into serious financial difficulties have been 'bailed out' by SOEID as funds have been made available during the course of a financial year. The SOEID has also made restructuring funds available to colleges seeking to reduce their staff costs and achieve a sounder financial footing. In a few cases a small number of staff have been made redundant in order to assist in this process. Colleges continue to rely heavily upon the public purse for the bulk of their income in spite of commendable efforts to earn income from other sources. Continuing anxiety and frustration about the reducing amount of available grant-in-aid, and about the method of allocating the funding, risks senior college staff becoming unduly distracted by such problems to the extent that the quality of the core function of teaching and learning could suffer. At a time when the colleges are still being urged to widen participation and enrol more students, their capacity to respond could be undermined by the effects of increasing complexities of a financial nature.

PATTERNS OF STUDENT RECRUITMENT

Information available from the SOEID (*Scottish Education Statistics Annual Review, 1997*) shows that the number of students registered in further education colleges has increased from 239,221 in the first year of incorporation, 1993–4, to 285,557 in 1995–6. Some 229,520 of the 1995–6 registrations are part-time. Over 60,000 students are studying at the higher education level. Only 18% are aged under eighteen; 54% are aged twenty-five and over. The proportion of female students rose from 47% to 52% over these three years. Part-time day studies (63%) and directed private study (including open learning) saw the biggest increases for 1995–6, in terms of mode of attendance. Enrolments on vocational further education courses were widely spread across subject groups, with the largest numbers studying Social Work, Personal Development, Business Studies and Computing.

Given the growing demand for short, part-time courses, the enrolment process continues right through an academic year in further education colleges. Most colleges open on three evenings a week or more, and some are opening on Saturdays or across a weekend. Likewise more courses and other services are being provided in what have been traditional holiday times for colleges. The flexibility and quick response of colleges to work at times preferred by employers and students partly accounts for the successful growth since incorporation, despite competition from private training organisations. The year 1995–6 saw provision for special educational needs students increase by 21 per cent.

A continuing challenge for colleges as they strive to widen participation is to sustain high levels of course completion. HM Inspectorate recently reported that whilst completion rates were generally good, there was a wide variation across departments and subjects. Discussions are currently taking place on the benefit of linking funding to quality when making grant-in-aid allocations to colleges. There is some concern that too significant a shift in this approach would encourage colleges to be more selective on admissions at the expense of those who may, initially, find learning a difficult experience.

CURRICULAR CHANGES: AREAS OF EXPANSION/CONTRACTION

Broadly speaking, areas of expansion and contraction reflect labour market changes, e.g. engineering courses have seen a decline, as well as changes reflecting the introduction of computer-controlled and automated equipment for production lines; the rapid growth in the electronics industry bringing a shift to assembly as distinct from manufacture, has also brought changes in curricula. Care in the community initiatives, and legislation/regulation affecting the care of young and old, has brought an expansion in numbers enrolling for qualifications in social work, social care, child care and personal services.

Various reports by employers, trades unions and government have sought to introduce core skills, such as communication, numeracy, information technology, inter-personal skills and problem-solving, into college curricula as a way of strengthening the capacity of individuals to readily transfer such skills from one work situation to another. Current college practice is to embed such skills into vocational subjects being studied and also to assess such skills in work placement periods. Experience of these changes is likely to support initiatives designed to widen participation.

Another area of expansion is where colleges are being contracted to deliver education and training in the workplace, as distinct from the previous traditions of day release and block release. Such provision might lead to accredited qualifications which are studied and assessed in partnership with work-based tutors and assessors. In other instances colleges may be called upon to deliver short, intensive courses, followed by the award of a college certificate. Whilst much of the focus on incorporation has been upon administrative changes, there is little doubt that colleges have responded positively, flexibly and professionally to the changing curricular demands. Such demands would have come irrespective of incorporation; the process of incorporation has better positioned colleges to be proactive and responsive.

ASSESSMENT AND CERTIFICATION: FROM SCOTVEC TO SQA

Scottish further education colleges held contracts with SCOTVEC, which met criteria to enable them to design, approve, deliver and assess a range of SCOTVEC National Certificate level modules and Higher National Certificate and Diploma units, in the form of free-standing modules and units and of group awards. Contracts were usually of five years in length, with all relevant systems subject to an annual audit by a SCOTVEC appointed systems verifier. Colleges appointed internal verifiers from their own staff to assist in the operation, and external verifiers appointed by SCOTVEC also audited the internal procedures and assessment as part of the process to maintain standards. Information technology was widely used to support the arrangement from initial registration at the college onto a SCOTVEC programme through to the despatch of certificates by SCOT-VEC. The contract also enabled colleges to take part in the delivery and assessment of SVQs, whether under simulated conditions in college workshops, laboratories and catering facilities for example, or in the workplace.

In April 1997, SCOTVEC and SEB were merged to form the Scottish Qualifications Authority (SQA), which organisation has taken up existing contracts and arrangements agreed with colleges by the predecessor bodies. The SOEID has been funding a major curriculum development and assessment project for post-sixteen school/college qualifications called 'Higher Still' with a view to introducing new courses and awards from August 1999. Reviews are also being conducted of Higher National qualifications and of SVQs. All this development work should lead to a new national qualifications framework for Scotland by the year 2000, especially if proposals for changes to higher education qualifications made by the recent Dearing Inquiry are put into place.

In spite of having to implement changes of systemic proportions, and of having to cope with the workload implications, colleges have welcomed these developments. They have been frustrated by delays in start dates, and concerned by the prospect of less flexibility in assessment diets, and the imposition of more external assessment. There is a feeling that the pace and direction of the changes is being unduly influenced by the schools and higher education sectors, with the result that the colleges' capacity to respond to employers, and to calls for widening participation, may be somewhat impaired.

ROLE OF ASC

The Association of Scottish Colleges (ASC) was formed in 1995. It has brought together under one body the roles of the former Employers' Association, created at the time of incorporation by the new boards of management of colleges, and of the former Association of Principals of Colleges (Scottish Branch). ASC now provides a single voice of advocacy, influence and support for the Scottish further education colleges, drawing upon the work of its Chairpersons' Forum and of the Principals' Forum. ASC is funded through annual subscriptions paid by colleges, scaled upon the size of grant-in-aid. The funds provide for a small team of staff, mainly specialising in policy advice, and for premises. ASC is located in a new building at Stirling managed by the Scottish Further Education Unit. It sees as its main objectives to:

- lobby policy and opinion-makers, and raise general awareness of the sector;
- develop the collective efforts of members and the sense of purpose of FE as a critical sector of education in Scotland; and
- provide information and support to members on matters of strategic concern to principals and boards of management.

LINKS WITH SFEU

The Scottish Further Education Unit is the principal support agency of the further education colleges sector in Scotland. It is designated as a non-departmental public body (NDPB) and it operates as a limited company with charitable status. Its members and chairman are appointed by the Secretary of State; they include college principals, a college board member from industry, HM inspector, an educationalist from higher education and an officer from SQA. SFEU re-located from the University of Strathclyde's Jordanhill Campus in 1995 to newly-built accommodation in Stirling. Its current programme of work is in the following areas:

- professional and management development
- curricular development and support
- information and information technology
- research
- organisation development for colleges.

In 1995-6 SFEU received £635,000 in the form of grant-in-aid income from SOEID, this sum being top-sliced from the FE funding available to the sector as a whole. In the same year it received £964,000 from other sources. As an NDPB the SFEU is subject to the government's quinquennial review process.

The SFEU has had to adapt rapidly to the incorporation era in undertaking its support agency role for colleges. It was particularly effective at the introduction of incorporation by providing training and information courses, and producing guidance manuals for the incorporation process. As colleges have since found their feet and developed institutional self-confidence and determination, the SFEU has had to re-define its role and strategic direction in close consultation with colleges. Its relocation, along with ASC, has given it a new focus and provided a centre of gravity for Scottish FE development and wider influence.

LIKELY PATTERN BEYOND 2000

The success of colleges since incorporation, in terms of growth and student achievement towards national targets, looks to have assured the future of the colleges as free-standing institutions. Their strong characteristics include localness, flexibility, speed of response, relevance, and an innovative approach. In addition they are rapidly building a capacity to work in partnerships with public and private sector organisations. All this positions the colleges well to strengthen their esteem in the changed policy environment of the present day whereby new local authorities came into being in April 1996 as a result of re-organisation, a Labour government came into power in May 1997 and in the September 1997 referendum Scotland voted to establish a Scottish parliament with tax-changing powers.

Yet Colleges will continue to face competition from each other, from schools, from community education, from higher education and from employers' own training centres as well as from other training providers. At the same time, the squeeze for efficiency in the public sector is likely to continue its relentless journey beyond the year 2000. Colleges which can reduce their dependency upon the public purse stand to have greater potential for reaching out to new opportunities. However, the great majority of colleges will continue to be proud, businesslike and effective public sector institutions, which will make significant contributions to the local and regional economies where they operate. The public will continue to expect higher standards from all education sectors; HM inspectorate are introducing a self-evaluation model of inspection and development which will lead to FE colleges becoming accredited institutions in the early 2000s. This should form another strand in the on-going distinctiveness of the FE college sector. Its central role in the present push to widen participation will be another reputation-building feature far beyond 2000, if colleges are given the funding to help achieve success in this campaign.

A key challenge is to sustain a distinctive FE college mission in the interest of the wide range of students and organisations which colleges serve. Undoubtedly this mission will be put under pressure as the further and higher education sectors come close together under a Scottish parliament, whether or not a single tertiary education funding council emerges as the preferred way forward. Some strategic planning and intervention seems inevitable, and some would say desirable, if a nation of five million people is to make the best collective use of its post-compulsory education institutions, and the available staff expertise, in order to reach those many citizens whose lives have not been touched by learning opportunities since leaving school. Colleges have made a good start along this path since incorporation. If they can go on to lead the way on the widening participation agenda, instead of waiting to be pushed, they can then achieve a level of public recognition and esteem, which will not only help keep the colleges open and local, but will bring about new investment on a scale not known for the past fifty years. If the FE sector does not take this lead, or is not allowed to, history has shown that local communities will suffer, in spite of job creation and inward investment initiatives, because the required skills will be imported from elsewhere, or the jobs will go elsewhere.

REFERENCES

Finlay, I., S. Holmes and L. Kydd Institutional boundary management: experiences of Scottish colleges since incorporation in R. Levacic and R. Glatter (1997) *Managing Change in Further Education*, London: FE Development Agency.

Howgego, J. (1993) *The Incorporation of Colleges of Further Education in Scotland – a personal account*, Edinburgh: SOED.

Leishman Management Consulting (1995) *Study into the Operation of Further Education Colleges Boards of Management*, Glasgow: Profiles Research International and Consulting Groups Limited.

Alex Neil and Roger Mullin Associates (1996) *Scotland's Colleges: Relationships with Business and International Sectors*, Report for the Association of Scottish Colleges and Scottish Enterprise, Stirling.

Scottish Office Education Department (1992) *Quality and Efficiency in Further Education Colleges in Scotland*, A Report by HM Inspector of Schools, Edinburgh: SOED.

Scottish Office Education and Industry Department (1997) *Standards and Quality in Further Education 1995–96*, A Report by HM Inspector of Schools, Edinburgh: The Stationery Office Limited.

6

The Scottish Universities: Character and Provision in Tertiary Education

Ronald Crawford

The Robbins Report of 1963 has finally been archived with the publication of the monumental report of the 1997 National Inquiry under Sir Ron Dearing. If Dearing and Robbins are the twin peaks of higher education in Britain this century, the key questions for Scotland in the long run are whether the traditional distinctiveness of the Scottish brand of higher education has been reinforced by Dearing (who had the advantage, denied Robbins, of a separate Scottish Committee under Sir Ron Garrick) and whether it is legitimate to claim that Dearing presages greater alignment of the Scottish 'system' with the rest of Britain; or, on the contrary, that the report anticipates the final act of repatriation of Scottish Higher Education (HE). These are important questions but unfortunately this chapter cannot, of itself, provide the answers and, in any event, it is much too early to try. What it can do is help fill out some of the background against which, in time, an informed response may be attempted. Together with the Dearing and Garrick Reports, the conclusive outcome of the referendum that took place on 11 September 1997 will also massively influence the future shape, size and direction of Scottish higher education but in ways that cannot yet be fully assessed. In a 1997 lecture (reproduced in part in *The Times Higher Education Supplement*, 12 September 1997, p. 14) Peter Scott speculated on precisely that theme but concluded that no one can yet predict whether the influence of a separate parliament will take the form of steering Scotland's universities in the direction of greater convergence with the higher education sector elsewhere in Britain or, on the contrary, that it will distance them further from their English (and Welsh) counterparts.

THE ROBBINS ERA

It is no longer possible, as it was in Robbins' day, to regard the British universities as a more or less homogeneous system, with broadly uniform missions and standards. Any modern account of UK universities has necessarily, therefore, to begin by distinguishing between an increasingly diverse number of discrete groups of which the Scottish universities form one of the most coherent. Even so, just as it has long ceased to be valid to separate English universities into Oxbridge and the rest, so in Scotland, too, it is no longer sufficient to regard the universities as a uniform group of institutions.

It is currently fashionable to assign the universities of Scotland either to the group of 'pre-' or 'post-1992' institutions – the obvious watershed being the Further and Higher Education (Scotland) Act of that year. Before 1992 it was usual to describe the eight Scottish universities, in terms of their provenance, as, more straightforwardly, the 'old' (or, even more venerably, the 'ancient') and the 'new' universities. Of course, even within that small group there exists a variety of provenance from the three Papal Bull foundations of St Andrews (1411), Glasgow (1451) and Aberdeen (1495) to the early civic model of Edinburgh (1583). And within the newer universities – i.e. those whose governance derives from Royal Charters – Strathclyde (1964) and Heriot-Watt (1966), though they originated as technological institutions, were by no means the same creatures as the pre-Robbins Colleges of Advanced Technology (CATs) in England.

The dominant theme of Robbins was, of course, the need for expansion of the system. In Scotland it was not only the number of universities that doubled. In 1963 Robbins reported an Age Participation Index (API) in Britain (universities only) of a mere 4 per cent. By 1980 (STEAC 1985, p. 131) the API for Scots entrants to the Scottish universities stood at 8.9 per cent. Nonetheless, with the benefit of hindsight and now with the advantage of being able to compare Robbins with Dearing, it can be argued that the expansion which characterised the university system in the immediate post-Robbins era was remarkably superficial. It scarcely affected young school leavers whose parents had not themselves been exposed to some form of higher education and it did almost nothing to eradicate the poverty of expectation among the lower socio-economic groups.

While, therefore, the justification for expansion as set out by Robbins tended to emphasise above all the advantage conferred on a civilised nation by a proper scale of investment in higher education, that is a far cry from the market-driven expansion of the early 1990s. It is fascinating to speculate on what a Scottish Committee of Robbins might have made of the aims and principles of higher education seen from within the significantly different university tradition Scotland takes for granted, with its more pragmatic, less ethereal attachment to the world of work and to a vision of higher education famously described by Adam Smith as a 'public and economic good'.

In the meantime, however, one has to be content with Dearing's vision of a learning society in which the special contribution that higher education can make will be driven by 'compacts' between the providers, the consumers (i.e. students), government and society at large. Significantly, in a Scottish context it is said (by Sir Ron Garrick in his Foreword, p. 3) that this ideal was interpreted by his committee to mean that 'as a first priority . . . we had to ensure that the quality and output of the [Scottish] system would be comparable with the best of the world.' For Scotland, in other words, more, uncompromisingly, must mean better. Such a message should please all but the most cynical of educational commentators for it is firmly in line with the Scottish tradition for excellence at almost any cost.

THE BEGINNINGS OF WIDER ACCESS – AND THE OBSTACLES

After Robbins the next great watershed for higher education in Britain was the publication of Sir Keith Joseph's Green Paper in May 1985 – *The Development of Higher Education into the 1990s* – the impact of which is still felt today. In a Scottish context, the report of the Scottish Tertiary Education Advisory Council (STEAC), published in September of the same year, was equally significant. Both reports attempted to solve the same basic conundrum: how to reconcile projected falling demand for places in HE with the Thatcherite premise that it must be national economic need dictating the future shape and size of the UK (and, within it, the Scottish) system at a price that justified its inexorably rising cost.

All the major commentators at that time – the University Grants Committee (UGC), the Committee of Vice-Chancellors and Principals (CVCP), the Royal Society, the Association of University Teachers and last but not least, the SED – were agreed that, effectively, the world had moved on since Robbins. Student demand projections were notoriously unreliable but it seemed possible that the falling birthrate would result in over supply within the HE system. As the Green Paper put it, 'it is not improbable that some institutions of higher education will need to be closed or merged at some point during the next ten years' (Cmnd 9524, p. 5). At no time had Scotland greater need of its own powerful sectoral mechanism for responding to STEAC and Keith Joseph. But in 1985 no such mechanism existed.

Like the Green Paper the STEAC report similary attempted to reconcile its own forecasts of a sharp decline in demand 'from traditional sources' with the country's skilled manpower needs, and wrestled with the organisational structures which the Committee thought necessary to secure a firm basis upon which the planning and funding of HE (and, remarkably, FE as well) could be founded. Though STEAC – in common, it has to be stated, with most other bodies at the time – seriously underestimated the latent demand for places in HE from all relevant sources and failed to anticipate the already manifest frustrations of the Scottish Central Institutions in aspiring to university status, it would be crass to accuse the Committee of misdiagnosing the ills of the system then in force. Certainly STEAC's lasting monument is the pragmatism of its vision: the report clearly documents the need for greater 'flexibility' in the provision of courses, retraining to meet the special challenge of the burgeoning knowledge society, the increasing importance of continuing and vocational education on the one hand, and of credit transfer on the other. It can fairly be said that, in many ways, Dearing's emphasis on the needs of the 'learning society' was anticipated by Sir Donald McCallum twelve years previously. Nevertheless, and admittedly with the benefit of hindsight, the lasting influence of STEAC has proved to be strictly limited.

THE DEBATE ON ENTRY REQUIREMENTS

One area of great public concern that STEAC clearly saw had to be urgently addressed was university entry and the criteria that universities used to determine their individual and collective admissions policies. Anticipating initiatives such as the government's Scottish Wider Access Programme of the early 1990s, STEAC boldly (but still tentatively) concluded that 'without wishing to advocate any general lowering of entrance requirements, we believe that they should be reviewed periodically *to ensure that they are not operated too rigidly*' (STEAC 1985, p. 43, author's italics).

A year previously, writing in *The Scotsman* (11 December 1984), the chairman of the Scottish Examination Board, Dr Farquhar Macintosh, appealed to individual universities and to the Scottish Universities Council on Entrance (SUCE) to embark on 'a liberal policy' on recognition of Standard Grade subjects and to 'give priority to the interests of the age group as a whole' by modifying what he believed were unnecessarily rigid attitudes to entry.

A few months earlier, and in the columns of the same newspaper (30 October), the Academic Registrar of the University of Strathclyde called attention to a 'growing crisis' in university admissions created by a combination of strictly controlled intakes, monitored for funding purposes by the University Grants Committee in the wake of the draconian cuts of 1981, and a growing suspicion that SUCE – far from coming across as an agent of enlightenment in facilitating entry – saw its role (as custodian of the General Entrance Requirement) more as that of lock-keeper and as the agent of maintaining standards. Expressing his dismay at the trend in favour of ever more stringent entry qualifications for a shrinking number of places in key subjects of national need, he doubted 'if the universities, at least in combination, are yet ready to consider the introduction of the radical, more liberal and more-open minded admissions policies that will be necessary to reform the system.'

Though few were aware of it at the time, these were the opening shots in a protracted war of words which only came to an end with the Forty Report (Committee of Scottish University Principals, 1989) and with the decision of the older universities to wind up SUCE in 1992. With the creation of initiatives designed to embrace wider access to higher education in general and to provide credit for learning undertaken outside institutional confines (promoted with missionary zeal by such as Sir Christopher Ball) and, last but not least, with the formal ending of the binary division with the 1992 legislation, it was generally acknowledged by the majority of senior university officers that things – at least in this context – would never be the same again.

Outside the higher education sector, on the other hand, it was not uncommon for the view to be heard expressed that the universities after the second world war had failed many of Scotland's able young people by stubbornly clinging to inflexible admissions policies that refused to acknowledge that fitness for entry often lay in more than formal paper certification. Certainly – whether by those inside or outside them – it could scarcely be claimed that the older established universities were at any time trailblazers in the devising of imaginative schemes conferring the second chance or the benefit of doubt in such matters. For them standards of input and output were absolutes and incapable of modification.

It took a very long time, and profound changes in the mentality informing entry to higher education, before a more enlightened policy predominated. Arguably, however, by then it was too late and the newest universities, in common with the established universities, found themselves inheriting a very different regime dominated by the Funding Councils, with their insistence on 'value for money', efficiency, productivity and an underlying philosophy pragmatically defined in terms of national need. A far cry indeed from the Robbins axiom of promotion of 'the general powers of the mind' and the production of 'not mere specialists but rather cultivated men and women.'

THE 1992 FURTHER AND HIGHER EDUCATION ACT AND ITS CONSEQUENCES

When the four ancient universities in Scotland were joined by four others of varying provenance from 1964 onwards, the Privy Council gave each of the latter a Royal Charter. The Charters laid down, in considerable detail, the form of governance they had to observe and prescribed the academic machinery by means of which standards could be protected in important areas such as approval of degree courses, the appointment of examiners (both internal and external), examination arrangements, first and higher degree awards and student appeals. Crucially, for a period of five years, each new university (until specifically remitted by the Privy Council) had to submit proposals for new degree courses, modifications to existing courses and recommendations for the appointment of external examiners before the critical eye of a predominantly external authority styled an 'Academic Advisory Committee', usually presided over by a distinguished professor from an established university and comprising four or five other persons of academic and/or lay distinction.

External oversight of the new universities in the 1960s also extended to non-academic affairs where provision was made for the composition of their Courts to include one member appointed from an established (usually neighbouring) institution. Strathclyde, for example, had a member of Court appointed by the University of Glasgow, Heriot-Watt a member appointed by Edinburgh and so on. While these arrangements succeeded in helping the nascent universities overcome the local and national scepticism they, perhaps inevitably, encountered in their fledgling years, the fact that the older universities were privy to the plans and future aspirations of institutions that would rapidly become their competitors undoubtedly rankled with most new Principals and their Courts and Senates.

It was a completely different story with the five new universities created in the wake of the Further and Higher Education (Scotland) Act of 1992. In contrast with the elaborate governance and statutory procedures attending the birth pangs of Strathclyde, Dundee, Heriot-Watt and Stirling, when Napier, Glasgow Caledonian, Robert Gordon, Paisley and Abertay Dundee were elevated from the status of Central Institutions to universities there was never any prospect of their receiving Royal Charters. Instead, they were incorporated by the simple expedient of Privy Council Instrument with the barest data relating to governance and without any of the transitional quality assurance arrangements imposed on the chartered universities in the 1960s.

Admittedly conditions were very different. Demonstrably – or so it seemed to the Conservative government in 1992 – the polytechnics and their Scottish counterparts had substantially met the prevailing criteria for university status and had already proved themselves according to the exacting standards laid down by the Council for National Academic Awards (CNAA), in whose name they awarded their degrees. In any case, the polytechnics had delivered increased numbers on cue and at an attractive price. Moreover, they had done so in areas of perceived national need, were committed proactively to the principles and practice of wider access and were encouragingly silent on issues like entry standards where successive governments had met with stubborn resistance from the established universities.

DEVOLUTION OF FUNDING AND THE CREATION OF SHEFC

Provided certain pre-conditions were secured STEAC had argued for the creation of a single 'overarching body' responsible for academic planning and the coordination of provision across the university and non-university sectors of higher education in Scotland and for allocation of resources within a system of funding at the disposal of the Secretary of State. Sir Donald McCallum was right when he predicted that not everyone would be pleased by his report and, indeed, it was not until 1992 that the Scottish Higher Education Funding Council (SHEFC) was created and the funding of the entire higher education sector became the responsibility of the Secretary of State. The failure of the university sector to achieve consensus in this most sensitive of issues was a major factor in the sectoral disarray that dogged higher education in Scotland in the years immediately after STEAC reported.

COSHEP: A NEW VOICE FOR HIGHER EDUCATION

It is sometimes overlooked that it was by no means inevitable that Scotland would be left to her own devices when it became clear that a means would have to be found to articulate a common voice on behalf of all of the higher education institutions funded by SHEFC. The austere – and, some would have said, ineffectual – London-based Committee of Vice-

Chancellors and Principals (CVCP) canvassed the possibility of opening a branch office in Edinburgh, serving the needs of its Scottish members. Undoubtedly this plan would have been implemented were it not for two important developments. First, anticipating the growing importance of being able to formulate a representative Scottish voice independent of the CVCP, the Committee of Scottish University Principals (CSUP) had re-organised itself in 1988 when it established its own permanent secretariat. More fundamentally, the first Chairman of SHEFC, Professor (later Sir John) Shaw made no secret of his desire that all of the Scottish Higher Education Institutions (HEIs) – not just the universities – to be funded by the new Council must devise a means of reacting in a coordinated way to the constant flow of consultation documents which, first, the SOED, then subsequently SHEFC itself, began to release in ever increasing volume throughout the sector.

When the Committee of Scottish Higher Education Principals (COSHEP) was set up it was quickly affirmed by all its members that it must be much more than a purely reactive mechanism; that it should be seen as a body that could rapidly earn respect as an innovative and reliable group; that it should come to be regarded as much more than a committee of Principals but, more purposefully, as the officially recognised common 'voice' of the totality of Scottish higher education. The achievement of COSHEP is that, by common consent, that objective was accomplished in a remarkably short period of time. Indeed, when the *soi disant* Commission on Scottish Education reported in 1996 they referred to COSHEP as 'the most effective regional organisation of its kind in the UK' (*Learning to Succeed in Scotland*, p. 89).

TEACHING QUALITY AND THE MAINTENANCE OF STANDARDS

The 1992 Acts required the Funding Councils to 'ensure that provision is made for assessing the quality of education' within the institutions to which they allocated financial resources. This is not the place to itemise the immensely detailed, complex and often inaccessible aspects of the process of quality assurance under which universities and colleges laboured from 1992. Given the responsibilities laid on SHEFC in that regard, perhaps it was inevitable that, for some, the experience was a more painful one than many considered strictly necessary. The results of Teaching Quality Assessment (TQA) exercises in the period 1993–6 are given in Table 6.1.

Table 6.1 Distribution of Scottish TQA outcomes – all HEIs

	Excellent	Highly satisfactory	Satisfactory	Unsatisfactory	Total TQA
1993–94	22	42	15	0	79
1994–95	5	28	19	1	53
1995–96	12	45	11	0	68
Total	39	115	45	1	200

Source: Garrick Report p. 53 Table 4.1

It is too early to say if the Dearing report will succeed in bringing order to quality assurance in higher education with his recommendations for less burdensome arrangements. It is also too early to predict how Scotland will fit into these proposals but the hope is that any new system that is informed by the Dearing principle of a 'lighter approach' will finally dispel institutional and sectoral concerns with the current system, founded, as many perceive it, on an over-bureaucratic zeal for conformity and, consequently, with an almost inbuilt capacity for confrontation.

THE PROBLEM OF RESEARCH FUNDING

The Principal of the University of Abertay Dundee is frequently quoted as an unofficial spokesman for the post-1992 universities in complaining about the absence of a level playing field in research funding. Their evident frustrations are conveniently summed up in the statistical fact (quoted in the Garrick Report, section 4.89, p. 57) that 'nearly 65 per cent of the funding stream allocated on the basis of the Research Assessment Exercise (RAE) conducted in 1996-7 was concentrated in three higher education institutions'. The three universities in question are, of course, Edinburgh, Glasgow and Strathclyde – as an extrapolation of Table 6.2 clearly shows. These three universities attracted SHEFC income of about £63.5 million in 1997-98 as a result of their combined RAE performance. That has to be set alongside a total figure of less than £3 million for all five of the post-1992 universities to form a picture of the scale of the problem the Principal of Abertay seeks to highlight.

Even more graphically, these three universities earned a total of c.£113 million from research grants and contracts in 1995-6 – or 60 per cent of the total of all such research income earned in that year in Scotland.

Table 6.2 Performance of Scottish universities in 1996 RAE

University	Total FTE academic staff	percentage staff active in research	RAE Scores					
			5*	5	4	5*+5+4	3a+3b	1+2
Edinburgh	1,367	94	2	12	28	42 (90)	12 (9)	1 (1)
St Andrews	364	88	1	5	15	21 (90)	2 (8)	1 (2)
Glasgow	1,407	76	2	5	27	34 (69)	19 (30)	2 (1)
Strathclyde	928	74	1	6	11	18 (61)	12 (35)	3 (4)
Dundee	622	76	1	3	9	13 (56)	10 (40)	3 (4)
Heriot-Watt	335	70	1	2	6	9 (62)	5 (38)	–
Stirling	355	76	1	1	7	9 (52)	9 (48)	–
Aberdeen	614	92	–	2	7	9 (27)	19 (72)	1 (1)
Napier	455	17	–	–	1	1 (5)	7 (78)	2 (17)
Glas Cal U	598	31	–	–	–	–	8 (60)	7 (40)
Robert G U	418	33	–	–	–	–	5 (59)	9 (41)
Abertay D'dee	220	35	–	–	–	–	3 (33)	9 (67)
Paisley	359	19	–	–	–	–	4 (30)	10 (70)

Note: The outcome for departments with ratings of 5*, 5 and 4 are summated as all of the ratings include considerable areas of international research excellence. The scores for departments receiving 3a and 3b have been summated as have those departments rated 1 and 2 since the former will receive funding whereas the latter will not.
Source: Garrick Report p. 25 Table 2.4

Dearing has done his best to try to resolve the issue by recommending a new funding stream for departments that choose not to participate in future RAEs. His formula, however, is unlikely to offer a permanent solution to the problem and, on closer examination, Dearing contains few words of comfort for the newest universities. Indeed, there are clear signs of an accelerating trend in the direction of yet further selectivity with a concomitant concentration of funding.

There is a specifically Scottish dimension to this UK-wide issue in that the Scottish higher education sector is increasingly being orientated in a research context by the twin drivers of commercialisation on the one hand (notably by the combined forces of Scottish Enterprise and the Royal Society of Edinburgh) and by successive governments' Foresight policy on the other. The newest universities can hardly be blamed for not wishing to lose out on the fruits of these initiatives although they are realistic to concede they face a long haul towards their goal of fair competition with their more senior rivals. Perhaps this is one area where Scotland could in future achieve a balance of interests which might not necessarily, in all respects, replicate the situation prevailing elsewhere in the UK.

GOVERNANCE AND ACCOUNTABILITY IN THE SCOTTISH UNIVERSITIES

Historically, an enduring feature of the Scottish universities is their greater interaction with the communities they serve than is commonly the rule in England or continental Europe. However, it was not always so. J. D. Mackie (in *The University of Glasgow 1451–1951*, Glasgow, 1954) and others have documented the intense rivalries and internal feuding which did incalculable harm to the University of Glasgow in the late eighteenth century and which presaged the inevitable reforms of the Victorian Age. Successive Royal Commissions from 1826 onward led to the Act of 1858 which permanently changed the constitutional framework of the Scottish universities and set in place a system of governance persisting to the present day.

The 1858 Universities (Scotland) Act substantially curtailed the absolute power of the professors in their hitherto unchallengeable control of university affairs and established a new body – the University Court – but it was not until the Act of 1889 that the general management and administration of the Scottish universities was transferred from the Senate to an enlarged Court.

Today the Court is the undisputed supreme governing body in Scotland's university system. While the students in the ancient universities continue to elect a Rector to plead their cause at meetings of Court, it had seemed that the days of the Rector chairing the Court were numbered, given the observation of the Garrick Committee that they regarded the practice as an unwarranted anachronism. However, the government does not agree and, without waiting for the end of the Dearing consultation process, have announced that, far from changing the tradition, they prefer to see 'greater democratic representation in all of our universities.' How, precisely, that faintly obscure goal is to be achieved – whatever it may mean in practice – remains to be seen.

Apart from Dundee – which chose to provide for a Rector but no longer with the power to chair the Court – all the other Scottish universities founded after Edinburgh have opted to dispense with the office of Rector and, more important, all including Dundee have sought to identify prominent individuals for appointment to their Courts and to provide for the Court itself to elect one of their number as chairman. It can fairly be argued that in that respect the Scottish universities had already anticipated the recommendation of the Jarratt

Committee (1985) on efficiency that University Councils (i.e. Courts in Scotland) should in future play 'a much more active role' in the governance of universities. (Indeed, Jarratt noted that 'over the past three decades the influence of Councils has weakened.') Certainly there is no doubt that Scotland was well ahead of the rest of the UK in recognising the importance of involving men and women of real distinction in the management and administration of her universities.

A strong governing body is vital to the success of any organisation but in a complex mixed economy which a university represents it is crucial that public confidence in an institution is maintained through a combination of sound professional expertise at officer level and, within the boardroom, mature judgement acquired in the professions, commerce and industry on the part of the essentially part-time practitioners who serve on Courts.

These qualities are, of course, all the more important given the determination of the Nolan and Neill Committees that probity in public service must extend beyond government and that educational institutions are no less exposed than other bodies in receipt of taxpayers' money to the duty to observe high standards of professional conduct and accountability. At bottom, however, the key word here is effectiveness as Dearing hands university and college governing bodies new responsibilities which ensure they maintain a competitive edge, domestically and internationally, in the learning society.

TENSIONS WITHIN THE SYSTEM: COOPERATION AND COMPETITION

Cooperation – or at least a spirit of working together to meet a common objective – has not been an obvious feature of higher education in Britain any more than it has been a priority in North America or Europe. And in Scotland, as in the rest of the UK, universities have been slow to sign up for inter-institutional cooperation, preferring to continue to compete, one with the other, in the open market for students as much as for research contracts. It is pointless to debate whether the new advocacy for cooperation (stemming on the one hand from the National Inquiry but, more important, virtually forced on institutions by pressure from the funding councils) is motivated by simple expediency or genuine insights into the real advantages purposeful cooperation can confer. The point is that it is clear that cooperation among academic institutions is here to stay. Government says it is important, SHEFC actively promotes it and Dearing says that institutions ignore its potential benefits at their peril.

The greatest challenge to making the principle of cooperation work in practice may well lie in the use and application of the new technology. Here, the advantages are plain for all to see – shared use of scarce resources, the opening-up of exclusive and often expensive facilities to a plurality of institutions and to the individuals who work within them. However, cooperation is often a thinly disguised form of rationalisation and can sometimes result in a genuine loss of autonomy. In the end, therefore, institutions may be unwilling partners so long as mutual guarantees fail to be established on the defined objectives of cooperation.

Of course, the ultimate form of institutional cooperation is merger. Since the inaugural meeting of COSHEP in October 1992 the number of institutions in membership of the Committee has decreased by four as a result of merger: Craigie College of Education (now merged with the University of Paisley), Jordanhill College of Education (now merged with the University of Strathclyde), Queen's College, Glasgow (which merged with Glasgow Polytechnic to form Glasgow Caledonian University) and Duncan of Jordanstone College of Art (now merged with the University of Dundee). Further mergers have taken place more recently affecting Moray House Institute of Education (with the University of Edinburgh) and the Scottish College of Textiles (with Heriot-Watt University). A merger between St Andrew's College and the University of Glasgow is due to take effect later in 1999. Northern College, which operates from two campuses in Aberdeen and Dundee, looks likely to divide its operations and merge with the Universities of Aberdeen and Dundee. Even the longer term prospect of inter-institutional mergers at the level of universities can no longer be ruled out.

REFERENCES

Crawford, R. L. (1984) Curing the ills of university selection, *Scotsman*, 30 October.

Committee on Higher Education (1963) Report (The Robbins Report), London: HMSO (Cmnd 2154).

Green Paper (1985) *The Development of Higher Education into the 1990s*, London: HMSO (Cmnd 9524).

National Committee of Inquiry into Higher Education (1997) *Higher Education in the Learning Society*, Report of the National Committee (The Dearing Report), Norwich: HMSO.

National Committee of Inquiry into Higher Education (1997) *Higher Education in the Learning Society*, Report of the Scottish Committee (The Garrick Report). Norwich: HMSO.

Scottish Tertiary Education Advisory Council (1985) *Future Strategy for Higher Education in Scotland*, Edinburgh: HMSO (Cmnd 9676).

7

Policy Making in Scottish Education

Walter Humes

Stephen Ball (1990), drawing on the work of earlier writers, defines policies as 'operational statements of values'. Both parts of this definition are important. The phrase 'operational statements' carries prescriptive intent and implies the exercise of power, which may be more or less legitimate. The word 'values' raises questions about the basis on which the values are formed and the groups in society whose aspirations are validated in particular policies. Moreover, in an advanced democratic society the process of policy making is rarely straightforward. At best, according to Ball, it is likely to be 'unwieldy and complex'; at worst, 'unscientific and irrational'. These observations point to the need to dig beneath the surface of policy statements and to interrogate their origin, justification and intent.

This chapter offers an account of the policy-making processes which are characteristic of the Scottish educational system. Following the approach suggested by Ball, this involves looking at the roles of individuals, groups and institutions in the generation and development of policies, including the values which they hold and the power which they exercise. In order to illustrate the general argument it will be necessary to refer to specific policies, for to separate process and substance in policy making would be artificial and potentially misleading: the nature of particular policies can shape the way in which they progress from conception to implementation. First, however, a conceptual framework will be offered based on 'official' and 'unofficial' views of what happens. Thereafter, attention will be focused on different styles of policy management and on the relation between political ideology, culture and educational reform. Finally, consideration will be given to the implementation stage of policy and the critical role of teachers in determining the success or failure of policy initiatives.

OFFICIAL VIEWS

At a meeting of the Scottish Educational Policy Forum held in Edinburgh in May 1997, Nisbet Gallacher, formerly Senior Chief Inspector within the Scottish Office Education and Industry Department (SOEID), gave an account of his perceptions of educational policy making in Scotland. Rejecting the definition of policy as 'a system of administration guided more by interest than by principle' (Chambers Twentieth Century Dictionary), he argued that no single model could account for the diverse routes by which educational initiatives arrived on the political agenda. Policy, according to Gallacher, is made in a variety of circumstances, in different ways, by a range of people. Sometimes it emerges after mature consideration and reflection, informed by evidence and research. At other times it is a response to an immediate event which is perceived as requiring attention. Furthermore, educational policy is not the exclusive province of one set of people. Many individuals and groups are involved. Within the Scottish Office there are politicians, administrators and inspectors, all with an important part to play. In addition, there are the collective interests of bodies such as the Educational Institute of Scotland (EIS), the Association of Directors of Education (ADES), the Convention of Scottish Local Authorities (COSLA), the Scottish Parent Teacher Council (SPTC) and Headteacher Associations to be considered. The only common features in all this, on Gallacher's account, are, first, that for policies to go ahead the agreement of the Secretary of State for Scotland, given in the context of United Kingdom government, is required, and, second, that the Secretary of State invariably reaches a decision having listened to advice from senior civil servants – both administrators and members of Her Majesty's Inspectorate (HMIs) – within the Scottish Office. Under-lying the whole process is the common goal of improving the quality of educational provision in Scotland.

Gallacher's account is interesting, based as it is on extensive 'inside' experience of the forces at work, not least because he was in post at a time when education was high on the political agenda (1987–95). In many respects it is consistent with other official views of policy making, evident in SOEID reports and material issued by the Scottish Office Information Directorate. These invoke the concepts of partnership, consultation and consensus to explain what happens. On this analysis educational provision depends on the cooperation of central and local government, teachers and parents, curriculum and assessment bodies and so, in the framing of new policies, it is essential that they work in partnership with each other. This requires that all those concerned have an opportunity to make representations and express opinions on policy proposals – thus the importance of consultation. As a result of this process, policies are adjusted and the outcome is a broadly agreed consensus which takes account of the legitimate concerns of a wide range of people. In all of this, the stewardship of those entrusted with formulating, developing and implementing policies is seen as unproblematic: they can be relied upon to act in the public interest.

These accounts are as significant for what they do not say as for the insights they offer. What is missing from them is an acknowledgement that within a democracy all policy decisions take place in the context of competing values and beliefs representing different visions of the good society. The consensus model seeks to minimise these conflicts by suggesting that differences can be reconciled and an agreement reached that is acceptable to all the major players. The fact remains, however, that 'agreed' policies do emerge and this raises important questions about how the processes of consultation and policy development are controlled. Three points are significant in this respect. First, power is differential. The individuals and groups who are involved in policy making do not all carry the same weight: the 'partners' are not equal. Second, the development of any policy has to be managed and this involves decisions about the allocation of responsibilities and the frame of reference within which those given responsibilities are allowed to operate. Thus questions to do with how and why people are chosen for particular tasks arise. And third, the currency in which these processes are conducted is language. Policy making involves the drafting and redrafting of documents, as well as verbal exchanges in committees and working groups. To understand the dynamics of policy making it is necessary to understand the power of language in determining perceptions and actions (see Ball, 1990). Language is not neutral: it is a verbal expression of social relations. Peter Cookson states: 'Words do not exist in a disembodied form; they have meaning within a social context that is class bound, conflictual and power driven. Those who control this symbolic world are able to shape and manipulate the marketplace of educational ideas' (in G. Walford, ed., *Researching the Powerful in Education*, London: UCL Press, 1994).

These points suggest that it is necessary to go beyond official accounts of educational policy in Scotland to look in more detail at the distribution and exercise of power, the management styles that are deployed and the forms of discourse that are used in advancing policies. Fortunately, there is a growing body of research literature which can help in addressing these issues.

UNOFFICIAL VIEWS

The most detailed source for educational policy making in Scotland remains Andrew McPherson and Charles Raab's excellent study *Governing Education*, first published in 1988. They employ the term 'policy community' to describe the network of people inside and outside government who, collectively, help to determine the educational agenda. At the centre of this process is the SOEID. Although all major decisions have to be approved by the Secretary of State, it is the Minister responsible for the education portfolio, together with senior administrators and HMIs, who carry out day-to-day responsibilities. The relationship between these three groups – politicians, administrators and HMIs – has been subject to change over time, as will be shown later. In terms of maintaining good lines of communication with outside agencies, HMIs are particularly important. They are some-times described as 'the eyes and ears' of the Secretary of State, indicating that they have a key role as sources of intelligence informing departmental decisions. They are undoubtedly adept at maintaining contacts throughout the system and this means that they are well placed to make recommendations when nominations are sought for membership of the working parties, committees and development groups which are used to plan and flesh out the details of policies. Their powers of patronage are substantial, but not unqualified, for they have to ensure that different constituencies (local government, professional associa-tions, interest groups) are represented. McPherson and Raab suggest, however, that expertise is not the only criterion for admission to the policy community. Recipients of patronage have to exhibit the qualities of 'deference and trust', including a respect for the traditional bureaucratic virtues of discretion and confidentiality, and a willingness to proceed through 'proper channels' rather than engage in public debate which might be politically embarrassing. The permitted discourse of the policy community is thus controlled from the outset.

In developing their analysis McPherson and Raab make extensive use of a contrast between 'pluralist' and 'corporatist' approaches to policy and suggest that at different points in the post-war period one or other has tended to dominate. Pluralist approaches are characterised by negotiation and bargaining, and are justified with reference to a rhetoric of democratic participation. By admitting 'outsiders' into the policy community the SOEID is able to draw on a range of skills, some of which it could not supply from within its own ranks (if only for reasons of number). These 'outsiders' are thus given an opportunity to influence policy but they are required, as part of the bargain, to operate according to the formal and informal rules laid down by the SOEID. They are, in other words, expected to come to share the 'assumptive worlds' of government officials.

Corporatist explanations of the policy process emphasise the differential power of those involved and, in particular, maintain that the state's control of the process, rather than the limited scope for democratic involvement, is what matters. Thus the 'legitimacy' of outside groups does not depend so much on the validity of the interests which they represent as on the fact that government actually chooses to accord them some recognition. That choice is informed by procedural as well as substantive considerations. It is not only the value of the contribution which particular groups can offer that matters: the extent to which they can easily be controlled and made to conform to established practices is also important. McPherson and Raab sum up the contrast between the two interpretations in these terms: 'Pluralist interpretations of policy communities emphasise their multiplicity, their indispensability to government, and their independence of it. Corporatist interpretations assert that government has considerable influence over the constitution of such communities, and over the issues they affect'.

The present writer has offered an interpretation which would suggest that the contrast between the pluralist and corporatist forms of policy management may be more cosmetic than real (Humes, 1986). On this view, the basic style is centralised but the degree of authoritarianism is disguised by various presentational devices or 'strategies of containment'. These include the following: careful control of the flow of information relating to policy initiatives; initiation of those admitted to the policy community into a conformist bureaucratic ideology; employment of a disarming rhetoric of partnership and empowerment; the marginalising of dissent; skilful circumscribing of the nature and scope of research enquiries; promotion of a cult of managerialism which encourages concentration on 'how' rather than 'why' questions. To put it this way may seem to overstate the case by attributing to the SOEID a degree of efficiency and unity of purpose that would be difficult to substantiate. Policies do not always go according to plan, demonstrating that the control function is not invariably successful. One example would be the failure of the attempt to change the pattern of teacher education by introducing mentoring in Scottish secondary schools in August 1995. This policy was first postponed and subsequently abandoned. An analysis of the episode suggests that there were serious weaknesses in communication both within the SOEID and between the SOEID and the Teacher Education Institutions (TEIs) which were given responsibility for promoting the policy. In a subsequent damage limitation exercise the Department sought to attribute blame to the TEIs for the failure. This was accompanied – at the point where postponement rather than abandonment was the preferred option – by a threat to re-consider approval of TEI courses if they did not in future incorporate mentoring. Such public embarrassment is rare, however, and threats are a last resort. Authoritarian measures are only invoked if quiet, behind-the-scenes, persuasive techniques fail to deliver the required goods. Behind the charm of pluralism lies the menace of corporatism.

MANAGERIAL STYLES

To make these points is not to suggest that the policy process in Scottish education has remained static and inflexible. There have been significant changes over the years in relation to the role of individuals and groups within the policy community, the function of institutions, the influence of political and ideological factors, and sensitivity to the cultural distinctiveness of Scottish society (discussed in Chapter 10). It will be instructive to illustrate these shifts with reference to the reform programme in curriculum and assessment over the last two decades (see Humes and MacKenzie, eds, 1994).

There have been four major curricular reforms in Scottish education since 1980 – Standard Grade, Action Plan, 5–14 and Higher Still. These had different origins and were managed in different ways. In the case of Standard Grade there was a recognition among teachers that the previous O-Grade examination was unsuited to a significant proportion of pupils. The policy, in other words, arose partly from professional (as distinct from political) pressures. In the development of new curricular materials and assessment instruments, teacher involvement was strong, albeit under the direction of HMIs, the Scottish Examination Board (SEB) and the (then) Consultative Committee on the Curriculum (CCC). There was extensive piloting of materials and refinement of ideas on assessment, especially in connection with grade-related criteria. Direct political involvement was minimal. The weakness of this approach was that it was demanding of time and resources and implementation was slow. Its strength was that it addressed the concerns of teachers and sought to involve them in developing solutions.

The managerial style of Action Plan was very different. Once again the policy did address a recognised problem – the need to rationalise all non-advanced Further Education (FE) courses via a single National Certificate in place of the existing plethora of certificates and diplomas. But whereas Standard Grade had been preceded by two major reports (Munn and Dunning, both published in 1977), Action Plan suddenly appeared on the educational agenda with little advance warning. Development was swift, with the Scottish Vocational Education Council (SCOTVEC) being established in 1985 to approve courses and establish assessment procedures. The principal impetus for Action Plan came from within the Inspectorate who were motivated by two factors. One was a genuine wish to improve vocational education: the other was a desire to limit the incursion into Scotland of the (then) Manpower Services Commission (MSC), an increasingly powerful offshoot of the Department of Employment in London. This could be construed either as bureaucratic self-interest or as an assertion of Scotland's distinct cultural identity.

The 5–14 Development Programme was different again, this time because of the degree of political control exercised in driving it forward. The key figure was Michael Forsyth who became Education Minister at the Scottish Office in 1987 (Humes, 1995). He set aside the CCC's 10–14 report and replaced it with a government paper *Curriculum and Assessment in Scotland: A Policy for the 1990s* (SED, 1987). Forsyth took a keen interest in the details of recommendations for particular curricular subjects, demanding changes and setting out his views in robust terms. Moreover there was a strong managerial drive behind the programme, with narrow remits for working groups, tight time-scales and an emphasis on accountability and delivery. W. A. Gatherer (in *Curriculum Development in Scotland*, Edinburgh: Scottish Academic Press, 1989) has described 5–14 as a 'totalitarian curriculum' indicative of a 'new authoritarianism' in Scottish education.

The most recent reform programme, Higher Still, aimed at the fifth and sixth years of secondary schooling, is (at the time of writing) not yet implemented, though the development work is well advanced. Implementation has twice been postponed, partly as a result of representations from teachers about workload pressures and 'innovation fatigue'. In terms of the management of the reform, there is evidence to suggest that the traditional policy community, in the shape of professionals and bureaucrats, has regained some of the ground it lost during Forsyth's term of office. Both in the early stages, when the policy proposals were being promoted among teachers, and in the current phase, when the push towards implementation is the priority, senior HMIs have adopted a high profile. Certainly there is political will to complete the restructuring of the secondary school curriculum but the first Labour Education Minister in Scotland (Brian Wilson) seemed content to leave the details to officials. What remains from the Forsyth era is an emphasis on operational efficiency with clear lines of responsibility within the bureaucratic structure which services the programme. The role of the Higher Still Development Unit (HSDU), for example, is clearly subordinate: policy direction comes from within the SOEID.

These examples show that the origins of educational reforms may be professional or bureaucratic or political – or some combination of these. To that extent, part of Nisbet Gallacher's characterisation of the policy process can be accepted. In both Standard Grade and Higher Still there was a professional recognition that existing certification systems were no longer meeting the requirements of sections of the pupil population. There was also a professional element in the emergence of Action Plan but in this case the real impetus was bureaucratic, in the sense that HMIs saw not only an educational opportunity but also a way of cutting off the encroachments of another government agency, the MSC. 5–14 was clearly political and was introduced quite deliberately to stop another professionally-led initiative, 10–14. Higher Still is probably the most difficult to classify because all three pressures – professional, bureaucratic and political – are in evidence to a degree. Teachers acknowledge the need to reform existing Highers but are concerned about resources and staff development. Politicians recognise the force of economic arguments which challenge the wisdom of a sharp division between academic education and vocational training. And officials see an opportunity to reinstate the centrality of their function in the policy-making process, using some of the managerial techniques which they were required to adopt during the Forsyth regime. An ability to adapt to changing circumstances and turn them to advantage is a mark of successful leadership groups, whether in education or any other field.

Clarifying the origins of educational policies is, however, not enough to explain the whole process. Whatever their origins, once policy options get on the agenda, their progress is directed from within the SOEID. That is why questions to do with the way in which consultation exercises are conducted, the selection of individuals to serve on committees, and the lines of responsibility between the Scottish Office and Non-Departmental Public Bodies (NDPBs) such as the Scottish Consultative Council on the Curriculum (SCCC) and the Scottish Qualifications Authority (SQA), are so important. These are issues of power, not just operational efficiency. The power dimension is even more apparent when recent changes in the governance of education are considered.

IDEOLOGY, CULTURE AND DISCOURSE

During the period of Conservative government (1979–97) a number of measures designed to alter the administrative structure of Scottish education were introduced. These included parental choice of school, enabling parents to send their children to schools outside their immediate catchment area, the establishment of School Boards, comprising representatives from local communities and businesses as well as parents and teachers, provision for schools to opt out of local authority contol, and devolved management, whereby schools have direct control of the greater part of their budgets. All of these measures involved weakening the traditional role of local government in education. Underlying the reforms were certain recurring themes characteristic of New Right ideology: consumerism, choice, accountability, standards, value for money. Parents were regarded as central actors in the reform programme, the aim being that they should act as a counterweight to self-interested professionals. Once again, Michael Forsyth was the prime mover in these developments.

However, there were conceptual confusions, even contradictions, in the raft of new measures. They were intended to release parents and schools from the alleged inefficiency and paternalism of local authorities and reduce the power of professionals. Ironically, in order to achieve this, a strong degree of central direction from government was required. And it soon became apparent that Forsyth had misjudged the public response. There was a lack of enthusiam among parents for School Board elections and virtually no take-up of the provisions of the Self-Governing Schools Etc. (Scotland) Act of 1989. Even stronger opposition to another of Forsyth's proposals – on national testing – emerged. He had a very formal and traditional conception of what testing should entail. Both parents and teachers were in favour of improved assessment and reporting procedures but regarded the Minister's approach as crude and unhelpful. What finally emerged was a more limited exercise relying heavily on the judgement of teachers.

This resistance is not surprising in view of the unpopularity in Scotland of Conservatism in general, and Thatcherism in particular, throughout the 1980s and beyond. What is interesting in relation to the making of educational policy is the cultural aspect of Scottish responses. The philosophy of individual consumerism ran counter to the image of civil society as an embodiment of certain principles (notably equality and social unity) valued in the national consciousness. That this image is as much myth as reality is not important. What matters is that people believe it. A history of relative poverty has meant that Scottish people have inherited a communal consciousness which stresses fairness to all as a guiding principle. Against this background, Forsyth's brave new educational world was unappealing. The risk inherent in educational consumerism – that it might encourage selfish individualism where parents pursue the interests of their own children at the expense of others – thus provoked a degree of cultural (and moral) revulsion in Scotland.

Forsyth seems belatedly to have recognised that both his policies and his style were fuelling Scottish discontent with New Right ideology and, when he became Secretary of State in 1995, he began to adopt a more conciliatory manner. This was aided by the less interventionist approach adopted by the Conservative Education Ministers who succeeded him (Lord James Douglas-Hamilton and Raymond Robertson). The traditional policy community saw an opportunity to regroup and reinstate themselves as the principal players in the policy process, in readiness for the election of a new government. Professionals and bureaucrats enjoy relative security of tenure in comparison with politicians and can afford to take a long-term view.

It would be misleading, however, to suggest that Forsyth simply represented a temporary aberration. He demonstrated how strong political will, fired by ideological zeal and backed by managerial drive, could make a major impact on the policy agenda in Scotland. Although he was unable to carry through all his intentions, what he did bring about was a change of discourse, whereby the language of choice, quality, standards and achievement has become part of the educational currency. In Cookson's terms, he transformed 'the marketplace of educational ideas'. New Labour shows no signs of abandoning these principles. Its commitment to tackling problems of 'failing schools' and 'failing teachers' and to ensuring professional accountability is, if anything, even stronger. To that extent, Forsyth's legacy survives.

The establishment of a Scottish parliament in the year 2000 will almost certainly bring about further changes in the way educational policy is conducted. At this stage projections can only be speculative. Lindsay Paterson has suggested two possible scenarios (cited in Clark and Munn, eds, 1997). One would involve an upsurge of 'civic activism' which would challenge the 'democratic deficit' in the traditional policy process. Instead of relying on selective consultation with favoured partners and on compliant quangos, a Scottish parliament would have to be more transparent in its dealings with 'a new active citizenry'. Where the impetus is to come from for this new activism is not entirely clear. The hope seems to be that the Scottish people will somehow be transformed by the simple fact of having a focus for political debate. This seems optimistic. Increased disenchantment with an additional layer of government is just as likely.

The alternative scenario is that the parliament will lead to 'the strengthening of the central Scottish state'. The checks on Scottish educational policy currently deriving from the Treasury and the Department for Education and Employment in London would no longer exist and this, combined with the weakened condition of local government, would ensure that SOEID control of the policy agenda would become more rather than less powerful. The natural tendency in Scottish education has always been to 'look to the centre' for leadership and, despite the self-image of Scots as forthright and challenging, they show remarkable passivity in the face of professional and bureaucratic authority. An Edinburgh-based elite, issuing prescriptive 'guidelines' on all aspects of educational policy might have some merit in terms of ensuring uniformity of practice throughout the country, but such an approach rests on the dubious assumption that there is always one best 'solution' for all educational problems. The most effective protection against this possible outcome is likely to be the proportional representation system on which elections to the Scottish parliament will be based. Even if 'civic activism' is uncertain in the short term, the election of substantial representation from opposition parties should ensure that there is a focus for resistance to an oppressive 'central Scottish state'.

THE IMPLEMENTATION OF POLICY

The ultimate success of educational policies depends on the extent to which the values and practices recommended in policy documents become operational at school and classroom levels. Attempting to achieve this involves the efforts of a wider range of people than those who might be regarded as central players in the policy community. It is necessary to establish strong lines of communication between central government, local government and individual institutions. Here the role of development officers, advisers and in-service trainers is important. All of the major programmes of reform – Standard Grade, Action Plan, 5–14, Higher Still – have depended on substantial inputs from 'intermediate' staff of this kind, often seconded from local authorities or teacher education institutions on temporary contracts, who have explained and promoted approved policies to groups of teachers up and down the country. Within local authorities, advisers and staff tutors attached to educational development services have also made vital contributions. It is at this stage that the 'unwieldy and complex' nature of policy implementation becomes particularly apparent. Levels of initial awareness among school staff vary, schools may be more or less receptive to new ideas, and demand for back-up in the form of equipment and resources is rarely matched by supply. The 'intermediate' staff generally do not have an easy task in their efforts to ensure that policy initiatives get off to a good start. Their power is limited and, while they can convey concerns at local level back to the central agencies, they cannot guarantee that there will be an adequate response. They thus occupy a somewhat ambivalent position, trying to satisfy two audiences – members of the policy community at national level and classroom teachers at local level. Their ambivalence serves as a reminder of the untidy, and sometimes frustrating, nature of policy development – a feature that official accounts tend to ignore.

In the preceding sections it has been suggested that both consensual-professional and rational-managerial interpretations of the policy process in Scottish education are inadequate. The consensual-professional model fails to address questions of how a 'consensus' is reached and assumes too readily that professionals know best and that traditional institutions always operate in the public interest. At worst, it is complacent, self-serving and inward-looking. Looked at from that perspective, Forsyth's assault on the practices which he encountered when he assumed office as Education Minister was justified. He sought to replace them with a rational-managerial model in which the hard-edged practices of business and industry were applied to education. On this model, policy moves logically through a series of clearly marked stages: conception, development, implementation, evaluation. Once the basic framework of policy is decided, the emphasis is on delivery and action: endless reflection on issues of meaning and purpose is seen as unprofitable, an intellectual luxury which cushioned professionals had enjoyed for too long.

But this approach too has its weaknesses. It fails to acknowledge that education and industry are profoundly different kinds of enterprise. The development of children is not the same as the manufacture of products. The former can never be reduced to a series of standard processes which will guarantee the desired outcome. It is an immensely complex undertaking, operating at intellectual, physical, social, emotional and moral levels, which interact with each other in subtle and often puzzling ways. It is the task of the teacher to interpret these messages and decide on the most effective form of pedagogic response. No policy document, however carefully formulated, will provide all the answers to the diverse challenges faced by teachers on a daily basis. Moreover, the job of teaching is not directly comparable to the role of an operative in an industrial enterprise, who is given a task and instructed in the stages which have to be gone through in order to complete it. Teaching is often a messy business which resists the clear-cut formulae of management theory. To attempt to reduce teachers to the role of operatives is to devalue the skill and judgement on which their work depends.

A sensitive understanding of what teaching involves is required if educational policies are to be implemented effectively. In the final analysis it is in classrooms up and down the country that the success or failure of educational policies is determined. Teachers can be provided with all kinds of support and staff development to acquaint them with the requirements of new programmes but that is not enough. They need to be convinced that the reforms which they are asked to implement are sound in principle and that time and resources will be provided to allow the work to be done to a satisfactory standard. There is no short cut or 'quick fix' in this process. Where teachers are not persuaded of the wisdom of what they are asked to do, they may pay lip service to the new requirements but continue to act much as before. Policy failure would thus be compounded by professional dishonesty, thereby deepening the cynicism and low morale which have characterised teaching throughout the United Kingdom in recent years.

One of the ethical principles for the teaching profession set out in the Code produced by the Universities Council for the Education of Teachers in 1997 is moral courage, which is defined as 'willingness to teach subject matter or use methods which are unpopular or officially frowned upon, if intellectual and/or vocational integrity so demand'. In other words, teachers have an obligation not only to those who employ them but also to their own consciences and, above all, to the interests of their pupils. It is entirely proper that teachers should reflect seriously on the deliberations of the policy community and should scrutinise their recommendations very carefully. Decisions about the nature and extent of educational provision in any society are inescapably decisions about the value system which that society is seeking to promote. Educational institutions embody social messages about fundamental principles such as freedom, authority, equality, justice and community. Thus policy decisions are never purely technical matters about the most efficient means of reaching stated outcomes. They are always expressive of a social philosophy which, in a democracy, should be contestable and open to debate. The perceptions of those who are at the sharp end of policy delivery – whether teachers or other public service groups (such as police officers, doctors, nurses, social workers) need to be taken seriously. Finally, this is true not only when new policies are being implemented but also when established policies are being evaluated. Within Scottish education there has been a tendency in the past for those who have been responsible for policy development (principally HMIs) to have had a significant part to play in the subsequent evaluation of policies. That is an unhealthy state of affairs. Research into the success or otherwise of policies needs to be fully independent if it is to inform future decision making in a constructive way.

REFERENCES

Ball, S. J. (1990) *Politics and Policy Making in Education: Explorations in Policy Sociology*, London: Routledge.

Clark, M. M. and P. Munn (eds) (1997) *Education in Scotland: Policy and Practice from Pre-School to Secondary*, London: Routledge.

Humes, W. M. (1986) *The Leadership Class in Scottish Education*, Edinburgh: John Donald.

Humes, W. M. (1995) The Significance of Michael Forsyth in Scottish Education, *Scottish Affairs*, no. 11, pp. 112–130.

Humes, W. M. and M. L. MacKenzie (eds) (1994) *The Management of Educational Policy: Scottish Perspectives*, London: John Donald.

McPherson, A. and C. D. Raab (1988) *Governing Education: A Sociology of Policy Since 1945*, Edinburgh: Edinburgh University Press.

8

The Politics of Scottish Education

Malcolm L. MacKenzie

It is not easy to define politics. One of the most famous attempts is Easton's 'the authoritative allocation of values'. However defined, the subject involves policies, decision making, political parties, ideologies and conflict, the implementation process and the micropolitics which take place in small groups in all organisations. Many educationists are wary of politics, not least because it can involve them in what Humes has described as 'getting their hands dirty'. Yet in recent years the study of the relationship between politics and education has been very prominent because of the obvious impact of political thinking on educational change. This is as true of Scotland as any other comparable country. It is particularly true in contemporary Scotland in terms of the relationship between the education system and the governance of Scotland.

THE WHITE PAPER: SCOTLAND'S PARLIAMENT

In July 1997 the newly elected British Labour government presented to parliament a White Paper containing its proposals for the creation of a Scottish parliament to which clearly defined powers would be devolved, including education and training. These powers incorporated school education, including pre-five, primary and secondary education; the functions of Her Majesty's Inspectorate of Schools; teacher supply, training and conditions of service; further and higher education, including policy, funding, the functions of the Scottish Higher Education Funding Council (SHEFC) and student support; science and research funding where supported through SHEFC and where undertaken in support of other devolved matters; training policy and lifelong learning, including all the training responsibilities which had been exercised by the Scottish Office; vocational qualifications, including the functions of the Scottish Qualifications Authority (SQA); careers advice and guidance. The White Paper proposed to reserve certain matters to the United Kingdom Parliament, including the United Kingdom Research Councils. It should be noted that, in the words of the White Paper, the UK Parliament 'is and will remain sovereign'.

Following the union of the Crowns of Scotland and England in 1603, the Union of the Scottish and English Parliaments in 1707 created a Parliament of Great Britain meeting in London. In its first chapter the White Paper provides a short historical account of the development of the government of education in Scotland. It points out that the office of Secretary for Scotland was created in 1885, and enhanced in 1926 to Secretary of State. St Andrew's House in Edinburgh became the headquarters of the Scottish Office in 1939 and functions of the Scottish Office in London were transferred to Edinburgh. It should be noted that this was administrative devolution as distinct from the parliamentary devolution now being advanced. The White Paper also indicated that in recent years further administrative devolution to the Scottish Office has taken place, resulting in the addition of major functions such as industrial support, training, higher education and the arts.

The central government of education in Scotland has, therefore, in pre-devolution times been conducted through the Scottish Office, headed by the Secretary of State for Scotland. The government department with the administrative responsibility for the Secretary of State's functions has been the Scottish Office Education and Industry Department (SOEID) usually headed by a junior minister accountable to the Secretary of State and a member of the team of ministers, all elected politicians, accountable to the Westminster Parliament.

It should be noted that while the SOEID has had national oversight of education and a major role in the inspection of schools, through Her Majesty's Inspectorate, the provision and delivery of school education is the responsibility of thirty-two unitary authorities which are known as education authorities. Factsheet 3 issued by the Scottish Office states that the education authorities have a statutory duty to provide adequate and efficient school education. The duty of providing further education was removed from education authorities by the Further and Higher Education (Scotland) Act 1992 (see Chapter 5) as a consequence of which further education colleges became accountable directly to the Secretary of State through a process known as incorporation. Other functions of education authorities include the making of provision for special educational needs and for the teaching of Gaelic in Gaelic speaking areas. They also have a duty to provide adequate facilities for recreational and sporting activities. They are responsible for the construction of buildings, the employment of teachers and other staff, and the provision of equipment and materials. As Factsheet 3 puts it, 'they exercise responsibility for the curriculum taught in schools taking account of national guidance'.

PARTY POLITICS

It should be noted that the Secretary of State for Scotland and his Ministers are politicians elected as candidates on behalf of a political party. At local authority level most elected councillors are party political although some stand on an independent ticket. Thus the governance and policy process of education in Scotland are imbued with the political debate. This is not to discount the vital role of professionalism in delivery of the education service, a professionalism for which Scottish teachers and lecturers have an international reputation and which is expressed not only in the classroom and lecture hall but through bodies such as the Scottish Consultative Council on the Curriculum (SCCC) and the General Teaching Council for Scotland (GTC) described and discussed elsewhere in this volume (see Chapters 17 and 110). The relationship between teacher autonomy, professionalism and politics is an important, controversial and increasingly sensitive one, not least in respect of curriculum and methods. One of the most notable developments in post-war Britain has been the growing importance which politicians of all political parties attach to education both in their policies and in their public pronouncements. Indeed the leader of the Labour Party, subsequently Prime Minister, Tony Blair announced before the 1997 British general election that the main theme of his campaign was to be 'Education, Education, Education'. This contrasts significantly with the position in immediate post-war Britain when education, although important, undoubtedly took second place in the minds of politicians to other issues such as the economy, foreign affairs and, in terms of the personal social services, health. The key importance now attached to education policy in respect of its contribution to the national economy, changing technology and the culture and fabric of society renders it necessary that students and practitioners of education make themselves familiar not only with the policies of the political parties but with their underlying theories and ideologies.

THE PARTY MANIFESTOS: THE BRITISH GENERAL ELECTION 1997

This chapter, and indeed most of this book, will inevitably focus on the education policies of the British Conservative and Labour Parties. There is no discourtesy here, intended or implied, to the other major parties which have represented Scottish constituencies at Westminster in the post-war era, notably the Scottish National Party and the Scottish Liberal Democrats. The reason why major consideration must inevitably be given to the policies of the Conservative and Labour Parties is that they, and they alone, have formed British governments at Westminster since the war so that it is their policies which have been implemented in Scotland and by whose study the evolution of the Scottish education system can be understood. Even when the Conservative Party's parliamentary representation in terms of Scottish M.P.s began to fall dramatically (ending in a wipe-out in the 1997 Election) under the Thatcher and Major administrations, the politicians who held ministerial positions in these governments in the Scottish Office were, inevitably, Conservative MPs implementing Conservative policy, emanating from thinking which did not necessarily originate in Scotland. It is this complex relationship between the Scottish education system and the British political system which students often find most difficult to understand and, hopefully, justifies the factual background with which this chapter has begun and which forms the backcloth to the political debate.

A term increasingly used in describing political policy in recent years is 'discourse'. Ball (1990), acknowledging his debt to the work of Michel Foucault, says that discourses embody meaning and social relationships, and constitute both subjectivity and power relations. As he puts it: 'Discourses are, therefore, about what can be said, and thought, but also about who can speak when, where and with what authority' (p. 17). The relationship between knowledge, language and power is central to any analysis of discourse. Individuals or groups who can change, control or 'set' the discourse are exercising real power. The source of the discourse may not be immediately apparent. The parameters of the discourse may, in fact, determine a person's perception and creation of reality so that, as Ball puts it, 'We do not speak the discourse. The discourse speaks us' (p. 18).

In the era of the government headed by Margaret Thatcher the discourse in education changed. In common parlance one might say that 'the goalposts were moved'. Whereas in the immediate post-war era the emphasis was on equality, the comprehensive school and educational expansion, a new language appeared and this is reflected in the manifestos put forward to the electorate by the political parties in the 1997 general election. Taken collectively, one notes in them a concern with standards and teacher appraisal, skill, school discipline, pre-school education, the rights of the consumer, usually defined as parents. The discourse is important not only for what it says but, sometimes even more important, for what it does not say. One notices the sparse reference to equality, structures, or social engineering of the kind endemic in the pre-Thatcher era.

The following are some examples of policy taken from the published documentation of the major political parties during and immediately prior to the 1997 election. It must be stressed that these are merely examples. They do not pretend to be fully representative or exhaustive. (It should also be indicated here that the author is aware of and notes with respect the existence of other political parties not only in Scotland but in Northern Ireland and Wales.)

As would be expected, the Scottish National Party stresses the conservation and appreciation of Scottish culture. A policy document states in regard to Scottish culture:

> An independent nation will wish its people to be aware of this heritage, and the curriculum at all levels of education will make available knowledge and experience of our history, languages, literature, arts, music and dance.

The Scottish National Party's general election manifesto committed the SNP to 'restoring' educational excellence. Its main thesis was that Scotland's 'crisis in education' was a result of under-funding and it committed a Nationalist government to provide, among other things, additional teachers and improved buildings, to replace the student loans system by maintenance grants, to improve training and skills development and to foster Gaelic-medium education.

The Labour Party pledged itself to cut class sizes to thirty or under in the first three years of primary school; to provide nursery places for all four-year-olds; to raise standards and tackle under-achievement; to provide access to computer technology. A new initiative to provide lifelong learning through a new University for Industry was promised. Stress was placed on a grounding in the three Rs, computing and a foreign language for all children and standards of appraisal for teachers.

The demands in the current discourse for improved standards and concern about poor teaching, combined with preparedness to be tough, may be seen to be reflected in the following commitment by Labour: 'We will enhance the role of the General Teaching Council in the accreditation and development of teachers. There will be speedy, but fair, procedures to remove teachers unsuited to the job'. It should also be noted that the aforementioned University for Industry is to be a public/private partnership developing the links to extend lifelong learning.

The Scottish Liberal Democrat Manifesto listed as its 'key priorities' increased funding for books and equipment in schools; the reduction of primary school classes; the tackling of the backlog of repair and maintenance to buildings; the boosting of the chances for all adults to improve their skills and obtain better qualifications. It pledged education for all 3–4 year olds whose parents wanted it; the raising of standards in schools, the strengthening of school inspection and school discipline; the publication by all schools of meaningful information on their standards, achievements and plans for the future; an 'increased role' for parents in education, the development of Gaelic medium education; support for the Scottish four–year Honours Degree; wider access for further and higher education; the reintroduction of the training levy to promote training in the workplace and the expansion of training oppor-tunities for young people.

The Scottish Conservative and Unionist Manifesto 1997 committed a future Conserva-tive government to extend testing in schools; to improve discipline and teaching standards; to provide parents with better information about school performance; to increase each school's control over its own affairs; to publish all school test results, including the results of tests of seven and fourteen year olds; and to extend nursery vouchers. The Manifesto also promised to ensure standards in schools by introducing an Educational Standards guarantee which would set national standards for children of all ages. This would involve all schools being given individual targets for achievement which took account of the characteristics and performance of each school. From these, national standards of achievement would be set. These standards, it was stated, would be increased each year to ratchet upwards the performance of schools. Schools failing to meet standards would be 'targeted' by the schools inspectorate. The Manifesto reflected with pride on the Conservative government's implemented policies of devolved school management and proposed, if elected, to ensure that devolved school management was introduced into all schools by April 1998 with 90 per cent of the schools' budget devolved to schools. It noted that 43 per cent of school leavers now went on to higher and further education.

The above is a partial review of policy commitments by the major political parties in respect of Scottish education in the general election of 1997. Yet by what route did they evolve? What do they tell about the relationship between education and society? To chart the road to the manifestos it is necessary to go back in time.

THE POST-WAR CONSENSUS

The notion that education is central to any concept of society and, above all, to any planned programme of political reform is embedded in Scottish history and consciousness. As early as the sixteenth century the Scottish religious reformer John Knox in *The First Book of Discipline* (1561) envisaged a public financed system of universal compulsory education as an essential component of his vision of an authoritarian, theocratic state which would create an ideal society intended to mirror the Kingdom of Heaven on earth. The notion that 'there is no such thing as society' does not resonate with the consciousness and history of the Scottish people. In pre-Reformation times Scotland could boast three great universities (St Andrews, Glasgow and Aberdeen); in mediaeval literature the notion of the Common Good, the Commonweal or simply society appears, for example, in Sir David Lyndsay's play *Ane Satyre of the Three Estaites*. Scotland's international reputation for educational excellence and a national commitment to educational improvement can be traced back at least to the Act for Settling Schools (1696) which, albeit with limited success (Smout, 1969), at least attempted to realise Knox's vision of creating a school in every parish. The point to note is that the use of education as an instrument to improve society, even to attempt to create an ideal society, is not foreign to the historical Scottish conception of politics.

This is most clearly illustrated in the years during and immediately after the second world war. At that time Scottish politicians, educationists and other thinkers participated in the creation of an educational/political consensus which had international dimensions. The foundation of the post-war consensus was laid not by the 1945–51 Labour government headed by Prime Minister Clement Attlee but by Winston Churchill's wartime co-alition in which Labour MPs such as Chuter Ede and Tom Johnston, Secretary of State for Scotland, played a prominent part. Its thinking contributed to the Education Act 1944 (the Butler Act) which applied to England and Wales and the Education (Scotland) Acts of 1945 and 1946, and its philosophy can be seen in its most brilliant, international dimension in two great reports, viz., *Secondary Education* (1947) by the Advisory Council on Education in Scotland and *General Education in a Free Society* (1945) (the Harvard Report) produced by an American team led by J. B. Conant of the University of Harvard. Both reports, although focusing on the needs and individual characteristics of their respective countries, essentially encapsulated the ideology of the Western democracies forged during the war. This ideology espoused the following principles:

1. Western democratic civilisation has both the right and the duty to socialise children in its cultural, political (broadly defined as democratic) values so that the breakdown in civilisation, which had led to the horrors of the Holocaust, should never be repeated. The Scottish report laid great stress on the need to foster human spirituality in its use of the term Christian Democracy.
2. Social reconstruction, social control and social engineering, liberally interpreted, are legitimate political methods for a democratic society, using the educational services as its most powerful instrument.
3. Such methods improve the quality of citizenship, a major aim of the education service. This, in turn, leads to democratic political stability.
4. The main contribution which schools can make is to provide a broad, general education available to, but not necessarily identical for, all. Such an education should be compulsory, not capable of being rejected by the wishes of either parents or children.
5. The education service has both the ability and duty to make a contribution to the economic well-being of society.

The above is a shorthand attempt to summarise the complex, theoretical thrust of two closely argued reports. As a consequence, it runs the danger of over-simplification. However, it may put the radical movement of right-wing ideas discussed below in a meaningful context. Perhaps it should also be noted that the Scottish Advisory Council's promotion of spiritual values through the development of Christian Democracy was intended to reflect Scottish history and culture. It was in no sense a dogmatic assertion that spirituality and morality can only be developed in terms of one particular religious commitment.

On the acceptance of this ideological base the political parties (in this case the Conservative and Labour parties) vied with each other in the post-war period in pursuing expansionary and compulsory policies, encouraged by their advisers in a series of official reports. For example, the school leaving age was raised to fifteen in 1947 and to sixteen in 1972. The high point of the era of consensus was probably the Robbins Report *Higher Education* (1963) which accepted the principle that all who could acquire the entrance qualification had a 'right' to higher education. McNay and Ozga in their book *Policy-Making in Education: The Breakdown of Consensus* (Pergamon Press, 1985) argued that the consensus was 'fragile'. This is true, but only up to a point. There had been considerable conflict between the Conservative and Labour parties about comprehensive schools, notably Labour's plan to end the selection of children into different types of secondary school by means of the eleven–plus examination in England and Wales and transfer tests, usually at the age of twelve, in Scotland.

The forthcoming debate and challenge to the consensus was to be more profound than debates about structure. It was to change, perhaps permanently, the nature of the political discourse with consequences for Scottish education and politics which it would be an understatement to describe as dramatic.

THE NEW RIGHT

The consensus cracked in 1968 although the cracks did not become clearly visible until the 1970s. An event of great significance, although few realised it at the time, was a speech made by Conservative MP Enoch Powell in that year to the Conservative Party's National Advisory Committee on Education. In his speech Powell claimed that, of all sacred cows, education was both the most sacred and 'the most cowlike'. He dismissed the conventional wisdom that there was a direct causal relationship between educational expenditure and economic growth as 'bunkum' and attacked 'the deceptive air of simplicity and obviousness' of the 'Robbins principle' that those with the requisite entrance qualifications had a 'right' to higher education. Powell accepted that education was a 'good' which society should distribute only to the extent that it wished or could afford to do so, not in anticipation of some measurable economic return or in accordance with some mythical right of the individual.

The following year, 1969, saw the publication of the first Black Paper. Edited by C. B. Cox and A. C. Dyson, it was a pamphlet, the first in a long series, containing articles by prominent literary figures, academics and politicians, which criticised the consensus in contemporary education. The first Black Paper entitled *Fight for Education* attacked, among other things, comprehensive schools, alleged falling educational standards, the end of selectivity, a perceived breakdown in discipline both in schools and higher education. The first shots in the battle about to be waged by the New Right had been fired. Scottish academics, politicians and members of various pressure groups were to participate in the battle, but its nature and effects can only be understood by looking at the Conservative Party in a British and international context.

Carr and Hartnett (1996) argue that the central aim of the New Right was to break the consensus about education policies. The crucial event was the election of Margaret Thatcher as leader of the Conservative Party. As Carr and Hartnett put it 'the real change came when Mrs Thatcher was elected leader of the party in 1975: that event allowed the educational counter-revolution to be staged' (p. 154). Levitas (1986) in her book *The Ideology of the New Right* (Polity Press 1986) identifies two strands in its thought. One is a neo-liberal, laissez-faire economism devoted to the principle of the free-market, associated with a wide range of authors including J. S. Mill, Adam Smith, F. A Hayek and Milton Friedman. The second strand Levitas identifies is the puritanism of the American 'moral majority' associated in the 1980s with spokespersons such as Irving Kristol and the Reverend Jerry Falwell, and in Britain with the emphasis on cultural transmission advocated by the Salisbury Group and *The Salisbury Review* edited by Roger Scruton.

In Carr and Hartnett's view the New Right coalition operated 'with consummate political, media and rhetorical skills' (p. 158). They refer to Knight's research (1990) which, they state, analyses how the New Right coalition 'moved from the periphery of educational policy-making to its centre'. Perhaps most important of all is what they say about discourse:

> The New Right, through its techniques of persuasion and, by hard work and the imaginative use of language and the media, created a new populist form of discourse based on pamphlets and the 'findings' of its think tanks. This discourse was directed not at educational experts or teachers but at parents and voters. It also developed and exploited close links with the media, especially newspapers and television. This gave far greater coverage to its claims, assertions, fictions, myths and proposed policies. (p. 159)

The impact of the new discourse is reflected in the manifestos of all the political parties quoted above. Scotland was not a mere recipient. Prominent Scots contributed to it and its pressure groups. One might mention Michael Forsyth (Humes, 1995), former Secretary of

State for Scotland, and ex-government Minister Allan Stewart. It should be noted that both had strong links with St Andrews University. Indeed more research is required into the contribution to New Right discourse and its impact on Mrs Thatcher and her advisers by ideas emanating from that great university.

THE IMPACT ON POLICY

The following policies might all be seen as evidence of the impact of New Right thinking on Scottish education: the Parents' Charter; the growing power of parents in Scottish school management encouraged by the School Boards (Scotland) Act 1988; the transfer to Scottish schools of power over their budgets by devolved management of resources; the opting out legislation contained in the Self-Governing Schools etc. (Scotland) Act 1989; the abolition of Strathclyde Region and the hostility directed towards it, for example, in Prime Minister John Major's description of it as a 'monstrosity'; the ending of the two-tier system of local government; the privatisation of services through 'contracting-out'; the encouragement via the curriculum of a risk-taking entrepreneurial culture; the emphasis on skill acquisition and wealth creation; positive school-industry links; national testing and the publication of school test results; a concern with standards and measurable outcomes reflected, for example, in the 5–14 Development Programme; a strong line on appraisal and the dismissal of incompetent teachers; an increased role for the GTC. These policies did succeed, through changing the discourse, not only in destroying the old consensus but in going some way towards creating a new one. The requisitioning of this discourse, albeit with adaptations, by New Labour, explains in part the landslide victory gained by Labour in the 1997 general election, the loss of all Conservative seats in Scotland and the likelihood of long-term Labour hegemony in Scottish political life whether at Westminster or in a devolved Parliament in Scotland. The new consensus, if one emerges, is likely to centre round the concept 'the social market'.

THE SOCIAL MARKET

In 1988 in the publication *The Social Market Economy* (published by the Social Market Foundation) Robert Skidelsky wrote:

> The most hopeful political development of recent years is revival of belief in the market system. It has become worldwide, uniting rich and poor, capitalist and socialist countries in a common language and the beginnings of a common practice. In Russia, China and Eastern Europe, the monoliths of state socialism have started to crumble; in the West the army of officials is in retreat. (p. 4)

Skidelsky argues that a social market economy is, above all, embedded in social arrangements regarded as 'fair'. This analysis may give a clue to the electoral success of New Labour and the abandonment by the Labour Party of state socialism, as witnessed by the excision of Clause 4, pertaining to common ownership of the means of production, distribution and exchange, from its constitution. The quest for social justice embedded in the social market approach may also explain the apparent paradox that, in a post-Thatcherite world, the worth of market forces has been accepted while the harsher, socially unconcerned aspects of classical liberalism have been rejected by the British electorate, above all in Scotland. The way forward for the Scottish Tory Party may lie in the revival of and adherence to its One Nation tradition, essentially a commitment to welfare capitalism, ensuring the maintenance of an economic and social safety net below which nobody shall fall. In education terms this means ensuring high standards of skill and general education for all. It does not mean, as Richard Pring has argued in his book *Closing the Gap* (Hodder and Stoughton, 1995) the creation of a 'helot' class, whose education is limited to short term skills, or of an 'underclass', whose value system is alien, even hostile, to that of the rest of society.

According to Skidelsky, the movement of ideas in favour of a more decentralised, competitive and entrepreneurial economy is driven by the force of new technology, as a consequence of which the 'social market economy' recognises the 'instrumental efficiency of decentralised decision-making'. The move to decentralisation, seen in the decision to create a Scottish parliament, raises questions about Scottish national identity and consciousness, and whether recent constitutional changes will inevitably trigger radical developments along nationalistic lines.

SCOTLAND: 'A FIGMENT OF THE IMAGINATION'

Scotland, as a nation, chose to merge its parliament with that of England in 1707. Now it is to have, not the restoration of that parliament, but a 'devolved' one, denied sovereignty which, for the time being at least, will remain at Westminster. Is Scotland still a nation? In their analysis of this question Brown, McCrone and Paterson (1996) describe Scotland as a 'civil society' partly because the Scots are a group of people who are aware of having a distinct identity from other groups around them. They argue that Scotland is not simply a piece of geography but a 'transcendent idea which runs through history, reinterpreting that history to fit the concerns of each present' (p. 36). Thus, Scotland, England and Wales, are 'figments of the imagination'.

That nationhood lies in consciousness more than law and economics can be readily agreed. Hence the importance of education because it, above all, forms consciousness. It is of course true that Britain, and the sense of being British, is also a figment of the imagination. The future of Scotland will be determined by which form of consciousness prevails. The Scottish Conservative Party may revive, especially it if returns to its One Nation compassionate tradition compatible with Scottish culture. Or it may cling to a neo-classical liberalism alien not only to the Scottish people but to its own traditions. New Labour, in many ways more akin to One Nation Toryism than to Socialism, may hold sway for a generation with a new social market philosophy. The devolved parliament may prove not a bulwark against but a stepping stone towards an independent, increasingly natio-nalistic Scotland. The Scottish 'policy community' and 'leadership class' may, like the Sicilian aristocracy in Giuseppe di Lampedusa's novel *The Leopard* continue to filter, interpret and re-group in face of the radical changes of New Labour politics, just as they did in response to the New Right. In any event, education, as Prime Minister Blair has stated, will remain centre stage in the political debate awaiting the next dramatic developments in what Winston Churchill described as 'the awful unfolding scene of the future'.

REFERENCES

Ball, S. J. (1990) *Politics and Policy Making in Education. Explorations in Policy Sociology*, London and New York: Routledge.
Brown, A., D. McCrone and L. Paterson (1996) *Politics and Society in Scotland*, London and New York: MacMillan Press Ltd., St. Martin's Press, Inc.

Carr, W. and A. Hartnett (1996) *Education and the Struggle for Democracy. The Politics of Educational Ideas*, Buckingham, Philadelphia: Open University Press.

Humes, W. M. (1995), The Significance of Michael Forsyth in Scottish Education, *Scottish Affairs*, no. 11, pp. 112–29.

Knight, C. (1990) *The Making of Tory Education Policy in Post-War Britain 1950–1986*, London: Falmer Press.

Smout, T. C. (1969) *A History of the Scottish People 1560–1830*, London: Fontana/Collins.

9

The Independent Sector

Keith Pearson

The independent sector in Scotland is best defined as comprising those seventy-five schools currently in membership of the Scottish Council of Independent Schools (SCIS). Since its inception in 1978, SCIS has been the principal vehicle through which the vast majority of Scottish independent schools have sought to express common interests and secure joint representation at national level. Much of the statistical information given below is taken from literature published by SCIS, and the assistance of its Director, Judith Sischy, is acknowledged in the preparation of this chapter; but it must be recognised forthwith that every independent school in Scotland is just that – independent – and that few general-isations can claim to be applicable to every single school.

Whereas in England and Wales some seven to eight per cent of pupils have for much of this century been educated in fee-paying schools, in Scotland the figure has consistently been much lower, around only three to four per cent. The difference is usually and persuasively explained by the fact that Scottish education has long been highly regarded and that the Scottish 'burgh' school is traditionally considered to have catered well for pupils of all abilities, including the 'lad' and more recently the 'lassie o' pairts'. Parents – even those who could afford it – have felt less need, therefore, to seek an alternative form of education for their offspring. Other factors, such as population density in the Highlands, Islands and Borders, militated strongly against the introduction of private fee-paying day schools, and the nation's low population also meant that only a limited number of wealthy parents could and might wish to afford a more expensive boarding education. Not surprisingly, therefore, the Central Belt and the larger cities and townships were the areas in which independent day schooling developed and has thrived; and, with few exceptions, the successful Scottish fee-paying boarding schools have been in or close to the townships or have enjoyed relative ease of access from them.

HISTORY

The history of the development of the schools within the sector is as interesting and as diverse as are the schools themselves. A handful claim to trace their origins back to the Middle Ages, though the links are rarely unbroken. For example, despite suffering temporary closure as recently as 1976, the High School of Glasgow is perhaps the oldest school in today's independent sector, as its history can be traced back to the twelfth Century. The High School of Dundee is also believed to have had religious origins and to have been founded in the thirteenth century by the abbot and monks of Lindores.

In the seventeenth Century several wealthy Scottish merchants followed the example of their English counterparts, leaving huge legacies to be devoted to the support, almost exclusively, of poor boys. The first of these was George Heriot, jeweller to James the VI and I, who was so impressed by Christ's Hospital in London that in 1623 he bequeathed almost his entire fortune for the founding of a similar 'Hospital' for fatherless bairns in his native city of Edinburgh. A mere eighteen years later the Hutcheson brothers showed similar beneficence in support of the children of Glasgow. Heriot's example was acknowledged in the establishment in Edinburgh in 1741 of George Watson's Hospital and a century later in Aberdeen of Robert Gordon's Hospital; in the meantime Mary Erskine had had the foresight to ensure that through her generosity the Edinburgh Merchant Company could make provision for the care and education of girls also.

In all these cases, the emphasis was charitable: young people who were otherwise destitute were taken into the care of the trustees and were given board and lodging, usually extremely spartan despite the wealth of the trust and, in some cases, despite the grandeur of the building in which they were housed. Their education was at first rudimentary and destined principally to secure for them valued apprenticeships and, hence, a safe livelihood; only the ablest would be prepared for further study at the local grammar or high school. Although these young people undoubtedly had cause to appreciate the generosity of their benefactor, they seem to have been regularly reminded of it and expected to celebrate it annually with the dignitaries of their city, who were usually also the trustees of the foundation. This allegiance often continued after the pupils had left the school, and from it developed the earliest former pupils' clubs, of which the Heriot Decorating Club, dating back to 1712, is almost certainly the oldest.

But most of today's independent schools have their origins in the last two centuries. Dollar Academy's literature claims it to be Britain's first coeducational boarding school: the school was established in 1818. Loretto – established in 1827 – is, however, the oldest school in Scotland to have been an independent boarding school throughout its history. In the absence of an adequate national system, around this time there began to develop a real interest in styles of education, and private schools were established in various parts of the country, often to satisfy the needs of a group of parents in a neighbourhood or to educate according to an explicit personal philosophy. One example of the latter is Dr Hely-Hutchison Almond, who purchased Loretto in 1862 and is described as having had no time for slavish adherence to custom or fashion but instead to have 'encouraged individuality of outlook, loyalty, integrity and service to the community' (see Mangan, 1979). In keeping with the times and acknowledging the importance of a classical education, many schools adopted Latin, even Greek, mottos: 'Spartam nactus es: hanc exorna' (Loretto); 'Labor vincit omnia' (Strathallan); 'ΑΙΕΝ ΑΡΙΣΤΕΥΕΙΝ' (Kelvinside); 'Industria' (Fettes). 'Ready, Ay Ready' (Merchiston) or 'Plus est en vous', the Kurt Hahn philosophy on which Gordonstoun was founded early in the twentieth century, may have a more modern ring but they too illustrate the ethos of encouragement to effort and achievement which continues to colour the work of Scotland's independent schools today.

SINGLE-SEX SCHOOLS

None of the existing Scottish private schools was involved in the creation in mid nineteenth century of the Headmasters' Conference – for boys' schools only – though twenty are now members of the newly-named Headmasters' and Headmistresses' Conference, which admits coeducational and boys-only schools into membership. Even as late as the end of the nineteenth century little importance had been given to any form of private education for girls. In 1867, the Argyll Commission had expressed the view that girls 'should be kept separate from the boys and under their own lady superintendent'. As the great debate raged about national provision, and as the original Hospital schools were forced by the conclusions of the Endowed Schools and Hospitals Commission of 1872 to change their statutes to allow expansion as day schools rather than as charitable hospices for orphans, so at last a number of schools opened in Scotland for the private education of girls. The list includes St Margaret's, Aberdeen (1846), St Leonards, St Andrews (1877), the Park School (now merged with Laurel Bank School), Glasgow (1880) and St George's, Edinburgh (1888). The last was originally modelled on a school established in Chelsea in 1873 by the Girls' Public Day School Company; it is interesting to note that, whilst Scotland was lagging behind in its provision, by the end of the nineteenth century that Company alone was responsible for the running of thirty-six schools in England and for the education of some 7,000 girls.

In the meantime many independent girls' schools were established in Scotland only to lose numbers to existing coeducational schools or to those many boys' schools which, reflecting the national preference for coeducation, welcomed girls. Nevertheless, whereas as a result of this process there remain just two boys-only schools, a dozen girls' independent schools (eight of them in membership of the Girls' School Association) continue success-fully to fly the flag at a time when the debate about academic attainment in single-sex schools has re-emerged as a national issue.

PREPARATORY AND JUNIOR SCHOOLS

The majority of preparatory and junior schools developed as the feeder schools either of the boarding schools (most often those known in times past as the Public Schools) or of the senior schools to which they were attached. Unlike their English counterparts, many of the longer-established schools have always been 'all-through', educating children of junior and senior school age on the same campus, though through time the age of admission has been lowered and in most cases now includes children of nursery age. The 'prep' schools, which used to prepare pupils almost exclusively for Common Entrance and Scholarship entry at age thirteen or fourteen to the senior boarding sector, have also adapted to circumstance and may now send pupils on to secondary schooling at age twelve, thirteen or fourteen. Some fifteen SCIS schools are affiliated to the Independent Association of Preparatory Schools (IAPS), though several are junior schools attached to senior schools and are also therefore affiliated to other Associations.

THE LAST THIRTY YEARS

One of the complications in writing of the independent sector in Scotland today is the diversity of methods of funding which has existed, mainly during this century, either directly from central government or indirectly through local authority grants. The topic is covered thoroughly in the Public Schools Commission (Second Report) of 1970 (usually referred to as the Donnison Report), which gives separate statistics for the 125 schools which were fully independent of all grant (many of them very small) and the twenty-nine grant aided schools (most typically the city-centre day schools). The development of fully comprehensive education had left selective grant aided schools in anomalous positions and some were to become fully state-maintained. The Assisted Places Scheme having been introduced in 1981 and all grant aid having finally ceased in 1985, in this latter year the then government sought to rationalise the situation, so that schools had either to register their status as fully independent schools or to become fully integrated in their local authority. In the event, most registered as independent schools and chose to participate in the Assisted Places Scheme.

Despite the changes in status of schools and the closure of many, the total number of pupils in today's independent sector in Scotland, and their geographical distribution, is remarkably similar to that outlined in the Donnison Report. In 1968 the grant aided and fully independent schools combined were educating almost 36,000 pupils (3.9% of the population); in September 1997 the total roll in SCIS schools was almost 31,000 (around 4% of the population).

The majority of independent schools are in or close to the cities of Edinburgh, Glasgow, Aberdeen and Dundee, though there is an unusual predominance in Edinburgh, where it is estimated that over 17% of school places are fee-paying. (Thirty years ago it was as high as 25%) The capital city already had more independent school places, and a greater percentage of its population were from the professions and therefore more likely to be able to afford to pay fees, but the snowball effect undoubtedly distorted the picture as parents came to realise that the maintained schools were losing a sizeable proportion of abler pupils and, in consequence, seemed to fare less well academically.

The geographical distribution of fee-paying places in the rest of Scotland also remains uneven. Twelve of the thirty-two unitary authorities have no fee-paying schools within them, and in four more fewer than one per cent of pupils are fee-paying. The apparently high figures in authorities such as Clackmannanshire (12.7%) and Perth and Kinross (11%) are most easily explained by the existence of boarding and/or preparatory schools in areas of relatively low population density.

COSTS

In comparing figures with thirty years ago, what is perhaps most surprising is that numbers have remained high despite the escalation of fees due to the loss of grant and to the increase in the cost of educational provision. In 1966 day fees ranged from £38 (primary) to £198 (secondary) per session in the grant aided sector and up to £225 for day schooling in the most expensive boarding school. In 1996 the equivalent costs were £1,578 (primary), and £5,283 (secondary) per session, with day fees in one boarding school as high as £8,655; fees for full boarding were between £6,363 (primary) and £12,810 (secondary). Much tightening of the parental belt, extensive use of the Assisted Places Scheme and the early return of mothers to work have been essential factors in the ability of many families to afford such spiralling costs; it has to be concluded that, for these families at least, a sound education for their children has a high priority and is worth the sacrifice.

BOARDING

The figures above do not reflect the trends in boarding, which now accounts for less than 15 per cent of the total. The recent decrease in the number of boarding pupils is not in any sense a purely Scottish phenomenon: it simply reflects the spread of wealth in the UK and, again, the increasing cost of education. The willingness of businesses whose employees live abroad, or of the Armed Forces, to subsidise the cost of boarding has also had a detrimental effect on numbers. In 1996 of the 4,357 boarders in SCIS schools almost exactly a quarter were from overseas and around 10 per cent were non-British passport holders; 640 were children from service families. The reduction in demand for 'full' boarding places has been alleviated by the provision of 'weekly' boarding (usually Monday to Saturday) and by the admission of many more 'day' pupils, i.e. pupils who are able to live at home but otherwise enjoy the benefits of the extended school day, most likely including prep and additional evening activities.

In order partly to shed once and for all the old image of cold showers and morning runs, which – opinion polls showed – the public had of boarding schools, most have also invested heavily in the improvement of accommodation and educational facilities. Several have, for example, outstanding facilities for craft, design and technology, including information technology. All offer small classes and specialist tuition, and all have reason to claim to be caring communities and to offer a vast range of valuable experiences to their charges.

CLASS SIZES

In May 1997 it was estimated that the overall pupil-teacher ratio in the independent sector was 10.6:1; in state primaries it was 19.1:1 and in secondaries 12.1:1. It follows that, although there will be exceptions, independent school pupils enjoy the benefits of smaller classes than their counterparts in authority schools. Primary classes in particular are likely to be smaller, and the vast range of subjects on offer in the fifth and sixth years of secondary education will almost certainly produce smaller average class sizes than those in their local counterparts, but classes in the early secondary years, when a more general curriculum is offered, may well be of a similar size, particularly in the larger day schools.

CURRICULUM AND ASSESSMENT

With independence comes the freedom to offer specialised curriculum and assessment arrangements, and this includes in-school innovation or importing systems in whole or in part from furth of Scotland. At the same time, schools are constrained in their choice of curriculum and subject-syllabus by the external examinations which their pupils sit. In practice, most junior school teaching in SCIS schools owes much to the Scottish 5–14 Programme; indeed, a number of independent schools developed the Programme more rapidly and with greater adherence than some maintained schools, and some continue to be well ahead at the 12–14 stage since they have the advantage of all-through schooling on the same campus.

At secondary level there is a wide variety of provision, some schools following a purely Scottish system, one or two concentrating almost exclusively on the English system and a number using a mixed economy borrowed from both systems. Although some have experimented in the past with the International Baccalaureate, none is believed to be doing so at the moment.

One obvious area of difference between most independent junior schools and their counterparts in the maintained sector is the amount of teaching done by subject specialists; this, too, is made possible by the fact that many schools share a campus and can, with relative ease, timetable their senior school subject specialists to teach junior age groups.

Thus an early start is made to specialisation in art, music and physical education, often using purpose-built facilities. The preparatory schools, driven by the demands of the Common Entrance examination, have long taught modern foreign languages, and some continue to include Latin. Some junior schools have also had modern language provision for many years and most others have recently introduced a foreign language, even as early as in the nursery. Similarly, in some schools, technical subjects, information technology and science are able to be taught to the older primary years by senior teachers in collaboration with their junior colleagues. In some independent junior schools setting is employed in the upper stages, particularly in mathematics, though for the most part a mixed-ability culture is preferred.

In the secondary schools, mixed-ability teaching continues to predominate for the first two years, though setting in mathematics is common and is being increasingly practised in other 'main' subjects; in the later stages, setting is the usual practice in all subjects where there is more than one class. In S3 and S4 the typical column-structure of the Scottish-oriented schools automatically includes mathematics, English and a foreign language with options to choose from four, possibly five, more columns. This is not markedly different from the typical national provision, though pupils may be allowed greater flexibility of choice, with less insistence that a subject from every 'mode' be studied.

The great majority of pupils in SCIS schools follow Higher and CSYS courses in S5 and S6. A five-column structure in S5 is most typical, though it is not uncommon for pupils to study as many as six Higher subjects in that year. In those schools offering GCSE courses and following a recognisably English curriculum, as many as ten subjects may be studied in S3 and S4. The ablest pupils in a few such schools may, in their last two years of schooling, study for three or four A Levels in preparation for university entrance, but Scottish Highers are offered and extensively used in all but Gordonstoun, each other 'mixed-economy' school offering its own solution in S5 and S6 to the debate over merits of the depth of A Level versus the breadth able to be achieved through Scottish Highers.

The sixth year is perhaps the one in which the difference between maintained school and independent school education is most marked. Once more, the reasons are not hard to find. Firstly, as independent schools are to varying degrees academically selective, most have a greater percentage of pupils of above average ability whose instinct is to stay on at school in order to achieve university entrance qualifications. They are more able, therefore, to offer to their S6 pupils a wide choice, including 'minority' subjects, often in very small classes.

EXAMINATION STATISTICS, UNIVERSITY ENTRY

Although the independent sector educates in total fewer than 4 per cent of the nation's children, this figure increases steadily in the older age groups: in 1993, as many as 40% of Edinburgh's sixth year pupils were in independent schools, though this figure is certainly not replicated elsewhere in the country. Numbers for national examination presentations are, therefore, disproportionate to the overall total. Scottish Qualifications Authority examination statistics for 1996 show that at Standard Grade just 4.1% of presentations were from independent schools; but 10.7% of Higher presentations in S5 and 13.4% of all CSYS presentations were from independent schools.

Independent sector representatives spoke just as vehemently against the introduction of the publication of national examination statistics as did their colleagues in the rest of the profession, and they have been just as relieved that the Scottish press has taken a more responsible attitude than the English press in the interpretation of examination results. Whereas league tables are common south of the border, any attempt to ape them in Scotland has been roundly rejected from all sides. Nevertheless, the published statistics consistently indicate that the independent sector as a whole outstrips the local authority sector at Standard Grade, Higher and CSYS. A Scottish Office Statistical Bulletin from July 1996 shows that in 1994–95 15.1 % of leavers from state schools held five or more higher passes compared with 47.1 % from the independent sector. (In addition 6.6% of the latter also held GCSE A Level qualifications.) Consequently, as the more recent SOEID report Leaver Destinations from Scottish Secondary Schools records, in 1996, whereas on average 28% of local authority pupils entered full-time higher education straight from school, the SCIS-schools equivalent figure was 74%. The comparison would be even more marked if it were possible to include in both totals the number of pupils taking a year out before going to university.

One myth worthy of explosion is that the independent sector's main aim is to send pupils to Oxford and Cambridge Universities. In 1996, only 64 Scottish pupils in total went to Cambridge; in the same year, of the 82 going from Scotland to Oxford 59 are known to have attended independent schools. Although it is the case that most SCIS schools have experience of Oxbridge application and that their pupils clearly gain a disproportionate number of places, that is merely a reflection of the lack of interest in Scotland in general in sending pupils to the supposed seats of English privilege: it most certainly does not reflect some sort of favouritism afforded by the Universities to pupils from the sector, who have to compete on academic and other merit with all comers.

Over the last decade there has been a small but increasing interest in travelling to non-Scottish universities, not just in the UK, but this, too, is a national trend in which, perhaps, independent pupils have shown a lead. Nevertheless, well over two-thirds of SCIS pupils going to university continue out of preference to attend Scottish universities; the equivalent UCAS figure (1996) for the comprehensive sector is 94%.

PASTORAL CARE AND EXTRA-CURRICULAR ACTIVITIES

In the paragraphs on boarding education, 'caring' was mentioned as an important aspect. The independent day schools also point to their history, often as charitable institutions of several centuries' standing, of caring for their charges. The expansion throughout British education in recent years of Guidance, and the demands made by recent legislation such as the Children (Scotland) Act 1995, have been more than met in the independent sector, and many schools would claim to remain ahead of the game and to view this as an important advantage.

If academic standards and the care for every child are two of the main strands in the claims of independent sector schools, a third and very important one – and one which, sadly, distinguishes it in the main from the state sector – is the breadth of extra-curricular activities and experiences on offer. For over a century, British schools have led the world in the provision of activities beyond the classroom, but during the 1980s many of them were lost in local authority schools (following industrial action by teachers) whilst being retained in the independent sector. Once lost, they are hard to resurrect, and the result is an imbalance of success and of representation at local and national level in a vast panoply of sports and other activities.

OBJECTIVE MEASURES

Examination statistics and sporting success apart, there exist few wholly objective measures of the differences between local authority and independent educational provision in Scotland today. Fortunately, however, all of Scotland's schools are subject to inspection by Her Majesty's Inspectors; their published reports have not been uncritical of individual independent schools, but as a general rule they have been very positive. In 1996 the Commission on Scottish Education gave only one page to consideration of the sector as a whole, but its findings, too, were very positive:

> 'Parents . . . are normally making assumptions about high academic achievement, a variety of extra-curricular activities, a strong and supportive ethos, high standards of behaviour and the development of such qualities as independence and self-confidence. By and large [the sector] meets the expectation of parents in turning out well qualified young people ready to take their place in adult society.

RECENT CHANGES; FUTURE PRIORITIES

Throughout its history, independent education in Scotland has had a remarkable capacity for survival against the odds, no more so than in recent times. In the 1980s the demographic curve was predicted to have a devastating effect on school rolls and the recession was expected to reduce the number of parents able to afford fees. Also in that decade, despite it being a time of monumental change in curriculum and assessment techniques, the sector had only limited access to national and local professional development initiatives. More recently the uncertainty about the continuity of external funding, mainly through the Assisted Places Scheme, has imposed financial strains on many of the schools involved. In 1997 – despite claims that the £12 million saved would make little or no tangible difference in authority schools – the incoming Labour government carried out its manifesto commitment to phase out the Scheme, which only the year before the Conservative government had proposed to double. Those schools heavily committed to it regretted not only the potential loss of funding as poorer parents no longer have any form of government financial support, but more importantly also the possible change in ethos as their clientele will by definition be only those who can afford the full fees.

In view of their long history of successfully coping with change, it is perhaps not surprising that the schools have survived the threats posed by the recession and the demographic curve. Future numbers have already been protected to an extent against the phasing out of the Assisted Places Scheme by the introduction of nurseries in most schools and, in some, by increasing the primary school roll. Nevertheless, only time will show the full effects of the loss of funding, and virtually every school acknowledges the need to continue to monitor closely its resources and to market its wares well, perhaps to a wider audience. In order to attract abler children from less affluent homes, it may be that schools will offer reduced fees through additional scholarship or bursary schemes; some already apply sliding scales and others are appealing for funds to put in trust to assist poorer parents.

The problem of professional development has also been overcome, largely because SCIS became a provider of in-service training for its own schools. Its teachers now also have relative ease of access to national and local training, and many are themselves heavily involved as contributors. They share with their colleagues in the authority schools a concern to see further professional development in preparation for the introduction of the Higher Still programme, and they, too, hope that the uncertainties currently surrounding progression to higher and further education can be rapidly resolved to the benefit of their pupils. The result of the Referendum of September 1997 will also surely have an effect on Scottish education in general, though it is too soon to predict what will be its long-term effects on the independent sector in particular.

Mainly as a result of their history and of the nature of their respective foundations, Scotland's independent schools have always maintained strong links with their local communities. Increasing attention has been paid to these links in recent years, and it would be surprising if they were not further strengthened in the future. Indeed, the Commission on Scottish Education recommended that this should be so.

In its brief piece on independent schools the Commission also concluded: 'We have no doubt that the sector will continue to have a place in the spectrum of educational provision.' It should not be doubted that schools themselves, and therefore the sector as a whole, have every desire to continue to adapt and to contribute in every way possible to the betterment of the education of Scotland's young people – in the twenty-first century and beyond.

REFERENCES

Mangan, J. A. (1979) Almond of Loretto: Scottish Educational Visionary and Reformer, *Scottish Educational Review*, vol. 11, no. 2, pp. 79–106.

Public Schools Commission (1970) Report No. 2 (The Donnison Report), London: HMSO.

Report of the Commission on Scottish Education (1996) *Learning to Succeed in Scotland*, Edinburgh: Commission on Scottish Education.

Scottish Council of Independent Schools, *Which School? A Directory of Independent Schools in Scotland*, Edinburgh: SCIS (published annually).

SOEID (1996) *Scottish Education Statistics*, Edinburgh: SOEID.

10

The Distinctiveness of Scottish Education

Walter Humes and Tom Bryce

It is instructive for any nation to re-examine from time to time the fundamental values which its major social institutions are said to embody. Education has traditionally been identified as one of the three institutions which mark the social and cultural life of Scotland as distinctive, especially when compared to England. (The other two are the law and the church.) With the election of a Scottish parliament in 1999 a new focus for the political identity of Scotland will be created, which is likely to strengthen the separate character of the nation's defining institutions. Scotland is thus at an interesting historical juncture and it seems timely, therefore, to take stock of the particular contribution which the educational system has made to the life of the nation in the recent past and, potentially, will make in the future. This will involve looking not only at the formal ways in which Scottish education is distinctive but also at the beliefs which underlie its institutional structures.

A useful reference point for the discussion that follows can be found in James Scotland's two–volume history of Scottish education, published in 1969. In his final chapter, Scotland attempted to define the Scottish tradition in education. He first identified a number of key components which helped to shape that tradition – e.g., pietism, poverty, militant democracy, academic bias, conservatism, authoritarianism, economy. None of these components, he acknowledged, 'has been entirely for the good of the people; each in its own way is open to severe criticism' (Scotland, 1969, vol. 2, p. 274). Nevertheless, 'the general impression is of a heritage worth remembering and building upon' (ibid., p. 274). He summed up his interpretation in six propositions which, he suggested, encapsulated the essence of Scottish attitudes towards education:

- education is, and always has been, of paramount importance in any community;
- every child should have the right to all the education of which he is capable;
- such education should be provided as economically and systematically as possible;
- the training of the intellect should take priority over all other facets of the pupil's personality;
- experiment is to be attempted only with the greatest caution; and
- the most important person in the school, no matter what theorists say, is not the pupil but the (inadequately rewarded) teacher. (ibid., p. 275)

Much has changed in the thirty years since this list was drawn up and a few of the items no longer seem persuasive, but some at least (the first three?) would still receive widespread endorsement. And although the pride which Scottish people traditionally have had in the quality of their educational system is now held less confidently, belief in the importance of education, its value both for the individual and for society as a whole, remains unshaken. Thousands of Scots, many from modest backgrounds, can testify to the power of education to enrich (in some cases, transform) their lives, and even those who have not themselves done particularly well at school are often anxious that their own children should take advantage of the improved opportunities now open to them.

These attitudes help to ensure that the position of education in the national consciousness remains strong. Moreover, belief in the worth and purpose of education is linked to the sense of national identity which is regularly invoked to draw attention to the differences between Scottish and English society (see Chapter 22). This takes the form of a story or 'myth', shaped by history but not always supported by historical evidence, to the effect that Scottish society is relatively egalitarian and meritocratic, that ability and achievement, not rank, should determine success in the world, that public (rather than private) institutions should be the means of trying to bring about the good society, and that, even where merit does justify differential rewards, there are certain basic respects – arising from the common humanity of all men and women – in which human beings deserve equal consideration and treatment. Taken together, these features can be summed up in the phrase used by George Davie for the title of his famous book, *The Democratic Intellect* (1961). To describe the democratic intellect as constituting a 'myth' is not to dismiss it as untrue. Gray, McPherson and Raffe make the point that a myth is a narrative that people tell themselves for two reasons – 'first, to explain the world and, second, to celebrate identity and to express values' (*Reconstructions of Secondary Education*, London: Routledge, 1983, p. 39). The extent to which the values are actually achieved in practice is a matter for analysis and interpretation. So too is the question of who promotes the myth and who benefits from it. These are crucial issues that will be re-visited later in the chapter.

First, however, it is necessary to ground the discussion in some factual information about those features of the day to day workings of the Scottish educational system which mark it out as distinctive. How are the differences between Scottish and English education reflected in the experiences of pupils, teachers and parents? What is the significance of these differences? And how do they connect with broader questions of consciousness, identity and values?

FORMAL DISTINCTIVENESS

Perhaps the most potent expression of the distinctiveness of Scottish education is the separate legislative framework which sets out the nature of provision and the agencies responsible for its delivery. Legislation is framed in the Scottish Office and formal responsibility for the system as a whole rests with the Secretary of State. Scottish legislation often (but not always) post-dates statutory provision in England, but it should not be assumed that it follows an identical pattern. A clear example is the legislation relating to parental choice of school enshrined in the Education Act of 1980 (England and Wales) and the Education (Scotland) Act of 1981. The Scottish Act gave stronger rights of choice to parents. Exceptions to the granting of parental rights had to be specific and had to relate to such things as the need to employ an additional member of staff or to alter school buildings. Furthermore, Scottish parents had the right to appeal to a sheriff and, where an appeal was upheld, the education authority was required to review all similar cases (Adler et al:

Parental Choice and Educational Policy, Edinburgh, Edinburgh University Press, 1989). Partly as a result of the Scottish experience, the rights of parents in England were strengthened in the 1988 Education Reform Act.

Other examples of important legislative differences can be seen in the arrangements for school boards in Scotland compared to governing bodies in England, devolved school management in Scotland compared to local financial management in England, and the circumstances which require the opening and maintenance of a Record of Needs for children requiring special educational provision in Scotland compared to the Statement of Needs in England.

Provisions for the testing of pupils are also different north and south of the border. The Conservative government tried to put national testing in place in Scotland as it did in England and Wales but considerable resistance from parents, teaching unions and local authorities (particularly Strathclyde Region) resulted in different legislation being enacted in Scotland. As described elsewhere in this volume, teachers carry out national testing at times of their choosing to check their classroom assessment judgements, and do so by drawing upon available national item-bank test materials. There is, therefore, no centralised capacity to assemble data such as has been used for league tables in England and Wales.

Further evidence of Scottish distinctiveness can be seen in the separate institutional apparatus which maintains the system. There is one national examination body, the Scottish Qualifications Authority (SQA), whereas in England there are several examination boards, ostensibly serving different parts of the country though schools are not confined to entering candidates in the board located in their geographical area. Other important bodies expressive of the separate character of the Scottish system include the Scottish Consultative Council on the Curriculum (SCCC) and the General Teaching Council (GTC). The SCCC advises the Secretary of State on all matters relating to the curriculum as they affect the age range 3–18. It issues guidance to local authorities and schools, carries out programmes of curriculum development and produces a wide range of publications covering many aspects of pre-school, primary and secondary education. In Scotland, unlike England, there is no formally prescribed national curriculum though, in practice, most schools follow closely the recommendations contained in national documents such as those deriving from the 5–14 Development Programme.

The GTC, established by statute in 1965, is a body containing a majority of teacher representatives, which controls entry to the profession, accredits initial training courses for teachers and has responsibility for the assessment of probationary teachers. Formally independent, the GTC has strong links with the SOEID and some teachers are sceptical of the degree of real autonomy which it possesses. Its very existence, however, is testimony to the relative status of teaching as a profession in Scotland, compared to England. Only now is an English GTC under consideration, with proposed powers that are significantly weaker than those enjoyed by the GTC in Scotland.

The way in which the institutional apparatus of Scottish education functions helps to explain a somewhat ironic feature of the system. Although the educational workforce consistently exhibits anti-Conservative tendencies (in a party-political sense), the process of educational advancement nonetheless reflects a kind of determined conservatism. As Brian Boyd's 1996 Herald Essay observes ('The Scottishness of our Schools', *Herald*, 28 January 1996), Scotland has never been extreme with its educational innovations; the Scottish approach 'has always been to integrate innovation firmly into traditional approaches'. Boyd's analysis is consistent with James Scotland's observation that a feature of the Scottish tradition is that 'experiment is to be attempted only with the greatest caution'. National bodies such as the SCCC and the SQA operate as bureaucracies with established ways of doing things and a concern to ensure that safeguards are built into the system. Their officers often have a strong commitment to particular areas of the curriculum and, although important cross-curricular developments are taking place in both primary and secondary schools, most developments start from existing practice rather than a radical review of the curriculum as a whole. This approach is strongly promoted by Her Majesty's Inspectors (HMI), a small but powerful group concerned to identify and disseminate 'good practice'. Through the exercise of their very considerable informal power, HMIs oversee many of the activities not only of SCCC and SQA staff but also of the diminishing group of teacher educators who contribute to educational reform by helping to develop and deliver programmes of staff training. For major initiatives, the coordinated efforts of all of these groups is important and the small size of Scotland is often seen as an advantage in this respect. People tend to know each other and a consensus is perhaps easier to reach than it would be in a larger, more anonymous system. This consensus is often presented as a distinctive and positive feature of Scottish education but it has a downside as well. It can lead to complacency and a failure to question existing practice in the fundamental way that may be needed. The 'practice-driven' approach to curriculum development helps to explain the relative conservatism identified by writers such as Boyd and Scotland.

Another feature of Scottish education for which claims are made in respect of distinctiveness is the breadth of the curriculum available to pupils in schools, and it would be fair to say that all the national programmes – Standard Grade, 5–14 and Higher Still – have preserved breadth of study. A common Scottish-English comparison has been between the number of Higher subjects taken by the typical S5/S6 pupil and the fewer subjects taken in England by the typical A-level pupil. A careful distinction should be made, however, between courses followed and actual qualifications gained. Too few Higher passes are achieved by the end of S5, and S5/6 courses are not genuinely two-year courses where they need to be (as the Howie Committee noted). Therefore breadth in opportunity to take Highers there may have been, breadth in achievement there has not. Pupils do study a broad range of subjects in Scotland but implicit claims for the benefits of that are somewhat exaggerated. It remains to be seen whether the Higher Still reforms to the post-sixteen curriculum will significantly alter the picture.

Compared with the school system, the formal distinctiveness of Scotland's universities is less clear cut. For most of the twentieth century Scottish universities were seen primarily as United Kingdom institutions and the body responsible for their funding – originally the University Grants Committee (later the University Funding Council) – was accountable to the Department of Education and Science (DES) in London. This position was reviewed from time to time but the consistent message from Scottish University Principals was that they were against the Scottish Office taking over responsibility. Part of the explanation was a desire to retain international standing and a fear that the Scottish Office might try to interfere with academic freedom. These attitudes began to change in the 1980s when, following a major financial exercise involving severe cutbacks, in which there was a feeling that the UGC's understanding of and sympathy for the Scottish dimension was deficient, demands for the establishment of a separate Scottish sub-committee of the UGC were voiced. These were initially rejected but the climate had altered and it was only a matter of time before the funding arrangements were revised. Since 1992 the Scottish Higher Education Funding Council (SHEFC) has been responsible for distributing grants for teaching, research and associated activities in all Scottish higher education institutions. Matters relating to quality assurance, however, continue to be adminstered on a UK-wide basis under the direction of the Quality Assurance Agency (QAA), a new body established in 1997.

UNDERLYING VALUES

The extent to which the various manifestations of formal distinctiveness embody a particularly Scottish vision of the nature and purpose of education is a matter of continuing analysis and debate. G. E. Davie (in *The Democratic Intellect*) argued that the special character of Scotland's educational system has been progressively weakened by a process of assimilation to English norms, notwithstanding the separate legislative framework. According to Davie, the Scottish university curriculum, with an emphasis on curricular breadth and philosophical enquiry, was steadily weakened during the nineteenth century by a narrow English empiricism which led to specialisation and fragmentation of knowledge. This process was aided by the introduction of English-style examinations and the appointment of English candidates to key university chairs in Scotland. Secondary schools were required to adapt to the changes in order to prepare candidates for university entrance and so the Anglicising tendencies gradually entered the whole system. One manifestation of the trend was the disparagement of Scots and Gaelic as legitimate forms of language for learning. A re-statement and updating of Davie's analysis was offered by A. L. Walker in his highly polemical study *The Revival of the Democratic Intellect* (Edinburgh: Polygon, 1994).

The pessimism of Davie and Walker would now be challenged. Cameron Harrison, writing about attitudes to Scots and Gaelic says that 'the age of hostility is past' (Harrison, 1997, p. 160). Similarly, it is possible to point to the development of curricular materials with a strong Scottish flavour across a range of subjects in primary and secondary schools. Scottish history is now well-established as a field of study in schools and universities, and the use of Scottish texts in drama and literature courses is widespread. Add to this the wider cultural renaissance in Scotland, which includes art, music and media, and the argument that Scottish society and Scottish education are dominated by English values and institutions seems hard to sustain.

It is, however, not a simple either/or issue, with the 'purity' of Scottish values being set against the 'contamination' from south of the border. A significant number of Scots feel themselves to be both Scottish and British (and in some cases European as well) and they want the next generation to enjoy the freedom to enter different cultural worlds. They certainly want Scottish identity and culture to be given proper recognition within the curriculum but they also want their children to be able to cope with the globalisation of knowledge. The international character of many areas of learning and the employment markets associated with them (e.g. technology, computing, economics, banking, law, government) is now recognised. These are cross-national trends which cannot be resisted. To the extent that any educational system must try to prepare young people for the future, Scotland cannot afford to construct a curriculum on the basis of romantic retreat to an imagined golden age of the past. Scottish distinctiveness has to be shaped and re-defined in a way that is compatible with the realities of the modern world.

This is not an easy task and it has as much to do with maturity and confidence as with knowledge. Evidence for such an attitudinal shift is patchy. It is perhaps strongest in those fields associated with the artistic renaissance referred to above. But in other spheres of activity there are still many instances of Scottish defensiveness, inarticulateness and embarrassment when faced with the seemingly greater social confidence of the English. Even worse, there have been a number of ugly examples of anti-English racism in different parts of Scotland. Self-confidence about one's own national identity should not be incompatible with tolerance of diversity in other people. That is a mark of cultural maturity. A useful first step would be a recognition of the diversity inside Scotland itself. There is, and always has been, considerable cultural variation within Scotland – between Highlands and Lowlands, Edinburgh and Glasgow, cities and rural communities, Catholics and Protestants. This diversity has often been submerged in a standardised and idealised model of Scottish life which, with staggering improbability, manages to combine elements of Knox, Burns, Hampden, Red Clydeside and a kailyard version of community life (Humes, 1984). Stripping away these internal mythologies may serve to counteract the easy recourse to demonising the English. Blaming England for Scotland's ills prevents the hard thinking that is needed at a time when Scotland is about to assume greater responsibility for its own affairs.

CRITICS OF THE SCOTTISH TRADITION

One way of extending the demythologising process is to examine what critics of the Scottish educational tradition have had to say. The accounts of that tradition which receive greatest attention and which help to shape popular consciousness tend to be those which are written by members of the educational establishment. James Scotland is a case in point. He was Principal of Aberdeen College of Education, Convener of the GTC, and a long-standing member of the policy community. It is not surprising that interpretations coming from such sources should give more prominence to the achievements of the system, rather than its shortcomings. However, there is a counter-tradition – albeit a minor one – of radical twentieth-century criticism which casts interesting light on the cherished principles identified by James Scotland. It is an interpretation, moreover, that raises important questions about the relation between schooling, society and values.

One early critic was Patrick Geddes (1854–1932), a botanist and environmentalist, who described elementary and secondary schools as 'prisons for body and mind' whose main function was to serve the needs, not of children, but of 'text-book perpetrators' and 'examination-machine bureaucrats' (quoted in P. Boardman, *Patrick Geddes: Maker of the Future*, Chapel Hill, North Carolina, 1944, p. 269, 266). Underlying this criticism was a profound awareness of the ways in which schooling, the provision of which was intended to open up opportunities, could become an oppressive institutional apparatus for stifling genuine interest in children. Geddes was a keen advocate of getting children out of the classroom and encouraging them to discover things for themselves: his advocacy led to the introduction of nature study in primary schools. A similar philosophy was evident in the writings of A. S. Neill (1883–1973) who became a key figure in the progressive movement, attracting enthusiasm and notoriety in almost equal measure for his school Summerhill. Neill left Scotland because he disagreed fundamentally with the emphasis on discipline and authority, and the centrality of the teacher rather than the pupil. Strongly influenced by Freudian psychology, he based his school on the principle of freedom and saw modern society as hostile to individuality and creativity. Yet another critic, R. F. Mackenzie (1910–87) tried, ultimately unsuccessfully, to establish a regime within the state system which challenged traditional ideas on curriculum content and pupil learning. Like Neill, he saw attitudes to schooling as symptomatic of wider social attitudes: 'The crisis in Scottish schools is a crisis in Scottish life . . . Scotland's schools are at the centre of Scotland's perplexity, one of its main causes' (*The Unbowed Head*, Edinburgh, EUSPB, 1977, p. 6). Mackenzie believed that for many Scottish youngsters the experience of schooling was largely negative. They were given few opportunities to explore and enjoy learning in creative ways that connected with life outside school: they were constantly reminded of their inadequacies and failures: and they were ill-equipped to meet the challenges they would face as adults. These deficiencies, Mackenzie believed, helped to explain the cultural malaise from which he felt Scotland suffered – a malaise evident in a lack of drive and intiative, a passivity in the face of officialdom and an impoverished sense of life's possibilities. It is a bleak picture of institutional failure and missed opportunities.

The current generation of teachers and headteachers would certainly dispute these accounts and claim that modern schools are much less oppressive places where pupil achievements are celebrated and the richness of learning in all its forms is recognised and encouraged. That may be so – though it would be a matter for debate – but it does not diminish the responsibility to confront past practices and to reflect on their significance for the present and future. The value attached to schooling in Scotland (identified by James Scotland as one of the tradition's defining characteristics) makes it doubly important to consider its wider social impact and here the need to confront uncomfortable truths remains strong. In a statement which resonates powerfully with the critics, the historian T. C. Smout comments:

> It is in the history of the school more than in any other aspect of recent social history that the key lies to some of the more depressing aspects of modern Scotland. If there are in this country too many people who fear what is new, believe the difficult to be impossible, draw back from responsibility, and afford established authority and tradition an exaggerated respect, we can reasonably look for an explanation in the institutions that moulded them. (Smout, 1986, p. 229)

Even if the radical educational philosophies of Geddes, Neill and Mackenzie are not accepted, it is possible to recognise the validity of what Smout is saying about Scottish society. Resistance to change in working practices, reluctance to take on new challenges, unwillingness to accept leadership roles, reticence in the face of professional and bureau-cratic authority – these are recognisable features of life in Scotland. They are by no means universal but they are sufficiently widespread to have attracted the attention of social commentators. In the Thatcher years they led to the phrase 'dependency culture' being coined, a concept that implied an expectation that the state would provide when personal responsibility failed. Under New Labour an attempt is being made to address the problems associated with passivity and defeatism through schemes such as 'Welfare to Work' designed to reduce dependence on state benefits and encourage people, particularly young people, to become active citizens, contributing not only to personal advancement and the economic life of the country but also to attitude sets in families and local communities. These are long-term projects and it will be some time before their effects can be evaluated.

Arguably a Scottish parliament could provide a positive focus for the kind of national self-confidence which would strengthen the attempt to reduce dependence and promote active involvement. For this to happen on the scale that is needed, however, would require a major social transformation encompassing not only education but a wide range of other public and private services as well. Schooling cannot be seen in isolation. The capacity of children to benefit from schooling is profoundly affected by issues of housing, employment, poverty and health. It is in the inter-connection of these forces that solutions to the sort of cultural defects which Smout describes must be found. A major test of the Scottish parliament, therefore, will be its preparedness to explore these inter-connections in an innovative and coordinated way. Prior to the reorganisation of local government in 1996 some of the larger regions (notably Strathclyde and Lothian) tried to do so but, with the fragmentation of services involved in the creation of the thirty-two new councils, some ground has been lost in terms of developing multi-disciplinary social strategies. It will be important, therefore, to move swiftly beyond the euphoria which will inevitably accompany the opening of the parliament to develop policies which locate educational provision in the context of broader social issues.

SOCIAL POLARISATION AND THE KNOWLEDGE UNDERCLASS

The sheer scale of the task should not be underestimated, as consideration of the case of a comprehensive school serving a disadvantaged housing scheme on the outskirts of Glasgow or Edinburgh will demonstrate. Such a school is affected by social polarisation, in the sense that it is cut off from the amenities of more affluent districts, and by the legacy of ill-judged housing and planning policies in the 1950s and 1960s. The community is likely to suffer from higher levels of poverty, unemployment, ill-health and crime than other areas within the city. What are the choices open to parents, teachers and politicians in such a case? Some parents might exercise the right of choice and send their children to a 'better' school further afield. That could have individual advantages but it might deprive the neighbourhood school of the children and parents who, potentially, could make the greatest contribution to its ethos and level of achievement. To the extent that that happens, the comprehensive principle – a central plank in Scottish distinctiveness – is weakened.

The teachers in such a school might make a strategic decision to offer a curriculum that is different from the mainstream curriculum in most Scottish secondary schools. This is unlikely to be as radical as that recommended by Neill or Mackenzie but it might well involve giving particular attention to issues which children will face outside school. Thus a programme with a substantial input on social education, covering topics such as health and diet, sexual behaviour, relationships, parenting skills, the use and abuse of drugs and alcohol, living within a budget and awareness of the law, might occupy a significant part of the timetable. A programme of this kind would be well-intentioned but it could, para-doxically, convey a message of social stereotyping and intensify, rather than reduce, the 'ghettoisation' of the community. Furthermore, insofar as it leads to a reduction in the amount of time spent on more conventional subjects, it could help to expand what has recently been called the 'knowledge underclass' – those who lack the understanding and skills to be able to function effectively in an information-rich environment.

For politicians, both local and national, the key question is what kind of social intervention is likely to pay the greatest dividends. The current government is committed to putting education at the top of its priority list. But might it not be that greater employment opportunities or improved housing would actually be a sounder investment in that they would improve individual and community self-esteem which, in turn, might encourage greater responsiveness to what education has to offer, in a way that schooling alone could not do? Once again, the inter-penetration of the various aspects of social policy is apparent.

There are, of course, no simple answers to these questions, but it is in schools such as these that the strongest test of Scottish educational principles is to be found. If democracy and equality mean anything, then they must offer hope to children and families experiencing multiple disadvantage. Around 40 per cent of pupils attending Glasgow schools live in poverty, as measured by their entitlement to free school meals, and the evidence is that this poverty is increasingly concentrated in a few areas. If the trend towards community segregation continues, the credibility of that part of the Scottish tradition in education which emphasises opportunity for all (never mind achievement for all) will be difficult to maintain.

COMPETING INTERPRETATIONS

In earlier sections of this chapter a contrast has been drawn between celebratory interpretations of the Scottish educational tradition (such as James Scotland's) and critical interpretations (such as R. F. Mackenzie's). To polarise these inevitably over-simplifies the forces at work, not least by failing to take account of the particular circumstances at any given time in the evolution of the tradition. Lindsay Paterson has claimed that an analysis of the ways in which Scottish education has been subject to reform suggests that a highly complex blend of traditional and radical thinking can be detected at various points in recent educational history (Paterson, 1996). He argues that it is misleading to interpret the development of Scottish education in terms of a crude dichotomy between control and liberation. Depending on the circumstances of the time, different educational philosophies were mobilised in a variety of ways. Referring to the introduction of comprehensive education, he states that 'the single act of abolishing selection [was] a real victory for progressive educational thought' and that its radical effect can be seen 'in the slow revolution it has brought about in the educational aspirations of the whole community'. Significantly, however, the switch to comprehensivisation was not a peculiarly Scottish development, though it is often claimed that comprehensive schools had their roots in the old 'omnibus' schools found in small towns and rural communities in Scotland. This claim ignores the extent of selection and streaming within omnibus schools.

A better test of Paterson's thesis would be to look at a specifically Scottish policy, such as Higher Still, which is represented as a bold attempt to address recognised weaknesses in upper secondary education. To what extent does it embody continuity with traditional values and to what extent does it break new ground? At one level, Higher Still can be seen as a strategy to extend the principle of equality of opportunity by making it easier for a larger proportion of the school population than hitherto to gain awards for achievement, in the form of national certificates, across a wider range of curriculum content. Furthermore, in its explicit rejection of a 'twin track' approach, which would have separated academic and vocational cohorts of pupils, Higher Still seeks to end the divisiveness of the stratification of knowledge. It aims to provide a unified system of post-compulsory education which offers a fair measure of flexibility and choice to users.

All this can be regarded as enlightened but, at another level, the Higher Still programme might be seen as driven by professional and bureaucratic interests rather than the interests of learners. It fails to challenge the autonomy of subject departments in secondary schools (see Chapter 4) and this might well make it difficult to achieve success in promoting cross-curricular core skills, which employers regard as valuable. The modular structure on which Higher Still is based brings with it a bureaucratic system which teachers are likely to find oppressive and pupils may find confusing (thus the heavy emphasis on guidance in negotiating the system). Moreover, the whole programme is assessment-led, a feature which some would see as fundamentally anti-educational. The emphasis on assessment and certification has produced what might be called a 'technical' approach to development and implementation. What is lacking is a wider vision of how Higher Still will impact on the lives of students and on Scottish society in the 21st century. There is, in other words, a philosophical vacuum at the heart of Higher Still. Any attempt at serious epistemological debate about the nature and structure of knowledge appropriate to the upper secondary school has long since been abandoned. Pragmatism has taken over. The task now, it seems, is to run with the plan that has been devised and get it into place.

The fact that Higher Still can be subject to alternative readings goes some way towards bearing out Paterson's point about the complexity and malleability of traditions. In a similar fashion, it is possible to tell the bigger story of the distinctiveness of Scotland's educational tradition in more than one version. New 'myths' can replace the old ones and the task of deconstruction is never-ending. What can be said is that the claims made for the quality of Scottish education, past and present, have been substantial and that they have sometimes led to an unjustifiable degree of complacency. Increasingly, international comparisons suggest that Scotland needs to do better on a number of fronts. The value attached to education, both by policy makers and by ordinary Scots, remains high but the ideals expressed in the official discourse need to be constantly tested against the realities as experienced by pupils, teachers, parents and employers. As devolution becomes a reality, Scottish education needs both its advocates and its critics.

REFERENCES

Davie, G. E. (1961) *The Democratic Intellect*, Edinburgh: Edinburgh University Press.

Harrison, C. (1997) How Scottish is the Scottish Curriculum? in M. M. Clark and P. Munn, eds, *Education in Scotland*, London: Routledge, pp. 156–69.

Humes, W. M. (1984) The Cultural Significance of Scotland's Educational System in D. McCrone, ed, *The Scottish Government Yearbook 1984*, Edinburgh: Unit for the Study of Government in Scotland, pp. 149–66.

Paterson, L. (1996) Liberation or Control: What Are the Scottish Education Traditions of the Twentieth Century? in T. M. Devine and R. J. Finlay, eds, *Scotland in the 20th Century*, Edinburgh: Edinburgh University Press, pp. 230-249.

Scotland, J. (1969) *The History of Scottish Education*, vol. 2, London: University of London Press.

Smout, T. C. (1986) *A Century of the Scottish People 1830–1950*, London: Collins.

III

The Administration and Control of Scottish Education

11

The Scottish Office Education and Industry Department (SOEID)

Sally Brown

The Scottish Office, at the time of writing, is still under the control of the United Kingdom (UK) government and headed by the Secretary of State for Scotland. This arrangement has resulted in Scotland sometimes being administered by a political party in power whose policies are at variance with the views of the majority of the Scottish people as expressed in elections. Such dissonance was the case for most of the two decades before this publication was prepared. In May 1997, however, a general election brought in a new UK Labour government which, on the face of it, should have a closer affinity with the electorate in Scotland. Inevitably this has meant that the pattern of activity in the Scottish Office is changing as this chapter is written. Furthermore, one of the earliest policies to be enacted by the new government was to establish legislation to devolve a great deal of political responsibility (including education) to a Scottish parliament and Scottish executive. While these changes will take a few years to come into effect, they clearly engender a considerable dynamism in speculative educational thinking about the future. The next five sections of this chapter, therefore, aim to map out the relationships which the Scottish Office has with other aspects of Scottish education in the context of working with the UK administration, while the last section looks forward to how things might be under a devolved parliament, executive and administration.

RESPONSIBILITY FOR EDUCATION WITHIN THE SCOTTISH OFFICE

Within the Scottish Office, during the period of the 1980s and 1990s, the department with responsibility for education has been variously called the Scottish Education Department (SED), the Scottish Office Education Department (SOED) and the Scottish Office Education and Industry Department (SOEID). This is not the place to examine the significance of these changes of title which took place under a Conservative administration, except to point to the significance of the latest grouping of industry with education. This has clearly brought together education and training, and has highlighted the political priority of education as preparation for work at the expense of other cultural, social and personal purposes.

Responsibility for SOEID within the Scottish Office rests with a Minister of State. As Members of the UK Parliament (MPs), both the Secretary of State and the Minister for education have to spend most of the week in London when Parliament is in session. This implies that only one day a week is spent in Scotland for official engagements and face to face contact with officials. The most senior Scottish Office civil servant is also based in London, but each department, including SOEID, has a very senior official as Secretary and Head of Department in Edinburgh with the major responsibility for that area of work.

During the 1980s and 1990s, education has been at the core of much government policy. Under both Conservative and Labour (from May 1997) administrations, Scottish Ministers with relevant responsibilities became much more directly engaged with educational issues than was the case in earlier decades. Within the Scottish Office there remained some dependence on advice from civil servants, but a much more 'hands on' approach was evident and a culture evolved in which consultation with the Minister, about matters which would previously have been left to the administrators, became a required feature. The politicisation of education, in comparison with the 1970s, has been all too apparent.

The position in relation to finance has been one which has seen the SOEID to be at something of an arm's length from the UK Treasury. On the one hand, the Scottish Office has been dependent on the block grant determined at UK level by the Barnett formula (currently about £14.5 billion per annum). On the other hand, the decisions about how the money should be divided up between education and other expenditure have been made entirely in Scotland.

The Secretary of State for Scotland is a member of the British cabinet and is bound, therefore, by cabinet decisions. During the 1980s and most of the 1990s, the political complexion of a large majority of the Scottish members of the UK Parliament and local government councillors was different from the Conservative government in power. The opportunities for SOEID to 'go it alone' in the educational field were somewhat constrained as a consequence of this. So, for example, the Conservative Secretary of State for Scotland and former Minister for education, Michael Forsyth, would have found it difficult, even had he so wished, to avoid implementing policies which enabled maintained schools to opt out of Scottish local authority control, or introducing an assisted places scheme for young people to attend independent schools in Scotland. Since these policies were being energetically pursued as cornerstones of educational progress in England (though not without opposition), it would have been unacceptable not to do the same in Scotland even though the political climate north of the border was very different and the opposition to such moves put low ceilings on their effectiveness. This is not simply a feature of the particular UK political party in power at the time, however. It is likely that the distinctive nature of the Scottish system could present a Labour minister with a comparable dilemma in relation to policies developed primarily in the context of England to solve a problem in that system.

COMPARING SOEID WITH DFEE

In making comparisons between the ways in which the SOEID and the Department for Education and Employment (DfEE) south of the border undertake their educational roles, a particularly striking difference relates to the much smaller staff of civil servants available in the Scottish Office. Important implications of this are that the individual civil servants in the Scottish Office have to shoulder wider areas of responsibility than their counterparts at DfEE, and they cannot afford to have such an hierarchical way of operating as those in the London department. So, for example, the educational work at senior levels of the SOEID is currently organised into two broad blocks; the first, 'School Education', includes educational matters for young people up to the age of sixteen and the second, 'Lifelong Learning', education and training from sixteen onwards. Within each of these blocks there are four divisions:

School education
1. Schools provision and organisation.
2. Teachers, curriculum and community education.
3. Sports policy.
4. Pre-school education.

Lifelong learning
1. Qualifications and skills strategy.
2. Further education funding.
3. Higher education.
4. Training, new deal and guidance.

In the DfEE, however, these broad categories are covered by many more strands each of which is the responsibility of a senior civil servant. Middle range responsibilities are similarly contrasted between the two departments and are less specialised in Scotland. For example, at the time of writing one person (a member of Her Majesty's Inspectorate) has the responsibility (among other responsibilities) for educational developments in new technology in the SOEID whereas the DfEE has a team of people. To some extent, the civil servants in Scotland rely on London for co-operation to supplement their expertise north of the border in specialist areas where the numbers of staff are low.

A second important distinction between SOEID and DfEE concerns Her Majesty's Inspectorate. In England the inspection function now falls to the Office for Standards in Education (OFSTED), a body which, at least in principle, is separate from the government department. In Scotland Her Majesty's Inspectors (HMIs) are part of the Scottish Office staff along with the administrators with whom they work very closely. Indeed, SOEID regards it as a strength of the Scottish system that in many instances these individuals can be used interchangeably. HMI have, of course, exclusive responsibility for the inspection of schools, but in other circumstances they (especially the Chief Inspectors) can function as senior civil servants on committees or in advisory roles. This has been a conscious strategy in order to make the best use of scarce resources in terms of the small cadre of people, and to ensure that the HMIs are engaged in both policy and practice developments. (It has been suggested that DfEE has regarded the loss of the inspection function to OFSTED as removing their main communication link to what is going on in practice on the ground.) A danger associated with this strategy, however, is that governments might see HMI as able to act as their tools during inspections.

An examination of specific aspects of Scottish Office policy areas shows that some (e.g. research, European matters, new technology) are, or have been, led by HMIs rather than administrators, but such leadership roles are regularly under review and can change from time to time. Research is a particularly interesting area. Since the early 1970s SOEID have had a Research and Intelligence Unit (RIU) which has had responsibility for commissioning and managing the research programme. The RIU has been headed by Chief HMIs since its inception and its staff have included other HMIs and research officers from the Scottish Office Central Research Unit (CRU). Administrators' roles in the RIU have been mainly those of involvement in the so-called 'trawls' for research priorities and in overarching decisions on finance. Over the last twenty years there has been a transition from a system where much of the research activity was reactive in response to ideas from researchers and others about the important issues to be addressed, to one where a procedure of strict tendering for contracts promotes those specifications which the SOEID and the Minister see as most urgent. A gesture towards the collection within the trawl of general ideas for research from others in Scottish education appears to have had little impact on this process. This transition has changed the research from what was essentially a policy-informing programme to one which is policy-directed. It has to be said, however, that RIU has had a reputation for close contact with the educational research community, for being prepared to leave the safety of their offices in Edinburgh to visit institutions and research conferences around the country and for regularly arranging seminars within the Scottish Office to inform HMI and administrators about research findings. The effect of this has been a much closer relationship between the research community and SOEID than is apparent between researchers and DfEE south of the border.

SOEID AND THE LOCAL AUTHORITIES

The current financial arrangements for local government funding enable central government to determine how much money is to be allocated to local councils but not how that money is to be spent. There was a time when, for example, there was a Buildings Division within the SOEID; that kind of decision making is now in the hands of the local authorities and the Scottish Office role is limited to such matters as concerns that the total amounts of borrowing are adequately controlled. These arrangements can thwart government plans. For example, the Conservative government from 1979 to 1997 had been politically out of tune with most of those in power in what were twelve regional councils until 1996 and thirty-two unitary authorities thereafter (most of these were controlled by the Labour Party). Various aspects of guidance and regulations promoted by the Conservatives were not welcomed with open arms by the local authorities, and there were no statutory mechanisms which allowed central government, in this relatively hostile environment, to insist on the implementation of its proposals. So, for example, the Scottish Ministers enthusiastically promoted developments like teacher appraisal, but within the regions its introduction was, to say the least, thin on the ground and remained a source of friction between central and local government. Similarly the plans for national testing of pupils were dogged by opposition from local authorities (reinforced by teachers' and parents' efforts).

Local authorities remained, therefore, in powerful decision-making positions, much more so than in England and Wales where there was less conflict between the political perspectives of local and central government and a more deliberate erosion of local education authorities' control of education. Local authorities' powers were substantially disturbed, however, by the Conservative government's decision to reorganise Scottish local government into unitary authorities in 1996. From education's point of view, the fragmentation into a much larger number of unitary councils, many with singularly small populations and resources compared with the former regional councils, led to considerable reductions in programmes of support for existing educational practice or the implementation of new creative ideas.

In May 1997, the election of a UK Labour government signalled a clear change in the atmosphere. Central government might be expected to be in tune with the political stance of local government with local authorities accepting the advice of the Scottish Office much more readily than in the past. The new government's ideas, however, have not all been universally welcomed at local levels, and the authorities still retain control over how their block grant is spent. It remains to be seen, for example, whether the current Scottish Office's plans to introduce targets for schools in the areas of literacy and numeracy within a tight schedule will be achieved in the face of substantial objections to the possibility of a narrowing of the curriculum, the demanding time-scale and what many see as a re-issue of the Conservative's approach to the publication of league tables of schools' performance.

SOEID, HIGHER EDUCATION AND FURTHER EDUCATION

The funding of higher education (HE) is channelled from the Scottish Office through the Scottish Higher Education Funding Council (SHEFC) to individual institutions. Like the local authorities, SHEFC has the responsibility of deciding how the funding is to be divided up and used. SOEID gives general guidance on the emphases that it would wish to promote and there are a number of statutory requirements placed upon the Council. So, for example, science, technology and quality assurance are all assured of very high profiles, but that is rather different from an attempt by the Scottish Office to impose a detailed blueprint on the programmes of either SHEFC or individual institutions. This is not unreservedly to confirm the Scottish Office's claim to adopt a completely 'hands off' approach to HE. In the area of pre-service teacher education, for example, the Labour government has re-introduced inspection by HMI, a course of action which was by no means endorsed within HE where quality assurance is already extensive and conceptualised on a very different basis.

On a rather larger scale, major issues have arisen which have profound implications for the structure and functioning of HE and strong political undertones on which central government has to take a stand. Sometimes these relate to rather specific matters such as the merging of institutions and the future of monotechnics (e.g. the teacher education colleges), the incompatibilities during the 1980s and 1990s of promoting competition between institutions at the same time as exhortation to collaborate, and the 'stop/go' pattern of encouragement to increase the proportion of the population who have access to HE. The Labour government, elected in 1997, will have to decide what its position is on the future of Scottish monotechnics, whether it is going to emphasise competition or collaboration among institutions and how it is going to plan for increasing access. All of these matters are of crucial importance to the institutions in Scotland, but they are essentially political matters which cannot be left to the funding council to decide.

At a more general level, the Conservative government commissioned an enquiry into HE which reported in July 1997 (the Dearing Report) and included a specific report for Scotland (the Garrick Report). The recommendations for the funding of HE elicited an immediate response from the UK Labour government, confirmed by the Scottish Office, which took a quite different line from the reports' proposals on the payment of tuition fees and the availability of maintenance grants for students. There was considerable public debate about the implications of this for HE between the Minister and the Committee of Scottish Higher Education Principals (COSHEP). A second recommendation, that there should be a common qualifications framework for HE across Scotland, which gave explicit credits on entry for school and Further Education (FE) qualifications, was readily accepted by the Scottish Office and the Minister publicly urged HE to take a common approach to acceptance of such credits. The effect of this kind of pressure, together with some of the moves being made by the Scottish Qualifications Authority (SQA), made a large number of the institutions very nervous about the possibility that the SOEID was moving towards a system which could incorporate a national curriculum for HE or a centrally determined validation system. The general point being made here is that the message promoted by the Scottish Office, that it adopts a 'hands off' policy towards HE, is fragile. The big political decisions which have to be made have a profound effect on the day to day processes of the sector and the future existence of some institutions. At least some of the decisions are illuminated in a government paper on lifelong learning published in 1998 (see Chapter 112).

In FE the circumstances are rather different and there was, until late 1998, no dedicated funding council comparable with SHEFC. Since 1993 colleges in this sector have been Incorporated. The duty of providing the FE Service passed from the local authorities to the Scottish Office, and new College Boards of Management assumed responsibility for strategic decision making, finances, property and personnel. As in HE, the Scottish Office sees itself as assuming a 'hands off' stance. The basic funding it provides is decided according to a formula (under review), but the ways in which it is spent by the colleges is a matter for the Boards of Management. Once again as in HE, however, there are issues where political decisions can have a crucial impact on the operation of this sector. The tension between competition and collaboration, both within FE and between it and HE, is one such issue. In circumstances where actions are driven by the need to get 'bums on seats' in order to survive, competition has led to considerable invasion of both geographical and sector territories. Scottish Ministers will have to decide whether Scottish education at degree or pre-degree level is best served by this approach. They also have to adopt a monitoring role which ensures that non-advanced FE continues to be well served in Scotland and is not dismembered by the colleges' enthusiasm to take on the work previously the province of the universities. The new Labour government's approach has been to leave the sectors alone, let them settle or drift and see how things develop. Just two years before the end of the century, there is a sense of HE and FE in Scotland being in something of a state of limbo.

From the student's point of view, an important aspect of the work of the Scottish Office has been that of the Students' Awards Agency (SAA). This has dealt with, among other things, student maintenance grants (including the associated means tests) and special allowances for students with disabilities. From the academic session 1998–9 there will be no maintenance grants for students entering HE though there will be a student loan system. At the time of writing the details of the loan system are as yet unclear, but there will remain a role for the SAA no matter what happens because the new requirement for students to pay for their own tuition fees will be means tested. How that will be done is also not yet clear, but it will require confidential information relating to families' tax returns and it is very unlikely that the Scottish Office under a Labour administration would allow this service to be privatised and so remove public sector control of such information.

SOEID AND THE SPECIALIST COUNCILS

There is a variety of bodies within Scottish education which have fairly close relationships with SOEID but are distinctively separate bodies. These include:

- Scottish Consultative Council on the Curriculum – SCCC
- Scottish Community Education Council – SCEC

- Scottish Council for Educational Technology – SCET
- Scottish Council for Research in Education – SCRE
- Scottish Qualifications Authority – SQA

The extent to which these bodies work closely with the Scottish Office depends on the priorities of the government at that time. So, for example, in the late 1980s and early 1990s there was a very close association between the SOEID and the SCCC as they developed and established a national curriculum for primary and early secondary school through the 5 – 14 programme. In the late 1990s, however, the spotlight moved to focus on the arrangements and assessments for the Higher Still programme for the upper part of the secondary school and FE Colleges, and on innovations in new technology. This led to firm and frequent links with SQA and SCET. SCRE has a responsibility to respond to requests to carry out specific pieces of research for SOEID which relate to the Department's current concerns and so its relationship has a rather more consistent pattern. SCEC is expected to undergo a review at the time of writing. Labour government policies on lifelong learning and social exclusion, which came to the fore in their first year of office after election in 1997, could well lead to a reformulation of the Scottish Office view of the role that the council with responsibility for community education should fulfil.

The formal framework for the relationships with the Scottish Office is similar for all these bodies. Under the Conservative administration the membership of the Councils moved to being by ministerial appointment. This power was considerably tempered, however, by the rules which emanated from the Committee on Standards in Public Life set up by the UK Conservative government in 1994 and chaired by Lord Nolan. Under these rules there is a substantial set of procedures by which posts have to be advertised and applicants approved by a panel, which is made up of people from both within and outwith the Scottish Office, before the final decision is made by the Secretary of State. There is considerable variation in the extent to which the work of the different Councils is funded by SOEID. This depends both on the costs of that part of their work which the Scottish Office regards as essential, and on the potential for the different bodies to earn money (contracts, grants, fees) in the educational market place.

A rather different kind of body is the General Teaching Council for Scotland (GTC). This council has a responsibility for standards of teaching in Scottish schools and for the accreditation and review of pre-service teacher education. It is financially independent of the Scottish Office and derives most of its income from the subscriptions of all registered teachers in Scotland (registration is required of all teachers working in Scottish schools). The Registrar and various members of the Council are frequently asked to serve on committees or ad hoc groups to consider matters of national importance to Scottish education. In particular, there is a great deal of interaction about the national needs for the supply of teachers and the quotas for teacher education institutions. The final decisions on these numbers are not made by the GTC, however, but by the SOEID (overall numbers) and SHEFC (distribution of institutional funded places). The GTC has been accepted by the SOEID as significant in its own sphere and as fulfilling the Labour government's commitment to a self-governing profession. However, the Scottish Office has in the past displayed some irritation at what it sees as attempts by the GTC to pontificate outside its remit and so to reduce its own credibility. It was perhaps significant that by the start of 1998 the Labour Minister, in post since 1 May 1997, had not found time to meet the GTC.

LOOKING FORWARD TO DEVOLUTION

It is important to emphasise that looking to the future is highly speculative. There is a characteristic inability of humans to predict what is going to happen, even in the short term. The best seers are frequently humbled by the misadventures of their stories about what is to come when what is to come actually arrives. Nevertheless, the issues of concern and interpretation that are of most importance to professional educators at this time are those of the impact of the devolution of political power over the next few years.

One of the most obvious changes that can be expected from devolution to a Scottish parliament is the removal of constraints imposed by what the UK government deems to be appropriate for education in the rest of Britain. The Scottish Executive will no longer have to worry about reflecting educational developments in other parts of the country and the Scottish system will have opportunities to diverge as it wishes. The financial relationships with the Treasury in the context of the block grant are likely to be similar to those in place at present; there will be tax raising possibilities, however, which the Scottish Parliament might choose to use for educational purposes.

With devolution there is likely to be a new pattern of interchange between civil servants and the ministers. Rather than having only one day out of five in Edinburgh each week and dealing with much of the education business on paper, memos and e-mails will be readily supplemented by face to face meetings with Scottish Office officials. Relationships will be expected to be closer and extend to a wider range of people, and ministers will have the opportunity to increase their 'hands on' approach if they so wish. It is unlikely, of course, that there will be any more civil service staff available for education and so the differences in numbers of people working in particular specialist areas north and south of the border are likely to continue. The Scottish Office may well still be seeking cooperation, therefore, with the rather larger groups of experts in the DfEE.

Perhaps the most interesting area of speculation about how things will be after devolution relates to spending decisions by local government. There are, of course, areas where there is a broad consensus among all levels of government about how resources should be used. For example, there was very little disagreement about the value of moving towards pre-school provision as a right for all four year olds (it has to be acknowledged, of course, that this policy was implemented by ring-fencing funding through a voucher system which was both controversial and at odds with the usual block grant system). However, a Scottish Executive, of whatever political persuasion, is unlikely to be happy in other circumstances where its ideas, guidance or regulations are ignored by the local authorities which have the responsibility for so much of the education system. For example, in the area of pre-school provision both Conservative and Labour Ministers exhorted authorities to develop partnerships with the private and voluntary sectors. Such partnerships have been very modest indeed; local authorities have not been eager to contribute to a system in which they are expected to provide support for their competitors, and the other sectors see their role as one of receiving, not of contributing to, such support. At the time of writing, there is ample opportunity in the immediate future for back-peddling at local level on the Labour party's plans for performance targets for schools. This kind of tactic will always be available in areas of tension as long as there is no requirement on local government to spend the block grant in ways which match the pattern hypothecated by a central Scottish administration.

There is likely to be a comprehensive spending review soon which will analyse value for money in education expenditure. This undoubtedly will focus attention on the absence of any mechanism to ensure that money, in education and elsewhere, is spent in the way central government wishes. Reconsideration of this state of affairs will exemplify the fundamental concern of a devolved administration with the balance of power between, on the one hand, the Scottish parliament and executive and, on the other hand, Scottish local government. This may well constitute a threat in the longer term to the latter's financial control of its own activities. It may reinforce the pattern of educational decision-making being in the hands of the SOEID and an inner group of 'partners' such as SCCC, SQA and SCET.

On the other hand, there are civic activists who have long protested about the opaqueness of, and lack of democracy in, this educational policy-making process. They seek much broader consultative action under a new Scottish administration with a major role for the lay population in local communities. Inevitably, that would lead to devolution of control away from the SOEID and to much more local variation in provision, curriculum and the ways that schools are run and held to account for their activities. There is no doubt that this scenario of invigorating civic activity and responsibility, for the future under a Scottish parliament, is encouraged by the increased awareness of the general population (especially parents) that it can and should have more say in the education service.

In the HE sector, devolution will bring a number of difficult issues into even sharper focus. One of these relates to the extent to which Scottish institutions use tax payers' money to educate students from elsewhere, particularly those from south of the border. For example, many more doctors are trained each year than are needed to practice in Scotland. In total, the excess of students coming into Scottish HE institutions over those leaving Scotland to study elsewhere is equivalent to the population of a large university. Because the financing of HE is in transition at the time of writing, and there is a complex set of arguments about the advantages that accrue from the presence of these students in Scotland, it is difficult to put a figure on the support which the Scottish taxpayer is paying for the education of students from other parts of the UK and beyond. Despite such difficulties, these are issues which a devolved parliament and the Scottish Office will have to address. Whether they do so successfully remains to be seen.

REFERENCES

Gibson, J. S. (1985) *The Thistle and The Crown: a history of the Scottish Office*, Edinburgh: HMSO.

Humes, W. (1995) The significance of Michael Forsyth in Education, *Scottish Affairs*, 11, pp. 112–130.

Humes, W. (forthcoming) State: the governance of Scottish education 1872–2000, in H. Holmes, (ed.), *The Compendium of Scottish Ethnology*, vol. XI.

McPherson, A. and C. D. Raab (1988) *Governing Education: a sociology of policy since 1945*, pp. 113–206, Edinburgh: Edinburgh University Press.

Paterson, L. (1994) *The Autonomy of Modern Scotland*, pp. 125–27, Edinburgh: Edinburgh University Press.

Paterson, L. (1997) Policy making in Scottish education: a case of pragmatic nationalism, in M. M. Clark and P. A. Munn (eds), *Education in Scotland: policy and practice from pre-school to secondary*, pp. 138–55, London: Routledge.

12

The Work of the Scottish Higher Education Funding Council (SHEFC)

Dugald Mackie

The Scottish Higher Education Funding Council (SHEFC) has existed since June 1992 as the responsible body for the distribution of Government funding to higher education institutions (HEIs) in Scotland. Funding mechanisms and the making of payments came into effect on 1 April 1993. What has been achieved in the five years since its establishment illustrates the work of SHEFC and provides a basis for a little speculation on how that work might develop in the future.

BACKGROUND

For many years, what little government funding went into higher education in Scotland was channelled through two main routes: either via the University Grants Committee (UGC) or via the precursors of the present Scottish Office Education and Industry Department (SOEID). The four 'ancient' universities of Aberdeen, Edinburgh, Glasgow and St Andrews, the Royal Technical College in Glasgow and Heriot-Watt College in Edinburgh were in receipt of funding from both sources but would clearly have preferred all funds to be routed via the UGC (Hutchison, 1992). The Scottish Education Department of the day (SED) was seen as heavy-handed and interfering by comparison with the rather cosy and gentlemanly University Grants Committee (see Shattock, 1994).

The SED looked after what were known as the 'Central Institutions' with a commendable degree of generosity, possibly stemming from the tradition of the Scots realising the worth of education. The Education Department formed a more potent force within the Scottish Office than the Department for Education did with its Whitehall counterparts as is evinced by the succession of powerful Departmental Secretaries in Scotland by comparison with their English equivalents. This relative strength of the SED was a continuing factor into the 1980s and early 1990s and helps to explain why there is a Scottish Funding Council and not simply a Funding Council for the UK as a whole.

Scotland was as much a participant in the development and growth of higher education as was England, starting with the Robbins Report and the creation of polytechnics by the post-1966 Labour government and proceeding through the transfer of control of the polytechnics in the 1980s to the rapid expansion of student numbers in the early 1990s. In Scotland, the by-now eight institutions funded by the UGC saw responsibility for government funding pass to the Universities Funding Council in 1987 while the 'old' SED-controlled Central Institutions were joined by polytechnic style colleges transferred from local authority control, of which two swiftly adopted the title of 'Polytechnic'.

Eight universities in receipt of funds from a body based in England and Central Institutions in receipt of funds directly from the SOED in Edinburgh was an anomaly in relation to the general position of Scottish affairs within the United Kingdom. Much of government in Scotland was (and is) the responsibility of the Scottish Office. Health, transport, environment and education were all the responsibility of St Andrew's House. However, these responsibilities did not extend to fiscal matters where the Treasury's fiat extended across the whole of the UK.

Because the University Grants Committee had been established in 1919 as a committee to advise the Treasury, responsibility for funding the six higher education institutions in receipt of Treasury funds rested in London rather than in Edinburgh. This arrangement persisted, despite, as mentioned earlier, attempts by the SED to 'repatriate' responsibility back to Scotland. The arrangement survived the transfer of responsibility for the UGC from the Treasury to the Department for Education, thus creating an anomaly whereby policy responsibility for higher education stopped at the Scottish border but where funding did not. It was therefore no great surprise when the Further and Higher Education (Scotland) Act 1992 rectified this anomaly by permitting the establishment of a body to fund higher education institutions in Scotland.

THE NATURE OF SHEFC

The Scottish Higher Education Funding Council was created as a 'Non-Departmental Public Body' (NDPB), colloquially known as a 'Quango'. While it was part of the governance of education, it did not form part of a government department. It therefore stood outside the Civil Service but not outside the influence of civil servants, given that it was required to have a 'sponsoring department' – unsurprisingly the Scottish Office Education Department. As quangos had rather gone out of fashion in the 1980s and early 1990s and as other seemingly new quangos such as Scottish Homes were essentially re-inventions of existing bodies, it was the first wholly new major NDPB to be established by the Scottish Office in almost twenty years. Its comparative novelty (and the fact that any experience of setting up an NDPB had largely disappeared from the Scottish Office) resulted in some initial operational tensions between the Higher Education Division of SOED and staff in the Council.

The first Chairman of the Council had been appointed by the Secretary of State in early 1992. A distinguished accountant, both as practitioner and as theoretician, Professor (and since 1995 Sir) John Shaw was already a member of the Universities Funding Council (and Chairman of its Scottish Committee) and a Board member of Scottish Enterprise as well as being a Deputy Governor of the Bank of Scotland. His initial brief in relation to SHEFC was to work with officials from the Scottish Office in establishing the Council both as a corporate body and as a functioning organisation. In this task, he was assisted by civil servants from SOED, particularly by Dr Paul Brady, then an Assistant Secretary with SOED and later Director of Finance and Planning at Scottish Enterprise. Council members were identified and appointed by the Secretary of State, premises were located, an initial budget was agreed and, importantly, a Chief Executive was appointed in May 1992.

Professor John Sizer CBE might have seemed an unusual choice as Chief Executive in that he was neither Scottish nor linked with a Scottish institution (although an earlier part of his academic career had been spent in the University of Edinburgh). However, he had had experience at senior levels of university management (as Senior Pro Vice-Chancellor and Acting Vice-Chancellor of Loughborough University of Technology) and, significantly, as a member and as Vice-Chairman of the University Grants Committee (UGC). His appointment was a clear signal to the suspicious eight ex-UFC institutions that the Council had no intention of being parochially Scottish and would have its work influenced by a person with experience of university management and of developing the transparency of government funding of higher education.

Firm commitments to corporate propriety (on the part of Professor Shaw) and to transparency and accountability (on the part of Professor Sizer) were important elements underlying the initial work of the Council which had been set out in a letter of guidance sent by the Secretary of State in June 1992. That letter was itself the product of discussion and of consultation within a framework set by the 1992 Act and the powers which it gave the Council and, importantly, the constraints which the Act also placed on it.

The Government had acceded to the concerns expressed in Parliament when the legislation was being debated. It had not given the Council explicit powers or responsibilities as a planning body, reflecting the anti-corporatist spirit of the times or, more mundanely, the unsuccessful and ultimately damaging attempts of the UGC to 'plan' subject provision across universities in certain high-cost subjects. Just as the legislation failed to mention 'planning', so the June letter from the Secretary of State did likewise, other than in relation to SHEFC's own corporate plan. Any moves by the Council, either overt or covert, in the direction of planning the HE system in Scotland would therefore be of its own volition and were not in any way required by the Government.

The Secretary of State's letter clearly laid out the Scottish Office's expectations in relation to the main areas of work of the Council. It also required SHEFC to work jointly in a number of areas with the Higher Education Funding Councils of England (HEFCE) and of Wales (HEFCW) and the Department of Education in Northern Ireland (DENI). Although good relationships existed at officer level and there was cross-assessorship on each other's Council, the tendency of the largest partner (HEFCE) to forget that it needed firstly to consult its fellow Councils and then actually to agree joint activities with them (such as the Research Assessment Exercise) was at times a source of some tension. As a caveat, it would be wrong to exaggerate the scale of difficulties which were operational and which went unnoticed by higher education institutions.

The Council's main areas of work fall into the following categories:

- Funding (of Teaching, of Research, and of Capital Works/Equipment)
- Quality Assessment of Teaching
- Teaching and Policy Initiatives
- Financial Appraisal and Monitoring

FUNDING OF TEACHING

SHEFC inherited the responsibility for the funding of teaching from the Universities Funding Council (UFC) and from the Scottish Office Education Department (SOED). Institutions funded by the UFC were the eight universities which, although different in size and scope, were all fundamentally involved in research and teaching and could therefore be described as a relatively homogeneous group. No such homogeneity existed on the part of the SOED-funded institutions which fell into the categories of urban polytechnic-type institutions which either had achieved University status (in line with the provisions contained in the Further and Higher Education Scotland Act 1992) or which had aspirations to do so, colleges of education, smaller and more specialised colleges, a music/stage conservatoire and art schools.

The Central Institutions had gradually shaken off some of the controls imposed by the SOED. One would like to say that this process of glasnost stemmed from flexible thinking within the SOED: the truth is, alas, more probably linked to polytechnics putting pressure on the DES in England and Wales which eventually filtered across the border. However, by 1992, the SOED had moved away from annual deficit funding (whereby institutions were required to return surplus funds at the end of the financial year to the Treasury) and compulsory approval of courses to a system of funding which closely resembled that of the Universities Funding Council. However, one important difference was that the SOED did not provide the basic funding for research supplied by the UFC.

The similarity of approaches using a 'unit of resource' (in effect a price) in a relatively small number of broadly defined subject areas enabled SHEFC to continue a method of funding which was robust, effective, transparent and flexible in its ability to incorporate changes in external circumstances. In essence, the 'contract' between SHEFC and each of the institutions in receipt of funds was that they would teach an agreed number of students at undergraduate, taught postgraduate or research postgraduate levels in any or all of a number of broad subject areas. The teaching would be assessed for its quality with the Council retaining the right to withdraw funding where it was judged to be sub-standard. The relationship was governed by a Financial Memorandum, similar to that between the Scottish Office and SHEFC.

By 1993, the expansion of student numbers in higher education had exceeded government expectations. The expansion had been driven by an incentive to institutions involving the fee element of the funding per student. If the totality of that funding is thought of as a 'gross unit of resource', the relationship between the two elements within it explains expansion and also illustrates what happened when the Government called a halt to the expansion. Element one is the funding provided to institutions through the Funding Councils. Element two is the fee, also paid to institutions but either through the Awards Branch of the SOED (now the Student Awards Agency Scotland), local Education Authorities in England and Wales or the Department of Education in Northern Ireland. A critical factor was the government policy which guaranteed fee and subsistence support to all British students studying for their first degree or advanced diploma at a recognised institution. Thus, while the number of students who brought with them elements one and two to an institution was limited by the funds allocated to SHEFC, the number of students who brought solely element two with them was in practice unlimited. Had the relationship of the two elements within the gross unit of resource remained at 80:20 in favour of element one, there would have been little incentive to expand numbers, even as 'marginal cost' students, bringing with them little more than £750 each. However, a relationship of nearer 50:50 made 'fees-only' students (at, say, £2,500) a much more attractive proposition as an adjunct to their 'fully-funded' brethren (at, say, £5,000). Thus there ensued the rapid expansion of student numbers.

SHEFC inherited this system of 'fully-funded' and 'fees-only' students but immediately met a change in government policy whereby the expansion was to be suspended in favour of 'consolidation' of what had been achieved largely because of the costs involved in guaranteeing support from the Treasury to all eligible students. The relationship within the gross unit of resource reverted to its traditional norm of around 80:20 with institutions being warned that they ran the risk of being penalised if they continued to take in excessive numbers of fees-only students. The Council was also faced with the dilemma of the funding of existing 'fees-only' students. A cut in funding for such students from £2,500 to £750 would have had a catastrophic effect on institutions which had, after all, been following government policy by expanding numbers. What followed was an elegant solution devised by the Council's Director of Funding, David Wann, which allowed both for a manageable withdrawal from dependence on students at the higher fees-only rate and for no loss of the expansion achieved through a gradual conversion of 'fees-only' students into 'fully-funded' students.

While institutions may have grumbled about other aspects of SHEFC policy, there has been a good relationship between SHEFC and the HEIs in the area of the funding of teaching. A change towards funding by output and/or to staged achievement during a course (i.e. only those who are eligible to proceed to the next year of a course or to graduate) was resisted by institutions during consultation and was therefore put to one side by the Council. However, it seems likely that this method of calculating students eligible for Council funding will re-appear and may be introduced.

Other areas for funding – in particular of adult and continuing education – have proved to be more controversial. The changes made by the Council in this area have, though, brought a needed professionalism in some institutions to an activity which is now seen as an important part of a process of 'life-long learning' rather than as a slightly shameful and essentially amateur activity.

FUNDING OF RESEARCH

The principal reward for the polytechnic sector in the 1991 White Paper and the subsequent legislation was the power to award degrees in an institution's own right and, in the process, to call itself 'university' if it so wished. The new title of university soon had heads of institutions seeking to emulate their older brethren in other ways, not least in their aspirations to be centres of research activity. Such aspirations came to be translated into calls to the new Funding Council for a share of some of the research funding which was 'unfairly' concentrated in the eight 'old' universities.

SHEFC was therefore faced with the need to keep everyone happy: not reducing funds for high-quality existing research activity while offering some encouragement to other institutions in which there could be found pockets of active research of a high standard. It was also faced with advice from the Secretary of State to encourage research but to concentrate funding on areas of high quality. Its funds were also limited, which was an important factor which some staff in institutions seemed not to understand. In other words, the research funding cake was the same size as before (c.£100m): the question was whether to continue to deliver large wedges to the Universities of Edinburgh and Glasgow and their pre-1992 colleagues, slivers to Paisley, Napier et al., and crumbs to the smaller colleges, or whether to even out the size of the slices.

Fortuitously for SHEFC, one of the periodic Research Assessment Exercises (RAE) had been run by the Universities Funding Council in 1992 which had included polytechnics and other non-UFC institutions for the first time. Such exercises existed in order to provide qualitative evidence about research being funded so that funds could be concentrated in areas of higher quality.

The results of the 1992 exercise (based on largely peer-review of work published by individuals), were published in time for use in the first funding allocations for research made by the Council. It decided that it did not wish all of its c.£100m to follow the results of the 1992 RAE but that it would retain £5m to be used for 'research development'. The remaining £95m was then allocated using quality (RAE scores of 5 down to 1), volume (i.e. primarily the number of research-active academic staff), size of the 'pot' of funds in that subject area and other factors indicating healthy research activity such as industrial research contracts.

This initial allocation set a pattern for research funding for the next four years (until the results of the 1996 RAE were known). The Council's main activity in relation to research was therefore primarily focused on research policy and on working with other bodies (the Royal Society of Edinburgh, Scottish Enterprise, and the Scottish Office itself) on exercises such as Technology Foresight. The Council was also able to use its Research Development Grant to good effect: evidence for this came in improved performance in a number of areas in 1996 RAE.

FUNDING OF EQUIPMENT AND CAPITAL WORKS

SHEFC inherited approaches to the funding for equipment and for capital works which were less clear-cut than the methods for teaching or research. The position with the ex-SOED institutions was clearer because of the interventionist way in which the Education Department had operated in the past. That control had allowed it to adopt a more planned approach than the UFC both to annual expenditure on capital projects and equipment and on the longer-term physical development of institutions.

The approach adopted by the SOED, based on appraisal of projects against Treasury guidelines on '6 per cent return on capital', meant that there were several 'approved' projects on the stocks when SHEFC came into existence. The position with the UFC was less clear, with institutions being unsure of where they stood in relation to outline plans which the Funding Council had encouraged them to develop. The UFC had inherited the UGC's approach to capital works which seemed to depend on informal understandings and on the permanent availability of capital funds, rather than their inexorable year-on-year contraction. It was easier for the Government to reduce the Public Sector Borrowing Requirement (PSBR) by freezing or cutting capital expenditure than by cutting recurrent expenditure.

In brief, the UFC had a number of proposals which had, alas, not been subject to the same appraisal as comparable SOED-funded projects for the simple reason that the UFC had never required such an appraisal. SHEFC, with an initial (and short-lived) tranche of capital funding, adopted the simple (if disingenuous and unfair) expedient of only being willing to consider 'fully appraised' projects. In other words, only ex-SOED proposals would be eligible. Of all the early decisions made by SHEFC, this one is probably the least defensible. Fortunately for the Funding Council, it has disappeared into the mists of the past, along with, it has to be said, the availability of large sums of money from whatever government is in power for capital projects in higher education or, indeed, in the public or quasi-public sector in any form.

Why did capital funds disappear? Firstly, they were a target for squeezes on the PSBR.

Secondly, the value for money (or, indeed, the added value) which they were purported to deliver often turned out to be more apparent than real. And thirdly, they were seen as one of the last manifestations of the discredited Welfare State. The successor to such funding was to be 'investment' from the private sector via the Private Finance Initiative (PFI). A whole new cottage industry sprang up virtually overnight of 'PFI experts' in the fields of law, finance, facilities management, design and construction. Large sums were invested to little effect, given that the costs of a PFI-funded project might well exceed the costs of a traditional Exchequer-funded project in view of the need for each of the interested parties to make some positive return on its investment. SHEFC staff were expected to master the PFI brief and to change their role from being 'funders' to being 'enablers'.

PFI has been partially adopted and partly abandoned by the current Government. It remains to be seen quite how SHEFC will develop its work in this area. It has certainly worked with institutions on major estates issues: the extensive backlog of essential maintenance of buildings (for which it has provided small but welcome sums of money to help redress problems built up during the 1980s when the buildings maintenance budget provided a soft target for short-term expedient cuts); the development of a more strategic and more planned approach to the 'estate' (as opposed to what many in institutions had seen simply as a collection of buildings); and investigating the applicability of PFI to capital projects in Scottish HEIs (through the provision of small 'pathfinder' grants where lessons learned in particular schemes were hoped to have generic application, thus avoiding the costs associated with 'reinventing the wheel' on every occasion).

Equipment funded was initially allocated and calculated according to a formulaic approach which was amended after one year to increase allocations in Computer Science. With the move to PFI, specific allocations for equipment are disappearing into overall grants for teaching and research.

TEACHING QUALITY ASSESSMENT (TQA)

SHEFC's work in the area of quality assessment of teaching has had a major impact both directly on standards of teaching and less directly but no less importantly on helping create a quality 'culture' within higher education as a whole. Starting in 1992, with the pilot assessments and finishing in 1998, its first cycle has seen all major and many lesser subject areas on offer in Scotland assessed using a method based on peer review of institutional self-assessments. SHEFC has also decided to 'sign up' with the recently established (in 1997) Quality Assurance Agency (QAA) such that that Agency will in future have responsibility for assessing teaching quality (and attempting to measure academic standards) in Scottish HEIs. In a major sense, therefore, the Council's direct involvement in quality assessment has come to an end.

Although TQA was a novelty for pre-1992 universities, it had been a major element in the 1991 White Paper, the 1992 legislation and the guidance from the Secretary of State. Some SOED institutions were already liable for inspection by members of Her Majesty's Inspectorate, the remit of the Inspectorate having gradually expanded from schools to cover colleges. Initial ideas on TQA came from Jim Donaldson, the Council's first Director of Quality Assessment, an HMI (with experience in and of higher education) on secondment to SHEFC. These ideas were developed and refined, both after consultation with institutions and after discussion within the Council itself. That latter discussion proved to be particularly influential in that the one Council member with extensive experience of the application of a 'quality culture' (in IBM), John McClelland, was able to show that self-assessment, tempered by peer review, was a highly effective means of gaining acceptance and ownership of the need to build quality into all aspects and stages of teaching students in particular and into institutional culture in general.

It was unfortunate for SHEFC that its TQA framework involved the production of much documentation by institutions (which helped ensure the fairness of the process). Quality Audit, which had been in place since 1990, also involved much documentation, as did validation of degree programmes by professional bodies such as the Institution of Civil Engineers. TQA was thus portrayed as a necessary evil (at best) or as an intolerable burden from which institutions should be freed. Principals were forever complaining about the burdens (especially in Graduation Day speeches) but were quite happy to accept the kudos and extra funding which came with an 'Excellent' rating.

TEACHING AND POLICY INITIATIVES

Pressures on funding from 1993 onwards meant that the Council pursued initiatives which were aimed at improving institutional efficiency and effectiveness, either through 'adding value' to a process or by allowing institutions to undertake it more economically. These initiatives were funded through a 'top-slice' of Council funds, set aside before grants were made for teaching, research and capital purposes. The amount of the top-slice (up to £23 million in 1994) was a source of aggravation to a number of Principals who failed to be convinced that it was money well spent.

Considerable sums were spent on schemes designed to improve the learning process for students. Some schemes (Teaching and Learning Technology Programme – TLTP; Computers in Teaching Initiative – CTI) were partly inherited from the UFC and were run in tandem with the other Funding Councils. Other schemes (Flexibility in Teaching and Learning Scheme – FTLS) were unique to SHEFC. There was often a link between the schemes and the quality assessment process, given that assessments revealed areas for improvement in the teaching process.

While often worthy in intention and in their development, the effectiveness of the schemes in their application remains a matter for debate. They were a means through which institutions benefited from additional SHEFC grants but at times in areas which might not have been high in terms of institutional priorities. Nonetheless, it is also true to say that the real advances made in developing computer-assisted learning (CAL) material would not have occurred so rapidly had there not been central funding. Indeed, it is this ability to add to the infrastructure underpinning the whole HE sector which is, and will continue to be, a major characteristic of SHEFC.

Unlike some initiatives where schemes lasted as long as the current enthusiasm of their protagonists, the Council's improvement of facilities and resources for students with disabilities will form a lasting legacy to its investment of small but significant sums in a planned and coordinated manner. The Council's interest in championing the lot of contract research staff (through its initiative in this area) is also noteworthy in that it has helped to improve the employment conditions of a group of staff who are fundamental to success in research.

One infrastructure initiative taken by the Council has been the development of four Metropolitan Area Networks (MANs) interlinked across Scotland. The decision to invest in networks was made because of a view in SHEFC that such facilities (high-speed, 'broad-based' fibre-optic cables linked using sophisticated 'routers') were going to be fundamental to future institutional success in a world of easy global communications. Edinburgh and Glasgow Universities were already pilot sites in a Joint Information Systems Committee initiative to test a high-speed version of the UK's Joint Academic Network (JANET). Interest and expertise in high-speed networking thus already existed, as did reasonable local area networks (LANs) within institutions.

SHEFC, which was a co-sponsor of the Joint Information Systems Committee (JISC), worked with its secretariat to ensure that the development of MANs was compatible with wider UK policy. It then engaged in a dialogue with the service provider (the UK Education and Research Network Association – UKERNA), which ran JANET, and then with institutional representatives of the four groups (based in the Aberdeen, Edinburgh, Fife/Tayside and Glasgow areas). Armed with adequate funding, the four groupings were able to negotiate a leasing deal with a fibre-optic network supplier (in all four cases, Scottish Telecom) to install the MANs. This success allowed staff within SHEFC to argue for further funds to extend the MANs, inter-connect them via dedicated links and to permit development of projects to bring greater use of the MANs to institutions. This work of developing the use of the MANs continues today and is likely to continue in the foreseeable future.

FINANCIAL APPRAISAL AND MONITORING

In relation to the pressures put on institutions to account for the use of the funds granted to them, ex-SOED institutions had either been used to decades of strict control of their finances by the Scottish Office and a regime of 'deficit funding' or to equally stringent control by local government. On the other hand, ex-UFC institutions guarded their autonomy jealously, enshrined as it was either in Acts of Parliament or in Royal Charters. While universities were content to accept public funding, mainly from the UGC/UFC, but also from research councils and government departments, they seemed at times to regard it as an impertinence that they should be required to account in detail for its use.

The relationship between a government department and an NDPB was governed, as mentioned earlier, by a Financial Memorandum. Replicated between SHEFC and the institutions, each university was required to designate an 'Accounting Officer' – in practice the Principal or Director – who could be held to account by Parliament for the use of public funds alongside the Chief Executive of SHEFC.

In practice, the Financial Memorandum has proven to be less onerous than was envisaged. While undoubtedly strengthening the need for institutions to be more externally accountable for the use of public funds (and in the process to be more accountable internally), it has not undermined the autonomy of those institutions. SHEFC has not had to resort to the approach of making a general requirement on all institutions or a particular requirement on a specific institution a 'condition of grant' and nor has it had to put any of the institutions in intensive financial care. The discipline of preparing realistic annual financial forecasts, scrutiny by the Council's financial appraisal and monitoring staff, and an active dialogue between the Council's audit team and both internal and external auditors of institutions, have helped to ensure that the higher education sector is financially well managed. That standard of management allows institutions better to weather hard financial times and the short-term uncertainties of the future.

STRATEGIC PLANNING

As a 'Non-Departmental Public Body', SHEFC has been required to produce both corporate and operational plans on an annual basis in accordance with Standard Cabinet Office guidance to sponsoring departments. In turn, the Council has required institutions to submit their own strategic plans (along with financial plans in the shape of annual financial forecasts and estates plans plus projections of student numbers). Institutions have had certain requirements imposed on them in order to try and strike a balance between consistency of approach (allowing comparison) and reflection of a particular institution's own characteristics and needs. Both sets of processes are relatively mature by now and have resulted in the production of plans which are helpful to government and to the higher education sector, as well as to the wider public.

INSTITUTIONAL COLLABORATION

The unpopularity of 'top-slicing' among the Principals and their lobbying against Scottish Office Ministers, brought an assurance from SHEFC in 1995 that it would limit such top-slicing in future and would concentrate it in a 'Strategic Change' funding stream involving collaboration among two or more institutions and only rarely to single institutions.

The 'Strategic Change' initiative is the closest the Council comes to overt planning of higher education in Scotland. After a rather shaky start which can probably be ascribed to SHEFC itself being unclear about its objectives in launching the initiative, there are signs that it is encouraging collaboration which will result in greater economy or will add value to the higher education sector. Whether it will result in the 'transformational' (sic) change so desired by the Chief Executive of SHEFC does, however, remain to be seen. It certainly represents a useful source of funds on which institutions can draw to invest in developing activities. In difficult times, such funds are not easily accumulated by institutions from within their own resources. If the attached constraints can be swallowed, this particular form of 'supping with the devil' may yet prove to be of greater benefit than first thought.

ROLE OF THE COUNCIL AND GOVERNANCE

Any examination of the work of SHEFC would be deficient were it not to cover the importance of the Council itself and the role played by Council members. Drawn from education (school and higher), business, commerce and public service, the members appointed by the Secretary of State have been fundamental to the success of SHEFC. Although 'quangos' have often been the target of accusations by political parties that they are full of 'political placemen', the Scottish Office has skilfully avoided any such fate befalling SHEFC. The common theme among members has been an interest in education and a genuine wish that higher education in Scotland should not simply succeed but should excel in a global market.

One particular interest of Council members (and of its Chairman, Sir John Shaw) has been in governance. It has also been a topic of interest to the National Audit Office, the Public Accounts Committee and the Committee on Standards in Public Life (the Nolan Committee). This interest on the part of the Council has manifested itself in the publication (jointly with COSHEP) of a guide for members of governing bodies and in annual meetings involving such members with members of the Council. If the principals of institutions have sometimes been uneasy at this active encouragement of members of courts and governing bodies, the end result has been an enhancement of the role played by such members in ensuring good governance within institutions. Some little local difficulties apart, the 'crisis of governance' (a phrase coined by Professor Peter Scott, now Vice-Chancellor of Kingston University) which it is claimed afflicts higher education in England seems unrecognisable in a Scottish context, not least due to the work undertaken by SHEFC working in concert with institutions.

THE FUTURE

This account of SHEFC has done scant justice to its considerable achievements in the period since its foundation. It has established itself as a body which, although beholden to the overall policies of government, has succeeded in being seen as slightly apart from it. Its success has itself meant that it is listened to by government ministers and is therefore able to influence policy-thinking and policy direction. The relatively small size of the higher education sector in Scotland has been one of the keys to this success in that it has allowed informal dialogue between SHEFC and representatives of all the institutions 'round the table'. This advantage has not been shared by its counterpart in England which, it must be said, does not enjoy the same esteem as SHEFC among institutions.

That esteem is not unqualified but, even in the areas which have brought forth criticism such as teaching quality assessment, it can be argued that the reasoning of principals was based more on prejudice than on an objective assessment of the success of the Council's work. Indeed, the Council emerges relatively unscathed from the pages of the Garrick Report when the opposite might have been the case, given the opportunity for any scores to be settled through the medium of the Dearing and Garrick Committees. The reports of the main committee and its Scottish offshoot have galvanised the Government into over-hasty action on the introduction of student contributions to the cost of tuition. At the time of writing, confusion is the order of the day on the part of potential students, parents and the institutions themselves. Contradictory statements from ministers and officials, inadequate performance on the part of the Student Awards Agency Scotland (SAAS) and broadsheet newspapers ever willing to inflame matters through selective reporting written on the basis of synthetic moral indignation have resulted in a debacle which the Scottish Office will no doubt look to SHEFC to unravel.

It may have been unfairly caricatured as 'the dullest quango in Scotland', but its influence and work look unlikely to diminish in importance, not least with the prospect of the Scottish parliament from 1999 onwards. It is likely that the members of this parliament will take a more active (interfering?) interest in Scottish higher education and, importantly, in Scottish higher education institutions. A successful Higher Education Funding Council which builds on its achievements since 1992 and which develops further the good relationships which it has built up with universities and colleges can do much to defend higher education from political interference of an unwelcome nature. Steered by a new chairman and with a fresh influx of members, the work of SHEFC and its executive seems set to be no less important in the next five years than it has been since 1992.

REFERENCES

Hutchison I. G. C. (1992) The Scottish Office and the Scottish Universities c.1930–c1960 in *Scottish Universities: Distinctiveness and Diversity* in J. Carter and D. Withrington (eds), Edinburgh.

National Committee of Inquiry into Higher Education (1997) *Higher Education in the Learning Society*, Report of the National Committee, Chairman Sir Ronald Dearing, Norwich: HMSO.

National Committee of Inquiry into Higher Education (1997) *Higher Education in the Learning Society*, Report of the National Committee, Chairman Sir Ronald Garrick, Norwich: HMSO.

Shattock, M. (1994) *The UGC and the Management of British Universities*, Buckingham.

13

The Scottish Inspectorate and their Operations

Nisbet Gallacher

Since establishment some 150 years ago the range of responsibilities and the manner of operation of HM Inspectors of Schools in Scotland (HMI) have changed continuously with the changing times, but always with a clear focus on the quality of education and the improvement of it. The development and refinement of role and responsibility has, however, accelerated significantly over the last decade or so in line with the rapid pace of change in education and in society generally, and in response to governmental concerns for greater accountability in public services.

HM INSPECTORATE: SIZE, STRUCTURE, RECRUITMENT

In recent years, the number of HM Inspectors has varied between about 90 and 110, with fluctuations both as a result of changes in duties and demand and in response to the availability of public finance. HM Inspectorate is led and managed by HM Senior Chief Inspector of Schools (HMSCI) who combines the role with that of principal professional adviser on education to the Secretary of State for Scotland.

HMSCI is supported by a senior management group consisting of a Depute Senior Chief Inspector (HMDSCI) and eight Chief Inspectors (HMCI). The Chief Inspectors share responsibility for leading and managing the inspection programme and follow-up of it and the Inspectorate's extensive contribution to educational development and policy advice and formulation. Three 'territorial' Chief Inspectors are responsible for inspection activity in schools and links with education authorities and other interested groups in the Western, Eastern and Northern Divisions into which the country is divided for these purposes; a further three have 'sector' responsibilities for educational development and professional policy advice and casework for pre-school and 5–14, secondary, and formal and informal further education (in this case including inspection which is organised nationally) respectively; one has responsibility for professional matters in teacher education, for developments in the use of technology and for educational research and intelligence; and one heads up the Inspectorate Audit Unit.

The Inspectorate's diverse responsibilities in pre-school, primary and secondary education, including independent schools where assessment for registration is a significant responsibility, informal and formal further education and teacher education, and their professional input to policy, quality and standards in education generally, present a challenging agenda in both scale and intensity of demand. Also, the Inspectorate operates without executive power, relying on the quality and credibility of its contribution to influence institutions, education authorities and other agencies, and fellow professionals. Recruits to the Inspectorate must therefore be highly respected and experienced professionals in their field. They are recruited to provide an appropriate balance of expertise across the various sectors and subject specialisms. They must offer an outstanding track record in teaching or lecturing or in informal education, have occupied one or more posts of responsibility in education or a relevant field with distinction, and demonstrate the ability and adaptability to extend their range of professional interests and sphere of activity.

ROLE AND RESPONSIBILITIES

A number of important national developments over the last three decades have significantly influenced the role and responsibilities of HMI. The establishment of the General Teaching Council in 1965 allowed HMI to shed their then remaining responsibilities for teacher qualifications, in respect of the final certification of probationer teachers and various endorsement qualifications, e.g. 'Infant Mistress'; and the creation of the Scottish Examination Board in 1963 allowed the transfer of the substantial responsibility of administering the then Scottish Leaving Certificate examinations at Higher and Lower levels. These developments paved the way for concentration in the work of HMI on the qualities and needs of the education system as a whole and of its component institutions.

There was a further very significant development in 1983 when, following a Scottish Office review of the role of HM Inspectors, the Secretary of State decreed that HMI reports on individual institutions, until then shared and discussed in confidence with the Head of the relevant institution and, as appropriate, with the Director of Education/Chairman of Governors etc., should be published. That presented a new and challenging set of circumstances for HMI, requiring absolute rigour in evaluation and the utmost sensitivity in reporting and in working relations with staff in schools and colleges, education authorities etc. Procedures for the publishing of reports, the inspection procedures which underpin them, the style of the reports themselves and arrangements for follow-up of inspection findings have all been systematically reviewed and refined over the intervening years.

Meantime, the developing importance and scale of provision of informal and formal further education required extensions of HMI responsibilities in these areas; and in more recent years, the increasing emphasis on pre-school education has necessitated greater attention by HM Inspectors.

The current nature and scale of HM Inspectors' responsibilities were set out in a statement to Parliament by the Secretary of State in 1992. That statement acknowledged and embraced the developments of the preceding twenty years or so. It cast HM Inspectors' responsibilities and operations firmly in the context of wider government policy requiring greater accountability of public services, and the need for openness and objectivity in the evaluation and reporting of them. Earlier developments in working practice had ensured that HM Inspectors were well placed to embrace these principles.

The statement, while affirming that HM Inspectors would continue to operate as an integral part of the Scottish Office Education Department, as it was then known, reinforced the independence of the Inspectorate in relation to evaluation and public reporting. It set out tripartite responsibilities for the Inspectorate viz:

1. evaluating and reporting publicly on the performance of a statistically valid sample of educational institutions, and thereby on the performance of the education system as whole;
2. identifying national developments needed in education and providing a leadership role in respect of them;
3. providing professional policy advice through the Senior Chief Inspector to the Secretary of State and Ministers and within the Scottish Office Education Department.

These responsibilities were seen to be mutually supportive with the first-hand experience and evidence from inspection informing advice and input on developments and policy. In line with Scottish Office practice, the Inspectorate's work is set out each year in an agreed management plan listing tasks to be undertaken and objectives, resource commitment and output measures for each task, together with an audit of the previous year's performance. About 60–65 per cent of HMI time in recent years has been devoted to evaluation and reporting with the remainder split among educational development, policy advice and casework.

LINKS WITHIN AND BEYOND THE SCOTTISH OFFICE

While HM Inspectorate operates independently in relation to evaluation and reporting, they work closely with others in the Scottish Office and in the field in educational development and policy matters. In relation to broad policy issues, senior members of the Inspectorate work jointly with their administrative counterparts in SOEID to serve the needs of ministers, bringing a professional dimension to the development of advice to ministers on policy issues and in discussion with ministers about them. Such advice might be in the form of a suggestion of the need for a particular initiative, and how it might be pursued, or in response to ministers' policy priorities, giving advice about desirability and practicability in educational terms. Specialist HMI contribute similarly in the Department and to ministers in relation to subject-specific issues. Inspectors at all levels also work closely with professional and other colleagues in the field – directors of education, headteachers, principals, teachers and lecturers, representatives of parents and from industry, and others – in national committees and working groups, and in individual contacts, in pursuing the outcomes of inspection and in identifying the need for educational developments and pursuing these.

THE INSPECTION PROCESS

As indicated, the processes of inspection and reporting have been developed progressively since the decision in 1983 to 'go public'. Over any two or three year period a statistically valid sample of institutions in each phase of education is inspected, leading to the publication of reports on these institutions and allowing extrapolations to be made and published about the qualities and needs of the system as a whole. Inspections are conducted by teams chosen to reflect the scale and range of provision in the institutions concerned in line with agreed inspection guidelines, performance criteria and reporting formats. Extensive use is made of electronic recording and analysis of data in the preparation of reports.

Typically, a full inspection of a small primary school might involve two inspectors spending two or three days in the school with time allocated for setting up and preparing for the visit, drafting the report, discussing it with key individuals and finalising it for publication. For a large primary school a team of four or five HMI would spend three or four days in the school with similar arrangements for preparation and follow-up. Evidence is collected from a variety of sources: discussion with the Head, staff, pupils and representatives of parents; reviewing documentation such as the school development plan, communications with parents and the community generally, and pupils' written work, tests and assessments; classroom observation; and generally absorbing the characteristics of the school, its ethos, pastoral care, behaviour etc. A cardinal principle is that no inspection leading to a published report shall be conducted by only one inspector – a minimum team of two is deployed in all cases to provide corroboration. In secondary schools and further education colleges a much larger team is needed for a full inspection to match the range of specialist provision. Increasingly, with the existence in all sectors of school/college development plans and evidence available from institutional self-evaluation, more limited, focused inspections are undertaken in some cases, usually following a number of 'audit trails' identified in part from the development plan.

Each inspection is led by a nominated reporting officer (HMI) who has responsibility for briefing staff, parents and participating HMI about the inspection, managing the inspection, preparing a draft report, agreeing it with senior colleagues, participating in discussion of it with the Head, Director/Chairman and parent representatives, and producing a final version of the report.

Once finalised, reports are published and made freely available to staff in the institution, authorities/boards, parents, local Members of Parliament and other interested individuals and agencies. The institution and managing authority together are then obliged to produce in four to six months an Action Plan to address the recommendations of the report. After some twelve to eighteen months a follow-up inspection, usually on a much smaller scale, is undertaken to assess the action taken to address the issues and recommendations of the report. While HM Inspectors have a clear responsibility to identify deficiencies and areas requiring attention, an important responsibility is to identify and describe, and thereby disseminate good practice.

To reinforce the openness and independence of both the inspection process and reports a lay member is included in each inspection team. These members are sought through public advertisement and selected following interview. Specific formal qualifications are not required but the person must be judged capable through experience and temperament of making a distinctive and complementary contribution to the inspection process. They must not have held professional positions in education as, for example, teachers or lecturers. Training is provided on both the education and inspection processes. Lay members are involved at each stage of the inspection and are asked to take responsibility for specific enquiries related to their experience, for example, into the efficacy of links with parents or local employers, behaviour and ethos. They are not asked to undertake tasks requiring professional expertise, for example, assessing teaching competence and effectiveness or pupil performance. Lay members have contributed well to inspection teams and after initial, understandable suspicions by schools are generally well received and the distinctive nature of their contribution recognised.

In a further development in the last few years, Associate Assessors have also been recruited. These are carefully selected staff of proven expertise from a variety of levels and subject disciplines in schools and colleges. Selection is made from nominations invited from education authorities, colleges and others. Training is provided and the assessors are then included in inspection teams as full participating members. Their inclusion has two main objectives: to diversify the personnel involved in inspection and to give key staff in schools, colleges and other educational institutions first-hand experience of the processes and techniques of independent inspection and reporting, and thereby to inform the development of institutional self-evaluation. The move has been welcomed by the assessors, who have found valuable the training provided and the experience of inspection gained, by the institutions inspected and by the institutions from which the assessors have been drawn.

The prospect of inspection inevitably generates apprehension in the institution but steps are taken to brief staff in advance about the processes, intentions and outcomes of inspection, and the feedback collected systematically from staff and parents at the end of each inspection usually indicates that, in retrospect, the inspection can be viewed as a positive and helpful experience with due recognition of good practice and realistic pointers to improvement. The systematic collection at the end of each inspection of the views of heads and others about the conduct and efficacy of the inspection and the validity of the report and findings is, from the Inspectorate's point of view, extremely valuable, with comments across inspections aggregated and analysed to inform and improve future inspection practice. Inspection reports on institutions and on aspects of education are generally seen to provide well informed, fair and helpful comment and assessment, and are almost invariably actively and positively followed up by the institutions concerned.

The evidence from inspection is collected in such a way that it can be aggregated to provide the basis of reports on the quality of education nationally or of aspects of education, and a number of such reports are published annually on topics such as quality and standards in schools, mathematics in the primary school, the use of new technology, student guidance in further education, youth work etc. These reports are also the subject of systematic follow-up in national seminars and in discussion with heads of institutions, education authorities and others.

Over the last decade, major changes have been made to inspection procedures designed to ensure consistency of approach and standards of evaluation across inspection teams, to focus attention more closely on evaluation in reports and to respond to developments in the education system. National inspection and reporting guidelines were developed, bringing together the best practice from the earlier Divisional arrangements. Perhaps most significant, however, was the introduction into inspection of performance indicators covering all the important aspects of school and college activity: curriculum and assessment; quality of teaching and teaching methods; organisation, management and leadership; the quality and use of accommodation and other resources; ethos and student guidance, etc. These indicators and the accompanying illustrative criteria defining four levels of performance were piloted and refined in successive inspection programmes in the late 1980s and early 1990s before being firmly embedded in inspection arrangements, and then published. The development and publication of the indicators had a dual intent: for the Inspectorate, to bring greater rigour, consistency, transparency and a focus on evaluation in inspection; and for the education community at large, to give a clear steer on expectations and promote and support developments in institutional self-evaluation.

PROMOTING A 'QUALITY CULTURE'

The encouragement and support of wider quality assurance arrangements have been a feature of Inspectorate activity in the 1990s. Hitherto, the combination of a teaching force of high quality, general expectations of performance set out by the Secretary of State, the expectations of the national assessment and examination systems administered by the

Scottish Examination Board and the Scottish Vocational Education Council, and the sample school and college inspections conducted by HM Inspectors had been relied upon to secure quality. In the late 1980s, however, the Inspectorate concluded that these arrangements were unlikely in themselves to stimulate or guarantee the level of performance needed to prepare the young, and not so young, in education to meet the increasing economic and social demands of the 1990s and beyond. HM Inspectors, therefore, set about the promotion of a wider 'quality culture' in Scottish education whereby the external evaluation provided by HM Inspectors would be complemented by institutional self-evaluation based on school and college development plans incorporating realistic but challenging performance targets; institutional review of performance; and reporting of achievements to school and college boards, parents etc.

The initiative was taken forward through a series of Inspectorate publications and an extensive series of seminars and conferences for senior personnel. The first step was to create an awareness among key personnel at all levels of the need to strive for more consistent and higher quality of performance, both individually and corporately. To provide models against which all institutions might examine their own effectiveness, a series of reports was published setting out what seemed to be the key characteristics of the most effective primary, secondary and formal and informal further education institutions on the basis of inspection findings of the previous few years. These reports proved to be highly influential, stimulating extensive discussion of school and college effectiveness and paved the way for further work on school and college planning, promoted and supported by further Inspectorate reports in 1991 and 1992. These reports proposed that all institutions should have a development plan which laid out short and longer term objectives and targets, priorities for development and an audit of performance against the stated objectives and targets. While caught up to some extent in concerns about the pace of educational change generally, development planning in itself was seen to be a useful management tool and a helpful means of articulating priorities. So much so that plans to legislate for compulsory development planning proved unnecessary.

It was recognised, however, that for the arrangements to be effective and credible, agreed and readily available performance criteria were required. The performance indicators already extensively trialled by HM Inspectors were therefore piloted further with a number of education authorities, schools and colleges, and after further development, the indicators with their performance criteria were published and circulated widely.

This initiative provides the basis for a total quality approach with a sharing of responsibility for quality among

- educational institutions, through internal planning and review;
- education authorities, college boards, etc., through systematic monitoring and evaluation of quality and standards;
- HM Inspectors, through their independent evaluation and reporting.

It also places the independent inspection and objective reporting by HM Inspectors within a wider quality assurance framework. It has required the Inspectorate to adjust further their inspection and reporting procedures to take account of the existence of the evidence of institutional self-review, leading to new, and helpfully more economic, forms of inspection.

THE AUDIT UNIT

In 1986 a new unit, the Management of Educational Resources Unit (MERU) was established within the Inspectorate Research and Intelligence Division, charged with assessing and promoting improvement in the use of resources, human and physical, in education. In 1992, in response to the demands for greater accountability in education, as in other public services, and to capitalise on the increased opportunities for recording, collating, analysing and reporting of data made possible by the new inspection procedures, the systematic use of performance indicators and the power of electronic technology, MERU was expanded to create a new Inspectorate Division – the Audit unit. Led by a Chief Inspector and drawing time and expertise from across the Inspectorate, it also incorporates statistical, accounting and computing expertise to provide a multi-disciplinary approach to the measurement of performance in education. The Unit has been the executive of much of the drive towards more thorough-going quality assurance arrangements in education and has been responsible for the highly influential series of publications on effective schools, development planning and performance indicators. It has also had responsibility for a new range of publications on quality and standards, based on national analysis of inspection evidence; performance in examinations; school attendance; leaver destinations and other topics.

NATIONAL DEVELOPMENTS

The Inspectorate's involvement in national developments in recent years has spanned not only quality assurance as described above but also a wide range of issues in relation to curriculum and assessment, institutional management and management training, pupil and student guidance and support etc. In each case, Inspectorate input was made at carefully calculated strategic levels. Among major developments to which the Inspectorate were key contributors over the 1990s are the 5–14 Development Programme, Higher Still, modern languages in the primary school, student guidance in post-school education, management training for headteachers, staff development and appraisal. The nature of the Inspectorate involvement in such work can be exemplified in consideration of its role in relation to the 5–14 Development Programme.

This development was designed to bring improved structure and consistency to curriculum, assessment and reporting to parents for pupils aged 5–14, and to 'bridge' the primary/secondary 'divide'. The genesis of the programme was in the concern by ministers and others in 1987 about evidence from inspection reports that although there were some excellent primary schools in Scotland, and others in which the quality of aspects of the curriculum was high, there was insufficient consistency in quality and standards and in balance of curriculum across primary schools; a need to review arrangements for assessment and for reporting to parents; and a need for greater continuity of experience into early secondary education. As in most such developments, senior members of the Inspectorate with counterparts from the administrative Group with responsibilities in school education in SOED had a key role in assisting ministers to shape the underlying policy taking account of current issues and circumstances, to articulate it and to develop appropriate plans for implementation.

The development itself was led by a national Steering Committee chaired by HM Senior Chief Inspector, which was supported by a number of Review and Development Groups on the various aspects of the curriculum, to which strategic specialist HMI input was made. The Inspectorate also had responsibility for promoting awareness and understanding of the development in schools and by education authorities; monitoring reaction in the field; finalising the various reports in conjunction with the Scottish Consultative Council on the Curriculum (SCCC), taking account of the views expressed in extensive field trials and consultation, and the requirements of ministers; and monitoring and reporting on the effectiveness of implementation.

The 1987 election proved something of a watershed in respect of government and ministerial interest in the detailed workings of the education system, for example, in curriculum and assessment, educational management. The 5–14 Programme, based on a policy document issued by the Secretary of State was among the first signs of this heightened ministerial interest. That document set out not only the aims for the development but also the structure of a Development Programme to be pursued at ministers' bidding through his civil servants, principally HM Inspectors. That required a new accommodation by SCCC, hitherto primarily responsible for curriculum development with HMI guidance and support, and by HM Inspectors; and inevitably led to some tensions in relation to role, ultimate responsibility etc., which had to be patiently worked through. It is greatly to the credit of those involved that these adjustments did not jeopardise the successful completion of the development.

POLICY ADVICE

In relation to policy and policy development, the Inspectorate must be both proactive and reactive. They must be prepared to bring forward proposals within the Scottish Office and to ministers whenever their first-hand experience from inspection, their wide range of contacts with senior professionals in the field and/or the distilled messages of inspection evidence, suggest the need for a policy initiative or shift, and be ready to justify their suggestions as both professionally sound and practicable in the context of prevailing circumstances. An important recent example of that role is in the review of provision in S5 and S6 by the Howie Committee, now being developed as Higher Still. In the late 1980s, the Inspectorate drew to the attention of senior colleagues in the Scottish Office and ministers the need to take action if a suitable range of courses and qualifications was to be available in the future to the growing number of youngsters, with increasingly diverse needs, staying in education post-16; and if an adequate range of skills is to be available in the workforce to meet the country's economic needs in an increasingly competitive world. That advice having been given, and accepted, the Inspectorate, as in 5–14, then made significant strategic contributions to the shaping and implementation of the development: providing assessorship advice and support to the Howie Committee; analysing the responses to the Committee's findings; assisting the Department and ministers to shape sound policy proposals which capitalised on the excellent prognosis and analyses of the Committee and the supportive and the constructively critical comments made in the extensive consultation responses; and taking a lead role in implementation. The national Steering Committee was chaired by HMSCI and key contributions were made by HM Inspectors to the deliberations of the various generic and specialist groups established; in many seminars and conferences for senior personnel from schools, colleges, education authorities and others; and in staff development.

Equally, the Inspectorate must be ready to respond to requests from ministers for confidential professional comment and assessment on initiatives they are proposing, and to help give practical educational shape to these taking account of current contexts. An example in recent years was in relation to the proposals for national testing in primary and early secondary education. These proposals were part of a UK-wide governmental initiative to introduce more systematic testing to national standards of pupil performance in key areas, specifically language and mathematics. The political imperative for rigorous testing arrangements had to be married to the need to customise proposals to the Scottish context and to produce an educational rationale which allowed justice to be done to achievement across the wide range of ability in the various school stages. The unpopularity of the measures made finding an acceptable solution challenging and several iterations were necessary before a defensibly sound educational arrangement was in place which, while satisfying for the most part Ministers' concerns, still did not prove widely acceptable.

In addition, too, to serving the immediate policy interests and concerns of government, the Inspectorate must attempt to be 'ahead of the game' in second guessing future policy directions and being prepared for these. A recent example was in pre-school education where through the late 1980s and early 1990s, while government attention in education was elsewhere, the Inspectorate maintained their interest and, for example, prepared a curriculum paper, ready for when pre-school became a political priority, as inevitably it did in the mid 1990s.

QUESTIONS ABOUT ROLE AND EFFECTIVENESS

The chapter would scarcely be complete without addressing two questions often put to the Inspectorate. Who inspects the inspectors? And, does the tripartite role of the Inspectorate not leave them open to the challenge of being both gamekeeper and poacher, responsible for evaluating the quality of a system over which they have considerable influence through their roles in educational development and policy formulation? On the first, the Inspectorate is probably among the most frequently reviewed groups in Scottish education, its operations having been subjected successively in recent years to independent reviews by the Scottish Office, the Treasury and the National Audit Office to name but three. The validity and effectiveness of its work is also monitored within government through scrutiny of its annual management plan and performance in its various tasks against the specific output measures agreed for each. On the second, there is no evidence of a conflict of interest having infringed the evaluative judgement of the Inspectorate – the time lag between policy inception and later evaluation in fact provides its own safeguards, with those originally involved almost certainly having moved on to something else – and the undoubted advantages of constructive interplay between the various responsibilities is seen to far outway any risk.

A NEW CHALLENGE

Over recent decades the Inspectorate has become a highly influential body in Scottish education, with a reputation for the quality, integrity and impartiality of its contribution, and for its stewardship of the distinctive Scottish educational tradition. This is indeed exemplified by its status and scope and mode of operation remaining largely unaltered in the 1990s as radical changes were made to its counterparts in England and Wales. An immediate challenge as the millennium approaches will come from the establishment of the Scottish parliament to which the Inspectorate will then be responsible. New relationships will require to be forged at national level and new trusts developed. It will be important, then, to ensure that the traditional independence of the Inspectorate and its ability to provide a leadership role and to continue to offer an objective view of the qualities and needs of Scottish education are not prejudiced in the new arrangements.

REFERENCES.

Hansard, (1992) HM Inspectors of Schools in Scotland – A Policy Statement by the Secretary of State for Scotland.

SED/SOED/SOEID (1983 onwards) 2000+ reports by HM Inspectors of Schools on individual educational institutions.

SOED (1992) *School Development Plans in Scotland – a report by HM Inspectors of Schools*, Edinburgh: HMSO.

SOED (1992) *Using Ethos Indicators in Secondary School Self-Evaluation – a report by HM Inspectors of Schools*, Edinburgh: HMSO.

SOED (1996) *Standards and Quality in Primary and Secondary Schools in Scotland – reports by HM Inspectors of Schools*, Edinburgh: HMSO.

SOEID (1997) *Standards and Quality in Scottish Further Education, 1995–96 – a report by HM Inspectors of Schools*, Edinburgh: HMSO.

14

The Local Governance of Education: A Political Perspective

Malcolm Green

LOCAL AUTHORITIES: PRE- AND POST-WHEATLEY

It is sometimes said of the English system of education that it is 'a national service locally administered'. This is a definition of the governance of education which would be strongly resisted by councillors and officials in Scottish local authorities. Ever since the advent of statutory and compulsory school education with the 1872 Act it has been clear that the primary legal duty to ensure that a child is educated rests with the child's parents and the corresponding duty to ensure that the necessary schools are provided to enable that statutory obligation to be fulfilled rests with the school authorities.

From 1872 until 1918 these authorities were School Boards based on parish boundaries. However, the rapid development of local authority structures and competence made the School Board system obsolete within a generation and directly elected education authorities were set up in 1918. These education authorities did not however take root, and lasted only until 1929. Then they were abolished, with their powers transferring to the City and County authorities. From that time on the education service was the statutory responsibility of the City Corporations and the County Councils, which discharged this function through an education committee.

Certain anomalies deriving from the originally independent existence of the education service nevertheless remained. There was a statutory requirement for education committees to contain representatives of the churches and of the teaching force within the authority, and a teacher could only be dismissed by a two-thirds majority of the education committee meeting with at least half of its full membership present. Currently, remnants of these special provisions remain: the churches are still represented as of right (though teacher representation is now at the discretion of the individual authority) and employment protection legislation (though no longer the education acts) continues to require that a proposal to dismiss a teacher be brought before the education committee before it can be implemented. After 1929 the next watershed in the governance of Scottish school education came with the 1975 reorganisation of local government following the Wheatley recommendations. The reform was far reaching in scale: 465 authorities became 65: 9 Regions, 53 Districts and 3 Islands Councils. Ironically, the only parts of Scotland which were equipped to realise the full range of Wheatley's principles were also the smallest and, in the case of Western Isles at any rate, financially the weakest.

The new authorities were required to plan corporately and strategically, and to be genuinely accountable to their electorate for their use of considerably enhanced resources. The office of Chief Executive was created in all authorities and, at elected member level, a Policy and Resources committee was everywhere instituted, to provide members and officers alike with an incentive to monitor and review the whole gamut of services for which the authority was responsible. Several other important changes came into being at about the same time. All committees of the authority were now open to the public, whereas previously the public had only been admitted as of right to the full Council meeting. Elected members now represented, universally, one electoral division each. Multi-member divisions were thus consigned to history. Council publications began to recognise for the first time that most elected members, in urban authorities at any rate, represent political parties and organise themselves within the Council into party groups with collective responsibility, and the term Leader of the Council came into being to describe the leader of the majority political group.

How did all these changes affect education? First, the education service lost some of its previous autonomy. The personnel functions, budgeting and property management and a host of minor functions were transferred to greatly expanded or newly created central resource departments. Education was no longer master in its own house, and loud and long were the complaints from Directors of Education in the years immediately after 1975 that these transferred responsibilities were being inefficiently or unfairly managed.

Second, by the mid 1970s it was also clear that the years of post-war expansion had come to an end. All experienced chief officials and councillors had grown up during decades of growth and expansion, with resources never enough, indeed, to meet the demands placed upon them, but steadily increasing nonetheless.

Some aspects of the local education service were, it is true, still growing. Secondary school rolls boosted by the raising of the school leaving age from fifteen to sixteen in 1972, were still rising, and would not reach their peak until 1979. Comprehensive education, decided upon by the old local authorities in the early 1970s in response to pressure from both Labour and Conservative governments, was in the process of implementation, bringing with it rising expectations and a steadily expanding cohort of pupils sitting 'O' grades and expecting to continue to higher grade examinations. The need for expanded vocational education had been recognised in the 1960s, and new colleges of further education (in those days still an education authority responsibility) were coming on stream.

What no-one fully understood, though the evidence was very apparent, was the dramatic decline in the birth-rate in the early 1970s which would almost immediately solve one major problem by creating another. The chronic shortage of qualified teachers which had plagued education authorities since time immemorial, was about to come to an end. More teachers were being trained and the ending of the boom years of the economy meant that there were fewer opportunities for teachers to pursue a career outside teaching. But what no-one had envisaged was the suddenness with which the surplus struck. In 1976, for the first time, many hundreds of new college primary education graduates found themselves without a job. The education world was scandalised. How could society tolerate such a waste of talent and resource? But the facts were inescapable. 1973 represented the lowest number of births in recent Scottish history and the projections for the future were that the birth rate would never recover to its previous levels. There were simply not the children there to teach. The

Government responded by taking powers to limit the number of entrants to colleges of education, and in due course would propose to close a number of them. Teachers themselves responded by hanging onto their jobs. From this point on fewer women teachers left the profession to raise a family, with the consequence that, a decade later they began to make their way in increasing numbers into senior management positions in schools and even into the education directorates – a process that has continued to the present.

COSLA AND THE SJNCs

At national level the new education authorities had organised themselves into a single local government organisation, replacing the plethora of previous institutions. The Convention of Scottish Local Authorities (COSLA) came into being as a unitary organisation representing Regions, Districts and Islands authorities – a remarkable and far reaching achievement, which was not possible at the time in England, and has only been achieved there as a result of the 1996 re-organisation.

The Convention, of course, has no statutory functions. It is a purely voluntary association of the local authorities themselves. Reference is occasionally made in statute to a requirement by the Secretary of State to consult 'a body representing the local authorities', which implies the existence of COSLA or something very like it. But it has no power to make decisions on behalf of the authorities who compose its membership, and a delicate balance is required in order to maintain the credibility of its role.

Consensus has therefore to be the rule, but at the same time that consensus must not become a meaningless common denominator. COSLA must be seen to be an effective advocate of the interests of Scottish Local Government as a whole. It must grapple with the most important issues facing Scottish education, but at the same time must not become partisan. Unlike the local authorities, however, COSLA has never felt the need to impose corporate working on its service committees. Only in respect of such matters as the annual revenue support discussions with government, pay negotiations with employees and (in the 1990s particularly) when legislation affecting the structure of local government was under consideration, did the Convention's leaders speak for the services as a whole. It is difficult to see how it could be otherwise, without either diluting COSLA's effectiveness or antagonising the minority.

The principle of consensus was applied equally to the national Pay and Conditions National Negotiating bodies, though strictly speaking it did not need to. The Scottish Teachers Salaries Committee (STSC) had been set up in the early 1960s by statute, and its decisions were therefore binding on education authorities. Conditions of Service were not, however, at that time thought to require a statutory base, and the Scottish Teachers Service Conditions Committee (STSCC) was thus a voluntary body set up jointly by the employers and the teaching unions. Both these bodies covered lecturers in further education as well as teachers employed in schools. By the late 1970s it was clear that conditions of service were just as important as pay negotiations and, moreover, that the further education sector had now expanded so far that it required more attention than a school focused body was likely to give it. Legislation in 1982, therefore, replaced the STSC and STSCC with two new bodies, one for school education and one for further education, each covering both salaries and conditions of service, thus permitting pay and conditions to be negotiated in the same forum – the Scottish Joint Negotiating Committees (SJNCs). SJNC responsibility for further education ceased in 1992 when legislation removed the FE sector from local authority control. The school teachers negotiating committee continues, however, to function as a statutory body, despite various threats from the Secretary of State during the last Conservative administration, Michael Forsyth, that its abolition was being considered.

Central government, through the presence of Scottish Office officials, has always exercised a strong influence on pay and even service conditions negotiations. But this influence never amounted to anything approaching a veto. The civil servants normally content themselves with reminding the Committee of government policy, whatever that might be at that time, and acting as a channel of communication between the Committee and the Scottish Office Ministers. Relationships on a personal level have always been excellent, and the kind of distance between the local authorities and Whitehall which has often been a feature of central/local government relations in England finds little parallel in Scotland.

GOVERNMENT PAY POLICIES AND THEIR EFFECTS

Government policy on pay did, of course, change radically from time to time, within governments as well as between them. The Conservative administration (1979–97), initially committed to the free market, became steadily more centralist and authoritarian so far as local government was concerned, and from 1981 onwards a whole range of new powers were put in place by statute which effectively placed the budget of each and every local authority under the direct control of the Scottish Office. Authorities were still, in theory, free to determine the pay levels of their staff, but they could not fund these increases by raising local revenue beyond what the government itself had previously determined was reasonable.

This policy was pursued more or less consistently from the early 1980s throughout the life of the Conservative government, and was indeed tightened in the 1990s, with no specific cost of living increase allowed for in the government's estimate of authorities' expenditure plans. Authorities would expect to fund cost of living pay increases by reducing their overall expenditure, e.g. by employing fewer staff. Inevitably, this led by 1997 to a significant reduction in the number of teachers employed and to a consequent worsening of pupil/ teacher ratios.

The Labour government elected on 1 May 1997 had made a pre-election commitment to maintaining the overall government expenditure plans for at least the first two years. But it had committed itself equally to prioritising education within that total, and the evidence since the Chancellor's Budget of July 1997 is that that commitment is being honoured. The consequences for other parts of the government's expenditure, notably in the area of welfare benefits, and for other areas of local government responsibilities, especially cultural services, are becoming a source of major political controversy within the Labour Party.

These powerful shifts in government incomes policy left their mark on the Scottish teachers' pay negotiations. The increasing downward pressure on pay settlements produced by the Conservative policy for local government led directly to the teachers' dispute of 1984–7, the most serious and prolonged labour dispute in Scottish educational history. It is a tribute to the effectiveness of the working relationships between the two sides of the SJNC that the teaching unions' demand was for government intervention to provide the authorities with extra money to meet an enhanced settlement, while the authorities from the outset supported the teachers' demand.

It was the style of the Thatcher government to 'tough out' such pressures, but by early 1986 (the teachers having foregone their pay claim for 1985), with no end in sight to the curriculum development boycott and with after-school activities and even parents evenings suspended for the duration, it was obvious that the government would have to move. The new Secretary of State, Malcolm Rifkind, persuaded the Cabinet in February 1986 to allow an independent review. This review body, under Sir Peter Main, recommended a 16 per cent increase when it reported in September.

This was accepted by the government, and, after a ballot, overwhelmingly by the membership of the teacher trade unions. The SJNC had then to tackle the difficult but challenging task of implementing the recommendations within the additional cash envelope. As the government noose tightened around local authorities in the course of the 1990s it became increasingly difficult for the Scottish local authorities to match the English and Welsh settlements, with the result that Scottish teachers' pay is now some 3 per cent behind that prevailing in the south. The consolation for Scottish teachers, and the factor which alone has made this situation tolerable for them, is that the staff reductions which have been severe in England and Wales have so far not been matched in Scotland. However, that situation began to change with the 1997/98 budgets. Glasgow, for example, cut its teacher work force by 3 per cent. Experience from the 1980s demonstrates quite clearly that it will be impossible for government and authorities to continue to constrain teachers' pay to a figure at or below the rate of inflation, while at the same time cutting teacher numbers and introducing major curriculum change in the form of Higher Still.

CONSERVATIVE GOVERNMENT HOSTILITY TO LOCAL GOVERNMENT

A fundamental principle, however, governing the attitude of Margaret Thatcher's and John Major's administrations was a consistent hostility to a sector of government that, because it had its own mandate from the electorate, could be regarded as an alternative centre of power. In fact, local government has never seen itself in this light, but it does expect to be treated with respect as a partner with its own statutorily guaranteed place in the governance of the nation. It was however no part of Conservative policy to make councillors more effective in their role. Rather, they wished to see them marginalised through obloquy and ridicule. The electoral consequences of this approach were devastating for the Conservatives. The last Scottish education authorities controlled by the Conservatives passed out of their hands in 1986, and in the unitary authority elections of 1995 the Conservatives emerged in control of not a single Council. Naturally, this gave great satisfaction to the other parties, but it was damaging for democracy, since the Conservative Party's base at local government level was constantly shrinking and their interest in the delivery of local services diminished accordingly. Consequently, there was no pressure during the eighteen Conservative years for councillors to examine and improve their own effectiveness.

COUNCILLORS AND MANAGEMENT

Essentially, the role of the elected member is three-fold. First, to act within the Council as an advocate for his or her own electorate and to represent their needs to the authority as a whole; second, to ensure that the services for which the authority is responsible are delivered efficiently, effectively and in accordance with statute; and third, to bring to bear on individual service decisions a viewpoint based on an understanding of the impact of those decisions on the community at large. The role of the chief officer, on the other hand, is to propose, advise and implement. The Conservative government's view was that the market should take care of the issue of public accountability. The councillors' role should basically be to ensure that the contracts for delivering services (whether held in-house or undertaken externally) were properly drawn up and secured to the lowest bidder. Everything else was a matter of contract compliance and should be left to professional officers to monitor. This simplistic view of local government, and of councillors' responsibilities in particular, could not, of course, be achieved anywhere, even in Conservative controlled authorities. It represents, however, an attitude of mind which hampered the appropriate evolution of local government practice to meet the enormous changes in the economy and in public expectation that the last twenty years have brought.

A major review of the structure of management of the education service in Strathclyde Region was undertaken in 1988 (by consultants Inlogov of Birmingham University) and heralded changes which spread nationally. The distinction between strategic and operational management was made explicit for the first time, and became an important element in disentangling and clarifying responsibilities which had become confused over the years. But the most far-reaching recommendation was that schools be given devolved management. It is worth recalling that in 1989 this concept had only recently been introduced in England and Wales, where it was widely felt to be aimed purely at depriving local authorities, and local councillors in particular, of their traditional control of schools. The policy was therefore bitterly resented within local authorities and in implementation led to serious financial dislocation for many schools. But Scottish Office ministers had not shown any interest in going down this road – presumably, they preferred to rely on the temptation of self governing status, the legislation for which was put in place in 1989.

It might have been expected that Labour-controlled Strathclyde, with its strong tradition of administering the service from the centre in the interests of securing equality of treatment for everyone, would find the encouragement of diversity distasteful. In fact, there was little difficulty in convincing councillors of the desirability of this step, and it was implemented in 1990. Perhaps they were influenced by the argument that it was better to implement their own system of devolved management rather than have the Government impose something worse. But it is doubtful if this was the prime consideration. It was, perhaps, an early indication that traditional Labour attitudes were already giving way to a more diverse culture. In fact, the tactical wisdom of this step was proved three years later, when the Scottish Office eventually got around to insisting that devolved management be implemented throughout Scotland and allowed the Strathclyde model, rather than the English one dictated from Whitehall, to become the standard pattern for the country.

THE NEW UNITARY AUTHORITIES

The years after 1992 were hardly normal, since everyone became increasingly caught up, first in the campaign to resist the dismemberment of the Regions and, when this became inevitable, with the process of disaggregation itself. The thirty two new unitary authorities, which assumed all of the previous District Council functions and many (though not all) of the former Regional functions, were elected in 1995 and, after a transitional year to organise themselves and appoint senior staff, assumed their statutory functions on 1 April 1996. The keynote of that year 1995/96 was continuity. The reorganisation had been carried through by a Conservative government by *force majeure*, without any basis of support for what it was doing, much less consensus. It was a totally different experience from the previous reorganisation in 1975, and consequently no-one could safely plan or promise to take the service forward. Apprehension rather than eager anticipation was therefore the order of the day as the Regions disappeared into history and the new authorities emerged.

The overwhelming atmosphere was one of gloom. No rationale for the reform was ever seriously argued, the government contenting itself with the simplistic statements that unitary authorities would bring local government closer to the people and thus be more responsive, and that confusion as to which authority was responsible for a local service would be eliminated. 'Simplistic' is fully justified as a description of these two supposed advantages. First, although the big Regions were being broken up, smaller districts were being amalgamated. The new authorities of North Lanarkshire and South Lanarkshire, for example, each represented an amalgamation of three former District Councils, while in the Highlands, Fife, Dumfries and Galloway and Scottish Borders the District Councils were abolished altogether and the new unitary authority had the same boundaries as the former Region. Quite apart from boundaries, the responsiveness of an authority depends crucially upon the resources available to it to deliver its services, and an authority which is too small or too poorly resourced to do the job cannot said to be 'local' in any meaningful sense whatever.

Second, the reform in no way eliminated confusion. Rather, it increased it. Many of the services run by the Regional Councils could only be run on a regional basis, and consequently were not transferred to the new authorities at all. Water and Sewerage services were handed to three newly created public bodies independent of local government. The Police and Fire Services were to be run by joint boards, composed of councillors drawn from a number of authorities but not answerable to those authorities. Strategic Planning and Valuation were to become joint committees serving differing geographical areas, and the Reporter to the Children's Panel became a government service based in Edinburgh. In the West of Scotland, the Strathclyde Passenger Transport Executive continued in existence, but as a joint board on which Strathclyde's twelve successor authorities were represented. Each of these bodies has a different secretariat, based in a wide variety of locations. It cannot possibly be said that this proliferation of adhoc arrangements has increased accountability or efficiency or has contributed in any way to public understanding of 'who does what'.

The most urgent issue facing the new authorities was not, however, the structural dislocation, but rather the government-imposed financial stringency. The budgets for 1997/98 had, of course, been set under the Conservative government, and embodied in virtually every case significant cuts, the most severe of them falling on the cities. Glasgow, for example, had to cut 6 per cent from its 1996/97 budget. But the new Prime Minister had declared at the previous Labour Party Conference that his first three priorities were 'Education, Education, Education'. The July 1997 budget of the new Chancellor, Gordon Brown made £1billion available over the lifetime of the government for additional revenue support for detailed priorities such as pre-five education and basic literacy and numeracy, and a further £1 billion for capital expenditure on the repair and modernisation of schools.

A corresponding sum of money was intimated by the Scottish Office a few weeks later. The gloom and depression which had characterised the first year of the new authorities now acquired a silver lining, so far as education was concerned. There was, and at the time of writing still is, a serious mis-match between these additional funds made available for the education service and the overall cut still being demanded by the government in local authority budgets as a whole. The government clearly expects the additional money to be used for development in line with its stated priorities (with which, in educational terms, the

Councils have no disagreement), and not to finance the cuts required in the total budget. If this were to be the case, it would an intolerable burden on other local authority services, since they would require to take a much heavier cut. To take Glasgow as an example: at an annual total expenditure of £300 million, the education service represents one third of the authority's total revenue budget. The 6 per cent cut required in that overall budget would mean that services such as Social Work and Roads would need to bear a cut of almost 9 per cent. The incompatibility between these two approaches will need to be resolved by the government very quickly if it is not to lose the confidence of the electorates – which are well aware that government and not the local council now fixes the authorities' expenditure and thereby determines the level of Council Tax for the year – ahead of the crucial elections of 1999.

GUIDING PRINCIPLES: DECENTRALISATION, PARTNERSHIP AND ACHIEVEMENT

Against this background, what have the new authorities taken as the guiding principles of their operation of the education service? The answer to this question must be sought in three main areas: decentralisation, partnership and, above all, achievement. Decentralisation of school management has already been referred to, through the delegation of control of school budgets to headteachers, so that schools can now vary the staffing complement (within limits), order supplies and utilise savings on absence cover and energy consumption for other purposes. This decentralisation was, as explained above, an initiative of Strathclyde Region, subsequently taken up by the Conservative government and made into a statutory requirement for every education authority.

The creation of School Boards was, however, an initiative of the Conservative government itself, and hotly debated when it appeared in 1987. The original consultation paper spoke of 'floor powers' and 'ceiling powers', the clear intention being that, once set, Boards would move steadily up the scale into the assumption of full management responsibility for their school. It was immediately clear from the public reaction that there was no group of parents remotely interested in managing their children's school themselves. Throughout the length and breadth of Scotland, in middle class and deprived areas alike, there was a universal thumbs down for the concept of School Board Management. Boards with consultative powers, however, received a cautious welcome, and were not unacceptable to education authorities which since 1975 had been running a system of school councils.

Decentralisation extends beyond School Boards, of course. Great strides have been made in the last twenty years in developing an attitude of openness and receptivity to parental opinion, and this openness is often characterised by the prominent 'Welcome' placed (sometimes in many languages) at the entrance of the school. Headteachers nowadays routinely allocate a great deal of their time to discussion with individual parents. On some issues, though, notably school closures, it will never be possible to reconcile the perspective of individual parents, which is limited to their own children's period of attendance at the school, with the responsibility of the local authority to plan for its area as a whole and over a much longer period. The most that can be achieved is that parents generally at least respect an authority's decision to close their school, even though they would have preferred it to remain open (at least until their own children had left).

The second theme underlying education authorities' policies in the late 1990s is that of partnership. For eighteen years authorities felt, with some justification, that the government lacked commitment to the public education service. Many of the specific initiatives the Conservatives put forward and funded, such as the Technical and Vocational Education Initiative (TVEI); the implementation of the Munn and Dunning recommendations through the introduction of Standard Grade; the Higher Still reforms of the upper secondary school curriculum stemming from the Howie Committee's report; the introduction of foreign language teaching in primary schools and its inclusion as part of the core curriculum in S3 and S4; and even School Boards themselves, were not unwelcome to education authorites and indeed often accorded with their own priorities.

But there was always a top-down approach to these initiatives. Indeed, the last Conservative Secretary of State, Michael Forsyth, made a virtue of not seeking consensus. He firmly believed that education professionals (including Councillors, as well as Directors of Education and teachers) were far too set in their ways and resistant to change to be worth his while trying to persuade them. In this he was quite mistaken. A consistent effort to take the education service into partnership with the government, backed by additional resources, would certainly have achieved far more of the government's programme than was actually the case. A spectacular casualty of this centralist approach was the timescale for the Higher Still reforms. Although the Higher Still programme was supported in principle by the teacher unions and by the local authorities, its detailed implementation was driven exclusively by HM Inspectorate, and consequently ordinary teachers (including headteachers) felt bewildered and uninvolved. The government was forced as a result, in 1996, to postpone the introduction of Higher Still for one year to 1998, and by the time the Conservative government fell, no-one outside St Andrew's House believed that even this was possible. Consequently, the new Labour government moved quickly to put the implementation date back a further year to August 1999. It has to be said that there are still grave doubts about the ability of the system to deliver Higher Still in a consistent fashion over the whole country by that date.

A fundamental principle of the approach of the Labour administration has been this same stress on partnership. Indeed the first Education Minister in Scotland, Brian Wilson, used the word so often in his speeches, that journalists and civil servants gave up counting the number of times the word was mentioned. Fortunately, more than rhetoric is intended. Meetings with councillors and senior officers of the Convention of Scottish Local Authorities are conceded more readily and more quickly than was ever the case previously, and the atmosphere at them is both purposeful and relaxed. There appears to be a clear recognition that educational reforms can only take root and deliver their intended results if the education authorities, as the statutory managers of the service, and the teachers, as the work force, are taken into confidence and are equipped to do the job.

The area in which the government's commitment to partnership is most evident is that of the raising of standards in a determination to improve achievement. As in so much else, the education service in England and Wales is being subjected to far more explicit and direct government intervention than is the case in Scotland. This process was fully evident in the 1980s during the Conservative administration, particularly after Sir Keith Joseph left the then Department of Education and Science in 1985. Under Kenneth Baker as Secretary of State for Education, the National Curriculum was introduced, City Technology Colleges financed by the private sector were set up, 'opting out' became a loudly trumpeted feature of Government policy, and the Burnham Joint Negotiating Committee machinery was abolished. Under Labour, David Blunkett's Schools Attainment and Framework Bill reinforces the right of the Secretary of State to intervene in 'failing' schools and Education

Action Zones, in areas of deprivation and incorporating in many cases under-achieving schools, are to be given special resources and management, possibly even by the private sector.

Fortunately, none of these central mechanisms envisaged in the Blunkett Bill have commended themselves to government ministers in Scotland. The commitment to improved achievement is, however, an increasingly important element in authorities' own business plans. Nowhere is this more evident, or more necessary, than in the City of Glasgow. Already in the autumn of 1995, the Education Blueprint laid before committee by the Director of Education placed attainment at the head of the list of priority commitments.

This may seen curious, since achievement ought, surely, always to be the first priority for an education authority. But in fact this has traditionally not been so. A generation ago education authorities spent most of their time struggling to put up enough schools, provide enough places, and secure enough teachers, to educate the steadily expanding number of pupils. Very little time was left over for monitoring the quality of the education provided in the schools. Similarly, examination results for individual schools (league tables) were unknown, even to the schools themselves. There was no cost breakdown for individual schools, so no-one knew how much it cost to run their school. And until the 1980s HMI Reports were seen only by the Director of Education and by the headteacher of the school in question. By 1990 all this had changed, and Strathclyde Region deployed expert personnel to devise a sophisticated means of measuring the attainment, not merely of individual schools, but of subject departments within schools. It thus became possible, for the first time, to see which departments were performing well or otherwise compared to what might have been expected.

Once this analysis became familiar and understood it gave rise to the debate about the fairness or otherwise of comparing schools by virtue of crude statistics of Scottish Certificate of Education (SCE) passes. Quite obviously, schools with a predominately middle class intake would be expected to produce a much higher proportion of good passes than a school serving an area of multiple deprivation. If comparisons were sought, they should surely be between schools serving comparable catchment areas. And the debate goes on about precisely how to measure this comparability. Strathclyde Region based its comparability graphs on the number of pupils receiving footwear and clothing grants, i.e. an index of poverty. More recently HM Inspectorate has suggested a comparison based upon the level of educational attainment in the area in question. It seems more than likely, however, that material and objective indices such as free meal entitlement will prove to be the only reliable index of educational comparability.

So the means now exist to assess the quality of teaching as evidenced by the attainment of the pupils who receive it. But the implications for action have been slow to emerge. It is generally agreed that the biggest single influence on a school's attainment is the headteacher. Yet no headteacher has ever been removed from office in Scotland for running a poor school. Likewise, and just as importantly, authorities have never been willing to replace a principal teacher whose subject department consistently under performs. The Labour Party's Education Manifesto was clear and forthright about the responsibility of headteachers and the need to remove those whose competence fell below an acceptable level. The Scottish Qualification for Headship has now been introduced and a government White Paper (January 1999) proposes a strengthening of the role of the General Teaching Council in monitoring the competence of serving staff.

Of course, the drive for improved attainment must rest far more on encouragement of professional commitment than on sanctions. Nonetheless it is difficult to envisage the public education service in Scotland continuing to function, in this new climate of emphasis on performance and attainment, without an effective means available to it for dealing with teachers whose standard of performance is consistently and unacceptably low.

THE FUTURE

The three themes of Decentralisation, Partnership and Achievement are likely to characterise the last years of the present millennium. A further development of schools' sense of responsibility for their own standard of attainment should be expected as well as a corresponding growth in their power to control the resources made available to them. It is also reasonable to expect to see education authorities (now much smaller than they used to be) cooperating more readily with one another, both on an adhoc basis – and it is remarkable how the authorities in the former Strathclyde Region have wanted to continue working together – and nationally through COSLA. Enhanced parental awareness of their own responsibility (anchored after all, firmly in statute since the nineteenth century) for their children's education and a determination by school and authorities alike not to accept second best is likely to be another continuing theme.

It is tempting, now that the Scottish Parliament is to be set up from the year 2000 with full educational competence, to leave everything on the shelf until then. This would be a big mistake. Whoever the members of that Parliament are to be and whatever party or parties form the Government of Scotland at the start of the next millennium, they will require to continue that partnership which has been so welcome a development over the past year or so and to recognise that the education service cannot be managed from a parliament building in Edinburgh. Just as teachers now have to work closely with parents and education authorities with teacher unions, so the new Scottish Government must work with local Councils to ensure that Scottish education retains and develops those classic features of which it has always boasted: equality of opportunity irrespective of background and a determination to work together as a community, so that no individuals or groups are excluded and everyone is stronger as a result.

REFERENCES

Blair, T. (1998) *Leading The Way: new vision for local government*, London: Institute of Public Policy.
Commission on Scottish Education (1996) Governance and Accountability, in *Learning to Succeed*, Report of the Commission on Scottish Education. pp. 111–18, Edinburgh: Commission on Scottish Education.
Humes, W. M. (1986) Local Democracy? in *The Leadership Class in Scottish Education*, Edinburgh: John Donald.
Midwinter, A. (1997) Local Education Spending in Scotland and England: Problems of Comparison in the LACE Study, *Scottish Educational Review*, 29. 2, 146–153.
Midwinter, E. and N. McGarvey (1994) The Restructuring of Scotland's Education Authorities: Does Size Matter? *Scottish Educational Review*, 26.2, 110–17.
Ross, D. (1986) *An Unlikely Anger: Scottish Teachers in Action*, Edinburgh: Mainstream.

15

The Local Governance of Education: An Operational Perspective

Keir Bloomer

DUTIES AND RESPONSIBILITIES

The overarching statutory educational responsibility of local authorities is contained in Section 1 of the Education (Scotland) Act 1980. The 1980 Act consolidated earlier legislation and the Section 1 responsibility has remained largely unchanged over a much longer period. Section 1 states that, 'It shall be the duty of every education authority to secure for their area the provision of adequate and effective school education.' 'School education' is taken to mean primary and secondary education and, where necessary, special education. Local authorities also have a power, but not a duty, to provide nursery education. Until 1992, they had responsibility for both formal and informal further education. Since then, however, further education colleges have become self-governing incorporated institutions funded directly by the Scottish Office. The responsibilities of local authorities for post-school education are now limited to less formal areas such as adult basic education and the provision of a range of opportunities in an informal, community setting.

Councils (sometimes known as 'authorities') have a range of responsibilities and powers which can be seen as supportive of the main duty of ensuring the provision of adequate and effective school education. Thus, they must maintain a psychological service, collaborate with parents in the recording of special educational needs, provide school catering (at any rate for those entitled to free meals), issue grants to poorer families for school clothing and footwear and arrange for the provision of school transport where children have relatively long journeys to school. They also have under Section 69 of the Local Government (Scotland) Act 1973 a fairly general power to take action which can legitimately be seen as supportive of their statutory responsibilities.

It will be apparent that the statutory responsibilities are, for the most part, stated in very general terms. The requirement to arrange free school transport is unusual in its precision: transport must be provided for children under eight years who live more than two miles from the school and for older children at a distance of three miles or more. It is thus relatively easy to establish whether or not an authority is carrying out this particular obligation. Conversely, the Council can calculate with reasonable accuracy the cost of fulfilling its duty. The same cannot be said of, for example, the main Section 1 responsibility. What is 'adequate and efficient education'? How many teachers does it require? What quality of materials or of buildings does it presuppose? This lack of precision is an important issue when Councils are deciding spending priorities in difficult circumstances.

The Act does, however, provide a mechanism by which the fulfilment of statutory duties can be judged. Under Section 70 of the 1980 Act, the Secretary of State has the power to determine that Councils are in default and to require that certain action be taken. The main recent use of this mechanism has been in relation to Records of Need (see Chapter 90). However, it is potentially applicable in much wider circumstances.

In recent years, there have been quite significant changes in the legislative framework. Councils have lost responsibility, not only for further education colleges, but also for the Careers Service. Under the Self-Governing Schools, etc. (Scotland) Act 1989 they also stood to lose control of individual schools although, in the event, only two schools (Dornoch Academy and St Mary's Primary in Dunblane) out of over 2,500 acquired self-governing status.

Running in parallel with this tendency to remove responsibilities from local authorities is a trend towards prescribing, both in primary legislation and through regulation, more precisely how they will carry out their responsibilities. Thus, most Councils always allowed some latitude to parents in choosing schools. The Education (Scotland) Act 1981 and subsequent regulations, however, prescribed a framework through which choice could be exercised. The same Act lays down in great detail how special educational needs should be assessed and provided for. The School Boards (Scotland) Act 1988 details a particular mechanism for consulting with parents and involving them in the affairs of the school.

In addition to the statutory framework there is a less formal set of prescriptions which represent further obligations and responsibilities. In a sense, given the small scale of the Scottish education system and the close relationships among leading figures in its various institutions, these constitute a more significant pattern of constraints than those imposed by law. It is, indeed, this system of informal regulation that accounts for the astonishing homogeneity of the Scottish education system. There is nothing in law to prevent Scottish Authorities setting up the wide diversity of infant schools, first schools, middle schools, sixth form colleges etc. that exists in England and Wales. Scotland, however, has to all intents and purposes only two types of mainstream school; seven–year primaries and six–year secondaries. A handful of exceptions in remote areas can hardly be said to challenge this uniformity of provision.

Similar conformity is apparent in relation to curricular arrangements. Unlike England, Scotland has no statutory basis for a national curriculum. In theory, Scottish authorities have a free hand. Provided the education they offer is 'adequate and effective', they can devise their own syllabuses and seek accreditation for their pupils' learning from wherever might seem appropriate. The international baccalaureat, for example, could be considered. In practice, however, the existence of a single national examination board, the Scottish Qualifications Authority, and of an extensive series of national curricular guidelines have created a de facto national curriculum. In practice, if not in law, education authorities and individual schools are obliged to conform.

MAINTAINING THE SERVICE POST-REORGANISATION

Local government in Scotland was reorganised with effect from 1 April 1996. The reorganisation involved no change in the three island areas where unitary authorities had been established twenty years before. However, in mainland Scotland, 29 new unitary authorities assumed responsibility for all local government functions. These 29 authorities thus replaced the 9 Regional Councils which had previously been responsible for education and 53 District Councils. Four of the new Councils have the same boundaries as the predecessor Regions. These include the 3 smallest in population terms – Borders, Dumfries and Galloway and Highland – as well as Fife. Central, Grampian and Tayside Regions were each divided into 3 new authorities; Lothian into 4 and Strathclyde into 12.

Thus, in about one-sixth of Scotland, the reorganisation necessitated only a fairly limited change so far as education was concerned. In the remainder of the country, existing large services had to be divided into much smaller organisations. The complexities of change were not, however, as great in the case of former regional services such as education as in the case of district services, at least in some instances. No new authority took over educational responsibilities from more than one predecessor regional council. By contrast, services were often acquired from two, three or even four predecessor districts.

As a result, the task of 'disaggregating' staff was, for the most part, relatively straightforward. All school-based staff – teachers, clerical staff, auxiliaries, librarians, technicians, etc. – simply transferred to the new authority within whose boundaries the school was located. Potential problems were almost entirely confined to the staff of regional or divisional headquarters and groups such as educational development officers and advisors.

In a sense, this pattern symbolised the evolving new relationship between schools and the centre. The service to the public continued uninterrupted and with little difficulty because the organisation at school level remained intact. By contrast, at headquarters level, such stability was largely lacking. Even the place of education within the corporate management structure was subject to change in a way that it would not have been during the previous twenty years.

Although no longer required to do so by legislation, all Councils retained a senior officer who could be broadly identified as 'Director of Education'. In some cases – for example Edinburgh or Glasgow – the education department retained essentially the same responsibilities. In other cases, such as Stirling, however, the scope of the department's responsibilities was reduced as community education was joined with libraries and leisure and recreation for form a new community services department. Other Councils – such as South Ayrshire – brought all of these services together with school education into a unified service in which education was clearly predominant. Such multi-purpose services were seen as offering increased opportunities for inter-department work.

Somewhat surprisingly, despite this variety of remits, significant similarities emerged in the internal organisation of education directorates. While titles varied, a widely adopted pattern was to establish three depute director or head of service posts with responsibility for schools and curriculum, non-statutory education (i.e. pre-five services and community education) and resources.

RELATIONS BETWEEN OFFICIALS AND ELECTED MEMBERS

Prior to the 1996 reorganisation, education authorities were under an obligation to establish a post of Director of Education. The Local Government (Scotland) Act 1994 which came into effect on 1 April 1996 removed this requirement. Nevertheless, as indicated above, each of the thirty-two authorities has a senior officer who can be identified as Director even though his/her responsibilities may extend beyond those traditionally identified with education departments.

In any theoretical model of accountability within the local government structure, the post of Director is particularly significant. Individual elected members cannot instruct officers. Only the Council or a committee to which it has delegated decision-making power has this capacity. Even then, instructions are, in theory, given to the Director who decides how they will be carried out and gives responsibility to other members of staff.

In practice, of course, relations between elected members and senior officers are less formal than this model would suggest. The link between the education committee convenor (or equivalent figure) and the Director is particularly important. In larger Councils with a more elaborate committee structure and several elected members having particular remits within education, the working relationships between them and the members of the directorate relevant to their particular remits are equally significant.

Local government reorganisation has, of course, brought about a significant reduction in the size of Councils responsible for education. Relationships between elected members and senior officers have become rather closer and less formal. In some cases, however, the nature of the parties and conflict within the Council makes it difficult for officers to form appropriate working relationships with members of opposition groups.

Over recent years, there has been much written about corporate management in local authorities and the strategic role of elected members. In theory, members make policy and officers implement it. In reality, the relationship is much more complex than this. While some members have strategic vision and are comfortable with a role as policy maker, many others are much happier functioning as an advocate for constituents' interests. At the level of the individual service, policy tends to originate with officers, frequently in response to government initiatives, with members functioning in an ombudsman role.

RELATIONS WITH HEADTEACHERS AND SCHOOL BOARDS

The efficient management of the education service is critically dependent upon the relationship between senior officers of the authority and headteachers. If the local authority tier of organisation within the service is to have any long-term future, it is essential that these relationships are strengthened.

Most recent writing on school effectiveness has laid great stress on the role of headteachers and the importance of good leadership in schools. At the same time, much of the debate on standards of education has focused on improvement at the level of the individual school, thus further reinforcing the significance of the post of headteacher. Initiatives such as devolved school management and school development planning have given the individual school greater autonomy but have, at the same time, made headteachers vastly more accountable. The relationship between the head and the authority requires to reflect these changes. In many cases, it would not yet appear to have done so.

The headteacher is accountable to the Council through the director of education for the quality of teaching and learning in the school. On the other hand, the director is, in a sense, accountable to the headteacher for the quality of the support services on offer. The relationship is thus not a straightforward line management one but involves a degree of inter-dependency.

SETTING PRIORITIES IN A CLIMATE OF FINANCIAL CONSTRAINT

Continuing severe financial constraint has caused education authorities to review their priorities in a more thoroughgoing way during the 1990s than at any previous time. This need has become even more pressing as Councils have gradually begun to understand that these constraints are not the result of short-term financial emergencies but an inescapable consequence of the prevailing view that economic success can be achieved only in a low tax environment. This flight from taxation has been accompanied by a growing belief, not only on the right of the political spectrum, that direct state provision of services has proved both less efficient and less egalitarian than was hoped. Against this background of contracting resources and influence, Councils have tended to take the view – some more willingly than others – that statutory obligations must be fulfilled and core services delivered, if necessary at the expense of other activities.

To an extent, the education service as a whole has benefited from this approach. Most of the new unitary authorities have attempted to ensure that major front-line public services, principally education and social work, have been allocated smaller savings targets than, for example, central support services and chief executive's functions. Within the education service, the same type of thinking has tended to protect primary and secondary schools at the expense of, for example, community education. Within the school service itself, teacher staffing has been seen as the key priority while 'extras' such as outdoor education and music instruction have been adversely affected.

There has thus emerged a hierarchy of priority in which greatest protection is given to statutory activities, followed by activities seen as supportive of statutory functions with all other areas of provision some distance behind. As a crude rule of thumb, this approach clearly has something to commend it. Its weakness lies in the fact that very few of the statutory obligations relating to education can be easily quantified. The provision of 'adequate and effective education' clearly requires suitably qualified teachers – but how many?

At a time when they are being asked to cut overall expenditure, Councils have naturally given some consideration to the possibility of increasing income. Education offers less scope than many other Council services. Nevertheless, significant increases in charges and the introduction of new types of charge have been features of many recent Council budgets. It is now commonly accepted that, for example, school meal prices and fees for music tuition should bring in a realistic proportion of the costs of providing the service. Along with this new emphasis upon income generation has come a desire to ensure that, where there is subsidy, it is targeted appropriately. For example, many Councils have reviewed their schemes for letting of Council premises with the intention of ensuring that better-off groups using school premises pay something approximating to the economic cost.

PARENTAL RIGHTS

Over the past twenty years or so, parental involvement in children's education has increased markedly. Two distinct influences can be identified.

First, there has been an increased recognition of the role of parents as educators. Many primary schools encourage parents to help in classrooms. Some education authorities and individual schools have run projects designed to help parents to help their children with homework and, indeed, with schoolwork in general. These kinds of involvement have given many parents a feeling of having a larger stake in the educational process and a greater right to be informed and consulted.

The second trend has been concerned with such rights. Section 28 of the Education (Scotland) Act 1981 indicates that, in general, children should be educated 'in accordance with the wishes of their parents'. The 1981 Act translated the principle of parental influence into practical effect in two important areas; special educational needs (SEN) and choice of school. The general principle has subsequently been paralleled by the Children (Scotland) Act 1995 which emphasises the rights of the child rather than those of the parent.

The SEN provisions of the 1981 Act involve parents in the process of drawing up and agreeing a 'Record of Needs'. The Record indicates the nature of the provision to be made, thus giving parents an ability to insist upon a particular level of service. Later ideas, canvassed by the Labour Party prior to the general election of 1997 but not yet given any practical effect, built on the concept of the Record of Needs by suggesting that each child should have an individually determined education plan. Whether the service could logistically support this degree of individualisation is clearly open to question.

The aspects of the 1981 Act dealing with choice of school have been, if anything, even more far reaching in their effects. Parents are not bound to use their local school but have the right to put in a placing request to the school of their choice. These requests can be rejected only in certain circumstances indicated in the legislation. In most cases, an authority would have to be able to demonstrate that enrolling the additional child would require significant, otherwise avoidable public expenditure, normally in the form of an additional teacher or extra accommodation. In practice, some 90 per cent of placing requests are granted.

Judged in terms of its own objectives, therefore, the legislation has been very successful. A substantial minority of Scottish families has been enabled to exercise consumer choice in relation to education. On the other hand, significant difficulties have arisen at a practical level. It has proved difficult to establish when schools – particularly secondary schools – can be considered full. Furthermore, it seems clear that families exercise choice for reasons other than the quality of teaching provided. The strongest observable trend is away from schools in deprived areas and towards those in more affluent districts. Underpinning this seems to be a desire to avoid perceived risks such as playground violence and drug abuse. Whether these parental perceptions are justified is obviously open to question: their effect on the pattern of educational provision, however, is not.

In the late 1980s, the then Conservative government sought to introduce a different kind of parental right. The School Boards (Scotland) Act 1988 allowed parents in primary and secondary schools to establish Boards which are, in effect, similar to but less influential than Boards of Governors in England and Wales. Although by no means the only interest group represented on Boards, parents were intended to be the most influential (see Chapter 19). Boards have fairly restricted powers including an involvement in the selection of senior staff and a general oversight of school spending but no locus in the curriculum or day-to-day management. Although Boards have the right to seek additional powers and to appeal to the Secretary of State if these are refused by the education authority, few have pursued this option. Thus, while many Boards appear to be frustrated by their lack of involvement in the real business of education, few have sought any remedy. In some areas dissatisfaction with Boards' remit, however, has led to a decline in their number as interest has waned.

In 1989, schools were given the opportunity to opt-out of local authority control. A move to opt-out could be initiated by the school board or by petition of the parent body. Parents then had to vote for a resolution that their school become self-governing.

This option did not prove popular with parents. Few ballots were held and even where it might have been expected that parents might support opting-out – as in the case of Paisley Grammar school in the aftermath of its attempted closure by Strathclyde Regional Council

– a majority often voted in favour of staying with the local authority. Indeed, the most common cause of opt-out ballots lay in a determination to frustrate a proposed closure rather than in any serious attempt to become self-governing. In the event, eight years of the opting-out legislation produced only two self-governing schools in Scotland.

The Conservative government's initiatives during the 1980s involving parents' rights can perhaps be seen as falling into two phases. The earlier phase, involving mainly the 1981 Act, enshrined the notion of individual choice and established free market mechanisms. The second phase, characterised by the 1988 and 1989 Acts, although considered by both supporters and opponents as a further development of the market philosophy, actually represented an attempt to involve parents in the management of schools. While undoubt-edly aimed at reducing the power of local authorities, this legislation owed little to the application of free market principles. The concept of empowering the local community through the establishment of School Boards belongs, in fact, to a totally different political tradition. Indeed one of the ironies of the last government's record is that it might have achieved more if it had understood its own philosophy better. In the education market it wished to create, the role of the parent had to be that of customer, not manager.

SCHOOL CLOSURES

During the 1960s and 1970s successive governments funded an extensive education Capital Programme. New schools and school extensions constructed during these two decades account for approximately half of the school accommodation in Scotland. This expansion took place shortly before a dramatic fall in pupil numbers. Indeed, much of the building programme of the 1970s took place after a steady decline in the number of births had already become a well-established pattern. From the mid 1970s onward, the total number of primary pupils declined significantly and from the early 1980s this decline, of course, spread to the secondary sector.

Other factors have, to an extent, offset this drop in roll. Staying on rates into the fifth and sixth years in secondary schools have greatly increased. The contractual limits on class sizes introduced in 1976 and the steady, slow, improvement in staffing ratios which continued for a further decade or so, have meant that accommodation is now less intensively used than it was twenty-five years ago. Nevertheless, the overall drop in pupil numbers over the past twenty years is almost 30 per cent leaving many schools with substantial surplus capacity.

In certain areas, migration and parental choice have compounded this trend. The total populations of the peripheral estates around the cities are now much smaller than in the 1960s. Furthermore, there has been a steady movement by placing request from such areas to schools in more affluent districts.

Since the early 1980s, there has been a widespread recognition that unused school accommodation constitutes a major waste of resources within the system. Underused buildings still require to be maintained: indeed, certain costs such as vandalism may actually increase as usage declines. Furthermore, small schools experience diseconomies of scale in relation to teacher and support staff costs. Most importantly, at least so far as secondary schools are concerned, decline in pupil numbers brings restricted curriculum choice, problems of differentiation and low expectations. Not surprisingly, therefore, education directorates and politicians, both local and national, have been keenly interested in closing underused schools. However, though the arguments in favour of closure are strong, they have not generally been found persuasive by the local communities involved. School closure proposals are almost invariably contentious and the amount of surplus capacity so far removed from the system represents only a small proportion of what exists.

The first serious attempt to tackle this issue on a large scale was made by Strathclyde Regional Council in the years 1986 to 1990. In an attempt to win community support for rationalisation, local review groups were set up to consider the available options on a neighbourhood basis. Each area review group undertook extensive public consultation. These efforts, however, only provided a platform for local opponents of closure who were assisted by various legislative changes. The Schools (Consultation) Regulations 1981 set up formal consultation procedures which exposed local councillors to considerable pressure. These regulations were amended in 1987 in a way which made it impossible for local authorities to close 'popular' schools without reference to the Secretary of State.

Most importantly, the Self-Governing Schools etc. (Scotland) Act 1989 unintentionally provided threatened schools with a means of impeding closure practically indefinitely. Parents in a school which was under threat could begin the process of 'opting out', thus preventing the local authority implementing any closure decision in the meantime. The process of balloting and subsequent decision by the Secretary of State imposed a considerable delay. As the period of delay neared its end, a further period of obstruction could be initiated by starting the opting out process in an associated primary school. This sequence could be repeated almost indefinitely.

Although it now appears unlikely that the opting out legislation will again be used, it remains on the statute book. Even if it were to be repealed, the consultation process would continue to expose local politicians to considerable pressure. The educational and financial issues posed by small and declining schools, therefore, remain largely unresolved. In this context, it is perhaps significant that the government has made available money for improving school buildings which can be accessed only by authorities prepared to carry through closure programmes.

DEVOLVED SCHOOL MANAGEMENT (DSM)

Experiments in the delegation of school budgets took place in London more than twenty years ago. Schemes were introduced by several other English authorities in the mid 1980s and financial delegation became one of the central planks of the English Education Reform Act of 1988.

It was against this background that Strathclyde Regional Council introduced its own scheme, known as Delegated Management of Resources (DMR) in 1990. This decision formed part of a broader strategy aimed at increasing the capacity for operational management at school level while emphasising the strategic role of the authority centrally. DMR was also, however, intended to pre-empt legislation in Scotland and, if possible, influence the form of any statutory Scottish scheme. Indeed, the national guidelines subsequently issued by the Scottish Office are considerably more flexible than the statutory arrangements in force in England. Whether this was because of the influence of the Strathclyde initiative or merely reflected the relatively weaker political position of the government in Scotland can only be a matter of conjecture. In the event, most of the Scottish education authorities developed schemes which owed more to the Strathclyde precedent than to Local Management of Schools (LMS) as the English system was called.

The Scottish schemes delegate to schools budgets made up of a large number of separate components, each allocated on a different basis. Pupil numbers, although obviously strongly influencing the size of the school's budget are not regarded as overwhelmingly the main determinant as happened in England and Wales. Thus, it remains possible to allocate additional resources to schools serving deprived areas. Property budgets normally reflect the extent of the premises and the actual costs of rates, thus ironically helping to sustain declining half-empty schools which would otherwise be unviable. The teacher staffing component is usually based upon average salaries rather than actual costs, thus avoiding the difficulty faced by many English schools of having to dispense with more experienced staff as they move up the salary scale. These approaches mean that the introduction of devolved school management did not significantly disrupt the resourcing of individual schools. On the other hand, it did not impose the same degree of financial realism and discipline as in England and Wales where funding follows the service user in a much closer relationship.

The 12 education authorities differed considerably in their approach to DSM. Some, such as Lothian, were enthusiastic while others, such as Central, tried to retain as much central control as possible. The attitude of the thirty-two unitary authorities has been similarly varied. Since 1996, some councils have attempted to reduce the extent of devolved control while others have removed existing restraints. The amount of genuine delegation now prevailing thus differs greatly from one part of the country to another.

A surprising factor has been the attitude of the Scottish Office, which appears to have been mainly concerned with the percentage of total expenditure notionally devolved to schools. Thus, a scheme which appears to delegate, say, 87 per cent of spending would be regarded as a good one while a scheme delegating 75 per cent would be considered not to meet the requirements of the national guidelines. The fact that the latter scheme might give a school wide discretion over the use of its resources while the former might allow only minimal virement does not seem to have been considered an important factor. As a result, some DSM schemes consist of little more than an elaborate book-keeping exercise, involving schools in considerable additional paperwork but doing nothing to transfer decision-making responsibilities to local level.

Nevertheless, where serious attempts at financial delegation have been made, significant changes have occurred. School management has been strengthened. Headteachers have been encouraged to look critically at long-established practices and judge their cost-effectiveness. Expenditure on, for example, absence cover which is seen as expensive but educationally fairly non-productive, have come under considerable pressure.

There is, of course, substantial scope for delegation within the school. Just as DSM enables authorities to empower headteachers, so heads can empower staff. There remains considerable scope for progress in this area.

THE KEY ISSUES

From the individual perspective of local government, perhaps the most significant issue is whether local Councils will have or should have any future role in the management of education. As the century comes to an end, there are perhaps two substantial reasons why this is a matter which is open to serious question.

The last Conservative government was clearly interested in weakening local government for overtly political reasons. It also, however, had a vision of education in which schools operated largely independently within a national framework. Parents would be encouraged to exercise choice with funding following the individual pupil. Competition in the quasi-market thus created would encourage efficiency and promote higher standards.

It is not yet wholly clear which parts of that agenda have any continuing significance under Labour. Strengthening devolved management at school level seems to be a continuing priority. There will, however, be a focus on collaboration rather than competition. It seems unlikely that parental choice will be seriously challenged despite the government's interest in reviewing the operation of the placing request legislation. Strong pronouncements on raising standards suggest that the centre will maintain, if not strengthen, its control of overall strategy. In short, the concept of the relatively autonomous school operating within a strong national framework seems likely to prevail.

The second potential force for change is the impending establishment of a Scottish Parliament. Supporters of the parliament, including government ministers, have emphasised the importance of strong local government within the new arrangements. However, ultimately the powers and functions of local government and its relationship with the parliament will be matters for the parliament itself to determine.

There are clearly reasons why the parliament might consider running education as a national rather than a local service. Such an approach might well be considered more compatible than the current arrangements with the strong centre/strong institution model of management set out above. Removing the burden of spending on education (and also possibly social work) would leave local authorities able to raise a more realistic proportion of their own budgets through local taxation and thus, arguably, allow them more freedom of action in relation to their remaining services. Furthermore, the idea of a national funding formula for education is clearly attractive to the largest teachers' union, the Educational Institute of Scotland, and it is uncertain whether teaching staff feel any strong loyalty to local authority control.

If local government is to withstand these pressures, it must be able to demonstrate that it contributes something valuable and distinctive. In 'Best Value-speak' what value does it add?

First, there is a question of democratic accountability. The establishment of the Scottish Parliament should ensure greater accountability for the actions of the Scottish Office Education and Industry Department. It is doubtful, however, if it could be an effective mechanism for overseeing the actions of management at local level, particularly the kind of decisions made in schools which have the greatest immediate effect on pupils and parents. There is an essential ombudsman role provided by local councillors which could not easily be replicated at Scottish level.

Second, schools are dependent on a wide range of support services, some specifically educational such as curriculum advisers and others, for example property maintenance, payroll facilities and legal advice, of a more general character. In theory, these could all be provided through the open market. In practice, however, some of the more specialist services are not readily available outwith the local authorities while others could only be independently accessed at a significant cost in senior management time. There is a limit to the time which headteachers can or should devote to dealing directly with clerks of works, banks or insurance companies. Schools have often had good reason to complain of the quality of the backup services which they receive. Nevertheless, the notion of a one-stop shop through the local authority retains significant attractions.

Third, there is a vital need for diversity in strategic management. Schools are rightly focused on operational concerns. A national monopoly in strategic management carries serious risks, as the history of major curriculum development programmes demonstrates. Local authorities, therefore, have an important role (which they have not always fulfilled effectively) as sources of alternative thinking and constructive criticism.

This point relates closely to the debate about standards in education. That debate can, perhaps, be traced back to James Callaghan's 1976 Ruskin College speech (which called for discussion of how to achieve higher levels of attainment) but it has become far more intense in the 1990s with both main political parties strongly committed to strategies for raising pupils' attainments. The debate now takes place in the context of a radical reappraisal by Scots of the quality of their education system.

Its separate education system is one of the touchstones of Scottish identity. For a century at least, Scots have taken it for granted that their education service was worldclass and certainly vastly superior to that of England.

Now, that view is being seriously challenged. The greater economic success of Pacific-rim countries is seen as reflecting the greater effectiveness of their education systems. Too many young people are leaving British, including Scottish, schools without the skills or qualifications to compete in the Information Age. Worst of all – at any rate from the point of view of Scottish self-esteem – the Third International Mathematics and Science survey suggests that Scottish performance is not better than average and has fallen behind that of England.

In some respects, these arguments are open to challenge. What is beyond question, however, is that Scotland's confidence in its education system has been badly shaken. There is a growing demand that those who manage the system, including local authorities, should answer some questions and offer some solutions.

In its triennial review of standards and quality in Scottish education, the Inspectorate offers the view that the great majority of teaching in Scottish schools is 'good' or 'very good'. This raises an important question. How can good teaching result in disappointing levels of attainment? It is hard to avoid the conclusion that the answer lies in poor management. Teachers try – and by and large succeed – in doing what is asked of them. Unfortunately, what is asked for has often been misguided as the recent policy U-turns in documents such as *Achievement for All* and *Mathematics Education 5–14* clearly demon-strate (see Chapters 4 and 44).

Replacing one set of discredited prescriptions with another is no answer. If they are to play an important role in raising standards, local authorities have to endorse wholeheartedly the government's emphasis on setting targets for the outcomes of education while resisting the tendency of its agencies to try to prescribe in excessive detail how those outcomes are to be attained.

Concentrating on ends rather than means is a powerful and appropriate strategy. It depends, however, on having a clear and complete notion of what the ends might be. After three decades in which the importance of success in learning has been grossly undervalued, a renewed emphasis on basic skills and success in obtaining qualifications is neither surprising nor out of place. Unless accompanied by a broader vision, however, it is certainly dangerous.

A final big issue facing local authorities, therefore, is how to maintain such a broader view in a climate where education is increasingly seen in utilitarian terms, with the priority being to raise levels of academic achievement. How can they ensure that appropriate emphasis is also placed on the social, emotional and physical development of young people? How, indeed, can they ensure that the pre-conditions for learning are put in place by supporting families in difficulty and providing a wide range of enriching activities which some children may not otherwise experience? Most fundamentally, how can they help to ensure that the process of transition from childhood into adult life is a well-rounded one?

In a sense, local government is well placed to try and answer these questions. Apart from health, it is responsible for most of the key services involved. It has a capacity to think corporately as well as strategically. Above all, it represents and can potentially lead a united community in action.

REFERENCES

SED (1988) *Effective Secondary Schools*, Edinburgh: SED.
SED (1989) *Effective Primary Schools*, Edinburgh: SED.
SOED (1993) *Devolved School Management – Guidelines for Schemes*, Edinburgh: SOED.
SOEID (1996) *Standards and Quality in Scottish Schools 1992–95*, Edinburgh: SOEID.
SOEID (1996) *Achievements of Secondary 1 and Secondary 2 Pupils in Mathematics and Science*, Edinburgh: SOEID.
SOEID (1997) *Achievements of Primary 4 and Primary 5 Pupils in Mathematics and Science*, Edinburgh: SOEID.

16

Educational Development Services

Alison Cameron and Vivien Casteel

Prior to April 1996, every local authority educational development service consisted of a team of advisory staff (variously named), drawn mainly from teaching backgrounds, who fulfilled a curriculum development and a staff development function for schools in that authority. Depending on individual interests and areas of expertise, their personal credibility and their local and national profile, these individuals might also provide professional advice to the directorate, help to shape policy, select staff and generally assist in the organisation and administration of the service.

The picture across Scotland was by no means uniform. The regional authorities had grown in individuality and power since their formation in 1975. Delegated management of resources, adopted early on by Strathclyde Region and in various stages of development elsewhere in Scotland, had meant that the traditional centralised model of an authority-run core group of stage and subject specialists, meeting the development needs of schools on the one hand whilst fulfilling a sub-education officer role for the authority on the other, was no longer as tenable as once it had been. And yet, despite differences in structure, in terminology, in funding base, and in function, by and large every authority had the equivalent of an educational development service.

Local government re-organisation in April 1996 created thirty-two unitary authorities where in terms of educational provision there had previously been twelve 'local' providers: nine regional and three island authorities. The implications for educational development services were profound. However unwieldy the regions had been in terms of size and geographical diversity – Strathclyde Region alone covered half of Scotland in terms of population – economies of scale had compensated for a certain lack of sensitivity to local need. Further, the very diversity in terms of socio-economic profile, geography and scale of regions such as Grampian, Lothian and Strathclyde had meant that resources could be dispensed more equitably across pockets of affluence and ghettos of deprivation. Given the cost of reorganisation as it impinged at every level and in every area of local government, any services which were non-statutory were going to be regarded as standing on extremely shaky ground. Even where the political will existed, the smaller unitary authorities simply could not afford to provide such services. And at the very point where co-operation and a sharing of resources might have been sensible, there was an equal and opposite pressure to 'go it alone'.

When the dust settled, a very uneven picture emerged across Scotland in terms of support services. Factors of geography, size, past history, funding base and political will influenced whether and/or in what degree a development service as such had been built into the new structures. To a certain extent, the individuals 'disaggregated' from their regional base to their chosen unitary authority determined the shape and function of the service. The unitary authorities may have been new, but the fact that their coats had to be cut from old cloth, and limited old cloth at that, had meant that some radical makeovers were probably necessary. This may not have happened to the extent it should have. Early signs are that in some cases, the holes show, despite the energy, enthusiasm and commitment of the individuals involved. Whether and to what extent the trauma of reorganisation has reinvigorated or obstructed the progress of the educational development service in Scotland towards meeting the challenges of education in the very late 1990s must be the subject of further reflection.

The rest of this chapter aims to progress this discussion, by reflecting on the forms in which the old 'advisory' services have risen from the ashes and currently operate within the new structures; by outlining the broader educational context within which educational development services were already reconstituting themselves prior to the political structures changing; and by examining a variety of possible responses to the need to support educational development in the face of continued under-funding.

EMERGENCE OF EDUCATIONAL DEVELOPMENT SERVICES

To understand current (and future) provision in terms of educational development in Scotland, a look at the emergence and history of the service and of the people who have traditionally provided the service is essential. Although there has never been uniformity of approach across Scotland, it is still possible to trace a discernible pattern of provision as developed in response to changing circumstances over the last thirty years.

Throughout the 1960s, specialists in 'practical' subjects (Physical Education, Technical Education, and Music) were increasingly employed to organise swimming venues, sports fixtures, concerts, or the deployment of specialist equipment across the authority. These 'organisers' also had a responsibility for health and safety issues, and had a major say in the appointment of staff in schools. With substantial resources at their disposal, they were seen as fairly powerful individuals.

It was not until the early 1970s, however, that the need became apparent for subject specialists to be appointed at local level in other 'non-practical' subjects, for the purposes of curricular and staff development. The introduction of the Primary Memorandum heralded major changes in the curriculum and in teaching approaches; at secondary level there was the development of 'O' Grade and the raising of the school leaving age. Teachers in schools needed support and advice to help them negotiate their way through new curricula and respond to new challenges. 'Staff tutors' and 'advisers', usually effective and innovative principal teachers, were brought in to develop the new subjects being introduced, and gradually the advisory service at secondary level came to replicate the departmental structure in schools. Primary advisers, usually drawn from the ranks of primary head-teachers, fulfilled a more generalist function, able to provide not only curriculum and staff development, but often management advice to their former colleagues.

By the mid-to-late 1980s, 'advisory services' were probably at the height of their power. Dependent on size, local authorities could count on fairly complete services, with teams of primary and secondary advisers, and at least one special needs and pre-five adviser. In Strathclyde, the largest of the authorities, each of the six sub-regional divisions replicated this pattern. This meant that there was potential across Scotland for cross-fertilisation of ideas and good practice, and national committees of advisers were formed to act as support networks and to influence the development of the curriculum at national level. At local level, advisers had a fair degree of control over the allocation of resources. By and large, their support was welcomed (if not always uncritically) by teachers struggling to survive the onslaught of continual development. Within local authorities, furthermore, a career structure was beginning to emerge. An adviser might graduate to a post as sector or 'senior' adviser within the service, to the directorate, to Her Majesty's Inspectorate or return to school as Head or Depute Head.

External influences, however, began to have an impact on the provision of this service within local authorities. It became clear that any service delivered 'free' from the centre would be viewed more critically once resources were delegated to schools. To survive, a more flexible and responsive service would be required.

The example of Strathclyde, where a major restructuring of the advisory service took place in the early 1990s, illustrates this development. In retrospect, the restructuring was at this stage largely to do with nomenclature – the 'Educational Development Service' replaced the old 'Advisory Service' – but an attempt was made to resolve certain issues which continue to be at the forefront of the debate. In addition to streamlining the management structure at divisional level, a clutch of regional advisers were appointed to cover cross-curricular issues such as Special Educational Needs, Health Education, Guidance, Religious Education, Outdoors Education, the Arts, Education-Industry Links and the European Dimension. This grafting on of a regional tier of advisers satisfied the demand at the centre for instant access to expertise on a range of policy issues although it also meant a lack of clarity in the management structure, with advisers relating operationally to their Divisional Education Officers as part of the divisional support structure, but strategically to their regional subject-related counterparts. Further, a substantial budget was made available for secondments in addition to permanent members of staff, reflecting the perception that the pace of educational change demanded a continuous transfusion of new blood into the service.

If the first restructuring within Strathclyde Region had been mainly about managing an increasingly complex service more efficiently, the second, which took place in 1993, carried much more radical and painful implications. The transfer of development staff salaries to schools may have been notional, but the conceptual shift it carried with it was profound. Schools started the year with an allowance of credits, which they could 'spend' on the purchase of services – centralised or in-house staff development, curriculum development, management consultancy – delivered by members of the development service. For the first time, there was a sense that schools paid the piper and could therefore expect to call the tune. In the new service delivery model, theoretically at least, the constraints of a market economy operated. The shift of emphasis was reinforced by the establishment of the title of 'Educational Development Officer' as the generic term for a member of the Educational Development Service. The days of 'advisers' determining the needs of schools and dispensing expertise and largesse as they saw fit were over.

The restructuring within Strathclyde Region was intended to achieve several things. First, it tried to resolve a tension inherent in every local authority advisory service, namely that of reconciling the adviser's responsibilities to schools with the vying demands of the administrative centre. The notional transfer of funds was designed to make it clear that the prime task of an adviser was school-based. Second, it attempted to make service provision to schools more equitable, ensuring that every establishment was able to gain access to the resource on offer, and encouraging less proactive establishments to take advantage of this and to be more discriminating in their use of it. Third, however, and most significantly, it attempted to preserve a service which was in danger of disappearing altogether by applying some reality therapy. Government pressure to delegate management of resources to schools was only part of a wider movement which would radically affect not only the delivery of services but the nature of the service to be delivered. This second major restructuring in Strathclyde mirrored the changes in the funding of the teacher education institutions (TEIs) vis à vis the specific grant made available from central government for the provision of in-service training for teachers. The substantial proportion of this grant previously ring-fenced to the TEIs had been transferred to authorities in a phased arrangement which gave staff in the TEIs a chance to adapt to meeting the needs of clients, and to compete in the market-place along with other providers.

So too, members of the advisory/development services were required to adapt to a changing economic climate. This meant adjusting to hard and (for some) unpalatable truths. The distress evident in long-serving and in some cases even recently appointed advisers to the change in title from 'adviser' to 'educational development officer' bore witness to the fact that the old title carried a prestige and a status which the new term did not. Losing the title seemed like a demotion. Similarly, the idea that development services had a cash value attached to them was a major culture shock to both advisers and schools. It offended the still prevalent view that education should be removed from such considerations, it disturbed the established client/provider relationship, and it imposed a bureaucracy (as well as a certain rigour) in which few could see any advantage. Yet although the 1993 restructuring of the Strathclyde service may have stemmed from financial imperatives, it set in motion a necessary transition from an increasingly unwieldy, permanent, secondary-dominated, subject-focused service to a flexible, needs-related and therefore more responsive service.

In most of the authorities which would be substantially affected by re-organisation, rationalisation of the existing provision had begun prior to 1996. The question of whether pre-1996 attempts to adapt the service to meet the needs of schools and hence to safeguard its existence have been built on or abandoned in the unitary authorities is highly significant, and will be returned to in the context of reviewing current provision and considering likely developments.

CURRENT PROVISION

As already discussed, the picture since April 1996 across thirty-two authorities is diverse, confused and, it may be assumed, fluctuating, as budget cuts bite deeper and as education departments find their feet within the new council structures. The Highland Council, less affected by reorganisation, has retained a large advisory team with subject specific remits, as have Glasgow and North Lanarkshire, where advisers offer curricular support in their subject specialism, have a functional responsibility within the authority, and have a pastoral role with regard to schools. In stark contrast, certain of the smaller authorities, such as Aberdeenshire, Moray and Midlothian, have no educational development service staff as such. In Aberdeenshire, development work is taken forward by 'Curriculum Networks' made up of practitioners in schools, and facilitated by Education Officers who are not themselves subject specialists but who act as lead officers for the authority.

A more typical picture lies somewhere in between. Many of the responses to a survey carried out by the Association of Educational Advisers in Scotland (AEAS) in August 1997 suggested that educational development services in Scotland comprise anything from three to ten individuals whose remits range widely across subject specialisms and age ranges, and include a myriad of authority tasks and responsibilities. In the smallest of these, three or four advisers/development officers act in a consultancy role with respect to schools, brokering staff development needs whilst also supporting the directorate. In the middle are a range of education development services whose members typically have many more generic responsibilities than would hitherto have been the case. An English Adviser might also be responsible for Drama, Modern Languages, and Personal and Social Development. This adviser might also have responsibility at a policy level for taking forward national developments such as Higher Still. Typically, he or she might also have a pastoral role in a number of schools, and be involved in development planning and in quality assurance.

A more exhaustive analysis of each of the thirty-two different responses to reorganisation goes beyond the scope of this brief overview, but some major themes emerge. Firstly, the terms 'adviser' and 'advisory service' are still popular. Out of nineteen authority responses to the survey, ten had retained (or reverted to) the job title, although the service was more usually referred to as 'educational development', 'quality development', 'curriculum support', or 'services to schools'. This may be an attempt to restore a status which was perceived to have been lost, or to suggest a return to a more ordered world amidst changing times. Given the greatly varying nature of roles and remits in the new authorities, however, it is unlikely that the selection of the term 'adviser' in preference to any other has any great bearing on the degree of responsibility assumed or the type of work undertaken. (The term 'adviser' will be used henceforward in this chapter as a generic term for a member of a local authority educational development service, or for someone undertaking a staff/curricular development role within an authority: no particular status should be attributed to the word in this context.)

A second theme which emerges in the smaller authorities is the tendency for named individuals to have responsibility for a wide range of curricular areas beyond their subject specialism, in addition to cross-curricular responsibilities. There seems little doubt that members of an educational development service are likely to have ascribed to them duties which are organisational in nature and have as much to do with running an education service as with improving teaching and learning. Too few people are doing too much. Even on paper, it seems obvious that something will have to give.

Thirdly, there is a sense of 'ad-hocery' in the survey returns, a year into reorganisation, reflecting both the enormity of the transition and the uneven distribution of resourcing. Indications are that educational development services in Scotland have been reformulated not so much in response to best practice as to exigency. The very issues which prompted the Strathclyde restructuring, prior to reorganisation, remain, as yet, largely unresolved and indeed may have been exacerbated by reorganisation.

THE ISSUES

One of the issues which has dogged educational development services has been the problem of identifying the correct locus for its work. Local authority advisers have traditionally had to respond to a number of different priorities. These include overarching national priorities, such as (currently) the phasing in of the 5–14 development programme, the implementation of Higher Still, or the introduction of guidelines for staff development and appraisal. Local authority priorities also impinge on the work of an adviser who may have a major role to play in implementing policy measures such as the council's social strategy or the education department's extension of early years provision. Individual establishments have priorities relating to their own development plans and in some cases clusters of schools might share priorities. There are also the priorities determined by functional groups relating to new developments in their specialist/sectoral/stage areas. Finally, as the notion of continuous professional development gains ground each staff member will be encouraged to determine their own development needs in relation to their current role and the evaluation of their performance, their career intentions and the school's needs.

Prioritising these various and varying development needs against a backdrop of ever more limited resources is problematic. Individual, group and establishment priorities identified through school development and departmental planning, and to some extent the staff development and review process, inevitably compete for time and attention with other group priorities established via adviser-led planning groups and related to the national specialist agenda. While service planning at local authority level determines priorities for the next three to five years, there is as yet no national development plan for education and the national education budget is only known on an annual basis. National priorities therefore emerge in a less ordered fashion, often in response to political influences. The introduction of staff development and review and the nursery vouchers scheme are recent examples of national developments which have major implications for local authorities. Trying to meet all of these competing needs poses a challenge to the best resourced service; in the current state of play, for many authorities, it is an impossibility.

A second major issue is the question of how best to support educational development. With increasingly sophisticated planning mechanisms in place at school level, and more recently at individual level, the traditional model of support – adviser-led, and centre-based – is no longer flexible enough to provide what is required. Many schools provide an increasingly effective range of development opportunities from their own resources. They have visibly increased their abilities to do this year by year as they have taken on more responsibility for the professional development of their staff, providing school-based courses, mentoring, tutoring, and various work-based learning opportunities.

Despite recognising and indeed supporting more diverse approaches to meeting staff development needs, the educational development services have continued (predominantly) to provide courses at school, cluster or local authority level. A menu of provision has been prepared on an annual basis and distributed to schools, and courses attracting sufficient clients have been calendared. While it has to be said that many schools rely on this kind of provision, and expect to be able to tap into what has been centrally determined as appropriate, too often attendance at such courses is seen as a one-off event rather than as part of a development process. Schools take responsibility to a greater or lesser extent for preparing their staff for courses and for providing follow-up on return. A further problem is that the 'menu' may in effect turn into a 'diet' of staple fare, offering endless runs of courses which appear relevant but do little to challenge people's thinking. Meanwhile the more esoteric and perhaps more 'cutting edge' offerings will have been removed as minority interests. Post-reorganisation, in fact, many of the smaller authorities have found that it is simply not viable to provide even the basics in this way. Calendared courses may attract only six or eight participants, and have to be cancelled. As a result, more and more centralised provision has to be generic in nature. For example, a course on 'effective learning and teaching' will be offered, as opposed to the subject-specific input which might have been justified in a larger authority.

Arguably, re-organisation with attendant budget cuts could and should have led to a reconsideration of this traditional model. In the City of Edinburgh, for example, the necessity to streamline educational development services has led to a potentially greater degree of 'democratisation', with local curriculum groups meeting with 'generic' advisers to determine needs and to respond to these needs. This model would appear to provide a solution to the charge sometimes levelled by practitioners that the centrally determined 'menu' has little to offer them, and early indications are that other authorities are similarly tapping into existing expertise.

A third issue is that of the blurring of roles between advisory staff and directorate staff. However unjustifiably, advisers and education officers have often been seen as requiring essentially different characteristics to perform their jobs well. Members of the advisory service have been seen as needing to be innovative and creative people, self-starters rather than team members, able to inspire others and to facilitate developments in their subject or sector specialism. Members of the directorate, on the other hand, have been seen as requiring to be more conventional and politically-minded, 'safe pairs of hands' when it came to delivering and being accountable for the statutory demands of the service.

Yet arguably, the skills developed and the nature of the experience acquired over time by both groups had much in common. The dividing line between advisory/developmental and directorate activities was often finely drawn, with advisers acting on the one hand in a pastoral capacity with respect to schools, and on the other performing a sort of sub-development officer role in respect of drawing up policies and attending meetings on behalf of the authority. Directorate members have traditionally found advisers to be useful field officers for them, investigating difficulties, managing projects etc. This meant that over a period of time a variety of different roles emerged for advisory service members which were little to do directly with the improvement of teaching and learning, but had quite a lot to do with running the service.

It is in this context that, for long serving advisers, the process of local government reorganisation came as a painful awakening. Apart from the uncertainty about where or whether a post would continue to exist in the successor authorities, there was a justifiable expectation from the more experienced and senior members of the development services that they would be able to compete on equal terms for the plethora of directorate posts which became available as a result of reorganisation. In the event, this was not borne out. Comparatively few were successful, and this did nothing to lessen the perception that experience in supporting the business of learning and teaching had not been seen as a particularly valuable commodity when it came to running the service overall.

It is perhaps ironic that in the new smaller authorities resulting from local government re-organisation the roles are likely to become even more blurred, with advisers assuming organisational roles in addition to their development role. Whether through time the distinctions will become less significant and the status gap will lessen remains to be seen. Early reports suggest, however, that while some members of the development service are enjoying the challenges presented, others see their more bureaucratic/administrative duties as encroaching on what they regard as being their fundamental role and find the pressure to represent the authority in any number of capacities frustrating and even demoralising. 'I used to attend meetings because I had something to contribute', said one development officer. 'Now, I'm a spectator.'

The fourth issue, namely the problem of attracting and retaining high quality staff to the advisory service, is very much related to the uncertain status attached to the role. At one stage, an advisory post was perceived as offering not only a high degree of job satisfaction, but considerable kudos as well. It represented for many the apogee of their career, and for others, the possibility of access to the national stage, to directorate posts, or to headship in a school. But changes in funding structures, in the balance of power between authorities and schools, and for many, a disenchantment with the way local government reorganisation was conducted has brought about a sea-change in the way advisers see themselves and in the way they are viewed.

Advisers, to be effective in the increasingly responsible and complex roles they perform – consultant, trainer, policy-maker, organiser, broker – must have a thorough knowledge of their specialist area, a good grasp of wider educational issues and the ability and willingness to take on a variety of generic roles on behalf of the authority. Most importantly, advisers have to have a high degree of credibility with their peer group and with headteachers. This presents an in-built paradox: credibility with teachers in schools relies on recent hands-on experience; to be able to perform all the other tasks, the experience of operating at authority and even perhaps national level is required. Both schools and the authority want continuity and both also want a continual infusion of fresh blood, new ideas, enthusiasm. The question of how to sustain a cutting-edge, energetic advisory service in a shrinking economy without any real career prospects to offer has exercised authorities in the past and will continue to do so. The traditional answer of secondments is proving less attractive than before, as School Boards demonstrate a marked preference for continuous school service over other kinds of experience in appointing senior staff.

At the same time, while the confusions and dissatisfactions continue to circulate, anecdotal evidence would indicate that those who have survived the rebirthing pains of reorganisation and who turn up to the endless rounds of conferences and meetings to reconnect with old colleagues in new roles, exhibit a mixture of feelings about the brave new world. Some have moved into an arena where their pseudo education officer role and the necessity to work in a different way within limited means, has given them a new lease of life. The challenges of operating in a smaller authority, in some cases in a less formal environment, are proving exhilarating. They are enjoying the challenge of covering not only early years, but 5–14 expressive arts, whilst taking charge of personal and social development across the age range and developing a role in supporting school self-evaluation. A reliance on specialist expertise is of necessity being replaced by an ability to be flexible, and to exhibit a range of interpersonal and generic skills.

For others for whom reorganisation has meant a reduction in profile and responsibility, or who have been effectively pushed into a variety of roles for which they do not feel qualified, the combination of career disappointment, lack of resourcing and/or an unrealistic workload is proving too much. Inevitably, the piling on of tasks leads to a sense that nothing is being done adequately. As one member of a small educational development service commented, 'It is dreadful to watch committed, enthusiastic professional people having to confront a sense of failure.' Their response varies: early retirement followed by new, more satisfying careers elsewhere; quiet/grim acceptance of the status quo; disillusionment and retrenchment until the next round of retirement packages makes escape possible. In cases where authorities retain a high proportion of staff in this category, or where authorities fail adequately to support staff faced with a well-nigh impossible workload, it is difficult to see how an educational development service can be sustained let alone developed.

LIKELY FUTURE DEVELOPMENTS

It might have been anticipated that the break up of the large regional authorities and subsequent financial constraints would have provided the ideal opportunity to resolve some of these major tensions and issues surrounding educational development services in the mid to late 1990s. And indeed there are signs that the new education authorities are grappling with the issues: the problem of keeping a large, unwieldy and permanent cohort of advisers to meet schools' demand for continuity and for specialist support; the need to develop more generic skills in place of subject or stage specialism; the problem of spreading limited resources too thinly; the changing culture of demands and expectations as schools became progressively adept at defining their own development needs; the requirement to rationalise provision in line with continuing budget cuts. The fact that the tensions and issues have not been resolved and in some authorities may be approaching crisis level is not necessarily a condemnation of either the personnel involved or of their management. Certainly, opportunities for radical restructuring may not have been taken, and the refusal or inability of the unitary authorities to share resources may prove regrettable. But while a greater degree of vision or imagination might have helped, under-funding is at the root of the problem. In the face of budgetary and political pressures, local authorities choose to defend front-line delivery at the expense of any non-statutory services: educational development is a soft target.

The inclusion of the specific grant in the block grant system for authorities (April 1998 onwards) has further destabilised the situation. The specific grant was introduced in Scotland in 1991 for the purpose of staff development in relation to national priorities. Its inclusion in the block grant has made it more difficult first to ensure that resources for staff development are safeguarded and second to ensure that the staff development resources take account of the national agenda. The absence of ring-fenced funding for professional development following the removal of the specific grant requires urgent address.

Meanwhile the demand for support for educational development at local level has if anything intensified in response to national pressures. The staff review and development mechanism entitles individuals to continuous professional development in relation to their identified needs. National curricular initiatives demand massive amounts of development work at authority level in order to be implemented. At institutional level, HMI inspections, school development planning and the pursuit of national standards such as the Charter-mark, Investors in People etc. give rise to a consistent need for establishment-focused, localised support.

The challenge which confronts local authorities in the late 1990s, then, is to provide a service which can offer this depth and breadth of provision in the context of devolved school management and of a strong national agenda. More accountability to schools means that sophisticated planning and consultative structures will have to evolve, with more partner-ship and less paternalism than hitherto. And a means has to be found of enabling local authorities to influence the development agenda for schools in terms of their distinctive priorities and in response to local needs.

One putative solution would be to resource educational development from the centre. As the influence of local authorities diminishes with increasingly more resources devolved to schools, the development of a number of major national initiatives and in the build up to the new Scottish parliament, it seems likely that the agenda for educational development will be increasingly nationally driven and managed. Over the years, Scotland has been comparatively centralised and consensual in its approach to development, and national models of educational development already exist in the form of training programmes for the introduction of staff development and appraisal or of Higher Still. A centralised agenda may be further taken forward by the restoration of specific grant at national level in order to direct resourcing to developments such as the proposed Scottish Qualification for Headship (SQH).

Another partial solution to the problems faced by virtually all of the new authorities in attempting to resource an adequate range of provision for a relatively small client group might be the formation of authority partnerships, perhaps in association with universities or other providers, to resource staff development. Prior to the break up of the regions, Strathclyde's management training unit or 'Staff College' operated an extremely successful model of provision which involved buying in associate staff as required rather than employing a large number of full-time staff. It charged schools the real costs of courses including staff costs in purely financial terms and did indeed make a profit. Over a region the size of Strathclyde, it was possible to offer a coherent and comprehensive management development programme which was not only viable financially but which enabled the fruitful exchange of views across more localised boundaries.

Certainly the ability of local education authorities to maintain educational development services as they did in the past has been severely depleted. As progressively less scope is offered for creativity and innovation at local level, and in default of all but the largest authorities being able to provide a comprehensive service, it may be that the development officer jobs of the future will increasingly come to be with central bodies or partnership agencies, with local authorities offering support for maintenance and inspection follow-up.

And yet, while such centralised or partnership arrangements might resolve some of the problems and tensions identified here, schools over the years have come to expect a comprehensive and localised service. National developments have seldom if ever translated neatly into local contexts, or been accepted as immediately and obviously workable. Post-reorganisation and a year into a new education agenda, the need for relevant, practical, up-to-the-minute support for learning and teaching, for mediating the national agenda, and for responding to the particular circumstances of establishments and teachers has not lessened. If this imperative is to be met, a safeguarding of funding along with new and creative solutions at local and at national level is going to be required.

REFERENCE

Scottish Councils Advisory Servise Information, collated by the Association of Educational Advisers in Scotland, August 1997.

17

The Scottish Consultative Council on the Curriculum (SCCC)

Hamish Ross

Established in 1965, the Consultative Committee on the Curriculum (CCC) was part of government-supported movements to develop educational provision among several advanced countries in the 1960s. In England and Wales, in 1964, the Schools Council was set up; New Zealand, in 1963, formed a Curriculum Development Unit. In Scotland, from its beginning, the CCC has been closely identified with the Scottish Education Department (SED). Its continuing existence, functions, its relationships with the Department and the efficacy of its work are themes in this chapter. Although now styled the Scottish Consultative Council on the Curriculum (SCCC), the practice of using the original acronym, sometimes prefaced with the word Scottish, widely obtains. Both CCC and SCCC will be used at different points in this chapter. The account has been informed by discussions with personnel, serving and retired, from SCCC, the Scottish Office, Her Majesty's Inspectorate of Schools (HMI), education authorities and other organisations.

CONSTITUTION AND REMIT

CCC's original remit was to oversee the whole school curriculum, advise the Secretary of State on areas which should be developed and maintain continuous review of the curriculum. It had no staff, it had no budget and its chairperson was the Secretary of the Scottish Education Department. In 1976, CCC assumed oversight of central committees and curriculum development centres. It created two important coordinating committees and a permanent secretariat was established, headed by a seconded Inspector of Schools who later became its first Chief Executive. Following the Rayner Review in 1980 – a government initiated scrutiny on effectiveness and value for money – it was determined that CCC should have an external chairperson. Its responsibilities grew until the late 1980s and it oversaw a large substructure which engaged hundreds of teachers in development. Retrenchment, relocation to Dundee and a new nomenaclature followed a further review (the Crawley Review, 1986), this time by the Department. The substructure was done away with; CCC became, in 1987, the Scottish Consultative Council on the Curriculum (SCCC) an incorporated organisation, a Non Departmental Public Body (NDPB) sponsored by the Department. Such bodies, in terms of the Department's practice, are reviewed every five years. After Crawley, SCCC was reviewed by Robertson (1993) and again at the time of writing this chapter by Alexander (1998). Members' responsibilites and the workings of the Council are covered by the Companies Act and the financial rules of the Scottish Office.

Scottish CCC comprises twenty members of council, appointed by the Secretary of State, Inspectorate and SOEID assessors, a staff of fifty-one with a Chief Executive, three Directors, six Curriculum Officers and technical and clerical support. Its budget for 1997/98 was £1.425 million, mainly from the Scottish Office Education and Industry Department (SOEID). In addition, it was allocated a special budget of £4 million to undertake development for the government's Higher Still Development Programme. As part of an international network of curriculum agencies, SCCC acts as secretariat to the Consortium of Institutions for Development and Research in Education in Europe (CIDREE). It is thus part of a movement involved in several projects including school self-evaluation, cross-curricular themes, early childhood education and one concerned with the development of broad competencies in upper secondary education. Within the UK, SCCC has contact with the other curriculum councils for England and Wales and Northern Ireland. In contrast to those bodies, its role remains focused on the curriculum; it has no oversight of assessment.

Corporate Plan 1997–2000

Scottish CCC at present has four sets of corporate goals: supporting the central role of schools in promoting learning and teaching; developing effective relationships with client groups; developing a better understanding of the principles which should underpin the curriculum; improving its effectiveness as an organisation. Those goals are supported by four broad programmes which include review activities and projects: monitoring of the whole school curriculum 5–14, including a review of Scottish history and Scottish culture; development of early education, special education, Level F in 5–14 and early stages of secondary education; a review of curriculum design for secondary stages and for the 14–18 area; learning and teaching, climate and ethos and a project entitled the 'Learning School'.

Methods of working

That the SCCC is described as the Secretary of State's principal advisory body on the curriculum tells very little about either the degree of freedom open to the Council to initiate a particular review or the extent to which ministers set the agenda for curricular change. Over the period of the SCCC's existence the balance in this regard has changed. However, three models of working can be discerned; the implications of their adoption will be discussed in subsequent sections.

The first could be called, *SCCC Initiated Review and Development* and this occurs where a need is identified – usually within the service: for example, ideas about a particular area of the curriculum, such as technology education, may be thought to require reconceptualising. SCCC would set up a group, often chaired by a member of Council, to explore and report. There would be prima facie agreement on the part of SOEID that the area should be examined, and if a consultation exercise were to be undertaken it would be carried out by SCCC. In due course, a final report, in the light of responses, would be published by SCCC, sometimes endorsed by the Minister as guidance to schools and education authorities. The genesis and outcome of the Munn Report (1977) and *Curriculum Design for the Secondary Stages* (1989), referred to later, exemplify this model.

A second model can be identified as *Government initiated – SCCC Supported*. In this case the Minister would request SCCC to construct a curriculum framework in an area which the government had decided should be developed. The 5–14 curriculum programme is perhaps the clearest example of SCCC as a subordinate partner of the executive of government, rather than the progenitor of change (in this particular instance having had its own proposals for the curriculum of the 10–14 age group earlier rejected by the Minister). In such a model the government may consent to the testing of SCCC's ideas through consultation which is undertaken by SOEID. And, in the light of the responses, the government would adopt a position, assume ownership and publish a final report as guidance to education authorities and schools.

Recently, a third method of bringing about innovation has become apparent which involves SCCC as a subsidiary. It could be described as *Government-owned with SCCC contracted to undertake development work*. The Higher Still Development Programme illustrates an approach which has remained in the hands of government from inception to implementation. First, a group would be appointed by the Secretary of State and commissioned to prepare a report; thereafter, consultation would be arranged by SOEID. A policy position would eventually be announced and a development programme set in train with a predetermined time-scale. In the case of the Higher Still Programme, the SCCC was contracted to undertake the development work and a unit was set up within SCCC, funded by SOEID and overseen by a strategy group, not the Council. Curiously SCCC's review of the curriculum for the 14–18 age group did not precede this development, but followed it. The emergence and predominence of models two and three for government programmes in the decade from 1987 to 1997 seems related to expediency for policy ends. It does, however, give rise to a number of problems: lack of clear responsibility for the publication of curriculum guidance, and ambiguity surrounding the precise role of SCCC.

REVIEW OF THE CURRICULUM

As its functions evolved, SCCC's remit of curriculum review, development and advice, enabled it to create and oversee a vast substructure. The zenith of its influence was in the mid 1980s. It was responsible for four Deliberative Committees, ten Development Committees and fifteen Central Committees. One of its reviews, the Munn Report (1977), along with a companion report commissioned by SED on assessment, the Dunning Report (1977), led to the Munn and Dunning Development Programme which in turn became the Standard Grade Development. In addition to the activities already listed, SCCC became involved in twenty-three Central Support Groups and thirty-two Joint Working Parties (JWPs) with the Examination Board.

Scottish CCC's review, *Education 10–14 in Scotland* (1986) – referred to below – was to become a watershed. The government felt that the proposed management of the development through groups of schools was flawed (although SCCC conceded an alternative strategy) and it did not believe that, 'its key recommendations would achieve the desired improvement in quality and standards' (*Curriculum and Assessment in Scotland: A Policy for the 90s*, SED, 1987, para. 10). Instead government initiated a reform of the 5–14 curriculum. In response to the Secretary of State's request to advise on the curricular framework, SCCC set up Review and Development Groups (RDGs) which made proposals on: English Language, Mathematics, Environmental Studies, Expressive Arts, Religious and Moral Education, Personal and Social Education. Groups also reviewed reporting and assessment, modern languages, Latin and Gaelic.

Review of the whole school curriculum did not proceed systematically but as a result of the circumstances of the time. Changes within the system, in some cases, provided the motive force for review; government policy, on other occasions, required it; and, in some instances, change was the outcome of new ideas within the service. The following documents and activities illustrate the changing contexts out of which review arose.

1. The Munn Report (1977). *The Structure of the Curriculum in the Third and Fourth Years of the Scottish Secondary School* (*The Munn Report*, 1977) proposed differentiated courses within a modal framework. This report provided the basis for a rationale of the 14–16 curriculum whose assumptions are still generally accepted.

2. Education for the Industrial Society Project (EISP). Initiated by the Minister for Education in 1977 to review secondary education in the light of the needs of the world of work, this project gave impetus to a range of work related initiatives. An outcome was *An Education for Life and Work* (1983) which gave a context for education/industry liaison.

3. More than Feelings of Concern (1986). This position paper attempted to promote guidance as a whole-school concern and clarify the management implications. Education authorities evolved their own practices but *More than Feelings of Concern*, as an influence, is still discernible.

4. Education 10–14 in Scotland (1986). This important, forward looking discussion paper was destined to incur the opprobrium of government ostensibly on grounds of management and cost but fundamentally on grounds of ideology (Boyd, 1994). Widely read, particularly in teacher education institutions throughout the UK, it became, according to its chairman David Robertson, wryly referred to by civil servants as 'the satanic verses' (Ross, 1993, p. 236).

5. Curriculum Design for the Secondary Stages (Revised 1989). These guidelines are most influential, followed, as they are, by all state secondary schools in Scotland. Their modal design, in large part derived from the The Munn Report (1977) based on ideas of realms of meaning or forms of knowledge, incorporating key skills as well as elements of personal and social education, stands in distinction to the subject based National Curriculum in England and Wales. They have been revised in 1997 and consultation is now awaited.

6. Working Papers of the 5–14 Development Programme. Review and development of the 5–14 curriculum in Scotland, it will be recalled, was of the Secretary of State's initiating. Between 1989 and 1992, the SCCC's Review and Development Groups (RGDs) produced working papers on structure and balance and components of the curriculum. The Department's final guidelines, nowithstanding amendments (of a significant nature in the case of Environmental Studies), largely reflect the design of the SCCC's development groups.

7. Committee on Special Educational Needs (COSPEN). The work of the standing committee on special educational needs spanned eleven years. Its role was three-fold: influencing SCCC and its structures on the extent of special educational needs; working with other bodies outside education; producing documents and materials on its own initiative or that of the Council. COSPEN became an important source of support and advocacy for teachers working in various specialist fields.

8. The Heart of the Matter (1995). This paper, outcome of a joint SCCC/SOED review of education for personal and social development, marks a new departure for SCCC as it moves into areas of school climate and ethos, exploring how contexts for learning can help promote personal and social development. Two years after its publication, 20,000 copies had been disseminated in Scotland and beyond. It is used by schools for staff and institutional development.

9. Teaching for Effective Learning (1996). This report reflects awareness that teachers need to be sensitive not only to how pupils learn but conscious of their own role as learners. It

takes a synoptic view of research findings, invites teachers to reflect on their own practice, and offers discussion and exploration. Follow up staff development in schools has been an outcome.

10. Technology Education in Scottish Schools (1996). This position paper is a reformulation of ideas about technology education, seeing it as a creative human activity capable of developing skills and understanding as well as moral awareness. It defines areas of technological capability and outlines discrete learning activities.

11. Supporting Learning in Schools (1997). Continuing an approach introduced by *Heart of the Matter* (1995) and *Teaching for Effective Learning* (1996), this report considers some of the implications of the idea of the school as a learning organisation. Attention focuses on the teacher as facilitator and supporter of learning, the importance of school policy and the need for evaluation.

12. Scottish History in the Curriculum (1997). Sensitivity on the part of Scottish CCC to wider issues in Scotland, some of them of a political nature, mark this document for mention. Described as a paper for discussion and consultation, it emerged at a time of much interest in matters relating to Scottish culture and history. Its endorsement by the Secretary of State duly followed.

RELATIONSHIP WITH EDUCATION AUTHORITIES

One might assume a close relationship between SCCC and the education authorities. It is, after all, the responsibilitiy of the education authorities to deliver the curriculum. Yet, no formal liaison mechanism existed until recently (see Chapter 15 in this volume). Directors and their staffs were certainly involved as individual members of SCCC and its sub-structure. But this did not happen at a strategic level. Reorganisation of local government in Scotland in 1975 into nine regional and three island councils enabled education authorities, collectively, to have large development services: Lothian Region created a Regional Consultative Committee on the Curriculum. Gatherer, then Chief Adviser of Lothian Region, canvassed the idea of a similar model for the education authorities linking directly to the Scottish CCC. The proposal was not seriously considered by the education authorities.

> Had it been put to the test, I am quite sure that it would have been received with a great deal of hostility because, quite understandably, they (education authorities) would not wish to be linked to St Andrew's House – the CCC, of course, was very much a creature of the SED. (Gatherer, in Ross, 1993, p. 223)

There were no regular policy meetings at officer level between the Scottish CCC and the Association of Directors of Education in Scotland (ADES).

Further reorganisation of local government in Scotland took place in 1996 increasing the number of education authorities to thirty-two; about the same time government policy required some 80 per cent of education authority budgets to be devolved to schools. Overall responsibility, however, remained as in successive education acts: to provide adequate and efficient education. Out of this new context, liaison between SCCC and the education authorities has taken on a more systematic and structured form. As one of the priorities in the Corporate Plan, each SCCC officer now has responsibility for a set of education authorities and meets with a member of the directorate – at second or third tier level – about three times a year. The reduced capacity of education authorities to undertake development work has led to two further outcomes. National networking for review and development is emerging in both generic areas of the curriculum, such as learning and teaching, and in specific subject areas. In addition, there is development carried out by SCCC staff – at present in the learning and teaching field but there is pressure to extend to other areas; whether SCCC has the capacity for this activity is doubtful.

RELATIONSHIPS WITH THE CENTRE

Scottish Office Education and Industry Department

The Department wanted a body that was flexible and responsive to control (McPherson and Raab, 1988). Chaired by the Secretary of the Department, SCCC was able to evolve to suit the prevailing circumstances and central policy makers' ends. Suiting the policy makers over time, however, involved different and conflicting strategies for SCCC. The Department's commitment to the principle of a body providing independent advice to the Secretary of State, on putting it forward as its (only) submission to the Rayner Review, was doubted. 'It was suspected that the SED offered the CCC to Rayner as a tethered goat, (Gatherer, 1989, p. 42). While it survived and emerged stronger with an external chairperson, and went on to be given an important role in the Standard Grade development, within seven years it was time, in the Department's view, to pull back power that had been ceded. The Crawley Review (1987) recommendations arose from a context of a Department thwarted in its development of Standard Grade by the teachers' industrial action. SCCC's substructure which relied on teacher cooperation and involvement was rejected as inefficient. While its position was apparently strengthened through the device of incorporation as a company limited by guarantee, it still retains its dependency on SOEID. Its core grant is SOEID funding and its corporate plan has to be agreed by the Department. Every five years it undergoes civil service review.

While Scottish CCC was involved in the 5–14 review, the Minister wrote announcing that it was to be relocated in Dundee. Sister Maire Gallagher, the chairperson, met what was felt to be insupportable with forthrightness and informed the Secretary of State that the development could not be undertaken in those circumstances, that the matter was a resignation issue for her, the Chief Executive and Council. The successor Council, in 1991, was reduced to fifteen. Its credibility was openly speculated on. The *Times Education Supplement Scotland* had sport, attributing obvious or obscure reasons for members' acceptability politically:

> Forsyth's [Education Minister] first XV: a selective guide to form. Spot the common factor . . . the director of education who ensured 100% testing in the Western Isles . . . the headteacher of one of the few schools in Scotland to be blessed by a visit from Margaret Thatcher . . . [the parent] who spoke up on testing at a public meeting in Dumfries attended by Government officials . . . the depute director from one of the Government's favourite regions, i.e. it pays its poll tax. (6 September, 1991)

Its precarious position was highlighted by the recommendations of the Robertson Review (1993). Lacking the insight of its predecessor into the needs of a modern education system, the review focused on administrators' solutions. Proposing hiving off the SCCC's development role to another body and retaining its advisory function, it argued that SCCC could be compromised if, having given advice to the Secretary of State which was rejected or heavily amended, it was then asked to undertake development of an area it had earlier advised against. The reviewer brought discussion full circle to where Scottish CCC began, proposing that the Secretary of the Scottish Office Education Department should again consider assuming its chair.

Her Majesty's Inspectors of Schools

Her Majesty's Inspectorate of Schools in Scotland constitutes a powerful body whose remit is to evaluate the system, engage in and give leadership to development and advise ministers. There is no concession to the quasi-market model, applying in other parts of the UK, separating specification, development and evaluation of the curriculum. Some would say that there is contradiction of function – HMI operating as judge and jury on its own development role. Whatever theoretical lack of clarity surrounds the Inspectorate's role, its position at the heart of a centralist model for change is clear; Scottish CCC's, on the other hand, is not.

At one time, SCCC was looked on by central administrators as a useful coordinating device, one preventing the Inspectorate from pursuing its own specialisms at the expense of general advances across the curriculum, which was a characteristic of subject led development. Innovation in secondary education, hitherto, according to Sister Maire Gallagher 'happened through haphazard development. The development of very powerful committees in particular areas which were regarded as important . . . and other areas had absolutely nothing' (Ross, 1993, p. 194). One of the first tasks that SCCC gave its newly created Committee on Secondary Education was to redress the balance.

The normally sure-footed inspectors intermediating between administrators and Scottish CCC failed in their involvement with the 10–14 Report. Three Chief Inspectors of Schools, at different times, acted as assessors during the group's deliberations and according to Smyth, one of the 10–14 Committee's joint secretaries, there was never any closure of communication between the work of the group and the Department.

> The critical difference seemed to be the change of attitude that was at least represented by the arrival of some hardline, strong, managerial – I think it is fair to say, Thatcherite – civil servants in key positions. And they changed the policy more or less overnight. It was they, of course, certainly with Mr Stewart's (Minister for Education) approval, who rejected the 10–14 Report and who turned the Inspectorate upside-down. It really did put the Inspectorate in a very embarrassing position. (Smyth, in Ross, 1993, p. 235)

Failure of whatever group in the Department to impress upon ministers that the pace of change in the Standard Grade Development was driving teachers towards industrial action (in contrast to Scottish CCC's advice to the Department to that effect), redounded to SCCC's detriment and led to the denigration of a model of curriculum development which is spelled out, administrator style, in the Crawley Review.

Moreover, SCCC found itself in tension with the Inspectorate with whose advisory and development functions it overlapped. In the 1960s, the Inspectorate had been very much associated with a movement towards empowering other bodies in the fields of national examinations, certification of teachers as well as curriculum development. When it was originally founded, CCC, for example, was strongly supported by the Senior Chief Inspector, John Brunton who wanted 'a relatively independent body giving powerful advice to the Secretary of State, (McPherson and Raab, 1988, p. 243). By the late 1980s, however, it was perceived within Scottish CCC that the Inspectorate wanted to marginalise it. Clearly there were tensions between the politics of the New Right and the older consensual order, and in the SCCC there was a view that the Inspectorate was in thrall to the Minister.

SCCC's position was further skewed with the government's 5–14 Programme where its contribution was restricted. The Executive Group overseeing the development was chaired by the Senior Chief Inspector and this pattern was to be repeated with the next major development, Higher Still. The problem for the Inspectorate is that it does not have the resources itself to carry out large scale national development work. However, it has access to top-sliced funding – possibly an amount greater than that allocated to SCCC – and individual inspectors can commission SCCC officers to undertake particular developments. This Inspectorate activity may have no place in SCCC's corporate plan; this is a similarly haphazard way of promoting educational innovation, as Sister Maire Gallagher observed twenty years earlier. The problem bedevilling relationships between SCCC and the Inspectorate is lack of clear definition between its role and that of the Inspectorate, and SCCC is not in a position to benefit from that ambiguity.

Scottish Examination Board

Friction and harmony have both marked the relationship between SCCC and the Scottish Examination Board (SEB). In its early years, SCCC's influence was felt more in the non-certificate areas of the curriculum which left the SEB as the dominant innovatory influence in the upper school curriculum (McPherson and Raab, 1988). The Board's subject panels were a powerful force and one of the first areas of conflict between the two bodies developed from the Board's desire to create an examination in Geology. Scottish CCC resisted, with support from the Department, but the Board was adamant and the Board won.

Its position in statute contrasted with that of SCCC. When, however, Standard Grade came along with reform of curricula and assessment, both worked together and were represented on Joint Working Parties (JWPs). This arrangement, however, has been open to question.

> [JWPs] were of extraordinary ambiguity in terms of the constitution because the Examination Board and the CCC have quite different constitutions. Yet, nevertheless, they were able to work together as bodies beyond the fringe and one never really knew what the products of the working parties represented. (McPherson in Ross, 1993, p. 231)

What is usually claimed for the device is that it worked in practice, but ambiguity surrounding areas of interest led to tensions again, this time during the revision of Higher Grade subjects. The Examination Board argued, for example, that revised Higher Maths would require 160 hours of study; SCCC was firm, in terms of its curriculum guidance, it should be 120 hours. A compromise was reached with perhaps SCCC claiming more of the field.

The demise of SCCC's substructure in the late 1980s posed a problem for joint working arrangements. Loss of the central committee structure put SCCC in a difficult position in relation to the Examination Board which had its subject panel system and access to a wide range of teachers. Informally, SCCC might ask the Board for suggestions regarding suitable personnel who would be its representatives – such were the circumstances of a curriculum body without development groups.

INNOVATION IN THE CLASSROOM

At a time when Scottish CCC had a developmental substructure, Gethins, Morgan, Ozga and Woolfe (Open University, 1979), comparing its working with the Schools Council in England, judged that the former did not encourage curricular innovation from the grass roots: 'There is very little of the lengthy process of experimental trial, feedback and evaluation which characterises the Schools Council approach to curriculum development' (p. 25). The Scottish CCC operated through working parties, issued reports which carried the authority of the Department and which teachers tended to accept. However, this method, Gethins et al. found, could be surprisingly speedy and efficient, for example, in the introduction of modern mathematics.

The dominant model for innovation in Scottish schools has been, and continues to be, external leadership by the centre. Summing up science curriculum development in Scotland – which is applicable generally – Bryce (1994) described it as being characterised by: 'Consultation and practice-driven consensus, efficiently maintained and cautiously (and somewhat conservatively) steered by relatively few, highly visible, key individuals.' This has certain strengths: change can be effectively brought about in a controlled way; conformity across the country can be anticipated; the approach is unquestioned; other stake holders, when the direction is set, tend to bend their shoulders to the wheel. However, the model has weaknesses: undue reliance on the centre; lack of teacher commitment to the development; failure to adopt a system-wide culture of change.

In the production of curricular materials for schools, Scottish CCC's position is unrivalled: market research shows that around 96 per cent of schools order materials from SCCC and during 1997, 52,000 resources were ordered from SCCC. An evaluation by a market research company into teachers' views on SCCC's mechanism for marketing centrally-produced materials found that 95 per cent of primary schools and 98 per cent of secondary schools examined the materials and the overall expression of satisfaction with SCCC's arrangements for the materials was 95 per cent.

Large scale development with which SCCC has been associated over the past twenty years has amounted to one government programme succeeding another. Any suggestion (for example, contained in the Dunning Report) that there should be a coordinating body promoting a whole system development is a threat to SOEID. Dependency tends to be the permanent state of the other partners in the process and there is fragmentation. Sister Maire Gallagher noted compartmentalising in earlier years, with Scottish CCC responsible for curriculum development and an SED committee sponsoring staff development.

> The remit of the CCC excluded it from in-service and staff development. The national committee drew up the priorities for staff development, took its advice from CCC but, literally, that was a poor exercise. (Gallagher in Ross, 1993, p. 194)

The situation was no different in the late 1980s. There existed for a few years a national staff development body – the Scottish Committee on Staff Development in Education (SCOSDE) set up by the SOED – and it had no formal links with SCCC. As recently as 1990 the SCCC did not see itself having a prime role in school and teacher development.

This has changed. Aspects of the Values, Learning and Teaching Programme have implications for school development. While echoes of *The Heart of the Matter* (1995) can be heard in, for example, the Higher Still development, explicit endorsement by SOEID/HMI of SCCC's growing contribution to ideas on school climate and ethos eludes the interested observer. A defence might be that too many innovations cannot be supported. However, this raises the question, whose agenda for change is the system designed to serve?

ISSUES AND CONCERNS

Advising policymakers

According to the Robertson Review (1993), SCCC is too distant from ministers. The truth may be that distance is not the problem, but lack of access. Administrators are the door keepers. And it is the administrators' autonomy due to their close contact with state power that dominates. The Scottish Office reviewer puts it bluntly: government policies have to be implemented; officials at the centre are required to give a national lead; SCCC's role is to advise on implementation. Advising on policy formulation, as a key requirement, is played down.

This raises a number of questions. Has the requirement for a consultative body offering advice to the Secretary of State been superseded by changes in educational policy making in the UK? Politicians, over the last decade, are much more involved in decisions on the curriculum; intended change is often signalled through political party manifestos. Is it not sufficient for administrators and professionals within the executive of government to advise ministers? This appears to be one of the conclusions of central administrators.

An alternative way for advising policy makers that may be suggested is to reconstitute the Advisory Council mechanism, for which statutory provision has existed since early in the twentieth century. Such a departure would take the wheel full cycle to the debate in the SED in the 1960s concerning the setting up of the CCC. The Department, at that time, did not want an Advisory Council with a prominent educationist as chairperson and run the risk of its providing advice which the Secretary of State would not accept. Such had been the result of the last Advisory Council on secondary education in 1947. Perhaps, however, the political climate is maturing to the point where such a scenario is unembarrassing. Constitutional changes in Scotland will require that some existing structures be re-thought.

Scotland's parliament and the implications for SCCC

Bringing policy making closer to elected representatives has been one of the arguments put forward for a Scottish Parliament. And one of the functions of that parliament will be responsibility for education. More scrutiny by politicians will be inevitable and there will be more opportunity for legislation. However, this need not mean that the curriculum has to be legislated upon: the Scottish framework for curricular design is claimed to rest on consensus and breaking with this – myth or truism – may not be deemed necessary. It is too soon to say what mechanisms may come about in the parliament: a Standing Committee on education may be set up. But whatever arrangements come into being, there will be closer interaction between politicians and officials; the autonomy of bureaucrats will be restricted.

Such a consequence brings with it the question whether there will be a requirement for SCCC in its present form. Some will say no: there will be an Inspectorate of Schools whose functions include advice to ministers; there could well be a Standing Committee of Members of the Scottish Parliament (MSPs); a third advisory body would surely be supernumerary. Others will say that the same basic issues in a democracy will still apply: it is insufficient to have only a professional elite close to the heart of power advising politicians; the major stake holders in the education sytem should be involved.

In any event, if there is to be a Scottish CCC, or successor body, its role will have to be clearly defined. Will it be a surrogate for the service – as it has been described in the past – or will it have a wider constituency? Openness and accountability have also been associated with the arguments for more devolved power. Invitation to join a consultative body may be scrutinised by MSPs; parliament may invite the main interest groups to nominate representatives.

Review and development

SCCC's review, advice and development role is clearly an issue. It is argued by SCCC that without involvement in development its advice lacks credibility. As has been said earlier, the loss of its central committee structure put it at a disadvantage in relation to the Examination Board with regard to joint working. An argument for the loss of this function relates to an old dilemma for civil servants throughout history: the perceived problem of an official's (here an organisation's) advice to the 'prince' having been rejected, the undertaking of an alternative course of action becomes the duty of that same adviser. Civil servants and HMI have no difficulty in rationalising the situation; why not a body of (mainly) professionals?

The anomaly of the Higher Still Development in SCCC – a state within a state – is cited as reason for removing SCCC's development role. But, on the other hand, some concerns have been voiced within the profession that the curriculum is too important for a body such as SCCC to be an NDPB and thus open to manipulation by SOEID. Relocating SCCC's development role to another group or to the education authorities would be possible. Re-allocating SCCC's development budget, for example, to the education authorities to undertake developments, of national rather than local significance, could have the effect of strengthening their development capacity – much depleted with the loss of advisory services since local government reorganisation in 1996. Alternatively, another group or individuals could be commissioned to undertake development work. The problem is that each of those options would have the effect of strengthening the centre, and in particular the Inspectorate, through its influence in stipulating the specification for development. And that raises the whole issue of the way innovation and implementation come about in the Scottish system.

The management of innovation

A report of an international comparison of innovative school systems published by the Carl Bertelsmann Foundation, Gütersloh (1996) was based on a scrutiny of seven educational systems including that of Scotland. One of the seven, the Canadian province of Ontario, found particular favour with an international panel of experts. The essential features of this sytem were the extent of devolved power to subordinate authorities combined with a central system for constant feed-back on the results of reform. The system was also characterised by an advanced degree of reform integration.

This can not be claimed of the Scottish system which, by contrast, is characterised by fragmentation. Curriculum development for national initiatives is led centrally by HMI. Staff development, though, now tends to be the responsibility of the education authorities and yet school development is influenced both by the local level through the setting of strategic targets and development plans, and centrally, by the promotion of school development planning and the creation of indicators for school self-evaluation.

What is sometimes said of the Scottish system is that it has a high degree of cooperation between the centre, the local level and the different agencies. This cooperation, however, confirms the leadership role of the centre and reinforces the dependency of the other parts of the system. Whether this arrangement and mind set encourage a flexible and adaptable learning system is doubtful.

Both education systems whose curriculum bodies were founded about the same time as CCC, and which are referred to in the introduction to this chapter have changed radically. The Schools Council for England and Wales has been disbanded due to the withdrawal of government funding; the curriculum is legislated on. The New Zealand educational system has cut out an echelon of governance: ten education district boards have been replaced by a central ministry which relates directly to school boards. But, as Scottish education takes stock for the future, greater specification from the centre should not be at the expense of a body such as SCCC interacting with all parts of the learning system.

REFERENCES

Boyd, B. (1994) The management of curriculum development: the 5–14 programme, in W. M. Humes and M. L. MacKenzie (eds), *The Management of Educational Policy: Scottish Perspectives*, pp. 17–30, Harlow: Longman.

Bryce, T. G. K. (1994) *Curriculum Development in Science in Scotland*, paper presented to a Consortium of Institutions for Development and Research in Education in Europe (CIDREE) conference in Edinburgh.

Gatherer, W. A. (1989) *Curriculum Development in Scotland*, Edinburgh: Scottish Academic Press.

Humes, W. H. (1986) *The Leadership Class in Scottish Education*, Edinburgh: John Donald.

McPherson, A. and C. D. Raab (1988) *Governing Education: A Sociology of Policy Since 1945*, Edinburgh: Edinburgh University Press.

Ross, H. (1993) *A Giant's Strength: An Analysis of the Management of Staff Development in Scottish Secondary Education 1975–1990*, PhD thesis, University of Aberdeen, unpublished.

18

The Scottish Council for Educational Technology (SCET)

Nigel Paine

A BRIEF HISTORY OF SCET

SCET's origins, in educational technology terms, disappear into the mists of pre-war history. The organisation started life as a film library dedicated to bringing what was then a new medium into Scottish schools: 16mm film. The Scottish Central Film Library in the 1940s, was the largest educational film library in Europe loaning, at its peak, 4,000 films of various shapes and sizes per week to schools the length and breadth of Scotland. For some children, in the remoter parts of Scotland, this would have been the first time they had ever seen a film. Its modern history, however, begins in 1974 when, following a government report, SCET was established out of a merger of the Scottish Film Council (which then became one of its divisions) and the Scottish Centre for Educational Technology and incorporated as a company Limited by Guarantee, and registered in Scotland. Later, it was recognised by the Inland Revenue as a charity. Its job has always been to help the education system use media effectively in the classroom or lecture theatre. What has changed is the particular selection of media that SCET focuses upon.

In the years since 1974, SCET has moved from film strip and acetate, to video and computer software. SCET is a learning organisation before it is a technology organisation and has always employed a unique mix of former teachers and lecturers, combined with those with particular technical and creative expertise.

In the late 1970s, SCET absorbed the Scottish Computer Administration and Management Programme (SCAMP) from Moray House College of Education. In 1980, the Scottish Micro-electronics Development Programme (an initiative to introduce Scottish schools to computers) was sited in SCET and later absorbed into its mainstream in the mid 1980s. In February 1998 MEDC (Micro-electronics Development Centre) based at the University of Paisley was absorbed into SCET thus extending its reach into the further education Sector.

CONSTITUTION AND REMIT

SCET's role, as described by its Memorandum and Articles, is broadly defined. SCET's objects are listed as:

- be expert in the application of educational technology to learning and be recognised as a source of expertise,
- be a source of information and advice on educational technology to central and local government,
- apply technology to the solution of educational problems related to curriculum, management information systems, provision of information, facilitating communication and exchange of information, and staff development and training,
- identify the needs of its customers and clients and be responsive to them,
- provide customer training and service, as necessary, to support effective implementation of projects and approaches which involve the application of educational technology, and
- operate prudently and efficiently to ensure optimum use of scarce resources.

SCET is run by its Board of Directors who are designated Governors. The Memorandum and Articles allow a maximum of thirteen Board Members, plus a Chairman, but currently there are less than this number. The Board was once an unwieldy council, of over thirty members representing every shade of Scottish education, but unable to take effective decisions and steer the executive. At the beginning of the 1980s it was cut back to approximately its current shape and size. Another difference between the council and the current Board is that those appointed now are nominated for their individual expertise rather than as nominees of organisations or institutions. The current Memorandum and Articles, incorporated within the last few years, following a SOEID review of SCET in 1992/3, allows the Scottish Office Education and Industry Department to appoint the Chairman and three further Board Members, while CoSLA can appoint one local government official or elected member. The remaining members of the Board are appointed by the Board itself. This makes SCET a slightly more autonomous animal than other similar Scottish education support organisations.

HOW SCET WORKS

SCET employs approximately ninety full-time equivalent staff. A few work as consultants, giving a few days a month to SCET, but most are full-time and based at SCET's large Victorian premises in the west end of Glasgow, a former teacher training college.

SCET's most recent turnover was £4.1 million of which £1.33 million was received in the form of grant-in-aid from the Scottish Office Education and Industry Department. The remainder was earned by SCET from the provision of services. An indication of how this breaks down gives an idea of the role and work of SCET. Approximately 15 per cent, £600,000, came from local authorities for the provision of support for their current management information systems. This is based around training, maintaining a telephone helpline, software upgrades, etc.

SCET is also the biggest provider of educational software in Scotland, having large contracts with Microsoft and CLARIS and many other educational software developers. This accounted for 12 per cent, £500,000. In addition, SCET develops its own software, and sales of SCET software accounted for £100,000. SCET also trains teachers to use technology effectively and this accounted for £100,000.

SCET participates in a number of European projects and has won contracts from a number of organisations for the provision of specific services ranging from the development of CD-ROM; consultancy reports; advice and guidance at both a strategic and tactical level. This accounted for £700,000 of income.

The final piece of the turnover jigsaw is related to the SCET building. This generates around £250,000 in rental and service income. It exceeds SCET's immediate needs and as a consequence sections are rented out to twenty-six tenants, the largest of whom is the Alliance Français, but there are numerous small video production companies and, of course, the former Scottish Film Council and its related organisations. SFC was once a division of SCET, but was floated off as a separate company Limited by Guarantee in April 1990, along with the Glasgow Film Theatre which was once a separate part of the Scottish Film Council. Many of these smaller organisations have been brought together under the banner organisation Scottish Screen to focus on encouraging and sustaining the Scottish film industry.

The SOEID grant is now virtually a Service Level Contract. The Scottish Office is 'buying' services to Scottish Education from SCET which are definable and auditable. SCET has set up Europe's largest Technology Centre which is essentially a hands on environment for teachers, lecturers and trainers with approximately 4,000 software packages and 1,500 educational CD-ROMs available for detailed study or casual browsing. This is next to the Training Suite, so forms a useful continuum from formal training to completely informal browsing with every stage in between catered for. The running of this centre accounts for a third of Scottish Office grant and other areas such as the provision of telephone advice and information; free publications into schools and briefing sessions for local authorities and the Scottish Office are financed directly from the grant.

SCET's staff of 90 (the salaries of which account for some 56 per cent of turnover) are made up of software developers (25); teachers, trainers and staff supporting use of technology in schools (15); dispatch, facilities, cleaning staff, etc. (approx. 15); our senior management (approx. 5); marketing (approx. 5); finance (5). Project Management and support staff account for approximately 20 full time equivalent staff.

As a company offering services to Scottish Education, it is a classic small to medium enterprise. What makes it unique is the nature of SCET. Fundamentally, it is a trading organisation earning its revenue by the provision of software and related services to the education sector. It lives in the twilight world between a fully independent company and a fully funded government organisation.

INFORMATION AND COMMUNICATIONS TECHNOLOGY (ICT)

SCET has the huge advantage or the permanent burden, depending on one's perspective, of working in an environment which changes far more rapidly than the education system to which it is attached. It has gone from an initial role as a unique focus for the introduction of both computer hardware and software into Scottish schools in the early 1980s to a relatively small player in a multi-million pound investment programme that comprises purchase of hardware, software and infrastructure. It has also gone from being a voice crying in the wilderness while emphasising the huge educational potential of ICT to an organisation sometimes drowned out in the shouting as government policy increasingly reflects the value system and priorities established by SCET over the last five years. This is not a reflection of SCET's extraordinary perceptiveness, but an indication of the changing educational perspective in the light of the growing information revolution.

If one focuses only on schools (and SCET's remit is far wider), there are five major issues surrounding the development of information and communications technology:

1. Ensuring that schools have an adequate access to contemporary computing power, i.e. with multimedia and Internet capability.
2. Ensuring that the computing resource is networked internally around the school and externally into the Internet.
3. That schools invest in the right software to run on those machines.
4. That once established, staff are adequately trained to use that technology effectively across the curriculum.
5. That its overall support and management is accounted for.

Scotland is now moving into an era where the government is prepared to invest new money into the provision of technology in schools and is making pledges to get schools Internet connected by the early part of the next century. There is clearly some kind of role for an organisation which has had these kinds of issues at its heart for a number of years but what that role is, is not clear as government not only defines government policy but operationalises it internally. One could also argue that SCET's trading position makes it difficult for the government to 'intercept' current SCET activity without having to pay for that access.

The danger in the headlong run to multiply the impact of technology in schools is that SCET's role will become increasingly ambiguous and its message, and the overall technology message, will become diluted. These are bigger issues for later in the chapter.

THE ADVANTAGES OF INFORMATION AND COMMUNICATIONS TECHNOLOGY (ICT) IN SCHOOLS

What educational or other benefits will accrue from greater exposure to ICT, for a pupil currently in either a primary or secondary school, during his or her school career?

If it is managed well, the pupil will be working increasingly in an environment which is information-rich and delivered through multimedia. This means that he or she will have access to more information than was previously available, in a more immediate and colourful way. It will encourage the pupil to analyse that information, to make sense of it, and to interpret it, and it will also give him or her a number of skills in searching and gathering relevant information from disparate sources.

The pupil will be able to use very simple technologies such as e-mail to contact other pupils, perhaps working on similar projects in different schools within Scotland or perhaps abroad. If he or she is learning a language, then communication will be possible in that language to achieve a sense of the reality and immediacy of multilingual societies. The pupil will also have access to networks of experts that would not have been contactable using other communication means. These experts could be all over the world.

WHAT DOES SCET DO?

In addition to developing its own hard coded software, SCET develops multimedia product using third party authoring packages such a Macromedia Director or Apple Media Tool. These products are distributed on CD-ROM and are either self-generated or commissioned by outsiders. McGraw-Hill, the publishers, for example, commissioned a complex multimedia CD-ROM for Business Studies students which took over a year to develop and required real ingenuity and technical expertise on SCET's part to fulfil the very specific demands of the customer.

SCET is also an expert electronic publisher in its own right, specialising in the education and training arena, with commissions to produce Scottish Qualifications Authority (SQA) and Higher Still Development Unit information on CD-ROM, as well as working with the Scottish Media Group to make the *Herald* newspaper available on CD-ROM. To do this, SCET developed its own indexing software – SCETDEX – and has developed extensive expertise in Adobe Acrobat (a software package which allows common format files to be issued and searched regardless of the software package that created them).

SCET has also developed a unique technique of building materials in Hyper Text Markup Language (HTML) and releasing them on a CD so that they can be read through a web browser without having to connect to the Internet. This is a cost effective means of development, is multi-platform, i.e. Macintosh and Windows, and allows relatively simple incorporation of animation, sound, video and other media.

The innovative Technology Centre is the largest and best regarded in Europe and is the ideal showroom for our products and expertise. Equally the Technology Centre hosts an increasingly heavily utilised telephone, fax and e-mail query service for all aspects of technology and education. In addition, its software catalogue offers over a thousand products sourced from all over the world. SCET is, therefore, a service company dealing with hundreds of customers a week from a strategic level on the one hand, to offering simple advice on software selection and purchase on the other.

TENSIONS: LEADING EDGE VERSUS TRAILING EDGE

SCET has to understand and interpret current technology developments which occur at a significant rate. It needs staff who are up to speed on critical new technologies such as those that drove the Internet. At the same time, it has to offer advice and guidance at a very basic level and understand the reality of both the knowledge, skill and equipment position currently in education. This can result in significant tensions concerning SCET's priorities.

Does SCET develop software that only runs on more recent high end computers, but which has extraordinary functionality, or does SCET develop for the lowest common denominator and sacrifice functionality? Does SCET train staff to support what exists, or learn about what is coming into being? Does SCET jump on board a new technology before it is proven with the risk that its endeavours will be wasted if the technology ultimately fails in the marketplace?

COMMERCIAL VERSUS PUBLIC SECTOR

It is very hard to charge economic rates to schools with low budgets on the one hand and expectation that things come free on the other. In the relatively small Scottish market, it is also difficult to cost expensive product development at a rate that will give any kind of reasonable return. Yet to operate uneconomically, spells financial disaster for the organisation. To attempt to get a fair return on all investment will lead to a lack of uptake on goods and services and the same kind of financial disaster.

NEUTRAL ADVICE VERSUS SELLING PRODUCTS

SCET has always been committed to supplying advice and guidance that is, as far as we can make it, balanced and neutral. SCET has never pushed people towards something that it sold if that were not in the best interests of the customer. It has never clamoured to take on training or consultancy which it was not competent to undertake. However, there is a pressure to focus on income at all times. The general perception is that SCET is an honest broker and that is a very important accolade and one that is significant for everyone who works in the organisation. There is, however, a thin line between what is ethically desirable for SCET's reputation and what is financially desirable for SCET's survival.

Schools have spent considerable time in SCET evaluating a whole range of products and have then been persuaded by slick salesmen actually to spend their money elsewhere. This is perfectly within their rights, but ultimately it is clearly not a tenable for the long term.

MAKING A DIFFERENCE

To maximise its impact on the education sector, SCET has to do things on a large scale. At its November 1996 conference, SCET pledged to make 5,000 teachers Internet-ready by the end of 1997. In spite of the fact that over 1,200 teachers had gone through its Internet training programme, largely in SCET, the only way to make a substantial impact on the entire teaching profession was to develop something that was exciting, multimedia, and dispatch it to schools. The result was that over 6,000 teachers benefited from that staff development programme. With only limited sponsorship, however, the resulting investment of SCET's own resources was high, but the impact great. There is inevitable tension between doing what is right in the circumstances and consequently making the greatest impact or being cautious in allocating resources so that endeavours are kept, as far as possible, within budget and with minimal impact.

RELATIONSHIPS WITH OTHER BODIES

SCET contrasts strongly with NCET, the National Council for Educational Technology, based in Coventry. NCET is a fully-funded government agency whose role is to implement government policy. NCET was reconstituted as BECTA (British Education and Communications Technology Agency) in January 1998 and will, as a consequence, move closer to the Department for Education and Employment (DfEE). It has the strength and security of that closer relationship with central government and guaranteed income. It has, arguably, the weakness of being far more removed from the needs, values and aspirations of classroom teachers. As an organisation, it is able to invest much more heavily in research, evaluation and general guidance in the field of ICT in education. Its publications are widely respected and, for the most part, distributed free. The route chosen for it is very different from SCET, but no less valid. In many ways, the two organisations represent contrasting approaches at central government level and there is no reason why the two cannot co-exist.

More controversial is the potentially uneasy relationship between what can be called the support organisations beginning with 'S' in Scotland. As technology becomes a bigger and bigger issue, everybody wants to be a technology organisation. In some ways the Scottish Office let hares loose and is now, with a series of reviews timetabled, attempting to rationalise. Just as in England and Wales where a number of organisations had come together, such as the curriculum, assessment and vocational training authorities, it is likely that a similar series of mergers or close alliances will occur in Scotland. How this will be handled and what the outcomes will be, are unpredictable.

It is also unclear whether the SCET model of substantial self support in the marketplace is workable in the long-term if it is competing with much bigger, more influential bodies tied more closely to government policy and finance. Interestingly enough, at a recent meeting in Denmark, a senior official from the Danish Ministry of Education explained that the government had rejected the concept of hybrid organisations working with government funding on the one hand, but expected to operate commercially on the other. She felt this had never worked well as the government was resentful of the fact that the organisation looked elsewhere for much of its direction but at the same time was not able to compete effectively in the commercial marketplace. She was very impressed by the position that SCET has reached (with approximately 30 per cent turnover attached to government grants) and was interested in the practicalities of how this worked out on a day to day basis.

TECHNOLOGICAL INNOVATION

In many ways, it is up to the people who run SCET to ensure that it keeps pace with technological innovation. SCET, like many other companies around the world, had to adjust to the huge impact the Internet was beginning to make on many aspects of work, leisure and education. It invested heavily to gain Internet expertise; bought a permanent leased line to the Internet; set up its own web site and began implementing web technologies.

It is conceivable that it could have misjudged that situation and been left behind in that technological advance. The fact that SCET was an early adopter has meant that its viewpoint is based on practice as well as theory, and its understanding of fundamental web technologies has meant that it can train others.

SCET is always investigating new software development environments. In a competitive and rapidly changing field it is important to pursue novel opportunities as they arise. As the industry develops new products, SCET has to decide which products will allow the development of more exciting educational software. Recently, SCET has investigated Java, Lingo and Pearl, as well as core Microsoft technologies. If SCET makes an error of judgement about which platform to invest in, there can be considerable wasted effort. Conversely, a timely judgement to move ahead can give important commercial, techno-logical and educational advantages. Any decision about whether to move in a particular direction is initially taken by senior staff working with the development teams and this is then endorsed by the Board.

Likewise, SCET decided to produce software for a low-cost laptop computer called the Apple eMate 300 because it saw its huge potential in education. It took advice and discussed the issues at Board level but the senior staff made the final decision. They were convinced that the product would be a success despite the fact that, when development started, the product existed only as a prototype. Since its launch it has performed strongly both in the US and the UK. The quality of the software produced and the fact it was ready at launch encouraged Apple to bundle the software with every product sold. This in turn meant that SCET's software for the eMate sold well, but in early March 1998, only months into the software cycle, Apple decided to move the eMate from its Newton antecedents to a Mac Operating system product making SCET's software investment obsolete. In some areas, therefore, SCET chooses its own destiny and is at the mercy of market conditions and changes which can impact immediately and painfully on its strategy. The working relationship established with Apple's headquarters in Cupertino during the development phase – unique in a non-US based developer – may still stand us in good stead for the future.

The advantage of being able to use its own resources to invest in its own future, is that it can advise others – central and local government – on contemporary developments in ICT and give a view which may be accepted or rejected. In these circumstances it is acting as a totally independent player.

On the other hand, there are areas where government policy drives innovation. The Scottish Office established a Superhighways Task Force in November 1996 and in effect operationalised central government activity. This is unusual for the Civil Service and illustrates the strategic importance of technology and the desire directly to influence its impact in the field.

SCET's relationship with the task force is essentially as a contractor being asked to carry out a range of predefined projects. It has been invited to comment on government policy such as the proposed National Grid for Learning and bid to implement the Scottish Virtual Teachers' Centre. However, SCET has clearly not been empowered to drive these initiatives forward. Its influential Cyberschools Project, putting training material into every school in Scotland, was its idea alone and the full responsibility for development, implementation and paying for this rested with SCET.

CURRENT PRIORITIES AND FUTURE TARGETS

SCET is undergoing structural change at the current time. Its product portfolio is altering and its relationship with the various sectors of education has changed considerably in the last two years. Its relationship with the Scottish Office is also very much under review. Out of this will emerge a new SCET which will be:

- much more autonomous. The NDPB status that SCET still carries will probably be dropped.
- focused more equally on the education sectors it serves, i.e. schools, post-school and training. Currently it is skewed towards schools.
- resourced with a new generation of senior managers driving those areas and generating enough revenue to make SCET stable and profitable.
- based around a completely new approach to software development, keeping the Council ahead of the game to allow more rapid and more design led software.
- backed up by an efficient customer sales and support department.
- generating a more global perspective with the organisation earning as much as 10 per cent of its revenue from overseas sales and activity.

It is unlikely that the staff in SCET will increase dramatically. It has always fluctuated around 100, but with the merger with the Micro-Electronics Development Centre (MEDC) and the absorption of twenty-two key staff from that organisation and new posts in SCET, the new energy generated will propel SCET from a turnover of £4.1 million in 1996/97 to £5 million in 1998/99. With government support unlikely to increase, this means that the SOEID element will decline to less than 20 per cent of turnover. At that point, SCET is surely in charge of its own destiny?

It launched its corporate plan for the year 1997/8 with the title Making a Difference and, in essence, the organisation will be judged by the impact it has both at the grass roots level, as well as strategically. It has competitors looking closely at every aspect of SCET's work and it can only survive by being fleet of foot. This, in turn, relies heavily on both the approach and the intelligence of its staff whose collective ear must be kept firmly to the ground.

SCET does not necessarily represent a model that can be replicated elsewhere. It grew in a haphazard and pragmatic way from its origins in the 1930s to embrace ICT in the 1990s. It grew in response to identified need as well as specific government policy. It deserves to flourish.

ACHIEVEMENTS AND SHORTFALLS

SCET's major achievement is to have survived the vagaries of central government funding to create a stable entity based largely on its own ability to generate income in a marketplace that generally assumed that everything SCET did should be provided free. There has been a systematic culture change whereby SCET has had to encourage its staff to see the world very differently from earlier perceptions, whilst simultaneously helping customers towards a new relationship.

The organisation in the 1980s gave away the software that it developed through a network of local authority distribution centres. It provided limited advice and information and offered a modest programme of audio/visual training. In the IT context, it began the 1980s with virtually a monopoly of software supply and expertise. Virtually no other educational software existed. By creating curriculum focused software and supplying it free, SCET built an enormous, dominant presence. By the end of that decade, it was a small player in the overall educational software market and its free software packaged in plastic bags, with photocopied notes and typed disc labels, looked cheap in comparison with what else was available and because it was free, it was often ignored.

SCET gathered vast amounts of information in catalogue form from manufacturers of audio/visual hardware which no one particularly wanted and where it had genuinely pioneered in innovative and exciting areas such as open learning, which everybody did want, no resources were allocated as all the money went elsewhere. So SCET became an expensive anachronism by the end of the 1980s. It spent its government grant largely maintaining the status quo and not reflecting customer need, demand or market context.

This came to a head when SCET began to lose money. As a trading organisation, this sapped morale, but as an organisation with no automatic access to government funds it was in severe danger of going out of business. In a sense, the catastrophic loss of £267,000 in financial year 1989/90 was the catalyst needed to jolt the company. There was a change of senior staff and the beginning of a major realignment. The key features of this were:

- Focus on producing product on time and to specific market need.
- Decision to sell software and all SCET services, apart from information and advice.
- Decision to terminate the relationship with Scotlander. This company had established a joint company with SCET – Scetlander – with exclusive rights to market SCET software firth of Scotland. SCET decided it could market SCET software world-wide better itself.
- To bring new blood into the organisation.
- To restructure around core product areas.
- To increase income wherever possible.

This process, painful in the early stages, created an organisation that listened to its customers in schools and colleges and was able to increase its turnover significantly year on year while sustaining small, but significant, cuts in grant-in-aid over the same period. Staff were turned from quasi civil servants to, in some instances, entrepreneurial individuals able to see and seize opportunities.

This has had a major impact. On the one hand, it has stabilised the organisation and given it a sense of purpose and mission and direction. On the other hand, it clouds somewhat its relationship with SOEID and puts a limit on the demands that SOEID can make of the organisation without quantifying, costing and paying for those additional demands. It also puts a limit on the activity that SCET undertakes which, although valuable to the education community is not cost effective.

The realigned SCET is still a major player in the educational software marketplace and is one of the biggest independent developers of educational software in the UK. It has extensive sales of its software in the US (between $500,000–$750,000 per year) and was selected by Apple in Cupertino to develop launch software for its brand new laptop product, the eMate 300. This was the first time Apple had gone outside the USA to commission launch products. In addition, SCET software sells in Australia and New Zealand and will soon be distributed in Italy and possibly other European countries. The revenue from this is ploughed straight back into Scottish education. It is a good deal all round. It also now means that SCET will not undertake a major software project without consulting American colleagues. SCET can make sure that it fits in Scotland, but SCET also has to nsure that it has a potential role elsewhere.

CONCLUSION

SCET has the potential to survive well into the next century. But survival is not mandatory. The challenges for the future are extensions of the pressures and challenges of the last few years. SCET has to decide how it will work with its customer base and offer the best quality and range of services. These will include the sale of software, staff development as well as advice and consultancy. It will require service level contracts to generate steady income from its main large account base (the local authorities and the further education colleges) while developing innovative software and training materials that have a life beyond Scotland. Its role, and the perception of its role by the Scottish Office, will be clear and unambiguous. In general, SCET will be perceived as an indispensable part of the education scene. It will make a difference where, ultimately, it has to count most: in the classroom or the lecture theatre; making learning more exciting, and helping build the generic skills for the twenty-first century to enable Scotland to flourish in the Information Age and the knowledge economy.

REFERENCES

Department for Education and Employment (1997) *Connecting the Learning Society: National Grid for Learning*, London: DfEE.

SCET (1997) *Annual Review*, Glasgow: SCET.

SED (1987) *Learning and Teaching in Scottish Secondary Schools: The Use of Micro-Computers*, Edinburgh: HMSO.

SOEID (1993) *Effective Learning and Teaching in Scottish Secondary Schools: Computing Studies*, Edinburgh: SOEID.

SOEID (1997) *Office Administration, Technology and Systems*, Edinburgh: SOEID.

19

The Parental Dimension in Scottish Education

Cameron Munro

The last thirty years have witnessed a remarkable transformation in the way the parental issue has been perceived. From a position best exemplified by the sign outside schools which read 'No Parents Beyond This Point', the education system has been required to develop on-going relationships with parents. The impact has been felt at all levels within the education system, but has been most evident at school level. Schools are now required to publish information for parents on school performance that was previously the exclusive domain of the professional educator and administrator.

This change has not emerged by chance. The pressures have originated from outwith the education system, driven principally by governments to promote specific social and economic aims. A feature of the period since the mid 1970s has been the degree to which politicians of both main parties have been prepared to legislate to alter the relationship between parents and the education system. Parental links are no longer a matter left to the discretion of an autonomous professional.

There remains uncertainty however, about the degree to which these changes have been no more than purely cosmetic (Vincent, 1996) and a concern that the rhetoric does not match practice. Parents now have a political voice, but usually at the invitation of the major players. Parents have proven a useful ally to promote or defend a particular cause. Governments have used parents as the guardian of standards but there has been a sting in the tale. Parental expectations about their power to change the system have increased as is evidenced by parental campaigns to save schools from closure.

PATHWAYS TO THE PRESENT

There have been a number of key landmarks which have set the style and direction of the links with parents in the last thirty years. The publication of the Plowden Report in 1967 was a a turning point in the history of home-school relationships, for it highlighted the important role of parents, identifying a link between parental attitudes and pupil attainment. The report signalled the development of a range of schemes and projects designed to involve parents in nursery and school. The related research findings which challenged the notion of intelligence as a fixed entity did more to shape the nature of these links with parents and to promote an interest in early intervention. Despite the good intentions of this approach, the theoretical bases and attitudes upon which the intervention programmes were built have been questioned. The approach compounded difficulties by defining pupils and parents as deficient and incompetent. Plowden did much to shape the relationship with parents in the next thirty years. Parental involvement is still seen as involvement in school and with the purpose of targeting those parents who need most help. The residue of this deficit model is still evident in the concerns of many teachers that they fail to see those parents whom they need to see most.

The proposals and recommendations of the Plowden Report were promoted at a time when there was a general expansion of education and an increase in public expenditure. It was the decline in the economy that resulted in a new role for the parent. The education system was the scapegoat for the country's economic failure and resulted in politicians challenging the professional autonomy of the teacher. The support of employers and parents was enlisted to ensure that the system was more effectively regulated. Many writers have marked Prime Minister Callaghan's speech at Ruskin College in October 1976 as signalling this new approach. The evidence from the election manifestos for the 1974 election suggests an earlier start, but this speech was the first time in which a Prime Minister had placed such an importance on the working of the system. Education ministers became less concerned about professional sensitivity and more prepared to use parents to pressurise the professionally led system.

A feature of the post-Ruskin era has been reduced belief in the school as an agent of social change. Schools during the early post-Plowden era were perceived as central to bringing about social change but by the mid 1980s schools were perceived as somewhat marginal, and the scarcity of resources awoke a parental interest in making demands on the system.

THE RISE OF THE PARENTOCRACY

The background to these changes was to be found in disciplines other than education. For Plowden the fields of sociology and psychology were central, but it was economics that provided the impetus for the changes in the 1980s. Milton Friedman, a prominent right wing economist, argued strongly in *Capitalism and Freedom* (1962) for a new role for government in education: 'The role of government would be limited to ensuring that the schools met minimum standards, such as the inclusion of a minimum common content in their programs, much as it now inspects restaurants to insure that they maintain minimum sanitary standards' (p. 89). This, he argued, would provide a new role for parents: 'Parents could express their views about school directly by withdrawing their children from one school and sending them to another' (p. 91). From analyses of this kind a number of key themes have emerged during the last thirty years.

Choice and Information

One feature of this period has been the way in which similar policy developments have been used for different purposes. Parental choice of school and information for parents were recommended in the Plowden Report and legislated for in the 1980s but for different reasons. The Plowden Report argued on the back of research which indicated that parental attitudes influenced pupil attainment. Choice and information were also cornerstones of the reforms in the 1980s; however they would be used to make schools more accountable and help to regulate the system with information intended to assist parents in choosing schools for their children.

In 1986, the University of Glasgow study, *Parental Choice of School in Scotland*, suggested that parental choice was often made for non-educational reasons and by parents across all social classes. The placing requests, however, were for schools within middle class catchments and this has had a considerable impact on the system. Despite the prominence given to parental choice its extent has always been rather limited. Parents have no choice over the curriculum, how it is delivered or how it is assessed. The only choice is that of venue, and in many urban areas this is not available and in rural areas not possible.

Parents have emerged from this change with new identities as clients, consumers and partners of the system, but it is questionable if they are sophisticated consumers and the political focus on school performance may have done more to generate parental anxiety than create support for the system.

The legislation has done little to provide parents with an influence in the classroom and has proven to be no guarantee that they will be welcomed in the school or be encouraged to have a role in homework etc. One reason for this has been that much of the information provided has not been accessible or relevant to many parents. This has been supported by much of the school effectiveness research which indicates that the more information parents receive, the more positive they are about the school, but that parents who receive information about classroom activities, children's progress and how to help at home, are even more supportive and more likely to talk to staff and visit the school.

Partnership

Partnership has been the key term to define the relationship parents have with the education system. The term, however, has become so overused that it has done little to assist clarity. Official documents are littered with references to partnership:

in general terms:

> If the school's links with parents are to be reviewed, a necessary condition for success is the establishment of a good working partnership. (*Effective Primary Schools*, SED 1988, para. 4.2, p. 28)

in relation to the individual child:

> In summary, parents valued teachers who involved parents as partners in their child's education. (*Teachers and Headteachers* MVA, 1989, para. 3.13, p. 9)

in relation to the PTA:

> Yet the potential for PTAs to act as stimulation-points for such a partnership is considerable. (*Scottish School Councils: Policy Making, Participation or Irrelevance?* HMSO, 1980, p. 32)

in relation to homework:

> Homework provides a way of enabling parents to see examples of the kind of work being tackled during the school day and this is important in encouraging a sense of partnership between schools and parents. (*Effective Primary Schools*, SED, 1988, para. 1.27, p. 8)

in relation to specific parents:

> And if they are to have an impact on children from disadvantaged homes, do they not have a professional obligation to take active steps to draw all parents into a partnership. (*Scottish School Councils: Policy Making, Participation or Irrelevance?*, A. Macbeth, M. MacKenzie and I. Breckenridge, 1980, p. 122)

It is often unclear what this partnership is designed to achieve and Sharp and Green in *Education and Social Control* (1975) describe it thus: 'the sort of partnership envisaged really amounts to parents helping teachers to achieve goals specified by teachers in ways specified by teachers.' The use of the term partnership has helped to highlight the importance of the relationship, but the continued use of educational jargon and the profession-led agenda has perpetuated a power imbalance that continues to place parents at a disadvantage.

Parental Involvement

The term parental involvement has also carried the mantle of overuse. It has been used most often to relate to involving parents in-school, usually in a helping supportive role. As David (1993) has pointed out, the social and demographic changes in the last twenty years have rendered this approach limited. Nevertheless, recent HMI Audit publications have continued to place a significant emphasis on this traditional role for the parent.

Standards and Quality 1992–95 (SOEID, 1996), outlined ways in which parents helped the schools directly:

- supporting school trips and visits
- organising resources
- helping with paired reading
- running art and craft sessions
- giving talks about interests and hobbies
- taking sports and clubs

The key features of this model of involvement are as follows:

- almost exclusively involves mothers
- focuses within the pre-school and early stages of primary
- targets 'safe' (non-curricular) areas of the school for parental participation
- parents fulfil a supportive, helping role

There has been concern that this approach to involving parents assumes existing levels of parental confidence and many parents who lack confidence remain unable to contribute to any school based programme.

Involving parents in school has, however, provided two benefits. First, an improvement in the general ethos of the school and second, a springboard for many parents to take a step towards developing their own skills with a view to future job hunting. This model does little to promote achievement and attendance across the school and, if parents are to be involved in these aims, then schools require to develop a range of more creative approaches. Parents are not a homogeneous group; a range of ways requires to be found to meet their diverse needs.

The model in Figure 19.1 recognises that parents can be involved with their child at home and in school and that this involvement can be 'soft' or 'hard'. Quadrants A and C offer the traditional approach. If the aim is to improve attendance and attainment, schools require to consider strategies moving into B and D.

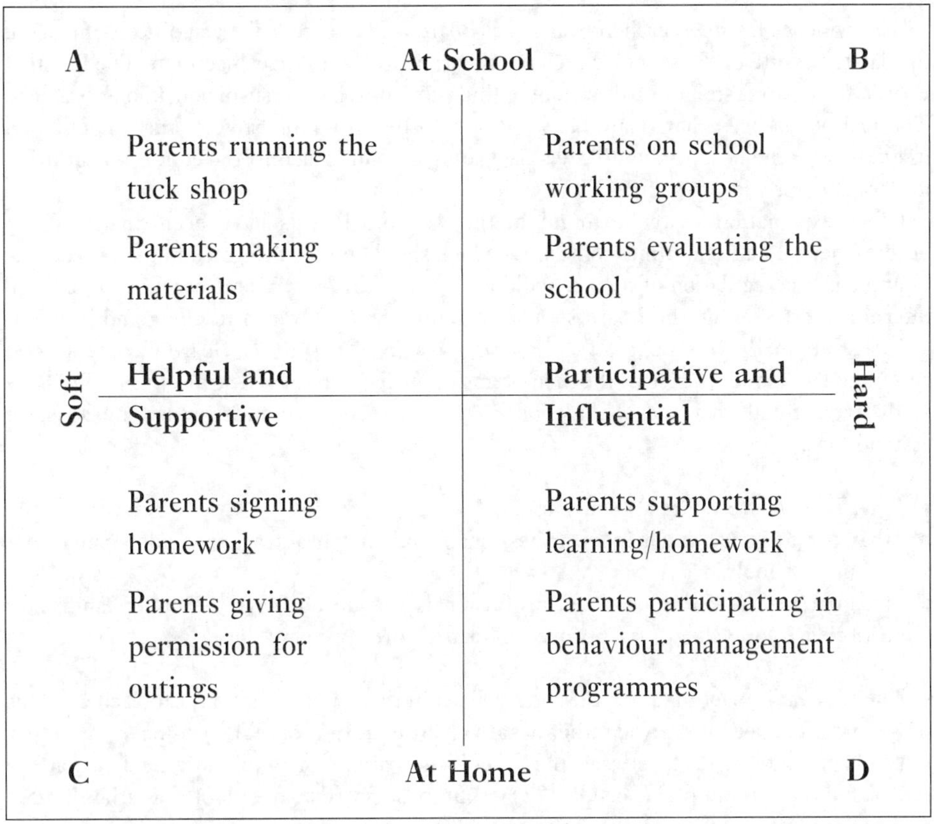

A At School		**B**

A At School B

Parents running the tuck shop	Parents on school working groups
Parents making materials	Parents evaluating the school
Helpful and Supportive	**Participative and Influential**
Parents signing homework	Parents supporting learning/homework
Parents giving permission for outings	Parents participating in behaviour management programmes

Soft ... Hard

C At Home D

Figure 19.1

Participation

The Local Government (Scotland) Act 1972 provided for the formation of School Councils with parental representation. Councils covered a large geographical area encompassing a large number of schools. Their functions were broad, and subject to the discretion of the education authority. Councils, for example, had no financial power and only in two of the twelve education authorities did they have any influence on senior staff appointments. The evidence from the major research in 1980 on the work of School Councils, *Scottish School Councils: Policy Making, Participation or Irrelevance?* by Macbeth, MacKenzie, and Breckenridge (1980) suggested that the work of Councils focused on matters that were more administrative than educational. The study found that only 8 per cent of the items discussed at meetings could be described as 'broadly educational' and less than 1 per cent concerned the curriculum. The same study also found that although parents wanted more information on what was taught in the school, the teachers seemed resistant.

Despite the widespread antagonism to Boards from within the education system, the powers outlined in the School Boards (Scotland) Act 1988 were limited. Macbeth (1990) in *School Boards: From Purpose to Practice* argued that the model chosen provided Boards with influence rather than power. Boards do have the option of asking for more powers to be delegated to them, but this has rarely happened and, despite concerns about Boards as a first stage to something else, opting-out was never a serious issue in Scotland.

The evidence from research indicates that Boards have yet to make a significant impact in the day to day life of the school. Much of this originates from their inception. The fear that Boards were a first step towards school opting-out led to a deep suspicion among teachers. The reality has been that Boards have proven to be very supportive of the school and a useful tool for the headteacher to galvanise parental opinion against the education authority in demands for more resources.

Other explanations may be found in the way the Boards have been 'managed' by headteachers. The Act outlines some areas which should not be delegated to the Board. One example is 'the regulation of the curriculum' (Section 15 (2) (c)). This has most often been interpreted as meaning the Board should have no role whatever in teaching and learning.

In a study in 1992, *Making School Boards Work* (SOEID, 1992), Board members listed accommodation and finance as the main items of business discussed at meetings. The same study highlighted that the attitude of Board members was underpinned by a set of assumptions:

- that schools are doing a good job,
- that parents trust teachers as professionals and that headteachers understand about running schools,
- that parents are not educational professionals and do not have the understanding or experience to evaluate or improve on what is already being done.

The greatest impact made by Boards has been in the appointment of headteachers. This power has often been perceived rather negatively by education staff. Boards have a statutory duty to 'promote contact between the school, the parents of pupils in attendance at the school and the community' (Section 12 (1)), but most Boards have adopted a rather limited approach to fulfilling this. Perhaps the most enduring conclusion on the work of Boards is that any suggestion for improving their effectiveness depends on the willingness of headteachers to encourage them to have a central role in the life of the school.

TEACHER ATTITUDES

Underpinning any change is the way it is perceived by teachers. In 1985, the Main Report, into teacher pay and conditions (*Cmnd 9893*) recorded an acknowledgement of the links with parents: 'All the teachers' associations acknowledged that parental liaison formed an essential part of the professional role of the teacher' (p. 65). There has been some concern about the negative impact of the legislative changes on senior managers and this was highlighted by the same report: 'The pressure on Headteachers from this source seems constantly to increase with the passage of legislation and the growing expectations and demands of parents' (p. 25, para. 2.8). However, the impact of the changes on class teachers is less clear. School effectiveness research has highlighted the important influence of attitudes. Reynolds (1991) in a study of twelve inner-city secondaries (*School effectiveness in secondary schools: Research and its policy implications*, in *School Effectiveness Research: Its Messages for School Improvement*, edited by Riddell and Brown), argued that schools could be distinguished as 'incorporative' or 'coercive'. The former are able to incorporate parents into the support of the school, but the coercive schools do not achieve this because teachers believe that parental support would not be forthcoming: 'Teachers regarded pupils as being in need of character training and control which stemmed from a perceived deficiency in their primary socialisation, a deficiency which the school attempted to make good by a form of custodialism' (p. 27).

In 1991, after the decade of the parent, the GTC published guidance on the parental issue: 'The development of relationships between teachers and parents is crucial to the success of the educational process, and the development of proper parent/teacher partnerships is to be welcomed' (p. 1). The partnership envisaged was rather limited in scope: 'Parental involvement in extra-curricular activities and school trips in co-operation with teachers is not uncommon and helps foster such partnerships' (p. 1). Teachers have safeguarded the areas for this partnership and in particular ring-fenced the curriculum as their domain. It is still assumed, for example, that parents can make the child's learning to read and write at school confusing by actively helping in the early stages. There is no research evidence that has shown this to be the case.

Sharp and Green (1975) in *Education and Social Control*, argue that teachers are happy working with the good parent. They argue, that for the relationship to be successful requires four things from parents. The parent should be:

- knowledgeable about the way the school operates,
- interested in their child's education,
- capable of cuing into the the teacher's system of relevancies, and
- able to play the role of the good parent in a way that is concordant with the teacher's definitions. (p. 198)

Hornby (1995) outlines a variety of skills teachers require to work successfully with parents. These include the important skill of listening, but it is the teacher's belief system rather than the technique which will determine the nature of the relationship.

Despite legislation specifically related to parents, the publication of national guidelines, the development of policies on parental issues by schools and education authorities, teacher attitudes continue to make the greatest impact. The view from the class teacher's desk is less attractive, with a landscape often littered with frustrations about condoned absence, non-completion of homework, complaints about bullying, demands for a Record of Needs etc. Within this context it is very difficult for class teachers to see that parents are partners and almost impossible for them to accept that parents should have a role in their child's learning.

THE TARTAN TINGE

The importance given to the parental issue has been evident on both sides of the border but with different emphasis. In Scotland there was no 'Great Debate' or William Tyndale school that would highlight the pitfalls of unchecked professional autonomy. The more centralised education system in Scotland did not lend itself to such sharp divisions. When legislation commenced in the 1980s, there was widespread concern about the 'Anglicisation' of Scottish education and a suspicion that Scotland was a guinea pig for changes to be introduced in England. This was an understandable view. National Testing was introduced in Scotland in advance of England. The work of the Parents Coalition did much to galvanise parental opposition to the first proposals for national testing.

It is sometimes forgotten that parental choice was operational in Scotland well in advance of the Education Reform Act 1988 in England. This had more to do with the wording of the

Scottish legislation than any ulterior motive, and interestingly did not lead to claims of a 'Scottishisation' of the English system.

More significantly, Scotland has led the UK on the parental issue. Scotland, for example, has been well served by the writings of researchers and academics, and high profile parent projects. The influence of education authorities has proven most lasting: a significant development in Scotland has been the way in which they introduced mechanisms to involve parents in decision making at authority level. The developments within Strathclyde Region were of particular importance (SCCC, 1992). At a time when National Testing was being introduced Frank Pignatelli, the Strathclyde director, in a speech to the Scottish Parent-Teacher Council (SPTC) annual conference in November 1991, launched three initiatives that were to provide a challenge to the notion of parents as merely clients of the system. These were as follows:

1.   the formation of a parent consultation group on the curriculum,
2.   the creation of a post of Regional Development Officer (Parents),
3.   the development of Strathclyde Parent Prompts, a set of curricular materials to inform and involve parents about the 5–14 curriculum.

These initiatives were the first of their type in the UK and set a benchmark that has moved the parental issue from the project to the classroom.

The Parent Consultation Group on the Curriculum within Strathclyde region brought together four different groups of parents; those who were members of School Boards, those who were members of PTAs, those who were not members of any school body, and parents from voluntary organisations. The group of thirty parents met on a regular basis with the director of education and senior officers.

Despite the reform of local government, many education authorities continued this trend. East Ayrshire was the first of the new education authorities to appoint a parent member of the education committee with full voting powers. Other authorities such as South Lanarkshire followed a similar approach. Many other authorities have introduced an annual conference for parents, and North Lanarkshire formed a Parent Consultation Group which meets regularly with senior officers. On the national picture, the SPTC and the Scottish School Board Association (SSBA) now regularly contribute to national committees including Higher Still.

Parents are influencing policy making at school, authority and national level, but it is still unclear if this is any more than tokenism. This has highlighted concerns, usually from the professional educator, about the representativeness of those parents involved and the danger of the emergence of the super-parent. It reflects the change in the political status of the parent, but says nothing about their influence over the individual child. Despite these considerable changes there is little evidence of a willingness by politicians and administrators to move from a political to an educational partnership.

THE NEXT STEPS

Two areas are emerging as priorities as the new millenium approaches:

Parents and the curriculum

The functions of home and school have traditionally been separated and the role of the home has been focused on socialising the child. The publication of the 5–14 national guidelines opened the secret garden and made public the range of learning being undertaken in school. It also highlighted that much of this learning is already happening out of school.

Following the publication of the 5–14 guidelines, a number of developments took place in Scotland which served to highlight the role of the parent in children's learning. These developments came together at a national seminar in March 1992. The seminar Parents and the 5–14 Curriculum was organised jointly by the University of Glasgow and the SCCC. This was a significant gathering, bringing together policy makers from all areas in the education system, including parents. The seminar explored a number of the developments such as parent prompts, the Dialogue game and Class Parent meetings which highlight the parental role in the curriculum: 'In particular it was thought that the parent prompts focus the issue of partnership in learning and teaching and challenge the power of professionals to establish ownership of the curriculum' (SCCC, 1992, p. 38).

Following the conference, the SCCC developed two guides on the curriculum for parents in the primary and secondary sectors. These recognised the different learning environments through which the child was moving each day: 'The home and the school are mutually dependent learning contexts, both of which are important influences on the lives of young people' (SCCC, 1996, Foreword).

The Task force set up by the Secretary of State to report on addressing underachievement, placed an importance on the parental role in the child's learning as a means of improving achievement in schools. The report, *Improving Achievements in Scottish Schools* (SOEID, 1996), highlighted the on-going learning already happening within the home:

> Learning theory points to the need to build on prior knowledge and understanding and to draw on the whole range of the child's experience. (p. 20, para. 5.35)

> A first stage in addressing parent-school partnerships is accepting that within their own home all parents are contributing to their child's learning and that this contribution is important. (p. 20, para. 5.35)

Hannon (1995) has also argued strongly for this need to learn more about the learning in the home and distinguishes between home learning and school learning, and concludes a review of recent research on the influence of the home with this challenging notion:

> One lesson to be drawn from these, and other studies of parental involvement in primary education, is that the quality of 'teaching' provided by parents can, in important respects, surpass that provided by teachers in schools.

> One implication of all of this could be that instead of getting parents involved in children's school learning, we should be getting teachers involved in children's home learning.

The professional educator and administrator continue to remain unaware of what learning is happening in the home and how this might impact on school learning. Most often teachers never ask. By placing a value on the monopoly of school learning, a system has developed where parents attend school at times suitable to the school, to discuss an agenda set by the school.

All of the studies and reports outlined above offer an opportunity to focus on the individual parent-child relationship and not the collective political power of parents. The evidence from school effectiveness research suggests that this can bring significant results.

Fullan (1991) in the *New Meaning of Educational Change* states that, 'The closer the parent is to the education of the child, the greater the impact on child development and educational achievement.' One challenge in the new millennium will be to end this 'learning apartheid' between home and school and to focus on the ways in which the school can better coordinate the different learning environments the child is passing through each day. Talking and listening to parents will be central to this and help shape the way in which parents and teachers interact. Hannon (1995) lists a range of everyday activities which encourage children's literacy development.

Parental Responsibilities

The election of a Labour government in May 1997 has led to a greater emphasis on parental responsibilities. After courting parents, politicians are now making them aware that they have responsibilities. The policy paper *Building Scotland's Future – Labour's Compact for Scottish Education* (Scottish Labour Party, 1997) avoids the use of the term home-school contract. Instead it proposes a Compact that places the student at the centre. But it is the emphasis on parental responsibilities that is a feature of the compact: for example their commitments to homework and hard work, regular attendance, good behaviour.

In return for the commitments and guarantees given by the school in this partnership, parents will be expected to fulfil their own responsibilities, e.g. supporting the school's aims and its policies, and supporting children's homework and attendance:

> Parents will know exactly what their children are expected to achieve, the programme that is available to support them, and the progress they are making towards achieving those targets. Pupils and parents will know exactly their responsibilities. (p. 8)

The new government has followed this commitment by the publication of a discussion paper *Parents as Partners: Enhancing the Role of Parents in School Education* (SOEID, 1998). This advocates the use of home-school agreements stressing that they should 'identify both rights and responsibilities of the school, parent and pupils' (p. 20). Among the possible parental responsibilities listed are completion of homework, participation in the extra-curricular life of the school, and acknowledgment and acceptance of school rules.

The paper does not advocate a legally binding agreement but does raise the issue of how this will be enforceable. Macbeth (1989) has been a sincere advocate of the use of home-school contracts. His approach is predicated on the notion of the parent as the school's legal client. A number of schools, principally within the secondary sector, e.g. St Machar (City of Aberdeen), Chryston High (North Lanark), Earnock High (South Lanark) and Carrick Academy (South Ayrshire), have developed a voluntary home-school agreement. This has focused on targeting parents whose child is starting S1 and has been written by the school. The perceived imbalance in power in favour of the professional has prompted considerable criticism that contracts simply reify the existing power differential in home-school relations (David, 1993; and Vincent, 1996).

The Elton Report (1989), *Discipline in Schools*, also considered the use of home-school contracts and concluded 'that it would be inappropriate to borrow the contract concept from civil law' (para. 158).

The final White Paper from the Conservative administration *Raising the Standard* (SOEID, 1997, Cmnd 3542) also argued for the use of contracts within the field of exclusions and requested opinions on the value of this carrying a statutory role. The forthcoming Scottish parliament may consider ways in which parental responsibilities may be clarified in law and could seek to amend Section 30 of the Education (Scotland) Act 1980. This outlines the parental duty to provide an education. Most often this is fulfilled by the parent sending the child to school. There is no obligation on the parent participating in any other way. Politicians may consider amending this to require parents to attend an annual conference with the school. Whether it is about parental rights or duties, the experience of the last thirty years suggests that it is time for parents and teachers to listen, talk, share and understand, and the use of legislation has proven to be no guarantee of that.

SUMMARY

Educational historians will debate the reason why, in the last quarter of the twentieth century, the education system has become interested, some might say obsessed, with the parental issue. The interest has been driven principally from outwith the classroom as part of a general interest in increased regulation of the system to fit the needs of the economy. The parental genie when unleashed, however, did not produce the results expected by the Conservative government. Far from regulating the system and exposing failing schools, parents have proven to be supportive of the local school and increasingly adept at using education law to force local politicians to abandon plans for school closure.

Parental involvement is now seen as a good thing and most studies have found that parents are generally satisfied with schools. Barber (1996) in *The Learning Game: Arguments for an Education Revolution* strikes a note of caution, arguing that there is no such thing as a parental view on anything. It is still early stages in this new relationship.

Despite a range of research and exhortations from central and local government, rather sterile models of parental involvement persist, often linked to the notion of the good parent. It is encouraging that in Scotland innovative models are beginning to emerge designed to go beyond the rhetoric of partnership and in particular to build on the learning in the home.

It is questionable what would have changed had governments not placed such an importance on providing parents with a minimum amount of information. It is apparent that much of this information is not impacting on large numbers of parents, partly because of the style of presentation and also because of concerns that it is partly designed to expose specific schools, often in areas of disadvantage. Although parents would agree with professional educators about the inaccessibility of the information, there often remains a reluctance on the part of schools to share information that parents want, in particular relating to the individual child, what the child is learning in school and how parents can help.

The future will involve acknowledging that parents are more central to the child's learning and require to consider new ways of developing this relationship and in delivering information about the school and the child. The increased development of communication systems offers the opportunity for this information to be more easily accessed in settings beyond the school.

The degree to which the disaffected parent, or the parent from an ethnic minority, can have the same quality of service as other parents remains an issue to tackle and resource. At the centre of this are the attitudes of teachers, and their belief in the value of working alongside parents. This has exposed the need to consider if the present teacher contract is commensurate with this change in emphasis on parental matters.

Much of the change in the role of the parent has emerged as a consequence of a restructuring of the education system and the role of the parent will continue to be affected by structural changes. Despite the uncertainties and tensions, Scotland has a proud record of interest and commitment in the field of parental involvement.

REFERENCES

David, M. E. (1993) *Parents, Gender and Education Reform*, London: Polity Press.
Hannon, P. (1995) *Literacy, Home and School*, London: The Falmer Press.
Hornby, G. (1995) *Working with Parents of Children with Special Needs*, London: Cassell.
Macbeth, A. (1990) *Involving Parents: Effective Parent-Teacher Relations*, London: Heinemann Educational.
SCCC (1992) *Parents and the 5–14 Curriculum*, Dundee: SCCC.
Vincent, C. (1996) *Parents and Teachers: Power and Participation*, London: Falmer Press.

IV

The Historical, Cultural and Economic Context of Scottish Education

20

The History of Scottish Education, pre-1980

Robert Anderson

Scottish education has been characterised by a peculiar awareness of its own history. Since 1707 its distinctness has been a mark of national identity to be defended against assimilation with England, and its supposed superiority has been a point of national pride. Two achievements were especially notable: the early arrival of universal or near-universal literacy, and a precociously developed university system; on these was founded the 'democratic' myth of Scottish education, later expressed in the literary and popular image of the 'lad o' pairts', the boy of modest social origins from a rural or small-town background climbing the educational ladder to such professions as the ministry, schoolteaching, or the civil service. Like other national myths, this idealises reality, but has a core of truth, though most historians would agree that it represented an individualist form of meritocracy, rather than reflecting a classless society. For all the virtues of the rural parish school, the chief features of modern Scottish education were created in the few decades following the Education (Scotland) Act 1872, and as a pioneering urban and industrial country Scotland was deeply marked by the class divisions of the nineteenth century. The 1872 Act was a political and administrative landmark, but (as we shall see) the basic task of schooling the new working class had already been largely overcome, and the increased intervention of the state was not so much a reaction against the previous dominance of religion and the churches, but rather a modernised and secular form of an ideal of 'national' and public education, aimed at imposing cultural uniformity, which can be traced to the Reformation, if not before, and which is itself a strong constituent of the Scottish tradition.

THE PARISH SCHOOL AND LITERACY

The leaders of the Scottish Reformation had an unusually clear vision of the role of education in creating a godly society. The First Book of Discipline of 1560 sketched out an articulated educational structure, from parish school to university, and aimed at providing basic religious instruction and literacy in each parish. Achieving this was the work of several generations, but it is today generally agreed that by the end of the seventeenth century the network of parish schools was largely complete in the lowlands, though not in the highlands. The Act of 1696 passed by the Scottish Parliament, which was strengthened in 1803 and remained the legal basis of the parish schools until 1872, consolidated this structure. The landowners (heritors) were obliged to build a schoolhouse and to pay a salary to a schoolmaster, which was supplemented by the fees paid by parents; ministers and presbyteries were responsible for the quality of education and the testing of schoolmasters. This was a statutory system, but one run by the church and the local notables rather than the state.

Schooling did not become compulsory until 1872, and attendance in the early modern period depended partly on the perceived advantages of education (which were greater for boys than girls), and partly on the pressure of landowners, ministers, and community opinion. Attendance was clearly not universal, and recent studies of literacy have challenged the traditional optimistic picture. Houston (1985, pp. 56–62) estimates male literacy (defined as the ability to write a signature rather than a mark) at 65 per cent in the lowlands in the mid-eighteenth century, and female at no more than 25–30 per cent. This put the Scottish lowlands among the more literate areas of Europe, but was not a unique achievement. As elsewhere, literacy varied regionally (the borders and east central Scotland being the most advanced), was higher in towns than in the countryside, and was correlated with occupation and prosperity, reaching artisans, small merchants or farmers before labourers, miners, factory workers or crofters.

It is very likely that the early stages of the industrial revolution, with the accompanying phenomena of urbanisation and migration from the highlands and Ireland, worsened overall rates of literacy. But exact figures are lacking until the official registration of marriages was introduced in 1855. At that time 89% of men and 77% of women could sign the registers – compared with 70% and 59% respectively in England. But signature evidence may underestimate the basic ability to read, for writing was taught as a separate skill, with higher fees, and many children, especially girls, did not advance beyond reading. Taken as a whole, the evidence on literacy suggests that by 1800 Scottish lowland communities had made the fundamental transition to written culture. Illiteracy survived, but was stigmatised and deplored by the church and the secular authorities, and the ability to read was broad enough to support the beginnings of a tradition of working-class self-education and self-improvement.

None of this applied to the highlands, where attempts to create schools suffered from adverse economic and geographical conditions, the slow penetration of the church's basic parochial organisation, and the resistance of an oral Gaelic culture. After 1715, and even more after 1745, church and state combined to enforce loyalty and orthodoxy, and it was axiomatic that this must be through the medium of English. Parish schools were supplemented by those of the Society in Scotland for Propagating Christian Knowledge, founded in 1709, but the refusal to teach in Gaelic (except initially as an aid to learning English) created a formidable cultural barrier between family and school. Nevertheless, by the early nineteenth century conditions in the more prosperous parts of the highlands and islands were not so different from the lowlands, though usually with scantier resources, and illiteracy was being driven into its last redoubts in the western isles.

A notable feature of the parish school was its connection with the universities. Schoolmasters were expected to have some university experience, and taught enough Latin to allow boys to pass directly into university classes. This system had evolved to encourage the recruitment of ministers, and there were bursaries to give promising pupils financial support. This was the origin of the tradition of the 'lad o' pairts', and though in practice most such boys came from the middle ranks – the sons of ministers, farmers and artisans – rather than the really poor, the educational opportunities offered in the countryside made Scotland unusual.

BURGH SCHOOLS AND UNIVERSITIES

The parish school legislation did not apply in burghs. It was normal for royal burghs to maintain burgh schools, whose existence can be traced back into the middle ages. Originally these were grammar schools, teaching Latin with an eye to the universities, but town councils began to appoint additional teachers for modern and commercial subjects, and by the late eighteenth century there was a move to consolidate the various schools in an 'academy', usually housed in impressive new buildings. The expanding middle class of the towns was thus well catered for, and outside the big cities the burgh schools and academies were open to both sexes, an unusual feature at the time. But town councils had no statutory duty to provide education for the mass of the population, and most basic education in the towns was given by private teachers. Although Scotland has a strong tradition of public education, private schools once had a vital role, in rural areas as well as in the towns, being squeezed out only in the nineteenth century by competition, from churches and charitable bodies as well as the state. These schools have been underestimated as they left few traces in historical records. They ranged from the 'dame school' where a woman taught reading to young children in her own home, through the 'private adventure' school which at its best could give the same sort of education as a parish school, to expensive boarding and day schools in the cities, training boys for the university or a commercial career, or 'young ladies' in the accomplishments expected of a middle-class bride.

The vigorous state of urban education by 1800 reflected the prosperity of the age of improvement, as did the striking success of the universities, of which Scotland had five. Three were founded in the fifteenth century (St Andrews, Glasgow and King's College Aberdeen), and two after the Reformation (Edinburgh and Marischal College Aberdeen), but the Reformation did not change their fundamental character, as inward-looking institutions teaching arts and theology, whose core task was the training of the clergy. The political and religious upheavals of the seventeenth century were damaging, but after 1700 the universities embarked on a notable revival culminating in the age of the Enlightenment, when Scotland was for a time in the van of European thought. The lecture-based curriculum had a broadly philosophical approach embracing modern subjects like science and economics, and directly expressed enlightened ideals of politeness, improvement and virtue. The universities could thus offer a liberal education to the social elite, while simultaneously developing professional training, especially at Edinburgh, in law and medicine. Medical education was especially important in securing the universities' reputation and in attracting students, as was to remain the case in the nineteenth century. Socially, the fact that all the universities except St Andrews were situated in large towns kept them in touch with contemporary demands and made them accessible to the new commercial and professional classes; the sons of the aristocracy and gentry, no longer sent abroad to universities like Leyden, rubbed shoulders with a more modest and traditional contingent aiming at the ministry or schoolteaching.

THE INDUSTRIAL REVOLUTION AND MASS EDUCATION

By the end of the eighteenth century Scots were aware of the distinctive character of their educational system, and already saw it as a point of superiority over England. But it had evolved within a predominantly agrarian society, dominated by its traditional elites, and committed to religious uniformity. Industrialisation, the appearance of modern class divisions, the rise of political democracy, and the growth of religious pluralism posed formidable challenges, and required far-reaching adaptations. The working of the Scottish system had not been affected by the union of 1707, but the practical and political response to industrialisation was inevitably similar in Scotland and England, and required legislation which brought them closer together.

The problems of educating the new urban working class were first tackled around 1810, initially by philanthropists advocating the 'Lancasterian' method of monitorial instruction, but mainly by the church. Supporting schools became a standard activity for church congregations, and there were many religiously-inspired committees and societies which promoted special types of school – infant schools, schools in the highlands, schools for girls, schools for the 'ragged' children of the streets, evening schools for factory workers. These activities were coordinated locally by the church's presbyteries, and nationally by the General Assembly's influential Education Committee. But hopes of a continuing partnership between church and state were shattered by the Disruption of 1843, after which the Church of Scotland was a minority church. Shortly afterwards, in 1846, state aid to education (which had started in the 1830s with building grants, and was supervised from 1840 by a Scottish inspectorate) was reorganised to give annual grants to schools which followed the state's curricular 'Code'. The grant system encouraged the professional training of teachers through the 'pupil-teacher' system of apprenticeship, linked with the 'normal' or training colleges run by the churches. In dispensing its grants, the state did not discriminate between denominations. The new Free Church threw itself into an ambitious educational programme, while Episcopalians and Roman Catholics concentrated on providing for their own adherents. The growth of Catholic schools, especially in Glasgow and the west, was fuelled by Irish immigration, and state support was especially important because of the poverty of the Catholic community. The Catholic system also had distinctive cultural features such as teaching by religious orders, and separate boys' and girls' schools.

There thus developed a dual system: the statutory parish schools, still limited to rural parishes, and a very diverse sector of denominational and voluntary but state-aided schools. Attempts to merge the two systems and achieve a more rational use of resources preoccupied politicians for many years, but always foundered on the rocks of party-political and religious dissension. The 1872 Act was thus a considerable achievement. It created a 'state' system by giving control of most schools to an elected school board in each burgh and parish, and persuaded the presbyterian churches to hand over their schools to the boards. This contrasted with the situation in England and Wales, where the Education Act 1870 inaugurated a bitter rivalry between board and church schools, requiring further legislation in 1902 and 1944.

The 1872 Act created two new agencies which, in different forms, were to share the direction of education thereafter. The school boards gave new scope to local opinion. They were elected by a form of proportional representation, and the franchise included women if they were independent property-holders; women could also be members of the boards, and made a distinctive contribution in the larger towns. School boards lasted until the Education (Scotland) Act 1918, when they were replaced by ad hoc education authorities on a county basis; only in 1929 was education transferred to the all-purpose local authorities. The second creation of 1872 was the Scotch Education Department (SED: not renamed Scottish until 1918). From 1885 the SED was attached to the new Scottish Office, and its early secretaries Henry Craik (1885–1904) and John Struthers (1904–23) turned it into a powerful bureaucracy, giving Scotland a more centralised and uniform state system than England. The balance between central and local control was weighted from the start towards the SED, since school boards and local authorities, despite their rating powers, still depended on state grants and had to meet the conditions laid down centrally.

BEFORE AND AFTER THE EDUCATION ACT 1872

The creation of state systems of popular education was a general feature of the nineteenth century, related to broader movements of democratisation (the franchise was extended to urban workers in 1867), to the needs of a developing economy, and to the rise of the nation-state and national rivalries. Legislation reflected the desire of the state to control a vital agency of citizenship and national efficiency, as much as to promote mass literacy. In fact both school attendance and literacy were already at a high level in Scotland, as the reports of the Argyll Commission in 1867–8 revealed. The practical significance of the 1872 Act was that it established common standards and filled the gaps which the voluntary system had been unable to reach.

The first gap was between men and women. In 1870 90 per cent of bridegrooms could sign their names, but only 80 per cent of brides. The idea that girls needed a less complete schooling than boys lingered, but in the mid-nineteenth century there had been a growth of separate schools for girls, which probably helped to accelerate female literacy. It was associated with the rise of the woman teacher, and although it was well after 1872 before women outnumbered men in the profession, the training colleges offered women a significant path to independence and social mobility. After 1872 school boards usually abolished the small girls' schools, and mixed education became the norm. By 1900, when formal literacy was virtually complete, there was only one point between men (98 per cent) and women (97 per cent), and girls stayed slightly longer at school than boys (Anderson, 1995, pp. 234, 305).

A second gap was within the working class. Under the voluntary system, skilled and 'respectable' workers, who could afford to pay the standard school fee of about threepence a week, had access to schools of reasonable quality, and their children could stay long enough to master the basics, as did nearly all children in the rural lowlands. But the urban poor usually had access only to inferior schools, charging a penny a week or giving a charitable free education. In factory and mining districts, and in the big cities, child labour was a major disincentive to education. Factory legislation, as well as compulsory schooling, progressively removed this obstacle, and though school fees were not abolished until 1890, school boards offered an education of equal quality to all their constituents. The huge urban schools which remain the symbol of the Victorian era in education became part of the homogeneous working-class experience which had evolved by 1900.

A third gap was between lowlands and highlands. The Argyll report revealed the poverty and backwardness of education in the western isles, Skye and some mainland districts, though these conditions were by now untypical of the highlands as a whole. For some years highland school boards were to struggle with inadequate resources, but the problems were overcome within a generation. Part of the price was a further retreat of Gaelic. The 1872 Act has often been blamed for this, and it is true that official policy made only minor concessions to the language; but there was nothing new in this, for highland educational initiatives had always insisted on the primacy of English. It was not until after 1945 that serious efforts were made to promote bilingualism.

A fourth gap, which the 1872 Act did not remedy, was the situation of Catholic schools. Illiteracy persisted in the Catholic community, and helped make the western counties a problem area. The religious settlement of 1872 was not accepted by Catholics or Episcopalians, and they continued to receive direct state grants, which covered running costs but not capital expenditure. The Episcopalian schools stagnated and eventually withered away, but the Catholic sector expanded, from 65 schools in 1872 to 226 in 1918; about an eighth of all Scottish children were in Catholic schools. Lack of resources meant that schools were under-equipped, teachers poorly paid, and secondary education under-developed. This was increasingly felt as an injustice, and the 1918 Act transferred Roman Catholic schools to the education authorities, to be supported on the same financial basis as other schools, with safeguards for religious instruction and the denominational affiliation of teachers. Protected and promoted by the hierarchy, often in alliance with the new Labour electorate, Catholic schools soon acquired an entrenched position in the public system (see Chapter 24).

The 1872 Act made education compulsory from five to thirteen, raised to fourteen in 1883. But this was theoretical, as children could leave earlier if they had mastered the 'three Rs'. From 1901, however, fourteen was enforced as the effective leaving age, and by then the elementary curriculum included subjects like history, geography, elementary science, physical training, and some semi-vocational elements: woodwork for boys, cookery and 'domestic economy' for girls. Once every child passed through the school, governments also saw its value as an agency of social welfare: school meals and medical inspection were put on a statutory basis in 1908. The daily routines of the elementary school were not to change fundamentally thereafter until the 1960s.

THE REMODELLING OF ELITE EDUCATION

While elementary education developed on its own lines, having an essentially working-class character which contrasted with the lack of sharp social differentiation in the old parish schools, secondary schools and universities were remodelled to meet the needs of the expanding middle class for professional qualifications and examination credentials. The movement for university reform began early, and was often controversial. There were royal commissions of inquiry in 1826 and 1876, and reforming acts of parliament in 1858 and 1889, which overhauled both constitutions and curricula. In the early nineteenth century the universities had no entrance examination, and although there was a recommended curriculum, many students stayed for only a year or two, chose which lectures to attend, and took no examinations – formal graduation had become the exception. But this no longer suited the needs of the age, and the outcome of reform by the 1890s was a standardised pattern of graduation, with the arts curriculum offering a choice between three-year Ordinary and four-year Honours degrees. Specialised courses, including separate faculties of science, replaced the old MA curriculum with its compulsory Latin, Greek and philosophy. The typical age of entry rose from fifteen or sixteen, as it still was in the 1860s, to seventeen or eighteen, and free entry gave way to an entrance examination equivalent to the school Leaving Certificate introduced by the SED in 1888. These changes were only possible because secondary schools had been reformed and given an extended academic curriculum.

A 'secondary' system (the term itself appeared only in the 1860s) was constructed from disparate elements. The 1872 act transferred the burgh schools to school boards, but otherwise did little for secondary education. Resources were found instead from endowments, and in the 1870s and 1880s many older endowed schools, including the former residential 'hospitals' like George Heriot's in Edinburgh, were modernised. Further gaps were filled by 'higher grade' schools, founded by school boards as extensions of elementary schools, especially in Glasgow. In 1892 the first state grants for secondary education appeared (ten years earlier than in England), and were used to build up schools in smaller towns as well as to strengthen existing ones. The result was that although schools differed in prestige and legal status, they formed an effective national network able to prepare both for the universities and for business careers. The Argyll commission in the 1860s had identified 59 public secondary schools with 14,879 pupils. By 1912 there were 249, with 38,312 pupils (19,611 boys and 18,701 girls). Of these 143 gave a full five-year course, and 106 a three-year or 'intermediate' one; 171 of the schools charged no fees (R. D. Anderson, *Education and Opportunity in Victorian Scotland: Schools and Universities* Clarendon Press, Oxford, 1983, pp. 134, 243–6). This pattern was to change little until the 1940s.

Two points were especially significant. First, though Scotland was not a pioneer in university education for women – because of legal obstacles, their admission was delayed until 1892 – mixed secondary education became firmly established, at least outside Edinburgh, Glasgow and Aberdeen, where high schools and endowed schools remained single-sex. Middle-class parents now had as good a choice of education for their daughters as for their sons, and this was reflected in the percentage of women students at the universities, which was high by contemporary standards: 23% by 1914, rising to 34% in the 1920s, though it fell again in the 1930s to 26–7%.

Secondly, the schools served a wide social range. The road to the university now lay only through the secondary school, but analysis of the social origins of university students suggests that opportunities for mobility were not narrowed. Although Scotland had a few English-style 'public schools' like Fettes College, and some exclusive day schools like Edinburgh Academy and its equivalents in Glasgow (see Chapter 9), the Scottish middle class were generally content to use their local schools. At the other end of the social scale, accessibility was wide because many secondary schools charged no fees, and bursaries were fairly widely available. Transfer from elementary to secondary schools around the age of twelve became an accepted if still limited phenomenon. The 1918 Act required education authorities to make free secondary education available to all, though they could and did retain fee-paying in designated schools.

THE TWENTIETH CENTURY: TOWARDS AN INTEGRATED SYSTEM

By 1900, the extension of the elementary curriculum and the increasing number of children staying at school after age twelve raised the question of relations between the two sectors. The SED was now using the term 'primary' for the early stages of education, but the underlying social conception was still that true secondary education was only for an academically gifted minority, and it was official policy (formalised in 1903) to draw a sharp distinction between secondary and advanced elementary education. A 'qualifying examination' at twelve identified the exceptional talents who might climb the educational ladder (a favourite image of the time), but the majority stayed on in the primary school and took 'supplementary courses'. After leaving school, they were encouraged to attend evening 'continuation' classes, mostly vocational. The reforming mood created by the First World

War raised hopes of an end to this dualism, especially as the 1918 Act proposed raising the leaving age from fourteen to fifteen. But financial crisis suspended this provision – and also plans for compulsory continuation classes for adolescents – and the SED resisted pressures for 'secondary education for all', continuing to insist that the different types of course should be rigidly separate. Its controversial regulations of 1923 renamed the supplementary courses 'advanced divisions', but these were denied secondary status, and most had only a two-year curriculum.

In practice the inter-war years saw a blurring of the distinction between courses. In smaller towns, both types were given in 'omnibus' schools which took all older children, and elsewhere the authorities usually grouped advanced education in 'central' schools, replacing all-age schools with a redistribution at age twelve (the 'clean cut'). The Education Act 1936 proposed raising the leaving age to fifteen in 1939, and although this was postponed because of the war (until 1947) the SED finally accepted that all post-primary courses should be called secondary, divided where necessary between 'senior' (five-year) and 'junior' (three-year) schools. This system was consolidated and developed in the 1940s. Most senior secondary schools were old-established secondaries, with superior buildings, equipment and staffing, while junior secondaries were either former central schools or new foundations. All-age primary schools finally disappeared except in remote rural areas. Thus apart from places served by bilateral omnibus schools, Scotland now had a selective secondary system based on the 'twelve-plus' examination, given new scientific authority by the intelligence testing developed in the 1930s.

Secondary schools were the most dynamic sector of Scottish education between the wars: numbers rose to about 90,000 by 1939. But low birth rates and the collapse of traditional industries had a generally negative and depressing effect. Despite a few initiatives like the creation of the Scottish Council for Research in Education in 1928, official thinking remained conservative. There was, for example, no vigorous promotion of scientific and technical education, of a kind which might have helped revive the Scottish economy. The Second World War changed this, directly by underlining the importance of science and advanced education, indirectly by creating long-term social aspirations which broke the fetters of the selective system. Even for the political left, selection seemed acceptable after the war as an expression of equality of opportunity, and the more idealistic vision expressed in the 1947 report of the Scottish Advisory Council on Education was rejected by the SED. But the breaking down of the old industrial economy, with its relatively small elite and its mass working class, undermined the assumption that academic education and examination qualifications could be reserved for a quarter or a third of the population. There was also a fundamental change in the career expectations of women. Thus by the 1960s there was an increasing demand to stay on at school, and to gain qualifications which the junior secondaries were unable to offer. One response was the introduction of the Scottish Certificate of Education in 1962, with a Higher Grade which was less university-oriented than the old Leaving Certificate, and a new Ordinary Grade offering a wider range of subjects for fourth-year pupils.

These pressures paved the way for the eventual raising of the leaving age to sixteen in 1973, and more immediately for the abolition of selection in 1965, a policy which aroused some controversy at the time, but which soon achieved wide acceptance, as it failed to do in England. The pattern of mixed, six-year comprehensives was almost universal in Scotland. Difficulties arose chiefly in the cities, where it meant the end of the remaining fee-paying schools, and where residential segregation strongly influenced the character and achievement of schools. A further consequence of the policy, also concentrated in the cities, was the withdrawal of the state's direct grants to old-established endowed schools, which now passed with their middle-class clientele into the independent sector.

The organisation of secondary schooling and its relation with primary schools was the most politically sensitive issue in Scottish education for much of the twentieth century. But primary education had its own revolution after 1945. An expanding birth-rate, and the shift of the population from central districts to suburbs and new towns, required a massive programme of new building and teacher training. So did the introduction of more child-centred educational methods, and the SED's Memorandum *Primary Education in Scotland* of 1965 gave these official sanction.

Expansion was also marked at the post-secondary level. Government policy after 1945 accepted the need for more students in both traditional universities and technical colleges, and the Robbins Report of 1963 only endorsed a trend already well under way. A new university opened at Stirling, and Strathclyde and Heriot-Watt universities were created from existing advanced technical colleges. Technical colleges had their roots in the nineteenth century, and the leading ones had been financed directly by the SED as 'central institutions' since 1900. Now full-time and degree-level work was encouraged, and local technical and adult education were combined in a network of 'further education' colleges. The old teacher-training colleges, renamed colleges of education in 1958, were also encouraged to expand their remit and award degrees. By 1980, therefore, the concept of a 'tertiary' education of which traditional universities were only one part was well accepted, and it attracted more than 15 per cent of the age-group; but the general extension of university status remained in the future.

CONCLUSION

The growth of secondary and higher education since 1945 can be seen as the latest stage in a continual expansion of education, and of its place in the lives of individuals, which began in the mid-nineteenth century and shows no sign of coming to an end. At its outset most working-class children, if they attended school at all, left at ten or eleven, while middle-class children, apart from a small minority who went to the universities, left at fourteen or fifteen. By 1980, the age of leaving full-time education, though still conditioned by social class, ranged from sixteen to twenty-two or more. In responding to the problems created by the industrial revolution, Scotland was given a good start by its tradition of national education and by a cultural disposition, with religious, political and social roots, to value educational achievement. But as other countries caught up, Scotland ceased to be so exceptional, though some indicators (notably the rate of participation in higher education) remained very favourable. Many historians would argue that while the system promoted meritocracy, and allowed individual Scots to move upwards into both Scottish and British elites, the education offered to the ordinary child was less impressive. The structure of schooling which developed after 1872 reflected class divisions in Scotland much as elsewhere, and twentieth-century progress towards greater equality of opportunity, though perhaps made smoother by an idealised conception of the educational past, had still to contend with social inequalities which the formal integration of educational institutions achieved by 1980 could not itself remove.

REFERENCES

Anderson, R. D. (1995) *Education and the Scottish People, 1750–1918*, Oxford: Oxford University Press.

Gray, J., A. McPherson and D. Raffe (1983) *Reconstructions of Secondary Education: Theory, Myth and Practice since the War*, London: Routledge.

Houston, R. A. (1985) *Scottish Literacy and the Scottish Identity: Illiteracy and Society in Scotland and Northern England, 1600–1800*, Cambridge: Cambridge University Press.

Humes, W. and H. Paterson (eds) (1982) *Scottish Culture and Scottish Education, 1800–1980*, Edinburgh: John Donald.

Scotland, J. (1969) *The History of Scottish Education*, 2 vols, London: University of London Press.

Withrington, D. J. (1988), Schooling, literacy and society, in T. M. Devine and R. Mitchison (eds), *People and Society in Scotland. I. 1760–1830*, Edinburgh: John Donald.

21

The History of Scottish Education, 1980 to the Present Day

Willis Pickard

LABOUR LEGACY, TORY AGENDA

Changes of government do not affect day-to-day teaching in schools and colleges. Yet over time they make a difference. It is convenient to start the most recent story of Scottish education in 1979 when a Conservative government led by Margaret Thatcher took over from Labour. The new ministers at the Scottish Office inherited an education system in transition and arrived with their own agenda. Decisions that had to be taken because of matters in the pipeline were at least as significant as those emanating from the Conservative manifesto.

The most poisoned chalice handed to Thatcher, in her own opinion, was the Clegg Commission which was studying UK public sector pay and which in 1980 recommended rises for teachers ranging from 17 to 25 per cent. The effects of wage inflation on economic policy and political direction were dire. They were also to lay the foundations for an intensifying argument about teachers' pay and conditions which in Scotland led to the long and bitter industrial dispute from 1984 to 1986.

A second inheritance from Labour was in the secondary school curriculum. The Labour government had reached no final conclusions about the Munn and Dunning Reports of 1977. Together these had recommended new courses and examinations for all S3 and S4 pupils to replace the Ordinary Grades which had been designed for 30 per cent of the school population and which were clearly unsuitable for a large number of the pupils staying on till sixteen following the raising of the leaving age in the early seventies. The new Secretary of State, George Younger, and his education minister, Alex Fletcher, decided in 1980 to pursue the Munn and Dunning agenda. By 1982 that took final form in a paper, *A Framework for Decision*, as the Standard Grade development programme.

The two year courses were based on the belief, enshrined in the report of the committee chaired by a headteacher, Sir James Munn, that all pupils should follow a curriculum based on eight modes of learning. Following the recommendations of the committee under Joseph Dunning, then principal of Napier College, they would achieve Standard Grade qualifications – partly assessed within schools – at three levels, Credit, General or Foundation. Although five years had elapsed between the original reports and the launch of the development programme, the speed with which teachers were then expected to implement changes and the reliance placed on them to develop suitable course-work were to have some unfortunate results. The government's strategy was to retain direction of the programme, coupled with extensive involvement of practising teachers. But the extra demands fuelled the wider discontents about pay levels and conditions of service. They also gave the teachers a weapon. Because Standard Grade needed their cooperation, it could be jeopardised by a withdrawal of goodwill that fell far short of a withdrawal of labour. The two-year dispute was to postpone full implementation for virtually the remainder of the decade.

Unusually for a Scottish education minister, Fletcher won legislative time in two successive parliamentary sessions. His 1980 Education (Scotland) Act restated longstanding principles such as the duty of parents to educate their children, but it also took forward another non-partisan legacy from the previous Government. The Warnock Report of 1978 had recommended sweeping changes at UK level in the education of children with special needs. Its principles had accorded with the views of the Inspectorate in Scotland and the upshot was legislation which established rights for parents and children to education within either a special setting or a mainstream school. Early identification and assessment of need were emphasised, and for children with more pronounced difficulties a Record of Needs would be opened and regularly reviewed.

The new ministers wanted to make their own mark as well as carry forward an inheritance. In 1978 Fletcher, along with fellow MP and teacher John MacKay, later himself to be an education minister and now member of the House of Lords, had published an Opposition pamphlet, 'Scottish Education – regaining a lost reputation'. It denounced standards in schools and demanded greater accountability to and more opportunities for parents. In government this had two immediate consequences. As in England, an assisted places scheme was instituted by which children of less well off families qualified for free or subsidised places in independent schools. Secondly, Fletcher, as an Edinburgh MP, had been influenced by parents who had brought court cases, such as one involving the 'Leith Ten', to challenge the rigid school catchment areas in Labour regions. So the Education (Scotland) Act of 1981 was framed to include the so-called 'Parents' Charter'. Those who did not want their child to go to the school in their catchment area could nominate another which was obliged to take a pupil unless it could show that it was overcrowded. Since the 1980s most parents who have sought a placing request have been successful. But some schools have become oversubscribed.

Yet the charter has stood the test of time. With some amendments to protect the rights of local parents who were finding themselves excluded while outsiders crowded into a popular school, the legislation successfully married the demands of parents with the local authorities' need to retain planning through designated catchment areas. The reform had an educational purpose but a political one as well.

SPEEDY ACTION

Less well remembered than the Standard Grade development programme but at least as important was the *Action Plan* launched in 1983. It charted the way to a curriculum for 16–18 year olds not going on to higher education. In effect it was a bold plan to transform the whole of further education, and the contrast has been drawn between how quickly the FE colleges responded to the challenge while the schools dragged their heels over Standard Grade.

The *Action Plan* led to the establishment of the Scottish Vocational Educational Council

(SCOTVEC) with a completely new system of curriculum delivery, assessment and certification. For the SCOTVEC National Certificate every course had to be redesigned in the form of forty–hour modules, each of which was accompanied by detailed 'descriptors', of which there came to be many hundreds. The advantage of modularised courses lay in their flexibility. They could be used to build coherent curricula of increasing difficulty and they gave students far greater choice. Experience with these courses, which soon came to be used in schools to complement the Highers, especially for less academic pupils, would influence later thinking about how to bridge the divide between academic and vocational education.

Whereas previous governments had had to tackle overcrowding of schools and lack of qualified teachers, the 1980s saw a different challenge: a drastically reduced birth-rate leading to smaller pupil numbers and pressure to close under-used schools in the face of parental opposition. But despite the reduced numbers, there was a growing tide of youth unemployment as unskilled jobs disappeared and traditional avenues from school to work, such as apprenticeships, had to be replaced by a succession of national measures starting with the Youth Opportunities Programme, which was intended to focus on training but looked more like a stop-gap response to unemployment. When the government launched the Youth Training Scheme in 1983, the Sheffield-based Manpower Services Commission, which was charged with UK training initiatives, appeared to have more clout at the summit of government than the national education departments.

Teaching children about business and preparing them for the world of work was not new, but it received greater emphasis from a government wedded to ideas of self-help and entrepreneurship. In Scotland teachers remained suspicious of the politics behind enterprise education but cooperated in, for example, the great expansion of work placements for pupils, especially in the final year of compulsory schooling. They also welcomed opportunities themselves to observe business in action, but regretted that their interest in learning from industry and commerce was rarely matched by business appreciation of what schools were trying to achieve. The Technical and Vocational Education Initiative which offered government cash to locally devised schemes was initially regarded with suspicion by the Scottish Office Education Department, but the pool of money was irresistible. TVEI schemes were especially beneficial to schools in deprived urban areas, and teachers became adept at making bids which found a vocational and entrepreneurial slant for almost any kind of secondary school project.

A 1981 report, *Teaching and Learning in P4 and P7*, by the Inspectorate showed how traditional had remained methods of teaching and curriculum content despite innovative thinking dating back to the Primary Memorandum of 1965. Having instituted changes in the middle years of secondary, the government and its advisers in the Scottish Consultative Council on the Curriculum turned their attention to the lower secondary and its relationship to the upper primary. After a starter paper in 1980 a committee was set up two years later under the chairmanship of David Robertson, director of education in Tayside. Its attempt to pilot ideas in schools was frustrated by the teachers' dispute, but in 1986 it published *Education 10–14 in Scotland*.

This was an ambitious and widely acclaimed attempt to find a philosophy that would unify the education of the age group and counter discontinuities between the generalist approach of primary teachers and the subject specialisms of secondary. The admirers of the report did not, however, include the government. The Inspectorate published a 'costing' of implementation, which the new minister of education, Allan Stewart, found excessive. The report was buried, but the belief remained that cost was less of an obstacle than the insistence by Robertson and his colleagues that every secondary and its associated primaries be involved in translating a recommended model for learning into a detailed curriculum. That would have placed too much power in teachers' hands, and they were already holding the whole system to ransom.

THE LONGEST DISPUTE

The teachers' dispute was to alter everyone's thinking. Both sides, government and unions, had much to lose during the two years, and after it was over, each vowed for different reasons never to let disagreement become a damaging stand-off. At root from the unions' point of view, and especially that of the Educational Institute of Scotland (EIS) whose dominant position with almost 80 per cent of school teachers in membership meant it controlled the teachers' side of the direct-bargaining Scottish Joint Negotiating Committee (with the local authority employers on the other side of the table) was a belief that the pay gains of the mid-1970s had been lost. The Clegg award of 1981 may have been too much for the Prime Minister, but it clearly failed to restore the position following the earlier inquiry, by Lord Houghton, in 1974. Restoration of Houghton-levels of pay award, coupled with refusal to trade off conditions of service for money, was the rallying cry.

The strategy was to call for an independent pay review. The government repeatedly rejected the demand. By 1984 the EIS was ready for action, and a rolling programme of short strikes was set in train. In addition, work on curricular development was halted. The annual timetable of preparation for the Scottish Examination Board's Standard Grade and Highers awards was threatened, and this was to cause particular anxiety for two years. In the event the external exams went ahead and were marked as normal. Whether any pupils got poorer marks because of disrupted teaching, no one could later prove.

The EIS, backed by the smaller Scottish Secondary Teachers' Association, neither wanted nor could have afforded an all-out strike. The teachers needed outside support. They had it in principle from the local authorities, the largest of which were Labour controlled. They had to ensure parental backing as well, and too much disruption to classes would have sacrificed that sooner rather than later. So a new form of action was devised. It concentrated disruption on schools in Conservative-held seats, especially those of Government ministers. John Pollock, the wily as well as charismatic general secretary of the EIS, knew the tactic was risky. It came close to contempt of parliament. But it limited the number of days' teaching lost and largely excused schools in poorer areas (most of which did not have Conservative MPs).

The public remained convinced the teachers had a case – that they were, in the view of a joint local authority-union study, over-worked, under valued and under stress. The government could only hope that the teachers' resolve would crumble under public pressure because the Prime Minister refused to budge. She was after all in prolonged and bitter dispute with trade unionists traditionally more militant and more capable of causing national damage. But it was a sign of a changed economy that a formerly moderate white-collar profession could retain public sympathy and remain undefeated while the miners found themselves isolated and ultimately powerless.

The deadlock was not broken until March 1986. Two events prompted a change of attitude by the government and allowed the unions to call off their action. The first was that

Malcolm Rifkind had replaced George Younger as Secretary of State. Allan Stewart lost his job as minister of education, the victim of the cabinet's no-surrender policy which he had defended manfully but with no effect on public opinion. The new team of Rifkind and John MacKay as his junior convinced the Prime Minister that the dispute had to be resolved well before the next election, which took place in the spring of 1987. They were helped by a second factor – the ending of a similar dispute with teachers south of the border. Mrs Thatcher reluctantly accepted a Scottish committee of inquiry headed by Sir Peter Main, former chairman of Boots.

If *An Unlikely Anger*, the title of a journalist's contemporary account of the struggle is correct, most teachers accepted that they had won an unlikely victory and could not count on continued public patience. Six months later the Main committee proposed limits on the hours teachers were contracted to work, a new grade of senior teacher to reward those who stayed in the classroom and a simplified pay structure. There was no recommended increase to compensate for previous losses. In other words the claims about pressure of work had had a more sympathetic response than those for a pay rise. Both sides in the dispute could accept Main without loss of face.

From the dispute the unions took two important lessons. Firstly, all-out, countrywide stoppages are no longer practicable, especially because of restrictions imposed by Conservative trade union legislation. Power should be devolved from union headquarters to local associations. The council reforms of 1996, creating thirty-two education authorities out of the twelve previous ones, encouraged the EIS to a more locally based structure. Secondly, winning public support had been the key to maintaining the dispute over two years. In future, sympathy would be turned into alliance. The government learned lessons, too. It felt it had been held to ransom because too much reliance had been placed on a profession which had behaved as a militant trade union. The relaunched Standard Grade programme now relied on centrally produced materials and not those devised (latterly, not devised) at classroom level.

Meanwhile the teachers had had to adjust to another expression of consumer pressure. In 1984 a bill was introduced to ensure that no child in a state school received corporal punishment if his parents objected. Due to take effect in 1986, the legislation did little more than recognise a fait accompli. The European Court of Human Rights had ruled in the 1982 Campbell and Cosans case that the philosophical convictions of parents against the use of corporal punishment had to be respected. To avoid further legal challenges all but four of the twelve education authorities had abolished the belt by the time the government introduced its bill. Teachers who had supported corporal punishment as the best last resort accepted that times had changed. But there was widespread concern about the effectiveness of alternative sanctions, especially exclusion from school.

IDEOLOGY TAKES OVER

The election of 1987 reduced the number of Scottish Conservative MPs to ten. Among the casualties was John MacKay. Malcolm Rifkind found a new education minister in Michael Forsyth, the right-wing young MP for Stirling. Immediately Forsyth, who had trained in public relations, set out to make his mark. His gospel was a pamphlet, *Save Our Schools*, which he and other members of the Thatcherite No Turning Back group of back-bench MPs had published during the last parliament. It argued the consumerist message for education. Schools should be removed from local authority control, power should pass from professionals to parents, and vouchers should be introduced to allow parents to 'buy' education where they chose.

Despite upsetting civil servants and even the Secretary of State by his impetuosity, Forsyth got his way. His first affront to the educational establishment came with legislation to create school boards. The measure could have been uncontroversial since all four political parties had included in their election manifestos a pledge to reform existing school councils. In most parts of the country a council existed for a secondary school and its associated primaries. It therefore was not felt to belong to an individual school. Had Forsyth limited his legislation to creating a board (or council) for every school, he would have had little opposition. But he cloaked his proposals in consumerist garb, arguing the case for parents to become involved in the practice of education as well as in supporting and working with the school as part of the community. Parents soon made it clear they had no wish to interfere with teachers' professional judgements or to take over the running of a school from its headteacher. In the first elections to boards in 1989, where parents formed a majority of members, most candidates stood on a minimalist platform, tacitly or explicitly rejecting the government's philosophy.

Politically, Forsyth made a strong impression but he showed himself an immature politician because he upset potential supporters. His distrust of teachers and particularly of their unions was by now shared by government officials bruised by the two-year dispute. But he bruised them in his own way, making brusque demands which were also injudicious. He alienated parents who had been fed up with the disruption to their children's education. He appeared to be working to an English agenda, which upset Scottish sensitivities and made him a target for MPs from all three opposition parties.

The Self-Governing Schools Act of 1989 illustrated the difficulty which increasingly became one of credibility for the Conservative Party north of the border. Following English example, the Scottish Office introduced legislation to allow schools to leave local authority control if parents voted to opt out. Such schools would then be funded directly by the Scottish Office. Forsyth was enthusiastic, the Secretary of State much less so. Opposition MPs found themselves wrongfooted by Forsyth's debating skills and the legislation was always destined to pass because of the weight of English Tory MPs. But the irrelevance of the measure to Scottish conditions was clear. Only two schools were to opt out compared with many hundreds in the south of England. The statute was used most by schools trying to resist closure proposals from their local authority. Since Conservative ministers regularly mocked the inability of Labour councillors to close underused schools and the profligacy in keeping them open, it was ironical that the Secretary of State was called upon to adjudicate between parents voting to opt out and councils at last making sensible attempts to rationalise provision. He always came down against parent power.

The self-governing legislation was a monument to irrelevance. The balance of power between local authority and schools was changing for another reason. In England local management, by which financial and administrative decisions were devolved from councils to heads and lay governors, became universal by the end of the 1980s. The Scottish Office followed suit with a scheme for devolved management of schools, but not before the Labour fiefdom of Strathclyde had embarked on its own scheme for 'delegated management of resources'. Frank Pignatelli, Strathclyde's director of education, determined not to wait for an imposed Scottish Office scheme and devised one which avoided many of the problems of the one south of the border, where funding formulas proved too rigid and encouraged school governors, for example, to remove experienced teachers and replace with them cheap young ones. The Scottish Office was unable to promote devolved management as a route to greater school efficiency and accountability to parents. But espousal of devolved powers within the local authority structure undermined the case for opting out.

A MORE NATIONAL CURRICULUM

The government also turned its attention to the primary and lower secondary. In a 1987 consultation paper, *Curriculum and Assessment – a Policy for the 90s*, it argued that there was a lack of precision in what primary schools offered and that parents were puzzled. Reflecting on the messages of the discarded 10–14 report it also pointed to discontinuity between primary and secondary. The Consultative Council on the Curriculum was asked to draw up guidelines, with priority for English, mathematics and environmental studies including science. Here was an example of the Scottish Office taking a firm lead. Primary schools had had little direction about what to teach. Inspectors had not been able to assess them against an agreed programme. The question was how far the new intervention stemmed from Scottish conditions – including ministers' resentment at teachers' autonomy and the power of education authorities – and how far it reflected a UK strategy. On the one hand it was argued that Forsyth was in thrall to the forces which produced a statutory national curriculum south of the border through Education Secretary Kenneth Baker's Education Reform Bill, which passed through parliament in 1988. On the other hand there was no attempt to base the 5–14 programme (as the new curriculum came to be called) on statute or to prescribe, for example, texts suitable for seven year olds or episodes of glorious history to be studied, as Thatcher insisted in England and Wales.

The 5–14 curriculum eventually evolved in five areas – English, mathematics, environ-mental studies (including history, geography, science and technology), expressive arts (including physical education) and religious and moral education. Was the generic primary teacher expected to become a polymath? There were concerns, especially about science and technology and religious education. But many teachers welcomed a structure to their curriculum and the detailed guidance offered. The Inspectorate emphasised repeatedly in the 1990s that not all aspects were to be introduced at once. The aim was to have schools comfortable in all five areas by the millennium.

If the philosophy and content of the changes were widely accepted, the proposals for assessment were not. The curriculum was divided into five levels. Most pupils were expected to achieve level A in the first or second year of primary, level E in S1 and S2. Forsyth insisted that parents wanted an external gauge against which individual pupils' progress could be measured, but he said he was not wanting league tables of primary schools or of teacher performance. National tests would be set for pupils in P4 and P7.

The response was national resistance. An alliance to boycott the tests sprang up. Teachers defied their local authorities, though some authorities were themselves in defiant mood. Parents withdrew their children on test days. The government was powerless, caught again by unexpected consumer support for the teachers' case, which basically was that the tests would tell them nothing they did not already know about their pupils and that the curriculum would be narrowed as inevitably pupils were prepared to face the banks of test items prepared by the Scottish Examination Board.

By this time Forsyth had gone off to chair the Scottish Conservatives. Ian Lang, his successor and later the Secretary of State, was more emollient but also less committed. He realised that compliance with government wishes was impossible to ordain. Winning the

1992 election was the priority. Unexpectedly the Conservatives not only held on to power but regained modest ground in Scotland. The government, with the gentlemanly Lord James Douglas-Hamilton installed as education minister, stopped defending the indefensible. Instead of every P4 and P7 child being tested, teachers would use the tests to check on every pupil as he or she moved from one 5–14 level to the next. So there would also be tests in secondary schools, though the introduction of these proved hard to achieve since teachers were reluctant and local authorities unwilling to apply pressure.

THE STANDARDS DEBATE

In 1988 the centenary of the Highers was celebrated, but it was clear that all was not well with the benchmark of dependability in the Scottish assessment system, preferable though its breadth was to the much criticised narrowness of English A levels. With increased number of pupils staying on at school, too many found the Highers an impossible or dispiriting challenge and the alternative diet of SCOTVEC modules lacked coherence and esteem. For all candidates there was too short a period between Standard Grade and Higher exams, with cramming taking precedence over education. For able pupils the sixth year offered too little challenge: they were accepted for university entrance on the basis of Highers, with the Certificate of Sixth Year Studies not being recognised. In 1992 a government committee chaired by John Howie, a St Andrews University mathematics professor, found that although Scotland continued to compare well with England in terms of school leavers qualified for higher education, we had been overtaken by other west European countries.

The Howie committee, much impressed by the Danish model in particular, suggested a twin-track system by which pupils would opt for an academic or vocational route with a common terminus in higher education entry for those who wanted it and with opportunities for transfers along the way. Able pupils would prepare for a Scottish Baccalaureat in sixth year. Although the report was initially welcomed, its academic-vocational division was soon declared divisive. In 1994 Michael Forsyth as Secretary of State produced an alternative model known as the Higher Still development programme, which retained the Highers but added an Advanced sixth-year version to challenge the ablest and established, for slower learners, access and intermediate levels. Further education as well as schools would use the programme which would seek parity of esteem between courses derived from the SCOTVEC experience and those from an academic tradition. The Scottish Examination Board and SCOTVEC would merge.

The thrust of the programme proved acceptable to most teachers, the short time for preparation and alleged lack of resources did not. Twice the government conceded a year's delay. The second postponement was among the first acts of the Labour administration in 1997. The first Higher Still exams will now be set in 2000 with Advanced Higher a year later. A large question was not fully resolved: the universities said they would continue to regard Highers as the benchmark for entry, but it was clear that some popular faculties would expect Advanced Highers. The debate, which was important both for the future of the sixth year and for the number of pupils reaching higher education entry level was bound up with the universities' concerns about the four-year honours degree. Retaining it meant accepting pupils on the basis of Highers rather than sixth-year study. Reducing courses to three years would mean a cut in university funding.

Concern about standards extended beyond S5 and S6. Michael Forsyth believed that schools should be publicly challenged. So tables of exam performance were published, though teachers said the results showed the social composition of the school rather than the 'valued added' between S1 and S4–S6. Tables of attendance and absence, leavers' destinations and school costs were also made public. Schools were expected to prepare and make available to parents their development programmes. Schemes of self-evaluation supplemented inspectors' reports which had been made public since the 1980s. Teachers were to be appraised by their seniors, although with the aim of enhancing staff development rather than identifying the incompetent. The agents of change were to be central government, through the Inspectorate, and school managers themselves. Distrust of education authorities continued even after local government reorganisation in 1996 saw the end of the large Labour regions and the creation of thirty-two councils, none of which returned a Conservative administration in the first elections.

Fittingly, the last major reform by Forsyth introduced parental vouchers, a cause he had propounded through the No Turning Back group. Across the UK universal pre-school education for four year olds was to be achieved by offering parents a voucher which could be used in a local authority, voluntary or private establishment. In the session 1996–7 four Scottish councils piloted a scheme which was then made national from August 1997. Parents welcomed an increase in nursery places but were unimpressed by the bureaucracy attached to vouchers. Labour opposed the scheme in the 1997 election campaign and on taking office announced its abolition, but the new Scottish Office team of Donald Dewar as Secretary of State and Brian Wilson as education minister said it should run for a year until an alternative could be devised. Wilson later made clear that local authorities should have responsibility for implementing the pledge that places would be available in one setting or another for all four year olds.

The Conservatives lost all their Scottish seats in 1997. Distrust of their education policies contributed to the debacle. A sign of looming trouble was the march and rally in Edinburgh in 1996 against cuts in school funding which attracted 40,000 parents and teachers. When Labour took office, the education community breathed a sigh of relief and the atmosphere lightened, but ministers made clear that money would remain tight. An early popular initiative was extra funding for a scheme to help young primary pupils who were struggling with reading. In opposing Conservative measures, teachers and parents had expressed satisfaction with school standards which were regarded as better than those south of the border. After the 1997 election complacency was diagnosed: international comparisons showed Scots pupils trailing in mathematics and science, being outpaced even by the English. Wilson made standards his priority. The small minority of incompetent teachers had to be removed. Schools should be grouped into categories, so that in aiming for better performance, those in privileged areas would not rest on their laurels while those with social problems were given appropriate targets.

Over twenty years the balance of power that influences classroom practice had changed. The role of central government and of parents had increased, that of local government and the teacher unions diminished. Further education shows more starkly than schools the shifting of power. In 1993 as a result of the Further and Higher Education Act, which also allowed central institutions to seek university status, the colleges of FE were removed from their local authorities and given a form of self-government. Their boards were expected to look for profit-making courses. Funding now came from the Scottish Office, which strove to find formulas that would reward enterprise and student success. The needs of the consumer, that is the student, reigned over those of the provider. National pay and conditions were challenged. The unions found themselves confronting individual boards and college managers rather than a nationally uniform structure.

Pupils and students are barely aware of how education is structured. For them as the century ended, the important issues were, as always, about teaching and learning. Scottish education, where traditions of imbibing dollops of instruction had died hard, showed continuing tension between advocacy of mixed ability classes and individualised learning on the one hand, and a reassertion of grouping pupils by ability and whole-class teaching on the other. But perhaps such debates belonged to the past. Sophisticated applications of information technology were widely available and becoming increasingly so, an area where Scotland remained in the vanguard. Learning how to learn and developing core skills – team working, for example, as well as literacy and numeracy – had moved centre-stage. Unforseeable changes more fundamental than those recently experienced in the curriculum and management of schools and colleges probably lie ahead.

REFERENCES

Clark, M. M. and P. Munn (eds) (1997) *Education in Scotland: Policy and Practice from Pre-School to Secondary*, London: Routledge.

Roger A. and D. Hartley (eds) (1990) *Curriculum and Assessment in Scotland: A Policy for the 90s*, Edinburgh: Scottish Academic Press.

Ross D. (1986) *An Unlikely Anger*, Edinburgh: Mainstream.

SED (1983) *16–18s in Scotland: An Action Plan*, Edinburgh: SED.

SOED (1992) *Upper Secondary Education in Scotland (Howie report)*, Edinburgh: HMSO.

SOED (1994) *Higher Still: Opportunity for All*, Edinburgh: HMSO.

22

Culture, Nationalism and Scottish Education: Homogeneity and Diversity

David McCrone

At the core of this chapter is a puzzle. Scottish education is central to Scottish national identity. The movement for statehood in most western countries was about mobilising a strong sense of national identity. Why, then, has it taken until the closing years of the twentieth century for a Scottish parliament to be re-established? How is this apparent Scottish exceptionalism to be explained?

EDUCATION AND SCOTTISH NATIONAL IDENTITY

The first premise can be stated simply: that education has been and is vital to the sense of Scottishness. In the words of the historian Robert Anderson: 'Education has become a marker of Scottish identity, associated with various supposed qualities of the Scottish character such as individualism, social ambition, respect for talent above birth, or "metaphysical" rationalism' (1997, pp.2–3). In many ways, education in Scotland has this capacity to be the carrier for so many and often contradictory meanings of who Scots are (McCrone, 1992). That is the first clue to the puzzle. It prompts a more detailed exploration of the ideas associated with education. What is involved here are myths. The term 'myths' does not mean the same as untruths, such as, for example, that the earth is flat. It can be proved that it is not. The point about myths, however, is that they are not amenable to proof. In the words of the United States Constitution, 'we hold these beliefs to be self-evident'.

Myths, in other words, operate on a different plane from 'facts'. By their nature they are a collection of symbolic elements organised to explain and validate sets of social institutions. The social anthropologist, Clyde Mitchell, defined them as follows: 'myths operate to record and present the moral system whereby present attitudes and actions are ordered and validated' (*A Dictionary of Sociology*, 1968, p. 122). Myths are general guides to help interpret complex social reality. They operate as reservoirs of beliefs and values which allow individuals to interpret the world and their place within it. All human beings are subject to this process. There is a natural human tendency to think of myths as something that other people require. Anthropologists or sociologists of religion show the ways sacred or transcendent beliefs act as guides for others, but most people think that as rationalists they have little need of such symbolic supports. Such a view would be mistaken. Everybody is affected, including academic writers who seek to uncover the myths others live by.

Consider again the case of the United States of America and its self-evident truths. One central one is the American Dream. This holds that the raw materials of success are hard work and talent. However, a critic might point out that success in the USA seems to come to those who have inherited capital, whether in material or cultural form. Cynically, it might be said that rich and successful people tend to have rich and successful parents. Rags to riches, it might be concluded, is a myth (to revert expediently and temporarily to the common-sense usage of the term).

THE LAD O'PAIRTS AND KAILYARDISM

In Scotland, there is an equivalent myth, the lad o'pairts, and it too is centred upon 'getting on', and education is central to it. The lad o'pairts (note that there is no 'lass o'pairts' in this pervasive myth: getting on is for boys to do) was, according to David Murison writing in the *Scots Dictionary*, a talented youth, usually the son of a crofter or peasant who had ability but insufficient means to benefit from schooling. Murison traces its usage to the late nineteenth century in a story 'Domsie', published in the collection, *Beside the Bonnie Brier Bush*, (1894) by the Kailyard novelist, 'Ian MacLaren' (in real life a Free Church Minister, the Rev. John Watson, born in Essex). The 'Domsie' of the title is the schoolteacher or dominie who skilfully wheedles sufficient capital out of the purses and pocket-books of local worthies to allow his talented charges to go on to university. Domsie is so successful that in MacLaren's words: 'Seven ministers, four schoolteachers, four doctors, one professor and three civil service men had been sent out by the auld schule in Domsie's time, besides many that had given themselves to "mercantile pursuits" '. Clearly, the professions are what matter – teaching, ministering and administering. Trade is of lesser importance in this scale of values (indicated by the quotation marks and the lack of precision in numbers). The short story is cut shorter by the early death of Domsie who receives this panegyric:

> Domsie, as we called the schoolmaster behind his back in Drumtochty because we loved him, was true to the tradition of his kind, and had an unerring scent for 'pairts' in his laddies. He could detect a scholar in an egg, and prophesied Latinity from a boy that seemed only fit to be a cowherd. (1894, p. 8)

It might, not unreasonably, be tempting to relegate such stories to sentimentalised history, issuing as they did from the popular literary style called Kailyard which flourished from about 1880 until 1914, and described by the *Penguin Guide to Literature* as consisting of 'minor writers who pursued Scottish country quaintness into whimsical middens'. This tradition is often blamed for sins much worse than affronts to literature; some saw it as laying down a distorted image of Scotland as a couthy, parochial backwater. Tom Nairn, in *The Break-Up of Britain*, commented:

> Kailyardism was the definition of Scotland as wholly consisting of small towns full of small-town 'characters' given to bucolic intrigue and wise sayings. At first the central figures were usually Ministers of the Kirk (as were most of the authors) but later on schoolteachers and doctors got into the act. Their housekeepers always have a shrewd insight into human nature. Offspring who leave for the big city frequently come to grief and are glad to get home again (peching and hosting to hide their feelings). (Nairn, 1977, p. 158)

At this point it may seem easy to dismiss Kailyardism and its narratives as of little importance beyond the cultural genre of the turn of the century. After all, as Willie Donaldson has pointed out in his book *Popular Literature in Victorian Scotland* (1986), even at its height it was by no means as hegemonic as was once thought, and took second place in Scotland to a much more popular genre of newspaper writing with a more radical and less complacent edge.

Kailyardism, however, cannot be dismissed so easily. First, it generated its own mythology in the second half of this century insofar as many critics blamed it for laying down a reactionary and defensive view of Scotland. Such a critique argued that Scotland's failure to strike out for a parliament of its own could be traced to the supposedly insidious effects of this dominant discourse. Quite simply, Scots were feart, and blame lay with the distorting imagery of cultural formations like the Kailyard. Critics spun their own versions. In the 1970s the historian Christopher Harvie identified two historical Scottish personality-types the 'red' and the 'black' (remember that it was a Scot, R. L. Stevenson who invented Dr Jekyll and Mr Hyde):

> The red Scots were cosmopolitan, self-avowedly enlightened, and, given a chance, authoritarian, expanding into and exploiting bigger and more bountiful fields than their own country could provide. Back home lurked their black brothers, demotic, parochial and reactionary, but keeping the ladder of social promotion open, resisting the encroachments of the English governing class. Together, they controlled the rate of their own assimilation to the greater world, the balance which underlay the Union. (*Scotland and Nationalism*, 1977, p. 17)

There was, in truth, little empirical evidence for Harvie's distinction, but it caught the imagination at the time (especially after the failure of the Devolution bill in 1979) of those seeking to explain why Scots for much of the history of the Union did not strive for political independence, or even a home rule parliament.

The second reason why the Kailyard mattered was that it captured and amplified the key social icon of late nineteenth- and early twentieth-century Scotland, the lad o'pairts. If and when the Kailyard declined, the iconography of the lad o'pairts did not. This was because it was embedded in a wider tradition of social egalitarianism. Few myths are more powerful and prevalent in and about Scotland than that it is a more egalitarian society than England, and that it is less class-bound. The late historiographer-royal Gordon Donaldson put it this way: 'It is true to this day that Scotland is a more egalitarian country than England, but as a result of class consciousness horizontal divisions into classes have become . . . more important than vertical divisions into nations' (*Scotland: the Shaping of a Nation*, 1974, p. 117). Scottish literature and culture have made considerable play of this set of ideas. Kurt Wittig in his book *The Scottish Tradition in Literature* (1958) made it the central motif from the poetry of the fourteenth and fifteenth century, through Robert Burns and even Walter Scott, and on into the 20th century with novelists like Neil Gunn and Lewis Grassic Gibbon. Wittig depicted the movement as follows:

> The democratic element in Scottish literature is one of its most striking characteristics. 'Democratic' is not really the correct word; it is rather a free manliness [the gendering of core values once more – author], a 'saeva indignatio' against oppression, a violent freedom, sometimes an aggressive spirit of independence and egalitarianism. (1958, p. 95)

This generic Scottish myth of egalitarianism has at its core the iconography of the lad o'pairts, and is the key to explaining why educational values appear so central to a sense of Scottish culture. In defining Scotland and its distinctiveness vis-á-vis the 'Other' – in this case, England – it helps to confirm a sense of identity by saying who Scots are and what they value. It connects, of course, with other typifications such as 'we're a' Jock Tamson's bairns'. David Murison gives the origin and meaning of this saying as 'the human race; common humanity; also with less universal force, a group of people united by a common sentiment, interest or purpose' (*Scottish National Dictionary*, 1986, vol. v, p. 337). 'Jock Tamson' also stands for whisky, and for 'John Thomas' with its sexual connotations.

THE AMBIGUITY OF TRADITION

Myths, like traditions, draw upon the past, but they have an active, contemporary significance which involves processes of selective inclusion and exclusion. Traditions and myths, as Raymond Williams observed, provide meaningful though partial interpretations of social reality

> Tradition has been commonly understood as a relatively inert historicised segment of social structure; tradition as the surviving past. [However] what we have to see is not just a 'tradition', but a selective tradition – an intentionally selective version of a shaping past and a pre-shaped present, which is then powerfully operative in the process of social and cultural definition and identification. It is a version of the past which is intended to connect with and ratify the present. What it offers in practice is a sense of predisposed continuity. (*Marxism and Literature*, 1977, p. 115)

Traditions, then, legitimise institutions, symbolise group cohesion and socialise others into appropriate beliefs and values (see Chapter 10). They do so in a complex and ambiguous way so that they lend themselves to a variety of cultural and political ideologies. This can be seen when the Scottish – egalitarian – myth is examined more closely. It has an asociological, almost mystical element (similar in purpose to the American Dream). Scots are deemed to be egalitarian almost by dint of racial or ethnic characteristics. On the other hand, social inequality – the actual distribution of society's resources – may well be, and of course usually are, unequal. The myth has, in fact, two versions, which might be labelled the 'idealist' and the 'radical'. In the former, the objective existence of social inequality matters far less than the shared common humanity of (in this case) being Scottish. Inequality is man-made, set against the basic egalitarianism. That, after all, is the point of Burns' poem 'A Man's a Man for a' that'. Social rank – the guinea's stamp – matters less than common humanity. There is, however, ambiguity in Burns' message. There is no calling for the end of social inequality, simply the proper appreciation of 'the pith o' sense and pride o' worth'. Indeed, 'a Man's a Man for a' that' is an appeal to the virtues of fraternity rather than equality in a sociological sense.

It is true that in the strong – the 'radical' – sense of the poem, Burns is making a revolutionary appeal to radical social change, and that is possibly the sense which those on the Left wish to give it. There is however the idealist version which implies that the objective facts of social inequality and rank matter far less than basic common humanity. Why change the superficial?

When the Scottish myth and its incumbent lad o'pairts is examined in this way, its sociological significance begins to emerge. Egalitarianism does not assume social equality. As Allan MacLaren pointed out:

> The egalitarianism so often portrayed is not that emerging from an economic, social or even political equality; it is equality of opportunity which is exemplified. All men are not equal. What is implied is that all men are given an opportunity to be equal. Whatever the values attached to such a belief, if expressed today, it would be termed elitist not egalitarian. (*Social Class in Scotland*, 1976, p. 2).

This is familiar territory. The two senses of the myth refer to, on the one hand, equality of opportunity – the idealist version, and equality of achievement – the radical version. The latter refers to measuring equality of outcomes: class, race, gender and so on. The former refers in essence merely to formal opportunity afforded to the able student to proceed through the educational system from school to university.

It can also be seen how the lad o'pairts would have been a creature of his time. In eighteenth-century Scotland a small elite was being catered for in a limited number of professions – schoolteaching, the law, the ministry and medicine. The failure of the 'lad' to make it could readily be explained in personal rather than structural terms: in short, it was his own fault. In this respect, egalitarianism was a conservative ideology which congratulated itself on the openness of Scottish society and its social institutions. It could even be employed, as it was in the 1970s, to defend fee-paying local authority schools on the grounds that they afforded the lad o'pairts an educational and social opportunity not given in the comprehensive sector.

To connect together the idealist and the radical versions of the myth is to give them a coherence which they do not normally have. Nevertheless, it can be seen more clearly how flexible, ambivalent and multi-stranded the myth is. It lends support to the conservative seeking assurance that existing institutions are for the best, while for nationalists it provides a vision of a Scotland which is democratic and different from its southern neighbour; while for socialists it confirms the radical predispositions of Scotland. The myth matters because of its framing assumptions rather than its substance. It confers legitimacy on both idealist and radical interpretations alike.

The myth is also addressing a former social order. As MacLaren points out: 'There is some evidence to suggest that the "Scottish Myth" is a product of a former rural paternalism rather than an urban industrialism in which class identity and economic individualism overruled a declining concern for communal and parochial obligations' (1976, p. 9). It largely derives from a typically pre-industrial, even pre-capitalist social order where social identity is conferred by community not class. In strict sociological terms, the lad o'pairts belongs to a defunct Scotland. Ian Carter in his analysis of the Kailyard school commented:

> MacLaren's novels share important features with the parish histories that poured off the presses in such numbers in the 1880s and 1890s. Both rest on an ideology of community – parish life as harmonious – and both tell pawky stories of local characters to demonstrate that sense of shared community. (*Scottish Journal of Sociology*, 1976, p. 1)

The egalitarianism bred of an attachment to peasant values and the social organisation of small towns could make little sense of the new urban industrial experience. Should then the iconography of the lad o'pairts be dismissed as a historical legacy of the Scottish conservative imagination? It cannot be simply this, because it consistently runs up against counter-evidence, and so is difficult to debunk. As Robert Anderson observes,

> Most observers agree that the myth of the lad of parts [sic] corresponds to some underlying reality, albeit idealized. It expressed a nineteenth-century ideal of meritocracy, which did allow for individual social mobility, yet also legitimized the reproduction through schooling of the inequalities of industrial society; even when meritocratic concepts challenged class barriers, they hardly acknowledged those of gender. (1997, p. 53–4)

Anderson's evidence (*Education and Opportunity in Victorian Scotland*, 1983) shows that as late as the third quarter of the nineteenth century, many students at Scotland's universities came from peasant or working class origins. Aberdeen admitted a large number from agricultural backgrounds (as many as 20 per cent in 1910), while Glasgow had a relatively high percentage of students from manual working class origins (24 per cent in 1910).

Myths do not survive and flourish unless they connect with the realities of life, or are at least not wholly contradicted by them. In the post-war period, there is evidence that educational opportunity was unusually present in Scotland. Keith Hope's re-analysis of the 1947 Scottish Mental Study led him to conclude that 'Scotland, as we would expect, is more merit-elective than the United States' (*As Others See Us*, 1984, p. 30). The surviving potency of the myth does not simply rely, however, on such evidence, but above all on the institutional carriers which sustained it. McPherson and Raab (*Governing Education*, 1983) have been able to show that Scotland's administrative elite gave it voice through the educational system. Andrew McPherson has spoken of the 'Kirriemuir Career' among the Scottish schools inspectorate to show how small-town Scotland predominated in these circles, to the detriment of the urban west. Robert Anderson uses McPherson's findings to conclude that the Welsh and Scottish 'democratic myths' had some substance, and that as members of the British elite they may have had broader social origins than their English equivalents. In other words, the Scottish myth is kept alive in large part because it was and is a key ideology to the Scottish education system and its cadres. It also helps to explain why a perceived attack on the Scottish education system is perceived as an attack on Scottish culture and identity itself.

EDUCATION AND NATIONAL IDENTITY

It will be instructive at this point in the argument to return to the puzzle with which the chapter began. We have tried to show how central education and its iconography is to Scottish national identity. Our next task is more straightforward, namely to show how this was in no sense unique to Scotland but a central feature of all western industrial societies. The late Ernest Gellner showed that nationalism is not the result of sentiment or historical folk-memory, but is an essential part of the modern condition. Being national is the modern condition, and the natural form of political loyalty. 'Every man is a clerk', in his words, because there is an assumption of universal literacy, and secondly, that clerks are not horizontally mobile because they cannot move from one language-zone to another very easily. The condition of language in which he/she is reared and operates is commonly the vernacular, the language of home, school and state, which in turn reinforces nationalist tendencies.

Modern loyalties correspond in large part with political units defined by language which is the dominant mode of instruction and expression in the education system. In other words, the state is in these terms a cultural system, but one in which the population actively attests to its nationality. This is a key point in Gellner's book *Nations and Nationalism* (1983), as it permitted him to argue that nationalism derives not from atavistic and sentimental attachment, but is made and mobilised by the conditions of modernity themselves. That is why Gellner had no truck with either pro- or anti-nationalists who wish to essentialise nationality, and why he is frequently associated with a modernist position which sees nationalism as a form of secular religion for the modern state.

Because change is the characteristic feature of such societies, people have to be ready for change, and the main agency for sensitising people to this is the education system which becomes the central institution in society. Modern society is both more homogeneous (everyone gets the same basic training), and yet more diversified (the complex division of labour). The key motor in all this is education which furnishes a generic training, and shapes society like an army in terms of its integrated and fine-tuned organisational features. However, the key difference in terms of social order is that modern society is largely self-regulating. At its centre is the professor, not the executioner; the doctorate rather than the guillotine is the emblem of state power. The monopoly of legitimate education is now more important, more central than is the monopoly of legitimate violence. Hence, nationalism grows in the medium of this rational, egalitarian ethos.

In the translation of society from rural to urban, peasants had to be turned into citizens. Eugene Weber in his book *Peasants into Frenchmen* (1977) shows why this was necessary so soon after a thoroughgoing revolution only a century before. The startling fact was that as late as the 1860s, fully a quarter of the French population did not speak the language. 'In short', says Weber, 'French was a foreign language for a substantial number of Frenchmen, including almost half the children who would reach adulthood in the last quarter of the century' (1977, p. 67). The key institutions which 'made Frenchmen', according to Weber, were the village school system of the Third Republic, the fact that education became useful as a means of social mobility up and away from the countryside, and above all, the sequence of wars with Prussia/Germany which induced conscription. The French state also supplied the first modern maps of the country soon after the Franco-Prussian war, so that 'by 1881, few classrooms however small, appear to have lacked a map' (1977, p. 334), and the image of the national hexagon began to be both recognised and hegemonic. Weber comments that the famous geographical icon can be seen as a colonising symbol reflecting a complex of internal territories conquered, annexed and integrated into the political and administrative whole.

The idea of 'France' which began as an elite concept was extended by a process akin to colonisation through communication (roads, railways, and above all by the newspapers – '*le papier qui parle*') so that by of the end of the nineteenth century popular and elite culture had come together after a break of two centuries. Three major cultural innovations had helped to bring this about: education – the development of the secular equivalent of the church, sometimes both competing with and complementing it; the invention of public ceremonies such as Bastille Day; and the mass production of public monuments.

SCOTTISH OR BRITISH?

How does Scotland fit into this model? Here the third and final part of the puzzle is encountered. The main purpose of schooling everywhere was to imbue pupils with the new patriotism rather than simply teaching them new technical skills such as reading, writing and counting. This can be seen in the mobilisation of 'national' history and geography, and the 'national' curriculum.

The social construction of history can often be seen in cases where there are competing accounts on offer, or changes over time. For example, as Robert Anderson shows, the curriculum for teaching (especially history) in Scottish schools in the late nineteenth century reflects these shifts rather well. The 1873 Code drawn up by (as it was known then) the Scotch Education Department (SED) had a greater emphasis on Scottish (over British) history than the 1886 Code which abandoned Scottish and local emphases. The political aims of at least one Schools Inspector was clear: 'one must question the value of a school history that lands a child in the midst of loose laws and looser passions, and unquestionably helps . . . to maintain sentimental Scotch antipathy to England' (Anderson, *Education and the Scottish People*, 1750–1918, 1995, p. 214). However, in the 1880s, there was resistance to the use of the term 'English' rather than 'British' in history textbooks, and by 1907, the SED was stressing that Scottish history was central to the curriculum, with an emphasis on Scotland's contribution to empire. The general message was that Scotland and England, once historic enemies, now formed the basis for a world empire (ibid., p. 219–20).

In like manner, the icons of history are redrawn according to the political and cultural needs of the day. For example, that icon of Scottish national identity, William Wallace, was resurrected in the 1990s by Hollywood and turned into 'Braveheart'. In many ways the survival of mere fragments of history is a boon to heritage makers, because it allows more easily the re-presentation of national myth. Graeme Morton shows how, despite his execution by the English state in 1305, Wallace could be refocused in the nineteenth century as the fusion of nationalism and unionism. During the age of nationalism, he argues, William Wallace secured his position as Scotland's most efficacious patriot, fulfilling the agenda of friends and foes of the Union.

The completion of the puzzle is now close. Why, if Scotland's identity was inextricably bound up with its education system, and it can be shown that in the nineteenth century similar processes were happening in Scotland as elsewhere, did education and national identity not generate the demand for self-determination? The short answer is that Scotland had already achieved this. In many ways it had little need for a formal parliament as long as its needs were met by other social institutions – what is called civil society – and as long as the British state did not interfere unduly with the internal mechanisms of self-governance.

AUTONOMY AND CIVIL SOCIETY

The term 'civil society' refers to those areas of social life – the domestic world, the economic sphere, cultural activities and political interaction – which are organised by private or voluntary arrangements between individuals and groups outside the direct control of the state. In other words, whereas the state can be treated as a unitary entity which functions externally (through warfare) and internally (through law), society is composed of an extensive though bounded network of self-activated individuals and groups. State and society are not wholly independent of each other, but are largely formed and maintained within the context of the other.

The concept of civil society is not without dispute, particularly concerning its relationship between state on the one hand and market on the other. As regards the first, civil society should be understood as the sphere of that which is relatively but autonomously private within a modern polity. In other words, given the way state and civil society operate across each other today, they cannot easily be differentiated. To take the Scottish example, institutional autonomy as regards law, education and local politics is now underwritten and managed by the state, albeit a Scottish 'semi-state'.

'Civil society' indicates that there is a sphere which is autonomous from the state. Neither is it simply the economy writ large. Similarly, what is meant by the state and society have themselves changed over time, as well as the relationship between them. The distinction between the two was probably much more meaningful to Victorians than it is to us today. That is because the last century or so has seen an increasing fudging of the boundary between state and society. Notably, the extension of the franchise has brought to bear new political and social pressures on the state, and increasingly the state is constituted to exercise rule over society. The state is required to address the concerns of its citizens more directly, and this presents the task of societal management for modern governments.

In short, for so long as Scottish civil society was in charge of its education system, and Scots found it worthwhile to compete in the British imperial labour market, then there was little need to mobilise a political nationalism to win what freedoms one already actually had. This was also the context in which educational reforms had taken place at the end of the nineteenth century. As regards the reform of university education in 1876, George Davie has famously argued in *The Democratic Intellect* (1961) that it was driven by pressure to anglicise the curriculum the better to compete in the wider British marketplace, and that in the process Scotland's 'democratic intellect' was sacrificed. Lindsay Paterson in *The Autonomy of Modern Scotland* (1994) points out that such a view does not explain why the universities never generated the same degree of nationalist agitation which took place elsewhere. In other words, the nationalist dog did not bark because it already had what it wanted. This is a view shared by Robert Anderson who argues that as a result of the reforms: 'Intellectual standards were raised, and the middle class demand for qualifications allowing Scots to compete for jobs on a British basis was well satisfied' (1997, p. 38).

CONCLUSION

What has brought this state of affairs to an end is that what Neil MacCormick called in his 1997 British Academy lecture, the 'Scottish anomaly' – the capacity of an archetypal 'nation-state' to operate in a federal way – can no longer be contained within the unitary state structure. Scotland's autonomy in educational as in other institutions of civil society can no longer operate in its traditional way. MacCormick observes:

> It is an autonomy that has made possible the continuing assertion of a submerged constitutional tradition of a distinct Scottish stamp. The continuing claim to a historically attested sovereignty of the people is part and parcel of that. It includes the implication that assent to the union involves a continuing '*plebiscite de tous les jours*'. So long as the will of the majority sustains it, it will continue. If it ceases to do so, it will cease.

And it has ceased: at least in its post-1707 Union form. The puzzle is solved. Scottish education is central to Scottish national identity. The movement for statehood in most western countries was about mobilising a strong sense of national identity. Only in the late twentieth century have people in Scotland found it necessary to defend and extend their civil autonomy with a parliament, albeit within the British state, at least for the time being. The old bargain – the marriage of convenience, as it were – which was struck in 1707 to give Scotland civil self-government but within the British state, and crucially its empire, has run its course.

REFERENCES

Anderson, R. (1997) *Scottish Education since the Reformation*, Studies in Scottish Economic and Social History no. 5.
Davie, G. (1961) *The Democratic Intellect*, Edinburgh: Edinburgh University Press.
McCrone, D. (1992) *Understanding Scotland: the sociology of a stateless nation*, London: Routledge.
McPherson, A. and C. Raab (1988) *Governing Education*, Edinburgh: Edinburgh University Press.
Nairn, T. (1977) *The Break-Up of Britain*, London: Verso.
Paterson, L. (1994) *The Autonomy of Modern Scotland*, Edinburgh: Edinburgh University Press.

23

Gaelic Education

Boyd Robertson

Gaelic is the longest-established of Scotland's languages. It was brought to Scotland by settlers from Ireland in the fifth and sixth centuries AD. These immigrants, known to the Romans as Scotti, gave the country its name and their Celtic language penetrated almost every part of Scotland and became, for a brief period, the language of the Crown and of government. From the twelfth century onwards, the status of the language was eroded by anglicising influences from the south and it became increasingly marginalised.

Today, only 1.5 per cent of Scots speak Gaelic. These 69,000 Gaelic speakers are to be found mostly in the Western Isles and on the western fringes of the mainland but there are also significant communities of Gaelic speakers in urban centres such as Glasgow, Edinburgh and Inverness. The last twenty years have, however, seen a remarkable renaissance of the language and culture, reflected in the arts, the media, the socio-economic sphere and education. Considerable progress has been made in meeting the educational needs and aspirations of Gaelic speakers and learners as will become apparent from the following account of current provision and recent developments.

PRE-SCHOOL EDUCATION

It is singularly appropriate to begin an overview of Gaelic education with the pre-school sector because this has been the seedbed for much of the regeneration and growth in Gaelic in, and beyond, education.

Increasing exposure to English and to Anglo-American cultural influences caused concern amongst parents and Gaelic activists about the detrimental effect this would have on young children's fluency in, and attitude towards, the language. It was considered essential to counteract this trend by seeking to associate the minority language with positive and enjoyable experiences and this led in the late 1970s to the formation of the first Gaelic playgroups and to demands for children's programmes in Gaelic on television. A national association, *Comhairle nan Sgoiltean Araich* (CNSA), was set up in 1982 to promote the development of Gaelic-medium playgroups. The existence today of over 150 pre-school groups throughout, and in a few instances beyond, Scotland suggests that CNSA has been successful in its mission. CNSA is a voluntary sector provider with limited resources and has not, hitherto, seen a major role for itself in delivering nursery education. This has been regarded as the province of local authorities and, up until 1995, there were only three Gaelic nursery units in the whole of Scotland. Development of provision has accelerated in the last two years and there are now ten units, six of which are located in schools with Gaelic-medium classes.

PRIMARY EDUCATION

Provision for Gaelic in primary schools has been transformed in the last three decades. Before the reorganisation of local government in the 1970s, Gaelic had a minor role in the primary curriculum. Even in schools in strong Gaelic-speaking communities, the teaching medium was almost exclusively English, the home language of most of the pupils being reduced to the status of a subject to be studied.

The position of Gaelic changed radically in 1975 with the launch of a bilingual education project by the newly-formed local authority for the Outer Hebrides, *Comhairle nan Eilean*. This initiative received government backing with the Scottish Office jointly funding the first two three-year phases of the project which sought to build on the home language of the majority of pupils and used Gaelic as a teaching and learning medium along with English. This was the first time that Gaelic was used officially as a medium of instruction in State schools and represented a major advance for the language in education. There was a favourable parental response to the project in its early years but, by the early 1980s, concern was being expressed about the level of fluency in Gaelic being attained by pupils in some schools after several years of bilingual schooling. Parents also voiced dissatisfaction with the progress being made by certain schools in implementing the bilingual model.

A similar bilingual scheme was piloted in 1978 in five Skye schools by Highland Regional Council and was eventually extended to all primary schools on the island. The lower incidence of Gaelic-speaking children on Skye required a rather different bilingual approach with greater emphasis placed on the needs of learners. Doubts about the ability of bilingual models to deliver fluency in Gaelic comparable to that in English and a growing awareness of the erosion of the language amongst the school age population made parents, educationalists and language activists realise that another approach was needed. Developments in Welsh and in other minority languages were studied and the findings suggested that use of the minority language as the medium of education had to be maximised to ensure language maintenance and transmission. The first Gaelic playgroups had demonstrated the viability of this approach and convinced parents that it should be continued in primary school.

Highland and Strathclyde Regional Councils responded to parental pressure for Gaelic-medium education and set up units in schools in Inverness and Glasgow in 1985. The success of these first units and the continuing spread of the playgroups, fuelled demand for provision in other areas. By 1997–8, fifty-five schools and 1,736 pupils were engaged in Gaelic-medium education. Most units are in the Highlands and Islands but there are several in non-Gaelic-speaking areas such as Aberdeen, Cumbernauld, Edinburgh, Kilmarnock and Perth. The largest units are in Portree, Inverness and Glasgow. English-medium education is the exception in some schools in the islands and even in Portree, a fairly anglicised administrative centre, half of the annual intake enters the Gaelic-medium stream.

In virtually all Gaelic-medium classes there is a mix of fluent speakers and learners. The proportions vary depending on the type of community the school serves. In rural, island schools, many of the pupils come from Gaelic-speaking homes while in urban, mainland schools few pupils have that home background. Research shows that factors which influence parents to opt for Gaelic-medium education include maintenance and development of the mother tongue, restoration to a family of a language that has skipped a generation or two, acquisition of a second language, the perceived advantages of bilingualism and access to Gaelic culture and heritage.

The Gaelic-medium curriculum follows the National Guidelines on Gaelic 5–14 produced by the Scottish Office Education Department in 1993. These guidelines set out attainment targets and programmes of study for five levels of primary and early secondary education. They provide teachers with a curricular framework that identifies 'the aims of study, the ground to be covered, the way that learning should progress and how pupils' attainment should be monitored and recorded' (Gaelic 5–14 Preface). The guidelines for Gaelic-medium education have been formulated along similar lines to those for English but there are significant differences between the two, especially in respect of the scheduling of attainments in certain linguistic skills. This arises from the fact that Gaelic-medium education begins with a two-year language immersion programme.

The immersion phase is designed 'to provide children from non-Gaelic backgrounds with basic oral competence in Gaelic' (1.3) and 'to reinforce the existing skills of Gaelic-speaking children whose competence in the language may diminish in a predominantly English-speaking environment' (1.3.) During this phase, the teacher uses Gaelic almost exclusively and the emphasis is on the development of listening and speaking skills. It is anticipated that 'pupils should be able to communicate with the teacher and other pupils in social interaction and classroom routines on a range of topics' (1.1) by the end of the two years. The emphasis on oral skills, which continues beyond the immersion phase, means that pupils in Gaelic-medium classes attain targets in these and in literacy skills in a different sequence and time frame to those in English-medium classes.

The 5–14 Guidelines state that Gaelic-medium education should aim 'to bring pupils to the stage of broadly equal competence in Gaelic and English, in all the skills, by the end of P7' (1.1). It is left to the discretion of local authorities and schools how this should be achieved. There is considerable variation in practice between authorities in the use made of English as a teaching medium beyond the immersion phase. The balance between Gaelic and English ranges from 60–40 through to 90–10 and there is concern amongst parents that the weaker Gaelic model inhibits the development of fluency. Most schools introduce reading and writing in English in P3 and increase the weighting given to English in P6–7.

There is little doubt that Gaelic-medium education has been a success. An HM Inspectors of Schools report on Provision for Gaelic Education, published in 1994, acknowledged that the Gaelic-medium approach had 'worked well' and was more effective than bilingual provision in achieving fluency. The increasing uptake of it and the continuing demand from parents for new units to be set up are clear indicators of satisfaction with the system.

Gaelic features in the curriculum of primary schools in another two forms. In the Outer Hebrides, some schools which do not have Gaelic-medium units offer pupils a form of bilingual education developed from the earlier project model. Schools which have units also provide a measure of bilingual education to pupils outwith the unit. In other schools, Gaelic is taught as a second language for a short time each week by a specialist itinerant teacher or by a member of staff with the appropriate skills. This type of provision has been offered in schools in parts of Argyll and Perthshire, in Inverness and in areas such as Lochaber, Skye and Lochalsh and Wester Ross for the best part of three decades.

Many educationalists are sceptical about the value and effectiveness of the language learning experience afforded by itinerant personnel, arguing that it produces little more than language awareness and a knowledge of basic vocabulary. It would appear that many parents take a different view judging by the reaction to a decision by the Highland Council to discontinue its visiting teacher service in 1997 as part of a cost-cutting exercise forced on the Council by a sharp reduction in government funding. The proposal was denounced by school boards and parental organisations and the Council was forced to bring forward a proposal for an alternative service utilising existing Gaelic-speaking staff and other teachers willing to undertake a ten-day course that would enable them to carry out a basic level of teaching in the language. Doubts have been expressed about the reach and application of the scheme and unfavourable comparisons have been drawn, in respect of training and resourcing, with the Modern Languages in the Primary School national development programme on which it seems to be modelled.

SECONDARY EDUCATION

The use of Gaelic as a medium of education in secondary schools has not kept pace with developments in the primary sector. The language was first used in the teaching of secondary subjects in 1983 when *Comhairle nan Eilean* set up a pilot project as an extension to its primary bilingual programme. The two-year pilot involved two small secondary schools in Lewis, Lionel and Shawbost, and concentrated on the social subjects. Pupils responded positively to the use of their mother tongue and the pilot was deemed a success by all concerned. The two, two-year schools continued to teach history and geography through Gaelic following the pilot phase.

The first Gaelic-medium unit on the mainland opened at Hillpark Secondary in Glasgow in 1988. Further provision was established in 1992 in Millburn Academy, Inverness and Portree High School thus ensuring that there was continuity of Gaelic-medium education for pupils of the three largest primary units. By 1997, Gaelic-medium education had been introduced into another seven schools.

The use of Gaelic as a medium in secondary is restricted to a few subjects. History is the only subject available in all schools. Geography, personal and social education, mathematics, science, home economics, technical education and art are the other subjects taught in Gaelic in one or more of the schools. Candidates may elect to sit Gaelic versions of Scottish Certificate of Education examinations in history, geography and maths at present and other subjects will be added as the system develops.

The development of Gaelic-medium education in secondary has been hampered by a number of factors. One of the most significant of these is the fragmented nature of the secondary curriculum with its specialist subject structure. To operate economically and effectively, this requires a substantial cohort of pupils in any one year. The typical primary school structure with one teacher per class lends itself more readily to a smaller cohort and the level of subsidy required is significantly less. It will be some considerable time before the Gaelic-medium cohort in most receiving secondaries reaches the point of economic viability in a range of subjects and expansion of provision will be contingent on central government funding being available.

Financial considerations were probably uppermost in influencing HMI to conclude in their 1994 report that 'the provision of Gaelic-medium secondary education in a number of subjects, determined by the vagaries of resource availability, is neither desirable nor feasible in the forseeable future' (1.12). This recommendation, which contrasted with the report's commendation of Gaelic-medium primary education, was accepted by the then

Conservative government and became Scottish Office policy. It provoked an indignant response from the Gaelic community which highlighted the absence of educational rationale for the decision, the disjunction it would cause in children's education and the illogicality and waste of abandoning a scheme in which so much had been invested. One of the earliest actions of the new Labour government was to overturn this policy and the Inspectorate was instructed by the Minister for Education and Gaelic at the Scottish Office, Brian Wilson, announcing a three-point boost for Gaelic education on 19 June 1997, to enter into discussions with local authorities about ways 'to support and extend Gaelic-medium teaching in specified subjects in the secondary curriculum'.

Pupils in Gaelic-medium classes also study the language as a subject. They take the *Gàidhlig* course which is designed for fluent speakers and will lead to certificate examinations at Standard Grade, Intermediate 1 and 2, Higher and Advanced Higher. In 1997, 101 candidates sat the Standard Grade exam and forty-six were presented for Higher. The fluent speakers cohort includes pupils who have been in bilingual programmes in primary, and a small number who may not have had access to Gaelic-medium education and had little or no exposure to the language in primary, but who come from Gaelic-speaking homes and begin formal study of the language in secondary.

A Gaelic (Learners) course leading to separate certificate examinations was instituted in 1962. This followed a campaign by prominent Gaelic teachers who highlighted the inequity of asking learners of Gaelic to sit the same examination as native speakers. The new course brought provision for pupils learning Gaelic broadly into line with that for pupils learning other modern languages.

Classification of pupils as learners or fluent speakers is a recurrent issue. The Scottish Examination Board (SEB) Gaelic Panel produced guidelines on categorisation but the interpretation and implementation of the guidelines is sometimes challenged by parents. This usually arises where a school has adjudged a pupil to be a fluent speaker and parents feel that categorisation as a learner would improve the child's chances of success in certificate examinations.

Less than 10 per cent of state schools offer the Gaelic (Learners) option. Most of these are located in the Highlands and Islands. The number of schools has remained at around forty for many years, although there have been regional fluctuations with expansion in the Inverness area and contraction in Glasgow. Four Glasgow schools have ceased to offer Gaelic in the recent past and there is now only one school where Gaelic is taught in a city with over 6,000 Gaelic-speakers. Some schools in the independent sector occasionally present pupils for SCE examinations. The number of presentations for the Gaelic (Learners) exams, though small in comparison with most other languages, shows an upward trend with 529 candidates at Standard Grade and 102 at Higher in 1997.

In schools in the Outer Hebrides, Skye and the western part of the Highland mainland, it is council policy that all first and second year pupils study Gaelic and another modern language. In most other parts of Scotland, pupils typically have to choose between Gaelic and French, or German, from first year or take Gaelic as a second language option in second or third year. These option arrangements militate against a large uptake of the subject.

The teaching of Gaelic has changed radically in the last thirty years. Where it was once a subject of study and analysis with an approach not unlike the classical languages, it progressed through a stage where the emphasis was on vocabulary, grammar and structure using English as the medium of instruction, to a methodology today which aims to produce learners with communicative competence in the language and uses the target language extensively in the classroom.

The last ten years have seen a marked improvement in teaching/learning resources. Before then, teachers had to adapt courses geared for the adult independent study market but now they have access to a substantial corpus of materials designed for learners in school. A similar advance has been made in respect of materials for the fluent speakers course, much of it produced by local authorities sometimes on an individual, but more often on a collaborative, basis.

In addition to the long-term courses outlined above, there are also short-term modular courses for both learners and fluent speakers. There are five levels of National Certificate (NC) modules for Learners which, in 1996, had an uptake of over 1,000 students. The Learner modules adhere closely to Modern Languages module specifications. Gaelic versions of eight of the NC modules in Communication are on offer to fluent speakers and were taken up by over 100 candidates in 1996. Short courses in Celtic or Gaelic Studies feature as pre-language or introductory courses in the first year curriculum of a few schools and modules in these topics could figure in the Higher Still menu of modules in more schools.

SUPPORT STRUCTURES

Recent developments have been facilitated and sustained by the creation of enabling mechanisms and support structures. Chief among these has been the Scheme of Specific Grants for Gaelic Education initiated by the government in 1986. Under this scheme, local authorities submit project proposals to the Scottish Office and receive 75 per cent funding for approved projects. Grants are only awarded for new or additional provision and authorities are expected to meet the full costs of developments after three years. The Scheme's initial budget of £250,000 had risen to over £2 million in 1996–7. Authorities can bid for funding on an individual or collective basis, but the Scottish Office Education and Industry Department (SOEID) expects authorities to allocate a proportion of total funding to collaborative projects.

The Scheme of Specific Grants and the impulse to collaborate created a need for coordinated action by local authorities and led to the formation of an inter-authority network. A structure, affording cooperation at political, managerial and curriculum development levels, was put in place by the three local authorities with the largest concentrations of Gaelic-speakers – Highland and Strathclyde regional councils and *Comhairle nan Eilean*. Other authorities with Gaelic provision joined the network's Management Review Group which prioritised development proposals submitted by Primary, Secondary and Community Education Review Groups. This review process resulted in projects such as the production of maths and science schemes for primary schools, a learners' course for secondary schools and the creation of a database for modern Gaelic terminology.

Despite the impressive progress of recent years, there is still an urgent need for more and better resources for schools. This is widely acknowledged amongst agencies involved in Gaelic and was made explicit in the HMI report referred to earlier. The SOEID, acting on the advice of the Inspectorate, is to establish a national resource centre in Lewis in 1998–9.

National agencies such as the Scottish Qualifications Authority (SQA), the Scottish Consultative Council on the Curriculum (SCCC) and the Scottish Council for Educational Technology (SCET) play significant roles in supporting Gaelic education. The SQA has a

Gaelic Panel which nominates setters, examiners, moderators and markers for national examinations and provides advice on matters relating to syllabus and assessment. The Panel, then under the aegis of SEB, instigated a wide-ranging review of Gaelic orthography and produced, in 1981, an authoritative set of guidelines known as Gaelic Orthographic Conventions. Panel members regularly participate with SCCC representatives in working parties which prepare subject guidelines and advice for national curriculum development programmes.

Teachers today have access to a range of computer programmes in Gaelic. Some are original Gaelic programmes but many are Gaelic versions of programmes produced in English by SCET. Teachers can also access a bank of radio and television programmes designed for use in school. Scottish Television, Grampian and Channel 4 have each produced schools programmes but the BBC is the main provider. It produces programmes on radio and television, caters for learners and fluent speakers and addresses various stages within both primary and secondary. The *Comataidh Craolaidh Gàidhlig*, the Gaelic Broadcasting Committee which administers an £8.5 million Gaelic Television Fund set up by the government in 1991, has recently indicated that it is to give a higher priority to educational output.

Language development bodies and community organisations also play a key role in bolstering and promoting Gaelic in education. The main language development agency, *Comunn na Gàidhlig* (CNAG), employs an education officer who participates in the inter-authority network referred to earlier and liaises extensively with community groups, service providers and national agencies. CNAG was instrumental in setting up *Comann nam Pàrant* (*Nàiseanta*), a national association of parents involved in Gaelic education which has branches in most places where there is a Gaelic-medium unit.

TEACHER EDUCATION

Three teacher education institutions (TEIs) make provision for Gaelic – the University of Strathclyde in Glasgow, Northern College in Aberdeen and St Andrew's College in Bearsden. Strathclyde's Faculty of Education, formerly Jordanhill College, is the only TEI that has consistently provided training in each of the main preservice courses with permanent specialist staff.

Each TEI offers some training in Gaelic within the BEd and Post-Graduate Certificate in Education Primary (PGCE(P)) courses. The University of Strathclyde and Northern College have Gaelic pathways in the BEd course and Gaelic-speaking students receive tuition in linguistic skills and teaching methods throughout the course. A period of school experience in a Gaelic unit is built into the pathway and into the training of students on the PGCE(P) course. Provision for Gaelic at St Andrew's College, which services the Roman Catholic sector, is more ad hoc but includes a Gaelic school placement. Most of the training in Gaelic at each TEI is optional and outwith core elements of the course. The concentrated nature of the one-year PGCE course affords little scope for additional classes and Gaelic input is, therefore, very limited. The number of Gaelic-speaking students in training seldom exceeds 3 per cent of any year group.

There is widespread dissatisfaction amongst teachers, education managers and parents about the nature and extent of training currently provided for Gaelic-medium teachers. Surveys have shown that newly-qualified teachers are highly critical of preservice arrangements and feel inadequately prepared for the Gaelic-medium classroom with its additional demands and specialised requirements. The present situation where students receive no certification or formal qualification for Gaelic-medium teaching is deemed increasingly anomalous and representations to this effect made to the General Teaching Council and the Scottish Office have set in motion a consultative process.

Preservice training arrangements for secondary teachers of Gaelic are more satisfactory. Gaelic is one of the subject specialisms in which students undertaking the Postgraduate Certificate in Education (Secondary) course (PGCE(S)) can qualify and they receive training in Gaelic teaching methods as a core part of the course. Their training enables them to engage in teaching both the *Gàidhlig* and Gaelic (Learners) courses. Strathclyde University is the only TEI that offers the PGCE(S) Gaelic course each year and it is also the sole provider of any training in Gaelic-medium secondary education, a field set to assume greater significance.

Most inservice training in Gaelic is organised and delivered at local authority and school level with occasional input from TEI staff. The inter-authority network arranges inservice courses annually and there are national training events as part of curriculum development initiatives like Higher Still. Teachers wishing to convert from secondary to primary or to gain a qualification to teach another secondary subject can do so by means of a one-term Additional Teaching Qualification (ATQ) course at a TEI. Several teachers have entered Gaelic-medium teaching by this route and the ATQ has helped authorities address staffing shortages more immediately than otherwise possible. Strathclyde University's plans to introduce inservice open-learning modules in Gaelic-medium education in 1998 should help redress deficiencies in current preservice training.

Strathclyde University and Northern College have responded to pressure from local authorities and SOEID to produce more teachers able to teach in Gaelic in primaries by allocating a certain number of places on courses to Gaelic-speakers or by giving some weighting to Gaelic in the selection process. They also participated, with local authorities and other interested parties, in a recruitment drive funded by SOEID and coordinated by CNAG. These measures have helped to reduce the gap between supply and demand but the throughput of trained personnel is still insufficient to sustain, let alone expand, the Gaelic-medium service.

FURTHER AND HIGHER EDUCATION

The use of Gaelic as a medium of education extends into the tertiary sector and is, indeed, at its most comprehensive in one Further Education (FE) college. *Sabhal Mòr Ostaig* was founded in 1973 as a Gaelic College in the Sleat area of Skye. Initially, the College ran a programme of short courses in Gaelic language and culture but, ten years on, it embarked on full-time provision.

Today, the College offers Higher National Certificate (HNC), Higher National Diploma (HND) and postgraduate courses in business studies, information technology, management, communications, broadcasting and the arts. All these courses, and others in Gaelic language and *Gàidhealtachd* Studies, are delivered and assessed in Gaelic and the administration of the college is also conducted in Gaelic. *Sabhal Mòr* has considerably expanded its portfolio of short courses and over 500 students enlist annually for tuition in a range of language and culture classes. The College campus houses a Gaelic research agency, *Lèirsinn*, a Gaelic theatre company, *Tosg*, and a marketing and communications company, *Cànan*, which publishes educational material. Towards the end of 1997, *Sabhal Mòr* also became home for the Columba Initiative designed to foster closer cultural, educational and linguistic links between Scotland and Ireland.

1997–8 saw the introduction of a full-time Gaelic immersion course at *Sabhal Mòr*. The first such immersion course, sponsored by CNAG, was piloted in Lochaber in 1995–6 by Inverness College. The pilot was adjudged a success and the 600 hour course was repeated in Lochaber, in Inverness and in Clydebank College the following session. The effectiveness of learning a language through immersion is now widely attested and demand for this model amongst adult learners is such that a further five colleges mounted the course in 1997–8.

Sabhal Mòr, Lews Castle, Inverness and other FE establishments in the north have joined forces in the University of the Highlands and Islands Project (UHIP) which aims to win university status for the federal, collegiate institution by the millennium. An award of £33 million from the Millennium Fund, supplemented by European money, is being used to upgrade facilities and to develop degree level courses at the thirteen participating colleges and institutes. It is envisaged that UHI will reflect the character and culture of the region and give Gaelic a higher profile and an enhanced role as a specialist subject of study and as a medium of learning and assessment. *Sabhal Mòr* is likely to be the main centre of Gaelic provision within UHI but Lews Castle will also play a prominent part.

At present, students wishing to study Gaelic at university have to go to Aberdeen, Edinburgh or Glasgow, each of which has a Celtic department. These three departments offer a range of undergraduate courses in Gaelic and Celtic Studies and students can take an Honours degree in Celtic or a joint Honours in Celtic and another subject. Celtic Studies encompasses the study of other Celtic languages, particularly Irish Gaelic and Welsh. Provision is made for those wanting to learn the language and Celtic Civilisation classes cater for those with an interest in cultural heritage. Some Celtic Studies classes are taught in Gaelic but the language is not yet deployed as a medium in other subject areas. Postgraduate study opportunities are also available in the discipline. The University of Strathclyde has, since its merger with Jordanhill College, established Gaelic classes for learners.

COMMUNITY EDUCATION

Time spent in school is but a fraction of the time spent in the home and the community, and the contribution of these domains to the education of the child is being recognised and addressed increasingly in the development of Gaelic education.

Local authorities throughout Scotland arrange evening classes for parents who wish to learn Gaelic and thereby assist, and keep in step with, the linguistic progress of their offspring. Some authorities also provide language packs for parents who are not Gaelic speakers so that they can help their children with homework. Reinforcement of the language beyond the school is regarded as a vital part of the Gaelic-medium education strategy, especially for children from non-Gaelic-speaking homes, and a nationwide network of Gaelic youth clubs has been set up by CNAG. Over 1,500 children between the ages of 5 and 12 attend the 40 *Sradagan* clubs.

Another community initiative, *Fèisean nan Gàidheal*, seeks to reinforce the link between the language and the culture. A *fèis*, or festival, is typically a week-long event which offers children tuition in Gaelic and in a variety of Gaelic arts including drama, storytelling, song and music. The *fèis* movement began in Barra and has evolved into a national agency which assists with the organisation of 29 separate *fèisean* in communities in, and beyond, the

Highlands and Islands. Two of the *fèisean* provide all tuition through the medium of Gaelic.

In addition to the classes for parents mentioned above, a number of agencies run classes and short courses for adult learners. The community education departments of local authorities and FE colleges continue to be the principal providers. Most of the classes are designed for beginners and follow an SQA modular scheme or have a less defined conversational format. University departments of continuing education also offer similar kinds of classes. Intensive short courses for learners are organised by a number of public and private agencies.

RESEARCH

While a great deal of research has been conducted on linguistic, socio-linguistic, demographic and literary topics by university Celtic departments, the School of Scottish Studies at Edinburgh University, the *Lèirsinn* Research agency at *Sabhal Mòr* and individuals such as Kenneth MacKinnon and Charles Withers, Gaelic education has not received the attention it warrants. There was, until lately, little available in published form.

The Department of Education at Stirling University has been the locus for three important research projects into aspects of Gaelic education in recent times. The first of these was an evaluation of the Western Isles Bilingual Project, led by Donald MacIntyre and Ros Mitchell, published in 1987. The findings were generally favourable to the Project and supportive of the bilingual scheme. There followed, in 1994, Professor Richard Johnstone's review of research on the Impact of Current Developments to Support the Gaelic Language. The report gave a comprehensive account and perceptive analysis of developments in education and other fields of Gaelic activity. The previously referred to HMI report on Provision for Gaelic Education in Scotland, also published in 1994, provided a more detailed review of each sector of education but was heavily criticised by the Gaelic community in respect of some of its conclusions and recommendations. Stirling University is currently engaged in a third SOEID funded project, a three-year programme of research on the attainment of pupils in Gaelic-medium Primary Education in Scotland. This project is being carried out in conjunction with the Scottish Council for Research in Education (SCRE) and *Lèirsinn*.

Like Stirling, *Lèirsinn* has been involved in a number of research projects concerned with Gaelic education. The agency was commissioned by the Inter-Authority Standing Group for Gaelic (IASG) to undertake a review and assessment of support and provision for Gaelic-medium education and produced two reports, one on Teacher Training and another on The Critical Skills in 1996. *Lèirsinn* has recently, at the behest of SOEID, investigated the supply of teachers able and willing to engage in Gaelic-medium teaching.

PROSPECTS

It will be apparent from the foregoing review that substantial progress has been made in Gaelic education, particularly in the provision of Gaelic-medium pre-school and primary education. Buoyant and burgeoning as the Gaelic-medium development would appear to be, it is, nevertheless, a tender and fragile flower. This was graphically illustrated in 1996 when cutbacks in local authority funding led to a proposal to close a thriving Gaelic-medium unit in East Kilbride. A concerted campaign by parents and language agencies averted closure but the proposal underlined the insecurity of provision for Gaelic and highlighted once more the absence of a national policy on Gaelic education and the associated lack of official status for the language.

CNAG is leading a campaign to win 'secure status' for the language. It is envisaged that this would consolidate current provision, confer additional linguistic rights on Gaelic speakers and lead to greater use of the language in official domains. Closely linked to this campaign is another CNAG initiative to persuade the government to adopt a national policy for Gaelic education. A plan entitled Framework for Growth was submitted to the government prior to the 1997 general election and was discussed at a meeting in September 1997 with the government minister with responsibility for Education and Gaelic, Brian Wilson. The minister's personal commitment to the language was translated into a positive programme of action with spending on Gaelic education increasing in 1998–9 by £1 million. It is likely that the Scottish Office's celebrated 'benevolent neutrality' stance in regard to bilingual education in the early 1980s will be transformed into a more enlightened progressive and facilitative role.

There is clearly a need for a closer partnership between local and national government in the delivery and development of Gaelic-medium education. Local authorities will have to devise, or refine, policies which articulate with a national framework and will require an assurance of government funding for new initiatives and projects. Further education colleges and higher education institutions also require specific funding for Gaelic if they are to meet the increased demand for training in the language in the face of diminishing budgets. This is particularly true of the TEIs where an extension of Gaelic-medium training would be costly because of the small numbers involved and the need to place students in schools some distance from the institutions.

Teacher recruitment and training has the highest priority in CNAG's discussions with SOEID and there is a growing recognition that a more coordinated and sustained approach is required to address the shortfall in recruitment and the deficiencies in current training arrangements. The training of subject specialists to deliver Gaelic-medium education in the secondary sector will assume greater significance and urgency following the government's decision to end the previous moratorium on development in this sector.

Impressive as the growth in Gaelic-medium education has been, a great deal remains to be done. Twelve years after the establishment of the first Gaelic-medium units in primary schools, there is still no designated Gaelic-medium school anywhere in Scotland. In this respect, Gaelic lags some way behind Irish and Welsh. Urban centres with concentrations of Gaelic speakers, such as Glasgow and Inverness, should be able to sustain an all-Gaelic primary school. Access to Gaelic-medium education needs to be facilitated by means such as the provision of school transport and attempts, such as that by Edinburgh City Council, to cap the number entering Gaelic-medium education need to be exposed and resisted.

Good practice in maximising the use of the language as the vehicle of instruction needs to be more uniformly adopted if the 5–14 target of attaining broadly equal competence in both languages by P7 is to be achieved. The government's proposals to make nursery education available to all four year olds should result in greatly enhanced levels of provision for Gaelic and the recommendation that it be integrated with Gaelic-medium primary provision should lead to a more coherent experience for children and a more systematic pattern of development. While the difficulties in establishing Gaelic-medium education in secondary schools should not be minimised, properly planned progression across sectors and incremental development of subject specialist teaching through the medium of Gaelic should lead to greater parental confidence in Gaelic-medium education as a whole, while continuity from pre-school to primary and from secondary into further and higher education will yield the throughput of trained personnel required to maintain and develop the system.

As a Scottish parliament comes ever closer to being a reality, it is a matter of regret that over 90 per cent of secondary school children in Scotland are denied the opportunity to learn Gaelic in their local school. Research, attitudinal surveys, audience figures for learners' programmes on television and the uptake of learners' classes in continuing and higher education suggest that there is considerable potential for the development of provision for learners within secondary schools. A partnership of central and local government could devise a strategy for a phased programme of development which might include identifying one school in urban areas which would offer tuition in Gaelic and measures such as harnessing information technology and open-learning to provide access in areas with little Gaelic tradition.

A strategy is also required to ensure that the Celtic and Gaelic elements of Scottish heritage, life and culture form part of the curriculum of every school child in Scotland. This, one hopes, will result from the Review of Scottish Culture and the Curriculum launched by Scottish CCC in 1997.

REFERENCES

Dunn, C. M. and A. G. B. Robertson (1989) Gaelic in Education, in W. Gillies (ed.), *Gaelic and Scotland*, Edinburgh: Edinburgh University Press, pp. 44–55.

HM Inspectors of Schools (1994) *Provision for Gaelic Education in Scotland*, Edinburgh: The Scottish Office Education Department.

Johnstone, R. (1994) *The Impact of Current Developments to support the Gaelic Language: Review of Research*, Stirling: Scottish Centre for Information on Language Teaching and Research.

MacKinnon, K. (1991) *Gaelic – A Past and Future Prospect*, Edinburgh: Saltire Society.

Robertson, B. (1995) Provision for Gaelic in Scottish education, in Vallen, Birkhoff and Buwalda (eds), *Home Language and School in a European Perspective*, Tilburg: Tilburg University Press.

The Scottish Office Education Department (1993) *Curriculum and Assessment in Scotland: National Guidelines: Gaelic 5–14*, Edinburgh: HMSO.

24

Catholic Education in Scotland

Tom Fitzpatrick

THE EDUCATION (SCOTLAND) ACT 1918

Ten days after the Armistice that ended World War 1 the Education (Scotland) Act 1918 was passed, initiating a complete reorganisation of the system established by the Education (Scotland) Act of 1872. It aimed at developing an educated community marked by religious tolerance and equal opportunity for all, and enshrined a concept of secondary education 'for all fit to profit from it'. It made available financial aid whereby that ideal could become a reality for a greatly expanded spectrum of the population. Religious education according to use and wont would be allowed within well-defined limits, but would not be fostered by the civil authority, and provision was made for a revision of the teacher-training system.

The Act was a generous and statesman-like measure that remedied long-standing grievances affecting the voluntary schools that had, in 1872, opted to remain outside the system. Two hundred and twenty-six Catholic schools transferred into the control of the Education Authorities set up under the Act. The vast majority were elementary schools managed by the parish priests, located for the most part in industrial areas of the south-west and west central belt, or in populous centres of the Lothians, Fife, Tayside and Aberdeenshire. A few existed in Speyside, Banffshire, Galloway and in the West Highlands and Islands, where Catholic communities had survived from pre-Reformation times. Post-primary education, apart from that given in supplementary classes in some parochial schools, was in the hands of religious teaching orders – the Marist Brothers, Christian Brothers, Society of Jesus, Benedictines, Ursuline and Franciscan Sisters, Sisters of Mercy, Congregation of Notre Dame, Society of the Sacred Heart, Faithful Companions of Jesus, and the Sisters of the Cross and Passion – who managed some fifteen independent schools in Glasgow, Edinburgh, Ayrshire, Renfrewshire, Dumbarton, Dundee, Dumfries, Bothwell, Fort Augustus and North Berwick. The number of secondary pupils was a very small fraction of the primary population. Other orders, among them the Vincentians, Sisters of Charity and Good Shepherd Sisters, contributed to the education of the community by work of a social nature including the housing of orphans, the supervision of delinquent children and teaching the deaf and blind.

Catholic Scotland had been generous in scholastic foundations. Before the Reformation three universities existed, and according to M. Lynch in *Scotland – A New History*, (London: Century, 1991, p. 106) 'the generations after 1560 saw the consolidation rather than the establishment of an elementary national system of education; in many cases, schools were refounded or recast rather than created as new foundations.' Catholic schooling however ceased until the end of the eighteenth century, when the population began to increase rapidly, particularly in the coalfield areas where demand for labour was greatest. New parishes were founded, often with a school attached. In the latter part of the nineteenth century an attempt was made to develop an independent Catholic schools system, but limited resources made it impossible to keep pace with the national system. The vast majority of the parochial schools were grossly overcrowded, ill-equipped and under-staffed. As Sister M. Skinnider has shown, in T. R. Bone (ed.) *Studies in the History of Scottish Education 1872–1939, SCRE No. 54* (London: ULP, 1967), in Glasgow where one third of the Catholic population was located, fewer than 3 per cent of pupils went on to any form of post-primary schooling. The position in other parts of the country was probably worse. There was a gross imbalance between the primary and secondary sectors, which contributed to a serious shortage of properly qualified teachers.

Studies in the *Innes Review* relating to the preparation and operation of the 1918 Act include: J. Darragh, *The Apostolic Visitations of Scotland, 1912 and 1917*, vol. XLI, no.1 (Glasgow: Scottish Catholic Historical Association, 1990), 7–118; Brother Kenneth FMS, *The Education (Scotland) Act, 1918, in the Making*, vol. XIX:2 (1968), 91–128; J. H. Treble, *The Working of the 1918 Act in the Glasgow Archdiocese*, vol. XXX1:1 (1980), 27–44. The settlement satisfied many of the aspirations of the Catholic community. It made possible the evolution of a Catholic sector within the national system, supported by public funds, in which the Hierarchy had a measure of control through its statutory power to approve teachers and appoint supervisors of religious education. Catholic teachers had to be qualified under the national regulations and also be approved by a bishop 'as to religious belief and character'. They would be the principal witnesses to the religious nature of the education to be provided.

BETWEEN THE WARS

After 1918 there was an upsurge in demand for secondary education. If the benefits of the Act were to be fully achieved, a new system had to be developed to meet the legal requirements and also satisfy the Hierarchy in respect of the nature of the education that would have to be provided to a wider spectrum of the population than before. In the parochial schools, the spiritual formation of the child lay at the heart of the educational process, whereas in the national system intellectual rather than spiritual formation and attention to utilitarian values took precedence. The associated problems, felt most acutely at secondary level, were exacerbated by the changes in school organisation introduced by the Act, and also by the rising standards of academic qualification that were being asked of all teachers.

In the next two decades some primary schools progressed to junior secondary or intermediate status, existing secondary schools expanded, and new ones were founded. A massive drive to meet the ensuing demand for teachers began. A second teacher-training college, for women, was opened at Craiglockhart in Edinburgh. Dowanhill College in Glasgow, also for women only, was already well established. Special provision for the training of Catholic male teachers had to be made. As well as following the prescribed course at a provincial centre, they had to attend a parallel course in Religious Education, provided by the Hierarchy, leading to the award of a Religious Teaching Certificate. All who sought to teach in Catholic schools were required to hold this certificate and be approved by the bishop of the diocese.

A new degree of social mobility was experienced within the community, with teachers the backbone of an emerging middle class. Progress was made in the expansion of the schools, particularly at secondary level, throughout Strathclyde and in Edinburgh, Fife and Dundee. The flow of Catholic students to the universities, previously minuscule, greatly increased. By 1939 the number of graduates had outstripped the provision of school places, and many newly qualified teachers found themselves surplus to requirements at a time when the need for more secondary places remained acute. The emphasis on producing teachers, which had had a restrictive effect on educational objectives, diminished, and more former pupils began to find their way into other professions and occupations. The outbreak of World War Two halted the progress.

THE WAR YEARS

The impact of war-time conditions on schools was severe. In 1939 some 70 per cent of the Catholic population was located in the most congested areas of the south-west of the country, with a majority in the city of Glasgow itself. When evacuation became necessary, most Catholic schools were situated in sending or neutral zones, with very few in receiving areas. One objective of the scheme, 'to match householders and evacuees according to social class and religion', was impossible of achievement, so that the disruption bore heavily on a major part of the Catholic sector.

As the war progressed the number of teachers completing training fell drastically. A significant proportion of the teaching force consisted of recently qualified young men, who were called up for national service. Staffs were depleted, and recently-founded schools were disrupted before becoming properly established. The following statement from the 1947 Scottish Education Department *Report on Education in Scotland* was particularly true of the Catholic sector: 'great efforts were made . . . to maintain ordinary standards at least in the basic subjects . . . this aim was not fully achieved . . . at the primary stage proficiency in written composition, arithmetic and power to comprehend was not yet up to pre-war standard.'

REVOLUTION

The Second World War ended, like the first, with the passing of a measure of historic significance, the Education (Scotland) Act 1945. The school leaving age was to be raised to 15 and later to 16; adequate and efficient provision of free primary, secondary and further education was to be made; Junior Colleges were to be set up for the compulsory part-time education of young persons aged 15 to 18; milk and meals were to be provided in all schools. Primary and secondary education were re-defined as progressive courses of instruction appropriate to the age, aptitude and ability of the pupils concerned. Secondary education was seen to be a stage in the schooling of every child, rather than a particular type of schooling provided for some but not for all. This changed view, stemming at least in part from the national experience of common suffering in war-time, required that a new type of schooling be evolved that would suit the majority of pupils as well as the old had fitted the few.

An expansion of school accommodation was urgently needed. The shortage of teachers, a legacy of war, was exacerbated by the demands following from the raising of the leaving age, and by a dramatic rise in the school population resulting from a greatly increased birth-rate.

Inevitably, the shortage would become progressively more acute as secondary and further education developed. In 1958 the regulations governing the training of teachers were revised. Training Colleges were given increased powers, and several new ones founded.

Through the 1950s and 1960s, as the children born in the immediate post-war years progressed through the primary, secondary and further stages of the educational system, these sectors experienced in turn rapid expansion followed by equally dramatic contraction. The resultant strains were compounded by large movements of population, the break-down of old communities, the emergence of new towns, an unprecedented explosion of knowledge and of communications technology, a decline in religious faith and practice, and a loss of certainty in previously accepted moral absolutes. The Catholic sector had to adjust also to the insights of the Second Vatican Council, which ended in December 1964. Its findings have implications not only for formal religious instruction, but also for all aspects of Christian education.

The traditional Scottish approach to secondary education, designed to provide a broad general education with a distinct academic bias, was not appropriate for the enlarged spectrum of the population expected to proceed to further rather than to tertiary education. In 1965 the Scottish Education Department abolished the distinction between junior and senior secondary schools and required county authorities to implement a comprehensive system. It was hoped this would minimise the divisiveness associated with the separate categories of schools of the former system. The Catholic community felt that the demands of social justice would be better met by a comprehensive than by a selective approach which ran counter to the Christian view of the value of every individual. It was also aware that its need for expansion at secondary level would only be met through the implementation of this government policy.

The schools had to adapt to this revolution while preserving their distinctive religious character. It has been argued that the ensuing problems, particularly the persistent shortage of teachers, were felt more acutely in the Catholic sector than in the national system as a whole. Scottish Education Statistics, *Secondary School Staffing Survey 1970, vol. 3* (1972) points out that in the industrial west Roman Catholic schools especially were understaffed by any reasonable standard, as evidenced by high pupil-teacher ratios, large classes, high turnover, curtailed curriculum and part-time education. It also notes that counties in the east fared better through their ability to attract non-Catholic staff.

As the pressures on the secondary schools mounted, their capacity to offer an adequate programme of religious education diminished. Periods of religious instruction were shortened, their number reduced and much of their time taken up with secular tasks. The presence of the religious orders in the schools declined, in line with a decrease in vocations to the religious life and in religious observance generally. The system of catechetical training broke down and the examination for the Preliminary Religious Certificate was abandoned. The difficulties were further aggravated when the school leaving age was raised to sixteen in 1972.

INCREASE

By 1972 the Catholic schools sector had expanded to a size almost commensurate with the population it served. A system of comprehensive education was emerging, albeit at varying rates in different parts of the country. In Glasgow, where the move towards a fully comprehensive system had started early in the 1950s, the seven full secondary schools of

1945 had increased to twenty-one comprehensives by 1972. Progress was also being made in Edinburgh and Dundee, and in the landward counties of the south-west.

The accompanying demand for teachers was met by an unprecedented expansion of the training colleges. In a major overhaul of teacher training beginning in 1967, men were admitted to the Primary Diploma course and new teaching qualifications were introduced, including a college-based Bachelor of Education degree in which academic development and professional training were carried out concurrently, validated in the case of Notre Dame College by the Council for National Academic Awards. The vast changes in curricular content required both by the explosion of knowledge and the particular needs of the comprehensive system were met by a wide range of courses for teachers in service.

The turbulence in the national educational community associated with the comprehensive revolution reflected a deep-seated spiritual malaise in society at large. A loss of moral certainty in the adult population, experienced nationwide, resulted in the erosion of parental authority and confusion in the minds of the young, and led to a crisis in moral and religious education which demanded responses from civil and ecclesiastical authorities. Following the publication by the SED of two seminal memoranda, *Guidance in Scottish Secondary Schools* (1968), and *The Structure of Promoted Posts in Scottish Secondary Schools* (1971), which outlined the underlying philosophy and dealt with the practical issues involved, a structure of personal, vocational and curricular guidance was introduced in all secondary schools. Because of its long involvement in Child Guidance, and its concept of education as necessarily concerned with the moral and spiritual as well as the intellectual development of children, Notre Dame College cooperated vigorously and gave a lead in this new departure. In 1971 non-denominational in-service guidance courses were created, which led to a widening of the commitment to pastoral aspects of the teacher's work, and prepared the way for the introduction, at the national level, of special qualification courses in this field.

In 1972 the Millar Report on Moral and Religious Education, for schools other than Roman Catholic schools, appeared. In 1974 a Teaching Qualification in Religious Education for Secondary Education was introduced, regulations governing qualification to teach religious subjects were formulated, and Specialist Teachers of Religious Education began to be trained to meet the curricular demands that followed. This led to the development of examinable Religious Studies, which required that the teaching was subject to inspection. Section 66(2) of the Education (Scotland) Act 1980, which forbade inspection of Religious Instruction by HMI, was repealed by the Education (Scotland) Act 1981, and in 1983 inspection of Religious Education began. Parallel with these developments the Catholic Education Commission, composed of representatives nominated by the bishop of each diocese, was instituted in 1972 to advise the Hierarchy on educational matters; full-time chaplains were appointed to secondary schools, diocesan catechetical centres were set up, and in-service courses in Religious Education were introduced. In 1976 an Advanced Diploma Course in Religious Education offered by Notre Dame College gained recognition as a teaching qualification. It developed into the Advanced Teaching Qualification in Religious Education (ATQRE) now provided partly by correspondence.

DECREASE

By the middle of the 1970s a fall in the birthrate, as dramatic within the Catholic community as in the nation as a whole, led to a decline in the primary schools population, with a similar consequence at higher levels to follow. The endemic shortage of teachers suddenly disappeared. The educational expansion of the post-war period went into reverse, and many primary and secondary schools contracted or closed. In 1981 the two Catholic training colleges were dissolved and a new institution, St Andrew's College of Education, was founded at Bearsden in the building formerly occupied by Notre Dame College. The rule that the principal of a Catholic college should belong to a religious teaching order was abrogated, and the way was open for a lay person to become head.

TRANSFORMATION

Between 1918 and 1980 Catholic education was transformed, mainly because of the greater understanding of the needs of the community shown by the civil authorities and a major shift in educational policy decreed by government. Children of an enlarged segment of the population were being taught in smaller classes and in better surroundings than ever before. Teachers were better qualified, and the shortage that had so long haunted the system had ended. The level of academic attainment was comparable with that of the non-denominational sector. The number of former pupils going on to higher and tertiary education had mushroomed, and was contributing to the common good in a multitude of ways, in medicine, nursing, the law, civil service and in the expanding world of finance, as well as in higher education, educational administration, politics, journalism and the arts. A Catholic middle class had emerged, the fruit of the expanded educational service, and the image of the Catholic layman as 'hewer of wood and drawer of water' no longer applied. Something, however, had been lost. Before 1918 the Catholic community had a unity of outlook based on a common culture, distinguishing it in many respects from the country as a whole. By 1980 this was no longer the case, and within the community itself there was evident a growing division based on social distinctions. The tradition of Catholic intellectualism of the 1930s had dwindled, and with it that integration of culture and faith which might be taken to be the hallmark of an educated Catholic community.

THE ETHOS OF CATHOLIC SCHOOLS

The ethos or characteristic spirit of any community is a function of its fundamental and essential beliefs, a reflection of its value-system and of its view of its place in the universe. It is related to the prevalent tone of the community, and is the result of the manner and degree to which practical expression is given to its beliefs. The ethos of an educational system can be understood only in relation to the community it serves.

Scottish Catholic schools have to be seen in the context of the history and spiritual disposition of the local Catholic community. They give expression to the Catholic view of the condition of the human person, as imperfect, redeemed, and of infinite value. The fullness of this expression may vary, depending on the degree of understanding of and commitment to that view.

By their transfer in 1918 Catholic schools accepted the academic standards and organisational structure of the national system, and subsequently absorbed many of its positive aspects, as for example recognition of the contribution of education to the common good, the right of young people to an education from which they are capable of profiting, and access to it unhindered by class, gender or other distinctions. However, Catholic schools also belong to an older, faith-centred tradition that aims to bring faith, culture and life into harmony, in which the rhythm of school life is in tune with the Church's liturgical year, and within which academic content is illuminated with the spirit of the gospel. This tradition holds that education must be directed towards the development of the moral as well as the intellectual faculties of the child, and that personal development is incomplete where spiritual and religious growth is neglected. It strives to achieve its aims through the implanting of the motives and practices of the Catholic religion. It is this religious dimension that gives the Catholic school its distinctive character. The Christian message should animate the school community and infuse secular teaching with religious awareness and understanding. This is what makes the difference between a school where education is permeated by the Christian spirit and one in which religion is regarded as an academic subject like any other. Teachers committed to this philosophy accept a responsibility for the moral and spiritual welfare of their pupils that extends beyond the satisfying of their intellectual needs.

In this tradition moral and religious education are inseparable. The distinctiveness of Catholic education therefore rests ultimately on the faith, doctrine and sacramental practice of the Catholic Church.

THE TRAINING OF TEACHERS FOR CATHOLIC SCHOOLS

In the natural order parents are the first teachers of their children and the source of authority over them. In the Scottish democratic system parents devolve some of this authority to the schools.

A religion is more than a philosophy, and education more than the passing on of an ideology. The consequence for teachers is spelled out in the Roman document *The Catholic School*. 'The achievement . . . of the catholic school depends not so much on the subject matter or methodology as on the people who work there . . . The extent to which the Christian message is transmitted through education depends greatly on the teachers, by whom the integration of culture and faith is mediated.' The demeanour and life-style of teachers proclaim their outlook and attitudes. It is the quality of integration of faith and life in the person of the teacher that ennobles the educator's task.

After 1918 Catholic men and women seeking a licence to teach had to meet the requirements of both civil and ecclesiastical authorities. Women could do this by training at either of two residential Catholic colleges. Men had to train at a provincial college, usually at Jordanhill or Moray House, and also follow a parallel course laid down by the Church. This involved obtaining, by written examination, a preliminary religious certificate at the end of the secondary school career, and attendance at a series of extra-mural lectures taken concurrently with a university or college course. A further series took place during the training college course with the cooperation of the authorities there. A full Religious Certificate was awarded on satisfying all these requirements, the complexity of which indicated the importance attached to the teacher's role. A detailed account of the system appears in T. A. Fitzpatrick, *No Mean Service* (Glasgow: St Andrew's College, 1995).

With the massive expansion of education in the 1960s the training system came under great strain. When in 1967 men were admitted to the non-graduate diploma Course in primary education, the Catholic colleges opened their doors to male students. Catholic men could now meet all civil and ecclesiastical requirements during their period of college training.

Notre Dame College expanded into a new building at Bearsden while retaining its original premises at Dowanhill, and Craiglockhart expanded. Degree-awarding powers were extended, and Notre Dame College sought validation of its degree courses from the Council for National Academic Awards. National qualifications for Specialist Teachers of Religious Education were introduced, and after discussions between the Scottish Education Department and the Catholic Education Commission it was agreed that HM Inspectors had the right to inspect professional aspects of religious education in Catholic schools.

In 1981 St Andrew's College of Education at Bearsden became the National Catholic College of Scotland, and all prospective Catholic teachers were required to follow the course in Religious Education provided there. To meet the difficulties of students unable for geographical or other approved reasons to undertake training there, Distance Learning courses in Religious Education are provided, backed by in-service courses at bases in Edinburgh and Dundee.

The matter of the approval of teachers to posts in Catholic schools has always been a particular concern of the Hierarchy. In view of the many changes that had taken place in the field of Religious Education, the Commission approached the government to discuss an amendment to the Education (Scotland) Act 1980 reaffirming the right of the local bishop to approve 'as to religious belief and character' any teacher to be appointed to a post in a Catholic School. This amendment became part of the Self-Governing schools etc. (Scotland) Act 1989.

When the fall in student numbers reached tertiary level, the organisation of higher education was again overhauled. The Council for National Academic Awards was wound up, and St Andrew's College, the national Catholic College became an Associate College of the University of Glasgow.

TOWARDS THE MILLENNIUM

After 1980 the rate of change that characterised the post-war educational scene accelerated. The presence of the religious teaching orders in the schools declined to near vanishing point. The historic convent schools of the Franciscan Sisters and the Sisters of Mercy in Glasgow, in existence since 1847, Sacred Heart Convent School in Girvan and the Benedictine Abbey School at Fort Augustus were among those that closed. St Joseph's College in Dumfries, a Marist Brothers boarding school for boys, became a comprehensive school controlled by the local education authority. In Glasgow lay men and women took charge of St Mungo's Academy and Notre Dame High School. Private schools in the Archdiocese of St Andrews and Edinburgh founded by the Ursuline Sisters, the Sacred Heart Society, the Christian Brothers and the Benedictines, all closed. The tradition of single-sex education that had characterised the catholic educational tradition all but disappeared. The independent Kilgraston Convent School, founded by the Society of the Sacred Heart, and Notre Dame High School in Glasgow, continued as schools for girls only, but St Aloysius' College, founded in Glasgow in 1859 and still under Jesuit management, began to cater for both boys and girls.

In 1918, 70% of the entire Catholic population was located in the south-west of the country, and of that total 70% were located in the city of Glasgow. Eight decades on, the fifteen independent schools then existing were reduced to three, and 59 Secondary, 360 Primary and eight Special schools replaced the 226 schools that had transferred into state control. Some 60% of Catholic primaries were situated in Strathclyde, about 40% of them in Glasgow. The number of schools in Edinburgh, the Lothians, Fife and Tayside increased, with notable gains also in Ayrshire and the Borders. These figures are indicative of some drift of the Catholic population from west to east, and also of a wider dispersal within the historic areas of high density in the west.

THE FUTURE OF CATHOLIC EDUCATION.

For the foreseeable future, Catholic education has to work towards a fusion of its two traditions, while remaining true to itself. Historically these had much in common. The Scottish pedagogical tradition, underpinned by the trinity of Home, Church and School, was consonant with the Catholic view that full educational development is a function, not only of the school, but also of the family and the whole Christian community. In consequence, in the inter-war period Catholic schools could follow the model of the non-denominational sector relatively easily.

Now the supporting pillars are being eroded, and cultural changes running counter to Christian values expose pupils to confusing and disturbing influences and endanger the ethos of the schools. The Catholic system has to operate in a structure in which secular education has priority over religious and moral aspects, and in a climate of scientific materialism unsympathetic to the values that it tries to propagate. The advances of modern science, buttressed by communication technology in all its forms, have produced a mind-set which finds it difficult to reconcile the truths of science and of religion. In this respect the obstacles faced by Catholic educators are shared by people of good will generally.

Catholic education is based on a view of reality, and of the nature of human beings, that will not change. It entails an acceptance of a transcendental view of the nature of the cosmos as in essence contingent, and of human beings as fundamentally imperfect. It holds that these views are not contrary to reason; but that they have more clearly and more certainly been arrived at through the revelation of God in history and finally in the person of Jesus, the embodiment of divine truth.

The mind-set of scientific materialism rejects these views, and until recently did so with an unjustified certainty in the strength of its position. The unfolding of the last century of the second millennium of the Christian era has undermined this confidence in a number of ways. The participation in two world wars by the most enlightened nations of the planet lends credence to the view of humanity's fallen nature, while within the once most firmly-held field of human knowledge, the world of physical matter, an uncertainty principle has raised its head. Science now accepts that the fundamental building-blocks of matter are at once solid and not solid; and in the realm of the human psyche has no clear understanding of how the supreme emotions and virtues, such as love, courage and self-abnegation can come about through purely material operations.

In 1988 the Catholic Education Commission considered ways of promoting the distinctive nature of the Catholic school. An extensive process of discussion and consultation resulted in the launch in 1992–3 of *Faith and Learning*, development programmes for Catholic primary and secondary schools. These were followed by *Affirms*, which offered spiritual support and an opportunity for reflection to those involved in Catholic education.

This initiative derives from the work of religious teaching orders. Although they were not omnipresent, their influence extended throughout the system. The great majority of teachers had been trained by them at some stage, and the religious schools they managed provided a generally accepted model of what a Catholic school should be. The responsibility for the continuation of the tradition devolves more and more on a lay teaching cadre, at a time when many young people are alienated from the mainstream churches. Should the present religiously indifferent cultural climate persist into the next millennium, the case for Catholic education as an alternative to other forms of schooling must strengthen.

REFERENCES

The Sacred Congregation for Education (1977) *The Catholic School*, London: Catholic Truth Society.

Abbott, W. (ed.) (1966) *The Documents of Vatican II*, London: Chapman.

Dealy, Sister M. B.(1945) *Catholic Schools in Scotland*, Washington DC: Catholic University of America.

Fitzpatrick, T. A. (1986) *Catholic Secondary Education in South-West Scotland before 1972*, Aberdeen: AUP.

McRoberts, D. (1979) *Modern Scottish Catholicism*, Glasgow: Scottish Catholic Historical Association.

Maritain, J. (1932) *The Things that are not Caesar's*, London: Sheed and Ward.

25

Education and the Scottish Economy

David Hartley

Scotland has a mature capitalist economy. In 1995 it contributed 8.5 per cent of the UK's gross domestic product. As in the UK as a whole, about 70 per cent of employees work in the service sector, and about 26 per cent in manufacturing industry. In 1996, their average gross weekly earnings were about 93 per cent of those for mainland Britain as a whole. Scotland's unemployment rate was just over 7 per cent, fractionally higher than that for the UK. The proportion of workers who are self-employed in Scotland is about 10 per cent, about three percentage points below that for Britain, and the number of so-called non-standard, flexible workers is rising, many of them women. Contemporary capitalism in Scotland reveals a growing divide between the 'haves' and the 'have-nots'. According to the Scottish Low Pay Unit's criteria, 42.6 per cent of all Scottish workers were low-paid, women more so than men. Almost one in five children are entitled to free meals; in Glasgow it is two in five.

Throughout the industrialised world, capitalism is being re-structured. There are two broad trends emerging: globalisation; and post-Fordism. Take globalisation. Transnational corporations constantly seek to increase their profitability by relocating to those parts of the world where the rate of return on their investment is maximised. The production and consumption of goods and services is becoming globalised. Capital now flows around the world almost instantaneously, in digital form, without regard for national boundaries. Speculators can cause a run on a currency which a national government would find difficult to curb. The Pacific-rim economies are developing rapidly, and they have access to capital, to an educated labour force, to very low wage-levels, and to vast domestic markets; and they are not overly burdened by the costs of a welfare state. They are in business, in competition among themselves, and with the more mature economies of the 'West'.

But there is a paradox: whilst the globalisation of markets proceeds unchecked, there is a tendency for cultural forms to assert themselves around the banner of national identity. Indeed one could say that this collection of essays is an example of that very assertion of national identity. A White Paper published in 1997 underlines the point. Its title, *Raising the Standard*, seems ambiguous: not only to raise standards in education so that the country can become economically competitive, but also to fly the flag, to raise the standard so to say, and assert national identity. Thus whilst at the economic level there is an internationalisation (or globalisation), at the cultural level there is a search for identity, and this can reveal itself in the affirmation of nationhood, or in the assertion of other community affiliations such as those based on religion, sexuality, gender, or ethnicity.

So much for globalisation. What of post-Fordism? This logically requires a prior statement about Fordism. In the first two decades of this century empirical studies of the work-process were undertaken – notably by F. W. Taylor in the United States – so that its elements could be defined, and best practice documented. Taylor's ideas were taken further by Henry Ford who built the moving car-assembly line. The raw material went in at one end of the factory and the car emerged at the other. But what was so efficient about Ford's process was that the control of the workers was built into the very technology, the assembly-line, whose speed could be set by management. But that was in the 1920s. Since the 1960s a new management style has emerged: post-Fordism. The workers must be flexible, able to multi-task, to come and go as the needs of the business dictate. Although flexibility means being adaptable while actually in work, it also requires a readiness to move in and out of work. At work, employees must be able to supervise themselves, and to display a repertoire of social skills in order to deal better with the public. So this is emotional labour, not just manual labour. These workers are said to be empowered, to have a sense of ownership about what they do. But this ownership is usually of the means – of the tactics – whereby they will achieve management's goals and strategies, on time, to specification, with zero-defects, all this while revealing a pleasant have-a-nice-day disposition. And this post-Fordist workforce is divided into 'core' and 'peripheral' workers. At root, post-Fordism is a managerial style which is aimed at maximising efficiency and effectiveness, without workers having to succumb to highly bureaucratic directives. The idea is that they manage themselves.

So much for the central shifts in the economy, namely globalisation and post-Fordism. How have these economic shifts impinged upon Scottish education in recent years? The response will be in two parts.

1. The first part considers the extent to which market forces have influenced Scottish education. There have been changes in the organisational arrangements for governing and managing Scottish education. This is referred to as the 'marketisation of education'.
2. The second part deals with curricular and pedagogical changes which both implicitly and explicitly are vocational in their purpose. This is referred to as the 'vocationalisation of education'.

These two strands, of course, overlap, both logically and chronologically, and the nature of this intersection will be indicated.

EDUCATION AND ECONOMY: THE MARKETISATION OF SCOTTISH EDUCATION

What is the nature of the relationship between education, economy and society? Take a few statistics. In a recent international study of standards in mathematics and science some of the so-called developed societies got a rude awakening. The Third International Mathematics and Science Study (TIMSS) compared the performance of 13-year-olds' average scores for mathematics and science across forty-one nations. When the data for South Korea is compared with that for Scotland, it suggests that there is no simple correlation between achievement and per-pupil expenditure. In mathematics, South Korea ranked second; Scotland, twenty-ninth. In science, South Korea ranked fourth; Scotland, twenty-sixth. But South Korea spent only $2,000 per pupil compared to Scotland's $4,300. The government's interpretation of data such as this has been that Scotland could well make large efficiency gains without necessarily lowering standards. Indeed throughout the 1980s, Conservative politicians in Scotland, led by Michael Forsyth, tried to devise ways of maximising effectiveness at the same time as increasing efficiency, thereby 'doing more with less'.

Most importantly for the analysis, the globalisation of markets has profound consequences for the welfare state. Before 1945 there was not much of a 'safety net' for those who had fallen on hard times. In the post-war egalitarian mood the welfare state was created. It took the roughness out of the justice which capitalism had hitherto meted out to its losers. Not only was the welfare state good for democracy, it was also good for business, because the costs of preparing an educated and healthy workforce were met through taxation. There were universal benefits, paid for and used by all, according to need. In a sense the welfare state has been too successful: the more education and health care people received, the more they wanted. The demand never ceases, and the costs continuously rise. In the 1970s, the capacity to pay for it was called into question. Economic recession, the increasing competition from the Pacific rim, the pluralisation of society, and the so-called tax-revolt of the rich all seemed to combine to cause a re-examination of the nature and funding of the welfare state.

Until 1979 governments had decided upon the social distribution of education, health-care and other benefits in society. Thereafter the New Right sought to subject the welfare state to market forces, for a number of reasons. In the first place it was said to be both inefficient and less than effective. Part of the reason for this was that there was too much bureaucratic interference, especially by local government, which was allegedly driven by petty politics rather than by the need to get the job done properly. In sum, the 'producers' – the professionals and bureaucrats – had allegedly 'captured' the welfare state for their own ends, leaving aside the needs of the clients, or 'consumers'. Under Thatcherism, however, consumers were to be placed in control. This meant that they had to be in a position to decide upon the best provider and product. Schools would have to compete for children, and in order to succeed in the market they had to be both efficient and effective, otherwise they might cease to 'trade'.

So the state would be rolled back, and quasi-autonomous nongovernmental organisations (quangos) were inserted between government and civil society in order to steer policy on the government's behalf. Individual freedom would replace social justice; quality would prevail over equality; business contracts would replace social contracts. In short, a completely new vocabulary began to suffuse education: gone were the egalitarian notions of the 1950s and 1960s; in their stead came accountability, consumer choice, audits, efficiency, effectiveness, enterprise, together with a range of metaphors drawn from industry. The story was being re-written. According to Mrs Thatcher there is no such thing as society; only individuals and families. Paradoxically, what individuals share socially is that they are self-interested and all-consuming. They are urged to become active citizens: ever-ready workers, lifelong learners and ceaseless consumers, purposeful and prudential, with a can-do demeanour.

During the 1980s the elements of the market slowly began to emerge: first, the 'raw material' (the pupil); second, the 'producer' (the school); third, the 'product' (the examination results); fourth, the 'marketplace' (as symbolised in the league-tables of results); and fifth, the all-important 'consumer' who 'shops around'. In education, however, the pupil is in the logically difficult position of being both a producer and a consumer: that is, pupils co-produce their learning with their teachers. Given all of these elements, what would ensue would be efficiency, effectiveness and excellence – in theory. But there is a caveat to be made about this market. It is rigged and regulated. As shall be argued below, its rules of exchange and currency are set by the government, and the 'players' are not evenly positioned to profit from it. It is not a free market; it is, as Le Grand states, a 'quasi-market', and it is represented below.

The Quasi-Market in Education

Consumer choice:
    Parents Charter
    Assisted Places Scheme
Involvement:
    School Boards

Process de-regulation:
    Devolved School Management
    Self-Governing Schools

Output quality control:
    National curriculum guidelines
    National testing
    School league tables

Process quality control:
    Teacher appraisal
    Reform of teacher training

The two columns seem to contradict each other. On the left are those policies which have helped to redefine the parent as a consumer. The consumer is involved in the school and in some of the decisions which can be taken about it – whether or not, for example, it remains under the control of the local authority. On the right are listed a series of measures which enable the consumer to compare objectively the 'output quality' measures of the different schools in the local market-place. Also on the right are those policies which might serve to ensure 'process quality' – that is, the quality of teaching. So, on the left-hand side there are appeals to choice and local democracy, and on the right-hand side there are measures which are controlled by central government. In a free market the controls put in place on the right-hand side would be absent. What emerges, therefore, is a quasi-market, a regulated market. Its two dimensions, choice and control, will now be examined.

Choice, involvement and process deregulation

A market requires consumers. Before 1979, 'parental involvement' had tended to mean that schools should establish a professional relationship with parents because research had shown that parental involvement correlated well with pupil achievement. In 1981, however, the professional relationship between home and school was redefined as more of a business or calculative relationship. Parents were to be consumers. They were enabled to choose a school which was not necessarily their local one. In a democracy, this notion of choice had a politically sound ring to it, and it resonated even more with parents who were part of a consumer society. Here, therefore, was the first dent in the 'social engineering' of the state education system which had been constructed since 1945. Now, calculation and self-interest would be the determinants of educational provision. There was, too, an impression given that the 'market' was somehow 'natural': that there was a Darwinian logic to it which saw the fittest survive and the weakest go to the wall.

Choice

The government assumed that parents would make rational choices on the basis of reliable information. In the early 1980s, league-tables of school attainment were not available, so a school-by-school comparison based on objective data was not easy to make. The government had assumed further that all parents had available to them the same range of choices. This was clearly not the case, especially in rural areas, or when the costs of travelling to a desired school were in excess of what parents could pay, or when the costs of moving house nearer to that school were equally prohibitive. So although parents had the same 'right to choose', the available choices were by no means equally distributed. Furthermore, a certain cultural capital is required of parents when they come to de-code the images and information which a school provides, and this capital – like financial capital – is not available equally to all. The ability to exercise a choice is therefore socially structured; it is not just a matter of rational choice.

The Education (Scotland) Act 1981 enabled open enrolment by allowing parents to express a preference for a school. This would be met if the local authority did not have to supply another teacher, or alter the architecture of the school, or if the incoming pupil was not overly disruptive. Even so, by 1995 about nine out of ten pupils in Scotland continued to enrol in their local school, the more so in rural areas, the less so in the city. Ironically, sometimes parents who entered a catchment area were unable to place their children in the local school because it was already full. In response, the Education (Scotland) Act 1996 has had to assign local authorities the right to retain empty places to meet this sort of eventuality, but they are unlikely to do so. Even when parents do exercise their right to choose, they seem to do so for reasons which were not intended by the government: proximity; the presence of family and friends; or perceptions about the social composition of the catchment area, the more up-market the better. And notwithstanding all of this, when the demand for a school exceeded the supply, then instead of the consumer choosing the school the school began to select the child.

A further policy which purported to widen parental choice was the Assisted Places Scheme (APS). This was introduced in 1981 and has been the object of much controversy. From the outset the Scottish Education Department was very careful in its rationale for the scheme not to imply a denigration of Scotland's much-esteemed comprehensive schools. Indeed, by claiming to widen educational opportunity, the scheme was said to complement the comprehensive system. It also had the convenient effect of injecting state funding into an independent sector which had been feeling the pinch in the wake of the demise of the grant-aided schools. In order to take advantage of the scheme, parents would have to be informed about it, but its availability seems not to have been widely known in the beginning, except, of course, if a pupil of limited means was already in the private sector. In 1994, only 45 per cent of pupils were receiving a full remission of fees in Scotland, and it is clear the poorest children were not taking up their full quota. Immediately before the 1997 general election, the Conservative government had proposed to nearly double the number of assisted places. The incoming Labour government withdrew the scheme.

According to Conservative thinkers in the 1980s, a market can only operate when schools are freed from the fetters of local authority control and placed in the hands of the parents and the staff. Only when local bureaucracy is by-passed can the schools be set free to perform as they would wish. To effect this, a conversion process was set in train. The first stage was to involve the parent in the school; and the second was to empower both the parents and the school by assigning to them greater financial powers in the hope that they would go on to opt out of local authority control.

Involvement and empowerment

This process began with the school boards, which were established in 1988. Unlike their English counterparts – the governing bodies – the Scottish school boards neither controlled the Budget nor did they have the right to hire and fire staff. And curriculum, pedagogy and assessment remained under the control of central government. The main power of the school board is that it can ballot parents who can decide whether or not to apply to the Secretary of State for self-governing status. This power was conferred by the Self-Governing Schools etc. (Scotland) Act 1989. The number of schools which have become self-governing is tiny, only two. Even those schools which thought that, by opting out, they could avoid closure were dismayed to learn that the Education (Scotland) 1996 Act prevented them from doing so. But schools which think that they might be set for closure could well move quickly towards self-governing status, thereby avoiding closure. The unwillingness of Scottish schools to opt for self-governing status may partly be explained by a curious procedural mistake by the government. In England and Wales, grant-maintained (or opted-out) status had been enabled at the same time as the legislation for local management of schools (LMS) was enacted, the reason being that schools should first have experience of managing their own budgets before seeking opted-out status. In Scotland, however, the government's policies for devolved school management (DSM, the counterpart to LMS) came nearly three years after the Self-Governing Schools etc. (Scotland) Act 1989. As the new Labour government enters office, it is unclear whether or not the road to the market of self-governing schools will be blocked. So much for the left-hand or 'choice' dimension of the marketisation model. Now consider the right-hand side of the Quasi-Market in Education outlined earlier.

Product and process quality control

A market needs a product for consumers to buy. But consumers have rights; they are to be protected. One way of protecting the consumer is to ensure that there is suffcient quality control exercised by an independent agency. There must be ways for the consumer to distinguish between the products on offer. There must be reliable and valid information which is readily available and simple to understand. For the government this 'product' was in the form of an 'output measure', namely the school's aggregate attainment level on national tests and examinations. Each secondary school was ranked on a league-table, thereby enabling the consumer to shop around. But before this assessment could take place there needed to be a standardisation of the curriculum so that national tests could be seen to be fair and comparable. One of the reasons – though not the only one – for the introduction of national curricular guidelines in Scotland was that it would allow for national testing across a given age-range. Its elaborate curricular structure facilitated the bureaucratic ordering of knowledge into discrete sections. In a sense, therefore, the national guidelines were assessment-driven. The point being stressed here is that the 'national curriculum' was a necessary pre-condition for the quasi-market in Scottish education.

What of process control? This is much more difficult to achieve. The process is in effect the pedagogical relationship, which is a social process, and which is not easily freeze-framed into discrete assessable units, unlike the national 'product' tests. More to the point, the pupil and the teacher co-produce the product, so it is difficult to disentangle the teacher's pedagogical input from that of the pupil.

The Conservative government was cautious about introducing teacher appraisal. It was first mooted in 1984 when the government was formulating its policy on staff development. Staff development was seen as the pre-condition of worthwhile staff appraisal: that is to say, unless the staff development needs of a teacher are known then it is difficult to define a worthwhile programme of professional development. Needs and programmes should be matched. By appraising the staff their needs would be made explicit. Needless to say, the teaching profession were less than pleased when in 1989 the Secretary of State proposed a hierarchical and somewhat judgemental system of staff appraisal, for they feared a link between it and merit-pay, a link which the Main Report had earlier denied, but which was later to be admitted by the government in January 1997 with the publication of *Raising the Standard*. More directly, the government has intervened in the colleges of education by defining the competences which must be taught. All that said, however, there is no counterpart in Scotland to England's OFSTED and Teacher Training Agency; not yet.

EDUCATION AND ECONOMY: THE VOCATIONALISATION OF EDUCATION

This relationship between the economy and education can be taken a little further. In addition to the organisational changes which have been made to facilitate the operation of market principles in education, there has also been a series of other changes to education which purport to render it as being functional for the economy. First, there was the vocationalisation of the curriculum; and second, there was the emergence of new learner-centred pedagogies which prepare the pupil for post-Fordist management regimes in the workplace and for service-sector jobs. Taken together these substantive curricular and pedagogical changes have been found mainly in secondary and further education. Perhaps most important have been the profound pedagogical shifts which have taken place since 1983. In that year, the *Action Plan 16–18s in Scotland* hurriedly and comprehensively rationalised further education. The various credentials and examining bodies were incorporated within a new National Certificate validated by a new examining body, SCOTVEC. Completely new modes of assessment and teaching styles were also initiated. The curriculum was modularised. In sum, a learner-centred pedagogy was called for, one which would enhance the self-esteem and autonomy of the learner. SCOTVEC, the examining body for FE, has now been combined with the Scottish Examinations Board (SEB) to form the Scottish Qualifications Agency (SQA). This reveals yet another strengthening of the relationship between the economy and education.

There were sound vocationalist reasons for these changes. The importance of the service sector of the economy was becoming more apparent as traditional manufacturing industries declined. School-leavers were more and more required to manipulate words rather than materials. They needed to be taught – implicitly and explicitly – a new repertoire of personal and social skills which would also be functional for these emerging service industries. So, although 'personal and social development' (PSD) courses had the expressed intention of contributing to personal development, they also had the added benefit of being functional for the economy. They could be seen as both therapeutic and as vocational: therapeutic in the sense that the learner was taught not to feel a diminution of dignity even if she or he had 'failed to find work'; vocational in that the emergent service-sector economy required a sophisticated repertoire of social skills – skills not taught by the entrenched didactic pedagogy of the secondary school. Put another way, the learner-centred classroom management style was supposed to anticipate a future self-managing style at work. Just as in the classroom, students were to take responsibility for their own learning, so later in the workplace they would work with minimum supervision. The mode of social control became more reflective, more inner-directed, less bureaucratic. Even the school league-tables have been redefined as an aid to self-evaluation and management. For example, when the latest school-league tables were published in November 1996, the Education Minister, Raymond Robertson, was reported in *The Scotsman* (11 November, 1996) as saying that the tables helped schools in their self-evaluation process, a theme echoed by Archie McGlynn, HM Chief Inspector of Schools, who went on to say that they enabled school 'self-analysis' rather than competition.

In sum, both SCOTVEC modules and the school-based Technical Vocational Educational Initiative (TVEI) adopted this new pedagogical style, especially for the lower academic achiever. They initiated curricular and pedagogical changes which were functional for the new service industries and for an emerging post-Fordist managerial regime. TVEI was also very well resourced, its funding controlled not by the then Scottish Education Department but by a quango – the Manpower Services Commission (MSC) – which was a UK-wide agency of the Department of Trade and Industry. Later, both north and south of the border, the education and industry portfolios of government were combined, thereby underlining the tightened bond between them. It was the MSC, too, which initiated the contract culture in education: a new payment-by-results approach to funding.

The Compacts Initiative in the early 1990s was another explicitly vocationalist policy. Unlike TVEI, it did not seek to 'buy' the formal curriculum; rather, it sought to remove what were perceived as shortcomings in the transmission of the hidden curriculum. Whereas under TVEI the school entered into a contract with the Training Agency (the successor to the MSC), under the Compacts Initiative the individual pupil, the school and a local business consortium or college entered into a joint 'contract'. Though not a legally binding contract – more of a commitment – the pupil was 'guaranteed' a job, or training leading to a job, provided that the pupil met stringent behavioural and achievement targets. But what was curious about the Compacts was their emphasis on rewarding what would be termed the 'work ethic' of old: neatness, time-keeping, diligence and deference. During a time of rising youth unemployment, the guarantee of a job seemed to be too good to be true; and it was, for there were no legal obligations on any of the parties to adhere to the 'contract'.

There have been other measures. The Scottish counterpart to the City Technology College (CTC), the Technology Academy, failed to materialise. Colleges of Further Education were incorporated, thereby becoming detached from the control of local authorities. The Enterprise in Higher Education scheme was launched. Tax relief for vocational course fees was allowed in 1993–4, and a system of Youth Credits was introduced. But perhaps the most important decision yet to be taken is the extent of the use of information technology in education. This, in theory, would have a number of economic effects: it would drastically reduce 'delivery' costs, thereby lightening the fiscal burden on the welfare state; and it would widen access and maximise flexibility. Given the relatively higher costs of teaching in higher education – especially in the sciences – there may be some move towards first implementing it there. The MacFarlane Report *Teaching and Learning in an Expanding Higher Education System* has already opened the debate on this in Scotland. (For a discussion, see Hartley, 1995.) However, if information technology is to be used as a pedagogical device, it would almost certainly require a standardisation of the syllabus in certain subjects, at a cost to academic freedom in higher education. The University of the Highlands and Islands is already being developed very much with a view to using information technology. The new Labour government seems set to continue to strengthen the link between education, with a White Paper on Lifelong Learning being planned for the autumn of 1997, and there is talk of a University for Industry.

CONCLUSION

The market-driven education policies of the Conservative governments between 1979 and 1997 have changed the metaphors and meanings of education. In Scotland, where education is held in high public esteem, there has been a mixed reception to them. So far as the *marketisation* of education is concerned, the attempt to produce a 'market' has been relatively unsuccessful. It has been argued above that, in order to bring about this quasi-market, the curriculum itself needed to be defined, and its transmission to be monitored by national testing, league-tables and teacher appraisal. Here the government's gains were greater. Although, unlike England, the curriculum in Scotland was not legislated, nevertheless any deviation from it is denounced. The *vocationalisation* of education, both in terms of curriculum and of pedagogy, was also considered. Except in further education and in the education of the lower achievers in secondary schools, the vocationalisation of the formal curriculum has not been great. (The *Higher Still* reforms may change this.) However, insofar as pedagogy is concerned, there are strong signs that Scottish education at all levels is shifting towards a learner-centred approach, except, paradoxically, in the primary school where the 'excesses' of child-centredness are to be curbed. Many of these reforms – modularisation and continuous assessment – have their roots in further education, a sector which has always been closest to the world of work. This pedagogy is functional not only for a service sector economy, but also for post-Fordist management regimes. But – and here the link with efficiency looks questionable – it is also a much more expensive pedagogy than the old didacticism. What is evident, therefore, is an emerging tension between this relatively expensive learner-centred pedagogy and the increasing use of standardised curricula and information technology which are meant to cut costs. In the interests of economic efficiency, governments can be expected to try and claim that both consumer choice and learner-centred pedagogy are compatible with the greater use of information technology and a standardisation of the curriculum.

REFERENCES

Hartley, D. (1992) The Compacts Initiative: values for money, *British Journal of Educational Studies*, 40(4), pp. 321–334

Hartley, D. (1995) Teaching and Learning in an Expanding Higher Education System (The MacFarlane Report) – a technical fix?, *Studies in Higher Education*, 20(2), pp. 27–38.

Hunter, L. C. (1993) The 'flexible' work force in Scotland? A discussion paper, *Scottish Economic Bulletin*, 48 (winter), pp. 15–24.

Munn, P. (ed.) (1993) *Parents and Schools: customers, managers or partners?*, London: Routledge.

OECD (1995) Education and training in the United Kingdom, *OECD Economic Surveys 1994–1995*, Paris: OECD, pp. 46–84.

Scottish Office (1997) *Raising the Standard: A White Paper on Education and Skills Development in Scotland*, London: The Stationery Office.

26

Vocational Education

Douglas Weir

CHANGING EXPECTATIONS

While it has never been an easy task specifically to measure the value of links between pupil attainments at school and a nation's economic performance, the existence of such links has been taken for granted. Therefore governments in most countries have sought to ensure that curricula and standards in schools matched the needs of industry and commerce. That pressure on schools has grown especially in the last twenty-five years and has become associated with the concept of 'vocational education.'

It is important, however, to bear in mind that a vocational education is 'not a narrow set of content, nor is it direct training for an occupation or occupational group, but more a general preparation for a life which is practical and relevant' (Weir, 1988, p. 3). Since each subject in the school curriculum may serve different purposes for different individuals, it is not necessarily the subjects which are vocational; since each individual goes through school with a variety of life experiences it is not school alone which determines job and career decisions; and since economic change is continuous, it is impossible to predict which elements of today's school curriculum will be of most value to individuals in tomorrow's labour market.

This chapter will therefore focus on secondary schools and on their role in vocational education. It will assume that all elements of the school curriculum, whether normally described as academic or vocational or general, can make a contribution to individual and national success. And it will attempt to show how the present view of the school curriculum as an integral part of Scotland's economic future has emerged.

From the standpoint of society at large, a number of factors have been used to legitimate the pressure on the education system to contribute more to the nation's economic well-being. The factors include:

- the ideological need of governments to manage unemployment statistics, since unemployment is seen to be electorally damaging;
- the changes in family structures in the developed world where it can no longer be assumed that extended families exist and play a significant part in inducting young people into social and occupational roles;
- the decline in the social and economic strength of local communities and the increased need for young people to take a wider geographical view of career and occupational routes;

- technicisation and globalisation in economies which places a higher value on the contribution of formal education and training to economic competitiveness;
- the growing tendency towards short-termism and casualisation in employment which demands that young people acquire skills and habits of flexibility and adaptability at an early age.

Increasingly, schools are being asked by employers, communities and parents to play a bigger part in the development of young people, albeit consistent with the classic definition of their role as described in the eighteenth century by Thomas Jefferson whose Rockfish Gap report asked schools to:

> inform pupils of their rights and duties as citizens;
> develop their basic skills and enlarge their minds;
> give them the ability to succeed in business and industry.

In other words schools must give young people a civic purpose, a personal purpose and a utilitarian purpose. The changed emphasis towards the end of the twentieth century, however, is that the civic and personal purposes are means towards the greater end of the utilitarian or economic purpose rather than legitimate, independent ends in their own right. In approaching the twenty-first century, therefore, schools are responding to a changed set of circumstances which include:

- significant increases in the number of 17 and 18 year olds who choose to remain in schools rather than enter work or further education;
- higher education participation rates at an historic high;
- curriculum guidelines from government where the study of English, Mathematics, Science and European languages is mandatory;
- pressure to ensure that all young people show competence in core or general skills such as communication, numeracy, information technology, problem-solving, and working with others;
- a recognition that the traditional division of curriculum between academic and vocational tracks is now redundant.

THE EVOLUTION OF CURRENT POLICY

The present emphasis on the vocational purpose of the secondary school curriculum has arisen from a number of phases in policy and practice. No one phase has been unique in itself but all have reflected the past and presaged the future. And all have attempted to reconcile a number of key concepts. Among the concepts which have been in dynamic tension are:

> differentiation – whether by study programme or institution
> esteem – whether in terms of achieving parity of esteem across subjects or positively dis-
> criminating in favour of vocational subjects
> access – for all learners to any programme or by fixing admissions quotas in terms of national
> priorities.

All this takes place in a context of improving national economic competitiveness by increasing competition between schools and between pupils.

The values given to the alternative positions in that conceptual map are of particular significance when the key political priority is to make schooling contribute more to economic success. Then it is of paramount importance that all pupils develop their abilities to the highest possible degree and especially in those subjects which have the greatest contribution to make to economic competitiveness.

Immediately after the Second World War, Scotland was preoccupied with setting up a secondary school system which conferred access to opportunity according to 'age, aptitude and ability'. Senior and junior secondary schools were created for different ability groups. This assumed that national manpower needs in the professional, managerial and technical occupations and in the craft, semi-skilled and labouring occupations could be predicted accurately, and that the curriculum in the two types of school could provide these two types of labour at ages 15 and 17 respectively.

By the late 1960s this approach was discredited by sociologists and economists, the former because it was elitist when egalitarianism was in vogue, the latter because it failed to cope with the dynamics of modern labour markets and led to mismatches in supply and demand. Government thus responded by a new type of school organisation, the neighbourhood comprehensive school (SED Circular 600, 1965). As an almost inevitable corollary to extending access to a full programme of secondary schooling to all, and as a response to growing demands for more skilled and credentialled entrants to the workforce, compulsory schooling was extended to age 16 in 1973 and certification at that stage was made universal as a consequence of the Dunning Report *Assessment for All* (1977). Similarly, through the Munn Report (1977) on the *Structure of the Curriculum in the Third and Fourth Years of the Scottish Secondary School* the attempt was made to divide the curriculum into eight modes spanning all of academic, general, and vocational domains and to ensure that every pupil had access to all modes and domains.

The first phase of universal, comprehensive, secondary schooling did not in itself solve the problems of esteem across subjects. It was perceived that too many young people were aspiring to the so-called academic subjects and seeking to pursue them at university. A change of focus was required and thus, from the mid 1970s, a shift towards more specialisation and diversification began. As a better understanding of how the British economy could compete internationally was growing, it was being argued that success would depend on providing specialist skills and expertise and on diversifying away from 'smokestack' industries such as coal, iron and steel, and other heavy manufacturing. The workforce needed to be more innovative and creative (what came to be called the 'enterprise culture'), to be leaders in the 'knowledge industries' by mastery of information and communication technologies, to maintain a leading role in financial services, and to be more effective in the classic service industries of retail, hotels and catering, travel and tourism.

But all of these changes required young people entering the labour market with relevant dispositions and skills. This need for young people of appropriate calibre coincided with mass young unemployment. Thus the Labour government made two major initiatives in the late 1970s. The first was a call from Prime Minister James Callaghan, in a speech at Ruskin College in 1976, to make the school curriculum more work-related, and the second was an extensive programme of remediation amongst the unemployed (or even unemployable) school leavers. The second was launched through a new Manpower Services Commission in the form of the Holland Report *Young People and Work* in 1977. That report and the Youth Opportunities Programme which it created, recognised that not only did young workers require vocational skills, especially at the technical end of the labour market, but that they also required social and life skills, especially at the service end of the labour market.

These initiatives of the Labour administration were continued and extended by their Conservative successors from 1979 and throughout the 1980s. This period has been described as 'new vocationalism' because it sought to give schools more direction through central government control; to make them more like businesses in their focus on products, customers and accountability; and to make their pupils more conforming and better matched to a national economic agenda. And the curricular programmes which were introduced in the UK to achieve these 'new vocationalist' goals included the Technical and Vocational Education Initiative (TVEI) in 1983; Compacts, in 1988; and Education Business Partnerships (EBP), in 1991 through the White Paper *Access and Opportunity*. These vocational programmes, mainly for 14 to 18 year olds, set explicit curriculum and achievement targets for schools and pupils in terms of standards to be reached, programmes of study to be followed, and of behaviours such as punctuality, courtesy and attendance to be exhibited. Unless they adhered to these targets, schools and local authorities would be denied access to the full range of central government funding.

But in each stage of development there was overlap with other stages; the seeds of change in one phase have often been sown in the preceding phase. Thus one culmination of the first era of specialisation by age, aptitude and ability was the Brunton Report of 1963 (*From School to Further Education*, Scottish Education Department) which advocated a 'vocational impulse' as the core of the curriculum for the early leavers (and the junior secondary school) just a few years before school reorganisation along comprehensive lines. Before this programme was properly tested, schools were shifting their values in accord with the comprehensive philosophy. Instead of more pupils having access to the vocational curriculum, success for comprehensive schools was being defined in terms of how many more pupils could be given access to the academic curriculum and the Highers.

Similarly the introduction of the Standard Grade of the Scottish Certificate of Education in the 1980s as a truly comprehensive route for all 14 to 16 year olds was being challenged before it was fully implemented by the more specialised TVEI programme (introduced to Scotland in 1984) and the differentiated curriculum of the Scottish Vocational Education Council (SCOTVEC). SCOTVEC was set up in 1984 following *16–18s in Scotland: An Action Plan* (SED, 1983), and quickly made its modular, vocational programmes available to schools as well as further education colleges and to 14 to 16 year olds as well as to its original target population of 16 to 18 year olds. Both TVEI and SCOTVEC were intended to raise the esteem of the vocational curriculum as a separate track which it was hoped would equal the esteem of the academic track in which Highers were the prize.

The influence of SCOTVEC became one of the crucial features of this phase of differentiation between tracks. Initially intended as a revision of the Further Education curriculum, the SCOTVEC programmes became increasingly attractive to schools as an alternative to Highers for the increasing number of S5 and S6 pupils to whom Highers were neither suitable nor attractive. To consolidate this influence, groups of SCOTVEC modules were put together as general Scottish Vocational Qualifications (gSVQs) from 1991, and claimed to be the equivalent of Highers. Government hoped that these parallel academic and vocational tracks in secondary schools would achieve equal esteem.

But the specialisation of the 1980s lasted no time at all. It was overtaken by a new philosophy which will accelerate from 1999 into the next millennium. No sooner had the Howie Report of 1992 on *Upper Secondary Education in Scotland* and a celebration of the twin tracks of Highers and gSVQs, of the academic and vocational, been published than a strong resistance to the two tracks approach arose from both lay and professional communities on the grounds that it was divisive and would never achieve parity of esteem between the tracks. The review of upper secondary education was thus taken back inside the Scottish Office, and re-emerged as the *Higher Still: Opportunity for All* programme in 1994 under which it was proposed that Scotland return to one, comprehensive, equal esteem, curriculum and assessment system, now extending up to age eighteen.

As David Raffe has said in the *Unified Learning Project, Working Paper Two* (1997) when talking about a range of countries including Scotland and England:

> Post-compulsory education and training systems have grown in functional complexity as well as scale. Not only do more young people continue, stay there for longer and reach higher levels of attainment; the system has a wider, and more complex, range of demands to meet. These demands cannot be met by tracks serving specific and distinct purposes; old forms of specialisation by sector, course or institution are no longer viable.

EXPLANATIONS OF POLICY VARIATION

While key notions such as differentiation, esteem, access, and competition have clearly all been in play at each stage in the evolution of the present structural harmony between academic and vocational dimensions of the school curriculum, the reasons for different combinations gaining the ascendancy at different times are complex. It is important to remember that UK economic and labour policies are interpreted differently in the different education systems in the UK. That tendency had been growing steadily in the post-1975 period and will be likely to accelerate following the pro-devolution vote in Scotland in 1997.

For a long time the intimate educational community in Scotland has been aware of its ability to subvert those intentions of a Westminster government which were not supported by the Scottish people. No matter what else changes, the Higher continues; no matter how strong was the intention that SCOTVEC modules be the preserve of FE, there would be some loophole found by some schools to allow them to use the modules with pupils; no matter how determined the government was to bring a 'manpower' solution to the secret garden of education via TVEI, there was an equally determined alliance of representative bodies of Scottish local government, trades unions and professionals which could ensure that the more acceptable features of Scottish education as represented in the implementation of the Munn and Dunning reports still dominated the school curriculum.

But another, equal, strength of Scottish education is its ability to tolerate local experimentation and then adapt it to national needs. Little change in Scottish education requires legislation when a circular from the Scottish Office will suffice. There is little desire in the Scottish Office to enforce uniformity of provision in all parts of the country. Most national, i.e. Scottish or UK, innovations in recent years have been more noted for the speed with which they have been adapted to local circumstances than for anything else. But then, when local practice is successful it can be very quickly communicated and adapted to the needs of many communities. There is thus a sufficient confidence among the local and national leaders of Scottish education that they can respond to the need for change through informal and evolutionary methods. Dramatic changes in schooling then become unnecessary or, at least, unpopular. And so, while one account of the educational developments since 1945 can be given in terms of policy landmarks, more persuasive is the account in terms of a conservative national consensus, where change is incremental and nudged forward by local experimentation.

THE RISE OF SOCIAL EDUCATION

As the nature of employment has changed away from notions of a job for life towards norms where individuals will have a variety of jobs, or none, so too have notions of how best schooling may equip young people for diversity and uncertainty. When William Bennett, US Secretary of Education, wrote in the *Vocational Educational Journal,* in March 1986, that the specifics of individual jobs change too quickly for schools to keep up-to-date but the benefits of teaching adaptability and flexibility can last for longer, he was reminding educationalists that social skills and the social development of individuals may well be the best contribution that schools can make to the health of the economy. In reaching the point where social development is recognised as a major contributor to occupational success the multiple purposes of education must be remembered. For any person to have the ability to contribute to their own and their nation's economic well being, the school curriculum must effectively transmit Jefferson's other two senses of civic purpose and personal purpose. And, while previous generations of school curriculum have had an apparent tendency to separate the civic and the personal from the vocational, in the present generation there is a determined attempt to integrate all three.

When there were separate schools for pupils of differing abilities, other crude assumptions were made about social class and career destinations. The senior secondary pupil was equated with a middle class background and a professional or managerial career. It was assumed that this pupil's personal and occupational socialisation would take care of itself and that the curriculum should deal with the academic and technical knowledge base required by the appropriate careers. The junior secondary pupil was equated with a working class background and, at best, a skilled or unskilled job. But since no great technical or vocational knowledge was required for entry to such jobs, the curriculum had other functions, which were predominantly social. Indeed the very term 'social education' was first used in the SED report of 1955 on Junior Secondary Education, and the school's function was described such that 'one of the prime duties of the junior secondary school as of all schools, is to produce boys and girls who are honest, responsible, persevering and self-reliant. . . .'

By the time of the comprehensive school movement, the focus had changed a little, mainly because the beginnings of family and community breakdown referred to earlier were requiring schools to play a greater part in the social education of all pupils. At this stage both means and needs were coinciding. A new post for teachers – the Guidance teacher – had been created in 1971 to coordinate personal, curricular and careers guidance for pupils, and these teachers needed tasks to undertake and 'subjects' to teach. And the school leaving age had been raised to sixteen in 1973 and subject content was needed to fill this extra year. Seen initially as a means of 'padding out' the curriculum for those lower achievers or poorly motivated pupils for whom SCE courses were inappropriate, a social education programme quickly became part of every pupil's diet. Schools were faced with demands from the community to take on roles previously undertaken by extended families in careers education, health education, rights and responsibilities, and so the social education 'period' accessed by all pupils became a convenient way of demonstrating that these demands were being met.

But social education as described here soon became quite distinctive from guidance and developed its own specialists (in FE and in schools) and its own rhetoric. By 1983 these specialists had an SCE Standard Grade subject – Social and Vocational Skills – to offer as a means of delivering social education in a vocational envelope. Also popular in linking the social and occupational strands of vocational education were the Skills for Adolescence packages and the Award Scheme Development and Accreditation Network (ASDAN), an attractive amalgam of social and educational ideas also found in the Duke of Edinburgh's Award Scheme and the Records of Achievement movement.

Many of these developments stem from concerns raised by employers (see *The A-Z Study*, Industrial Training Research Unit, Cambridge, 1979) that young entrants to the labour market lacked key attributes such as adaptability, pride in their work, the ability to use their initiative and good interpersonal skills. Not only, therefore, did schools enlarge their curriculum for all in response to community pressure, they also legitimated this social dimension of the curriculum by reference to demands from business interests.

As John MacBeath said when summarising the growth and purpose of social education in *Personal and Social Education* (Edinburgh: Scottish Academic Press, 1988):

> Personal and Social Education might, for example, be seen to have a pay off in terms of job interview skills acquired, the learning of effective letter writing or phoning, management of time, of study, or of lifestyle. It might even derive its value for young people because it has tangibly made them more aware of themselves, more demonstrably confident, or significantly better at handling themselves in social situations. (p. 116)

A further dimension of the vocational responsibilities of schools called 'key skills' in England and 'core skills' in Scotland then emerged. As the demands which employers placed on schools have grown, schools have been obliged to demonstrate that pupils reach externally-prescribed levels of performance in literacy, numeracy and information technology. While some attention had been given in the early 1990s to the need to give special treatment to these areas and while core skills were an integral part of the curriculum of Higher Still, it was the incoming Labour government of 1997 that made them a particularly prominent part of the educational agenda.

What remains uncertain, however, is the context within which the core skills and the social competences are to be demonstrated. While ostensibly the school curriculum in Scotland encourages access to core skills and to social education for all pupils from S1 to S6, there is still significant differentiation by level and element of courses. Especially in the upper secondary school there is a separation in both core skills and social education between different categories of pupil. Those who are highest achievers in traditional terms (four or five Highers from the old academic menu), can overtake core skill and social education requirements within their Highers, but those who are less high achievers (few or no Highers and following more ostensibly vocational programmes), generally take core skills and social education as separate study units, to be certificated independently and to count towards Group Awards. A complete vocational package is now more easily accessible by all learners but it remains perceptibly distinctive from the academic package.

When the Scottish Consultative Council on the Curriculum produced its overview on Educating for Personal and Social Development (*The Heart of the Matter*, 1995) it became apparent that those skills central to EPSD – Personal and Interpersonal Skills; Communication Skills; Problem Solving Skills; Learning Skills – were not only at the heart of social education in serving the civic and personal purposes of schooling. They were also those most in demand by employers to provide the contemporary underpinning to the occupational or utilitarian purposes of schooling. So while there remains some doubt whether academic and vocational programmes of study can ever be esteemed as of equal worth, the vocational programmes have now become more all-embracing in curricular terms by the integration of subject content, core skills and social competences.

THE PRESENT AND THE FUTURE

At present there is an explicit message from the Scottish Office that education for work is one of the cornerstones of the school curriculum. Schools are asked to transmit this message in a variety of ways from the earliest stages of secondary education through to S6. At one level the message is communicated through key elements of the general curriculum such as personal and social education, careers education, work experience for all, and enterprise education, and through a wide range of education-industry links. In most respects these key elements are delivered in an undifferentiated manner in an attempt to give every pupil access to them and be made aware that they are held in high esteem by the school. At another level the message is communicated through the specific subjects in the curriculum. In both explicit and implicit ways each subject conveys an image of its values, its uses, its challenges and the employment or further study options available to those who achieve mastery in that subject. But access to each subject is restricted, often by prior achievement in general or in similar subjects. And opportunities to master the subject are differentiated year by year so that only a small number of pupils gain entry to the highest level of study in each subject. Furthermore, the esteem in which each subject is held depends on a number of factors including the values of a school, the opinions of peers, the entry requirements of universities and the wage levels and employment prospects in particular jobs. So, whether academic and vocational terms are used to distinguish subjects by esteem, or not, there are still significant status distinctions prevailing in school education.

The Higher Still reform recognises a need to broaden pupil experiences in upper secondary education, not simply because of economic necessity but even more because of changes in school intakes. Secondary schools are now catering for large numbers of 17 and 18 year olds who previously would have been in employment or training or further education. (The percentage of S4 pupils staying on to S5 rose from 41% in 1978 to 70% in 1995; the corresponding figures for S6 were 14% and 42%.) Schools therefore are being expected to deliver parts of the curriculum which previously resided in training establishments or FE colleges, and, in addition, to meet employer demands that young entrants to the labour market have basic skills in literacy, numeracy and IT, together with social competence in terms of interests and motivations.

In the response to these needs through Higher Still, the whole S5/S6 curriculum will now be delivered and accredited in a single manner. While there will be differentiation by level of achievement – ranging from Access to Advanced Higher – that differentiation will not be in terms of the academic or vocational origin of subjects. Every subject will have the same curriculum structure of forty hour units of study; the same scheme for assessment based on carefully-described performance standards; the same award from a single examining body – the Scottish Qualifications Authority. Labelling by general or social or vocational or academic competences will be replaced by the more comfortable Scottish rhetoric of 'omnibus' or 'comprehensive' education.

But there then remains a set of questions as to how far the apparent harmonisation of academic and vocational routes is real and does make a significant contribution to economic success. For example, the school curriculum all but ignores work-based training and learning. Work-based learning is a central part of European thinking about vocational education but has barely impinged on 'official' Scottish thinking. As David Raffe (1997) reports, not only will the work-based programmes of Skillseekers and SVQs be impoverished, but Higher Still will be diminished by not being able to draw on the rich seams of workplace learning.

A further question derives from Raffe's reference to SVQs (Scottish Vocational Qualifications). Here we have government rhetoric disguising reality in a disturbing way. As part of the skills revolution in the 1990s, government determined that our national economic success could be gauged by how many people achieved vocational qualifications at specific SVQ or equivalent levels. These targets were meant to encourage more training to occupational standards and more workplace demonstration of competence, with SVQ3 being the central benchmark of minimum skill required to fill most of the key technical grades in the labour force. But noting that the SVQ3 equivalence is three Highers and that three-fifths of the Scottish achievement of the year 2000 targets is already accounted for by these credentials raises the question of whether the move towards merging academic and vocational curricula is a convenient smokescreen. If there is no distinction between academic and vocational Highers then there is no way of telling whether the curriculum is actually shifting in a vocational direction.

A third concern relates to the divisions between secondary and further education. The Higher Still programme awards the same overt esteem to Caring, Engineering and Construction as it does to the Arts, Sciences and Social Sciences. But the first set of courses will run in FE colleges where the equipment and staff resources exist, and the second set of courses will run in schools. If there is significant movement of young people between sectors because the esteem of different types of course is made more equal, then there is little to fear. There will continue to be a healthy number of people in the 14 to 18 age range accessing the more vocational studies. But if the trend to stay on at secondary school continues and the schools only offer the more academic studies, for financial and staffing reasons, then the disturbing lack of young people with the appropriate 'subject' background to meet the needs of industry will remain.

Arising from Higher Still there is then a final question about the appropriateness of the renewed emphasis on core and social skills. If success in life and in employment is heavily dependent on basic competence in a number of technical and social areas, can that competence be acquired out of context? Is 'working with others' on a production line the same as 'working with others' in a shop and are the skills transferable? Is the IT competence acquired in a design studio equivalent to the IT competence of a 'direct sales' operative and can these be transferred? And, of even more concern, is there any way in which the community of a school resembles a work community in its structure, norms, and routines? Because unless the skills are transferable, unless they can be acquired in contexts which are relevant and realistic, and unless it can be shown that the school is an appropriate setting for acquiring these skills, a different rhetoric prevails. Instead of pretending, as has been the case with all governments over the past twenty years, that core and social and vocational learning in schools directly fits young people to enter the labour market and function well, we must admit instead that these forms of learning are essential in order to provide a rounded and complete experience for 14 or 16 or 18 year olds. In other words, answering the question of what is a relevant curriculum for boys and girls of 14 is much more important than asking how 14 year olds can be made ready for work.

CONCLUSIONS

While there seems to be some curricular harmony in Scottish school education entering the twenty-first century, that harmony has only a slight connection with the persistent debate over the academic/vocational divide.

At one level the debate is based on false impressions. In 1932 A. N. Whitehead wrote in *The Aims of Education* (London: Williams and Norgate) that 'the antithesis between a technical and a liberal education is spurious. There can be no adequate technical education which is not liberal and no liberal education which is not technical; that is, no education which does not impart both technique and intellectual vision'. And Richard Pring (1995) confirms today that both subject knowledge and practical skill can be combined as well for academic development as for vocational development.

At a second level the debate is unnecessary. Irrespective of curricular choices, young people have access to a wide range of post-school destinations compatible with the general level of their school achievement rather than the specific subjects in which they have achieved. And with growing recognition for all subjects as admissions criteria to higher education; with more attention being paid by employers and universities to personal skills, not just intellectual or practical skills; and with a rising tide of part-time and flexible patterns of education and training, few barriers to occupational and certification progress confront motivated individuals.

At a third level, however, the debate seems to be perpetual. A Stirling University team (Turner, 1993) suggest that no matter how many initiatives are tried by government, education-industry practices still only comprise a small enclave of activity in most schools. Government is concerned that international measurements of Scottish pupil achievements in Mathematics and Science show a declining standard by comparison with our significant competitors. Examination statistics show that the take-up of the most vocationally relevant subjects in the school curriculum remains stubbornly low by comparison with the more academically or professionally relevant subjects. Schools will therefore continue to be pressed to become more vocationally relevant whenever the economy is performing less well than government requires.

But Scottish schools are not particularly susceptible to government interference. There are strong professional networks which enforce a conservative approach to curricular change. There are also strong community pressures to retain a broadly-based school education leading to university and thus to social and economic mobility. And Scots have not expected their schools to meet all of society's needs, but have retained a strong sense of community and a desire to support the development of their young people not only through schooling but also through many other social, family and community networks.

Within that philosophy, the fundamental vision of schools in Scotland is that they are community-based, with a broad curriculum, and postponing selection as long as possible. What has therefore been happening in the last twenty years is that, as society and employment have become more fragmented, the education service has contributed to the national consensus about purpose by extending access and reducing differentiation throughout the secondary school. The vocational, the social and the academic elements of the curriculum are all recognised as legitimate parts of every pupil's education to age 18 just as previously they were up to the age of 15, and before that up to the age of twelve. Holding on to that sense of purpose is more likely to enable the country to cope with a dynamic future than the continual striving to match the school curriculum to short-term labour market needs which characterises some other education systems.

REFERENCES

Finegold, D. et al. (1990) *A British Baccalaureate: Ending the Division between Education and Training*, London: Institute for Public Policy Research.

Pring, R. (1995) *Closing the Gap: Liberal Education and Vocational Preparation*, London: Hodder and Stoughton.

Raffe, D. (1997) *Higher Still in European Perspective*, Edinburgh: Centre for Educational Sociology.

Toffler, A. (1970) *Future Shock*, London: Pan.

Turner, E. et al. (1993) *Plotting Partnership: Education Business links in Scotland*, Stirling: University of Stirling.

Weir, A. D. (1988) *Education and Vocation: 14–18*, Edinburgh: Scottish Academic Press.

27

Access to Scottish Education

Angela Roger

WHO HAS ACCESS TO SCOTTISH EDUCATION?

Scottish education has achieved a great deal in terms of access in recent years. Primary and secondary education are a realisable expectation for the vast majority of young people. However, beyond the compulsory stages of education in Scotland, comprehensive access to education is far from a reality. Although government policy has put mass participation in further and higher education on the political agenda, the participation rates in Scotland still fall short of other developed Western nations. Nevertheless, the century has been characterised by expansion of educational provision. This chapter considers mainly the extent to which Scotland has succeeded in expanding access to post-compulsory education, with a particular focus upon higher education, for it is here that there is still much to be done. In the second part of the chapter, some of the issues arising out of the existing pattern of progress are considered and it is argued that despite the expansion of provision, pride in the success to date may mask continuing inequalities in access to education. Furthermore expansion may be resource-limited by under investment in universities rather than likely to progress into the new millennium.

Background to expansion

Expansion in post-compulsory education at school level has been promoted by successive governments assiduously during the 1980s and 1990s. Two main sets of arguments have been used to advocate the increase in numbers of students sought for recruitment to further and higher education: an aspiration for economic competitiveness and an appeal for social justice. The first set of arguments holds that Scotland as a nation requires to participate in a global market which is premised less upon manufacturing and more upon marketing of information in which competition is fierce. Education is seen to be a crucial component in success. Nations with whom the UK competes in the global market, such as Germany and Japan, have higher participation rates in education than the UK and it is therefore believed that there is a causal link between economic success in those countries and the high numbers in their populations achieving higher levels of education. A simple causal link is, of course, open to dispute, though in the past it has been possible to show that higher achievement in education leads to greater success at an individual level in terms of job opportunity and professional status.

The social justice argument holds that access to education is an individual's right and that there are long-term benefits for society in having a well-educated citizenry, for educated people are more likely to participate in democracy and better able to contribute to the cultural life of the nation. In addition, under-representation in higher education of some groups of people – women, disabled people, minority ethnic groups, older people and people from lower socio-economic groups – suggests a waste of talent since it is indefensible in the enlightened 1990s to believe that talent resides exclusively or even primarily in young, white, able-bodied, middle-class men.

The thrust of government policy has been driven more by the economic competitiveness argument rather than by appeals to social justice, but there is a convenient convergence of aspiration among advocates of each argument which has permitted considerable progress to be made in providing greater access to higher levels of education.

Extent of provision

Paterson (1997) traces the expansion of secondary education in what can be seen as an unprecedented period of change. Four indicators are used: Ordinary and Standard Grade attainment; staying-on rates; attainment in Highers; and rates of entry to higher education. (The Standard Grade examination was first set in 1986 and was accompanied by a revised curriculum framework; it fully replaced the O-Grade in 1994.) At Standard Grade the attainment rate for five or more passes at levels 1–3 has reached 70 per cent compared to 54 per cent achieving five or more O grades at levels A–C in 1981. In particular, the performance of girls has improved beyond the rate of boys. Notably, also, the gap between the performance of socially advantaged young people and socially disadvantaged, has narrowed, though not at the top end of achievement.

Persistence in secondary education has also improved. By 1994, the staying-on rate had risen from 52 per cent in 1983 to 70 per cent, with reduced social class inequalities and girls being more likely to stay on than boys. Achievement at Higher, measured at three or more passes, the traditional entry qualification for higher education, has also improved. This has risen from 20 per cent in 1981 to 29 per cent in 1995. Clearly, the introduction of comprehensive education made a positive impact on social class inequalities during the early 1980s. Once again, girls have increasingly outperformed boys.

Entry to Higher Education

The most dramatic expansion in Scottish education has undoubtedly been in participation in higher education. From a 6 per cent participation rate by the age of 21 in the 1960s, the rate rose to 45 per cent in 1995. Between the years 1988 and 1993 a very rapid rise in participation took place. Social class differences in entry rates have now begun to diminish though participation by young people from homes where the father is in manual work is still less than half that of children of professional fathers. Once again, females are more likely than males to enter higher education with the female participation rate now over fifty per cent. Another hitherto under-represented group has also achieved a considerable turn-around: participation in higher education by students from minority ethnic groups outstrips that of white students' participation by more than two to one. As Paterson (1997) shows, some substantial inroads into social inequalities have now been made in Scotland in the last forty years, especially in gender but significantly also in social class and ethnicity.

However, there is no cause for complacency. It appears to be the case, for example, that middle class girls are achieving entry to higher education while the participation of working class boys remains low. Some of the backlash school of thought seek to interpret the success of girls in terms of evidence of discrimination against certain groups of boys and say that middle class girls achieve their places in higher education 'at the expense of' working class boys. It is important, however, to recognise that an analysis of achievement by gender is insufficient in itself to address the multiple inequalities which affect some groups in society.

Key access documents

Since the Education (Scotland) Act 1872 paved the way for universal secondary education, various government and non-governmental initiatives have been directed at further improving access to education. Whilst it might be argued that the battle for comprehensive access had been won in secondary education by the 1980s using such evidence as quoted above, participation in further and higher education required new impetus because of the demographic downturn in the number of young school leavers. The Action Plan (*16–18s in Scotland: An Action Plan*, SED 1983) called for renewed efforts to increase participation in further education. The Action Plan restructured the further education curriculum into a modular system and introduced a unified system of certification for post-compulsory education (the National Certificate). The reforms had far-reaching effects not only on the further education sector, but also in post-16 education in schools in Scotland. The Action Plan brought further education a more dynamic profile than had been the case before. These reforms have also attracted a great deal of interest in the rest of the UK and from further afield. It also had a significant impact on preparation for higher education, providing an alternative set of qualifications to the Higher for under-qualified school leavers and adult returners.

More recently, the Scottish Office embarked on an ambitious programme of reform of upper secondary education. The Howie Committee which was charged with a review of upper secondary education argued for a twin track of vocational and academic qualifications, the 'ScotCert', a course which was primarily vocational in orientation, and the 'ScotBac' which was primarily academic in focus. However, Howie's proposed solution to the problems of upper secondary education, though not the analysis underpinning it, was rejected in favour of the Scottish Office's alternative programme, Higher Still (*Opportunity for All*, SOEID, 1992). The Higher Still reforms of curriculum, due to be implemented in Autumn 1999, propose an integrated set of courses throughout the upper stages of secondary schooling and the introduction of a new examination, the Advanced Higher, to replace the Certificate of Sixth Year Studies. It is the intention that both academic and vocational subjects should be offered to pupils and that the vocational subjects should have 'parity of esteem' with academic. It is also to be possible that pupils can study for 'group awards' comprising a cognate set of courses. At the time of writing, some two years before the introduction of the Advanced Higher, it is feared in some quarters that children in schools in small centres of population may be disadvantaged by the inability of small schools to provide for a full range of Advanced Highers. Fears have further been expressed that the need to pool resources to provide a wide range of subjects may spell the end of the all-through six-year comprehensive school. One further development envisaged in the system, which will have an effect on higher education, is that pupils with Advanced Highers may be permitted entry into the second year of a degree course.

Access to further and higher education

The most significant new recruiting ground for students for higher education is not from among the school leaver population at all. The numbers of adult students gaining access to higher education have been increasing rapidly since the early 1980s showing a 193 per cent increase in over 25s during the years 1982 and 1986. As a response to the 1987 White Paper *Meeting the Challenge* (DES, 1987) which called for widening participation in vocationally relevant education, the Scottish Office announced a new initiative in April 1988, the Scottish Wider Access Programme (SWAP). SWAP was intended to 'stimulate developments aimed at increasing the number of mature students and those without traditional entrance qualifications entering higher education' (Scottish Information Office, 0643/88). Later in that year, the particular needs of employers facing the demographic decline in young workers was cited, together with the needs of the teaching and health-related professions for women graduates, as further reasons for those in higher education to adjust their attitudes to non-standard entry to higher education (Scottish Information Office, 1968/88). Significantly, SWAP arrangements provided guaranteed places in higher education for those who successfully completed their further education courses. At the same time, many further education colleges had already developed courses which would provide access to higher education institutions.

Universities' own dedicated access summer schools for adult returners have been in existence since 1981. However, the difference between the SWAP courses and universities' access courses lay in SWAP's use of recognised national qualifications, especially the National Certificate. After completing a SWAP course, people could theoretically proceed to any course of higher education and not be confined to one particular institution.

As a result of these various initiatives, during the period 1987 to 1994, the increase in over 21s entering full-time undergraduate and sub-degree courses was almost double (201.7 per cent) that of the overall increase (104.7 per cent overall). Adult returners have more than compensated for the demographic downturn in numbers of school-leavers.

Whereas most of these special courses were organised for mature students, normally those over 21 and who had experienced a significant break between school and return to study, a new departure in university access summer schools has recently taken the form of summer schools for young people who have been educationally or socially disadvantaged during their final years at school. Traditionally, these young people would have had to follow a further education course in order to gain access to higher education. However, the new access courses seek to speed up entry to higher education through an intensive, university-based summer school with guaranteed places offered to those who successfully complete the course.

Institutional polices

Motivated in part by the competition for students upon which funding is based, most Scottish universities now have policies in place which permit socially or educationally disadvantaged students to enter courses of study. It should be said that the pre-1992 universities have had a worse record of admission of students from previously disadvantaged groups. It should also be noted that some the 'ancient' universities are less likely than the 1960s-established or later established institutions, to admit non-traditional students. Although the data of Osborne et al. (1997) are selective, they cite figures for 'non-standard' entrants as 1.7 per cent of 'standard entrants' in one 'ancient' university compared to 15.2 per cent 'non-standard' as compared to 'standard' entrants in a 1960s-established institution. It is clear that some universities have found it more in their interest to recruit from previously under-represented groups than the others which have never experienced any lack of well-qualified traditional applicants to fill their places.

Radical alternatives to HE institutions

Higher education in Scotland is not the exclusive preserve of higher education institutions. Students in many further education institutions follow courses of higher education aiming not for a degree but, for example, a Higher National Diploma. The proportions of students studying full-time in higher education courses in further education colleges in 1987 was 19.1 per cent of overall numbers, whereas in 1994 it had grown to 33.1 per cent. The corresponding proportions of undergraduates in HEIs declined from 80.9 per cent to 66.9 per cent in the same period, clearly indicating that the growing significance of the further education sector in the higher education 'market'. The Open University in Scotland also provides opportunities to study to degree level for some 2,000 students. A more recent development, the University of the Highlands and Islands Project (UHI), an initiative launched in 1996 with generous government funding, is based upon a consortium of further education colleges serving the north and north-east of Scotland. The UHI aims to develop a radical alternative to institution-based higher education. Both the UHI project and the well-established Open University provide a model of remote-access education to challenge the status quo both in terms of student access and the funding of higher education. It is no longer necessary, although it may continue to appear desirable, for a student to attend classes for face-to-face teaching in order to obtain a degree.

Support for adult returners – changing patterns of learning and the achievement of 'access' students

The tendency among institutions to identify an increasingly large proportion of the HE student population as 'non-traditional' and their entry routes as 'non-standard' speaks volumes about the view of these students as departures from the norm, often with the implication of some deficit on their part. This perspective conveniently masks the implications for institutions of the need for the institution and those who teach in it themselves to adapt as they admit new groups of students. Ball (1990) pointed out the responsibilities of those in higher education to recognise that new groups of students (by which he meant anyone not fitting the traditional profile of young, white, middle class men and women) in higher education would create new demands in terms of learning and teaching methods and pastoral care (*More Means Different: Widening Access to Higher Education*, London: RSA/Industry Matters). Most universities take the young, full-time undergraduate as the norm and have been slow to adapt by providing new modes of study, flexible teaching, additional support for people with child-care responsibilities or people with disabilities. Initial predictions that 'more means worse', that is, that students hitherto denied a place in the academy would perform poorly if admitted, have not, however, been borne out. Although research in this area is only in its infancy, the indications are that students gaining access by non-traditional routes are just as likely to succeed in gaining a degree as their more traditional counterparts. Some further fears have been articulated that degree standards have fallen and therefore that a degree is now easier to obtain. Universities deny this and cite as evidence the various quality assurance processes which will now be considered.

Standards and quality

The impetus in higher education to attract new groups of students coincided with the accountability movement which introduced into HE various quality and accountability measures such as student charters and the teaching quality assessment process (TQA). Driven by government's drive towards efficiency and value for money, TQA sought to assure the tax payer that higher education was maintaining standards and ensuring quality. The Lindop Report (Department of Education and Science, 1985) first raised the suggestion that 'standards' for Access students were lower than for traditional students, although *Meeting the Challenge* (DES, 1987) reported that no evidence could be found to substantiate the fear of a drop in standards. However, in part due to the relative novelty of non-traditional access routes to higher education, little empirical evidence yet exists. The research which has been completed suffers from problems of comparability since systematic collection of statistics by the Higher Education Statistics Agency by mode of entry, which would allow comparisons to be made, has only just begun. The most extensive review to date of the research into the performance of non-traditional participants in higher education in Scotland is that commissioned by SCOTVEC (Gallacher and Wallis, 1993). This study concluded that 'non-traditionally qualified students perform at least as well as, and in some cases better than, traditionally qualified students'. There were, however, some subject differences. Over-21s performed better than their younger counterparts in arts and social sciences, but this was less marked in science, engineering, medicine and health studies. Whilst no national study of the performance of students entering higher education with non-traditional qualifications exists, studies in individual universities (such as the University of Dundee and the University of Stirling) confirm these trends. However, as Osborne et al. (1997) recognise, a significant gap in the research evidence about the performance of these new groups of students is an analysis of any factor other than route of entry, such as socio-economic status, on performance. Student finance, for example, now a more complex business than ever, and expected to become more fraught following the findings of the Dearing Report (National Committee of Inquiry into Higher Education 1997 *Higher Education in the Learning Society*, HMSO), continues to be a very substantial barrier to access.

Future provision

Perhaps the most significant event in the past three decades in higher education has been the setting up and reporting of the Dearing Committee of Inquiry into Higher Education. Its report, *Higher Education in the Learning Society*, signals significant changes for Scottish education in the years to come. The Dearing Report states as one of its main principles that higher education in the future must 'encourage and enable all students whether they demonstrate the highest intellectual potential or whether they have struggled to reach the threshold of higher education – to achieve beyond their expectations'. In so saying, the Dearing Report appears to re-state Robbins' comprehensive ideal for higher education and apparently denies any pretensions to an elite system of education. The report recognises both the economic and social justice arguments for continuing to widen access. However, at one and the same time, Dearing has turned the clock back on the principle of higher education which is 'free at the point of entry' with a recommendation to introduce fees for study (see Chapter 12).

THE ISSUES

In the second part of this chapter, some of the issues arising out of the pattern of progress which has been traced above will be considered. It can be said with confidence that comprehensive compulsory secondary education has been achieved and schools have been successful in achieving a 70 per cent participation rate in post-compulsory stages. Much of this achievement is due to the efforts of teachers and schools themselves and this is more readily recognised by the Scottish public than by their cousins south of the border. Some of the explanation for the improved participation rate also lies in the success of government policy which has effectively insisted on school-leavers remaining in some form of education or training until the age of eighteen. More negatively, an explanation lies in the difficulties young people would experience in finding work if they were to leave school, and the inflation in qualifications required to achieve most kinds of employment. Nevertheless there are encouraging signs that staying on at school may be more than a good thing in itself. Achievement, for example, has kept pace with the higher participation rates. This means that young people derive a positive educational benefit out of staying on at school, though persistent social class inequalities in performance at the top end of achievement at Standard Grade can be distinguished.

New gender inequalities are, however, now apparent. Whereas in the early part of the century it was the case that girls were at a disadvantage in educational terms, as we approach the end of the century, boys appear to be under-performing compared to girls. While explanations for these differences vary and some would have us believe that advocates of gender equality have over-stepped the mark and are in danger of visiting discrimination against boys, the most plausible explanation seems to lie in peer pressure for under-achievement among boys and their poor perception of prospects in the labour market.

In terms of participation in higher education, significant inroads have been made into the achievement of mass participation. If we take as a marker of a comprehensive ideal for access to higher education Robbins' notion of a place for anyone with the ability and aptitude to benefit from higher education, Scotland is not far short of the mark. However, there is no room for complacency. The likelihood of children of fathers in manual work being twice as unlikely to participate in higher education as children of professional fathers, gives grave cause for concern. Though Scotland is now a better educated society than ever before, unacceptable social class and other inequalities persist.

The overall picture of positive progress in higher education in overcoming inequalities does also mask some persistent problems. There exist significant pockets of under-representation in some subjects. In science, technology and engineering there are substantial gender differences in participation which are not wholly accounted for by schools' preparation of young people for access to higher education. Girls are less likely to choose these subjects and are less likely than their male counterparts to persist in them if they do choose them. Entry qualifications do not present a barrier to participation since girls are achieving good grades in mathematics and science, but there may be hidden, cultural barriers, both in society at large and within higher education itself, which conspire to dissuade them from participation in science at university. Research into the factors which affect women's experience of higher education in science, engineering and technology, for example, suggests that the social context of these subjects, and the culture of the departments in which they are taught, are constructed according to a white, male, Euro-centric set of attitudes and values which is not conducive to the participation of excluded groups (E. Byrne, 1993, *Women and Science: The Snark Syndrome*, London: Falmer Press).

Despite schools' success in better preparing young people for higher education, the expansion of higher education provision and enhanced opportunities for adult returners to education, significant structural barriers exist – the costs of participation in terms of maintenance, family responsibilities (especially for mature students) and now the intro-duction of individual liability for fees – and must be overcome. An additional factor lies in the location of a suitable course and the feasibility of living away from home base which means extra resources. The quantitative increase in access provision continues to mask the underlying inequalities for those who are disadvantaged either by life chances or family circumstances of taking advantage of the increases in provision. Increased access does not necessarily meaner wider access.

The question of whether access to higher education affords the same opportunities in terms of quality of provision and future reward as heretofore must also be posed. While the numbers of students in higher education have doubled over the last twenty years, this rapid rise has been achieved against a background of a reduction of more than 40 per cent in funding for higher education over the same period. Furthermore, expansion may be confined to the past by under investment in universities rather than be likely to progress into a new period of expansion in the new millennium. It was precisely this crisis of resources which prompted the government to commission the review of finance in higher education published in the Dearing Report. The raising of fees from students turns around the principle of higher education which is free at the point of entry – a principle which Scotland has long espoused. While it is a popular argument that those who benefit most from higher education should contribute most, and that therefore students and their families should pay for it directly, the category of 'those who benefit' also includes employers from whom no new funding is being sought. Even the idea that the individual graduate will benefit most because their job will attract a premium salary is based upon a scarcity model of graduate employment, not one where the majority of job-seekers are graduates. It is to be feared, therefore, that the outcome of the Dearing review is not a comprehensive package of opportunity, but may result in strengthening existing barriers and in raising new ones. Many so-called full-time students are already working substantial numbers of hours in order to supplement their grants and loans with consequent effects on the amount of time available for study and even attendance at classes. Further encroach-ment into full-time study is likely; indeed, full-time study may become the exception rather than the norm as students in the UK adopt the mode of study prevalent in other countries such as the US, where 'working one's way through college' is commonplace.

Bernstein's definition of the university as 'an institution based on talk' may be all but gone. It can no longer be assumed that the undergraduates of the future will leave home to immerse themselves in study at an institution of their choice with all the social and cultural benefits this may bring. Although study at a home university appears more economical as the cost of maintenance is privatised within the family, it may reduce choice of course and relevance of qualification for an individual. It may also place a burden on them which is unsustainable.

The opportunities offered by information technology for remote teaching and study such as those provided by the Open University or promised by UHI have the potential to change the dominant, full-time mode of study. The Open University has long recognised the benefits of face-to-face interaction with tutors and peers and has organised for it. Cheaper distance-learning providers are less likely to arrange for this kind of communication which may diminish the educational experience of students.

The need for employment to supplement income may demand more flexible modes of study including modular degrees and the type of sandwich courses more familiar in vocational further education. While these modes of study offer an apparently economical alternative to full-time study, there is necessarily a loss of coherence and consistency in this fragmentation of experience which may be detrimental.

Scotland's traditional and much-prized four year degree is also under threat from three distinct directions. One of the aspirations for the new Advanced Higher is that it will permit entry to the second year of a degree programme thereby reducing the university experience for some students to three years. The Dearing report advocates the wide-scale re-introduction of a general three year degree. At the same time, the increased bill for maintenance costs for the fourth year of the Honours degree, (though not for Scots-domiciled students) may render the Scottish Honours degree less attractive.

These factors all promise to shape the higher education of the future in a new and unfamiliar way and it cannot be assumed that the progress of the last forty years will continue. Institutions themselves are changing. The competition for scarce research and teaching funds bring closer the prospect of a new two-tier or even three-tier higher education system in which an elite group of universities specialise in research and teach only an elite group of students; a middle-ranking group who strive to provide quality research and teaching; and a lower rank who cannot compete for research funding and only teach. Under the current climate of competitive individualism and diminishing resources, the prospect of a comprehensive higher education system run on the same basis as the comprehensive school, that is, equality of opportunity, becomes more and more remote.

It appears then, that social justice is a prize which is as yet beyond the grasp of a country which nevertheless has high aspirations for its education system. While the economy of Scotland remains in the doldrums, appeals to economic competitiveness will continue to be made and pressure on institutions to produce more and better graduates will be renewed. But further expansion is likely to be increasingly resource-limited and competitive, and it is more than likely that a return to increased selectivity – of and by students – will be seen. Increased selectivity spells a diminution of opportunity, not expansion. Until the economic position permits, social justice will probably have to wait.

REFERENCES

Dalgarno, M. and L. Hart (1987) Access courses to higher education, in Johnstone, R. (ed.) *Access by Mature Students to Higher Education*, Edinburgh: SIACE.

Department of Education and Science (1987) *Higher Education: Meeting the Challenge*, London: HMSO.

Department of Education and Science (1985) *Academic Validation of in Public Sector Education: the Report of the Committee of Enquiry into Academic Validation of Degree Courses in Public Sector Education*, Cmnd, 9501, London: HMSO.

Gallacher, J. and W. Wallis (1993) *The Performance of Students with Non-traditional Qualifications in Higher Education: a review of research literature commissioned by SCOTVEC*, Glasgow: SCOT-VEC.

Osborne, M., J. Leopold and A. Ferrie (1977) Does access work? The relative performance of access students at a Scottish university, *Higher Education*, 33: 155–76.

Paterson, L. (1997) Student Achievement and Educational Change in Scotland, 1980–1995, *Scottish Educational Review*, 29:1.

28

Values Education in Scotland

David Carr

VALUES AND VALUES EDUCATION

The recent enormous growth of interest in education in values and so-called values education in the UK and elsewhere itself undoubtedly calls for comment; as well as producing a rash of professional conferences, books and papers on the theme this interest has also drawn commentary from such official educational quarters as the NCC, Ofsted and SCAA and has also been a focus of widespread political and media attention. However, given that on certain fairly uncontroversial accounts of the meaning of 'education' and 'values', the expression 'values education' is little more than a pleonasm – what else could education be but a matter of communicating values – it seems well worth asking what this particular fuss about values might be about. Briefly, it seems likely that three distinguishable but related reasons lie behind this current educational movement.

The first reason reflects a degree of public panic at what is widely regarded as the breakdown of traditional mores under the influence of liberal individualism and economic consumerism; this is thought to be generally evident in a decline of discipline among the young – exhibited in the drug or crime oriented hedonism of this or that youth culture – but it has been highlighted for many by a number of unsavoury, if more sporadic, recent outbursts of individual murder and mayhem. A second related reason, however, seems more expressive of a professional concern that recent politically-driven educational reforms have focused more on the economic than the moral benefits of education: that recent emphases on raising standards have been upon the academic or vocational goals of schooling to the serious neglect of more fundamental issues concerned with the humanisation of young people. But, at a more theoretical level, some would regard latter day political preoccupations with the raising of academic and vocational standards as simply one expression of those consumerist values of contemporary economic liberalism which have been (allegedly) directly responsible for the spread in western society of selfish materialism and hedonism. Hence a third reason echoes a filtering down of concerns – long a source of controversy in contemporary social and moral theory – about how a degree of common social cooperation and purpose might be sustained in that problematic fusion of cultural pluralism and liberal individualism which, by and large, conditions both the social reality and the political ideology of developed democracies.

Thus, despite an apparent cross-curricular concern throughout the values education literature with a broad range of human values – with the social, intellectual, aesthetic and spiritual as well as the moral – the main focus has undoubtedly been upon the ethical dimension of human development; the values education movement seems to have been above all concerned to emphasise that some responsibilty for the moral formation of their pupils is an inalienable aspect of teachers' professional lives – there being a strong presumption here that this means all teachers, not just specialists in Religious Education or Personal and Social Development – in the interests, primarily, of producing individually responsible, law-abiding and socially attached citizens.

But, of course, whilst it would be outrageous to suggest (as some recent scapegoating of teachers for the moral ills of society has perhaps come near to suggesting) that teachers have in general been unaware of this responsibility, this emphasis does squarely confront educationalists with a web of conceptual and practical problems about the very character of moral education which have been a source of rich debate since Socrates. And, though there is not space here to rehearse the moral philosophical complexities required to understand these problems in any depth, it may be useful to identify a few interrelated issues around which the main controversies concerning moral education largely pivot. To begin with, there is an issue of freedom versus authority in relation to moral life; since people are naturally inclined to think of morality in terms both of obedience to some sort of law or rule and of free independent choice – what, then, should be the proper balance of freedom and authority in morality? But now, recognition of moral freedom raises the difficult question of the precise nature of this liberty. And here, whilst some moral theorists have denied that morality is at all a rational matter, most have argued that the capacity to grasp moral reasons is an important precondition of free moral choice.

This, however, raises questions about the logical status and authoritative force of these reasons. Whereas some moral theorists would be inclined to regard moral reasons as deriving from recognition of one's place in a socio-culturally determined network of attachments and responsibilities which sharply define one's moral identity, others – particularly so-called *non-cognitivists* – have regarded moral reasons as little more than personal constructs by virtue of which individuals are entirely free to form *ab initio* (subject only to requirements of rational consistency) their own commitments and attachments. And this, of course, leads to the issue of whether moral conduct should be construed primarily in terms of individual autonomy or social responsibility; in the terms of a very sweeping distinction of contemporary moral and social theory, those who place a large premium on individual freedom are often called *liberals* whereas those who strongly emphasise the social dimensions of morality are sometimes referred to as *communitarians*. Finally, for now, it may be noted that all these considerations intersect in interesting and complex ways over the issue of whether there can be any such thing as moral education as opposed to moral indoctrination – and it is a perennial, if not always clearly justified complaint of liberals that those who locate moral authority in the received socio-cultural values of community are hard put to sustain this distinction.

At all events, given the obvious moral educational relevance of these difficult conceptual issues – which continue to be the focus of much heated controversy in the often demanding literature of modern moral and social philosophy – it seems that at least some working knowledge of contemporary ethics is a *sine qua non* of any serious professional interest in moral education. However, insofar as modern empirical psychology has also been a source of highly influential ideas about the processes of moral formation, it is also arguable that teachers *qua* moral educationalists also need to be knowledgeable about the psychology of moral development. It is also likely that the single individual who has exercised the greatest influence on thinking about moral education in the post-war period is the cognitive psychologist Lawrence Kohlberg who, under the initial influence of Piaget (and through him Kant), developed a complex theory of moral formation which attempts to track the growth of moral reason through a series of cognitive stages from infancy onwards. Briefly, Kohlberg's cognitive psychology is a constructivism of the kind philosophers would regard as morally 'non-cognitivist' – and, as such, it has strongly liberal individualist leanings.

All the same, Kohlberg was from an early stage sensitive to criticisms that his account seriously neglected the social and interpersonal dimensions of morality and, in response, supplemented the psychology with a kind of moral sociology focused on the development of so-called *communities of justice*. However, in drawing for this upon ideas in the contractarian tradition, Kohlberg did not significantly depart from a basically liberal position and his ultimate account is a highly unstable mix of ideas from Dewey, Rawls, Habermas and, as mentioned, Kant and Piaget; it is thus doubtful whether his various amendments adequately address the kinds of objections that have been raised over the years by, for example, communitarians, post-analytical social philosophers, virtue-theorists and feminists of the 'ethics of care' school. Of more recent challenges to Kohlbergian ideas perhaps the largely American *character education* movement has been the most widely influential – though the ideas behind this movement have often been conceptually crude as well as strongly associated with various forms of right-wing reaction to the alleged permissivism of contemporary liberalism. A philosophically more sophisticated response to cognitive developmentalism might, however, be expected from the Aristotle inspired ideas of modern *virtue theorists*; but whilst there is evidence of growing interest among educational philosophers in virtue theory, such interest is relatively embryonic and it is rather too early to assess its practical impact and implications.

VALUES EDUCATION IN THE SCOTTISH CONTEXT

Whilst attention to the sort of questions which are currently exercising the current proponents of values education seems always to have been high on the agenda of Scottish educationalists – it may be worth noting here that Scots (A. S. Neill and R. F. McKenzie to name but two of the more famous) have been very much in the vanguard of 'progressive' attempts to give education a more 'human face' – serious Scottish interest in 'values education' as such is, as elsewhere, a relatively recent phenomenon. To be sure, serious interest in questions of moral, social, spiritual and religious formation have long been a distinctive feature of major Scottish educational initiatives – and it is noteworthy in this connection that whilst these aspects of education were from the very outset regarded as crucial components of Scotland's own 5–14 Development Programme, much of the official values education documentation produced south of the border seems to have been by way of compensation for a lack of explicit recognition of these issues in English national curriculum. But, be that as it may, Scottish interest in 'values education' in its current form is probably due in no small part to the timely appearance on the scene of the Aberdeen based Gordon Cook Foundation in the early nineties.

Thus, whilst the Gordon Cook Foundation did not in and of itself create the widespread interest among Scottish teachers and academics in educational values and values in education, the emergence of an extraordinarily well heeled charitable trust dedicated precisely to the promotion of better personal and social values among the young – at the extremely generous behest of the late Aberdeen industrialist for whom the trust is named – has proved an enormous shot in the arm to research and development in fields that have perhaps not always been prime targets for funding from more conventional sources. Moreover, whilst one cannot be sure that Cook grants have been awarded to projects which would have been wholeheartedly endorsed, had he known about them, by their benefactor – and whilst there is always bound to be, in the nature of an enterprise of this sort, some controversy and disagreement about the worth of this or that enterprise – there can be no doubt that the Foundation has supported a rich variety of theoretical and practical projects under the broad heading of 'values education'. It is therefore worth taking some space here to draw attention to some of these projects – especially those which have involved collaboration with major Scottish educational institutions and organisations otherwise invoved in research and development in relation to the value dimensions of education.

Perhaps the best place to start is with the work throughout the nineties of the Scottish Consultative Council on the Curriculum (SCCC) which seems to have been one of first beneficiaries of Cook largesse. Whilst the Council (formerly the Committee) had certainly been exercised by questions about values in the curriculum in the natural course of its professional involvement with major Scottish curriculum initiatives from the seventies onwards, its interest in value aspects of education certainly seems to have intensified with Cook Foundation stimulus and support, and a constant stream of challenging and some-times controversial papers have greatly helped to keep important issues of educational values and ethos in the spotlight during the present decade. Thus, beginning with the publication in 1991 of the discussion paper *Values in Education* the SCCC has gone on to produce, either with Cook Foundation assistance or under its own steam, a number of significant documents – such as *School Climate and Ethos* (1994), *A Sense of Belonging* (1995), *The Heart of the Matter* (1995) – all addressed to important issues concerning personal and social development, school climate and ethos and so on. In addition, the Council has also commissioned individual authors researching into questions of values and moral education – including Elliot Eisner, Bart McGettrick and the present writer – to write for a wide ranging series of essays entitled *Perspectives: Occasional Papers on Values and Education*.

Given the concern of the Cook Foundation with research and development into aspects of education, it is hardly surprising that Scottish institutions directly concerned with educational research and the professional training of teachers have also received generous Cook funding – and, indeed, two Principals of Scottish colleges of education are on the board of trustees of the Foundation. At one time or another, then, all major Scottish teacher training institutions (many of which have now become university faculties of education) have been engaged in Cook funded projects concerned to investigate this or that aspect of values education – with specific reference to such areas as secondary education (Northern College 1990, Moray House 1991), primary education (St Andrews College 1990), nursery education (Craigie College 1991), professional teacher education and training (Jordanhill 1991, Northern 1990, St Andrews 1990) and further education (Jordanhill/Strathclyde 1994). But, at an academic level somewhat removed from professional concerns with teacher training and basic schooling, the Cook Foundation has also supported some valuable university projects concerning various aspects of values education in Scotland and else-where. A particularly noteworthy initiative in this connection has been a very impressive series of *Victor Cook Memorial Lectures* organised by the Centre for Philosophy and Public Affairs at the University of St Andrews; this has already featured papers on values and education from Lord Quinton and Professor Anthony O'Hear (1992), Baroness Warnock and Professor Richard Pring (1994), Sir Stewart Sutherland and Rabbi Jonathan Sacks (1996) – and more of these appear to be in preparation. With additional Cook assistance the Centre has also produced further short booklets (each containing two papers on philosophical aspects of values and values education) entitled *Values and Values Education* (David Carr and John Haldane, 1993) and *Values, Education and Responsibility* (Elizabeth Pybus and Terence McLaughlin, 1995).

In addition to its sponsorship of prestigious university lectures, however, the Foundation has also supported the mounting of significant university and higher education conferences on aspects of values education in Scotland and elsewhere. Besides its support for recent key conferences on moral and spiritual education outwith Scotland – not strictly within the scope of this chapter – the Foundation in 1991 assisted the prestigious University of Edinburgh Centre for Research in Child Development to mount a conference on the moral development of the child which brought together an international group of leading scholars in the field. On the subject of conferences, however, it should certainly not go unremarked here that several significant conferences have also been organised with Cook sponsorship in recent years by the colleges of education – Northern College (1995), St Andrews (1996), Moray House (1997) – for the express purpose of at once celebrating and monitoring the progress of Foundation funded projects; once again, many of these have featured presentations and addresses from leading local, national and international lights in the fields of values and moral education. These Cook Foundation conferences seem also to be planned to occur on an annual basis.

It would be impossible, in the available space, to do anything like full justice to the breadth and extent of Cook funded work; much assistance has been to individual educational and/or teacher researchers often operating relatively independently of major research agencies, institutions and organisations in Scotland and elsewhere. Indeed, as already noted, much Cook funding has gone to projects conceived and implemented well beyond the borders of Scotland; and these cannot, as such, really be included within present purview. Thus, having no choice other than to round off this brief Cook's tour in fairly short order, mention may be made of a few notable associations and/or collaborations between significant Scottish agencies and the Foundation. One such important continuing collaboration has been with the Scottish Council for Research in Education (SCRE) located on the premises of the Moray House Institute in Edinburgh; moreover, as well as supporting a number of professional research projects into values aspects of education, particularly concerning parents perceptions of values education (1991) and values in the primary school (1992), the Foundation has sought the assistance of SCRE in the process of evaluating the effectiveness of its own activities as a funding agency (1996, 1997). Some of the work associated with SCRE, as well as other research and development initiatives inside Scotland and beyond, were usefully highlighted in a special pull-out feature of the *Times Education Supplement Scotland* – also supported by the Cook Foundation – in June 1995.

Other instances of collaboration between the Foundation and official and/or Scottish civic organisations have included support for values education initiatives mounted by the Scottish Environmental Council (1995), the Scottish Community Education Council (1996), the Scottish Parents Consultative Forum (1996), Glasgow City Council Education Department (1995), the Highland Award Project (1993), Grampian Police (1995) and the Scottish Office Education and Industry Department (1995). This last collaboration is noteworthy insofar as the Scottish Office Department of Education has ever been – in the very nature of its leadership and overseer role with regard to educational provision in

Scotland – the author of many values implicated school initiatives. In this connection, one most important educational values related initiative involving the Scottish Office, has been the recent development of a set of *Ethos Indicators* (1992) for use in self-evaluation by primary and secondary schools. Thus, with the assistance of professional teacher-researchers, the SOEID has sought to utilise the longstanding experience of the Schools Inspectorate in assessing quality of school ethos and relationships, to the end of developing tools which might be effectively self-employed by schools to monitor the value dimensions of their work.

One could not possibly conclude even a brief survey of the current state of values education in Scotland without appropriate recognition of the important role that the religious communities (of all major world faiths) have continued to play in the moral and spiritual formation of young people, both in the course of daily religious witness and via more particular church-based initiatives. However, given the history of Scotland's cultural development – not least the major formative influence that patterns of imigration, particularly from Ireland, have had on that development (see Chapter 97) – it could hardly have been otherwise that the most substantial communities of faith in Scotland fall either side of the main western Christian confessional divide. Several leaders of values education iniatives and projects in Scotland are active Catholics or Protestants; but, more importantly, the main Christian denominations have continued to exercise a significant influence on values education in mainstream state and independent schooling. What, of course, is immediately distinctive about Catholic values education in Scotland is that it has long been pursued in a relatively separate sector of state maintained schooling which continues to be a matter of some controversy. Nevertheless, there can be no doubt that the Catholic church has in this context sought in both policy and practice to remain faithful to a particular vision of the inseparability of moral and other human values from the religious and the divine which continues to present a powerful challenge to contemporary secular materialism (see Chapter 24).

CRITICAL EVALUATION OF RECENT VALUES INITIATIVES

Nothing, of course, has so far been said about the overall character and quality of all these diverse values education initiatives. The most general thing that might be said, however, is that there is no overall character and the quality appears to have been extremely variable. A fair proportion of the work – that which, one may suppose, comes most readily under the heading of research – seems to have been fairly straightforwardly descriptive or fact-finding, though usually with a view to the information or formulation of school or other educational policy proposals. Some other work has been of a more academic or theoretical kind focused primarily upon the conceptual clarification of this or that aspect of moral and evaluative discourse, though there has been a degree of hesitance on the part of the Cook and other research funding agencies to target such work for support, given a questionable assumption that such investigations are of less urgent practical import than direct developmental work in schools. Apart from any consequences such an assumption might have for the coherence of practical work undertaken without benefit of conceptual clarification, however, it is arguable that it also presupposes a questionable view of the actual relationship of moral philosophy, discourse or 'theory' to moral practice.

At all events, much recent work does seem to have been of a practical developmental rather than research or philosophically orientated kind. Some of this work seems to have been concerned, perhaps in the light of empirical research, to try to change or modify aspects of the educational environment – school discipline policies, teacher-class relationships or patterns of pupil motivation – in the interests of 'improving' institutional ethos or reducing what are perceived to be 'negative' aspects of young people's behaviour. To that extent, however, it might be said that at least some values initiatives have operated according to a more or less manipulative agenda of social engineering or behaviour modification, no matter how well-intentioned this may have been. But, by contrast, other work seems to have focused less on environmental conditioning or behaviour shaping and more – via the development of curriculum and pedagogy – on the education of moral reason and understanding. But such work raises rather different problems, of equally familiar and just as intractable kinds, concerning the very character, point and purpose of moral and evaluative deliberation.

Given the previously mentioned post-war influence of the cognitive psychologist Lawrence Kohlberg, it is hardly surprising that many values education initiatives focused upon the development of moral reason, in Scotland as elsewhere, have pursued a quasi-Kohlbergian strategy of moral dilemma exploration broadly aimed at the resolution of moral problems. It is probably safest in most cases to speak of a 'roughly' Kohlbergian strategy, since it may be doubted whether much teacher initiated work of this kind is very methodologically pure; many other pedagogical approaches employed in values education, such as *Values Clarification* and Matthew Lipman's *Philosophy for Children*, utilise techniques of dilemma exploration and it seems likely that much street level values education pedagogy is a theoretically loose blend of ideas drawn from somewhat disparate (and not necessarily mutually consistent) sources. But the truth is that, mixed or pure, all such work raises familiar difficulties about the precise point and purpose of moral deliberation.

One point on which there is much agreement is that moral dilemmas are of a significantly different logical character from scientific or artistic problems, and therefore that moral reason does not operate in relation to moral problems as scientific or artistic reasoning function for the resolution of theoretical or technical problems. Indeed, if it is a hallmark of a dilemma or conflict of moral value that it is precisely unsusceptible of any theoretical or technical solution (for if it was it would not be a moral but a theoretical or technical problem) then it becomes difficult to see how moral reasoning – construed either as a moral decision procedure or as a form of values clarification – could have much, if any, rational or educational point. The trouble is that it is liable to collapse either (on a values clarification interpretation) into a form of moral subjectivism or relativism, or (on a Kohlbergian constuctivist interpretation) into some kind of non-cognitivist personal commitment to self-legislated principles, which is just subjectivism by the scenic route; none of these provide much of a basis for genuine education in moral enquiry. What would therefore seem to be required for this purpose – as a whole legion of contemporary communitarian, virtue theoretical, ethical realist and feminist critics of liberal individualist moral theory have, in their different ways, argued – is a quite different conception of the economy of practical reason in human affairs from any one finds in liberal moral educational theory of either cognitive developmental or values clarificatory kinds.

But a rather more general problem with the current spate of new values education activity – one which may well already have been discerned from what has been said so far – arguably lies with the extraordinary diversity of educational and other aims which seem to be entertained within its overall compass. From one point of view, of course, the diversity might be welcomed as a good thing; the garden of values education might be seen as one in which a thousand flowers bloom (and the fact that a few weeds also flourish might be considered a price worth paying for the diversity); it seems to be in some such spirit of openness that the Cook Foundation claims to eschew allegiance to any particular values agenda. But unwillingness to co-ordinate a set of diverse practical activities or to bring them in line with some overall strategic plan is liable to become a serious logistical problem if the normative and evaluative underpinnings of different projects and initiatives differ to the point of practical inconsistency.

Thus, while it may seem not just unexceptionable but entirely laudable that a values education initiative attaches great importance to the production of morally principled, law abiding citizens who are also able to identify with some sort of community, it may also be that there is not inconsiderable tension between these praiseworthy but different aims. There does seem, for example, to be an enormous unresolved confusion at the heart of the values education movement between education and social control; it has already been seen that whilst some programmes seem to place emphasis on getting young people to think for themselves in the interests of forming their own personal values, others seem more concerned with reducing deviance via this or that form of social engineering. Again, it would seem that whilst some values education researchers are busily engaged in trying to create some sense of cultural attachment for the promotion of a greater sense of human fellowship, others are just as busy trying to heal those social divisions which are, at home and abroad, in part the result of such attachment. Briefly, then, it is not obvious that moral education (in any robust sense) would be the best route to crime reduction, it may be that the most effective ways of reducing crime or producing socially conformist behaviour may well be inimical to moral development, a strong sense of cultural identification might inhibit rather than foster greater moral reflection, and so on. It therefore remains at least a danger that any large scale movement towards values education which does not sytematically address the normative and conceptual questions underlying these potential conflicts of interest is liable, however much good otherwise comes of it, to spend some of the time falling over its own feet.

REFERENCES

Carr, D. (1996) *The Moral Role of the Teacher*, Perspectives on Values 3, Edinburgh: SCCC.

Haldane, J. (ed.) *Education, Values and the State*, (Victor Cook Memorial Lectures by Baroness Warnock and Professor Richard Pring) University of St. Andrews: Centre for Philosophy and Public Affairs, 1993.

Halstead, M. and M. J. Taylor (eds) (1996) *Values in Education and Education in Values*, London and Washington DC: Falmer Press.

Haydon, G. (1997) *Teaching about Values: A New Approach*, London: Cassell.

SCCC, (1995) *The Heart of the Matter: A Paper for Discussion and Development*, Edinburgh: SCCC.

SCCC (1993) *Religious and Moral Education: 5–14*, Edinburgh: SCCC.

V

Pre-School and Primary Education: Organisation and Management

29

Pre-five Education

Joyce Watt

Pre-five education is a much wider concept than is implied by its institutional settings: the home and community are by far the most pervasive educational influences on young children. This chapter, however, confines itself to a discussion of pre-five education in organised groups outside the home. It should be read in conjunction with Chapter 30 which discusses public provision for pre-fives in nursery schools and classes and also examines the fundamental questions about learning and teaching which lie at the heart of pre-five education in any setting.

Pre-five education in Scotland is non-statutory and its development has therefore been spasmodic, diverse, and variable and characterised by both government and public ambivalence. This chapter tells the broad story of how pre-five education has developed in Scotland and highlights some of the contemporary issues which reflect its chequered history.

CONTEXT: TO THE EARLY 1990s

Pre-five education in Scotland in the twentieth century has been characterised by government uncertainty in the face of one broad unanswered question: what is pre-five education outside the home for and how can it be justified? With no clear answer to that question, the result has been low levels of provision, fragmented services and a lack of direction. Government uncertainty is rooted in its changing attitude to four subsidiary questions: whether 'education' and 'care' are to be viewed as different or as 'integrated' services; whether pre-five education can be justified for all children or only for those in social need; whether pre-five education is a legitimate contender for limited educational resources; and whether, in the provision of pre-five education, there can be a satisfactory 'partnership' between the public, voluntary and private sectors. Each is examined in turn.

First, 'education' and 'care' were traditionally assumed to be different. Within local authorities, 'education' was provided for three to four–year-olds in nursery schools and classes through education departments and was part of a continuous service with schools. Social and physical 'care' was provided for children in special need throughout the pre-five age range in day nurseries, first by health departments, then from 1969 by the new social work departments. There were few links between the two. 'Education' was, for the most part, based on a free play curriculum which, at its best, provided a flexible, child-centred but structured approach to children's learning and development. The curriculum of early day nurseries was very limited.

Second, government ambivalence to pre-five education as a public universal service has revolved round its cost and its potential threat to the family. Given its professional staffing and adult:child ratios, pre-five education is a costly service to provide and, although fifty years have now passed since the first official recognition that all children can benefit, the focus has traditionally been on children from disadvantaged homes. This has long been reflected in national policy statements and local authority strategic planning. Pre-five education might well benefit all children, but the public purse could afford to loosen its strings only for the few. That position was justified on the grounds that at least the 'care' elements of pre-five education should be, for the great majority, a family not a state responsibility.

Besides, was pre-five provision not a threat to the coherence of the family and, in particular, to the mother-child relationship? In the post-war period government enthusiasm for day nurseries with their long hours of parent-child separation was lukewarm and the number of children in day care continued to fall, a policy supported by then current theories of child development which highlighted the dangers of mother-child separation at critical periods in the pre-school years. Such thinking, though often misguided, contributed more positively to a reassessment of the nature and conditions of day care, subsequently incorporated into the Social Work (Scotland) Act of 1968. Within nursery education the same thinking was a potent influence on the widespread development of part-time provision at the time.

In this same period there was an unequivocal answer to the third question, whether pre-five education as a non-statutory service could be a strong contender for scarce educational resources. At a time of massive social and educational reconstruction, a huge rise in the birth rate and a severe shortage of teachers, priorities clearly lay elsewhere. Indeed in 1960 there was a complete government ban on any expansion of state nursery education, a ban which remained in force, with minor concessions, until 1972.

By the 1960s there was, however, increasing research evidence on the critical influence of social background on educational achievement and the importance of the early years. In a decade when arguments for equality of opportunity were gaining ground internationally, 'compensatory education' was promoted as an investment not just for children but for the nation, and a number of pre-five initiatives were launched in disadvantaged areas. Provision was still, however, heavily selective.

In 1972, the Conservative government, under heavy public pressure, announced a major programme of expansion for nursery education. But the international oil crisis which hit the country the following year changed the position yet again. Throughout the 1970s and beyond, as the economic crisis bit deeply into resources, few authorities were able to invest in pre-five education on the scale envisaged in 1972.

By the late 1970s the educational spotlight certainly shone elsewhere. In 1976 the Labour government launched its 'Great Debate' on education and, with the election of the Conservative government in 1979, the still ongoing concern over school effectiveness and standards of achievement was at the centre of the educational stage. Pre-five education was relegated to the sidelines.

Most local authorities however expanded their nursery provision steadily if slowly, sometimes with funding from the Urban Aid Programme, and provision increased in more affluent areas. A number of social work departments replaced their traditional day nurseries with family centres which, as well as providing day care, put a new focus on the family as a unit and the inter-related needs of all its members, and a few local authorities invested in the joint provision of 'children's centres' which catered for the whole pre-five age range.

In 1985 Strathclyde Region made a major investment in pre-five education through the radical reorganisation of all its pre-five services under its education department. The 'flagship' of that policy was the 'community nursery', planned to cater for the entire pre-five age group and to act as a social and educational resource for children, parents, families and communities (Wilkinson et al., 1992). In the 1980s then, while nationally pre-five education lost the battle for public recognition and funding, a few local authorities continued to see it as an important investment.

The fourth question relates to the possible partnership between public and non-public provision. To examine this issue it is important to look back to the 1960s when local authorities first had to accommodate a rapid growth in alternative forms of pre-five services.

Thwarted by the ban on the expansion of nursery education in 1960, mothers themselves launched the pre-school playgroup movement as a self-help organisation which focused on children's play and gave a central role to parents. The Scottish Pre-school Playgroup Association (SPPA) was founded in 1967. The movement was originally seen and saw itself as a short-term expedient until nursery education could be adequately funded, but that position had changed even by the early 1970s as playgroups became a viable and distinctive alternative offering play facilities for large numbers of children, a new role for parents and a focus for community development through young families. Inevitably, however, given the pattern of nursery provision, playgroups developed first in more affluent areas and in rural communities.

National voluntary organisations by the 1970s were also making their mark. Barnardos, the Aberlour Trust, Save the Children, and Stepping Stones in Scotland, for example, funded independent family centres and community-based nurseries which reflected their own distinctive philosophies. These were predominantly in disadvantaged areas and a significant element in many was the promotion of educational, training and employment opportunities for women, some funded more recently through the European Social Fund.

New social patterns also demanded some rethinking. Changing norms within family life and the development of the Women's Movement meant that increasing numbers of women wanted employment, either because of economic necessity or because they felt they had a right to work, or both. Child care became a major issue and, given all the pressures on public provision, the private sector grew rapidly. Creches, childminding, and nurseries run in commercial, business and adult education establishments as well as in private homes began to burgeon. For many, of course, the private sector was no solution as child care costs are notoriously high, but for those who could afford it, the private sector offered what few public sector groups could match: extended flexible hours, provision for under-threes, and no regular demands on parents' own time.

Throughout this period the relationship between the public and voluntary sectors remained largely cooperative but detached, although local rivalries were common. Nursery teachers sometimes resented playgroups as 'cheap alternatives' which allowed governments off the financial hook of providing universal nursery education and playgroups were often resentful that their distinctive contribution was undervalued. In Strathclyde, relationships were particularly difficult given the region's determination that trained teachers would not necessarily be appointed to key roles in the new integrated service. Throughout Scotland there were also, however, innumerable examples of mutual help and cooperation between the two sectors: grant support to playgroups, sharing of premises and joint informal training. Relationships between the private and other sectors were at this stage generally weak.

THE LEGACY

In the early 1990s, the legacy of long-term government ambivalence was obvious. Except in Strathclyde, formal administrative distinctions between 'care' and 'education' persisted, frustrating the genuine attempts to see them conceptually as inseparable. Levels of provision were still woefully inadequate. Although there were wide regional variations, only 36 per cent of all pre-five children were in some form of provision (Scottish Office Statistical Bulletin SWK/DC/1996) and only 20 per cent of three-year-olds and 54 per cent of four-year-olds were in nursery education (Statistical Bulletin Edn/B1/1997). The playgroup movement was still very active but overall no longer expanding, except in certain sectors such as Gaelic medium playgroups. In 1994 the fastest growing provision was registered childminding which in a decade had risen by 500 per cent (Statistical Bulletin EDN/A2/1995).

There was still a strong emphasis on social disadvantage not surprisingly since, even in 1996, over 40 per cent of under-fives both urban and rural were living in poverty. Public provision dominated urban areas, the voluntary sector rural areas. Few groups offered the hours needed by women in employment, and there was a huge unmet demand for provision for under-threes. Like the rest of the United Kingdom, Scotland lagged far behind most of its European counterparts. The European Commission Network on Child Care estimated that, in the mid 1990s, over all pre-five groups, the UK had one of the lowest levels of public provision available among member countries and provision for under threes was particularly poor (*A Review of Services for Young Children in the European Union*, 1996).

Another legacy was the vast army of under-fives workers in the voluntary and private sectors with no formal training or qualifications for the work. A network of informal training courses had been available from the 1960s through local authorities and the voluntary sector, but these did not lead to recognised qualifications. Two outstanding problems ensued. The first was the danger of low quality provision where those who ran pre-five groups either chose not to pursue training or had no opportunity to do so. The second was the frustration of many dedicated and able women with impressive experience of working with children who wanted to make a career in pre-five education but were denied the opportunity.

Other legacies were more positive. One was the play curriculum which is discussed more fully in Chapter 30 and which was, to greater or lesser degrees, adopted by all sectors. Another was the role played by parents which, given the fragmented way in which pre-five provision had developed, varied considerably. The first pre-war nursery schools included parents as part of their efforts to improve the social conditions of families by giving them opportunities to learn practical child-rearing and domestic skills. With the recognition of the educational importance of the early years, teachers and others had been urged to help parents take part actively in their children's learning both at home and at school. A few developed home-visiting schemes and most encouraged parents to be involved in the life of the school, sometimes as participants in the classroom.

The first day nurseries also emphasised parents' 'skills'. However, the function of the day nursery was seen largely as relieving parents temporarily of responsibility. To-day's day care and family centres acknowledge that many parents need a break from their children but, recognising that parents are central to their children's long-term, future they also try to involve them as appropriate: working alongside their own children in the nursery, participating in family counselling or pursuing their own educational or training opportunities.

Parents are at the heart of the playgroup movement. They founded it, developed its rationale and ran it for their children, for themselves and for their community. Parents are employers (of the supervisor), managers through the committee structure, and participants in children's play as helpers. Because of this diversity of roles, the playgroup movement, perhaps more than any other sector, has put the parent in the dual role of 'teacher' and 'learner'. In contrast, parents in the private sector are consumers of a service for which they pay and in which, for the most part, they do not expect to play an active role.

All pre-five groups, however, including the private sector aim for a 'partnership' with parents, but the nature of that partnership inevitably and rightly is different. The most radical is probably that epitomised by the Stepping Stones projects in disadvantaged areas where it is the parents who decide what the nature of the partnership will be. Partnerships with parents have come a long way since parents came to learn to make soup in the nursery schools of the 1920s.

The diversity of the 'parent legacy' has therefore had positive outcomes, opening up a range of possibilities for involvement which might never otherwise have been considered. It has made a significant contribution to an understanding of the relationships among child, adult and community learning, a legacy not yet sufficiently valued.

A NEW VISION: QUALITY AND PRE-SCHOOL EDUCATION FOR ALL

The new vision for pre-five education is linked with other wider national trends from the late 1980s. Examples are the formal recognition of children's rights (United Nations Convention on the Rights of the Child, 1989) and the insistence on quality in all public services. 'Quality' and 'children's rights' came together in two pieces of child care legislation, the Children Act (1989) and the Children (Scotland) Act (1995). Both were committed to the principles of children's rights, inter-agency collaboration and partnerships with parents.

The 1989 Act made it mandatory on local authorities to establish quality assurance procedures for all voluntary and private pre-five groups registered with their social work departments and to bring their social work and education departments together to review and report on all services for children aged 0 to 8 every three years from 1992. The 1995 Act required local authorities to provide day care for 'children in need' and to prepare, consult upon and publish plans for children's services by 1998. Both Acts made it clear that 'pre-five' was an artificial distinction and the term 'early years' was increasingly used to cover the 0 to 8 age range.

Alongside the legislation came quality guidelines for all sectors. The Scottish Office Education Department (SOED) in 1995 issued *Using Performance Indicators in Nursery School/Class/Pre-Five Unit Self Evaluation*; SPPA published its *Code of Practice* (1994) followed by *Standards and Indicators of Good Practice for Sessional Playgroups* in 1997; and the Scottish Independent Nurseries Association (SINA) commissioned a self-evaluation study, *Evaluating Ourselves*, from the Department of Education, University of Glasgow (1992).

The new emphasis on quality in pre-five education has also brought a welcome impetus to training for pre-five workers particularly in the voluntary and private sectors. While training remains patchy and expensive, some new structures are at last in place. Since the early 1990s Scottish Vocational Qualifications in early childhood care and education have made it possible to have relevant skills and understanding accredited on the basis of practice in the employee's own workplace. SVQs at Levels II and III are now available and Level IV is in preparation. From 1997 a new Modern Apprenticeship in early childhood care and education is available as part of the government's Skillseekers initiative which aims training programmes at the young unemployed. The scheme aims to combine the best features of traditional apprenticeships, employment and training on the job, with new features based on a partnership among the apprentice, the employer, the Local Enterprise Company and the National Training Organisation. The level aimed at is SVQ III. The new BA in early childhood studies, discussed more fully in Chapter 30, is also significant in opening up academic training to those to whom it was previously denied. Its great strengths for those in employment are in the opportunities it provides for distance learning and for variable access and exit points.

One of the most significant developments of the 1990s has been the growing recognition of pre-five provision as 'education' and its place in the long-term improvement of educational standards in the statutory sector. This was helped hugely by a series of national publications. First came *Learning to Succeed*, the National Commission's Report on Education in England and Wales (1993), then its counterpart *Learning to Succeed in Scotland* (1996). Both argued strongly for a major expansion of pre-five education as the foundation of all later learning. The Royal Society's highly influential report, *Start Right* (Ball, 1994), also made a soundly argued and costed case for the long-term benefits of investment in high quality nursery education. Questions were asked in the House of Commons and a strong political lobby emerged. By 1995 all major political parties, with an eye to a general election in 1997 at the latest, were committed to supporting the idea of a publicly funded high quality universal service at least for children in their pre-school year.

For the Conservative government, the mechanism was the voucher scheme announced in July 1995. Pilot schemes were planned for Scotland from 1996 with full implementation from 1997. This scheme entitled each four-year-old to a place where available in an 'accredited' pre-five group in the public, voluntary or private sector for up to five part-time sessions of at least 2½ hours each per week. Accreditation was awarded at national level and was automatic for the public sector. For voluntary and private groups it was based on a profile of the service offered and an assessment of its quality. Each voucher was valued at £1,100, money for the scheme coming from local authority funds already allocated to pre-fives with £3 million of new money.

The Scottish consultation, launched in August 1995, provoked strong initial criticism on the grounds that it was concerned only with the implementation not the principle of the scheme. It was alleged that it ignored the wishes of parents who had consistently shown an overall preference for expanded public provision, threatened provision for younger children in need, and encouraged unhealthy competition among providers. Despite the criticism, the scheme went ahead in four pilot areas in August 1996.

Stirling University's national evaluation of the pilot (Stephen et al., 1997) shows that, while not covering full costs, the scheme has enabled pilot areas to expand local authority provision considerably and has given all sectors a new impetus to re-examine what they provide and to plan new strategies. Quality as a result is seen to have improved. Parents have been largely indifferent to the mechanism of the voucher but very positive to the opportunities it opened up. On the debit side, the voucher scheme seems to have led to a substantial decrease in the involvement of parents in both the voluntary and public sectors. The evaluation also highlights the anomalies of a system based on the competition of the market place in which participants were also exhorted to work in partnership. Whatever the merits and demerits of the voucher scheme, the evaluation concludes that the pilot has certainly put pre-school education in the public spotlight: it has provided a 'spark' which 'has changed the world of pre-school provision in Scotland' (p. 8).

That world is now changing very rapidly indeed. In opposition, the Labour Party committed itself to the abolition of the voucher scheme, describing it as 'a tragic missed opportunity' (Scottish Shadow Circular, *Early Years Services*, December 1996, p. 2) and promising alternative strategies to bring the benefits of pre-school education closer for every four-year-old immediately and for every three-year-old as resources allowed. In May 1997, however, the Labour government in office conceded that, for practical reasons, the voucher scheme would have to be retained throughout Scotland for session 1997–8 but again repeated its promise of an alternative strategy within a wider vision of pre-five education.

That strategy was heralded in a ministerial statement in September and a full Consultation Paper was published in November (SOEID, 1997). The terms of the paper are too comprehensive to cover in detail but it brings together many of the ideas foreshadowed in the Labour Party's pre-election manifesto as well as in more recent government circulars and statements. The paper is explicit about the importance of pre-school education, its distinctive nature and the government's commitment to it. That commitment is first to four-year-olds all of whom will be entitled to a pre-school place in an accredited group by session 1998–9. Universal provision for three-year-olds will follow but at the time of writing no target dates are given.

Funding will be controlled by local authorities but a major priority will be the development of integrated services. While scathing of the voucher scheme as a mechanism for the expansion of provision, the Consultation Paper acknowledges that the pilot exercise highlighted the importance of the voluntary and private sectors and the high quality of what some of their groups provide. Local authorities are urged to work in partnership with other sectors and with parents in a variety of ways to plan, build on and deliver quality services which are flexible and reflect the particular needs of their own children, families and communities while providing best value from public funds. The aim is a national framework of educational provision which will reflect local needs and priorities and will be coordinated with a national childcare strategy subsequently to be announced.

The Consultation Paper stresses the importance of the document *A Curriculum Framework for the Pre-School Year*. Launched originally for consultation under the Conservative government in 1996 in parallel with the voucher scheme, this document was published in its final (not very different) form under the new Labour government in September 1997. Its significance is discussed in Chapter 30 but here it is important to note that, given its origins in policies for universal provision for four-year-olds, and that both Conservative and Labour governments (if for different reasons) are encouraging the involvement of the voluntary and private sectors, this document will be the definitive source of curriculum thinking for four-year-olds across every sector. The Consultation Paper of November goes a step further, announcing that plans are already in hand to develop a parallel curriculum strategy for children in the 'ante-pre-school' year which for the youngest children will start at the age of 2½.

In the mid to late 1990s then, pre-five education in Scotland has probably never been so vibrant nor as high on the educational and political agenda. As the century draws to a close is there at last some kind of answer to the question: what is pre-school education for and how can it be justified?

TOWARDS THE MILLENNIUM

Even in a period of such rapid change, the subsidiary questions posed at the beginning of this chapter are still relevant. Few to-day argue for a conceptual distinction between education and care but administrative distinctions are still widespread and even under the new unitary authorities traditional committee structures largely prevail. Stirling Council's new 'Children's Committee' is one of the few new initiatives aimed at blurring administrative boundaries. The recent Consultation Paper (SOEID, 1997) expresses a very strong commitment to the principle of integration but also makes a distinction between 'education' as planned learning within a recognised curriculum framework and the informal learning which is an integral part of good quality child care. 'Education' has its own agenda.

The battle to see pre-five education as a universal service has now been won for four-year-olds and provision for all three-year-olds is now a real possibility. Questions about the funding of pre-five education in the face of claims from the statutory sector have been answered in part by 'ring fencing' funds within local authorities for the education of children in their pre-school year.

The diversity of pre-five education remains: the public, voluntary and private sectors all have a strong stake in its future. It is a diversity encouraged in the public rhetoric within a framework of partnership. 'Partnership' is knitted into the legislation of the Children Act of 1989 and the Children (Scotland) Act of 1995 and is reflected in recent government thinking which includes the pre-five sector in the joint strategic planning expected of local authorities through 'early years forums' as they plan for 'children's services'. 'Early excellence' should also be acknowledged and promoted wherever it is found (SOEID, 1997).

Inevitably the nature of the 'partnership' will vary given that funding will come through local authorities which will not only provide but coordinate and commission services. It remains to be seen whether it will be a partnership of equals which recognises diversity as a strength or one driven by the public sector towards long-term uniformity. And, ironically, might a partnership develop among 'accredited' groups across all sectors and a two-tier system of 'accredited' and non-accredited groups result within the voluntary and private sectors?

These issues are too complex and too new for the present discussion but two brief observations illustrate the move towards possible uniformity. The first relates to the curriculum. While the *Curriculum Framework for the Pre-School Year* targeted at four-year-olds will be the basis of the curriculum for accredited groups across all sectors it is clearly modelled on the public sector with its professional staff, its nursery classes composed almost entirely of 4-year-olds and its implicit although not explicit notion of laying a foundation for primary school. Voluntary and private sector groups will be under pressure to formalise their curriculum in terms of national guidelines and while this may in some cases raise standards, it may also sacrifice their freedom to be different and they may become more formal in their approach to the curriculum than was ever intended by the guidelines themselves. The Scottish Pre-school Play Association is already on record as regretting that it has to persuade some of its members of the value of play. The potential danger is even greater if a curriculum framework for under-fours is to be developed.

A second observation concerns the role of parents. It has already been argued that one of the compensations for the chequered history of pre-five education was that different roles for parents had evolved. But again this diversity is being compromised as the consumer model of education comes to dominate. For some time the playgroup movement has been losing its traditional involvement of parents increasingly reluctant to share actively in the group. The voucher initiative confirmed this but also showed a worrying move away from involvement by parents in the public sector.

The diversity of pre-five education in Scotland has been a great strength where it has exemplified a range of high quality but different services which have pursued their own distinctive objectives. In the immediate future it is clear that diversity will remain, but whether it will be a vibrant strength or a fatal weakness in the pre-five system will depend on how the partnership is handled by local authorities which now have an unprecedented opportunity to determine how a comprehensive integrated service should operate.

This chapter began with the assertion that pre-five education in the twentieth century has been characterised by low levels of provision, fragmented services and a lack of direction. The major changes of the last few years, however, suggest the century may end with relatively high levels of provision and integrated services justified by a comprehensive policy framework which puts a high priority on children's achievement.

The twentieth century has also shown us, however, that pre-five education can have many purposes reflecting different times and contexts as well as value systems which ask different questions about how children, adults and communities learn, and about what is worth knowing. Perhaps the most valuable legacy of pre-five education from the twentieth century would be the acknowledgement that not only is there no one answer to the question: 'what is pre-five education for and how can it be justified?' but that a wide range of people have the right to ask the question and the right to come to their own conclusion.

REFERENCES

Ball, S. (1994) *Start Right: The Importance of Early Learning*, London: Royal Society for the Encouragement of the Arts, Manufacturers and Commerce.

Scottish Office Education and Industry Department (1997) *Education in Early Childhood: The Pre-School Years*, A Consultation Paper, Edinburgh: SOEID.

Stephen, C., L. Low, S. Brown, D. Bell, P. Cope, B. Morris, and S. Waterhouse (1997) *Pre-School Education Voucher Initiative: National Evaluation of the Pilot Year*, Stirling: Department of Education, University of Stirling

Watt, J. (ed.) (1994) *Early Education: The Quality Debate*, Edinburgh: Scottish Academic Press.

Wilkinson, J. E., B. Kelly, and C. Stephen (1993) *Flagships: An Evaluation Research Study of Community Nurseries in Strathclyde 1989–1992*, Glasgow: Department of Education, University of Glasgow.

30

Organisation and Management in Nursery and Infant Schooling

Anne Hughes and Sue Kleinberg

This chapter focuses on three to eight year olds in nursery and infant schooling. It may seem puzzling to have Chapter 29 on pre-five education and then to find this one overlapping by its inclusion of 3 to 8 year olds. The overlap, and there will be some, is part of an historical and continuing debate about early education. The debate rests on the extent to which children in this age range have distinctive ways of learning and therefore might require specific educational provision. Firstly, the nature of the distinctiveness will be outlined within the context of what is known about young children learning. Secondly, educational provision made by local authorities, now councils, will be described. Thirdly, recent developments in curriculum and management in the two sectors will be examined including issues related to continuing professional development. It will be argued that Scotland now has an infra-structure of curriculum guidelines and assessment practice which make it likely that there will be increasing links between the two sectors and issues about these links will be raised

THE DISTINCTIVENESS OF YOUNG CHILDREN'S LEARNING

Why has early childhood been seen as special? Traditionally it has been seen as a time of rapid development in all areas of learning. The acquisition and development of language, social, physical, emotional, moral and spiritual intelligences/capabilities are seen as inter-related, equally valuable and to be fostered, indeed nurtured, by a curriculum which is responsive to the child. Whilst not discarding the role of direct verbal instruction, recognition was given to the motivational power of curiosity, play, activity, interest, first-hand experience and the creation of meaningful contexts. The subject-centred curriculum and transmission models of pedagogy were seen as less appropriate for an age group which had not acquired the symbol systems used by older children. Propositional, 'know that', knowledge was deemed less important than process, 'know how', knowledge in laying the foundations for such learning. The environment should be health promoting, safe but challenging and leading to positive attitudes to learning, the self, and others.

Support for the views held by pioneers in the field of practice came from the work of Piagetian psychologists. This suggested marked changes in the nature of logic a young child used which were seen as based on age-related stages. Whilst Piaget did not underestimate the influence of the environment on development, his work was interpreted by many as indicating that a loosely structured curriculum with varied and rich resources to explore was sufficient for such development to occur.

Such a view of early education might well have led to separate provision for the age group. This did not occur as the emerging concept of early education would have required a radical reorganisation of existing structures at a time in the post war period when supporting and staffing the mandatory sector faced resourcing problems. In Scotland, post war experiments in extending the primary 1 class to become a nursery infant class were undertaken, particularly in rural and small town settings, but these did not take root. The pressure to provide pre-five places and the influence of the ideology of compensation for early disadvantage was tied to the increase in nursery provision per se. An increase in the number of children accessing provision was achieved by moving from full-day attendance to part-time half-day attendance with exceptions only for priority needs. Expansion was slow, rising from 59 nursery schools and 28 classes in 1946 through 100 schools and 46 classes in 1968, to the Scottish Office of Industry and Education figures for 1996 of 245 publicly funded schools and 606 departments attached to primary schools and a further 61 schools and departments in the independent sector (Scottish Office Statistical Bulletin Edn/B1/ 1997/3). Increasingly the provision has been in classes rather than separate nursery schools.

The SED Memorandum, *The Primary School in Scotland*, (Edinburgh: HMSO, 1950) recognised the distinctiveness of the infant years. Discussion centred on the appropriate organisation for primary one and two. The memorandum advocated play, interest, integrated projects, activity, independence, purposefulness, and a flexibility in the timetable to cope with infant learning. It acknowledged that although nursery education was already seen as separated from infant provision both sectors should subscribe to these principles, stating that it should 'in practice make little difference whether a child spent the two years, five to seven, at the top of a nursery school or the bottom of a primary school' (p. 130).

Two research traditions have helped build knowledge about how young children learn. The first were studies relating to the impact of provision and types of provision, the second to child development. Research in the first sought evidence of measurable and lasting gains for the disadvantaged, but many findings were difficult to generalise because of the designs of the studies. Much of the work in Scotland focused on examining learning in different pre-school settings – with very little work on learning in the infant class (see M. Clark, *Children Under Five: Educational Research and Evidence*, London: Gordon & Breach, 1988, for Scottish and other studies). The influence of American studies was probably greater than indigenous ones in establishing a sound basis for supporting early education. Sylva (1994) for example, argued that the impact is not necessarily in cognitive gains but in 'life skills, social and economic outcomes rather than tests of formal intelligence' (p. 84). Quality was seen as resting on parental involvement and cognitively oriented programmes which were associated with positive attitudes to learning, self esteem and task orientation. Recent new wave American early intervention studies, like the Tennessee Star project, which span the pre-five and primary sector have also suggested that reducing class size to an average of fifteen leads to persistent gains on reading and mathematics tests over a period of five years, providing teachers change their style to cope with smaller classes. It may be as Clark (op.cit.,) suggests the infant class does not provide opportunities to continue with the pursuit of challenging and creative activities because of its size as well as for other reasons.

The significance of recent work in child development cannot be neglected. The work of Donaldson in *Children's Minds* (London: Fontana, 1978) showing the contextually embedded nature of children's learning, and Tizard and Hughes in *Young Children Learning* (London: Fontana, 1984) showing the competence of children in the home context are perhaps best known. A growing influence has come from Vigotsky's concept of the zone of proximal development. This is the zone within which there are things which the child can do with guidance and scaffolding help from a more expert person which they could not do alone. Similar ideas are contained in the metaphor of the child as an apprentice.

Whilst such work in child development can be seen as endorsing the principles of early education, it can also be seen as showing the importance of the parent/carer in promoting learning. Studies show how, in the home context, the adult's contribution is more likely to be initiated by the child and be more readily interpreted through a shared culture and intimate knowledge of contexts. This work gives additional support to the concept of the parent as key educator providing continuity and having implications for partnership with schools.

The growing recognition of the importance of active adult participation poses a problem for teachers given the ratio of adults to children in both the nursery school and class and in infant classes. The teacher-pupil ratio in the nursery school is 1: 24.7 though this differs throughout the country. The ratio in the primary school is currently 1: 19.3. The difference may not be that great but it can mean that the contact with a teacher may be less in the pre-five settings given the management responsibilities teachers undertake.

In the 1990s there is a sounder knowledge of why good practice might be so. This knowledge reinforces the largely intuitive knowledge of earlier early educators. However the new knowledge has to be disseminated to a range of contexts which have their own traditions and frameworks.

PROVISION MADE BY LOCAL COUNCILS

Provision has two distinct forms, non-statutory nursery education for children under five years of age and statutory infant education in primary schools for four and a half year olds to eight year olds. Nursery schools are usually free standing with the most common size being up to fifty children. Nursery classes are, in the main, attached to a primary school with its headteacher assuming overall management responsibility. All nursery provision is non-denominational but on transfer to primary school parents may choose a Roman Catholic or a non-denominational school. Scotland's dominant pattern of an all-through primary school is unlike the English tradition of combining nursery and infant schooling as the first school and then moving to the junior school.

In 1996, 37.9 per cent of the population of three and four year olds were in nursery education. 35.7 percent of the age range were in part-time places. In both nursery settings, the majority of children were attending part time, usually five mornings or afternoons. Just under 1 per cent of the children had a record of needs or were in the process of being recorded (see SOSB op.cit.). Small numbers of children, with special priority needs, can attend full-time.

Provision varies across the country both in terms of the number of places and the type of provision. Council provision has been absent till recently in some areas and in others is solely in classes. Nursery schools have been a feature of urban areas. Some councils operated priority entry criteria. In some areas the criteria have been linked to economic and social factors such as support for single parents, the prevention of reception into care, whilst other areas have prioritised educational grounds such as the pre-school year, second language learners or special needs.

Entry to primary school occurs once a year. In Scotland all children who are 5 before March 1 enter school in the preceding August. This results in an entry age between 4½ and 5½ years old. The average school size is 188 children with the average class size being 24.7 and the pupil teacher ratio being 19.3. There is considerable variation in this sector with, for example, an average school roll of 59 in the Western Isles (SOSB op.cit.). Parents can request early entry for children. However, these placing requests are low in number with 861 being made in 1994–5 and only 20 per cent gaining admission.

Depending on parental choice and provision available, two children of the same age could be attending different types of provision. Will they be having the same experiences?

DAILY LIFE

The 4½-year-old in a nursery class or school is likely to have a staff ratio of 1:7 children and a pupil-teacher ratio of 1:24.7. The staff will include at least one teacher but the majority are nursery nurses. Only 1 per cent of the teachers are male in the nursery sector compared with 8 per cent in the primary. The teacher, in both primary and nursery settings, is now likely to have gained a B.Ed (Hons) degree qualification in teaching through a four year university level course and may have then taken a specialist qualification in early education; the nursery nurse is likely to have undertaken two years of Further Education leading to a Higher National Certificate in Child Care and Education. The nursery school headteacher is likely to have an additional qualification in early education. The promoted staff in the primary school which houses the nursery class will not necessarily have such a qualification.

Entrants to both sectors will spend an initial time settling in, but the primary school child will soon attend full time for twenty-five hours a week. The nursery class and school child is likely to attend for fifteen hours a week. There may be additional staffing by Special Needs Assistants in both sectors.

In the nursery provision resources are play and activity based. Space is mostly open plan with freedom to move between different areas/resources, and a common pattern is to have periods of free choice of activity and grouping interspersed with small group or whole group activities determined by the adults. There have been differences across the country in terms of the model used. In some areas the degree of adult determined activities through themes and topics has been more marked than in others. Overall though, the nursery play way enables the child to construct their own curriculum to a considerable extent choosing resources to explore their concerns.

In contrast primary provision is structured by the 5–14 subject areas and suggested time allowances, as well as by commercial texts and schemes adopted as school policy. In the infant classes, time for free choice is more limited and progressively so across the three years. Where play does occur it is more frequently structured by the teacher rather than selected or initiated by the child. The capacity to follow up an interest is undoubtedly made harder by the number of children and the press to cover the agreed curriculum in this setting. The infant child is likely to spend a large part of the day working alone on individual tasks assigned by the teacher. Such tasks are carried out whilst seated in groups of four to eight. The child is periodically withdrawn to work with the teacher in small groups, commonly ability groups for mathematics and reading. This may then be followed up by differentiated tasks. Times for the whole class to work together are provided particularly for activities to do with news, story time and phonics. In many schools the morning is still given over to language and mathematics activities. Most classrooms are self-contained and hold one age group, but composite classes made up of two or more age groups may be formed depending on the size of the school roll.

PARENTAL INVOLVEMENT

Parents of children in primary school have certain rights to information and to representation on school boards. No such rights exist in the nursery sector. However the involvement of parents in early education has been a feature across the sector possibly because of the close proximity of staff and carers as young children are brought to and collected from the establishment. The role of parents is more fully discussed by Watt in Chapter 29, suffice to say here that most schools provide a range of ways to ensure the information flow from school to home. Innovations in the form of pre-entrant visits, workshops on specific curriculum aspects and parental assistance with classroom activities, materials and visits are now well established. However, it is probably true to say that genuine involvement in decision making and participation in curriculum and assessment remain largely a professional concern.

RECENT DEVELOPMENTS IN CURRICULUM AND MANAGEMENT

Although the nursery sector is inspected and has set performance indicators, the curriculum has been largely structured and interpreted locally. The 5–14 Guidelines made no reference to this sector. What advice there has been nationally, in 1971 and 1994, (SED *Before Five*, and SOED *Education of Children Under 5 in Scotland*, respectively, Edinburgh: HMSO) was couched in terms of broad learning experiences. It was not until the 1990s that local authorities tackled curriculum issues in a way which offered advice which could be applied directly to planning for a school or class. By 1995 all authorities making provision had produced guidelines which, whilst broadly following national advice in subscribing to play and process approaches, also framed the curriculum in broad content areas. Increasingly such guidelines have sought to recognise the relationship with the 5–14 content framework. In contrast there has always been national guidance which covers the curriculum of the infant classes.

The recent introduction of two sets of curriculum guidelines create the possibility to forge links across the sectors. These are the raft of 5–14 Curriculum and Assessment guidelines (SOED, 1994) and the 1996 draft and subsequent final version of SOEID's *A Curriculum Framework for Children in their Pre-school Year* in 1997. Both can be seen as defining nationally appropriate content and assessment procedures.

The framework for HMI inspections is based on schools realising the 5–14 targets. Children in Primary 1 to 3 are now subject to the expectation that they will cover and achieve level A targets for all curriculum areas and meet national test thresholds for mathematics, reading and writing. The infant curriculum is further linked to the upper primary age through the expectation that some children will have attained level B. Indeed, recent concern with national mathematical attainments has led HMI to suggest that schools should seek to have most children reach level A in primary 2 and this may well increase the pressure downwards.

The 1997 pre-five guidelines contain some significant differences to the draft version. Four will be outlined. Firstly, the five-fold curriculum framework was reorganised to put emotional, personal and social development first. Secondly, the document recognised that young children will develop at different rates and that some may have had 20 per cent more life experience than others. These two changes can be seen as recognising the distinctiveness of young children. Thirdly, the number of outcomes of learning were increased with more detail on the literacy and numeracy items. Fourthly, the 5–14 model of assessment was inserted as advice on planning. The intention to make links between the pre-five curriculum and that for five to fourteen year old can be seen in Figure 30.1.

Figure 30.1   Transition from pre-school framework to 5–14 curriculum

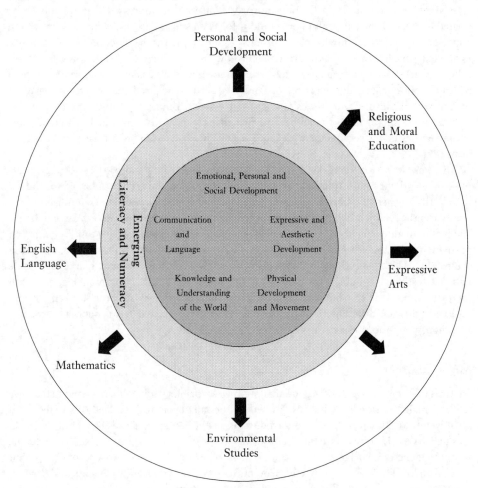

Source: SOEID (1997) *A Curriculum Framework for Children in their Pre-School Year*, Edinburgh: HMSO

Two related concerns about early education may well have been influential in promoting such overt curriculum links. Firstly, there has been a long standing educational concern about the possible lack of continuity and progression between the phases of early education, with the primary one child's prior learning being too often unrecognised and, even if recorded, largely ignored. Secondly, and recently, the new government has pledged itself to raise literacy and numeracy levels and put substantial specific grant funding for early intervention programmes to raise standards in primary schools.

Moves to link may be beneficial but they can pose problems. The potential conflict between the traditional responsive curriculum of early education and the subject-centred nature of the 5–14 reform has not gone unrecognised. In 1992 the Scottish Consultative Council on the Curriculum produced *Reflections on Curriculum Issues – Early Education*. This document still used the term early education to cover pre-schooling and the infant stages but raised questions such as, should future advice focus on the 3–8 age group or pre-fives? How can continuity in learning in early education be addressed? Should advice be related to areas of the curriculum or should it focus on specific issues, e.g. play, motivation and learning, parental involvement in early education? In the document HMI Boyle expressed concern that, 'There are dangers now in beginning to accept the term "pre-school", particularly in terms of it suggesting a downward extension of the primary school instead of an outward development of family education, with all that means in terms of differences in culture and values' (p. 25). In essence Boyle's warning was that as the curriculum of the primary school became increasingly centrally controlled this could have an impact on the nursery sector with more control being exerted on at least the pre-school year.

There are now two frameworks in place to ensure continuity and progression across the pre-school/primary transition both expressed in terms of objectives to be worked to. Indeed the SOEID paper, *Education in Early Childhood: The Pre-School Years* published as a consulation paper in 1997, states that the framework for the pre-five year might be 'extended in due course to provide advice on an appropriate curriculum for children receiving two years of pre-school education (i.e. from about the age of three)' (p. 5). Given the role of HMI inspections in operating with such guidelines as benchmarks, alongside national testing, it would seem likely that the pressure to talk a common language will increase. Indeed, it can be suggested that the concept of 3–8 has been broken up and replaced with the different resonances of age and grade related terms such as the ante-preschool year, the pre-school year, level A, level B etc.

MANAGEMENT

Implicit in immediate post-war documentation was a primary school management structure led by a male headteacher who was advised by the infant mistress. Indeed this lasted from 1950 well into the late 1960s. The introduction of the Assistant Head Teacher role (SED Circular 819, 1972) increased the number of promoted posts in primary schools and the move to generic management was subsequently evident in the erosion of the infant specialism. In 1980, a study by the Committee on Primary Education entitled *Primary School Organisation: A Study of the Nature and Extent of the Role of the Assistant Headteacher* (Edinburgh: SCDS), showed the retention of an early years remit in the sample of schools surveyed, but that the range of responsibilities varied enormously. The specific age link/concern of the infant specialist was diluted within the new AHT post as wider school experience became the route to further promotion.

The influence of a management ideology via developments such as the Whole School Development Policy, Staff Appraisal and Management training alongside changes in school posts in some ways contributed to the erosion of the distinctiveness of the infant stage. The development planning movement gathered momentum in the early 1990s. This was based on the process of auditing to manage school effectiveness using collective responsibility, teamwork and commitment. Progression, continuity, breadth, balance and coherence were to be realised and evaluated by a whole school perspective rather than a stage approach.

The move to conceptualise the headteacher as manager grew in the 1980s and culminated in the SED funded Management Training Modules for Headteachers produced in 1990. Seven modules were produced with each designed to be taken over a period of twelve to fifteen weeks. No formal assessment was linked to the modules at this point. The initial suite of modules were not designed for the nursery sector and the heads there were dependent on local authority initiatives. The existence of credit systems in Higher Education has seen many councils now continuing and extending such professional development linked to accreditation. Ongoing proposals are to move towards a national Scottish Qualification for Headteachers which would cover all sectors and be open to aspirant heads not just those in post. The contents of such a qualification are likely to be generic in terms of the materials rather than relate to specific sectors.

PLANNING AND MANAGING THE CURRICULUM

The 5–14 framework provides clear remits for the responsibilities of the headteacher and other teaching staff with respect to the curriculum. All are to be involved in the process of audit: reviewing current practice, identifying gaps between practice and the guidelines advice, devising a plan and incorporating that within the school development plan so as to have the curriculum and assessment reforms in place by 1998–9. The advice on planning for 5–14 is tied to the school development model.

The SOED Document, *5–14 A Practical Guide* (1994), suggests that curriculum policy making is less onerous because the major elements are now provided in the guidelines. Indeed the role of the school staff seems to be restricted in policy making to:

- how the flexibility allowance is to be used,
- the role of integration across subject areas,
- special circumstances of the school in general,
- any extra advice on a specific curriculum area, e.g. the core mathematics scheme and how to apply mathematical skills, or the reading scheme and how it should be used.

But such decisions are not perhaps simple as they raise the argument of how best young children learn as well as what they should learn. The debate on these issues was not tackled as a coherent section within the 5–14 documentation though the extensive cross referencing of attainment targets at level A suggests some appreciation of how young children learn.

Once the whole school audit for a curriculum area has been made, the individual teacher's role is seen as 'keeping the existing strengths of your classroom practice while trying to develop aspects which may be new or in which you lack confidence' (p. 9), and engaging in long and short term planning. Long term is linked to the school year and framed by strands. Short term is framed by a topic or block of teaching-linked targets and fleshed out to show if it is for class, group or individual and what will be assessed and recorded.

The role of the headteacher currently is to monitor and evaluate the implementation of the curriculum ensuring that within each classroom each strand is addressed, that teaching and learning builds on what was learned in earlier years and that children are making satisfactory progress in achieving the standards indicated in the attainment targets. The headteacher is to oversee and monitor progression and continuity throughout the seven years of the school's provision in a curricular area and similarly to ensure breadth and balance in any one year and through a programme. The collegiate nature of the audit and development plan process is somewhat diluted with the head taking on an increased evaluative role. The teacher's role is to work within the ensuing school framework and ensure coherence and balance for her or his class.

Unlike primary schools, staffing in nurseries consists of both teachers and nursery nurses, two distinct groups with different training and possibly different beliefs about what each is aiming to do and responsible for. *Before Five* indicated some differences in both level of responsibility and roles for different categories of staff. The headteacher was perceived to be the instigator of policies, ensuring that staff understood and carried out school aims and to be heavily involved in the admissions procedure. The assistant teachers would plan situations and activities, observe interests, abilities and progress, which would form the basis of their teaching, and ensure that provision was varied and differentiated. The nursery nurse was to play a part in these experiences by participating with children and taking responsibility for caring routines.

Increasingly there has been a blurring of aspects of the teacher's and nursery nurses role in practice and policy documents. The HMI report, *Education of Children Under Five*, adopted the generic term educator to refer to those holding professional qualifications relating to the education of children and made few distinctions in role descriptions between staff other than to observe that some members of every staff team require 'depth of knowledge' (para. 7.2).

Powney and colleagues (1995) observed twenty-eight staff interacting with children only three of whom were teachers. It indicated that despite different training, 'it could be difficult to distinguish between the practices of nursery nurses and teachers, even when they were explaining their practice and justifying it to researchers' (section 14.4). However, the generalisability of this finding is recognised as questionable because of the methodology employed.

CONTINUING PROFESSIONAL DEVELOPMENT

Changing roles and career development aspirations of staff in early education have created a context in which access to continuing professional development has become a key issue.

Post-graduate courses at certificate, diploma and masters level which emphasise practitioner reflection have been developed in higher education. The multi-professional background of staff and their involvement in a range of provision for three to eight year olds is an innovative and enriching feature of these courses. The newer courses exist alongside or incorporate parts of the traditional infant and nursery teacher special qualifications. Recently the needs of nursery nurses for continuing professional development have been recognised by the proposed establishment of a Professional Development award beyond the level of HNC in the FE sector.

Innovative modular BA degrees in Early Childhood Studies have been introduced in 1997 in the University of Strathclyde and in Northern College. For the first time early years staff who are not teachers have the opportunity to access graduate level study in early childhood care and education. Both courses are modular and part-time to offer opportunity to those in work. The course at Northern is a distance learning course which provides access to anyone working with under eights at Scottish Degree Level 1. The Strathclyde course aims to build on and extend learning previously achieved by starting at Scottish Degree Level 2 for students who are already qualified to HNC level in Childcare and Education.

Indeed routes are potentially there from an HNC to a Diploma on to a BA and then to Masters level.

Individuals have been keen to undertake this training and some employers have supported it financially. However, it is not clear what career development will be available to those undertaking these awards or what impact their increased expertise will have on practice.

The 1997 consultation paper is seeking advice on the 'broad issue of teacher involvement in all pre-school settings' (p. 27) and questioning if there is a need to 'review the coherence and the future of training and qualifications for the early years' (p. 38). The outcomes of such consultation will have a significant financial impact on the public, the independent and the voluntary sector as the government seeks to move towards more integrated services in the early years.

ISSUES

Dynamic times with an unprecedented period of rapid change seems to be the current situation facing early education and the effects of devolution are still to come!

The concept of 3 to 8 as a distinctive period of learning has been eroded by the content press of the 5–14 reforms. Whilst the links may promote continuity and progression in content terms, which may be desirable, there remains a danger that the distinctive methodology of early education could be hard pressed by an emphasis on assessment and standards. The aim for early education may be stated as 'preparation' but the government itself recognises that this intent could be subverted into 'an early start'.

Indeed, the curriculum may become narrowed, given the increased attention to literacy and numeracy for both sectors. The introduction of base-line assessment with its value added dimension may well have a similar impact if it leads to 'teaching to the test'. Recent work on the English reception class and key stage 1 has voiced similar concerns, with Pollard (1997) suggesting that the impact of the National Curriculum in England is that 'the extent of content specification and its assessment structures may unwittingly be undermining positive dispositions to learn.' The fear expressed here, and by others, is that an introduction to the technical rules/subskills of say reading, without first understanding the cultural rules and purposes of the skills, may lead to surface not deep learning and perhaps an earlier chance to fail. Early Education professionals will need to be vigilant.

The current situation is probably not different to that in many countries. Bruner (1997) has recently drawn attention to the emphasis developed societies are placing on basic skills in order to compete more effectively on world markets. But, he warns, a limited emphasis on this can conflict with other needs such as threat of tackling social exclusion and 'unjust distribution of wealth'. His conclusion may strike a chord with Scottish practitioners for he asks that we reconceptualise schools as communities of learners,

> on the basis of what we have learned in recent years about human learning, that it is best when it is participatory, proactive, communal, collaborative and given over to constructing meanings rather than receiving them. (p. 15)

REFERENCES

Bruner, J. (1996) What We have Learned about Early Learning, in *The European Early Childhood Education Research Journal*, 4. 1, pp. 5–15.

Pollard, A.(1997) *The Basics and an Eagerness to learn: A New Curriculum for Primary Schooling*, mimeo, Graduate School of Education, University of Bristol.

Powney. J. et al. (1995) *We Are Getting Them Ready For Life: Provision for Pre-Fives in Scotland*, Edinburgh: SCRE.
SCCC (1992) *Reflections on Curriculum Issues – Early Education*, Dundee: SCCC.
SOED (1994) *5–14 A Practical Guide*, Edinburgh: HMSO.
SOEID (1997) *A Curriculum Framework For Children in Their Pre-school Year*, Edinburgh: HMSO.

31

Ethos, Management and Discipline in the Primary School

Eleanor Gavienas and Graham White

Ethos and discipline are two closely related but separate aspects of the management of schools. Ethos, or the habitual character of primary schools, is quickly apparent both to professionals involved in education and to parents. Indeed the casual visitor to a school can rapidly gain an impression of the ethos of the establishment by merely observing playground behaviour, relationships between pupils and staff, relationships among staff members and the overall presentation of the building. Eisner (1994) usefully summarises what he considers ethos to be 'Ethos for me is a term that refers to the underlying deep structure of a culture, the values that animate it, that collectively constitute its way of life' (p. 2).

To those outside education, discipline, in the sense of control and regulation, has long been regarded as an important part of a school's ethos and a key area of concern for teachers and school managers. Indeed, politicians are very quick to blame the ills of society on a supposed lack of discipline in our schools. Yet this naive causal link ignores the complex and changing relationship between schools and the populations which they serve, and, more critically, fails to recognise that if the ethos of an establishment is good, then discipline is much less of a problem.

In Scotland, during the last twenty years, there has been a shift in thinking about discipline and ethos in primary schools. Formerly teachers saw discipline as something to be imposed upon children if learning and teaching were to be productive. Teachers felt they had the right, indeed the duty, to impose particular rules and to ensure that these rules were adhered to by the pupils. When these rules were broken teachers saw it as part of their professional duties to punish the miscreants. Such punishments were devised to fit the misdemeanour rather than the child. Scottish teachers felt comfortable that this approach to discipline was fair, rational, logical and that it was sanctioned by the pupils' parents in particular and by Scottish society in general. Despite changing attitudes, the term 'ethos' was not in common currency until the 1980s when research into this aspect of school life burgeoned.

Before outlining current approaches to developing a policy on ethos and discipline and how schools put policy into practice there are important background factors to be considered which are particularly relevant to the Scottish context. These include cultural traditions, social changes which impinged upon schools, and the requirement for parental consultation and involvement.

THE SCOTTISH CONTEXT

Cultural traditions

The historical link between ethos and discipline can be explained, in the first instance, if one examines the development and traditions of Scottish primary education. Scotland has a long history of valuing education not just for an elite but also for the wider population, which stretches back to the time of John Knox. As documented by Cruickshank in the *History of the Training of Teachers in Scotland* (London: ULP, 1970), there was a democratic tradition in Scottish elementary education which preceded the demand for an educated workforce evident in other rapidly industrialising countries across Europe. Indeed the brightest pupils were encouraged to aspire to a university education, if possible, irrespective of ability to pay. Education was seen as the key to advancement in life, an attitude which permeated society at all levels. This resulted in considerable respect for teachers and the authority invested in them.

In the nineteenth century large classes were the norm and, in order to ensure control, rituals and routines were thoroughly established in schools. Discipline was strict, a fact acknowledged by Hunter in *The Scottish Educational System* (Oxford: Pergamon, 1972), but, generally, there was very little conflict with parents. This tradition of accepting that authority is largely in the hands of teachers can be witnessed in the attitudes of some parents over a century later. An historical legacy of support for the school and discipline is still there, to some extent, in the Scottish psyche.

Social changes

By the 1960s, the writings of philosophers such as Montessori and Froebel and the evidence from research into learning by Piaget and others was beginning to influence mainstream primary education. These changes were formalised in the Scottish Education Department's publication of the watershed report *Primary Education in Scotland* (SED, 1965). To some extent this report was a product of its time. The 1960s was an era of great social change with, in particular, the emergence of individual freedom of expression and a questioning of traditional power structures. Freedom and respect for the individual, which starts in childhood, is a common thread in the writings of the great educational philosophers and, critically, was in tune with the prevailing mood of the decade. The ethos of society at large was reflected in recommendations made to schools.

Teachers were liberated from what was seen as too structured a curriculum, with too much central control of education, and were encouraged to adopt a child centred approach to learning. The official view, as set out in the report, was that when such reforms were achieved children would assume much greater responsibility for their own conduct and discipline. Teachers in consultation with their professional bodies, for example the Educational Institute for Scotland and the General Teaching Council for Scotland, were also encouraged to review the use of corporal punishment in primary schools. The notion that learning should be pleasurable, with schools being places to which children would want to go, was actively upheld by Her Majesty's Inspectorate (HMI). To a considerable extent this has been one of the lasting legacies of the reforms. Most primary children now declare that they like school and are most anxious to attend.

Parental involvement

The changes in schools in the 1960s became characterised under the generic term of 'progressive education' and left many experienced teachers feeling uncertain about their role. They had responsibility for the curriculum but only general guidance on its content and structure. Parents also seemed to lack an understanding about what schools were trying to achieve. As far as some teachers were concerned the whole process was made doubly difficult with the abolition of corporal punishment in 1981. Without physical sanctions, discipline had to be achieved using other systems of control such as deprivation of privileges. The ethos envisaged in the 1960s of teachers and pupils and parents working together in an atmosphere of mutual respect had not developed in many schools.

However, the traditional trust and respect, built up over the past century still lingered, but it could be argued that the decade between 1970 and 1980 was a time when increasing numbers of parents began to doubt some of the methods and activities within primary schools. In most schools parents were not consulted, nor even informed, about changes to the curriculum or to the discipline policy. The deficiencies of the situation were accurately summarised by the Committee on Primary Education (COPE, 1983) when reflecting upon the previous ten years. The authors of the COPE document wrote, 'Neither the teacher nor the curriculum exists in a vacuum,' and further suggested that all of the members of a school community should accept the purposes and intentions of the organisation and 'work together in attempting to achieve the purposes.'

In the 1970s schools did not actively encourage parents to question teachers. The prevailing attitude at the time was exemplified by notices, displayed prominently at the door of primary schools, instructing parents to report directly to the headteacher, thereby discouraging any direct contact with a class teacher. Such an attitude was not conducive to the creation of the community spirit envisaged by COPE.

As a response to the uncertainties of the 1970s, the 1983 COPE document was indeed important. Deliberately, it put considerable emphasis on the role of parents in the education process:

> formal arrangements for school parent contact cannot replace a school ethos which encourages a parental interest and encourages parents to come to the school at other times than those set aside for the formal transmission of information. (p. 61)

Schools were also encouraged to be more aware of the wider community which they served and to recognise that education would not necessarily lead to full employment:

> the situation in which children could be encouraged to do well at school so that they could do well in terms of a job and lifestyle is rapidly changing. Schools more than ever need to be seen to be relevant to the needs of the community and able to cope with a changing society. (p. 67)

The formal participation of parents was important for two reasons: firstly to play their part in school life and, secondly, to encourage parents, some of whom the educational system had failed, to look again at what schools were trying to achieve. However, a minority of schools were subject to parental pressure in the areas of discipline and control, with teachers challenged to explain why certain actions had been taken against their children. In this crucial area of school management and community liaison it was recognised that work had to be done.

It is now almost universally accepted by Scottish teachers that the level and nature of parental involvement will have a profound effect on a school's ethos. Many primary schools offer a range of opportunities, over and above the statutory parents' evenings, for teachers and parents genuinely to collaborate in their children's education. These often include the provision of a parent's room, interest classes, opportunities for parents to assist in classrooms and in outdoor activities, regular newsletters where the tone reflects a real partnership between home and school, and home visiting schemes whereby teachers visit parents in their homes to discuss their children's progress. The nature of opportunities will vary from school to school, but the quality of parental involvement will be characterised by the teachers' willingness to appreciate the concerns of the parents and to enter into truthful and non-condescending dialogue with the first educators of their pupils. There can be little doubt that the quality of the home-school relationship should mirror the quality of teacher-pupil relationships which is at the very heart of a school's ethos.

APPROACHES TO DEVELOPING A POLICY ON ETHOS AND DISCIPLINE

By the mid-1980s there was a general acceptance by teachers that effective learning can occur only when certain conditions exist. It was recognised that children learn best in a relaxed atmosphere where they feel free to question teachers in order to clarify their thinking. Teachers, and society in general, began to appreciate the reasons behind children's unacceptable behaviour, where it existed, and sought to understand rather than condemn. In such a climate inflexible rules and punishments would have no place and schools would now have to find other means of establishing and maintaining discipline. Schools, therefore, began to examine their discipline policies in light of this more enlightened thinking and sought to reach a common understanding of the issues.

Some senior management teams began this process by considering the 'hidden curriculum' of their schools. If the ethos of a school is the value system that underpins all the practices within a school then the hidden curriculum is a subset of this and refers to all the practices related to the transmitting of the formal curriculum. It could be said that the hidden curriculum makes manifest, perhaps unintentionally, the value system that underlies the curricular policies of a school. It might, therefore, include such things as the means of delivering the curriculum (e.g. class/group/individualised programmes of work), the manner in which it is delivered (e.g. whether the teacher takes a didactic/discursive approach), the condition of the resources, and the way in which the teachers address the pupils when teaching. The hidden curriculum, therefore, refers to the way the pupils are treated during lessons and could be said to be the aspect of school life that is, ironically, least hidden from pupils.

Examination of policies, both curricular and more general, is currently the overall responsibility of headteachers. Increasingly over the last ten years they have been charged with overseeing the planning and implementation of all school policies of which ethos and discipline were but two. A key to this process was the introduction of Development Planning, whereby staff together would analyse the strengths and weaknesses of a school and as a result establish priorities for action. Action could include formulation or revision of school policies, appropriate staff development and the purchase of any materials considered to be necessary to support the changes. Discussion of Development Planning was instigated by HMI who highlighted the importance of a team approach and of a consultative management style. To assist further in this process *Using Performance Indicators in Schools*

Self Evaluation (SOED, 1992) was produced and circulated to all schools. This working document contained advice on procedures for whole school development planning with one major section of the document entitled Ethos. Within this chapter there were subheadings entitled climate and atmosphere, pastoral care, effectiveness of staff and team work, partnership with parents, with school board, and links with other schools and agencies.

However, the most popular and accessible publication to date on the subject, which is currently widely used in Scottish primary schools, is *Using Ethos Indicators In Primary School Self Evaluation* (SOED, 1992). This document identifies twelve ethos indicators related to different aspects of ethos and discipline in primary schools. The indicators identified are: pupil morale; teacher morale; teachers' job satisfaction; the physical environment; the learning context; teacher-pupil relationships; equality and justice; extra curricular activities; school leadership; discipline; information to parents; parent-teacher consultation. This useful publication also contains sample questionnaires for pupils, parents and teachers to be used to audit/monitor the development of a school's ethos. The extremely thorough approach to the analysis of a school's ethos from a range of standpoints has proved a useful starting point for many primary schools.

The two earlier documents of 1992 were, to some extent, brought together by HMI when they produced *How Good is Our School: Self Evaluation Using Performance Indicators* (SOED, 1996). Within this publication, there are performance indicators relevant to ethos and discipline under the subheadings of Support for Pupils and Ethos. This latest document is now the starting point for school inspections by HMI, therefore making reflection upon ethos and discipline an important part of the quality assurance process, to be undertaken both within the school and by external assessors. A positive atmosphere for learning and teaching is now a vital aspect of every school. The way in which schools create it will now be considered.

POLICY INTO PRACTICE

Many schools have recognised the part the physical appearance of a school can play in enhancing a positive climate and have endeavoured to create and maintain a clean, warm, bright, welcoming environment for all who work in or visit the building. This basic but important aspect of school life is often one of the first tackled by headteachers and senior management teams wishing to improve the ethos of their schools as change to the physical environment may be simple and relatively inexpensive. Such things as displaying children's work imaginatively, decorating rooms and corridors with pot plants and artefacts, ensuring that curtains/blinds are in good condition, all help to send the message that the people who run this school care for the comfort and aesthetic sensibilities of those who work there.

The presence of pupils' and parents' noticeboards in a school helps to create a climate where people's views and interests are valued. In the same way, 'Best Work Boards', where children's achievements are displayed in a prominent way, indicates that pupils' individual successes are important. Clear and friendly signs, in several languages, which direct people to the headteacher's room or school office, give the impression that those who work there recognise the possible insecurities of visitors and that they wish to put people at ease.

The environment immediately outside the school has also recently received much attention, in particular how the condition of the school playground can affect the climate of a school. As the Scottish Consultative Committee on the Curriculum has shown, in *Climate for Learning* (Dundee: SCCC, 1996), the physical environment of the playground can have an effect upon children's self esteem and therefore their behaviour. In the accompanying audio tape, entitled *Grounds for Learning*, the issue of the design of the playground is discussed and the conclusion reached that fights and bullying are often an inevitable consequence of the physical design of the space. The same research has shown that children value quiet peaceful places in the school playground and many schools now provide areas with tables and benches where children can spend time chatting, reading or simply watching the world go by. The curtailing of football games to specified areas of the playground must count as one of the major blows for equality in recent years; in the past the football players (traditionally boys) dominated much of the space in playgrounds.

Perhaps the most fundamental shift in the practice of effective discipline in Scottish schools has been away from punishing unacceptable behaviour towards rewarding conduct which is acceptable.

Regular assemblies where pupil successes are celebrated by the whole school is now a fairly common means of raising pupils' self esteem and of creating a sense of belonging as well as reinforcing high expectations. This celebration of success is compatible with a system of discipline which rewards rather than punishes. Some schools have very precise means of rewarding children which entail tangible objects such as plastic tokens which can be 'cashed in' for symbolic rewards such as points or merits. Those pupils gaining an agreed amount of symbolic rewards are often then given some sort of treat at the end of the week such as a longer playtime or more time playing computer games. An accompanying 'certificate' is often given to reinforce the school's approval and to inform parents of the success of their children. In other schools those pupils gaining the desired amount of symbolic rewards are simply offered a certificate.

Exactly who rewards pupils also varies from school to school. Some may decide that only the class teacher should do this while in other schools all adults, including non-teaching staff, are encouraged to reward acceptable behaviour in all pupils. The definition of acceptable behaviour is also variable. Some schools reward those pupils whose behaviour has been exemplary whilst others reward those whose behaviour has improved over a period of time. The setting of very individual and focused goals (e.g. managing not to call out in class from 9 o'clock until the morning interval) and then rewarding such behaviour, is now fairly common.

Some schools which have used extrinsic rewards for good behaviour are also giving attention to how they might develop the intrinsic values in children which go alongside behaving acceptably, which ultimately should be the aim of any positive discipline policy. This entails giving much time to listening to pupils' explanations of their actions and to explaining teacher actions to pupils. Such an apparently simple approach has been found to be effective in dealing with instances of bullying in schools. Pupils who are being bullied will confide in teachers if they know they will be listened to and those who are bullying will be more likely to change their behaviour after discussing the effects of their actions on others. The inclusive school which attempts to serve all pupils, including those who bully, also attempts to develop its pupils' ethical and moral sensibilities. Without devoting time to such development any reward may be only superficially successful in that it may modify children's behaviour but may not instil in pupils values such as justice, integrity and honesty.

Where rewarding acceptable behaviour has not been sufficient to ensure appropriate conduct, schools often enforce sanctions. In the past, practices such as denying children their interval or lunch breaks, although illegal, were fairly commonplace. It has been standard practice for many years for teachers to ask pupils to write lines, although both teachers and pupils recognise that this practice is usually ineffectual. In some schools the practice of sending pupils to a member of the senior management team is used frequently although precisely what the result of this course of action might be is often never discussed amongst staff. Perhaps this approach does have some merit in that it provides 'time out' for the pupil, his/her classmates and the teacher. The severest sanctions might include the withdrawal of some pleasurable experience such as attending class parties, end of term trips or playing for the school's netball or football team, but perhaps the action that works best when pupils behave unacceptably is the involvement of the child's parents, as verified by Munn et al. (1992):

> A letter home to parents, a parent being asked to come to the school, or a child being placed on 'report' with a parent having to sign a behaviour card, are examples of actions heartily disliked by pupils. (p. 104)

When this misdemeanour is deemed to be very serious schools can consider temporary exclusion for up to three days or, ultimately, permanent exclusion, the latter being fairly rare in Scottish primary schools. Temporary exclusions require the involvement of parents in that they are required by law to accompany the child on return to school and to enter into discussion with the headteacher on how the child can be encouraged to behave appropriately in future. This exercise will be of greatest benefit when the ongoing relationship between home and school is based on mutual trust and respect. The quality of home–school relationships is therefore crucial to the discipline policy which constitutes a very important part of the ethos of a school.

The role of the promoted staff will be crucial in monitoring the implementation of any policy and teachers have the right to expect practical support in this. Support from the senior management team may take many forms, from modelling the agreed desired behaviours, to picking up the pieces when things go awry, as well as adapting the strategies to accommodate new or unforeseen situations.

Headteachers and their senior management teams may also be in need of support in establishing a positive ethos in their schools. The Scottish School Ethos Network was established by the Scottish Office in order to provide such support. This network provides teachers with a platform to share ideas about how exactly they are improving the ethos of their schools and to offer advice and support to those who are finding the process of change difficult. The network provides regular newsletters and an annual conference helps to keep members in touch with the latest successful strategies for the creation and maintenance of a positive school ethos. The sharing of practices regarding positive discipline policies may be a part of the network's function but it is not its sole function. The Promoting Positive Discipline Initiative has been established to allow teachers to share their philosophies and the actual day to day strategies they use in effecting positive and humane discipline in their schools. The initiative encourages teachers to write about their practices in order that good practice in relation to discipline is recorded and disseminated.

Another widely used set of materials for staff development has been a pack entitled *Promoting Positive Behaviour in the Primary School* (Strathclyde Regional Council, 1991). This pack contains a video, case studies and structured tasks to help teachers analyse their current practices and to consider strategies for the development of policies on ethos and discipline.

CURRENT ISSUES

The all embracing nature of the concept of a school's ethos can act to both complicate and to oversimplify what is meant by the term. The staff of one school may wish to view it as a complex set of messages which it sends to pupils, parents and the community. The staff of another may view the ethos of their school as being determined by how decently teachers and other adults behave towards pupils. Both definitions may be deemed appropriate but neither make it easy to offer clear and unambiguous advice on how a positive ethos can be achieved. Ethos indicators merely indicate desired states, they do not define the routes to success. If teachers view the indicators as a recipe to be followed it is doubtful if a positive ethos will result. Each school must debate its own route to this end. That is the difficult part. Sharing a vision of what constitutes a positive ethos means examining personal values and being prepared to enter into genuine debate with colleagues about how exactly it can be achieved and maintained in a school. The quality of the debate will be dependent on the level of commitment that each member of staff can bring to the process. The complex nature of building a positive ethos and discipline system means that the process will be continuous and ever changing – not an easy or comfortable position for those teachers or headteachers who seek absolutes.

Although many teachers are sharing the details of their policies and practices regarding ethos and discipline across Scotland through the Promoting Positive Discipline Initiative and the Scottish School Ethos Network, it is recognised that no two schools will share the same policy or practice in relation to ethos and discipline. The very different contexts of Scottish primary schools, particularly with regard to location, class and race, defy blue-prints for success in the field of discipline and ethos. There can be little doubt that teaching children in areas of deprivation, where they are in receipt of free school meals and clothing grants and where the levels of unemployment are high, can be a very different job from teaching children in affluent suburbs. Children's poor living conditions will no doubt affect their self esteem and their motivation to do well at school. In such situations the primary school must offer understanding and compassion with no lowering of its expectation that children will succeed with the appropriate support. Teachers in schools in deprived areas of Scotland may find it more difficult to create and maintain a positive climate for learning and teaching and therefore deserve a high level of support from their senior management teams who deserve the same from their education authorities.

Perhaps one of the most important aspects of current thinking about discipline concerns the examination of how teachers' behaviour can influence the discipline and therefore the ethos of a school. In *Teaching for Effective Learning*, SCCC (1996) states that:

> In the classroom the way teachers behave, determines the way learners behave. How teachers establish their authority, the tone of their voice, the little things they continually say and do on a daily basis, determines the climate in their classroom. (p. 19)

A common understanding of exactly how teachers should behave towards children, in order to facilitate effective learning and teaching, has not been achieved. This is not surprising and should not be viewed as disappointing. Schools which seek such recipes have missed the point. If a school is serious about improving discipline and its general climate, then the teachers must enter into debate about how and why they behave the way they do towards children and how their behaviour affects the learning and teaching process.

The difference between treating all pupils equally and treating all children equitably is still to be fully explored by all teachers. The fact that some children, by dint of their differing capacities to behave acceptably, may require slightly different rules or may require to be treated differently by teachers, is not fully appreciated by those teachers who seek easy answers. However, the notion of the inclusive school which demonstrates the desire to involve, care for and cater for all its pupils, not just those who present few challenges to teachers, is slowly gaining ground in Scottish primary schools. In turn, the senior management team must recognise and accept the differences there will be amongst staff in implementing any policy, and should not be disappointed when common purposes are interpreted slightly differently or when common strategies are executed in a variety of styles. Teachers can only work within the limitations of their personalities and to expect otherwise is to expect too much. It will be the duty of the senior management team to monitor the day to day procedures and to discuss any difficulties that individual teachers may have in putting the agreed policy into practice, before offering advice and practical support. This is not to say that any teachers should be exempt from attempting to establish good quality relationships with their pupils, far from it. All teachers should be willing to show care and concern for their pupils, and this should not be seen as something added on to the business of teaching effectively but as an integral and pivotal part of teaching and learning.

The manifestation of a primary teacher's care and concern for pupils takes many forms. She or he will be prepared to listen to pupils not merely to assess whether the key points of a lesson have been absorbed but to determine the pupils' opinions, misgivings, fears, misconceptions about the subject matter. She or he will ensure that all resources are carefully planned to meet the different needs of pupils. She or he will accept responsibility for the social and moral well being of pupils. In short, many Scottish primary schools attempt to get to know their pupils and will give something of themselves in return. As the SCCC document states: 'Giving of yourself to establish and maintain quality relationships in a classroom situation is one of the most challenging and stressful aspects of the job of teaching' (p. 16). The Scottish primary education system whereby teachers are in constant contact with their pupils for most of the school day, week, term, session offers tremendous opportunities for teachers to model decent and compassionate behaviours. Such behaviours from teachers are a prerequisite for the nurturing of the same behaviours in pupils.

Despite all the difficulties, it would appear that many Scottish primary schools are successful in their attempt to create a positive ethos in their schools. A great number of HMI reports contain evidence that Scottish primary teachers are aware of the multifarious aspects that constitutes a school's ethos and are working to improve the pupils' experience of school life. The following statement exemplifies this:

> The school has a very positive ethos. The atmosphere was welcoming, morale was high and there was a pervading sense of common purpose. Pupils' achievements were highlighted prominently through awards and displays and at weekly assemblies. There was a great range of extra-curricular activities. Older pupils often accepted responsibilities for aspects of the life of the school. (David Livingstone Memorial Primary School, HMI, 1996)

REFERENCES

Committee on Primary Education (1983) *Primary Education in the Eighties: a COPE Position Paper*, Edinburgh: CCC.

Eisner, E. (1994) *Ethos and Education*, Dundee: SCCC.

SOED (1992) *Using Ethos Indicators in Primary School Self-Evaluation*, Edinburgh: SOED.

SOED (1996) *How Good is Our School: Self-Evaluation Using Performance Indicators*, Edinburgh: SOEID.

Munn, P., M. Johnstone and V. Chalmers (1992) *Effective Discipline In Primary Schools and Classrooms*, London: Paul Chapman.

SCCC (1996) *Teaching For Effective Learning*, Dundee: SCCC.

32

Primary-Secondary Liaison

Margaret Mitchell

At present there is no clear national policy or guidelines concerning liaison procedures for the transfer of pupils from primary to secondary school. As a result there is neither consensus on a definition of primary-secondary liaison nor a statement about what its constituent parts are. Renewed interest in transition from primary seven to secondary one is evident in the 1997 report by Her Majesty's Inspectorate (HMI) *Improving Mathematics Education 5–14* (Edinburgh: SOEID) and in ongoing work by the Scottish Consultative Council on the Curriculum (SCCC) on the operational arrangements of primary-secondary liaison. This chapter will look at current understandings, identify emergent areas of interest and suggest issues for potential development. The area of primary-secondary liaison is itself in transition.

UNDERSTANDINGS AND CONCERNS

Primary-secondary liaison is a tool in the form of procedures that anticipate, smooth, and influence the transition from primary to secondary school. The term transition suggests a passage from one state to another. In music, transition refers to the movement from one key to another. In the development of language the term transition is applied to the interval between one form of the language and the next and to the transitional form of the language during the interval. Likewise the movement from primary to secondary is a transition period in which the experiences undergone allow change to take place in the child. The liaison procedures within the transition process are crucial events which define the child's experience of the passage from primary to secondary. Well-planned liaison allows the passage from one school context to another to gather momentum and should create the possibility of an enriched experience. Schools have an opportunity to raise children's awareness of change in their lives and to reflect on that experience as a progression.

Derricot (1985) states that, 'the process of transition is accompanied by.liaison procedures' (p. 15). He identifies five key concepts in primary-secondary curriculum continuity: transition, liaison, continuity, consistency and structure. These concepts should be viewed as discrete and any overall plan should take account of them all. The concepts suggest a need to take account of how to combine the child's experience with curricular, organisational and administrative arrangements. Derricot draws a distinction between transition and liaison and suggests that the transition process will be smoother if there are procedures covering 'the exchange of documentation about pupils; the organisation of activities for pupils and teachers, (and) staff' (p. 15).

Similar ideas were implicit in *Education 10–14 in Scotland* (1986), a Consultative Committee on the Curriculum (CCC) discussion document, which identified four organisational arrangements related to transition:

1. Administrative procedures.
2. Familiarisation.
3. Curricular liaison.
4. Supply of information at transfer.

The purpose of transferring information and records is to aid continuity of experience for the pupils with the assumption that information of a curricular and pastoral nature is useful to the receiving school. The form of the information transferred varies but generally includes class lists of pupils, written information on attainments using recording and reporting procedures linked to the *5–14 Guidelines* and the child's primary file, including all class reports from Primary 1 to Primary 7. The use of a Record of Achievement profile, which was initially a secondary recording method, is increasingly being introduced in primary schools. These records cover a wider range of achievements and seek to do so in a positive way. The record may, for example, detail involvement in extra-curricular activities and can include the child's view of his or her progress. Additionally the child's strengths and areas for development may be conveyed in written form or orally at staff exchange visits.

The extent of use of transfer information and the degree to which it influences secondary practice is of interest. In *The Education of Able Pupils P6–S2* (1993) HMI state that the extent to which transfer records were used was questionable. This was expressed more strongly by Lance who, in an article on 'The Case for Continuity' in *Forum* vol. 36, no. 1. (1994) called transfer a 'bone of contention' between teachers in the two sectors involved. Similarly, the Scottish Office Education and Industry Department (SOEID) publication *Interchange 35* which looked at 'Putting 5–14 in Place: an Overview of the Methods and Findings of the Evaluation 1991–95' noted that the 'lack of interest in records and work sent by pupils' previous teachers remains a cause for some concern' (p. 11). Jones (1995) in the article 'Continuity in the Curriculum' in *Forum* vol. 37, no. 2 recognised that there had been little progress in the use of transfer records and raised key questions about how teachers use transfer information and what the most useful information to transfer might be.

The message gathering momentum in recent years is that transfer of information from primary to secondary school has taken the form of an exercise completed by primary school staff without much significant influence on how secondary schools organise their learning and teaching. Many schools have upheld the 'fresh start' approach to pupils transferring into first year in Secondary. This has continued in the face of mounting evidence reviewed by HMI in 1993 that the 'fresh start' is untenable. In schools where Secondary 1 is regarded as a fresh start it was 'not until pupils were well into their first year that teachers were ready to make confident judgment about their abilities, and then only over a limited area of the curriculum' (p. 16). The importance of progression and continuity for all was stressed. Along with the stance that significant evidence from primary schools should not be neglected, patterns of emerging strengths should be identified and activities where continuity of experience ought to be preserved should be properly recognised.

This does not only relate to the able pupil but to all. *Interchange No. 40: Criteria for Opening Records of Needs* (Edinburgh: SOEID, 1996) found that there is a surge of Records opened during the period prior to moving to secondary school. The extent to which this smoothes transition for the children concerned is questionable. While teachers in the secondary school familiarise themselves with the pupils and their attainments, the establishment of good learning and teaching is delayed.

Interchange 35 found some positive developments in the schools surveyed, stating that 'The various effective strategies for improving communication and continuity in the type and level of work across the transition that were being put into place were grounds for optimism' (p. 11). However there were also reservations expressed about the extent to which these organisational arrangements were impacting on the rate of progress of the pupils. This concern had been highlighted earlier by Fouracre in the Scottish Council for Research in Education's (SCRE) *Autumn Newsletter* (Edinburgh: SCRE, 1993). In an article on 'Pupils' Expectations of the Transition from Primary to Secondary School', Fouracre's survey of Primary 7 children showed that 80 per cent of them agreed that work would be more difficult in secondary school but that only 50 per cent found their expectation met after transfer. Furthermore there was a drop in progress after transfer which was particularly significant for language skills such as spelling and punctuation. Pupils found secondary work rather like revision, mentioning English, Mathematics, Geography and Modern Studies in particular. Perhaps not surprisingly the 1996 HMI report *Achievement for All* (Edinburgh: SOEID) discouraged the 'fresh start' philosophy and the 1997 HMI report on Mathematics also rejected a 'fresh start' approach in favour of building on prior attainment.

These areas of concern have grown in the last ten years, so that at present there are managerial, organisational, curricular and pastoral concerns which all seem to have discrete functions yet also impinge on each other to the extent that boundaries are blurred. This confusion must be recognised and acknowledged.

EMERGENT DEVELOPMENTS

The way forward begins with the recognition of a clear distinction between transition and liaison. An understanding of the connection between teaching approaches and effective learning forms a major part of the unravelling required to arrive at a liaison model which performs the function of smoothing transition. Primary and secondary school structures and approaches to teaching and learning differ. The organisation of the curriculum into five main areas in primary school then up to fifteen subjects in S1 and then eight modes in S3 does, as Jones suggests, move the emphasis 'from learning to teaching and from child to knowledge base' (op. cit., p. 44) and highlights the level of managerial, curricular and organisational programmes required to guide and support children through the experience.

Changes in management such as more records and information being handed on, changes in curricular materials with less individualisation, and changes in organisation through setting and whole class approaches, have been suggested as ways to address the disquiet about transfer from primary to secondary. The result may well be a different set of experiences for children but, in terms of addressing the needs, these changes may only end up as a re-arrangement of the furniture. It may be that shifting the focus in response to one concern creates a confounding variable within another concern.

Surveys carried out in connection with the documents *The Education of Able Pupils P6–S2* (1993) and *Achievement for All* (1996) have shown that in most schools P6/7 and S1/2 are taught in mixed ability classes. *Achievement for All* stated that primary mixed ability classes often have attainment groupings, social groupings or mixed ability groupings as the sub-groups within the classroom. The reasons for continuation of mixed ability in S1/S2 were:

> commitment to perceived social benefits, the prevailing culture of S1/S2, the common course, the idea of secondary providing a fresh start, and the reluctance of teachers to take account of the evidence of prior attainment. (p. 24)

In May 1997 at the SCRE Forum on Educational Research *Equity in Education* the work of Harlen and Malcolm was presented. While children of all abilities appear to gain from within-class ability groupings, the evidence shows that it is the provision of differentiated experiences that is important. Within-class ability grouping is only one method to achieve progress as noted in *Interchange No. 30 – Studies of Differentiation Practices in Primary and Secondary Schools*. Here the conclusion was that no particular method of organising material or pupils in itself leads to improved learning. The factors summarised as the key to the level and quality of learning were: quality of interaction, quality of explanation, quality of support and assistance with identified problems.

If the child is looking for interaction with the teacher and a feeling of being supported, then the teacher's success in conveying this would significantly influence the child's experience of learning. The factors of interaction, explanation, support and assistance with identified problems may well appear to be the factors involved in *The Education of Able Pupils P6–S2* when it stated that, 'The concept of individual needs was rarely thought to apply to able pupils who, it was generally assumed could be relied upon to cope' (p. 16). The tension between meeting different needs and abilities of individual pupils and giving quality teaching time to individuals, groups and whole classes was recognised in *5–14 A Practical Guide for Teachers in Primary and Secondary Schools* (1994). The achievement of a harmonious balance between the two factors involves making decisions on which methods ensure the most effective learning.

The 1997 HMI report on Mathematics supports the recommendation in *Achievement for All* that a move towards broad band setting in secondary school should take place. Furthermore, schemes of work based on individualised methods should be reviewed and group or whole class lessons be increased. What is also highlighted is the requirement that teachers become more interactive with pupils, suggesting that they 'engage pupils actively in learning'. Explaining, asking questions and asking pupils to explain their thinking are methods suggested which require more lesson time from teachers.

Evidence such as this suggests a move towards a change in methods of grouping and materials used. Pupils who currently experience the S1 curriculum as revision might then be replaced by pupils who experience stimulating classrooms. Brian Boyd of the Quality in Education Centre at Jordanhill Campus, Strathclyde University has highlighted and questioned the tendency in Scottish education to view a change in structure as a means of addressing concerns and making improvements. This connects to the findings in *Interchange No. 30* where it was concluded that the quality of relationships between pupils and teachers was the most significant factor in effective learning and teaching. It is how transition is experienced that is the key factor in the movement from primary to secondary school.

AN EXAMPLE

Successful primary-secondary liaison requires both a sound structure and a sensitive consideration of processes and quality relationships. One example can be drawn from the work of St Aidan's High School in Wishaw where the Headteacher, Rosemary McDonald, has made primary-secondary liaison a priority for over a decade. The current liaison programme is a result of development and refinement of the approaches used. Assistant Headteacher Stephen Campbell has responsibility for 5–14 in his remit and sees the liaison programme as an important part of this. The inter-school collaboration with eight associated primaries aims to 'support learning by recognising achievements, attainments and previous experiences in order to build on these by providing appropriate and challenging goals for every child.'

The sharing of information on pupil progress through personal liaison is identified as the most effective means of developing good understanding between the primary and secondary school. Teachers from the secondary and primary schools, pupils and parents are all involved in a comprehensive plan which encompasses all that is currently required of best practice. Figure 32.1 shows the elements of the programme which address the overall aim.

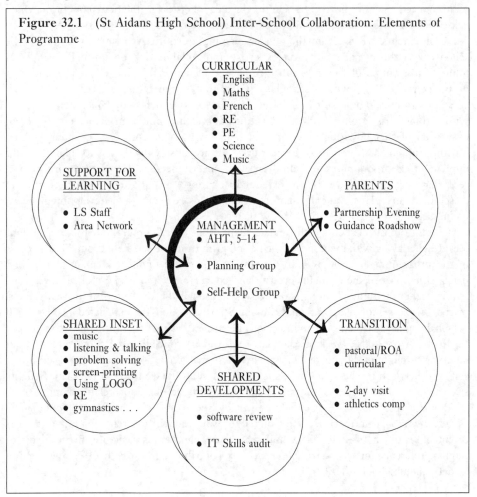

Figure 32.1 (St Aidans High School) Inter-School Collaboration: Elements of Programme

A strong curricular link is made as the subject departments give a commitment to the associated primaries and are timetabled to visit. Secondary staff work in the primary classroom on an agreed area of work. The departments involved may change slightly each year depending on staffing issues.

Primary 7 parents are invited to a partnership evening in St Aidan's. Parents are introduced to staff and then participate in a series of workshops which simulate the experience which their own child will have. The result is that parents have some direct understanding of how their child feels moving from class to class. Positive evaluations from parents is evidence of the success of this event. The Guidance Roadshow involves Guidance staff visiting each primary school to meet parents. This serves as an introduction to the guidance staff and is an opportunity to clarify the guidance teacher's role in the transfer of pupils and to explain the nature of continued contact in secondary school.

A Record of Achievement for each child starts in primary school and the secondary guidance staff use this as a means of encouraging the child to be proud of his or her achievements. At a meeting of guidance staff and groups of Primary 7 children the Record of Achievement is used as a means for pupils to introduce themselves. Children in Primary 7 have a three-day visit during which they experience a secondary school timetable and some of the subjects they will have in S1. On the third day there is an athletics competition which is a social event that brings children, parents and staff together.

Developments arising from the cluster meeting are initiatives which provide all the schools with the means of sharing expertise and collaborating on mutually beneficial topics. An example of this is a software review identified by the self-help group as a useful exercise. This involves schools writing about any materials used and doing so to an agreed format. The result is a shared reference text which is updated each year. In-service topics arise from the cluster meetings at which common priorities emerge from discussion of the individual development plan for each school. The secondary school learning support staff and the area network staff are closely involved with planning and implementing programmes for children with special needs in both the primary and secondary sectors. There is an extended learning support team whose members disseminate any plans and information on children's strengths and development needs to the secondary departments.

Central to all the elements is the management of the overall programme by the Assistant Headteacher along with members of the liaison group and the self-help group. The success of the programme is seen by staff as heavily dependent upon good management and personal liaison. All the elements are running concurrently and purposeful planned visits require tight scheduling. Emphasis on personal liaison as the key factor means that value is placed by the senior management teams at St Aidan's and the associated primaries on personal contact between staff and pupils. The strength of that commitment is apparent in the thirty-two periods a week of secondary and primary time allocated to curricular liaison on-going throughout the session. The quality of interaction between primary and secondary staff and between teachers and pupils is the focus of all the elements in the plan. Benefits stretch far beyond Secondary 1 as a result of an early emphasis on relationships.

This example fits well with the findings of Spelman (1979) in *Pupil Adaptation to Secondary School* (Northern Ireland Council for Educational Research) who found that the extent of liaison between primary and secondary schools was a significant predictor of pupils' preference for secondary school and also contributed towards the lessening of pupil anxiety about school.

Other examples are available in *Sharing Good Practice: Prevention and Support Concerning Pupils Presenting Social, Emotional and Behavioural Difficulties* (Edinburgh: SOEID, 1997) edited by Lloyd and Munn. This includes a chapter by Sharp on a primary–secondary transition programme planned for children considered likely to experience difficulty in the transition period. Secondary and primary teachers and home link workers cooperate with parents to develop and deliver a coordinated programme aimed at smoothing transition. The programme provided includes consultation with the children, discussion groups and a range of planned visits to secondary school. Staff are also involved in home visits and information exchange. Factors in the success of this programme and essential in the plan for future development are the joint working between schools, interagency work and involvement of parents.

It is clear that the successful interaction of adults and children during liaison procedures is emerging as the main factor in a productive experience. All arrangements must be viewed in terms of how they aid the process of change. Many factors are involved, all of which move at different paces and at different times and are differently experienced by children. The range of experience is highlighted in *The Education of Able Pupils P6–S2*: 'Pupils who had shone in the primary school setting sometimes drifted into anonymity in the more complex world of the secondary school. Others who had been unremarkable as primary pupils showed unsuspected talents' (p. 15).

What must be of concern is how children react to the process and how liaison procedures could help create a more positive outcome for more children. While *Interchange No. 30* concludes that there is no particular method of organising materials or pupils which is connected to improvement in learning, *The Education of Able Pupils P6–S2* suggests that there are 'factors in the organisation of learning and teaching which themselves create or conceal difficulties for some able pupils' (p. 16). It is evident that changes in structures will not necessarily produce improvements. Equally, whilst the value of relationships is not in doubt, it is becoming clear that there is a need to know more about the child's experiences of transition.

Qualitative research into children's perception of transition by Brown and Armstrong (1982) entitled 'The Structure of Pupils' Worries During Transition from Junior to Secondary School' (*British Educational Research Journal*, vol. 8, no. 2 pp. 123–31) identified three emergent areas of concern – social relationships, schoolwork and discipline. They further indicated that these change quantitatively and qualitatively during the transition time. Spelman's (1979) findings mentioned earlier indicate the importance of identifying qualitative factors at work in the process of transition. References to interactive teaching (*Improving Mathematics Education 5–14*, 1997), the quality of relationships (*Interchange* No. 30, 1994) and personal liaison (St Aidan's liaison programme, 1997) are all indicators of a modern move towards looking more closely at the nature of relationships as they exist in the classroom.

ISSUES

It has already been demonstrated in this chapter that there are a number of texts and practical approaches which are useful in the context of primary–secondary liaison and transition. What is needed is a coherent approach which draws on established good practice, recent research and responds to current concerns. Over the last ten years evidence has accumulated from research in education, psychology, biology and medicine which indicates the existence and importance of emotional intelligence. The time has come to incorporate this into approaches to the managerial, organisational and curricular issues arising during transfer.

The construct of emotional intelligence was developed by Goleman (1996). It is based on the identification of part of the brain known as the amygdala which is 'a storehouse of emotional memory' (p. 15). The importance of this storehouse rests in the speed with which it operates, which means that the emotional response occurs prior to, and independently from, the cognitive response. The implications of this for education, and for primary-secondary liaison in this instance, lie in the need to give due weight to the emotional dimension in planning and operating procedures. There is a growing body of knowledge on emotional development and the conditions needed to promote it. The findings on resilience in children are one example. In *Young Children* (Washington: National Association for The Education of Young Children, November, 1984) Werner indicates factors which are related to resilient children who grow into stable adults despite having to recover from misfortune or sustained life stress as children. Such resilient children have an active approach to solving life's problems, have a tendency to use painful experiences constructively, have an ability from early in life to gain other people's positive attention and have a strong ability to see positive meaning in their lives.

The characteristics of resilience appear to come about as a result of factors within the child, such as pronounced autonomy and strong social orientation as pre-school children, sociability and a remarkable sense of independence as school age children, e.g. finding a refuge and source of self esteem in hobbies and creative interests. In middle childhood and adolescence, experience of 'required helpfulness' was an important factor. This is involvement in a task which is understood to be crucial to the functioning of the family unit they live in, for example, managing the household. Resilient children also seem to find surrogate parents or minders in the extended family or outside the family circle. The powerful models identified are a favourite teacher, a good neighbour and a member of the clergy.

Hints of these factors can be found in documentation and practice in relation to primary-secondary liaison. Salient issues in *The Education of Able Pupils P6–S2* include those connected with progression and continuity. Section 4.8 of the document, for example, states that a whole school policy is required in order to encourage talent to reveal itself and to develop the use of extra-curricular activities to exploit the possibilities for fostering talent. In St Aidan's the school liaison plan involves the music department working in P5. This takes account of the emergence around middle childhood of 'comparative self concept'. Around this age children who until then had enjoyed an activity or sport in relation to the fulfilment experienced begin to compare their performance with others' and experience feelings towards themselves based on comparisons with others. Targeting middle childhood allows the experience of music to enhance the child's self concept.

Confidence, curiosity, intentionality, self-control, relatedness, capacity to communicate and cooperativeness have been identified as emotional predictors of school success and these are outlined in *Head Start: the Emotional Foundation of School Readiness* (Arlington Va, National Centre for Clinical Infant Programmes, 1992). The factors emerging from studies of resilient children and emotional school readiness indicate the kinds of characteristics which should be fostered in children. Individual assurance and interpersonal awareness are common areas which emerge. These were presaged in the *10–14 Report* which set down a statement of conditions which were essential to the 10–14 curriculum. These included individual learners interacting with their environment; encouraging independent learning; promoting problem-solving skills; enabling children to think through answers and evaluate their own learning; reflecting on learning strategies and encouraging decision-making and choice.

Effective teachers are required to develop the above characteristics in children and create the essential conditions for progress. Burns (1982) in *Self Concept Development and Education* (Eastbourne: Holt, Rinehart and Winston) states that effective teachers show flexibility, an easy, warm manner and an appreciative reinforcing attitude. The national guidelines on *Personal and Social Development 5–14* (1993) state that there are 'three inextricably linked approaches to personal and social development' which have 'implications for all concerned and for each teacher's classroom organisation and practice' (p. 2). Personal development is concerned with self awareness and self esteem and social development is concerned with interpersonal relationships and independence and inter-dependence. These require to become a natural part of school life through the whole school, cross-curricular and special focus approaches. *Interchange No 27 – Effective Support for Learning: Themes from the RAISE Project* mentions the well documented associations of positive self-esteem and the self as learner with optimum attainment and progress, and raises concern that there seems to be little awareness of its importance. Emotional response to school experience is an extremely important factor which is currently overlooked. At SCRE's *Equity in Education* conference in May 1997 Julie Allan's research into how children with special needs experience inclusion takes forward the question of how children experience each other. She uses the idea of the 'pupil's governmental regime' and suggests it can be experienced as pedagogic, transgressive, pastoral or punitive – further suggesting a world of daily experience which is untapped by teachers.

These ideas and findings are critical to the teacher's understanding of what is going on in the classroom. It is in areas such as these that further work is required in order to understand the child's experience of transition. Personal and social development has a central role in primary-secondary transition. Allowing children time to explore, identify and describe feelings about the process, is a major part of their development through the experience of transition. Liaison procedures must take account of this. Goleman's work suggests that feelings should be on the agenda for discussion with children in school. The child's experience becomes a subject of the curriculum, the aim of which is to help the child know, understand and develop tools to work with his or her own emotional responses. In primary-secondary liaison the foci become feelings about, for example, an impending visit to secondary school, or feelings about how children are dealing with the change in their lives. Incorporating the emotional dimension involves auditing current practice to see if it meets these needs. It does not mean throwing out the good things already in place, rather it is looking at them from the perspective of emotional intelligence. This has implications for teacher education, both pre-service and in-service, and requires teachers to look at themselves and their relationships to others.

Nationally, a comprehensive review is required to cover current models of liaison which work and are evolving. Good practice can only be imported to a limited degree. As has been shown in the St Aidan's example, practice evolves on the basis of establishing relationships, planning responsive developments and constructing intentional plans and visits. To transfer anything of the St Aidan's model to another context would require an understanding of the quality of the development process. Simply transposing the model's practical arrangements into another school would leave behind the key factor – the personal liaison.

The potential to look afresh at what is in place and re-define it in terms of fostering personal development and social relationships is the way forward. Current concerns relating to transition and liaison are well documented and now is the time to collate these from different sources. The current orthodoxy is the expectation that children will grasp change and assimilate its effects in a short time and with little acknowledgment or support. The strategy is to develop a model which combines both stability with change and established practice with innovative work, yet keeps as the central focus the child's own experience and reflections.

The author would like to thank Rosemary McDonald and Stephen Campbell for their help.

REFERENCES

CCC (1986) *Education 10–14 in Scotland*, Dundee: CCC.

Derricot, R. (1985) *Curriculum Continuity–Primary to Secondary*, Windsor: NFER.

Goleman, D. (1996) *Emotional Intelligence*, London: Bloomsbury.

SOED (1993) *The Education of Able Pupils P6–S2*, Edinburgh: SOED.

SOED (1994) *5–14; A Practical Guide for Teachers in Primary and Secondary Schools*, Edinburgh: HMSO.

SOEID (1997) *Improving Mathematics Education 5–14*, Edinburgh: SOEID.

VI

Pre-School and Primary Education: Curriculum

33

5–14: Origins, Development and Implementation

Frank R. Adams

ORIGINS

The Curriculum and Assessment 5–14 Programme can be seen as having two linked but distinctive origins. One was the political circumstances which led a government to seek central control over the school curriculum and the other was the professional imperatives which have led to the curriculum for the primary and early secondary stages being more explicitly formulated than in the previous forty years. It is difficult to disentangle these two sources given the commonality that exists between them in the professional role of the Inspectorate in advising the Secretary of State for Scotland on the school curriculum.

Political priorities for the Conservative government, coping with the backlash from a damaging teachers' strike in the mid 1980s, were an increase in parental choice and in the provision of information on schools. The frequent expression of traditional concerns about alleged falling standards and the ideological distrust of so-called 'progressive' methods created the context for the introduction of a programme to provide a centralised initiative on the curriculum which would simultaneously limit teacher autonomy, promise clearer definition of the curriculum and better communication with parents, and exercise greater control over standards through national testing, thus creating a comprehensive, appropriate political response. The appearance of the Secretary of State's Consultative Paper (SED, 1987) has been described as, 'a shift in policy-making style in Scotland from debate followed by consensus to consultation followed by imposition' (Roger in Hartley and Roger, 1990, p. 1).

The professional context for 5–14 can be traced through the range of reports produced by HM Inspectorate and the Scottish Education Department (SED) in the period from 1965 to 1987.

DEVELOPMENT

The starting point of the SED's *The Primary School in Scotland* (SED, 1965) is not arbitrary. The Memorandum, as it came to be commonly called, was widely described, up to 1987, as the benchmark against which all progress in primary education was measured. It pre-dated by two years the English Plowden Report, regarded as the epitome of child-centredness, and set out a philosophy of primary education which started with the needs and was responsive to the interests of the child, was appropriate to age, aptitude and ability and which saw pupils as active in their own learning.

The document emphasised consultation and debate: 'The memorandum avoids prescription of either subject–matter or methods' (ibid., p. viii), and variety rather than conformity:

> Much of the content of the curriculum will vary from school to school, from class to class within the same school, in certain instances from pupil to pupil within the same class . . . it is for each headteacher and his [sic] staff to determine . . . precisely what is to be included . . . (p. 38).

It challenged teachers, and perhaps more significantly headteachers, to reconceptualise their approaches to the education of primary school age children. This is in stark contrast to the prescription of the present centralised arrangements.

Six years after the publication of the Memorandum, the SED published *Primary Education: Organisation for Development* (SED, 1971) which was a 'progress report' on the guidance for teachers in implementing the Memorandum's suggestions offered by education authorities, colleges of education and headteachers.

The 1965 Memorandum had left the provision of guidance on the curriculum to the education authorities but the wide variability found in the quality and impact of that guidance was ascribed to failure to take full account of school circumstances, being over-general in the advice given and even to the providers sometimes having lacked 'the opportunity to practise in the classroom the theories they were advocating' (p. 8–9). A need for schools to have 'clearly defined curricular policies' was identified because of the evidence that 'few headteachers [had] done anything to formulate a policy for the planned implementation of the approaches suggested by the Primary Memorandum' (p. 16).

Significant weaknesses in primary–secondary liaison were identified with secondary teachers unable to appreciate the nature of work in primary and some primary teachers asking secondary teachers to tell them what to teach in upper primary leading to advice which was 'ill-advised and [which] has had a restricting effect on the curriculum of the primary school'. Contemporary with the primary report, the SED published *The First Two Years of Secondary Education* (SED, 1972) which reported on a survey of just under half of secondary schools in Scotland and which commented on 'a disconcerting absence of a clearly defined policy' on new forms of organisation and with the common course for S1 and S2 (p. 18).

Between 1972 and 1980 a number of SED reports were circulated to schools, developing specific aspects of the curriculum the most significant of which was *Primary Education in Scotland: Mathematics* (SED, 1973). Known as Curriculum Paper 13, the document is presented as an updating and consolidation of the work outlined in the Primary Memorandum and might be seen as the first national guideline in a curricular area for primary schools. Advice was offered in relation to three stages, P1–3, P3–5, and P5–7, with two short paragraphs on links with the secondary with a foretaste of the attainment targets and levels of 5–14:

> The test of where a child should be at the end of P3 is his ability to understand and deal with the work he is doing, not his age nor the length of time he has been in school. The brightest pupils will have covered more than is suggested here, while the slowest will not have reached the final point in the progression. (p. 5)

Learning and Teaching in P4 and P7 (SED, 1980) was a survey of primary education in 152 schools at P4 and P7 which also assessed, through the Scottish Council for Research in

Education (SCRE), national standards in reading and mathematics. Rather than the broad, active curriculum proposed in 1965, *Learning and Teaching in P4 and P7* found a narrow curriculum comprising reading comprehension, language exercises and formal aspects of maths with little or no science, spoken English and art. The Inspectorate suggested that the curriculum was not meeting the expectations of 1965 and, in some cases, not even extending to the standards of the 1950 guidance to schools or the 1956 Code. Teachers favoured closed responses from pupils, very little discovery learning, open-ended questioning and discussion. Curricular integration was not common:

> The Scottish primary school teacher insists on making her pupils literate and numerate. . . . The acquisition of a variety of modes of learning and a potential for creative activity appears to go largely unchallenged by the present curriculum. (p. 7)

In 1980, only seven years before the Curriculum and Assessment 5–14 Programme, the need for consensus appeared to be still a major concern of policy makers. In calling for a major review of primary education, the SED felt that 'it would be unwise to undertake it without regard to a wider consensus about the nature and content of primary education' (pp. 49–50). Nevertheless, for the first time since 1965, the necessity, desirability and extent of national monitoring of standards is raised, setting the scene for battles to come over national testing.

The questioning of the extent and desirability of teacher autonomy in determining the curriculum appears to have been founded on a concern for the narrowing of the curriculum but, taken with Curriculum Paper 13 and later with the SED report on *Learning and Teaching: The Environment and the Primary School Curriculum* (SED, 1984), the clear signal is that official thinking in the 1980s was moving in the direction of increased central direction of the curriculum.

The Inspectorate's response to *Learning and Teaching in P4 and P7* was published as *Learning and Teaching: The Environment and the Primary School Curriculum* (SED, 1984) which focused on the confusion surrounding Environmental Studies and evidence of the lack of 'disciplined learning'. Unlike *Learning and Teaching in P4 and P7*, the new report found considerable evidence of curricular integration with projects and centres of interest in 75 per cent of classes in the survey. The 1984 paper tried, therefore, to reconcile a desire for more disciplined learning with multidisciplinary work resulting in a very complex and not particularly helpful paper.

An important stance taken in the report was the need for advance school planning in Environmental Studies rather than teacher autonomy to decide topics in response to children's particular interests, a dilemma allegedly set up by the child-centred approaches of the Memorandum. The need for continuity and progression in the curriculum and methodology throughout primary and into secondary was emphasised. The Environmental Studies report provides an insight into developments in Inspectorate thinking in the mid 1980s and how this must have coincided with the emerging political/educational views of the government.

An account of the origins of 5–14 would be incomplete without reference to the alternative proposals for a reconceptualised primary and early secondary curriculum developed by the Consultative Committee on the Curriculum's (CCC) Education 10–14 Programme (CCC, 1986). Challenged with the task of reconciling primary and secondary approaches to the curriculum, the Education 10–14 Committee proposed the same basic principles of continuity, progression, breadth and balance as the Curriculum and Assessment 5–14 Consultative paper would do only eighteen months later, but the 10–14 concept of guidelines was combined with a recognition of the professional commitment of teachers and proposed 'autonomy within guidelines'. As commentators have noted (Boyd in Humes and McKenzie, 1994; Hartley and Roger 1990), 10–14 was the victim of a change in the political climate.

This change was reflected in the fact that the concept of guidelines in *Curriculum and Assessment in Scotland: A Policy for the '90s* (SED, 1987) was based on the threat that 'the Secretary of State would not rule out introducing legislation to ensure the proper implementation of national policy' (SED, 1987, para. 54). The consultative paper suggested that there were weaknesses in the curricular and assessment practices of primary and early secondary schools identified as poor school policies for the curriculum, lack of definition of the curriculum and curricular discontinuity, insufficient challenge for pupils especially at P6 and P7, inconsistent assessment practices and poor communication with parents.

The paper set out a strategy to meet these weaknesses which was, in essence, to produce detailed guidelines on the aims, objectives and content for each aspect of the curriculum for P1–S2 and to put into place improved assessment practices and a national testing programme to give 'assurance about the progress that is being achieved.' (SED, 1987, p. 9). HMI reports, mainly on primary education, from 1973–84 contained the elements of the official advice that was eventually crystallised in the conjunction of professional advice and political ideology that was represented by the 1987 consultative paper.

Continuity and progression between P7 and S1 was a major objective of both the Education 10–14 Report and the 5–14 proposals. It is significant, however, that the 5–14 programme in seeking to achieve linkage between two sectors of school education, traditionally different in rationale and assumptions, proceeded without any contextualising rationale or philosophy. This has been discussed elsewhere (Adams, 1988; Adams in Kirk and Glaister, 1994) and is common with events which have surrounded the development of the National Curriculum in England, Wales and Northern Ireland. In that context, particularly following the Dearing Review of 1994, there was a concerted effort to keep advice to schools as slim as possible in response to politicians' suspicion of so-called 'theory' and their more pragmatic fears about the impact on teacher workload. In Scotland, the response of politicians and some civil servants to the length of the Education 10–14 Report was rejection of the prolixity of professional educators and an apparent lack of confidence in the ability of the teaching profession to cope with the analysis of complex ideas in favour of a short, sharp, simple set of instructions presented as guidelines, a view disputed by many practising teachers.

Among the short, simple instructions of 5–14, the advice on the complex notion of balance in the primary curriculum stands out. In 1983, the National Committee on Primary Education (COPE), in *Primary Education in the Eighties* (COPE, 1983) had acknowledged the importance of the issue of balance and breadth in the primary curriculum but had rejected a simple arithmetic approach to balance: The idea of balance involves not just a balance of modes or curricular experiences, but balance of skills, activities, social experiences, . . . balance of teaching approaches of different types,' (pp. 18–19). This kind of complexity was rejected by 5–14 where, late in the development process, a precise definition of balance as 'appropriate time . . . allocated to each area of curricular activity', was set out in *Structure and Balance of the Curriculum 5–14* (SOED,

1993). The overriding need to find a way of describing the primary curriculum balance that articulated with the existing timetabled structure of S1 and S2 appears to have forced this kind of simplistic approach to a complex issue. The recommended balance is set out below in Table 33.1.

Table 33.1 Balance of the Allocation of Time in 5–14

	Primary	Secondary 1 and 2
Mathematics	15%	10%
Language	15%	20%
Religious and Moral Education	10%	5%
Expressive Arts	15%	
Environmental Studies	25%	
Scientific Studies & Applications		10%
Technological Studies and Applications		10%
Social & Environmental Studies		10%
Creative and Aesthetic Activities		10%
Physical Education		5%
Flexibility	20%	20%

The guidance emphasises that the allocations of time are minimum allocations. Early criticism based, for example, on the problems of specifying the 15 per cent of the curriculum that is exclusively language development as distinct from the language development that takes place elsewhere have continued. (See, for example, Adams in Kirk and Glaister, 1994, pp. 4–6) Four years on from the publication of the time allocations there is evidence to suggest that, even given the flexibility factor, the profession is not satisfied that global allocations of time can be made. Differences between the needs of P1–3 and P4–7, for example, raise doubts about the minimum allocation of 25 per cent to Environmental Studies throughout the primary years. Growing emphasis on, for example, early literacy have caused some education authorities to issue guidance on balance which is different from the official line.

The 5–14 Programme applies only in Scotland while the National Curriculum is the statutory guidance on the curriculum in England, Wales and N. Ireland. There have been marked similarities in the process of production of the national curriculum guidance in Scotland and England. In both cases subject based working groups were set up. In Scotland each Review and Development Group (RDG) produced its 'ideal' curriculum, the sum of which is a vastly complex map of the primary curriculum, while in England syllabus overload resulted from curriculum decisions made by isolated working groups using the strategy of include everything and cross-reference among curricular areas. Other similarities include the confidentiality of the working groups (lack of public access to minutes and working papers), tight time scales, tokenistic consultation and rapid introduction to schools.

Despite these similarities, the English National Curriculum has been a more centralised development than 5–14. A fundamental difference has been in the overt political influence that has been exerted on the development in England arising from Conservative policies and the active involvement in curriculum policy of various political figures from Sir Keith Joseph through to Kenneth Baker. However, the lack of clear and consistent approaches to the content and assessment of the National Curriculum between 1988 and 1993 led to the review carried out by Sir Ron Dearing and the School Curriculum and Assessment Authority (SCAA) which resulted in the so-called 'slimmed down' National Curriculum which was to be implemented from August 1995.

The 1995 English National Curriculum differs principally from the Scottish 5–14 Curriculum and Assessment programme in its separation of the primary stages from the secondary through presentation of curriculum at Key Stages 1 and 2 (5–7 years and 7–11 years) for primary and Key Stages 3 and 4 (11–14 years and 14–16 years) for secondary. While 5–14 occupies the longest timespan in the Scottish curriculum made up of 5–14 years (P1–S2), which includes attainment targets grouped at five levels of progression A–E, followed by Standard Grade (S3/S4) and Higher Still (S4–S6), there is no overall perception of the Scottish curriculum as a seamless garment from P1 to S4. Differences also exist in the curriculum coverage at each of the stages. The 5–14 Programme covers all of the areas of the curriculum and does not prescribe a core curriculum, while the English National Curriculum labels English, mathematics and science as core subjects with technology, history, geography, art, music and PE as foundation subjects at Key Stages 1 and 2 and, with the addition of a modern language, as foundation at Key Stage 3. There are similarities in terminology within both structures but differences in interpretation of the terms used is set out in Table 33.2, below.

Table 33.2   Definitions of Terms used in the National Curriculum (England & Wales) and the Curriculum and the Curriculum and Assessment 5–14 Programme (Scotland)

Terms Used	National Curriculum (England & Wales)	5–14 Programme (Scotland)
key stage	Key Stage 1: 5–7 years Key Stage 2: 7–11 years Key Stage 3: 11–14 years Key Stage 4: 14–16 years	not used in 5–14
attainment outcome	not used in the National Curriculum	broad competences in each curriculum area
strands	not used in the National Curriculum	key constituents of an attainment outcome
attainment target	expected standards of pupil performance	specific learning goals
levels	eight level descriptors (not in art, music, PE)	five level descriptors (all curricular areas)
programmes of study	what pupils should be taught	advice on appropriate forms of learning and teaching

The nature of the 'programmes of study' in the two educational systems is of particular interest. The English National Curriculum is prescriptive in what is to be taught at each Key Stage while the Scottish 5–14 Programme expects schools to use the information and advice contained in the 5–14 guidelines to review existing school programmes and to develop appropriate responses.

IMPLEMENTATION

It is a moot point as to when any development programme is complete and full implementation of the changes should be expected. The 5–14 Development programme is no exception to this since final versions of the national guidelines appeared over a three year period (1991–94) and then had to find their place in the existing development plans of schools. The order of publication also played a part in the implementation in schools as Table 33.3 shows:

Table 33.3 Publication Dates of 5–14 National Guidelines

1991	1992	1993	1994
English Language	Expressive Arts	Structure and Balance of the Curriculum	5–14 A Practical Guide
Assessment	Religious and Moral	Personal & Social Development	
Mathematics	Latin	Environmental Studies	
	Modern Languages	Gaelic	
	Reporting		

There are three current sources of evidence about the extent and nature of the implementation of 5–14. One is the official SOED funded evaluation programme co-ordinated by the Scottish Council for Research in Education (SCRE). The second source is evidence from school inspections summarised in *Standards and Quality in Scottish Schools 1992–95* (SOEID, 1996). The third is the Economic and Social Research Council (ESRC) funded research project carried out by Swann and Brown of the University of Stirling into how 5–14 had affected teachers' thinking about their classroom teaching.

The official evaluation of the 5–14 Programme (Harlen, 1996) focused initially on the years 1991–5 and was subsequently extended to take in the period 1995–7. Evidence from the primary school evaluation indicates that 5–14 documentation appears, increasingly, to be used as the main tool for curriculum audit and, as familiarity with the details of the documentation grow, 5–14 takes on the dominant role in forward planning. The overall tone of the SCRE evaluation suggests there is acceptance of the 5–14 framework by the profession despite some initial difficulties caused mainly by the apparent complexity of the documentation and the pace of change (Harlen, 1996, p. 32). Evidence from the secondary sector, however, indicates that there is less enthusiasm to adopt the national guidelines as the basis for continuity from primary to secondary:

> in terms of continuity of progress for the individual pupil, the entrenched preference for a 'fresh start' and lack of interest in records and work sent by pupils' previous teachers remain a cause for some concern. (Harlen, 1996, p. 31)

The preliminary public reports in the educational press (Simpson and Goulder in *Times Educational Supplement Scotland*, 12 September 1997) on the surveys carried out in 1995–96, indicate that implementation of the English and Mathematics guidelines is regarded as 'well under way' in most secondary schools but that other curricular areas are at 'the earliest stages of implementation, that of discussion and awareness raising' in half of the schools surveyed by the researchers. Clearly the existence of the 5–14 Guidelines is not sufficient in itself to guarantee that there will be continuity between the primary and secondary stages.

5–14 is an essential plank in the 'quality initiative' that has been promoted by HM Inspectors in Scottish schools. The 1987 consultative paper did not rule out legislation to ensure the introduction of 5–14 and expected HMI to 'pay particular attention in their inspection of schools to the extent to which schools and education authorities have had regard to the national curricular policies' (SED, 1987, p. 7). *Standards and Quality in Scottish Schools* (SOEID, 1996) reported on standards of attainment in English language and mathematics in both primary and S1/S2 against the 5–14 attainment targets (with other curricular areas to be the subject of future reports). While the majority of schools had reached the minimum targets in English and mathematics set out in the national guidelines, the Senior Chief HMI points out that:

> substantial improvement is needed in some important areas of the primary curriculum . . . pupils were not attaining appropriate 5–14 targets in writing in 30% of our schools . . . in number, money and measurement in 25% of schools . . . courses for S1/S2 gave concern in 35% of schools. There was a particular need to accelerate the implementation of the 5–14 curriculum and assessment guidelines to take better account of pupils' primary school experience. (pp. iii–iv)

The ESRC funded research carried out by Swann and Brown is different in nature from the official implementation studies and the HMI monitoring of national standards in that its focus was the teacher's thinking rather than the 5–14 guidelines themselves. The research suggested that, in 1995, there was very little evidence of the 5–14 concepts being apparent in teachers' thinking about their classroom practice. The researchers argue that the complexity of 5–14's structure made it difficult for practitioners to incorporate into their thinking at classroom level and:

> while teachers are able to engage in 5–14 discourse on staff development days, in the writing of school development plans, or in answering structured questionnaires it does not inevitably follow that the ideas have been or will be internalised into their classroom thinking. (Swann and Brown, 1997, p. 109)

This is an important issue given the lack of independent studies of the impact of 5–14 on overall classroom practice ten years after the beginning of the Programme. While one might feel that the teachers in the study had had relatively little time to internalise 5–14's structure in 1994–5 there has been no subsequent comparable attempt to carry out similar research. As more and more students in initial teacher education have become familiar with 5–14 and subsequently entered teaching, the 5–14 structure is no longer decontextualised innovation but has itself become the practical, familiar and intuitive way of approaching teaching for new teachers. Clearly more detailed research could be fruitful in this field.

ISSUES

The 5–14 Development Programme has given rise to many issues for practitioners in both schools and teacher education institutions as well as those in education authorities. The final section of this chapter will identify some of these issues which remain problematic and which will continue to form the basis for considerable debate.

The 5–14 Programme was promoted by SOEID as being 'founded on widely accepted principles' (SED, 1987, p. 3) and 'built on the advice and teaching materials already available as a result of the work of the CCC.' (p. 18). English Language 5–14, for example, could draw on the extensive work done in the 1980s on children's writing by the Scottish Committee on Language Arts (SCOLA) in the primary context and on similar work which had been going on in the secondary context but, even then, the resulting guidelines were open to criticism by the former chair of SCOLA:

> the neat curricular tabulations of the 5–14 documents are . . . a denial of the innate complexity of learning and teaching. English Language 5–14, as a model, bears little if any relationship to how children acquire language. (Macdonald in Kirk and Glaister, 1994, p. 57)

This kind of criticism reflects the problem that the totality of the experience of pupils in primary or early secondary schools is much more than the assurance that the curriculum is broad, balanced, continuous and progressive, important as these concepts may be. Their importance is, perhaps, only matched by their problematic nature when attempts are made to turn them into day to day classroom experiences for pupils and teachers. The apparently straightforward presentation of the content of the national guidelines belies the complexity of the daily professional judgements required in teaching and neglects to emphasise the role of competent, reflective practitioners in the successful application of any guidelines.

Where the basis of curricular agreement did not already exist the potential for the exercise of professional judgement might be seen to be greater, giving the teacher more flexibility and freedom to act. However, the complexities of the professional disagreements over Environmental Studies (see Adams in Kirk and Glaister, 1994, pp. 11–16) are such that more than four years after the publication of the national guidelines there is a continuing lack of consensus on the preferred curricular organisation, particularly at the S1/S2 ages.

In particular, the extent to which integration should exist in the primary curriculum remains problematic (see, for example, Macdonald, pp. 50–68; Adams, p. 15–16) for both schools and teacher education institutions seeking to prepare students for the often apparently conflicting demands of the modern primary school. One source of insight into the 'official' stance on integration is contained in ex-Depute Senior Chief HMI McClelland's *Scottish Education 5–14 – A Parents' Guide* (Edinburgh, 1993):

> The national guidelines have been written in a way which enables this area of the curriculum (Environmental Studies) to be taught either as an integrated whole or as a series of separate, although interrelated, subjects. In either case the aim is to achieve studies which are coherent, continuous and progressive. (p. 18)

Unfortunately the problem is more complex than whether to link subjects within a curriculum plan. The Committee on Primary Education (COPE) issued a 'starter paper' *Some Aspects of Thematic Work* (COPE, 1987), at the same time as, and subsequently swamped by, the consultative paper on 5–14, which emphasised the centrality of the processes of learning and the contexts in which learning took place. The 5–14 programme, while endorsing the modes of teaching first established by COPE in 1983, did little to examine the relationship between the processes of learning and the planned curriculum and it is in this vacuum that the issue of integrated work exists. Patrick Whitaker, in *Primary*

Schools and the Future (Buckingham: Open University Press, 1997), identifies the attempts
to reconcile the separation/integration issue as a constant struggle for primary schools:

> It is perhaps beyond possibility to capture it in guidelines and plans, since it exists as praxis – the
> continual interplay between what we do and how we experience it . . . the crucible is the learning
> activity and all that involves in the heat of the moment, not the curriculum statement or the
> development plan. (Whitaker, 1997, p. 48)

The fundamental issue for primary practice is not about how the curriculum is organised,
described or reported on. It is about the conceptions of knowledge and how it is constructed
and, in particular, the role that the teacher plays in partnership with his or her pupils in
constructing that knowledge. It is to do with the relationship between the teacher and the
taught; between teaching and learning.

The fundamental nature of this issue has been recognised by the initiation of a national
debate on learning and teaching led by the Scottish Consultative Committee on the
Curriculum (SCCC), released from the burden of the 5–14 programme, through the
publication of *Teaching for Effective Learning* (SCCC 1996) and the associated activities of a
network of interested professionals. While 5–14 endorsed the 'modes of teaching' –
expository, discursive, activity and enquiry – first proposed by COPE in 1983, it is clear
that discussion of the methodology of teaching has not been explicit in curricular guidance
issued to schools. Scotland, unlike England, did not experience a New Right backlash
against child-centred methodologies. Methodology was not listed as a 'weakness' in the
1987 consultative paper and it can be argued that the effective implementation of the detail
of 5–14 depends upon the employment of the full range of the modes of teaching. An
analysis of the issues relating to methodology and organisation (Skinner in Kirk and
Glaister 1994, pp. 26–49) highlights the lack of consistency and confusion that exists in the
national curriculum guidelines and suggests that, 'Viewed as a whole, the guidelines cry out
for a comprehensive, co-ordinated review of teaching methodology, classroom organisation
and differentiation, interesting ideas on which lie scattered among the guidelines' (p. 38).
SOEID guidance since 1994 has not advanced the issue beyond the situation described by
Skinner. *5–14: A Practical Guide* (SOEID 1994) suggests that 'variety' and the 'balance' of
methodology over time are important without any rationale for this statement leaving, by
default, a genuine engagement with this complex issue to the SCCC.

The impact of 5–14 on teachers' professionalism has been alluded to earlier and is an
issue that received most attention in the earliest days of the development of 5–14. For
example, the SCRE response to the 1987 consultative paper that 'Teachers are no longer
professionals but employees, hired assistants who have no necessary commitment to the
curriculum aims and objectives which they have to meet' (quoted by Gatherer in Hartley
and Roger 1990, p. 73). The need for teachers to maintain a professional, reflective role has
been proposed earlier, in relation to primary practice in general. This kind of professional
attitude remains vital even for 5–14 itself to succeed in its own terms. If the relatively top-
down model of curriculum development represented by 5–14 has the effect of making
teachers believe that the curriculum has now been 'sorted' for the foreseeable future and
engenders in the profession a reluctance to consider change then the Programme will have
done education little service. The process of school development planning should engender
feelings of ownership on the part of the staff for the curriculum of a school, but as long as
that curriculum is measured by externally derived means the feeling of ownership is likely to
be compromised.

Recent indications are that teachers are working at understanding 5–14 and putting it into practice but public perceptions tend to be coloured by the negative presentation of teachers' achievements. For example, the need to re-interpret the levels (level A by the end of P2 rather than P3; most pupils beyond level D by the end of P7) proposed for mathematics in *Improving Mathematics 5–14* (SOEID 1997) may be justified but it is presented to the public as the failure of teachers to challenge pupils sufficiently, echoing the negative tone of much of the curriculum direction of the mid to late 1980s. The continuing top-down approach to curriculum development with the consequent reinforcement of the blame culture sits uncomfortably with the official stance (in SOEID, *How Good is Our School?*, Edinburgh, 1996) that the key to school improvement is teacher self evaluation.

The message of the late 1990s sounds depressingly similar to that of the era of the New Right and the professional status of teachers remains a fragile thing.

REFERENCES

Adams, F. R. (1988) Curriculum Framework for the Primary Stages, in *Scottish Educational Review*, 20.2, pp. 93-96.

Harlen, W. (1996) *Four Years of Change in Education 5–14*, Edinburgh: Scottish Council for Research in Education.

Hartley, D. and A. Rodger (1990) *Curriculum and Assessment in Scotland: A Policy for the 90s*, Edinburgh: Scottish Academic Press.

Humes, W. and M. MacKenzie (1994) *The Management of Educational Policy*, Essex: Longman.

Kirk, G. and R. Glaister (1994) *5–14: Scotland's National Curriculum*, Edinburgh: Scottish Academic Press.

Swann, J. and S. Brown, S. (1997) The Implementation of a National Curriculum and Teachers' Classroom Thinking, in *Research Papers in Education*, 12.1, pp. 91–114.

34

English Language

Sue Ellis and Gill Friel

Language is a key curricular area in Scottish primary schools and constitutes 15 per cent of the timetable but many schools allocate a proportion of the 20 per cent flexibility factor to English Language. *English Language 5–14* (SOED, 1991) was the first of the national curriculum and assessment guidelines to be published and was received with remarkably little debate. Implementation has been almost universal and it frames policy development, planning, teaching, assessment and reporting to parents.

English Language 5–14 identifies four attainment outcomes; listening, talking, reading and writing. Strands describe the aspects of learning in each outcome and detail progression in the form of attainment targets as shown in Table 34.1. The Guidelines also emphasise diversity of language and culture; knowledge about language, and Scottish culture. This has improved awareness of bilingualism, mother tongues and Scots language. Scottish Consultative Committee on the Curriculum publications such as *Languages for Life – Bilingual Pupils 5–14* (Dundee: SCCC, 1995) and *The Kist/A' Chiste* (Dundee: SCCC, 1996) pack on Scots languages support policy and practice in these areas.

Table 34.1 Attainment Outcomes and Strands in English Language 5–14

	ATTAINMENT OUTCOMES			
	Reading	Writing	Talking	Listening
S T R A N D S	Reading for information	Functional Writing	Conveying information, instructions & directions	Listening for information, instructions & directions
	Reading for enjoyment	Imaginative Writing		
		Personal Writing	Talking in groups	Listening in groups
	Reading to reflect the writer's ideas and craft	Handwriting & Presentation	Talking about experiences, feelings & opinions	Listening in order to respond to texts
	Awareness of genre	Spelling Punctuation & Structure		Awareness of genre
	Reading aloud	Knowledge About Language	Talking about texts	Knowledge about language
	Knowledge about language		Audience awareness Knowledge about language	

MONITORING AND ASSESSMENT

Her Majesty's Inspectorate (HMI) monitor the implementation of the Guidelines and standards of attainment through inspection reports of individual schools. They produce summary reports and reports on aspect inspections which highlight general issues.

National tests for all children in Primary 4 and Primary 7 were strongly opposed by parents and teachers when they were introduced in 1991. Parents withdrew two-thirds of the eligible pupils from the test trials and the programme was changed. Now, all children sit national tests in reading and writing, but only when the teacher considers them to have attained the next level. Reading tests are selected from a bank of items by the teacher who administers and marks them. Writing tests are marked against national criteria. Test items are designed to reflect classroom practice and the reading tests are particularly well regarded.

A programme of Scottish Office Education and Industry Department (SOEID) funded surveys, known as the Assessment of Achievement Programme (AAP), monitors national standards at P4, P7 and S2, enabling comparisons between stages and over time. English Language surveys were carried out in 1984, 1989, 1992 and 1996. From 1997, externally contracted curricular specialist teams will be replaced by one general team, employed by SOEID.

POLICY AND PRACTICE PRIOR TO 5–14

Major influences prior to 5–14 were the 'Primary Memorandum' (SED, 1965, *Primary Education in Scotland*, Edinburgh: HMSO), which promoted an integrated, contextualised language curriculum over rote learning and book-based exercises, and the Bullock Report (1975). The Scottish Central Committee on Primary Education (SCCOPE/ COPE) and its sub-committee for Language Arts (SCOLA) were remitted to investigate and advise on teaching methodology and content (SCOLA, 1975). Key problems concerned poorly focused teaching and progression in topic-based language work. From the start, COPE and SCOLA publications report poor awareness of talking and listening and concern about the lack of good classroom resources and advice in this area.

In reading, the concern was over 'unit studies' (class novels intended to develop higher-order reading and comprehension skills) which often degenerated into general topic work; the scant attention paid to promoting reading for pleasure and the haphazard nature of much assessment and recording. The debate on reading was vigorous and productive. United Kingdom Reading Association (called the West of Scotland Reading Association in Glasgow) meetings were large and frequent. Classroom resources such as the *Edinburgh Reading Test* (London: Hodder and Stoughton, 1977), the *Scope for Reading* series (Edinburgh: Holmes McDougall, 1975) and COPE documents such as *The Reading Habit* (COPE, 1978) illustrate the desire to develop skills beyond the infant stages.

In writing, the narrow range of tasks and exclusive focus on secretarial skills was problematic. Three COPE documents *Hand in Your Writing* (Dundee: SCCC, 1981) *Mr Togs the Tailor* (Dundee: SCCC, 1982) and *Responding to Writing* (Dundee: SCCC, 1986) promoted context and purpose, audience awareness and redrafting. However, concern that such contextualised tasks would lack a clear teaching focus meant that assessment continued to be based strictly on the written product. This focused teachers' attention on the communicative adequacy of children's writing rather than on how children become writers or on the writing process strategies they needed to be taught.

READING AND WRITING

Currently, over 97 per cent of primary schools use a commercial reading scheme and most have programmes for teaching phonics. Beginning readers commonly take words and reading books home to practise. Many schools use class and group novel studies to extend, or in the upper primary stages, to replace the reading scheme. Schools also supplement reading schemes with a variety of reading activities structured around the 5–14 strands.

Reading schemes are used in attainment groups, but whole class activities include reading stories, discussing big books and some phonics teaching. Many classrooms have book corners, although the quality and use of these varies. Reading for Information is taught through language schemes and topic work and, according to the AAP and HMI reports, is weaker than other areas.

AAP and HMI reports indicate that reading standards have remained stable over the past ten years and the debate about teaching reading is less politicised than in England. However, the proportion of children leaving school with unsatisfactory reading competence has not declined and the variable success rates of schools with apparently similar catchment areas hints at hidden under-achievement. In 1997, education authorities were given SOEID funding for 3-year early intervention projects. These should prompt healthy debate on literacy; baseline assessment; pedagogical knowledge; staff development and policy into practice. Most authorities appear to be targeting schools in social priority areas, which may limit the range of issues addressed and the projects' ability to promote wide reflection and change.

Handwriting, spelling, punctuation and grammar have always been important and feature routinely in school policy documents and teacher's planning. Many schools have coordinated programmes for teaching these aspects, frequently using commercial schemes to ensure coherence across stages.

Much writing is taught as a whole class activity in which children work individually. Functional writing is often derived from topic work and is discussed in terms of formats: letters; instructions; posters; reports etc. This means that teaching tends to focus on layout rather than genre. In imaginative writing, many see the teacher's role as 'helping the children get ideas' by creating a context, often through class discussion. Stories are commonly written into jotters and marked by the teacher. Desk-top publishing is becoming popular but it is comparatively rare for children to write extended stories or to choose their own writing topics. The purpose and teaching focus of personal writing often remains vague.

In infant classes, it is becoming less common for P1 classes to all copy one child's news from the board, but many schools still separate the composing and transcribing processes. Teachers often transcribe until the child is proficient in forming letters. This approach has recently been criticised for not encouraging emergent understandings of print and for ignoring the children's understanding that writing should be about ideas that are personally important to the author. Early writing tasks tend to be 'news writing' and vary in the degree to which they promote real purpose and meaningful choice.

Despite recent advocation of process approaches (SCRE, 1995), the role of the teacher and nature of the teaching input in writing continues to be problematic. Although the AAP reports increased use of planning pages, there is little evidence that children are being introduced to a variety of rehearsal, planning and drafting strategies, or that these help individual children develop their own 'voice' in writing. Teacher awareness of how to sequence and structure lessons, making judicious use of collaborative work, overnight thinking time, and non-writing activities to support the writing process remains low.

National testing was heavily inserviced and focused attention on the written product rather than the process, the child, or on writing to learn. Issues such as the children's sense of authorship and ownership; their knowledge of the craft techniques used for different genres; their understanding of reading-writing links and of writing to learn remain largely unaddressed.

Traditionally, nurseries have not been associated with, and were frequently discouraged from, literacy teaching. Research showing the link between pre-school knowledge of literacy and school success has caused a re-examination of this policy and recent advice (SOEID, 1997) promotes knowledge of print, stories, phonological awareness and home-school links.

TALKING AND LISTENING

The emphasis on talking and listening in *English Language 5–14* was greeted with genuine surprise in schools, despite policy documents since 1965 advocating the importance of planned contexts for talk and of accepting and developing the language children bring to school. Improved standards in talking and listening, measured by AAP surveys and a selection of HMI school reports, came when teachers corrected the mismatch between their practice and the balance required by the Guidelines.

Now most schools have policies for talking and listening and often timetable the use of audio-visual materials and listening laboratories. Most infant classes have a 'news' or 'circle' time and implement the listening and group discussion activities of reading schemes. Some schools use published schemes on oracy, others plan it into topic work, using assemblies and class presentations as opportunities for children to address a larger audience. Burns Day celebrations and local festivals promote poetry recital, Scots language and choral speaking.

Group discussion, particularly skills of listening to and including others, remains problematic. The current framework of the Guidelines splits oracy into talking and listening which deflects attention from the relationship between talking, listening and learning. A deeper understanding of collaborative group-work and of how to adapt task structures to develop specific types of learning would ensure more effective use of group tasks. Without this understanding, teachers perception of what is important in the language curriculum may be unduly influenced by the exclusion of talking and listening from national testing and future AAP reports.

ISSUES OF CONCERN

English Language 5–14 presented a welcome return to a focus on the content of language teaching. However, unless sympathetically interpreted, it presents a skills-based and reductionist model of language which does not capture and promote the rich model that underpins best practice in Scottish schools. Although language as a vehicle for learning is recognised in the rationale of the Guidelines, this is rarely exemplified in the strands, targets and programmes of study. In practice, the Guidelines promote the view that language is used to communicate and transmit knowledge but only rarely and incidentally to explore and re-frame ideas to create new understandings.

If the Guidelines were used merely to audit and highlight gaps in teachers' planning this would not be a serious problem. However, teachers are invited to use the 5–14 strands and targets as a basis for planning their teaching programmes. Thus, whilst the 5–14 framework undoubtedly supports weaker teachers, it can divert average teachers from developing more complex models and simply frustrate the best.

The pressure for accountability created in the wake of the Guidelines ensured that talking and listening was taken seriously and aspects of attainment have improved. However, it may also have led to an over-emphasis on forward planning and on schemes and worksheets to ensure coverage. This could encourage fragmentation of the curriculum and limit the opportunities for children (and teachers) to follow their interests and devote time to understanding things in depth. It is an approach which sits uneasily with the notion of a flexible curriculum in which teaching input is adapted to meet the children's needs and produce language work that is intellectually and emotionally satisfying. In reading, where teachers were already working to reasonably sophisticated models, this is less of a problem than in writing, where it militates against a shift in the teaching focus from the product to the writer.

The early intervention projects may encourage headteachers to see that promoting effective language teaching is a cornerstone of quality management and leadership. This would help to create a climate in which good management is seen as helping teachers acquire the knowledge to use the Guidelines appropriately and creatively rather than mechanistically. Staff development initiatives of the future may be driven by this need to develop a rich and broad understanding of language, teaching and learning.

REFERENCES

Napuk, A., B. Normand, S. Dickie and N. Entwistle (1997) *Assessment of Achievement Programme (Scotland) English Language Monitoring, 5th Round*, Edinburgh: SOED.

Scottish Committee on Language Arts (1975) *The SCOLA Survey*, Edinburgh: COPE.

SCCC (1998) *Learning to Write, Writing to Learn – Teaching Writing 5–14*, Dundee: SCCC.

SCRE (1995) 'Taking a Closer Look at Reading' and 'Taking a Closer Look at Writing' in *SCRE Publication 123 (English Language Pack), Edinburgh: SCRE.*

SOEID (1991) *English Language 5–14: National Guidelines*, Edinburgh: HMSO.

SOEID (1997) *A Curriculum Framework for Children in their Pre School Year*, Edinburgh: HMSO.

35

Environmental Studies

Rae Stark

Environmental Studies is one of the five broad areas of the curriculum within the 5–14 Development Programme, the national guidelines for curriculum and assessment in Scottish schools between the ages of 5 and 14 years (SOED, 1993). The term 'environmental studies' was given currency in the policy document *Primary Education in Scotland* (SED, 1965) where it was stated that:

> they [environmental studies] have in common the twofold aim of fostering in the child a desire to know more about the world around him [sic] and of training him in the skills he needs to interpret it. (p. 126)

This document, usually referred to as the 'Primary Memorandum', defined environmental studies as the integration of a number of curricular areas (primarily history, geography and nature study but also mathematics), advocated working in groups and promoted the 'project' as an important approach to learning and teaching. It advised focusing on the needs of the individual child and active learning rather than the acquisition of 'exhaustive factual information' (p. 37), i.e. a child-centred rather than a subject-centred philosophy. While the place of environmental studies in the primary curriculum was thus established in policy, classroom practice responded slowly, if at all.

POLICY INTO PRACTICE

In 1980, fifteen years after the Memorandum, Her Majesty's Inspectorate of Schools (HMI) reported that only 25 per cent of Scottish primary schools visited displayed high standards of learning and teaching in environmental studies (SED, 1980). Group methods of working were not commonplace and clear links to other areas of the curriculum had not been established. Indeed in 75 per cent of schools, environmental studies received 'scant attention or were ineffectually taught' (p. 25).

Pupils were not receiving a balanced experience of the three subject areas (now history, geography and science rather than 'nature study') with science faring particularly badly. According to HMI, many teachers appeared unconvinced that an integrated approach could be made to work and experienced considerable problems in planning, organising and managing topic studies. It was considered that, unless adequate support was provided, teachers would be 'tempted to settle for something less demanding' (p. 23).

Other contributory factors listed included: the absence of any coherent policy at primary school level, particularly one which had relevance for the associated secondary school; a lack of coordination across stages within the primary school; and a lack of confidence, and a need for guidance in the primary teachers themselves. However, they also noted that 'there is a danger that too much detail, too many objectives, may simply overwhelm and frustrate them' (p. 26). While broadly endorsing the main themes of the Primary Memorandum, HMI concluded that there was a need to review the whole notion of environmental studies, its aims and constituent parts and its relationship to other subject areas. The report also noted that there was pressure to introduce new subject areas to the curriculum and questioned whether these could be accommodated without decisions on priorities and balance.

The 1980s saw a flurry of reports and activity, with environmental studies increasingly regarded as embodying important aspects of education with long term implications for Scotland's economic position in the world. In 1983 the Committee on Primary Education (COPE) identified environmental studies as an area of the curriculum requiring a major initiative. Soon after the Primary Education Development Project (PEDP) was launched with the aim of producing support materials for the learning and teaching of environmental studies which, by this time, had expanded to include health education. A number of topic packs, advocating practical activity within a problem-solving approach were produced and trialled in schools. In 1987 COPE was disbanded and the PEDP was phased out in favour of the whole curriculum approach of the 5–14 Development Programme, under the management of the re-structured Scottish Consultative Council on the Curriculum (SCCC). The Review and Development Group (RDG 3) which was set up to develop guidelines for environmental studies had a membership of twenty-three and included representatives of all relevant areas of the curriculum, in both primary and secondary sectors. The resultant draft document, *Working Paper 13*, was issued for consultation by the The Scottish Office Education Department(SOED) in 1991, the last of the five curriulum area RDGs to report.

That it took so long to produce, longer than any other curriulum area, may well reflect the difficulties of achieving a consensus in such a diverse group. However, *Working Paper 13* also caused greater debate than any other RDG publication, primarily because it contained a foreword by the then Minister for Education in Scotland, Michael Forsyth. In this, he set out his views on education in general and environmental studies in particular. Much of his comment was at odds with what was regarded as 'good primary practice' by practitioners, with a rejection of integration and topic work, particularly in the later stages of primary school, an emphasis on a subject-centred approach and the suggestion that 'some form of specialism' in teaching should be introduced at the upper primary stages (p. iii).

The ensuing debate focused on this statement and the values which seemed to underpin it, diverting attention from the actual content of the guidelines. While there was some concern amongst secondary specialists that individual subject areas were inadequately represented, much of the argument from the primary sector echoed the philosophy of the 1965 Primary Memorandum. The final version of the environmental studies guidelines emerged in 1993, without further consultation and in a much altered form.

The three main components, with eight attainment outcomes, reflected 'the different forms of knowledge and ways of thinking within Science, Social Subjects and Technology' (SOED, 1993, p. 3). Five strands, arranged in age-related levels, identified the knowledge, skills and attitudes to be developed. Where *Working Paper 13* had attempted to indicate commonality amongst subject areas and promote integration through the terminology used, this was considerably reduced in the final version. The science component, for example, contained three attainment outcomes which, while not called such, were effectively biology, physics and chemistry. Guidelines on Health Education formed the fourth component and Information Technology (intended to be regarded as integral to the other four) completed the document. The allocation of time for Environmental Studies was set at 25 per cent.

A distinction has been made between environmental studies as the integration of a number of traditional subject areas, and environmental education, where the focus is on society's responsibility for the health of the environment and related concepts such as pollution and sustainable development. In the guidelines, environmental education is regarded as permeating the learning experiences of pupils, adding yet another dimension to environmental studies, and all pre-service primary teacher education courses are required to include some preparation for teaching in this area.

A METHODOLOGY FOR ENVIRONMENTAL STUDIES

In 1984, the Scottish Curriculum Development Services (SCDS) published *Learning and Teaching: The Environment and the Primary School* curriculum which encouraged teachers to consider the environment as 'something to learn from, learn about and be responsible to' (p. 10) where an active methodology and first hand experience of the environment were important. Three kinds of approach were advocated: the subject specific topic, where a single area of the curriculum was the main focus for learning; the general topic, involving a number of subject areas; and the provision of a series of planned learning steps for the direct teaching of specific skills and processes. In each, a 'theme' was identified and pursued through a range of activities, drawing on knowledge and skills from language, mathematics and the expressive arts.

The first of these, the general topic, has tended to be the most widely adopted approach. Topic studies can vary significantly in length and in the degree of integration with other subject areas. In nursery and early primary, 'mini-topics' provide contexts for the acquisition and development of concepts and skills across the curriculum. These tend to reflect events in the wider community, such as seasonal changes and festivals, or relate to the immediate experiences of the pupils, within their families or the school. There is evidence however of a move towards subject-specific topics, particularly in the upper stages of the primary school (Harlen, 1995).

Unfortunately topic studies, or 'projects', have tended to be used as a means of organising the curriculum so that a number of subject areas are 'covered' within them rather than the development of learning opportunities where links are natural and relevant. In addition, activities (things to do) rather than learning outcomes (things to learn) dominate the planning. *Some Aspects of Thematic Work in Primary Schools* (SCDS, 1987) illustrated this with the topic 'The Sea' where the Vikings were listed alongside the Romans (history), seashells (mathematics and art), the fishing industry (geography) and Fingal's Cave (music): high on coverage, low on coherence!

Traditionally Scottish primary teachers have tended to structure the school day so that English language and mathematics are tackled in the morning when the children are more likely to be alert and receptive, while the other curriculum areas are scheduled for the afternoon. Text books and published schemes of work within the core areas provide a degree of coherence and progression which is rarely present in the learning and teaching of other elements of the curriculum. These factors serve to militate against a strong, structured, integrated approach to environmental studies in the primary curriculum.

ASSESSING ENVIRONMENTAL STUDIES 5–14

Concern over the limited attention given to assessment by primary schools grew during the 1980s; one of the main criticisms of the PEDP materials was the lack of guidance on assessing progress. Since the introduction of the 5–14 Programme, teachers have been expected to undertake the assessment of pupils' progress in all areas of the curriculum, including environmental studies, and to report that progress in terms of the five Levels.

This is demanding on primary teachers who have tended in the past to rely mainly on their own judgement of the day-to-day progress of pupils in their classrooms as evidence of performance and progress. The 5–14 Programme demands a more structured approach and teachers are expected to assess conceptual understanding, practical and process skills and attitudes in areas of the curriculum where they lack confidence in teaching, far less assessment (Harlen, Holroyd and Byrne, 1993). As a result, there are important staff development implications if reports of pupil progress are to be reliable and valid.

General guidance on assessment is included in the 5–14 documents and the SCCC has produced materials designed to support teachers in implementing environmental studies. In addition, the SOEID's Assessment of Achievement Programme (AAP) provides advice on assessing science, as well as English language and mathematics. However the inclusion of science only in the national monitoring programme might be construed as an indication that it is of greater consequence than other aspects of environmental studies, again at variance with the integrated approach traditionally advocated.

DISCUSSION

Environmental Studies 5–14 occupies an uneasy position in the Scottish primary curriculum. On one hand it has been presented as a way to integrate areas of the curriculum in a way that reflects the child-centred approach cherished by many primary teachers. Now, whilst the environmental studies label has been retained, the guidelines are sub-divided such that science, social studies, health education and technology are set out independently, albeit with some indications of potential linkages. The introduction of time allocations for each curricular area and the increasing pressure to show performance and progress against national levels of expectations may mean that, in order to meet the demands of the Programme, teachers will similarly sub-divide their practice, disaggregating environmental studies into its constituent parts.

Since 1965 there has been considerable expansion of what constitutes environmental studies, putting pressure on (generalist) primary teachers to have a command of a greater number of knowledge bases. In addition, integrating these subjects to provide a coherent learning experience for pupils has been a challenge that only a small proportion of teachers has been judged as meeting effectively. Given that HMI were reporting difficulties with three subjects in 1980, the need to acquire even more and deeper knowledge of environmental studies let alone the management and organisational skills to provide integrated learning experiences, poses considerable challenges for teachers (and the preservice and inservice agencies).

The Primary Memorandum introduced environmental studies in the belief that an integrated approach held greater relevance for children and reflected the ways in which they learned, not in discrete subject areas but as a series of inter-related concepts, growing from what they already knew and could do. Such a view is in accordance with what a constructivist approach would advocate today. However, government concerns about performance levels and standards and the pressure to meet targets and progress through the 5–14 Levels, across an increasingly diverse curriculum, cannot be readily reconciled with such a philosophy.

REFERENCES

Harlen, W. (1995) *Interchange 35: Putting 5–14 in Place*, Edinburgh: SOEID.

Harlen, W., C. Holroyd and M. Byrne (1995) *Confidence and Understanding in Teaching Science and Technology in Primary Schools*, Edinburgh: SCRE.

SED (1965) *Primary Education in Scotland*, Edinburgh: SED.

SED (1980) *Learning and Teaching in Primary 4 and Primary 7*, Edinburgh: HMSO.

SCDS (1987) *Some Aspects of Thematic Work in Primary Schools*, Edinburgh: CCC.

SOED (1993) *Curriculum and Assessment in Scotland: National Guidelines: Environmental Studies 5–14*, Edinburgh: SOED.

36

Expressive Arts

Pam Robertson

The Expressive Arts in pre-school and primary education in Scotland currently comprise four elements: art and design, drama, music, and physical education. The history of these subjects within Scottish primary education is well documented: Maura Hanlon's summary (1993) offers the reader a detailed description of the historical pathway and philosophies. Today, however, teachers are asked to ensure a broad and balanced programme in these four areas, together allocated 15 per cent of the total curriculum time in primary, which offer pupils new ways of knowing – essentially in the four subject areas – and which can also support, stimulate and enhance learning in other curricular areas. The 5–14 Guidelines (1992) seek to rationalise planning and teaching expressive arts, and the document identifies three attainment outcomes which all four subject areas share. These are: using materials, techniques, skills and media; expressing feelings, ideas, thoughts and solutions; evaluating and appreciating. Additionally, each subject area has six strands (within the attainment outcomes) which further analyse or describe the activities in which pupils should participate; these are to do with investigation, the use and application of media and material concerned with each subject, creation and design, communication, and finally critical observation.

THE TENSIONS BETWEEN 'LEARNING IN' AND 'LEARNING THROUGH'

Prior to 5–14, hard-hitting statements were made regarding the quality and content of teaching in the arts and reinforcing the generally held views that art was used merely to illustrate the class topic, music and PE were too often performance/competition dominated and that drama was virtually non-existent. The 1980 publication *Learning and Teaching in Primary 4 and Primary 7* (Edinburgh: HMSO) contains evidence of sporadic and unsatisfactory practice in art and music, and to a lesser extent, physical education, whilst in 1986 the Consultative Committee on the Curriculum (CCC) dubbed drama the 'Cinderella' of the arts in its report *Education 10–14 in Scotland* (Edinburgh: CCC). In 1987 COPE produced *Some Aspects of Thematic Work in Primary Schools* stating, 'We certainly mean serious consideration of the expressive arts as tools for learning rather than victims of trivialisation' (p. 27), and exhorted class teachers to use the arts as powerful ways of learning.

Things did improve, and many teachers began to understand how to use the arts as tools for learning (see Jordanhill Storyline Packs: Rendell and Bell: 1980s); indeed many publications still contain material and ideas packaged to meet these needs. The bonding aesthetic principles were more in evidence, and class teachers tackled the idea of interlinking work in one arts subject with another. What was lacking, though, was the progressive skill development needed for each subject in order that the pupil was able to progress, and not merely to revisit the same skills, changing only with the topic title. Many class teachers argued – and still do – that because of their own lack of confidence and knowledge in the arts, they were unable to fulfil this requirement.

As exemplified in Her Majesty's Inspectors reports *Learning and Teaching in Primary 4 and Primary 7* (op. cit., p. 34) and *Visiting Teachers in Primary Schools* (Edinburgh: HMSO, 1993), Scotland has a history of regional arts specialists being employed to teach in primary schools. Subject specialisms have included the arts as described above, and additionally home economics, fabric craft, and knitting. Staff were employed according to local needs and enthusiasms, and were initially fairly autonomous regarding actual curriculum content. Additionally, most authorities also employed music instrumental instructors who taught small groups of pupils to play, for example, brass, string and woodwind instruments. These pupils then fed into the regional orchestra or ensemble network, affording regions shop-windows of musical excellence of which they were justly proud. Recent legislation regarding funding and employment arrangements for specialist staff has begun to change the picture; some headteachers are now in a position to choose the specialists they employ, and the terms under which they are employed. The results of these idiosyncratic arrangements mean that the quality and nature of children's education in the arts is increasingly dependent upon geographical location and specific school enthusiasms.

As all teachers continue to grapple with the demands of 5–14, what has become clear is that although the concept of the arts as a generic area is embraced in the Guidelines, the fact that the four subjects are treated individually has meant that a greater emphasis on learning in the subjects has taken place, and the concept of the arts as enabling processes, enhancing other aspects of learning – learning *through* – has been minimised. Class teachers look to the attainment targets to plan and assess, and to the specialists to plot progressive skills-based courses, whilst continuing to use the umbrella notion of the theme or topic to foster links in learning. A wealth of material has been generated to support teaching in the subject areas, for example: *Pathways to Action 5–14* for physical education (Dundee: SCCC, 1995); the CD Rom, *5–14 Music* (Scottish Council for Technology, 1995); *Drama 5–14: A Practical Guide to Classroom Drama* by Rankin (London: Hodder & Stoughton, 1995), and *A Policy for Art and Design* produced by Grampian Regional Council in the same year.

STATISTICAL EVIDENCE, RECENT TRENDS AND DEVELOPMENTS

Analysis of findings from a random sample survey of 450 classes in eighty-nine primary schools documented in the Audit Unit report, Standards and Quality in Scottish Schools (Edinburgh: SOED, 1993) showed that 15% of schools needed to give more emphasis to both music and drama; but that good attainment in expressive arts was seen in 80% of physical education lessons, 75% of art and design, 70% of music, and 45% of drama lessons. A recent trawl through a random sample of 99 extended HMI reports of primary schools from thirty regions in Scotland (dated from June 1995 to March 1997) revealed very similar statistics. Specifically, work in expressive arts was deemed satisfactory, good, or very good in the following subjects: 81% in physical education, 70% in music, 65% in art and design, and 48% in drama. Broadening the picture, recurring comments included: excellent opportunities for pupil self-expression in art and design, but greater rigour required for the upper age group; drama programmes needed greater cohesion across the school; music continued to be dominated by singing, and more opportunities for creative work still needed to be afforded to pupils; and that physical education is the most consistently well-developed area of the expressive arts with many teachers using assessment and recording procedures.

Impressions given by the same trawl reveal the following trends:

- teachers are addressing the demands of 5–14 and many pupils are being offered a wide variety of activities in the arts;
- the emphasis is shifting from the arts serving the topic to skill-based courses;
- a wide variation and combination of visiting specialist teachers are still being employed: certain regions, for example, Highland, and the Scottish Borders are still well served by visiting specialist teachers;
- where visiting teachers are still employed, then work by the pupils tends to be of a higher quality when collaboration with class teachers has taken place;
- schools without specialist help evidence class teachers planning their own programmes, some of which are of excellent quality, but programmes throughout the school lack cohesion and progression;
- the area which remains the least secure in all four areas is that of critical reflection.

Over the past fifteen years, the notion of artists' residencies in schools has taken off: Scotland has witnessed the growth of fully fledged education outreach programmes in many regions, with artists, sculptors, story-tellers, drama groups, members of orchestras (notably the Scottish Chamber Orchestra), composers, and dancers working in a variety of ways with a mixture of pupil-clientele. There is evidence (see McKinnon, 'Theatre at the Growing Stage', *Times Educational Supplement Scotland*, 15 August 1997) to suggest that headteachers are beginning to look outwith the regional authorities for help and guidance in the arts – possibly to replace the visiting specialists with independent artists or companies. However, the problems which arise from this situation are under current scrutiny by Eileen Crawford at Stirling University in an ongoing project, *The Arts Education Interface in Transition: Evaluating Quality* (1996-98). Clearly, whilst many experiences offered to pupils are entertaining, it is vital that the precious hours afforded to expressive arts activities on the curriculum are educationally viable, and are also of high standards in terms of artistic and aesthetic demands.

The area of assessment used to be anathema for the arts (the notion of subjective assessments being shunned for fear of upsetting the pupils or indeed inhibiting expression), but as arts professionals we are coming to terms with the objective view of assessment being an integral part of teaching, and are developing much clearer criteria in planning, teaching and assessing. For example, skill development in mixing and applying paint, using a hand puppet, keeping a steady beat, and choosing a pathway through which to move are beginning to be assessed objectively. Additionally, more formal assessment is now taking place regarding processes of working, perseverance, motivation, and levels of cooperation. Thus, pupil attitude and 'steps along the way' in the processes of working have begun to be noted, recorded, and progression charted.

ISSUES

Whilst much excellent work goes on in both nursery and primary contexts, there is a real dilemma confronting teachers with regard to expressive arts: spontaneity versus linear progression, enjoyment versus accountability. Take, for example, this advice from the Guidelines: 'A school's expressive arts policy should seek to further this curiosity and excitement in learning; to encourage this positive attitude to trying and the sheer enjoyment of doing' (p. 11); the sentence bubbles with the enthusiasm it is seeking to engender. Whilst teachers endeavour to retain this type of approach to the arts, many will, like their English colleagues in a recent study by Ross and Kamba (1997) 'see themselves as battling against a hard-nosed, market-led tendency to boil the aesthetic way of knowing into little nuggets of cognitive gains which can be ticked off for assessment.'

Here, in a nutshell, is a problem: in primary schools, for many years, the expressive arts area of the curriculum has provided challenges for children in the enjoyment, interaction, fulfilment and sharing experiences which were not overtly part of their learning elsewhere in school. Despite the principle throughout 5–14 of exhorting teachers to place emphasis on enjoyment, the analysis brought about by the documentation, whilst helping with articulation and progression, has had the effect of narrowing and suppressing experiences for children. This is partly due to the additional pressures on teachers generally brought about by increased accountability, and partly because of endeavours to meet curricular needs: there is a danger of sidelining pupil needs, and losing the spontaneity, risk-taking, and open-ended characteristics which feature in successful expressive arts activities.

The quality of learning and teaching which can take place in pre-school was well exemplified in the recent exhibition of work from Reggio Emilia, Italy, (*One Hundred Languages of Children*, Edinburgh: June 1997) which showed how far Scotland has to go to use the arts to develop learning powers in children. The emphasis placed on listening to children, which in turn leads to interacting and negotiating with them remains an area of growth. The arts in particular stimulate and offer the means through which these qualities may develop. Whilst pupils are being given good experiences in the expressive arts in pre-school and primary, aspects of listening and reflecting are taking second place to more active forms of learning. This mirrors the cluttered, fast-moving, video-productions supplied by much media coverage to the detriment of personal interaction and peer discussion, which pupils need in order to grow effectively in the sensitive dimension of aesthetic responding.

In essence the main issues associated with expressive arts in pre-school and primary may be summarised as follows:

- continuing tensions between teaching and learning in or through the subjects, and the use of the arts to support and bring learning to life in other curricular areas;
- the emergence of political and market pressures which encourage the skewing of the arts curriculum towards performance;
- the reliance upon an uneven and decreasing distribution of visiting specialists;
- an uneasy balance between performance and product and process and reflection;
- difficulty in ensuring that staff have confidence and competence in all the arts.

Finally, and perhaps most importantly, there is the problem of the erosion of the education of the senses and of the development of children's understanding of feeling.

REFERENCES

Committee on Primary Education (1987) *Some Aspects of Thematic Work*, Edinburgh: SCDS.
Hanlon, M. (1993) 5–14 and the Role of Expressive Arts: 1950–93, in *Scottish Educational Review*, 25.2 pp. 97–104.
Ross M. and M. Kamba (1997) *State of the Arts*, School of Education: University of Exeter.
SOED (1980) *Learning and Teaching in Primary 4 and Primary 7*, Edinburgh: HMSO.
SOED (1992) *National Guidelines: Expressive Arts 5–14*, Edinburgh: HMSO.

37

Mathematics

Effie Maclellan

CURRENT POLICY

The framework within which the mathematics curriculum is delivered and assessed in primary schools in Scotland is quite explicit. The Mathematics 5–14 Programme (SOED, 1991) describes the kinds of learning which are to be achieved and the aspects of mathematics which are to be covered. Furthermore, the guide suggests that mathematical experience should extend across the curriculum so that pupils understand the nature and purpose of mathematics. Although the guidance suggests that pupils should work on a wide range of mathematical concepts, following a fairly familiar line of progression, there is no curriculum prescription as such. Schools are free to structure and develop their own mathematics programmes so long as these foster meaningful and comprehensive mathematical learning. However, according to available evidence (Robertson et al., 1996), most primary schools deliver a curriculum which uses the commercial scheme, Heinemann Mathematics (SPMG, 1992) which, according to its authors, addresses the content and pedagogical requirements of the framework document. In the practice of adopting a commercial mathematics scheme, Scottish schools are conforming to a worldwide phenomenon.

INFLUENCES ON EVOLVING PRACTICE

The official curricular guidance offered is claimed to derive from the existing good practice which has allegedly developed during the last thirty years. Prior to 1965 the mathematics curriculum was exclusively concerned with practising and perfecting numerical computations. But in 1965 the Scottish Education Department recommended both a widening of the field of mathematics and an approach to mathematics which espoused the availability of concrete materials, calculators and computers and the provision of a wide variety of practical problem-solving contexts to support learning. Indeed such was the strength of the SED's (1965) conviction that mathematics is a means of understanding, and acting upon, the world that mathematics was classified not as a discrete curricular area but as one element of environmental studies.

The recommendation that mathematics should permeate the primary curriculum never really gained full acceptance. In 1980 Her Majesty's Inspectors noted that arithmetical computation dominated the mathematics curriculum with as much as seven hours per week being spent on pencil-and-paper exercises from textbooks (SED, 1980). This is far in excess of current recommendations which suggest that 15 per cent of the available time be spent on mathematics. Although nowadays schools do give proper attention to the wider aspects of mathematics, it can be inferred from the Inspectorate's independent audits that mathematics is principally delivered as a discrete subject with applications to other curricular areas, notably environmental studies. Perhaps the most sincere interpretation of the Memorandum's recommendations was to be found in the early stages where an infinite range of play situations was seen as potentially sustaining concepts such as sorting, matching, comparing and ordering shapes and objects. But even this informal, serendipitous approach to early mathematics is currently being formalised through Her Majesty's Inspectors of Schools specifying in *A Curriculum Framework for Children in their Pre-School Year* (Scottish Office: Edinburgh, 1997) what children might achieve, mathematically, in the year prior to the commencement of formal schooling. It is seen as reasonable, for example, that not only should children be able to sort, match and count objects (up to ten in number) but that they should, further, be able to apply these processes to mathematical problems.

Just as teachers found it hard to broaden the mathematics curriculum, so they found it hard to implement a differentiated approach to teaching. In 1980 HMI noted that many teachers were still not disposed to group methods and even those who were, had difficulty in catering for the different achievement levels within their class. More recently, in *Improving Mathematics Education 5–14*, HMI (1997) report that group methods are now used much more effectively but that the value of whole-class teaching should be recognised, as should the practice of setting pupils (since this would allow greater use of whole-class teaching). The renewed interest in whole-class teaching gives primacy, once more, to the benefits of direct instruction (such as clear explanation by the teacher, direction by the teacher as to what elements of the mathematical task to focus on); to the value of corporate engagement by the pupils (such as explaining to their peers their line of reasoning, observing alternative methods of solution); and to the essentially abstract nature of mathematics which is mastered through the construction of mental meaning. The return to a teacher-focused pedagogy can be seen as replacing, at least in part, the activity-based pedagogy which has dominated primary practice in recent years and may ameliorate some of the worst excesses of the progressivism advocated in the 1960s.

MATHEMATICAL PERFORMANCE

The intention to provide a meaningful mathematical curriculum and the considerable effort which goes into trying to realise this intention, yields disappointing results in terms of pupil performance. The recent study by Robertson et al. (1996) is one of a series of surveys conducted to describe national levels of attainment in Scottish schools. Large numbers of pupils are sampled at Primary 4, at Primary 7 and at Secondary 2. The data produced from the surveys are extensive and only one or two examples will be offered here. In relation to the basic algorithmic operations which are deemed (SOED, 1991) to be attainable by most pupils in Primary 4, 70% of the sample were accurate in their computation of addition and subtraction while 59% were accurate in multiplication and division. When these operations were applied to realistic situations, accurate performance dropped by about 10% in addition and subtraction and by 3% in multiplication and division. At Primary 7 about 70% of the sample were accurate in their computation of whole numbers though this fell to 49% when fractions of numbers were included in the assessment tasks. As compared with earlier AAP Surveys (Robertson et al., op. cit.) the 1994 Survey showed that there was no improvement in mathematical performance in Scottish primary schools and indeed in some respects performance was declining.

Poor, and possibly declining, performance is confirmed in the Third International Mathematics and Science Study (Scottish Council for Research in Education, 1997). The achievement of Primaries 4 and 5 pupils in relation to that of nine–year-olds in more than forty other countries is well below the international average, particularly in relation to number. However, the comparison is slightly unfair in that the Scottish pupils were the third youngest in the sample. (Children may start school in Scotland when they are 4 years of age, and so will not be nine years of age by Primary 4.) Since the performance gain between Primary 4 and Primary 5 by the Scottish pupils was above the average performance gain for all the other countries, it could be argued that inclusion of the younger children depressed the Scottish rankings. Despite the methodological problems of conducting international comparisons, however, the relatively poor performance of the Scottish pupils cannot be denied.

WHAT IS PROBLEMATIC

The reasons for this state of affairs are not altogether clear but the following two suggestions may offer insights. Firstly, although there is an expressed desire in all the seminal documents that pupils learn that mathematics has meaning, value and utility in the real world, pedagogical practices may militate against this. For example, one of the main tasks given to pupils to enable them to develop connections between arithmetical operations and the real world is the solving of word problems, such as 'Petrol costs 60.9 pence per litre. How much will 24.5 litres cost?' This kind of task is well established in the mathematics curriculum. But pupils have typically found word problems difficult, and indeed continue to do so (Robertson et al., op. cit.). Perusal of Heinemann Mathematics (SPMG, 1992) would suggest that word problems are provided merely for additional computational practice. It is assumed that if the appropriate computational skill has developed, that skill can be applied without difficulty. Despite evidence to the contrary, the role assigned to word problems continues to be limited and ignores the complex relationship which obtains between a hypothetical real world situation and its notational representation. Thus, in spite of good intentions, opportunities for learning that mathematics is both powerful and meaningful are not really being provided.

Secondly, in terms of curriculum content there would seem to be a simplistic and misleading assumption that increasingly more complex mathematical concepts are merely the sum of previous, simpler concepts. However, multiplication, for example, is not simply repeated addition. Although some aspects of addition form the basis of multiplication, it is unhelpful to treat the teaching of multiplication as a rather complicated form of addition because even the crudest understanding of multiplication involves appreciation of the sometimes constant and sometimes co-varying relationship between the elements in multiplicative situations. Equally, the introduction of fractions should involve pupils in a major adjustment of the meaning of number. Fractions are not merely ordered pairs of integers. Fractions are indeed numbers in which the numerator and denominator may represent some configuration of the whole (as in two thirds of the cake) but equally the numerator and denominator could represent different units (as in two dustbins for every three houses). Competence with these more sophisticated concepts is not a smooth continuation from earlier and simpler concepts but represents a fundamental change in understanding of what is meant by the concept of number. That performance in multiplication/division and fractions was poorer than performance in addition/subtraction and whole numbers (Robertson et al., op. cit.) should not be surprising since the children were being required to grapple with ideas which were inherently more abstract than previous learning had been. At the same time, the cognitive restructuring demanded by the more abstract learning assumes certain prerequisite skills and knowledge, which in reality may not exist (because the child, for example, is still grappling with basic ideas such as counting or place-value). The significance of moving from addition/subtraction to multiplication/ division and from moving from whole numbers to rational numbers is huge, but is largely unrecognised in the curriculum documents which advocate the provision of challenging and exciting mathematical experiences.

The task of enabling effective mathematical development is probably more difficult than has been hitherto acknowledged, although publications such as *Taking a Closer Look at Mathematics* (1993) and *Taking a Closer Look at Number* (1995) produced by SCRE tacitly acknowledge that mathematics is epistemologically complex. Learning to make sense of mathematics is a cognitively demanding and protracted process in which the teacher's sensitive and focused intervention is critical: on the one hand the conceptual and procedural knowledge of the mathematics curriculum is too complex to expect pupils to develop this knowledge spontaneously; on the other hand no teacher can deliver the knowledge pre-packaged in a completed form since pupils must construct their own knowledge. The demand which this places on Scottish primary teachers (many of whom will acknowledge their own understanding of mathematics to be naive) is enormous and forces us to consider what particular conception of mathematical knowledge is to underpin the mathematics curriculum. For more than thirty years the official documents have advocated breadth and eclecticism in mathematics ignoring, until very recently, the possibility that pupil performance may be disappointing because the curriculum is overloaded. Now, however, the government is explicitly supporting (through additional resources) the development and implementation of early intervention programmes on numeracy, and *Improving Mathematics Education 5–14* (HMI, Edinburgh, 1997) is suggesting that there be a much sharper focus on all pupils developing a robust concept of number. In these initiatives there is no suggestion that the achievement of pupils be limited. Indeed there is an expressed desire that a firm conceptual grasp of number, thoroughly developed from the earliest years, would allow increased and accelerated mathematical achievement. Such positive suggestions for improvement are most welcome.

REFERENCES

Robertson, I., R. Meechan, D. Clarke and J. Moffat (1996) *Assessment of Achievement Programme: Fourth Survey of Mathematics (1994)*, Glasgow: University of Strathclyde.

Scottish Council for Research in Education (1997) *Achievements of Primary 4 and Primary 5 Pupils in the Third International Mathematics and Science Study (TIMSS)*, Edinburgh: Scottish Office Education and Industry Department.

SED (1965) *Primary Education in Scotland, (The Primary Memorandum)* Edinburgh: Her Majesty's Stationery Office.

SED (1980) *Learning and Teaching in Primary 4 and Primary 7*, Edinburgh: Her Majesty's Stationery Office.

SOED (1991) *Curriculum and Assessment in Scotland: National Guidelines on Mathematics 5–14*, Edinburgh: Scottish Office Education Department.

Scottish Primary Mathematics Group (1992) *Heinemann Mathematics*, Oxford: Heinemann Educational.

38

Modern Languages

Lesley Low

THE REINTRODUCTION OF A MODERN LANGUAGE INTO SCOTTISH PRIMARY SCHOOLS

The reintroduction of a modern foreign language into Scottish primary schools as part of national education policy took place in September 1994 when the first cohort of 370 specially trained primary teachers began teaching a foreign language (FL) to P6 and P7 children within their schools. Four further cohorts of primary teachers have been trained thus far and it is anticipated that by the start of the 1998–9 school session, well over 3,500 primary teachers will have completed the training and 75 per cent of Scottish primary schools will have at least one teacher capable of introducing a FL into the curriculum of P6 and P7 children. The predominant primary FL is French although a minority of teachers have been trained in German, Spanish or Italian and the main pattern of FL teaching consists of twice-weekly blocks of 30–40 minutes.

This phased national introduction of modern languages in primary schools (MLPS) followed on from a successful pilot stage initiated in 1989 by the then Minister for Education, Michael Forsyth, as part of a package of measures to expand the teaching of FLs in Scotland's schools. The main impetus behind this political interest was the need to prepare for the European single market in 1992 by ensuring a pool of young people with good FL skills to help Scotland take advantage of this economic opportunity. The measures to achieve this, set out in January 1989 in the Scottish Office Circular 1187, included making a FL part of the curriculum of all secondary pupils up to the age of sixteen and piloting the introduction of MLPS.

The impetus then for the reintroduction of a FL into the curriculum of Scottish primary schools came from government. There had been no call for such a development from teachers in either the primary or secondary sectors, nor from the Scottish Consultative Council on the Curriculum (SCCC), Her Majesty's Inspectorate (HMI) or parents. The evaluations of the experiments in the 1960s and early 1970s had found no evidence of a lasting advantage to pupils who had begun their foreign language learning in primary (see Johnstone, 1994, pp. 43–44 for a review of these findings), but foreign languages had continued to be taught in the preparatory schools and primary departments of the independent sector and there was some informal teaching going on in a small number of primary schools in the form of after-school language clubs. However, a FL was not included in the 5–14 curriculum guidelines for primary and so was not part of the experience of mainstream primary pupils.

In setting up the twelve pilot projects (secondary schools and their associated primaries) HMI had two main priorities. The first was to opt for a language acquisition rather than a language awareness model. The aim was to give pupils an extra year or two in which to develop their foreign language competence rather than develop insights into the general patterns and structure of language or cultivate positive attitudes towards the future learning of another European language. The second priority was to avoid the mistakes which had led to the failure of the earlier experiments by ensuring an appropriate primary methodology and continuity of learning experience into secondary school (see Giovanazzi, 1992). The partnership model of secondary visiting FL teachers and primary class teachers which characterised the national pilot phase of MLPS and which was replicated in regional pilots across Strathclyde, Lothian and Fife seemed to fit these requirements more than adequately.

The most accessible pool of FL teachers was to be found in the modern languages departments of secondary schools and the Scottish Office Education and Industry Department (SOEID) funded one extra full-time equivalent teacher (FTE) in each of the twelve pilot secondary schools to enable secondary FL teachers to act as visiting teachers to their associated primary schools. This option was taken up by eleven of the twelve participating secondary schools but in the twelfth a primary specialist with a background in the FL was appointed as a tutor-trainer to the primary schools. The visiting teachers made twice-weekly visits of up to forty minutes to each P6 and P7 class. In all cases, the primary class teacher was present in order to advise on appropriate strategies and content for primary age pupils and be in a position to conduct follow-up work with the class in between the visits of the FL teacher. The secondary schools chose to use the FTE in a way which permitted several members of the modern languages department to act as visiting teachers to primary, thereby seeking to ensure a smooth transition from primary to secondary FL learning for pupils.

The approach to the piloting phase was a pragmatic one with no common theoretical framework across the schools. Each of the pilot projects was free to develop the MLPS programme within the parameters of the partnership model but, in the event, one particular approach emerged which quickly assumed the status of best practice. This approach became known as embedding and advocated the use of the context of the primary classroom and the areas of the primary curriculum as the basis for the FL content. Everyday routines such as taking the register and dinner numbers, doing mental arithmetic, talking about the date and the weather, and a range of class topics involving, for example, the body, healthy living, food, animals, clothes and sports, could be exploited as a means of introducing and reinforcing the FL (see Johnstone, 1994 for a fuller discussion of this approach). HMI and the two national development officers employed specifically to support the pilot projects produced a set of Guidelines for Teachers (November 1990, revised January 1992) which identified common areas of language and topics well suited to the embedding approach and advocated activity-based, non-linear teaching methods which would maximise pupil participation whilst making the target FL the predominant mode of communication in the classroom.

The national pilot for MLPS ran until the end of the school session 1994–5 and was subject to independent research in an evaluation funded by SOEID from 1991–5. In its first phase, researchers found evidence of an advantage in linguistic attainments at secondary school for pupils who had begun their FL learning in primary over those who had begun in secondary. This advantage was most evident in pronunciation, intonation, readiness to use communication strategies and ability to sustain patterns of initiation and response (see Low et al., 1993).

The huge popularity of the MLPS pilot with pupils, parents, teachers and national and regional officers, and the positive picture of pupil attainments and enjoyment emerging from the early stages of the national evaluation no doubt led to the then Conservative government's 1992 election manifesto pledge to extend the teaching of a FL to all Scottish primary schools. In January 1993, the Minister for Education, Lord James Douglas Hamilton, duly announced a consultation process on training arrangements which would enable primary class teachers to develop the necessary linguistic skills to introduce a FL into the primary curriculum. The pilot model for MLPS could not be replicated on a national scale because of the high staffing costs and the insufficient supply of secondary teachers of modern languages available to work in both sectors. The main justification given for the changes was, however, an educational one according to Staff Inspector for Modern Languages, J. Boyes, and Strathclyde Regional Council Director of Education, F. Pignatelli, who argued in *Scottish CILT Info 1: Modern Foreign Languages in Primary Schools* (Scottish CILT, Stirling, 1993) that the primary class teacher was the best-placed person to deliver the embedded approach to MLPS, given appropriate training and support.

The authors of the national training programme for MLPS had been very involved in the pilot phase of the initiative and drew extensively on their experience to compile a list of ten competences which primary teachers would need to acquire. Emphasis was placed on gaining a confident command of key areas such as the sound system and basic structures of a particular FL, core language (personal, descriptive and affective) and language for the classroom (including daily routine, organising activities), as well as the language required to deliver some basic art, craft, home economics, science, technology, drama and PE activities through the medium of the FL, and an appropriate methodology for young FL learners including games, songs and story telling. The primary teacher would also develop the ability to use a FL dictionary appropriately, and to write labels and captions accurately and acquire an awareness of the culture and background of the country whose language was being taught (MLPS – The Training Programme, 1993). These areas were covered in the twenty-seven days of the training programme which took place over one year in groups of up to twenty primary teachers based in each local authority and led by a teacher-trainer and native speaker of the FL.

ISSUES OF CONCERN

The national training programme has proved popular with primary teachers and so far demand for places has outstripped supply. The original estimate of four phases to achieve one trained teacher per primary school has proved inadequate, not least because some regions chose to use their allocation of places to provide two trained teachers for every three P6 or P7 classes in the larger primaries. Even the fifth phase of training is unlikely to achieve national coverage because of the natural wastage of primary teachers moving on or out of post. The staging of the training programme over twelve months means it cannot respond quickly to plug such gaps, putting in jeopardy the whole FL provision within a particular school.

Two main principles guided access to places on the national training programme – that it should be undertaken voluntarily by the teachers concerned and that, wherever possible, it should be done on a cluster basis, that is, one teacher from each of the associated primaries of a particular secondary school, the latter as a means of guaranteeing maximum impact on the receiving secondary school. However, the excess demand for places on the training courses has masked an underlying problem of individual schools and clusters where teachers have no wish to become involved. Given such resistence, national coverage of MLPS may only be achieved once a FL has become an integral rather than a voluntary part of the pre-service training of all primary teachers.

There is also the question of continuing support for the primary teacher once trained, for although a wealth of teaching and other support materials may be available to primary FL teachers, such as the *Advice to Schools* handbook (SOEID, 1996), they can often feel isolated. The decision to continue with a competence model for MLPS means that primary teachers are dependent for their FL support on colleagues largely operating outside their own sector. Such colleagues are not as readily available as in the pilot phase. The two part-time national development officers have to cover the whole of Scotland; the post of modern languages adviser has all but disappeared since local government re-organisation; and secondary colleagues are no longer directly involved in MLPS. Under such circumstances it is easy for the trained primary teachers to begin to lose confidence and interest in teaching the FL.

There are management problems associated with having only one trained teacher per school. As well as teaching her or his own class, the primary FL teacher may have to 'drop-in' on the classes of other colleagues and this may have implications for class cover and time-tabling arrangements. The drop-in arrangement also has an effect on the management of time within the busy P6/P7 curriculum as embedding the FL into the daily activities of the class is not feasible. Two thirty-minute sessions a week can represent a significant chunk of time with no clear indication from SOEID about from which aspect of the curriculum it should be drawn. In other European countries, the time for MLPS tends to come from the language dimension of the curriculum, but this particular form of 'embedding' has not been a feature of the Scottish development at either phase (see Hirschfeld, Boffey, King and Cooke in Low ed., 1996 for a discussion of the above issues).

SOEID has argued the need to wait and see how the primary-led model for MLPS develops before attempting to crystallise it in the form of revised 5–14 Guidelines for modern languages. However, there are moves at national and local authority level to begin to evaluate the success of the new model, particularly given the large sums of public money which have been invested in the training programme. There is a paradox here in that formalising the place of the FL in the primary curriculum through, for example, inspection or the assessment of pupils' linguistic attainments, is perceived by teachers and trainers alike as potentially damaging, particularly to the confidence of primary FL teachers, who are still getting to grips with a new skill and extra responsibility. Yet to leave the FL outside those formal arrangements may leave it vulnerable both in terms of the time devoted to it within the primary curriculum and any future demands for accountability from central and local government.

REFERENCES

Giovanazzi, A. (1992) *Foreign Languages in Primary Schools, Sense or Sensibility – The Organisational Imperatives*, paper given to the British Council Triangle Conference, January 1992: Paris.

Johnstone, R. (1984) *Teaching Modern Languages at Primary School, Approaches and Implications*, Edinburgh: SCRE.

Low, L. et al. (1993) *Evaluating Foreign Languages in Primary Schools*, Stirling: Scottish CILT.

Low, L (ed.) (1996) *MLPS in Scotland; Practice and Prospects, Proceedings of Two Conferences on Modern Languages in Primary and Early Secondary Education*, Stirling: Scottish CILT.

Scottish Office Education and Industry Department (1993) *Modern Languages in the Primary School, The Training Programme*, Glasgow: Strathclyde University, Jordanhill Campus.

Scottish Office Education and Industry Department (1996) *Modern Languages in the Primary School, Advice for Schools 1996*, Edinburgh: SOEID.

39

Personal and Social Education

David Betteridge

> There are few things which I can desire to do . . . which do not depend upon the
> active co-operation of others. We need one another to be ourselves.
>
> John Macmurray, *Persons in Relation*, (London: Faber, 1961)

STATUS, DOCUMENTS AND RECOMMENDATIONS

Personal and Social Education occupies an important position in current thinking about the
aims and curriculum of Scottish schools. It had considerable status and publicity given to it
when, in 1993, the Scottish Office Education Department (SOED) issued a set of national
guidelines devoted specifically to it (SOED, 1993a), and when, in 1995, the Scottish
Consultative Council on the Curriculum (SCCC) published its aptly titled *The Heart of the
Matter* (SCCC, 1995), reviewing and reflecting on emerging policies in this core aspect of
education.

Looking back, there is an interesting history to tell. MacBeath (1988) usefully documents
the variety of banners and labels and initiatives under which Personal and Social Education
was treated in Scotland in the decades prior to the launching of the SOED's guidelines. He
identified the Advisory Council on Education's report on *Secondary Education* (1947) as
being particularly significant and eloquent. An essential purpose of all schools, according to
this often cited but under-implemented report, is the provision of a setting conducive to
young people's 'progress towards social selfhood'. These last two words nicely encapsulate a
notion that is central to a form of personalist philosophy running, sometimes subterra-
neously, through Scottish policy debates. No dualism, no contradiction between the
individual and society is seen. Rather, as *The Heart of the Matter* restates and updates it:

> An understanding of what caring for self . . . means . . . is an essential pre-requisite for an
> understanding of how to care for others . . . [Our] well-being as individuals and as a society
> depends on our living interdependently . . . [Human] beings are social animals. (p. 4)

The SOED's (1993b) strategic outline of aims and curriculum, *The Structure and Balance
of the Curriculum 5–14*, also gave prominence to personal and social matters, but,
interestingly, did not count them as constituting one of its five main areas for curriculum
planning. Rather, the personal and social development of pupils was seen as being a
fundamental aim of education to which work in the framework areas of Language,
Mathematics, Environmental Studies, the Expressive Arts, and Religious and Moral

Education should contribute. Not only the content of these five areas, including values and an understanding of the pupils' place in the wider world, but the very experience of learning were deemed to be a proper vehicle for promoting development.

Originally, when the Research and Development Group charged with the remit for Religious and Moral Education was set up, it was intended that it should incorporate aspects of social education in its work. However, it rapidly became apparent that the complexity of the field could not effectively be addressed in this way. A case was made to the Scottish Office for a separate set of guidelines for Personal and Social Development, and this was agreed. The fact that the resulting guidelines were among the last to be published thus reflects the manner in which the status of Personal and Social Education came to be recognised and the time required to give attention to it.

The guidelines differ from those provided in other curriculum areas in that they do not use an A to E format for the grading of levels of targets. Rather they propose a framework of three broad developmental stages as an aid to understanding how children progress in four necessarily overlapping areas, viz. self-awareness, self-esteem, inter-personal relationships, and independence/ inter-dependence. The active, educative role that schools need to adopt if their pupils' progress is to be fostered is emphasised. Significantly, the guidelines seek to establish a timetable niche for the teaching of personal and social work against any possible superficiality or marginalisation that the *Structure and Balance* document might encourage in the unwary or uncommitted. So, whilst reiterating and endorsing the point that 'personal and social development is embedded in all learning', the guidelines urge the management team of a school to ensure, not only time for cross-curricular approaches, but also for what it calls the special focus approach. By 'special focus approach' is meant concentrated work on 'issues which pupils have identified and raised as being important, or which others have identified as being important for the pupils' (SOED, 1993a, p. 3).

Besides the special focus and cross-curricular approaches there is a third that the guidelines identify, namely the creation of 'a warm, caring, supportive atmosphere in which all individuals, pupils, staff and parents, know that they are valued' – the whole school approach. Other sources than the guidelines brought the whole school approach to the attention of schools. In place of the guidelines' 'atmosphere', the term 'ethos' began to gain currency, becoming a focus of concern in Her Majesty's Inspectors of Schools reports and in their Audit Unit's set of performance indicators for schools' self-evaluation, *How Good is Our School?* (Edinburgh: SOED, 1996). This document, as well as teasing out educative measures aimed directly at the pastoral care of pupils and the development of certain personal and social skills, lists eleven 'themes' for attention, including a sense of identity and pride in the school, equality and fairness, a welcoming environment, good discipline, pupil and staff morale, high expectations and the use of praise.

PRACTICES, ACHIEVEMENTS AND DEVELOPMENTS

It is unlikely that any two schools arrive at the same set of practices in Personal and Social Education, even given an equal commitment to the sorts of recommendations reviewed above. Schools can only progress from the contingencies of their present positions, 'taking account', as the 5–14 guidelines acknowledge, 'of local circumstances, priorities and resources' (SOED, 1993a, p. ix). Further, as perusal of HM Inspectors of Schools reports suggests, school staffs' own views vary, leading to the giving of different degrees and kinds of priorities. Thus some schools will favour the special focus approach referred to in the guidelines, whereas others include a cross-curricular approach; and in special focus work it may be the case that some teachers choose to pay more attention to the negative and dysfunctional – to 'problems' – than to the positive. In a context of bullying and drug-taking, racism and sexism, and the physical, sexual and emotional abuse of children, such attention is, of course, readily justified, though still running the risk of imbalance.

A growing body of useful resources is available for special focus work. A Scottish Consultative Council on the Curriculum (SCCC) catalogue provides an impressively long list of books, packs, posters, videos, etc. and of contact addresses (Ashton, 1996). One of the best known and widely used sources of support is TACADE (The Advisory Council on Alcohol and Drug Education). It is important to note, however, that the SCCC and TACADE go far beyond the focusing on single issues. They also address, and urge schools to address, broader, deeper concerns of rights and responsibilities, caring and sharing, community and communication, self-esteem, feelings, friendships and values, as, for example, in TACADE's *Skills for the Primary School Child: Promoting the Protection of Children* (1990).

Thus enabled, teachers can increasingly turn to whole school and cross-curricular approaches, seeking to find in their schools' day-to-day activities appropriate learning contexts for their pupils' personal and social development. It is a helpful feature of the SOED's guidelines that a variety of learning contexts are identified and their appropriacy to particular aspects of development clearly shown (SOED, 1993a, pp. 8–15). Even 'being a messenger' or 'handing out resources' has its value as a learning context, along with the more ambitious 'negotiating school rules' or 'developing enterprise initiatives'.

The most successful practice appears to be achieved when a school's development plan and its routine curriculum planning devices guarantee a specific time allocation for Personal and Social Education, when rich and relevant resources are available, and when regular evaluations are undertaken by staff, including the headteacher, to ensure that whole school, cross-curricular, and special focus approaches are all employed in a judicious mix. Further, as Luby (1993) argues in his study *Democracy and the Classroom* (M.Phil thesis, University of Strathclyde), the ethos of a school needs to be such that it fosters and protects a measure of self-direction on the part of pupils. Teachers, too, if they are to extend the scope of their work, and thus encourage their pupils to do the same, benefit from a supportive school ethos, and, where such exists, from a network of friendly and critical fellow practitioners. One network showing some of the attributes described by Luby is the Ethos Network coordinated from Moray House Institute of Education, Edinburgh.

Two initiatives to be noted as constituting practical attempts by an increasing number of schools to involve all of a school's community in its Personal and Social Education are partnership with parents and circle time. The first entails possibly far-reaching clusters of activities, pastoral, recreational and/or curricular, in which parents have a role. The second, circle time, is a particular form of group work designed to optimise the involvement of pupils. Derived originally from work by Moreno, Lewin, and others, circle time provides emotional space in which pupils can express and explore their thoughts and feelings freely, and, crucially, can be listened to. A detailed account of how one school adapted circle time to meet a wide range of purposes is given by Campbell and Dominy in *Sharing Good Practice*, edited by Lloyd and Munn (Edinburgh: Moray House Publications, 1987). Here the authors describe how circle time evolved from being a tactic used initially to tackle particular social difficulties to 'a key plank in our general personal and social development programme'.

SHORTFALLS, DIFFICULTIES AND CHALLENGE

The extent to which schools can approach a full programme of Personal and Social Education depends on their capacity to address a number of daunting difficulties. With mounting demands from government and public for schools to be accountable in particular ways, the temptation is to give more and more attention to the more formal parts of the five 'framework' areas of the curriculum, and in particular to the more readily tested aspects of Language and Mathematics. If single-discipline programmes of study gain in status and time-allocation, then it follows that cross-curricular work, including work that incorporates a personal and social dimension, correspondingly suffers. Primary schools seeking to develop flexibility can build on and extend the best practice in the nursery sector, where aims relating to personal and social development have long been a prime and explicit focus, and where all aspects of a day's activities are regarded as a fit means for delivering them.

Questions concerning values constitute a further set of difficulties to be addressed. In a survey of teachers' perceptions of values, a Scottish Council for Research in Education team concluded that 'there is not an established discourse for values education' and that many teachers spend little time with their pupils considering 'the processes involved in acquiring knowledge and understanding and reaching a personal values stance' (J. Powney, 1995, p. ix). It also appeared that there was a tendency to concentrate on those values that 'encourage pupils' development as social beings, especially so as to fit in to the social context of the school'. Promoting debate and discussion addressed to long-term issues and values appeared to be less common.

It is clear that there is a long way for schools to go before they meet the full challenge of Personal and Social Education. One necessary aspect of their task is to undertake the sort of values clarification called for by Powney, and sketched out by the SCCC in its *Values in Education* (Dundee: SCCC, 1991). Work done under the aegis of the Gordon Cook Foundation also proves useful here. After such clarification, there remains the matter of appraising and reforming the approaches to teaching and learning that are employed.

The so-called hidden curriculum of schools, often far from hidden as far as pupils are concerned, is the subject of a discussion paper of considerable interest and optimism published under the title of *Teaching for Effective Learning* by the SCCC in 1996. Three questions from the many posed in the paper will serve to illustrate the ambition of its challenge to Scottish Education:

- How often do I encourage learners to think for themselves and to try out new ideas?
- In what ways do I demonstrate to young people that I respect and trust them?
- How do we promote, recognise and value the achievement of all young people? (p. 33)

A further, more pessimistic, question remains to be put: Is Scottish, and British, society at large not so anxious, unequal and authoritarian that it massively limits schools' ability to realise the aims of Personal and Social Education?

The author would like to acknowledge the value of discussions with Lynn Bennett and Jim Callery, Tormusk Primary School, Glasgow; Mary Doyle, Headteacher, St Bride's Primary School, Bothwell; Bryce Hartshorn and Tony Luby, University of Paisley; and Margaret McGhie, Assistant Director, SCCC.

REFERENCES

Ashton, T. (1996) *5–14 Catalogue: Personal and Social Development*, Dundee: Scottish Consultative Council on the Curriculum.

MacBeath, J. E. C. (1988*) Personal and Social Education*, Edinburgh: Scottish Academic Press.

Powney, J. et al. (1995) *Understanding Values in the Primary School*, Edinburgh: Scottish Council for Research in Education.

Scottish Consultative Council on the Curriculum (1995) *The Heart of the Matter: Education for Personal and Social Development*, Dundee: SCCC.

SOED (1993a) *Personal and Social Development 5–14*, Edinburgh: SOED.

SOED (1993b) *The Structure and Balance of the Curriculum 5–14*, Edinburgh: SOED.

40

Religious and Moral Education

James C. Conroy

> . . . if at the Church they would give us some Ale,
> And a pleasant fire, our souls to regale;
> We'd sing and we'd pray all the live-long day,
> Nor ever once wish from the church to stray.
> William Blake, *Songs of Innocence*

The authors of the Curriculum and Assessment guidelines for Religious and Moral Education in Scottish Primary schools (SOED, 1992) might well have penned Blake's words for him in so far as they wished to retain a healthy attachment to traditional forms of Christianity while recognising that socially, culturally and religiously many of their students have already 'left' for the Ale-house.

This chapter attempts to delineate the evolution, purposes, nature and distinctive qualities of religious and moral education in the Scottish primary school as well as comment on some of the complexities and most evident contradictions etched into the national framework.

HISTORICAL INFLUENCES

The 'modern' era for religious education in Scotland can be traced back to the Scottish Education Department report (SED, 1972) on Moral and Religious Education in Scottish Schools commissioned by the then Secretary of State for Scotland. Subsequently known as the Millar Report it both diagnosed the state of religious education then available and offered a prescription for future development. Prior to this, provision in Scottish schools was based on notional assent to the legislation first enacted in the Education (Scotland) Act of 1872, and re-affirmed in subsequent Acts and Memoranda between 1918 and 1980, which required that religious education be the only compulsory subject on the curriculum. Unlike its English progenitor it did not preclude religious education from being taught in accordance with a particular denominational formulary. Thus an inspectoral report of 1878 quoted in the SED, 1943 *Memorandum with Regard to the Provision made for Religious Instruction in the Schools in Scotland*, could state that 'The public schools are to all intents and purposes denominational schools. Public and Presbyterian are practically interchangeable terms' (p. 7). Despite subsequent Education Acts, Religious Education remained effectively denominational up to and beyond the publication of the Millar Report. Catholic schools and 'non-denominational' schools taught Religious Instruction in accordance with the tenets of Catholicism and Presbyterianism respectively.

The Millar Report, on non-denominational education, indicated that the vast majority of Religious Instruction at the beginning of the 1970's continued to focus on biblical knowledge. This practice largely ignored the emerging insights of scholars such as Ronald Goldman and Ninian Smart. Goldman applied the insights of developmental psychology to the study of religious attitudes in the young and realised that they were frequently taught from texts which they were certain to misconstrue because of their stage of growth. Smart wished to promote a 'scientific' study of religion which relied on the student being a dispassionate observer rather than a participant in the religious experience and discourse.

At the time of the report 78 per cent of schools indicated that they never or rarely used any text other than the Bible in their religious education lessons. Little or no provision was made for any religious education which was not scriptural and not Christian. Paralleling developments in England, the Millar Report opted to promote a more developmental and child-centred approach. It also distinguished the task of the school from that of the home and other (church) institutions in children's religious development. Nevertheless religious education was to continue to serve a social function with a continuing emphasis on the fundamental and formative place of bible stories in the growing moral life of children. Thus it came about that religious education in public primary schools was no longer to be seen as 'denominational'. It was, instead, to reflect and promote a generally ethical form of Christianity as the basis of the public good. Indeed the explicit wedding of moral and religious education by the curriculum planners in Scotland marked out a continuing distinction between the Scottish and English approaches to curriculum development. This may simply have been a consequence of the more distinctively religious character of Scottish civic life as shown in G. Davie's work *Religion in Britain since 1945* (Oxford: Blackwell, 1994).

Religious education in Roman Catholic Primary schools during the 1970s came under the influence of a Belgian based journal, *Lumen Vitae*. While the focus remained on preparation for participation in the sacramental life of the Catholic church, changes mediated through *Lumen Vitae* were largely concerned to improve methodology and not to re-shape aims. The aim of Catholic religious education remained unequivocally to nurture pupils as believing members of the community. New methods, paralleling those evident in non-denominational schools, were developed to ensure that the proclamation of the 'word of God' would be relevant to the pupils' life experiences. Further, the new and important distinction adumbrated in the Millar Report between the school on the one hand and the parish and home on the other was not replicated in the thought patterns of Catholic primary educators. Rather, school-based nurture was seen as a fulfilment of one's obligations to the church. Syllabuses were generated locally at diocesan level and approved by the bishop so that significant variation in the quality of provision was to be seen across Scotland. One syllabus produced by the diocese of Paisley demonstrated the anxiety felt by many in the Catholic community that the 'modern', less doctrinally focused approaches were leading to confusion. To counteract this the syllabus juxtaposed the 'new modern text book complete with work books . . . [with] a compendium of doctrine extracted from the Catechism of Christian Doctrine' (Diocese of Paisley, undated).

THE MODERN ERA

Despite the clear distinctions in approach between denominational (largely Roman Catholic) and non-denominational schools there was Roman Catholic representation on the new Scottish Central Committee on Religious Education (SCCORE) established in 1974. Although the systems were, and remain, discrete there has been more traffic in ideas between the two than is often acknowledged. The Catholic sector has learned much from developments in the professional management of religious education while the non-denominational sector has begun to rediscover the place of the interior life and narrative in the study of religion which has always been maintained in Catholic approaches to religious education. The first SCCORE publication (HMSO, 1978) promulgated a view that the common ground across all sectors should be that whatever was provided should be 'educational'. This merely served to suppress an issue which was to re-emerge in the early 1990s with the advent of the National guidelines for 5–14 Religious and Moral Education (SOED, 1992). The issue was and remains centred on a disagreement as to what is to count as 'educational'.

For non-denominational education, the view which emerged from SCCORE Bulletin One was that the Bible should continue to hold a significant place but should be approached developmentally. The example offered explored three ways of examining the life of David. For the early stages the focus was to be on David's becoming King, for the middle years pupils were deemed to be interested in David's warrior/guerrilla phase and pupils in the upper phase might wish to discuss why David refused to kill Saul. While such an approach begs as many questions as it answers, taken with the more general recognition of the importance of rooting conceptual and religious development in children's growing yet actual experience, the methods advocated were similar to those which might be seen anywhere in the curriculum.

A number of major national courses on religious education held in the late 1970s and early 1980s helped establish the practical force of the 'scientific' study of religion. The approach in primary schools, as seen in a variety of local authority policy guidelines and materials, was to bring about understanding and not commitment, yet the undertow was unequivocally Christian with the, still compulsory, requirement for religious observance being characterised as an opportunity for the school to affirm its Christian identity. Thus a confusion of purpose remained, however subliminally.

Parallel developments in Catholic education saw the replacement of diocesan syllabuses by a nationally approved programme published by the Irish ecclessial publishers, Veritas. This programme, *Leading Our Children to God*, by Melody et al. (Dublin: Veritas, 1987) was more systematic and extensive than anything heretofore used in Scottish Catholic education. Veritas too deployed the insights of developmental psychology in constructing the material. It was also consistent with the catechetical principles centred on revelation (God's gift) and faith (the human response) laid down in the documents of the Second Vatican Council. The developmental element was manifest in the choice of annual themes which covered Life, Friendship, Community, Growth, Building/Creating, Communicating. These themes were used at each stage to communicate Christian revelation experientially, doctrinally, morally and sacramentally.

On 1 January 1983 Religious Education was opened to inspection across all sectors of Scottish education, though in Roman Catholic schools the inspection could only deal with structural and systemic issues and could not refer to the content of what was being taught. This major change to religious education resulted in a number of insightful and studied reports by both Her Majesty's Inspectors of Schools and local education authorities on the state of religious education during the 1980s and 1990s. The first of these (SED, 1986) indicated a general lack of awareness of the issues raised by the Millar Report and SCCORE Bulletin One even among a majority of headteachers. Where religious education did occur, which was by no means universal despite its statutory position, the most frequently used method and content were represented by whole class teaching of bible stories; the other staple being 'moral' lessons. The introduction of Veritas as the nationally approved syllabus appeared to offer Roman Catholic schools a more coherent approach to religious education, but here too the report found that all was not as it should be since many were using the Veritas programme as a basis for a more traditional catechetical approach which failed to reflect the spirit or structure of the original. In neither sector was there seen to be any significant attempt to address the teaching of faiths other than Christianity.

In the years following the publication of the 1986 report, local authorities provided guidance and materials for primary schools which generally laid stress on an implicit religious approach through the study of life, living and growing in the early years. A more systematic and explicit approach was taken in materials developed for the upper primary school with the emphasis remaining on Christianity though some material was being developed by local authority advisers for the study of other faiths, mainly Judaism and Islam.

The 1991 SED consultative paper, *Curriculum and Assessment in Scotland: A Policy for 90s: Religious and Moral Education* showed that staff development had received significant attention from local authority advisory services and that a majority of schools had policies on religious education and observance which derived from parent documents developed by the local authority. Nevertheless confusion as to purposes and practices remained with considerable variation in the quality of planning and monitoring of religious education. 'Religious education was commonly seen as an area of difficulty and uncertainty' (p. 15).

CURRENT ISSUES

The development of the national guidelines in religious and moral education (SOED, 1992) marked a further decisive moment in the development of the subject in the primary school. In the debate leading to the publication of the draft guidelines much had been made of the need to grapple with religious education as process rather than product as well as with the need to develop a more rigorously 'scientific' approach which demanded no personal commitment. Yet in the end the attainment targets and programmes of study were heavily content laden. The guidelines indicated, for the first time, that 10 per cent of class time should be devoted to religious education. They also structured the attainment outcomes in terms of knowledge and understanding, skills and attitudes in relation to Christianity, Other World Religions and Personal Search. Thus Other World Religions takes a central place in the primary curriculum for the first time and general dispositions take the place of personal commitment. Given the importance attached to the role of religious education in the personal development of pupils in the guidelines, assessment emerged as a crucial issue. Some suggested that it should provide opportunities for reporting on the individual's growth in matters moral and religious; others perceived this to be both impossible and inappropriate. For now the latter view holds sway though the discussion continues.

Inherent contradictions re-emerge since it is not at all clear what such general dispositions might look like; pupils are invited, as a central aim of the programme to develop their own beliefs and attitudes, moral values and practices while at the same time appreciate common values. Carr (1995) and others suggest that it is difficult to hold that there are common values to which presumably everyone should subscribe and at the same time suggest that all values are a matter of personal clarification and preference. The explicit alignment of moral and religious education, the continued emphasis on Christianity, the preserving of religious observance all point to a culture which knows not its own mind.

On the publication of the guidelines it was generally thought that the Roman Catholic sector, which had been represented on the original research and development group, would accept the guidelines as being applicable to Catholic schools. However, in June 1992 the Catholic Education Commission rejected the SOED guidelines and the Catholic Church in collaboration with the Scottish Office Education Department drafted a parallel document (SOED/CEC, 1994) which reflected the structure of the original while replacing the aims and content with others more consistent with the wishes of the Scottish Catholic educational community. Other World Religions remained in the Catholic document but with a reduced emphasis. Nevertheless the inclusion of the study of other faiths represented a significant development in Catholic primary religious education. A further important difference was the omission of moral from the title of the Roman Catholic document since it was unequivocally held that the moral life could not be divorced from ultimate beliefs.

The more focused approach offered by the guidelines has resulted in primary religious education dealing with some of those areas in the study of religion which were traditionally the domain of the secondary phase, especially in the teaching of other faiths. This may say something about educators' perceptions of fundamental changes in the developmental patterns of our pupils as well as changes in our wider political and social culture. *A Gift to The Child*, developed by Hull et al. at the University of Birmingham (Hemmel Hempstead: Simon and Schuster, 1991) is indicative of a contemporary approach which draws on story, song and meditation from different religious traditions as a basis for an affective as well as a cognitive approach to religious education. Utilising artefacts, videos and visits to places of worship, religious education also provides a place where other's festivals and celebrations are both re-enacted and understood.

CONCLUSION

Many confusions and contradictions remain in religious and moral education. Some of the most important which have yet to be resolved include the indecision about the purpose of moral education. Is it to introduce students to the 'good life' or to promote good behaviour? Related to this is the insecurity about whether or not a moral education programme should or should not be attached to a religious education programme. Further, despite differences from English models Scottish religious education continues to draw heavily not only from the same insights but also from its structures. There remains an opaqueness about whether or not the aims are religious or educational and confusion as to what extent the stance adopted makes any difference. All these and the other issues raised here represent the contrary forces manifest in Blake's poem which make the task of the primary school religious educator in Scotland a challenging one indeed.

REFERENCES

Carr, D. (1995) 5–14: A Philosophical Critique, in G. Kirk and R. Glaister (eds), *5–14: Scotland's National Curriculum*, Edinburgh: Scottish Academic Press.

Scottish Central Committee on Religious Education (1978) *Bulletin 1: A Curricular Approach to Religious Education*, Edinburgh: HMSO.

SED (1972) *Moral and Religious Education in Scottish Schools*, Edinburgh: HMSO.

SED (1986) *Learning and Teaching in Religious Education: An Interim Report by Her Majesty's Inspectors of Schools*, Edinburgh: HMSO.

SOED (1992) *Curriculum and Assessment in Scotland: National Guidelines: Religious and Moral Education: 5–14*, Edinburgh: SOED.

SOED/Scottish Catholic Education Commission (1994) *Religious Education: 5–14 Roman Catholic Schools*, Edinburgh: SOED.

VII

Secondary Education: Organisation and Management

41

Organisation and Management in the Secondary School: Chosen or Imposed?

Andrew Bruce

In a recent article, Dick Staite, one of Scotland's foremost headteachers, describes the complexity of school management thus:

> the running of a school is a big business with a large formalised bureaucracy. The bureaucracy itself, the planning and resourcing, requires considerable management energy, management systems, and management focus. Imagine yourself as manager of a company, fixedly focused to task, resisting all distractions for the quality of the 'good'. Then imagine yourself as a school manager surrounded by pupils with their endless capacity and ingenuity for distraction. (GTC Link, No. 27, 1997)

In the course of the last thirty years the nature and complexity of secondary school management has changed radically, a fact reflected both by the practice of headship itself and by the impact of the major educational initiatives of the last three decades.

BUREAUCRATIC ORIGINS AND THE UNASSAILABLE POWER OF THE HEAD

In Scotland the 1970s were characterised by a multitude of reports, by thinking and reflection, by discourse on the nature of learning. Bullock, Munn, Dunning, Pack; substantial reports which stimulated dialogue and debate. How vividly the present writer recalls a Dunbartonshire headteacher addressing his colleagues from behind an astonishing pile of reports most of which he had received in the course of one session alone. His symbolic presentation induced considerable fun and laughter, for the seventies was still very much the era of the autonomous 'heidie', the man (women were a rarity) who could poke fun at the planners and centralists secure in the knowledge that he could return to his school and do very much as he wished.

The 1980s on the other hand saw the beginning of changes which are still being felt today. These changes were to affect both the nature of the curriculum and the style of school management. The eighties were characterised by problems of financial stringency, falling rolls, unemployment and increasing central political direction. Following a period of bitter industrial action which often placed headteachers in an uncomfortable middle position between teachers and employers, thinking and talking began to give way to radical centralised planning typified by *16–18s in Scotland: An Action Plan*, the Technical and Vocational Initiative (TVEI), and the introduction of School Boards. In different ways, each of these initiatives started to challenge the traditional role of headteachers heralding as it did both a more centralist role for educational change and a more accountable role for headteachers themselves.

It is important to recognise that the history of management in general, and school management in particular, is comparatively brief. The organisation of the Scottish secondary school in the seventies was based on a simple hierarchical model little different from the type of structure which had supported the British Army or the Indian Civil Service from the time of their inception. The key personnel in the structure were Head, Depute, and Principal Teachers, the group of subject specialist teachers who carried responsibility for managing departments. Heads taught, dealt with pupil problems and administered the school timetable. Deputes (there was for some time in some places one male and one female, the latter often called Lady Adviser) dealt with discipline and routine administration. Principal Teachers (often autonomous power barons) implemented the curriculum very much as they pleased. In fact, the impetus for creative, radical change often came from this key 'middle management' group rather than from senior managers.

Management style itself attracted little reflection and virtually no research. Belief in the unassailable power of the head was largely unquestioned, as was 'top-down' decision making. There were few explicit policies, few meetings of any sort (staff meetings took place once a year on the first day of the session); the commitment was to continuity, stability, maintenance of the 'status quo'. Significantly, it is hard to find the word 'leader' anywhere in the literature of school management in the seventies and early eighties. Bureaucratic structures headed by autonomous managers led to the evolution of two types of head-teacher, those (the vast majority) who saw their role as perpetuating the status quo, and a very few who pursued radically new approaches to management and learning.

In purely structural terms, the 1970s did however begin to anticipate later changes largely because of a significant growth in the size and complexity of the bureaucracy. The introduction of a whole new middle management tier came with the creation of the Guidance structure in Scottish schools, followed quickly by the introduction of new posts of Assistant Headteacher. However, while the bureaucracy increased in size, management style hardly changed. The new posts were simply absorbed into the existing structures. In fact it became the norm for secondary schools to have more promoted than unpromoted teachers!

With hindsight, it is surprising that the style of management which prevailed remained almost unchallenged, a reflection perhaps on the absence of significant research interest. This was after all an era of dramatic change in political and educational thinking. The introduction of the six year comprehensive school was a defining moment. For many younger teachers the comprehensive ideal was about valuing all young people equally, not stigmatising them at age twelve as first or second class citizens; it was about enhancing the self image, promoting the learning potential of all students. It was about dignity and respect. How strange then that this commitment to a new, more egalitarian system for young learners was not reflected in a similar shift with regard to teachers themselves and their role in the management of schools. Even in schools like Summerhill where the new radical educational ideals were most publicly revered there was little evidence of genuinely open management.

Senge describes what can be accepted as the prevailing headteacher role of the late seventies and early eighties thus:

our traditional view of leaders – as special people who set the direction, make the key decisions, and energise the troops – are deeply rooted in an individualistic and nonsytemic world view. Especially in the West, leaders are heroes – great men (and occasionally women) who 'rise to the fore' in time of crises. Our prevailing leadership myths are still captured by the image of the captain of the cavalry leading the charge to rescue the white settlers from the attacking Indians. So long as such myths prevail they reinforce a focus on short-term events and charismatic heroes rather than on systemic forces and collective learning. At its heart, the traditional view of leadership is based on assumptions of people's powerlessness, their lack of personal vision and inability to master the forces of change, deficits which can be remedied only by a few great leaders. (*The Fifth Discipline*, New York: Random House, 1990)

There is little evidence of challenge to Senge's view though, with some courage, HM Inspectors for Schools did suggest that the emphasis on organisation should shift 'to positive management of the curriculum . . . a major reappraisal of the roles and contributions of principal teachers (subject) is required' (SED, 1988). This treatise on Secondary School Management explored the wish to restrict 'traditional independence' by arguing for wholescale creation of 'whole-school policies covering all the areas of development that can be foreseen', an ambitious undertaking which was to absorb the energy of senior management teams for some years to come before it was accepted that paper policies did not necessarily reflect the reality in the institution!

NEW CONCEPTS: LEADERSHIP AND CONSULTATIVE, PARTICIPATIVE MANAGEMENT

All this was about to change. In his 1989 SERA Lecture, David Hargreaves presented a persuasive account of the growth of the school effectiveness movement and the impact this had on school management as well as on the local authorities to whom school managers were accountable. Hargreaves (1990) identified three publications which set the tone for what was to follow.

The first, in 1977, was written by Shirley Williams and called *Education in Schools: a Consultative Document*. In this paper Williams says;

> schools must have aims against which to judge the effectiveness of their work and hence the kinds of improvement that they may have to make from time to time . . . [there is a need] for schools to demonstrate their accountability to the society which they serve . . . LEAs need to be able to assess the relative performance of their schools.

Here, succinctly stated, are the themes which were to become significant in the late 1980s and which, by the nineties, were dominant. The status quo was being challenged by the politicians.

The second influential publication was Rutter's famous *Fifteen Thousand Hours* (1979). This very ambitious research established the highly significant fact that schools did in fact make a difference and that improvement was possible, issues which have come to dominate educational research, local and national politics, and school management practice and philosophy.

The third publication which set the agenda was a report by HM Inspectors of Schools called *Effective Secondary Schools* (1988). Starting with a chapter called 'The Need for Evaluation' this report linked school evaluation with effective learning and teaching – and directly with the management of schools. Nailing its colours to the mast the report states 'leadership and ethos are important' and, while conceding that leadership is to an extent a personal quality, 'certain common features can be identified in the practices of many good school leaders'. The reports records the following imposing list of features:

- consulting staff on significant issues while retaining the ultimate responsibility for decisions
- being personally involved in the school and its community
- maintaining a high and purposeful profile in the school
- setting up good lines of communication within the school
- being open to personal approaches from pupils and staff
- launching initiatives, or encouraging appropriate initiatives suggested by others, and monitoring progress
- establishing a team based approach to management
- creating appropriate expectations
- monitoring teaching practice
- following individual pupils, or groups of pupils, to sample their everyday experiences
- attending staff working groups.

Elsewhere in the report there is reference to the importance of delegation, consultation, participation, teamwork, the importance of trust, support, ethos, planning for development!

Publication of this seminal report was accompanied by the launch in the same year of the SOED Management Training Initiative for Headteachers (MTHT). The intention? 'To address the main issues of management.' The first of nine new modular training programmes for headteachers in Scotland was *Principles of Management*, the main message of which was clear; following *Effective Secondary Schools*, school management should be underpinned by a management style which was consultative and participative, a style which recognised that the most important asset which schools possessed was the people who worked in them. This was a management style which sat comfortably (though the connection was seldom made, or even recognised – was it even understood?) with the new drive to introduce Total Quality Management (TQM), following the work of Deming and others, in many of the most effective business companies worldwide.

While Head of the Lothian Region Management Development Unit the present writer was charged with the responsibility for presenting the SOED training programme to headteachers. Staff involved devoted considerable energy to blending the impact of the modules with the international perspectives gleaned from the work of such as Mortimore (in England) and Fullan (in Canada). The aim was to promote this style of management and to stress the importance of building a culture to initiate and support change; of involving all staff in establishing values, reviewing strengths and weaknesses; of developing staff; and of strategic partnership between LEAs and schools (see Bruce and Kerr in Knowles and Wight, eds, 1995).

PERFORMANCE MANAGEMENT AND A NEW SCHIZOPHRENIA

However, unremitting political pressure quickly changed the message. The reports which soon followed promoted a distinctly different approach to management. In 1992 came the establishment of the Scottish Office Education Industry Department Audit Unit, a unit which was to be responsible for a wide range of reports over the next six years. This was also the year in which the same Department published a report which was to affect the role of the headteacher radically; *Devolved School Management: Guidelines for Progress*. This report announced the delegation of around 85 per cent of the total budget for the secondary school directly to headteachers, thus adding a very substantial new responsibility for financial planning and accounting to an already large and varied responsibility. Unfortunately, the new workload brought with it few additional resources of any significance, nor have the implications of this change been subject to sufficient analysis or research.

More was to come; *The Education of Able Pupils* (1993), *The Role of School Development Plans in Managing School Effectiveness* (1993), *Towards Quality Assurance in Scottish Schools* (1996), *Improving Achievement in Scottish Schools* (1996) to name but a few. Never in the history of Scottish education have so many reports been generated and directed at headteachers. What was it all for? The agenda was, at least, clear. Headteachers were accountable. Schools had to improve. Audit, planning, quality, efficiency, effectiveness were the key concepts. In retrospect, it is instructive to reflect on the impact of all these reports on a cadre of headteachers whose first experience of management had largely been under the traditional top-down, heroic model of management, many of whom had just undertaken training courses promoting consultative, participative management. It is also instructive to reflect on this 'educational schizophrenia' which, almost simultaneously, promoted differing philosophies of management.

Effective Secondary Schools and *Principles of Management* advocated a style of management which was consultative and participative. To cope with this, headteachers did develop new structures of management even while continuing to operate within the old bureaucratic system. Senior Management Teams consisting of Head, Depute and Assistant Headteachers met at least weekly to discuss policy, plan development and deal with routine administration. Guidance Teams were created which took responsibility for pupils' pastoral and curricular development. Development Planning Teams were appointed to involve staff in the planning process and to consult effectively. Finance Teams and Staff Development Teams were formed with broad staff representation to improve participation. While power, in the form of ultimate responsibility for decision making, still largely resided with headteachers, the early nineties saw a clear and deliberate move to involve staff, teachers and support staff – and sometimes students and parents – in the overall management of the school. There was, of course, no more time available within the teachers' contract for those committees to operate with the result that pressure to meet often began to undermine the good intentions of enlightened managers.

But while heads were being urged to devote time to a consultative, participative style of management the new push for accountability finally arrived with a vengeance. Fairley and Paterson (1995) describe what they saw as the pressure to introduce a 'new managerialism', a concept which in their view has just as great an impact as changes in the curriculum. They see the new managerialism as focusing on value for money, performance indicators, a shift in emphasis from accountability to voters towards accountability to users and, ultimately, to the denial that professional experience is needed to manage a school at all; in other words the skills of management are generic and apply equally to a bank, a department store or a school. The influence of the Management Charter Initiative (MCI) on educational management training was a new, if peripheral, feature of this trend, efforts to introduce educational management competences proving elusive.

There is no doubt that performance management is now being demanded both by politicians and employers. A style which successive Conservative governments sought to impose is now being evangelically pursued by New Labour replete with the regalia of performance indicators, target setting, and the enhanced role of parents in managing schools. The impetus for this approach to management is overtly and unashamedly economic. New Labour's view is that education is essentially to do with what Adam Curle described as 'competitive materialism'.

'Scots Schools Damned Again' screamed a headline in *Scotland on Sunday* (7 December 1997) in a story which claimed that 'Scotland and the rest of the UK are trailing behind most of our 29 industrial competitors around the world'. Tables of comparative statistics from the Organisation of Economic Cooperation and Development (OECD) showed Scotland far down the international league tables for the sciences, mathematics, and for the amount of homework done. Ironically, little media or government attention was devoted to the equally shocking fact that Scotland was placed 22 out of 24 when it came to the percentage of GDP spent on education.

Faced with a sustained centralist drive towards the new managerialism many head-teachers find themselves struggling with managerial schizophrenia, a fact reflected in the relatively small numbers of applicants coming forward for such posts. Apart from the scale and intensity of the many changes forced through from the late 1980s onwards, very few people have taken time to recognise that the management style currently demanded by the new managerialism conflicts with the style demanded by *Effective Secondary Schools* and recommended by international researchers such as Fullan. Present government statements stress the importance of 'partnership' while demanding that 'rates of improvement over the most recent three years be doubled in each target area.' Headteachers are literally being asked to face in different directions simultaneously. Staite in GTC Link No. 27 (1997) alludes to this when he says, 'the sheer scale of change in recent years however makes for real contradictions'. He argues that school improvement takes time, that the running of a school 'is a big business . . . the bureaucracy itself, the planning and resourcing, requires considerable management energy, management systems and management focus'. Echoing Fullan, he reflects on the fact that those who develop the change policies are seldom those who actually deliver them, and are thus deprived of genuine understanding of the nature of the institution. Elsewhere, Williams writes of the LEA inspector having 'an obligation to myself and to the school I work with to really examine the worth of my own wisdom, opinions, directives and advice . . . Do I really understand the situation, the culture, the aspirations, the needs and demands of the school I am working with? This approach demands sensitivity, uncertainty and humility' (*The Adviser*, March 1993).

There is no place for sensitivity, uncertainty and humility in the new managerialism. Nor do these qualities abound amongst those controlling, directing and assuring policy. The result is that many headteachers simply survive instead of practising the fearlessness, vision and enterprise which real improvement demands.

VALUES AND CHANGE MANAGEMENT

While Fairley and Paterson succinctly and compellingly demolish the 'new managerialism', there are, however, two other major weaknesses in the present drive to impose performance management on schools which deserve attention.

The first is that performance management completely ignores the value base on which any organisation must depend. And second, performance management pays scant attention to the need to be aware of, and informed about, the impact which change itself imposes on school organisation.

Bruce (1995) describes how the best companies throughout the world recognise the need to define a clear set of core spiritual values which enable organisations to perform in a superior way and to endure over time. Pascale and Athos (in *The Art of Japanese Management*, Harmondsworth: Penguin, 1986) argue that to be effective British companies have to look hard at their ethical and spiritual fabric, and not just at their systems and structures. The message is reinforced by Peter Drucker talking of the qualities required of leaders in the future:

> every one of the education builders – from Confucius to Arnold of Rugby – knew that there is no education without moral values. To slough off moral values, as modern educators propose to do, only means that education conveys the wrong values. It conveys indifference, irresponsibility, cynicism. (*The New Reality*, London: Mandarin, 1990)

While the Scottish Consultative Council on the Curriculum (SCCC) recognised this crucial fact with the publication in 1991 of a short paper *Values in Education*, little importance has been paid to the the need for a clear and unequivocal value base overtly and explicitly stated, as the bedrock for managing our schools. Cormack concluded his talk to the Lothian Quality Forum by stating:

> what we see in Scotland is not the result of a deficient skill base, what we see is the result of self-centred values rather than other-centred values. Our values have set manager against manager, department against department, customer against supplier and management against union. (Address to the Lothian Quality Forum, September 1990).

He could have added school against school, school against local authority. Performance management is the latest 'fad' which will fail until collectively and deliberately teachers, headteachers, parents, local and national government together address the importance of values in a market led economy and not just the economic implications of success or failure.

Unfortunately, there is little evidence of serious research into the effects of change on school management and organisations. Judith Brearley, an organisational consultant who has carried out a great deal of work with health professionals and, unusually, some schools, is an exception. In an unpublished article, 'The Impact of Change on Organisations, their Staff and the People they Serve', she states:

> Sudden fundamental change is the hardest to cope with, because it does not allow for adjustment, mourning for what has gone before or preparation for what is next. For what reasons is the change being made? If the values underpinning it are perceived to be alien, then both the anxiety and the resistance will be greater.

With rare insight Brearley goes on to argue that the manner in which change is perceived to be implemented significantly affects those experiencing the demands of the change:

> on a wider scale, we can see how those features of central government policy which are experienced as persecutory or devaluing tend to be contagious, somehow being replicated at local government levels or even closer to home in one's own management approach, despite the best intentions to behave in a more benign way.

It is my view that until clear and explicit attention is paid to the importance of values and the need to understand and manage change, to search for and discover afresh 'structures of meaning', school managers will continue to struggle to come to terms with the impatient and relentless demands of the centralists.

MANAGEMENT FOR THE MILLENNIUM: NEW LABOUR PHILOSOPHY

In the approach to the twenty-first century the impact of the SOEID Audit Unit on Scottish schools has been immense. Working in the habitual Scottish manner of directing change with the cooperation of a carefully selected education and business élite (an approach increasingly attacked by the Scottish media as 'consensual' and therefore, by implication, weak) the Audit Unit has made a very strong public commitment to the concept of school self-evaluation. The publication *How Good Is Our School?* (SOEID, 1996) sets out a very clear description of a system of improvement based on self-evaluation using performance indicators very similar to those used by HM Inspectors of Schools in the course of school inspection. The theory is sound; inviting each school to assess strengths and weaknesses recognises that schools are unique and improvement strategies, likewise, will be unique to meet the circumstances of the school. Equally, inviting the school to assess and review provides strong motivation for improvement. The school can create its own agenda for change within the national framework.

Unfortunately school self-evaluation sits uneasily with the new managerialism and with central demand for change. Despite the stated philosophy the hidden New Labour agenda of school management, expressed by a member of an authority Quality Assurance team, is quite different; 'Schools have had plenty of chances to change and haven't taken them. Now they are going to be forced to change whether they like it or not.' Publications such as *Achievement for All, Standards and Quality in Scottish Schools 1992–95*, and *Achieving Success in S1/2* all present insightful evidence from school inspection of problems within the present first two years of secondary education without offering anything but generalised solutions. There is scant analysis of the real problems which do exist in the first two years; an overcrowded curriculum, fragmented teaching, lack of detailed knowledge of the learning styles of individual young people, lack of effective differentiation, inadequate guidance time, a historical focus on S3 to 6, and so on. Nor is there even any explanation for the 'significant strengths' which are acknowledged, 'including generally good teaching, a positive ethos and an improving trend in the achievement of qualifications at S4 and beyond' (SOEID, *Achieving Success in S1/2*, HMSO, 1995).

New Labour's flagship report further confuses the picture. *Setting Targets – Raising Standards in Schools* (SOEID, 1998) sweeps away the old 'league tables' approach to comparison of school examination performance, offering instead a framework for setting 'simple, clearly expressed and quantifiable targets' which take account of 'a school's current performance and, where appropriate, the performance of schools with similar characteristics.' This approach, however, presents school managers with a number of problems relating to development planning, the concept of school improvement, the nature of language and with simple honesty.

In contradiction to the universally stated belief in the importance of the development plan, Jenkins advises headteachers 'don't put too much trust in planning.' Jenkins argues that account must be taken of the contingency nature of planning and the need for flexibility, of the fact that the development plan will be limited and will undergo change. He states; 'the difficulty of rational planning is in making assumptions about the future – assumptions which can be undermined by external factors that foul up the planning process'

(*Getting It Right*, London: Blackwell, 1991). *Setting Targets* exemplifies this dilemma neatly by, at one and the same time, advocating the importance of planning while imposing change to existing plans. It is a feature of the new managerialism and the new centralist, interventionist approach that development plans are being stripped of individuality and reduced to a universal, standard content.

The problem with this is that schools are uniquely different and that real improvement, as distinct from superficial, does take time. There is a great deal of research evidence to support this. Anning (in P. Easen, ed. *Making School-Centred INSET Work*, Open University, 1985) describes the way in which many headteachers move post after about seven years when the real, as opposed to the superficial, problems of managing the school come into sharp focus. The work of Mortimore and the Quality in Education team in Scotland lends support to this. There is a very real danger that introducing the target setting framework will in fact divert energy and attention from the need to continue to explore the nature of genuine, lasting improvement in schools. A school which honestly and courageously assesses its strengths and weaknesses as recommended in *How Good Is Our School?* and then prepares an agenda for improvement has real chance of success. There is an ironic, and hopefully unintended, danger that the current nature and scale of central directives will put such improvement at risk.

The language of *Target Setting* is instructive. Much of the report is written in the familiar Scottish philosophical style. There has been 'wide consultation'. Scotland has 'a highly professional and committed teaching force.' 'The framework builds on existing approaches to self-evaluation and development planning.' 'Improvement will be achieved only if all those with an interest in raising standards work together in partnership.' 'Schools are at the centre of the drive to raise standards.' The impression given is of open, seamless and uncontroversial evolution. The reality is somewhat different. There is very little open debate about, or analysis of, the implications of this initiative. Few education authorities, themselves recent victims of severe financial reduction, are in any position to 'support the plans schools make for improvement.' There is no statement which shows what can and will be done to help those schools which apparently fail to achieve the targets set. There is no mention of resources. There is no recognition of what Staite described as the daily unpredictability of school management. In short, there is no real honesty about the complexity of management, of improvement and the need to continue to search for long-term solutions.

MORE CHOICE, LESS IMPOSITION: COLLABORATION FOR REAL CHANGE

There is no doubt that changes are necessary. The statistical evidence about achievement and underfunding are deplorable. But improvement will not come about through the imposition of performance management on headteachers nor through continuing emphasis on short-termism 'rather than on systemic forces and collective learning'. At the very time when less choice and more imposition is the centralist credo, the reverse is precisely what is required.

Hand-in-hand with recognition of the vital importance of values and the need to understand and manage change there is an absolutely imperative need to address the outdated nature of the secondary school bureaucratic structure; a fact which the Teacher Unions also must accept. The present structure is top-heavy and inappropriate. Senior managers need quality time to do their jobs (private sector business managers are aghast at the realisation that an Assistant Headteacher is required to spend half the week teaching and marking and the other managing guidance, or staff development or the 5–14 Curriculum). Headteachers require appropriate quality support to assist with the management of devolved responsibilities, especially in the areas of building management and financial management.

As the authors of the National Commission on Education have pointed out, this is a vital debate at a defining moment in our understanding of the nature of schools and learning in the not too distant future:

> in time the organisation of schooling is likely to be more diffuse, with the boundaries between schools, the workplace, the community, and continuing education and training providers becoming much less marked than at present. Even so, schools will remain the central focus for young people's education, though increasingly working in partnership with other educational institutions, as well as with a range of organisations and people outside the school. (*Learning to Succeed*, London: Heinemann, 1993)

In a book of extraordinary vision, Drucker argues that 'new knowledge is no longer obtained from within the disciplines around which teaching, learning and research have been organised in the nineteenth and twentieth centuries.' (*The New Reality*, London: Mandarin, 1990). Scotland needs a bold, not half-hearted, vision of the school of the future based on the work of the National Commission, a vision which takes real account of the nature of learning and the potential of technology to free young people to learn in their own time and at their own pace while also freeing teachers to direct their teaching in a far more individualised and meaningful manner. Now is the time to weld a very real partnership between schools, parents, local and national government and research institutions to address these real issues in a deliberate, sustained and collaborative manner. New Labour's discussion paper *Parents As Partners* (SOEID, 1998) offers a quite unrealistic and unfocused scatter of proposals for substantially increasing the power of School Boards where much more detailed focus and development of the concept of 'personal targets for each pupil' could be so much more productive.

It is precisely in areas such as this that genuine collaboration, innovation and research can be so valuable. There is considerable evidence that imposing change leads to disharmony, stress, anxiety, lack of control, wastage, absenteeism and creative avoidance. Collaborative, shared change on the other hand produces commitment, drive, energy, creativity, responsibility, dignity and continuous improvement. Fullan and others have argued that the key role of the headteacher is not in implementing innovations but in transforming the culture of the school. Handy rightly says that 'schools need to become learning organisations, places where change is an opportunity, where people grow where they work.' This will not be achieved by imposition but by genuine and meaningful openness and collaboration. As top companies know, those who lead must model the behaviour which they wish to see throughout the organisation. It is no surprise that in a training manual on the Process of Management, Hewlett Packard introduced the programme with the following statement:

> The key to making all this work is trust. You can't lead without trust. The technical part is trivial. You're dealing with human beings. The key question is, are you wishing to invest in building trust? Are you willing to explain yourself – who and what you are – your values?

It is time to recognise the power of the collective will to develop and sustain a vision of the future which will involve school managers meaningfully in a genuine collaborative, leadership role rather than as treating them cynically as ciphers required to do what they are told.

REFERENCES

Bruce, A. (1995) Quality and Values: an Account of a Journey in A. Rodger and J. Squires, eds, *A Handbook for School Values Education*, Aberdeen: Northern College.

Bruce, A. and J. Kerr (1995) Developing Management Development in I. Knowles and J. Wight, eds, *High Hopes or Hemlock? Assuring Quality in Schools*, Edinburgh: Moray House Institute.

Fairley, J. and L. Paterson (1995) Charter for Democrats, Article in Platform series, *The Times Educational Supplement (Scotland)*.

Hargreaves, D. (1990) Making Schools More Effective: the Challenge to Policy, Practice and Research, in *Scottish Educational Review*, vol. 22, no. 1.

SED (1988) *Learning and Teaching in Secondary Schools: School Management*, Edinburgh: HMSO.

SOEID (1996) *How Good Is Our School? Self-evaluation using Performance Indicators*, Edinburgh: HMSO.

42

Ethos and Discipline in the Secondary School

Pamela Munn

Imagine the following scene. An English teacher is meeting her class of thirty fourteen-year-olds for the first time. It is August 1997 and the start of a new school year. She begins: 'Hello, everyone. My name is Mrs Brown and I'm really looking forward to getting to know you all. I've heard great things about you from Mr Black, about the play you wrote and produced last year and about the terrific poetry you can write. Now we are all going to need a bit of time to get to know each other, and it is important that we work well together. So the first thing we need to decide is the four or five rules that we are all going to stick to. Can you divide into five groups of six and we'll spend ten minutes deciding what these are.'

This vignette contains several elements that are known to contribute to positive relationships and hence to good discipline. A key feature is Mrs Brown's high expectations of the standard of work she will encounter – 'I have heard great things about you.' Equally important is her pleasure at meeting the class for the first time. She is looking forward to getting to know her pupils – signalling that they are people as well as pupils. Finally, she wants to involve class members in decision-making about classroom rules. Their decisions about rewards and sanctions would no doubt follow. Mrs Brown's approach is based on the well founded belief that if she transmits her interest in and liking for her pupils, involves them in decision-making and takes their views seriously, she is likely to motivate them to work hard and to behave well. While the scene is idealised, in that few teachers would embark on group work with a class they didn't know, it nevertheless is not too far removed from the practice of many teachers. There has been a growing realisation of the importance of feelings of self-esteem in pupils if they are to be motivated to learn and there has been an increasing awareness of the influence of the so-called hidden curriculum on pupils' (and on teachers') learning and behaviour. Thus school customs, routines and physical environment send messages, intentionally or not, about who and what is valued. Encouraging teachers to explore these features and to gather views about them from pupils, parents and members of the local community is a recent feature of Scottish schools. The days when pupil-teacher relationships were characterised by intimidation and fear through the use of the belt and other degrading punishments are gradually disappearing.

This chapter begins with a brief consideration of the importance of school ethos and discipline before going on to describe discipline in Scottish secondary schools today. It outlines the main sanctions and punishments used by schools but also draws attention to efforts to promote positive discipline, locating these in an increasing understanding of the ways schools themselves influence pupils' behaviour for good or ill. It concludes on an optimistic note but warns against the stigmatising of pupils displaying troubled or troublesome behaviour and their segregation from mainstream schools.

THE IMPORTANCE OF DISCIPLINE

School discipline is generally regarded as having two related purposes. One purpose is a means to an end, to provide a necessary condition for learning. Thus good order in the classroom is often seen as a necessary, though not a sufficient, condition for learning to take place. Children cannot concentrate on the academic curriculum if there are, for example, unacceptable levels of noise, rowdiness or verbal or physical aggression in the classroom. A second purpose is that of socialising pupils to behave in certain ways. In this sense discipline is an end in itself, an outcome of schooling. Its purpose is to instil in pupils values such as honesty, respect and diligence. Furthermore, such values can be seen in the notion of subject disciplines, which have their own rules of evidence, of what counts as knowledge and so on. The inter-relatedness of the ideas of socialisation into generally accepted values, academic learning and of conforming to rules of behaviour is captured by Bertrand Russell's comment that 'the valuable intellectual discipline of close research into a limited topic . . . needs the discipline of hard work and early rising'.

A description of school discipline then, tells us a great deal about a society's values as well as about the behaviour of young people and their teachers. The little that can be gleaned about discipline in eighteenth-, nineteenth- and even twentieth-century Scotland, for example, paints a rather depressing picture. The main features seem to be an emphasis on conformity, typified by the widespread use of rote learning by pupils and payment by results for teachers; respect for authority through intimidation of pupils by corporal punishment and of teachers through inspection of their competence by local presbyteries and the Inspectorate; and moral rectitude as evidenced by the teaching of the catechism, the Bible as the main text in use and the emphasis on the religious orthodoxy of teachers.

Thus discipline can be seen as instilling values not only about acceptable social behaviour but about the very nature of learning. Teachers were the embodiment of both moral virtue and of academic learning. Their job was to transmit these accepted virtues and bodies of knowledge to the next generation, who were expected to absorb them unquestioningly or be punished.

DISCIPLINE IN SCHOOLS TODAY

A number of key developments in contemporary Scottish schooling provide the context in which discipline should be understood. First, the raising of the school leaving age to sixteen in 1972–3 (ROSLA) stimulated a concern for truancy and indiscipline, leading to the setting up of a national committee on these issues. It was recognised that part of the discipline and attendance 'problem' related to the inadequacy of curricular and assessment provision for those now obliged to stay on at school. Indeed there was a more general concern about the curriculum for 14 to 16 year olds which resulted in a radical overhaul of curriculum and assessment for this age range and the replacement of O Grade by Standard Grade in the 1980s. This reform, followed by the 5–14 programme introduced between 1987 and 1993, provided a common curriculum and assessment for all. Secondly, corporal punishment was abolished in state schools in the United Kingdom as a result of a legal action. Thirdly, the conceptualisation, categorisation and treatment of children seen as having special educational needs changed. There was encouragement for these children, including those who might be classified as having social, emotional and behavioural difficulties, to be educated in mainstream schools rather than in separate specialist provision. Thus teachers in contemporary Scotland are teaching a wider range of pupils than has been the norm. Fourthly, legislation was enacted giving local authorities power to exclude children from school on very general grounds.

The Pack Report of 1977 on truancy and indiscipline was unable to report on the extent and nature of indiscipline in schools because of the slippery concept of indiscipline and confined itself to the itemising of contexts likely to create problems for teachers. However, concern about indiscipline continued to be voiced by teacher unions, the press and others, and in 1987 the Scottish Office commissioned research on understanding effective discipline in schools. Part of the study included a survey of secondary school teachers' perceptions of indiscipline, involving almost one thousand teachers in 112 secondary schools (Johnstone and Munn, 1992). A follow-up survey was commissioned in 1996 by the Educational Institute of Scotland (EIS), the largest teaching union (Johnstone and Munn, 1997). This survey included primary as well as secondary teachers. Both surveys revealed that it was the wearing effect of constant minor disruption which concerned teachers. The most frequently encountered misbehaviours were 'talking out of turn', 'hindering other children from working', 'eating in class' and in primary schools, pupils getting out of their seats without permission. Physical or verbal aggression towards the teacher were reported as rare. However, 69 per cent of primary teachers and 50 per cent of secondary teachers surveyed reported encountering physical aggression towards other pupils at least once during the week specified by the survey, and around two-thirds of both primary and secondary teachers reported encountering verbal abuse towards other pupils at least once during the week. Although the most commonly reported behaviours could be seen as relatively minor, they could nevertheless convey troubled classrooms, especially given pupil-pupil verbal and physical aggression. The cumulative effect on teachers was summed up by this typical comment from a primary teacher:

> Major incidences of indiscipline, I find, are usually the easiest ones to deal with, eg pupils can be excluded, referred to a senior member of staff, parents can be called to the school. It is the continuous minor infringements during the normal day-to-day running of the class which probably cause the most disruption and take most time. . . . Almost any method of trying to deal with and improve poor behaviour over a long period of time takes a significant amount of time and adds to the workload. (Johnstone and Munn, 1997, p. 10)

This comment also indicates the range of the reactions to bad behaviour that is now available. No one punishment is universally effective, and there is now a greater awareness of the need to prevent disruption in the first place. This is part of the rationale underlying the promoting positive discipline initiative launched by Scottish Office Education and Industry Department (SOEID) in 1997 and in the establishing of the Scottish Schools Ethos Network in 1995.

Worries about pupil-pupil verbal and physical aggression were reflected in the prominence given by the government to the development of anti-bullying policies and strategies in schools. Research by Andrew Mellor, a Principal Teacher of Guidance, revealed that 50 per cent of a sample of 942 pupils surveyed had been bullied once or twice during their school careers and a quarter said they had been bullied more frequently. These findings, together with the tragic deaths of a small number of young people reportedly because of bullying, resulted in the Scottish Office funding the development of anti-bullying support packs for schools and the establishing of the post of Anti-Bullying Development Officer in Scotland. Most secondary schools now have anti-bullying policies in place. More importantly, most recognise that bullying is a serious issue which schools can tackle productively. The attitude that bullying is a normal part of growing up and doesn't do any harm is on the way out. There is recognition, however, that with multiple demands on schools, it can be difficult to keep concerns about bullying high on the list of priorities. The reorganisation of local government, bringing new single tier authorities into existence in 1996, has generally reduced the number of advisers who could support schools in their anti-bullying work. This, together with the disappearance of the Anti-Bullying Officer post, has meant that this aspect of school discipline and ethos has perhaps been neglected.

PROMOTING POSITIVE DISCIPLINE

Our understanding of the causes of and hence the 'cures' for troublesome and troubled behaviour has grown over the years. In the past most explanations were rooted in the individual child who was seen as either mad or bad. Thus in the Advisory Council report 1950–2 dealing with the education of handicapped children, four residential child guidance clinics were suggested as meeting the needs of 'pupils who are maladjusted because of social handicap' (quoted in Petrie, 1978). The treatment provided by these clinics was in terms of psychiatric or psychological approaches. A different emphasis was that of the biological causes of disruption, of children who showed an abnormal incapacity for sustained attention, restlessness, and 'fidgetiness'. There is much debate about the meaning, cause and treatment of this condition which is currently called attention deficit and hyperactivity disorder. A contentious treatment is the use of drugs to aid concentration and attention span. More recently, however, sociological explanations of pupil disaffection have drawn attention to the role schools and teachers play in promoting positive behaviour in pupils. Areas such as curriculum organisation in terms of setting or streaming, curriculum provision, teaching approaches, systems of praise and rewards for positive behaviour and pupil involvement in decision making about school and classroom rules, rewards and punishments have all been highlighted as ways in which schools and teachers influence discipline. These sociological explanations, then, focus attention on things which school can do to promote positive behaviour and provide a counterbalance to medical and psychological explanations which see the causes of bad behaviour as located firmly in individual children.

Two initiatives launched by the Scottish Office in the 1990s are underpinned by the notion that there are steps which schools can take to promote positive discipline. These are the Scottish Schools Ethos Network and the Promoting Positive Discipline in Scottish Schools Initiative. Both these initiatives have as their starting points a belief in the importance of positive relationships between pupils and teachers, in the benefits of pupils, teachers, parents and others being actively involved in policy development and in pupils of all abilities being valued.

The Scottish School Ethos Network was established to encourage schools to share ideas and experiences about developing a positive ethos. A range of research studies has highlighted the importance of school ethos in the context of raising standards. The studies include the large scale, statistically robust, quantitative work on school effectiveness and smaller scale case studies of individual schools. The findings of all these studies suggest that without attention to the culture and organisational conditions of the school, real improvement is unlikely. The Scottish Office commissioned a group of researchers to identify key aspects of school ethos and to help schools investigate these aspects taking account of the views of the staff, pupils and parents. This work has been reinforced by the Scottish Office publication *How Good is Our School?* which identifies a number of features of ethos. Thus ethos can be broadly conceived as encompassing the entire school culture and relationships, or it can be subdivided into features such as the physical environment, the way learning is organised, relationships, leadership style, belief systems and the policy framework. The key point is that schools are now being encouraged to evaluate their ethos, taking account of the views of pupils, teachers, parents and others, and to identify aspects for improvement.

The network grew out of the schools' use of the Scottish Office ethos indicators, their desire to share experience of using them and to exchange information about strategies for bringing about change and improvement. The network has over 1,000 school and local authority members. For a small fee, members receive a regular newsletter, case studies of school experiences of improving their ethos, and can attend regular seminars and an annual conference. There is also a database of members which individual schools can access to make their own direct contacts. An important aspect of ethos is the disciplinary climate and schools have shared experiences about, for example, using 'buddy systems' whereby older pupils befriend younger pupils to induct them in the school; pupil councils as a way of involving pupils in decision-making; anti-bullying strategies; using praise and reward systems to recognise positive and caring behaviour; and developing the playground to encourage constructive play, thereby helping to avoid anti-social behaviour.

The Ethos Network includes school discipline in its activities but it is not its sole focus. The Promoting Positive Discipline Initiative focuses on strategies adopted by schools to combat the low level, minor disruption which teachers report as a feature of life in most schools. Working with local authorities, the Initiative encourages schools to write brief case studies of positive and successful practice, to reflect on key features of their culture which promote good discipline and generally to raise awareness within authorities and nationally about innovative developments. The Initiative recognises that good practice in promoting positive discipline takes place in many schools but that there is no obvious method for disseminating and discussing it. Small amounts of funding are made available through the Initiative to release staff to write about the ways in which their school promotes positive discipline, to visit other schools, and to take forward new approaches.

Both these initiatives stress the importance of positive and inclusive approaches to promoting good discipline rather than a negative regime of a hierarchy of sanctions to punish unacceptable behaviour. Such sanctions exist, of course, and it is to these that we now turn.

PUNISHMENT AND SANCTIONS

The typical form of punishment for unacceptable behaviour for most of the history of Scottish schooling was corporal punishment. The 'tawse', 'belt' or 'Lochgelly' – the town famous for the manufacture of the strap used to inflict punishment – was a feature of the school system until the 1960s and 1970s. In the writer's own school days the class of eleven-year-olds were belted by a music teacher because no one would 'own up' to some minor misdemeanour. In secondary, a French teacher habitually wore his belt over his shoulder, under his gown, and flourished it at any pupil making impertinent remarks. The conventional wisdom is that corporal punishment had little beneficial effect on 'real trouble-makers' although it intimidated the majority of pupils, pupils unlikely to misbehave in the first place.

The abolition of corporal punishment brought reliance on a wider range of sanctions to punish unacceptable behaviour. These included a telling off from the teacher, extra homework, lines – for instance, writing a hundred times 'I must behave well in class', detention – staying in school over break, lunchtime or after the end of the school day, withdrawal of privileges such as being refused a place on a school outing, reference to a higher authority in the school, and involving parents. As reported above, surveys of teachers reveal that no one sanction or punishment is seen as universally effective. Indeed teachers report using punishments such as extra work or lines knowing that they do not work. The most effective reaction to misbehaviour is seen as using humour to defuse the situation, thus avoiding the escalation of minor incidents into more serious confrontations.

The 1975 Education (Scotland) Act and subsequent regulations defined the local authority's power to exclude children from school. Exclusion was justified if the pupil or his parents refused to comply with school rules or if the pupil's continued presence in the school posed a threat to the safety and welfare of others. Unlike England and Wales, the Scottish legislation does not stipulate minima or maxima for fixed term exclusion; nor does it endorse permanent exclusion whereby the pupil is refused re-admission to his or her original school. Indeed research has demonstrated considerable diversity in local authority policy and practice in regard to exclusion in Scotland. There are thus no comparable statistics between Scotland and England in terms of the number of pupils permanently excluded from school. There is growing concern south of the border at the number of permanently excluded pupils, estimated to be over 11,000 in secondary schools and 1,800 in primary schools in England. The absolute numbers are worrying in themselves, but of greater concern is that numbers are growing with a 45 per cent increase between 1993–4 and 1995–6 in primary schools and an 18 per cent increase over the same period in secondary schools.

Scottish research (Cullen et al., 1997) revealed that in a sample of around 200 schools, of the 4,500 pupils who were excluded in an eight-month period, most were excluded only once and for three days. Nevertheless a substantial minority, 30 per cent, were excluded for longer and over 1,000 young people had been excluded for six days or more. The kinds of offences for which most pupils were excluded seem relatively trivial, or low key. They include the rather general categories, breaking the rules and insolence. More dramatic offences were recorded in a minority of cases. For example, 26 pupils were excluded for physical assault on staff; 19 for possession of an offensive weapon and 45 for the use or sale of drugs. These pupils came from 41 different schools. Provision for long-term excludees varies across the country and ranges from the minimum of an hour a week home tuition to placement in a day or residential establishment for pupils with social, emotional and behavioural difficulties. Thus, for some schools, a short-term exclusion might be seen as replacing corporal punishment, while longer-term exclusion might represent a lack of expertise in meeting the needs of children with social, emotional and behavioural difficulties, and perhaps an unwillingness, in some cases, to recognise how the school itself might be contributing to these difficulties.

This is not to deny that troubled children cause problems for schools. A number of local authorities now adopt an inter-agency approach to children evincing serious behavioural problems, whereby social workers, educational psychologists and doctors collaborate with teachers in diagnosing the causes of such problems and suggesting ways forward. The evidence is overwhelming that, as with other social ills, poverty and other forms of social disadvantage are associated with children excluded from school on a long-term or permanent basis. Lawrence and Hayden (1997) found that in a sample of excluded primary school pupils almost all had experienced one or more than one of the following: family breakdown; time in care; multiple moves; disability/bereavement; violence/abuse; major accident/incident; special needs; previous serious exclusion; no member of household in paid work. Thus school discipline inevitably bumps into issues of social welfare and there are clearly limits of resources, expertise and sometimes will, to tackle these. Some schools recognise that they can be a haven for troubled children and hold on to them; others are less willing to do so. We once again encounter the importance of school ethos in explaining the differences in exclusion rates from schools with very similar kinds of pupils. Schools can be identified as 'inclusive' or 'exclusive' in culture. For example inclusive schools tend, among other things, to emphasise social as well as academic development and have a senior management team who believe in the duty to educate all children not just the well motivated and well behaved. It is generally accepted that the 1,150 pupils in mainstream schools currently recorded as having social, emotional and behavioural difficulties are only the tip of the iceberg.

CONCLUSION

Discipline in secondary schools has gradually been transformed as understanding about the 'causes' of and 'cures' for disaffection increases. The days of harsh, oppressive and authoritarian regimes are all but over and it is easy to forget how far we have come in a relatively short time in establishing more positive and constructive relationships between teachers and pupils.

A series of major changes in the 1970s and beyond have begun to influence the way we view schools and teacher-pupil relationships. The most important of these changes have been those in curriculum and assessment whereby there is now a common curriculum for all pupils between the ages of five and sixteen; the abolition of corporal punishment; the inclusion of children identified as having special educational needs in mainstream schools; and more diverse teaching methods including projects, investigations, group discussions and individual study as well as whole class teaching. These changes have been accompanied by a growing realisation of the importance of feelings of self-esteem in pupils if they are to be motivated to learn. This has been combined with an understanding of the contribution of school ethos to pupils' personal and social as well as academic development. Thus most schools in Scotland are now more relaxed and friendly places than they used to be. Relationships between pupils and teachers are generally positive, based more on mutual respect than on fear and intimidation. The trend is to involve parents and pupils more in decision making areas such as school rules, dress codes, anti-bullying strategies and the like. Furthermore there is increasing awareness of the need to recognise and value positive behaviour as well as having systems of sanctions and punishments. Thus many schools now have 'pozzies', statements by teachers about the positive behaviour of pupils, merit certificates and awards for positive behaviour, and 'I am special' badges for younger pupils to celebrate particular achievements.

Furthermore, techniques such as social group work and anger control originally used with severely troubled and troublesome youngsters are being recognised as having educational value for all pupils.

Optimism is tempered with concern, however, about continuing social inequality and poverty in Scotland. Clark (1997) notes that there are high levels of poverty in some areas:

> In 1995 about 20% of the school population were entitled to free school meals; this varied from about 6% in Borders region to about 40% in the City of Glasgow. In Glasgow in 1993 one in three children lived in households dependent on income support and one in two of all primary-school children received clothing grants.

It can be difficult to motivate and involve parents, living in such circumstances, in their children's education. It is easy to label parents, who do not attend parents' evenings, or who do not assure their children's regular attendance at school, or who fail to respond to their children's exclusion from school, as inadequate and/or uncaring and to write them off. Many schools are aware, however, that they provide an important source of stability and security in the lives of troubled youngsters and resist the provocation to excluded them which is sometimes offered. Such schools work with their local communities and with other agencies such as social work and community police to maintain an inclusive ethos and to prevent the ratcheting up of the spiral of disadvantage for their pupils.

The balance between a welfare approach and one which emphasises a 'get tough' response to indiscipline will continue to be a major dilemma for government, education authorities and schools. An exclusive emphasis on an attainment culture, whereby schools are judged only by the numbers of pupils achieving particular numbers of passes in public examinations, may encourage an undue reliance on punishment. Scotland has managed to avoid some of the worst effects of a quasi-market approach to schooling evident in rising numbers of children permanently excluded from school in England and Wales. It is clearly important that, in a drive to improve standards of attainment, schools are not placed in direct competition with each other. If they are, the temptation to exclude children with special needs involving social, emotional and behavioural difficulties will be strong. These pupils will be seen as depressing a school's position in performance tables and as making a school an unattractive choice for parents.

Scotland prides itself on its commitment to high quality education for all and comprehensive education has strong roots. Moreover there are numerous examples of successful inclusive approaches across the country. Such approaches need to be widely disseminated and built on so that positive relationships between teachers and pupils are the reality experienced by all pupils and teachers in our schools.

This chapter draws on P. Munn (forthcoming) 'Discipline in Scottish Schools' in H. Holmes (ed.) *An Ethnology of Scotland*, vol. 11, Edinburgh: Scottish Ethnological Research Centre.

REFERENCES

Clark, M. (1997) Education in Scotland: Setting the Scene in M. Clark and P. Munn (eds) *Education in Scotland: Policy and Practice from Pre-School to Secondary*, London: Routledge.

Cullen, M. A., M. Johnstone G. Lloyd and P. Munn (1997) *Exclusion from School in Scotland: Headteachers' Views*, Edinburgh: Moray House Institute of Education.

Johnstone, M. and P. Munn (1997) *Indiscipline: A Survey of Scottish Primary School and Secondary School Teachers*, Edinburgh – Confidential Report to the Educational Institute of Scotland.

Johnstone, M. and P. Munn (1992) *Discipline in Scottish Secondary Schools*, Edinburgh: SCRE

Lawrence, B. and C. Hayden (1997) Primary School Exclusions, *Educational Research and Evaluation*, 3:1, pp. 54–77.

Petrie, D. S. (1978) The Development of Special Education in Scotland Since 1950, in W. Dockrell, W. Dunn and A. Milne (eds) *Special Education in Scotland*, pp. 1–15, Edinburgh: SCRE

43

Guidance and Personal and Social Education in the Secondary School

David McLaren

THE ORIGINS OF GUIDANCE

Many would argue that the system of guidance we have today originated in 1968 with the publication of the Scottish Education Department's paper *Guidance in Scottish Secondary Schools* (SED, 1968), and to some extent that argument has some currency in that the issue of 'pupil guidance' had come to the fore as a result of the move away from Junior/Senior Secondary education towards the comprehensive model. Historians might well argue that schools had always been concerned with the welfare of their pupils. The 'dominie' tradition, with its emphasis on academic excellence and intellectual ability, was all-powerful at least until the mid twentieth century (and some of this tradition ramains strong even today), but the move to comprehensive education in the 1960s was the first time that the education system had had to face up to the challenge of S1–S6 all-through secondary schooling. There had always been such schools in rural areas of Scotland, but throughout the country many large secondary schools were created which catered for a much wider ability range and socio-economic mix than ever before – contentious issues, then as now.

Embedded in the notion of comprehensive education itself was the commitment to ensuring the best provision possible for the individual, meeting individual needs and recognising that pupil 'potential' was a much wider concept than academic achievement. By offering the wide and varied curriculum which larger schools could offer at the appropriate levels and by encouraging a wider social mix, elitism and divisiveness would become things of the past and there would be a new emphasis on equality of opportunity.

Leslie Hunter, in his book *The Scottish Educational System* (Oxford: Pergamon, 1972), observed at the time that where a curriculum was characterised by variety and flexibility, 'the need for guidance of pupils arises'. He noted that some large schools had introduced a House system, 'where house masters are expected to know every pupil in their house – his or her abilities, weaknesses, interests, family circumstances, proposed career and so on' (Hunter, 1972, p. 20). Many schools had had a House system before this time, but Hunter was echoing the spirit of the SED's paper which also identified 'personal', 'vocational' and 'curricular' guidance – terms still used today. In 1968, 'personal' tended to mean discussing vital problems of the day, while 'vocational' had to do with careers information (as opposed to work experience, self-assessment etc.) and 'curricular' tended to focus on option choice at

S2. Each pupil had the right to receive advice or help from a teacher who had 'a special and continuing responsibility for him' and, most importantly, guidance was for all pupils, not only for those who had problems. The guidance system might be organised vertically (house groups) or horizontally (year groups) and staff would require training. Little or nothing was said about the appropriateness or otherwise of having potentially competitive House groups in the new system.

In anticipation of the raising of the school leaving age in 1972, a promoted post structure was introduced as a further recognition of the importance of guidance in dealing with increasing numbers of pupils who were having to stay on at school (SED, 1971). It is highly significant that the guidance promotion structure was exactly the same as the subject promoted post structure introduced at the same time, both of which are still in existence, although the additional senior management post of Assistant Head Teacher (AHT) Guidance was created.

However, there was still enormous confusion as to what exactly guidance was all about, not least among newly-appointed guidance staff themselves. By the mid-1970s, HM Inspectors had become involved and, while they reiterated the importance of curricular, vocational and personal guidance, they stressed the need for other, non-promoted members of staff to become involved. There was also a growing recognition that the formal subject curriculum was insufficient preparation for the world outside school and that 'Social Education' classes were required to deal with such matters as relationships, health, work etc. Guidance staff, with their cross-curricular approach and their concern for the whole pupil, were seen as appropriate staff to devise and deliver Social Education programmes.

By far the most important influence on the aims, objectives and practice of guidance was the SCCC position paper *More Than Feelings of Concern* (SCCC, 1986). This was the first real attempt on a national scale to define aims and objectives for guidance. It tried to identify the characteristics of a 'caring' school. It argued that guidance was more than just good intentions: it was, or should be, an active, on-going process which required planning and eight objectives were suggested as an aid to such planning. In addition to reinforcing earlier messages about personal, social, vocational and intellectual development and the need to ensure that each pupil was known personally by at least one member of staff, it included objectives covering the following areas:

- raising pupil awareness of and responsibility for their own development
- identifying and responding quickly and appropriately to individual pupil needs
- good teacher/pupil relations
- liaison with home/support and welfare services
- effective record-keeping

The paper also attempted to define the remits of promoted guidance staff and, on a wider level, it discussed the relationship between guidance and the discipline system, assessment, the subject curriculum and careers education. Inevitably, it emphasised the need for more time and training for guidance staff and was at pains to point out that all staff have a guidance responsibility.

This report was a seminal piece of work, not necessarily for its intellectual depth or its great vision, but for its practicability. It provided a major stepping stone into the educational world of the 1990s and gave guidance an enhanced status and a much surer footing on which to contribute to important contemporary issues such as school ethos,

quality and performance in guidance, school effectiveness, profiling, inter-agency collaboration and education for personal and social development – issues which the 1986 paper
could not be expected to envisage. It is a testament to its durability that its eight original
objectives were described by HMI in 1996 as being 'as relevant today as they were 10 years
ago'.

WHAT DO GUIDANCE TEACHERS DO?

Based on their guidance inspections in some 250 Scottish schools, HMI outlined a
'Guidance calendar' of whole school or year group activities.
    Year specific activities included:

- S1/S2 Primary/Secondary Liaison Programme, reception of S1 intake and S2 course
  choice process;
- S3/S4 Careers information, monitoring subject progress, SCE presentation checks and
  post-exam consultation, post-16 option, S4 leavers;
- S5/S6 Advice on study skills/decision making, monitoring, 16+ progress, UCAS
  applications.
- Whole school [S1–S6] activities – pupil interviews, profiling/National Record of
  Achievement (NRA) activities and reporting to and meeting with parents.

    It is obvious that any one of the above activities involves a great deal of time and effort
from guidance staff. For example, the reception of S1 intake is often a process which begins
in P7 and extends throughout the first few months of S1 and involves (or should involve)
frequent individual interviews and group activities with new pupils. Similarly, option
choice programmes at S2 will often require guidance staff involvement in PSE classes on
self-evaluation, in collating subject reports, interviewing pupils, arranging careers information and further interviewing of pupils and parents. So complex has this process of option
choice and career planning become at S4, that a major investment of time and training will
be required to implement the Higher Still guidance proposals.
    The calendar above can reveal only some of the many and varied activities involved in
guidance – a fact recognised, to some extent, by HMI. One or two examples will illustrate the
point. Guidance staff spend an enormous amount of time dealing with matters relating to
attendance and latecoming. While these tasks might appear to be mundane (if time
consuming), they point to the larger issue of the involvement of guidance staff in creating
and maintaining a positive school ethos and in supporting individual pupils – in helping
pupils to feel valued by the institution. Guidance staff also spend a lot of time (some would say
an inordinate amount of time) dealing with 'crisis' guidance, i.e. helping young people cope
with the whole range of traumatic experience which may be part of their lives – family
traumas such as separation, divorce and bereavement, relationship issues, health matters etc.,
and while these are unlikely to feature in an annual calendar, they feature heavily in guidance
work. It is also essential to note that most schools see guidance staff as the first point of contact
for parents and for the support agencies. The Principal Teacher of Guidance may have
responsibility for some 200 pupils, S1–S6, and is quite properly expected to deal not only with
parental enquiries but to be pro-active in liaising with parents. In addition, many pupils may
have involvement with one or other of the support agencies, e.g. social work, psychological
services, or the Reporter to the Children's Panel. Liaison with these agencies, including case

conferences, pupil contracts, individual pupil support, action planning and target setting, are all crucial if a pupil is to benefit from a coherent inter-agency approach and, while it is true to argue that these issues affect every teacher in every classroom, they are the specific responsibility of the promoted guidance staff.

Guidance staff require to liaise closely with other members of staff in this respect. There is little point, for example, in school, psychological services, and social work agreeing a strategy on behaviour management or special needs provision if guidance staff do not make subject staff aware of the issues and discuss with them how this strategy might operate in the classroom. While this may be particularly true of the relationship between school and social work/psychological services, it is equally important in relation to other support agencies such as the careers service. Research indicates that careers officers have felt excluded from the S2/S4 options process.

THE STRUCTURE OF GUIDANCE

The number of promoted guidance posts varies from school to school, although as a general rule most schools still follow the guidelines in the 1971 paper, i.e. one promoted post per 150/200 pupils on the roll. It is worth noting that the variability has increased in the last few years as schools have accepted greater responsibility for the management of resources previously controlled by the local authority. A management team which wishes to emphasise the work of the guidance team may well appoint more than the recommended minimum number of staff and may recognise the contribution of guidance to a positive school ethos by allowing more time for unpromoted staff to work with guidance staff in such areas as NRA, option choice, or work experience. However, the converse may also be the case, depending on the priorities of the senior management team.

Normally, the overall responsibility for guidance will rest with an AHT or Depute but nowadays guidance will only form part of such a remit, the post of AHT with sole responsibility for guidance having largely disappeared in the state sector. (Some independent schools retain the post of AHT Guidance within a structured guidance system, while others have no recognisable guidance system at all.)

In very large schools, a horizontal or year group system may operate, where guidance staff are responsible for age stages and may follow their pupils through the school. In such schools, assistant heads can be responsible for guidance in S1/2, S3/4, or S5/6. In smaller schools, horizontal systems will be managed by guidance staff only, responsible to one AHT/DHT. However, many schools operate a vertical or House system, where each House comprises pupils from S1–S6, usually grouped by alphabetical order of surname and again managed by one or more AHTs. There are hybrids of these systems and much depends on the number of pupils on the roll, but more schools tend to favour the vertical system. This system has several benefits. From a parental viewpoint, all members of the same family will be in the same House and so parents will have to deal with only one member of staff who will know the family circumstances. From a staff perspective, a vertical system offers a wider range of guidance work and a more even spread of workload. It is difficult, but not inconceivable, to imagine a horizontal system in a school of, for example, 1,200 pupils coping effectively with a development such as Higher Still where only one or two members of the guidance team were directly involved. A vertical system ensures that all guidance staff are involved in the major elements of guidance work, while still allowing individuals to develop specialisms or additional management responsibilities.

These additional whole-school or cross-curricular management responsibilities are often undertaken by Principal Teachers of Guidance, as distinct from APTs, although remits vary enormously from school to school. Some schools distinguish PT/APT remits purely in terms of numbers of pupils, while others attempt to separate functions and activities. Remits have always been something of a grey area, particularly given the emphasis in recent years on guidance as a whole-school responsibility and the increasing role of first-level guidance staff, i.e. register or form teachers. Added to this must be the important pastoral and spiritual role played by the school Chaplain, most obviously in denominational schools.

Staff development, training and time allocation will be discussed later, but for the moment it is sufficient to note that guidance staff in most schools are employed first and foremost as subject staff and spend the majority of their time teaching the school subject for which they were trained. In 1994 the School Census indicated that there were 1,123 principal teachers and 1,072 assistant principal teachers of guidance and that in each category only one-third had a guidance-related qualification (Certificate, Diploma, or Masters), although it should be noted that the vast majority of guidance staff will have some experience of in-service training, often provided by the local authority (SOEID, 1996, p. 5) There is no statutory allocation of time for guidance but a generally accepted minimum is forty minutes per fifteen pupils for whom guidance staff have a direct responsibility. What is clear from recent research is that many schools do not even reach this minimum allocation (Howieson and Semple, 1996, p. 5) and the competing claims of guidance work and subject teaching continue to increase stress levels.

PERSONAL AND SOCIAL EDUCATION

Most whole-school guidance policies will indicate a strong guidance commitment to PSE, variously referred to as Personal and Social Development (PSD), or Education for Personal and Social Development (EPSD). It is worth noting in passing that, while the commitment may be strong, the relationship between the guidance process and PSE is often unclear, at least beyond the timetabled PSE element.

The Scottish Office's 5–14 document noted that PSD was 'essentially concerned with the development of life skills. . . . All aspects of a child's experience at home, in school and outwith school contribute to PSD' (SOEID, PSD 5–14, 1993, p. 1).

More recently, the SCCC's *Heart of the Matter* offered the view that education for personal and social development had to do with:

> developing certain qualities and dispositions which will help them to make sense of an increasingly complex world and to respond in a pro-social way to the diversity of circumstances, systems and working environments they face in their lives. (SCCC, 1995, p. 1)

These (personal) 'qualities and dispositions' tend to refer to positive regard for self and others, increasing responsibility for a pupil's own life, self evaluation, target-setting and decision-making skills, although the list is potentially endless. The 'social' element tends to include such factors as social responsibility, participation in a democratic society and moral and ethical decision making.

Guidance staff, with their close involvement in individual pupils' personal, social and vocational development can clearly have a major impact here, particularly in individual interviews and in the process of recording achievements for the NRA document.

On a wider level, any school has to consider how it might achieve these and many other PSD objectives, taking into consideration the socio-economic context of the community in which the school operates and, just as importantly, the ethos of the school and its staff. A few schools deal with PSE by 'embedding' certain PSE topics (e.g. health education) in certain curricular subjects and they try to ensure that other PSE qualities and dispositions (e.g. core skills) permeate classroom teaching.

While it is desirable that the aims and objectives of PSE should permeate all aspects of classroom life, it is a difficult way to organise a structured, coherent and progressive PSE programme and most schools opt for timetabled PSE, (interestingly still referred to in some schools as 'the guidance slot'), usually one period per week, S1–S6. Topics covered are many and varied and will reflect the needs of the pupils in their local community. Most schools will cover topics such as health education, careers education and study skills, and the classes will normally be smaller than subject sections with a more active, learner-centred methodology.

Guidance staff are seen to have a particular role to play in PSE. In addition to the personal guidance mentioned above, the guidance team is often responsible for devising and delivering the PSE programme although, since this is timetabled time, many other staff will be involved. There are clearly important issues here regarding staff development for all involved, since PSE/Guidance issues are not afforded much time in the initial teacher education process, despite the fact that a very large percentage of beginning teachers will take classes in PSE within a few weeks of first appointment or during supply work. The issue of certification of PSE in Higher Still also raises major questions. For example, how appropriate is it for schools to be grading pupils (with the inevitable norm-referencing which will occur) on their personal awareness and development? If a pupil has a Higher in PSE is s/he more aware and developed as a person than a pupil with Intermediate 1?

CURRENT ISSUES IN GUIDANCE/PSE

It is clearly impossible to discuss all of the major issues in any great detail. The issues which are outlined below represent only a few of those which guidance staff might identify. They are all inter-related and, while some are relatively new, some are old favourites.

Higher Still

For many, the most immediate and pressing issue is the whole process of guidance in S5/6 and the fulfilment of the Higher Still guidance entitlement. The Higher Still Development Unit are at pains to emphasise that the guidance process in S5/6 is merely an extension of current good practice. According to this view, there will be no substantial change in the guidance teacher's job – merely a re-prioritising to ensure that Higher Still (with its particular emphasis on curricular and vocational guidance) is placed at the top of the list. Inevitably, in the current system, if Higher Still is prioritised then other guidance work must be downgraded. Even if this were an acceptable argument in an era ostensibly concerned with quality provision, the logic of it is destroyed when guidance staff read between the lines in recent SOEID documents and discover that 'de-prioritising' S1/S2 is not acceptable, and that areas such as PSE, expertise in profiling and first level guidance, to name but a few, are all priorities. Thus, areas for improvement are to be remedied, not by re-thinking the time allocation given to guidance or the training of guidance staff but by better time management within existing resources – an argument which fails to impress many guidance practitioners.

Higher Still, then, may appear to many guidance staff as a missed opportunity in that it fails to provide an opportunity to debate the possibility of reducing subject commitment, of grouping together guidance, PSE and learning/behaviour support, of offering a truly cross-curricular approach and of re-thinking a promoted post structure which is almost thirty years old and which has almost certainly outlived its usefulness.

Nevertheless, even in its present form, Higher Still has raised a number of guidance (and guidance-related) issues. In particular, it has helped to identify the need for a closer understanding of and relationship between the process of guidance, PSE, Core Skills and the NRA. To some extent, concerns about the guidance entitlement and how to deliver it have brought these to the surface. Guidance staff will clearly have a pivotal role in ensuring that the PSE programme includes Core Skills at the appropriate level for each pupil. They will also require to ensure that pupils have an increased role in choosing courses and they will need to advise on appropriate career paths and monitor individual action plans. Pupils will require additional help in recording improved skills, knowledge etc. for the NRA document.

For many years, guidance, PSE and profiling have often run along parallel lines – albeit in the same direction but never quite meeting. The Development Unit have recognised some of the problems which the entitlement now poses for schools and with the certification of PSE and the inclusion of Core Skills, work is being undertaken to 'map' areas of current provision against the entitlement (and vice versa). For example, many PSE units and courses might help structure and deliver some of the entitlement. It is not yet clear the extent to which this mapping process will include the NRA recording process, but it is a welcome aspect of Higher Still.

The Inspectorate

HMI are recognised as established, authoritative figures in Scottish education and are seen by many teachers as being experts in their field. Inspectors themselves often prefer to be seen as identifiers of good practice and as 'enablers'. This enabling function has been increasingly emphasised in the last few years by the development of guidance performance indicators for use in the process of school self-evaluation and development planning. This desire to have schools evaluate themselves does not always sit comfortably with the inspection/reporting role and the expectation by guidance staff that HMI provide leadership by clearly identifying national priorities (Howieson and Semple, 1996, p. 64). This potential or actual conflict between enabling, inspection and leadership is not helped when HMI identify nearly all the major areas of guidance work as being priorities, or at least worthy of development, but only within the traditional guidance structure.

At times, it seems that the Inspectorate are reluctant to provide a clear lead at national level (e.g. identifying everything as a priority and adopting a 'hands off' approach to problem solving), preferring to leave it to individual schools to identify needs. At other times, HMI do seem to want to identify individual issues (e.g. PSE) as being of national concern, but even here recommendations as to improvement are often confined to rather vague exhortations to do better or are constrained by a failure to debate alternatives to the existing guidance structure. The conflict between inspection, enabling and leadership may well come to a head in the next few years as the pressure increases on the traditional guidance structure.

Staff development

Every guidance document in the last thirty years has called for improved training for guidance staff. Despite the fact that improvements have been made, this remains an issue. As has already been indicated, only one third of promoted guidance staff have a recognised post-graduate qualification in guidance from a university or college – and this at a time of increasing diversity and complexity in guidance work.

There is, as yet, no requirement for newly-appointed guidance staff to have any formal qualification in guidance, although an increasing number of headteachers are insisting on such qualifications. This is not, of course, to deny the importance of local authority in-service provision in this area but, by its very nature, it cannot offer the range and depth of a Certificate or Diploma, and on a national level local authority provision in this area is inevitably variable. The old adage about getting the job and then getting the training is still true to a large extent. In-service training is an essential part of guidance but it is unlikely to be sufficient in itself, given the increasing demands of the job. The time may well be right to phase in a requirement for guidance staff to have a formal qualification.

It is quite possible for the Teacher Education Institutions (TEIs) to offer qualifying courses in guidance during Initial Teacher Education (ITE) but our current system will not recognise this as a 'teaching' qualification because guidance is not a classroom subject. It is to be hoped that the General Teaching Council (GTC) will take a more enlightened view and face the issue of the subject/guidance dilemma.

A similar situation exists for PSE. Despite the fact that many (subject and guidance) staff will be asked to deliver PSE, not all will have much in the way of in-service training (although a good school will have involved them in the process and will have undertaken in-house staff development sessions). Fewer still will have any formal qualification. Those who do have a formal qualification may well have studied only one area of PSE, e.g. health education or careers education. As with guidance, the TEIs could certificate students in PSE during ITE if there was a will to do so among the educational establishment.

National Record of Achievement

There remain some unresolved issues around the recording of achievement for the NRA document. At the moment, most research evidence points to the fact that staff and pupils in schools generally value the document and, more importantly, the process which leads to its completion. Pupils are encouraged to believe that the NRA will be a positive account of their years at school and will serve them well in seeking employment and/or FE. The same research indicates that FE colleges use the NRA in their student selection process. However, conflicting evidence emerges from HMI in this respect. They found that very few colleges in their survey used the NRA in the selection process.

Guidance staff already know from experience and from documented research that many employers have little understanding of the NRA document and that universities have been unenthusiastic. Staff therefore have to ask some important questions about NRA. It is almost certainly true that the process of positive reporting, identifying strengths and encouraging positive self-image etc. is more important than the final 'product'. These elements might be better emphasised in a strengthened S1–S6 PSE course and in a much stronger emphasis on recording achievements/strengths/skills in subject classrooms and on how guidance staff might capitalise on this and integrate it into a personal profile without the need for a standardised final document. Some may feel that a final document is still required and that better marketing is required.

In any event, it seems clear that any such document may have a limited use unless pupils are able to use it and develop it. Rather than viewing it as a final product to be shown to an employer or college, greater emphasis could be given to it as a document which pupils require to discuss and expand upon with a potential employer. Some schools attempt to tackle this through mock interviews and this might be the starting point for this shift in emphasis, providing that interviewers themselves saw the document as a basis for discussion and not as an end point. It is to be hoped that the re-launch of NRA will address at least some of these issues.

Time allocation

If there is one issue which permeates all of this, it is the question of time allocation for guidance. Guidance staff are well aware of the strengths and weaknesses of guidance in Scottish schools. They would almost certainly identify the issues raised above as being important and they would wish to tackle them. They might also point to a host of other concerns – first level guidance, transition points, counselling skills, lack of time given to able or 'non problem' pupils, anti-racist education, the evaluation of guidance and many more.

However, the overarching concern and the reason they would give for being unable to do everything required of them is not, as HMI would argue, poor time management but a lack of time itself. They are trained as subject specialists and spend some two-thirds or more of their time as subject teachers in a system which appears to value, or at least desire, guidance and PSE but which at the present moment seems unable to create time and space for both, preferring instead to emphasise the traditional subject areas. That is not to say that all guidance staff wish to relinquish all subject teaching, but it is true to say they have never been encouraged on a national level even to consider the possibility of reducing subject commitment in favour of more PSE work (including PSE classes), of increasing involvement with small groups working on self-esteem, careers and other guidance related work and of initiating and delivering projects with learning/behaviour support, support agencies, and so on. Scottish education, it seems, is not yet ready for such an apparently radical move, although one or two areas of the country have experimented with the idea.

Thus the time issue itself is only superficially about hours and minutes. It has to do with priorities, the structure of the curriculum and the structure of promoted posts designed to deliver that curriculum. Ultimately it is about attitude – attitude which filters down from the educational establishment into schools and which schools help to engender in young people.

The historian Christopher Smout notes that schools are the key to many aspects of modern Scotland:

> If there are in this country too many people who fear what is new, believe the difficult to be impossible, draw back from responsibility and afford established authority and tradition an exaggerated respect, we can reasonably look for an explanation in the institutions that moulded them. (T. C. Smout, 1987, *A Century of the Scottish People, 1830–1950*, Fontana, p. 229)

On the one hand it might reasonably be argued that guidance, PSE, NRA and positive school ethos are all designed to equip pupils to deal with what Smout calls 'the more depressing aspects of modern Scotland'. At the same time, however, there is still this fear of the new – the clinging to subject fiefdoms and rigid timetabling in a competitive, knowledge-based system. There is a fear of spending too much time on 'marginal' activities. It is time we realised that guidance and PSE are crucial elements in modern education before we ourselves are marginalised in that respect by the rest of Europe.

REFERENCES

Howieson, C. and S. Semple (1996) *Guidance in Secondary Schools*, Edinburgh: Centre for Educational Sociology.
SCCC (1986) *More than Feelings of Concern*, Dundee: SCCC.
SCCC (1995) *Higher Still Guidance Arrangements*, Edinburgh: SCCC.
SED (1968) *Guidance in Scottish Secondary Schools*, Edinburgh: HMSO.
SED (1971) *The Structure of Promoted Posts in Secondary Schools in Scotland*, Edinburgh: HMSO.
SOEID (1996) *Effective Learning and Teaching: Guidance*, Edinburgh SOEID.

44

Classroom Management in the Secondary School

Margaret Kirkwood

The issue at the heart of effective learning and teaching is differentiation. Through using differentiated approaches teachers seek to address the individual learning needs of pupils to enable them to reach their full potential. The task of identifying individual learning needs and addressing them effectively presents a considerable challenge to the secondary teacher. Pupils often attend classes for relatively short periods (in some cases for only fifty-five minutes per week) and the teacher has to get to know and respond to the needs of pupils across a range of classes and age groups. This is an important distinction between the organisation of the primary and secondary school.

Adopting a particular form of class organisation will not, in itself, create the conditions for effective learning and teaching. Schools must establish an ethos of achievement which permeates to the classroom, and the tasks which pupils are allocated must be stimulating and appropriately challenging. Teachers must establish a climate for learning which will support all pupils to achieve success and which is not undermined by misbehaviour or by some pupils being labelled as 'swots'. Pupils must be encouraged to take responsibility for their learning to enable them to become self-directed as learners, since schools have a crucial role to play in promoting lifelong learning. Above all, it is necessary for teachers to be caring and to establish relationships of trust with pupils to ensure that pupils' emotional and cognitive needs are met, and that learning and teaching become a genuinely shared enterprise.

WHAT HELPS PUPILS TO LEARN?

The task of identifying and responding to individual learning needs would be impossible if pupils did not share some common characteristics. Researchers who have asked secondary pupils about what makes a good teacher get consistent responses. For example, when Sally Brown and Donald McIntryre investigated what it is that S2 pupils say their teachers do well, the pupils' statements showed a considerable appreciation of what their teachers were trying to do (*Making Sense of Teaching*, Buckingham: Open University Press, 1993). The different things which pupils mentioned were: creating a relaxed and enjoyable atmosphere in the classroom; retaining control; presenting work in a way which interests and motivates pupils; enabling pupils to understand the work; making clear what pupils are to do and achieve;

judging what can be expected of each pupil; helping pupils with difficulties; encouraging pupils to raise their expectations of themselves; developing personal, mature relationships with pupils; and displaying personal talents (subject related or other). In a recent study conducted by John MacBeath and colleagues on school self-evaluation the consensus which emerged amongst pupils, teachers and parents is that classrooms should be places where learning was fun and was stimulating and where achievements of all kinds would be celebrated. The pupils in this study listed many characteristics of good teachers, amongst which were: likes teaching children; likes teaching their subject; takes time to explain things; doesn't give up on you; has faith in you; treats people equally; cares for your opinion; has time for you; and makes you feel clever (see Boyd in Kirkwood, ed., 1997, pp. 7–10).

Research into learning, conducted in laboratories as well as natural settings, has identified a number of key conditions which optimise learning (Simpson, 1997):

- New learning happens best when it is related to what individuals already know, understand and can do.
- Learning is enhanced when individuals are clear about its purpose and about their specific learning goals.
- Learning happens best when individuals are confident and motivated.
- Learning can be enhanced when individuals are enabled to take more responsibility.

Unfortunately, Mary Simpson observes, these conditions are very seldom met in secondary classrooms. In her study on differentiation in Scottish secondary schools (Simpson and Ure, 1993) the factors which pupils mentioned as making a difference to how well they did at school turned out to be remarkably similar to those identified by the research. Nine teaching strategies emerged from discussions with pupils on what their good teachers were doing:

- identifying and responding to a range of needs;
- building on strengths and addressing weaknesses;
- promoting the belief that attainment can improve (by the teacher demonstrating that by applying certain agreed procedures pupils can become good learners and achieve something);
- identifying targets and criteria for success;
- setting realistically high expectations which pupils can achieve, with support;
- giving feedback on attainments and problems (praise and encouragement are important, but pupils also want to know where they are performing badly and how to put it right);
- using a self-referenced rather than norm- or criterion-referenced approach to enable pupils to see how they are progressing;
- employing a range of sources of support, including older pupils, parents, learning support teachers and library staff;
- sharing the management of learning (but pupils must also be given the information and support to cope effectively with responsibilities).

THE IMPLICATIONS OF DIFFERENT CONCEPTIONS OF LEARNING

From all of this evidence it is clear that there is a great deal the teacher can do to enhance learning and therefore to raise pupils' achievements. This contrasts markedly with the traditional view of school learning, in which variations in attainments between pupils are 'explained' as a natural consequence of pupils having different amounts of general ability, and general ability is perceived as something intrinsic to the pupil and beyond our influence (Drever, 1985). Benjamin Bloom has dismissed this explanation as 'no explanation'. Eric Drever explains Bloom's ideas as follows:

> But how do we know that they differ in ability? As a rule we infer this from the differences in attainment. The 'explanation' is no explanation. But what it does is important: it allows us to take for granted the quality of our *instruction*. (ibid., p. 60)

Bloom substitutes a different model in which the idea of general ability is abandoned in favour of specific abilities. He argues that a pupil's chance of success on a learning task will depend on three things: whether the pupil has already learned the specific skills and knowledge that the task requires; whether the pupil has an interest in learning from the task; and on various aspects of instruction. The attainments that result from the task add to the pupil's stock of specific abilities and raise the chances of future successes.

The important point about Bloom's model is that it deals with variables that can be altered rather than with a fixed quantity (general ability). He argues that if we can identify the alterable variables that can make a difference to children's learning, this will do much to explain the learning process and even more to directly improve the teaching and learning processes in schools. Bloom's view is therefore an optimistic one.

Eric Drever has investigated Bloom's model with S1 and S2 pupils in relation to mastery learning. In spite of teachers' well grounded concerns about Bloom's 'utopian vision' (for example, that it does not give adequate recognition to the affective dimension of learning and overplays the formal, cognitive curriculum), he concluded there was no reason to doubt Bloom's central premise. Also whenever teachers could be induced to suspend belief in 'general ability' and act instead on Bloom's hypothesis, they began to look critically at curriculum and assessment and to experiment creatively in their classrooms, and they reported an improvement in pupils' motivation and performance.

When Mary Simpson and Jenny Ure investigated differentiation in Scottish secondary schools they identified two models of differentiation (Simpson and Ure, 1993). One of these models (labelled by the researchers as 'measure and match') had as an assumption that a stable, underlying characteristic of pupils is the key determinant of pupils' competencies (for example, intelligence or mathematical ability), and that this characteristic can be reliably measured at a point in time. A further assumption was that a match could be made between the competency of the pupil and the level of difficulty of the curricular materials or course, and that this match could subsequently be fine-tuned by summative assessment. This model was found not to deliver good differentiation, according to pupils' perceptions. The second model ('pick and mix') worked on different assumptions. It assumed that the competencies of pupils are determined by a complex range of factors (motivation, classroom relationships, past learning experiences etc.), and that these competencies would continue to be influenced by these factors, and therefore measures at any one point in time are useful, but not critical. Furthermore it assumed that a range of learning needs has to be taken into account when allocating work or responding to learning outcomes, and that differentiated materials should cater for this range and be accessed as and when appropriate for individuals or groups. Not surprisingly, this model was found to be far more successful by pupils.

It has been found that pupils also hold different conceptions of ability or 'theories of intelligence' which affect how they approach learning tasks and what they hope to gain from them (Dweck and Elliott, 1983). The first theory (the 'entity' theory of intelligence) involves the belief that intelligence is a rather stable, global trait that can be judged to be adequate or inadequate. This trait is displayed in one's performance, and the judgements of that performance can indicate whether one is or is not intelligent. The second theory ('incremental') involves the belief that intellectual competence consists of a repertoire of skills that can be endlessly expanded through one's efforts. While most older children understand both views of intelligence it appears that different children, independent of their actual ability, tend to favour one or the other. As one would predict, entity theorists prefer tasks that afford opportunities to avoid mistakes and to be judged competent, whereas incremental theorists prefer tasks that afford them opportunities for learning, and they will happily immerse themselves in enquiry ('How can I do it?' 'What will I learn?').

Teachers can influence pupils towards holding an incremental view of intelligence by treating pupils' errors as natural and useful events rather than as evidence of failure, providing opportunities for pupils to engage in problem solving and enquiry, acting as a resource and guide rather than as a judge, and applying flexible and longer-term performance standards which enable progress towards targets to be recognised. Unfortunately, the imperative to 'cover ground' in relation to prescribed syllabuses which are often content-packed, and the presence of national examinations create pressures which prevent many pupils from experiencing the satisfactions of learning for its own sake.

Howard Gardner's theory of multiple intelligences has been very influential in shaping thinking about learning. The theory identifies that there are at least seven relatively autonomous intellectual capacities – each with its own distinctive mode of thinking – to approach problems and create products. In addition to linguistic ability (using words and language, both written and spoken) and logical-mathematical ability (working with numbers, recognising abstract patterns and thinking and reasoning in a logical and deductive manner) there are abilities of other kinds which traditionally get less emphasis in schools: visual-spatial, musical, interpersonal (which operates through person-to-person relationships and communication), intrapersonal (which is concerned with self-reflection and self-awareness) and kinaesthetic (which is related to physical activity). The implications of Gardner's theory are far reaching:

> We should spend less time ranking children and more time helping them to identify their natural competencies and gifts and cultivate these. There are hundreds and hundreds of ways to succeed, and many, many different abilities to help you get there.
> [This quotation, by Gardner, is taken from a recent (1996) Scottish CCC publication, *Teaching for Effective Learning*, which discusses a range of influences on thinking about learning.]

Daniel Goleman's book, *Emotional Intelligence* (1996, London: Bloomsbury) has helped to raise awareness of the role of emotions and feelings in children's education:

> when too many children lack the capacity to handle their upsets, to listen or focus, to rein in impulse, to feel responsible for their work or care about learning, anything that will buttress these skills will help in their education. (p. 284)

Goleman suggests that emotional lessons can be woven into the fabric of school life, through, for example, getting teachers to rethink how to discipline students who misbehave.

Such moments present ripe opportunities to teach children skills they are lacking – impulse control, explaining their feelings, resolving conflicts. The school ethos and classroom atmosphere are important to establish the conditions for emotional intelligence to develop. Goleman defines emotional intelligence as:

> abilities such as being able to motivate oneself and persist in the face of frustration; to control impulse and delay gratification; to regulate one's moods and keep distress from swamping the ability to think; to empathise and to hope. (ibid., 1996, p. 34)

Many Scottish secondary schools are now seeking to tackle indiscipline through promoting positive behaviour. This has to be a better alternative to exclusions where, in many cases, excluded pupils are not receiving any formal education at all and are free to roam the streets. The discipline referral system which replaced corporal punishment in the early 1980s is not effective if it only serves to document pupils' misdemeanours, without any sustained interventions to educate pupils about appropriate behaviour and to equip them with the skills to regulate their behaviour. Nor will a system of rewards and sanctions (and this is how some schools are currently seeking to promote positive behaviour) be effective if there is no real attempt at timely intervention.

Emotions and feelings do not only come into play in relation to pupils' behaviour at school. John Nisbet, in his introduction to the research literature on teaching thinking (published by the Scottish Council for Research in Education, Edinburgh, 1990, as *Spotlight* No. 26), stresses their importance for learning:

> We need to build on the satisfactions of thinking, not be preoccupied with the difficulties or the shame of failure. Resolving a difficulty, understanding a complex topic, the flash of insight in solving a problem: these are (or should be) deeply satisfying experiences. Confusion and inability to comprehend are frustrating and quickly erode the will to learn or even to try. (p. 4)

Enabling all learners to succeed in worthwhile tasks is vital for motivation and self-esteem. This point is well illustrated in the findings of a case study on teaching and learning in computing studies (Kirkwood et al. in Kirkwood ed., 1997, pp. 22–28) which involved one Standard Grade class. Pupils' sense of satisfaction and of growing intellectual competence were very evident when they succeeded in solving a difficult problem:

> I enjoyed working on this problem mainly because it required a lot of thinking and testing. It took me a bit longer than some other programs . . . but was a lot more interesting. Every time I ran the program I would discover another bug but eventually I managed to . . . get the program working. I learned that (to) have a detailed design to work from really does help, and I think that had I not used a design I would have had a lot more errors. (Carol)
>
> I felt that it was really MY (underlined twice) work. I would not have felt this if the program had been in the book and I had only copied it. (Carol again, discussing a different problem)

The advice that the case study pupils offered to younger learners embarking on Standard Grade was very insightful:

> Don't expect it to be easy.
> New things may seem hard, but they become clear after a few tries.
> Go through it (the problem) one step at a time, don't try to do the whole thing at once.
> Try to solve problems yourself first to help you later, instead of giving up and asking the teacher.
> Be prepared to accept help from other pupils . . .

Inevitably, difficult work will provoke anxiety amongst pupils who are not confident about their abilities:

> like compared to a lot of the people in the class – everyone is away on topic . . . I don't know – I'm just a bit behind, I think. (Marie)
>
> You're more (further on) than me! (Annette)

Annette's willingness to empathise with Marie is striking in this brief exchange. The main factor that enabled pupils such as Marie and Annette to cope with anxiety and to achieve good grades was the support – both practical and emotional – that pupils gave to each other (which came about by design through the teacher's active promotion of collaborative learning) and the individual support provided by the teacher. The other important commodity was additional time, secured through a variety of means, to enable pupils' understandings to emerge naturally without attempts to rush the process.

HOW SECONDARY CLASSROOMS SHOULD BE MANAGED

Classroom management has been a major focus of recent official reports: *The Education of Able Pupils P6–S2* (SOED, 1993); *5–14: A Practical Guide* (SOED, 1994); and *Achievement for All* (SOED, 1996).

Achievement for All examines the efficacy of current arrangements at S1/S2 with reference to findings from school inspections and national and international surveys of achievement. The evidence from school inspections indicates that pupils are not being stretched, insufficient account is being taken of their primary school experiences, there are weaknesses in attainment (notably in aspects of English language and mathematics), better assessment is required including the use of national tests, and homework needs to be used more effectively. The evidence from national surveys of achievement in English language, mathematics and science indicates a consistent decline in some aspects of pupils' attainment in mathematics since 1983, and insufficient progress in learning for all three subjects between P7 and S2.

HM Inspectors observe that organisational structures frequently get in the way of effective teaching:

> Frequently the organisational structures adopted in schools complicate the task of teaching and restrict teachers' opportunities for direct teaching. Too much of teachers' time is consumed managing resources and explaining what is to be done. (SOED, 1996, p. 22)

The report examines critically three forms of class organisation – streaming, mixed-ability and setting, and a range of 'within class' organisations. It recommends that grouping by attainment should be the preferred form of organisation for most teaching purposes in S1/S2.

This departs from the more neutral stance of *The Education of Able Pupils P6–S2* where it was recognised that clear planning and good classroom management, well-designed materials, and regular assessment and monitoring of progress could together provide the conditions in mixed ability classes to meet the needs of all pupils, including the more able (SOED, 1993).

STREAMING

Streaming was a form of organisation common in the 1950s and 1960s which was used both to assign pupils to secondary schools and to group them into classes. Pupils would be in the same class for all subjects on the basis of an overall assessment of their ability arrived at through testing. The aim was to provide each stream with appropriate educational experiences. Pupils in the top streams were given what was regarded as a more academic curriculum and they were expected to learn at a faster pace. The curriculum for the top streams was also better resourced and planned.

Streaming is now rarely found in Scottish schools. The main challenge to streaming was on social grounds and came with the introduction of comprehensive education in the late 1960s, which was founded on the desire to have equality of educational opportunity and to provide a shared educational experience for all pupils. Other challenges arose in the following areas:

- it came to be understood from research that cognitive skills can be highly specific and unrelated to each other, and therefore pupils in a given stream could contain a very wide range of abilities;
- the tests used to stream pupils ignore the broader range of human abilities such as creative and aesthetic skills;
- there was a lack of consistency in allocating pupils to streams and it was difficult to move pupils between streams;
- the motivation and self-esteem of pupils in the lower streams was adversely affected as a result of being labelled;
- teachers held inappropriate expectations of pupils in the highest and lowest streams which affected pupils' performances. In particular, lower streams provided less educational opportunities since teachers expected less of these pupils.

There is no recommendation in *Achievement for All* for any return to streaming.

CURRENT ORGANISATIONS – MIXED-ABILITY VERSUS SETTING

The two main forms of class organisation currently in use in secondary schools are mixed-ability, in which pupils within a year group are assigned to classes to create a mix of ability in each class, and setting, in which pupils within a year group are assigned to classes for a given subject on the basis of their prior attainment in that subject. A consequence of setting is that pupils may be in different sets for different subjects, and an assumption underlying setting is that learning and teaching in each set will be different, particularly with regard to the pace of learning which is expected of pupils. A variant of setting is broad-banding where pupils are assigned to classes for a given subject which are within an upper or lower band (or within a top, middle or bottom band if there are three bands). The classes within any band are created to be equivalent in terms of attainment. Broad-banding is sometimes used in subjects where there is limited assessment information available to guide the process of allocating pupils to sets (Computing Studies at S3 is a typical example).

The vast majority of classes across all subjects in S1/S2 are organised as mixed-ability, irrespective of the size of the school. However as pupils begin their Standard Grade courses in S3, the proportion of schools opting for setting increases markedly, particularly in mathematics.

The main argument which HM Inspectors advance in favour of setting is as follows:

> In secondary schools, setting offers teachers the opportunity to reduce significantly the time spent on organising and managing learning for a wide range of attainment within one class. It also eases the pressures of having to be constantly responsive to very wide differences of pupil demands and needs. . . . The efficiency gains can be spent on direct teaching and on ensuring that pupils work effectively on tasks which challenge them appropriately. (SOEID, *Achievement for All*, 1996, p. 22)

However, in spite of the perceived gains to efficiency, it is difficult to see how setting would avoid many of the pitfalls associated with streaming. Brian Boyd has expressed his disquiet, shared by many teachers, at the prospect of more setting being introduced:

> Differentiation is a set of strategies designed to ensure that 'teaching for effective learning' takes place. It assumes a belief that all pupils have the potential to be effective learners, and, like Bloom, that if we can provide 'a courteous translation' then they will be able to learn more successfully than at present. Above all, it is a means to the end of 'achievement for all' – not achievement for some at the expense of others. (Boyd, 1997, p. 10)

He concludes: 'we need to invest our energies, not in arid discussion about classroom organisation, but in unlocking the doors to the barriers which prevent pupils from being successful learners' (ibid. p. 10).

The conclusions of a recent review of research on setting and streaming do not support the increased use of attainment groups in secondary schools: 'There is no consistent and reliable evidence of positive effects of setting and streaming in any subjects or for students of particular ability levels' (Harlen and Malcolm, 1997, p. 40). Effective differentiation emerges from the review as the key issue:

> The challenge is to find some way of catering for pupils' individual needs. The research . . . shows that for many, ability grouping reduces both their motivation and the quality of the education they receive. On the other hand, mixed-ability teaching which denies the differences between high- and low-ability pupils is not the answer. (SCRE Newsletter, Spring 1997, pp. 8–9)

The authors recommend that urgent action is needed to identify and study methods of adjusting the content, pace and support of classroom work to suit individual needs.

WITHIN CLASS ORGANISATIONS

A range of within class organisations is to be found across subjects and stages. Mary Simpson and Jenny Ure observed the following organisations in English, modern languages, science and mathematics at S1–S4:

- In English and modern languages during S1–S4 a common organisation is whole class teaching which has been observed to involve high levels of interaction between teachers and pupils.
- In science during S1/S2 there is widespread reliance on resource-based learning in which pupils work independently on set tasks and the teacher maintains comprehensive records of their attainment levels in the units of the common course.

- In mathematics during S1/S2 pupils work on highly structured individualised learning schemes, on which they are placed according to their individual rates of progress and their attainments in end-of-unit criterion-referenced tests.
- In the sciences and mathematics at S3/S4 the Standard Grade courses contain elements of whole class teaching which entails the use of differentiated materials. (Simpson and Ure, 1993)

Whole class teaching is a well established practice in every subject area, and indeed its over-use has been criticised in the past (SOED, 1993). In the upper school the pressure for coverage at Higher Grade often leads teachers to resort to it because it gives them more control over the pacing of instruction. If whole class teaching is properly differentiated it can be very successful (Simpson and Ure, 1993).

Using ability groups is a less common practice in secondary classrooms than in primary. Observational studies of primary classrooms seem to indicate that a vicious circle can be created when ability groups are used:

> pupils in low-ability groups feel stigmatised and demotivated; teachers are less motivated to teach them and have lower expectations of them; in turn this reduces the opportunities for achievement and pupils in low-ability groups tend to stay there. (Harlen and Malcolm, 1997, p. 21)

5–14 A Practical Guide contains advice for teachers on working with groups, which includes: identify one group at a time as the teaching group and give each group a turn of being the teaching group, and give the other groups clear instructions for working on their own (SOED, 1994). While this advice makes group work more manageable for the teacher, it can only work successfully if pupils are given quiet work to do which can be accomplished without further input from the teacher.

Using ability groups for mathematics in upper primary classrooms has been found to raise achievements, with low achievers appearing to gain the most (Harlen and Malcolm, 1997, p. 18). There could therefore be benefits to extending this organisation to S1/S2, so long as it is not over-used.

Three common criticisms of resource-based and indivisualised learning are that the management of the materials consumes the teachers' time, monitoring of pupils' progress is complex, and pupils tend to work in isolation from each other and the teacher (SOEID, *Achievement for All*, 1996; Simpson and Ure, 1993).

These problems are mainly located in the design of the materials and the learning environment, and it is apparent that many existing 'schemes' are not well designed. Many are over-elaborate and therefore difficult for both the pupil and teacher to manage, collaboration may not have been planned for so that pupils lose the benefits of learning from each other, and teachers may attempt to do all of the checking of pupils' work during the lesson, which is neither desirable nor practicable.

Eric Drever has identified a number of other issues which need to be tackled if resource-based and individualised learning are to be successfully implemented:

- Time appears to be critical. Attempts to speed up to fit the available time can undermine the whole approach by preventing proper self-pacing, cutting off learning before mastery has been achieved, and causing teachers to restrict their resource-based teaching to a minimum.

- The design of materials should be to engender fruitful interactions between pupils, resources and the teacher, rather than to enable pupils to work unaided.
- Research evidence shows that pupils may simply 'go through the motions' of one activity after another.
- A strength of traditional teaching is that teachers can lend coherence to a topic. This can be lost, and with it, retention ('they do it, check it, forget it') if resource-based materials are designed on an instructional objectives model. (Drever, 1988, pp. 94–5)

An important missing element in the overall equation has been training for teachers on the design, appraisal and use of such materials. Two important benefits of these organisations are that they enable pupils to work at a pace that is suited to their needs, and pupils gain a measure of independence from the teacher which is necessary for developing skills in self-regulation.

CONCLUSIONS

Grouping pupils by attainment is not the solution to the differentiation 'problem', but there may be circumstances where it is appropriate to do this, for example, targeted intervention to address a specific problem that is preventing certain pupils from making progress in learning.

To fully address the problems of under-achievement and indiscipline (which must be viewed holistically) schools need additional resources. Research funding should also be directed towards these areas to extend understanding of the issues and to guide policy and practice. These measures will be cost effective for society in the long run if they prevent some youngsters from wasting their life opportunities.

Differentiation and classroom mangement should become major focuses of pre-service training and teachers' professional development. It would be highly regrettable if 'direct teaching' became equated in teachers' minds with whole class teaching and the current advice from HM Inspectors led to a narrowing of teachers' skills and an abandonment of mixed-ability teaching and resource-based and individualised approaches.

Teachers need time and more opportunities to examine their beliefs and assumptions, and to appraise the research, ideas in the literature, existing policies and practices. It is only through such thoughtful engagement that real and lasting improvements in learning and teaching processes will occur.

REFERENCES

Drever, E. (1985) Mastery Learning in Context, Theory and Practice, in S. Brown and P. Munn (eds) *The Changing Face of Education 14 to 16: Curriculum and Assessment*, Windsor: NFER-Nelson, pp. 58–68.

Drever, E. (1988) Resource-Based Teaching: The New Pedagogy?, in S. Brown and R. Wake (eds) *Education in Transition.*, Edinburgh: SCRE.

Dweck, C. S., and E. S. Elliott (1983) Achievement Motivation, in E. M. Hetherington (ed.) *Socialization, Personality and Social Development* (Vol. IV of P. H. Mussen (ed.) *Handbook of Child Psychology*) New York: Wiley pp. 643–92.

Harlen, W. and H. Malcolm (1997) *Setting And Streaming: A Research Review*, Edinburgh: SCRE.

Kirkwood, M. (ed.) *Differentiation S1 to S4: The Ways Forward, Report on a one-day conference at Jordanhill Campus, Strathclyde University*, Glasgow: University of Strathclyde.

Simpson, M., and J. Ure (1993) *What's The Difference? A Study Of Differentiation In Scottish Secondary Schools*, Aberdeen: Northern College.

VIII

Secondary Education: Curriculum

45

The Structure of the Secondary Curriculum

Tony Gavin

BACKGROUND

The introduction of comprehensive secondary schooling in the 1960s was a fundamental influence in shaping the Scottish secondary school curriculum in the ensuing decades. Those responsible faced the very real challenge of providing quality education for 12–18 year olds of all abilities and of diverse aspirations. Education Authorities were ill prepared to meet this imposed change, teachers had little real understanding of its likely impact, many were less than enthusiastic and few understood its potential benefits.

Recognition of the increasing need for pastoral and vocational support to sustain pupil learning resulted in the introduction into schools of guidance staff. These are subject specialist teachers who undertake additional remits for providing pastoral, curricular and vocational support for pupils. Faced with the real and practical task of providing for all young people, schools expanded their range of subjects. Courses in economics, accountancy, modern studies, drama, personal and social education, outdoor education and, later, computing, graphic communications and technological studies became more common. New specialist departments were often established to accommodate these new courses.

In 1972 the raising of the school leaving age from fifteen years to sixteen years significantly increased the pressure to introduce new learning experiences relevant to meeting the perceived needs of these new clients. This usually meant courses of a vocational nature as opposed to the established core of academic subjects. The inadequacies of provision created a demand from teachers for an agreed curricular rationale, particularly for the third and fourth years of secondary school, together with a national curricular and assessment framework to provide for all pupils.

These tasks were addressed by two committees set up by the Scottish Education Department (SED). The committee chaired by James Munn addressed the curriculum and that chaired by Joseph Dunning examined issues relating to assessment and certification. Their reports were published in 1977 (SED, 1997a and b) and were to shape the post 14–16 secondary curriculum leading to the introduction of Standard Grade courses and certification for all within a commonly accepted curricular framework based on eight modes of learning.

In 1986 the Scottish Consultative Committee on the Curriculum published a discussion paper entitled *Education 10–14 in Scotland*. This report identified the desirable outcomes of education over the 10–14 age range expressing them in terms of behavioural and attitudinal characteristics of young people. The 'fresh start' philosophy for pupils transferring from Primary 7 to Secondary 1 was firmly rejected and the report challenged the widening gap between the primary and secondary sectors caused by their different approaches to curricular innovation. In rejecting the more widespread use of middle schools for the 10–14 age group the report supported the retention of the established primary and secondary sectors whilst emphasising the need for these sectors to work more closely together.

The report was influential in nurturing a national debate which, in turn, influenced and shaped the 5–14 development programme. A number of innovative ideas proposed in the report quickly became normal practice in schools and colleges. The committee's proposals regarding the use of criterion referenced assessment to promote learning, and for improved forms of recording pupil progress and reporting to parents, found a place in school development planning in the 1990s. Recommendations regarding pupil care which clarified the roles of teachers, parents and support agencies were later reflected in education authority schemes designed to support vulnerable children through the use of inter-agency groups involving teachers, social workers, health officers, psychologists and community education personnel.

Pupils entering the S1 stage of a typical Scottish secondary school are faced with an exciting but sometimes bewildering diet of different subjects, teachers and learning experiences. In the majority of schools between twelve and sixteen different subjects contribute to the S1 curriculum. Usually this is organised and delivered through a timetable by allocating a number of periods each week to the discrete subjects. This results in pupils being taught by up to 16 different teachers.

The curriculum modes common throughout the S1–S4 years and within which the various subject specialisms provide courses of systematic and active study are defined in the guidelines published by Scottish Consultative Council on the Curriculum (SCCC).

At the S1/S2 stages of secondary school, English, mathematics, modern languages and science usually have a more generous time allocation than other subjects. Some schools also include one or more additional elements from modern studies, drama, celtic studies, economics, classical studies and outdoor education. Schools which provide these additional elements may choose to leave them until the S2 stage or provide them by a process of extracting pupils from the timetabled courses for short periods of time. Some schools, recognising the obvious disadvantages of such a fragmented learning experience, use timetabling devices such as rotations of history and geography, music and art and craft design and technology and home economics in order to reduce the number of different teacher contacts experienced by the individual pupil during the course of a week. This situation creates a tension between the advantages of increased choice, which in turn creates a fragmented learning experience, and the pursuit of the educational advantages of personalised pupil teacher relationships.

Schools use the term common curriculum when describing that range of subjects, determined by the school, which is provided for all pupils. Its introduction in the late 1960s was in keeping with a philosophy which promoted equal access for all and rejected any notion of curricular elitism. New ways of addressing issues arising from the introduction of the common curriculum such as effective differentiated learning, the individual pace of learning and appropriate use of prior attainments in primary school are still to be resolved.

THE CURRICULUM IN THE FIRST AND SECOND YEARS

The SCCC guidelines suggest that the S1/S2 curriculum should allow opportunities for pupil choice. In practice this can be limited to selecting one from a choice of two modern languages and some project activities within some subjects. The curriculum for pupils in S1 and S2 is seen mainly as a continuum but with some degree of increasing subject specialisms becoming more distinctive. Some schools, for instance, which offer an integrated science course in S1 move to discrete biology, chemistry and physics during S2.

The 5–14 initiative seeks to promote the curriculum as a number of broad areas of learning. For the primary stages and the first two years of secondary these are identified as English language, mathematics, environmental studies, expressive arts and religious and moral education. What pupils should gain from the study of these broad areas is expressed in the general terms of desirable outcomes. The way in which the curriculum is organised so that pupils can reach towards these outcomes is signposted for teachers by identified strands which focus curricular activities on relevant knowledge, skills and attitudes. Attainment targets, which are specific statements of what pupils should know or be able to do, are set at five different levels: A to E. Some recognition of the individual's pace of learning is indicated in ascertaining when pupils are expected to reach particular levels. This national initiative also provides examples of programmes of study for each of the five areas of learning.

To date this initiative has had some impact in the secondary sector in S1 and S2 by rationalising what is being taught and assessed in English, languages and mathematics and, in some instances, religious and moral education. The impact of this programme is less clear in the areas of environmental studies and expressive arts. There is a need to address the question of how far the 5–14 initiative helps resolve the problems inherent in the use of the common course in S1 and S2.

THE CURRICULUM IN THE THIRD AND FOURTH YEARS

The S3/S4 curriculum is designed to meet the general aims of the development of knowledge and understanding, the development of cognitive, interpersonal, psychomotor and social skills and the acquiring of behavioural attitudes and insights into the world of work. Pupils have an increased element of choice when embarking on their two year course of study in S3 and S4. A typical pupil aged 14 to 16 years will study seven or eight subjects leading to Standard Grade awards selected from a curriculum framework designed to ensure a broad and balanced education. This is done in accordance with the SCCC guidelines which recommend that subjects are grouped into categories representing eight modes of learning.

At the S3 and S4 stage languages and mathematics are allocated a minimum of 20 per cent and 10 per cent of the available time. The language component includes the study of another modern European language as well as English. Scientific studies, social studies, technological and creative/aesthetic activities each receive 10 per cent of the time with physical education and religious and moral education each receiving a minimum of 5 per cent. This leaves the remaining 20 per cent for student choice. In practice the freedom of choice for any individual is limited to the range of subjects offered in their particular school.

In addition to the subjects which make up the eight modes of learning, pupils commonly follow a course in social education devised by the school. This accommodates careers education, aspects of health education, care of the environment, learning about rules, rights and responsibilities and guidance relating to living and employment. Schools also use the device of syllabus inserts or permeation across subjects to deliver these elements of the curriculum. Religious and moral education can be provided through the use of permeation, syllabus inserts and special courses. The majority of S4 pupils in Scottish secondary schools undertake a period of planned work experience. This is organised by extraction from the school timetable for a continuous period of between five to ten school days.

SCOTTISH EDUCATION DEPARTMENT'S 16–18 ACTION PLAN (1983)

This initiative, which came from the Further Education sector, successfully rationalised much of the non-advanced post-16 provision in colleges of further education into modular form and established a national system for modular course assessment and certification under the newly formed Scottish Vocational Education Council (SCOTVEC). In secondary schools the arrangements for Higher Grade and the Certificate of Sixth Year Studies remained unaffected. However, with post-16 school staying-on rates rising and schools searching for courses appropriate to the increasingly diverse needs and aspirations of the growing student population, most secondary schools introduced modular courses leading to SCOTVEC certification. Schools working both collectively and individually began to develop and offer a range of modular courses derived from the SCOTVEC catalogue, frequently using the new system to certificate pupil attainment in areas such as work experience which had not previously enjoyed national recognition. In schools modular courses were used to create progression routes from Standard Grade levels 3, 4 and 5 to provide for some students a suitable bridge between Standard Grade and entry to Higher Grade courses in their second year of post-16 education, normally in S6.

Curriculum planners were concerned that indiscriminate use of the modular course catalogue was leading to fragmentation of the curriculum and a lack of coherence in some students' learning experiences. Some schools then offered modular courses within a framework of the General Scottish Vocational Qualification (GSVQ), a type of group award, in an attempt to bring some coherence and progression into post-16 modular provision. The Action Plan Programme placed great emphasis on the autonomy of students in their choice of programmes of study and this was not always compatible with the limited range of modular programmes schools could offer and with the requirements of the GSVQ awards.

The disadvantages of having two distinct examining bodies, namely the Scottish Examination Board and SCOTVEC, became increasingly frustrating to students and teachers as well as creating some confusion among parents and employers. The system accentuated the academic/vocational divide and it proved difficult to arrive at clear agreements on such matters as credit transfers across the two distinct systems. In some instances this meant students having to repeat elements of courses in order to satisfy the different examining boards. By the late 1980s the need for one examining authority to cover all post-16 non-advanced education in Scotland was very evident, but, as thinking progressed, moves to create such a system awaited the implementation of the Higher Still Programme.

In the early 1980s, as the recommendations of the Munn and Dunning Committees were being translated into acceptable curricular guidelines and assessment and certification for all in S3 and S4, the impact of computer technology began to influence the thinking and practice of teachers. Clearly the use of such technology will continue to impact on society and has exciting possibilities for learning and access to learning.

The implementation of the Standard Grade programme brought benefits to all pupils in S3 and S4. Paradoxically this led to increased dissatisfaction with school provision for the post-16 age group. Despite innovative efforts by many schools in using modular courses, the system lacked recognition by many employers and gatekeepers to further education and training. In 1992 the Scottish Office Education and Industry Department (SOEID) established a committee under the chairmanship of Professor John Howie of the University of St Andrews to review the aims and purposes of courses and of assessment and certification in the fifth and sixth years of secondary school education in Scotland. This committee reported in February 1992 (SOED, 1992) proposing two broad post-16 routes, namely that of the Scottish Certificate (SCOTCERT) with certificated exit points at the end of a one or two year programme of study, and the Scottish Baccalaureate (SCOTBAC) with students following a three year programme to a higher level. This latter route to higher education was to be accomplished at a more measured pace with an increased chance of success compared to the one year post-16 dash to Higher Grade. SCOTCERT would provide progression routes to SVQ courses in further education and employment with the SCOTBAC route leading to entry to higher education.

Schools agreed strongly with the need for change and the rationale underpinning the report. Considerable disquiet was expressed at the potentially divisive nature of the proposed progression routes and the absence of coherence with provision in further and higher education. Taking cognisance of the responses to the Howie report, the SOEID produced in 1993 further proposals for post-16 provision. This time the vision was for one structure to provide for all post-16 non-advanced education in Scottish schools, FE colleges and adult centres catering for all ages, abilities and aspirations and leading to awards from one newly formed examination board to be called the Scottish Qualifications Authority (SQA). With school staying-on rates rising and pressure from central government to meet the targets set by the Advisory Scottish Council for Education and Training Targets (ASCETT), the prevailing mood was for action.

THE CURRENT CURRICULUM IN THE FIFTH AND SIXTH YEARS

On entering the fifth year of secondary school, which, for the majority of students, is their first year of non-compulsory education, the time allocation for subjects is increased with a corresponding decrease in the number of subjects chosen by the individual student. The current model of post-16 curricular provision commonly found in Scottish secondary schools consists of three main variants: Higher in S5 and Certificate of Sixth Year Studies (CSYS) in S6; modules (40 hour courses) in S5 followed by Highers in S6; modules in both S5 and S6. The majority of students negotiate an individual curriculum appropriate to their needs, interests and aspirations from a combination of these variants. Using this approach, schools go some way to providing for all their students and, to some extent, ensure that those who choose to leave school at December or June in their fifth year do so having acquired certification appropriate to their levels of attainment in their chosen subjects.

SCCC guidance to schools on the S5/6 curriculum recommends a design that incorporates key skills and elements as 'critical structural features' of the curriculum in terms of specific courses. Schools commonly structure S5/6 provision around the development of communication and mathematical skills, the key elements of technological, creative and critical thinking, together with personal, moral and social development. This approach provides some desirable progression from S3 and S4 while maintaining flexibility in the choice of subjects to be studied. Two examples of curricular framework used by schools to provide both progression from the S3/4 stage and choice for post-16 students are provided in the SCCC guidelines *Curricular Design for the Secondary Stages* (1989). A further revision of these guidelines has been completed and is currently awaiting a response from the Secretary of State for Scotland.

In late 1993 the SOEID established the Higher Still Development Programme. This programme for development sets out to revise all current Higher and Certificate of Sixth Year Studies courses together with all additional courses provided at levels between Standard and Higher Grades. Following completion of Standard Grade in S4 there will be five levels of courses: Access, Intermediate 1, Intermediate 2, Higher and Advanced Higher. The aim is to provide opportunities for all to continue with relevant and successful study after completion of Standard Grade and at a level appropriate to the individual student. The programme stresses the importance of core skills to the development of the individual. In Higher Still these are defined as communications, numeracy, problem solving, information technology and working with others. Student achievements in these skills are to be assessed and certificated. Group Awards, both general and specific, are to be devised to minimise the academic and vocational divide. The new Scottish examining board, the Scottish Qualifications Authority, is to take responsibility for all assessment arrangements and certification for all courses within the new framework.

Considerable efforts are being made to engage teachers, employers, administrators and parents in the implementation of this programme now due to commence in August 1999 with the first examinations due in 2000.

Concurrent with these formal curricular changes there have been a range of focused external influences which have impacted on teaching and learning within the secondary school curriculum. Schools and businesses across the country have affirmed in recent years that significant mutual benefits are to be found in working together.

EDUCATION-INDUSTRY LINKS (EIL)

The importance of Education-Industry Links has been highlighted in national policy statements (SCCC 1995). The extent of these activities within Scottish schools varies from the occasional school visitor from the world of work to well managed and developed school programmes which influence both the content and nature of the learning experienced by secondary pupils. EIL programmes designed to impact on the curriculum encompass a range of activities such as enterprise projects, mock interviews, work experience and work shadowing, placements for teachers with corresponding business personnel placements in schools and joint projects which enrich specific subject courses through using industrial and business contexts and examples for teaching.

The demands from employers to provide young people with the language skills needed by business and commerce in a developing European Common Market led to a radical rethink on the place of modern languages in the curriculum. Very quickly French, German and other European languages lost their elitist status and ceased to be regarded as only for the most able, becoming a core learning experience for all between the ages of 12 to 16 years.

All of these are genuine attempts to influence and shape the curriculum with a view to providing all young people with an understanding of the world of work and equipping them with social and personal skills to function in the increasingly complex and changing scene of business, commerce and employment. Innovative schools seek employer support for business enterprise projects. These are generally optional and 'bolt on' learning experiences for students, the absence of any means of providing national certification creating a barrier to their acceptance as an integral part of the curriculum.

THE TECHNICAL AND VOCATIONAL EDUCATION INITIATIVE (TVEI) (1984–96)

TVEI was a programme through which education authorities throughout the United Kingdom could access funding from the Department of Employment (later the Department of Industry) to promote change in the education of 14–18 year olds. The aim was to effect changes in the school curriculum designed to better equip young people for the demands of working life in a rapidly changing technological society. This was to be done by relating what is learned in schools and colleges to the world of work by improving skills and qualifications in the areas of science, technology, information technology and modern languages. The programme criteria required that young people be provided with real work experience and supported by counselling and individual action planning.

The intention was to facilitate change in the curriculum in the secondary stages S3/4/5/6, not by offering an alternative curriculum, but by influencing the focus of developments and pace of change within the agreed national curricular framework.

There is evidence to show that the TVEI programmes significantly influenced the curriculum (SOED, 1994) through enhancement of technology, problem solving inserts, the development of personal and social development (PSD) courses, work experience and enterprise education and the introduction of national records of achievement. Teachers have identified TVEI as having a major influence in bringing about changes in teaching methods, and, by promoting pupil centred learning, differentiation and flexible learning.

SOME CRITICAL ISSUES FOR THE FUTURE

Managing change in the secondary curriculum

In any education community change is an essential part of growth. Such change is necessary to ensure the stability and the survival of the institution as an organisation capable of achieving its aims and objectives. The idea that a period of no change within a school will provide stability is dangerously misleading. Change is a natural state in human affairs. Schools exist within dynamic communities and to fulfil their functions change is both endemic and essential. If a 'no change until we are ready' stance is adopted then, increasingly, the clients of education will see what schools offer as irrelevant to their needs and to their futures. This will certainly not make the job of the teacher any easier. While clearly the needs of teachers must be addressed these cannot be met by refusing to meet the needs of pupils, parents and employers. Practising teachers are continuously changing their approaches in order to meet their perceptions of the needs of their pupils. The origins of change derive from a range of sources including the school classroom, the partnerships between schools, parents and employers and from the wider interface between the education establishment, education authorities and central government. All of these groups initiate and influence change to varying degrees. Successful change in secondary schooling requires these key players to come together, to negotiate the change programme and jointly to take responsibility and accountability for the change process. The real issues for schools are those relating to the direction, pace and management of change. Schools exist to serve people and are staffed and managed by people. Even though they desire a degree of change, the participants are often cautious. While in theory teachers may agree with the vision of the future which is to be achieved through change, their immediate concerns often relate to their own present and special interests. Successful implementation in schools requires, therefore, a high level of professional management of people including the ability to maintain the confidence and commitment of students, teachers, parents and employers during the change process. For the parties involved this process is never risk free. It is important, therefore, to learn from our successes and failures over the past decades.

Successful programmes for change include the introduction of Standard Grade, the TVEI Programme in Scotland and the implementation of the 16–18 Action Plan. These were all characterised by a number of common features. To manage change successfully it is important to provide a clear and easily understood rationale for the change and to focus the nature of the development in such a way that the people involved understand their role within the process and are clear as to the expected outcomes. People grow and develop within this change process.

Change invariably requires additional resourcing but usually not as much as might be supposed by teachers and administrators. More important is the careful targeting of resources to promote change and the attention and time given to monitoring and reviewing. The involvement of practitioners in the whole process of planning, developing, monitoring and reviewing is essential in reflecting ownership, in maintaining confidence and in influencing the direction of change. Change is a natural state in human affairs but it neither adopts a linear pathway nor is it a one issue phenomenon.

Any programme which sets out to bring about change has to challenge the status quo and, in doing so, will attract criticism. These critics should be heard and their views carefully examined. Valid criticism may well offer perspectives not previously considered and may challenge assumptions so encouraging the proposers of change to clarify their thinking. It should also be recognised that some critics represent vested interests other than the well being of young people in our schools.

The subject centred promoted post structure in secondary schools

A typical secondary school of 900 + pupils is staffed with approximately sixty-six teaching staff, more than half of whom hold a promoted post within the school. About twenty of these promoted posts are allocated to principal teacher subject (PT) and assistant principal teacher subject (APT). The remaining promoted posts will be allocated to guidance support (six), senior teacher posts (five) with four or five positions being occupied by the assistant headteachers, one depute headteacher and the headteacher. This arrangement, whereby the majority of promoted posts are created within the subject departments, has existed since the 1950s and 1960s and was further expanded as new courses found a place in the secondary curriculum. During this period the structure has served the development of the secondary curriculum reasonably well with new courses in areas such as business studies, computing and religious education all being accommodated and supported by the appointment of new subject PTs and APTs. However, this predominantly subject centred promoted post structure is unlikely to prove effective for the delivery of a coherent and progressive secondary school curriculum in the coming decade.

In the secondary school the present structure has not proved to be sufficiently flexible to respond to the 5–14 development programme. Cross curricular courses such as health studies, social and vocational skills, media studies and personal and social education have been slow to become established within the secondary curriculum. One reason for this is that they have not proved attractive to many teachers since the teacher career routes are through principal teacher (subject) or through principal teacher (guidance). What is needed is a structure which motivates teachers and principal teachers to embrace curriculum management responsibilities across a number of subject specialisms.

It could be argued that the present structure has not only hindered the development of the 5–14 programme, particularly in the areas of environmental studies and the expressive arts, but has also contributed to the fragmentation of the curriculum in S1 and S2. The structure does not fit easily within the modal arrangements in S3 and S4; indeed ensuring a technological entitlement for all pupils in S3 and S4 could not be guaranteed through the established core courses in science and mathematics. The present subject centred structure has underpinned the development of individual Higher Grade subjects. However the future at the post-16 stage is now likely to be one of wider access to modular courses and units with students building credits across a range of these. This will require co-ordinated planning and development with student needs and progression routes central to this process.

The role of the Scottish Qualifications Authority

There is frequently a healthy tension between the aspirations of curriculum planners and innovators and the demands of the examining board. Society rightly expects that pupil attainments are recognised through the award of qualifications approved by a national body which commands public confidence. However, an examination board's course arrangements can determine not only the content of a course but, on occasions, the methodologies deployed in the teaching of the course. For example, in a science course any change in the examination board's arrangements to increase or decrease the weighting given to the assessment of practical skills can lead to significant changes in the teaching of that subject for all pupils. These changes are not necessarily in the best interests of all pupils in terms of their motivation and attitudes to learning. Many teachers take the view that a major factor in the perceived declining standards of arithmetical skills among Scottish pupils is directly related to the former Scottish Examination Board's decision to remove arithmetic as a separate course leading to a national award for pupils at the end of their fourth year in secondary school. Clearly it is important that curricular planners and examination subject panels enjoy a shared and collective understanding of each other's aims.

Subject choice within the secondary curriculum

The SCCC Curricular Guidelines (SCCC, 1989) place considerable emphasis on opportunities for pupil choice in S1 and S2 with an increasing element of choice in the succeeding years. Many teachers and parents regard pupil choice as an important factor in sustaining motivation and in meeting career aspirations although it is debatable whether or not such a view can be substantiated. The practice of presenting pupils with increased choice can lead to uncertainties and even stress among pupils and parents listening to the competing claims from subject specialists. Increasing choice creates resourcing problems for all but the largest of schools and these are exacerbated as students seek to pursue subject specialisms in S5 and

S6. Do we know that increasing pupil choice in secondary schools results in higher quality education? Given that the school curriculum from S1 to S4 as laid out in the SCCC guidelines guarantees breadth and balance together with core skills development and personal social education, does subject choice really matter?

A case can be made for rationalising the S1/S2 curriculum to achieve less emphasis on individual subject specialisms and for reducing the range of subjects available in S3 and S4 while still meeting the principles of breadth, balance and coherence. Such a curriculum could also be sufficient to ensure the maintenance of post-16 progression and career routes. Is the way to quality education not more a question of how learning and teaching takes place within a broad and balanced curriculum rather than that of pupil choice from a widening range of subject specialisms?

With school post-16 staying on rates in excess of 80 per cent and, in some cases, approaching 100 per cent, then would it not be more sensible to target limited resources towards improving the quality of teaching and learning even if that means reducing pupil choice from S1 to S4? At the post-16 stage extended student choice could then be provided through the use of the Higher Still framework and the imaginative application of flexible learning supported by technology.

Parents and the secondary school curriculum

The past decade has witnessed a raft of initiatives to promote partnership between parents and school. Some, like the publication of examination results, attendance figures and school costs statistics have become established practice while school boards are promoted, regulated and even constrained by legislation. Although many of the traditional barriers to school-parent partnerships have been lowered the initiatives themselves are not widely supported by parents and are viewed with some suspicion by some local councils.

The significant focus for school partnerships with parents must be to further effective teaching and learning. Some radical thinking is required with a view to engaging the attention, cooperation and participation of all parents in the education of their children.

Statistics relating to attendance at school parent evenings, to parental involvement in homework and extra curricular activities might prove a useful starting point for reflection. There are now untapped skills and resources among the over-50 age group in all our local communities. These could be harnessed and directed to assist our young people to be enthusiastic learners. The curriculum must not be the sole prerogative of the education professionals nor should employers have undue influences. The curriculum, to be effective, must belong to everyone.

REFERENCES

SCCC (1989) *Curriculum Design for the Secondary Stages – Guidelines for Headteachers*, first revised edition, Dundee: SCCC.
SCCC (1995) *Education Industry Links in Scotland 5–18 – A Framework for Action*, Dundee: SCCC.
SED (1977a) *The Structure of the Curriculum in the Third and Fourth Years of the Scottish Secondary School*, Edinburgh: HMSO.
SED (1977b) *Assessment for All*, Edinburgh: HMSO.
SOED (1992) *Upper Secondary Education in Scotland* (The Howie Report), Edinburgh: HMSO.
SOED (1994) *School for Skills Report*, Edinburgh: SOEID.

46

Art and Design Education

Stuart MacDonald

DRAWING THE LINE – ANTECEDENTS

Originally called 'Design', then 'Drawing', then 'Art', art and design has been an integral part of Scottish education since the Scotch Education Department was founded in 1872. In those days a prescribed course of instruction, arranged to suit children in graded standards, was laid down by the Department. The aim was functional not cultural. The art curriculum was designed to develop hand and eye training and to equip the scholar for mechanical work in the factory. The government also hoped that drawing lessons would help improve the standard of British industrial design. At the turn of the century the Department began to lessen its grip and hand over responsibility to specialist teachers. The decision by the Department to abandon formal schemes of work after the Second World War and official encouragement to develop more experimental, child-centred courses, created considerable progress, especially in junior secondary schools. The most significant development was the introduction of 'divided classes', and led to Scotland being almost unique internationally, in having small practical classes in art taught by specialist teachers.

FROM SHEEPS' HEADS TO CRITICAL STUDIES

At the beginning of the 1970s an attempt was made to enshrine the successes of the junior secondary school in the guidance for the new comprehensive and its expanded cohort. *Art in the Secondary School – Curriculum Paper 9* (1971), however, like its counterpart in England and Wales, merely codified visual analysis, free exploration of the environment and other process-based approaches into arrangements for the 'new' Higher Art Examination. The result was an orthodoxy, colloquially referred to as the 'sheep's heid syndrome', in which investigation of the environment was interpreted as the detailed observation and rendering of natural form. Annually, this culminated in the submission of thousands of drawings and paintings of sheeps' skulls (as well as trainers and Coke cans) to the Examination Board. One major casualty was the use of fantasy and imagination, elements synonymous with post-war child-centred creativity.

It was not until Standard Grade that the necessary broadening of the art and design curriculum took place. It balanced the essentially expressive nature of fine art practices like painting, printmaking or sculpture with the problem-solving constraints of designing, and sought to contextualise both these practical activities with a critical, reflective approach.

That development, the integration of the productive aspects of art and design with what is known throughout the UK as Critical Studies, was and remains contentious amongst art teachers – a profession whose training is predominantly practical. As well as demonstrating historically the influential role of the examination system, Critical Studies is also part of a larger international contemporary debate about art and design both in education and society. Understanding that debate is not only crucial to appreciating the current status and role of art and design education, but also its future rationalisation.

PHILOSOPHIES OF ART AND DESIGN

In philosophical terms, for most of the twentieth century, art and design education in Scotland could be largely characterised as Modernist in its approach. That is, teachers have either been concerned with imparting the subject's disciplinary essentials – using representational modes of drawing and developing skills in traditional media like painting and printmaking – or with child-centred expression. Both have been seen as inimical to the wider introduction of cultural contexts and issues into the art and design curriculum.

Lately, the subject repertoire has been extended with design activities like graphics and textiles, and with new media like computing and digital imaging. According to the 1996 Scottish Examiners' Report, for example, Design Activity in Standard Grade was 'well organised and supported' and was improving in scope. Equally, HMI reports have observed that Critical Studies has been introduced successfully, albeit conventionally, focusing largely on historical figures from the history of Western Art. Nonetheless, within this convention Scotland is distinctive in the UK in having its version of Critical Studies as a mandatory element within the courses and examinations at Standard Grade and Revised Higher Grade (MacDonald, 1996).

Indeed, inherent within the advice for art and design within Expressive Arts 5–14, the recommended approach for S1 and S2 includes designing as part of a broad approach to communication, as well as 'Evaluating and Appreciating'. The latter again differentiates Scottish art and design education from developments elsewhere in the UK and is potentially more culturally diverse than its English/Welsh counterpart in which the study of Western Civilisation is pre-eminent (MacDonald, 1993).

AFTER MODERNISM

Despite the changes of recent years it could be argued that Scottish art and design education remains predominantly Modernist, namely, the focus has been either discipline-centred or child-centred. The exclusivity of both has been perceived as eschewing the plurality of contemporary culture. If this were so Scotland would be no different from many other countries. According to international commentators on art and design the 'juggernaut' of curriculum reform is universal and shares commonalities such as an emphasis on skill development at the expense of wider theoretical concerns. The present analysis of Scottish art and design education indicates that this has been persistent historically. Certainly, if the art and design work submitted by senior secondary students for national examinations around the world were lined up together it would be impossible to distinguish one country from another. The antidote, a Post-modern art and design curriculum – an idea which is gaining international momentum – would celebrate, it is claimed, such things as cultural diversity, gender difference and local contexts, and over-ride what is seen as the Modernist hegemony of child-centred expression and discipline-focused debate (Efland et al., 1996).

METHODOLOGY

Whilst sharing many of the international characteristics contingent upon examination-led curricula, art and design in Scotland can nevertheless lay some claim to being identifiably different, in terms of methodology at least. For example, the development of Critical Studies brought with it an emphasis on flexible learning strategies such as Supported Self Study, underpinned by national and local staff development packages. All of this has been embodied in more recent developments relating to Higher Still.

Further, the national interest in differentiated learning applies as much to art and design as to other subjects in the curriculum. This has been facilitated by art and design being given a secure role in the 14–16 secondary curriculum within the Creative Aesthetic Mode, and this is reflected in Expressive Arts 5–14. In sharp contrast to the situation in England and Wales, it has allowed art and design teachers in Scotland to put a focus on the learner instead of being diverted by consuming debates about the status of the subject. The result, therefore, despite little superficial change in student work, has been an interest by some practitioners in evolving underpinning methodologies, increasingly aided by new technology. As well as contributing to 'core skills', this has helped democratise the subject, and in that respect at least Scotland can lay some claim to a Post-modern curriculum.

ASSESSMENT

Changes in methodology and classroom practice apply equally to assessment. 'Portfolio' assessment, now common to many subjects, has long been practised in art and design. This practice has increased as a result of the emphasis on internal modes of assessment in Standard Grade but more especially by SCOTVEC module work. To that has been added an interest in self assessment – now recommended in subject guidelines for all stages – (including Higher Still) – aided by the informal atmosphere of many artrooms. A greater role for the learner in national assessment systems is advocated by Post-modern reformers. However, the reliance placed by many classroom practitioners on the traditional format offered by a national examination would appear to melitate against any immediate change in policy.

CULTURAL INNOVATION

No analysis of art and design education would be complete, however, without an acknowledgement of its contribution to wider cultural initiatives, bridging the gap between school and community. This can best be seen in relation to artistic festivals which have involved the education sector: European City of Culture; Photofeis; The Edinburgh Children's Festival and Glasgow UK City of Architecture and Design. Another example is the number and range of artists (and, indeed designers and architects) in residence schemes. Underlining such innovations, the Scottish Arts Council has stated that:

> The professional artists who work in education constitute a remarkable live and lively pool of knowledge, information, stimulation and resource which can bring a life-changing experience to a pupil, a teacher, a class or a whole. They bring into the school the living, breathing world of art and ideas, and they leave behind a lingering sense of excitement which can last for long after the visit. (Scottish Arts Council, 1994)

The relationship of art and design education in schools to the wider issue of cultural regeneration is therefore strengthened by such initiatives. Brian Wilson, the Education Minister, in a keynote address to the Fourth European Congress of the International Society for Education Through Art (InSEA) held in Glasgow in 1997, outlined the breadth of art and design, highlighting its promotion of:

- visual awareness and aesthetic understanding
- the creative use of media and technology
- creative thinking, innovation, problem solving and enterprise

Underscoring the importance of innovation as a central theme within the development of art and design in Scottish schools, the minister indicated that effective progress depended upon consensual working partnerships and declared his interest in fostering 'this spirit of co-operation and collaboration among teachers, the local authorities, the Scottish Office and other agencies both in this country and abroad.' Apart from lending governmental endorsement to its role in the secondary curriculum, Wilson described art and design as 'essential' in supporting 'our cultural and economic frameworks' and thus helped underpin its broad-based rationale.

DEVELOPMENT AND PARTNERSHIP

Staff development has been a key feature of the attempt not only to develop the curriculum but also to contextualise the subject by making links with the world outside school, especially with the professional worlds of art, architecture and design. As part of the background to the 1997 InSEA European Congress the SOEID contributed towards the production of a teacher development package. That package contained case studies of innovation, many involving artists or designers in residence in Scottish schools (SOEID, 1997), and which integrated Critical Studies, testifying to the growth of activity in that area.

The need to share information at a national as well as international level and to discuss contemporary developments has been recognised by the Scottish CCC which has established an 'Art and Design Forum' with the active involvement of one of the colleges of education. The Forum offers teachers opportunities to participate in an annual programme of seminars, presentations and exhibitions which focus on good practice in art and design. The Scottish CCC has also established *The Scottish Network for Art and Design Education*. With a site on the Internet, in one sense this virtual network seeks to compensate for the demise of subject advisory support concomitant with the 1996 reorganisation of local government. Its audience is the Scottish local authorities and members from the independent sector. In another sense, its pragmatic response to an actual contemporary problem about information and ideas sharing, represents a considerable shift from the previous CCC whose previous role in relation to art and design – outwith major curriculum developments like Standard Grade – was, in the 1980s, lastly and mostly confined to the production of position papers that had little discernible impact on practitioners.

FUTURE TENSE

If Standard Grade is any indicator art and design would appear to be flourishing. There is a steady growth in the uptake of the subject, which now has in excess of 21,000 candidates presented for annual examination. With the implementation of the Higher Still Programme and a wider range of routes to FE/HE qualifications, the trend in the numbers studying art and design beyond age 16 is likely to grow. At another level its status is assured by being one of the four areas of the Expressive Arts in the National Guidelines 5–14, and is also seen as central in delivering creative aspects of Technology Education as perceived by the Scottish CCC (SCCC, 1995).

Equally important, however, is that art and design responds to the Post-modern condition and concepts of diversity and cultural identity. The categories of culture are bleeding into one another. As the boundaries between art, architecture, design and media become blurred a new narrative is being created, and Scottish artists and designers are at the forefront of that development nationally and internationally. A high quality art and design education needs to draw on art and design itself. By the same token, involvement in education leads to enhanced quality in the world of art and design. A fresh agenda is being posed for art and design education in Scotland.

REFERENCES

Efland, A., K. Freedman and P. Stuhr (1996), *Post-modern Art Education – an approach to curriculum*, Virginia USA: National Art Education Association.

MacDonald, S.W. (1993) A National Curriculum or National Guidelines, *Journal of Art and Design Education*, vol. 12 no 1.

MacDonald, S.W. (1996), Critical Studies and Critical Issues – The Scottish Context, in L. Dawtrey et al., *Critical Studies and Modern Art*, Yale University Press and the Open University.

Scottish Arts Council (1994), *Now to Create – Arts and Education in Partnership*, Edinburgh: SAC.

SCCC (1995), *Technology Education in Scottish Schools*, Dundee: SCCC.

SOEID (1997), *Art@ed.uk – Scottish Case Studies*, National Society for Education in art and design, Edinburgh: HMSO.

47

Biology Education

Nicky Souter

The emergence of biology as a major subject in the Scottish secondary curriculum has been remarkable. Prior to the publication of the 'new' syllabus for biology in 1968, fewer than 1,000 candidates were being submitted for examinations in various combinations of botany, zoology, agriculture and horticultural science, chemistry and physics. The 1996 SEB report indicated that biology was sixth in popularity at Standard Grade (c. 23,000 candidates) and third at Higher Grade (c. 14,000 candidates in biology and human biology). This apparent success masks, however, a disturbingly progressive gender imbalance within the subject. Clarke et al. (1974) reported that the ratio of girls to boys was 2:1 at Higher; by 1996 the proportionate presentations had moved to 2.3:1, figures that are mirrored at Standard Grade (trends that are, incidentally, reversed for physics). Although plausible suggestions might be offered, science course selection may be a case of gender inequality and an extended enquiry into this is overdue.

The expansion of biology may be due to one or more of the following factors: nature of subject; graduates from UK Universities; international and domestic climate; primary teachers' confidence and understanding.

NATURE OF SUBJECT

Biology is a heterogeneous subject with more than one million original research papers published each year. The traditional divisions of zoology, botany and microbiology that relied on observational and morphological studies have been supplanted by disciplines that bring together characteristics, instrumentation and techniques of other sciences, enabling previously unimagined biological insights. One consequence of these is public concern about social, moral and economic issues such as biodiversity, global warming, food quality, and genetically modified crops and livestock. According to the Institute of Biology, 'the pace of biological research and the potential impact of recent discoveries show that biology will play an increasingly important role in wealth creation and improved quality of life.'

GRADUATES FROM UK UNIVERSITIES

During the 1960s increased numbers of biology graduates entered teaching at this time of curricular expansion. An enthusiastic and recently qualified teaching force undertook the implementation of the 'new biology' course, coinciding with the introduction of an

'Integrated Science Course', based on Curriculum Paper 7, *Science for General Education*, HMSO 1969, that gave parity to the three sciences, formalising the scope and extent of biology taught in the first two years of secondary school.

INTERNATIONAL AND DOMESTIC CLIMATE

Perrott et al. (1968) acknowledged the impact of the American Biological Sciences Curriculum Study that provided impetus to the 1962 Nuffield Science Teaching Project, 'a British curriculum study which was initiated by the desire of many individual school teachers and organisations for renewal of science curricula and for a study of imaginative ways of teaching science subjects.' Such was the climate that led to the publication of the syllabus for biology by the Scottish Certificate of Education Examination Board in 1968.

PRIMARY TEACHERS' CONFIDENCE AND UNDERSTANDING

Traditional primary school 'nature study' has been assimilated into primary science and subsequently into the national guidelines for Environmental Studies, 5–14, (SOED, 1993). These have defined the scope and range of life science for that age range. The subject area has some advantage and Harlen et al. (1995) reported that in the primary school, 'teachers were reasonably confident that they had the knowledge needed to develop pupils' under-standing of "Living Things and the Processes of Life", but . . . . . one-third of teachers said they needed significant amounts of help.'

ORDINARY AND HIGHER GRADES

These courses were based on 'the establishment of concepts and principles which are common to all life' (Biology, Ordinary and Higher Grades, SCEEB, Edinburgh, 1968). This syllabus design principle facilitated integration of the existing botany and zoology courses. The syllabus, continuous from Ordinary into Higher Grade, demanded a commitment towards experimental and investigative approaches. It focused a laboratory and field based 'systems approach' to biology, which, rather than studying the 'whole organism', involved the applications of biological principles to a variety of organisms to establish generalisations about each system. These included modes of nutrition, gas exchange, osmosis, transport, sexual reproduction, responding to the environment.

The syllabus gave a representative introduction to the breadth of biology. In the duration of these courses the subject accelerated to its current level of popularity.

Ordinary Grade was assessed by two compulsory papers; the first, lasting an hour, included forty multiple-choice questions; the second with structured questions and limited choice, on knowledge and understanding and on manipulating information, lasted one and a half hours. The multiple choice item bank remained confidential and with one exception were not released to presenting centres. Concern was repeatedly expressed by teachers regarding their inability to respond to and prepare candidates for a public examination without appropriate insight into the assessment instruments. An analysis of the content of each paper was published towards the last few years of Ordinary Grade.

In its latter stages the Higher Grade examination involved a multiple-choice assessment paper which was followed by a two and a half hour examination including structured questions on content and process, data handling of written and numerical data and two essays. The emphasis of the examinations, especially at ordinary grade, changed during its final years towards the problem solving approaches that were to be introduced with Standard Grade. This robust syllabus prevailed, with minor amendments, from 1968 until the implementation of Standard Grade in 1988. During its final years it was evident that syllabus revision was required due to subject advances, notably in the fields of molecular biology, biotechnology and genetics.

CERTIFICATE OF SIXTH YEAR STUDIES

CSYS Biology was introduced in 1977, somewhat later than other CSYS subjects, but has shown a steady growth and by 1996 had become the fourth most popular subject at this level with more than a thousand candidates from around half the presenting centres. CSYS biology involved students following study units on a range of topics, including microbiology, behaviour, and the soil. Syllabus revision, alongside Higher Grade, reduced the number of topics. Candidates currently select two from; chemistry of life; developmental physiology; behaviour; microbiology; diversity of life; man; organisms and environments. Assessment involves an examination incorporating data handling and essays contributing towards 50 per cent of the award. Practical abilities are assessed by a suitable laboratory or field investigation, providing 30 per cent of the total marks and forming the basis of an oral examination by an external assessor. A laboratory notebook on each topic studied supplies 20 per cent of the total marks.

SCIENCE FOR ALL

Munn's curriculum (SED, 1977), which demanded a scientific mode of study and the 'distinctive methodology depending heavily on an empirical approach, based on hypothesising and experimentation' determined the shape of Standard Grade courses. Munn also suggested that the social impact of science be a component of Standard Grade courses.

STANDARD GRADE BIOLOGY

The derivation of Standard Grade from Ordinary Grade courses is evident with significant content retention. Standard Grade biology includes a more detailed specification of the anticipated learning within the course elements of knowledge and understanding; problem solving; practical abilities; and attitudes. The first three of these elements are assessed formally. Suggested leaving activities at General and Credit levels indicate appropriate contexts, resources and approaches for learning and teaching. The 'learning outcomes' described at each level form the basis of examinable content. This close specification restricts examiners' and teachers' choice in syllabus interpretation.

Standard Grade biology includes seven discrete topics, derived from three general aspects: the biological basis for life; relationships; applications of biological principles in work, health and leisure activities.

Each topic covers a domain of the subject: the biosphere; the world of plants; animal survival; investigating cells; the body in action; inheritance; biotechnology. The 'systems approach' was not incorporated and fewer opportunities arise within Standard Grade biology to generalise fundamental processes. HMI generally comment that the level of resources within biology departments is considered to be realistic to suit modern needs and that field work is performed within school grounds, the local environment, on day trips and on residential experiences. Teachers report that this is limited by time, financial and training constraints.

ASSESSMENT AT STANDARD GRADE

Internal assessment involves grading practical abilities and estimating performance for 'knowledge and understanding' and 'problem solving'. Two components of practical abilities are assessed; 'practical techniques', laboratory and field procedures, for example tasks with microscopes, food tests and sampling biotic and abiotic factors; 'investigations' in biological content are performed in structured tasks that are derived from the TAPS investigative skills objectives (Bryce et al., 1991). Each structured investigation conforms to a prescribed format. It is disappointing that field based investigations are not supplied within published exemplars. Practical abilities assessment will be unified for all science subjects from 1999. 'Techniques' and 'investigations' will be assessed with reduced weighting from 33 per cent to 20 per cent. This measure risks diminishing the status of practical abilities. External assessment involves written examinations combining knowledge and understanding and problem solving with separate papers at general and credit levels, each lasting one and a half hours and including multiple choice, short answer, extended answer and interpretation questions. Working parties throughout the country developed a range of support materials including worksheets, games, simulations, computer software, and some guidance on management, teaching and learning. Teacher's guides provide useful analysis of each and supply a foundation for suitably varied classroom experience. The topic resources were designed to be used flexibly by departments and to promote a range of learning approaches. Revised versions remain widely used throughout the country.

REVISED HIGHER GRADE BIOLOGY

Arrangements for Higher Grade were published for first examinations in 1991 and clear progression of content and problem solving from Standard Grade was indicated. The course consists of topics on cell biology, genetics and evolution, control of growth and development, regulation of biological systems and adaptation. The practical abilities promoted through Revised Higher Grade sit somewhat uncomfortably between the structured investigative approaches of Standard Grade and the extended open-ended investigation of CSYS with the inclusion of compulsory practical work of the course which is assessed by mandatory questions in the final examination. This provides limited opportunities for individual competence to be demonstrated beyond a formalised, procedural response to set questions.

Assessment consists of two formal papers, the first lasting one and a quarter hours includes forty multiple choice items selected from the national bank, and the second lasting two and a half hours with structured questions on knowledge and understanding, data interpretation and compulsory practical, and extended essay questions. Academic quality in higher biology, reviewed in Devine et al. (1996) suggested that: 'There were some statistically significant differences in individual skill areas between years, but no consistent pattern to indicate any overall change in standards.'

HIGHER GRADE HUMAN BIOLOGY

A parallel course on Human Biology was introduced in 1992 to replace a previous course in Anatomy, Physiology and Health. It consists of topics on cell function, continuation of the species, life support mechanisms, the biological basis of behaviour, and population growth and the environment. Presentation reached more than 2,100 candidates in 1996.

BIOLOGY TEACHERS

It is evident that the age profile of the teaching force has changed. Clarke et al. (1974) reported that in 1974, 35 per cent of teachers had ten or more years experience and that 45 per cent had less than five years of experience. The 1994 SOEID school census indicated that less than 6 per cent of teachers have five years teaching experience and that more than 90 per cent have more than ten years teaching experience. Figure 47.1 also illustrates proportionately greater numbers of women below forty-five and the converse above that age. The recent low numbers of recruits is about to reach a point where a crisis may arise in the capacity to train sufficient numbers of biology teachers to meet demand.

Figure 47.1   Biology teachers in Scotland by age and sex (1994)

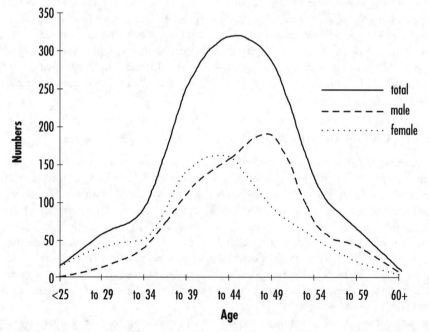

Biology teachers are active across a full range of extra-curricular activities with conservation, outdoor, health education and horticulture groups being amongst the most popular.

INTO THE FUTURE

Biology at all levels of Higher Still will build on existing provision and offer pupils a suitably challenging range of experiences. The SCCC discussion paper *Science Education in*

Scottish Schools (1996) has already presented innovative and challenging postulates within the five aspects of 'scientific capability' (curiosity, competence, understanding, creativity and sensitivity); biological education must accept these and provide a responsive and progressive curriculum that can contribute to pupil achievement as well as remaining a popular choice, and for all pupils.

REFERENCES

Bryce, T. G. K., J. McCall, J. MacGregor, I. J. Robertson, R. A. J. Weston (1991) *How to assess open-ended investigations in biology, chemistry and physics*, Oxford: Heinemann Educational.

Clarke, R. A., G. Cruikshank, J. F. Haddow, H. Sloss, D. G. Taylor (1974) *Biology in Scottish Secondary Schools*, Dundee: Dundee College of Education.

Marion Devine, John Hall, Jacqueline Mapp, Kerry Musselbrook (1996) *Maintaining Standards: Performance at Higher Grade in Biology, English, Geography and Mathematics*, Edinburgh: Scottish Council for Research in Education.

Harlen, W., C. Holroyd and M. Byre (1995) *Confidence and Understanding in Teaching Science and Technology in Primary Schools*, Edinburgh: Scottish Council for Research in Education.

Perrott, Elizabeth, E. Martin, I. Campbell (1968) *Biological Sciences in Scottish Secondary Schools*, Stirling: University of Stirling.

SED (1977) *The Structure of the Curriculum in the Third and Fourth Years of the Scottish Secondary School*, Edinburgh: SED.

48

Business Education

Barry Finlayson

DEVELOPMENT OF BUSINESS EDUCATION IN THE SCOTTISH CURRICULUM

The opportunity to learn about 'business' has been available to young people in Scottish schools for over a century, the courses on offer reflecting the needs of the business sector over time. In the first half of this century the focus was on providing young people with the skills and knowledge that would equip them for clerical functions within the world of commerce and so emphasised the development of office skills. Thus school courses concentrated on typewriting and shorthand, commercial arithmetic, and bookkeeping. The department in the schools responsible for delivering 'business' courses was the Commercial department and, latterly, the teachers working there were often referred to by colleagues as 'the typing teachers'. Pupils were almost exclusively female.

However, during the 1960s significant changes enhanced the status and position of Business Education in the Scottish secondary school curriculum. These changes not only increased the menu and scope of subjects available to young people but also began to provide opportunities for both genders to participate. The development of single subject 'O' grades in Economic Organisation (later to become 'O' Grade Economics), Principles of Accounts, and Secretarial Studies, with progression through to respective Higher grades in Accounting, Economics, and Secretarial Studies, set in place the foundation for the current Business Education curriculum. The final pieces in the jigsaw were laid in place during the late1980s and1990s.

As a result of the revision of the S3/S4 curriculum, Standard Grade courses were developed in Accounting and Finance, and Economics. A new course, Office and Information Studies, was developed to replace Secretarial Studies and reflect the importance of Information Technology in the modern office. Both Accounting and Finance, and Office and Information Studies, aimed to offer pupils a wider view of the business world than their respective 'O' grades had done. The revised courses sought to equip young people with knowledge and understanding of the subject area but were also designed to help develop process skills in, for example, using information to solve problems and take decisions.

In 1987, a very important review group was established which would once more change the direction of Business Education in the last part of the century and provide a sound future for it in the curriculum. The Review Group in Business Education was set up 'to identify the areas of knowledge, understanding and skills which were directly relevant to *business management* in industry and commerce and which should be embodied in the modern school curriculum'. Among a range of recommendations, the Review Group confirmed the existing subjects, Accounting and Finance, Economics, and Office and Information Studies, as key disciplines and relevant to business management and also argued for the development at Higher Grade of a new course, Management and Information Studies. This Higher would offer young people an insight into the role and function of management in modern organisations. The Review Group further recommended the ending of Higher Grade 'Secretarial Studies with Word Processing'. However, in the face of strong representations from the profession, this subject was retained.

Finally, curriculum development for post-16 young people embodied in the Higher Still Development Programme will make further adjustments to Business Education. A wide provision for young people of all abilities will be available from 1999 and will include a menu of four subjects, all of which articulate with the appropriate Standard Grade subjects: Accounting and Finance, Administration (as the replacement for 'H' Grade Secretarial Studies), Business Management (the replacement for 'H' Grade Management and Information Studies), and Economics. The absence of courses to provide articulation into Business Management and Administration has resulted in the development of two new Standard Grade courses: Business Management and Administration. A chart of the current position of the Business Education curriculum is shown below:

Adv Higher	Accounting and Finance	Administration	Business Management	Economics
Higher	Accounting and Finance	Administration	Business Management	Economics
Inter 2	Accounting and Finance	Administration	Business Management	Economics
Inter 1	Accounting and Finance	Administration	Business Management	Economics
Access 3	–	Business	Business	–
'S' Grade	Accounting and Finance	Office & Information Studies (To be replaced by Administration 1999/2000)	Business Management	Economics

THE CONTRIBUTION OF BUSINESS EDUCATION TO THE SCOTTISH CURRICULUM

Business Education is an optional element in the secondary school curriculum which pupils can choose at the end of S2. This means that a large number (around 60 per cent of the school population) will leave school with little structured understanding of the important business component of society which affects their daily lives. Where support from the senior management team is present and where staffing permits, a number of Business Studies departments do offer useful inputs into their school's common course at S1 and S2 – often short courses in Keyboarding and general taster courses in 'business' – which make use of Information Technology. Further opportunities currently exist to bring appropriate elements of Business Education to all pupils in S1/2 through the 5–14 Development

Programme, particularly in the curricular areas of Environmental Studies and Information Technology. The current interest in including inputs of Enterprise Education in the secondary curriculum offers further possibilities for the involvement of Business Education departments whose staff have the knowledge and skills to deliver such courses.

Under the Higher Still development programme, a Specialist Group in Business Education, set up to review the provision of business education subjects, identified the aims of business education as:

- developing a broad understanding of the role, purpose and operation of business and enterprise activity in contemporary society;
- preparing pupils for a wide range of employment opportunities through the acquisition of relevant knowledge and generic skills;
- preparing pupils for entry to a broad range of further, higher and professional education; and
- contributing to the preparation of pupils as active citizens.

In its own particular way, each of the Business Education subjects seeks to achieve these broad aims and helps to develop in pupils an understanding of 'business' as well as contributing to their general education. However, until the development of the Standard Grade and Higher Grade courses in Business Management, no one course provided a general study of business activity but, instead, viewed 'business' from the subject's own perspective, e.g. Accounting and Finance, Economics, and Office and Information Studies.

Business Education in many schools usually comprises some form of short course for S1/S2, two or three courses at Standard Grade from Accounting & Finance, Economics, or Office and Information Studies and, in S5/S6, at least two courses from Higher Grades in Accounting & Finance, Economics, Management & Information Studies, and Secretarial Studies.

The total numbers of pupils presented for the SEB examinations in Business Education at Standard Grade has declined from 33,135 in 1987 to 24,517 in 1995, representing a 29% overall fall in the numbers taking the courses. Accounting and Finance fell by 49% over the period, while Economics and Office and Information Studies recorded falls of 43% and 10% respectively at a time when the number of pupils in secondary schools fell by 19%. With regard to Accounting and Finance, and Economics, both subjects were popular with S5/S6 pupils who often took them as a one-year 'crash' course. However, the introduction of Standard Grade and the consequent barring of S5/S6 pupils from taking Standard Grade examinations has had the effect of significantly reducing the number of presentations.

At Higher Grade, the total number of presentations in the SEB examinations has remained fairly constant at 13,005 pupils in 1987 and 12,887 pupils in 1995. While the most popular subject is Secretarial Studies (4,219 pupils in 1995), both Accounting and Finance, and Economics, have shown a decline over the period. This has not been the case for Management and Information Studies, a less specialised course, where, from a modest base of 292 pupils taking the first examination in 1992, the course had attracted 3,307 pupils by 1995 and thus had largely offset (and at the same time probably contributed to) the declining numbers in the other subjects.

CURRENT ISSUES IN BUSINESS EDUCATION

A number of common issues continue to concern both curriculum developers, senior management in schools and teachers as they each try to ensure the delivery of a meaningful, relevant and viable Business Education curriculum to pupils. Not least of these is the dynamic nature of the subject area and the need to ensure that what is taught to young people should reflect what is going on in the world of 'business'. Alongside these external pressures for constant change are those which rightly advocate a more process based and experiential form of learning for pupils. To satisfy these demands requires the regular updating of syllabuses, teaching content, and often significant changes to learning and teaching approaches. Such changes have been endemic in Business Education for many many years and teaching staff have recognised the inevitability of such changes and responded positively. However, the last twenty years has seen a quite radical reappraisal and reconstruction of the secondary school curriculum which began with Standard Grade, continued with the Action Plan and the 5–14 Developments and currently shows no sign of easing as the Higher Still programme is introduced. These developments have placed enormous strains on Business Studies departments that have had to cope with and gain confidence in teaching new courses often using approaches for which they have not been adequately prepared and lacking in the support and hardware resources which are needed if meaningful learning experiences are to be created. This issue is currently worrying Business Studies teachers as they begin to consider the significant changes envisaged for Business Education under the Higher Still proposals due to be introduced in 1999. While a certain amount of staff development is being provided by the Higher Still Development Unit, the changes are coming at a time when the reorganisation of local government has reduced, and in many cases removed, the direct support that teachers received from specialist Advisers. As a result, many staff feel isolated and lack the confidence to tackle certain aspects of the proposed course content contained in some of the new courses, e.g. Administration. In particular the whole area of assessment, especially the administering and recording of internal assessment, is causing much concern among Business Studies staff.

Another curriculum issue concerns the provision and resourcing of Information Technology inputs to Business Education courses. The importance of IT to modern day business cannot be underestimated and is reflected in the Business Education curriculum which not only prepares pupils to use IT confidently themselves but also shows how 'business' can gain significant benefits from using IT for decision taking and problem solving. While appropriate aspects of the uses and application of IT are built into all Business Education courses, similar approaches are taken in Computer departments so that, in the absence of coordination between the two, pupils taking Business Education and Computing courses often experience a degree of overlap. This issue has prompted a growing number of schools to appoint a principal teacher of IT to replace the PT Business Studies and PT Computing, thus ensuring a more coordinated and coherent delivery of IT (and also saving the salary of one principal teacher!). At present the number of such departments is not large, but, at a time when schools are pressed for resources, a restructuring of this kind must have its attractions. (As this article is being written and with the emphasis that is currently being placed on 'Enterprise Education', another departmental alignment is emerging – the Business Enterprise department!) To a lesser but nevertheless important extent, elements of the Business Education curriculum are being appropriated by colleagues in other subject areas who seek business contexts and use/abuse business ideas to deliver their own subject.

Perhaps the most important curriculum issue facing Business Studies departments today is that of deciding the menu of subjects to be offered to pupils both at S3 and at S5 (see earlier chart).

With a future curriculum containing four Standard Grades and four Higher Grades and typical departments of two/three members of staff, it is not likely that many Business Studies departments will be able to offer the complete range. Further pressure is coming from senior managers in schools, many of whom look longingly to the day when Business Studies departments can be persuaded to offer just the one Standard and Higher grade course. Hard choices will have to be made between continuing to offer two or sometimes three familiar specialist subjects at Standard Grade (Accounting and Finance, Economics, and Office and Information Studies), or moving towards the more general Business Management course at Standard and Higher grades or, more likely, a mixture of both. At the end of the day the decision should be based on the needs of the pupils and their parents, the trend of demand for each subject in the Business Education range, the longer term curricular objectives of the school as expressed in its development plan and, where appropriate, the needs of the local business community. Faced with such decisions, principal teachers of Business Education will require to think hard about the direction they wish their department to take. Decisions taken about the nature of the S3/S4 curriculum will affect what is offered at S5/S6, although the popularity of the one-year Higher Grade course for able S6 pupils is likely to continue.

The one subject within the Business Education curriculum that is perhaps under the most threat is Economics. The trend among Scottish pupils away from taking Economics mirrors a similar trend in England which has been present for a number of years. The contribution that Economics can make to pupils' general education is not always appreciated by senior management in schools, and the competition that it faces from other social subjects coupled with the fact that the subject has no substantial presence in the S1/S2 curriculum, all conspire against pupils opting for Economics in S3. Often they do so to default from another social subject. A knowledge of Economics is essential to the study of business and this is reflected in its inclusion in all HNC and HND Business courses in Further Education. For that reason, and to allow articulation from business courses in school into Further Education, a place is assured for Economics within the school curriculum. However, its future there depends on the enthusiasm and commitment of teachers to promote the subject, a recognition by senior management of its importance to general, vocational and higher education and a desire on the part of pupils to study its ideas. Further development of the subject is not likely to be helped by the fact that the annual supply of newly qualified teachers in Economics coming from the Teacher Education Institutions is low, as student teachers see greater opportunities for employment if they qualify in Business Studies or Computing as their second subject rather than taking Economics. This, coupled with the fact that the regulations for entry into teacher training for the year 2000 will increase the graduating courses required by a student wishing to train for Economics from two to three, will make the recruitment of appropriately qualified teachers of Economics very difficult indeed and so further compound the problem.

In conclusion, the view is sometimes expressed that Business Education is a 'Cinderella' subject, worthy, but neglected in the power politics of the Scottish secondary school. The Business Education department is also often seen by some senior managers as being merely reactive and unwilling to become actively involved in setting, or at the very least influencing, the agenda for its own future. In order to counter these views it is important for principal teachers of Business Education to stand tall and actively ensure that parents, pupils, senior management and other staff recognise what the Department does and its overall contribution to the secondary school curriculum.

At the present time when important choices affecting the very future of Business

Education in the secondary school have to be made, there is a definite need for many departments to 'market' their curriculum more widely and effectively than they have done in the past in order that senior management, parents and pupils recognise the value added for pupils who opt to study in the department .

A relevant, interesting, and challenging Business Education curriculum does exist and, if resourced adequately in terms of both human and material resources, there is the opportunity for Business Studies departments to continue to make a very worthwhile contribution to preparing young people for their future whether that be in the workplace or in Higher or Further Education.

REFERENCES

CCC (1987) Review Group in Business Education in Schools, Final Report, Dundee: CCC.
SOEID (1997) *Effective Learning and Teaching in Scottish Secondary Schools: Business Education and Economics*, Edinburgh: HMSO.

49

Careers Education

Cathy Howieson and Sheila Semple

DEFINITION

There is no agreed current definition of careers education. Recent official publications simply offer general statements such as: 'All pupils need to prepare for their future after they leave school . . . Careers education is therefore an essential part of guidance provision' (SOEID, 1996 p. 61).

Schools are challenged further by the introduction, as part of Higher Still, of a guidance entitlement which focuses to a large extent on the vocational implications of curricular choice (Higher Still Development Unit, 1995).

Some would define careers education as simply 'helping young people to come to a decision about their career after school'. However a more subtle definition might be 'giving young people the chance to practise the career management skills they will need in the future'. This takes account of the expected need to change career direction several times in a working life, to spend time re-training or out of the labour market and to develop the skills necessary to enable career planning over an individual's lifetime. The content and approach of careers education will differ depending on the definition in use, but, having said that, it is still uncommon for a school to have an articulated definition or 'mission statement' for careers education, and rare for its implications for the careers programme to have been systematically thought through.

EXPECTATIONS

Most young people think that a key role for secondary education is helping them to prepare for their future role in working life (perhaps after time spent in college or university). This view is shared by their parents. Many see it as the clear justification and motivation for being at school, and research suggests that it is a key area of anxiety for both parents and young people; not enough, they say, is being done (Howieson and Semple, 1996).

For governments, careers work in schools is critical for the economic performance of the country: the economy needs well motivated young people with a sense of direction, who can make appropriate choices, be able to manage career development and who will be committed to learning and training throughout their lives.

COMMON CONTENT AND DELIVERY PRACTICE

A common model for considering careers education is the DOTS framework. This was developed in the 1970s as an analytical tool for both careers education and guidance (Law and Watts, 1977).

It sets out four broad areas, each with sub-elements:

Decision making: post-16 decisions; decision making styles; appropriate and inappropriate influences on choice (including parents, family, friends, teachers, careers advisers, etc.).

Opportunity awareness: local and national labour markets and employment trends; job studies; careers conventions and employer visits; careers library and careers computers; courses in FE and HE; equal opportunities.

Transition skills: applications and interviews; getting and keeping work; preparing for changed status (e.g. as a student, worker or trainee); reviewing plans and seeking help; preparing to leave home after school.

Self awareness: how interests, abilities and values develop; life style and career choice; changing career plans as the individual changes and develops; community and personal values; links to records of achievement and profiling.

In practice, only a minority of schools will have developed a consistent programme which covers all the content listed above and which has clear progression in its content and approach. However virtually all will have some form of careers education input which will address the DOTS framework to a certain extent. Most schools deliver careers education as part of a rolling programme of Personal and Social Education (PSE), with a number of weeks devoted to careers education, followed by some weeks covering health, records of achievement etc.; some have a discrete careers education programme and a very small number deliver careers education through the curriculum. Overall the extent to which careers education articulates with other parts of PSE is often limited.

In practice, the main focus of careers education is S2 (when Standard grade subjects are being chosen) and S4 (when post-16 choices are being considered). A clear difficulty for schools is the design and delivery of careers education in S5 and S6: the variation in students' academic attainment, career intention, choice of post-school route and vocational maturity is very noticeable and careers education is difficult both to design and also to deliver. Ideally it requires a short compulsory programme combined with a choice of subsequent inputs based on the individual's needs. This requires a clear identification of needs which is likely to be a complicated and time-consuming task; and a more individualised programme is difficult for schools to deliver within the twin constraints of resources and the timetable.

In most schools, careers education is delivered in a variety of ways. A great deal is presented through classroom work, with discussions, worksheets and, in some cases, video material used. A key part of the programme is often the preparation, and debriefing, of one-week's work experience with a local company.

Of course, the key point is whether work experience is supported effectively, as it requires this support to ensure that the full and most appropriate use is made of this powerful experience for young people.

LINKS TO WORK-RELATED TEACHING AND LEARNING

Work experience is only one aspect of education/industry links. Also included is work shadowing, mini-enterprise activities, industrial inputs into subjects in the curriculum and events such as Industry Awareness Days, Challenge of Industry and Challenge of Europe Days. National guidelines for education/industry links in Scotland (SCCC, 1995), due to be updated in 1999, indicate that a key strand is provided by careers education and careers information, but in practice it is rare to have these links made apparent within the secondary school.

LINKS TO THE CURRICULUM, TO GUIDANCE SYSTEMS AND TO THE CAREERS SERVICE

As has been noted above, it is rare in Scotland to deliver the whole careers education programme through subjects: however it is common to have particular topics covered in subject teaching, e.g. applications and interviews in English. Subject teachers do also have a direct impact on young people's career thinking: they are most likely to discuss post-school choices with pupils thinking about entering university, but may also be involved with pupils considering other options (Howieson, Croxford and Semple, 1993).

Although a member of the school's senior management team will have overall responsibility for the careers education programme (normally within the context of the whole PSE programme), individual guidance teachers are likely to have responsibility for different aspects, e.g. the S2 PSE programme, work experience, the S5/S6 careers input. The extent to which guidance teachers deliver careers education to their own guidance caseload is variable, and it is often the case that non-specialists (volunteer or non-volunteer) are timetabled to teach parts of the careers programme.

Careers service companies provide a professional careers guidance service to schools, focusing mainly on individual specialist interviewing of pupils at key transition points in S4, S5 and S6. But pupils' readiness for, and their ability to make the most progress in, their careers interview is dependent on the quality of the careers education in the school. Careers education could be defined as providing the context in which individual career decisions are made.

Because of the importance of careers education to informed decision making, careers advisers work with schools to review and develop careers programmes; and when this joint approach works effectively, there is evidence that young people make more progress in their career thinking.

ARTICULATION WITH PRIMARY, FURTHER AND HIGHER EDUCATION

The development of career thinking starts very early, continuing throughout adolescence and being refined and reviewed in adult and working life. At one end, primary schools can begin to extend pupils' knowledge of the working world beyond that of their family and community through project work and visits; at the other end, further education colleges include careers education modules (previously SCOTVEC, now SQA accredited) in many courses; and some universities now run career development classes as part of undergraduate and postgraduate courses.

However, these inputs rarely link to each other or provide recognised progression. This is partly because of the lack of Scottish guidelines: England and Wales have targets for careers education and guidance at the key stages of the national curriculum (including Stage 1, roughly 7 years old), and from April 1998 learning outcomes will be identified in England and Wales for careers education from 5–18. Another reason for a lack of articulation may be a failure to understand the long-term nature of career choice, and to realise the need for careers input throughout young people's educational experiences.

KEY ISSUES

The lack of a policy framework for careers education has been referred to above. TVEI units and local education authorities in the past issued guidelines for careers education, but the ending of the TVEI initiative and the restructuring of local authorities has meant the loss of much policy guidance. In particular, national guidelines at a Scottish level are lacking. The Advisory Scottish Council for Education and Training Targets (ASCETT) has recommended to the Secretary of State for Scotland that a framework for all-age careers education and guidance be produced for Scotland. Such a framework would provide a basis for the integration of careers education, education-industry links and recording achievement, but this has yet to happen. Without such guidelines, each school will continue to 're-invent the wheel' in designing careers education and will have no template against which to evaluate its programme. There will continue to be no baseline provision to ensure that pupils from one school are not disadvantaged in making the transition out of school, compared with pupils from the neighbouring school. It is also possible for a school in Scotland to offer no or minimal careers education, unlike schools south of the border where legislation makes careers education compulsory in the National Curriculum. However, plans recently announced by the Scottish Office indicate that, by the end of 1999, a strategic policy framework for careers education in Scottish schools should be in place.

Over the three-year period from 1995 to 1998, the Scottish Office allocated £750,000 pounds to the training of teachers in careers education. This is evidence of the importance of careers work to government, and it has resulted in greatly increased inservice training, primarily to promoted guidance teachers. A key issue remaining is to support and inform those teachers without a guidance background who are delivering careers education: such teachers typically lack confidence and tend to fall back on safer methodologies of delivery such as worksheets and videos (less popular with pupils and less effective). The impact of the training has also been limited to a certain extent by the lack of a framework. What precisely are teachers being trained to deliver? Against what standards are they being trained to evaluate their programme?

The aims of careers education need continuing review in the light of the changing nature of work, training, education and vocational routes. Careers education programmes need to reflect the world as it is and will be, and not as it was. A related issue is the extent to which the careers education programme challenges pupils' views of their choices and their aspirations rather than merely reflecting pupil interests and ideas (which may be limited by prejudice, narrowness or limited experiences and expectations).

Not only does the content and balance of careers education need review, but so also do the methodologies used. Young people respond well to special events (such as equal opportunities days), open discussions and case studies, work experience, outside speakers (especially those with credibility, such as previous school-leavers discussing their experiences and revisiting their career decisions) and to computer-generated information and guidance. They respond less well to class-based worksheets, and to heavily teacher-centred approaches. There are clear issues here relating to the design of careers activities and lessons; to training in student-centred methodologies; to the provision of appropriate classroom accommodation to allow flexible teaching; and to the availability of computers capable of handling the range of careers guidance and information databases, including those produced to support the Higher Still programme.

There is an issue about the balance between the acquisition of knowledge and the learning and practising of skills within careers education. Careers education cannot be only about 'learning facts about how many exam passes you need to be an accountant' but about the gathering of employability skills and career management skills. Following the elections of 1997, the new government has emphasised the importance of 'education for work' and of 'social inclusion' as twin strategies for development. By ensuring that all young people access the support of careers education and guidance and by developing employability skills (and better links between the world of work and education), careers programmes have a key role to play for the individual and for society.

REFERENCES

Higher Still Development Unit (1995) *Guidance Arrangements Consultation Document*, Edinburgh: Higher Still Development Unit.

Howieson, C., L. Croxford and S. Semple (1993) *Choices in a Changing World: A Report to Scottish Enterprise*, Edinburgh: Centre for Educational Sociology.

Howieson, C. and S. Semple (1996) *Guidance in Secondary Schools*, Edinburgh: Centre for Educational Sociology.

Law, B. and A. G. Watts (1977) *School, Careers and Community*, London: Church Information Office.

SCCC (1995) *Education Industry Links in Scotland 5–18: A Framework for Action*, Dundee: SCCC.

SOEID (1996) *Effective Learning and Teaching: Guidance. A report by HM Inspectors of Schools*, Edinburgh: SOEID.

50

Chemistry Education

Douglas Buchanan

THE PRESENT SITUATION

In the first two years of most Scottish secondary schools, chemistry forms clearly identifiable sections of an integrated science course, still predominantly based on Curriculum Paper Number 7 (SED, 1969). The recent publication of the national guidelines for Environmental Studies 5–14 (SOED, 1993) has provided a framework to support primary teachers with the introduction of aspects of chemistry to programmes of work and, in turn, has given secondary teachers the opportunity to review learning and teaching in science up to age fourteen.

In years three and four, in line with national policy for all students to study at least one science subject, chemistry can be taken as a two-year Standard Grade course (SEB, 1992). Unlike science but in common with biology and physics, chemistry at Standard Grade is on offer at Credit and General Levels only, which results in the absence of lower ability students in the uptake. Progression is to a one-year Higher Grade course for students in fifth year and then the Certificate of Sixth Year Studies (CSYS). The Higher Grade course is usually also available for students in sixth year who wish to improve on their fifth-year performance or who elect to study at that level for the first time. These courses are described in the Arrangements documents produced by the Scottish Examination Board (SEB), now the Scottish Qualifications Authority (SQA). As with the other science courses, they are highly popular with close to 25,000 students taking chemistry at Standard Grade (approximately 38 per cent of the cohort compared with 23 per cent in 1973), over 11,500 studying at Higher Grade and just under 1,900 taking CSYS, making chemistry at this level second in popularity to mathematics.

Internally assessed Scottish Vocational Education Council (SCOTVEC) modules provide alternative provision; in chemistry these tend to be taken by students who are likely to experience difficulty with the kind of end-of-course external examinations employed at Standard Grade and Higher Grade. Each of the more popular modules attract approximately 1,300 candidates.

FROM THE 1960s TO THE 1980s

In the early 1960s, practical work by students tended to be limited and there was a heavy emphasis on theory combined with illustrative demonstrations by teachers. Copying from the blackboard, taking down dictated notes and memorising facts were common student activities. However, public interest in science, aroused by events such as the early achievements of space exploration, led to support for the reform of chemistry education at the classroom level. Of the many influential initiatives, three were to prove to be particularly significant:

1. The 'Chemistry Takes Shape' textbooks, published by Heinemann, promoted a more active approach to learning;
2. Memorandum Number 43 (CCC, 1980) encouraged teachers to consider how the effective use of language could help students with their learning of chemistry;
3. The raising of the school leaving age from 15 to 16 in 1972 led to some teachers starting to introduce more pupil-centred learning and teaching approaches in an attempt to cater for the wider range of ability taking chemistry in the third and fourth years.

THE IMPACT OF THE STANDARD GRADE DEVELOPMENT PROGRAMME (SGDP)

Few would disagree with the assertion that the SGDP provided the catalyst for the 1980s revolution of chemistry education in Scottish schools. What has been the effect of the key aspects of the innovation on classroom practice?

1. The acquisition of knowledge and understanding of essential chemical theory, processes and reactions continues to be an important activity. However, in view of the other two assessable elements (see below) there has been a significant reduction in content compared to the previous SEB 'O' Grade course.
2. The decision to make problem solving a separate assessable element of the course has given much greater prominence to the development and assessment of 'conventional' problem-solving skills such as concluding and explaining, generalising and predicting, as well as 'related' skills, e.g. selecting, presenting and processing information. In the classroom, students engage in practical problem-solving which is likely to involve designing and planning investigations and evaluating results as well as paper-and-pencil exercises which require students to decode written information about unfamiliar chemistry. Where appropriate, many students use problem-solving approaches to acquire the essential knowledge and understanding.
3. In a similar way, the Practical Abilities assessable element has given added importance to both 'basic' chemical techniques, e.g. producing and collecting a precipitate, volumetric titrations, and practical investigative work (see above).
4. Theoretical chemical knowledge and understanding is made more relevant by giving prominence to social, economic, environmental and industrial applications. For example, students study topics on fossil fuels, acid rain, corrosion, fertilisers and plastics and synthetic fibres. A project jointly sponsored by Understanding British Industry and British Petroleum was a particularly exciting initiative; this involved industrialists working with teachers to produce a wide range of audio-visual support materials which emphasise the links between classroom chemistry and industry.
5. To cope with the wider variety of student needs and abilities, chemistry teachers have extended their range of methods to include more pupil-centred approaches. Worksheets, generated as part of the course materials by different teams of teachers, are now commonly used in many classrooms to support learning and teaching. These refer students, usually working in groups, to a range of resources; as a result, students make regular use of textbooks, leaflets and posters, as well as models and video facilities, and schools are

encouraged to use microcomputers in a wider variety of ways, e.g. to simulate experiments, for self-teaching programmes and to interface with scientific equipment. It says much for the commitment and ingenuity of chemistry teachers that there is such a wide choice of course materials; indeed Chemcord, RISE and Complete Chemistry are three examples of 'cottage industries', set up by teachers to produce and distribute a range of resources on a commercial basis, which have become familiar features on the chemistry landscape.

6. Chemistry teachers have always taken a commendable interest in their role in the development of 'core' skills for their students and the SGDP further sensitised this interest. Many teachers give more careful thought to communication skills as well as numerical work and word processing opportunities. In addition, the increasing use of group methods has promoted the development of personal skills.

Such practice is not just confined to learning and teaching in third and fourth years. Although problem solving and practical abilities are not assessed separately as at Standard Grade, the balance and style of questions in the external examination at Higher Grade helps to ensure that there is continued emphasis given to these areas, and relevance is stressed when appropriate. However, the time constraints tend to result in teachers making greater use of whole-class methods.

The popularity of the project and the practical work contributes to the success of the CSYS course. The project allows students to study a selected topic and can make a major contribution to the development of practical and investigative skills as well as promoting independent learning. These two aspects, which are both internally assessed and externally assessed by a visiting examiner, make a significant contribution to the overall award. Approaches to the learning of the content aspects of the course tend to be different from those of other courses, often being based on a combination of lectures and self-study.

The SCOTVEC modules are usually taught in conjunction with SEB courses. A consequence is that learning and teaching tends to embrace the previously described characteristic features of chemistry classrooms.

THE IMMEDIATE FUTURE

Just as the influence of the SGDP dominated thoughts on chemistry education in the 1980s it would appear that the Higher Still Development Programme (HSDP) is having a similar impact in the 1990s. For fifth year students, courses at different levels will provide opportunities for all students to continue with their studies of chemistry as well as catering for 'fresh-starters' (HSDU, 1997). The same courses will also be available to students in the sixth year with the Advanced Higher designed for those who wish to progress from achievement at Higher. One should not be surprised that the principal aspects of developments in chemistry at Standard Grade form a basis for course structure and delivery within Higher Still. In addition, the initiative has provided an important opportunity to recognise the wish of the majority of chemistry teachers to update post-16 courses. For example, the Higher course includes the study of such new materials as Kevler, poly(ethanol), poly(vinyl carbazol) and biopolymers as well as covering the general principles of the modern chemical industry.

CURRENT CHALLENGES

Among the many issues which have generated lively debate within the chemistry community in Scotland there are perhaps two which stand out – the assessment of practical work and the use of appropriate methodology.

Given that practical work is an essential part of all science courses, it is difficult to argue that practical work should not be assessed. But, keeping in mind such factors as validity, reliability and work-load and management demands for teachers, by what means? At Standard Grade the model for the assessment of both techniques and investigations requires a measure of direct observation of pupil experience. This has led to the production of lists of criteria to help teachers to make judgements rather than the use of a more holistic approach. Although the principles of this model are supported, there is a general view that the administration is found to be time-consuming and the final outcome is 'hollow'. Within Higher Still a new model is to be employed; the practical outcome is stated in terms of writing reports for set practicals which then become the focus for the assessment rather than the actual practical activities. Further differences to Standard Grade include firstly, the inclusion in the external examination of questions which draw on the experience of the set practicals and secondly, the emphasis given to practical investigations as a vehicle for the development of problem-solving skills, also to be assessed externally in the examination but which are not to be assessed internally. It would appear from consultation with chemistry teachers that this approach will prove to be less problematic.

An exploration of the methodology issue is equally interesting. The Arrangements document for Standard Grade recognises that to cater effectively for the wide range of ability 'variety in teaching and learning approaches and resources becomes almost a necessity'. However, many schools appeared to take this message as a signal to move away completely from more traditional teacher-centred approaches towards pupil-centred methods heavily based on the use of worksheets. While this transformation of classroom practice has resulted in classrooms becoming 'busier' places with pupils generally benefiting from being given more responsibility for their own learning it is now agreed that effective teaching requires judicious use of the complete range of methods; there will always be a place for exposition and whole-class question-and-answer sessions, accompanied by memorable demonstrations of illustrative practical work. The relationship between trends in methodology and current achievement in the different aspects of the subject is thought-provoking. Consider the following extract from the brief report on Higher Grade Chemistry in the SEB Annual Report for 1996. 'Problem solving questions were generally well done. However, there were signs of weakness in questions assessing knowledge and under-standing.' Readers are free to draw their own conclusions. Undoubtedly, as the HSDP is introduced, the issue will continue to provide a major challenge for chemistry teachers in Scotland.

A LOOK INTO THE CRYSTAL BALL

The innovations which started in Scottish chemistry education in the 1970s and 1980s have continued into the 1990s and it is difficult to foresee other than further change in the next century. In the classroom of tomorrow, the range of resources used by students is likely to be extended to include interactive video, interactive compact disc and the internet. The increasing number of effective science programmes in primary schools is likely to lead to further reform in the first and second years; this may well have an impact on current Standard Grade provision as may the new and attractive Higher Still courses. However, perhaps the safest prediction relates to the effectiveness of the practitioners. This is highlighted in a recent report by the Scottish Office Education Department (SOED, 1994): 'The substantial rise in the popularity of the sciences over the last three decades owes much to the determination of dedicated teachers to create courses which are interesting, relevant and accessible to all pupils.' There is little doubt that chemistry teachers will continue to cope with subject developments and meet the needs of the students in the new millennium.

REFERENCES

CCC (1980) *Memorandum Number 43, Language in Chemistry*, Glasgow: Consultative Council on the Curriculum.

HSDU (1997) *Arrangements for Chemistry*, Edinburgh: Higher Still Development Unit.

SEB (1992) *Amended Arrangements in Standard Grade Chemistry*, Dolkak: SEB.

SED (1969) *Curriculum Paper Number 7, Science for General Education*, Edinburgh: SED.

SOED (1993) *Environmental Studies, 5–14*, Edinburgh: SOED.

SOED (1994) *Effective Learning and Teaching in Scottish Secondary Schools: The Sciences*, Edinburgh: Scottish Office Education Department.

51

Classics Education

Tony Williams

Classics is the object of more hostility and indifference than any other subject in the Scottish curriculum. Behind these two attitudes lies a swathe of ignorance about Classics and its syllabuses currently available to pupils. This chapter should therefore begin with a clear definition of what Classics means.

Classics comprises the three subjects of Latin, Greek, and Classical Studies. Classical Studies is a study of the great civilisations of Greece and Rome which represent the cultural ancestry of modern day Western European civilisation. It can include literature, drama, politics, social issues, science and philosophy, art and architecture and all things that a whole society embraces. Latin and Greek are the languages in which were written the great literatures of Rome and Greece. Latin in particular has a massive influence both on English (for which it is the single largest source of words) and modern European Romance languages, but both languages open the door to a study of the great literatures of the civilisations which are our cultural heritage.

The account which follows covers Latin and Classical Studies. Greek is a very small (though very precious) subject in the Scottish curriculum and most of what is said about Latin can be taken to apply to Greek also.

THE FIRST CHALLENGES

There were two main challenges which comprehensive schools posed for Classics Education. The first arose because of the 'common course' rationale of S1 and S2 which dictated that no pupil could study any subject that was not studied by all pupils. It could be stated thus: 'If Classics was to have a place in the first 2 years of Secondary schooling, Classicists would need to produce material which avoided the intrinsic difficulties of Latin and was accessible to all.'

The second challenge emerged because linguistically able pupils who might have been expected to pursue Latin with success were a much smaller proportion of the cohort than in grammar schools, thus rendering class sizes too small. In addition, the most commonly used beginners' Latin course book of the late sixties, *Approach to Latin* (published 1939!) was based on the faulty assumption that the prior learning of grammar automatically developed the skills of translating and reading. The second challenge could be expressed thus: 'If Classics was to be viable even after the common course, Classicists were going to have to produce beginners' course book material in Latin both more accessible to pupils and better designed to promote reading skills.'

1970 – THE CHALLENGES MET

The answer to the first challenge – to produce material which was accessible to all pupils in S1 and S2 – was so very simple – or so it seems now. If it was hard to envisage pupils of the whole ability range enjoying the languages of Greek and Latin, it was very easy to imagine them caught up in the worlds of Greece and Rome – especially since young children respond so well to stories of the Gods, Heroes, and Monsters of Greek mythology. Thus it was that Classical Studies was born. Just as the main challenge to Classics in S1 and S2 had come in the west of Scotland, so it was in Strathclyde Region that Classical Studies' foundation material was now produced. The main sources of the material were the civilisations of the Minoans and Mycenaeans. This meant that not only could pupils discover the myth of Theseus and the Minotaur and the legend of the Trojan war but they could be introduced to archaeology as well, including the palace of Cnossos on Crete and the Mycenaean sites on mainland Greece and Turkey. Thousands of pupils worked at this material over the years. The first challenge seemed well and truly met.

As for the second challenge – to produce beginners' course book material in Latin more accessible and more relevant – a new course emerged in England at the end of the sixties that seemed purpose designed to meet the challenge – the Cambridge Latin Course. It was very closely followed both in time and philosophy by its Scottish counterpart – *Ecce Romani*. The writers of the Cambridge Course rejected activities such as learning grammatical tabulations and translating English sentences into Latin as irrelevant to the development of reading skill. In both these courses it was evident that pupils almost immediately had the satisfaction of reading a continuous story in Latin. Grammatical analysis was minimal in Cambridge and not much more than that in *Ecce Romani*. Both courses rejected Roman history in favour of a Roman family as the focus of their continuing storyline. The effect – both North and South of the border – was startling. Latin teachers found they were able to attract and retain more pupils in their classrooms. The second challenge seemed also to be met.

THE PROBLEMS OF THE 1970s

Alas, the very solutions which answered the early challenges themselves proved problematical.

Strathclyde's Classical Studies material comprised a series of information sheets and accompanying worksheets. The latter made it very clear that the whole point of the material was to fill pupils up with facts and then to check that these had been learned. Pupils were asked what a Minotaur was, how many Athenians Minos fed to the Minotaur each year, how Ariadne helped Theseus to kill the Minotaur and escape the labyrinth – and so on. Opportunities to use the myth to stimulate imaginative responses ('how do you think Theseus would feel as he left his old father in Athens for the dangers of Crete?') or arouse intellectual curiosity ('how might the archaeological discoveries at Cnossos suggest that "Theseus and the Minotaur" is more than just a good story?') were nearly always lost.

As for the Cambridge Latin Course and *Ecce Romani*, whilst few people criticised the attractiveness of the material or the storylines, doubts were emerging about the lack of structure in the presentation of language material. In the present writer's view, the new courses had been right to suggest that the reading of Latin should normally come before grammatical comment but wrong to believe that pupils did not require the grammar to be structured at all if they were to read the literature of an inflected language. Even the Scottish course, *Ecce Romani*, which was more explicit about grammatical rules and even occasionally presented a grammatical tabulation after a reading passage, failed to ensure that the bits and pieces of the tabulation occurred sufficiently in the reading passage for the teacher to make the vital connection between grammatical knowledge and reading skill.

Other problems at this time concerned Scottish Examination syllabuses.

- as yet there was no certificate (O grade) examination in Classical Studies which remained a subject confined to S1 or S2.
- the O grade examinations in Latin and Greek had been designed on the assumption that pupils would begin study in S1. As has been explained the common course meant that in the maintained sector an S2 or even an S3 start was becoming the norm. As a result the examination was proving too difficult for many pupils. Not surprisingly this was particularly the case with the unseen passage of Latin for translation into English. The effect was very demoralising for pupils and teachers alike.
- prescribed literature was assessed either by the requirement to translate a block of lines (which some pupils – without the ability to translate – coped with by learning a translation of the whole prescription by heart) or by the requirement to answer factual questions on another block (which suggested that the author had written a mini-encyclopaedia rather than a piece of literature.)
- finally, the last section of the O grade Latin and Greek papers was a 'Classical Studies' section in which pupils answered questions from a choice of topics such as 'Hadrian's Wall' or a book of Ovid's Metamorphoses in translation. Here there were two problems. Firstly the questions were depressingly factual again (e.g. 'What was the width of Hadrian's Wall?'). Secondly, teachers were uncertain about the coverage required in some topics. For instance, they may have spent a lot of time introducing pupils to the design of forts, mile castles, and turrets on Hadrian's Wall only to find that in the examination paper the questions required a knowledge not of the shape of a fort but of the particular troops which manned it.

THE TRIUMPHANT 1980s AND 1990s

In view of the solutions which soon emerged to solve the problems just listed, it does not seem an exaggeration to use the adjective 'triumphant' of the years from 1981.

It was in that year that the first candidates took O grade Classical Studies. The Examination Board had finally agreed that an examination in the subject could proceed. Candidates had to answer questions on a whole range of topics but the most important thing about the examination was that questions demanding factual recall ('What law had Antigone broken?') were at long last balanced by questions which demanded some analysis and evaluation by candidates ('What is your view of the arguments which Antigone uses to justify her action?'). There was criticism as well as great praise for the syllabus and examination. Some teachers felt that the style of questions made the examination too difficult for S4 pupils. Unfortunately the examination had to meet the standards of a certificate (O grade) which had always been geared to the top 30 per cent of pupils academic range. However, O grade's days were numbered (Classical Studies was one of the last syllabuses to be approved) and Standard Grade was already on the horizon. Any discontent would not last for long.

It was also in 1981 that a first consultative panel for Classics was set up within the Consultative Committee on the Curriculum in Scotland (now the SCCC) and reported in the following year (CCC, 1982). It had set out the four main skills developed by the learning of a Classical language:

- translation (of Latin into English)
- interpretation (of Latin literature)
- investigation (into the Roman world)
- language awareness (insight into English and modern Romance languages on all of which Latin was the chief influence)

The working party devising the Standard Grade Latin syllabus adopted the first three of these as its main elements, correctly regarding the fourth as an excellent by-product of the learning of Latin. Because of this and the fact that it was offered at Foundation, General, and Credit levels (and so to a far wider academic range of pupil than ever before) the following solutions to previous problems were almost automatic:

- translation would be assessed by the requirement to turn an unseen passage of Latin into English. The passage would be rigorously controlled so as to be translatable by pupils after only 2 years of Latin. Passages in English would cue pupils into the context, and a Standard Grade vocabulary was produced to inform teachers and pupils about the words to be known.
- interpretation skills would require pupils not only to understand what a writer was saying but to appreciate how he was saying it ('Why does Catullus use the words lux (light) and nox (darkness) to refer to life and death in poem V?') and to give their own opinions on the result. Prescribed literature was being treated as literature for the very first time and those privileged to mark papers could see how much pupils were enjoying it.
- investigation skills were defined not simply as gaining knowledge of the Roman world but as evaluating evidence, making comparisons with the modern world, and presenting results. Since it was felt that an examination could not easily assess such things, the natural decision was to require an investigation or report from pupils produced as a piece of their own research under teacher supervision. Immediately pupils could choose a topic that they found interesting and teachers no longer had to worry about predicting the questions that would be asked in an examination room. It is hard to overestimate the enthusiasm created by this element alone.

Standard Grade Classical Studies was to follow, and this preserved the balance between knowledge and evaluation first demonstrated by the O grade exam but now came with the advantage that it was available at Foundation and General as well as Credit levels – in fact to pupils of the whole ability range. Needless to say, the S grade skills or elements of Latin, Greek and Classical Studies were continued into Revised Higher and CSYS syllabuses – thus ensuring progression.

In 1992, the Latin 5–14 report was issued (SOEID, 1992) – setting out the standards to be achieved by pupils in the first two years of Secondary schooling. Not surprisingly the working group returned to the very elements of Latin identified by the consultative panel of ten years earlier. However, since it was right that interpretation as well as translation should be developed even on the synthetic Latin young pupils were reading, these two elements were brought together for this age group. And since many of these pupils would end their study of Latin before reaching real literature, the knowledge about language element was elevated to a main aim. Thus the three outcomes were: translating / interpreting texts, knowledge about language, the Roman World.

In view of the educational value of Classics – especially with the changes of the last twenty years described above – it is hardly surprising that the Scottish Office has reinforced its position within the Scottish curriculum.

The following examples illustrate this support:

- Classical Studies is now included within the social subjects mode of the Scottish curriculum. This means that it can be taken by pupils as part of their core curriculum up to S4.
- Classical Studies is now, like Classical languages, available at all certificate levels in schools.
- As for Classical languages, the Secretary of State – in a circular of 22 January 1988 – made it possible in certain circumstances for a Classical language to replace a modern European language as the compulsory foreign language to be studied by pupils up to S4.
- Another SOEID policy document issued in July 1988 by the Secretary of State included the following statement:

> The classical languages . . . represent an important part of our heritage and provide a valuable educative experience. It is right that opportunities for their study should continue to be available and encouraged. I shall therefore be asking education authorities to ensure that *some schools in each area* [my italics] continue to offer these languages.

Thus, the position of Classics in Scottish schools as far as the expressed wishes of the Scottish Office are concerned would appear to be well secured for the future.

CONCLUSION

Alas, the actual position of Classics in maintained schools is desperate. In Grampian Region and Dumfries and Galloway, there are no schools with Classics departments. In Highland and Lothian regions, the subject can hardly be found anywhere, and it maintains only a precarious hold in Central Region. Most dramatically Classics has declined to the point where it is available in only four schools out of more than forty in Glasgow.

The reason for this stark contrast with the government's own policy is the hostility and indifference mentioned at the start of this chapter. It seems that just a single individual – be it a headteacher or someone of influence in a local authority – can on personal whim just remove the subject from school curricula. This means that whole cohorts of pupils in widespread areas of Scotland do not have the opportunity even to decline to opt for the subject – it does not appear on their menu of choices at all. It is very regrettable that even in a system that is not centrally controlled, the government can only look on as its policy statement is flouted everywhere in the land.

Classical Studies can now be taken like Classical languages as a main degree subject at many universities including St Andrews, Edinburgh and Glasgow. The next logical step is that it should become a recognised subject for teacher training in Scotland (as has been the case for many years elsewhere). This would mean that the Classics department at Strathclyde University's Jordanhill Campus would not each year have to reject applicants with degrees in Classical Studies and another subject who, at the moment, can only train to teach in one of their specialisms. Regrettably, the Scottish Office has so far resisted the urgent requests for this development.

Maybe there is still some ground for optimism. Classics has had two development officers and two specialist groups in the Higher Still programme – one for Classical Studies and one for Classical Languages. At the time of writing a report produced by the Scottish Inspectorate on Effective Learning and Teaching in Classics (to parallel one produced in England in 1989) is at press but has not yet been released for publication.

There is approval for using technology to create a flexible distanced learning system which would enable a single teacher in one school to teach classes in schools many miles away. This might achieve something, but it is difficult to imagine a school which gave up Classics when there had been a Classicist on the staff, restoring it in the absence of any personality at all.

There is also the possibility of a pendulum swing. This seems to be happening in Classics south of the border where until only a few years ago the position of the subject was far weaker than in Scotland. As for continental Europe, it seems to appreciate fully Classical subjects and what they can do for the linguistic and cultural heritage of children. Classics is going from strength to strength there. It is to be hoped that urgent action can be taken soon in Scotland. For it is not Classics which is the loser but the educational experience and enrichment of all Scottish pupils.

REFERENCES

Consultative Panel on Classics (1982) *The Needs for Development in Classics in the Secondary School* (A report to the Committee on Secondary Education), Dundee: CCC.

HSDU (1997/8) *Higher Still arrangements for Classical Languages and Classical Studies*, Dundee: SCCC.

Scottish Classics Group (1971, 1982) *Ecce Romani*, Edinburgh: Oliver and Boyd.

SEB/SQA (1986–93) *Revised Arrangements in Latin, Greek and Classical Studies at Standard Grade*, Dalkeith/Glasgow: SQA.

SEB/SQA (1988–94) *Revised Arrangements in Latin, Greek and Classical Studies at Higher Grade*, Dalkeith/Glasgow: SQA.

SOEID (1992) *Latin 5–14*, Edinburgh: HMSO.

52

Computing Studies

Tom Conlon

Computing Studies barely existed in Scottish secondary schools until the second half of the 1980s. Then came a period of vigorous growth. New courses were devised by the Scottish Examination Board (SEB) at Standard Grade (1986), Higher Grade (1989) and CSYS (1993). These are summarised as they stand at the time of writing in Figure 52.1. SEB statistics show that by the early 1990s, Standard Grade Computing was studied by around 30 per cent of all S3/S4 pupils. Most schools had by that time created computing departments, typically consisting of a Principal Teacher and one or two (possibly part-time) assistants. In addition to the SEB courses, computing departments have usually provided introductory courses in S1/S2 and short modular courses in S5/S6. Considerable controversy surrounded the early development of Computing Studies (Conlon and Cope, 1989). This chapter will demonstrate that plenty of scope for debate remains today and, indeed, that the subject's future is far from being assured.

STANDARD GRADE

Computing Studies is situated in the 'technology mode' of the S3/S4 curriculum. There it competes for recruits with subjects such as Office and Information Studies (OIS), Craft and Design, Home Economics, and Technological Studies. Computing presently dominates this group but it is coming under increasing challenge, especially from OIS which also offers a large practical IT element. SEB statistics show that an average secondary school in 1996 presented forty-four candidates for Standard Grade Computing. Such a figure would be envied by some other subjects but for Computing it actually represents a continuation in the gentle decline of recent years (see Figure 52.2). Of course, schools vary tremendously. In some, Standard Grade Computing has almost swamped its rivals; in a few, the course has disappeared.

CONTINUATION INTO HIGHER AND CSYS

Computing Studies has a problem retaining the pupils it recruits. National statistics show that only 14.6 per cent of 1994 Standard Grade Computing candidates continued with the subject into Higher in S5 and only 1.4 per cent continued beyond that into CSYS. For comparison, the corresponding figures for Biology (a rather successful science subject) were 33.0 per cent for Higher and 5.3 per cent for CSYS.

Figure 52.1 Computing courses with study hours shown in brackets.

	Standard Grade	Higher Grade	CSYS
Core topics	• Computer applications (60) • Computer Systems (20) • Programming (40) • Discretionary time (10) • Project (30)	• General Purpose Packages (20) • Computer Systems (25) • Programming (30) • Investigation (20)	• Project: specify, design build and evaluate (part of) a computer system (80)
Optional topics		*Select one from:* • Communications (25) • Knowledge Based Systems (25) • Interfacing (25)	*Select two from:* • Artificial intelligence (40) • Communications (40) • Software development (40) • Interfacing (40) • Computer Systems (40)
Assessment	*Grades 1–7 awarded for each of:* • Knowledge & Understanding (by examination) • Problem Solving (by examination) • Practical Abilities (by Project and coursework)	• Examination 70% • Investigation 15% • Programming coursework 15%	• Examination 50% • Project 40% • Practical competence 10%

Source: SEB 1997

Figure 52.2 Percentages of S4 presented for Standard Grade, 1992–6.

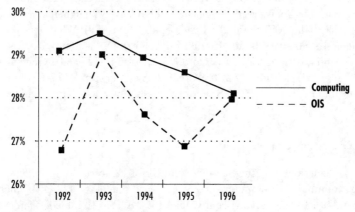

Source: SEB Examination Statistics, 1995 & 1996

To see how this affects a typical school, consider that forty-four pupils presented for Standard Grade Computing in 1994 would have yielded a Higher class of only six or seven pupils in 1995. No more than a single pupil would have reached CSYS in 1996. By contrast, had the typical Biology department started with the same number of Standard Grade pupils then its continuation rates would have produced a healthy-sized Higher class of fourteen or fifteen and perhaps three students for CSYS. It is not certain why Computing loses so many of its pupils after Standard Grade. Teachers point to a variety of factors, including disillusionment caused by a lacklustre Standard Grade course; the antipathy which university computing departments display towards the Computing Higher; the reputation for dourness and difficulty which the Higher course has acquired; and the profile of pupils whom the subject attracts.

PROFILE OF PUPILS

Two trends have become clear in the profile of pupils who are attracted to Computing Studies. First, more boys are recruited than girls and between S3 and S6 the gender skew becomes more extreme. Boys made up 65%, 75%, and 85% of the subject's 1996 candidates for Standard Grade, Higher Grade and CSYS respectively. There are other subjects that disproportionately recruit boys, including most technology mode subjects (although not OIS which is 83% girls). However SEB research shows that Computing does worse than most in failing to retain those girls whom it initially attracts. Interestingly, it seems that at Standard Grade level females actually perform better, although the same is not true at Higher. Among Standard Grade Computing candidates in 1995, 38.0% of females gained Credit awards compared to 32.1% of males. Among S5 Higher Computing candidates in 1996, 39.0% of females gained an 'A' or 'B' compared to 42.2% of males. Computing's gender problem has been partly researched. Cole et al. (1994) identified several possible causes, including boys' domination of home computers and video games machines from an early age, lack of female role models, and a perception by girls that Computing Studies undervalues skills in teamwork and communication.

The second trend concerns the educational achievement of pupils who take Computing. At Standard Grade the subject attracts large numbers of low-achieving candidates. In 1996, 39.7% of candidates gained awards only at lower General level or below (the corresponding figures for OIS and Biology were 29.7% and 20.6%). In contrast, Higher Computing candidates seem to be above-average achievers. They pass 3.7 Highers in total, equal to the figure for Biology (the average for all Higher candidates is 2.9). What does this mean for a typical school? Its Standard Grade Computing cohort of 44 contains 15 girls. The cohort may well be taught as two classes: a Credit/General group of 27 and a General/Foundation group of 17. The girls are mostly in the Credit/General group. Perhaps 5 boys and 2 girls will continue into Higher. The CSYS candidate, assuming one emerges, will very likely be a boy.

HARDWARE AND SOFTWARE

A 1996 survey conducted by the Scottish Council for Educational Technology found that the average number of computers per secondary school is 123, of which 34% are Macintosh, 23% BBC, 14% IBM compatible, 13% Acorn Archimedes, and 8% Amstrad PCW. It is certain that these figures conceal huge variation between schools. Schools in wealthy areas generally have a superior stock. Consider the average school with its 123 machines. Perhaps half of these are held in three dedicated computer rooms maintained by the Computing department. The department's key software resource is *Claris Works*, a package which combines word-processor, database, spreadsheet, and graphics functions. This program is installed on most machines. A variety of other programs are in use but if the school is typical, funds for software are extremely limited. Teachers wage a constant struggle to keep the hardware and software running. They have almost no technical support and spend a large amount of time on routine maintenance.

TEACHING AND LEARNING

The literature on teaching and learning in Computing Studies is meagre. Researchers have not been very active in this area. The Inspectorate has produced just one report (SOED, 1993). Although generally reassuring, its contents are bland (for example: 'Pupils are generally well motivated', 'Staff and pupils are punctual and hardworking'). In the author's experience, however, some features of a typical school can be predicted with confidence. Standard Grade classes are characterised by a large amount of 'hands-on' activity and considerable use of resource-based learning materials. A high proportion of lessons feature either *Claris Works* or some kind of business software (e.g. simulations for stock control or ticket-booking). For programming, the once mandatory *COMAL* language has been replaced by an authoring system (perhaps *HyperCard*). SEB data indicates that many teachers avoid project work that would involve programming, which is regarded as difficult. Projects done with packages like *Claris Works* are believed to produce better grades.

Higher Grade classes are more likely to feature whole-class teaching, often of a rather didactic kind. Lessons are based on some rather elderly (dating from 1989) booklets produced by the Consultative Committee on the Curriculum. Pupils are expected to learn a large number of technical definitions, with few opportunities to apply or integrate the ideas. In programming, which could use the *Pascal* language, the level of difficulty is dauntingly far beyond that encountered at Standard Grade. In some years a solitary CSYS candidate sits at the back of the Higher class. He or she works through another set of CCC booklets. These seem even more out of date than the Higher materials and they make many unfamiliar references: unfortunately the teacher can provide very little assistance.

STAFF DEVELOPMENT

Currently, prospective Computing teachers must have an academic qualification containing two undergraduate courses in the subject. During the 1980s the requirement was for just one course but even so the supply of eligible teachers fell far below the numbers needed to satisfy the subject's growth. In response the education colleges ran part-time Diploma courses through which hundreds of teachers gained qualifications. The previously mentioned HMI report states that in 1990, Scottish schools contained 798 qualified computing teachers. 27 per cent of Computing classes were being taught by the unqualified.

Teacher education institutes today recruit into their initial training programmes students of Computing alongside students of other subjects. High-quality applicants, with the right kinds of commitment and interpersonal skill, are scarce. An imminent increase in the eligibility requirement to three courses could produce difficulties, especially if headteachers expect, as many do at present, that new teachers will come qualified in a second subject in addition to Computing.

In the typical high school the principal teacher became qualified in the late 1980s through a college Diploma. He or she is troubled that since that time, opportunities to keep abreast of developments have been few. There is no contact between the school department and higher education. Following the abolition of regional councils, the IT advisory service disappeared and nowadays even meetings with teachers from other schools have become rare.

FUTURE PROSPECTS

It will be clear even from this brief account that Computing Studies is not short of issues of concern. It seems fitting to end this contribution by offering the author's own interpretation of the subject's prospects.

SEB computing courses presently justify their existence by three types of rationale. It is claimed (with varying emphases) that the courses:

1. teach IT skills essential for education, life and work;
2. introduce learners to the rich new disciplines of Computer Science and Artificial Intelligence;
3. provide a novel basis for developing important abilities of a general kind, for example in problem-solving, communication and teamwork.

The first type of rationale now looks very shaky, for four main reasons. First, advances in computer interface design make the concept of 'IT skills' increasingly nebulous since the thrust of most of these advances is to deskill computer operation. Second, many children now make frequent and effective use of IT through their 5–14 education and at home, suggesting that intervention at Standard Grade is less relevant. Third, research indicates that practical computer skills are best learned not through formal computer courses but through guided exploration in contextualised tasks (Carroll, 1990). Fourth, the pursuit of vocationally-oriented IT brings Computing Studies directly into conflict with established vocationally-oriented subjects, such as OIS and Craft and Design. The demarcation disputes are already simmering.

The future of Computing Studies may depend therefore upon its ability to develop courses of broad appeal which rest upon a rationale of types (2) and (3) rather than (1). That this is feasible is suggested by the analysis undertaken by Bird, Conlon and Swanson (1996). Challenging courses, which situate the learner as 'tool-designer' rather than 'tool-user', could attract those pupils who look with dismay at what is presently offered by the technology mode of the S3/S4 curriculum. The development of such courses could also serve to invigorate the subject's teachers.

Sadly, the prospects do not look good. Peter Cope in Conlon and Cope (1989), lambasted the subject's unimaginative and oppressive top-down control by the Inspectorate and its nominees. That regime still holds firm and the damage it wreaks has been most recently demonstrated in the Higher Still programme which, far from invigorating computing teachers, has alienated them to an unprecedented extent by imposing a framework that looks to be narrowly skills-oriented, outdated and inflexible. Even the normally compliant Computing Studies panel of the SEB expressed impotent rage at the manner of this development. Meanwhile, no review is planned for the ageing Standard Grade course and the subject is at best uncertain about its role in the curriculum in S1/S2.

Scottish teachers toiled mightily to construct Computing Studies in the 1980s. Thanks to their efforts, a generation of children whose education might otherwise have made little reference to it was introduced to computing. However, the subject's future place will be assured neither by past momentum nor by the present widespread (and surely temporary, in the era of increasingly ubiquitous technology) preoccupation with 'IT skills'. What is required is a return to fundamental questions: What exactly is the content and pedagogy of Computing that justifies its continuing distinctive existence as a school subject? Unless Scottish teachers can summon the energy, expertise and professional freedom to reconstruct their subject then the decline of Computing Studies in the coming decade could be as rapid as was its growth in the last.

REFERENCES

Bird, D., T. Conlon and S. Swanson (1996) Computing and Information Technology in Higher Still: Let's get it right, *Scottish Educational Review*, vol. 28. 1, p. 3–15.

Carroll, J., (1990) *The Nurnberg Funnel: Designing Minimalist Instruction for Practical Computer Skill.* Cambridge, Massachusetts: MIT Press.

Cole A., S. Jackson, T. Conlon and D. Welch (1994) Information Technology and Gender: Problems and Proposals, *Gender and Education*, 6:1, p. 78.

Conlon, T. and P. Cope (Eds) (1989) *Computing in Scottish Education: the first decade and beyond*, Edinburgh: Edinburgh University Press.

SOED (1993) *Teaching and Learning in Computing Studies*, Edinburgh: SOED.

SEB (1997) *Arrangements in Computing Studies: Standard Grade, Higher Grade and Certificate of Sixth Year Studies*, Dalkeith: SEB.

53

Drama Education

Paul Dougall

DEVELOPMENT AND AIMS

Drama as a teaching discipline is influenced by two competing ideologies:

> the utilisation of Drama method to develop interpersonal and social skill;
> the development of aesthetic understanding as mediated through theatrical performance.

The attempt to encompass both ideologies in a coherent and progressive curriculum will be discussed in this chapter.

Drama as a specialist teaching discipline in Scottish secondary schools was introduced in the late 1950s, when the whole philosophy and practice of secondary teaching and learning was entering a period of radical review and revision. The impulse to create a curriculum which would be more pupil centred than previously produced the necessity to seek ways in which the nurturing of the pupils' social and emotional development became a necessary complement to the development of intellectual skills.

The earliest proponents of Drama in the curriculum such as Way (*Development through Drama*, Harlow: Longman, 1967) defined the essential purpose as the development of the whole person, which would:

- encourage pupils to explore the variety of human emotions;
- assist pupils to gain confidence in their own abilities, particularly to communicate verbally and non-verbally;
- develop in pupils the capacity to work together to solve human and practical problems;
- permit pupils to explore the differences between right and wrong in simple moral dilemmas posed through Drama.

Thus, Drama can be seen as being in the vanguard of a progressive ideology which sought to encourage pupils to negotiate possibilities actively with their peers and their teachers. One definition of the central intention of Drama in the curriculum is the development of personal competence and social awareness in pupils. Having established the essential principles, it became necessary in Drama, as in other subjects which shared the same progressive impulse, to develop a methodology. The problem in seeking to customise the curriculum to the developmental needs of the pupils, is that pupils have quite frequently different developmental needs; and the educational process is ultimately a socialising system which is required to operate within relatively rigid boundaries of space, time and finance.

Throughout the 1960s and 1970s teachers of Drama in secondary schools sought to sustain the principles of active negotiated learning while accommodating to the need to construct a curriculum which could define the particular skills that would be developed through activity in the Drama room. One particular problem confronting the teacher was offering evidence that the Drama process had verifiable learning outcomes. The nature of the Drama process results in important developmental activity happening in the Drama room but the outcome remains ephemeral. The formative nature of teaching and learning in Drama has created a measure of ideological conflict among specialist teachers of the subject.

In the initial development of Drama methodology the necessity to sustain the purity of the driving principles resulted in the subject remaining on the margins of the school system. The formative developmental process became associated with those pupils who would not be able to cope with the academic curriculum and thus Drama became, to a degree, colonised as a teaching methodology which had a social value but lacked the intellectual dimensions of other more traditional subjects. Those additional dimensions were clearly cited in the assessment practices of the national certificate programmes in which Drama as a subject was excluded. Advantageously, even the most traditional of most secondary subjects by the 1970s were actively seeking ways to reflect pupil centred activity in their teaching and learning patterns. The challenge to Drama teachers was to refine the formative teaching programme to incorporate the more flexible summative assessment instruments that were being incorporated into the national examination systems. By accepting this challenge Drama has in the 1990s moved from the periphery to a more central position within the school system. The opportunity afforded to pupils of all ability ranges to undertake a variety of certificate awards in Drama has greatly enhanced the status of the subject.

Conversely, many of the principles and methodological practices incorporated into the teaching methods of other disciplines have been derived from the principles and practices that define Drama methodology, especially its exploratory, experiential approach to learning. Drama has made a signal contribution to teaching methodology across subject boundaries and has, in return, developed a more pragmatic sense that a curriculum must be taught and not merely caught (cf. Heathcote and Bolton, 1995). The tension between ideological purity and pragmatic necessity informs the ongoing dialogue in Drama as in other subjects.

The opportunity for the pupil to experience the Drama process has increasingly been understood in terms of the necessity for discrete skills to be defined, developed and evaluated. The emotional shock to many Drama teachers, when they realised that to be more firmly rooted within the secondary sector required of them a comprehensive review of the principles and practices that were driving what they were doing in their classrooms, was palpable.

There was a realisation that a key aspect of the process of teaching and learning was to differentiate between pupils within defined frames of reference, and not merely accommodate to the needs of all pupils by negotiating acceptable synergy with the group.

METHODOLOGY

Since all teaching and learning operates within finite space, time and finance, the teacher of any subject designing a curriculum must address the following questions: who does what? with whom? where? when? why and for how long?

While Drama existed on the margins of National Certificate assessment the curriculum framework was, as noted above, formative in nature, and located within a number of exploratory opportunities which became defined as the Drama process.

At this time limited attention was placed on the aesthetics of Theatre performance since that would entail critical commentary and an interpretation of texts. Essentially, the study of Theatre as a performance discipline was regarded as extraneous to the needs of the particular pupils undertaking Drama programmes. By extending the client base, the subject has had to extend the locus of activity to incorporate the study of Theatre as an aesthetic discipline as a complement to the study of the Drama process.

The key thing to note about the distinction between Drama process and Theatre process is that although they might share similar vocabularies their purposes are actually quite different. In the Drama process, acting out the improvisation by the group is a sharing of the exploration with the peer group. The improvisation is designed to address the social and emotional dynamics of the dilemma which becomes the point of focus for the pupils undertaking the task. The evaluation of the activity resides in the interplay of the engagement and exploration by the pupils. Have they been supportive of each other in the task; have they addressed the task demand appropriately? Essentially, the process of exploration is more important than the performed statement.

In contrast, when pupils engage in developing the skills that pertain to theatrical representation, the evaluation relates to the pupil's capacity to represent the appropriate stylistic feature of movement, voice, characterisation in interpreting the part being acted.

STAGE BY STAGE

In S1 and S2 the primary purpose is to introduce pupils to the Drama process through improvised activity. As noted above, the Drama form is utilised to mediate the social or moral theme being explored.

The pupils explore the concept of dramatic tension through role play activity. Again it should be stressed that role play is not an end in itself but a means of exploring different attitudes and behaviours. The participants develop an imaginary situation either as self or as another person in order to explore behaviours and values in a safe and constructive environment. The development of role play activity aligns the intention to assist the pupil to explore the social and imaginative world from a number of perspectives with the developing capacity to take on and sustain a number of roles using appropriate language and movement. Integrated with the role play activity, there are discrete lessons which focus on developing skills in voice, speech and movement which will assist the pupil to work more confidently in the different registers which inform the role play activity; and create the basis of technique which will be necessary in the later years when the focus becomes the interpretation of dramatic text.

By the end of S2 pupils should be able to develop convincing roles in specific situations; create and take part in improvised scenes in order to explore particular issues which could have a practical, social or moral dimension; carry out dramatic intentions with a clear but unforced control over movement and voice.

By the S3/S4 stage there is the further consolidation of the basic skills in voice and movement and a more formalised and sophisticated structure to the improvised activity. Groups of pupils are given more autonomy over the construction of the dramatic narrative they develop through working on characterisation, which is the investigation and portrayal in depth of a specific role.

Characterisation is the bridge between the role play activity of S1/S2 and the acting skills necessary in S5/S6. The movement from drama form to theatre form is articulated through developing pupil skills in characterisation (Neelands, 1990). In addition, the improvisatory work on characterisation is complemented by the interpretational study of text in order to strike a balance between the construction of a more sophisticated group improvisation and the deconstruction of theatre texts; and latterly theatre performances.

The assessment of both modes of activity informs the Standard Grade Certificate which incorporates the three dimensions of: Creating, Presenting, Knowledge and Understanding.

By the end of S4 the impetus towards interpersonal development has merged with an understanding of the essential conventions of theatrical representation. The pupil will, it is hoped, have enhanced his/her interpersonal skills and performance skills. In summary, the pupils should be able to appreciate dramatic ambiguity (i.e. when language and action work in opposition), call on a range of subtle skills in voice, posture, movement and gesture in order to sustain, and develop, dramatic action.

The bridge between the interpersonal and the performance is difficult for some pupils and philosophically problematic for some teachers. There is ongoing debate between those who feel that training in theatrical representation (i.e. acting) should begin at an earlier stage while others claim that the ideological purpose of working in the drama form is corrupted by the sudden switch to developing theatre performance skills (Hornbrook, 1989).

By S5/S6 the focus is on Theatre and the development of critical skills in relation to specified texts. This theoretical approach is complemented with practical workshop activity which seeks to exemplify the key stylistic features of performance skills directed to designated audiences, and theatre skills which monitor the pupil's ability in theatre arts and technology. Role play has become acting; improvisation has become investigative drama towards a performance; and exploration has become critical commentary and literary analysis.

In summary, the pupil should be able to understand the main characteristics of different kinds of drama, have practical experience of suitable classic and contemporary examples and use appropriate structures to control dramatic action. Drama teachers have been very imaginative in designing assessment frameworks which will contain the two, perhaps competing, ideologies; but there is continuing pressure to push the balance towards theatre studies since pupil performance is more amenable to auditing than pupil development.

The recent pressure to articulate coherent and progressive curricula across the primary, secondary and tertiary sectors will continue to give teachers of drama methodological problems to address and resolve. However, in a mere forty years the subject has influenced both general progressive pedagogy and established its place and purpose as a discrete teaching discipline (Taylor, ed., 1996). The future holds more challenges than fears.

REFERENCES

Heathcote, D. and G. Bolton (1995) *Drama for Learning: Dorothy Heathcote's Mantle of the Expert Approach to Education*, Portsmouth: Heinemann.

Hornbrook, D. (1989) *Education and Dramatic Art*, Oxford: Blackwell.

Neelands, J. (1990) *Structuring Drama Work*, Cambridge: Cambridge University Press.

O'Neill, C. (1995) *Drama Worlds; A Framework for Process Drama*, Portsmouth: Heinemann.

SCCC/SFEU (1997) *Subject Guide: Drama*, Higher Still Development Unit, Edinburgh: SCCC.

Taylor, P. (ed.) (1996) *Researching Drama and Arts Education, Paradigms and Possibilities*, London: Falmer Press.

54

English Language Education

James McGonigal

HOW SECONDARY TEACHERS APPROACH ENGLISH TEACHING: PHILOSOPHIES AND PRACTICE

The teaching of secondary English Language in Scotland differs from the teaching of the same subject south of the border much as Scottish English differs from Standard English: it is at once recognisably similar and radically different. Projects set up to deal with perceived problems in the teaching of English in England are responded to here with a different inflection; and even new critical understandings of the subject itself (in terms, for instance, of the ideologies implicit in texts) must be re-articulated for Scottish classrooms and culture.

Scottish teachers of English, of course, do share a broad rationale with their counterparts elsewhere. Briefly, every English teacher endeavours to 'bring texts to life', by creating an active engagement between pupils' growing minds and hearts, on the one hand, and the meanings (explicit or implied) in the words or images of the text in question, on the other. Choice of text and also teacher performance in enactment and exploration are crucial to effective learning here.

But English teachers must also 'bring life to texts', by structuring active and social responses to what is read or heard: pupils' first reactions are refined through being expressed in group or whole-class discussion; a more reasoned or reflective individual response then follows, frequently in writing, which may itself become the occasion for further discussion, or redrafting, or publication. Such writing, of course, can take a variety of forms, often literary or personal, less frequently transactional or functional. Ideally, both formative and summative assessment are natural elements in this dialogic process, as learners develop towards more confident self-awareness and control in language.

Such broad similarity of aims in English teaching can mask quite deep differences, however. The very term 'English Language' is problematic, where Scottish English, Scots Language and, in some areas, Gaelic are spoken in the local community, a linguistic mix enriched by ethnic minority languages such as Urdu or Punjabi. Such dialects and languages are not merely spoken alongside Standard Scottish English in the context of groupwork, but also read or written about: classroom texts by Scottish authors often include linguistic and cultural features which would be misunderstood in England, and are selected for study precisely because they do provide opportunities for insight into Scottish experience, urban and rural, past and contemporary.

This was not always so, when for example the Scots 'invented' English as a subject of study. Almost a hundred years earlier than in England, eighteenth-century Scottish professors of Rhetoric began to use such near contemporary English writers as Addison or Swift, rather than classical authors, as suitably elegant models for analysis and imitation by rough Scots. Adam Smith, rhetorician as well as economist, clearly intended that his students should not be linguistically, and hence economically, disadvantaged in their postgraduate pursuit of free trade in England and the Empire.

There has remained in Scotland something of this desire to support linguistic competence in Standard English as much as personal growth: the supposed 'creative writing' movement of the 1960s (which English traditionalists seem to have blamed ever since for declining standards in spelling and good manners) never appeared to overwhelm English teaching here, which has always sought to enable movement beyond dialectal boundaries. A national assessment system offering ready comparison of results between classes and schools, and generally close links between schools and their local communities, have also maintained a traditional stress on the English skills needed for written academic work. And yet those links also keep many classrooms open to the voices and rhythms of local and national literature, using Scottish Arts Council support for visiting writers.

METHODS AND ASSESSMENT S1–S6

Pupils in such schools and classrooms in the 1950s or 1960s can still recall the hierarchical, academic lines on which they were organised, and how many of their English teachers adhered to that Scottish rhetorical tradition of canonical texts of (chiefly) English literature, combined with model compositions for imitation and decontextualised grammatical exercises. Current methods and assessment developed in reaction to such rigidities, and aim to right the balance between directive teaching and active learning.

Most S1 classes in English are now taught in mixed-ability sets of about thirty, often subdivided into friendship or ability groups for discussion activities. During their three to four English lessons a week (about 200 minutes in total) pupils often experience a two-stage lesson, with initial teacher recapitulation or context-setting leading to individual or group follow-up on a focused task or diversified project. Group talk can also be used quickly at the start, to involve pupils in the day's agenda by eliciting initial reactions to the topic, which the rest of the lesson will unpack or refine.

Contexts for both talk and writing are most frequently created from a literary text appropriate to the pupils' level of maturity, with subsequent discussion arising from its conflicts and characters. Such texts are mainly by twentieth century authors, although often set in a recreated past or imagined future. (There have been recent Inspectorate reminders of the range of older classic texts, including Scottish texts, being neglected in the process.) Quite often a social or personal issue, such as Growing Up, is explored thematically, combining a variety of factual or autobiographical texts and media resources with literary genres to explore its different facets. Teaching and learning are normally structured in units of work, developed by departmental or local authority staff, with photocopiable worksheets linked to a variety of language purposes.

Within such mixed-ability English classes, the teacher's role in making texts and tasks accessible is vital. Differentiation may occur simply through accepting variation in the response of individuals to the same task; or by the creation of a hierarchy of tasks for different groups; or by additional texts or assignments to be tackled in extension work; or by the level of support offered through simplified worksheets, word-processing, or increased teacher contact, including cooperative teaching by learning support staff in the classroom. A recent Scottish study of differentiation (Simpson and Ure, 1993) found positive pupil reaction to the kinds of interactive support which feature in English classrooms more frequently than the tightly differentiated tasksheets of more 'linear' subjects. Nevertheless, group approaches to the reading of different novels, graded in terms of difficulty but clustered round common themes, have allowed some teachers recently to stretch more able readers while supporting the less able.

Evidence of pupil attainment in S1–2, increasingly gathered into folios reflecting a range of language purposes and skills, is used to set them in S3–4 into classes aimed broadly at Foundation/General or General/Credit levels in the Standard Grade examination. Differences between sets now become more evident in the depth and complexity of texts studied, and the techniques of close reading taught, which will include literal, inferential and stylistic understanding at varying levels, as well as reasoning skills. Assessment of Talk, both solo to an audience and in group interaction, will count towards the final grade along with Reading and Writing, so more opportunities for practice are given, sometimes using video tapes of pupil performance to help clarify skills and also the grade-related criteria being applied.

Much pupil (and teacher!) effort in S4 goes into the drafting and redrafting of a Folio for external assessment, which contains both discursive/informational and imaginative/personal writing together with three extended responses to literary or media work in different genres. This Folio, presented in Term 2, is internally and externally assessed, and combined in Term 3 with external examinations in Writing and Close Reading, and the internal assessment of Talk, to give a final award. The past ten years have seen a steady rise in attainment in this examination, which is taken by almost the complete cohort of secondary pupils, including some in special schools and secure units.

Normally, a Credit grade in English is followed by a one-year Higher course, and a General grade by a two-year course, which combines SCOTVEC modules in S5 in preparation for a Higher English in S6; or such modules can be taken on a free-standing basis. The complication of this 'system', which has developed gradually in response to increased numbers continuing their studies post-16, has led to current Higher Still developments towards a truly unified system with a staged modular approach, ranging from Access courses for those with special educational needs, through two Intermediate stages to Higher English and Advanced Higher (replacing the present Certificate in Sixth Year Studies).

In planning Higher Still in English and Communication, real ideological divisions have surfaced between the vocationally oriented and skills-based modular SCOTVEC approach, and the more literary emphasis valued by school teachers of Higher English, where depth and complexity of texts and critical analysis have been central. Shakespeare and other classic texts have traditionally been taught alongside such twentieth-century works as *Lord of the Flies* and *The Crucible*, the choice determined by individual teachers or departments. When Higher English was revised in 1991 to take account of Standard Grade advances, optional 'set texts' were included, with some initial teacher resentment at this 'right wing revision' of a liberal curriculum. But certain advantages of set texts were gradually recognised, in the preparation of candidates whose aptitude and motivation were more varied than formerly, and in the range and variety of new texts encountered.

Scottish works have regularly been set at both Higher and Sixth Year Studies level, and this has given wider currency to the use of Scottish literature in the classroom and in the substantial Review of Personal Reading which forms part of the Higher Folio, and also in the Dissertation of some 4,000 words which has been a feature of guided individual study and research in the Certificate of Sixth Year Studies. Although candidate numbers are small (6.1 per cent of the year group in 1997), CSYS has been innovative in its Creative Writing paper and critical exploration of literary, linguistic and media studies. Its influence is discernible in Advanced Higher arrangements, which now offer papers in Scottish as well as English Literature, and Scots as well as English Language. Set texts have been abandoned in Higher Still modules, but at least one Scottish literary work is now compulsory at every level below Advanced Higher.

INNOVATIONS AND CHANGE OVER THE PAST TWENTY YEARS

The last twenty years, then, have seen almost continual 'assessment-led curriculum development', in which traditional teacher concern for examination results has been used to extend classroom strategies and materials. An early and successful focus on the less able has swung in the 1990s towards the need for teaching that extends and challenges all, including those gifted in language.

Curriculum development was underpinned from the mid 1960s onwards by an influential series of Bulletins issued by the Central Committee on English, which set forth clear principles on which effective teaching of both language and literature could be organised at different stages of schooling, both in individual classrooms, in which teachers had some autonomy, and in coherently organised English Departments. By the early 1970s, a Centre for Information on the Teaching of English had begun to disseminate good practice through publications and projects.

Such initiatives provided a rationale for developments that were to occur powerfully through the central provision of exemplar materials for the Standard Grade developments of the early 1980s: units of work to illustrate how the 'new' purposes were to be addressed and assessed; inservice work and national publications on the development and assessment of talk, or listening, or drafting and redrafting in writing, or group methodologies. Imaginative resources were also created at regional level, and through BBC and ITV Education Officers, working with school colleagues.

The Scottish Examination Board brought out graded exemplars of talk, reading and writing, so that teacher confidence and skills in assessment grew steadily. This openness to sharing of criteria has had a powerful impact at many levels: from national conferences on the HMI's *Effective Learning and Teaching in English* (1992) which outlines the findings of some 200 departmental inspections in the previous ten years, to classroom interaction with a particular pupil aimed at improving performance in a Folio item.

Yet this progress in professional awareness has also paradoxically made the introduction of the 5–14 curriculum in the mid 1990s less welcome in secondary than in primary schools. Whereas primary teachers appear generally to have welcomed the formulation of a Language curriculum in terms of key outcomes, strands and stages (while suffering from conscientious attempts to track pupil progress across the whole range of curricular targets), many secondary English departments considered that the progress they had made in structuring the subject coherently (in terms of Standard Grade modes and purposes) was being disrupted by new terminology and assessment procedures. The perceived loss of progression from S1 to S4 clearly ought to be counterbalanced by greater (and probably more vital) continuity from P6 to S2: but that is happening slowly and patchily across the country; and is being further delayed as the focus of change now shifts to the upper stages with Higher Still developments in post-16 curriculum and assessment.

What may also have broken down is the consensual approach that enabled that earlier achievement. The break-up of larger regional authorities has often led to a loss of English subject advisors, who could link policy and practice in an identifiable way. Such changes have in turn led to a greater use in local authorities and schools (and hence English departments) of written policies and target-setting to achieve planning aims.

Will pupils be lost sight of in this more highly professionalised 'management culture'? The Assessment of Achievement Programme, set up to monitor pupils' progress in 5–14 language attainment, provides interesting feedback to teachers on the standards of reading and writing, most recently highlighting underachievement by boys in almost every area assessed. The Scottish Examination Board has regularly published analysis of results at age 16–18. What is surprisingly lacking is some public forum in which teachers can discuss such issues. The termly journal *Teaching English*, published by the Scottish Curriculum Development Service, lost government funding at a time in the late 1980s when teachers were coming to grips with Revised Higher arrangements and 5–14 English Language developments. Attempts at founding a distinctively Scottish association for the teaching of English have struggled to make widespread impact, when teachers' time and energies are already fully committed.

Yet the Consultative Council on the Curriculum, at least, continues to respond to the Scottish *zeitgeist*, with school-focused publications on such current issues as using information texts (*Into Print*, 1991), Talking and Listening (video, 1992), Scottish language and culture (*The Kist/A' Chiste*, 1996), and language awareness (*Knowing About Language*, 1999). These offer vital opportunities for reflection on current practice through sharing that of others. In any debates concerning the scope of a language curriculum for the new millennium, it would surely be damaging for teachers in individual English Departments to be talking to no-one but themselves.

REFERENCES

Crawford, R. (1992) *Devolving English Literature*, Oxford: Oxford University Press.
MacGillivray, A. ed. (1997) *Teaching Scottish Literature: Curriculum and Classroom Applications*, Edinburgh: Edinburgh University Press.
Northcroft, D. (1984) *Hearsay*, Edinburgh: Scottish Curriculum Development Service.
Peacock, C. (1990) *Classroom Skills in English Teaching*, London: Routledge.
SOED (1992) *Effective Learning and Teaching in Scottish Secondary Schools – English*, Edinburgh: SOED.

55

Geography Education

Donald MacDonald

CONTEMPORARY PATTERNS

Curricular Change

Secondary school geography has been a curricular element in Scotland since the latter part of the nineteenth century. When the Scottish Leaving Certificate examination was first instituted in 1888, geography appeared at both Higher and Lower Grades, although responsibility for its teaching lay with non-specialists, often members of the English department (MacDonald, 1989, p. 60). Throughout much of the twentieth century, geography has not been a high status subject, partly because of the naive rationalism on which it was founded, and partly because of the ossification which quite quickly pervaded the subject. Testimony to that process lies in the remarkable longevity of the pioneering textbooks produced by Scots such as Archibald Geikie or A. J. Herbertson, whose *Man and His Work*, first published in 1899, was still in print into the 1960s. Geography lessons were for the most part what one English HMI described in 1904 as 'a dreary recitation of names and statistics', with a major emphasis on rote learning of facts, some of them highly questionable, about world regions, around which the geography curriculum was organised.

By the mid-1960s, however, the quantitative approaches which were becoming prevalent in academic geography, particularly in Sweden and the USA, began to influence inservice courses for secondary school teachers. The 'new' geography elicited a divided response in the pages of professional journals, but the geography panel of the Scottish Certificate of Education Examination Board, as it then was, tended to support the waxing positivist paradigm, with its emphasis on data collection, hypothesis testing and model building. In 1972, syllabus reforms based on these novel notions were circulated to all Scottish secondary schools, in the form of a proposed Alternative 'O' Grade examination syllabus, followed a year later by suggestions for an Alternative Higher. In subsequent years, quantitative elements, such as descriptive statistics, have discreetly vanished from the geography syllabus. Meanwhile, pedagogic innovation has taken precedence over academic innovation during the Standard Grade revolution and during the introduction of 5–14 Environmental Studies.

Current philosophies

Contemporary documentary evidence about geography in Scottish secondary schools suggests two major influences. The first is an epistemology which is rationalist-empiricist, concerned with amassing facts, while the second is learning theory of the associationist or behaviourist variety. At the core of the subject lies the assumption that one can recognise human and physical factors operating together on the surface of the earth, and that the interactions between these factors can usefully be studied, as the Effective Learning and Teaching Report (ELTR) indicates (1995, p. 2). What results from such study, it is claimed, is an understanding of the world. But whether any such understanding can be formed without some detailed knowledge of specific places is, at the very least, debatable. Traditionally, geography used the regional approach to amass descriptive data about countless places, but offered no accompanying structure of comprehensive explanation. Yet, since the demise of that form of geography over the past three decades, various reports by organisations such as the Gallup Poll have indicated an alarming absence of place knowledge among the general public. Partly in response, the National Curriculum in England and Wales has statutorily re-instated knowledge of locations and of the character of different places. No such move has occurred in Scotland, where the syllabus focuses simply on describing and explaining selected physical and human themes, rather than on the diverse nature of particular places. Yet whatever understanding of the world is thus developed, it is done through the acquisition of knowledge and skills (ELTR 1995, pp. 3–4). Knowledge, in school geography, is still viewed as propositional and largely unproblematic. As ever, textbooks present data as 'objective evidence to be accepted by pupils, and not as something constructed and selected by people' (Healey and Roberts, 1996, p. 296). Meanwhile, the subject does also aim to contribute to the development of certain general transferable skills, including those of enquiry, analysis, evaluation and communication, the latter incorporating mapwork, widely held to be the only skill peculiar to geography.

Methods and strategies

Geography teaching has progressed considerably from the heavy didacticism of the 1960s, although the ELT Report (1995, p. 26) was still noting a 'divergence in approach' between student-centred activities and more teacher-directed methods. However, it is on the former that we will focus here. Most teachers of geography acknowledge that different pupils have different learning styles, and that a variety of learning experiences must therefore be organised, under the general label of enquiry or investigative activity. Yet it has to be conceded that enquiry is not always as active a process as it may superficially appear. After all, it is the teacher who is likely to choose the question for enquiry, to identify the sources from which data will be drawn and to organise the use of time. On the other hand, teachers are free to slacken control over those aspects of enquiry, whether cognitive or organisational, within which they wish to maximise opportunities for learning.

Student-centred learning depends heavily on a wide range of resources, including maps, atlases, textbooks, televisual aids, and fieldwork sites external to the school. Microcomputers have appealed strongly to a minority of geography teachers, while the majority make rather cautious use of information technology, though that technology can support the enquiry approach by providing access to secondary sources, including CD-Rom data on countries, digitised Ordnance Survey maps and electronic atlas pages. Again, investigations into weather phenomena, for example, can use data from automatic weather stations or from MetFax satellite images. As Robinson (1996, pp. 223–7) has shown, students working with data-handling packages can create their own maps and diagrams to illustrate geographical concepts and themes within specific regions.

Classroom organisation

The emphasis on student-centred or enquiry approaches brings its own advantages and disadvantages. Not least among the latter is that some teachers have put the role of resource organiser ahead of that of stimulating pupils' thinking processes. As a result, lessons can occasionally, as Leat (1997, p. 144) has described, become a mindless plod through seemingly endless worksheet questions linked to exercises in class textbooks. Where repetitive and time-consuming tasks induce neither motivation nor challenge, the result can be a tacit conspiracy in which the pupils work rather than mutiny, while the teacher accepts minimal standards of completed work.

On the other hand, the student-centred classroom offers commendable opportunities for different forms of classroom organisation. Individuals, at their own pace, can interpret maps, whether on the larger local scale or on the small scale of the atlas. Group work, by contrast, encourages pupils to accept shared responsibility for their own learning, but places a correspondingly greater onus on the teacher to differentiate the learning activities. Differentiation has been one of the major advances in geography over the past decade. In some cases, groups of pupils move around a set of resource stations, each station linked to tasks organised at core and extension levels. Acknowledging variations in the manner and also in the rate of learning, geography teachers routinely differentiate by expecting different responses to similar tasks, by organising graded tasks or by providing different sources to support a single common task.

Assessment, recording and reporting

Throughout most of the twentieth century, the dominant form of assessment in geography has been psychometric, dictated by external examinations and emphasising knowledge outcomes. In recent years, however, classroom practitioners have moved rapidly towards more authentic educational assessment, in which learning and assessment are integrated, rather than kept apart. On the other hand, formative assessment for diagnostic purposes has been encouraged, albeit indirectly, by the criterion-referenced attainment targets now identified for pupils in the first four years of secondary geography. Diagnostic tests have been most fully developed in those areas of geographical learning, notably mapwork, where a sequential development of skills can be clearly outlined. On the other hand, the programmes for Standard Grade Geography and for 5–14 Environmental Studies have encouraged teachers to assess samples of course work on a regular basis, without recourse to specially devised tests. In practice, some teachers keep a day book in which they enter brief descriptive comments about the performance of individual pupils. Observing and interacting with pupils, teachers gather evidence to supplement the annotated checklists and the marked collections of course work which all combine to produce a valid record of attainment.

Meanwhile summative assessment continues as a key feature of Standard Grade and Higher courses, in which geography ranks as one of the options most commonly followed. The external assessment of these courses remains the responsibility of the Scottish Qualifications Authority, as does the modular programme of post-16 courses which will be the basis for entry into higher education in the early 2000s (Hunter, 1996 p. 243).

CONTEMPORARY ISSUES

The 1995 Government Report on Effective Learning and Teaching in Geography identified a number of issues concerning the future development of the subject. One is an improvement in knowledge of place, which is arguably the central concept of all geographical study. Another is the concern that continuity of learning experience be maintained in the transition between primary and secondary school programmes. Alongside these, one might also consider the four which follow:

Relevance

Topicality and immediacy are sometimes suggested as factors which can motivate learners, particularly those who attain least. It is no doubt the case that much of what goes on in geography classrooms (and most others) has little bearing on the everyday concerns of pupils. But, for learning to become more relevant, it would have to shift somewhat from its mainly behaviourist stance, based on the transmission and replication of facts. At the same time, it would have to make more use of pupils' existing frameworks of informal geographical knowledge, upon which more formal structures could usefully be developed.

Relevant learning can also be that which examines controversies relating to the learner's circumstances. In a consumer-oriented society, divergent views emerge over the siting of supermarkets, for example, the extension of airport runways or the increasing commodification of Scottish culture for the tourist trade. Each of these is no doubt dealt with in any one academic year in at least some classrooms, but there is little to suggest that, in these studies, awkward questions are asked about capitalist values or about the political processes which underlie all locational decisions. Some geography teachers, it seems, prefer a stance of neutral impartiality towards controversial issues, while others believe that through critical discussion geography can contribute to a wider social education for future citizens of a pluralist democracy.

Environmentalism

Environmental education has been identified, over the past forty years or so, as that area of educational endeavour which raises awareness of environmental issues, while seeking means to effect improvements. More recently, it has mutated towards the formation of a sense of personal responsibility for living in a sustainable fashion. Geography and environmental education have much in common, since both are concerned with interactions between society and the biophysical environment. Yet, while environmental education is prepared to recognise an ethical component in learning, whereby some human actions can be seen as less justifiable than others, geography teachers have been generally reluctant to go that far. Thus, questions about acid rain, greenhouse gases, atmospheric lead and toxic dumps are routinely examined in class, without much reference to the rights and duties of the human agents involved or to the political contexts within which such problems arise. Similarly, where environmental education draws attention to, inter alia, individual behaviour and to the cumulative repercussions of personal choices, geography has been slow to follow. The result is that, where secondary geography might have been the main vehicle for learning about sustainable living, that area is but patchily developed.

Schools and Higher Education

There was, at one time, a discernible cycle of events in geography teaching. Senior pupils underwent a curriculum which, for a tiny minority, led on to a comparable but more advanced curriculum at university. From there, some students went on to practise selected aspects of the curriculum in teacher training courses, before proceeding to teach the same themes in secondary schools. Some, indeed, returned to their own original schools, fitting in seamlessly to an unchanging curricular fabric.

But no more. School geography became decoupled from higher education during the 1980s. University courses became more esoteric. Physically geography studied palaeoclimatic patterns, for instance, or the modelling of glaciotectonics, while in human studies emerging specialisms included electoral and entrepreneurial geographies. Pupils proceeding to university found themselves following lines for which school had not prepared them, and conversely some student teachers found their new repertoires of knowledge to be inadequate for classroom purposes. One price of these discontinuities is that there has been, during the 1990s, virtually no university-led conceptual development in school geography, to balance the plethora of pedagogic developments.

Teacher training

There has been a major decline in the role of geographers in teacher training over recent decades. Where once there were nine college of education departments staffed wholly or partly by a total of fifty geographers, there are at present only two university departments and four specialist staff involved in the initial training of secondary teachers. Meanwhile, the number of geography teachers, according to the Scottish Education Department Census of 1991, was 1,175, and their average age was forty-one. Since that census, the total number had declined further, while the average age has increased. These gloomy patterns have been exacerbated by the demographic decline in secondary school intakes which, coupled with local education authority financial constraints, have effectively reduced the annual recruitment of new geography teachers to a handful.

In those teacher training programmes which survive, the perennial tensions between theory and practice continue. But as training becomes more school-oriented, it may be that faculty tutors, teachers and student-teachers can resolve some of these tensions by sharing more of the critically reflective paradigm (Lambert, 1996, p. 239), emphasising the thoughtful, open-ended reconstruction of classroom experiences, viewed from the different perspectives of teacher and learners. That paradigm will, in turn, be more workable when the classroom experiences of student-teachers become part of schools' ongoing improvement plans.

REFERENCES

Hunter, L. A. (1996) Geography in the Scottish School Curriculum, in E. M. Rawling and R. A. Daugherty (eds) *Geography Into the Twenty-First Century*, Chichester: John Wiley & Sons, pp. 235–45.

Lambert, D. (1996) Understanding and Improving School Geography: The Training of Beginning Teachers, in M. Williams (ed.) *Understanding Geographical and Environmental Education*, London: Cassell, pp. 230–41.

Leat, D. (1997) Cognitive Acceleration In Geographical Education, in D. Tilbury and M. Williams (eds) *Teaching and Learning in Geography*, London: Routledge, pp. 143–53.

MacDonald, D. (1989) Values in Geography Teaching, unpublished M.Ed. Dissertation. Glasgow: University of Glasgow.

Robinson, A. (1996) Interactive Computer-Assisted Learning in Geography in Scottish Schools, in T. Van Der Zijpp et al. (eds) *Proceeding of the Commission on Geography Education, 28th Congress of the International Geographical Union*, Amsterdam: The Free University Press, pp. 253–7.

SOEID (1995) *Effective Learning and Teaching In Scottish Secondary Schools: Geography*, Edinburgh: HMSO.

56

Health Education

Joan Forrest

FROM HYGIENE TO HEALTH PROMOTION

Since the beginning of the century, there has been a focus on physical aspects of health in schools and the Scotch Education Department (as then known) ensured that teachers were prepared by adopting a course in Laws of Health within the training colleges. Part of the syllabus focused on the 'Evil Consequences of Intemperance to the Individual, to the Home and to the State', while other aspects introduced trainees to the physical and mental illnesses that children may have had which would impair their progression in school.

The report of the Advisory Council on Secondary Education in Scotland in 1947 provided a starting point for health education being introduced into the curriculum by suggesting that schools provide a 'healthy physical environment and care for well-being which would include "that simple but effective teaching of physiology and hygiene, of nutrition and regimen, which brings home to boys and girls the extent to which personal happiness and use of society alike depend upon bodily fitness and favouring environment"'.

It is rewarding to note that health education in schools has changed considerably since the days of instructions about washing under the arms and other unmentionable places, although many would agree that such a task must still remain highly desirable! It was only in the late 1960s that a more holistic approach began to emerge where the physical, social and mental aspects of health were considered inextricably linked. Prior to the 1970s, health education was seen as a component of preventive medicine with the emphasis on negative warning messages for those who were sick or considered 'at risk'.

There was a clear shift in the 1970s towards an approach which recognised that, to some extent, individuals could take responsibility for their own health. While it was agreed that social and environmental changes would have an impact on the prevention of illnesses, the emphasis fell on the need to consider lifestyle factors. With young people, psycho-social pressure related to sociability, independence, growing-up, etc. meant that alcohol, tobacco, drug use and early sexual behaviour became more common and therefore schools tended to focus on these factors. They had to be addressed more appropriately and with the development of the guidance system and an emerging personal and social education curriculum, moral and health issues started to find a place. Enabling young people to explore their feelings and emotions and share experiences and issues which were of real concern to them, meant that the learning and teaching approaches had to move from a didactic to a more interactive mode. Health education could no longer be limited to information-giving.

In the 1980s, the emerging concept of the health promoting school signalled a whole-school approach to health education where every aspect of school life contributed to pupil and staff well-being with community partnership becoming an important element. *Promoting Good Health: Proposals for Action in Schools* (1990) has been influential in changing attitudes to health education in primary and secondary schools. The report contained proposals for planning health education programmes in schools and indicated the three key elements of the health promoting school, i.e. the health education curriculum, the 'hidden' curriculum and links with the health and caring services.

INCREASING THE PROFILE

The profile of health education in Scotland in the 1990s has gradually increased and two reports from the Scottish Office signalled further commitment. *Health Education in Scotland: A National Policy Statement* (1991) determined health targets for Scotland and briefly described health education in schools. However, it was *Scotland's Health, A Challenge to Us All: A Policy Statement* in 1992 which highlighted the importance of health education in schools. It emphasised the view that health and well-being were inextricably linked to physical, social and mental factors and that changes in the environment as well as personal behaviours were required. However, according to Tones and Tilford (1994) schools are perhaps a little slow in recognising the importance of social and environmental causes of health and the need to promote awareness of a collective approach to solutions to ill health.

In 1993, health education was given a secure place in the school curriculum through the development of the 5–14 national guidelines on Environmental Studies, and schools were considered to have a role to play in promoting health in the wider community.

THE ROLE OF PERSONAL AND SOCIAL DEVELOPMENT

The importance of recognising a holistic view of health has led many schools to consider health education as part of the pupils' personal and social education. Concepts of self esteem and empowerment are central to education in this area and so health education has evolved into a model which incorporates life skills development, value clarification as well as the development of knowledge and understanding.

In 1993, the national guidelines *Environmental Studies 5–14* were introduced. The purpose of the guidelines was to provide pupils with a continuous and coherent programme which highlighted the interdependence between people and the environment. The health education component's attainment outcome *Healthy and Safe Living* produced three broad themes under which a series of contexts and content was described. The themes were as follows:

- looking after oneself
- relationships
- health and safety in the environment

In addition to the *Healthy and Safe Living* component of *Environmental Studies* there are good opportunities within other parts of the document for the development of health education.

The development of life skills and the role of values and attitudes as an integral part of health education has meant that the national guidelines *Personal and Social Development 5– 14* (1993) and to a lesser extent, aspects of *Religious and Moral Education 5–14* (1993) contribute to the overall health education provision.

While the guidelines are not fully implemented at this time, schools are using a number of subject areas to address health issues. Generally, social education incorporates aspects of health related to, for example, alcohol, tobacco, drugs, relationships and sexual behaviour. One potential weakness of a topic approach is that there is less likelihood of connections being made between, say, alcohol and sexual behaviour, or healthy eating and exercise.

Specific subjects such as science, home economics and physical education address health-related issues within their curriculum and in many schools religious and moral education, drama and English provide opportunities for debate and discussion. The range of teachers involved is increasing and schools are moving towards a genuine cross-curricular approach to health education.

COURSE PROVISION

In 1988, formal curriculum provision for pupils in S3 upwards was offered in the form of a series of short courses in Health Studies. This was part of the Standard Grade development and provided pupils with the opportunity to study specific aspects of health such as relationships, food choices, risk-taking, exercise, consumerism, parenting, technology and the holistic concept of health. The short course model was seen as a flexible way to introduce education for health to all pupils. The courses could be taught through a variety of disciplines such as science, home economics, physical education, religious and moral education, etc. They could enrich other Standard Grade courses or be part of the personal and social education programme. Each short course provides for forty hours of work; assessment is based on a pass/fail basis and pupils require to demonstrate that they have met the performance criteria for all the learning outcomes stated.

Curricular provision for post-16 is found within the Higher Still Development Programme. *Personal and Social Development* (PSD) has three principal contexts of *Personal, Social and Vocational* which are mandatory. Within each context or unit, students will be allowed a choice and *health-related issues* is offered as part of the *Personal* context. The focus is on improving personal well-being and developing awareness of the health needs of the wider community. While there is ample opportunity for students to develop personal and interpersonal skills throughout the entire programme, the health focus is fairly limited.

There are clearly several initiatives offering curricular provision. The coordination and coherence of that provision, however, is an extremely difficult task for schools. The health-promoting school concept means that aspects such as school meal and snack provision, a clean environment and less tangible factors such as positive relationships between staff and pupils have to be regularly monitored. This 'whole-school' approach is highly desirable but requires firm, practical management.

With a growing awareness of the importance of health education in young people's lives, the Scottish Office Education Department (SOED) recommended in 1993 that all schools should appoint a health education coordinator. Education authorities and schools should have clear policies on health education and staff development should be widely available on a regular basis. This was the start of a series of reports which highlighted good practice in both primary and secondary schools in Scotland and provided schools with guidance on a number of pertinent issues. In addition, a joint initiative between the SOED and Strathclyde Regional Council Education Department produced the Health Education for Living Project (HELP) which provides a health education framework for all stages from pre-5 to S6.

MEETING YOUNG PEOPLE'S NEEDS

One of the greatest difficulties for schools is ensuring that health education provision is relevant to their pupils' needs. Too often, adult perceptions of needs do not match those of the young people. Planning and implementation of health education requires to be within the context of the pupils' family life and the wider community. Research over the last few years has demonstrated that young people believe that important issues such as sex education and drug education are not being addressed early enough or appropriately enough. When one school, which wished to provide a relevant programme for their pupils asked what they felt they needed in terms of sex education, one fifth year girl, said: 'I wish I had known that sex isn't the most important thing and I wish I had known this before I had sex for the first time'. This simple but startling statement illustrates the need for relevant and realistic sex education. Society has changed greatly over the last twenty years; social and media pressures are quite different and more complex; peer pressure may be present but often young people experiment and take risks because they want to. Thus peer preference, i.e. where young people make a conscious choice to do what others are doing, is a concept to be considered. However, while the focus on risk factors is important, there is a need to emphasise the positive aspects of lifestyle and the contribution young people can make to a caring environment. This can be achieved through an integrated approach where the underlying philosophy is about promoting self esteem, exploring values and developing skills.

THE CONCERNS OF TEACHERS

For many schools, sensitive issues such as sexuality and relationships, HIV and AIDS and drug use can be problematic. Many teachers lack confidence for a number of reasons. Often embarrassment, lack of knowledge and parental views impinge on effective learning and teaching. However, it is a concern over conflicting values and the parameters for personal disclosure which contribute to teachers' anxieties. How do they handle questions from pupils about their views and their personal life? How open can they be? What about the religious, cultural and parental contexts for their work? Staff development support is patchy and for many teachers, insufficient. However, in recent years collaboration with area health boards has provided teachers with advice and support and in some cases enabled teachers to work in partnership in the classroom with health promotion officers.

LEARNING AND TEACHING APPROACHES

If teachers are to provide opportunities for young people to discuss their feelings and share experiences on a range of health issues, learning and teaching approaches have to reflect a more open and interactive mode where activities are designed to engage the pupils in learning together and reflecting on their learning, in a supportive and safe environment. Often, this student-centred approach can create difficulties for teachers who have a relatively didactic style for their own subject and who are expected to switch to a facilitative role for personal, social and health education.

HEALTH EDUCATION FOR ALL

Health education has emerged from the days of hygiene talks and dire warnings about smoking and drinking. Curriculum provision is more secure and the Scottish Office Education and Industry Department (SOEID) has gradually moved health education up the ladder of priority. However, the pressures of an increasingly overcrowded curriculum means that health education runs the risk of being marginalised. Social education has a full agenda and after second year, only those pupils undertaking short courses or the Higher Still PSD course may have opportunities to consider health issues. Health education must be seen as an entitlement for every pupil and not a luxury; the health promoting establishment must become a reality for all schools and reflect all aspects of health in order to give young people a real basis for life which is coherent and progressive.

REFERENCES

Scottish Health Education Group and Scottish Consultative Council on the Curriculum (1990) *Promoting Good Health: Proposals for Action in Schools*, Edinburgh: Scottish Health Education Group.

Scottish Office (1992) *Scotland's Health: A Challenge to Us All*, Edinburgh: HMSO.

SOED (1993) *Health Education in Scottish Schools: A Study of Provision in a Sample of Schools and Education Authorities*, Edinburgh: The Scottish Office Education Department.

Scottish Office Education Department and Strathclyde Regional Council Education Department (1995) *Health Education for Living Project (HELP)*, Dundee: Scottish Consultative Council on the Curriculum.

Scottish Office Home and Health Department (1991) *Health Education in Scotland: A National Policy Statement*, Edinburgh: Scottish Office Home and Health Department.

Tones, K. and S. Tilford (1994) *Health Education: Effectiveness, Efficiency and Equity*, 2nd edition, London: Chapman and Hall.

57

History Education

Peter Hillis

RECENT DEVELOPMENTS

The introduction of Standard Grade History in 1988 marked a radical departure from the traditional methods of teaching history in Scottish schools. Prior to 1988 history teaching emphasised the acquisition of knowledge and understanding but Standard Grade History moved the focus towards developing the historical skills of knowledge and understanding, evaluating and investigating. The syllabus defines evaluating as: 'evaluating sources with reference to their historical significance, the points of view conveyed in them and to the relevant historical context' (SEB, 1993, p. 9). The sub-elements of planning, selecting and recording information and presenting the outcome comprise investigative skills demonstrated within the Standard Grade Course by an individual investigation into an issue chosen by the pupil. The issue must relate to developments in Scottish history in the context of Scotland or Britain, or to connections between Scotland and other countries. The normal method of presenting the outcome of the investigation is a written report.

Standard Grade History concentrates on the middle two years of secondary education but its influence has radiated to other stages in the secondary school. The national 5–14 development programme lays down general curriculum and assessment guidelines for primary schools and the first two years of secondary school, pupil ages five to fourteen years. History is contained within the overall curriculum category, Environmental Studies, which emphasises similar skills to Standard Grade History. Within the 5–14 programme history, or understanding people in the past, should develop knowledge and understanding alongside the skills of planning, collecting evidence, recording and presenting, interpreting and evaluating and developing informed attitudes (SOED, 1993).

Similar features appear in courses designed for the upper secondary curriculum. Higher History, the Certificate of Sixth Year Studies and National Certificate Modules each emphasise knowledge and understanding, evaluating and investigating but with slightly different approaches. The 'investigation' within Higher History takes the form of an extended essay where pupils research an issue of their choice and prepare a plan for a related essay of approximately 2,000 words. Pupils write this essay under examination conditions. The 'investigation' within the Certificate of Sixth Year Studies is a dissertation of 4,000 words on a topic relating to the syllabus. Despite the variation in approach, each of these 'investigations' incorporates planning, collecting evidence and presenting the outcome. Developing evaluative skills involves, at every level, the extensive use of primary and secondary historical sources. The current Higher Still reform of the upper secondary curriculum will not alter the emphasis of knowledge and understanding, evaluating and investigating, but this emphasis has substantially altered the ways in which history is taught and assessed.

INFLUENCE OF RECENT DEVELOPMENTS

Course content

Here the impact has been less radical. Environmental Studies 5–14 lays down general guidelines for history courses. These must cover each of the main historical eras, but not necessarily in chronological order:

> The Ancient World
> Renaissance, Reformation and the Age of Discovery
> The Age of Revolutions
> The Middle Ages
> The Twentieth Century

In addition to the historical investigation pupils study three units at Standard Grade. These units focus on modern history and cover Scotland and Britain, International Cooperation and Conflict and People and Power. Within each unit schools choose from a range of contexts. For example, within International Cooperation and Conflict one of the following contexts is studied:

> A – 1790s–1820s; B – 1890s–1920s; C – 1930s–1960s.

A substantial part of course content in Standard Grade developed from earlier syllabuses but Higher History provides the opportunity to widen the chronological framework. Within the Higher course one of three periods must be studied: medieval, early modern or later modern. Each option contains a combination of prescription and choice as illustrated by Option C, Later Modern, where Britain 1850s-1979 must be studied alongside at least one other unit from either Growth of Nationalism or The Large Scale State. Moreover, one special topic must be selected from a choice of six units. The most popular special topic is Appeasement and the Road to War, to 1939.

The Certificate of Sixth Year Studies provides a choice of twelve fields of study one of which is studied alongside a study in depth. Germany: Versailles to the Nuremberg Trials is the most popular field of study with the associated study in depth, The Weimar Republic.

The teaching of History

The emphasis on evaluating and investigating has considerably influenced the teaching of history. In order to develop evaluative skills history teachers use a wide range of primary and secondary sources including written sources, photographs and cartoons. These are interspersed with the more traditional teacher–led explanation to develop both knowledge and understanding and evaluating. Lessons on housing conditions use a range of sources which might include the following extract from the *London Evening Standard* (1936):

Many of the houses in Methyr-Tydfil (Wales) contain only two rooms, one up and one down, joined by rickety wooden staircase which was rotting into holes. The ceilings of the lower rooms are simple, the loose floorboards of the upper. Windows are small and low and at two in the afternoon it is dark inside these houses. Ramshackle sheds, shared by several cottages, are the only sanitation.

Using this and other sources pupils discuss housing conditions and the source itself. One possible evaluating question based on the source could analyse the extent to which it accurately describes housing in British towns in the 1930s. Pupil answers must refer to key features of the source, notably date, authorship, content, possible bias and the extent to which it relates to their knowledge of housing conditions.

The use of primary and secondary sources encourages a variety of teaching strategies. The majority of lessons combine teacher-led discussion and pupils working on related materials either individually or in groups. The stations approach offers a variation on this strategy since it allows pupils, usually in groups, to examine a range of evidence on a particular topic. A lesson on conditions in the trenches during the First World War could utilise a range of sources including poetry, archive film, war diaries, textbook accounts and photographs, each allocated a particular station. Groups of pupils would move round each station answering specific questions to compile a profile of life in the trenches.

Developing the skill of investigating provides an opportunity for individualised learning at every stage within the secondary school. Given the importance of the Investigation at Standard Grade most history departments incorporate 'mini' investigations in secondary years one and two. The process allows a similar pattern at every level with pupils choosing an issue to investigate, carrying out the necessary research and writing a report of their findings. One important part of the final report is the conclusion which should relate to the original issue. The changes to the Investigation at Standard Grade, outlined later in this chapter, will modify this approach in order to ensure that 'mini' investigations which satisfy the 5–14 guidelines also prepare pupils for the amended procedure for investigating at Standard Grade.

Information technology has begun to influence teaching methodology especially in primary schools. Programs relevant to Scottish History incorporate primary sources such as census information within a database so allowing pupils to develop their research and IT skills by carrying out relatively complicated search routines. With access restricted to one or two computer systems the use of IT necessitates pupils and groups of three or four working at a specific task at the computer, returning to a whole-class exercise while another group moves to the computer. The teacher becomes a facilitator in addition to the more traditional role as a source of information. Given the expense of some software and use of the Internet the school library provides additional access to IT. Pupils use the library to search for specific information, for example, an article from *The Times* CD-Rom on the First World War.

Assessment

Resulting from moves away from a solely knowledge based curriculum, methods of assessment examine the newer skills of evaluating and investigation. In Standard Grade, Higher and the Certificate of Sixth Year Studies the investigation, extended essay and dissertation count towards the final award, so giving 'course work' a greater role in assessment. However, external examinations assess knowledge and understanding and evaluating with examination papers containing two broad categories of question. Knowledge and understanding is tested by questions requiring pupils to write a short paragraph or an essay, with the exception being Foundation Level at Standard Grade where a list of points or short sentences is accepted. The examination tests evaluation skills by incorporating a range of primary and secondary sources, including cartoons and photographs, with questions relating to the content, point of view, accuracy and reliability of the source or sources. As a means of preparing pupils for the external examination, the internal methods of assessment used by history departments reflect those used in the examination.

STANDARDS OF PERFORMANCE

Reports from Her Majesty's Inspectors of Schools record a generally high standard of history teaching with particular emphasis on a balanced approach between whole-class teaching and more active methods.:

> Across the department there was a variety of methodology especially in S1/S2. Video tapes, tape slide presentations, debates, individual projects and maps were used along with effective class teaching to enliven pupils' experience. A second year class were achieving a high standard of discussion in deciding whether Mary Queen of Scots was guilty of the murder of Lord Darnley. Individual projects from topics being studied involved pupils in conducting their own researches from an active range of books borrowed from the library and the resource centre. (SOED, 1992)

At Standard Grade in 1994, 24 per cent of candidates gained a Credit award, compared to 25 per cent in Geography and 26 per cent in Modern Studies (SEB, 1994). This marginal difference is explained by the difficulties caused by some evaluating questions, especially those asking for a comparison of points of view between sources. However, as pupils and teachers have become more familiar with evaluating, the results for this element have improved. Furthermore, a relatively high percentage, 33 per cent, of pupils gaining a Level 3 award at Standard Grade go on to pass Higher History. The percentage in most other subjects is below 33 per cent with History's relative success partly explained by high standards of pupil work in the extended essay.

KEY ISSUES

A National or A World View

A 1995 survey into pupils and trainee teachers' knowledge of Scottish history revealed an apparent knowledge gap in many key areas. This survey sparked considerable debate about Scottish history's place in the curriculum and a review group under the auspices of the Scottish Consultative Council on the Curriculum was asked to report on the teaching of Scottish History. The report advocates a balance between local, Scottish, British, European and global themes, but the draft framework for Scottish History is biased towards Scottish and British themes with one exemplar containing thirteen history topics between Primary 1 and Secondary 2. Eight of the topics feature Scottish and/or British History. The exceptions include: The French Revolution, The British Empire and Russia from Revolution to the Cold War (SCCC, 1997). This debate raised the profile of History but the Scottish Association of Teachers of History made strong representation for a balanced, rather than a nationalistic, approach to the history curriculum. At the time of writing this chapter the debate was on-going and is intrinsic to history teaching.

Investigations with particular reference to the Standard Grade Historical Investigation

Teachers raised three concerns over the Investigation at Standard Grade, namely, workload, authenticity and fairness. Many Standard Grade subjects require the completion of pupil folios and/or investigations so placing considerable demands on pupils especially towards the end of their Standard Grade courses. The Standard Grade Historical Investigation places specific demands on pupils since the process of historical research involves gaining access to a range of primary and secondary sources, many of which are difficult to read and interpret. The guidelines for the Investigation recommend a word limit of 1,200 words for each report, but this is not compulsory and many exceed 3,000 words, representing many weeks' work. Completing the Investigation involves a combination of classwork and homework and evidence exists that some pupils receive considerable help from parents and/or home tutors. This, it has been argued, favours pupils from more supportive home backgrounds.

Responding to these concerns, the Scottish Examination Board/Scottish Qualification Authority embarked on a consultation exercise with history teachers between 1996 and 1997 on the future of the Standard Grade Investigation. History teachers were asked to mark in order of preference three alternative proposals, viz. amendments to the present arrangements, a circumscribed investigation with the final report written under examination conditions, and incorporating investigative skills into the external examination. The majority of schools voted for the last option which embraces evaluating and investigating under the heading of enquiry skills. From a selection of source extracts, and using their own recalled knowledge, pupils will write a conclusion to a given issue. Consequently, from 1999 the external examination will contain two sections, knowledge and understanding and enquiry.

The Higher Still Programme

Given the propensity for historians to disagree with one another there has been a surprising degree of consensus over syllabus content within Higher Still history courses. In many schools a relatively small proportion of pupils opt for history in secondary years 5 and 6 which will prevent the formation of separate classes for each level of Higher Still course. Consequently, history teachers have expressed considerable concerns over 'multi-level' teaching, defined as the teaching of different levels and courses within the one class whereby a history class could combine pupils studying Intermediate 2, Higher and Advanced Higher. This will influence the choice of units to be taught as indicated in draft course outlines which recommend overlapping units of study to cater for these multi-level classes. For example, pupils opting for modern history at Higher level must study Britain 1900s–1979. Intermediate pupils in the same class are likely to study the equivalent unit, Campaigning for Change: Popular Attempts to Alter the Political Identity of Britain 1900s–1979. However, many teachers have indicated that the overlapping units are not necessarily the most suitable for pupils studying Intermediate Courses. There may be a danger that pupils will be made to fit the course, rather than the educationally desirable objective of courses being responsive to pupil needs.

CONCLUSION

Emerging from decades of communist rule many East European countries are re-examining their history syllabuses and look to Scotland as one example of how to develop historical skills. Part of this re-evaluation involves discussions on how best to incorporate into their history curriculum the interpretation of primary and secondary sources. Here Scotland can point to relative success, but difficulties with investigative approaches should warn against the example of the Standard Grade Historical Investigation being copied elsewhere. Nonetheless, over the past decade history teaching in Scotland has moved a considerable distance from Thomas Gradgrind's assertion in Charles Dickens' *Hard Times* that, 'facts alone are wanted in life'

REFERENCES

SEB (1993) *Standard Grade, Amended Arrangements in History*, Dalkeith: SEB.

SOED (1993) *National Guidelines: Environmental Studies 5–14*, Edinburgh: SOED.

SEB (1990) *Scottish Certificate of Education, Higher Grade and Certificate of Sixth Year Studies, Revised Arrangements in History*, Dalkeith: SEB.

SOED (1992) *Effective Learning and Teaching in Scottish Secondary Schools, History*, A Report by H.M. Inspectors of Schools, Edinburgh: SOED.

SEB (1994) *Scottish Examination Board, Annual Report*, Dalkeith: SEB.

SCCC (1997) *Scottish History in the Curriculum*, A Paper for Discussion and Consultation and Draft Frameworks for Scottish History in the 5–14 Curriculum, Dundee: SCCC.

58

Home Economics Education

Frances Gallagher

RATIONALE AND AIMS

Home Economics is concerned with using and managing human and material resources for the benefit of individuals, families and society. The aims of an education in Home Economics have evolved in response to changing circumstances and reflect the rapid and fundamental change in technological and scientific knowledge and in the social attitudes and conditions which have characterised life in the late twentieth century. The promotion of good health is closely linked to quality of lifestyle. In a country which has the worst incidence of diet-related disease in the developed world and mounting evidence of poor parenting skills affecting all strata of society, a good home economics education is needed as never before (MacFarlane, 1996). Emphasis on practical nutrition, how to achieve a balanced diet, along with the skills to support economic regeneration in a creative way, are very high on the curriculum agenda in Scotland.

The realisation of what is required for young people has resulted in an evolution in Home Economics education in Scotland from simple but disparate cooking skills and sewing skills to a highly developed and realistically focused understanding and acquisition of technological capability. This training gives young people the ability and skills to 'make things happen', 'get things done' and 'privilege the practical' (SCCC, 1996). Rigour and intellectual challenge is not simply a matter of the acquisition of knowledge. The conversion of theoretical knowledge into a practical reality, especially in terms of various aspects of lifestyle and health, e.g. food, food security, food hygiene, health, parenting and caring, are often perceived by many people to be something everyone can do and no one needs to learn.

This is not borne out by recent events. There is a large rift between behaviour and knowledge as indicated by the Pennington Report (1997) on *Food Safety and Hygiene*. The document *Scotland's Health* (subtitled A Challenge to us all – Eating for Health, Scottish Office Department of Health, 1996) recommends that all schools move towards making nutrition a focus of their health promoting initiative and consider the setting up of Schools Nutrition Action Groups (SNAG) as well as offering all post-S2 pupils a course in practical food preparation in healthy eating. The value of employing Home Economics teachers and professional Home Economists to take a high profile in this initiative is strongly recommended.

SOCIO-ECONOMIC FACTORS

David Alton (former Member of Parliament) has stated that 'We live in a society in which people sleep on the street and whole families are abandoned in a spiral of debt and poverty'. Likewise, Moira Macfarlane says that 'the nature of how to build student's self esteem along with the capability and will to promote health and well being on scarce resources presents home economists with the biggest challenge of all' (Macfarlane, 1996).

The socio-economic background of pupils is reflected in lifestyle and informs the approach taken in the classroom regarding the focus of course provision. National guidelines apply to all courses and ensure entitlement to a full range of learning experiences suitable to the needs of the pupils. It is, however, sometimes challenging for staff to relate in a meaningful and practical way to national guidelines, especially those relating to dietary goals. Society has not always kept pace with the changes in the modern curriculum particularly relating to those which have occurred in Home Economics. This knowledge gap has given rise to many popular misconceptions regarding the validity and reality of good home economics provision. Documented evidence from Scotland concerning diet related disease, *The James Report* (SOHHD, 1993), employment opportunities in the hospitality and care industries and entrepreneurial training experiences, all clearly support the requirement that Home Economics should be an essential learning experience for all.

Home Economics provides a progressive pathway to careers at all levels in various employment sectors. The hospitality and caring professions are two of Scotland's major employers and as such are critical to the wealth and well being of the nation. Other industries involving food technology, fashion and textile design, crafts and enterprise training can all be supported by a cohort of people trained as Home Economists skilled in critical and analytical thinking, practical application of knowledge and review and evaluation techniques.

THE CURRICULUM

In the Scottish curriculum model there are three main stages, 5–14 (including S1, S2), Standard Grade S3, S4 and the senior years of S5, S6. Home Economics forms part of the common course in secondary years S1, S2. It shares its position with Technical Education, as a core contributor to the Technological Activities and Applications mode of the curriculum, as defined by the SCCC's *Curriculum Design for Secondary Stages*. Courses in this mode can be described as being the vehicle for the development of the technological and practical skills, designing, making and using artefacts and resources, and practical problem solving. An ability to adapt knowledge and learning (effectively and confidently) to the reality of using a full range of high and low technology in an ergonomic manner is an entitlement for young people. The minimum percentage of class time assigned to this mode in the secondary sector is 10 per cent over two years.

The introduction of the Sex Discrimination Act (1975) accelerated equality of curricular provision for boys and girls in Scottish schools. Courses at S1, S2 underwent fundamental change in an effort to remove both gender and cultural bias. However the low uptake by boys in S3 shows that more remains to be done in this regard (SOEID, 1996). The role model of having an all female teaching staff is at long last changing, and although the balance is still predominantly female, several men now hold positions as teachers of home economics and in one case a male home economics teacher holds a high profile position of responsibility in several national curriculum and assessment areas.

The understanding of technological capability by many people is still bedevilled by conceptual confusion. People both within and outside the field of education would relegate yesterday's technological achievements to the category of standard tools and equipment and reserve the title of technology exclusively for the new. The publication and progression of the SCCC document *Technology Education in Scottish Schools* (1996) has done much to address this misconception. Several local councils are actively progressing a highly focused policy in partnership with the SCCC relating to Technology Education and this will positively influence the direction and status of the subject in Scottish schools during the next ten years. Home Economics plays a major part in this development while at the same time it raises awareness of global issues.

The 5–14 national guidelines Environmental Studies with sections on understanding and using the design process, understanding and using technology and taking action on health, is the main curricular foundation for course provision in S1, S2 Home Economics. Courses drawn up by each department have to allow for differences in course choices pupils make over the longer term. On the one hand the curriculum has to provide a free standing learning experience for all, laying secure foundations in essential life skills. On the other hand, the curriculum must lead progressively into Standard Grade in S3, S4 for those who opt for further study. It is possible for pupils to undertake study in Home Economics to the level of Higher via the Standard Grade route or as a direct entry. The present Standard Grade and Higher Grade provision in Home Economics is clearly laid out in Arrangements documents published by the Scottish Qualifications Authority (SQA).

In the S3, S4 provision at Standard Grade there are seven course objectives covering knowledge and understanding, handling information and practical and organisational skills. At Higher Grade level the course is divided into three parts. Topic A allows candidates to make a general appraisal of the needs of individuals and families in relation to materials and resources in the home. Topic B allows candidates a specialist study of diet, the factors which affect an individual's choice of food and the relationship between this choice and good health. The third part, the Independent Study, allows candidates the opportunity to further study one aspect of the course from a range of options set by the SQA.

The present range of course provision from Standard Grade and Higher Grade Home Economics is supported by a programme of short course certification on various aspects of health, care and design-related topics. There is also a range of SCOTVEC modular provision (continued by the SQA). This provision will be superseded by the introduction of the Higher Still programme in 1999. Home Economics departments will provide certification across the full range of qualifications post-16 from Access 3 to Advanced Higher. There will be a choice of courses in health and food technology, fashion and textile technology and lifestyle and consumer technology. There will also be an opportunity for students, should they so choose, to achieve qualifications in hospitality and care. Care qualifications post-Intermediate level 1 will be progressed in conjunction with Further Education Colleges. The nature of all courses as proposed in this new development underpins the philosophy that applied practical skills development must go hand-in-hand with the understanding of appropriate concepts.

ISSUES

A number of wider educational issues are impacting on the work of Home Economics teachers. Pupils with special needs have entitlement to educational provision which meets their needs in terms of acquiring life skills and empowering them to become technologically capable within their potential. This will assist the promotion of equal opportunities for all with regard to employment, independence and the ability to contribute to economic regeneration. Where need arises the level of certification is available from Access level 1.

It is essential for teachers in the secondary sector to relate closely with colleagues in both the primary and tertiary education sectors to ensure coherence and progression in pupils' learning, particularly in relation to technology and health education. Many schools have good established links with associated primary schools, especially in the context of nutrition and health education, and with further education centres in the context of care, hospitality and the technologies of food and textiles. The present restrictions on timetabling and staffing may or may not motivate teachers to extend their vision in the field of innovation.

There are some interesting pilot programmes based on a partnership model involving Education and Industry. Such initiatives give a meaningful reality to course provision for senior pupils and a sound training experience enabling them to make more fully informed career decisions, especially those relating to the Hospitality and Tourism industry.

In order to provide opportunities for effective learning to take place, the methodology used in many departments is of a varied nature. 'Effective teaching involves organisation and management, but no single style or approach to classroom organisation is best' (SCCC, 1996). Pupils working to a design brief or as a mini enterprise exercise tend to work as a group, while the acquisition of specialist skills through more focused tasks is acquired via an individualised learning programme. Core skills as presented in the Higher Still framework include problem solving and these may be met within Home Economics.

Varied classroom methods, using a partnership model (where target setting at both group and individual level develops decision making skills), encourage technological capability. The personal interaction of pupil and teacher is still seen as one of the most effective learning strategies. In Home Economics the support of technicians is also vital. This enables teachers to devote focused time for teaching and not divert their energies to non-educational but essential organisational tasks.

ASSESSMENT

Assessment evidence which is criterion referenced is in many departments effectively used to monitor pupil progress and attainment and, to some extent, evaluate the effectiveness of learning and teaching. Pupils are made aware of the objectives and learning outcomes of their courses and are often involved in teacher/pupil/peer discussion with regard to progress and attainment. Assessment in S1, S2 is based on the assessable strands of 5–14 Environmental Studies (knowledge and understanding, planning, collecting evidence, applying skills and presenting solutions and interpreting and evaluating, all underpinned by Developing Informed Attitudes). This gives a pupil profile built up over two years and can contribute to progression in further areas of appropriate study in S3 and beyond. This profile links the assessable elements of knowledge and understanding, handling information and practical and organisational skills at Standard Grade level and to the six course objectives at Higher grade. Motivation is often acquired as part of the assessment procedure where pupils record their own progress and set further targets for themselves in conjunction with a teacher and clearly understood course or task outcomes. At Standard Grade the double weighting of the practical and organisational skills element is an enlightened feature. This element is internally assessed and externally moderated on behalf of SQA. At the

Higher level the Independent Study completed by the student with initial teacher support is allocated 40 per cent of the total marks awarded. This emphasis is to be commended.

TEACHER TRAINING

The age profile of teachers continues to rise and it will require the imagination and commitment of senior level decision makers to ensure that a replacement cohort of suitably qualified teachers is available. The present difficult situation of scarce availability of training places gives cause for concern. Demand for Home Economics, which has always been considered a minority subject, is increasing. This reflects wider employment trends in a country where the maximum growth is in the hospitality and care industries.

The next millennium might well see a change of structure and values as they affect family and society but people will always have the need for the knowledge and skills which Home Economics can provide. The subject has a vital part to play in empowering people and enabling them to achieve a quality lifestyle according to their needs and aspirations.

REFERENCES

Macfarlane, M. (1996) *Home Economics Institute Newsletter*.

SCCC (1996) *Teaching for Effective Learning*, Dundee: SCCC.

Scottish Office Department of Health (1996) *Scotland's Health: A Challenge to Us All – Eating for Health*, Edinburgh: HMSO.

Scottish Office Home and Health Department (1993) *Scotland's Health: A Challenge to Us All – The Scottish Diet*, Report of a Working Party to the Chief Medical Officer for Scotland ('The James Report'), Edinburgh: HMSO.

SOEID (1996) *Effective Learning and Teaching: Home Economics*, Edinburgh: SOEID.

59

Information Technology

Bob Munro

Information Technology (IT) is not a subject in the Scottish secondary school curriculum – rather it is an ubiquitous resource which comprises an expanding set of sophisticated, powerful, yet increasingly easy-to-use tools which can be applied right across the curriculum, in any subject area. This 'toolset' can help teachers and pupils access, collect, manipulate and make sense of information and then present and communicate the conclusions of their examination of this information in a range of effective ways.

This integral relevance and importance to all areas of the curriculum is evidenced by the inclusion of IT as a key component area within the National Guidelines for Environmental Studies 5–14 (SOED, 1993), as one of the core skills within Higher Still (HSDU, 1995) and as underpinning the emergent National Grid for Learning.

FROM EC TO IT TO ICT – THE CHARACTERISTICS AND CONSEQUENCES OF RAPID GROWTH

Information technology burst onto the educational scene less than twenty years ago and has attracted unparalleled attention, debate, activity and expenditure in every sector of education. Evolution has been rapid, originating in the 'primeval soup' of educational computing, forming a distinctive identity as IT and metamorphosing into information and communication technology (ICT) – a recent recognition of the synergistic benefits and increased range of potential uses and applications afforded by the fusion of information technologies with communication technologies.

This rapidly changing technological evolution has spawned previously unimagined applications – word processing, spreadsheets, computer aided design, e-mail, hypermedia, videoconferencing, the Internet, the World Wide Web (WWW) – all new, powerful tools for education. The hardware platforms on which these applications are delivered seem, almost weekly, to develop greater capability and sophistication and link to a burgeoning array of external devices. Software development, driven by commercial rather than educational criteria, has been characterised by a desire to enhance performance and versatility – leading to short-lived software cycles, a plethora of outdated packages and the creation of ultra-sophisticated resources overloaded with facilities seldom relevant to, or fully utilised by, teachers in schools.

Not surprisingly, many teachers have found it difficult to respond effectively to such rapid change and to incorporate the best aspects of IT into their teaching and learning strategies – far less to rigorously assess and evaluate their use. Despite this, educationalists have been enthralled by IT and promote its continued and expanding use in schools. They are convinced that information technology has greatly extended the range of learning and teaching strategies which teachers deploy in classrooms, has enhanced the flexibility of these strategies to accommodate pupils with diverse learning difficulties, and has stimulated the exploitation of distance and open learning opportunities. Few question that ICT will enrich the learning experience for pupils in schools.

It cannot be said, however, that all the IT-oriented experiences offered within the secondary curriculum have been enriching, that all schools offer the full range of these experiences, nor even that all pupils have benefited thus far. IT use in Scottish schools, following the vanguard deployment of twenty microcomputers in 1979, has been un-coordinated, patchy, often uninformed and frequently inappropriate. The period has been one of radical, unplanned experimentation, constantly overshadowed by waves of innovation.

TWENTY YEARS OF EXPONENTIAL GROWTH – PLUS THE ODD QUANTUM LEAP

IT was introduced courtesy of a government initiative in 1981 aimed at putting a microcomputer into every school. A 50 per cent grant helped finance the purchase of one of three supported microcomputer systems – Sinclair Spectrum, BBC or Research Machines 380Z – together with an educational software pack. Short training courses were offered to selected teachers who were charged with cascading expertise throughout their school. The systems represented the cutting-edge technology of the day and were extremely expensive, yet schools, parent-teacher associations and local authorities, concerned they might miss out on the widely publicised IT revolution, invested heavily in this unproven, rapidly obsolescent technology. Today some newer, enhanced BBC microcomputers survive but generally the vanguard generation of technology has long been superseded in Scotland by Apple Macintosh, PC and, to a lesser extent, Acorn Archimedes equipment.

Early educational software producers – commercial publishers, educational organisations, subject bodies and even enthusiastic amateurs – created a range of largely subject specific programs. Most had clear educational objectives and were targeted at specialised areas of the curriculum – *Pathway to Bearings, How we used to Live, Running the British Economy, Diet Analysis, Transverse Waves, Election Simulation*. For teachers lacking IT experience but expected to integrate IT into classroom teaching as 'just another resource' such classroom focused and group oriented software resources were invaluable and were widely used.

To be of any real value in teaching and learning other, more 'open-ended', software had to be used in conjunction with a range of support files – data handling packages needed comprehensive datafiles on, for example, countries of the world, residents of villages long ago, elements of the atomic table or British kings and queens. Despite alleged classroom potential many open-ended packages, particularly databases, failed to enthuse teachers and pupils. Creating datafiles was incredibly time consuming and the query interface – the way questions had to be constructed to extract information from the database – was too complex for many pupils. However, other software like *Front Page Extra* and *Writers' Toolkit* offered templates into which children could enter creative ideas. Such software was more enthusiastically adopted.

As the hardware advanced so the software focus changed. Easy to use subject-based, curriculum-specific software was overtaken on one front by the open-ended generic package – increasingly an integrated package perhaps incorporating word processor, database, spreadsheet and graphics functionality. On another front a technological quantum leap brought sophisticated topic-based software on CD-ROM. This allowed huge amounts of digital information, drawn from many diverse sources – text, graphs, charts, maps, pictures, sound, video, even software – to be welded into complex multimedia/hypermedia resources for the classroom, or, increasingly, the library. Packages like *Encarta*, the *Grolier Encyclopaedia*, *How Things Work*, *World of the Vikings* and *World Atlas* emerged as important resources for investigative activity.

By 1995 communication technologies occupied centre stage. The Internet with its World Wide Web component emerged as the information delivery system of the future. Schools were encouraged to join the communications revolution, get on-line, enter cyberspace and surf the Web. Key proposals of the Stevenson Report (Independent School Commission, 1997) were adopted as policy by the incoming Labour government. In October 1997 the government committed £100 million to schools to buy advanced computers and software to facilitate access to the National Grid for Learning, 'powered' by a website delivering educational resources to schools, colleges, universities, libraries, museums and galleries throughout the UK. This website went live in January 1998. A deal with British Telecom could ensure that all schools have ten hours of Internet access per day at an estimated cost of £1 per pupil per day. Eventually all Scottish secondary schools should have established Internet links confident that problems associated with copyright, pornography and cost have been resolved.

To complement these initiatives all student teachers will be expected to be ICT literate when they leave teacher education establishments and, from 1999, up to £25 million of National Lottery funding will be available to enhance the ICT skills of teachers in Scottish schools.

THE SCENE TODAY – A MOSAIC OF DEVELOPMENT

This rapid and uncontrolled development has resulted in a disparate picture of IT use across secondary schools in Scotland. While all schools have a considerable number of computers and a selection of associated peripheral equipment, these resources vary widely in type, in age and in capability, and are unevenly distributed, both across the country and within individual schools. Software availability is similarly uneven and, while access to communication technologies is expanding (with 440 schools on-line in early 1999), it will only be available in a limited number of locations within individual schools for the rest of this century.

Given this maldistribution of resources it is heartening that much good IT use exists, generally due to individual teacher interest in IT and a desire to integrate its use into their subject specialism rather than to the influence of school policies on IT. The 5–14 Guidelines identified the key aspects of IT which schools should address in S1/S2:

> text handling
> information handling
> position, movement and control
> modelling (including simulations and adventures)
> image and sound handling
> applications of IT in society

This undoubtedly stimulated uptake and use in many schools. A subsequent document, *Describe IT* (SCET, 1995), offered a comprehensive framework on which schools might develop a progressive and coherent IT policy. Unfortunately it had little impact on the secondary sector.

In some departments – Computing Studies, Business Studies and Craft, Design and Technology – use of IT is prescribed by the syllabus. Consequently these departments attract a disproportionate share of school IT resources and are often lavishly equipped with the latest, and most powerful hardware.

Other subject departments frequently have limited and aged hardware. Their constrained budgets inhibit software purchase. Many lack a critical mass of IT resources, restricting their ability to incorporate meaningful IT experiences into their teaching and learning. Despite this paucity of resources, some teachers imaginatively and creatively integrate a variety of IT into curriculum work. In many Geography departments, for example, pupils create integrated, word processed reports, explore databases (on population, countries of the world), model aspects of industrial location and production on spreadsheets, evaluate farming problems via simulation software, investigate multimedia CD-ROMs (atlases, volcanoes, the weather) and trawl the WWW to support investigative work on the Amazon rainforest, El Nino or global warming. These uses support and enhance the development of geographical skills in a structured, progressive way.

Unfortunately such a planned integrative approach is not the norm, although ICT resources can be deployed to advantage in every curricular area and new sophisticated software has opened up fresh possibilities – creative opportunities in drawing and design in Art, inventing and composition in Music. Biology fieldwork and aspects of exercise in Physical Education rely increasingly on dataloggers and digital cameras.

THE SCENE TOMORROW – EXPLORING NEW FRONTIERS

While many schools are working to establish or consolidate a solid foundation of ICT curricular activity some are exploring innovatively. These trailblazers have a critical role in advancing the educational ICT paradigm and can provide models for future good practice. Since 1996 an HM Inspectorate task force has monitored these initiatives with a view to disseminating guidance to all educational establishments.

In selected locations, evaluation of expensive Integrated Learning Systems (ILS) has taken place. Although many educationalists question the desirability of deploying computer resources in this way, research suggests pupils on ILS programmes make considerable progress in the basic subjects of Mathematics and English.

In 1995/6 the UK Education Departments' Superhighways Initiative (EDSI) evaluated tweny-five projects, two of them Scottish. The Modern Communications for Teaching and Learning in Argyll and Bute project particularly explored the potential of video-conferencing. Northern College led the Superhighways Teams Across Rural Schools (STARS) project which used computer conferencing to involve able children, drawn from small rural schools (from Perthshire to the Shetlands), in a range of collaborative activities based on the development of critical and creative thinking.

The Scottish findings (SOEID, 1997) confirmed that electronic communications can benefit teaching and learning, especially where the technology is integrated into the curriculum and where electronic networks build upon shared interests. Evaluators found that rural areas could derive great benefits from ICT through linking of small schools, shared approaches to topic work and the collaborative activities of pupils of similar age and interests. They concluded, however, that rural schools risk being left behind as ubiquitous narrowband technology is replaced by intermediate or broadband networks which are expensive to place in remote or sparsely populated areas. It will be interesting to see whether these alleged benefits can be sustained in rural environments and whether urban areas can derive similar benefits from exploiting the information superhighway.

Also in 1995 St Andrew's High School in Kirkcaldy was selected as one of three European sites for the Apple Classrooms of Tomorrow (ACOT) project, with the mission statement 'To change the way teachers think about using technology for teaching'. Work has focused on the integration of ICT in Maths, English, Science and Modern Languages in S1 and S2. Four upgraded classrooms have been equipped with multimedia computers, laptops, digital cameras, Internet access and selected licensed software. A teaching team collaborates and innovates with ICT to assist pupil learning. Subsequently the project will involve all pupils and the school will become an in-service focus for Scottish teachers.

PROBLEMS, ISSUES AND SOLUTIONS

The development of IT or ICT in Scottish secondary schools has been eventful and, in many respects, unsuccessful. To date the full potential has certainly not been realised. Education must urgently address, and resolve, four key issues – as without their prompt resolution the expanding potential offered by ICT will never be achieved and our education process will be the poorer.

A vision for ICT is essential. Development has been patchy, hasty and reactive. Education has failed to articulate where pupils should be on an ICT skills and competences continuum during, and on completion, of their secondary school education. No progressive, coherent set of ICT skills and competences has been identified for secondary school pupils, far less a specific framework illustrating where and how they should acquire and might refine them. Teachers need to know how exactly ICT can support the curriculum and how best it should be deployed in classrooms.

Achieving this vision requires the creation of an educational environment where all pupils would have the opportunity of using ICT as desired in all aspects of curricular activity. Not that all pupils should have their own computer – rather that adequate, appropriate ICT resources are available and accessible in all classrooms. Formerly under-resourced departments should receive the bulk of this resourcing – not the established hot-beds. Local authorities can not underwrite this massive investment – joint initiatives with government and commerce are essential.

There is a desperate need for ICT-related staff development in secondary schools and teacher education institutions. Aforementioned Lottery funding should be specifically targeted at enhancing the pedagogic skills of the teaching force and must be used wisely and effectively. All staff should examine and evaluate their use of ICT more rigorously. ICT is but one, admittedly vital, facet of secondary school education and should always be used purposefully – where it complements, or preferably enhances, traditional educational methods or processes, where it more effectively establishes conceptual understanding, or where it offers an unique tool or experience to the pupil. Partnerships between schools, teacher education institutions, colleges and universities should seek to identify how best ICT could support secondary school education.

Finally, a development programme to create fresh educational software resources, which support and complement those currently available and which would maximise the benefits from Internet-sourced information, should be established. Schools lack curriculum relevant software. Much of that available often lacks educational rigour or fails to utilise the capabilities of the technology (Broadway, 1997). Scottish curriculum software development is principally the responsibility of SCET, though SITC at Moray House (particularly CD-i resources) and the SCCC (currently steering production of a History CD-ROM and a Modern Studies website) are also involved. All would welcome greater investment in software development and more precise articulation of teachers software needs.

The Millennium target for Scottish secondary school education must be the realisation of the potential of ICT. If all pupils have unfettered access to information and all facets of ICT are used imaginatively within teaching and learning strategies, pupils really could transform base information into the gold of knowledge.

REFERENCES

Broadway, J. (1997) Towards the Interactive History Classroom, in *CRAFT*, CTI Centre for History Archaeology and Art History, No. 17, University of Glasgow, Autumn 1997.

Higher Still Development Unit (1995) *Core Skills – Consultation Document*, Edinburgh:Higher Still Development Unit.

The Independent ICT in School Commission (1997) *Information and Communication Technology in UK Schools 1996/7*, London: The Independent School Commission.

SCET (1994) *Describe IT – the Essential Guide to Information Technology Across 5–14*, Glasgow: SCET.

SOED (1993) *Environmental Studies 5–14*, Curriculum and Assessment in Scotland – National Guidelines, Edinburgh: SOED.

SOEID (1997) *Superhighways to Learning*, Issue 1, Edinburgh: SOEID.

60

Mathematics Education

Lindsay Logan and Alan Starritt

The present position of mathematics education in Scotland derives largely from a number of national curricular initiatives which have taken place in the last two decades.

PRE-STANDARD GRADE PROVISION

In the early 1970s pupils could follow courses leading to the national qualifications of Ordinary Grade in Mathematics, Arithmetic or Statistics in S4, Higher Mathematics in S5 and a range of mathematical specialisms in CSYS in S6. About half the population in S4 achieved O-Grade Arithmetic with about half of these also achieving a pass in mathematics. Linked to a mathematics curriculum which was very abstract and theoretical in nature mathematics in the secondary years was for many a process through which they learned that they were 'no good at maths'.

Following the publication of the Munn and Dunning reports in the late 1970s and national feasibility studies which sought to establish a suitable curriculum and related assessment procedures to include provision for the lowest attainers, Standard Grade mathematics was introduced. For the first time, pupils of all attainment levels were offered opportunities to study a course suited to their abilities in mathematics and to have their achievements recognised nationally at the end of compulsory schooling in S4.

THE INTRODUCTION OF STANDARD GRADE

Standard Grade confirmed the pattern of 'setting' by the beginning of S3 with pupils following courses expected to lead to an award at Foundation, General or Credit level mathematics at the end of S4. Those students who had performed satisfactorily in their Standard Grade course were then able to proceed to study Higher mathematics in S5. A range of options were available at CSYS, though these were most suited to the needs of students intending to continue the study of mathematics or mathematics related subjects at a tertiary level. It is worth noting that suitable provision at Higher and CSYS levels for able students who will not subsequently specialise in mathematics is still an issue to be tackled.

The development of Standard Grade involved little discussion about the content of courses particularly for the highest attainers. In contrast there was considerable debate about the way mathematics should be viewed and the ways in which it was thought that students should learn the subject. Where previously maths had been seen as a body of knowledge, concepts and techniques to be acquired, Standard Grade courses sought to promote mathematics as a problem solving activity supported by the body of knowledge referred to above. The Arrangements for Standard Grade expressed the view that, 'The essential aim of mathematical education is to help pupils to learn how to describe, tackle and ultimately solve problems which require the use of mathematical knowledge and techniques' (SEB, 1987, p.4).

This view of mathematics was shared generally throughout the Western world. In England and Wales, for example, the Cockcroft Report (p. 73) stated that, 'Mathematics is only useful to the extent to which it can be applied to a particular situation and it is the ability to apply mathematics to a variety of situations to which we give the name "problem solving".'

Acceptance of these views of mathematics led, in Scotland, to greater use of contextualisation and a broadening of the range of ways in which pupils were expected to learn mathematics. More emphasis was placed on the use of investigative approaches to learning new skills and concepts, and more contexts were used in the practice and consolidation of these. Practical work and discussion were also encouraged to complement the traditional use of teacher exposition. There was perhaps less emphasis given to the practice of skills. and this has been suggested as a cause for a claimed decrease in, for example, manipulative algebra.

These changes were accompanied by a widening of the range of assessments used, with elements of practical work and investigations being assessed for the first time. There was concern amongst teachers about the workload implications of the assessment proposed and some found it difficult to accept that mathematics could be viewed other than as exclusively a study of abstract relationships.

Though there was reference to the use of calculators and computers their use was not widespread at that time – though very cheap calculating power was to appear very soon – and the implications were largely ignored. Their use in examinations was allowed without restriction, a fact which was later to be cited as cause of a reduction in mental arithmetic skills since that time.

MATHEMATICS AT 16+

A review of Higher Grade mathematics followed, but it was decided that this should be restricted to that which was needed to allow progression for the most able from Standard grade and to take account of views expressed by the Scottish universities. No courses were specifically designed for those students in S5 and S6 for whom Higher was unsuitable. Gradually in the years which followed, schools came to use SCOTVEC provision, originally designed for use in the vocational sector, for the increasing numbers staying on in S5.

THE USE OF INDIVIDUALISED MATERIALS IN S1 AND S2

While these changes were being implemented from S3 onwards there had been no corresponding curricular review of S1 and S2. Most schools continued to arrange their S1 pupils into mixed ability classes often motivated by a desire to offer pupils a 'fresh start' in secondary school. Individual schools had to decide how best to tackle the difficult challenge of teaching mathematics to classes consisting of children with widely different levels of attainment. Some schools retained mixed ability classes throughout S1 and S2 and set pupils for the first time at the beginning of S3, but many introduced an element of setting sometime during the second year, often because of the difficulties posed by mixed ability teaching in mathematics, especially where a common course and whole class teaching were the norm. However by the early 1980s many schools sought to prepare for the setting which they felt was necessary for Standard Grade courses in S3 and to answer the pressures coming from the inspectorate and others to meet a wider range of needs, by adopting published schemes of individualised materials for use in S1 and S2 mathematics classes.

These courses were largely resource- or workcard-based and were designed to allow each pupil to work at a level and pace appropriate to his or her own needs. Such an approach has, however, recently fallen out of favour. Individualised work was described, in a recent HMI report as having serious disadvantages. Lack of sufficient individual attention, some pupils working too slowly whilst others were insufficiently challenged, lack of opportunities for learning through discussion and poor retention of the content met, were cited as short-comings of this type of material, leading to the conclusion that, 'The weight of evidence is now firmly against the continued use of individualised methods . . .' (SOEID, 1997, p.12).

PRESENT TRENDS IN S1 AND S2

At present a variety of organisational structures in S1 and S2 are to be found in operation throughout Scotland. Some schools still retain their individualised materials for all or part of these two years. Others operate a mixed ability system using one or more textbooks, but there is an increasing tendency, encouraged by the Inspectorate, to set classes at the beginning of S1, so that the resulting classes, whilst still undoubtedly of mixed ability, do not contain such wide differences of attainment as they did previously.

THE 5–14 NATIONAL GUIDELINES

This change towards setting classes at the beginning of S1 has been facilitated by the most recent curricular development in Scotland – the implementation of the 5–14 development programme, one of the aims of which was to try to provide greater curricular continuity between primary and secondary schools. It was thought that this would be facilitated by having clearly defined levels of attainment throughout primary school which could be used by the secondary schools to plan for and provide appropriate education in S1.

The 5–14 National Guidelines in Mathematics also revised the curriculum in Mathematics for all children up to the S2 stage. Lists of attainment targets were specified within the three broad outcomes of Number Money and Measurement, Information Handling and Shape, Position and Movement. The targets were also defined at each of five levels A-E corresponding to a minimum set of expectations of what children could achieve from P1 to S2. A fourth outcome – Problem Solving and Enquiry – sought to ensure the development of the kinds of investigative and enquiry skills which had previously been introduced into the S3–S6 curriculum. Other innovations in the 5–14 Mathematics development included recommendations on the uses of the calculator and the computer, a greater emphasis on the use of context in mathematics and a reconsideration of the relative emphasis given to each of the written, mental and calculator methods of calculating.

Some of the recommendations in the 5–14 Mathematics Guidelines have yet to be implemented by secondary mathematics departments. The use of spreadsheets and databases, for example, are still often seen as the responsibility of other subjects and there has been less than total commitment to the use of National Tests in Mathematics in secondary schools. Secondary mathematics teachers are now having to accept the reality of having children in their classes who may be operating at a level achieved by many pupils in P2. For some teachers this makes new demands on their ability to teach mathematics at a very basic level.

One of the benefits of the 5–14 programme can be seen in the greater degree of communication and hence understanding between the primary and secondary sectors. Some primary schools now introduce their older pupils to the materials used in their associated secondary school who in turn are now making increasing use of what were previously seen as exclusively primary methods and materials. The use of group work and a greater variety of practical materials in S1 and S2 are two examples of changes in secondary practice which have been encouraged by 5–14.

THE HIGHER STILL PROGRAMME

The latest national development to influence the teaching of mathematics in schools and indeed in further education colleges is in the process of being implemented. From 1999 provision developed through the Higher Still programme will be used to plan and certificate achievement for all students at the post-16 stage. This will result in a more coherent system of progression at that stage. The increasing numbers staying on in education past the compulsory stage has led many to question the need for a national examination at the end of fourth year of school. It may be that the Standard Grade courses which were the stimulus for much of the change in mathematics education in the last part of the twentieth century will prove to be past their sell-by date.

In response to a range of interests including industry and higher education, Higher Still seeks to encourage the development and certification of core skills across the curriculum. One of these skills, numeracy, involves the use of graphical information as well as number. Evidence, however, suggests that number is not widely used across the curriculum. The debate on national standards might need to address this fact.

As with earlier developments at this post-16 stage, little change in content or methodology is being proposed though once again concern is being expressed at the possible workload for teachers in carrying out assessment. However, questions are being raised nationally about the implications of both computers and advanced calculators for the content and nature of the mathematics curriculum. The need for such a review has been recognised for some time but, in spite of having been recommended in an HMI report (SOED, 1993), has been largely ignored.

THE DEBATE ON STANDARDS

Just as the implications of advanced calculators which can carry out symbolic manipulation are being raised at the senior end of schools the influence of the calculator in the claimed fall in standards of numeracy is also being considered. Recent studies comparing attainment in Scotland with, for example, that in some Pacific rim countries has led HM Inspectorate to suggest that a more cautious attitude to the use of calculators for basic arithmetic should be adopted.

Such studies, taken along with Scottish ones which suggest a diminution of standards in some aspects of mathematics attainment, are giving rise to major public concern and debate.

In contrast, the nation seems to be less interested in other evidence that increasing numbers of students are achieving success in national examinations at 16 and 16 plus.

Considerable national effort has gone into measuring attainment by, for example, the Assessment of Achievement Programme (SOEID, 1996), HM Inspectorate and the 5–14 Assessment Unit, but less attention has been given to properly researched analysis of the reasons for this allegedly poor national performance. Depending on authors' insights or prejudices, any of the factors such as class size, calculators, lack of drill and practice, class organisation, teaching methods or individual schemes may be accountable. Whilst these issues are undoubtedly a cause of real concern they should not be allowed to deflect from the benefits of the curricular changes introduced over the last two decades, which have in most cases resulted in vastly improved provision for all Scottish pupils. Looking forward, however, the mathematics education community will now have to address the fundamental question of how to define 'numeracy' for citizens of the twenty-first century.

REFERENCES

Cockcroft, W. H. (1982) *Mathematics counts: report of the ccommittee of Inquiry into the teaching of Mathematics in Schools*, London: HMSO.
SEB (1987) *Standard Grade: Revised Arrangements in Mathematics*, Dalkeith: SEB.
SOED (1993) *Effective Learning and Teaching in Scottish Secondary Schools: Mathematics*, Edinburgh: SOED.
SOEID (1996) *Assessment of Achievement Programme: Fourth Survey of Mathematics 1994*, Edinburgh: SOEID.
SOEID (1997) *Improving Mathematics Education 5–14: A Report by HM Inspectors of Schools*, Edinburgh: SOEID.

61

Modern Foreign Languages

Richard Johnstone

The backcloth to modern languages in Scottish secondary schools features two conflicting forces. One is the seemingly irresistible advance of English, the dominant language of globalisation. This influences attitudes to all other languages in Scotland including minority languages (e.g. Gaelic, Scots, Punjabi) and foreign languages. English is the most widely taught foreign language in continental schools and is prominent in business and the media. The other and opposing force arises from the determination of policy-makers, academics and others abroad to ensure that the identity of the emerging Europe is shaped by a firm commitment to cultural and linguistic diversity.

The tension between these two forces makes it impossible to forecast how the 'languages game' will be played in the new millennium. Will all Europeans eventually share a common language (an evolved form of English)? If so, what will this mean for French, German and other national languages (these will not go away), and how necessary will it be for speakers of English to learn another language at all? Or, will all Europeans, Scots included, need to master at least three major languages, as is argued in an EC White Paper (1996)?

It is against this unpredictable backcloth that the major thrust of languages policy for Scottish secondary schools over the past thirty-five years has taken place: the attempt to make a foreign language accessible to the full range of pupils attending comprehensive schools. Before the mid-1960s it was taught to an academic elite, with emphasis on grammar, translation, writing and literature rather than on spoken language. Reflecting this view, the 1950 SED report on Modern Languages in Secondary Schools stated that the process of language learning should provide a general linguistic training which would give pupils a surer appreciation of the value of words and help them to use their own language more effectively.

By the end of the 1960s, however, most S1–S2 pupils except for a so-called 'remedial' minority were learning a foreign language. To confront the challenge of teaching this wider social range, including pupils living in areas of major social deprivation, languages teachers turned to language laboratories, audio-lingual courses and worksheets. Unfortunately, these generally drew on a psychology of language learning that (with Chomsky's attack on Skinnerian behaviourism) had been discredited at the very point at which they were being introduced to schools. In consequence, throughout the 1970s, pupils' learning was based on the repetitious drilling of situational dialogues. In addition, S1–S2 course books tended to feature a family (white) with parents (married), a boy (mischievous, sporty) and a girl (well-behaved, good at school) living in a house (middle-class, detached), and presented thereby a travesty of the cultures in which the particular foreign language was spoken.

It was not surprising that this first attempt to cater for all pupils had run out of steam by the end of the 1970s. An SED-funded research project (Mitchell et al., 1981), found that in S1 over 98 per cent of the French spoken consisted of 'practice language' with less than 2 per cent consisting of 'real communication', and the Munn Report (1977) could not justify a place for a foreign language in its core curriculum for all pupils in S3–S4.

A second attempt was launched in the late 1970s through the CCC national French project and regional initiatives. With encouragement from the Council of Europe, teaching became more functional, with the foreign language used for everyday purposes and pupils expressing their real selves, often in interaction with their peers. Differentiated materials offered a chance of success at some level. Another SED-funded research study by Mitchell in 1988 confirmed that by the early 1980s teachers had assimilated tactics such as paraphrase, simplification, L1–cognates and mime for communicating meaning through the foreign language. Drawing on inspections from 1984–88, HMI (1990) stated that many of the new-style course-books lacked cross-reference material and that many schools were not allowing pupils to take their books home, thereby failing to support them adequately in their learning. However, it also identified 'clear signs of greater participation and enjoyment on the part of pupils who are showing increasing capability in using and understanding the spoken language. These are distinct gains which accord with present-day needs' (paragraph 9.15).

STANDARD GRADE

Standard Grade was welcomed because it allowed the new approach to be extended to S3–S4. The 1987 SEB Standard Grade Arrangements saw the primary objective as 'real language in real use'. This meant confronting pupils with authentic rather than contrived texts and encouraging gist extraction, inferences, use of a dictionary, confidence, self-reliance and social strategies for dealing with others, as well as 'proper attention to appropriate grammatical structures'. The same objectives formed the basis of the modern language modules in the National Certificate. To create and implement a Standard Grade framework of three levels embracing six grades required national support, provided through exemplar materials in five languages for Standard Grade and beyond.

As the end of the 1980s approached it could be claimed that these developments had achieved much progress towards enabling the full range of pupils to profit from foreign language study. Despite this, SCCC (1989) remained 'persuaded that the study of a foreign language should not be a compulsory part of the curriculum post S2 now or in the immediate future'. They believed that to make it compulsory 'would not find favour with parents or with a broad range of professional interests within and outwith education' (p. 12), though research was not commissioned to inform this assumption.

However, a major policy-change occurred soon after, resulting from a 'campaign for languages' by teachers but also endorsed by political will. In Circular 1178 (SED, 1989) the Secretary of State for Scotland's wish was stated that 'the study of at least one language other than English, and preferably a modern foreign language, should normally be pursued by all pupils throughout the third and fourth years of compulsory secondary school.' (paragraph 7). Political will also legitimised the re-introduction of modern languages in primary schools. Within a short space of time, therefore, the ultra-cautious view of SCCC had yielded to an ambitious prospect of six years study (P6–S4). Behind politicians' thinking was the advent of the Single European Market (due in 1992) where languages skills would be vital for exports. To encourage larger numbers to maintain their language beyond Standard Grade, a Revised Higher was introduced that dispensed with prose translation and brought greater authenticity and relevance into assessment tasks.

POST-16

Although no research has been published on languages in schools post-16, there are undoubtedly problems of articulation between Standard Grade and Revised Higher, and the numbers presented for Higher show a steady decline, despite the substantial rise in numbers presented at Standard Grade as a consequence of Circular 1178. The Minister for Education and Industry has expressed his concern publicly and SOEID are funding research into the underlying factors. Beyond that, however, conflicting signals for languages post-16, as for pre-16, have been given by the educational establishment. The Howie Report on the upper secondary recommended that a foreign language should be taken by all students, though on two very different programmes, but when Howie was superseded by Higher Still a foreign language was not a core communication skill. Fluctuations of this sort reflect the uncertain backcloth for languages mentioned earlier and have sustained a lack of consensus and clarity about languages in schools.

ISSUES

In reviewing developments from the mid-1960s to the late 1990s, it is fair to cite a number of strengths. These include the professionalism and commitment of many teachers; the gradual implementation of a 'language for all' policy to age 16; strong national support for materials, methods and developments from S1 to Higher; the advent and impact of a Scottish Centre for Information on Language Teaching and Research; and a series of SOEID-funded research projects that have given Scotland an international reputation in this field.

Before turning to weaknesses, it is appropriate to consider two factors which make a language teacher's job particularly demanding. First, foreign languages are not used much in Scotland, whereas the raw material for most other subjects is available in society. Teachers have direct access to things geographical, technological, artistic and historical but it is difficult for teachers and pupils to engage in daily contact with languages. The languages teacher in Scotland therefore has a double task of not only teaching the language but also of providing the exposure to it that elsewhere in Europe is provided through English by their media. Second, the process of acquiring a language is not the same as the process of learning anything else. In particular, the relationship between the development of first, second and foreign languages in any individual is highly complex, varying according to age and other factors. Most teachers, advisers and teacher educators know little of the international research informing these processes and can fall victim to an alluring idea propounded by one expert who may in fact not represent the research consensus – ideas on whether or not to teach grammar being the best example.

Undoubtedly several weaknesses may be identified. Among them would be the financial constraints now operating on local authorities which make it difficult to provide foreign language assistants. There is a lack of clear support from the business community, despite the Scottish Council Development and Industry's indication in 1996 that of the top ten countries to which Scotland exported manufactured goods in 1995, only one was English-speaking, with France and Germany well ahead of all others. The national 5–14 Guidelines for Modern European Languages are not linked to 5–14 English, and other countries greatly surpass Scotland in helping pupils to grasp key concepts about language which benefit them in all of their languages: first, second and foreign. The documentation for Standard Grade over-emphasises speaking at the expense of comprehension (where progress can be made much more quickly). Indeed, for English-speakers, comprehension of a foreign language may in future prove more important than speaking because many Europeans may possibly need to speak one of (say) English, French or German but to understand all three. However, despite national reports (1971, 1985, 1989) recommending diversification of foreign language in order to reduce the dominance of French and to promote the learning of a second foreign language, the hope remains far from realisation.

If the above weaknesses are attributable to 'societal' or 'policy' factors, there are also weaknesses in 'teaching'. Research on modern languages at primary (cf. Lesley Low in the present volume) indicates an urgent need for secondary teachers to take better account of what pupils have learnt at primary. The teaching of grammar requires re-thinking, especially what to teach it for. Researchers elsewhere (e.g. Van Patten and Cadierno, 1993) suggest that learners' language may develop better when grammar focuses more on comprehension than on production, but in several Scottish schools fragments of grammar have been taught in relation to spoken or written phrases. Others suggest that learners comprehend better if they have been taught a range of intervention strategies that break up their teacher's flow of foreign language. At present, many Scottish teachers work hard to make the foreign language meaningful but very few have sufficiently taught their students how to intervene in order to negotiate their own meanings.

What of the future? Three possibilities suggest themselves that will increase 'time' and 'intensity', the two key factors. First, by teaching other subject-matter through the medium of a foreign language: in 1994, over 140 German secondary schools were teaching biology, geography, history and other subjects through the medium of English, French, Spanish, Portuguese or Russian. The same is beginning to happen in England with students taking Business Studies to GCSE-level through the medium of Spanish. The gains in motivation and proficiency appear to be substantial. Second, by exploiting the Internet and e-mail in order to sustain links all over the X-speaking world: this will afford learners and their teachers increased exposure to and interaction in the language. Third, by exploiting EC programmes such as Comenius which enable schools to engage in transnational collaboration for various educational purposes. If increases in 'time' and 'intensity' such as these do not happen, there is no reason to believe that gains arising from improvements in 'teaching' will be anything other than short-term, as usual. If on the other hand such developments do take place, then foreign languages will have broken their mould as a school subject and become instead part of the culture and everyday processes of schools, contributing to and benefiting from these aspects – in which case they might well fly.

REFERENCES

Consultative Council on the Curriculum (1985) *The Diversification of Foreign Language Teaching in Scottish Secondary Schools*, Dundee: CCC.

Mitchell, R., B. Parkinson, and R. Johnstone (1981) *The Foreign Language Classroom: an Observational Study*, University of Stirling, Educational Monograph 9.

SCCC (1989) *The Provision of Languages other than English in Primary and Secondary Schools*, Edinburgh: SCCC.

SED (1971) *Alternatives to French as First Foreign Language in Secondary Schools*, Edinburgh, HMSO.

SOED (1990) *Effective Learning and Teaching: Modern Languages*, Edinburgh: HMSO.

Van Patten, W. and T. Cadierno (1993) Explicit Instruction and Input Processing, *Studies in Second Language Acquisition*, 15, 2, 225–41.

62

Modern Studies Education

Henry Maitles

In a relatively short time, some thrty-five years, Modern Studies has had a marked effect on the curriculum in most Scottish schools, being seen by educators, pupils and parents as a meaningful addition to social subjects. Indeed, it has in many schools and areas achieved parity with the two other major social subjects, History and Geography and, taking FE college presentations into count, there are now more presentations at 'Higher' level in Modern Studies than in History or Geography. Although it is not yet taught as a discrete subject in all schools at S1/S2 (about 40 per cent in S1 and about 60% in S2), as far as Standard Grade, Higher Grade and university entrance are concerned, it is regarded as equal to the other social subjects. The crowded curriculum in S1/2 has meant that some 40% of schools do not teach Modern Studies in the junior school, although the 5–14 proposals will make the subject area compulsory.

WHAT IS MODERN STUDIES?

The subject initially was an amalgam of History and Geography with some Politics thrown in, as the early exam papers showed. In the first 'O' Grade in 1962, as well as questions of topical interest, there were some on the Great Depession, the rise of the Nazis, the Bolsheviks and map work questions. In its infancy, the subject was seen as being of most value for the less able as it related more directly to their immediate experiences, but fairly quickly the subject was seen as having value for all pupils. By the time, though, of the first 'H' Grade in 1968, the emphasis had shifted towards current affairs. The massive expansion of Politics and Sociology in the universities and the realisation that these subjects were central to an understanding of the complexities of modern societies has meant that since the 1988 Standard Grade Arrangements, the subject has as its main aim the teaching and development of political literacy, 'through a framework of analysis and a core of concepts adopted from the social sciences of politics and sociology.' Indeed it was this aim of giving the pupils and students the tools to analyse complex societal questions that most Modern Studies departments saw as being particularly distinctive about the subject in a series of national consultation exercises organised by the HMI in 1994. The report of these consultations suggested that the distinctive role of Modern Studies in the curriculum was to enable pupils to:

- develop social and political literacy;
- develop skills which will enable pupils to access, handle and evaluate information about the society and world in which they live;

- understand the society and world in which they live;
- promote citizenship, responsible participation in and respect for democracy;
- foster open-mindedness, participation and cooperation within society;
- develop an interest in and an understanding of current local community, national and international affairs;
- develop social skills;
- develop the ability to arrive at informed opinions and to reflect critically on society.

With these aims at its heart, Modern Studies has been seen as important by Scottish educationalists, particularly as there seems to be so much disaffection by young people towards politics as such, or at least organised democratic politics, despite a marked increase in involvement in single issue campaigns. It is fair to say that the least apathetic, most politically interested young people in the school will be likely to have taken Modern Studies. That is not to say that there has been universal agreement over how political literacy should be taught in the schools, indeed whether it should be taught in the schools at all, as a glance at the debates of the early 1980s would show; there were those who believed that teaching political/sociological material would destroy democracy and others who believed that teaching it would bolster capitalism! Indeed, the whole area of bias is one that has led some to believe it should not be taught to younger children as there is left-wing bias inherent in the subject (Scruton et al., 1985), although others have argued that areas of politics should be introduced as early as possible (Ross, 1987) and the Scottish Office appears to have endorsed this thinking through its 5–14 Environmental Studies proposals.

Modern Studies as presently organised is structured around a number of key concepts, seen as central to the development of the subject. These concepts – equality, rights and responsibilities, ideology, participation, need, power, representation – are believed to be the core of the subject and give the scope for analysing the subject and events in the real world. As pupils progress, there is a move from relatively simple to much more complex content. Whilst there is Scottish Qualifications Authority prescribed content at 'S' and 'H' (albeit with choices at 'H'), mainly of a sociological/political nature, a survey of departments shows a wide range of content in S1/S2, most of it now relating to the 5–14 guidelines. Topics such as representation and laws, participating in society, media bias, human rights, multicultural society, the USA, developing world, law and order, Europe, comparison of local area with another country or culture, United Nations Organisation are typical, and have an obvious relationship to both 'S' and 'H' grades and are clear content areas in terms of the development of political literacy.

THE DEVELOPMENT OF SKILLS IN MODERN STUDIES

The skills developed in the subject are now encapsulated in the term 'enquiry', involving both evaluating and investigating. Evaluating is the promotion of pupil ability in the critical appraisal and evaluation of information about social and political institutions, processes and issues through:

- recognising lack of objectivity
- making comparisons and drawing conclusions
- expressing support for a personal or given point of view
  (SEB, 1988, Standard Grade Arrangements in Modern Studies, Dalkeith: SEB, p. 7.)

These are clearly central to the development of political literacy at any level; progression from S1 to S6 involves the use of increasingly complex, subtle and abstract sources. For the 'Higher', pupils are expected to critically analyse and evaluate complex sources and to show, through a decision-making exercise, how their evaluating skills can be applied in other specific contexts. Investigating involves the processes of planning, recording, analysing/synthesising and reporting and again is a vital skill for political literacy.

In addition, Modern Studies has a distinctive and important role in attempting to develop positive attitudes amongst pupils/students. This should include at all levels:

- respect for truth and reason
- willingness to accept that other views and beliefs can have validity
- willingness to accept the possibility of, and limits to, compromise
- confidence and enterprise in pursuing information and communicating views. (ibid., p. 8.)

This is often seen in pupil activities and course content towards issues such as poverty, the elderly, development issues and civil and equal rights. Where dealing with controversial issues, Modern Studies teachers should be allowing pupils to examine evidence relating to a range of views.

This summary of what is taught in the subject misses out a central feature of the subject – its dynamism in the classroom. The teaching and learning of modern studies has since its development as a distinctive sociological/political subject been characterised by the enthusiasm of the teachers and novel methodologies. Central to this has been the use of 'dialogue' in the classroom. Indeed, debate, role-play, dialogue, group work, stages work and the varied use of media and IT have been central to its delivery in the classroom, especially around elections and participation, in particular. Modern Studies teachers are aware that the content of the subject means that many pupils will be coming to the classroom with some experience that they can input to the lesson. As the HMI noted in 1992: 'Most teachers encouraged a classroom atmosphere in which open questioning and challenging of opinion was common-place' (SOED, 1992).

ISSUES OF CONCERN AND DEVELOPMENT

The real world and change

What then of the future? The world is an ever changing and increasingly complex phenomenon and this offers tremendous opportunities and excitement for a subject like Modern Studies. It is a constant challenge to up-date content and, indeed, whole curricular areas depending on events in the real world. The fall of the dictatorships of eastern Europe, the ending of eighteen years of Tory government in Britain, the development of constitutional change in Britain, involving Scottish and Welsh assemblies, the ending of apartheid in South Africa, privatisations in the Welfare State and other political events mean that Modern Studies teachers are having to revise course content regularly, something that adds greatly to workload but also keeps the subject relevant, dynamic and interesting and goes a long way to explain the popularity of the subject with S6 pupils and FE students.

Curricular developments

There are widespread curricular developments covering every area of schooling – the new enquiry skills (amalgamating evaluating and investigating skills) at 'S' grade, the development of the Higher Still programme and the 5–14 'People in Society' guidelines. All of these offer great opportunities but also have potential difficulties.

The 5–14 proposals throw up the possibility of Modern Studies issues being taught from P1 to S2 and, in particular, those secondaries who have refused so far to implement Modern Studies in S1 and/or S2, whether for reasons of crowded curriculum, perceived unsuitability for young people or inertia to change, will now have to find ways of doing so. Modern Studies teachers and the MSA are arguing hard that this should be done through the appointment of Modern Studies specialists where there are none at present, preferably organised in Modern Studies departments, although there is a worry that in some of these schools there will be a temptation, for reasons of staffing, to deliver the Modern Studies elements through History and Geography.

The 5–14 Environmental Studies document does introduce Understanding People in Society into the primary school, where explicit Modern Studies themes will be taught, based around the following key ideas of:

- Social groupings, social needs and how they are met
- Social rules, rights and responsibilities
- Conflict and participation in decision-making in society
- Economic organisation and structures

This offers tremendous opportunities for Modern Studies. Apart from collaboration between feeder primaries and secondaries which will be in itself fruitful, Modern Studies departments in the secondaries will be able to expect pupils arriving with some experience and knowledge of the subject, hopefully meaning that planning and progression can be enhanced. For all departments, though, there will be the necessity of auditing courses, throwing out some parts and developing new units to fit the guidelines but, as argued earlier in the chapter, most departments have already started this process and are finding that much of what is in the courses is relevant.

The 'Higher Still' developments have been generally welcomed, although there are, in common with other subjects, worries over assessment, workload and the issue of more bi-, or even multi-, level teaching and consequent poorer learning experiences for pupils.

Expansion and limitations

Whilst it is undoubtedly true that Modern Studies is expanding in some areas and developing anew in some schools, there are a few schools where Modern Studies has been virtually eliminated as a subject in the middle school (S3 and S4). Worryingly, this has tended to be in schools with a larger percentage of lower ability pupils and is justified on the somewhat spurious educational basis of reducing choice and improving quality for these pupils by creating larger groupings in Geography and History. Fortunately, the practice is not widespread.

Common Social Subjects course in S1/S2

Another area of concern, in common with the other social subjects, although also with some positive features, is the trend in some schools to have a social studies course in S1 (and sometimes in S2) where History, Geography and Modern Studies is taught by a single teacher, often uncertificated in one or two of these subjects. This can work well in situations where there has been full discussion, timetabled meetings and committed teachers with ownership of the course, and has the added advantage of reducing the number of teachers with whom each pupil has contact. But often, when staffing is the major consideration, there is a lowest common denominator effect leading consequently to poorer courses on offer.

HMI findings

The detailed HMI reports outline many strengths in Modern Studies teaching, particularly in terms of methodology, as outlined earlier in this chapter. They also raised areas of concern that needed attention, such as the issue of progression in skills and content, planning in relation to assessment, ensuring that pupils have a clear awareness of what is expected of them and are thus able to plan schemes for improvement. At least part of the problem of these areas relates to an earlier concern – the fact that not all schools have Modern Studies PTs with the management time to deal with these weaker areas; there is plenty of evidence that where there is a Modern Studies department and structure the weaknesses are far less and where existing are much more easily eliminated.

Into the Millennium

The future is thus one of optimism tempered by realism. The subject is tremendously popular with pupils, parents, FE students and professionals alike and this is very important. The 1980s and 1990s have seen the development of a conservative consensus by governments over the direction of education in general and this has fuelled a rethinking of exactly how political literacy can be taught, and within this perspective, Modern Studies clearly has an important central role.

REFERENCES

Dunlop, O. J. (ed.) (1977) *Modern Studies; Origins, aims and development*, London: Macmillan.
Morrissett, I. and A. Williams (eds) (1981) *Social/Political Education in three Countries – Britain, West Germany and USA*, Colorado: Social Science Education Consortium.
Ross, A. (1987) Political Education in the Primary School, in C. Harber (ed.), *Political Education in Britain*, London: Falmer.
Scruton, R., A. Ellis-Jones and D. O'Keefe (1985) *Education and Indoctrination*, Harrow: Harrow Education Research Centre.
SOED (1992) *Effective Learning and Teaching in Scottish Secondary Schools; Modern Studies*, Edinburgh: SOED.
SOED (1993) *National Guidelines: Environmental Studies 5–14*, Edinburgh: SOED.

63

Music Education

Mark Sheridan

The contemporary music curriculum in Scottish schools is based on the simple premise that music is a practical activity and that it is open for all to study. These are obvious notions, but they have taken some time to establish. The publication of Curriculum Paper 16, Music in Scottish Schools (SED, 1978) was the dividing line between past practices and future developments which unequivocally and irrevocably changed the way in which music was taught. It was the one identifiable event amidst a time of experimentation and debate which clearly focused music teachers' and educators' energies and ideas. It encapsulated many of the ideas and innovations which had been forming in Britain through the work of Paynter and Aston (1970), Witkin (1974) and in the USA since the 1960s (Choksy et al., 1986) and placed them not only into a Scottish context but also into Scottish schools. The challenge to teachers was clear: a root and branch overhaul of the curriculum was called for which would reshape music in the classroom into an action-based experience, open to all children no matter their ability.

Previous generations of children had followed a diet of class-singing, solfah deciphering and music appreciation (occasionally with single-stave guides) in classes of forty pupils. The standard resources of the music classroom were the piano, the Curwen modulator, numerous sets of song and sight-reading books and a record player. Classes were usually single gender to enable class singing to take place. More enlightened teachers would have some percussion instruments or recorders in the classroom and the appearance of guitars in the 1970s heralded new directions for a minority. The Scottish Examination Board Ordinary Grade examination at the end of year 4 was designed to be overtaken by pupils who had expertise on an instrument or voice to the equivalent of Associated Board Grade 5, tuition on which was given outwith the classroom and more often by private teachers outwith the school. Historical study, rudiments and analysis were the order of the day. Music was an elitist subject and the growing disillusionment by pupils and many teachers who experienced a different world of music in their private lives was one of the key propellants towards an effective change which would ensure music's presence in the curriculum beyond the 1980s. In the contexts of both primary and secondary schools, Curriculum Paper 16 recommended syllabus content and teaching and learning strategies, the review of assessment approaches and most significantly, staffing, resource and accommodation requirements to enable the new music, 'music for all', to be implemented. These recommendations gave teachers and headteachers the tools and impetus to make demands on local authorities to fund the developments appropriately. Interestingly, no other report or guidance on music education since then has done so.

CURRICULAR OVERHAUL

The next ten years was a time of radical change and revolution in the classroom, of experimentation with different types of music and alternative approaches to teaching and learning against a backdrop of serious industrial unrest and anxiety for teachers. Teachers were encouraged to introduce practical music-making activities, giving the majority of pupils hands-on music for the first time in their lives. Ensembles of pitched percussion instruments, recorders and guitars were being heard across the country, playing home-grown material and a few published arrangements available at that time. 'Creative music' experiments were sprouting in schools and teachers were genuinely seeking positive ways to enliven and brighten the musical diet of their pupils. A Central Committee on Music oversaw a number of national courses for teachers and educators and produced numerous 'Occasional' papers and other texts written by practising teachers which raised awareness of techniques and approaches and of the relevant issues. These papers were disseminated to all secondary schools, colleges and universities and enabled a broad ranging debate to take place. Following the recommendations of the Munn and Dunning Reports in 1977, the SEB in consultation with the Scottish Education Department began the task of redesigning the curriculum at the hub: the reframing of the old 'O' Grade examination. From this cauldron of debate and discussion, the final distillation of the curriculum produced the Standard Grade Arrangements in Music (SEB, 1988) in which the aims of practical music-making for all pupils were enshrined. The activities of performing, inventing and listening taught in an integrated manner, with conceptual learning as a touchstone, were set at the core of the syllabus. An assessment strategy based on grade related criteria for all the elements ensured that pupils were recognised for their positive attainments rather than their failings and shortcomings.

Controversy, however, raged as it had done in 1978. Many teachers were unhappy about a variety of matters including assessment for all pupils on two instruments (in both solo and group performance which were included as separate components), the necessity to teach across a wide range of abilities in the same classroom, and the compulsory teaching and assessment of inventing. The latter was the most contentious area of the new curriculum and one which would remain so for a number of reasons, perhaps most significantly because of teachers' lack of training in composing and improvising, both in their own school days and as undergraduates. Traditional teaching and training in music in the UK did not encourage students in the art of creation, concentrating on performing or recreative skills, historical study and musical analysis. The reasons for inclusion in the curriculum were encapsulated in the text of the Standard Grade document: 'Inventing develops ideas principally through imaginative response . . . It offers pupils a training in discrimination and perception and in the words of the Munn Report provides for "deep imaginative satisfaction"' (SEB 1988, p. 10).

The persuasive arguments of the members of the Joint Working Party (1984) which produced this report and by subsequent descendant bodies such as the Central Support Group (1986) and the Working Parties on Revision of the Higher (1988) and the implementation of the Certificate of Sixth Year Studies (1990) ensured the continued strong role of inventing in the integrated curriculum. Parallel to these developments, the process of modularisation of vocational courses by SCOTVEC created a similar diet of music courses for students at colleges of Further Education, and some schools, based on a building block approach. The elements of music could therefore be studied separately and assessed by means of diaries and recorded attainment strategies rather than by examination.

The result of all of these changes was the rapid growth of numbers taking music in middle school, transforming the school music department's sound-world from a largely classical environment to one which resounded with folk, rock, pop and jazz riffs. The multi-instrumental nature of the classroom activities and the mixed ability range of the pupils made further demands on music teachers, many of whom were ill-prepared to deal with the new order. The Central Support Group, set up under the direction of the Scottish Consultative Council on the Curriculum, in collaboration with local authorities produced a significant body of materials to aid teachers in their task. Both curricular and staff development materials gave teachers at least the basis on which to plan and implement the new course. The main thrust of development was to ensure that the philosophy of an integrated, practical approach with conceptual learning was achieved. This was to be the most difficult aspect of the new syllabus to implement.

PHILOSOPHY?

It is likely that the teachers in the 1970s and early 1980s (a number of whom were architects of Standard Grade) who were experimenting in the classroom and gleaning ideas from a range of sources such as those writers previously mentioned and others such as Swanwick (*A Basis for Music Education*, 1979) and Regelski (*Teaching in General Music*, 1981), were not aware of some of the precedents which had been set in creating an integrated curriculum. The American approach and philosophy for teaching music called Comprehensive Musicianship would appear to be the main, if somewhat indirect, influence on the Scottish framework. Stemming initially from the Ford Foundation's funding of the Young Composer's Project (1959) and the Contemporary Music Project (CMP) for Creativity in Music Education (1963) the resultant seminar at Northwestern University in 1965 sponsored by the CMP spawned Comprehensive Musicianship. The fundamental aim of the first two projects was to enhance and develop the teaching of contemporary music in the American classroom, but the refocusing of the direction of the project at Northwestern University towards a broad based all-encompassing music curriculum created Comprehensive Musicianship.

David Woods (1986) writes: 'A CM approach to music study from preschool through university advocates that students develop personal musical competencies through a balance of experience in':

Performance:	reading and recreating music written by a composer
Analysis:	describing the music through perceptive listening
Composition:	understanding and utilising compositional and improvisational techniques.

(in Choksy et al.,1986, p. 110)

The Scottish experience over recent decades would indicate an adherence to a somewhat parochial approach to planning. While teachers and educators would have been well aware of, and to a little extent practised, the classroom approaches of Kodaly and Orff and Jacques Dalcroze, the tendency had been to assimilate and draw on these approaches and philosophies within the individual classroom. This created a dynamic and colourful national picture, but one which was hard to pin down to a particular approach or philosophy. Perhaps hard-pressed teachers, faced with such a sea of change in the last twenty years, ignored or dismissed debate on the philosophy and basis of the curriculum in favour of quick fix remedies designed to help them cope with the needs of the classroom. The philosophy, of a kind, exists however and having implemented the dramatic changes required of them, teachers may now be better placed to address some of the broader educational issues which would doubtless support their understanding of the processes in which they are involved daily.

FRAMEWORK: COMPLETING THE TASK

Having set the cornerstone of the new curriculum in Standard Grade, the creation and articulation of the Revised Higher (1990) and Certificate of Sixth Year Studies (1992) reinforced the integrated approach, while a greater degree of choice and specialisation gave senior pupils the freedom to develop skills and interests best suited to their own aspirations. This curricular choice is possible through selection of extension work in one of the three elements while maintaining core provision for the other two. Performing predominates pupils' selection at this level of study, while listening and inventing appear to be less popular although still present in the pupils' experience. This integrated building block approach enabled the music education community to deal with the task of realignment demanded by two further national initiatives. The far reaching 5–14 National Guidelines on Expressive Arts (SOED, 1992) looked towards primary school and the necessity to more effectively bridge the gap to secondary. Despite the heavy handed nature of the report and the contrived nature of its language, attempting to encompass all of the arts with one set of terms and phrases, the programmes of work and the assessment strategies proposed effectively paved the way towards a clear articulation with Standard and Higher Grades.

The process demanded by the Higher Still development programme (1995–8) also gave teachers and educators the opportunity to revisit some of the issues which arose during the process of curricular overhaul. Literacy and the study of rudiments, for a long time areas of controversy (deemed to be means to ends in the new approaches in 'S' Grade), have been addressed in Higher and Advanced Higher levels. Similarly, effective preparation of able pupils for entry to higher education (which seemed to be one of the aims of the original elitist Higher Grade) was for some regarded as a casualty in the new order. Greater collaboration and communication between Higher Education institutions and schools helped alleviate some concerns in this area. The impressive flourishing since the 1980s of the use of a broad range of highly sophisticated technological and computer facilities in music for performing, composing and recording has greatly expanded pupil access and enhanced achievement in the classroom. The advent of MIDI and advanced digital multi-media hardware has probably been the most significant development in music this century, and while many of its uses and applications still need to be rigorously examined and researched, this revolution has opened up new frontiers and experiences in music for all pupils. On the other hand, a major area of the curriculum undoubtedly damaged by rapid change in the classroom was singing. Teachers have argued that the implementation of a largely instrumental based approach, the reduction in size and the creation of mixed gender classes (most welcome for contemporary purposes) have created difficulties which almost extinguished singing in many schools. It may also be true that, as one of the most taxing aspects of the musical diet, it was easy prey for teachers to expel it from the curriculum. The result, however, is that community and church choirs have suffered in recruitment of young members and despite efforts by bodies such as the British Federation of Youth Choirs and local authorities to address the problem, the plight of singing in schools still needs to be addressed.

Highlighted previously as an area of concern, the inventing element is the one which appears to have been least successful in implementation. Research has shown that the Standard Grade examination results since 1991 to 1996 reflect a worrying trend:

> Pupil attainment in performing which has traditionally been well taught and learned, with awards at Credit level in Solo . . . and Group . . . now reaching 63% (from 53%) and 60% (from 45%) respectively. Attainment in listening has been improving steadily . . . (45% to 50%). The percentage of pupils achieving grades of 1 or 2 for . . . Inventing are the lowest, starting from 36% in 1991 and rising slowly to a peak of 43% in 1996. (C. Byrne and M. Sheridan 1997. *Music: A Source of Deep Imaginative Satisfaction*, unpublished paper presented at the SERA Conference)

Much work has still to be done in this and in other areas to overtake the challenges set in the 1980s. The trends however are encouraging, with more and more young people voting with their feet and taking up music in school with the result that demand for music teachers and places in higher education courses are greater than in the past. Clearly, music in Scottish Education has been a success story.

REFERENCES

Choksy, L., R. M. Abramson, A. E. Gillespie and D. Woods (1986) *Teaching Music in the Twentieth Century*, Prentice-Hall: Englewood Cliffs, New Jersey.
Paynter, J. and P. Aston (1970) *Sound and Silence*, London: Cambridge University Press.
SED (1978) *MUSIC in Scottish Schools, Curriculum Paper 16*, Edinburgh: HMSO.
SOED (1992) *Curriculum and Assessment in Scotland, National Guidelines, Expressive Arts: 5–14*, Edinburgh: SOED.
SEB (1988) *Scottish Certificate of Education: Standard Grade Arrangements in Music*, Dalkeith: Scottish Examination Board.
Witkin, R. W. (1974) *The Intelligence of Feeling*, London: Heinemann.

64

Physical Education

Bob Brewer and Bob Sharp

> There is no doubt about the fact that PE is not its own master. It is not unique among subjects, it is open to the influences of major national developments, of curriculum change, of political will, of parental pressure, just like all the others. (B. Fryer, 1991)

It should come as no surprise that a chapter reviewing Physical Education in Scotland opens with a treatise by a former specialist subject HM Inspector. His summary of the sentiments associated with the teaching of Physical Education during the 1990s is not without some irony, particularly as the inspectorate's influence might be considered an integral part of the shaping of policy in an increasingly centralist form of curriculum development. This, as Gatherer (1989) asserts, may be indicative of the 'new authoritarianism' of government-led initiatives with Physical Education striving inexorably to achieve recognition and status as the school curriculum is re-organised (*Curriculum Development in Scotland*, Edinburgh: Scottish Academic Press).

As a consequence, Physical Education has changed in a number of fundamental ways and this chapter presents a selective view on the nature of these changes, the sources that have inspired them and their effect on teacher and pupil practice.

THE POST-MUNN ERA AND THE DRIFT OF PHYSICAL EDUCATION TOWARDS CERTIFICATION

A key development in Physical Education over the last twenty years has been the rise of formally assessed and certificated courses. This trend could not have been anticipated easily from the Munn Report's ringing endorsement of 'physical activity' as one of eight 'modes of activity' in the S3/S4 secondary school curriculum. Reference therein to the educational currency of physical activity in terms of skills, enjoyment, personal interests and physical well-being were statements of intent well appreciated by Physical Education teachers. In particular, Munn's view that physical activity should have a firm place in the curriculum was reassuring to a profession traditionally preoccupied with concerns for status and educational justification.

While these statements were significant, they could barely anticipate the way courses for Physical Education were to evolve in the next two decades, nor could they have forecast the trends towards curricula more closely prescribed by an assessment agenda outwith the formal control of the school Physical Education department. Scotland's first examinable two-year course in Standard Grade Physical Education (SGPE) which was piloted in 1984/

6, acknowledged the challenges awaiting teachers. Accounts of piloting the experimental 'Guidelines for Physical Education' in 1984, provided a very timely snapshot of a curriculum being shaped and nudged by an externally set protocol (Macdonald, 1986). As recent HMI reporting has indicated, 'many Physical Education teachers were, for the first time, directly affected by influences on the curriculum which they had not previously encountered' (SOEID, 1995).

The significance of SGPE should not be underestimated for a number of reasons. Firstly, it heralded the move towards certification in Physical Education. This gathered apace despite various comments of caution. The document 'Framework for Decision' noted that, 'subjects like . . . Physical Education will continue to make their main contribution through non examined courses' and this tended to endorse the view expressed by the Educational Institute of Scotland Central Advisory Committee on Physical Education that core provision for all pupils in Physical Education was being jeopardised by the prioritisation given to resourcing minority courses like SGPE.

A second issue of significance arising from SGPE and other courses that followed in its wake, was the model adopted for supporting teachers in curriculum development. Centrally produced support materials for SGPE (partly inspired by a newly achieved conditions of service agreement), were distributed to all secondary schools to aid in-service arrangements and add substance to the fulfilling of 'Planned Activity Time' for teachers who were now required by headteachers to designate time specifically to agreed educational needs. This latter condition was to have a telling effect on the commitment of Physical Education teachers to the extra-curricular dimensions of school life. Arguably, it was a defining moment for the way Physical Education teachers perceived their professional role in the life of the school and the fact that their involvement in extra-curricular sport decreased during this period, and has been slow to recover ever since, bears testimony to such a view. This was itself the subject of significant reporting by other agencies such as the Scottish Sports Council. Nevertheless, the 'cascade' model for in-service work (described in other chapters) was typically adopted around the country and remains something of a template for the way Physical Education teachers engage in curriculum development in the 1990s. It is contestable whether this represents a genuinely sympathetic support service for teachers, or acts as a further step to what some have argued is a form of teacher de-professionalisation through the need to implement schemes devised and approved 'from above'.

A corollary of the drift towards formalised course guidelines for Physical Education throughout a child's school life, were the concerns about time allocation and the degree to which the various claims for the inclusion of Physical Education in the curriculum could actually be fulfilled. This was compounded by the definition of time-scales prescribed in the SCCC's *Guidelines for Headteachers*. Such a combination of factors reflected a harsh but pragmatic view that Physical Education as a certificated subject at least had a place in the timetable!

The implications of these three factors, viz., prioritising elective courses (notably SGPE) as compared to core; support for teachers with centrally-produced resources in a new climate of contracted working hours and conditions of service; reduced time available for Physical Education, did impinge markedly on the practice of Physical Education.

TEACHING AND LEARNING IN PHYSICAL EDUCATION

Current documentation for Physical Education makes frequent reference to the influence of teaching approaches on pupil learning. For example, the promotion of 'learning how to learn' and 'self reliance' strategies are consistently endorsed in the programmes of study for Physical Education at 5–14 and in statements framing the Higher Still initiative in Physical Education. Reference to process objectives, learning experiences, critical and imaginative practice, practical and experiential learning have been some of the enduring terms characterising the descriptions of teaching and learning in recent years. It is clear that the need to engage pupils in their learning through a variety of teaching approaches is implicit in course design. It is also an explicit aspect of HMI school inspection and the assertive reporting of what is 'observed good practice' (SOEID, 1995). The extent to which such references have been informed by research into successful teaching is not so evident, but the questions raised by research are an important focus of reflection for the day-to-day practice of Physical Education teachers.

The impact of these formative statements for pedagogy has evidenced itself in a number of ways. For example, it has helped the decision making associated with the content of teacher support materials for 5–14 'Pathways into Action' project and also provided the momentum for a BBC series based on SGPE. Similarly the concern for independent study as part of Higher Grade Physical Education (HGPE) was the starting point for developing interactive video programmes.

Case study reporting also suggests that the teaching of Physical Education has been fundamentally reviewed in light of some of the initiatives described above. For example, Macdonald (1986) contended that SGPE demands a radical change in teaching style from the traditional teacher led, teacher dominated lesson, while Lobban (1994) argued that the organisation of learning for HGPE has to be less dependent on the teacher as the main source of knowledge and judge of progress.

This sort of evidence encourages an optimistic view of the way teachers of Physical Education have responded to the demands of curriculum review. However, there are two elements of unease for Physical Education to which reference is briefly made.

UNEASE IN PHYSICAL EDUCATION

The first element of unease is the extent to which statements made about Physical Education have reassured the profession about its purpose and place in the curriculum. It is difficult to summarise adequately here what is a complex debate, but essentially the rationale for Physical Education remains a 'site of struggle'. There is a long history associated with this issue. It is illustrated most clearly in the way Physical Education is described as fulfilling intentions associated with an expressive arts curriculum at 5–14 which then becomes transformed at 16–18 to a rationale based on performance and the analysis and investigation of it. No doubt there are points of continuity and progression between the curricula but, as Reid (1996) has argued, this separate categorisation of Physical Education into 'arts' and 'science' is symptomatic of a reductionism in official policy documents at odds with the pluralistic vision of Physical Education described by Munn ten years before. The danger here (and hence, the unease) is one of distorting Physical Education and its practise on the basis of what Reid has described as a quest for some form of 'theoretical tidiness'.

The extent of this unease cannot be quantified. Sharp's (1991) data, however, on teachers, aims for Physical Education and how they rank order these, begs a view that, in their prioritising of 'motor skills' and 'physical development' objectives, the profession seems clear about the orientation of its subject matter. Sharp showed that teachers in

Scotland were remarkably focused and united in their view about the importance of skill learning, performance and physical development. On this count, the unease relates to a difference between teachers' perceptions about why they teach and the curricula they are asked to implement.

The second element of unease is associated with the effects of external assessment procedures on Physical Education. There can be very little doubt that the nature of assessment and the relative weighting given to the component parts of both SGPE and HGPE, have had a marked influence on teachers' practice. Despite statements that extol knowledge and understanding arising out of (pupil) practice, and the general endorsement of standards of performance being developed in tandem with analysis and investigation skills, there are tensions with the practicalities of teacher delivery. The tendency to fulfil the knowledge and understanding obligations of SGPE and HGPE syllabi in detached class-room contexts has become something of a pragmatic reality, even to the extent of warranting comment approaching rebuke from HMI reporting on 'chalk and talk' teaching (SOEID, 1995). Understandably, it is hard for teachers to reconcile the competing claims of a rationale proclaiming the practical, experiential nature of Physical Education while at the same time supporting an assessment culture that has a minimum 50 per cent weighting towards written forms of examination. It is perhaps indicative of an ongoing theory/practice conflict for Physical Education. If anything, this is likely to be compounded by the unitised structures of Higher Still courses, especially as teachers seek ways of improving pupil results in a school reporting system that takes a more public account of Physical Education achievements in nationally certificated courses.

CHALLENGES TO COME FOR PHYSICAL EDUCATION

Physical Education has attempted to meet the challenges of recent curriculum doctrine in Scotland in two major ways. Firstly, it has been obliged to re-shape its philosophy on the basis of a radical re-organisation of the 5–14 curriculum. Secondly, it has developed formally certificated courses under the externally moderated arrangements of the Scottish Qualifications Authority. While some aspects of these developments have been encouraging, such as the continuing rise of pupil/student enrolment in SGPE/HGPE and National Certificate courses, there is sufficient critique from within the profession to warrant caution on the degree of progress that can be stated for Physical Education.

It is important to acknowledge by way of a concluding comment, that the initiation and development of pupil motivation for regular physical activity remains an enduring and critical part of the Physical Educationalist's agenda. The need for regular levels of exercise as part of a healthy lifestyle and the role that Physical Education can play in this, is well supported by a vibrant research literature. If this can be achieved, it may also help slow down the drop-out rate from active participation in sport acknowledged by the Scottish Sports Council and National Governing Bodies of Sport. This latter issue continues to invite animated advice, especially in the way opportunities are afforded to girls, whose lack of participation and lower achievements in certificated Physical Education concerned the Scottish Examination Board to the extent that they have supported research in seeking some further explanation of the matter. The imminent introduction of Higher Still Physical Education will no doubt re-invoke this significant debate.

REFERENCES

Fryer, B. (1991) *Recent trends, future directions . . . Pragmatist's Progress*. Scottish Physical Education Association Conference Papers: Special Edition, pp. 2–5.

Lobban, D. (1994) Thoughts on the first year of Higher Grade Physical Education: Westhill Academy, *Scottish Journal of Physical Education*, 22.3, 16–19.

Macdonald, W. (1986) Standard grade Physical Education and what it means for the teacher, in *Trends and Developments in Physical Education*: Proceedings of the VIIIth Commonwealth and International Conference on Sport, Physical Education, Dance, Recreation and Health, London: E. & F. N. Spon Ltd.

Reid, A. (1996) The concept of Physical Education in current curriculum and assessment policy in Scotland, *European Physical Education Review*, 2.1, 7–18.

SOEID (1995) *Physical Education: Effective Learning and Teaching in Scottish Secondary Schools*, A Report by HM Inspectors of Schools.

Sharp, R. H. (1991) Physical Education in Scottish secondary schools (Part 1). *Scottish Journal of Physical Education*, 19.1, 10–15.

65

Physics Education

Drew McCormick

PHYSICS FROM 1960 TO THE 1980s

In 1962, science as a curriculum subject was split into discrete elements. There was a sense of change in the air. Bruner had said that:

> The schoolboy learning physics is a physicist and it is easier for him to learn physics behaving like a physicist than doing something else. (*The Process of Education*, Cambridge: Harvard University Press, 1960, p. 14)

This adage was used as the basis for the developments in America which followed from the beginnings of the space race. It led to the Nuffield scheme in England and parallel reforms in Scotland. The aim of the changes was to produce 'physics for all,' and a 'physics for the educated citizen' (Woolnough, 1988, p. 96).

There was an attempt to reflect the changes which had occurred in the world of physics. The topics were still very traditional but with an insight into modern physics. There was an increased emphasis on pupil practical work rather than just teacher demonstrations. During the 1970s the syllabus experienced slight changes and there were changes in assessment. During the 1980s the physics being taught became increasingly dated by comparison to syllabuses elsewhere and to developments particularly in electronics and in communications. The delay in the introduction of Standard Grade had meant the optimism of the authors in the 1960s had resulted in a fairly traditional syllabus.

A number of features required attention:

- The course was seen as too mathematical for many pupils.
- Some concepts were seen to be too difficult for the majority of pupils and would need to be removed completely or moved to a higher level.
- The majority of pupils who took physics were boys despite attempts to change the balance significantly.
- Physics was not seen as relevant to the real world. It was perceived as causing problems such as nuclear waste rather than helping people in detecting and treating disease such as cancers.

Despite the electronics industry and the growth in communications and leisure, the basic physics behind such topics was not reflected in school courses.

PHYSICS FROM 1990

Standard Grade

The aim in Standard Grade was to provide a course that was seen as being both relevant and useful to people in their normal lives. There was a need to encourage more pupils to choose physics or at least show no decrease. In physics, as with biology and chemistry, there was no Foundation level, therefore a pupil taking mathematics at Foundation level would not be advised to choose physics.

Based on developments in Holland, the course was designed as an applications-led course where the applications came first, followed by the principles. As an example, the operation of an electric motor would be followed by the principles of electromagnetism. The topics were: communications; using electricity; health physics; digital electronics; transport; energy matters; space. These topics were a mixture of the traditional and the modern.

The simpler concepts were assigned to General level and the more advanced ones to Credit although there was no research into the assignment of concepts to each level, merely a consensus by the working group. This has led to anomalies with some concepts being possibly wrongly assigned to Credit level (SQA, 1997).

Higher Grade

To update the syllabus, a revised Higher was introduced but the basic content remained broadly the same. The ideas not in Standard Grade were now in Higher. However, the reverse of Standard Grade occurred with the principles being taught and then the applications (SEB, 1991).

CSYS

CSYS consists of a taught course which contributes half of the final grade together with a project. The course is rather conventional but there are also option topics (SEB, 1991). The project can be entirely original or merely a re-working of tried and tested experiments which are new to the pupil. The pupil can seek advice from any source, including industry or universities. This part of the course captures the pupil's interest compared to the written part.

ISSUES

Standard Grade has been successful: the total number of pupils taking the subjects has been maintained but the percentage of the cohort has risen from 21.1 per cent in 1972 to 35.8 per cent in 1992. The number of girls has remained at one third of the cohort. At 'H' Grade, physics is the third most popular subject after English and mathematics although the reasons are unclear. One possibility is that these subjects allow entry to a wide range of courses such as science, engineering and medicine. Indeed the three sciences are almost equal in terms of entries to the exam. However, the applications-led approach has not been followed through and certainly at CSYS the content is still largely traditional. The rapidly changing applications, particularly in communications, have led to continual changes in the syllabus and this has necessitated an updating of teachers' knowledge. The Inspectorate have observed that 'authorities need to address the needs of science teachers in regard to updating and extending their knowledge base of their subject' (SOED, 1994, p. 22). The situation has been exemplified by the age distribution of teachers: 87 per cent are over 30 but 61 per cent are over 40. This can cause problems with both teaching and examining since many teachers are unfamiliar with the rapid changes in aspects of health physics and electronics. Despite some attempts to overcome the problems, the pattern looks set to remain like this for some years.

External Assessment

With Ordinary Grade and Higher there were multiple choice questions and structured questions covering the syllabus and which allowed pupil choice; this made comparisons of papers and candidates difficult. Now there is no choice at Standard Grade and both papers include a wide range of different types of questions and the Credit paper has more demanding questions. There is no Foundation level in any of the discrete sciences.

In the 1960s the type of questions was very conventional with a description of an experiment, followed by a calculation or explanation. Now there is a better balance of knowledge and understanding together with problem solving. The evidence from the examination board is that elements involving problem solving situations are improving. In the first reports of Standard Grade, questions involving knowledge and understanding were competently tackled (SEB Annual Report, 1990).

However, in the following year's Annual Report it was stated that 'candidates had less success in providing explanations of ideas and of physical phenomena'. Despite the introduction of the revised Higher, the report in 1992 concluded that 'a number were unable to cope with the demands of the examination.'

Internal Assessment

With both Standard Grade and CSYS there is an assessment of practical work. At Standard Grade until 1998 this constituted one third of the overall grade. After that the practical assessment will reduce to one fifth. The assessment has two parts, one of which is based on eight basic techniques required in the course. The pupil has to complete two investigations based on the TAPS 3 research programme (Bryce et al., 1991). Only one investigation was required from 1990 to 1998, but to harmonise the sciences all pupils must now attempt two complete investigations. The investigations are based on specific criteria and the process is moderated by the SQA. This aspect of assessment has been a contentious area with teachers. There was concern, especially from head teachers and others, about the high grades obtained for the practical element. Pupils could obtain low grades for written elements and high grades for the practical element, giving high grades overall. However when pupils are being advised about proceeding to Higher Grade, the grade for practical work is ignored. It could be argued that the pupils are good at attempting practical work and teachers are in danger of downgrading this type of work rather than encouraging it. This certainly goes against the spirit of the ideas of 'S' grade. There was no attempt to examine the nature of the investigations and extend the justifications which the pupil must make, which would be similar to that of GCSE in England.

Instead, there has been a move to an easy solution which will satisfy those concerned about the grades but will not extend the nature of practical work in schools. A typical feature is the reduction in weighting from one third to one fifth which was done to make the determination of the final grade easier. The CSYS has a project which is graded by the teacher and is subjective; however, each candidate is given an oral examination by an external examiner.

Teaching approaches

The first approaches in the 1960s were whole class teaching with a mixture of demonstrations and pupil experiments. The change has been a move towards more pupil-centred pedagogy. This involved the use of worksheets and, for a minority of schools, resource based learning. Over time, such teaching has been characterised as 'death by a thousand worksheets'. Standard Grade introduced a more pragmatic approach with whole-class teaching coupled with short sections of limited pupil-based learning. It was argued by a senior HMI that:

> teacher exposition, used in conjunction with questioning and discussion, is the most effective means of delivering the knowledge and understanding component of courses. Problem solving and practical activities lend themselves to a more resource based approach.

This approach has been used in most physics laboratories.

The use of different strategies has been described by Inspectors in the following terms:

> The aims of science education cannot be fully achieved through the use of any one learning and teaching approach. In successful departments teachers planned to make use of a variety of tactics in appropriate ways. These approaches included: exposition, discussion, consolidation, practical investigation, problem solving, homework and diagnostic and summative assessment. (SOED, 1994)

Resources

Materials (both paper and disc) were developed by local authorities for both Standard Grade and Higher but the increased cost of photocopying has reduced the use of consumable sheets. The small size of the Scottish market has meant a restricted choice of textbooks compared to England and a recent trend has been to take books written for another market and adapt them to Scottish courses – with varying degrees of success.

Computers have been increasingly used with some specially written software for the Standard Grade course. Developments in interfacing, that is using computers to measure physical quantities, and in data logging for lengthy experiments, also figure.

PHYSICS FOR THE FUTURE

Higher Still promises a new look at vocational and academic courses. At Intermediate 1 the physics course is aimed at those who have not taken physics before and who have a reduced level of mathematical skills. At Intermediate 2 the course will cover the work of Standard Grade Credit level and take some concepts to a more advanced level to act as a bridge to Higher. At Higher, the course will be almost the same. For each stage there are a number of units which will have practical work assessed. The time spent on this assessment will be lengthy and it will have no weighting on the final grade. Concern remains about the time and the quantity of resources. Tests will be provided, but any teaching materials will have to be developed in schools or purchased – a prospect which is creating some apprehension for many teachers.

Overall, physics has changed over the last twenty years both in content and teaching approaches. Undoubtedly the largest challenge facing the subject and the profession, is to reflect the enormous changes in the applications of physics in the real world while continuing to emphasise the basic principles.

REFERENCES

Bryce, T., J. McCall, J. MacGregor, I. J. Robertson and R. A. J. Weston (1991), *TAPS 3 Assessment Pack: How to Assess Open-ended Practical Investigations in Biology, Chemistry and Physics*, Oxford: Heinemann Educational.

SEB (1991) *Arrangements for Higher Physics*, Dalkeith: SEB.

SOED (1994) *Effective Learning and Teaching in Scottish Secondary Schools: the Sciences*, A report by HMI. Edinburgh: SOED.

SQA (1997) *Arrangements for Standard Grade Physics*, Dalkeith: SQA.

Woolnough, B. (1988) *Physics Teaching, 1960 to 1985*, London: Falmer Press.

66

Religious Education

Alex Rodger

PHILOSOPHY

In 1970 the goal of helping young people 'to come to a personal faith in Jesus Christ as Saviour and Lord' (Scottish Joint Committee on Religious Education) was regarded as broadly acceptable for religious education in both non-denominational and Roman Catholic schools. An important sub-theme of development since then concerns how these two sectors have negotiated the dialogue between educating young people for understanding and living within a modern pluralist society and equipping them to be reflectively committed within specific traditions and communities of faith.

In 1996 the Scottish Joint Committee on Religious Education was reconstituted as the Scottish Joint Committee on Religious and Moral Education. Its previous membership representing educational organisations and the churches was extended to include the different faith communities as full members. These changes can be seen as marking significant developments affecting religious education in the last quarter of the twentieth century.

This chapter deals mainly with mainstream developments. These justify the comment that 'Since the 1970s religious education has benefited from a much more professional approach and now has an educational value that is recognised in all major national developments that have taken place since that time' (SOED, 1994).

The dramatic development during that period was precipitated by the Millar Report (SED, 1972). Its statements, 'Religious education is no longer aimed at producing assent to one particular faith' (5.1); and 'The teacher is not there to convince pupils of specific religious beliefs . . . children should be exposed to a number of different attitudes and beliefs without the weight of "authority" being ultimately thrown behind any one of them' (5.3); signalled a radical shift in the understanding of the subject.

Important distinctions were marked also between the contributions made by the home, the church and the school to the religious education of young people. The goals were to be 'enlightenment rather than conversion, understanding rather than discipleship' (3.3).

The phrase 'rather than' safeguards the educational purpose against indoctrinative or proselytising intention. It has not, however, helped to resolve the important question as to how religious education can be both educational and religious: that is, how it can foster the kind of understanding which can appreciate a religion's attraction for its adherents, without influencing the learner to embrace it personally; in other words, without closing the issue either way. In various forms this issue continues to preoccupy those involved with religious education in Scotland.

The present working consensus as to the aims of religious education derives from the work of the Scottish Central Committee on Religious Education (1974–1986), expressed in its Bulletin 2, 'Curriculum Guidelines for Religious Education' (1981) as follows:

1. to help pupils to identify the area of religion in terms of the phenomena of religions and the human experiences from which they arise
2. to enable pupils to explore the nature and meaning of existence in relation to the questions religions pose and the answers they propose
3. to encourage pupils to develop a consistent set of beliefs, attitudes and practices which are the result of a personal process of growth, search and discovery (3.2)

This represents the general view which is embodied in national curriculum guidance for the subject in the last two decades of the twentieth century.

The distinction between two interrelated aspects of (and objectives for) the subject – 'those related to religions and other stances for living, and those related to the pupil's search for meaning, value and purpose in life' (4.2) – proved to be important in identifying what are called the 'assessable elements' of the subject and, therefore, in developing examinations in religious education.

INNOVATION AND CHANGE

In addition to providing an educational view of religious education, the Millar Report generated activity and reflection which were to transform religious education in the last quarter of the twentieth Century. It led to:

- the appointment of local education authority advisers in religious education
- the introduction of a teaching qualification in religious education for secondary teachers
- the inspection of the subject
- certificate examinations

These developments were crucial in enabling religious education, for the first time, to become integrally a part of the curriculum provision in Scottish schools. That principle was established by the Scottish Education Department's response to the Millar Report. The outworking in practice of its implications constitutes the greater part of the subject's development in the last quarter of the twentieth century, in the professionalising of religious education. The removal of the ambiguous benefit of its previous 'special' status has enabled it to establish the worth of its educational contribution to the learning and development of young people.

Prior to 1974 there was no secondary teaching qualification in religious education, the subject being taught by 'volunteer' teachers of other subjects. In 1997 the vast majority of secondary schools have at least one registered teacher of religious education; a small proportion of schools have more than one; and in many schools – particularly Roman Catholic schools – the religious education teacher leads a team of non-specialist teachers each devoting a small amount of time to teaching the subject.

HMI reports reveal an accelerating development in professionalism among religious education teachers since 1986, as indicated by departmental subject handbooks; course planning which takes account of balance, continuity, progression and coherence of courses to reflect the subject appropriately for pupils at different stages; awareness and use of a wider range of resources to enhance subject learning; differentiation of courses to match pupil needs and abilities; use of open learning and resource-based learning approaches, with corresponding adaptation of teacher role; the introduction of procedures for monitoring, evaluation, review and development of courses; an increasing uptake of certificate exam-inations in religious education and religious studies, with consequent transfer of (teacher) learning to benefit non-certificate courses in religious education.

The inspection of religious education, introduced in 1983, has had a dramatic effect on the professionalisation of the subject – supporting teacher development, spreading good practice, ensuring that curriculum principle increasingly shapes its planning, content, methods, assessment and development – bringing balance, continuity, progression, differ-entiation and coherence towards the realisation of the vision of a subject provided systematically and developmentally throughout the pupil's school career; addressed to educational and personal search needs; assuming a broad understanding of religion as the human search for meaning, value and purpose in life; and ensuring that content is broad and balanced and the approach open and disciplined.

Curriculum Design for the Secondary Stages prescribed for religious and moral education the following time allocations (actual provision shown in brackets):

S1/2   5% of curriculum time (in 1991, taught in 93% of schools – 82% in 1983; range 2.5%-4.0% of time)

S3/4   80 hours over the two years (in 1991, included in 88% of schools – 73% in 1983)

S5/6   a continuing element within the context of personal and social development (in 1991 in 53% of schools – 56% in 1983)

At each stage, Roman Catholic schools consistently provide at least the minimum recommended allocation of time. It follows that the provision in non-denominational schools is significantly lower than these percentages suggest.

With the caveat that by no means all schools are yet providing all courses, the published 'menu' for religious education in secondary schools is currently as follows:

S1/2   Courses based on the National Guidelines for religious and moral education 5–14. Each school to devise its own course to meet the attainment outcomes 'Guidelines' in relation to Christianity, Other World Religions and the pupil's Personal Search; in a framework of outcomes for knowledge and understanding, skills and attitudes. Roman Catholic schools have much more detailed diocesan syllabi.

S3/4   Scottish Examination Board short courses in religious and moral education. Standard Grade Religious Studies.

S5/6   Higher Grade Religious Studies
SCOTVEC modules in religious studies
CSYS in religious studies.

It is worth noting at this point that classroom practice in religious education in the secondary school has benefited from the upward influence of the 5–14 programme, where primary school experience and insights have helped to enrich the approaches and increase awareness of cross-subject links; and from the influence of certification – particularly the Standard Grade examination in religious studies – in affecting the awareness of teachers and extending their skills in such things as course construction, differentiation, variety of method, individual and group work and whole class teaching, assessment, the use of pupil investigative activities and the development of effective study skills in pupils. In the mid-1990s, by contrast, the pressure of content to be covered was reportedly stifling such innovations in the Higher Grade religious studies course.

The introduction of certificate examinations provided the justification for HMIs to inspect religious education (disallowed by statute from 1872–1983). In the event this may prove to have been the single most effective catalyst in accelerating developments in many aspects of the subject. Inspectors' reports created expectations and produced changes, as local education authorities ensured that their recommendations were implemented in the schools. Thus a new and sustained impetus was given to such matters as educational aims for the subject, leading to course planning and actual provision reflecting more adequately the view of the subject as fully a part of schools' educational provision, subject to the same educational obligation and deserving of the same resourcing and other support as other subjects.

Assessment raises peculiar issues for religious education, with fears of any 'test of faith' or intrusion into pupils' personal convictions. SCCORE's view of the dual nature of religious education – dealing with the phenomena and with the learner's personal search – opened the way for the identification of 'assessable elements' which avoided that charge, while still involving the learner's reflective activity and evaluation of things studied. Few would claim that this is altogether successful as yet in avoiding both uncritical acceptance and premature, ill-informed or insensitive judgements being made. Yet credit must be given, both for the courage to tackle such issues, which have been too long shirked, and for the determination to pursue them in the face of inevitable criticism.

It is perhaps realistic to recognise that a range of such interacting changes as is sketched above will be uneven in their introduction and their effects, difficult to predict and more difficult to control. On current evidence, however, it is reasonable to anticipate a continuing progress in the direction of a coherent and developing whole school experience which enhances the academic and personal development of young people in religious and moral understanding.

UNFINISHED BUSINESS

The vigour and commitment directed to the development of religious education in the last quarter century encourages, rather than disallows, the following comments. They are premised on a job well begun, rapidly advancing, but yet to be consolidated.

There is a suspicion that, even for some of those actively involved in implementing 'the new religious education', a holistic vision of the subject which internalises its root principles is lacking. Sometimes this is betrayed by lack of awareness of the contribution a specific course makes to the balance and range of pupils' experience and learning of the subject over one session: more often, in a failure to see the opportunities for continuity and coherence over the pupil's secondary school experience (far less its progression from learning in the primary school). To have a firm grasp of the approved framework for the subject within the curriculum is not the same thing as to have a coherent philosophy of the subject, or a clear and generous view of its potential and proper contribution to the human development of the learner. Important as the former undoubtedly is, over the course of a teacher's career, it is the latter two which inform the teaching which conveys life and engenders growth in both learner and teacher.

It is hard to avoid the conviction, try as one may (and does!), that there are criteria we should seek in a teacher of religious education which are not similarly required in teachers of others subjects (though there may be parallels in some subjects). The requirement is not that the religious education teacher be better (morally) or more religious than other people: and not that s/he be a Christian, or committed to some other specified faith. The requirement, in addition to appropriate academic and professional insight and competence, has to do with the teacher's own commitment to 'the search for meaning, value and purpose in life' in some recognisable form, and a corresponding commitment to let the view of 'the nature of things' (s)he holds have appropriate expression in her/his life.

The interaction of educational and religious interests in religious education has, over the last twenty-five years, been much more positive than negative; and it would be unrealistic to expect more than we have witnessed. Yet a question has to be raised as to the ambiguous acceptance of the requirements of an educational approach to the deepest convictions of human beings. Schools professing to cater for the educational needs of the children of all citizens in a pluralist society (even – and perhaps particularly – a predominantly Christian one) are compromised in their educational integrity if they provide religious education, or insist on participation in worship, of a kind which presupposes that Christianity (or any other faith) is 'correct' – with the unspoken corollary that others are wrong.

Scotland has moved away from the indoctrinative intention for the subject now called 'Religious and Moral Education'. It has not yet been possible to reach a position which removes grounds for legitimate complaint from those of faiths other than Christianity – particularly in relation to the specious claim that the new understanding of the subject can, on educational grounds, support the legal requirement for a compulsory act of worship within non-denominational schools.

The recognition that the search for meaning, value and purpose in life is not the monopoly of religions, but a fundamentally human preoccupation, raises questions for the onset of the third millennium, which must include:

- What is the purpose, nature and place of this subject in an education for living in a modern, open and pluralist society?
- What is the nature and range of the subject matter with which this subject is concerned? And what are its natural links with such other subjects as Social Education, Health Education and Personal and Social Development?
- What is the appropriate balance between traditional insight and new discovery in the education of the spirit?
- What is the wise contribution to this of public schools catering for the children and young people from families of a variety of religious and non-religious faiths?

A persisting difficulty in finding helpful answers to such questions arises from the fact that, despite the recent resurgence of interest in spirituality within education, society remains largely religiously and spiritually illiterate. The sins of the fathers have been visited on the children; the unresolved problems and conflicts of teachers are part of their legacy to their pupils. Thankfully, the damage inflicted on the education of the human spirit in the twentieth-century western world by the conflict between doctrinaire philosophical dogmas and doctrinaire religious reaction is now widely recognised as something to be lamented. Yet it will take time for any healthily mature outlook to prevail, whereby children are educated to a sensitive understanding of those stances for living in which human beings have found faith to live fully and courage to die well. Nothing less can discharge the school's responsibility to contribute to the education of human beings for the challenge of living humanely in relationship to themselves, to each other, to the world they inhabit and to the cosmos they wonder at, even while they are a part of it.

In addition to time, such an outcome will require that individuals listen to each other more than has been the case; that they listen to the world's faiths and its ancient wisdoms and to their contemporary expressions; and that they listen to their own experience of what it is to live in this mysterious world. In the community of learners people may thus find words which help them to engage with their too-often inarticulate experience, and be helped to recognise for themselves insights and experiences which give new life to dead words inherited from others. Such attention to what is the case, without attempting to constrain it into an existing outlook, is, by any reckoning, at the heart both of education and of religion when they are worthy of their names. How else can teachers be fit to serve those they teach?

REFERENCES

SED (1972) *Moral and Religious Education in Scottish Schools* (The Millar Report), Edinburgh: HMSO.

SOED (1992) *Religious and Moral Education 5–14*, Edinburgh: HMSO.

SOED/SCEC (1994) *Religious Education 5–14: Roman Catholic Schools*, Edinburgh: HMSO.

SOED (1994) *Religious Education: A Report by Her Majesty's Inspectors of Schools*, Edinburgh: HMSO.

SCCC (1995) *Religious and Moral Education: 5–14 Exemplification*, Dundee: SCCC.

Kincaid, M. (1991) *How to Improve Learning in RE*, London: Hodder.

67

Science Education

John MacGregor

SCIENCE AND THE INDIVIDUAL SCIENCES

It would be fair to say that Science teachers in Scotland tend to regard themselves as exponents of biology, chemistry or physics who also teach 'general science' rather than the other way round. However, over the past twenty years or so the emphasis has shifted towards the development of process skills as opposed to the acquisition of factual knowledge. Consequently teachers today ought to feel more comfortable wearing a 'science hat' than they did previously and more attuned to the notion of 'scientific capability' as advanced by the Scottish Consultative Council on the Curriculum in their discussion paper *Science Education in Scottish Schools – Looking to the Future* (SCCC, 1996).

S1–S2 SCIENCE

All pupils take science for the first two years of their secondary schooling. The majority of pupils are taught in mixed ability classes and follow a course which has a balanced coverage of key facts and ideas from biology, chemistry and physics.

Integrated science, for S1 and S2 pupils, was strongly advocated by the Scottish Education Department in the influential *Curriculum Paper Number 7 – Science for General Education* (SED, 1969). Science was to be taught, not as the separate disciplines of biology, chemistry and physics, but as a fully harmonised science course delivered to a class by one teacher rather than three: this format, it was argued, reinforced the unity of the subject and created the opportunity for consistent teaching and assessment. Since then the vast majority of schools have subscribed to this policy, although a significant number 'disintegrate' in second year in order to give pupils, they claim, a more clearly focused specialist preparation for S3.

The original integrated science course is gradually being phased out in order to accommodate the Science component of the common syllabus for all pupils from age 5 to age 14, as set out in the *National Guidelines – Environmental Studies 5–14* (SOED, 1993). In Science 5–14, knowledge and understanding is grouped under the broad headings of Understanding Living Things and the Processes of Life, Understanding Energy and Forces and Understanding Earth and Space. The general process skills to be developed and assessed are Planning, Collecting Evidence, Recording and Presenting, Interpreting and Evaluating and Developing Informed Attitudes.

Pupils entering S1 in future years should have received a broadly similar experience in science, at least in terms of subject content and emphasis on investigative skills. They will differ in the progress they have achieved so far and this will be reflected in the assessment levels to which their primary teachers have assigned them in the various categories. In the past teachers adopted a 'clean slate' approach to pupils entering secondary school. It was assumed most pupils would have relatively meagre knowledge of science and a fresh start was appropriate. This will no longer apply as pupils are systematically exposed to science from the age of five years when they enter primary education.

The introduction of Science 5–14 has stimulated a review of existing practice in S1–S2 and reappraisal of methodology. If there is to be natural progression in science skills and knowledge across the primary/secondary interface, teachers will have to decide whether the current policy of wholly mixed ability classes in S1 is now appropriate. In Her Majesty's Inspectorate (HMI) report *Effective Learning and Teaching in Scottish Schools: The Sciences* (SOED, 1994) it was suggested that 'teachers should consider the formation of ability sets as a means of narrowing the range of levels of understanding in one class, thus allowing a more ready focus on the needs of individual pupils.' It is also important that pupils moving from P7 to S1 do not experience an abrupt change in methodology but benefit from the sharing of good practice.

S3–S4 SCIENCE

Science, or at least one of the individual sciences, is a compulsory subject for pupils in S3–S4. Pupils are assessed in S2 and advised as to the most suitable courses for them to follow in S3. About one third of the S3 cohort takes Standard Grade Science. Course content consists of four compulsory core topics, namely, Healthy and Safe Living, An Introduction to Materials, Energy and its Uses and A Study of Environments.

While Biology, Chemistry and Physics offer certification at General and Credit levels only, Science caters for the full spread of ability and includes certification at Foundation level. Standard Grade Science classes tend to be composites; Foundation/General or General/Credit.

Standard Grade Science is the only option available for pupils who were relatively unsuccessful in S2 Science. As a result Science has to overcome the perception that it is the 'poor relation' of the individual sciences in order to attract the more able pupils who would be candidates for Credit level awards. A second factor which has dissuaded the more academic pupil from the option of a Credit Science course has been the lack of a genuinely appropriate follow-on course. There is no Higher Science course. When the SEB consulted teachers on providing such a course the proposal received a lukewarm response and had to be shelved. Specialist teachers were not convinced that a Higher Science course was sufficiently desirable to warrant the extra training and effort which would be needed to equip them with the necessary knowledge and expertise.

SCIENCE BEYOND S4

Higher Still developments have redesigned and brought together the various SEB academic courses and Scottish Vocational Educational Council (SCOTVEC) modules (more than fifty with a science bias) to form one coherent framework for the Sciences.

Implementation of the proposals ought to redress the problem of Standard Grade

Science being a course with a 'dead-end'. In future pupils with that particular qualification can progress into Intermediate 1, Intermediate 2 or even Higher courses depending on the grades which they achieved. An Intermediate 1 course in a science subject is the natural progression for a student with a Foundation award from Standard Grade Science. In some cases a more appropriate step would be into Access 3 Science, a coherent group of modules comprising Telecommunications, Practical Electricity, Health and Technology and Everyday Chemistry.

METHODOLOGIES IN SCIENCE

Most Science courses are organised, within the classroom, around a resource based learning (RBL) model. The movement to a child-centred rather than teacher-centred mode, received its initial impetus with the publication of Curriculum Paper 7 (CP7) and the subsequent national worksheet scheme which was produced to support the Integrated Science Course (ISC). The introduction of worksheets was intended to relieve the teacher of much practical instruction and to create the opportunity for differentiated teaching and learning. It was envisaged that each pupil would progress smoothly through a programme of work at a level and at a pace commensurate with his/her ability.

The ISC worksheet system was structured on the 'core and options' model and assumed classes consisted of basically three types of pupil; the 'average' pupil followed a preset programme of activities; 'less able' and 'more able' pupils could be diverted from the core into remedial or extension work as and when appropriate.

RBL self pacing methods feature quite strongly in Standard Grade Science courses. Clearly in composite classes it is essential to have a worksheet scheme which allows pupils to follow the different learning pathways and at different rates of progress. Teachers also consider it important to have a resource-based setup in order to cope effectively with classes where pupil attendance, and consequently continuity of teaching learning, can be irregular.

Over the years concern has been expressed at the increasing dependence on the worksheet as the major learning resource at the expense of other methods. However a note of optimism was struck in the HMI report *Effective Learning and Teaching* (SOED, 1994) which suggested that 'the problem of unselective use of worksheets at Standard Grade has largely receded and most departments are now adopting a better balance of approaches, a policy which is also affecting S1/S2 course.' Such a trend is very encouraging.

INNOVATIONS AND CHANGES

One of the significant developments over the past few decades has been the change from norm-referenced to criterion-referenced assessment. The listing of specific objectives for each of the fifteen sections of the Integrated Science Course signalled a change towards a scheme where pupils were given clear learning outcomes to achieve rather than having their performances graded by comparison with their colleagues.

The Dunning Report (HMSO, 1977) further supported the notion of criterion-referencing. Learning outcomes were identified for the Standard Grade Science course and set out by the Scottish Examinations Board in Arrangements for Standard Grade Science (SEB, 1987) .

Learning outcomes are not confined to knowledge and understanding but include objectives for process-based skills in the problem solving and practical abilities domains.

The internal assessment of practical abilities has been a feature of Standard Grade Science from the outset. Initially the emphasis was on basic skills with assessment based on items produced in the research project Techniques for the Assessment Of Practical Skills in Science (TAPS 1). Later inference skills were added to the practical assessment requirements using a bank of inference item-sets. These two developments were finally subsumed within the assessment of open-ended practical investigations, based on fourteen TAPS 3 objectives (Bryce et al., 1991)

For several years the desire for autonomy within each SEB Subject Panel led to the four Standard Grade Sciences operating slightly different schemes for assessing the same investigative skill objectives. Happily that anomaly is now being removed and a common assessment scheme will apply in the future. In addition to carrying out two formal investigations, pupils in Standard Grade Science are also expected to demonstrate mastery of eight basic laboratory techniques.

ASSESSMENT, REPORTING AND CERTIFICATION

There is no national external assessment of pupils in S1–S2 Science. Schools administer continuous assessment for the purposes of recording progress and reporting to parents. With the gradual implementation of Science 5–14, pupils' achievements will be monitored and reported in terms of levels of attainment, A – E. The average pupil would be expected to attain level E by the end of S2.

A pupil's performance in Standard Grade Science is assessed under three distinct elements: Knowledge and Understanding (KU), Problem Solving (PS) and Practical Abilities (PA). Questions in the external examination papers are weighted equally between KU and PS. A candidate can be entered for two external examination papers: either Foundation and General or General and Credit. The pupil would be awarded the higher grade achieved.

Pupils tend to score more highly on the internally assessed Practical Abilities element. This is hardly surprising, given the clearly specified nature of the exercise and the opportunity for extended practice. It was felt however that the typically higher grade obtained in PA distorted the overall profile, which included KU and PS, and thus produced an aggregate grade which was possibly a misleading measure of the pupil's capacity to handle more advanced study in the subject. As a result of consultation with schools and discussion between Scottish Qualifications Authority (SQA) Science Subject Panels it has been decided that the Practical Abilities element be reduced in weighting to one fifth of total marks rather than one third.

EVIDENCE OF THE LEVEL OF PUPILS' COMPETENCE IN SCIENCE

National surveys such as the Assessment of Achievement Programme (AAP) in Science help to provide a continuous monitoring of standards. The most recently published Report (SOEID, 1997) confirms that S2 pupils do not generally reveal the improvement in science skills which one might expect beyond P7. Why there should be this slowing down of progress is not clear but it is obviously an issue which needs to be addressed.

The Scottish edition of the Third International Mathematics and Science Study (TIMSS) Report (SOEID, 1996) compared the science knowledge and understanding of S1 and S2 pupils with that of 13-year-olds in other countries. Overall Scotland's ranking was 25th out of 38 countries at S1 and 25th out of 40 countries at S2.

One contributing factor may be a more casual attitude to systematic homework in Science compared to that in the individual sciences. According to TIMSS, the Scottish pupils spent less time doing science homework than their counterparts in almost every other country. In the case of Standard Grade Science set pupil study outwith school is even rarer: an HMI study reported that homework was an 'unusual' occurrence (SOED, 1994, p. 8).

On a more encouraging note the TIMSS study revealed that Scots 13-year-olds were relatively good on practical skills and came fourth out of a field of nineteen countries. Clearly the emphasis which is placed here on practical work in science is paying dividends.

While there is much admirable teaching and effective learning being carried out in various schools throughout the country there is clearly still no room for complacency. All concerned with Science education in Scotland have continuing 'homework' to do.

REFERENCES

Bryce,T. G. K., J. McCall, J. MacGregor, I. J. Robertson and R. A. J. Weston (1991) *TAPS 3 How to Assess Open-Ended Practical Investigations in Biology, Chemistry and Physics*, Oxford: Heinemann Educational.

SCCC (1996) *Science Education in Scottish Schools – Looking to the Future*, Dundee: SCCC.

SED (1969) *Curriculum Paper Number 7 – Science for General Education* Edinburgh: HMSO.

SEB (1987) *Standard Grade Arrangements in Science*, Dalkeith: SEB.

SOED (1993) *National Guidelines – Environmental Studies 5–14*, Edinburgh: SOED.

SOED (1994) *Effective Learning and Teaching in Scottish Schools: The Sciences*, Edinburgh: SOED.

68

Technology Education

Michael Bain

CURRICULAR DEVELOPMENT

Historically, Technical Education has been largely perceived to be the exclusive territory of less academically inclined boys. The development of the subject over the past thirty years has involved challenging this perception.

In the early 1970s core Technical Subjects consisted of Woodwork, Metalwork, Technical Drawing, Building Drawing and Applied Mechanics. In response to the report *From Secondary School to Further Education* (SED, 1963), extensive vocational courses were also offered in an effort to meet the requirements of industry and further education. The vocational elements were sometimes taught by 'instructors' from industry.

The wind of change really began with Curriculum Paper 10, published in 1972 by the Scottish Education Department (SED). It recommended the term 'Technical Education' should replace 'Technical Subjects' and suggested that the five subjects be reduced to three:

- Engineering Science replaced Applied Mechanics
- Integrated Craftwork replaced Woodwork and Metalwork and added Plastic Craft
- Technical Drawing remained
- Building Drawing was discontinued

The paper also provided encouragement for the introduction of co-education. This development was welcomed by teachers of Technical Education. Since that time, Technical teachers throughout this country have fought long and hard to promote the positive benefits of Technical and subsequently Technological Education for all. Curriculum Paper 10 contained thirteen recommendations, all of which were implemented.

It was not until 1979 that the first 'O' Grade in 'Integrated Craftwork' was introduced, the 'H' grade following in 1980. With this subject came the first introduction of design, albeit in a limited form. Following a report from the Design Council, the design factor in Technical Education became increasingly important. The report *Design Education at Secondary Level* was produced in 1980 by a working party consisting largely of designers and academics and chaired by Professor David Keith Lucas. The problem for teachers was in persuading pupils that there was indeed a designer within them. Many teachers have found it necessary to build a stock of core ideas, differentiating content and pupil input, particularly where traditional attitudes limit the clientele. There are, of course, a number of departments which now accommodate a full ability range amongst their pupils. For those pupils who develop a design capability, the rewards, in terms of personal development and satisfaction, have proved to be very great indeed. Integrated Craft later evolved to become Craft and Design.

One stated aim of the government's proposal for implementation of the Munn and Dunning reports entitled *Framework for Decision* (SED, 1982) was to improve the Technical and Vocational Education of young people. Circular 1107 was published in December 1983 by the SED. This circular announced that, acting on advice from the Scottish CCC, a further 'Technological activities' mode, although strongly argued for by the Committee on Technology (COT), would not be added to the eight proposed by the Munn committee. Instead an increased emphasis on technological activities should be pursued within the existing curriculum.

Circular 1107 announced the government's intention to introduce the new Standard Grade Craft and Design in 1985, with certification in 1987. A course in Technological Studies would be developed to replace the old Engineering Science 'O' Grade. The reason was simply that the old course content did not meet the requirements of modern society. The new Technological Studies course would include Pneumatics, Computer Numeric Control, Computer Aided Drawing, Electronic Systems, Electronic Control, and Robotics. The course would be driven by an integrated systems approach to problem solving.

The Scottish Examination Board proposed the phasing out of Technical Drawing. It was thought that drawing and graphics could be incorporated in Craft and Design and Technological Studies as required. Strong reaction from the Technology Teachers Association (Scotland) with support from industry reversed this decision. A new course with different emphasis, called Graphic Communication, was subsequently developed.

TEACHER TRAINING

Responding to a request from the SOED, and the need to prepare progressive teachers of Technological Education, Jordanhill College, as it then was, formed a partnership with the University of Glasgow to provide the Bachelor of Technological Education four year degree course to replace the Diploma in Technical Education. Similarly, Moray House developed the Bachelor of Education (Technology) with Heriot Watt University. These courses were established in 1987. In 1993 Jordanhill College became part of the University of Strathclyde and introduced the B.Ed. (Design and Technology) and the University of Glasgow formed a partnership with St Andrew's College to introduce a new Bachelor of Technological Education degree course. Although the SOEID are now asking for more and more graduates to teach in Technological Education many new graduates are forced to accept part time work and temporary contracts. Until this fundamental failure of educational provision is addressed it will be difficult to attract a continuing stream of suitable candidates. On the positive side more women than ever before, currently about 20 per cent of the total intake, are attracted to initial teacher education courses in Technological Education. Many believe these graduates will become role models for future generations and will go some way towards attracting more girls to study technological subjects.

IMPLICATIONS OF THE NEW TECHNOLOGICAL EDUCATION CURRICULUM

The introduction of Technological Studies was possibly the most significant development in Technical Education this century. It required the acquisition of much new knowledge amongst teachers. Pupils were given an opportunity to use their own initiative and ideas to develop solutions to problems. Indeed pupils were encouraged to bring real life problems to the class and there, under the guidance of the teacher, to explore and develop possible solutions, using and integrating all aspects of the new technologies. The development of the new Technological Studies course took some three years of hard work and dedication. Expertise was drawn from HMI and experienced teachers to form a Joint Working Party. The Scottish Schools Science Equipment Research Centre (SSSERC) provided much of the support material for teachers of the new Technological Studies programme. The role of SSERC (Science was dropped from the title in 1989) should, however, in no way detract from the vital contribution of both Jordanhill and Moray House in providing high quality inservice training for an enthusiastic vanguard of teachers of Technological Education. Along with the new Standard Grade Courses the SEB produced some excellent short (forty-hour) courses in order to make technological education more accessible to all. These ran alongside numerous SCOTVEC modules.

Graphic Communication began to replace Technical Drawing in the early 1990s with the first Standard Grade Graphic Communication examination being offered in 1993 at Foundation General and Credit level. The first Higher came in 1994. Engineering Drawing continues to form part of the syllabus as does Geometric Drawing. The addition of presentation skills and Computer Aided Drawing (CAD) at once broadened the relevance and appeal of this subject area. Initial Teacher Education (ITE) institutions met the challenge of providing inservice training for the new aspects of Graphic Communication. Additionally the existing expertise in school Art Departments was recognised and widely used to provide some very valuable in house inservice. Whereas Technological Studies provided a bit of a breakthrough in the gender barrier, it is Graphic Communication which seems to have captured the imagination and gained the approval of girls. A ratio of 60 per cent boys to 40 per cent girls is common in Graphic Communication classes.

TVEI

The Technical and Vocational Education Initiative (TVEI) was sponsored by the Government's Manpower Services Commission (MSC). TVEI was phased into Scottish Education via the local authorities from 1984. Its philosophy was to stimulate the provision of Technical and Vocational Education for 14–18 year olds. Initially seen as a potential threat to the comprehensive education system, TVEI's financial backing, some £14 million nationwide (SOED, 1989), served to persuade the sceptics. Eventually all departments found that they had a technological or vocational perspective and joined the initiative. Although this was not the sole source of funding, Technological Studies was one of the beneficiaries. The basic set-up cost of just one 'Technology Room' was in the region of £20,000.

RESOURCING IMPLICATIONS

Technological Studies began in 1988. The first Standard Grade Technological Studies examination was offered in 1990 at Foundation General and Credit level. The first Higher came in 1991 with the Certificate in Sixth Year Studies (CSYS) available from 1992. Again a great deal of excellent support material was developed by SSERC working in concert with the teachers and ITE institutions. Coursework was developed at regional, local and in many cases, individual school level. After the BBC micro-computers a variety of platforms including

Acorn, Apple Mac, R. M. Nimbus and other PC systems were purchased independently by schools. The opportunity of large scale savings on hardware and software by introducing or even recommending a single national platform was missed. The success of Technological Studies continues to depend, very much, on individual teachers and enlightened school administrations. Of course Technological Education, by its very nature, has always required a significant capital expenditure. Keeping abreast of current technology requires discerning investment and is not always popular with school administrators. During the late 1980s and early 1990s devolved management of resources (DMR) and school development planning, like twin carburettors of change, fuelled subsidiarity from regional and local authorities to individual schools. The result, for Technological Education, was to give more choice to schools on the degree to which they would be prepared to meet the initial set up cost which would enable them to offer the new technological curriculum.

TEACHING AND LEARNING STYLES

The old Woodwork and Metalwork classes generally took the whole class along making the same models and doing the same thing at approximately the same time. Craft and Design was the first major innovation resulting from the substantial changes in curriculum content. It had a significant impact on teaching and learning styles. A pupil centred, resource based approach evolved to support design. Pupils were required to pursue individual 'design and make' projects, and thus individual and group teaching became necessary. Teachers, for whom differentiation referred to that part of a vehicle drive system which allowed it to drive two wheels at different speeds round corners, found themselves introducing the principle to their teaching and learning strategies.

Engineering Science had lent itself to a didactic teaching style with the odd group investigation activity. Technological Studies provided impetus to review teaching and learning. For reasons both pedagogical and pragmatic it just had to be pupil centred. Scarcity of expensive resources encouraged paired and, occasionally, group learning in rotation. The educational success of such strategies soon became apparent. Didactic methods are all but replaced by activity-based teaching and learning now. The opportunity to put learning into context for pupils has added to the excitement and relevance of the subject.

Graphic Communication, while retaining some whole class teaching, which was the predominant strategy for teaching Technical and Engineering Drawing, has been developed to promote a range of teaching and learning styles. Collaboration between pupils is encouraged, leading to the production of individual folio presentations. The particular issues associated with computing skills are addressed through a range of methodologies including individual and group teaching as well as resource based learning packages.

STANDARD GRADE ASSESSMENT

Common to all the new Standard Grade courses was the introduction of internal assessment. Craft and Design requires that 'Designing' and 'Practical Abilities' are both assessed internally with the possibility of external moderation. Only one-third of marks in the form of 'Knowledge and Understanding' are externally assessed. In the case of Graphic Communication 'Illustration and Presentation', in the form of a folio presentation, represents just one-third of the marks and is assessed internally with the possibility of external moderation. Both 'Knowledge and Interpretation' and 'Drawing Ability' are assessed externally. Technological Studies internally assesses 40 per cent of the marks by a 'Problem Solving' report. A further 60 per cent of marks is allocated for 'Knowledge and Understanding' and 'Technological Communication'. These are addressed together in the final examination paper. Internal moderation has been well supported by the introduction of extended grade related criteria (EGRC). Diligent use of EGRC not only works as an excellent guide for marking but can also help pupils to focus on assessable elements.

THE FUTURE OF TECHNOLOGY EDUCATION

The introduction of 5–14 Environmental Studies (ES) continues to concentrate minds in both primary and secondary education. ES encompasses Science, Social Subjects, Technology, Health Education and Information Technology. Some secondary schools looked to existing practice to see if adjustments could be made. ES, however, embraces a whole new cross-curricular philosophy for Technology based on two outcomes. These are 'Understanding and Using Technology in Society' and 'Understanding and Using the Design Process'. While both these outcomes lend themselves to a discrete approach they also require examination of the relationship between technology and its associated components. Much work has already been undertaken by both primary and secondary school teachers.

In 1996 a Technology Review Group produced a document entitled *Technology Education in Scottish Schools*. The group comprised some twenty people from diverse backgrounds but included just one teacher of Technological Education. In the event the document provided a framework designed to complement existing provision and to extend Technology Education to every corner of the curriculum so that children might access the greatest possible diversity of perspectives on technological capability. Essentially the report defines technological capability and recognises the importance of preparing future generations to live purposefully in and to contribute to a society which shapes and is shaped by technology.

Higher Still has provided an opportunity to re-examine the structure and, to a lesser extent, the content of the three discrete areas of Technological Education. There has been more consultation with teachers and their associations, such as the Technology Teachers Association (Scotland), for this initiative than ever before. It was decided to retain three discrete subject areas and to add Practical Craft Skills. All courses will now have a modular structure. The recommendation that there should be an Advanced Higher in all three subject areas and an extra layer, in the form of Intermediate II, makes bi-level teaching, at least, seem a very likely development in the future. Of the three subjects currently on offer only Technological Studies offers a Certificate of Sixth Year Studies (CSYS) equivalent to the Advanced Higher. Since Higher Still will develop a modular approach throughout, previous short courses will become obsolete and all future qualifications will be awarded by the Scottish Qualifications Authority (SQA)

The future of any society depends now, as never before, on its technological capability. No part of the school curriculum will be more important to future generations than technology. The nation's future role, not just in Europe, but in the world, will depend on getting it right.

REFERENCES

CCC (1985) *The place of technology in the secondary curriculum*: final report of the CCC's Committee on Technology, Dundee: CCC.
Design Council (1980) *Design education at secondary level*, London: The Design Council.

Lindsay, W. J. and G. J. Murdoch (1996) *The Scottish experience*, in Proceedings of the ACET
    conference, Perth, Western Australia: Australian Council for Education through Technology.
SCCC (1996) *Technology education in Scottish schools*: a statement of position from Scottish CCC
    Dundee: SCCC.
SED (1972) *Technical education in Scottish schools*: Curriculum paper 10, Edinburgh: HMSO.
SOED (1989) *Learning and teaching in TVEI in Scotland*: a report by HM Inspectors of Schools
    Edinburgh: HMSO.

IX

Further and Higher Education

69

Current Priorities in Further Education

Joyce Johnston

THE CINDERELLA SECTOR?

The further education sector is of relatively recent origin. Founded largely in the earlier part of this century to meet the apprentice training needs of Scottish manufacturing, technical colleges have metamorphosed in the latter half of the century into institutions offering continuing education for all of the post-16 population. With approximately half of their activity accounted for by full-time students, and offering educational provision ranging from basic literacy and numeracy skills through to degree and post-graduate courses, the forty-three colleges now offer a local, accessible, 'second chance' for post-school education and training. Because of their focus on vocational education, delivered through the National Certificate (NC) and Higher National Certificate/Diploma (HNC/HND) curriculum, colleges constitute an alternative to S5 and S6 in school for many young people. Similarly, because of a rich network of articulation agreements, which permit students to progress from HNC/HND courses into the later stages of degrees, the colleges constitute a local and accessible alternative to undergraduate years 1 or 2 at university. Colleges are also increasingly extending their mission to help those in the community who need a second chance to learn.

This continuum of educational provision offered by Further Education (FE) colleges is one of their strengths. Conversely however, it presents one of their major challenges, as the overlap with other sectors means that the FE sector has little distinct identity in the national consciousness. Given also that education policy-makers are in the main products of the university sector, it is perhaps understandable that those in the FE sector often believe their comprehensive role to be unrecognised and under-valued.

Colleges however point to the successes of the sector in the last ten to fifteen years – a new, competence-based, accessible curriculum satisfactorily introduced, major contributions to government skills targets being made, access to higher education hugely increased, efficiency and effectiveness improved, local communities supported in their regeneration – and look with excitement, and a growing sense of identity and destiny, towards their future. This chapter considers some of the principal issues and priorities which at present confront the further education sector in preparing for and shaping its destiny (see also Chapter 5).

PARTNERSHIPS

Further education is unusual in the Scottish education system in that, while it offers a continuum of vocational education and training opportunities for the post-16 population, all parts of its provision overlap with other sectors. It therefore operates within a complex pattern of relationships, within which it has been beneficial to develop collaborative alliances. These partnerships are generally predicated on mutual benefit, and a need to rationalise the use of scarce resources. The pattern of relationships is illustrated and described below in terms of types of provision and main providers. (See Figure 69.1)

Figure 69.1 Relationships in Further Education

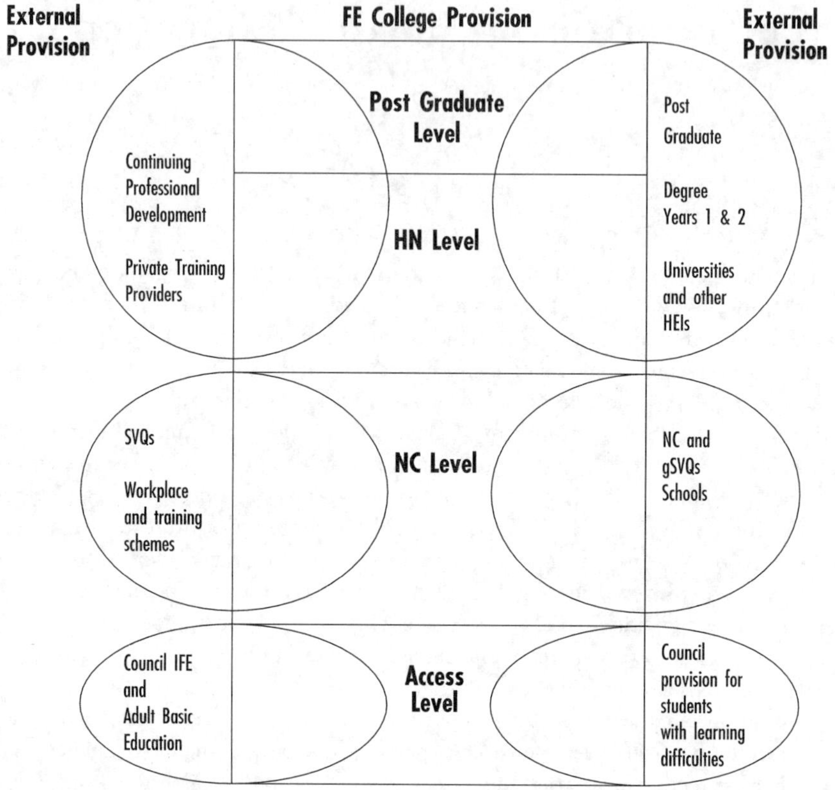

The maintenance or development of the partnerships is a priority for the sector. Each is now examined in its context.

PARTNERSHIPS – SCHOOLS

Vocational education and training as offered by further education colleges was radically altered in the 1980s by the introduction of the National Certificate (NC) – a competence-based, modularised curriculum which permitted colleges autonomy to develop courses to meet local needs, and which encouraged internal continuous assessment and student-centred teaching methods. Approximately one third of the volume of learning activity delivered by FE colleges is now based on the NC – although the proportion varies widely among colleges (SOEID, 1997).

National Certificate is also provided in schools for pupils aged sixteen and over as an alternative to 'O' or 'H' Grades, and colleges and schools have worked together to use NC modules to enrich the school curriculum. In many parts of Scotland strong partnerships have been established between schools and colleges, with pupils attending a portion of their week in the local college to undertake modules not available at school. General Scottish Vocational Qualifications (gSVQs), introduced by the Scottish Vocational Education Council (SCOTVEC) in the late 1980s, continued this trend. They provided a common framework for full-time courses across the country, incorporating core skills, with delivery often in part in school and in part in college. This shared delivery model will be built upon to assist with the delivery of the Higher Still curriculum.

School/college partnerships were tested by the incorporation of colleges in 1993, and the transfer of funding responsibility for colleges from regional councils to the Scottish Office Education and Industry Department (SOEID). The disappointment of some local authorities over the removal of colleges from their domain led to a degree of cooling in relationships, which in some instances was exacerbated by uncertainty over future college funding arrangements. Once it became clear however that colleges would continue to be funded for school pupil participation in their provision, colleges generally worked to strengthen the partnerships. The value of the extended resource which colleges could add to the post-16 curriculum was recognised by both parties. The value of introducing school pupils to the possibility of study at college was also recognised.

Funding and other arrangements for colleges (and schools) however now create further potential tension in the partnership. Staffing structures in schools are related to pupil numbers; the recurrent funding of colleges depends upon their success in attracting students. School staff are required to be registered with the General Teaching Council (GTC); college staff are not so required (although many have registered), and this can complicate issues of who teaches what and where. It is to the credit of both sectors in the partnership that generally the patterns of school/college attendance are determined by the needs of students, rather than such difficulties.

Higher Still, the major reform of the upper secondary curriculum to be introduced in 1999, will pose an additional challenge to these partnerships, as well as an implementation challenge to colleges. Colleges face substantial curriculum development, and must attempt to retain the present flexibility of internal assessment within new joint external arrangements under the auspices of the Scottish Qualifications Authority (SQA). Joint school/college programmes for S5 and S6 pupils are being planned. Colleges will have an important role in providing access to expensive training resources for school pupils, to ensure the possibility of a robust vocational alternative to the hitherto academic Higher Grade qualification. It is upon the success of school/college partnerships that the achievement of parity of esteem between vocational and academic routes post-16 will depend.

PARTNERSHIPS – HIGHER EDUCATION (HE)

The relationships between Higher Education Institutions (HEIs) and FE colleges are also at a significant point in their development. It has been a phenomenon of the last ten years, when SCOTVEC introduced local flexibility for the development of unitised HN courses, that colleges have responded to increasing demand for higher education by a large-scale development programme at HE level. At approximately the same time the Scottish Wider Access Programme (SWAP) facilitated growth in the extent of FE/HEI links. From these activities a rich network of articulation agreements between the two sectors has developed.

At the present time, it is common for any one FE college to have articulation links with several universities, such that students from HN courses have the opportunity to progress into the second (from HNC) or third year (from HND) of a degree course at a choice of universities. In addition, some FE colleges have obtained validation from a university to deliver degree level work. This is usually at Ordinary degree level, as a third year following successful completion of an HND. Such provision operates under the university's quality assurance mechanisms.

The quantity of full-time HE work undertaken in FE colleges now constitutes some 21 per cent of all HE in Scotland, and a considerably higher percentage (51 per cent) in part-time modes of attendance (SOEID, 1997). Its high rate of increase, and consequent increase in the cost of student support, led to a cap on full-time growth which was instigated in 1994–5 academic year, and which persists to date. Part-time numbers have continued to increase.

In some instances, articulation developments such as those described above have led to the creation of formal, even exclusive, association agreements between a university and an FE college, and it has been mooted that such agreements might be the precursor to a future merger of institutions, and in time of the two sectors. The University of the Highlands and Islands is an interesting model of development in this context, as it is planned that the University will be created from the combined HE activity of a consortium of institutions, mainly FE colleges.

It was within such a context of FE/HE relationships that the Committee of Inquiry into Higher Education, chaired by Lord Dearing, was established in 1996. The report of this committee gives substantial and significant support to the role of FE colleges in providing a cost-effective alternative route into and through higher education, and recommends that the cap on HN growth be lifted immediately in FE. For Scotland, the Report also recommends the creation of a Further Education Funding Council (SFEFC), which is envisaged as sharing a common executive and some membership with the Scottish Higher Education Funding Council (SHEFC). This is viewed as possibly an interim arrangement, leading to the eventual creation of a tertiary education funding council.

These recommendations of the Committee have generally been welcomed in the FE sector, and a current priority is to influence government to remove the growth cap as soon as possible. Action on this item will need to take account of a further Dearing recommendation for a national framework of qualifications, and of a current SQA review of HN qualifications. Subsequent development of HN provision will be related to the needs of industry in any one college's locality, but may also be shaped by government policy on student support, which is discussed below.

Proposals by the Scottish Committee of the Dearing Inquiry to create a SFEFC have also been welcomed, but the future possibility of a tertiary funding council is viewed with some caution. The role of FE colleges in meeting the educational and training needs of all sectors of their local community is central to their mission, and there is concern that their role in widening participation among the less able would be under-valued and under-resourced in a tertiary system.

The recommendation of the Dearing Committee that FE colleges should not develop further degree-level provision is also relevant to the development of FE/HE partnerships. Colleges which have an interest in developing such provision to meet local demand are presently arguing that further limited growth should be permitted, particularly for part-time students. There are at present twenty-five further education colleges located in Scottish towns which have no degree-awarding higher education institution.

Government policy decisions on these issues will be major determinants of the shape, structure and nature of FE and HE provision in Scotland in the next millennium. Many senior staff in further education in Scotland see potentially strong parallels with the 'two-plus-two' structure of higher education in the United States, where community colleges provide the first two years of HE for local students, who can then progress to a regional university for the remaining two years of a degree.

PARTNERSHIPS – INDUSTRY, UNITARY COUNCILS, AND LOCAL ENTERPRISE COMPANIES (LECs)

Local industry, local Councils, and LECs constitute the other major agencies with which colleges work in partnership.

The Further and Higher Education (Scotland) Act 1992, under which incorporated colleges operate, requires that at least half of the members of college boards of management be representatives of local employers. Colleges, since the days of apprentice training, have a long history of close links with industry in planning and delivering programmes to meet employers' needs. Colleges often operate through a strong structure of advisory committees to seek involvement by local companies in course review and development. It is common also that they actively seek involvement in the development and support of the small business sector through representative organisations such as Chambers of Commerce and the Federation of Small Businesses. Development of course provision to ensure that successful students are equipped with the knowledge and skills required by employers is a constant priority for colleges. It is also a requirement for SQA approval of courses.

The Investors in People standard is a kitemark awarded to companies and organisations which can demonstrate successful investment in business development through staff development. Its introduction has heightened companies' focus on training, and increased industry professionalism in seeking best value and quality in their training purchases. A recent study (Neil and Mullin, 1996) into the purchasing pattern for training by companies has shown that there is significant competition for colleges from the private training sector in this commercial market. The challenge for colleges now is to respond to this competition.

The re-organisation of local government in Scotland in 1996, and subsequent election of a new government, have accorded greater significance to colleges' relationships with local authorities. Colleges increasingly identify themselves as having a major role in local economic regeneration and development, and seek to cooperate with councils in community development initiatives. Activities in support of regeneration can include support for small business development, provision of 'incubator' units for new businesses, enterprise elements in course curricula, participation in inward investment initiatives, and the provision of training for community activists.

Councils are also often major employers in a college's locality, and hence significant customers, as well as continuing since pre-incorporation days to be providers of services such as payroll, legal and property maintenance. The development or maintenance of a harmonious and mutually-helpful relationship with the local council is therefore of importance to any college.

Similarly LECs are significant agencies for colleges. As organisers of major national training programmes for young people and for unemployed adults, LECs are a source of business and hence finance for many colleges. The cordiality of relationships between colleges and LECs however varies considerably across Scotland, and strategic partnerships are rare. Colleges generally believe themselves to be under-valued by the local enterprise network, and even where there is significant joint endeavour, colleges seek to strengthen and improve the relationship.

In the case of both local councils and LECs, legislation demands cooperation. It is a required part of colleges' development planning procedures that they consult with both agencies when drawing up the strategic plan for the college for the next three years. Similarly legislation requires that there be a LEC representative on the Boards of Management of colleges. These requirements however may well be overtaken by the stated aim of the new government in its 1997 manifesto to establish a 'strategic framework to improve co-ordination between colleges and maximise access to all courses without needless competition'.

COMPETITION, COLLABORATION, AND A STRATEGIC FRAMEWORK

In the period since incorporation colleges have developed considerable autonomy, and have responded dynamically to the pressure to expand. This pressure has been exerted partly by demand for their services, but also by a new funding methodology designed to smooth the wide variation in levels of funding discovered when colleges emerged from local authority funding. Recurrent funding is now determined on a historical basis by colleges' success in attracting and retaining students, and convergence of the level of funding has largely been achieved. Colleges are now considerably more efficient, delivering a higher volume of work at a lower unit of funding. A search for financial stability during this period of declining funding has caused many colleges to revise, and in some cases reduce, their portfolio of courses.

In these first years since incorporation, and in the absence of any controlling influence as had been exerted by local authorities, pressure to increase the volume of activity in colleges resulted in considerable inter-sector competition. This has been particularly the case in some areas of Scotland where several colleges are in close proximity, such as Glasgow. However in many instances colleges have also sought to collaborate in joint developments (e.g. Glasgow Telecolleges Network, Fife colleges in FAST-TRAC – the local variant of SkillSeekers), and at national level have formed the Association of Scottish Colleges. The Association is increasingly active in providing a national voice for the sector, and in coordinating its influence on policy.

There remains however, at government level, a concern that a greater measure of control or at least influence over the development plans of colleges is required. Ministers have publicly expressed disquiet over what they perceive as the negative consequences of excessive competition, and concerns have also been expressed by agencies such as the Construction Industry Training Board about the balance of subject-related provision across the country.

The need for the number of colleges which now exists has been questioned. There have been forty-three incorporated colleges since 1 April 1993, and it has been argued that the sector could achieve greater efficiencies if the number of colleges were reduced. Expenditure by each college on an administrative staff structure to manage finance, personnel etc. is cited as a possible opportunity area for savings. Some collaboration between colleges in these areas has been achieved, and it is now generally accepted that in the major cities some collaborative models, perhaps even full merger, will emerge. However there continue to be concerns about the danger of damage to diversity and accessibility (particularly in rural areas) which would result from the loss of a locally accountable FE presence.

The response of ministers to these concerns has been, in addition to the manifesto statement described above, to announce the creation of a Strategic Initiatives Fund through which colleges can access some funding to assist with collaborative ventures. The creation of a strategic framework will however constitute a significant steer for the operation of FE colleges in Scotland in future. No further details on this are available at the time of writing.

To provide a better sense of direction and purpose than the sector has to date received since incorporation, such a framework will need to address many of the issues identified in this chapter, in particular:

- coordination between colleges
- collaboration with schools, particularly in Higher Still developments
- the role of FE colleges in HE, and relationships with HEIs
- relationships with Councils and LECs
- the size and structure of the sector, and collaboration within it
- the role of the sector in widening participation in lifelong learning
- funding arrangements to support and encourage the above priorities.

NEW GOVERNMENT TRAINING SCHEMES

Further education colleges have an extensive record of involvement in government training schemes, particularly those directed at raising skill levels and tackling unemployment in a period of rapid social and technological change. From the early days of the Training Opportunities Scheme in the 1970s (a programme for unemployed adults), through the Youth Opportunities Programme and the Youth Training Scheme in the 1980s, and Training for Work and Skillseekers in the 1990s, to name but a few, colleges have played a significant role in working in partnership with government agencies to modernise the country's skills base. This has been at a cost.

The brief list above gives a flavour of the short-term nature of all government training schemes; the accompanying funding arrangements have often meant that colleges have had to take a short-term view of investment in human and material resourcing. Capital funding in particular has been miniscule. Despite these resourcing difficulties, however, colleges have been responsive and provided a large proportion of the off-the-job training needs of trainees on a variety of schemes.

It is therefore not surprising that, in announcing its plans to reduce the numbers of young people and adults dependent on welfare, the new government acknowledges the important role to be played by further education colleges. The Welfare to Work Programme, which includes a New Deal for unemployed young people aged 18–24, a New Deal for adults unemployed for more than two years, and New Deals for lone parents and disabled people, calls upon colleges to provide a full-time education and training option for participants, as well as providing underpinning learning for the other options of the schemes. Other elements of the government's policy – a new youth training scheme for 16–18s at present titled Target 2000, and a right to study one day per week for young people in work, will also require significant participation by colleges. Indeed, without the volume of training able to be delivered in colleges, the programmes could not happen.

Government's preferred model for the delivery of Welfare to Work programmes is one of partnership between all the agencies involved, on a regional basis. Agencies in any one locality are likely to include council, LEC, private industry, chambers of commerce, careers and guidance services, and voluntary organisations. The challenge which lies ahead for these partnerships is one of designing high quality programmes to create sustainable employability among trainees who may well be reluctant participants. This task of course has to be carried out in a context where the partnerships themselves do not create jobs.

THE MISSION OF WIDENING PARTICIPATION

There is ample research evidence to show that education and training post-school has been largely demanded by and provided to those who have already achieved reasonable levels of qualification (Steedman and Green, 1996). Clear links exist between lack of educational achievement and social disadvantage. Moreover, low levels of economic activity are linked to low expectations of or plans for future participation in learning (NIACE, 1996). It is argued in the Kennedy Report that the social case for widening participation in learning is irresistible, both because of the transformative power of learning to the individual, and because of the damage to the fabric of the community from the existence of a growing underclass (FEFC, 1997).

Together with community education services, further education colleges constitute the sector of the education system which can and does address this issue. Colleges have long made provision for disadvantaged groups in the community – disabled people, women returners to education, ethnic groups – and many operate outreach centres in community facilities which are designed to create an unthreatening and welcoming first step back into learning activity. The National Institute for Adult and Continuing Education (NIACE) report noted above however shows that there is enormous unmet national need – with 53 per cent of individuals in social classes D and E taking no part in learning since leaving school, compared to 19 per cent in social classes A and B. While many in the further education service cherish this societal service aspect of their role, the difficulties for colleges in expanding activity to meet needs lie in the high financial cost of such provision (often necessarily delivered in small groups), and the financial problems of the students themselves.

STUDENT SUPPORT

Financial support for students attending a further education college at present may come from bursaries administered by the college, student grants administered by the Student Awards Agency for Scotland, student loans administered by the Student Loans Company, access funds provided to colleges for disbursement to needy students, local council and other hardship funds, Job Seekers Allowance, Income Support, Disabled Student's Allowance, housing benefit, and other benefits. To this list must be added the support arrangements still to be finalised under the New Deal, and the Workskills pilot which in Glasgow is affording an interesting test of the effects of allowing unemployed people to stay on Job Seekers allowance while engaged in full-time FE.

While no one student is eligible for all of the above, for any one student there is often a confusing range of potential sources of finance. These interact on one another, sometimes, because of their regulations, in unexpected ways. Leaving to one side the adequacy of support in terms of amount of money, the confusion of arrangements constitutes a significant disincentive for adults to return to learning, particularly if they have dependants. It is greatly to their credit that so many adult students do attempt to penetrate this maze by returning to learning.

It has been announced that from 1998, full-time higher education students in further education will be required to contribute towards the cost of their tuition, on a means-tested basis. At the same time, student grants will be phased out and replaced only by means-tested loans. There are serious concerns within the FE sector, as elsewhere, that this requirement will be a further major disincentive for adults to return to learning. It may also make continuing education much less attractive to school-leavers choosing between short-term jobs and a longer-term commitment to higher education. Colleges will seek to address this issue by curriculum delivery patterns which allow for part-time employment and part-time study to a greater extent than before. Unfortunately, neither the Dearing Committee of Inquiry nor government has offered much incentive to part-time participation.

The government has announced a tax and benefits review to be undertaken as part of the New Deal. It will be a priority for colleges to work with government to simplify arrangements, and develop a more streamlined student support system which encourages wider and increased participation.

THE FUNDING OF FURTHER EDUCATION – STABILITY/INSTABILITY AND INADEQUACY

In 1993, on incorporation, further education colleges moved from funding by local authorities to funding by the Scottish Office Education and Industry Department. Due to the wide variation in funding levels provided by the authorities, (from £140 to £280 per SUM in 1993–4), it was necessary to develop a new funding methodology based on a common unit of measurement – the SUM (Student Unit of Measurement – equivalent to forty hours of student study time). The methodology is a distribution mechanism, allocating shares of the total quantum of funds available for FE according to each college's share of the national total SUMs in the previous academic year (e.g. allocations for 1997–98 were based on SUMs delivered in 1995–6). Given the historical variation in funding levels described, the immediate and full implementation of this methodology would have resulted in a major redistribution of resources across the sector, with catastrophic consequences for some colleges. Ministers of the previous government therefore adopted a cautious and gradual approach to implementation, over a period of five financial years.

During the five-year period of implementation, the funding of colleges has been affected in four main ways. Firstly, the relative generosity (or stringency) of previous local authority funding affected significantly the extent to which a college would gain or lose funds under the new system. Secondly, this effect was either compounded or mitigated by the success of the college in increasing its volume of activity at a rate higher than the average. Thirdly, the extent of any growth in the overall quantum could act to lessen losses, and, finally, a decision to apply a 'safety net' in the final stages of implementation, to protect colleges from major losses, had a smoothing effect.

While aiming to achieve, and obtaining, stability in the sector as a whole – i.e. no college closures – the implementation of the methodology has created instability for individual colleges. One of the effects has been to create heavy pressure for growth, with consequent demands on staff for higher productivity. In this regard policy makers would regard the methodology as successful, with substantial increases achieved in the volume of work undertaken by colleges. For many however this pressure applied at the same time as the need to cut costs, and industrial relations throughout the sector have suffered from the unrelenting drive for efficiency.

Systematic planning for the medium to longer term has proved impossible, as the outcome of each funding round depends not only on a college's efforts, but on the success of all other colleges too, and is impossible to predict. A fundamental review of the methodology is now underway, and the sector seeks as a high priority a move towards a contractual basis for funding, related to each college's development plan, and a more reliable level of funding per SUM, in order to provide a firmer base for longer-term planning.

The quantum of funds available for further education is a major cause of concern. Table 69.2 illustrates the declining amount of funding per unit of activity.

Table 69.2   Funding in Further Education

	Recurrent Grant	Total SUMs	Funding per SUM (delivered in same year)
1994–5	£223,950,000	1,528,369	£146.53
1995–6	£229,700,000	1,667,040	£137.79
1996–7	£232,948,000	1,767,062	£131.83
1997–8	£231,160,000	1,873,086	£123.41

Note: 6% increase in SUMs assumed in 1996–7 and 1997–8 – actual figures may be higher

While recurrent grant has been in substantial decline in real terms, capital grant, other than for UHI, has reduced sharply – from £16 million allocated in 1994–5, to £5.4 million for just four projects in 1996–7. Although the amount of recurrent grant per SUM has reduced by 16 per cent in cash terms since incorporation, SOEID now assumes that it will cover the capital as well as recurrent costs of colleges. The decline in the overall quantum of funding for FE since incorporation is therefore even greater than that illustrated above.

Capital work is now expected to be resourced from recurrent grant, or the Private Finance Initiative, or by borrowing – with its attendant risk. Some assistance from other sources such as the European Regional Development Fund may be available. Meanwhile many further education colleges are housed in buildings with substantial refurbishment and repair needs. Student facilities continue to be suitable only to the needs of the former part-time population of colleges, rather than to the present full-time, often mature, substantially HE, population. From the crumbling concrete of 1960s buildings, to the rotting windows of Victorian edifices, there exists an extensive catalogue of unaddressed need. The modernisation of college estates, within a context of disappearing funds, is one of the major challenges for college management.

Another is the need to generate investment in IT in order to keep pace with technological change, to enhance flexibility of provision, and to establish wider networked links to the home and workplace. These will be essential for the delivery of learning as indicated in the government's plans for a University for Industry.

USE OF ICT IN DELIVERING LEARNING

Teaching practice in further education colleges is on the brink of considerable change, fuelled in part by the need to increase efficiency, but also by the rapid development of new information and communications technologies (ICT). These are underpinning significant developments in flexible learning. Colleges have long been involved in open or distance learning, and since the mid-1980s have operated in consortia to produce (mainly paper-based) open learning packages. Flexible learning approaches are now in use to combine distance learning with resource-based learning in college, often provided in drop-in units.

Developments in ICT, and particularly widespread use of the Internet, have now made possible the telematic delivery of learning – i.e. the delivery of multi-media learning packages 'down-the-wire', with tutor support available by e-mail or by video-conferencing. In some innovative pilot projects, employees in small companies are studying from computers on their desks at work, and similar facilities are being placed in libraries and homes for individual use.

The FE student of the future will have a much wider choice of methods of learning. These might include inputs from a computer or other media at home, or in a drop-in resource base, or from tutorials and formally taught classes. Tutor support may be available face-to-face, by e-mail, video-conference, correspondence, or telephone. New methods of delivering learning require changed behaviour from teaching staff; many colleges are presently engaged in major staff development activity to underpin these new developments (see Chapter 72).

BUSINESS-LIKE PRACTICE WITHIN A PUBLIC SERVICE – EFFICIENCY, EFFECTIVENESS AND QUALITY

Incorporation has brought many challenges to colleges and their managers. As noted above, pressure for growth within a diminishing quantum of funds has resulted in increased efficiency, often achieved by adopting business-like practices – for example, benchmarking, using competitive tendering procedures to buy in services, contracting out services, collaborating in bulk purchase schemes. However it has equally been vital to ensure that increased efficiency was achieved with no lessening of the quality of a college's provision. Competition within the sector, and rising expectations from an increasingly consumerist customer base may themselves have been sufficient to ensure no diminution of the quality of college provision. Audit by a multiplicity of agencies however has been added to these forces. Colleges are subject to regular inspection by HMI, whose comprehensive reports on a college's provision are made available to the public. LECs and SQA also regularly audit quality in colleges, using the Scottish Quality Management System – a tool designed in a (vain) attempt to reduce the audit burden. Quality auditors or assessors from the European Social Fund, European Regional Development Fund, National Audit Office, SHEFC and HEIs also visit colleges. The sector has estimated that any one college will on average be hosting a visit from quality auditors/assessors for two days in every week.

Colleges have been able to demonstrate to all of the above agencies that they place considerable emphasis on maintaining and improving the quality of their provision. A recent HMI report on the sector confirmed that national standards are secure. Extensive internal quality assurance systems have been developed which check upon and assure assessment standards, and curriculum review and development are continuing processes. Performance indicators, including customer satisfaction, are calculated, used internally as part of the process of curriculum review, and published externally in college annual reports. The increasing maturity of quality assurance mechanisms in colleges has been recognised by HMI, who are now placing greater emphasis on self-evaluation in the inspection procedures.

The continuing challenge for college managers, who now lead business-like organisations that provide a public service, is the task of achieving even greater efficiency while at the least maintaining existing levels of customer satisfaction and continuing to operate to rigorous academic standards. This challenge has implications for management and institutional development.

INSTITUTIONAL DEVELOPMENT, MANAGEMENT AND GOVERNANCE

As Government funds for FE have reduced, colleges have become increasingly entrepreneurial in their efforts to widen their income base. In addition to the core activity of ensuring quality provision of training and education to appropriate standards, colleges are entering into contracts for other activities – e.g. employment-related services, and business development consultancies. The organisational structures of colleges, and the portfolio of qualifications and experience of their staff, are changing as institutions develop in these new directions.

The role of managers in further education colleges is considerably different from pre-incorporation. Financial pressures, and the need to operate in a business-like manner, mean that much management attention is now devoted to marketing, accounting issues, human resource considerations, information presentation and interpretation, and estates management. These are all activities which in the past were provided by local authorities and which now require attention in addition to the core activity described above. Almost all senior managers in colleges have reached their positions from a background in FE teaching, with no planned national programme of management development to assist them in preparing to discharge these responsibilities. It is currently a priority for the sector to implement such a programme, and provide for succeeding generations of managers.

The strategic management of a college is the responsibility of its Board of Management, a group of twelve to sixteen individuals who are deemed to be representative of the local community, and who employ the staff of the college. It is a legislative requirement that at least half of the board members are representatives of employers, and it is also essential that there be at least two staff and one student representative. Given national hostility towards quangos, and the concerns about standards in public life that led to the establishment of the Nolan Committee, it is unsurprising that the operation of boards of management in colleges has been scrutinised several times since incorporation. The most recent such study (MVA Consultancy, 1997) found that generally boards were operating satisfactorily, and discharging their strategic role of directing colleges with integrity. It is often difficult for colleges to attract appropriate senior industry personnel into involvement on boards, but the standing and continued development of the sector require that this must happen.

CONCLUSION

This chapter has analysed the current issues and priorities for the further education sector. Emerging themes from the analysis are the accessibility, diversity and flexibility of provision within the sector, the wide range of partnerships within which colleges operate in order to secure this provision, and the unrelenting pressure for efficiency which has been applied by government.

Two major and related strategic deficits for the sector have been identified – the lack of a national identity, and the need for a strategic framework for the sector's development. It could be argued that the absence of the latter has been the cause of the former.

With the concepts of lifelong learning and a learning entitlement for all gaining policy credence, an increasing belief that a degree is not the only worthwhile qualification, the view that education can be both liberally enriching and vocationally useful, and the advent of a Scottish parliament to turn these principles into policies, there is a prospect that the distinctive mission of the further education sector could be clarified, firmed, and accorded the value it deserves.

REFERENCES

FEFC (1997) *Learning Works – Widening Participation in Further Education – a report for the Further Education Funding Council* (The Kennedy Report), Coventry: FEFC.

Steedman, H. and A. Green (1996) *Widening Participation in Further Education and Training: A Survey of the Issues*, London: Centre for Economic Performance.

MVA Consultancy (1997) *Survey of Further Education College Boards of Management*. Report commissioned by SOEID. Edinburgh: MVA.

NIACE (1996) *Creating Two Nations?* Leicester: NIACE.

SOEID (1997) *Scottish Education Statistics – Annual Review*, Edinburgh: SOEID.

Neil, A. and R. Mullin (1996) *Scotland's Colleges – Relationships with Businesses and International Communities*. Report commissioned for the Association of Scottish Colleges and Scottish Enterprise. Stirling: Association of Scottish Colleges.

70

Liberal and Vocational Strands in Further Education

John Halliday

Policy in Scottish Further Education (FE) is presented mainly in the form of circulars and letters to college principals issued by the Scottish Office Education and Industry Department (SOEID). Her Majesty's Inspectors of Schools (HMI) also publish reports from time to time which give indications of certain aspects of policy and occasional White Papers and Acts of Parliament set out major changes to the framework within which FE operates. A scrutiny of policy documents published post 1980 indicates an over-riding concern with efficiency and quality of procedures in FE. Little is written in these documents about the fundamental aims and values of this sector of education. For example a recent letter sent to college principals set out the 'key purposes of FE' (SOEID, 1997) under the headings of participation, efficiency and quality. According to this document FE should increase student numbers with particular regard to 'local labour markets and economic development strategies'. This increase should be achieved within 'a culture of continuous quality improvement' by seeking 'efficient use of resources' and by maximising 'non-grant income'.

The absence here as elsewhere of mention of those fundamental values that should inform a further education might be attributed to there being a consensus on such evaluative matters. If there was such a consensus then it would be pointless to rehearse what everyone knows. Alternatively, this absence might be attributed to the dominance of neo-liberal thinking about further education in which it is assumed that, through market-mechanisms, the values of the sector are equivalent to what potential and actual students want to learn. This attribution roughly coheres with the belief that any form of learning should be supported for those over the age of 16 providing that resources are available to provide that support. Finally this absence might be attributed to a general worry that conflict is inevitable when fundamental evaluative concerns are put at the centre of policy formulation.

While all three attributions are reasonable, the latter worry is particularly important in a country in which consensus within a policy-making community is valued highly. As Humes has pointed out on a number of occasions but most notably in *The Leadership Class in Scottish Education* (Edinburgh: John Donald, 1986), this community does not tend to encourage inclusive evaluative debate about fundamental aims, values and purposes. Yet as college Principal Leech warns, 'F. E. has got to get to grips soon with the question of its role and purpose'. He goes on:

If as a sector we do not have a curricular philosophy we will be in a position of drift, exposed to the possibility of becoming training centres, with universities and schools picking off the cream of our present work. (*TESS* 17.11.95. p. 24)

Such drift might be the result of a failure to face up to inevitable disagreement that arises when answers are sought to the fundamental question 'what is a further education for?' The question might appear innocuous enough until it is realised that the rational allocation of limited funds is bound to favour those colleges that best satisfy the preferred answer.

It is not hard to see why concern might be focused on means, methods or techniques as these seem to be amenable to objective determination in the light of prescribed inputs and outputs. Yet further education no less than any other sector of education is centrally concerned with values. Ongoing evaluative deliberation is logically necessary not only for the rational allocation of resources within the sector but also to inform debate about the kind of society that Scots want to develop. Operational efficiency within accepted criteria for quality is only important insofar as it contributes to what actually is believed to be the most worthwhile aims, values and purposes for the sector. Learning is an under determined concept and cannot constitute an end in itself. One can learn to be a bricklayer or a thief and thieves can operate efficiently and effectively. Deliberation about what ought to be learnt in the light of what can be afforded cannot be avoided.

VOCATIONAL STRANDS

Many of those who have taken part in debates about research in further education see this strategic question – 'what is a further education for?' – to be in urgent need of sustained consideration (Coffield, 1996). There is widespread agreement as illustrated in the quotation above from the SOEID that a further education is in many cases a vocational education – an education primarily designed to prepare people for employment or to increase their abilities and aptitudes in employment. If all that there was to further education was to induct people into certain practices so that they can earn a living however, then it might be expected that further education would decline as more employers offered training to employees directly. Mechanisms are available for employers to secure grants from the Local Enterprise Companies to help them with 'on the job' training and employees can be awarded Scottish Vocational Qualifications (SVQs) as they develop their vocational competence. Private training agencies too offer lower cost routes to qualifications validated formerly by the Scottish Vocational Education Council (SCOTVEC) which is now part of the Scottish Qualifications Authority (SQA). Such agencies are often able to undercut colleges of further education because they pay their trainers less than further education colleges pay their lecturers. The economic advantages of 'on the job' training seem obvious. Despite this competition however, most further education colleges continue to attract an increasing number of students year on year, as they are encouraged to do through the funding methodology used by the Scottish Office Further Education Funding Unit.

There might be a number of reasons why students are attracted to further education and it would be wrong to assume that they expect to get something other than a narrow vocational preparation. Further education is notoriously under-researched and it is simply not known what attracts students to the colleges, where they go after college and whether their expectations of further education were realised (Coffield, 1996). Nevertheless it seems reasonable to assume that they have a right to expect a further education to do more than prepare them for a specific employment opportunity which might or might not materialise when they leave college. To prepare people for just one occupation without being able to guarantee that employment opportunities will arise within that occupational area is unwise and probably ethically indefensible. Moreover as Howieson et al. (1997) point out, the desire for a high skill-base within the Scottish economy requires all workers to have a high level of general education rather than an ability to practise in one limited area.

LIBERAL STRANDS

The ability to move beyond what is most immediate and particular towards what might be possible and generalisable is a characteristic liberal strand in education. As recent research (Halliday, 1998) illustrates, there are a number of people working in Scottish FE who demonstrate a commitment to a form of liberal education which attempts to enable students to see beyond the instrumental aim of achieving prescribed statements of vocational competence. At the same time these people do not denigrate the vocational – far from it. What they are seeking to do in different ways might perhaps best be summarised by Pring who writes:

> There seems no reason why the liberal could not be conceived as something vocationally useful and why the vocationally useful should not be taught in an educational and liberating way. (Pring, 1995, p. 183)

Virtually everyone who is employed in colleges of further education has been employed previously in industry and commerce. Many of them are suspicious of those modes of reasoning that seem to neglect economic considerations in education. They believe that public sector institutions, no less than private institutions, should be concerned with economic realities. The analogy that colleges of further education share some similarities with service or production industries is attractive to many of those who have earned their living in such industries. They value commercial and industrial enterprise as a necessary part of liberal democratic society and have little time for suggestions that such enterprise is necessarily illiberal.

Some of those who work in FE have earned their livings by engaging in manual work. The dignity of such work and the dignity of those who perform it informs an egalitarian sense of inclusion for them. Hospital cleaning, for example, has intrinsic value for those who do it well in addition to the extrinsic benefit that such work brings to those who benefit from it. Hospital cleaners no less than solicitors can value work for its own sake in addition to the increased private freedom that remuneration in employment brings. To communicate the intrinsic value of doing a job well is a central aim of some people in FE. The logical point behind this aim seems obvious. Unless students come to appreciate that there is something other than the monetary exchange value of their employment then they are bound to perform at the lowest level that is consistent with their being paid. If they do perform in this way then they require constant monitoring and the set of human relationships that might sustain their work disintegrates. This logical point applies equally to those who work within colleges of further education too, and many managers realise that it is not wise to ignore it.

There is a deeper reason for coming to recognise the intrinsic value of practices however. Without such recognition students remain bound by what must be an incomplete chain of instrumental reasoning. They are impoverished not only because they cannot recognise what intrinsic goods might be within a particular practice but more especially because they cannot understand the kind of deep practical engagement that others seem to enjoy. To come to understand such engagement is a form of moral education for some of those who study in FE (Halliday, 1996).

FE offers a second chance to those who for whatever reason were unsuccessful at the primary opportunity to become engaged in learning at school and to take the first steps on the road to a job. Of course, a further education cannot increase the number of jobs that are on offer unless it enables people to start businesses which do not lead to the closure of other business. The use of technology might be seen to be important here and it is worth remembering that many colleges were called colleges of technology at one stage. Now such titles have been dropped although the idea that colleges are sites where people have access to new and old technology remains important even if such access is difficult to resource.

The funding methodology for Scottish further education does make some allowance for the differential costs involved in keeping different sorts of technology up to date. These differentials do not in many cases accurately reflect the difference between classroom-based and workshop-based study. Consequently academic drift results as students are encouraged to write about doing something rather than actually doing it (Halliday, 1996). Such drift might be more of a problem in Scottish FE than its English counterpart because there is much more Higher National Certificate and Higher National Diploma work in Scottish colleges. This Higher work has tended to be associated with an increasing ability with the pen rather than more refined practice in wider and more varied contexts that require deeper thought and more refined skills. Academic drift has also been encouraged by the tendency for Higher National courses to form the entry to study at university which often does require higher levels of writing skill. There has been a tendency as illustrated in the white paper *Raising the Standard* (SOEID, 1996) to suggest that the value of a further education is determined by the extent to which it is an entry to a higher education.

Those areas of the further education curriculum that have been able best to resist academic drift are those areas where the cost of technology can be subsidised through the business ventures that serve also as vehicles for study at higher national level. For example, departments of hospitality studies may purchase advanced restaurant and hotel facilities to provide both a realistic context for learning and funds to update those facilities. Without such commercial ventures within further education and without the idea that a further education is valuable in itself and not only the means to a higher education, academic drift might continue unchecked.

Prior to *Action Plan* (SED, 1983) which introduced a modular curriculum in FE, every course with a vocational aim included some 'liberal studies' to reflect the view that narrow vocationalism was mistaken. As Connelly makes clear in Chapter 71, such studies were never entirely satisfactory and they began to disappear as *Action Plan* was implemented. It was not clear what the content of liberal studies should be, these studies were not examined and many students saw them as a distraction from their aim of securing permanent employment. It is hardly surprising that students did not choose liberal studies when they were given the opportunity to select a programme of study from a catalogue of modules and when the economic climate was such that the securing of permanent employment seemed paramount.

Of course curriculum designers were well aware that something important had been lost in the demise of liberal studies and that something more general needed to be added to the cafeteria-style curriculum of the modular catalogue. While the terminology has shifted over the years, the notion of core skills has come to the fore as a vehicle for preserving something of the general and liberal in a further education. In addition students on general SVQ courses are required to complete a project in which they show that they can integrate the various modular components of their study along with these core skills into the design of a project of their own choosing. Again there is scope here for some imaginative teaching that goes beyond the immediate and particular competencies that are prescribed and which encourages students to design projects which are actually useful to them and their communities.

The language of core skills does not immediately suggest a liberal strand in FE. Skills such as personal effectiveness, problem solving, communication, numeracy and information technology which are preferred core skills within FE do not immediately suggest that students should be encouraged critically to engage in a broad range of educational activities. Nevertheless the notion of critical thinking which is embedded within problem solving skills provides a vehicle for some students to see their predicament as something more complicated than a search for a job. While the desire for employment might be uppermost in many students' minds, skilled teachers can encourage students to see their predicament against a wider background of educational possibilities and institutional constraints.

Finally, it is worth noting that all colleges encourage those with learning difficulties to attend. Some of these students follow the same programmes of study as those presumed not to have learning difficulties. The curriculum in this 'mainstream' is prescribed. Others follow 'special programmes'. According to the Secretary of State's annual reports in FE, the numbers of students on 'special programmes' increased by 21 per cent between the 1994/5 and 1995/6 academic years. The corresponding figure for all students in FE was 9 per cent. These special programmes involve the production of individualised learning plans which are not, in many cases, designed to lead to immediate paid work. The contrast between these and mainstream programmes has prompted some to question whether a perception of particular learning difficulties is an adequate basis upon which to treat people differently. Such questioning has led some in further education to challenge deep-rooted conceptions of what personal autonomy is and how these conceptions might be reflected through liberal strands in curriculum design.

INSTITUTIONAL CONSIDERATIONS

A number of developments have conspired against the further development of these liberal strands in a further education. First, in some quarters there is a corrosive cynicism which is based on the view that these strands are no more than window-dressing for a deep-seated managerialist culture which values only that which can be measured and funded. Thus some might argue that growth in the number of students with learning difficulties in further education is not so much the result of a general belief in inclusion and community. Rather, according to these cynics, the growth is due to the fact that students with learning difficulties are funded at twice the rate of students deemed not to have such difficulties. Such cynicism might be more widespread in England rather than Scotland although in both countries there have been a number of industrial relations problems. Referring specifically to England, Coffield notes:

> All is far from well in a system where a Memorandum entitled 'Twenty Ways to Harass your Staff' is circulated from the Employers Forum to College Principals with the aim of coercing lecturers into signing contracts which reduce their terms and conditions. (Coffield, 1996, p. 6)

A second constraint upon the liberal strand in FE might be attributed to some of the literature and statements put about by SQA which is the sole body in Scotland responsible both for accrediting awards and validating programmes of study. Despite the best intentions of some of its senior officers, this body is often perceived to be caught between the aim of encouraging diversity in provision and the aim of ensuring consistency in standards. These aims are not necessarily incompatible but they are easily misinterpreted by those obsessed with the idea that the statement of standards precludes forms of teaching that encourage anything other than the stated performance criteria. Previously SCOTVEC not only prescribed curriculum outcomes but also made recommendations about the time that it should take to teach those outcomes and the teaching methods that should be used. These recommendations were accepted in most colleges and formed the basis of the lecturers' contractual obligations. Thus many lecturers felt that they had no room for manoeuvre as both the product and the process of their work seemed prescribed by one awarding body. The legacy of this sentiment lingers on. Yet paradoxically there is far more diversity in the Scottish FE curriculum overall than in the English counterpart where there is a multitude of awarding bodies. The course in Applied Christian Theology at Edinburgh's Telford College and the course in Rock Musicianship at Perth College are good examples of how SQA has enabled colleges to respond to what students want to learn.

It is interesting to consider some possible reasons for this apparent paradox. SCOTVEC was set up by government to encourage competition between different educational providers of which the colleges were just one. Therefore it needed to specify pretty tightly what providers were supposed to do in order to try to standardise the curriculum product, as it were, and to enable an educational market-place in FE. There is also an equity consideration in the drive to standardise. Plainly it is unacceptable for students to be deceived into believing that courses and qualifications are equivalent when in reality different providers teach and assess in quite different ways. Whereas in the case of the academic curriculum, the use of set examinations administered and marked under strict conditions at set times is often perceived to ensure standardisation, this option is not available for further education. In FE, practical assignments and projects are often the most valid forms of assessment and assessment takes place at various times to suit those who are treated increasingly as customers and clients.

SQA does not operate in isolation from other validating and awarding bodies in the UK. It would be very odd if SVQs and English National VQs in the same curriculum area were wildly different. It is not plausible to suggest that vocational competence in Scotland is radically different from that in England. Moreover, the VQ competence framework was developed partly in response to European requirements for trans-national mobility of labour based on equivalence of qualifications. It would also be odd if two countries sharing a common language could not agree on equivalence arrangements. SCOTVEC might have been dragged along in the wake of what were predominantly English concerns over the roles of the Employment and Education Departments within government. It is possible to argue too that the liberal vocational distinction was itself much more relevant to England where a tradition of specialism and disdain for manual work might support the academic interpretation of a liberal education. In Scotland the desirability of breadth in knowledge and practical skill remains influential.

Liberal strands in further education seem not to have been encouraged by the current funding methodology either, although at the time of writing this methodology is under review. Early indications are that the era of competition between further education colleges might be coming to an end as a result of this review (SOEID, 1997). In addition it seems that funding might be tied to some measure of quality in the future. Thus there is the possibility that through collective action and through appropriate quality criteria, liberal strands in FE might again be encouraged. That is not to romanticise about a pre-incorporation era in which it might be imagined that liberal strands flourished. In that era there was always a suspicion, at least in some political circles, that colleges served the interests of their staff rather than their students and clients. After all since most college lecturers were on permanent contracts to teach vocational areas in which they had some expertise, it was highly likely that courses in those vocational areas would be offered whether or not they were actually needed. For example, if a vocational preparation for shipbuilding was no longer required, shipbuilding lecturers would either have to made redundant, retrained or inappropriate courses offered to students. The latter option was both managerially and personally for the lecturer the least disruptive option.

Following incorporation moves were made in circulars following Circular 9/92 towards formula funding that would reward those colleges that were best able to attract more students and to be more efficient in teaching them. What some regard as the rather dowdy image of further education began to change as colleges took a great deal of effort in making their facilities and courses more attractive to students and in making their whole operation more businesslike and efficient. The current formula is based on the idea of a weighted sum. In essence the amount colleges receive is based on the number of students attending for 25 per cent of their programme of study multiplied by a weighting which varies from subject to subject and whether or not students have learning difficulties. Fuller details are given in Circular 9/96. HMI reports progress in meeting certain performance indicators but that progress does not affect the funding a college receives from SOEID. Indeed the present methodology seems to encourage colleges to ensure that students do not complete their course. It is as if students should be attracted to college irrespective of any ethical considerations about their long term interests. In reality it seems unlikely that any college would encourage non-completion in this way. Three per cent of college funding is given to cover the fixed costs of providing pre-entry guidance to students to try to ensure that they study the most appropriate courses.

CONCERN WITH QUALITY

In many ways a move now to include some measure of, and reward for, quality could provide a focus for debate about an appropriate balance between liberal and vocational strands in FE. It is clear that the SOEID has been aware for some time that such inclusion could be desirable. A research project was commissioned from Coombe Lodge, the then staff college and predecessor of the Further Education Development Agency (FEDA) to explore the mechanisms by which high quality provision could be recognised, encouraged and rewarded. Responses to the findings of this research were invited in Circular 8/95 but no clear consensus emerged from the consultation (Circular 21/95).

The Coombe Lodge research raised a number of issues which have not as yet been resolved. For example which approach to measuring quality should be adopted – quality management processes or educational processes? Should HMIs assess quality on an annual basis? Should any reward be based on value added or actual achievement? It is on this issue of quality that value concerns become most apparent and the flight to an apparent value neutrality becomes most attractive to those wishing to discourage evaluative deliberation. In Circular 21/95 it was reported that:

> any of the methods of measuring quality were seen as being fraught with methodological problems and value judgements, and therefore unlikely to underpin a system perceived to be objective and fair.

This circular is revealing because in it value judgements are associated with subjectivity and unfairness. So long as such association persists, it seems likely that there will be a proliferation of quality audits that are mainly paper-based attempts at objectivity. Yet as the Coombe Lodge report makes clear, if the views of students are taken into account then it seems preferable that colleges are judged on the presence or absence of a systematic process rather than a simplified summary of its results. In other words colleges might be rewarded if they had instituted a process of quality assurance rather than collected data about perceptions of quality.

An analogy might be useful here to illustrate an apparent confusion in further education between its incorporated status and the centralisation of quality audits. On the one hand, one might expect colleges to follow providers of goods and services in instituting their own quality assurance procedures. Such procedures would meet their customer demands and would include guarantees and compensation payments. Yet in fact it seems that colleges are simply required to collect some statistics according to a prescribed procedure. If this is compared to the situation in car manufacturing, then what is found is that quality is defined and determined by the customer and that unless those working for the manufacturer understand this, or their performance can be controlled absolutely, then the manufacturer would go out of business. If colleges are expected to be responsive to their customers and clients as car manufacturers are, they would need to institute procedures that were sufficiently open for all involved in the college to voice their concerns without fear of recrimination and with the expectation that any deficiencies would be rectified quickly. Plainly the performance of educators cannot be controlled absolutely and students cannot be expected to complain too readily about those who have the power of assessment over them. An ethos of openness and genuine respect for persons might be the best way to encourage 'quality' in the longer term. Such an ethos could extend into the process of student assessment and the process of pre-entry guidance through the provision of 'taster courses' which enable students to sample the breadth in curriculum that is offered.

It is widely believed that the distinctions between academic, vocational and liberal are deeply damaging and that the enhanced status that academic awards presently enjoy is a product of an outdated class system which privileged a leisured elite. It has also been argued here as elsewhere (Pring, 1995) that everyone has a right to a liberal education which is concerned to develop the ability to think, understand and appreciate the best that has been said and done by others. Howieson et al. (1997) identify three broad strategies for unifying the academic and the vocational. Paradoxically one of these seeks to preserve and emphasise what are seen to be distinct characteristics of academic and vocational tracks. A variant of this strategy was adopted in the Report into Upper Secondary Education in Scotland known as the Howie Report (SOEID, 1992) and this report was widely rejected. A second strategy adopted by England links the academic and the vocational through credit transfer arrangements. The third strategy favoured in the report, *Higher Still: opportunity for all* (SOED, 1994) attempts to unite the academic and vocational.

Typically further education prepares people to be hairdressers, builders, joiners, computer technicians, laboratory assistants and other forms of employment in which the use of tools other than pens is central. In this way a vocational education is contrasted with an academic education in which the use of the pen is central. The contrast may be misleading however in some contexts. That is because the distinction between academic and vocational may sometimes be based on the purpose for which the tools are being used. Thus it is possible to study law as part of a vocational practice through which people earn their living, but also as part of what might be a disinterested and academic pursuit of truth. Similarly, people might learn to be joiners primarily to earn their living or because they simply like doing joinery and some joiners enjoy earning their living through what for them is a kind of 'calling' or vocation.

There is nothing logically necessary about the practice of chemistry for example, which makes it either vocational, academic or liberal. Rather it is the primary purpose of chemistry students at any particular time which determines the appropriateness of the adjective. Pragmatically it makes little sense to induct people into the same practice in two separate streams, as it were, and this pragmatism has informed thinking about Higher Still which was referred to earlier. On egalitarian grounds too there are good reasons for designing an inclusive curriculum framework which suggests that carers, cooks, hairdressers and plumbers are just as important members of society as chemists, theologians, philosophers and linguists. There is also the economic argument that high skill economies require workers who are adaptable, flexible and good at working in teams. All these arguments indicate the desirability of curricular breadth for all students so that they can identify with others who have different special interests. Such breadth might encourage them to be able to make connections quickly between different practices. Arguably in an age in which specific information is available 'at the touch of a button', as it were, people do not so much need to know specific facts associated with particular practices. Rather they need to know how to make connections between those practices and to be able to get on with one another both at work and as citizens.

The title of this chapter indicates that a further education ought to be concerned both with enabling people to earn their living in useful ways and to look beyond what is immediate and obviously useful. Such a conception has both the advantage that it enables a high skill economic base, the social cohesion that is necessary for individual private flourishing and the ability to take part in political democratic debate. It may be that what Wolf calls *The Tyranny of Numbers* (Institute of Education, University of London, 1997) will always deem certain qualifications to have less status than others, but that is not immediately an educational concern. In the long term however people are both formed by and form the society of which they are a part. The privileging of academic qualifications and the balancing of liberal and vocational strands are not logical matters. They are centrally concerned with the values embedded within the liberal democratic state.

REFERENCES

Coffield, F. (1996) Introduction and Overview, in F. Coffield (ed.) *Strategic Research in Further Education*, Newcastle: University of Newcastle.

Halliday, J. S. (1996) Values and Further Education, *British Journal of Educational Studies*, 44:1, pp. 66–82.

Halliday, J. S. (ed.) (1998) *Values in Further Education*, Stoke on Trent: Trentham.

Howieson, C., D. Raffe, K. Spours and M. Young (1997) Unifying Academic and Vocational Learning: the state of the debate in England and Scotland, *Journal of Education and Work*, 10:1, pp. 5–35.

Pring, R. (1995) *Closing the Gap: Liberal Education and Vocational Preparation*, London: Hodder and Stoughton.

SOEID (1997) Funding Methodology Review Group: letter to Principals dated 5.6.97. (ref VEY/ 37/ 2) with attachments FMRG 97/1, Edinburgh: Further Education Funding Division.

71

Curriculum Development in Further Education

Graham Connelly

> If they hadn't learnt much from him, he had been able to go home in the evening with the
> knowledge that he had gained something from them . . . (*Wilt on High*, by Tom Sharpe, 1984).

Wilt muses that in twenty years' teaching Liberal Studies in a technical college, he has been
unable to get anyone to tell him clearly what he is supposed to be doing. His dilemma neatly
summarises the identity crisis of further education during the 1960s and 1970s expansion
and highlights the precarious position of non-vocational subjects in the curriculum of
technical and commercial courses. In Scotland, following the adoption of a modular,
outcome-based approach to the further education (FE) curriculum in the 1980s, the post-
Wilt generation of lecturers – vocational and non-vocational – are more likely to complain
about an unduly restrictive curriculum and domination by assessment. This chapter
explores the genesis of this change, from the immediate post-war years through the *Action
Plan* of 1983 to the modular curriculum of the 1990s. The chapter ends with a commentary
on issues of concern.

CURRICULUM DEVELOPMENTS POST-1945

In the immediate post-war years, theory evening classes for craft apprentices and office
workers were conducted mainly in school classrooms under the auspices of local education
authorities. In the mid-1950s, the FE college building programme expanded amid concerns
that workers were not equipped with skills required by industry. Employers were
encouraged to release young apprentices and trainees on a day per week basis or for
longer blocks of study, a voluntary arrangement later to become a requirement after the
formation of Industrial Training Boards in 1964. The new colleges had better practical
facilities and students were prepared for external examinations of the English-based City
and Guilds of London Institute (CGLI) and Royal Society of Arts (RSA), and the Scottish
Council for Commercial Education (SCCE). The syllabuses were strongly vocational,
emphasising expertise in practical skills. (See S. L. Hunter, *The Scottish Educational
System*, ch. 10, Pergamon, 1971.)

The Brunton Committee (SED, 1963) examined the effect of FE expansion on secondary
school provision. The committee's members were asked to recommend ways of better

coordinating the last year of compulsory schooling with FE programmes. Two concerns were identified: avoiding students having to 'waste time on work with which they are already familiar'; and integrating general education within vocational courses, 'aimed at all round development of the individual.' Students were increasingly remaining in school beyond the minimum leaving age and may have taken Ordinary Grade examinations or started vocational courses at school. The aim was to complement vocational education with teaching in literacy, numeracy and 'general studies', in a way that was relevant and not detached from the student's life experience. The language of Brunton now seems at best quaint, at worst stereotypical and uninformed. For example, FE students were said to be, 'not interested in academic learning and [to] prefer physical activity to thinking'; teachers were advised to keep in mind the 'verbal limitations' of their students. Vocational courses were in familiar occupational areas, such as building, agriculture and fishing, but also included 'girls' occupations', mainly retail and office work. The authors seemed content to leave the curriculum in vocational areas to the awarding bodies, like CGLI, but they did attempt to describe the general studies curriculum. All students, they argued, should be helped to become more proficient in written and oral English, to develop the capacity to understand instructions, convey information, and make notes and other types of records. They should also know about 'industrial relations, personal finance and budgeting, personal relations in an adult world, and about the local community and the facilities and opportunities it affords for the development of personal interests and for service' (ibid., p.32). Committee members acknowledged resistance from employers to general studies in the curriculum, particularly if the subjects seemed to have no immediate utility in the workplace. The report concluded, somewhat liberally, that teachers should identify their own and students' interests and, thus, 'it would be fruitless to prescribe a detailed syllabus in general studies.'

In 1962 the Scottish Association for National Certificates and Diplomas began to administer post-school technical education and the Scottish Council for Commercial, Administrative and Professional Education was established in 1966. These bodies reviewed National Certificate courses and standardised entrance qualifications. The Industrial Training Boards also influenced the curriculum of vocational courses, their work funded by a levy on firms. (See I. Robertson: *Recurrent Education and the Work of the Industrial Training Boards*, ARE Occasional Paper 3, 1979.)

The Scottish Technical Education Council (SCOTEC) and the Scottish Business Education Council (SCOTBEC), formed in 1975, together provided a broader range of vocational certificates and diplomas. (See Chapter 81 for a fuller discussion.) Courses were written in the then fashionable language of 'behavioural objectives', essentially statements of the behavioural changes in the learner. FE became embroiled in a vigorous debate about its contribution to national economic prosperity. The decade of the 1970s was a time of growing youth unemployment and the government responded with a series of short-term, and largely unsuccessful, initiatives, such as the Youth Opportunities Programme (YOP) and Work Introduction Courses (WICs). It was also a time of change in assumptions about employment, an acceptance that adults would no longer remain in a single occupation for life and a growing awareness that students should learn transferable skills. (See A. C. Ryrie, *Changing Student Needs in Further Education Colleges*, SCRE, 1984.)

FE, created to provide qualifications for specific jobs and particular industries, now found it had little to offer students requiring a more general preparation for eventual work, assuming the economy improved, or, pessimistically, long-term unemployment. There were structural problems in the system too. SCOTEC and SCOTBEC had different entrance requirements for courses, different programme lengths and different standards for their qualifications. Finally, the uneasy relationship with general studies remained un-resolved. The examination bodies seemed content to leave teaching in art, physical education, music and English to colleges but students and employers continued to question the value of these unexamined elements of the curriculum. There was considerable variation in practice between colleges and in many cases the standard of provision was poor and under-resourced. College lecturers of general and aesthetic subjects felt isolated from their secondary school colleagues and had limited access to in-service training. In some cases, the standard of teaching was appalling and in my experience it was not uncommon for students to endure an unconnected diet of propaganda films and unplanned discussions.

THE MODULAR CURRICULUM

In 1979 the Scottish Education Department began an extensive consultation exercise culminating in the publication of the *Action Plan* report, which radically changed the nature of FE provision in Scotland (SED, 1983). What had been initially concerned with the first two years of post-compulsory education in Scotland and the preparation for life of 16–18 year olds, paved the way for a radical revision of further and higher education for young people and adults of all ages. The Action Plan's authors squared up to the old debate about the education and training divide and concluded that 'there should be no abandonment of broadly-based education, and where specialisation is necessary it should be sought through appropriate emphases' (SED, 1983, p. 9). They envisaged a broad curriculum, emphasising personal and social development, with strong vocational influences supporting the applica-tion of theory and skills and helping to maintain student motivation. Flexibility became a byword and students were to be offered choice in putting together programmes of study, incentives to achieve and increased freedom to move between programmes and institutions.

The consultation indicated a major problem in FE concerning the independent con-struction of courses largely based on occupational disciplines like engineering. This meant there were separate syllabuses for fundamental subjects like science and mathematics in different vocational programmes. Apart from being wasteful, this made it difficult for students to move between courses and colleges, and between part-time and full-time education. The solution adopted was a framework based on a curricular component with standard design characteristics. This 'modular' curriculum was to be based on forty–hour blocks of course time and modules would be available at different levels of attainment to facilitate progression, with students entering at the level appropriate to their existing attainment or experience. Modules would be taken as free-standing units of study, combined to form unique programmes for individual students, or grouped to make up vocationally-recognised awards. Finally, module 'descriptors' would contain statements describing student outcomes and these would form the criteria against which performance should be assessed. This process of 'criterion referenced' assessment was advocated because attainment could be reported 'not in relation to the better or poorer performance of others, but in relation to success in achieving what the course was intended to provide' (SED, 1983, p. 40). The assessment process was to be applied internally by teaching staff, subject to external monitoring.

In 1985 the Scottish Vocational Education Council (SCOTVEC) assumed responsibility for developing the National Certificate programme, based on modules and in 1989 extended the modular principles to Higher National Certificate (HNC) and Higher National Diploma (HND) courses. (See Chapter 81.) An important influence on modular curriculum development was the work of the newly established Curriculum Advice and Support Team (CAST) in producing teaching packages and running workshops for lecturers. This centralised activity was designed to reduce duplication of effort and was arguably highly influential in speedily moving the FE curriculum – in general studies and communication at least – from a fairly permissive position to one characterised by a high degree of prescription.

In the National Certificate the basic component of learning and certification is known as a 'module', while at advanced levels the term 'unit' is used to avoid confusion, but design features are shared. A 'descriptor' of the kind illustrated below details the learning outcomes, performance criteria and assessment procedures and contains advice on preferred entry level, content and learning, and teaching approaches.

Extract from a National Certificate 'descriptor'
Module Title: Graphical Engineering Communication

Learning Outcomes:
The student should:
1. draw components in first and third angle projection;
2. construct isometric and oblique views and practical tangencies;
3. construct sectional and auxiliary views in one plane.

Performance Criteria (outcome 2):
The student:
(a) draws a component in isometric and oblique projection including the following features: (i) horizontal; (b) vertical; (c) sloping; (circular).
(b) produces practical tangencies which contain: (i) arc to arc (internal and external); (ii) line to arc.

Instrument of Assessment (outcome 2):
The student will be presented with two practical exercises to test the ability to construct isometric and oblique views and practical tangency drawings. The student will be given an orthographic drawing showing two to three views of a component. The student will then be required to draw an isometric view and an oblique view on plain paper. The student will then be given a drawing which requires reproduction to show the following tangency construction: (1) correct scale; (2) all construction lines; (3) outline; (4) tangent points.

When HM Inspectors conducted a review of the National Certificate, they concluded the unified modular system had been a major achievement: 'the National Certificate can be used to provide a delivery system which offers flexibility and choice in content and in mode and pace of learning' (SOED, 1991, p. 54). They found the planning of learning and teaching had improved and teaching had become more student-centred. Most students appeared to enjoy their college experiences and this satisfaction was attributed to a combination of increased choice, more active learning and units of study with clear, short-term targets.

Nevertheless, this initial review identified problems. The move to internal assessment presented several professional and organisational difficulties. Designing assessments and interpreting standards had become major activities for lecturers and assessment began to overshadow the learning process. HMI advocated 'approaches which integrate the assessment of a number of learning outcomes or which embed assessment in learning and teaching, so as to counter over-use of a "teach-test" approach to module delivery' (ibid., pp. 55–6). They also noted a need for more effective internal moderation to ensure consistency of standards between staff and within colleges, and staff development in assessment for new and part-time staff. Teachers and students had apparently adopted the culture of modules with enthusiasm, but the inspectors called for more 'coherent integrated programmes', an aspect of curriculum planning they felt had been neglected.

INFLUENCES ON THE CURRICULUM

In pre-module days, vocational elements of the curriculum were prescribed in syllabuses published by awarding bodies, in consultation with trades unions, employers, professional bodies and confederations of industrial and commercial interests. Teaching was left to college lecturers, qualified in their subject or trade, who might have gained a teaching qualification by part-time secondment. After 1985 several factors together influenced both the view of the curriculum and course design in further education, of which one important factor was undoubtedly the influence of SCOTVEC. (See Chapter 81 for more detail.)

Occupational competence and vocational qualifications

The Conservative government initiated an ambitious Standards Programme in 1987 to establish levels of achievement on youth and adult training programmes in the UK. Their research claimed that many employers were unable to define explicitly what was expected of employees and a massive development programme to specify statements of occupational competence began. The rationale for this complex exercise was twofold. First, changes in workplaces meant that an increasing proportion of workers could expect to change jobs in their working lives and therefore needed skills, transferable between different jobs, even in quite different industries. Second, if common definitions of competence in skills could be agreed, then it might be possible to facilitate credit transfer between qualifications and encourage recognition of competence in different occupational sectors.

The process by which statements of competence were written involved analysing job functions of experienced employees, a cumbersome task typically undertaken by consultants. This work was overseen by UK-wide committees, known as 'lead bodies', representing significant occupational groups. The Employment Department advised lead bodies to express standards of competence in 'unit' form – influenced by the Scottish experience of modules – ideally describing a separate role or function within an occupation, to encourage credit transfer. Lead bodies were discouraged from writing units specifying competence in generic skills like the use of information technology, which had already been developed by other lead bodies. The tasks of monitoring the quality of unit writing, avoiding duplication and standardising statements of competence in broad skills, were given by the government to SCOTVEC and the London-based National Council for Vocational Qualifications. The bodies cooperated to approve units of occupational competence, identical throughout the UK. Scottish Vocational Qualifications (SVQs), and their counterparts in the rest of the UK, National Vocational Qualifications (NVQs), made up of lead body units which assess students or employees against standards of performance recognised by employers, were introduced in 1989. (See Chapter 81.) SVQs are awarded at five levels, corresponding to an increasing degree of autonomy in the employment context. Units at level I describe competence requiring a minimal degree of independent work, skills typically needed by operatives, while level IV units describe the competences of professionals in work generally associated with degree-level entry qualifications. An example of an SVQ at level III (skilled craft qualification) is *Safety Services: Offshore*, which has eight mandatory units, including 'Contribute to the Reporting, Investigation and Follow-up of Accidents and Incidents', with two performance criteria: 'Assist with workplace reporting and investigations' and 'Contribute to the analysis of workplace accident and incident reports.'

General Scottish Vocational Qualifications (GSVQs), which SCOTVEC began piloting in 1991, were introduced widely in schools and colleges in 1994. They are made up of core skills in key curricular areas, identified as communication, numeracy, information technology, problem solving, interpersonal skills and vocational competence based on industry standards. Assessment of competence takes place in the workplace during a student placement, in simulated workplace conditions and in the classroom. GSVQs are available at three levels, the lowest providing a broadly-based vocational qualification, while higher levels are awarded for skills demonstrated in occupational areas, such as business administration. The SQA hopes employers (and higher education institutions) will regard the highest level of GSVQ as equivalent to traditional academic 'Highers', and these are planned to coordinate with the Scottish Group Awards (SGAs) in the proposed Higher Still framework, which will reform the curriculum for senior pupils in secondary schools from 1999.

The interface between further and higher education

The Scottish Wider Access Programme (SWAP) was set up in 1988, in response to the 1987 White Paper, *Higher Education: Meeting the challenge*, which invited higher education institutions to attract more adult students. SWAP set out to improve participation by older students and those lacking qualifications, to target traditionally under-represented groups in higher education and encourage collaboration between further and higher education. The Scottish Council for Research in Education (SCRE) studied the work of SWAP and found access courses were succeeding in opening up higher education to people who might otherwise have missed out, but had limited success in attracting students from traditionally under-represented groups (Munn et al., 1993). For example, they noted success in attracting students from working class households, but only around a third of students were unemployed on entry, only slightly more than half were women, just 2 per cent had disabilities and an estimated 1 per cent came from minority ethnic backgrounds. The authors make the important point that since neither SWAP nor the Scottish Office had specifically identified recruitment targets for under-represented groups, it was difficult to judge the success of the access programme on this criterion. A companion study considered the effectiveness of access courses through the eyes of students and their teachers (Munn et al., 1994). The research team found overwhelming evidence of the value of access provision in raising confidence in learning amongst students from traditionally marginalised groups in society, though, sadly, limited evidence of higher education changing to accommodate the needs of an increasingly different student population.

What is unquestionable, is the success of the FE system in attracting adult students in general. Table 71.1 illustrates the rise in non-advanced vocational FE over a seven-year period. A striking feature is the dramatically increased involvement by the over-25s, particularly in full-time courses.

Table 71.1   Participation in Vocational Further Education in Scotland

	Full-time		Part-time	
	All students	Age 25 +	All students	Age 25 +
1985–6	29462	3885	148004	40359
1992–3	36750	11482	170305	69679
% Change	+ 24.7	+ 195.5	+ 15.1	+ 72.6

Source: Scottish Office Statistics Branch

Also noteworthy is the involvement of FE colleges in advanced level HNC/D courses. Between 1985–6 and 1995–6 the number of candidates enrolled for HN 'Group Awards' more than doubled. There are many reasons for this increase, including the proliferation of qualifications across a broad range of vocational areas from golf course management to rock music performance, an unstable job market forcing young people to continue in full-time education, and the development of agreements on credit transfer aiding progression within higher education. (See Chapter 104 on SCOTCAT.) The widespread development of advanced courses in FE has helped students lacking traditional university entrance qualifications and those living in rural areas to access higher education. Many HNC/D students are now recruited from non-advanced courses in the same college. In 1995–6, 21 per cent of FE college students were on higher education courses (including SVQ levels 4/ 5). Part-time higher education courses have grown by 15 per cent from 1994–5 to 1995–6, compared to a 5 per cent increase in full-time provision in the same period.

Many colleges have made 'articulation' arrangements with universities, allowing transfer from HND to the final year of a degree programme. In some cases an entire degree is taught by college staff. Degree-level work in FE increased by over 12 per cent between 1994–5 and 1995-6 (compared with a 6 per cent increase for HNC/D work), though it accounted for only 1 per cent of the students seeking qualifications.

The most controversial higher education development in the FE sector has arguably been the project to establish a University of the Highlands and Islands (UHI), based on existing further education colleges and research centres using advanced technology to share teaching resources and intellectual expertise. (See *The Scotsman*, Tuesday, 1 October 1996, p.10.)

ISSUES OF CONCERN

FE teaching

The UHI project is controversial partly because it depends heavily on teaching by staff in FE colleges. Critics have described this arrangement as a second-rate university staffed by second-rate teachers. (See, for example, *The Scotsman*, Monday, 7 October 1996, p. 13 and Monday, 27 January 1997, p. 15.) This comment may show a misunderstanding of both the recent history of university-level education and the extent of variable provision in the current post-school system. The Robbins' expansion of the 1960s gave former Central Institutions degree-awarding status through the external moderation of the Council for National Academic Awards, in an arrangement not unlike the SCOTVEC/SQA quality control of FE colleges. The highly respected Open University depends on a backbone of tutorial staff drawn from a much broader set of backgrounds than is common in older universities. The flexibility of the modular approach allows adults with modest attainment to achieve with limited initial targets and to build up credit, moving seamlessly to more advanced study. The criticism also ignores the fact that the colleges in the UHI network have been developing vocational courses influenced by research in sustainable development, including fish-farming, gamekeeping and forestry. Relationships with ecological research institutes in the network and internet links to university departments in North America and Scandinavia with similar interests have been set up, and should lead to the kind of research and intellectual exchange which characterises good university education. Some criticisms may, however, be justified. Much faith is placed in the significance of new technology linking FE colleges to create a university. Capital grants for purchasing sophisticated equipment and transmitting lectures by video-conference links may not in themselves be sufficient; a new-style university is likely to require a radical re-think of curriculum and its presentation. At the time of writing, students in one college in the UHI network were reported in the press criticising video link teaching by a teacher based in another college.

Staff development and curriculum development

Unlike most university teachers, over 80 per cent of further education lecturers are trained, having qualified through the in-service TQFE run by the Scottish School of Further Education (SSFE) at the University of Strathclyde's Jordanhill Campus, a qualification which gives entitlement to register with the General Teaching Council for Scotland (GTC). Registration is not compulsory and therefore a teaching qualification is not mandatory, as in schools, an anomaly which concerns many observers who point out that the Higher Still framework should ideally lead to extensive school-college links, including sharing teaching resources. The SSFE monopoly will end after 1997–8, when institutions will be accredited, on a competitive basis, by the Scottish Office and GTC to provide training based on new competences for FE teaching. A major concern is the training and support of the growing number of part-time staff, very few of whom are teacher-trained. An HMI inspection of around 1,300 teaching sessions in Scottish colleges, found most were good or very good, while 18 per cent were fair and 1 per cent unsatisfactory (*Standards and Quality in Scottish Further Education 1995–96*, SOEID, 1997). The report does not indicate whether untrained teachers were responsible for most of the poor lessons, but faults were found in planning teaching and the development of quality learning and teaching packs, both of which are key aspects of the teacher training curriculum.

The Scottish Further Education Unit (SFEU) was set up in 1991, initially to support management training for senior FE staff in advance of 'incorporation' of colleges in 1993. The SFEU was formed by re-focusing the activities of the former Curriculum Advice and Support Team (CAST) in the SSFE at the former Jordanhill College to support the new modular curriculum. The SFEU is an independent agency, supported by government grant and income from commercial activities. It operates through a team of specialist develop-ment officers, from a base in Stirling, running tailored staff training, conferences and overseas study visits, maintaining a database of information and originating publications and curriculum materials in vocational further and higher education.

The SFEU has been unquestionably influential in FE provision because of its mission to respond to organisational development and staff training needs, but its physical relocation finally severed the weakening link between the pedagogical education of lecturers and development of the FE curriculum. This division had come about partly by circumstances (the merger of Jordanhill College with the University of Strathclyde in 1993), partly because of the prescriptive nature of the modular curriculum, and also, apparently, through the combined action of missed opportunity, personal rivalries and politics. (See *TESS*, FE Focus, February 16, 1996, p. 27.) Ironically the SFEU's predecessor, CAST, grew out of the experience of TQFE students' curriculum projects supervised by SSFE staff. Increasingly, colleges found it impossible to resource a pattern of training with staff released in blocks of ten weeks. The SSFE developed more flexible provision, but this stretched its resources and meant it could not also meet the growing curriculum and staff development needs of the colleges. CAST, and subsequently SFEU, responded to these needs by developing curriculum 'packages' for modules and units and the SSFE concentrated on providing the teacher training qualification. The curriculum packages, written by SFEU staff, consultants or working groups of FE lecturers, contain teaching and assessment materials, professionally presented, and are in wide use across Scotland. The materials are popular amongst hard-pressed lecturers faced with teaching many new classes and most are excellent resources, prepared by experienced and gifted practitioners. Nevertheless, many FE staff and observers are critical of the prominence of a packaged response to curriculum needs. The modular approach is highly prescriptive and the 'notional' forty hours has become established as the norm, leaving little room for teachers and students to negotiate variation of the programme, one acknowledged way of encouraging deeper learning. Packages tend to perpetuate prescription rather than support individualised responses. The assessment stranglehold remains relatively unchallenged, to the extent that in some courses, particularly in evening classes which are typically fighting for time, a whole teaching session can be given over to assessing a 'learning outcome', based on content covered only the previous session. As a result, many lecturers complain of feeling like acquiescent technicians, rather than autonomous professionals.

The rapid pace of change in the FE sector has undoubtedly forced both SSFE and SFEU to react to national initiatives and research has mainly been limited to evaluative studies of their implementation. More philosophical studies of the FE curriculum are required and lecturers' justifiable concerns need to be addressed.

Student guidance and support for learning

The success story of further education is the development of a system that encourages student progression. A negative effect is confusion about the plethora of courses, programmes and schemes, and their appropriateness for individual students given their aspirations and the local employment situation. The need for incorporated colleges to market their courses aggressively has produced a degree of tension between guidance advisers and teaching departments anxious to fill course places. Nevertheless colleges have become adept at providing pre-entry and on-course support, but HMI inspections suggest they are much less good at providing guidance about progression opportunities outwith their own institution. Considerable attention has been given to learning support since the

Further and Higher Education (Scotland) Act 1992 confirmed the responsibilities of colleges to provide adequate support services, but HMI have criticised colleges for not identifying students' difficulties early enough (SOEID, 1996).

The effectiveness of Scottish vocational FE

The system has become highly flexible during the 1990s, with collaboration between further and higher education, credit transfer and accreditation of prior learning. There are arguable benefits for students, particularly adults with family commitments, and employers. Nevertheless, problems exist. Many colleges have concentrated on developing higher level courses at the expense of lower level vocational programmes. This is due partly to market demand but probably also to the status and funding associated with HNC/D teaching. As a result, there is a shortage of skilled workers in some areas and, arguably, over-provision of advanced courses in FE. The 1995 report of the Advisory Scottish Council for Education and Training Targets (ASCETT) showed that around 27 per cent of school leavers lacked minimum qualifications and less than half the adult workforce had acceptable qualifications.

There are problems too with SVQs. The language of competence statements is overly-complex, unclear and gives difficulty in interpretation of standards, a complaint also frequently levelled at module and unit descriptors. A related issue concerns the use of the language of vocational competence to define the learning requirements of non-vocational disciplines like sociology and English literature. This is a particularly acute problem, since the vocational requirement to demonstrate competent performance against all the specified criteria and in a range of contexts may be inappropriate in arts and social science study. Some critics argue this approach is inappropriate in any subject area. Assessment has come to dominate further education in a clamour to award credits for small components of study. This approach leads, paradoxically, to inflexibility – the laissez-faire approach of 1960s and '70s general studies has been replaced by an overly-prescriptive curriculum. Efforts to meet ASCETT's training targets are based on an act of faith about the relationship between qualifications and economic prosperity rather than established causal connections. Ironically, one attempt to integrate core skills like problem solving with knowledge – a mandatory project for level II and III GSVQ courses – is itself festooned with the language of outcomes, evidence statements and portfolios. A justification for the additional project is to make it easier to award 'merit', an irony in a system rooted in the ideology of competent performance.

The FE curriculum occupies a key position in Scottish education not only because of its bridging role between school and university but because as Halliday (Chapter 70) points out, it is worthwhile in itself for many students. A greater proportion of the adult population can now enter higher education because of flexible access and college-university agreements, and FE colleges have also become adept at understanding the needs of adult students and helping them to succeed. In these ways they make an important contribution to the development of the notion of lifelong learning.

REFERENCES

Munn, P., M. Johnstone and K. Lowden (1993) *Students' Perceptions of Access Courses: A survey*, Edinburgh: Scottish Council for Research in Education.

Munn, P., M. Johnstone and R. Robinson (1994) *The Effectiveness of Access Courses: Views of Access Students and their Teachers*, Edinburgh: Scottish Council for Research in Education.

SED (1963) *From School to Further Education* (the 'Brunton' Report), Edinburgh: SED.

SED (1983) *16–18s in Scotland: An Action Plan*, Edinburgh: SED.

SOED (1991) *Six years On: Teaching, Learning and Assessment in National Certificate Programmes in Scottish Further Education Colleges*, Edinburgh: HMSO.

SOEID (1996) *Equally Successful: Provision for students with learning difficulties and disabilities in further education colleges in Scotland*, Edinburgh: HMSO.

72

Teaching and Learning in Further and Higher Education

Rebecca Soden

The profound social and economic developments of the last decades have brought about far reaching changes in further education (FE) and higher education (HE). Students numbers have increased dramatically and the content of education has had to take account of changes in the requirements put upon it by society. All this has demanded a new approach to questions of teaching and learning and given rise to a new wave of research into the ways in which students learn, as well as to an important inter-disciplinary discourse on the nature and purposes of post-school education; how it is and how it ought to be conducted.

Traditionally, teaching in universities was dominated by the mass lecture and follow-up group tutorials, with the expectation that students would engage in a good deal of self-directed reading and analysis whereas in the further education sector students passed their courses mainly by participating in classes which typically included exposition, questions, discussion and supervised tasks. The picture is much more complicated now. Increasingly, students in both sectors are expected to direct their own learning, often through engagement in project work.

THE CHANGING NATURE OF FURTHER AND HIGHER EDUCATION

By 1997, around 45 per cent of the relevant age group were undergoing higher education in Scotland (compared with about one third in England); participation is expected to exceed 50 per cent within ten years. Economic requirements and demands for social justice require institutions to include people who were previously under-represented to participate in further and higher education. Details of these changes can be found in 'Trends in Higher Education Participation' in Scotland, (Paterson, 1997, *Higher Education Quarterly*, volume 51, No. 1, January, 1997). This increased participation means that there is now a diverse group of students in Scottish further and higher education who might be expected to learn in different ways and at different rates. The Further and Higher Education Charter for Scotland has empowered students to demand that their different learning needs are met. At the same time per capita funding has diminished and the content of further and higher education has been affected strongly by the idea that education should prepare people for the world of work. This idea is reflected in the move to competency based courses throughout further education, parts of higher education and in initiatives such as the

Enterprise in Higher Education project. Most recently, the Dearing report (see Chapter 12), continued this theme of equipping students to contribute to an advanced, adaptable, knowledge-based economy. The traditional Scottish three year ordinary degree might change to reflect growing emphasis by employers on generalisable abilities (key skills). The suggestion that this degree might include components from arts and science faculties and from Higher National Certificate/Diploma (HNC/D) programmes is part of the same theme.

Related to these changes is the impact of technology, particularly Information Technology, on the educational process in particular and on society in general. The Scottish Higher Education Funding Council (SHEFC) has continued to support the development of learning packages involving web-accessed input, computer based assessment, electronic support mechanisms and tutorial groups established on the world-wide web. Such application of technology has already altered the role of staff in some departments from lecturing towards preparing course materials and monitoring student activities. It seems likely that very soon there will be a sharp increase in technology assisted, interactive, self-paced learning materials providing a combination of text, questions, repeatable experiments, work based simulations and tasks to provoke independent thinking about content. These materials will be supported by video tutorials and accompanied by more frequent monitoring of students' progress against learning tasks. Techniques such as video-conferencing will open up possibilities for students to discuss their ideas with people around the world who have made significant contributions to a shared area of interest.

THE BLURRING OF THE DIVISION BETWEEN FURTHER AND HIGHER EDUCATION

One consequence of all the changes is that Scottish higher education is no longer confined to degree courses in universities. It includes HNCs/Ds awarded by the Scottish Qualifications Authority (SQA). These courses are almost all located and taught in colleges of further education whereas degree provision is almost all in universities. However, provision in further education colleges also includes post-graduate programmes intended to prepare students for particular occupational areas such as marketing. The traditional distinction between the two sectors is becoming increasingly blurred as more and more higher education is provided in further education colleges and courses once classified as further education now fall within the definition of higher education. The first half of the 1990s saw a dramatic growth of higher education in the further education colleges. By 1994–5 one third of the further education colleges had 50 per cent or more of their students registered for higher education awards. In the same year over 40 per cent of students living in Scotland entering higher education were doing so in further education colleges; the trend is expected to continue. Further information appears in Norman Sharp's paper, 'FE/HE Links: Scotland in a UK context', presented at the seminar on 'The Further Education/Higher Education Interface in Comparative Perspective' (Centre for Research on Higher Education, Queen's University, Belfast, 17 June 1997).

The challenge for teaching and learning of this breaking down of institutional boundaries is in reconciling the consequences of the different curriculum philosophies which inform the design of HNC/D courses and degree courses provided by universities, particularly the pre-1992 universities. The idea that further education colleges and universities could provide the integrated and flexible network of work-related and academic opportunities, envisaged by the Dearing report, would entail clarification of, and agreement about, the values and purposes of further and higher education.

The Scottish Credit Accumulation and Transfer Scheme contributes to the development of an 'articulated' network by allowing students credit towards a degree for their achievements in programmes such as HNCs/Ds and work experience provided in further education colleges. The practical implications of different curriculum philosophies in HNC/D and degree courses are to be seen in the difficulties which sometimes arise in the 'articulation' arrangements enabling students to move from the competency based education provided in HND programmes to complete their degrees in a university. One response by the newer universities has been to design competency based degree programmes. 'Articulation' arrangements are the predominant form of further/higher education links in Scotland whereas 'franchising' is the dominant mode in the rest of the United Kingdom. 'Franchised' degrees are validated by a university but the teaching takes place either wholly or partly in a college of further education.

PEDAGOGICAL PRACTICE

Both university and college staff tend to adopt a theoretically eclectic approach influenced by a concentration on the content of their discipline, especially in the first two years of degree courses. Plainly, assessment methods such as course work, final examinations, oral presentations, essays and project reports encourage different approaches to learning. With the exception of final examinations, all these assessment methods are used widely in both sectors. In SQA accredited programmes, which account for the vast majority of provision in the further education sector, students are assessed continuously, with no final examinations. Although much of the methodology remains 'traditional' in the universities, practice in both sectors is changing and reflects to varying extents the better ideas in the burgeoning literature reviewed in Marton and Ramsden's chapter, 'What does it take to improve learning?' (in P. Ramsden ed., 1988, *Improving Learning: New Perspectives*, pp. 268-86, London: Kogan Page) and in Ramsden (1994). These ideas are discussed later in the chapter.

There is considerable variation in the extent to which any of these ideas influence practice, depending on the lecturer's training and experience of teaching, institutional encouragement, and the sense the lecturer makes of each approach. In as far as they do influence practice, the ideas tend to be realised in different ways in further and higher education colleges and in universities. They are realised in universities mainly in lecture/tutorial mode, with workshops in applied science courses, supported by individual library work. In the further education sector approaches are realised within a national competency based curriculum, with outcomes which reflect the job functions of experienced employees and which has mechanisms designed to ensure across-the-board standards. This is not the case in the higher education sector.

Prior to the further education curriculum initiative known as *Action Plan* (SOED, 1983) further education lecturers combined exposition, questions, discussion and written work in ways that resembled secondary school teaching but conducted in an atmosphere of much less formal staff/student relationships. There are still elements of this approach, practicable because the class numbers are often under twenty-five and popular with students because it offers them opportunities to seek clarification while the information is being presented. One unintended consequence of *Action Plan* development work was that many further education lecturers abandoned this approach altogether, believing that 'chalk and talk' was always bad practice.

Action Plan guidelines encouraged lecturers to use more 'practical', 'active', 'student centred' approaches such as project methods, simulated work tasks (for example, a 'training office') and small group discussions. These ideas were disseminated through Development Officers who encouraged lecturers across a section or department to produce for each module a pack containing learning, teaching and assessment materials. The *Action Plan* guidelines on learning and teaching reflect changes in society which seem to imply that students should be encouraged to develop a lifelong capacity for self-managed learning as well as strong communication and teamworking abilities.

Theories which implied that 'student centred' approaches were likely to promote these aims became influential. The methods to be used for achieving these ends, such as small group discussion, were more amenable to description than the nature of the ends themselves. While it is increasingly acknowledged that lecturers in both sectors should help students to think well in work related contexts, just what this means has not been clearly delineated. That this lack of clarity has had consequences for practice is implied in *Six Years On* (SOED, 1990): the authors report that while examples were found of programmes with a strong emphasis on problem solving this was not characteristic of the system.

Traditionally, further education students have been expected to attend far more classes or workshops than university students. This difference is beginning to diminish but this has as much to do with resourcing as with learning theories. Increasingly, students learn from packages, with access to lecturers, many of whom are on part-time, temporary contracts. There are signs of enthusiasm in some parts of the higher education sector for approaches encouraged by the *Action Plan* initiative. Issues surrounding these approaches are discussed in the final section of this chapter.

STAFF DEVELOPMENT

In neither the FE nor the HE sector is initial training a requirement of employment, although the further education sector has a history of encouraging its staff to complete an accredited programme of initial teacher education. This has not been a feature of the university sector. The changing nature of further and higher education has inevitably stimulated developments in staff training. The Dearing report recommends that all new higher education lecturers undertake teacher education and proposes the setting up of a National Institute for Teaching and Learning in Higher Education. This body would also have a role in the preparation of further education lecturers teaching on higher education courses. In 1997 the Scottish Office Education and Industry Department published *National Guidelines on Provision Leading to the Teaching Qualification Further Education (TQFE) and Related Professional Development* which set out occupational standards purporting to encompass the competences required of a further education lecturer.

The National Guidelines commit the providers of teacher education for the further education sector to a national competency based curriculum. There is no such commitment in the Dearing report to this form of competency based training for higher education staff, which, as has been noted, is intended to include those further education lecturers who teach HNC/D courses.

In discharging its statutory responsibility for Teaching Quality Assessment (TQA) in higher education institutions, SHEFC has funded a range of initiatives in teaching and learning which fall loosely into four categories not intended to be mutually exclusive, but rather to indicate the main emphasis of the various schemes and programmes. The four categories are quality, access, technology and flexibility. Examples include the Practice Dissemination Initiative, the Staff Development Initiative, the Teaching and Learning Technology Project, the Flexibility in Teaching and Learning Scheme, the Effective Teaching and Assessment Programme and the Staff Development Videos Project. The latter consists of five video programmes and accompanying materials providing a wealth of useful information and raising interesting questions on the following topics: effective learning, curriculum and resources, student support and quality control, teaching and assessment. These resources are intended to encourage further discussion within Scottish higher education on the issues of quality improvement and assessment. The messages seem to make sense to lecturers, possibly because they are based on a coherent set of ideas within constructivist psychology which are summarised in the Marton and Ramsden chapter (cited in the previous section) and in Entwistle (1994). Constructivist psychology holds that learning is most effective when students try to relate ideas to their current understandings and in the process transform these understandings into ones which help them to make better sense of the world. The Scottish Office also initiates and funds an ongoing programme of projects concerned with innovation in teaching and learning and assessment in further education colleges. These initiatives encourage lecturers to apply ideas from a range of theories within constructivist psychology.

It seems that in both sectors the extent to which theories about learning become influential depends not only on their overall coherence and explanatory power, but also on other factors such as their congruence with society's conceptions of the overall purposes of education and the resources which can be allocated to pursuing these purposes. In both sectors there has been a tendency in staff development provision to present fragments of theories about learning together with their specific applications. Pressures to make staff development activities 'relevant' and the many other calls on lecturers' time, pre-dispose designers of such activities to choose those parts of theories which seem to promise a quick pay-off. Such an approach seems to dilute the explanatory power of theories and to have little potential for suggesting to lecturers conceptions of learning which have wider scope and plausibility than their own narratives. In their article 'Conceptions of teaching and their relationship to student learning', in the *British Journal of Educational Psychology* (Vol. 63, pp. 20–33), Gow and Kember (1993) review research which suggests strong relationships between the sophistication of lecturers' conceptions and the effectiveness of their teaching. It seems important therefore that lecturers are helped to engage in theoretically informed reflection on their own day-to-day teaching practices.

RESEARCH ON TEACHING AND LEARNING

In such a brief account it is possible only to indicate the recurring themes in the vast literature on teaching and learning. Significant developments in the discourse of research on learning and teaching were already taking place before audits of teaching and other accountability mechanisms were introduced. The bibliographical volume of the MacFarlane Report (Committee of Scottish University Principals, 1992) provides an excellent source of further references in this area.

Over the last two decades, discussion about learning and teaching has more and more centred on students' approaches to learning and the lecturer's role in facilitating more effective approaches. One of the most important and influential research findings has been a description of deep approaches to learning and conditions which encourage or impede development of such approaches. Students adopting a deep approach make effective efforts to understand and transform content through critical engagement with ideas: they appraise the evidence offered and the conclusions associated with it; they offer arguments and conclusions. The research suggests that the factors which influence students to adopt a deep approach are the student's own purposes in studying, his or her previous experiences of education and beliefs about learning, together with the teaching and assessment encountered on the course. If students feel overburdened with work, if assessment requirements are inappropriate, and if authoritarian relationships between tutors and learners prevail, students tend to adopt ineffective surface approaches to studying (Entwistle, 1994).

This strand differs from the 'learning styles' literature. Harvey and Knight (1996, p. 125) say that 'learning styles' is a seductive construct which suggests that people have preferred styles of learning regardless of the task. They report studies which cast doubt on this idea. Students may be adopting a particular style which is not appropriate for dealing with the concerns of their chosen discipline and (as noted above) the students' perception of what is required by their course may account for inappropriate 'learning styles'. It may be more beneficial to help them to extend their existing repertoires. Perhaps students should be involved in departmental discussions about such matters.

Much of the research that has been described is based on the premise that teaching approaches which encourage learners to be more self-directed – often represented as student autonomy in learning – enhance abilities appropriate to life-long learning and to employment. Harvey and Knight report research which suggests that the main factor determining student learning is individual study outside the classroom and that teachers should give much more attention to supporting students in working independently and purposefully on worthwhile tasks. Sometimes this approach is described as active learning, a description which raises the question of whether it is possible to learn anything effectively other than through engaging in some sort of mental activity.

A particular type of programme, commonly described as Independent Study (for example, see Harvey and Knight, 1996; Goodlad, 1995), seems to encompass many of the elements of these teaching approaches. It is claimed that Independent Study provides a way of developing and demonstrating abilities which employers appear to value. Three stages are common in Independent Study programmes: a study proposal; fulfilment of the proposal; assessment. [This is followed by a proposal for the next year's study]. The emphasis is on the development of critique, analysis and interpretation. The subject-specific knowledge identified in the students' own study plans is used as a vehicle for development.

Another related and very influential approach is one described as problem-based learning. It starts with a problem rather than with disciplinary knowledge and uses stimulus material to engage students in considering a problem which, as far as possible, is presented in the same context as in real life. This approach often means that traditional discipline boundaries are crossed. What has to be learned is identified by addressing the problem and by reference to resources, some of which may have been provided, and some have been located by the students themselves. The MacFarlane Report bibliography provides references to leading researchers in this area such as David Boud. The value of these approaches could be contested. In their favour is evidence that employers value the qualities associated with the independent learner. They also seem to provide possibilities for encouraging deep approaches to learning in the student.

The emphasis on work preparation in recent policy statements has encouraged research into abilities which improve performance at work. Such research suggests that the most suitable graduates are those who are flexible, adaptable and quick to learn, and who can use skills such as analysis, critique and synthesis to the benefit of their organisations. These attributes, often summarised as the capacity and the disposition to engage in good thinking, are increasingly represented as being required of all employees. They also seem to be attributes which have the potential to empower people as citizens.

As has already been noted, demands for more flexibility in the workforce have led to calls for further and higher education to promote the development of so-called general, transferable skills. A number of problems arise, not the least of which is establishing what is to be included in and what is to be excluded from, the concept of transferable skills. It is worth noting that, in a recent review of studies of the transfer of learning (cited in Harvey and Knight, 1996), it was concluded that any transfer is usually within the domain in which the skills were learned. Central to this discourse has been the notion of metacognition, that is knowing and thinking about one's own knowledge and thinking processes. Three aspects of metacognition have been distinguished; metacognition about people, about tasks and about strategies. Examples of these aspects of metacognition would be: knowledge that one's own rationality and that of others is affected by emotions; knowledge that many academic tasks require information to be marshalled into arguments; knowledge that the quality of information available and the quality of conclusions are related; knowledge of the range of one's own cognitive resources which are appropriate for the task. The latter includes knowledge of effective strategies for different tasks, knowledge that enables adaptation of strategies, and monitoring and control of one's own progress with the task in hand.

Overall, current research suggests that there is considerable scope for developing lecturers' and students' conceptions to include the idea that learning involves transforming their views of their subject and of themselves.

ISSUES

By and large the consensus is that lecturers should develop an orientation to helping students with their learning rather than committing themselves to a specific set of teaching techniques. Many writers argue (for example, Goodlad, 1995) that it is difficult to demonstrate a direct link between a specific technique and a particular learning outcome. There is considerable enthusiasm for self-managed, technology-assisted learning. Students will benefit more from such innovations if they are carefully initiated into all that is involved in informed analysis and critique. This requires sufficient time for face-to-face interactions which offer opportunities for a tutor to judge a student's current state of understanding, to form some notion of what it might become and to engage the student in dialogue aimed at achieving the transformation. Peer tutoring and peer critiquing also have a part to play in this process, but they are not a substitute for tutorials. There is great scope for research in these areas.

However, it is possible to overstate the importance of help with learning and to ignore other crucial factors influencing the effectiveness of the educational process. Taking together government concerns about the low participation of disadvantaged groups in post-school education and the research which indicates strong relationships between students' conceptions of learning and their achievements, it seems worthwhile to encourage research on social and cultural influences on the formation of students' conceptions.

A new 'cultural psychology' is turning away from the exclusive concern with individual, intrapsychic processes of knowing and ways in which they can be assisted by pedagogy, towards the development of an approach which takes account of the concept of 'situated' cognition, situated in the sense that it is a product of shared activity in a context and culture where it is developed and used. It is not necessary to accept the new cultural psychology to recognise that students' motivation and perception of the social significance of their studies – and the strategies they adopt in coping with their studies – are not fully described by research on learning. It is probably also the case that, for some students, there are shared socially and culturally determined strategies that reject the stated aims of post-school education and the 'needs of post-industrial society' in favour of an instrumental accommodation to minimum course requirements. These phenomena have to be taken into account if student learning is to be understood fully and unrealistic expectations of the benefits of improved learning environments avoided.

An important contribution of the theoretical discourse has been to demonstrate that the concept of good teaching is highly contestable. It is now widely recognised that there are weaknesses in most approaches to judging good teaching. But even if it is to be judged by student progress, a reasonable criterion, there is the difficulty that assessment of learning is itself problematic, more so in some disciplines than in others. For instance, the procedure for the assessment of essays in Arts and Social Sciences subjects frequently includes up to seven discriminations (grades A to G) in each of perhaps five aspects of performance (say knowledge of topic, reading, quality of argument, quality of ideas, structure and critical sense), all of which involve thirty-five separate judgements, none of which is purely objective. Criteria which appear to be objective often conceal this subjectivity.

Then there is the question of the selection of the criteria themselves, also fraught with similar problems. Student satisfaction, another measure sometimes advocated, may be reassuring, or otherwise, to lecturers and has a place in any genuine evaluation of teaching and learning, but it is not, in itself, a reliable guarantee that learning has taken place. This is not to say that there are no sound suggestions about criteria for judging teaching such as those which are discussed by Diana Laurillard in *Rethinking University Teaching* (London: Routledge, 1993). These suggestions include the ideas that teaching approaches should address the students' conceptions of topics, help them to understand the key concerns, the mode of discourse typical in the discipline and the ways in which knowledge is constructed. It will also address the development of students' ability to conceptualise their own thoughts and those of others. Attempts to write more specific criteria often result in failing to capture these significant outcomes of teaching and do not avoid subjective judgements. At the same time, these criteria would also be appropriate ones for judging the adequacy of teacher education provision.

As well as paying attention to cultural psychology and the problems of assessing effective learning, a pedagogy for further and higher education needs to address the contradiction between the need for specialised knowledge in a particular domain and the demands for general skills said to be essential for the modern world. The development of so-called transferable skills is a key concern in policy documents. Yet funding for research aimed at elucidating the nature of these abilities has not been given sufficient priority. There are weaknesses in characterisations commonly used and consequent difficulties in teaching and assessing what has not been adequately described (for example, see M. Bonnett 1995, 'Teaching Thinking and the Sanctity of Content,' *Journal of Philosophy of Education*, vol. 29, 3, pp. 295–309).

One significant weakness is that the concepts commonly used in curriculum documents to describe the abilities overlap: communication, numeracy, problem solving, critical thinking, interpersonal 'skills' and enterprise. Another is that not enough account is taken of research which suggests that competency in exercising the abilities assumed to be transferable is likely to be strongly affected by the individual's knowledge of the domain in which they are to be exercised. At the very least cognitive research implies that course design should enable students to interrogate knowledge for particular purposes right from the beginning of the course, with no separation of knowledge acquisition and knowledge application.

Cognitive research on expertise implies that thinking is intimately bound up with the individual's knowledge of fundamental ideas from relevant disciplines and the inter-connectedness of these ideas. Such knowledge enhances and accelerates further related learning. For example, people in senior administrative posts probably communicate and think effectively in their jobs because they build up deep understanding of the broad issues on the agenda of various committees, not because they have had quick-fix training in the so-called transferable skills. The idea that mental skills transcend contexts is probably only tenable when the contexts require only generally familiar knowledge. The kind of transfer claimed in policy documents is likely to be realised through practice in performing generalisable activities (such as evaluating evidence) in different disciplines, and through discussion which enables the student to become aware of them as cognitive actions or strategies (metacognition). Further and higher education as at present constituted, with their bias towards specialisation, are likely to render the process harder to achieve, but proposals in the Dearing report suggest that this may be changing and that a more favourable regime may emerge in coming years. The reservations expressed here can be usefully summed up by saying that good thinking and good knowledge are intimately related.

Plainly, teaching and learning in further and higher education are informed by con-ceptions of the purposes of these forms of education. Serious attention needs to be given to clarifying the purposes of post-school education. It could be assumed that the purposes of further education should not be significantly different from those of higher education, in the sense that both should equip students to act on the basis of reasoned judgements. Such a purpose implies that students should be offered opportunities to contest knowledge as well as to apply it. Recent research on employers' requirements suggests that these competences are likely to be more occupationally relevant than the narrower knowledge and procedures which have had priority in further education programmes. While no-one would deny that employees need to learn to apply specific knowledge and procedures, it can be argued that these are probably best learned in a specific work context.

Although the development of good thinking is implicit in the stated aims of SQA accredited programmes, this is not given priority in performance criteria and accreditation and the practical emphasis is on the transmission and application of knowledge, a policy resting on false assumptions about what is occupationally relevant and about human potential for development. An untenable assumption is that people have a fixed amount of 'academic' ability. Current psychological literature no longer supports the idea of fixed ability but rather suggests that intellectual development is related to the kind of activities in which people engage. If students' achievements on entry to further education imply underdeveloped capacity for good thinking it would be logical to give greater rather than less emphasis in the further education curriculum to the development of good thinking. This is not to say that university lecturers are better than their further education counterparts at facilitating the development of their students' thinking but rather that it is easier for them to do so when assessment criteria are written in a way that allows students to earn substantial credit for good thinking.

A prior condition for the convergence in practices between higher and further education which seems desirable is commitment to a common curriculum philosophy. With a shared philosophy, a better curriculum articulation could be achieved in practice through share-able, possibly technologically based, learning materials. Learning/teaching packages pre-pared by course teams are commonplace in further education. In so far as current differences in curriculum philosophies allow, it may be possible for teams from universities and further education colleges to collaborate in preparing packages which cover HNC/D and the third year of the new-style general degrees recommended in the Dearing report.

Psychological literature suggests that lifelong intellectual development is possible. What seems to be required is opportunities for staff to develop their understanding of how cognitive development might be enhanced through the teaching of a discipline and through work-based learning. There is a vast body of sound research on conceptualising and encouraging the ability to engage in good thinking. Many writers, for example, believe that Vygotskian Development Theory provides powerful and appropriate theoretical tools for helping further and higher education lecturers to develop such understanding.

The challenge now facing post-school education is that of designing courses promoting the integration of what students learn not just in colleges and universities, but in work experience and in pursuing their lives in the wider community. What has been argued in this chapter is that the effectiveness of learning environments which help students to transform themselves and society is intimately related to the purposes of post-school education and that their design should be informed by research which takes proper account of social and cultural factors that influence individual values and cognitions. What is likely to improve learning and teaching is research which goes beyond finding out how policies can be implemented efficiently and engages in critical analysis of the conceptions, assumptions and values underlying proposed policies.

REFERENCES

Committee of Scottish University Principals (1992) *Teaching and Learning in an Expanding Higher Education System* (The MacFarlane report), Edinburgh: SCFC.

Entwistle, N. (1994) Recent research on student learning and the learning environment. Paper presented to the International Symposium *Independent Study and Flexible Learning*, Cambridge, 6 September 1994.

Goodlad, S. (1995) *The Quest for Quality: Sixteen Forms of Heresy in Higher Education*, Buckingham: Society for Research into Higher Education and Open University Press.

Harvey, L. and P. Knight (1996) *Transforming Higher Education*, Buckingham: Society for Research into Higher Education and Open University Press.

Marton, F., D. Hounsell and N. Entwistle (1997) *The experience of learning*, Scottish Academic Press.

Ramsden, P. (1994), Using Research on Student Learning to Enhance Educational Quality. Griffith University; Occasional Paper No. 1.

73

Institutional and Curricular Structures in the Universities of Scotland

Richard Shaw

Classification is a means of bringing order to a subject; classification by structure and purpose is indeed frequently illuminating. Refining classifications to incorporate detailed sub-classifications and ever more dimensions may bring either further illumination or, conversely, create obscurity. In this chapter the approach will be to use broad and hopefully simple categories but with the reminder that differences in ethos may differentiate just as effectively as differences in formal structures.

OLD AND NEW UNIVERSITIES: MISSIONS AND CHARACTER

The simplest categorisation is that between the old universities – those created pre-1992; and the new universities – those created as a result of the Further and Higher Education (Scotland) Act 1992. The latter group, the post-1992 universities, share similar missions and many structural features. The former group, the pre-1992 universities, while being readily identified as distinct from the new post-1992 universities, are in practice much more diverse in their history and character.

The pre-1992 universities

As indicated in Chapter 6 this group may be sub-divided into the four 'ancient' universities: St Andrews, Glasgow, Aberdeen, and Edinburgh founded between 1411 and 1583, and the four 1960s universities: Dundee, created by demerging from St Andrews; Strathclyde and Heriot-Watt evolving from their previous status as Scottish Office funded Central Institutions, and the one completely new 1960s university, Stirling, established on a greenfield site in 1966.

All eight pre-1992 universities, as well as being arguably still primarily teaching institutions for undergraduate and postgraduate students, regard themselves as being research universities. In the latest 1996 Research Assessment Exercise (RAE), 70 per cent or more of the academic staff of each of these institutions were included in their submissions as being 'active in research'. There is a clear expectation that all, or at least most, academic staff will be active researchers and an aspiration that they should contribute to assessment ratings denoting international research excellence. As is clear from Table 6.2 in Chapter 6 their success in achieving that aspiration inevitably varies.

While emphasis on research is a common characteristic differences in history, location, size, subject profile and academic structure make for substantially differing institutions. Put simply Edinburgh, Glasgow and Strathclyde are very large (over 15,000 full-time equivalent students) city based universities covering the vast majority of subject disciplines. At the other end of the spectrum Stirling and St Andrews are much smaller (around 6,000 students) universities situated in smaller towns and covering a wide but nevertheless relatively restricted range of subject disciplines. Only Aberdeen, Dundee, Edinburgh and Glasgow have full medical faculties with pre- and post-clinical medicine, while Stirling and St Andrews do not have engineering faculties. Heriot Watt and Strathclyde retain a strong emphasis on science and engineering reflecting their origins as technological institutions. Although some other institutions have recently adopted a modular structure within a semester system, Stirling began life in the 1960s as a modular university and as such was unique in Scotland until the 1990s.

In any sketch of the pre-1992 universities it would be wrong not to refer to both their Scottish character, built on a tradition favouring a broad general education, and their commitment to being also United Kingdom and international universities. Recent statistics show that around 22,000 students from elsewhere in the UK are enrolled at Scottish higher education institutions. These students are largely concentrated in four universities: Dundee, Edinburgh, Stirling and St Andrews. In addition overseas students add a distinctive character to most of the pre-1992 universities.

The post-1992 universities

The five post 1992 universities were created from existing institutions. Prior to the abolition of the binary line they were all degree and postgraduate level institutions with their awards being made under the Charter of the Council for National Academic Awards (CNAA). Up to the creation of the Scottish Higher Education Funding Council (SHEFC) the five post-1992 universities were all funded directly by the then Scottish Office Education Department (SOED) which strongly encouraged them in their commitment to vocationally oriented programmes of study and to widening access to higher education.

While all five institutions were committed to, and engaged in, research and scholarship broadly defined by CNAA, their essential character was defined by their vocationally relevant teaching mission. Most of the institutions' research was applied and targeted at being relevant to the needs of local and regional industry, commerce and public services. SOED, as the funding body, did not explicitly fund research in these institutions and indeed discouraged research activities unless they could be shown to be in support of the vocationally relevant teaching mission. This history is reflected in the submissions to the 1996 RAE in which between 17 and 35 per cent of academic staff in the five post-1992 universities were included as being 'active in research'. Thus, while the post-1992 universities are expanding their research activities, by comparison with the pre-1992 universities, the new universities are focused much more clearly on learning and teaching and much less on academic research.

INSTITUTIONAL STRUCTURES: FACULTIES, SENATE AND COURT

Although there are significant differences in detail, the formal academic management and governance structures in the Scottish universities are generally very similar. The supreme body responsible for the overall character, mission, and management of the universities is the Governing Body, in most cases called the Court. The formal responsibilities of the courts are laid down in the constitutional documents of the universities, legislation, and in some particulars reinforced by the 'Financial Memorandum' between SHEFC and the individual institutions. Although not part of the management and governance structure all the universities have a titular head, the Chancellor. The office of Chancellor is primarily ceremonial involving presiding over degree awards ceremonies and other formal functions. The Chancellor may also act as an ambassador for the University, assisting in the promotion of external contacts.

As the supreme body the Court, or Board of Governors, is ultimately responsible for the good management and financial health of the University. Although the detailed composition varies between universities the general pattern is of a Court of between twenty-five and thirty people with a majority of lay members but including, as well as the executive head of the University, the Principal, other appointed or elected members of staff, and students. In the four ancient universities: Glasgow, St Andrews, Aberdeen and Edinburgh, a lay Rector elected by students chairs the Court. In the other universities, pre- and post-1992, the chairperson is appointed by Court itself and is always a lay member. The lay members are largely drawn from the business, commercial and professional world and will also normally include at least one representative from local government.

The Court, or Board of Governors, is supported by a committee structure which generally includes finance, audit, senior staff remuneration, and nominations committees. Not surprisingly, given the differing histories of the institutions, there is some variation in the committee structure though it is now a condition of funding through the Financial Memorandum with SHEFC that all institutions have audit, and senior staff remuneration committees. Following the Nolan Committee reports on standards in public life there is also a strong recommendation that there is a nominations committee relating to membership of the Court. While formally supreme, the Court shares the responsibility for the University with the chief administrative and academic officer, the Principal and Vice Chancellor, and with the Senate, the senior academic committee. The nature of this 'partnership' has varied from time-to-time and from institution to institution. This will be the subject of later discussion.

The academic government of universities is formally the responsibility of Senate, or Academic Board (Council). This body normally has overall responsibility for the academic programmes of study, the admission of students, the assessment of students, and the granting of degrees and other awards. The Senate, or Academic Board, is chaired by the Principal. Senates vary enormously in size – from around 25 to over 200. This variation, as well as partly reflecting the size of the University, mainly results from the number of professors since in the older universities all professors may be members of Senate by right. In the newer universities, as well as there being far fewer professors they do not always have an automatic right to membership of Senate. In addition to professors senates have ex-officio categories of membership including the Principal and some other senior officers, heads of academic departments and deans, student representatives and elected members.

Senate, or Academic Board, like the Court is supported by a committee structure. The normal pattern involves two strands: subject based and specialist committees. The latter will include committees with special responsibility for University wide functions such as the library and information services, and monitoring academic standards. The subject based committees include faculties responsible for groupings of academic subjects such as medicine, business, humanities, science, and engineering, and academic departments responsible for particular subjects. Naturally, there is considerable variation in the detailed arrangements including the number of tiers involved in academic government. Thus, one of the post-1992 universities, Abertay Dundee, has abolished faculties as an intermediate tier between Senate and academic departments, and reorganised the latter into small groups of schools. In others, faculties have increased in importance following the devolution to them of increased financial responsibility.

THE JARRATT COMMITTEE: RELATIONSHIPS BETWEEN ACADEMIC STRUCTURES, COURT AND EXECUTIVE MANAGEMENT

As educational institutions all the universities share the common mission of seeking to provide their students with a high quality educational experience across the range of subject disciplines. With varying emphasis the universities endeavour to develop and sustain research excellence whether it be in pure or applied research.

An inquiry into the management of universities chaired by Sir Alex Jarratt, *Report of the Steering Committee for Efficiency Studies in Universities* (1985), accepted the central role of Senates as 'the main forum for generating an academic view', playing 'an essential role in decisions affecting academic questions', and 'coordinating and endorsing the detailed work carried out on their behalf by Faculty Boards, departments and committees' (p. 24, para. 3.50f). The Jarratt Committee endorsed the role of committees in 'academic matters (e.g. curricula, examinations)' . . . 'decision taking by committees is both desirable and necessary for sound functional reasons' (p. 25, para. 3.53).

However, the Jarratt Committee was concerned that the collegiate structure, heavily dependent on committees, was inadequate to sustain successful universities in an era of change. The Jarratt Committee, which was concerned with pre-1992 universities throughout the United Kingdom, wished to see a stronger role for Courts (Councils in England) with their lay membership in the sphere of strategic and financial planning. It questioned the role of committees concerned with 'non-academic functions (e.g. catering, residence),' arguing that 'decision taking might normally be assigned to individual managers or officers either with or without committee involvement or aided by consultative committees' (p. 25, para. 3.53). The Jarratt Committee noted that 'the tradition of Vice Chancellors [Principals] being scholars first and acting as a chairman of the Senate carrying out its will, rather than leading it strongly, is changing. The shift to the style of chief executive, bearing the responsibility for leadership and effective management of the institution, is emerging and is likely to be all the more necessary for the future' (p. 26, para. 3.58).

While acknowledging the central academic purposes of the universities, the Jarratt Committee pointed to the need for strategic academic and financial planning, and for the use of professional management structures and techniques to manage complex institutions responsible for thousands of staff and students and millions of pounds of public and private money. The Committee was concerned that what they identified as 'the relative decline in the exercise of influence by Councils [Courts] has increased the potential for Senates to resist change and to exercise a natural conservatism' (p. 24, para. 3.50h).

The Jarratt Committee recommendations were taken seriously not only in the pre-1992 universities but also through the Scottish Office in the higher education institutions it funded. In addition there was a developing agenda for government in increasing the professionalism of management throughout publicly funded institutions. As a result, and strongly aided by an increased pace of change in higher education, there were pressures to increase the chief executive officer role of principals, and to expand the role of courts relative to senates. Among the changes which enhanced these pressures were a series of major switches in government policy creating turbulence, uncertainty and financial pressure. The government first created financial incentives to universities to expand student numbers and then suddenly imposed a period of consolidation with student numbers capped. The government also implemented a continuing policy of squeezing real funding per student leading not only to efficiency savings but also to what ministers have recognised as a crisis in higher education funding. In addition there has been a process of dismantling student maintenance grants and their replacement by student loans; and most recently from 1998 the introduction of a contribution to student fees.

The changes outlined have been accompanied by others which have sharply altered relationships between the institutions. In the 1980s government policy towards higher education embraced the competitive model: universities were encouraged to compete firstly for public research funds from both the research councils and through competitive research assessment exercises, and then for students, and also for private funds to support research, teaching, students and buildings projects, and indeed any university activity. In this competitive environment the government moved to a position of encouraging mergers emanating from the institutions themselves. While SHEFC is now, in the mid-1990s, strongly emphasising the merits of collaboration, including mergers and strategic alliances, the competitive ethos has become deeply embedded in the psyche of higher education.

In these pressured circumstances it is not surprising that both executive managements, led by principals, and courts have seemed to exert more influence and authority relative to senates and the academic committee structure. Courts in particular have been encouraged by SHEFC to use their authority. Despite this much of the collegiate ethos of academia survives as indeed it must in support of the central teaching, learning and research purposes of the universities. It is on those central academic purposes that attention is next focused.

THE MANAGEMENT OF ACADEMIC AFFAIRS

As already indicated, the Senate sits at the top of the academic committee structures. Generally senates are concerned with broad matters of policy and academic regulation, with the detailed matters concerning individual students, assessments, curricula delegated firstly to faculty boards and then to academic departments, subject committees and examination boards.

As suggested by Jarratt, committees play a crucial role in debating and deciding on academic issues. Deans, who lead faculties, and heads of department normally chair the main faculty boards and departmental meetings. However, the deans and heads of department are also managerially responsible for their faculties and departments. In securing the effective management and administration of their respective responsibilities they will generally assign duties among academic staff so that academic management is shared with several or indeed many colleagues. Thus there may be admissions officers, examinations officers and examination board chairpersons, course leaders, subject area leaders, research convenors, etc. drawn from the teaching and research staff within the faculty and department.

While there is considerable similarity in the general approach between the pre- and post-1992 universities, there are at least two major differences. The first arises from the historically much greater academic autonomy of the pre-1992 universities with their own degree awarding powers contrasting with the original dependence of the post-1992 universities on the authority of CNAA. In the latter CNAA regulations governed academic procedures and practices prior to the achievement of the universities' own degree awarding powers under the Further and Higher Education (Scotland) Act, 1992. The second arises from differing employment contracts in the two groups of universities: fixed term 'rotating' academic management posts in the pre-1992 universities contrasting with 'permanent' academic management posts in the post-1992 universities. The effect of the two differing practices are examined in turn.

Academic autonomy has meant that universities decide for themselves the structure of their degree and other programmes, the regulations and practices under which individual programmes may be developed and offered, and of course the curricula and teaching and learning approaches. At the most general level the University, through Senate, determines the regulations for the award of degrees, honours degrees and the various postgraduate awards. Within those regulations academic programmes are normally developed by or between academic departments subject to approval by faculty boards and/or senate. In the pre-1992 universities this has traditionally meant that there has been little or no external to the university scrutiny of individual academic programmes prior to their being offered to students except in cases involving preparation for membership of professional institutions, for example, in accounting or engineering. In the post-1992 universities, on the other hand, historically new academic programmes could not be offered until they had been validated or approved by a process involving external scrutiny in accordance with CNAA regulations. Despite their newly gained academic autonomy the post-1992 universities have retained this tradition of external scrutiny as part of the approval process required before offering a new academic programme. This general approach is reinforced by the vocational education mission of the post-1992 universities which has led to a higher proportion of academic programmes than in pre-1992 universities also leading to membership of professional institutions. The latter naturally impose their own external to the university scrutiny before accrediting an academic programme as part or whole of the requirements for professional membership. This, of course, applies to pre- and post-1992 universities alike. Notwithstanding the influence of the professional institutions there remains a difference in ethos between the pre- and post-1992 universities with the latter accepting external involvement of both employers and other academics in the design and approval of programmes more readily.

A more subtle effect of both the CNAA inheritance of the post-1992 universities and their vocational character has been the emphasis on programme rather than subject discipline. Since each academic programme is approved, monitored and periodically reviewed the academic management structures typically are based on the programme or course. Thus there are course leaders, course committees and examination panels linked specifically to each programme. In contrast in the pre-1992 universities the emphasis has been more on the academic discipline and its subject health. Correspondingly course management structures, while clearly important, have a less prominent role in the academic management of departments.

The differences in programme approval and management outlined above were very clear in the early and mid-1990s; however, more recent developments suggest some measure of convergence in the practices of the pre- and post-1992 universities in the later 1990s. This is considered below in the context of other changes after a discussion of the differing academic management employment practices in the pre- and post-1992 universities.

In the pre-1992 universities the deans and heads of department do not hold permanent appointments. Typically they hold office for around three years, possibly with reappointment, and then revert to their substantive post of professor or senior lecturer. In the post-1992 universities historically the heads of department, and in most cases the deans, have held permanent appointments. The managerial style of these permanent office holders obviously varies from those emphasising a collegiate approach to those emphasising a more hierarchical approach. Of course, within the pre-1992 universities the apparent collegiality of 'rotating' heads of department may not be so real in cases when one or more senior staff dominate particular departments. Nevertheless, the presence of permanent officers from Vice Principal through deans to heads of department in the post-1992 universities creates a more managerialist ethos and practice than exists in the pre-1992 universities.

Whatever the ethos pressures have grown in recent years to develop more effective leadership and managerial approaches in all universities. These include the advent of the research assessment exercises and teaching quality assessments together with increasing financial pressures, and the rapid developments in information and communications technology. Put simply, the performance of colleagues in publishing research, in the effectiveness of their teaching and support for their students can no longer be a matter of mild interest. The reputation and financial health of the department and the working environment for individuals within it depend on the effectiveness of its members. Instead of being administrative units within which academics exercise their freedom and skills to teach and research, departments have become in pre- and post-1992 universities alike closer to businesses. Departments seek to succeed academically through their recruitment of students and teaching and learning strategies, and through their research, both supported by the attraction of external funds where possible. Success may be assessed formally or informally against a series of performance indicators. These may include: student numbers; completion rates; proportion of students attaining a 'good' degree classification; research assessment grading; teaching quality assessment grading; external income; net financial surplus; cost per student; employment rates for graduates.

The pressures outlined are common to all universities and, just as importantly, the externally managed mechanisms and criteria for teaching quality assessment and audit, and research assessment are identical for pre- and post-1992 universities. Inevitably identical external processes and criteria of assessment and audit have led to convergence in internal procedures and practices in response.

While the detailed responses vary between universities, and indeed between individual departments and faculties within universities, there are some common themes. The pre-1992 universities have developed a much more coherent teaching and learning quality management framework at university and faculty levels than had existed prior to the existence of teaching quality assessments and academic audits in the early 1990s. The post-1992 universities already had university-wide frameworks with, for example, an academic standards committee as part of the quality assurance requirements of the CNAA. Conversely, both the teaching quality and research assessments have created pressures for the post-1992 universities to move towards pre-1992 university practices in giving greater emphasis to subject health rather than focusing more narrowly on individual course or programme management. It is likely that this process of convergence will continue.

Two other developments may reinforce this process. These are, firstly, a trend towards modularisation of academic structures and programmes designed to increase flexibility and student choice; and secondly the associated development of credit accumulation and transfer both within institutions and as a national framework. Both modularisation and credit accumulation and transfer developments strengthen the need for university-wide strategies and regulations. While not all Scottish universities have adopted these developments those that have cross the pre- and post-1992 university divide. Furthermore the Dearing and Garrick reports of the National Committee of Inquiry into Higher Education endorse the development of national credit accumulation and transfer frameworks. The funding body, SHEFC, is also leaning towards the development of funding based on modules.

CURRICULAR STRUCTURES

Any discussion of curricular structures in Scotland must start with the recognition of the traditional emphasis on breadth of study, particularly in the early years, and the distinction between the Scottish 'ordinary' degree which seeks to retain breadth in later years and the Scottish honours degree involving both an extra year of study and normally a greater emphasis on specialisation in the later years. Within these traditions students may study between three and five different subjects in their first year before opting for continuing breadth or increasing specialisation. These are powerful traditions with continuing support within both pre- and post-1992 universities. Both the Dearing and Garrick reports added their support as is clear from one of the recommendations in the Dearing Report (Recommendation 15, p. 132):

> We recommend that all institutions of higher education should, over the medium term, review the programmes they offer:
>
> • with a view to securing a better balance between breadth and depth across programmes than currently exists;
> • so that all undergraduate programmes include sufficient breadth to enable specialists to understand their specialism within its context.

Breadth of study is cherished both for its educational value and increasingly for the flexibility it affords students to taste before choosing or indeed to change direction. However, it would be wrong to overemphasise the current place of breadth in the curriculum as many students choose vocational and professional courses in law, medicine, nursing and professions allied to medicine, accountancy, engineering, teacher education etc. In such cases the curriculum may or may not be broad depending on the requirements of the professional institutions as well as on academic views. While achieving breadth may be a consideration the main focus tends to be on the preparation to enter a particular career path. Nevertheless, the Garrick Committee were anxious to promote the merits of broad based degrees and recommended that institutions should develop a new Scottish Bachelor's Degree combining breadth of study with a strong emphasis on the skills required by employers.

One trend, whatever the nature and structure of the degree programme, has indeed been the increasing emphasis on its merits as a preparation for employment. This reflects pressure from both the student 'market' and the employer 'market'. Both the expansion in numbers of graduates and diplomates and higher general unemployment levels have created a much more explicit concern among school leavers and mature entrants to higher education for the employment prospects arising from successful completion of particular programmes at the different universities. This trend has almost certainly been given a further boost by the decline in student maintenance grants, the increase in student debt and the planned elimination of grants and introduction of contributions to fees. Employers, too, have become more demanding and increasingly asking not only for traditional graduate accomplishments such as the ability to analyse, to think critically, and work independently, but also for other transferable skills in communication, team working, numeracy, information technology and problem solving. Certainly, universities have responded to these growing demands as the Dearing Committee acknowledges, but they make their view clear: 'All institutions of higher education should aim for student achievement in key skills – communication, numeracy, the use of information technology, and learning how to learn – to become an outcome for all programmes' (Dearing, p. 135, para. 9.25).

Consistent with their advocacy for key skills the Dearing Committee also strongly endorsed the value of work experience as part of academic programmes. There has been a long tradition of work experience in Scottish higher education particularly in the professional and vocational areas such as engineering, computing, and business, where in the post-1992 universities sandwich degrees including one year in relevant employment have formed a major part of course provision. In other areas such as nursing and midwifery, social work and teacher education professional work placements are compulsory parts of the academic and professional qualification awards. However, as both the universities and the Dearing Committee recognise, the constraint on developing and implementing work experience programmes can be the lack of opportunities offered by the employers. This is ironic since employers are often the first to stress the value of work experience in academic programmes.

A particular feature in the majority of the post-1992 universities is the existence of Higher National Certificate (HNC) and Higher National Diploma (HND) programmes. These are typically vocational programmes with designed sub-degree exit points after one year, HNC, or after two years, HND. However, there has been an increasing tendency for the successful students to progress to a third year leading to a first degree. Importantly, the awards of HNC and HND have been made, until recently, through the Scottish Vocational Education Council (SCOTVEC), and are now made through the Scottish Qualifications Authority (SQA). Accordingly, these HNC and HND programmes are subject to the regulations imposed by first SCOTVEC and now SQA.

Aside from the delivery of HNC and HND programmes in the post-1992 universities there is the very important trend of increasing numbers of students completing HNCs and HNDs in the further education sector transferring directly into the second and third years of degree programmes in the universities. This trend reflects an increased commitment to improving access to higher education in the universities.

So far the discussion has focused on the curriculum designed primarily to meet the needs of school leavers entering universities to study full-time for three, four years, or even longer in the case of dentistry, medical and veterinary students, prior to starting their careers. In 1995–6 approximately 100,000 students fell into this category. However, the total number of all students in the Scottish universities, including those taking short courses either part- or full-time was over 300,000 in that year. It is difficult to do justice to the variety of programmes offered to meet the diverse needs of the broad spectrum of people involved. Nevertheless, a brief review will seek to draw out at least some of the main features.

The first main group are the 27,500 postgraduates. These divide into research students and those studying on taught postgraduate courses. For the 7,300 research students the core of their work is directed to individual research programmes leading up to the presentation of a thesis. A relatively recent development has been the institution of taught research preparation or 'training' courses as part of the master's and doctoral programmes. These courses may be offered at departmental, faculty or university wide levels.

Taught postgraduate programmes may be designed as advanced courses for those already having studied the subject, or a closely related subject, to first degree level. Alternatively, the programmes may be designed as 'conversion' courses for graduates from a wide range of disciplines. In the former category examples include an MSc/Diploma in Actuarial Science for graduates in mathematics (Heriot-Watt University), and an MSc/PgDip in Electrical Power Engineering (Strathclyde University) for honours graduates in electronic and electrical engineering or related subject. In the 'conversion' course category the largest groupings are in business and information technology. Somewhere in between come the postgraduate certificate teacher education courses which build on the graduate's first degree subject but whose primary function is to prepare the student for entry into the teaching profession. Indeed a key characteristic of most taught postgraduate programmes is their role in preparing graduates either to enter the employment market or to advance their careers through professional development.

For the very large numbers of continuing education students – over 200,000 – there again have been at least three different traditions. Firstly, in the pre-1992 universities, the continuing education departments have offered a vast range of part-time non-credit-bearing and non-assessed courses, often of short duration, in the liberal arts tradition. Secondly, and particularly, but not exclusively, in the post-1992 universities, there have been clearly vocational short continuing professional development courses. Typically, these too have been non-credit-bearing. Finally, there has been the development of continuing education using the SCOTCAT credit accumulation and transfer framework. This development pioneered in the post-1992 universities is increasingly being adopted as a way of providing a very flexible approach of accessing credit-bearing courses to suit both the liberal arts and the professional development needs of mature students. While many students are content to study individual modules as either a hobby or for a specific career development need, many others are using credit accumulation and transfer also as a way of progressing to the award of a degree, honours degree or even a postgraduate award.

The SCOTCAT credit and accumulation framework (see Chapter 104), to which all the universities are signatories, forms the basis of the qualifications framework for Scotland recommended in chapter 4 (pp. 36–39) of the report by the Garrick Committee. How this will impact on the structure of academic awards in universities remains to be seen, but there seems little doubt that the Dearing Committee's desire for a better balance between breadth of study and depth will be a source of argument among the curriculum designers for years to come.

FINANCIAL AND RESOURCE MANAGEMENT

According to the Jarratt Committee (1985) 'it is in the planning and use of resources that universities have the greatest opportunity to improve their efficiency and effectiveness' (p. 16, para. 3.27). Despite, in the intervening years, very large real cost reductions per student, impressive growth and adaptation, significant achievements in research, earnings from overseas students and attraction of private funding the Garrick Committee believes that further progress is possible.

Both the Jarratt and Garrick Committees highlighted issues such as formal structures and responsibility for planning and decision taking, quality and extent of management information including benchmarking against other institutions, and the importance of the effective and efficient use of resources. The latter include most importantly staff but also the estate and equipment.

The Jarratt Committee (1985) was concerned that 'there is still a strong emphasis on maintaining the historic distribution of resource. Planning and resource allocation tend to be incremental rather than dynamic' (pp. 21–2, para. 3.40). Other criticisms included a lack of long term planning; lack of systematic use of performance indicators; lack of awareness of the full cost of activities; fragmentation of budgets and inadequate coordination to ensure resource allocation takes account of the full picture.

The force of the Jarratt Committee (1985) recommendations was generally recognised. Both the pre-1992 universities, to whom the report was addressed, and the institutions which were to become the post-1992 universities developed long term planning processes and indeed are required by SHEFC to submit strategic plans to the Council. These plans involve not only issues of strategic direction but also an integration of the academic, financial and physical (estates, space, equipment) aspects of university development. In addition SHEFC have strongly promoted effective planning in areas such as estates, equipment purchasing and management, and information technology. For example, all institutions were required to develop a five year strategic estate plan in 1994 and are expected to update this plan continually.

Similarly, although as anticipated by the Jarratt Committee solutions have varied, universities have reviewed their financial allocation mechanisms. There has been a strong tendency to adopt more devolved budgetary practices with faculties or planning groups becoming responsible for the whole of their budget including staffing, running costs, space costs and non-recurrent equipment expenditure. Aside from giving scope to faculties, or planning groups, to adjust their expenditures to meet local needs the central allocation procedures have had to become more transparent. Indeed the explicit student numbers based formula funding model adopted for teaching and the formula driven research funding allocation adopted by SHEFC have substantially undermined tendencies to historical distributions of resource.

Nevertheless, the Garrick Committee expressed disappointment that 'ten years on, "awareness of costs and full cost charging", appears to have progressed slowly in institutions' (p. 74, para. 5.18). Particular areas indicated for further improvement included: greater collaboration between institutions 'ranging from administrative services to research facilities and teaching and learning materials and programmes' (p. 76, para. 5.27); communications and information technology also involving collaboration through the use of Metropolitan Area Networks (MANs) 'which make it possible to share electronic libraries, course materials and, particularly in research' (p. 77, para. 5.30); and 'making use of the summer period for credit-bearing teaching' (p. 77, para. 5.33).

The external pressures exerted by SHEFC and reports such as those of the Jarratt and Garrick Committees, together with the 'continuing funding crisis in higher education' (COSHEP, 1997) are causing the universities to review carefully their procedures and practices in financial and resource management. The universities are only too aware that their deteriorating financial situation requires a continuing search for improved effectiveness and efficiency in the use of resources. The universities, however, are concerned that without additional resources the vision of 'higher education in the learning society' painted by the Dearing and Garrick Committees will be unrealised.

REFERENCES

COSHEP (1997) *Response to the Report of the National Committee of Inquiry into Higher Education*, Committee of Scottish Higher Education Principals, Glasgow.

Farrington, D. J. (1994) *The Law of Higher Education*, London, Dublin, Edinburgh: Butterworths.

National Committee of Inquiry into Higher Education (1997) *Higher Education in the Learning Society*, Report of the National Committee, Chairman Sir Ronald Dearing, Norwich: HMSO.

National Committee of Inquiry into Higher Education (1997) *Higher Education in the Learning Society*, Report of the Scottish Committee, Chairman Sir Ronald Garrick, Norwich: HMSO.

Shaw, R. W. (1997) Catch 22: The Newest Universities, in R. Crawford (ed.), *A Future for Scottish Higher Education*, The Committee of Scottish Higher Education Principals, Lasswade: Polton Press.

Steering Committee for Efficiency Studies in Universities (1985), Report for the Committee of Vice Chancellors and Principals, Chairman, Sir Alex Jarratt, London.

74

Beyond Ivory Towers: The University in the Community

Drummond Bone

CIVIC PRESENCE AND COMMUNITY RESOURCE: AN OVERVIEW

The civic importance of the Universities of Edinburgh and Glasgow, Aberdeen and St Andrews has been an unquestioned fact at least since the eighteenth century. If golf is perhaps the first thing that springs to mind when a visitor thinks of St Andrews, anyone living in the town will quickly realise that the University is in fact the more dominating presence. The spire of Gilbert Scott's building on Gilmorehill is as much an emblem of the city of Glasgow as it is of the University itself. From 1557 the burghers of Glasgow city supported their University. There is a long tradition of classes being open to the public. The idea of universities as 'community resources' rather than as civic institutions is perhaps a new one however.

The model of a civic body would include the trade guilds, the burghers and the governing body where these were to be distinguished from the guilds, and the religious bodies or their secular successors including the universities. Each of these bodies would be a limb of the civic being, with responsibilities to the totality, but would not serve another body to which it did not belong. The resource model sees the citizen as the irreducible fact of the civic, rather than any institution. Accordingly the institutions become servants of a population defined by political 'rights' and commodified 'expectations'. Where continuity was central to the civic model, responsiveness to demand is central to the resource model. The paradigm shift marks a change from higher education as a provision available only as a privilege within a governed and walled structure to a provision available as a right for everyone likely to benefit from it, and from a model of the universities as autonomous collegiate bodies to state-funded managed organisations with a responsibility to their tax-payer funders. This essentially twentieth-century shift was rapidly accelerated both by the creation of new universities in the Robbins era – these new institutions frequently having a self-consciousness of place and local responsibility (Warwick for example was located in Coventry as part of that city's post-war regeneration project) and more rapidly still by the dissolution of the binary divide in 1993, which brought into the HE sector colleges with a tradition of local service and local funding .

To see universities as community resources is not quite the same thing as to see them as major drivers of the local economy, and indeed there are some tensions in these two visions as shall be seen below, but it is closely related. The universities provide employment to large numbers, even if the largely middle-class and often cosmopolitan academic staff are excluded. These employees have access to a great deal of career and personal development opportunities. People unconnected with the universities also have access to lectures, cultural events and cultural provision (galleries and museums for example), and perhaps even to sports facilities which are part of the epiphenomena of universities. The universities also provide space for local activities, in much the same way as the church hall does in a village context. And this is all without consideration of the provision of extra-mural courses run by the institutions, with the express aim of addressing community as opposed to university needs. Increasingly capital projects have an eye to the 'local resource' model – the new Gilmorehill Centre at the University of Glasgow, for example, includes not only a public theatre but also a public cinema, which has been integrated into the local cinema on a commercial basis. The fact that the lottery funding crucial to the project enshrined public access as a condition (the project was in any case never conceived in other terms) only serves to underline the connection between funding source and service responsibility. No university in Scotland could now function without an eye both to the obvious needs and the developing possibilities of its local community. The taxpayer has a very clear stake in higher education, and that stake is tangible at a local level.

LOCAL COMMUNITY RELATIONS

The stress on locality can be exemplified by Glasgow University's production of a Newsletter for the immediate surrounding area – some 60,000 copies are delivered to local households, to inform them of what the Goliath in their midst is up to, and to draw attention to the publicly available resources the University has to offer. The University also plays a fundamental role in the now annual West End festival (which itself may be seen as an example of an attempt to reinject the notion of community into an accident of geography), providing both space and financial input. More importantly perhaps, in the recent reorganisation by the City Council of schools provision, the University was involved in collaborative talks at a very early stage to discuss local planning and estate development issues. Indeed planning matters are often a node of tension in community/HE relations, in so far as the universities are large property owners whose changing needs directly impact on the physical environment. The development of the new playing fields at Garscube in a residential district of Glasgow and on a site of considerable natural attractiveness is a case in point – trees had to be cut down (many more were in fact planted), and there was a great deal of local concern. Civic hauteur must inevitably give way to community partnerships.

At the same time, the fact that the big 'civics' in the Higher Education (HE) sector function on a global stage is a source of local community pride. Here perhaps the distinction between the civic and the communal breaks down, though it is an interesting observation that the perceived activity of a university is sometimes coloured at civic level by its location in a particular kind of community. Thus the much greater commercial activity (in absolute terms) of the University of Glasgow is softened by its location away from the heart of the city's business on the leafy and middle-class heights of Gilmorehill when compared to Strathclyde, whose city centre presence throws into sharp focus its commercial activities. But both of the big Glasgow Universities, as of course Edinburgh, receive considerable national and international coverage for their research activities, particularly where these involve overseas clients or partners (Dolly the sheep is world news). This psychological boost to the community is usually mentioned long before the economic factors which benefit a local area – the spending power of thousands of students in shops, bars, restaurants and cinemas, and the provision of relatively cheap labour to help run these businesses in the shape of the same students who are the customers. This activity is often actually perceived in negative terms, since the numbers of students involved tends to swamp the residents and wildly skew the age profile of the area. Moreover those students have only a transient relationship to the community in which they live. This might be less true in the West Coast than in the East, where there can be considerable strain between non-indigenous students with high spending power who may see the local community as mere providers of a service, and the locals for whom the community is anything but a commodity. The facts and the perceptions do not always coincide: the universities increasingly see it as part of their own role to correct any mistaken perceptions.

EDUCATIONAL OUTREACH

The traditional extra-mural classes which catered for a wide range of local need have somewhat changed their character in recent years, since government decided that funding should only follow those courses which could provide a monitorable output in the shape of a 'qualification' of some sort. This has led to an increasingly close relationship between universities' outreach classes and their 'mainstream' classes through the provision of 'credits'. But it has not always meant that there is a closer relationship between the community and the university. Some popular courses have been withdrawn because they do not lead to a 'qualification'. The change in funding has professionalised what was previously something more personal and intimate. However, a whole host of initiatives have helped redress the balance. The work of the Science and Technology Regional Organisations (SATROs) (collaborative regional resources for bringing science and technology into the community) bring university activities to the communities and to the schools. Moreover they are themselves partnerships of universities and business interests. Exhibitions, inter-active workstations, and highly imaginative workshops make the day-to-day work of the research laboratory a familiar but still exciting activity in the community. In the hope that this will encourage the next generation of students, universities put relatively large sums of money into the SATRO organisations. Industrial partners have their own interest in encouraging a technological culture in the young. Other outreach activities have different apparent ends, but are often in the last analysis (arguably like the SATROs) a means of enhancing recruitment. Glasgow University runs a number of musical and artistic events for the young and very young to help fund its programmes for disabled access, but these events also bring pupils into the University and help overcome the 'fear factor' of HE, particularly amongst families where there is no tradition of university education. Most universities now tackle this problem directly by running summer schools for those prospective pupils from disadvantaged backgrounds, or those who are approaching uni-versity from a non-standard route – usually mature students. These access programmes have a notable effect on retention rates, so once again a public service brings a tangible benefit to the universities, in the shape of a decrease in the loss of fees from students who withdraw mid-year. The rapid development of distance learning through the use of Information Technology (IT) might also be seen as providing a link to the community beyond the campus boundary, but it is a virtual rather than a real one. Glasgow University is exploring a new route in the setting up of a satellite campus at Crichton College in

Dumfries, which will certainly make use of IT, but will also directly embed a human presence in the 'distant' community. The University of Paisley already has a number of 'campuses' in the West, and both Stirling and St Andrews have in the near past at least expressed an interest in expanding their geographical base. These additional sites have very specific local objectives, and although they have an institutional backer or owner, their character is very much more that of service provider than of institutional producer. This is a crucial distinction, though it is one which cannot be made definitively in any one case. The civic institutions have a determining effect on the civic body; the new campuses are reactive to their surrounding community. How far the institutions themselves will follow or are already following the reactive model they have themselves floated is a matter of debate. Too reactive an approach by major research engines is a recipe for long term stagnation; on the other hand no university can afford to ignore local demand, nor be allowed to be irrelevant to the needs of its funders.

Universities are now heavily involved in work placement schemes, some funded locally, and some from Brussels. These can be in-house or they can be run by companies in which the universities have a financial or personnel interest. The clients may be individuals with or without degrees, though they are typically graduates seeking new or more marketable skills, or they may be companies in search of outsourced training. In both cases the links between university and workplace are strengthened through the transfer of personnel.

LOCAL PARTNERSHIPS

It is becoming acknowledged that the Scottish universities make better use of shared resources than their English counterparts. There are some notable examples of teaching cooperation, such as the Scottish Doctoral Programme in Economics, and in the very near future a similar venture in Scottish Studies and in the Social Sciences. There are innumerable examples of research collaboration, particularly involving IT, quite a few of which have been driven by Scottish Higher Education Funding Council (SHEFC) bidding rounds, and backed by government resources. There are two main drivers – first to cut cost by efficient use of resources spread across a number of institutions, and second, to react to changes in the intellectual endeavour itself, which has typically spread across what was once conceived as the boundaries of two or even more disciplines, and thus requires a new matrix of skills to develop and deliver. The ability to react is certainly partly a function of the size of the sector, and of a shared community or national spirit. Recently the World Bank expressed the view that the Scottish university sector is uniquely 'cohesive', and comments from global pharmaceutical companies, not to mention the recent arrival of the Cadence project, conditional as it was on the cooperation of four universities, underscore the same point about cohesion. The Cadence example is particularly powerful. This major player in electronic 'system-on-a-chip' design is placing a new Research and Development facility in Scotland (with 1,800 highly paid employees) on the basis that Edinburgh, Glasgow, Heriot Watt and Strathclyde will provide a high level training and ultimately research institute as part of the inward investment package. The West Coast universities collaborate on commercialisation where possible, including Development Bank projects. All of the major Universities collaborate in Connect, an organisation to facilitate the passage of research ideas into the commercial world. All but one collaborate in the Scottish Biomedical Research Trust, which has seen a notable inward investment success from Japan. Strathclyde and Glasgow are in the planning stage of widescale collaboration on research.

And all of these initiatives stand outside of a recent spate of discussions over the merger of teacher training institutions with partner universities, which have their academic aspects, but which are arguably primarily financially driven. Here it is important to distinguish between short term financial issues, and longer term market driven issues, and not to be too concerned about an academic versus financial distinction. All of these changes are the result of the increasing privatisation of the universities, running in parallel with the globalisation of sophisticated business markets. As the universities are more and more dependent on contract research income, so they must become ever more efficient and flexible to meet a competitive and fast moving market. Strathclyde has set a ten year target of reducing its reliance on government funding to under 50 per cent. Glasgow currently only receives 53 per cent of its income directly from government, and fully 16 per cent directly from industry and commerce. On the other hand there is a danger in the pursuit of the year-end bottom-line, at the expense of long-term development.

This market imperative has the effect at a local level not only of increasing collaboration between universities, but of growing closeness between business institutions and the universities (in some ways a return to the civic links of previous years). Thus Chambers of Commerce and universities meet regularly. The City Council joins with a university in overseas promotional activities. The Scottish Council for Development and Industry has many university members. Organisations such as the Glenrothes University and Industry Development Initiative thrive. Again the existence of the Scottish Enterprise Network gives the Scottish universities an edge over the scattered Training and Enterprise Councils in England, though things may be currently changing in that country, in providing a common resource for development with local industry and overseas investors. Networks beget networks, and different kinds of collaborations grow – whether the relatively straightforward cooperation on conference-development between Tourist and Convention bureaux in the cities and the universities, or more complicated partnerships on archival storage and retrieval.

The structural interweaving of local health provision and the medical faculties can often be forgotten by the outsider. The National Health Trusts and the universities are, for better or worse, inextricably tangled in shared personnel and shared physical resources. The difficult part of the relationship is the financial. The wholly positive part is the provision of healthcare supported by the latest in research and technique. The threat of cuts in university staff for financial reasons impacts directly on clinical work, and the universities are acutely aware of their responsibilities in that regard, but it is a difficult circle to square, and the community is not obviously concerned unless there are problems, or spectacular successes (such as the West of Scotland Coronary Prevention Study). But it is not only the medical faculties that are involved in local health initiatives – the World Health Organisation Healthy Cities Initiative is interdisciplinary, and is a partnership of local councils, other local groups, and many university departments, including but not exclusively medical ones – environmental studies, policy studies, urban studies, psychology, to name a few.

Few of these relationships are without their tensions. The community tends to see the local university as a free resource, rather than a commercial partner. This can be particularly awkward in commercial negotiations where government intermediaries are involved. While in another context those intermediaries press the universities to maximise commercial gain, in this context they strive to present the university as a public resource in the service of industrial development. Similarly businesses have been known to claim that universities have been unenterprising, when what they mean is that the universities have not been prepared to risk their own resources for the business person's profit. But universities are a gateway to the global knowledge base for small and medium enterprises, and while the major research partners of the major research universities are almost certain to remain the multi-nationals, it is in the long term interest of the universities to have a healthy local economy, and therefore in their interest to nourish local business.

This positioning of the universities between the local economy and the global economy would appear to be behind what some supra-governmental institutions (the European Commission, the Development Banks) see as the universities' role in providing strategic analysis and leadership in local, and now, in the context of the Scottish parliament, national, government. In this view the universities play a role as a bulwark against a too narrowly local outlook. In an odd way this returns them to their function as institutions (this time of a global rather than a civic body) and moves away from the 'resource' model.

But whether the perspective is global or local, the universities' role in regional economic development is now an accepted fact by all parties concerned, and regional development no longer simply means the local science park. Whether a university should be the servant of local need, or the agent of global change, is probably a question which cannot have an absolute answer. It is a question however around which a lot of political tension is likely to build as the Scottish parliament grows into a reality.

THE FE SECTOR

The Scottish system of close relations and easy articulation between the FE and HE sectors was made much of in the Dearing and Garrick Reports. It certainly goes some way to providing that seamless transition from advanced school level to university level and onwards that lies at the heart of Dearing's vision of the learning Society. Its existence grows partly from the tradition of broad rather than specialised entry into university which makes access in general easier in Scotland than England (47 per cent of the age cohort are in the tertiary sector in Scotland as compared to 35 per cent in England), but probably even more from the tradition of viewing education as a chance to escape poverty, rather than as a means to preserve a social hierarchy. It is noteworthy that in a relatively flat society such as New Zealand the privatisation of the universities has proceeded at a much faster pace than in the UK, where government control of the market is seen as a necessary device to ensure access from disadvantaged population groups and from those with no university tradition. In Scotland the same effect has made the move from FE to HE a relatively easy one. That is not to say that it could not be better managed yet.

THE 'SCOTTISHNESS' OF SCOTTISH UNIVERSITIES

Although there is something to the idea of the 'democratic intellect', and something certainly distinctive about the breadth of Scottish education and the two tier degree system, it is possibly a little too easy to see these as a product of 'Scottishness'. Education as a highway to escape from poverty, as opposed to a method of reinscribing a hierarchy of privilege, is certainly a fondly held Scottish belief. There is of course some reality to it, and moreover the cohesiveness provided to a society by a wide dissemination of an expanding knowledge base has a virtue of its own (acknowledged by the Dearing Report and the present government). The current Scottish system provides a choice (between three–year general and four–year specialist degree) unavailable in England. This choice may be crucial to the sound functioning of a mass education system with its widely differentiated clientele, and has of course profoundly influenced the American mass system. The choice at university level is dependent on the range of subjects available at school level, and this is a function of time available, as much as of skills available. An increase in specialisation at school level inevitably reduces the time available for 'other' subject areas. This is an area of intense debate. Industry claims to want generalists, but Human Resource Directors tend to hire high-flying specialists, and thus themselves deter high quality students from entering general degree courses. This combines with the government's desire to save money into a pressure on the four-year specialist degree – not towards the logical three year general degree but towards the illogical and restrictive three–year specialist degree. To be fair the Scottish Office has recently started to advertise posts without specifying an honours degree. This is a case where the identification of the current system with a national characteristic (the 'democratic intellect'), no matter how tenuous, might be very much to the good in the political context of a Scottish parliament.

The Chief Executive of SHEFC is not a Scot, and SHEFC is as much to do with the way the universities conduct themselves as most things! Of course SHEFC is conditioned by the political environment in which it exists, and that in turn is conditioned by the cultural environment in which it exists, but to a large extent SHEFC's differentiating factors – its insistence on cooperation and its own cooperation with the Scottish Enterprise Network for example – are driven by economic rather than cultural imperatives. SHEFC has been involved in both Connect and the Cadence projects. SHEFC is also profoundly influenced by the size of the sector. This makes things easier in many ways to manage, but it also makes attempts to manage more transparent and therefore less politically acceptable. It favours institutional autonomy. While this might seem to be unequivocally a good thing, SHEFC can also use it to pass difficult funding decisions, which might have national significance, down the line to the institutions, and thus put them in the firing line. The level of medical funding is a case in point – universities have to choose between cross-subsidising from other areas of their activity, or being 'guilty' of running down medical care. It is surely not appropriate that this kind of decision be cascaded.

The movement to a mass education system has certainly favoured what already existed in Scotland. The fact that more of the Scottish universities have deep historical roots in their local civic structures probably helps guard against the town/gown polarisation still found in the two ancient English universities, which kept their governance much more independent for much longer, and the relative indifference of some civic-academic relations in the red-bricks. But it is easy to overstate a Scottish character in the way in which the universities reach out to their surrounding communities. It is not the subject of this chapter to dwell on the differences in governance between English and Scottish institutions, but with the signal exception of Oxbridge, it is rather hard to see how these affect relations with the community. Geography however, and the political fact of a boundary from Solway to Berwick most certainly do make a difference. They provide an apparently natural unit of a most convenient size (leading to what has been called the 'Switzerland effect'). The boundary provides a psychological sense of unity, which however illogical under scrutiny, is very real and facilitates cooperation; the size means that it is easy physically to meet, and a sense of shared community is built on real contact. The odd thing then is that the Scottish universities are relatively poor at maintaining alumni relations. Most are now making very conscious efforts to improve, but are still a long way behind Oxbridge. The very practicality of the Scottish approach to education seems to militate against emotional attachment. No doubt the non-residential nature of the traditional Scots university profile (though this has changed and is continuing to change, despite financial pressures to the contrary) has a lot to do with it too. But it could also be that that very closeness to the local community which seems in so many ways such a good thing, also deprives the universities *per se* of the loyalty of their students. There are fewer walls to feel safe inside. That said, there is a remarkable degree of what one might describe as passive sentimental loyalty – there is a community of Scottish graduates out there in theory, eager when questioned to assert their community membership, but curiously reluctant to wave their flags. Perhaps there is after all an element of Scottishness in universities in Scotland.

REFERENCES

Amin, A. and N. Thrift (eds), (1994) *Globalisation, Institutions, and Regional Development in Europe*, Oxford: Oxford University Press.

Crawford, R. (ed.) (1997) *A Future for Scottish Higher Education*, The Committee of Scottish Higher Education Principals, Lasswade: Polton Press.

Davie, G. E. (1961) *The Democratic Intellect*, Edinburgh: Edinburgh University Press.

Goddard, J. B., D. R. Charles, A. Pike et al. (1994) *Universities and Communities*, London: CVCP.

National Committee of Inquiry into Higher Education (1997) *Higher Education in the Learning Society*, Report of the National Committee, Chairman Sir Ronald Dearing, Norwich: HMSO.

National Committee of Inquiry into Higher Education (1997) *Higher Education in the Learning Society*, Report of the Scottish Committee, Chairman Sir Ronald Garrick, Norwich: HMSO.

75

Current Priorities in Higher Education

Stewart Sutherland

EXTERNAL AND INTERNAL PRESSURES

Priorities come from two sources, external and internal. If they are really serious they come from both directions simultaneously.

The major priority facing Scottish Higher Education is serious in just that way: the need to define its corporate and several individual identities. In the United Kingdom over the last twenty years or so a process of displacement has been sweeping through Higher Education and what has been displaced is the sense of worth and identity. The old certainties of what universities and colleges were, and were for, have been washed out of the system by successive tides of change and revolution. With these certainties have gone the sense of self-direction and self-definition. Whether this is good bad or indifferent is not the point: all three terms apply to different aspects of the process. What is clear, however, is that in this respect, the experience of Scottish Higher Education institutions has been no different from that of cousins south of Hadrian's Wall.

The changes which have brought this about are well documented elsewhere in this volume. The expansion of the number of Scottish universities in one lifetime from four to thirteen, plus the Open University and another in the offing, is dramatic. In the same post-war period, the age participation rate measuring the proportion of the eighteen-year-old cohort experiencing higher education has increased from just over two per cent immediately after the war to just under fifty per cent in Scotland currently. The size of the largest individual Scottish university now tops twenty thousand students.

These changes in themselves, largely driven from outside, but compliantly accepted, have had several significant but often unnoticed implications which affect the internal character of the institutions. It is now impossible for members of staff, academic or otherwise, to know more than a minority of colleagues by appearance, let alone as fellow members of a recognisable collegiate community. If Newman's account of the 'Idea of a University' ever had wide application, it is virtually unrecognisable now.

The consequences for self-regulation and what has now come to be recognised, albeit reluctantly, as the need for management, has inevitably changed the character of internal relations. Significantly increased student to staff ratios have altered the once reasonably intimate nature of teaching, and research has become too closely identified with the funds necessary to carry it out.

Basically, the higher education system in Scotland and the United Kingdom has become mass higher education. The people affected have yet to adjust fully to the meaning of this – and 'people' includes universities, employers, parents, and governments and their funding agencies. The central current priority is to adjust to this changed situation and in essence this means reconstructing a sustainable account of what a university is, what a higher education system is meant to be as well as to do.

Universities have become increasingly reactive over the last twenty years or so. Instead of helping to form national and international agenda they have reacted to the place defined for them in these agenda by others. In part this is a result of having to pay the price of becoming heavily dependent on the public purse, and in part a result of the corollary of what came to be seen as the burden which this created – a steady but compound slicing of the unit of resource. Gradually the focus of university activity was adjustment to downward financial pressure which took the form of an academic version of genteel middle class decline, patching a tutorial programme here and stitching together the overstretched laboratory budget there. In such a situation survival in one form or another rather than vision founded on a strong sense of identity becomes the order of the day. In fact most universities became rather street-wise and within those limitations moderately successful in adapting to harder times. In the process, however, the acquired skills of coping with a little bit of this and a little bit less of that became the replacement for a self-confident participation in national agenda-setting.

REDEFINING THE PURPOSE OF HIGHER EDUCATION

If the central priority for now is definition of the nature and future of higher education, what is the detailed shape of the questions which that raises? A visual aid which bears some resemblance to a completed game of noughts and crosses may offer some help.

T   R   X

R   N   I

T   R   C

Old hands at the game of university acronyms will recognise the first line, T, R and X. These are the letters used by David Phillips in the mid-eighties to open up a debate about the academic focus of various universities and university departments. Some, it was implied, would be research-led (R), some would lay particular emphasis upon teaching (T), and others (X) would have a mixed focus of, in the case of institutions, having some departments research-led and others focused primarily on teaching.

Part of the search for definition must be for each institution, and each sub-section, to define themselves and their aspirations against such benchmark terms and realities. That has difficulties of its own: but even more difficult, although at least as necessary in a Scottish context, is to take a view of the emphasis of R, X and T across the system. The advantage which Scotland has is that, granted the size of the system, this is an achievable aim. The fundamental questions are essentially of definition. What should a Scottish Higher Education system be? and then, What should it look like? In part those questions come with increasing force from the system. But equally importantly they should and do come from within. It is necessary to ask how academic staff and activities should have altered as the system increased the number of degree awarding institutions from four universities to thirteen plus several other colleges. Equally should the menu offered to nearly fifty per cent of the age cohort be uniformly the same throughout the system, and simply a cheaper form of what was offered to three per cent of the age cohort fifty years ago?

Such questions should be asked of itself by any respectable higher education system, as well as of themselves by each of its members. One thing is sure: the questions will be pressed from outside as will unsuitable answers if there is a failure of resolve to tackle them. Another certainty is that individual universities as well as faculties and departments will have to set priorities which define roles and individualities. It is not best use of scarce resource and talent if everybody tries to do everything.

REGIONAL, NATIONAL AND INTERNATIONAL ROLES

This leads appropriately to the second line of noughts and crosses. Here (R) stands for Regional, (N) stands for National and (I) stands for International. Universities must define themselves in terms of regional, national and international focus. Whom do they serve? Where do graduates seek employment? What are the continuing education and professional development activities which should be part of the institution's profile? Where should research and development activity find its external partners? Is the profile realistic and compatible with what else is on offer in the region or city?

The issues of regional and national strategies and roles have been shuffling steadily to the forefront of the stage over the last ten years or so. In one sense they are not unannounced, for old and new universities and colleges have played important local roles for, in some cases, hundreds of years. But there is a new edge to this as the political frontiers of both Scotland and the United Kingdom change. In Scotland, the rebirth of the Scottish parliament will bring renewed focus and scrutiny to the contribution which the totality of higher education makes to the health and well-being of the Scottish nation and its economy. The answers already given are very positive, but there is no doubt that the questions will become sharper and more insistent. Some questions may even be misdirected, but for institutions to say so and be convincing will require a stronger sense of self-identity than they possess now.

Each university in Scotland has a regional focus: all have a national role and the variations in the forms which each of these takes will be complemented by an even wider variation of international profiles. The process of self-definition which is the precondition of a sense of identity will involve institutions clarifying, department by department, whether the nature and extent of regional and national commitments does or should include international dimensions. They cannot all be, indeed perhaps none of them can be, the Harvard of the East Atlantic, but areas of some institutions should have the aspiration and confidence to set such benchmarks against which to measure progress and development.

What Scotland certainly does have is the mass higher education system of the East Atlantic and the corollary of that is that there is a need for the variety and diversity of the most experienced and successful mass higher education system in the world. One startling statistic from there: of the three thousand or so accredited degree awarding institutions in the USA only ten per cent are licensed to award doctoral degrees. Now that is diversity with attitude. It is not being suggested that the same proportions would be transportable to Scotland, but at least there is a question to be asked.

COMMUNITY

The third line of the crossword puzzle has a different set of questions, but a set which none the less encompasses much that has gone before. (T) stands for teaching and (R) for research, and these are the two terms around which most academics would seek to construct a redefinition of institutional identify. These surely lie at the core of higher education activities and hence of institutional identity. Of that there is no doubt, and what remains is to define individually for each institution where the balance between these lies.

However, to restrict the enquiry to these two categories in self-definition has perhaps been one of the ways in which institutions have played a part in side-tracking themselves from broader involvement. 'Involvement in what?' is a reasonable rejoinder to that claim. The answer is contained in (C) – (C) for community.

There are several key points here. The first is that in focusing upon (T) and (R) in the account of identitfy, universities abstract themselves, or at least seem to do so, from context. There is no context-free social institution. To leave space for such a misconception – either internally or externally – is to leave room for all the tedious, but dangerously alive metaphors of ivory towers. Aristophanes' portrayal of a philosopher living in a barrel on top of a long pole was meant to be a joke, not a model for academic success! In reality a philosopher who lives on top of a pole is not long for this world: the same is true of institutions which sought to be ivory towers. The fact that universities, after cathedrals, are European civilisation's most enduring institutions shows the fallacy of the ivory tower jibe.

However, if an attempt is made to define identity without reference to the communities in which universities are located – by reference to teaching and research alone as if they were abstract and abstractable activities – they give credence in many minds, including some within the institutions themselves, to the view that they exist outside or above society. This shows itself in a number of ways. Most rampant at the moment is the wish to bring universities to heel. This is a widely shared perception amongst some politicians who regard universities as too aloof, amongst some industrialists and officials of, for example, such Quangos as Scottish Enterprise, who would wish to blame universities for any perceived weaknesses in the Scottish economy.

It is a perception which universities have shared as they have responded to the parallel external wish to clip wings by cutting public resources, by defining the relationship to communities in terms of 'Them' unjustly denying 'Us' the necessary funds to carry out teaching and research in a traditional manner. That way lies increasing isolation and poverty.

The counter proposal is once again to recognise as one of the planks in the platform of self-definition that universities belong to communities and that the only healthy future lies in dialogue and conversation, no doubt robust at times, as members of that community. The University of Edinburgh, for example, was founded as the 'Tounis' university as was the University of London a creation of citizens of London in the 1820s, self-consciously drawing upon the Edinburgh experience of two centuries and more earlier. Each university can recount relevant chapters in its own history and the point is that these chapters are not historical accidents, they are founding and defining events.

It is not, of course, being argued that the way to redefine identity is to become some sort of academic fundamentalist, with universities defining themselves purely historically by what has been. Quite the reverse. The stress on community is stress upon what is living, moving and changing. A university must define itself within, as well as over against, that community.

The trick, in part, is to decide what for any institution counts as 'its' community. (R), (N) and (I) are all selectively relevant here and again the mix will vary for each institution and in some cases for each department. The point is that in the model which has been offered, (C) is a variable, but it is not an optional extra.

The fundamental plea as a first and almost all-consuming priority, is for a restatement of the identity of institutions as members of a community with a distinctive contribution to bring to that community. That contribution is in part defined as helping the community and its members to flourish, but not simply as providing the means to predetermined ends: rather also to take part in the continuing debate about ends and means and in the definition and setting of ends. Universities have lost their place in such a discussion and this is a sign of the extent to which they have been complicit in their own gradual devaluation. They must start regaining that place not by standing off and shouting, but by first reassuring themselves about their own identity as they move into a new millennium which includes in Scotland uncharted political waters.

76

Adult and Continuing Education in Scotland

Paul Standish

DEFINITIONS, HISTORY AND CURRENT PROVISION

For many readers of this chapter the picture of educational practice that the title brings most readily to mind will be that of the university extra-mural department. This is an arm of the institution reaching out beyond its body of mainstream courses to extend educational opportunity at university level to members of the wider community. In some respects this has seemed an epitome of liberal education – non-examined, subjects pursued for their own sake, committed university teachers sharing their enthusiasms. It will be evident to some that this is a paradigm under threat, but equally that this is but one of the range of ways that adults are, and have been, educated in Scotland. To bring this broader picture into view it is necessary to consider the terms of this discussion and the potential problems they raise, and this will lead beyond the university to other types of provision.

What is adult education? How appropriate is it to write about adult education as a discrete entity? Before considering the importance of adult education, or the desirability that it should be 'continuing', it should be recognised that the categorisation raises two kinds of problems. The first is both conceptual and practical: how clear is it as a category? The category of adult itself is problematic: the legal definition of the age of majority does not correspond with the various distinctions that have commonly been made in educational practice. There is a vast range of circumstances in which adults are engaged in education and the gap between this and the way that adult education is often understood needs to be emphasised. (Statistics in this field should then be regarded with a degree of caution.) The second, however, is ethical and political: how desirable is it to maintain the use of the category? What's in a name, one might be inclined to say. But inasmuch as this and the range of related overlapping terms are names for institutional practices, this stabilises and strengthens differentiations of funding, organisation, pedagogy, and self-conception. So the terminology does have a bearing on how adult education ought to develop. Where different terms are linked with different organisations, disputes about who is in control and who-is-to-pay-for-what can become critical. It is worth asking who has the responsibility and who has the power, and this needs to be done in terms of the evolution of the practice.

The early history of adult education in Scotland reveals a variety of developments. In the early eighteenth century an important role was played by small local libraries and by night classes in parish schools. In the universities pioneering work was done first by John Anderson at Glasgow University and then by George Birkbeck at the Andersonian Institute (now Strathclyde University). While Birkbeck's lectures for artisans did not always receive due recognition from the universities themselves, it is clear that there was an enthusiastic response from his students. After four years Birkbeck moved to London to continue his work, and the continuing reputation of Birkbeck College in the University of London, whatever financial difficulties it currently faces, is a tribute to his success. In 1821 the first independent Mechanics' Institute (later to become Heriot-Watt University) was established to 'afford instruction to the labouring classes'. By 1850 there were fifty-five such institutes (compared with 610 in England – significantly less in proportion). According to Birkbeck, Scots were theoretically in a better position to take advantage of adult education than the English. They were more likely to have had a sound basic education (through the parish schools) and there was a stronger tradition of adult learning. For example, more than one-tenth of Gaelic school pupils in the Highlands in 1849 were over twenty years of age. In the middle of the century there were 438 evening schools in Scotland catering for around 15,000 adult pupils. Two other Scots, James Stuart and Patrick Geddes, also played important roles in the development of university extra-mural education. Stuart, while at Cambridge, established the University Extension Movement. Geddes organised the first international summer school in Europe which was held in Scotland in 1887. Later growth in adult education was slow, relative to that in England and Wales, perhaps in part for reasons of geography and accessibility. This needs to be seen, however, in the light of the surprising difference in participation in university education between Scotland and England and Wales. In 1868 the Argyll Commission found that in Scotland proportionately six times as many students received a university education, one-fifth of all Scottish university students having working class origins.

In the latter half of the twentieth century, the climate has become progressively more favourable to adult education, although this progress has not been without its setbacks and distortions. Generalisation here is difficult because of the diversity. In the decades following the Second World War adult education was offered by a wealth of smaller voluntary organisations with developing services on the part of museums and art galleries, the library service, and public broadcasting. But four main providers stand out. Local education authorities' provision constituted the largest share of the work, while this was consistently complemented by the Workers' Education Association and the university extra-mural departments. The Education (Scotland) Act (1945) led to the evolution of the youth and community service, which attempted to offer a comprehensive service for young people and adults. This service developed outside of and as a complement to the main-stream provision of schooling, further education, higher education, and many aspects of adult education. The relationship between these providers and the Community Education Service has not always been harmonious. This is partly because of difficulties of demarca-tion and disparate administrative structures. But the difficulty also reflects in part a difference in outlook, the Community Education Service being committed more to setting up programmes within the community and building on community initiatives. This illustrates well the way the use of a term can be pivotal for practice, as indicated at the start of this chapter, and it suggests the kinds of consequences that may follow too insistent an emphasis on 'adult education'. For all the considerable merits of the practices of the Community Education Service, certain uses of the term 'community' undermined the possibility of more inclusive conceptions of community involving mainstream provision through schools and colleges (see Chapter 94).

The new and diverse opportunities that have emerged in recent decades represent the passage of adult education from margin to mainstream. Adults have come to be welcomed in all sectors of secondary and tertiary education. Adult guidance services have developed. Company training has extended and broadened. Tax relief has been provided for non-advanced vocational education and career development loans for those training on their own initiative. Research into adult education has become a major priority for public funding. Perhaps most dramatic of all has been the increase of adult participation in mainstream university courses.

It is worth pausing to consider how and why this recent growth has come about. A key document that laid the way for change is the Alexander Report, *Adult Education: the Challenge of Change* (1975). Appointed in 1970, the Committee was given the following brief:

> To consider the aims appropriate to voluntary leisure time courses for adults which are educational but not specifically vocational; to examine the extent to which these are being achieved at present; and with due regard to the need to use available resources most effectively, to make recommendations.

When the Committee reported in 1975, it had had twenty-four full meetings and numerous meetings of sub-committees, with wide consultancy. Indeed the Committee was careful to recognise the range of agencies involved in the field and, alert to the problems that had been generated by inter-agency conflict, stressed the need for collaboration and cooperation.

A starting point for the Committee was the recognition that, while there had been increases in participation in the preceding two decades, many people, and certain sections of the population especially, were not benefiting from adult education. Between 1953 and 1973 enrolments had increased from 104,000 to 217,000. But the latter figure still represented only 4.45% of the adult population. Most of the students were female and there was an imbalance between young and older adults (15% were under 25 while 25% were over 55 years old). Put in its most stark terms, only 0.2% of young working class males attended adult education classes. Perhaps most significant was the fact that over 80% of participants were in the top three socio-economic classes, with most students having educational qualifications higher than average. And the 'iron law' of adult education was demonstrated: that those who receive it come back for more, with many attending year after year. The restricted nature of that participation was something the Committee wanted to address. Much attention was given, therefore, to finding ways in which barriers to access to education might be removed – barriers to do with location and accommodation, with style of teaching, with subject matter, with the timetabling of classes, with lack of crèche facilities, with lack of marketing, and with traditional prejudices.

The Committee recognised the need to address the issue of adult education in the light of a changing world. Technological change suggested the need for adult education to help people to adapt to the increasingly technological environment that they found themselves in. This would include the need for a more highly trained – and trainable – work force but also the need to understand and make good use of the technologically advanced features of our world. Modern computer applications in some ways illustrate these factors. Adult education needed to respond, it was argued, to changes in demography – for instance, by offering courses appropriate to the growing numbers of retired people. Similarly, and partly as a result of technological change, the availability of increased leisure time was seen to provide new opportunities. The Committee also judged it desirable for people to be enabled through adult education to play a fuller part in democracy. This would go beyond the ballot box to include participation in local community and workplace organisation. In addition to the above the significance of change in education itself was recognised. This included the increasingly prevalent conception of education as continuing and as being something broader than a training of the intellect. The child-centred progressive movements of the 1960s (and before), and perhaps growing awareness of the work of Paolo Freire, had laid the way for a new commitment to learner-centredness in adult education. Against the subject-based curriculum, the possibilities of a broader approach that would enhance the learner's capability and flexibility were stressed. Furthermore the increasing demand for higher education – and the need to enhance access to this – was acknowledged. In the light of the dehumanising aspects of work and the impact of the mass media, more attention should be given, it was judged, to the reaffirmation of individuality through education, and this was thought to call especially for programmes relating to recreation, the family, the elderly, the disadvantaged, the handicapped, and remedial education. Increasing bureaucracy and technology were recognised as warranting such measures as consumer education and health education, the better to enable adults to benefit from society's changing resources. At a time of increasing pluralism, with society less certain about the values it should uphold, it was thought desirable to release funding to support educational institutions and initiatives of a variety of kinds. Varied provision, including education in industrial relations, courses for immigrants and foreign workers, and the participation of a variety of voluntary groups, would, it was held, reflect democracy in action. Furthermore, education for change was thought necessary to equip people to deal with the increasingly unpredictable nature of their lives and with the expanding arena for choice. The growing desire for that choice was again seen as a healthy reflection of democracy. A more rounded sense of what this might amount to, however, was evident in the Committee's emphasis on community development and on a social and political education promoting consideration of the environment, bridging the educational gap between the younger and older generations, bringing together different professional groups, and advancing the public understanding of technology and society. It is not surprising that in their recognition of the challenge of change the Committee advocated a raised profile for adult education staff with 200 additional full-time posts, better career and training opportunities, and wider awareness of adult education through B. Ed. programmes.

In concluding its statement of aims, the Committee quoted the words of Sir Eric Ashby's William F. Harvey Memorial Lecture in 1955:

> We live in a society which confers on the worker (irrespective of whether he is manual or clerical and irrespective of the amount of education he has) political responsibility, civic rights, and leisure. The contemporary problem in adult education is that among many people at all levels of education the leisure is without purpose, the civic rights are without significance, and the political responsibility is assumed without understanding. We are learning the hard way that social emancipation without personal emancipation is of little value. In a world noisy with the organs of mass communication and riddled with propaganda, modern man is hard put to it to preserve his status as an individual. To help preserve this status is the contemporary task for adult education.

The Committee judged that in the twenty years since these remarks had been made the imperative for change had intensified. It was with some zeal, therefore, that the Committee opposed the prevailing view of adult education as a marginal enterprise and stressed the need for a national policy committed to lifelong education.

When one looks back at the recommendations of the Alexander Report from the vantage point of the late 1990s, they seem for the most part unsurprising. Many of its recommendations were for practices that are relatively familiar today, ones that adult educators have come to regard as their stock in trade. Yet this perspective is misleading on two counts. First, it does not do justice to the extent to which the report did have a visionary element about it, arising as it did in a context that was very different. But second, it would be equally wrong therefore to conclude that the Report immediately ushered in a period of reform. The truth is that there ensued a period of disappointingly slow development. An early setback was evident when Robert Hughes, speaking for the Secretary of State for Scotland, asked those involved to consider particularly those recommendations that did not require additional expenditure (*Scottish Journal of Adult Education*, 1975). The economy was indeed the underlying reason why the ten years following the Report provided a relatively bleak climate for adult education. During those years attendance at LEA traditional adult classes declined, partly because of increases in fees and the lack of subsidy for non-vocational education. Scottish Office funding was withdrawn from university continuing education departments and from Newbattle Abbey, Scotland's only residential college for adult education. Central Government funding for Adult Basic Education stopped. Voluntary organisations came under increased financial pressure. Nevertheless development was seen in some areas: there was a new drive to combat adult illiteracy, in which the BBC played a prominent part; adult participation in formal education – especially university education – increased; and, although the Open University had existed for a number of years, open learning came onto the wider scene as an important innovation and a signal for later developments.

Since 1985 the picture has been brighter. Generally the ambience and attitudes of colleges of further education have been adjusted to the needs of those who were previously excluded. Practical measures such as the provision of crèches and the timetabling of classes to suit the needs of parents of young children have been taken. More subtly many institutions have altered their style and their presentation – at reception, in the classroom, in the library, in the canteen – to attract students who lack confidence or who would otherwise find the institutional environment alien. Participation rates have increased substantially with growing provision of adult educational guidance. Research has expanded – especially into such areas as access, open learning, the participation of women and ethnic minorities, staff development, learning effectiveness, and the relationship between industry and further and higher education – notwithstanding the closure in 1991, as a result of a reduction in the funding for voluntary institutions, of the Scottish Institute for Adult and Continuing Education. If courses promoting access to higher education have been the flagship of development during this period, achievements in extending continuing education at lower levels should not be underestimated, even if there remains much to be done.

The government document most clearly focused on adult education during this period was the HMI Report *The Education of Adults in Scotland*, published in 1992. This report noted approvingly the increased level of collaboration and cross-sectoral cooperation amongst providers, and was particularly influential in bringing to wider attention the importance of regional integrated networks for adult guidance. It encouraged the flexibility of delivery that was becoming more apparent, seeing this as a key factor in the further removal of barriers to access. The report did not set out to comment on vocational education but, in a language that would have come less naturally to the authors of the Alexander Report, it did affirm that 'Investment in wider access is likely to be cost-effective' (p. 2).

Moreover, progress in terms of flexibility and collaboration was explicitly attributed to improvements in 'marketing, planning, delivery and evaluation of provision'.

It is very much this rhetoric that characterises the 1997 Scottish Office White Paper *Raising the Standard*, proclaimed by Michael Forsyth as 'a radical vision of an education and training system in which schools, colleges, universities, teachers, and training providers focus on quality and standards' (p. 1). Rather than being especially radical, however, the report is characterised by its endorsement of familiar trends. Regarding adult education it follows the 1992 document in stressing the importance of adult guidance and in advocating collaboration between sectors to establish a 'complex grid of relationships making up a forward-looking community education service' (p. 44). Community education here comes to be seen more clearly as part of the common enterprise of the different institutions. In the rhetoric, however, the idea of community education is increasingly subordinated to that of lifelong learning, and this tends to be seen in terms of an emphasis on skills acquisition and qualifications that partially displaces liberal aims. While the boundaries between the functions of different providers are progressively blurred, so too there is an extension of learning into the work place with the establishment of work-based qualifications and the promotion of flexible delivery, especially through Scottish Vocational Qualifications. The Paper notes approvingly the 2,200 organisations committed to Investors in People and describes measures already taken to help Local Enterprise Companies work towards their targets. It goes without saying that all these developments are conceived with a view to the extended use of new technology in teaching and learning.

It has been seen then that, contrary to claims of radical change, there has been a steady trend towards the flexible delivery of a curriculum that is, if not vocational, orientated towards the economy, and delivered by institutions whose roles are less clearly demarcated. Change has been radical, however, in the incorporation of the colleges of further education, in the rapid expansion of participation in further and higher education, and in the current changes in the financial support of full-time students in higher education. What are the implications of these changes and what issues does the broader development of adult education raise?

CRITICAL ISSUES

The question asked at the start of this chapter of how far it is appropriate to write about adult education as a discrete entity points to two broad ways in which key issues can be identified and addressed.

The first of these involves locating developments in the education of adults within a larger picture of changes in education. This approach can be illustrated by way of an example. There seems little doubt that traditional liberal adult education, where subjects are studied or other activities pursued for their own sake, is in danger of marginalisation – the paradigm under threat referred to at the start. A clear index of this is the financial pressure on universities and colleges to shift resources away from uncertificated programmes. But this emphasis on certification is not isolated: it is a reflection of the more general credentialism that increasingly characterises educational policy and practice at every level. Credentialism in turn needs to be understood in terms of the pervasive demand for accountability. This dovetails with the climate of instrumentalism to create the preoccupation with efficiency and effectiveness nicely evoked by Lyotard's term 'performativity'. These problems are obviously not exclusive to adult education, and any attempt to understand the education of adults will be severely skewed if it does not take this broader background into view.

The second way in which critical understanding can be brought to bear is to focus on the distinctive features of adult education and to treat adult education in a more or less isolated way. Adult education researchers and practitioners have sometimes seen it as important to delineate the special characteristics of this field and to stress its distinctiveness from wider aspects of education. What distinguishes adults from younger people is their experience, it is said, and this has a bearing on the way that they learn and on the kinds of curricula that are appropriate to them. A leading idea in this way of thinking has been Malcolm Knowles' theory of 'andragogy', while other significant influences have been Paolo Freire's liberation pedagogy and the humanistic psychology of Carl Rogers. With these ways of thinking the emphasis is often on the therapeutic and consciousness-raising potential of adult education, possibilities that are perhaps implicit in aspects of the Alexander Report. This approach has surely been motivated in part by the failure of educational institutions adequately to respond to adults – their tendency to confront them again with the oppressive and authoritarian regimes from which many of them have in the past fled, and with an inflexibility of organisation and curriculum delivery that makes no concessions to their different practical circumstances, needs and aspirations. There is no doubt that elements of this alienating regime persist, yet there is a temptation to caricature this the better to affirm the cogency of alternative practice and to legitimate adult education as a discrete area of educational research.

Of course, these two approaches are not mutually exclusive and the challenge must in part be to find a way of recognising and responding to the broader changes in education that remembers those characteristics and needs of adult learners that have often been over-looked.

Whatever the cogency of this second approach, its practical application is inevitably complicated and likely to be reduced where the education of adults is integrated with the education of young people. The growth of access and adult returners' courses has provided new contexts where adults are educated separately, and the implication of the learning society that education will continue throughout adulthood and often through work again extends the contexts of adult education. Yet as these examples are considered, the distinction becomes increasingly blurred. With the dramatic increase in participation in further and higher education, it is not so much that adults are assimilated into the mainstream as that the mainstream changes to become partially adult. And adult education has expanded beyond its own mainstream through the Community Education Service, the Local Enterprise Companies, Investors in People, and a wealth of voluntary and private agencies.

The evolution of practice and institutional coordination encouraged by policy documents in recent decades makes the categorisation of 'adult' more porous than must have seemed to be the case in 1970 when the Alexander Committee was first convened. Adult education has always been diverse and it is becoming ever less easy to generalise about the kinds of curricula adult students follow and the contexts in which they learn. To some extent the difficulties over terminology and identity here have been superseded by 'lifelong education' and 'lifelong learning', terms that for all their current vogue date back at least to Philip Virgo's 1981 Bow Paper 'Learning for Change: Training, Retraining and Lifelong Education'. What do the terms signal? Although some understandably take them as being nothing other than fashionable surrogates for 'continuing education', adult education by another name, a more generous reading might find in them an exaltation of education throughout life, perhaps in the manner that Dewey advocated – education from the cradle to the grave. That education must be something that people return to repeatedly in the course of their working lives gives the term a slightly different weight, however, while the cognate idea of 'the learning organisation' heralds a world where the work-place itself has become a learning environment, where much education is related to work, and where the vocabulary of corporate finance is humanised (cf. Investors in People).

The evolution of the learning society through this terminology is related very much to questions of funding, questions crucial to the future education of adults. How are access programmes to be funded? How about adult basic education? What of undergraduate study? Whatever the short-term effects of current changes in policy, the problems of funding further and higher education are likely to lead to a situation in which more post-compulsory education becomes part-time, especially as students pay their own fees. (The distinction between full and part-time is, of course, itself equivocal, being subject to the inconsistent criteria of different funding bodies.) The numerous differences that need to be drawn here are sometimes glossed over. It is common now to hear of the glaring disparity that has existed between undergraduates with maintenance grants and their fees paid and further education students who pay for themselves. While in principle it has only been students in full-time higher education who have had their fees waived, the reality has been that many have attended further education colleges on a more or less full-time basis but without payment. Waiving fees for students has made financial sense where the same students could be registered as full-time equivalents, as has commonly been the case. Juxtaposing full-time undergraduate education against the vast range of part-time further education and generalising about these matters smacks more of sectarian interests than a contribution to equity and social justice.

In tandem with the concern for efficiency, a rhetoric of greater choice and ownership of learning provides the rationale for replacing anomalous systems of public funding with individual learning accounts. Students will then be able, it is claimed, to budget to meet their individual needs whatever their course preferences or academic level. Thus, it seems, education is added to a portfolio of personal financial planning and investment as people increasingly take responsibility for their own development. But how far does this apparent autonomy deflect attention from a reduction in public commitment? Freire wanted to liberate people from the 'banking' conception of learning; ironically today's students may come to rely on the learning bank! How likely is it that those from the lowest socio-economic groups will avail themselves of such opportunities? People from these groups are the most likely to be deterred by the prospect of long-term investments and debts, especially those arising from a good as intangible as education.

The cultural change that appears to have made unacceptable the kind of increase in taxation necessary for sustained public support is also, however, one that may be newly susceptible to marketing initiatives in education. As traditional educational institutions will have neither the expertise nor the goods to market in this way, their place may be usurped by providers more centrally located in the computer industry, with all its alertness to the knowledge economy and its marketing panache. New markets may be created.

If these measures do succeed in helping more students to pursue their education as adults, they are very much to be welcomed. But some questions need to be raised. The individuation and commodification of learning here can undermine aspects of learning that, precisely because they are not easily recorded, are easily overlooked. For all the systems of advice and guidance and learning support there is a potential isolation of the learner: the kind of friendship that can arise in the shared pursuit of a subject is eroded in favour of the supposed independence of the individual and the displacement of subject content by an emphasis on skills. Such friendship, and the larger sense of the common good of which it may be a part, are not incidental to learning. Learning that is shared – with teachers, with fellow students, and with what is studied – suggests a form of relationship for which 'community' may seem too woolly and 'stakeholder' too contractual, and for which the more recent notion of 'shared convoy' seems more apt: those studying together share a kind of journey, and the journey is enriched and made different by the company that is kept. This is not to eulogise exclusively liberal pursuits: the joint projects that arise with networks of trust and expert teams, and upon which industry's Research and Development can thrive, can equally occasion this kind of convoy. There are elements in this shared experience that individualised learning cannot replace.

If this is right it gives all the more weight to the idea of the educational institution as a locus of community. The change in student populations and diversified modes of attendance consequent upon changes in funding may require the university to become more like a college of further education in certain respects – less 'a place apart' and rather more a focal point for the local and regional community, a hub for a region's further education, continuing professional development, and Research and Development. Such an institution might extend through its satellite stations and outreach provision, and to virtual locations on the Net through its cybercafés or 'village halls'. Inevitably there are worries about what must seem a dilution of university life and inevitably there are concerns about the erosion of standards. But the potential gains are easily underestimated – not only of the academic benefits of the highly committed and able adult part-time students but of the democratic counterbalance to globalisation that cooperation with local industry might provide.

This section began by considering the fate of liberal education in terms of decisions about funding in a climate of efficiency and effectiveness. But in certain respects the liberal is in conflict with a number of paradigms that currently dominate policy-making and the training and professional development of practitioners. Progressive theory such as that alluded to at the start of this section has supported a therapeutic conception of practice, in many ways typical of late modern reflexivity. Student-centred learning has been partially subverted, however, by a different set of assumptions emphasising a consumerist conception of choice within an extensively managed and systematic curriculum. A second paradigm, which has partly been responsible for this and which tends to shape issues of policy and funding, is the vocational/instrumental. A third, equally involved in this subversion, is the application of information technology. There are immense gains to be made through the imaginative and efficient application of new technology. Such is their seductiveness, however, that there is a danger that artificial intelligence can come to provide the dominant model for human learning, with all the ramifications for curriculum and its delivery that this implies.

It is a mistake to think of these approaches as simply misguided. What is necessary is to dispel the hold that certain pictures have on policy-makers, researchers, and practitioners and against which the claims of liberal education are apt to sound reactionary, ill-defined, and perhaps rather dull. To redress the balance then it is worth ending this chapter by affirming the importance of the continuing liberal education of adults.

It may be that, contrary to vocationalist assumptions, the needs of industry are best served by liberal education because this can provide the breadth and imaginative resourcefulness that employers increasingly seek. It may be that personal growth, contrary to the expectations of many progressive educators, is best realised where students engage their attention in those intrinsically valuable practices and forms of enquiry that are part of the cultural inheritance. But these potential pay-offs are not the point of a liberal education. Indeed it has no point, if this is taken to be something external to its pursuit. There is no doubt, however, that the advantages offered by other paradigms seem more immediate and that they are better understood. The task of those concerned with the education of adults must be to reaffirm a central liberal commitment, whatever extrinsic benefits this may have and whatever other activities are also rightly promoted. The picture of the extra-mural class evoked at the start of this chapter may be tinged with nostalgia but the spirit that it implies is to be realised across the broad range of adult education. There are resources within the Scottish tradition for this to be sustained.

REFERENCES

Alexander, K. et al. (1975) *Adult Education: the Challenge of Change*, Report of a committee of enquiry appointed by the Secretary of State for Scotland, Edinburgh: HMSO.

Government White Paper (1997) *Raising the Standard, a White Paper on Education and Skills Development in Scotland*, Scottish Office.

HMI Report (1992) *The Education of Adults in Scotland*, Edinburgh: SOED.

Scottish Journal of Adult Education (1975) 1:4.

Virgo, P. (1981) *Learning for Change: Training, Retraining and Lifelong Education*, Bow Paper.

77

The Open University in Scotland

Bob Glaister and Ronnie Carr

THE OPEN UNIVERSITY – A UK PERSPECTIVE

The Open University (OU), which was granted its Royal Charter in 1969 and admitted its first students in 1971, has been widely hailed as the most important innovation in UK higher education in the last thirty years. Its underlying philosophy is illustrated by its commitment to be: 'open as to people . . . open as to places . . . open as to methods . . . and open as to ideas' (Crowther, 1969).

Established as the 'university of the second chance' and 'the university of the air' – the titles used by Harold Wilson when he first mentioned the idea in public at a Labour Party rally in Glasgow in 1963 – the OU has now developed into the largest university in the UK. It offers more than 400 courses and resource packs to well over 200,000 people every year both in the UK and, increasingly, in mainland Europe. It also presents programmes further afield (e.g. Singapore) and some of its materials are used, with local adaptation, in the Open University of Hong Kong. In total, over two million students have now studied with the University, and its impact spreads well beyond its student body as the weekly viewing figure of 3.5 million for its TV programmes attests.

It is hardly surprising that what was then such an innovative concept met with scepticism, even hostility, in some quarters in its early days, particularly because of the generally poor reputation of correspondence education and doubts about the viability of its open access policy. Most of these concerns have long since abated as a result of the recognised quality of its materials and the exit standards demanded of its students. The quality of the OU's integrated multi-media learning materials, which encompass advances in information technology, is assured by the course teams' consideration of several 'drafts', by the testimony of external assessors and, increasingly, by some form of professional accreditation. The standard of student performance, maintained by a comprehensive system of external examiners, is illustrated by the acceptance of OU graduates for post-graduate study in 'traditional' universities around the UK.

While the learning materials have been the focus of attention for academics in assessing the quality of the OU's provision, there is little doubt that, for students, the locally-based tutorial support assumes equal importance. There is a network of thirteen Regional Centres in the UK which support and supervise the work of nearly 8,000 part-time associate lecturers (ALs) in 300 Study Centres (and another forty or so elsewhere in Europe). ALs mark assignments submitted by students, provide written feedback, meet students at Study

Centres, and offer additional personal support through correspondence, telephone and in many cases, computer conferencing.

The OU is making a very significant contribution to mass higher education (HE) in the UK by demonstrating that the possession of traditional entry qualifications is not a prerequisite for successful university study; over one-third of the OU's 150,000 graduates did not match the entry requirements for conventional universities when they enrolled. It has shown also that learning and employment can be combined: three-quarters of OU students are in full-time jobs while they study. National, and indeed international, objectives for lifelong learning are made practicable. While scale and quantity are defining features of the OU, they are not attained at the expense of quality and scholarship. Indeed it may be that the first pair have been achieved because of the existence of the second. The OU has come through strongly in the comparative assessment exercises with British universities on teaching and research. For example, to date eight research areas have been recognised as producing research of international excellence with another eleven rated at national excellence.

The OU was for the first twenty years or so funded directly by government, through the DES, latterly DfEE. However, after the 1992 Higher Education Act, it moved into the mainstream of HE funding. Although it is a UK body, it was resolved to reduce complexity and have it funded by only one of the funding councils – the Higher Education Funding Council for England (HEFCE). Another outcome of the 1992 Act was the abolition of the Council for National Academic Awards (CNAA) whose role in validation and quality assurance for other institutions was given to the OU, as the only UK-wide institution of HE. The University, therefore, contributes to the widening of access to HE through its own provision and by the validation of others.

THE OPEN UNIVERSITY – A SCOTTISH PERSPECTIVE

The OU in Scotland is one of the 13 Regions mentioned earlier – Region 11 – with an office in Edinburgh. There is a core staff of 74, including the Scottish Director, one depute, three Senior Counsellors, 17 Staff Tutors or academic managers, two advisers, five adminis-trators and 45 secretaries and clerical staff. There are approximately 700 part-time associate lecturers offering tuition and counselling at the 36 Study and Location Centres.

The OU in Scotland's application rates initially fell below Scotland's proportion of the UK population – 8.5% of applications compared with approximately 9% of the population. However, this rose steadily to 11.3% in 1988 and 11.4% in 1993 – until 1996 when it dropped to 9.3%. Perhaps more significantly, the slight decline in actual student registra-tions was accompanied by a significant reduction in its share of Scotland's part-time student market – from 43% to 39%. There is no doubt that a partial explanation for this dip is the increased access to HE provided by other universities which are 'modularising' and offering part-time routes, placing them in clear competition with the OU for an audience for which it had previously been the only option. In this context the most serious threat could have been the project to establish a University of the Highlands and Islands, which would have removed a substantial number of OU students across a large swath of the country. A collaborative approach has now been agreed upon however, in which OU validating services are a key part of the project.

One of the most distinctive features of the OU in Scotland's student enrolment in the early years was the lower percentage of teachers than south of the border. Among the first ten cohorts of OU graduates, 44% were teachers, but only 37% in Scotland, which presumably reflects the fact that Scotland has traditionally had more graduate teachers. Also, some OU students already hold a degree and when one looks only at teachers graduating who had not previously held degrees, the Scottish difference was even more marked: UK 41%, Scotland 29%.

More recently, the OU has expanded into the continuing professional development and Master's degree sectors. While the OU in Scotland has a very strong record in the undergraduate market, it has fared less well at postgraduate level. The two longest running OU Master's degrees, the MBA and MA in Education, each recruit over 3,000 students annually in the UK, but Scotland attracts only some 5 per cent of the total. One explanation of this phenomenon must be the level of competition: Scotland has some very strong business schools, and the four cities have offered part-time MEds (originally EdBs) to Scottish teachers for three-quarters of a century. Another possible factor which is considered more fully in the last section is that the content of these general vocational/ professional awards lack 'Scottishness'.

Interestingly, some of the University's newer and more specialised Master's degrees, with smaller total numbers, have recruited well in Scotland – reflecting a technological and scientific interest which has been matched over the years in the undergraduate programme where the OU in Scotland has attracted above average percentages for these areas. In 1992 Scotland had 13.2% of Mathematics students and 10.8% of Science students, and in 1995 these figures had risen to 15.4% and 13.0%. It is not clear whether this feature has something to do with the total provision of HE in Scotland (more Higher National Certificates/Diplomas, as noted in the Dearing Report on HE) or with some aspect of Scottishness or Scottish students. The distribution of Scottish student courses by faculty or academic unit in 1996 is shown in Table 77.1.

Table 77.1   1996 OU student courses in Scotland

Arts	1,937
Management	1,238
Social Science	2,890
Education	681
Health/Social Welfare	457
Languages	256
Mathematics	2,281
Science	1,874
Technology	2,246
Courses validated at other institutions	339
Total	14,199

In 1971, only 27% of the new undergraduate students were women, but across the university the number of male and female students is now almost equal (49% women, 51% men). Over the years Scotland's share of women students has always been slightly smaller, but in 1996 it too reached 49%.

Although Scotland contains only some 9 per cent of the UK population, they are dispersed over an area which amounts to more than a third of the total UK land mass – including four major clusters of inhabited islands. This means that approximately 20 per cent of Scottish OU students are geographically remote, so that the OU's distance teaching 'package' has had to be augmented in the Scottish context. In addition to Study Centres (teaching accommodation located in a school or college/university), there are Location Centres in the more isolated areas, particularly the islands, staffed by at least one member of the OU part-time staff with an enhanced range of resources – such as a small library of course materials, administrative documents, careers guidance information, and in some cases a fax and a loud-speaking telephone. Significant use has also been made in Scotland of telephone conferencing; ALs talking with groups of students gathered round loud-speaking phones; or conference calls whereby half a dozen students and an AL can be linked so that they can talk together no matter how widely scattered geographically. There have also been pilot projects involving video conferencing, electronic whiteboards and computer-mediated conferencing.

Whether students are geographically isolated or not, the OU attempts to offer the same quality of support across the UK and, indeed, to provide access to the same range of courses. At present, the only exceptions to the latter point are some professional qualifications in Education and Law. All other courses are available – even in prison, where there are 40 OU students in 1996.

The OU in Scotland has successfully adapted the OU provision and systems to meet Scottish geography over the last twenty-five years and, while it has generated student registrations on a scale that matches any other Scottish university, it is still a university in Scotland rather than a university of Scotland – and that is the principal issue which needs to be addressed in its future development.

ISSUES

Competitive pressures have been generated in all areas of HE – in Scotland as well as the UK generally. Most institutions of HE have developed part-time routes: many have entered the OU's preserve of distance education; all are making more intense use of accommodation so that there is more limited access to it by the OU for Study Centres, residential schools, exam centres, etc.; and staff have less time to spare to teach part-time for the OU. The OU's strength is that it has always adopted a collaborative approach, and while it has been threatened by the competitive ethos, that approach is the means by which it could make an even more effective contribution to HE in Scotland in the new millennium.

Being governed by remote bodies has always been a source of discontent in Scotland. The Shetlands do not welcome Edinburgh control but, even more so, Scots have been suspicious of Westminster government and a Scottish parliament is imminent. Government of the OU from Milton Keynes has been a major factor impeding the further development of OU provision in Scotland, and indeed has often been a source of frustration for the staff of the OU in Scotland. How Scottish is the OU in Scotland? How Scottish might it be? How Scottish need it be?

Through its Scottish staff, the OU has developed strong links over the years with all relevant Scottish bodies so that the general OU provision could be best exploited. Of course, some OU provision, for example in mathematics/science/technology, straddles national differences (which might explain why Scotland has had a slightly higher success rate in these areas). However, in some other areas, specific initiatives have taken place to recognise a Scottish difference: Scottish supplements for some Education courses; Scottish assessors of proposals and draft materials; and resource materials on Scottish history and culture. Also, collaborative arrangements have enhanced the provision – for example, with Colleges of Education to offer Scottish modules in the Reading Diploma; with Scottish Power for an SVQ; and with Dundee University to develop courses in Scottish history.

All of these ventures have been welcomed and they have been effective, but they are ad hoc and piecemeal; they can appear as gestures by a predominantly English body. Two trends are of extreme importance for the OU in Scotland: firstly, the move from general to vocationally-relevant education; secondly, the increasing desire of Scots to support things Scottish. It is very significant that the three major developments in the School of Education in the 1990s have been funded by English bodies to meet specific English requirements: the PGCE (the initial teacher training qualification), a certificate for Specialist Teacher Assistants, and the supported open learning route to the National Professional Qualification for Headship. None of these is offered in Scotland. The MA in Education operates at a conceptual and theoretical level such that contextual/national differences are less significant and the degree stands fair comparison with Scottish MEds. (Indeed one might be astonished at how much Scottish MEds focus on English education.) But the trend is clearly to support more professionally and practically focused courses and the OU will not manage that on its own in Scotland; collaboration, if not partnership, with Scottish institutions will be essential. From the other perspective, distance education will remain a key element in Scottish provision and, because scale is essential to this mode, one can anticipate that OU expertise, if not necessarily all of its provision, will be essential to the Scottish effort.

Finally, all of these questions might be answered by funding. As noted earlier, the OU is funded for the UK by HEFCE. It cannot be long before the Scottish Higher Education Funding Council (SHEFC) decides that it wants to integrate more fully the 13,000 OU part-time students in Scotland funded by HEFCE. It seems unlikely that SHEFC will continue the current funding arrangements. The important questions seem to be:

- Does Scottish education wish to adopt the OU as a Scottish institution?
- Does the OU wish to accept the challenge of developing genuine partnerships in Scotland to meet smaller scale national needs?

REFERENCES

Anderson, D. (1982) The Open University Experience, in *Distance No Object*, Edinburgh: HMSO.

Carr, R. and R. Glaister (1981) Information Paper 7: the Open University in Scotland, *Scottish Educational Review*, vol. 13, no. 1, pp. 58–61.

Crowther, G. (1969) Inaugural Address, Royal Society.

Dearing Report on HE (1997) Report of the National Committee of Enquiry into Higher Education, chaired by Sir Ron Dearing, Norwich: HMSO.

Perry, W. (1976) *The Open University: a personal account*, Buckingham: Open University Press.

Two additional sources are the journal *Teaching at a Distance* (1974–85) which became *Open Learning* in 1986, and the annual reports of the Vice Chancellor of the Open University.

X

Assessment and Certification

78

Could Do Better? Assessment in Scottish Schools

Tom Bryce

A CHANGE FROM THE PAST

People remember their teachers for a variety of reasons, not least in their roles as assessors of what they did in school; as evaluators of their learning, and for that matter, much else besides. A scurrilous jibe ascribed perhaps to the previous generation, would have it that teachers wrote 'could do better' upon pupils' work, thereby neither indicating what they had achieved, nor whether it was any good at all. The remark carried with it a variety of messages: that teachers judge achievement, capability and worth (as professionally they must) and as such are gate-keepers to future prospects and employment; that assessment was easy to do and therefore required little effort. Perhaps most of all, in that bad old past, that really very little of substance was conveyed by such 'assessment'. And of course the tone of such remarks could provoke resentment; teachers would be seriously disliked if in the eyes of their pupils there was no recognition of their value and potential as a consequence of being so assessed. At worst, assessment could fail its very purpose if pupils were turned off learning as a result. How many adults harbour such feelings . . .?

In contrast however, the present generation will have quite different views of assessment, because what teachers actually do now, how they assess and report upon pupils' work, has become the subject of detailed prescription. Such has been the attention paid to assessment and reporting in the national developments of the last two decades that teachers cannot get away with 'could do betters'. Through the requirements of Standard Grade, SCOTVEC modular courses, the 5–14 Development Programme, and now Higher Still, central government has steered 'good practice' and uniformity in assessment along with changes to the curriculum. The criteria which teachers should use to assess pupils have been made much more explicit. Some of the changes to assessment stem from the accountability movement, with monitoring, standard-setting and the like influencing how achievement should be described, monitored and conveyed to parents and employers. In years to come, perhaps even more changes will result from international comparabilities and the need for easier movement of people, throughout Europe and beyond.

For many, the changes have made assessment even more conspicuous than curriculum. Assessment is more visible and serious now, and therefore more demanding of teachers. Scotland has not been alone in introducing such changes, however, and other developed countries have endeavoured, in broadly similar ways, to improve what goes on in the name of assessment (see J. Nisbet 1993, Issues/Questions Chapter in OECD Document, *Curriculum Reform: Assessment in Question*, Paris: OECD). However, some things are particularly Scottish and it is tempting, as the millennium approaches, to ask whether policies and practices in assessment in Scotland are sound and satisfactory or whether the system as a whole 'could do better'? The remainder of this chapter reflects on the distinctive shifts in emphasis which have taken place.

First, and with an eye to secondary schools, whereas assessment was once confined to an elite (the academic achievers, more or less) it is now required for all. Significantly, much of the associated thinking and some of the practice has moved from secondary to primary as a consequence of the order in which the national developments took place. Whereas in the past assessment had only formal characteristics and was dissociated from classroom learning, it is now rather more informal and internal. Furthermore, some claims can be made that it is more integrated with ongoing work, thereby guiding and informing teaching (and therefore earning the label 'formative'). Second, and perhaps most important, in the past both assessment and reporting were 'norm-referenced', that is they focused on how pupils compared with one another and standards were (at best) only implicit in descriptions such as 'average', 'below average'. . . . The focus is now on what pupils are able to do and criteria for achievement (for 'passing' or for particular grades) are now made explicit; assessment is said to be criterion-referenced. Third, and as a consequence of this, assessment has become tied up with grading everything and the concept of an educational ladder, where grades are labels for rungs, is the predominant metaphor (see Bryce, 1994). Thinking in grades or levels is sometimes helpful, but it can lead to difficulties, as will be shown.

FORMAL VERSUS INFORMAL: EXTERNAL VERSUS INTERNAL: ASSESSMENT FOR AN ELITE OR ASSESSMENT FOR EVERYBODY

A generation ago, assessment was a rather formal affair. It was the prerogative of the more able in secondary schools; written examinations dominated schooling and teaching was the preparation for them. Following the demise (in the 1960s) of the 'qualifying' examination at the end of primary P7, assessment remained low key in primary schools and did so until the advent of 5–14 in the 1990s. The important secondary examinations, as today, were externally set (by the Scottish Examination Board) and teachers could enjoin pupils to work with them against the unknown, external examiner, second-guessing what would come up this year, and so forth. Old memories are therefore dominated by the nervous anxiety associated with exam halls and cramming for the fateful day. In this sense, assessment had formalities and rituals; even when not external in the sense of a certificate examination such as a Higher Grade, school examinations were often seen as an end point, and somewhat external to, the processes of class work and teaching.

Preparation for certificate examinations meant preparatory examinations (prelims) and together these are often the only formal examinations which pupils take in today's secondary school. (In some schools there are end of year exams in S1–S3.) Rather more informal assessment characterises modern life in school. Some of this has come about through the recognition that it is not valid to try to check certain achievements by formal paper-and-pencil examinations. What you can write about is not the same as what you can actually do; the former can be rehearsed on the basis of rote learning, the latter offers greater opportunities and having it checked 'live' is a more valid process. Investigations and projects, problem solving, reading, listening and practical skills, most obviously require alternatives to written test papers and the assessment of such achievements are now properly located in class time and classroom locations with teachers assuming responsibility for the assessment as a matter of routine.

Two things are evident about this. The first is that while encouraging more internal, and therefore inevitably rather more informal assessment by teachers, the system has brought greater rigour and systematisation into classroom assessment than was formerly the case. Ensuring that everyone does the same thing and exercises judgements against the same standards has not proved easy, but has raised widespread professional debate amongst teachers where previously there had been little. That is a good thing and it has meant in the long run that how things should be judged permeates discussion with pupils. Assessment is thus beginning to be an integral part of the ongoing teaching and learning process (as predicted by Sally Brown, prior to the Standard Grade developments: S. Brown 1980, *What do they know? A Review of Criterion-Referenced Assessment*, Edinburgh: HMSO).

However the shift to greater internal assessment has made more demands of teachers and these are as onerous as they may be productive. A decade ago, Standard Grade course developments looked poised to permit individual subjects to determine the number of assessed elements which would apply to S3 and S4 courses and to allow a wide range of internal assessment strategies to be adopted. Teachers balked at what they saw as unreasonable burdens and an official 'simplification' took place. *Assessment in Standard Grade Courses: Proposals for Simplification* (The SGROAG Report, Scottish Education Department, Edinburgh, 1986) ordained that there would be only three elements per subject and curtailed the structured internal assessments to be carried out by teachers. Since then, developments in assessment have tended to indicate (if not labour the point) that what teachers do by way of on-going, informal assessment need only be made explicit and contribute to judgements made as the internal assessment required for certification or formal achievement.

Assessment 5–14 (SOED, 1991) is a carefully argued document and one would be hard-pushed to fault its philosophy of assessment, though criticism can be levelled at the lack of detailed advice as to how such laudable intentions might be realised. It outlines how assessment should be considered professionally, firmly identifying it as part and parcel of a teacher's planning, teaching, recording, reporting and evaluating. These five elements are not to be thought of as separate or sequential; 'assessment is an integral part of learning and teaching' (p. 12). Indeed right at the start, the guidelines endeavour to reassure teachers (particularly that they need not fear additional workload) thus: 'While some aspects of the 5–14 Development Programme are new for teachers, assessment itself is not. Teachers should approach this assessment with confidence' (p. 3). However, the assessment and reporting demands of 5–14 are quite considerable. Teachers are required to prepare detailed descriptive reports for parents on their children's progress; strengths and developmental needs (weaknesses) must be spelled out and many schools now issue a one or two page report per pupil in advance of the annual or biannual parents' night.

Thus pressure has been applied to shift the system towards an increase in internal, more informal assessment (where assessing is part-and-parcel of teaching) but has had to back pedal carefully to avoid the impression that it is too difficult to do.

The second thing which is evident about these changes, re-focusing here on secondary, is that despite satisfactory techniques of moderation (checks made by examination boards of the procedures adopted by teachers) internal assessment retains a minority weighting as far as certification is concerned. Indeed that weighting continues to be reduced following early enthusiastic innovations. For example, in the science subjects at Standard Grade, the internal assessment of practical abilities was, for six years, one third of the total. From 1999 onwards this will reduce from one third to one fifth (*New Arrangements for all Sciences*, Dalkeith, SQA, 1997). Once again the change was brought about in response to the concerns of some teachers about the overall burden of assessment. In this context, it might be said that there is a natural conservatism about teachers' views of their assessment roles – or at least what they are prepared to do in circumstances where very significant additions to workload have been put in place without compensatory gains of any sort. It is interesting also to reflect on the context in which decisions about the balance of internal to external assessment are made. Retaining the largest component of assessment as external to schools might have seemed the safe bet when Standard Grade was launched. With the recent steady increase in staying-on rates beyond S4, some doubts have been raised about the need for national certification at 16 years. Yet recent revisions to the system have not been to increase the school-based component, rather the reverse! Concerns about cheating in project work (see Bryce, 1994) have also been used as a justification for a reduction in internal assessment.

With regard to the future and the single framework of qualifications being evolved for Higher Still (S5 and S6 and in FE: see Chapter 82), part of the rationale is the proposed mix of internal and external assessment. Internal assessment will be expected of teachers for the units of each award; external assessment will be used for courses and group awards. The Scottish Office promised that by June 1998 a national assessment bank would be published, enabling teachers to draw upon prepared test items for their internal, classroom assessment of units. (Some 1,000 units require banks of test items.)

In parallel with the systematic evolution of assessment strategies in the 1980s and 1990s, Scotland has also participated in the UK-wide National Record of Achievement (NRA) initiative. A record of achievement is a document drawn up by a pupil/student, in collaboration with a teacher or teachers, which sets out in summary form that individual's overall achievements. It is deliberately wide in compass; academic achievements are but a sub-set of what is normally included. As a recent evaluation reveals (Somekh et al., 1996) the process of drawing up such a record is more important for the learner than the product. The cycle of activities where pupils review and record their achievements, assess their own strengths and weaknesses and set targets, significantly contributes to motivation. The recommendations from the report by Somekh et al. include aiming for the NRA 'to become a standard part of practice in assessment and recording in educational institutions'. However, it is evident that in Scotland (as elsewhere) there is a significant gap to be closed between conventional academic assessment procedures and those associated with best practice in the integrated use of NRA in teaching (see Chapter 79).

NORM-REFERENCED VERSUS CRITERION-REFERENCED ASSESSMENT

Probably the most striking feature of modern assessment is the existence of published criteria by which judgements are to be made of pupil work. A considerable amount of development time and effort has been spent on the articulation of criteria in all of the recent national initiatives. This first began during the 1980s for Standard Grade with the development of grade-related criteria; followed by the specification of SCOTVEC module assessment criteria; and finally during the late 1980s and early 1990s with the identification of targets for 5–14 achievements. It is interesting to reflect on what preceded those periods of intense educational activity; when there were no written criteria, did teachers assess pupils without reference to any standards of acceptability? While the answer to this must clearly be no, it is apparent from history that concerns about variation between teachers and between classes in secondary schools became serious during the 1960s and 1970s. Experienced teachers set tests of subject knowledge and understanding largely on the basis of their own subjective judgements of comparability to what had gone before; on the previous year's paper; on tests used elsewhere. Serious drift occurred when something novel was set in a certificate paper, and it was commonly noted that that particular topic or its demands became emphasised in the years which followed. Class examinations, including those for the years prior to certification, experienced a backwash effect with demands altering as a result. Were any particular year group to be brighter or more able in a teacher's judgement, then of course this would present difficulties for the proportions of pupils getting certain marks or grades. The tendency overall must have been for some constraints to be imposed upon year groups' justified 'achievements'.

During the 1970s, when first year intakes to secondary schools were rather higher than they are now, difficulties of comparing subjects (which pupils inevitably encounter, especially at the end of S2 when they seek to choose 'their best subjects' for S3 and beyond) were reduced by the advent of computer programmes for test mark analyses. Prior to the advent of personal computers, computing facilities in local teacher centres and teacher education institutions developed user-friendly programmes to permit norm-referenced computations to be carried out with ease. Typically, raw marks across a set of school subjects could be scaled to a chosen, common average and chosen common spread of marks. Thus a school could submit sets of subject marks with varying raw averages and varying spreads (left uncalculated of course) and have these computed as scaled marks all averaging, say, 55 per cent with common spreads in each subject (say a standard deviation of 15 per cent). Teachers simply chose the desired parameters and had returned to them printed lists of scaled scores. The hard bit was to explain to pupils why their marks had been reduced in those instances where exam questions had been set 'easy' or where marking had been 'generous', relative to other subjects. As well as introducing perceived fairness and the labour-saving facility of printed lists (which could have grades attached, merely by specifying grade-mark ranges: Grade A = 85% +; Grade B = 84% − 75%; etc. . . .) this disguised the 'real' standards being achieved by pupils in subjects and the diversity and variation among those subject demands. It was, however, a period where the philosophy of norm-referencing held sway. Such procedures mimicked what the Scottish Examination Board did with national data, ensuring commensurate proportions of the national population achieving A, B, C . . . at Higher or Ordinary grade, year on year. (See also Chapter 86.)

Two important developments took place in assessment during the 1980s. The first, which sought to replace norm-referencing, was initiated in response to the recommendations of the Dunning Report, *Assessment For All* (Scottish Education Department, Edinburgh, 1977) and produced assessment and certification strategies based on pre-determined targets for learning. These were devised by subject groupings of teachers, led centrally by the Scottish Examination Board. The second, related development was the imposition of grade levels to the outcomes of Standard Grade achievements (either in recognition that only limited progress had been made towards the certification of 'mastery learning', or more plausibly, as a political expedient to match the expectatations of the users of future certificates). Neither of these completely diverted teachers from their traditional thinking about test scores and marks out of 100; but they did build criteria, grades and grading into the heart of the assessment system.

During the development of the Standard Grade curriculum, not only was the content of the curriculum (content in the widest sense) extended and developed to span the entire ability range, but much effort was expended upon setting out descriptive statements of what pupils should know and be able to do. The various working parties which developed these statements inevitably got bogged down in considerable detail, since it is pretty nigh impossible to be both precise and terse. Rather than settle for description associated with a pass requirement for a Standard Grade subject, a compromise was struck to match more closely the traditional thinking of parents, of employers (and of teachers?), that is to preserve the notion of a scale of achievement from the most to the least able. What resulted was a system of grades 1 to 7, with 1 and 2 representing the Credit band, 3 and 4 the General band and 5 and 6 the Foundation band of Standard Grade (with 7 as 'no award'). Detailed criteria for what pupils should be able to do were distinguished by grade levels and were labelled extended grade-related criteria (E-GRC). Though not frequently used, the more general GRC are claimed to be meaningful to parents and employers. The SEB, and now the SQA, publish the detailed E-GRC as part of the Arrangements document for each subject. As teachers are at pains to say, these 'bibles' set out what has to be achieved by the end of S4. (Figure 78.1 illustrates the differences between Grade 4 and Grade 3 for Close Reading in English language.) The differences between criteria for different grade levels are sometimes quantitative in character, sometimes qualitative; and there are instances where the distinction is forced and not particularly helpful to the classroom teacher. Furthermore, the thinking which lies behind criteria and targets is to some extent in conflict with current approaches to learning and mental growth: see, for example, Bryce (1993).

Figure 78.1 EGRC for Close Reading in English for Grades 3 and 4

Nature of Texts
The candidate can read texts that are accessible as a whole, mainly related to personal interest and experience, dealing with concrete human relationships or containing clearly presented ideas.

As the nature of the text permits, the candidate can:

make a clear statement of the main concerns of the text;

state accurately in his or her own words (where appropriate) individual items retrieved from the text;

draw a precise inference from a key statement in the text;

comment relevantly on a clearly defined aspect of the author's point of view, and justify the comment from personal experience and knowledge and from evidence in the text;

identify individual features of the author's technique and explain their effects.

FACTORS DIFFERENTIATING GRADES 4 AND 3

Grade 4	Grade 3
While displaying as appropriate the characteristics essential for General Level the candidate's responses are less consistent, less apt in illustration and explanation, and less successful in retrieving, paraphrasing, explaining and justifying than at grade 3. Overall the performance is more uneven than at grade 3.	The candidate demonstrates a clear understanding and a sound appreciation in responding to particular questions on the various aspects of purpose. The responses are more consistent, more relevant and more successful in retrieving, paraphrasing, explaining and justifying than at grade 4.

From paragraph 7.9.2 of Standard Grade. Revised Arrangements in English at Foundation, General and Credit Levels in or after 1989, Scottish Examination Board (1987)

Broadfoot has noted the emergence of criterion-referencing in the assessment policies of many advanced countries, detecting flux and tension between the emerging 'pre-occupation with the attestation of competence rather than the regulation of competition as the principal focus for assessment' (Broadfoot, 1996, p. 51). She sees the new demand on teachers to operate internal, criterion-referenced systems for all pupils across the age range as being considerable, though there are significant differences between countries – depending upon what they implement and how they do it, with Scotland faring rather better than England. And so she notes the growing and powerful lobby in favour of 'retaining and indeed strengthening traditional pass/fail certificate examinations, evidenced by recent (English) government moves to reduce coursework assessment.' (Broadfoot, 1996, p. 53). The 'confirmatory' use by teachers of national tests in Scotland (teachers drawing upon the national test bank when they choose) is identified by her as one positive feature, compared with England's mandatory requirements. While the culture of assessment has changed, she does opt for 'oscillation' as a metaphor. Things are swinging back and on a somewhat pessimistic note she states that 'these changes have come about to defuse potential conflict and frustration while at the same time enabling schools to continue their traditional role of selecting and channelling pupils to different levels of the occupational and social hierarchy' (Broadfoot, 1996, p. 62).

GRADES AND LEVELS

While the incorporation of pupil performance criteria into the assessment system has made for great complexity, the definition of grades 1–7 across the entire ability range for all subject matter can be regarded as a success, at least at school level. SCOTVEC's national modular system did not take its cue from Standard Grade; it did not adopt grades for modules nor did it make distinctions between students. Instead it opted for a set of outcomes per module all to be mastered or non-mastered (thus taking no account of the reality of variations between students in possession of the same module).

The development of Standard Grade was so demanding of the system that when the policy of national curricula spanning the compulsory school years was introduced (and implicit in that the idea of targets in ascending order) Scotland was compelled to retain Standard Grade and confine its 'national curriculum' to 5–14. This resulted in serious mismatches in attainment descriptors at different stages. Pupils move upwards through levels A to E (E 'high' therefore) and must then switch to grades 1–7 (1 high) for S3 and S4. Grades or levels then have rather different meanings. In Standard Grade, achieving a grade level 3, say, by the end of S4 may be understood by scrutiny of the E-GRC so indicated. 3 is a final position on a seven point scale. In 5–14, a level is defined by a collection of the targets which should be attainable by a certain stage of schooling; thus level B targets should be met by most pupils in P4, level D by most pupils in P7, level E by most pupils in S2 (See Figure 78.2). While there are thousands of targets in the 5–14 Guidelines, it is intended that a teacher recognise the stage reached for any pupil through scrutiny of the numbers of targets reached.

The intention of such assessment using grade levels is that parents should receive reports on their children which indicate their progress up the sequential rungs of the national curriculum ladder. However, it also allows comparisons to be made to the achievements of the majority. Thus for example D is where most pupils should be by the end of primary school.

Figure 78.2   Targets and Levels

In each of the 5–14 Curriculum documents, the attainment outcomes have been sub-divided into strands, or main aspects of learning. Each strand is set out in terms of targets at five levels, A-E, where:

Level A	should be attainable in the course of the first three years at primary school by almost all pupils
Level B	should be attainable by some pupils in P3 or even earlier, but certainly by most in P4
Level C	should be attainable in the course of P4 to P6 by most pupils
Level D	should be attainable by some pupils in P5 or P6 or even earlier, but certainly by most in P7
Level E	should be attainable by some pupils in P7 or S1, but certainly by most in S2.

(See, for example, SOED, 1991. Mathematics 5–14 p.9)

Thus in Mathematics, for example, the attainment outcome 'Information handling' has four strands (collecting, organising, displaying and interpreting information). In respect of the strand 'display information' pupils should be able to display:

at level A	by using real objects, by using pictures; and by drawing simple diagrams
at level B	by using tables, charts or diagrams (such as mapping one to many); by constructing a bar graph (with axes graduated in units and with discrete categories of information)
at level C	by constructing a table or chart; by constructing a bar graph (with axes graduated in multiple units and discrete categories of information)
at level D	by constructing graphs (bar, line, frequency polygon) and pie charts (in-volving simple fractions or decimals; involving continuous data which has been grouped)
at level E	by constructing straight line and curved graphs for continuous data (where there is a relationship such as direct proportion – travel, temperature, growth graphs); by constructing pie charts of data (expressed in percentages).

The last statement is not as simple as it looks and it is not simply hair-splitting to note that the precise wording in any of the 5–14 Guideline documents is '. . . by most in P7'. Why and where does this matter? The point is that in trying to steer national assessment through grades and levels, the consequences of some ambiguity of terminology must be lived with. Grades or levels are not easily or sharply defined entities.

The 5–14 Curriculum developers opted to attach two years of schooling to each level through their selection of five levels for nine years of schooling (P1–S2). Two years usually constitutes a significant gain in a pupil's knowledge and skills; the many hundreds of targets associated with one grade vary greatly in their compass, difficulty and depth; grade levels such as D therefore cannot constitute some sharply defined end-point. Furthermore, when national test setters try to ascribe test questions to levels or where researchers try to work with levels to estimate the national proportions of children so achieving, difficulties are encountered. In the case of national tests (at the time of writing, set only for English language and Mathematics: see Chapter 83) when test items are judged to be appropriate to assess the attainment of a particular target, they inevitably vary in difficulty. The rule of thumb which seems to have evolved is for the easiest task to be incorporated into the test bank materials as applicable for the particular 5–14 level. In the Assessment of Achievement

Programme (see Chapter 85) researchers who have developed assessment tasks linked to the 5–14 levels have worked out different strategies. They too have had to operationalise some of the more vague terms from 5–14. Thus, for example, the team who conducted the fourth science survey in 1996 interpreted 'most' and 'almost all' as 75 per cent and 90 per cent respectively of the national sample; they used indices of achievement of 0.8 and 0.35 (proportions of scores on tasks assessing particular targets) to judge the extent to which national samples of pupils had or did not have 'secure understanding' or were making 'steady progress' respectively, these being the terms used in 5–14 Environmental Studies (Stark, Bryce and Gray, 1997). In short, terms adopted for targets and levels may appear attractively straightforward (and no doubt give some flexibility and freedom as far as curriculum guidelines are concerned). In practice assessors, whether classroom teachers or more formal 'national testers' or 'national monitors' have much interpreting to do. 5–14 documents may offer Curriculum guidelines; they do not present Assessment blueprints.

The whole question of standards in mathematics is an interesting case in point here. The 1997 report by HMI *Improving Mathematics Education 5–14* (Edinburgh: SOEID) sets out the concerns for pupils' maths attainment indicated by school inspections, national (AAP) and international (TIMSS) surveys of pupil achievements, and puts forward recommendations for changes to practice. Part of the argument is developed through comparisons made between teaching methods used in high achieving countries and teaching methods used in Scotland. Scottish teachers are urged to expect more of pupils, to increase the pace; schools are encouraged to set themselves realistic but challenging targets 'beyond national minimum expectations'. Thus HMI now declare that schools should interpret 5–14 targets as *minimum expectations* (para. 2.2, p. 3). They have observed that schools have used D as marking the end of P7. Can't D mark the mid-point of P7, they ask? Whereas the targets set out in 1991 were for level A to be attained by almost all in P3, level D by most in P7, the disappointing standards (and especially the international comparisons) lead to HMI arguing by 1997 that

> Most schools should aim to complete Level A as soon as possible and expect most of their pupils to have reached it by the end of P2. (Para. 2.3)

> There are also many P7 classes where teachers aim only to complete Level D by the end of the session even though significant numbers of pupils should have attained this minimum level sooner, perhaps in P6. By the end of P7, most pupils should be working beyond Level D and some should be well on the way towards completing Level E. (Para. 2.4, SOEID, 1997)

One has to paraphrase this as 'moving the goalposts' but it would be unfair to argue that it is improper in the long run (though it does pin much hope on the idea that people do always rise to expectations). It is professionally defensible for the system to adjust targets, in so far as a wide range of evidence is taken into account, particularly that deriving from well-conducted surveys like AAP. It is for another chapter to look at the arguments about teaching methods and standards, but it is interesting here to note that HMI observe that school guidelines provided in some other (high achieving) countries, like Switzerland, provide better, more detailed guidance to primary teachers about mathematics programmes. Might one deduce that more effective detail is supplied than that which has been built in Scotland around the 5–14 target colossus?

Perhaps we should conclude that the whole criterion-referencing paraphernalia with targets has been over-ambitious as an assessment device to advance standards and to tackle the primary/secondary interface difficulties. As many have observed, outcomes and strands and targets do not constitute linear sequences of advice to teachers; they do not translate into action in real time. Is that what the system sought to avoid by regarding teachers as professionals able to interpret a complex of target milestones strung across the (st)age-range? Would greater progress have been made by simpler, admittedly more directive, advice? Certainly, as far as assessment is concerned, a great deal has been asked of the profession. (Someone has estimated that by dividing the total number of 5–14 targets by the duration of time spent, one can reckon that a child should be achieving a target every 14½ minutes of their 5–14 school life!) The grade level mentality may be here to stay; if it is, all those involved in assessment are wielding a hefty club upon their own backs.

REFERENCES

Black, P. and D. Wiliam (1998) Assessment and Classroom Learning, *Assessment in Education*, vol. 5, no. 1, pp. 7–74.

Broadfoot, P. M. (1996) *Education, Assessment and Society*, Buckingham: Open University Press.

Bryce, T. G. K. (1993) Constructivism, Knowledge and National Science Targets, *Scottish Educational Review*, 25.2, 87–96.

Bryce, T. G. K. (1994) Challenges to the Management of Assessment. Chapter in Humes, W. H., and M. L. MacKenzie (eds) *The Management of Educational Policy: Scottish Perspectives*. Harlow: Longman.

Somekh, B., T. Tinklin, L. Edwards and R. Mackay (1996) Evaluation of the National Record of Achievement in Scotland. *Interchange No 44*. Edinburgh: SOEID.

Stark, R., T. G. K. Bryce and D. Gray (1997) Four Surveys and an Epitaph: AAP Science 1985–1997, *Scottish Educational Review*, 29.2, 114–120.

79

Diagnostic and Formative Assessment in the Scottish Classroom

Mary Simpson

INTRODUCING A NEW FORM OF ASSESSMENT

In the mid-1970s, the Dunning Committee was charged with reviewing assessment and certification strategies in S3/S4 within secondary schools. Its recommendations, which were accepted, led to a significant change in the form of assessment in the public examination system, in particular the replacement of norm referencing with criterion referencing, a system within which assessment items are written to match the pre-specified learning outcomes for each course. The new criterion referenced system readily fulfilled the then commonly accepted two main purposes of assessment – the measurement of the achievement of pupils, and the consequent guidance and advice as to the suitability of future courses or careers. However, the Dunning Report also recommended consideration of a third element which it was felt should be present within an effective assessment system – diagnostic assessment for the purpose of informing the teaching and learning:

> It is insufficient to devise curricular objectives and to find out if they have been attained by each pupil; for those who are not successful the reasons for misunderstandings require to be identified and alternative methods adopted. (The Dunning Report, *Assessment for All*, SED, 1977)

Thus, criterion referencing was not to be regarded as simply a replacement for norm referencing as a method of judging pupils' progress against intended outcomes, but also as a means of contributing to the improvement of educational attainment – difficulties were to be diagnosed and instructional action was to be taken when pupils failed to reach specified attainments.

Although this recommendation appeared reasonable and sensible, there was at that time a lack of clarity both in theory and practice on how diagnostic assessment might operate. Was it the case that tests which were criterion referenced to intended outcomes could serve not only the summative function of giving an account of what pupils had learned, but also diagnose the causes of learning difficulties? And what particular instructional action should be taken following pupil failure? In some subjects, notably science and mathematics, 'remedial loops' had already been incorporated into instructional materials but many teachers found these difficult to incorporate into the lock-step delivery which was typical of the time, and there was no convincing evidence that the pre-set remedial activities actually addressed the learning difficulties experienced by the individual pupil within the particular learning task in hand. Clearly, considerably more work was needed to inform any changes in practice.

This chapter outlines some of the subsequent interactions between policy, research and practice which have resulted in the forms of diagnostic assessment found in Scottish classrooms in the late 1990s.

INITIAL CONCEPTIONS OF DIAGNOSTIC ASSESSMENT

It was soon acknowledged that while a criterion referenced test could undoubtedly help a teacher to identify exactly what had not in fact been learned, this did not necessarily diagnose why the learning had failed and what remediation was therefore appropriate. There were suggestions that special diagnostic tests needed to be developed. The diagnostic tests available as models in the late 1970s were typically formal, standardised tests designed by psychologists to identify patterns of deviation from developmental age norms, or particular difficulties with such generic skills as reading; there was little or nothing related directly to the curriculum which could be applied by subject teachers in their classrooms to assist an individual pupil or class who were evidencing failure to understand and attain particular subject related information and skills.

In response to the Dunning Report's suggestion that 'diagnostic assessment as an aid to pupil learning' should be further investigated, the educational community in Scotland embarked enthusiastically on a programme of research, largely funded by the Scottish Office, and by February 1983, a full edition of the journal *Programmed Learning and Educational Technology* was devoted to reports of a range of Scottish initiatives. For example, two teachers wrote up a case study, in which they sounded a cautionary note on the amount of work involved, and the necessity to undertake 'a long campaign to inform teachers about diagnostic assessment and of the advantages that can accrue from its use' (p. 8). A group of teacher trainers reported on the development of test items which, they argued, 'can be used to provide both diagnostic and summative information' (p. 11). There was a description of the use of a package of mastery learning materials devised by researchers and tried out by teachers – the researchers noted that 'the teachers' general attitudes and expectations seemed little affected by their participation in this study' (p. 43). One article fired the opening shots in what became a long standing debate between Scottish researchers on the relationship, in theory and practice, between formative and summative assessment, on the nature and origin of learning difficulties and on the appropriate form of assessment which would contribute effectively to their resolution:

> Many learning difficulties can be attributed not to pupil limitations, but to major deficiencies in the subject presentation, e.g. inconsistencies, anomalies and ambiguities, and to inadequacies in instructional strategies, e.g. the failure to provide adequate instruction in pre-requisite concepts, to monitor their development, to detect the incorrect information acquired by pupils, or to define precise teaching objectives. (p. 36)

And in a percipient and prophetic overview, the guest editor for that edition, Harry Black, identified the range of problems which could be anticipated in trying to promote the understanding and adoption of this form of assessment in schools: 'Unless a favourable environment is created within which these problems and tensions can be dealt with, diagnostic assessment is likely to be misunderstood and misused' (Black, 1983, p. 58).

Both in Scotland and in the wider educational research community, interest had been growing in the underlying causes of pupil learning difficulties, particularly in science and mathematics. It had increasingly become recognised that these were commonly traceable to misconceptions which pupils had acquired, undetected, and therefore uncorrected, during their schooling or in the course of everyday life experiences. Such misconceptions were notably persistent, making the understanding and retention of correct information extremely difficult. Exemplar diagnostic tests were compiled by Scottish researchers, covering topics in science and geography in which research had revealed the patterns of typical misunderstandings and difficulties, but although these had the merit of being framed within the model of assessment best understood to teachers – that of the set test comprising objective items, there were practical and theoretical reasons why it was argued that the further development of such diagnostic tests was not a profitable way forward. For example, their coverage of the range of learning difficulties was limited and inflexible; time had to be found to apply them; and teachers tended to aggregate scores and treat them as summative tests (Black, 1983). Their use also tended to reinforce the idea that the causes of learning difficulties were located primarily within the heads of the pupils, and hence that the remediation should be directed wholly towards the actions of the pupils, who would be enjoined to listen, revise, read and practise more than previously. An alternative view suggested that key contributing deficiencies might lie not in the pupils, but in characteristics prevalent in instruction; remediation of the learning failure might thus require the teacher to change, to revise or restructure their whole teaching strategy and, in particular, to listen and pay more attention to the pupils' ideas (e.g. M. Simpson and B. Arnold, *Diagnosis in Action*, Northern College, 1984).

Key areas of difficulty were thus identified and discussed at an early stage: the reconceptualisation of the nature and origins of pupil learning difficulties and professionally appropriate and manageable ways of identifying and dealing with them; resolution of the tensions in the perceived relationship between formative and summative assessment; the identification of ways of successfully introducing innovation; the time and effort required for significant change to take place in teachers' thinking and practice; and the complexity of the professional context within which the changes were to take place.

The staff in schools were interested in and clearly stimulated by the debates and publications which were prompted by the policy exhortation and the dissemination of research findings (e.g. Brown and Munn, 1985) but, daunted by the range of unresolved difficulties of putting largely untested theory into practice, they turned their attention to the other massive requirement set upon them in the early 1980s, the task of putting criterion referencing into place in both the national certification system and in their own internal testing. Nevertheless, the term 'diagnostic assessment' had been introduced into the professional vocabulary and had sown the seeds of the idea that ways round learning difficulties might be found, complex and difficult as the route might seem, and that assessment had a key role in this.

By the early 1990s, when policy requirements associated with the 5–14 Development Programme again focused the attention of practitioners on the use of assessment as a tool to inform teaching and learning, the effects of changes in acceptable forms of assessment and in understanding about the complexities of learning had introduced a number of new factors into the arena.

DEVELOPING A FRAMEWORK FOR FORMATIVE ASSESSMENT

At the time the Dunning Report was written, the dominant form taken by assessment was that of formal objective testing. Over the two decades since then, the constructs around which the traditional testing edifice was erected have been gradually undermined as new ideas and requirements have developed and permeated throughout education. As employers have become much less concerned to know who is better or worse than average, and more concerned to know exactly what their new employees understand and can do, criterion referenced assessment has become widespread, and intended outcomes are routinely set for secondary school courses. There has also been a growing awareness of the extent to which the acquisition and display of certain complex skills and knowledge are determined by context and cannot be reliably demonstrated by paper and pencil tasks undertaken within the examination hall. The assessment by teachers of practical work and of the application of knowledge through extended project activities embedded within courses have increasingly become a feature of formal internal assessment requirements. There has been, therefore, a growing need for teachers to generate or learn to apply procedures for 'assessment in context' within their classrooms.

These developments concerned summative assessment, designed to measure attainment and grade pupils' performance. The requirement to use assessment to inform instruction was claimed by teachers in both sectors to be largely met by informal assessment based on their routine, on-going observations of pupils' attainments and difficulties. But, because these activities were intuitive, unsystematic and unrecorded, they went largely unexamined and unevaluated, and the traditional concepts of reliability and validity were not applied. The secondary teachers' acquisition of the skills of criterion referenced assessment related to authentic tasks performed within the classroom, workshop or laboratory offered an opportunity for the development of more systematic strategies for assessment which identified learning difficulties and informed teaching. Within the primary school, the informal modes of assessment had long predominated, and the requirement to relate teaching and learning activities to the learning outcomes within the curricular guidelines of the 5–14 Development Programme gave primary teachers experience of setting specific targets for pupils, against which their actual attainments could be systematically gauged and failure responded to (see Chapter 78).

Thus, in Scotland, the past two decades have seen an evolution of the concept of that form of assessment which has as its main purpose the promotion of learning. The initial assumption that criterion referenced assessment, which identified particular areas of pupil failure, was in itself sufficient to point towards appropriate remediation was challenged and soon abandoned. The use of the term 'diagnostic testing' set the thinking about learning difficulties within the framework of a medical model, but promoted the idea that investigations were necessary to diagnose the nature of the difficulties. The identification of the intended outcomes of the learning activities and of the current knowledge and understanding of pupils – including an exploration of their misconceptions – were seen as key components of this investigative activity. These investigative processes and the informed reactions to the identified difficulties and needs of the pupils, rather than the application of test items, came to be seen as central to diagnostic assessment as a process. In contrast to the use of standard formulae for the determination of validity in traditional tests, the validity of this contextualised assessment was determined by the success of its outcomes in accurately informing the teacher how to assist the pupil to overcome the identified learning difficulty.

These processes of investigation and remediation match fairly well with the standard model of the teacher as the skilled professional who has sole possession of the required specialist knowledge and who determines and controls the transactions within the classroom. However, there has been increasing acknowledgement of an additional, and potentially more problematical requirement, if formative assessment is to fulfil its full potential – that of the informed and active participation of the pupils.

It is now clear, in the present period of rapid technological change, that school leavers need more than basic knowledgeability, it is also essential that they gain the capacity to learn throughout life and to adapt to new environments. They have, therefore, to be motivated and committed to continued learning, to be self-determined, to feel they have the power to promote their own development, and to have confidence that they can succeed and continue to progress. This requires the learner to develop attributes of self-motivation, self-monitoring, self-reflection and self-reliance. In order to promote these characteristics, teachers have been enjoined to give pupils a more active and responsible role in the management of their own learning. However, giving pupils responsibility which is effective and meaningful necessarily involves the sharing of professional knowledge and skills – including full and informed participation in the processes of assessment which are central to the guidance of learning. As Black (1993) noted:

> The development of self assessment by pupils and students is still in its early stages, but within the framework of formative assessment as an integral part of learning, it seems a natural, almost essential development, as well as a potentially powerful source for the improvement of learning. (p. 82)

And he identifies the key characteristics of an effective self-assessment scheme which include: clear, shared criteria; giving students more responsibility for determining their own learning goals; and assessment procedures and recording schemes which are sufficiently clear and economical that students can work them for themselves. Ideas derived from research, and increasingly made accessible to teachers, also suggest that children are born with much greater potential than hitherto acknowledged and that considerable limitations on school learning outcomes may be set by the standard practices and expectancies of the classroom settings. The implications of these ideas go far beyond the fine tuning of current assessment strategies or the simple replacement of one assessment scheme by another. Thus, in Black's view:

> To incorporate formative assessment into their teaching would involve teachers in far more than acquisition of the necessary skills. Their view of the aims of the teaching of their own subject might have to change if they are to be close to their students in guiding them. The changes in their classroom practice might also involve profound changes of role, even for teachers regarded by themselves and others as already successful. (Black, 1993, p. 79)

It is thus clear why formative assessment has proved difficult to implement in the classroom. What it requires is that assessment is reconceptualised as a process central to the teaching and learning interaction rather than as a procedure at the end of instruction directed judgementally towards the pupil; there must be changes in the teachers' conceptions of pupils' abilities and potential leading to the adoption of the view that all pupils can learn more effectively given the appropriate context, knowledge, and support; there must be an articulation of the learning goals considered appropriate for pupils in general and for individuals when engaging in particular classroom activities; and finally, there must be a change from pupils being passive recipients of educational instruction, to being knowledgeable and proactive in the pursuance of successful learning strategies. Clearly, the introduction of formative assessment requires significant changes to take place in the thinking and practices of many teachers, and a redefining of their roles and of the relationships between them and their pupils. What incentives, models and support have Scottish teachers been offered from policy makers and from researchers to assist and promote development activities of this type?

PROMOTING THE USE OF FORMATIVE ASSESSMENT IN CLASSROOMS

If teachers are going to engage with the demands and difficulties of developing innovative assessment systems, then certain conditions need to be met. Teachers need to have the new strategies explained in professional language which they understand and trust – they abhor 'technical jargon'. They need to be clear about the aims of the new strategies and they have to perceive the changes as having the potential to solve current problems and deal with present professional concerns – and not as creating more difficulties which are just as formidable as the existing ones. They need to have models of what the new strategies might actually look like in practice, preferably along with examples already in use in classrooms and developed by other teachers. And finally, they need to have enough of a grasp of the underlying principles involved to customise with confidence the strategies already available in order to make them manageable and effective within their own context. To what extent have policy and research provided some of these key ingredients?

The SOED *Guidelines on Assessment 5–14* (SOEID, 1991) were developed independently from the guidelines on national testing and they promoted many of the characteristics of formative assessment outlined above. They presented assessment as an integral component of learning and teaching; indicated that the purposes of the learning tasks should be shared with pupils; proposed that the intended outcomes of the teaching should be clarified and planned in the light of knowledge of what the individual child had already attained; and suggested that if the outcomes in terms of learning fell short of expectations the teaching itself should be questioned and reviewed. They anticipated that engagement in these processes would lead to some indication of the next steps in learning appropriate for the pupil. They presented the ideas in the context of language and processes familiar to teachers – planning, teaching, evaluating, recording and reporting.

In essence, these guidelines reiterated many of the aspirations of the Dunning Report. Although a few years after its publication some exemplar materials had been provided for teachers in secondary schools, both by HMI and by researchers (for example in geography, by SCRE and in science, by Northern College), given the early stage of thinking of the majority within the educational system and the pressing demands of developing alternative summative systems for certification, their impact on practice had been fairly limited. However, there were some early initiatives linked to certification which have prevailed and which have been further developed within the secondary sector. For example, one of the major innovations in assessment in the sciences at Standard Grade has been the assessment of 'Practical Abilities' in the science subjects (TAPS). During the period 1980 to 1991, in collaboration with teachers, researchers developed a strategy whereby progress towards the achievement of the prescribed objectives could be noted, with successes recorded, early failures overtaken and so discounted, on a mastery learning model. Thus, for the practical investigations, assessment is based on one set of investigative skill objectives, but several authentic investigative tasks are engaged in by each pupil before decisions are made about what has finally been achieved. (T. G. K. Bryce, J. McCall, J. MacGregor, I. J. Robertson and R. A. J. Weston, 1991, *How to Assess Open-ended Practical Investigations in Biology, Chemistry and Physics*, Oxford: Heinemann Educational).

In the 1990s, almost twenty years after the Dunning Report, with many more in the profession at an advanced stage in their thinking about the interaction of teaching, learning and assessment, the Scottish Office again funded the production of practical exemplification of how the processes of assessment could be deployed in the classroom to serve the purposes of promoting effective learning, this time within the framework of the 5–14 Development Programme and therefore largely directed towards and accessible to primary teachers. The materials produced, which were developed by teams of researchers and teachers, were made available to all schools in the form of a series of curriculum focused booklets (relating to mathematics, reading, writing and science) entitled *Taking a Closer Look* (e.g. Hayward and Hall, 1995). These incorporated the key characteristics of formative assessment indicated above and promoted and exemplified the use of the professional knowledge and skills of the teacher as the central feature of the assessment process rather than the use of formal schemes or sets of test materials.

To what extent have teachers seen the strategies of formative assessment as contributing to the resolution of other pressing professional difficulties? One of the focal points for the development of formative assessment has been that of differentiation. Emerging from a number of recent Scottish policy initiatives has been a growing concern amongst teachers to develop differentiation – strategies for dealing with pupils who have different levels of attainment, but which are effective and acceptable within the non-selective and equitable philosophy of the Scottish educational system. Traditionally, the focus of differentiation has been the curriculum, either through its presentation at different levels of difficulty, or the requirement for different pupils to respond in different ways to the same task. Research projects set both in primary and in secondary classrooms indicated that the prevailing practices were of limited effectiveness in matching the pupils' levels of attainment to the curricular tasks which teachers allocated, and that the key differences between pupils which were influencing attainment, and of which teachers had to take account, had to go considerably beyond the narrow consideration of attainment levels as measured at a specific point in time.

Teachers were eager to hear of the research findings and, in particular, of the models of differentiation which focused on the central role of the teacher as responder to the varied needs of learners, rather than as merely a curriculum organiser. However, not surprisingly, many were uncertain as to how to proceed in the development of their practice. A number indicated that while they clearly needed more extensive and detailed information on pupils' attainments and difficulties in order to differentiate more effectively, the amount of necessary information would very quickly swamp them. Pupils themselves indicated that they would be more motivated and that improvements to their learning would be likely if they were made more aware of what they were supposed to be learning, if they knew not only what their problems were, but how to overcome them, and if they could track their own progress and see evidence of their improvement and progression. It became increasingly clear that mechanisms for identifying and sharing with pupils the key information on the intended learning, the actual outcomes, the difficulties encountered and possible ways forward – in other words, strategies for formative assessment – would fulfil the needs identified by both teachers and pupils (Simpson, 1997).

It would seem then, that despite powerful pressures within the educational system with respect to the development and use of summative assessment, a consistent set of policy initiatives, research information and practical support has prevailed over the past twenty years, all of which, in different ways, have been promoting the adoption of formative assessment. What evidence is available that classroom based developments in formative assessment practices are now beginning to meet the aspirations for its development and use?

CLASSROOM BASED DEVELOPMENTS

It is difficult to quantify the current extent of its classroom application since formative assessment can take a variety of forms in different contexts and is only reliably identifiable at the intimate interface of teaching and learning. However, there are positive indications of change at a number of levels.

In their report on *Implementing the 5–14 Development Programme in Secondary Schools: Continuity and Progression* (Aberdeen: Northern College, 1997), M. Simpson and J. Goulder suggest that in the secondary schools the 'technical jargon' of assessment has clearly entered the vocabulary of many staff. In their national survey conducted in late 1996, they found that 58% of science teachers, 62% of mathematics and 92% of English language claimed to be implementing assessment procedures which have a 'high formative element'. From their whole school perspective, the learning support staff indicated that since the introduction of the Assessment Guidelines there has been more integration of assessment into teaching (55%), and an increase in a learner centred approach to assessment (32%).

In the data presented by H. Malcolm and U. Schlapp in the parallel report *5–14 in Primary Schools: a continuing challenge* (Edinburgh: SCRE, 1997), there are indications that practice has changed there too: half of the primary headteachers surveyed felt that the guidelines have had a very strong influence on practice in their schools; 40 per cent of primary teachers indicated that they are now giving more feedback to pupils, and 45 per cent that they have increased the extent to which they use assessment to identify areas where pupils need help.

However, it is possible that teachers are claiming to be applying formative assessment when, in a fairly traditional manner, they use any information derived from summative assessment to inform the teaching process. For example in the studies noted above, some of the problems identified by primary teachers appeared to be of a fairly traditional type – 'Are they not listening properly? . . . Am I going too fast? . . . Maybe they've forgotten'. In the secondary schools, many English language teachers appear to have a clear vision of the formative nature and value of assessment in which interaction with pupils, rather than the use of tests, forms the central element. In contrast, for many teachers in mathematics, 'assessment' continues to mean 'testing'; tests are still a matter of pass or fail, and continuous assessment is little more than a staccato form of terminal assessment. For these teachers, sharing the management of learning means allowing pupils merely to mark their own tests and to track their progress by means of the wall chart that directs them to the next set unit of work; self-assessment means asking the relatively uninformed pupil 'do you think you did well in this piece of work?' Despite the elaboration of multi-levelled material within mathematics, pupils considered that their needs and abilities were better met and matched within English lessons (Simpson, 1997).

Nevertheless, it is increasingly possible to identify a range of innovative developments which, in very different ways, exemplify the key characteristics identified earlier. For example, although it is the case that, as Patricia Broadfoot noted in the 1993 SERA lecture, 'The *Pupils in Profile* project did not have a great impact in Scotland' (Exploring the Forgotten Continent: a traveller's tale, *Scottish Educational Review*, 26.2, 1994), there is evidence that, sixteen years after that initial project, some teachers are not only engaging comfortably with the recent promotion of pupil profiling, but are incorporating strong elements of formative assessment into its frameworks in the form of indications of what is to be learned, criteria which will indicate success, difficulties evidenced by the pupil in the work submitted, and ways in which difficulties can be overcome. Teachers have taken on the responsibility of linking their advice to a variety of 'help sheets' or other forms of support and pupils are encouraged to consult their records before starting new tasks in the same area.

Teachers involved in a number of classroom-based research and development projects have provided evidence of the variety of strategies which have been devised to share knowledge of the intended learning with pupils, and to help them monitor their own progress; these clearly signal a change in the culture of dependency of the pupil on the teacher: 'One feature of this approach is that pupils will have more freedom to get involved in their own learning. And as a direct spin-off from that, we as teachers have to trust them and have confidence in their ability to do that' commented one science teacher who had developed a particular format of progress sheets for managing differentiation as part of an SCCC development.

While the recording of attainments within the 5–14 Programme is seen by some teachers as a significant, and perhaps unnecessary chore, others, rather than just keeping records of progress in the traditional manner, have devised ways of promoting their active use by pupils and learning support staff, for example one English departmental plan noted:

> Pupils' record sheets have been introduced, which focus both the teacher's and the pupil's attention on areas of achievement and areas requiring support. Pupils are encouraged to consult their own progress sheets before beginning a piece of work. The progress sheets are used in Learning Support consultation time. [This] encourages the attitude that *all* pupils have areas which can be improved.

There are signs in many secondary subject departments of the erosion of traditional roles as teachers begin to question their previous well-established practices and share with pupils information about tests – such as the item codes which indicate which skill is being tested – which was once regarded as exclusively within the purview of the teacher, and the strategy of applying only end-of-unit tests is beginning to be seen to be inadequate. In the primary classrooms, a range of strategies based on a partnership approach has been devised which incorporate many of the key features outlined above and some teachers have skilfully turned Circle Time to the service of assessment through information exchange and the promotion of confidence, learning strategies and self-esteem. All of these are indicators of small but significant steps in the right direction.

FUTURE DEVELOPMENTS

Not surprisingly, given the fairly radical nature of the requirements, the rhetoric somewhat exceeds the reality of the application of formative assessment in Scottish classrooms and it is too early yet for the classroom initiatives to show real returns in terms of widespread improvements in pupil attainment. However, key aspects of the developments which have already taken place give rise to considerable optimism for the health of the concept in the future. It is auspicious that the assessment strategies illustrated above were initiated by teachers in response to difficulties they themselves had identified in their traditional practices, but they are clearly informed by ideas about learning and teaching cognate with those in the research literature and are in harmony with, and supported by, policy documents on assessment.

There is clearly an understanding of the importance and educational potential of formative assessment throughout a critical mass of professionals in all areas of the Scottish educational system – teachers, teacher educators, researchers, local authority staff, school inspectors and civil servants – and a commitment to promote and protect it against the domination and encroachment of summative assessment for accountability which has been given priority in England and Wales.

REFERENCES

Black, H. D. (1983) Introducing Diagnostic Assessment, *Programmed Learning and Educational Technology*, 20 (1), pp. 58–63.

Black, P. J. (1993) Formative and Summative Assessment by Teachers, *Studies in Science Education*, 21, pp. 49–97.

Brown S. and P. Munn (eds) (1985) *The Changing Face of Education 14 to 16: Curriculum and Assessment*, Windsor: NFER-Nelson.

Hayward L. and J. Hall (1995) *Taking a Closer Look at Reading – Diagnostic Procedures*, Edinburgh: Scottish Council for Research in Education.

Scottish Office Education Department (1991) *Guidelines on Assessment 5–14*, Edinburgh: SOEID.

Simpson, M. (1997) Developing Differentiation Practices: meeting the needs of teachers and pupils, *The Curriculum Journal*, 8 (1), pp. 85–104.

80

The Scottish Examination Board

Hamish Long

DEVELOPMENT AND STRUCTURE

The establishment of a Scottish examination board to have responsibility for the administration of the Scottish Leaving Certificate (SLC) examinations was first mooted on their introduction in 1888. However, this proposal did not find favour with the (then) Scotch Education Department and for the next seventy-five years or so, the Department itself conducted the examinations through Her Majesty's Inspectorate (HMI).

With the introduction of the Ordinary Grade of the SLC in 1962, it was anticipated that the work involved in administering the examinations would increase by several magnitudes and the establishment of an examination board was recommended by the Knox Committee in its report on *The Post-Fourth Year Examination Structure in Scotland* (Advisory Council, Scottish Education Department, 1960). Not only was the intention to free the Inspectorate for their principal duties and future involvement in large scale curriculum development, but also to give 'the teaching profession . . . a fuller part to play in our national examination'. Accordingly, the Scottish Certificate of Education Examination Board, later to be called the Scottish Examination Board (SEB), was established by the Education (Scotland) Act, 1963 (HMSO, 1963).

The Board's principal functions were to advise the Secretary of State on matters relating to examinations for pupils receiving secondary education and to conduct the examinations each year for the Scottish Certificate of Education (SCE). To oversee this, thirty-eight Board members were appointed, including representation from the universities, education authorities, central institutions, colleges of education, directors of education and teachers' associations. Under this was established a significant structure of committees, subject panels and examining teams. Servicing of the organisation, the examiners and the operational side of the annual examination was overseen by a permanent administrative and professional staff establishment, supplemented by temporary and seasonal staff during the examinations.

With some variation, and appropriate updating, this structure and *modus operandi* remained throughout the lifetime of the Board until it was succeeded by the Scottish Qualifications Authority (SQA) in 1997. However, the financing of the Board was significantly altered by the Education (Scotland) Acts of 1980 and 1981 (HMSO, 1981). Prior to these, the Board and the examinations had been financed by subventions on the local authorities with overall budgetary control resting with the SED. From 1982, the financing of the Board was founded on presentation charges with budgetary approval given to the Convention of Scottish Local Authorities (COSLA).

Within what proved to be a most stringent financial regime the Board was nevertheless able to operate successfully, given the wholehearted and unstinting support of teachers, lecturers and their employers – the independent schools, local authorities, colleges and universities. Teachers, lecturers and advisers constituted the subject panels which, for over thirty years, carried out examination and syllabus review and had annual oversight of their subject's examinations without any significant financial recompense. At the same time, an annual team of some six thousand examiners organised, set, marked and standardised the examinations at all Grades for fees well below what was generally considered to be the appropriate professional rate for the work concerned.

The Board ran annual examinations at three Grades, latterly Standard, Higher and Certificate of Sixth Year Studies (CSYS), as well as certificating Short Courses. It also carried out a demanding research and development programme and, from 1990, prepared and administered national tests for the 5–14 age group. In 1959, when the Knox Committee was established, there were some 15,000 candidates with 73,000 subject presentations. In 1996, over 126,000 candidates were presented in 668,800 subject presentations at SCE with, additionally, almost 12,000 presentations at CSYS and 43,000 awards in Short Courses. The actual costs of running the examinations in 1959 were about £45,000; in 1996, £11,000,000.

COURSE PROVISION AND PRESENTATION PATTERNS

The SEB inherited an extensive course provision from the Scottish Education Department (SED). This not only included the major subjects of the curriculum at Ordinary and Higher Grades but also a number of minority subjects, some offered for historic and cultural reasons, such as Swedish and Norwegian, others because of some specific demand, such as Portuguese. Navigation was provided to fulfil the demands of the coastal fishing communities; Agriculture and Horticulture for the rural areas.

During the lifetime of the Board several significant changes took place. The first was the introduction of the Certificate of Sixth Year Studies in 1968,

> to assist the schools in promoting study in depth and the capacity for the independent pursuit of a subject, in advancing the educational maturity of those who already have attained a recognisable proficiency in a subject discipline and in giving direction and focus to study undertaken by pupils in the sixth year of Scottish Secondary Schools. (Scottish Examination Board, 1968–97)

The second was the introduction from 1986 of Standard Grade to replace Ordinary Grade with a three-level system of examinations at Credit, General and Foundation which covered the whole ability spectrum at the age of sixteen. Thereafter, the Higher and Certificate of Sixth Year Studies were substantially reviewed to articulate with Standard Grade. Table 80.1 shows the presentation patterns in the Ordinary, Standard, and Higher Grades of the SCE, and the CSYS throughout the Board's lifetime as extracted from its Annual Reports (Scottish Examination Board, *Annual Reports*, 1965–96).

These figures reveal the rapid rise in presentations at Ordinary and Higher Grades through the 1960s and 1970s; the virtually unchanging level of CSYS presentations from 1971 to 1996; and the phased switch from Ordinary Grade to Standard Grade. Masked,

Table 80.1   Changes in presentation levels 1965–96

Year	Ordinary	Standard	Higher	CSYS	Total
1965	199,160		74,170		273,330
1966	210,255		78,412		288,667
1967	225,089		86,076		311,165
1968	246,339		97,566	1,993	345,898
1969	264,786		109,266	3,835	377,887
1970	276,457		124,039	6,357	406,853
1971	291,373		134,928	9,923	436,224
1972	314,971		144,702	11,043	470,716
1973	335,617		149,137	11,753	496,507
1974	392,921		151,485	11,433	555,839
1975	406,936		149,170	9,666	565,772
1976	422,396		154,049	9,571	586,016
1977	426,028		153,254	9,671	588,953
1978	431,194		146,900	9,582	587,676
1979	429,809		146,574	9,148	585,531
1980	456,790		154,001	10,107	620,898
1981	472,376		164,895	11,305	648,576
1982	483,903		173,269	12,148	669,320
1983	475,084		177,533	12,675	665,292
1984	459,564		172,220	12,637	644,421
1985	446,008		168,309	11,200	625,517
1986	444,888	32,095	166,403	10,393	653,779
1987	449,862	41,080	165,936	10,918	667,796
1988	415,789	68,729	169,818	11,073	665,409
1989	334,607	126,415	166,845	11,619	639,486
1990	204,457	256,895	158,191	11,240	630,783
1991	84,647	375,719	155,794	10,638	626,798
1992	23,952	424,763	157,995	11,586	618,296
1993	5,740	441,679	159,548	11,482	618,449
1994	75	464,675	160,646	11,942	637,338
1995		490,112	160,925	12,092	663,129
1996		504,098	164,701	12,273	681,072

however, are the changes to the size of the year cohort during this period which increased steadily throughout the 1970s until it reached a plateau of around 96,000 pupils in S4 in each of the years 1980 to 1982. Thereafter it slumped dramatically. In 1983 it was 89,000; in 1985, 84,000; by 1988, 74,000; and by 1992, only 59,000. By 1996 there was a gradual recovery to 67,000 but the later presentation figures in Table 80.1 have to be judged against a potential candidature which was only two-thirds of that of a decade earlier. Table 80.2 shows a selection of data to indicate the trends in candidates, and by awards, in relation to the age cohort over the period.

Of course, most of the changes which took place between 1965 and 1997 were evolutionary rather than revolutionary. New subjects, such as Modern Studies, Computing Studies and Graphic Communication were introduced; old ones such as Hebrew, Applied Mechanics and Anatomy, Physiology and Health were discontinued. However, such changes could not be made speedily. For any introduction or termination of a subject recommended by the Board, consultation with the educational community had to take place and the Secretary of State had to approve.

Table 80.2   Distribution of candidates by awards, 1973–96

Year	%S4 Cands	%S4 Awards	%S5 Cands	%S5 Awards
1973	52.1	37.3	31.6	14.4
1974	70.5	38.6	32.6	14.2
1975	71.9	38.6	32.9	14.1
1976	74.7	40.1	34.3	13.8
1977	72.6	40.8	35.1	14.6
1978	72.4	40.8	33.5	14.1
1979	73.7	40.9	33.3	14.3
1980	74.1	41.3	33.9	14.8
1981	76.3	43.0	36.8	15.2
1982	76.5	42.9	40.6	15.9
1983	78.1	44.0	42.2	16.0
1984	78.0	43.5	42.1	16.1
1985	80.0	44.9	42.6	15.5
1986	87.5	46.7	43.8	16.1
1987	91.5	48.6	45.9	16.6
1988	95.4	49.6	48.3	17.4
1989	96.7	50.3	50.9	18.2
1990	97.0	49.1	50.2	18.3
1991	97.2	52.7	50.6	18.9
1992	97.3	58.4	50.6	19.3
1993	97.4	60.9	52.2	21.1
1994	97.5	62.8	52.7	22.2
1995	98.7	65.2	52.2	22.2
1996	97.1	65.0	52.2	22.3

In table 80.2 the second column shows S4 candidates as a percentage of the age group; the third column shows the number of candidates achieving awards in 3 or more Ordinary Grade or Standard Grade subjects at grades A-C /1–3 as a percentage of the age group. Column 4 shows S5 candidates as a percentage of the age group, while column 5 shows the number of S5 candidates achieving passes in 3 or more Higher Grades (bands A-C) as a percentage of the age group.

EXAMINATION PROVISION AND STANDARD SETTING

With such a wide variety of subjects it is not surprising that the Board's examination arrangements were diverse and tailored to the needs and structure of each individual subject. There was, however, a common set of principles and examination operational procedures designed to provide the fairest and most accurate assessment and certification possible within the limits of financial provision and the state of the art.

The Board was always anxious to maximise the validity and reliability of the examination process. Differences between subject arrangements arose from the former. Thus, for example, there was always a significant place for tests of listening and speaking in the Modern Languages and this was further enhanced when Standard Grade was introduced.

Practical assessment ranged from boat-handling and ropework in Seamanship and Nautical Knowledge, to performance in Music; from pottery and painting in Art and Design, to advanced practical work in CSYS Chemistry. The basic examination provision, however, comprised written assessments, ranging from multiple-choice through structured question/ answer formats to the traditional open-ended essay question. Additionally, project work, assignments and investigative work were also required when validity considerations demanded. Wherever possible, examinations were designed to present all candidates with the same tasks, under examination-room conditions, and with external marking. Thus reliability was maximised. When practical testing was involved the same principles also applied, but, where external assessment was impracticable, internal assessment was used, supported by external moderation.

To ensure that the best quality examinations were provided for candidates, work on each paper started some two years before the examination diet with the appointment of a Principal Examiner and question paper Setters. Each paper was drafted, moderated by an expert panel, finalised, and then subjected to various quality checks before and after printing and also after distribution to the Chief Invigilator for each centre. Examining teams were appointed from markers of proven reliability and the marking teams themselves selected on the basis of providing marking of optimum quality. No marker was permitted to mark without attending a markers' meeting in which every detail of the paper and candidates' answers were considered. This was followed by a stringent review of each marker's work through sample re-marking by the core examining team and a detailed computer analysis of all marking. The strength of the Scottish system in this respect was that each marker was allocated a random sample of packets of question papers rather than whole school allocations. Where markers were consistent but slightly generous or severe, standardising factors were applied to their marked scripts; where markers were inconsistent or showed marked variability, their scripts were completely re-marked and they were not re-employed. In the latter years, a more sophisticated procedure was introduced using modern technology to identify all those scripts which, on the basis of the measured characteristics of the marker, might have resulted in a wrong grade. All of these were then re-marked, rather than having standardising factors applied.

As regards standard setting itself, or, to use the old terminology, 'pass mark determination', this was always examiner-referenced (i.e. the Principal Examiner determined the performance standard required for a pass). Though critics of the Board occasionally accused it of operating only norm-referenced procedures, this was never true. Statistical norms were nevertheless used as one of the sources of basic information for the decision-making process. The Board had a prime duty to maintain award standards each year and followed the principle that the year in which a candidate sat an examination should not influence his or her result; the attainment demonstrated should always receive the same grade regardless of the performance of other candidates or the particular question papers set. Accordingly, in setting the awards' standards each year, it was necessary to take into account all available information including the performance of candidates, markers' reports, changes in the examination population, diffi-culties in the question papers, and pre-test information. Each year there were two variables, the candidates and the question papers. The art of standard setting was to determine the contribution of each variable to the observed performance in the examination. At the final stage, awards in each subject were determined at a series of meetings of the Principal Examiner and other professional officers. These meetings were all chaired by the Director (Chief Executive) of the Board who was also Chief Examiner. There were only three Directors of the

Board throughout its life and, as most Principal Examiners gave many years of service in their posts, the maintenance of continuity of standards was virtually guaranteed.

In its standard setting procedures the Board was unique in many ways and also innovative. One significant innovation was the implementation of subject comparability indices based on SEB-commissioned work by Alison Kelly (Kelly, 1976). These indices enabled the Board to compare the relative difficulty of subjects within any one year and within a subject from year to year. Latterly, these played a significant part in the standard setting process. The SEB was fortunate in that, unlike the English examining Boards, it assessed virtually the whole national cohort each year; the use of the 'Kelly indices' would otherwise have been fraught with difficulty (see Chapter 86 for further details).

INTERNAL ASSESSMENTS AND MODERATION ARRANGEMENTS: APPEALS

As long ago as 1903, it was decided that teachers' estimates based on school assessment should play a significant role in the Scottish Intermediate examinations. In the report on the 1906 examination it was stated that 'No candidate for the Intermediate Certificate was rejected, and no candidate at all doubtful was accepted, until his school mark in each subject had been carefully scanned and collated with his written mark'. Such was the perceived success of this system that it was extended to the main Leaving Certificate leading to its 'unique reputation . . . by which the award of a pass is determined not solely by the results of the written examination' (SED, Annual Report, Edinburgh, 1951).

The SEB built upon this tradition during its stewardship although, in its early years, the use of internal assessment as a component of the actual examination mark, rather than as a back-up to be used in the case of appeals, was somewhat restricted. Its main application was in subjects with a practical or oral component where validity considerations outweighed reliability concerns. It was more extensively used in Ordinary Grade than at Higher and a principal determinant in this was the attitude of the Scottish Universities which laid down limits on the percentage of internal assessment beyond which recognition for the purposes of university entrance would not be granted.

The introduction of Standard Grade advanced the use of internal assessment. Most subjects had three elements, one of which was wholly internally assessed with the achieved grade appearing on the candidate's certificate and taken into account in an overall subject grade. To give external control and public confidence it was necessary to have a credible moderation system. Previously, at Ordinary Grade, all internally-marked components were moderated centrally or by visitation; any variation from the national standard was corrected by the application of a standardising factor to the candidate group concerned. Now, a new approach had to be developed given that internally assessed grades, not marks, would be submitted. This brought about a more collaborative method, in which teachers were informed of any differences in their assessment standards from the national standards and then carried out their own re-assessment. This approach ended the need to moderate every subject in every school every year, a procedure no longer feasible in terms of the available human and financial resources.

The Appeals procedure had always been based on teacher assessment. The underpinning principle was that the candidate had produced evidence of attainment at a better grade than that achieved in the formal examination. This evidence had to be acceptable in terms of both validity and reliability and the Board regularly issued guidance to teachers on the criteria necessary to satisfy the examiners that their evidence met the Board's requirements. Until the late 1980s, this evidence was always balanced against the external examination result and had to significantly outweigh it before any improvement was made to a candidate's grade, generally by averaging; latterly, however, if the evidence clearly demonstrated achievement at a higher grade than that of the examination the former was awarded, regardless of the actual examination result. It goes without saying that a candidate's original scripts were always re-checked for marking accuracy before any appeal was finally rejected.

In the 1990s, advanced technology enabled the computerisation of a significant part of the appeals process, that of the comparison of teachers' estimates with the grades achieved by their candidates. This increased the consistency of the procedure across subjects. Thus the SEB developed one of the most forward-looking and sophisticated appeals systems in the world, exploiting fully the advantages of using both external and school-based assessment and their inter-relationship.

THE SUBJECT PANELS

It was at its earliest meetings, held in 1964, that the Board considered and approved the establishment of Subject Panels under its Examinations Committee. Board members themselves were excluded from Panel membership, since the Board itself was the final arbiter on all matters. The Panels were given responsibility for the Board's syllabuses and their review. In particular, they had to ensure that the examinations each year met the syllabus requirements; additionally, they nominated the examining teams, appointed from their own membership small committees for the annual moderation of question papers, and reported to the Examinations Committee on each year's examination.

Basic Panel membership comprised three school teachers, a university or further education member, a college of education representative and one of Her Majesty's Inspectorate. Only a few of the Panels remained this size, with those Panels responsible for many examinations such as Modern Languages or Technical Subjects, adding to their numbers to cope with the duties. In later years, an advisorate category was also added to Panel membership and in the early 1990s, at the request of the SOED, the HMI members were reclassified as assessors, rather than members. Many Panels were also supported by an observer nominated by the Scottish Universities Council on Entrance (SUCE). The question-paper moderation committees normally comprised one practising teacher, the University member and the HMI. This combination was extremely successful in giving a high level of academic accuracy in the examinations, tempered by a thorough understanding of classroom teaching and what could be expected from school pupils at that stage.

Panel members were unpaid, other than for question paper-moderation, and there is no doubt that Scottish education owes all of those involved a tremendous debt for their unstinting input over a period of more than three decades. By 1997, there were thirty-one Panels which included five Short Course Committees and two Panels responsible for 5–14 Language and Mathematics assessment. It should also be noted that, for almost the entire history of the Board, these teachers, lecturers and others were released from their ordinary duties in schools, colleges and universities without any compensatory reimbursement being required by their employers, such was the generally perceived importance of the work of the Panels. The outcomes of this considerable commitment of experience and expertise were courses and examination papers of exceptionally high quality and national standing.

Shortly after the Panels became operational, it became clear that they had substantial power and influence regarding the secondary school curriculum. The examinations at Ordinary Grade related to courses which covered S1 to S4 and Higher Grade examinations were based on five-year courses. Thus the content of any subject in the secondary curriculum which was examinable was set out in *Conditions and Arrangements* and was subject to review by the Panel in question. No major changes were ever introduced without consultation since the Board always acted as a consensus body, taking the views of all interested bodies into account before revised arrangements were issued, normally two years before implementation (Scottish Examination Board, 1965–1997).

Nevertheless, the SED lost little time in establishing the then Consultative Committee on the Curriculum (CCC) in 1965 to advise the Secretary of State on general curricular matters (see Chapter 17). This led to some confusion about the relative areas of responsibility of the two bodies, but increased cooperation brought about an agreement in the 1970s to conduct all major syllabus review through the medium of Joint Working Parties of the Board's Panels and the Central Committees of the CCC. Consultation and responsibility for approval of the examination arrangements nevertheless remained firmly with the Board and its Panels operating through the Examinations Committee, although the SED gradually took more and more direct control of the development process. This was evidenced first in Standard Grade, where the Joint Working Parties worked to what was basically an HMI programme, and most recently in the Higher Still programme, where there was no pretence of either the Panels or the SCCC being responsible for the development of the syllabus or examination arrangements.

THE ANNUAL REPORTING PROCEDURES

One of the requirements on the Board as a statutory body was to report annually to parliament on the examinations and their conduct.

For the examinations from 1965 to 1996, a substantial annual report was produced, laid before parliament, and then widely distributed throughout the education community. All aspects were covered, from the strategic decisions of the Board itself, to detailed reports on every subject examination. Also included were reports on the guidance issued to teachers, liaison with other bodies, changes and proposed changes to examinations and research and development. A detailed financial report was also given, as well as information on the membership of Committees and Panels (Scottish Examination Board, *Annual Reports* 1965–96). This was supplemented by a substantial set of statistical details providing information on candidates and their performance across all subjects and Grades. These reports varied in detail over the years, but the general tendency was to provide more, not less, information to meet requests received from teachers' organisations, government and others. Latterly, following one of the regular quinquennial reviews of the Board by the SED, performance indicators were introduced to show how well the Board was performing in key areas of its work, both in terms of value for money and maintenance of standards.

Although the Annual Reports provided the summative account of the Board's work, parliamentary procedures meant that they could not be issued until the summer of the year following the examination. To provide necessary information for teachers and others, much more detailed examination reports were produced and considered answers were provided to comments submitted by the teachers' organisations and the SUCE. On the curriculum development side, schools and other educational bodies were provided with reports both of proposals and of decisions made, including reports on comments received and action taken. In these communications, the Board was always open; some proposed revisions were never introduced because they did not receive support and the Board always provided details on the reasons for such decisions.

In addition to providing the Annual Report, the Regulations governing the operation of the Board required it to 'submit to the Secretary of State reports on such matters as may be referred to them by the Secretary of State'. It also had to 'comply with any requests from the Secretary of State for information relating to the examinations conducted by the Board or to the work of the Board otherwise'. The Secretary of State in effect had powers of direction over the Board, after due consultation. Happily, throughout its lifetime, the Board was always able to satisfy government with regard to its work and the power of direction was never used.

SEB EXAMINATION RESULTS

When public examinations were introduced into Scotland, the intention was to provide a qualification of integrity and standard for entry into the professions. This intention was never lost. The main role of the Board's SCE at Higher Grade was to provide results which could be used for entry into Higher and Further Education and they very soon replaced the University Preliminary Examinations. While Ordinary Grade was also used in this context, Standard Grade was designed to be a certificate of achievement to guide future education choice and progression.

At all Grades, the qualifications issued by the Board were certificates of attainment. The Board never conducted tests of potential nor claimed that performance in the SCE could predict future success. Given the nature of learning and the level of maturity of sixteen- and seventeen-year olds it is not surprising that there are no particularly good predictors of future academic achievement for these cohorts. The overall performance of candidates in the SCE examinations did, however, appear to be the best there was, and it is hardly surprising that these examinations retained the central role in selection at the completion of secondary education.

The results, of course, had to be credible and reliable within the known limits of accuracy of this form of educational measurement. The Board was successful in achieving this throughout its tenure. It was sometimes difficult, however, to convince parents, and others, that candidates who were considered to have had a raw deal through long absences, poor teaching or the calamitous effect of some external factor on their education should not receive credit for what they might have achieved had things been different. The Board always operated very sensitive absentee and adverse circumstances procedures, intended to give credit to the candidate who failed to perform at the examination, but only up to a level already demonstrated and supported by evidence.

The results themselves were always deemed to be those of the candidate, though full information was provided to the presenting centres, to the education authorities and to UCAS (Universities and Colleges Admission System) and its predecessors. The SED also had full access to the results and in latter years this provided support for its school performance indicators programme.

STRENGTHS AND DIFFICULTIES

There is no question about the success of SEB and the credibility of its certification systems. Nor is there any doubt regarding its international recognition as a leader in the development of robust procedures for the combination of external and internal assessment. What criticisms there were, were usually founded on misunderstandings, either of the statutory limitations on the Board, or of the nature and limitations of the field of educational measurement in which it operated.

The Board's major strength, however, was the annual involvement of thousands of practising teachers in its work; indeed it was this dedication and enthusiasm which was the backbone of its success. Regrettably, such commitment was never fully rewarded financially although the Board took every opportunity available to improve the fees it offered. Indeed, it was the financial basis for the Board's operations which caused it the greatest difficulty. Although it was thought by some that it had direct central government funding, this was never the case. After 1980, it had to raise all of its funding through examination fee income, supplemented where possible with consultancy and other income. The governing statute prevented it from borrowing capital for the purchase of premises or equipment, nor was it permitted in practice to build up any reserve funds for development, for the acquisition of new technology, or indeed, for any purpose. It also found itself in the position of having to implement central government policy, but with its budget subject to local government control. Everything had to be funded from revenue income on a year-by-year basis. This created significant difficulties for long term strategic planning.

As far as major policy decisions regarding assessment and certification were concerned, for example, the development of Standard Grade, in practice these still resided within the SED. Indeed, it is difficult to see how it could have been otherwise. The Board was always anxious that the examinations and assessment should serve the Scottish curriculum, rather than the reverse. By statute, the Board had the power to develop major policy and advise the Secretary of State when it considered significant change to be needed. However, its normal strategy on such occasions was to advise that studies be carried out and recommendations developed by specially commissioned groups. Such advice led, for example, to the establishment of the Dunning and Howie Committees. It would have been interesting, nonetheless, had the Board itself devised a complete strategy for assessment and certification in the secondary school and beyond, something it was entirely capable of doing, given the breadth of expertise and experience of its membership. It did, for example, submit a plan for Vocational Highers to the SED in 1982, but since the government's report *16–18's in Scotland: An Action Plan* (SED, Edinburgh, 1983) and the HM Inspectorate Report, *Teaching and Learning in the Senior Stages of the Scottish Secondary School* (SED, Edinburgh, 1983) were on the point of publication, that initiative came to naught.

THE FUTURE

The establishment of the Scottish Qualifications Authority (SQA) in 1997 brought to fruition one of the long-standing aspirations of the SEB (see Chapter 82). In response to the Secretary of State's 1984 consultative document entitled *School and Further Education: A Single Examining Body?* (SED, Edinburgh, 1984) the Board indicated that it was strongly in favour of a single organisation, rather than the creation of the twin-track of the SEB and the proposed Scottish Vocational Education Council. There was, however, a lack of consensus in Scotland on this issue and the idea was put on ice. In retrospect, there seems little doubt that the amalgamation of the so-called 'academic' and 'vocational' courses into a single system would have been achieved by the early 1990s had the Board's view been accepted and a single examining body formed in 1985.

It is this single system that 'Higher Still' is setting out to design, although such an integrated system will not be easy to achieve. What makes it feasible is the establishment of SQA. A single body which has responsibility for all assessment from early school through to all but Higher Education degrees has every opportunity and facility to make this a success, given that it has no requirement to ensure the cooperation of other examining bodies. 'Higher Still' is nevertheless a government, not an SQA development. Thus, like the SEB, the SQA will require ingenuity, creativity and vision so that it can mould the outcomes of the Higher Still Development Programme into a reliable and credible system. One can have every confidence that this will indeed be the case and that in the field of national assessment Scotland will remain a world leader.

REFERENCES

Kelly, A. (1976) *The Comparability of Examining Standards in Scottish Certificate of Education Ordinary and Higher Grade Examinations*, Dalkeith: Scottish Examination Board.

Philip, H. L. (1992) *The Higher Tradition*, Dalkeith: Scottish Examination Board.

Scottish Examination Board (1965–97) *Scottish Certificate of Education Examination Conditions and Arrangements*, Dalkeith: Scottish Examination Board.

Scottish Examination Board (1968–97) *Certificate of Sixth Year Studies*, Dalkeith: Scottish Examination Board.

Scottish Examination Board Regulations 1981, (1981) No. 1562 (S.163) Edinburgh: HMSO.

81

The Scottish Vocational Education Council

Tom McCool

The Scottish Vocational Education Council (SCOTVEC) which was established in 1985 was wound up in 1997 when its responsibilities and those of the Scottish Examination Board (SEB) were combined in the remit of a new body, the Scottish Qualifications Authority (SQA). Over its relatively short lifespan, SCOTVEC made a significant contribution to the expansion and growing prestige of vocational education and training in Scotland. Modular qualifications were introduced to respond to a changing environment which put increased emphasis on the relevance and flexibility of qualifications as well as their credibility. The new vocational qualifications attracted new client groups, including school pupils, and their uptake exceeded all expectations. Qualifications were also designed for workplace delivery, encouraging fresh approaches to training and opening up new routes to qualified status.

This chapter charts the progress of SCOTVEC and the evolution of a framework of vocational qualifications in Scotland up to the point where the next logical step became the integration of vocational and academic qualifications under a single awarding body.

SCOTVEC'S PREDECESSORS

The Scottish Technical Education Council (SCOTEC) and the Scottish Business Education Council (SCOTBEC) had been created as a result of the need to ensure uniform national standards in the vocational qualifications offered in Scotland's Further Education colleges. SCOTEC awarded a range of qualifications at ONC, HNC and HND levels, mainly in scientific and technical fields, while SCOTBEC offered a similar range of qualifications in business related areas and general studies. Although both organisations operated – and generally competed – mainly in the Further Education colleges, a growing interest in schools in vocationally relevant courses and in qualifications which would recognise the achievements of pupils who were unsuited to SCE work, led to collaboration in 1982 in the development of the Scottish Certificate in Vocational Studies, a qualification for schools which, although short-lived, turned out to be an important indicator of future trends. Other awarding bodies also operated in Scotland, most notably the City and Guilds of London Institute (CGLI) and the Royal Society of Arts Examination Board (RSA), offering syllabuses and qualifications in a wide range of disciplines mainly at craft and non-advanced level.

The picture in Scotland, pre-1985, therefore was one of competing awarding bodies offering a variety of qualifications and courses which were driven by syllabuses and external examinations. Their requirements regarding modes of attendance were relatively rigid and the syllabuses were slow to change in response to new technologies and business practices.

THE ACTION PLAN

The consultation document *16–18s in Scotland: An Action Plan* (Scottish Education Department, Edinburgh, 1983) was seminal in introducing change. It resulted in a development programme which brought about rapid and dramatic reform of the vocational qualification system in Scotland which ultimately ended the independent existence of SCOTEC and SCOTBEC.

The Action Plan proposed a new approach to vocational qualifications in Scotland, a key feature of which was a modular structure. A range of modules, short bursts of learning, notionally forty hours in length, would be designed to cover all of the main vocational areas. Each module would include a clear statement of the required learning outcomes and performance criteria against which achievement of the outcomes would be measured; the outcomes would be competence based and refer mainly to demonstrable skills. In addition, the 'module descriptor' would provide guidance on suitable teaching and learning approaches and on the selection and use of appropriate criterion referenced assessment instruments, to be applied internally, with external monitoring and verification. 'Qualifications' would be formed by accumulating modules drawn from a national catalogue according to the requirements of particular users, e.g. employers, apprenticeship councils. A new National Certificate recording each successfully completed module was to be the responsibility of a new body the Scottish Vocational Education Council (SCOTVEC) to be formed by merging SCOTEC and SCOTBEC.

THE EMERGENCE OF SCOTVEC

Following extensive consultation on the Action Plan, the Secretary of State announced his decision to set up SCOTVEC as a company limited by guarantee, having a Memorandum and Articles of Association. The Chairman and fourteen of the twenty-eight members were to be appointed by the Secretary of State and the remaining members drawn from a range of organisations, some of which, e.g. COSLA, had a right of nomination and others, e.g. professional bodies, which could nominate potential members but without any guarantee of appointment. The new Council held its first full meeting on 29 April 1985. Like its predecessors, it was representative of a wide range of interests including FE colleges, schools, universities, local authorities, the Scottish Chambers of Commerce, the CBI, the STUC, together with assessors from the Scottish Education Department, the Manpower Services Commission and the Department of Education and Science. It was intended that SCOTVEC would become self financing through fees levied on its qualifications and services; to facilitate this, its remit and constitution gave it the freedom to widen its portfolio of activities without reference to the Secretary of State.

In its Memorandum of Association, SCOTVEC was required, as its main objective, 'to develop and encourage the advancement of vocational education and training in the context of national educational policy.' The design and delivery of high quality vocational qualifications was to be the main instrument for discharging this remit. However, throughout its existence, the Council also accepted an influential role in the wider aspects of the national vocational education and training enterprises and committed its members and officers to play a part in an extensive range of external organisations, working parties and committees. In its own operations, the Council quickly established a network of committees and groups which drew a widely representative group of contributors into its work. In addition to inviting external representation on to some of its major policy determining committees, eighteen sector boards representing particular occupational areas were set up to oversee the design of qualifications in their sector, thus drawing an additional 400 individuals with expertise and enthusiasm into its work.

The early decisions on the constitution, funding and modus operandi of SCOTVEC were to prove sound; over the next decade any changes were more a matter of refinement and adjustment to new circumstances than radical reform. By 1993, the Council which had started with an annual budget of approximately £4 million, of which 60 per cent was externally funded, had expanded its operations and, with an annual budget of over £10 million, had become financially independent.

NATIONAL CERTIFICATE MODULES

SCOTVEC inherited the National Certificate modular structure in a relatively raw state from the Scottish Office Development Team which had been responsible for its introduction and this, together with the advanced courses at HNC and HND level inherited from SCOTEC and SCOTBEC, were its main starting products. Both types of qualifications were extensively developed over the years and their increasing popularity, together with the introduction of new qualification types referred to later, not only contributed to the Council's financial security but also produced a considerable expansion in its headquarters based staff (from 160 in 1986 to approximately 350 in 1996). The number of teachers and lecturers employed on short term work increased significantly and the range of providers with which SCOTVEC interacted grew from approximately fifty Further Education (FE) colleges and Higher Education establishments to more than 1,000 schools, colleges, universities, training providers and other centres. The geographical pattern of the Council's activities showed similar development, spreading from Scottish based institutions to the provision of services in, for example, the Middle East, Africa, Russia and Eastern Europe.

The initial inheritance from the Scottish Office Development Unit was approximately 500 modules and the early work of the Council concentrated on extending the range of occupational areas covered until eventually the National Certificate catalogue contained about 3,000 modules. The Council also put in place a process of continuous review and refinement of module descriptors to improve the quality of their presentation and their relevance to workplace needs. Modular programmes gradually replaced most other qualifications in Further Education, including those of CGLI, and considerable effort went into promoting understanding and acceptance of the new programmes among students, employers and other users, including Higher Education.

CERTIFICATION

The original concept of the National Certificate, that modules achieved would be recorded without any other categorisation, did not stand the test of time. Colleges, responding to consumer preference, successfully marketed a variety of informal 'group awards'. SCOT-VEC, responding to the same market forces, but also recognising the benefits of a uniform certification structure across all its types of awards, decided to introduce Group Awards within the National Certificate. A grouping of modules which met specified criteria would be recognised as a 'National Award'. A grouping which failed to meet national criteria, but met more local requirements, could be recognised within the certification process as a 'Tailored Award'.

The Record of Education and Training (RET), a computer based document listing all modules, units and group awards within the new structures, became SCOTVEC's main vehicle for certification. It could be updated regularly to give a cumulative record of all of an individual's achievements, at any stage or age, and put SCOTVEC at the forefront of the application of information technology in national certification. The availability of this highly sophisticated certification process served SCOTVEC well when the movement to modular based group awards became even more formalised and widespread, initially through the introduction of General Scottish Vocational Qualifications (GSVQs) and later Scottish Group Awards (SGAs), both of which will be referred to later in this chapter.

ENSURING QUALITY

National Certificate modules, which were greeted with the caution which faces most new educational products, met the additional hurdle of fairly widespread suspicion associated with the reliability of internal assessment for the purposes of national certification. These reservations existed not only among potential users of the qualifications, but also among the teachers and lecturers who delivered them. Their concerns included the possible adverse effects on the teacher-student relationship if the teacher had responsibility for assessment decisions, and anxieties about the feasibility of establishing a recognised national standard and ensuring a uniform approach to its application across many different locations.

SCOTVEC's approach to quality assurance was based initially on a combination of three elements: approving centres, verifying assessment and validating awards. Further Education colleges were granted automatic approval as National Certificate centres, as it was considered that the supervision of the local authorities would ensure their fitness. Private training centres however, were only approved following an inspection process conducted by SCOTVEC. Verification, which applied to all centres irrespective of their status, was the main instrument of quality assurance. External verifiers, mainly teachers and lecturers, but some also from industrial and commercial backgrounds, were recruited by SCOTVEC on short term contracts and deployed to centres to check the quality of teachers' assessments. The process employed a sampling system which endeavoured to ensure that a proportion of all cognate groups of modules in any centre were verified in any one year. The third element, validation, consisted of a scrutiny applied to award design to ensure that new modules or awards entering the system were thoroughly examined before being given entry to the national catalogue, to check evidence of need, conformity with SCOTVEC's design criteria and the quality of the proposed teaching and learning procedures.

Undoubtedly, the change from a national external examination system to one based on internal assessment involved a learning process for SCOTVEC. The procedures introduced were robust, but unrefined, and never previously attempted on a national scale. It is remarkable then, that although there were worries and criticisms, there was never at any time a crisis of confidence in the new approach. The HMI report *Six Years On: Teaching, Learning and Assessment in National Certificate Programmes* (Scottish Education Department, Edinburgh, 1991), whilst commenting on the continuing need for staff development in assessment, nevertheless recognised that student performance was being assessed to national standards 'with reasonable consistency'. Much of the credit for this can be attributed to the effort made by schools, colleges and centres to support staff training and to develop sound internal processes for quality assurance. In its early management structure SCOTVEC, as one of its four directorates, had created a directorate for Quality Assurance thus affirming the high degree of priority which, from the outset, SCOTVEC accorded to its responsibilities for setting and maintaining a national standard.

The processes of approval, validation and verification remained key elements in quality assurance throughout SCOTVEC's existence but became increasingly sophisticated with the refinements that experience allowed. Gradually, module descriptors were reviewed and refined to remove ambiguities, to provide greater clarity of expression of the required outcomes and standards, and to give improved guidance on assessment. Training of verifiers was intensified and their deployment improved by the adoption of systems to allow prioritisation of verification visits and adequate overall coverage. Principal verifiers were appointed in key cognate areas to give leadership to verifier teams and, in due course, systems verifiers were appointed on a full-time basis with a remit which had less emphasis on direct verification and more on providing advice and assistance to colleges on assessment and quality assurance issues. Encouragement and support were given to centres to develop their own quality assurance systems, including procedures for conducting internal verification among the teachers and lecturers involved in a particular module or award. Eventually, it became a requirement for centres seeking approval to offer SCOTVEC awards to provide evidence that satisfactory internal verification procedures were in place; subsequently steps were taken to introduce a requirement for teachers/lecturers to hold qualifications in assessment and verification. The growing effectiveness of these quality assurance measures and in particular the growth of a quality ethos in centres, led SCOTVEC to consider delegating greater autonomy in quality assurance matters to centres and in 1992 it introduced its quality audit system which took quality assurance to a new level of sophistication. However, before discussing this development, it would be appropriate to look beyond National Certificate modules at other awards which entered the SCOTVEC portfolio.

SVQs AND NVQs

The introduction of National Certificate modules was a major revolution in the vocational qualification system in Scotland and the name of SCOTVEC is most closely linked with this development. However, other major qualification developments also took place under SCOTVEC's leadership.

In the report *Review of Vocational Qualifications in England and Wales* (Manpower Services Commission, 1986), the establishment of a National Council for Vocational Qualifications (NCVQ) was recommended in order to develop a new framework of vocational qualifications which would address the perceived lack of relevance and coherence of the vocational education provision in England at that time. NCVQ was not to award qualifications itself, but to determine criteria which, if met, would allow awarding bodies to have their own qualifications accredited as National Vocational Qualification (NVQs) and included in a national framework within which all qualifications would be classified by occupational area and level (I to V). These new qualifications were required to be relevant, credible, accessible, cost effective, and based on the assessment of competence.

Although the working group's remit did not extend to Scotland, it nevertheless proposed that there should be full Scottish participation. In Scotland, however, the view was taken that existing developments, i.e. National Certificates, should be built on and that SCOTVEC should be the accrediting body for Scotland, determining its own criteria and responsible for the accreditation of its own Scottish Vocational Qualifications (SVQs), but liaising with NCVQ to ensure UK wide compatibility of their qualifications.

NCVQ was also charged with the responsibility of giving recognition to the role of effective and appropriate industry bodies in developing their own standards. This led to the setting up of a large number of 'industry lead bodies' (ILBs) which were given responsibility for standard setting in their own occupational sectors. SCOTVEC participated fully in the subsequent research programme into the development of techniques for assessment in the workplace, undertaking major projects in competency testing, the accreditation of prior learning (APL) and the assessment of work-based learning (AWBL). The findings, although based on National Certificate, made a significant contribution to the development of assessment practice in NVQs and SVQs (The Training Agency, 1988). The emergence of industry-defined standards and the development of new approaches to assessment supported the design and delivery of the new NVQs in which the emphasis was on workplace training and assessment. These qualifications were not merely reformed versions of what had previously existed, but a new kind of qualification which added to the existing range and in many cases broke new ground by providing vocational qualifications in areas where none had previously existed.

The direction taken by the NVQ initiative had a significant impact on the development of the Scottish vocational qualification system. The learning outcomes of National Certificate modules, although competence based and designed with industry involvement, were less oriented towards delivery in workplace conditions than the standards produced by the industry lead bodies. The use of existing modules for SVQs therefore would have resulted in significant differences north and south of the border. SCOTVEC did attempt to adapt the outcomes of many of its modules to incorporate the new standards and a number of SVQs were created using revised National Certificate modules as their component units. However, there was a limit to the extent to which this could be done without compromising the suitability of modules for college delivery. In order therefore to match the provision of workbased qualifications which was resulting from NCVQ's work, SCOTVEC had to develop new modules drawing on ILB standards. The SCOTVEC portfolio of award types was therefore enlarged to include SVQs as a separate category of awards, some of which were based on NC modules, but most of which were eventually to draw on a new set of workplace assessed units.

The introduction of NVQs and SVQs was a ground breaking development which attracted widespread interest nationally and internationally. Nevertheless, sustained criticism was directed towards NCVQ concerning not only implementation issues such as costs, bureaucracy, and the overly complex language of standards etc. but also against the concept itself, with respect to both the emphasis on workplace skills, allegedly at the expense of the development of knowledge and understanding, and the assessment arrangements, which were claimed to lack the reliability essential for the purposes of national certification. Similar criticisms voiced in Scotland were at a much lower level and tended to be constructively directed towards specific issues within an overall atmosphere of acceptance and support. The greater confidence of the Scottish community, derived from experience of competence based internally assessed qualifications in the National Certificate, appeared to carry over to SVQs which were recognisably similar to National Certificate qualifications. A different situation existed in England where traditional vocational qualifications had remained the dominant provision and NVQs were seen as radical newcomers.

Nevertheless, NVQs and SVQs have a very close relationship and, although the levels of criticism were different, many of the concerns voiced over NVQs applied also to SVQs. The comprehensive review of NVQs and SVQs which was heralded in the Department of Trade and Industry White Paper *Competitiveness – Helping Business to Win* (HMSO, 1994) therefore also applied to Scotland and SCOTVEC contributed fully to the review, the findings of which were detailed in the report *Review of 100 NVQs and SVQs* (Beaumont, 1995). In addition to a reduction in bureaucracy and improved marketing and delivery of the qualifications, the review recommended strengthening the place of core skills, clarifying the specification of knowledge and understanding required, and invited further investigation into the choice of assessment methods, including the consideration of an element of external assessment. Perhaps the most significant conclusion, in view of the criticisms that had been levelled, was that 80 per cent of respondents to a consultation supported the NVQ/SVQ concept and 85 per cent of employers confirmed that NVQs/SVQs gave their employees competence.

The Beaumont Report prompted the government to introduce a programme of action to meet the main recommendations and to confirm its support for NVQs and SVQs as a continuing element in its vocational education and training policy. By 1996, the Scottish SVQ catalogue contained 750 SVQs and candidate registrations reached 30,000 per annum, suggesting that SVQs had acquired a recognised role in training and development plans. In the continuing reform process, it is to be expected that the more refined SVQs which will emerge will develop a clearer relationship with other qualifications and be imbedded more firmly in an overall qualification system within which credit transfer is routinely available.

HNC AND HND

Throughout the period that SCOTVEC was developing NC modules and SVQs, it was also modernising and expanding the range of HNC and HND awards it had inherited from SCOTEC and SCOTBEC. These awards, at levels approximating to Years 1 and 2 of Higher Education, were highly regarded by the business and industrial world and were also recognised by many HE institutions for entry with advanced standing to degree courses. Courses leading to the awards were offered in Further Education colleges and in the Central Institutions, a number of which subsequently became universities. The courses were syllabus driven, assessed by external examinations set by SCOTVEC, and required success in a pre-determined group of units for completion of an award. Alongside its innovative NC developments therefore, SCOTVEC was operating in the traditional role of examining body. However, in 1987, following consultation on the future shape of its advanced qualifications, the Council initiated a development programme to create a new system for HNC and HND built largely on the same principles which had been adopted for the National Certificate. Programmes would be built up from modules known as HN units designed around competence based learning outcomes and performance criteria. Each unit, which would be internally assessed, would carry a credit value and although individual units would be separately certificated, the emphasis would be on achievement of a full 'group award' of HNC or HND through the accumulation of a pre-determined number of credits. A further clear departure from National Certificate was the decision to introduce a merit level group award based on satisfying criteria beyond those required by the pass level.

One of the major objectives of the Advanced Courses Development Programme (ACDP) was to widen the range of awards and to make them more relevant to the needs of employers. To that end, colleges were encouraged to design units and awards for validation with the result that the National Catalogue of HN units contained not only units designed centrally by SCOTVEC but also locally produced units. The enthusiasm with which colleges took up this opportunity resulted in the appearance of many more college designed units than units designed centrally, an outcome which gave SCOTVEC some concern about proliferation and possible duplication of units. However, a compensating factor was the increase in uptake from approximately 15,000 candidate enrolments in 1986 to over 50,000 candidate enrolments for HN units a decade later.

The flexibility afforded by the new system meant that not only could local needs be more readily satisfied and innovative programmes introduced with consequent expansion in the market, but also that programmes could be designed to articulate more readily with other courses in FE and HE. Consequently, the period since the ACDP has seen the widespread introduction of HNC/HND/Degree programmes offered in FE colleges and universities. The HNC/D, whilst still retaining status as a qualification in its own right, is rapidly becoming an integral and important part of a wider post-16 qualification framework.

THE GROWING INFLUENCE OF MODULES

The enormous increase in the uptake of HNC/D courses over a period of 5 years is testimony to the attractiveness and flexibility of the modular approach and to the enterprise and inventiveness which can be released when centres are free to design their own programmes. Further evidence, if any is needed, can be found in the history of the uptake of National Certificate modules. By 1990, uptake had reached 1.1 million modules per annum and continued at approximately that level thereafter.

Although, not surprisingly, Further Education students were one of the biggest client groups, modules were adapted for a variety of other learning purposes. The Scottish Wider Access Programme (SWAP), a government funded initiative to promote wider access into Higher Education, negotiated modular based access programmes with universities, to bring students from non-traditional backgrounds, including mature students, up to admission standard. NC modules provided an alternative to SCE examinations which was more suited to the diverse backgrounds of access candidates and several thousand students eventually entered the Scottish universities through this route. A spin-off from this programme was the contact with modular qualifications experienced by university staff, which helped to improve understanding of modules in Higher Education. Modules also found their way into an expanding range of client groups including community education, government training programmes, company training schemes and the armed services.

However, the biggest expansion outwith FE colleges was in schools. An uptake of 24,000 modules in 1986 had grown to 419,000 by 1996 and the number of school students involved in modular studies overtook the FE level of participation. One of the main reasons for this highly significant development was that the flexibility of short programmes of learning, without the constraints of a national examination timetable, suited the needs both of those fifth year pupils who would leave school at the end of the first term and of pupils who had gaps in their timetable due to taking a limited number of SCE studies. The clearly defined outcomes of the modules and their vocational relevance also provided motivation for pupils of a less academic bent, as well as challenging some of the most able pupils who took modules in areas such as Information Technology to expand their range of skills. There can be no doubt that NC modules helped to fill a gap which existed in the secondary curriculum and they became significant ingredients in the menu available to pupils in most of Scotland's secondary schools.

GENERAL SCOTTISH VOCATIONAL QUALIFICATIONS (GSVQs)

One of the major problems of the 1980s was the inappropriateness of offering only an SCE Higher based curriculum designed for 30 per cent of the post-16 population at a time when the staying on rate was approaching 75–80 per cent. This was a problem which the availability of NC modules helped to alleviate. However, the juxtaposition of two different systems, although providing wider choice, also attracted criticism not only of the administrative difficulties of working with two separate awarding bodies, but also of the perceived lack of coherence in the educational experience of many pupils. Although many schools did in fact monitor module choice closely, SCOTVEC itself had recognised the desirability of providing incentives for a less random and more structured choice of modules and had introduced the concept of modular 'clusters', groups of three related modules carrying a single title and recorded under that title on the certificate. Work also started on the design of larger groupings of modules built on a core plus options model which would ensure a coherent experience for students and carry an 'added-value' for users. Although some of this work was carried to fruition, two significant developments changed the course of events.

In the White Paper *Education and Training for the 21st Century* (Department of Education and Science, 1991), NCVQ had been asked to develop qualifications within the NVQ framework which would be of a more general character than NVQs, preparing the holder for working life rather than a specific occupation. In all probability, this request stemmed from a realisation that NVQs, although filling an important gap in the qualification system, had done little to reform the system as a whole and, in schools in particular, the need for a vocational alternative to the academic route was unfulfilled. Scotland already had NC modules meeting the needs which the new General National Vocational Qualifications (GNVQs) were designed to meet, however the GNVQ design features of group awards on a core plus options model containing core skills and within the NVQ framework of levels were not replicated in Scottish awards. The Scottish Office White Paper *Access and Opportunity* (Scottish Office, 1991) therefore invited SCOTVEC 'to develop more broadly based vocational qualifications within the SVQ framework'. Essentially this request gave formal blessing to the movement towards group awards which had already begun and SCOTVEC began the process of developing General Scottish Vocational Qualifications (GSVQs) based on NC modules at three different levels corresponding to levels I, II and III of the SVQ framework.

THE SCOTTISH VOCATIONAL QUALIFICATION FRAMEWORK

The appearance of GSVQs completed SCOTVEC's contribution to the development of a Scottish vocational qualification framework which had started with the 'Action Plan' in 1983 and which latterly comprised a sophisticated arrangement of inter-related modular and group awards at various levels (Figure 81.1).

Figure 81.1   The structure of SCOTVEC vocational qualifications in 1996

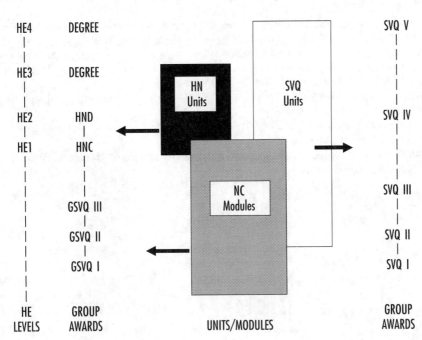

A SINGLE AWARDING BODY

The second development which was to change the course of events started with the appointment of the Howie Committee in 1990 and the subsequent government proposals in the form of 'Higher Still', for a single curriculum and assessment structure based on modules drawn from both SCOTVEC and areas of SEB provision (for details, see Chapter 82). Inevitably, this development led to an examination of the relationship between the two bodies. The decision to merge them was taken following consultation and enacted in the Education Act 1996 which set up the new Scottish Qualifications Authority (SQA).

SCOTVEC bequeathed to the new body not only a healthy financial legacy, but a robust portfolio of qualifications with a wide-ranging customer base. The early suspicions about the quality of qualifications based on internal assessment had long since been allayed and the system had acquired a level of maturity and sophistication which had allowed SCOTVEC to delegate responsibility for major elements of its quality assurance to centres which satisfied a rigorous quality audit process and which entered into a quality contract with SCOTVEC. The SCOTVEC approach had also attracted international attention and SCOTVEC staff had exported SCOTVEC ideas and qualifications to Australasia, the Middle East, Africa and Eastern Europe.

A decade of innovation and development had brought widespread recognition to SCOTVEC's qualifications, helped to raise the status of vocational education and training in Scotland and made SCOTVEC itself into a household name. It is left to SQA to fulfil the aspiration for a single unified qualification framework for all elements of the Scottish education and training system.

REFERENCES

Manpower Services Commission (1986) *Review of Vocational Qualifications in England and Wales: a report by the working group*, Sheffield: Manpower Services Committee.

The Training Agency (1988) *Credit Where Credit's Due: an investigation into the accreditation of work based learning, utilising assessment in the workplace, and relating to the SCOTVEC national certificate provision in Scotland*, Dalkeith: SCOTVEC.

Beaumont, G. (1995) *Review of 100 NVQs and SVQs: a report*, Department of Education and Employment: Evaluation Advisory Group, London: HMSO.

Department of Education and Science (1991) *Education and Training for the 21st Century, Vols 1 and 2*, (Cmnd 1536), London: HMSO.

Scottish Office (1991) *Access and Opportunity: a strategy for education and training*, (White Paper), Edinburgh: Scottish Office.

82

The Scottish Qualifications Authority

Ron Tuck

The Scottish Qualifications Authority (SQA) came into existence on 18 September 1996 and on 1 April 1997 took over all the functions of the Scottish Examination Board (SEB) and Scottish Vocational Education Council (SCOTVEC). It has responsibility for the development, assessment and certification of all types of qualifications in Scotland except degrees.

To appreciate the raison d'etre of the SQA, it is necessary to understand the key features of the debates and developments leading to its creation. The proposal in the consultation paper, *Options for the Future Relationship between The Scottish Examination Board and The Scottish Vocational Education Council* (SOEID, 1995) to create a single awarding body received overwhelming support. However, a similar consultation in 1984 had not elicited this response. Why was this? What had happened in the intervening years to create such a different climate of opinion?

The answer is that, whereas throughout the 1980s the concerns of upper secondary education and vocational education and training had been relatively distinct, by the early 1990s these had begun to converge. Through this convergence, the idea of a unified qualifications framework and a single qualifications body was born. The first part of this chapter outlines relevant features of the debates of the 1980s and 1990s; the second part describes the foundation of the SQA; the third part expands on the concept of a unified qualifications system in Scotland.

UPPER SECONDARY EDUCATION

From the early 1980s, concerns began to be expressed about the upper secondary curriculum and qualifications, notably in the HMI report, *Teaching and Learning in the Senior Stages of the Scottish School* (SED, 1983). There were two key issues here: the so-called 'dash and drift' problem, and the question of provision for 'middle ability pupils'.

Dash and drift

This referred to a situation faced by the relatively high achievers in fifth and sixth years. The time available for courses leading to Higher Grade examinations was little more than two terms hence the expression 'two term dash'. This was thought to have adverse effects on the quality of learning as well as making it difficult for many candidates to reach the required standards. Nevertheless, many pupils achieved well in their Highers in S5. Although possessing the requisite entry qualifications for higher education, an increasing proportion of the most able pupils stayed on into S6, probably because of a growing feeling that it was better to have an extra year to mature before commencing higher education. For many of these pupils, 'S5 dash' turned to 'S6 drift'. What exactly was the purpose of this sixth year if progression to university was already assured?

Provision for middle ability pupils

A fifth year curriculum based solely or mainly on Highers was best suited for pupils achieving Credit level in a significant number of Standard Grade subjects. Currently, around 40% of the age cohort achieve three or more Credit awards at Standard Grade. However, the percentage of pupils staying on into S5, and indeed S6, steadily grew from the mid 1980s. Staying on rates into S5 increased from 59% in 1985 to over 76% in 1996/97. Over the same period, staying on rates into S6 increased from 21% to over 42%. Many of the 'new S5' had Standard Grade passes mainly at General or Foundation level. What courses were these pupils to take? In many cases, pupils attempted to make the leap from Standard Grade General level to Higher Grade in one year; the usual outcome was failure, sometimes followed by a repeat experience in S6.

From about 1985 onwards, the so-called 'middle ability pupils' had an alternative to Highers: National Certificate modules, developed by SCOTVEC following *16–18s in Scotland: an Action Plan* (SED, 1993). There is no doubt that these qualifications performed a very valuable function in schools. However, they were not the whole answer to the problem. The question was: where did they lead? Some schools used National Certificate modules as preparation in S5 for a Higher in S6, a purpose for which they had not been explicitly designed, and success with this approach appears to have been mixed. Furthermore, there were difficulties with the currency of National Certificate qualifications gained in schools. Whereas in further education (FE) colleges, modules were grouped in coherent programmes (with titles such as National Certificate in Business) which had currency with employers and through the Scottish Wider Access Programme with universities, the often apparently random group of modules gained by school pupils did not normally attract the same recognition.

Thus, there was in most Scottish schools the growing problem that the curriculum on offer to a high proportion of fifth and sixth year pupils was inappropriate and did not lead to qualifications which provided a good basis for progression beyond school. Although the problem associated with Highers received more public comment and press attention, there is little doubt that for most headteachers, the problem of the 'middle ability pupils' was of far greater significance.

Developments in vocational education and training

Meanwhile, the world of vocational education and training had its own concerns. Dating from Callaghan's Ruskin speech in October 1976, there had been growing acceptance of the contribution of education and training to economic competitiveness. The key theme was the rapidity of social, economic and technological change and the need for individuals (both for their own sakes and for that of the economy) to be able to respond to such change.

The link to competitiveness gave rise to the identification of a number of challenges for vocational education and training: to develop the skills and knowledge actually required in employment; to develop the transferable or core skills deemed to be essential in all forms of employment; to enhance the flexibility of the qualifications system in order to open up access to a wider range of learners; and to end, or at least reduce, the 'academic/vocational divide', so as to create parity of esteem.

Developing job-related skills and occupational competences

There was a concern in the early 1980s that vocational education was not necessarily close enough to the world of work. Part of this concern was that there was an overemphasis on what students knew rather than what they could do. This led to a desire to focus more clearly on the outputs of vocational education – to specify qualifications on the basis of outcomes and to move to criterion-based assessment. This was one of the key features of the Action Plan. Later in the 1980s, and on a UK-wide basis, this emphasis was to be taken further in the development of work-based qualifications (NVQs and SVQs) based on standards of occupational competence defined by employer-led bodies.

Throughout the 1980s, there was a growing awareness that because specialist knowledge and skills became outdated ever more quickly, it was essential to develop those core skills which are necessary for all forms of employment and which are unlikely to become obsolescent. This was linked, to some extent, to more traditional concerns about the 'three Rs'. Core skills first featured in the Youth Training Scheme following the *Report of the Youth Task Group* (Sheffield: Manpower Services Commission, 1982). However, the current model of five core skills – communication, numeracy, information technology, problem solving and working with others – originated in a paper to the Howie Committee (*Core Skills By Design*) which traced the origin of core skills in the school curriculum in Scotland, demonstrating that this was not just a 'vocational issue'. Despite general acceptance of the concept, implementation of the core skills agenda was slow.

Flexibility

There were two principal ways in which the vocational qualifications system of the early 1980s needed to become more flexible. First, rapid economic and technological change required that qualifications should be able to be updated quickly. Second, the qualifications system needed to change to allow for more flexible forms of delivery to meet the needs of an expanded range of learners who would not necessarily be taking full-time programmes of study. These aims led to the adoption of wholesale modularisation – a key feature, of course, of the 1983 Action Plan which introduced National Certificate modules. The principle of modularisation (and of outcome-based, criterion-referenced assessment) was extended into the reformed Higher National qualifications, introduced from August 1988 (see Chapter 81).

FROM THE HOWIE COMMITTEE TO HIGHER STILL

The convergence of the hitherto separate debates on upper secondary and vocational education had its first significant expression in the work of the Howie Committee.

The Committee's remit had been to review the aims and purposes of courses, assessment and certification in the fifth and sixth years of secondary schools and there was some surprise that its analysis and recommendations extended into further education. While the Committee deserves credit for its breadth of vision in seeking to improve coherence and progression across school and further education, it is also probably true that they were driven beyond their remit by the fact that National Certificate modules had gained a strong foothold in schools. In considering how to meet the needs of pupils for whom Highers in S5 were not appropriate, they had to take National Certificate modules as their starting point (or face the unwelcome prospect of starting again from scratch). However, such proposals were bound also to impact on FE, in which the National Certificate was the basis of most non-advanced provision.

It is interesting to speculate that if SEB had been permitted to develop its own provision to meet the full range of needs in S5, the two systems might have remained separate and the SQA would not have been created, or at least not at this time (see Chapter 80).

The Howie Committee identified a number of problems to be addressed: low levels of achievement and a lack of breadth of achievement; little opportunity to study in depth or develop effective learning and study skills; an uneven gradient of progression (dash and drift); lack of coherence; and lack of esteem for vocational education.

One of the key concepts of the Report was the idea of educational pathways to establish continuity and progression. Two types of pathway were proposed: a more academically-oriented three year Scottish Baccalaurate and a more vocationally-oriented Scottish Certificate, (although the former had vocational variants and the latter had general education variants). While the pathways were distinct, they shared common design features: the same framework of core skills; criterion-based assessment; the use of a mix of internal and external assessment; and certification through group awards. More-over, both types of pathway had routes to higher education as well as employment, both were to be available in schools and colleges, and both were to be jointly administered by SEB and SCOTVEC. In all of these features, the future shape of Higher Still could distinctly be seen.

The Howie solution was decisively rejected in consultation, partly because of an aversion to making Standard Grade an S3 examination in order to make room for a three year Scottish Baccalaurate, but principally because the two types of education pathways were seen as divisive (twin-tracking) and consultees were not convinced about the prospects for bridging between the two. The consultation process also revealed concerns about compulsion in post-16 qualifications and a preference for guided choice.

The task for policy makers in the Scottish Office, following the Howie consultation process, was clear: solve the problems identified by the Howie Committee, drawing on a number of elements of the Committee's preferred solution, while avoiding the danger of 'twin-tracking'. The way forward was announced in *Higher Still: Opportunity for All* (SOEID, 1994). There were four key elements in the Higher Still solution: a single system of levels; the merging of assessment and certification arrangements; 'core skills for all'; and the development of group awards (all described in greater detail below). It was now clear that the hitherto distinct certification systems of the SEB and SCOTVEC were to be unified.

FROM HIGHER STILL TO SQA

Higher Still: Opportunity for All was published in March 1994. The task of developing the principles into concrete proposals and preparing for implementation was given to the Higher Still Development Unit, directly accountable to the Scottish Office but with a structure of steering committees which had broad-based representation from all education sectors and interested parties.

The Higher Still Development Programme had to grapple with a number of very significant issues and concerns, some 'political' and many technical. The former included: a perceived threat to breadth (would five Highers in S5 still be possible?); a fear that Higher Still was all about 'fast tracking for able pupils'; a concern about the implications for the Scottish four year honours degree; and suspicions that the core skills proposals represented an intrusion of training into education. The technical challenges included: devising a framework of progression in each subject area; unitisation of existing courses; description of what was to be learned in the form of outcomes and criteria; defining the five core skills at a number of levels and using these definitions as a tool to audit Standard Grade and Higher Still courses; devising external assessment arrangements which were sufficiently flexible to meet the needs of further education; and designing group awards which were coherent, fit for purpose, equivalent in demand at a given level, and, where appropriate, capable of being timetabled in schools. A further challenge lay in explaining the detailed proposals to a wide range of interested parties most of whom had difficulties with Higher Still's system-wide perspective, because their experience or interest lay primarily in one part of the system.

At the time of writing, the significant outstanding issues include: concerns about over-assessment and assessment workload; questions about bi-level or multi-level teaching groups; the currency of the Advanced Higher; and resource issues generally.

More could be written about the challenges faced in translating the Higher Still design into a reality, but that would be the history of the Higher Still Development Programme, rather than of the SQA. The important point, from a SQA standpoint, was that Higher Still set out a vision for the unification of academic and vocational qualifications which – notwithstanding heated debate on much of the detail – was widely welcomed. Despite early reservations on the part of the Scottish Office as to whether it would be feasible simultaneously to implement Higher Still and merge SEB and SCOTVEC, it was eventually decided to propose the creation of a single awarding body. This proposal was overwhelmingly endorsed in consultation.

CONSTITUTION AND GOVERNANCE

The SQA was established by the Education (Scotland) Act 1996 and became a legal entity on 18 September 1996. David Miller, Chairman of both SEB and SCOTVEC, was appointed as first Chairman of the SQA. The Chief Executive took up post in January 1997. From 1 April 1997, the SQA assumed all the functions of SEB and SCOTVEC.

It is therefore responsible for the following: 5–14 National Tests, Short Courses, Standard Grade, Higher Grade, Certificate of Sixth Year Studies (CSYS), National Certificate modules, General Scottish Vocational Qualifications (GSVQs), Higher National Certificates and Diplomas (HNCs and HNDs) and Scottish Vocational Qualifications (SVQs), as well as some other qualifications and services.

In addition to its functions as an awarding body, the SQA also inherited from SCOTVEC the function of accrediting body for SVQs. This function involved regulating the activities of all awarding bodies (including SQA itself as an awarding body) who offered SVQs. This role was analogous to that performed originally by the National Council for Vocational Qualifications (NCVQ) and now by the Qualifications and Curriculum Authority (QCA).

In 1997 the Scottish Qualifications Authority employed around 500 full-time staff and around 13,750 appointees to carry out duties such as setting, marking, moderation, verification and invigilation. The Authority had a budgeted expenditure of just under £25 million, met by income, over 90 per cent of which came from presentation and enrolment charges or charges for commercial services.

The SQA Board of Management has twenty-five members, twenty of whom were appointed by the Secretary of State for Scotland and five co-opted. The membership of the Board is representative of schools, further education colleges, education authorities, universities, employers, training organisations, parents and teaching unions. The Board is supported by six senior Committees: Finance, Planning and General Purposes Committee; Audit Committee; Accreditation Committee; National Qualifications Committee; Higher National Qualifications Committee; and Scottish Vocational Qualifications Committee. 'National Qualifications' is the name given to all qualifications which are below higher education level and are not SVQs. The National Qualifications Committee's responsibilities also include 5–14 National Tests.

The Scottish Vocational Qualifications Committee has oversight of SVQs for SQA as an awarding body. SQA's responsibilities for SVQs as an accrediting body are handled by the Accreditation Committee. Great care is taken to separate the management, funding and staffing of accreditation and awarding body functions so as to avoid any perception of conflict of interest. At the time of writing, the structure of specialist Panels and Committees has yet to be determined.

The organisational structure of the SQA is as shown in Figure 82.1.

MISSION AND CORPORATE GOALS

The mission of the Scottish Qualifications Authority is to 'enhance education, training and lifelong learning through the provision of high quality qualifications which meet the needs of the individual and society, and be recognised internationally as a centre of excellence in the design and assessment of qualifications.'

The SQA Board agreed to five Corporate goals, intended to be relatively enduring statements of the aims of SQA. These are:

- develop and maintain a coherent and relevant Scottish qualifications system;
- ensure that the award of all SQA qualifications is based on a consistent application of standards;
- consult and respond to needs of users and promote our qualifications and services, nationally and internationally;
- create an organisational ethos which supports individual development and teamwork and which enhances corporate performance;
- enhance operational effectiveness and maintain financial viability.

Figure 82.1 The Organisational Structure of SQA

ESTABLISHING THE SQA

In the minds of the Scottish education community, the establishment of the SQA was associated primarily with the development of a new integrated qualifications framework (of which more below). However, the establishment of the SQA as a new organisation taking on the functions of its two predecessor organisations required the attainment of other key objectives:

- the creation of a unified organisational structure;
- the harmonisation of pay and grading and terms and conditions;
- the development of an integrated and enhanced IT system to deal with candidate enrolment and awards processing;
- the harmonisation of a wide range of administrative procedures and practices;
- the development of new corporate and financial planning arrangements;
- the provision of effective information and publicity about the SQA and its qualifications and services;
- the building of effective liaison arrangements with all SQA's stakeholders;
- the fostering of a distinctive SQA culture drawing on the best features of the predecessor organisations;
- the implementation of an extensive training and development programme to prepare staff for their roles in SQA.

A common thread running through many of these objectives is the need to bring together two organisations with different traditions and cultures. While the qualifications of both bodies were used both in school and FE sectors, it would be true to say that the SEB was closer to the culture of schools and SCOTVEC to the culture of FE and of employers and training providers.

Creating a common culture involves the development of shared professional values about how qualifications are defined and developed and about assessment and quality assurance procedures. This aspect has proved surprisingly easy, partly because many of these questions had already been debated and consensus achieved through the Higher Still development programme. It is also a reflection of the keen desire of SQA staff to make unification work. However, while SQA aspires to a unified culture, its key stakeholders will remain very different. SQA staff will need to learn to be 'multi-lingual' and become equally at ease in the different worlds of school, further education and employment/training.

Perhaps the most significant cultural difference was that SCOTVEC – because of its more diverse and rapidly changing qualifications portfolio – had been more externally-oriented than the SEB. It should also be noted that the SEB rarely had the resources for extensive promotional activity; SCOTVEC had greater freedom in this regard. The SQA will operate in an environment where it will be very important to listen and respond to the views of stakeholders – candidates, centres, education and training staff, parents, employers, higher education, representatives, organisations, government and other national agencies, and SQA staff.

Again however, there is a general acceptance of the need for change. Throughout the early life of the new organisation there has been an attempt to consult with and involve staff in decisions about the development of SQA as a unified organisation.

THE SCOTTISH QUALIFICATIONS FRAMEWORK

The concept of a single Scottish Qualifications Framework lies at the heart of the SQA's raison d'étre. The role of the Howie debate and of Higher Still in moving educational and public opinion towards the idea of unification has already been traced. However, notwithstanding the importance of Higher Still, there were other significant factors and influences. First, Scottish Vocational Qualifications (SVQs) were now becoming an established part of the qualifications system, valued by the employers who used them because of their distinctive characteristics of being based on national occupational standards of competence and assessment in workplace conditions. However, just as Higher Still sought to unify academic and general vocational qualifications, so it was felt that SVQs – while preserving their distinctive characteristics – should become part of the wider qualifications framework by the establishment of clear progression routes and credit recognition.

Second, the *Report of the Scottish Committee of the National Committee of Inquiry into Higher Education* (HMSO, 1997) – the Garrick Report – recommended a single system of credit accumulation and transfer, embracing all SQA and higher education qualifications in Scotland. This proposal built on earlier work by the Higher Education Quality Council, SCOTVEC and SOEID, and was therefore generally welcomed.

Third, the implications of both Higher Still and the Garrick Report for Higher National Certificates and Higher National Diplomas had now to be taken into account. The recommendations of a SCOTVEC Review of HNCs and HNDs, culminating in March 1997, had been put on ice, pending clarification of the implications of these two other initiatives. The time was now right also to consider harmonisation of the successful Higher National qualifications system both with National Qualifications and with degree provision.

The Scottish Qualifications Framework was, therefore, a logical culmination of many years of development in which various qualification streams became progressively more integrated. Why was a single qualifications framework seen as a desirable objective? Perhaps three reasons may be advanced:

Continuity and progression

Particularly in an era of lifelong learning, it is imperative that learners should be able to build on previous achievement in a continuous and progressive way, without constraints caused by artificial barriers between different types of qualification.

Parity of esteem

Vocational qualifications had not hitherto enjoyed the same status or esteem as academic qualifications. It was thought that a single qualifications framework based on a series of levels and with common approaches to assessment and certification could do a great deal to create 'parity of esteem'.

Simplicity

The existing range of qualifications, many of them relatively new, was not well-understood by parents, employers and the general public. There was a growing desire for a simple and coherent system capable of being described in plain English.

The framework (see Figure 82.2) may best be understood by reference to four key elements: a system of levels; harmonisation of assessment and certification arrangements; core skills; and group awards.

The system of levels

The proposal to base the non-advanced post-16 qualifications system on a system of five levels was a central plank of Higher Still. The intention was to cater for the needs of all pupils (thus attempting to address both the 'dash and drift' and 'middle ability' problems).

Figure 82.2   The Scottish Qualifications Framework

Higher Degree	SVQ V
Honours degree	
Degree	SVQ IV
Year 2 / HND	
Year 1 / HNC	
Advanced Higher	SVQ III
Higher	
Intermediate 2	SVQ II
Intermediate 1	SVQ I
Access	

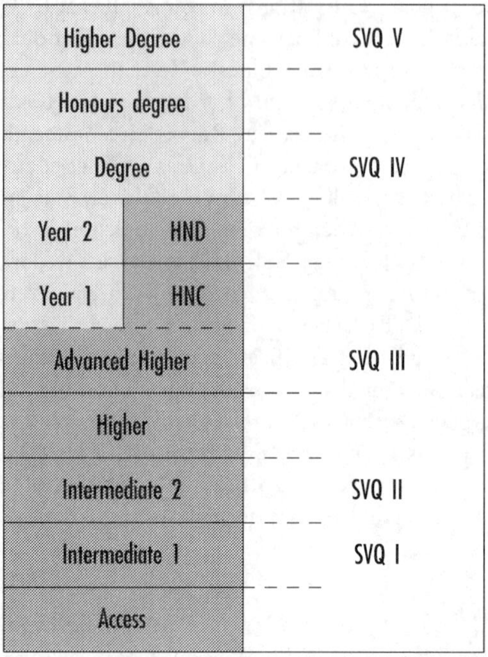

The left hand side of the diagram shows all SQA qualifications (except SVQs) and degrees organised in a series of levels. The SVQs, on the right hand side of the diagram are based on occupational – rather than educational – levels. These two concepts of level have yet to be reconciled.

Within the Scottish Qualifications Framework, all qualifications (with the exception, for the time being, of SVQs) are placed on a series of levels, from Access – largely for students with learning difficulties – through Intermediate 1 and 2 – for post-16 students not ready to progress immediately to Higher level – to Higher – the level of attainment required for entry to higher education – and Advanced Higher – a new level to stretch the most able school students. The pre-higher education levels flow into the subsequent levels of higher education, including HNCs and HNDs.

The system of levels should provide for continuity and progression in every subject area; students should be able to access a course at the right level for them, given their previous level of achievement and gain recognised qualifications. The levels system applies to all subjects from Mathematics to Mechatronics, and from History to Hospitality. The SQA's quality assurance system will ensure that all qualifications at the same level are broadly equivalent in level of difficulty, (although the nature of the 'difficulty' will of course be quite different), thus providing an objective basis for 'parity of esteem'.

Harmonisation of assessment and certification

The Higher Still proposals on harmonised assessment and certification arrangements were both principled and pragmatic. It had been argued by Howie – and accepted in consultation – that a combination of internal and external assessment was more effective than either in isolation. Internal assessment, combined with modularisation, would motivate learners by providing short-term targets, and reward them for partial success as well as helping teachers and learners to identify learning difficulties. It also ensured that all key outcomes were assessed. External course assessment ensured that the learner was required to retain knowledge and skills and demonstrate the capacity to integrate learning. It also provided a valued means of quality control. The pragmatism lay in the fact that unitised courses were an obvious way of bringing together the two systems without one being seen as 'dominant' over the other. This was important in terms of gaining support in both school and college sectors.

The proposals on unified assessment and certification arrangements were designed to achieve two aims: first, to create a qualifications system which contained a high level of flexibility and an emphasis on rigorous standards and public credibility; and second, to provide parity of esteem between 'academic' and 'vocational' qualifications by creating a common approach to assessment and certification.

Essentially, the system is unit-based with all units being written to a common format and awarded on the basis of internal assessment. While there are a large number of adult part-time learners who will seek to gain free-standing units, most learners, especially full-time, will aim to achieve courses or group awards.

Courses are qualifications comprising three units and an external assessment. The external assessment may take the form of an examination or of externally assessed practical work or some combination, depending on the nature of the subject matter. Courses have always been the normal form of qualification in Scottish schools. However, the range of courses is now being extended to include most vocational subjects taught in FE. It is believed that many part-time FE students building up a group award over two or three years will wish to achieve courses as interim qualifications with high status.

The Higher National qualifications are also unit-based (using the same format as National Qualifications) and are internally assessed. The possibility of using overall integrative assessments with a higher degree of externality is currently under review.

Core skills for all

A key aspect of the Higher Still proposals was that all students should have opportunities to develop core skills and that attainment of these should be certificated. Part of the rationale was that students in schools and colleges were already developing core skills in a range of ways and, given the significance of these skills for users (higher education as well as employers), it was important to provide a means of formally recognising these achievements in a standardised way. This alone would have been a relatively limited aim. However, it was also hoped that this new emphasis on core skills would heighten awareness among staff and students, leading to more sustained attempts to teach in ways which developed core skills, a conscious 'ownership' of the skills, and an awareness of their transferability.

The core skills to be certificated through National Qualifications are: communication, numeracy, information technology, problem solving and working with others. The core skills are specified at a number of levels, currently from Access to Higher, so as to offer all learners appropriately demanding targets.

The *Report of the National Inquiry into Higher Education* also made recommendations about core skills. The place of core skills within HNCs and HNDs will take account of the outcome of these deliberations as well as the implications of the Higher Still core skill position.

Group awards

The responses to consultation on Howie's proposals for group awards had been equivocal, largely because of fears about compulsion and loss of flexibility. Higher Still proposed a system of group awards, including not only the GSVQs introduced by SCOTVEC but more general group awards, suitable for use in schools by students who wished to keep their options fairly open. The aim was to encourage coherence in programmes of learning and to introduce common benchmarks of overall attainment across 'academic' and 'vocational' studies.

Scottish Group Awards (SGAs), available at all levels from Access to Advanced Higher, are qualifications made up of courses and units and broadly equivalent to a year of full-time study, although the number of credits required is less at Access and Intermediate than at Higher or Advanced Higher. To gain a group award, the student must pass a required number of units and, depending on level of SGA, two or three external course assessments. Up till now, group awards have not been much offered in schools. It is expected, however, that SGAs will become popular in schools.

SGAs serve the same purpose at the pre-higher education stage as degrees do in higher education. They indicate that the learner has succeeded in a coherent programme of study (and that could mean the coherence of a broad programme of general education or of a well-defined vocational purpose). They also indicate that the learner has reached a certain overall level of attainment. Thus any SGA at Higher level will be broadly equivalent in its demands, regardless of subject matter. The equivalence of level of attainment includes set requirements for core skills attainment. While free-standing core skill units are available, most learners will gain certification of core skills through the normal range of subjects taken.

While there will be one multi-purpose SGA at Access level and at Intermediate 1 level, a range of named SGAs will be available at other levels, e.g. Arts and Social Sciences or Construction. To allow for innovative developments, particularly in FE, there will be the facility to validate as SGAs locally-devised programmes which meet the required design criteria.

The introduction of group awards within National Qualifications brought these qualifications into line with the rest of the Scottish Qualifications Framework where group awards – degrees, HNC/Ds and SVQs – are the norm.

SCOTTISH VOCATIONAL QUALIFICATIONS

SVQs are the Scottish equivalent of the National Vocational Qualifications (NVQs) offered elsewhere in the UK. They are based on the same National Occupational Standards and share the same design characteristics as NVQs. At present, SVQs are linked to the rest of the Scottish Qualifications Framework, rather than being fully integrated into it. SVQs are different from other Scottish qualifications in two key respects: they are based on occupational levels rather than educational levels, and do not use external assessment. The goal is progressively to integrate SVQs into the Framework, while retaining the characteristics which employers value about SVQs: the fact that they certificate actual job-competence assessment in workplace conditions. Work has started to explore ways of giving SVQs a credit rating, so that attainment of SVQ units carry credit towards Scottish Group Awards, HNCs and HNDs, and – if Scottish higher education institutions agree – degrees, and to establish progression routes from SGAs to SVQs so that the Framework becomes seamless from a student point of view.

PARITY OF ESTEEM

At the heart of SQA's mission is the creation of a unified qualifications system in which academic and vocational qualifications have 'parity of esteem', or rather where the current sharp distinction between the 'academic' and the 'vocational' is no longer drawn.

As far as National Qualifications (i.e. all SQA qualifications except HNC/Ds and SVQs) are concerned, the hope is that the new common arrangements for assessment and certification will completely blur the academic/vocational distinction. The way university degrees are perceived is interesting in this regard. While people may confer varying levels of esteem depending on the awarding institution or the prestige of the subject, there is no obvious categorisation of degrees as 'academic' or 'vocational'. Moreover, we still talk generally about 'graduates' with the implication that there are certain features or qualities common to all degree programmes.

The SQA will seek through its literature and in contacts with stakeholders to promote a similar view of pre-university qualifications. The general message will be that while different qualifications at a given level may have different specific purposes, they are all broadly equivalent in the level of demand placed on candidates and in the rigour of the assessment and are therefore worthy of the same esteem. As SVQs mature and become recognised and accepted as valuable qualifications, they should also benefit in terms of esteem from being part of a single framework of qualifications.

THE FUTURE

The Scottish Qualifications Authority has more of a future than a past, but the future is harder to write about. The one certainty seems to be the lack of certainty. As for most organisations, the ability to cope with a complex environment and to respond flexibly is likely to be paramount for SQA.

Many significant challenges lie ahead. Merging two organisations is a process that will take a number of years to complete successfully. All areas of SQA activity and all aspects of working practice have to be reviewed and harmonised, while maintaining 'business as usual' for candidates and centres. This would be challenging enough. In addition, however, the SQA must play its part in the successful implementation of Higher Still, with a great deal still to be done to ensure the feasibility of delivery and to promote understanding and acceptance by stakeholders.

While the mission of the SQA is firmly rooted in Scotland, it is unlikely fully to flourish without taking account of UK, European and wider international contexts. The mobility of labour across the UK and the European Union and the mobility of companies on a world-wide basis makes it necessary that Scottish qualifications are understood and accepted beyond Scotland. The globalisation of the economy will create a trend towards the globalisation of qualifications, the first expression of which is likely to be a growth in international benchmarking.

SQA has decided that it must measure itself in the wider international arena. It will be important for it to test the quality of its ideas and practices through international consultancy. In a rapidly changing environment, the SQA must also aspire to world-class standards of business practice, through adherence to a clear set of values, an emphasis on continuous quality improvement, and the development of empowered and competent staff.

REFERENCES

SED (1983) *Teaching and Learning in the Senior Stages of the Scottish Secondary School*, Edinburgh: HMSO.

SED (1983) *16–18s in Scotland: an Action Plan*, Edinburgh: SED.

SOEID (1994) *Higher Still: Opportunity for All*, Report of the Scottish Committee of the National Committee of Inquiry into Higher Education, Edinburgh: HMSO.

SOEID (1994) *Options for the Future Relationship between The Scottish Examination Board and the Scottish Vocational Educational Council*, Edinburgh: SOEID.

83

National Testing

Lillian Munro and Peter Kimber

5–14 NATIONAL TESTS

National tests in English (reading and writing) and mathematics are designed to assess the competence of pupils in primary school and the first two years of secondary school. They comprise a large bank of materials at five levels of difficulty, from which teachers may request units of their choice at any time during the school year. A catalogue, giving brief details of each unit, is circulated to all primary and secondary schools in Scotland at the start of each school year. The tests have both a summative and a diagnostic value within certain specified limitations. These tests correspond roughly to Key Stages 1–3 in England, Wales and Northern Ireland but have greater flexibility in their use and administration. An additional level (F) is currently being developed which will extend the range of existing tests particularly for pupils in the first two years of secondary school.

NATIONAL TESTING AND THE 5–14 DEVELOPMENT PROGRAMME

In 1987 the Secretary of State for Scotland published a consultative paper *Curriculum and Assessment in Scotland – A Policy for the 90s* (Edinburgh: Scottish Education Department). This document acknowledged that while there was much good practice in learning and teaching in Scottish schools, there were a number of aspects of curriculum and assessment which required to be strengthened. The paper sought a redefinition of the curriculum from age five, when a pupil starts primary school, to the end of the second year of secondary schooling at age fourteen, recognising the need for a more coherent and consistent framework for the curriculum, and for assessment and recording policies and their implementation. The ensuing five years saw the development of a series of national curriculum guidelines addressing the five curricular areas of English Language, Mathematics, Environmental Studies, Expressive Arts and Religious and Moral Education.

The guidelines set out advice to teachers on planning the curriculum and on appropriate programmes of study, defining expected pupil attainment at five levels of increasing demand from A to E using a common framework of attainment outcomes, strands and attainment targets. Attainment outcomes are similar in concept to attainment targets in the English national curriculum, while attainment targets accord to statements of attainment; there is no equivalent to strands which represent different aspects of learning within a curricular area, for example, 'reading for enjoyment' and 'reading for information' within the area of reading. While the national curriculum in England and Wales is a statutory curriculum, which all schools are required to deliver, the curriculum guidelines in Scotland continue a long-standing tradition of education by consensus, albeit under the guiding influence of Her Majesty's Inspectorate.

For the first time, explicit, if somewhat generalised statements were made about expected levels of attainment. Thus, Level B was defined as being attainable by most pupils in P4, Level D by most pupils in P7 and Level E by most pupils in S2. Level A was somewhat more loosely defined in terms of the attainment of pupils 'in the course of P1–P3', and similarly Level C by most 'in the course of P4–P6'. Alongside the guidelines for each curricular area, additional guidance was developed on the structure and balance of the curriculum, on assessment and on reporting. The overall assessment strategy sought to ensure that pupil progress at the 5–14 stages would be systematically assessed by teachers in relation to the stated outcomes, strands and targets in the curricular guidelines. Testing at a national level in the key areas of English language and mathematics was introduced as an integral part of these new assessment procedures, to help inform judgements about the progress of individual pupils in relation to the five levels of attainment and to do so in relation to nationally agreed and understood standards.

Originally, testing was confined to all pupils in P4 and P7, paralleling to some extent Key Stage 1 and Key Stage 2 testing in England and Wales. A pilot round of national tests was carried out in March and April 1991 with the first proper round scheduled for the academic year 1991–2. In the wake of the first pilot round, a moderation of the test procedures and of the marking of test units was undertaken in a sample of schools. Given the extremely negative attitude to testing which prevailed, the overall response was surprisingly positive. The report *National Tests 1991: Report of Moderation* (Scottish Office Education Department, 1991) approved the main principles of the testing arrangements and endorsed the quality of the test materials. The workload, bearing in mind the novelty of the procedures, was not considered to be unduly onerous and could be expected to diminish with familiarity. Furthermore, pupils seemed not to bear the emotional scars prophesied by the critics. The major area of difficulty identified was in the application of criteria to assess pupils' writing. However, teachers were not questioning the validity of the criteria so much as their inexperience and lack of competence in using them and the consequent time taken to mark writing tests. In response to representations made by teachers, changes to the testing arrangements were made. The main change, which was included in the testing arrangements for 1991/92, was to enable teachers to determine when pupils in P4 and P7 should take the tests during the school session. (In the pilot round, testing had been restricted to a six week 'testing window' in March/April.) The layout and content of the writing criteria were also simplified. Despite these changes, opposition to statutory testing at particular stages continued. Following a boycott by a large proportion of teachers and the withdrawal of pupils from the testing process by many parents, the system was reviewed and the arrangements for national testing were amended. Revised proposals were set out in a consultation paper by the Scottish Office Education Department in May 1992.

POLITICAL BACKGROUND

Opposition to national testing amongst teachers and parents has already been alluded to and any review of national testing in Scotland must also include reference to the political background to its introduction, as this impinged heavily on the first few years of its development. It was in 1988, during the Conservative government's second term in office, and with Michael Forsyth as Under-Secretary of State with responsibility for education, that the government first announced its intention to introduce testing in primary schools in Scotland. It had already announced plans to introduce end of Key Stage testing in England and Wales and was determined to extend to all areas of the United Kingdom some form of external assessment system to cover the early years of schooling which had previously been assessed only by teachers with no external input.

Under the chairmanship of HMSCI Nisbet Gallacher, the Joint Committee on Assessment and Testing was given the task of taking forward both the wider aspects of assessment across the 5–14 curriculum and the narrower concerns of national testing. Subject subcommittees in language and mathematics were also set up to develop the curriculum and assessment in these key areas. Early in 1989 the Scottish Examination Board (SEB) was given the task of developing test materials and implementing the testing process under the policy initiatives of the various committees set up to oversee the system. A small unit called the Primary Assessment Unit, comprising an Assistant Director, a Research and Development Officer, two Development Officers, and approximately six administrative/support staff, was established.

As indicated above, the basic requirement for testing was a set of test units in reading, writing and mathematics at five levels of difficulty, where Level A was the easiest and Level E the most demanding. The guidance to the SEB was that Level B should be attainable by 'most pupils in P4' and Level D 'by most pupils in P7'. For practical purposes the Primary Assessment Unit understood 'most' to mean that about 80 per cent of the age cohort would be successful in a unit. This reflected general feelings about 'mastery levels' in criterion level testing, but it was emphasised by the Department that very tight statistical criteria were probably not appropriate.

REACTIONS TO TESTING

There was a good deal of hostile interest from the media, the teaching profession, the teaching unions and from parents and parents' associations. There was also a great deal of criticism of the proposals from the research community. This scepticism was directed towards the notion of setting national standards and the effects this might have on pupils taking the tests. Prior to the introduction of comprehensive education in Scotland in 1968, the Qualifying Examination had been taken by all pupils in P7 to determine which type of secondary school they would attend. Among parents and teachers, the word 'testing' awoke atavistic memories of the 'Qualie' and the personal and social traumas which it created. Many of the Education Authorities resented the implication that their own methods for monitoring and communicating standards were inadequate. Parents frequently said that they wanted direct access to class teachers for information about their children rather than an explicit comparison with a notional national standard. The resentment of teachers was also directed at the expense (around £600,000 initially) which, they maintained, could be better spent on materials and new teachers and the fact that the tests were being introduced before the curricular guidelines were properly in place, was seen as a 'cart before the horse' situation. The other objection was to the time taken administering and marking the tests to arrive at a judgement which usually confirmed their own more subjective one. This resentment against testing took many forms and SEB officers attended numerous public meetings to explain the testing proposals and to hear what the grounds for complaint actually were.

Beneath all the specific complaints there was a recurrent feeling that testing was an English response to a specifically English problem. Standards of performance in English schools were perceived by politicians to be seriously low, but there was no such vocal complaint in Scotland. Resentment against a Conservative government, for whom a substantial majority of the electorate had not voted, was fuelled by testing which became the educational equivalent of the Poll Tax.

DEVELOPMENT AND PILOTING

Serious work to develop tests began in October 1989 with a weekend training course attended by some 130 teachers and other individuals. Education Authorities had been asked to nominate suitable people, but the hostility towards testing meant that in some cases teachers came as reluctant appointees of their Authorities. Some advisers offered their services but many maintained an attitude of censorious detachment.

There was widespread hostility among local politicians. Only one of the twelve Education Authorities at that time raised little or no objection and cooperated positively in piloting. Some Authorities allowed an approach to be made to their schools so that piloting could progress but few schools agreed and of those which did, some later withdrew in face of hostile criticism in the media and from the Educational Institute of Scotland (EIS), the main teachers' union. Other Authorities simply would not give permission for their schools to be approached. Consequently, the first round of piloting in the year 1990–1 was somewhat restricted.

At this time, the EIS issued a document for parents which spelt out their opposition to the whole idea of testing. During 1990 and 1991, Peter Kimber, the Director of the Primary Assessment Unit and Douglas Osler, the Depute Senior Chief Inspector at the Scottish Office responsible for the 5–14 Development Programme, were involved in a long-running series of meetings with local authorities, teachers and parents, often with EIS representatives present to articulate opposition to testing. Formal opposition from parents was channelled through the Scottish Parent Teachers' Association and in particular through Diana Daly in Aberdeen and Judith Gillespie in Edinburgh who took up the cudgels in opposition to the government. Together they raised a very considerable degree of parental awareness, fostered by the EIS and the more hostile Education Authorities. In the academic year 1990–1 hostility to testing gradually increased. The government tried to persuade Authorities to cooperate voluntarily but they flatly refused to do so. The government therefore decided to introduce Regulations to ensure that testing would take place. This is the only time in the history of Scottish education that such a measure has been taken.

The Regulations requiring Authorities to implement testing came into force in August 1991. Strathclyde Region responded by pointing out a conflict between the Regulations and the Education Act which required Authorities to educate children in accordance with the wishes of the parents. If parents did not wish their children to be tested, presumably they had the right to withdraw them. Many Authorities took this opportunity to avoid testing children where the parents formally asked for them to be withdrawn. At least one Authority provided printed letters to this effect and gave them to children, suggesting that parents should sign and return them. At the height of the opposition, it was reported that 66 per cent of parents nationally had withdrawn their children. This was the position in the run-up to the 1992 general election, when it was widely expected that a Labour government would be returned, with the promise that national testing would be withdrawn.

In the event this did not happen and the returning Conservative government, with a change in the minister responsible for education, quickly negotiated new agreements with Authorities. In return for greater flexibility of administration and professional judgement on the part of teachers, Authorities and unions would agree to cooperate and implement the tests as soon as teachers could be prepared. *Circular 12/92* issued by the SOED in November 1992 became the agreed basis for the implementation of national testing, following which testing was gradually introduced.

CURRENT ARRANGEMENTS FOR NATIONAL TESTING

Three significant changes were made to the arrangements for national testing as a result of *Circular 12/92*. Firstly, the statutory regulations governing national testing were rescinded. Secondly, instead of pupils being tested only in P4 and P7, pupils were to take a test when the teacher's own assessment indicated that the pupil had largely achieved the attainment targets at one level and was ready to move from that level to the next. Thirdly, the new testing arrangements were also to apply to pupils in secondary schools in S1 and S2. These revised arrangements, set out in *The Framework for National Testing* (SEB, 1993), were implemented in primary schools from January 1993 and in secondary schools from January 1994.

Instead of testing being age or stage related, the principle which now underpins national testing is that of 'testing when ready'. In effect this means that before a pupil can be tested in reading, writing and mathematics at a particular level, the teacher has to be satisfied that the pupil has engaged in a programme of work for the level being tested and that the pupil's class work is of the standard described in the attainment targets specified for the level. Teachers decide not only when to test individuals or groups of pupils, individual schools themselves decide how best to organise testing to fit in with its particular needs. In the majority of cases, this means that testing is carried out as a normal classroom activity, which has some particular requirements, in line with the principle that these are confirmatory tests and not formal examinations. It is intended that there should be as little disruption as possible to pupils' programmes of work and that in most instances, groups of pupils are tested within the classroom while other pupils are engaged in appropriate tasks within the context of their normal activities. In some circumstances it may be appropriate for pupils to be taken out of class for testing, or to consolidate across classes, but such instances are the exception rather than the rule. Teachers decide not only when, and to some extent how to test pupils, they also select the specific units they wish to use for national test purposes. The *Catalogue of National Test Units*, issued annually to schools by the Scottish Qualifications Authority, provides a range of test contexts for national tests from which teachers choose test units to suit the interests and level of maturity of their pupils (e.g. Scottish Qualifications Authority, 1998).

THE TEST MATERIALS

From the outset, the type of test materials used for national test purposes has remained essentially unchanged, although minor changes have been made in response to comments from teachers and others involved in the testing procedures. It is the responsibility of the 5–14 Assessment Unit (FFAU) within the Scottish Qualifications Authority to develop, pre-test, print and distribute national tests (see Chapter 82). In developing the test units, two guiding principles are expressly followed, namely that they are rooted in good classroom practice and that they are as user-friendly as possible. The test units are developed by teachers, in their own time, for which they receive a modest fee. The units are vetted by appropriately experienced personnel before pre-testing in schools. The purpose of the pre-testing is to identify deficient items and to provide statistical information in order to set a threshold score for each unit.

As stated previously, for practical purposes the Primary Assessment Unit understood 'most' as in 'most pupils in P4' and 'most pupils in P7' to mean that about 80 per cent of the age cohort would be successful in a unit at levels B and D respectively. Threshold scores were set initially for levels B and D in relation to the definitions for these levels. Those for level C were designed to set a standard mid-way between B and D, while A and E extended the range at either end. Ever since the original standards were set on the basis of the results from the first trial of units, the aim has been to maintain the same standard from year to year. Each subsequent trial has included old units to serve as a benchmark for the new units at each level. Threshold scores for the new units have been set to give the same standard as the threshold scores of the old units. In technical terms, this has been achieved by Rasch equating, choosing as the threshold scores those scores which indicate Rasch abilities approximately equal to the average of those indicated by the threshold scores of the old units.

The pre-test results, including comments from teachers conducting and marking the pre-tests, are scrutinised by specialist panels comprising teachers from both primary and secondary schools, college lecturers, education advisers and members of Her Majesty's Inspectors of Schools before inclusion in the national test catalogue. The catalogue contains some sixty reading units, forty writing units and one hundred mathematics units, covering the five levels of difficulty and providing a variety of contexts and tasks. A significant proportion of the units in the catalogue are replaced each year, to provide new contexts for testing and to ensure that fresh material is always available for testing. Schools may order test units at any time and test orders are generally dispatched within 1–2 weeks.

A Reading Test comprises two units at the appropriate level: one 'Narrative Reading' and one 'Reading for Information'. Each unit has a text for the pupils to read and associated activities, and is designed to take about 20–25 minutes to complete. A Writing Test comprises two units covering either levels A to C or D and E; one unit is an 'Imaginative/Personal Writing' task and one a 'Functional Writing' task. A Mathematics Test comprises four short, contextualised units at the same level. In each unit the items follow a storyline or a theme within a context. Each unit is designed to take about 15–20 minutes to complete. The majority of the items in the reading and mathematics units are of a 'quick answer' variety, making the marking as simple and objective as possible, although, where appropriate, open ended questions may be used. Each unit in reading and mathematics has a threshold score for attainment of the level it represents. This is the lowest number of marks a pupil must obtain to be judged to have reached the level in that unit. Pupil scores are aggregated for the units taken (i.e. two reading or four mathematics units) and compared to the total threshold scores for these units to determine whether the level has been achieved for the test. Threshold scores are determined through pre-testing. In writing, level A-C tasks are distinguished from D/E tasks in terms of the amount of support given. At levels A-C pupils are given help with the choice and use of language, content, planning and layout; at levels D/E, given general headings, pupils are expected to be responsible for these aspects of writing. In writing, a pupil's response is judged against a set of task-type specific criteria to determine the level awarded. Where the level awarded differs between the two tasks, the teacher will decide which level should be awarded on the basis of evidence collected in the classroom during the rest of the year.

Test units are printed in bulk and stored in a warehouse facility run by the FFAU. Orders received from schools are sent directly from the warehouse. Each year, the FFAU distributes test catalogues to some 2,400 primary schools and 500 secondary schools. In 1996/97 almost one and a half million test units were issued. The annual operating cost for the same period was approximately £800,000 which means that the cost of each national test was in the order of 60p. The cost of the system is funded directly by SOEID.

MODERATION

Unlike the testing at the end of key stages in other areas of the United Kingdom, national testing in Scotland is not designed to provide comparative or summative information on levels of achievement throughout the country. There is no central collection of test results and consequently there can be no comparisons between schools, or between Authorities. The monitoring of standards over time is carried out within the context of the *Assessment of Achievement Programme*, a three year rolling programme of research funded by SOEID, which measures the attainment of representative samples of pupils in P4, P7 and S2 in English language, mathematics and science (see Chapter 85). Information collected from schools by the SQA for its moderation purposes is of a quite different nature and is principally concerned with the validity and reliability of the test instruments, not with measuring levels of attainment.

From the beginning, it was envisaged that systematic checks would be applied to the tests to ensure consistency of standards from year to year and within units at each level. As testing was implemented, a sample of schools was moderated each year, giving additional data for analysis. The primary purpose of this moderation was to confirm – or otherwise – that the tests were providing a consistent level of difficulty as old tests were deleted from the catalogue and new units were added, and to confirm the validity for operational tests of threshold scores set on the basis of pre-testing. By and large, the evidence confirmed the achievement of consistency. In a very few cases the moderation showed a difference between the expected cut-off score, as provided by the pre-testing, and the effective one as shown by the operational tests. Where this was the case, no action to change the cut-off scores was taken but the unit would be deleted from the catalogue as soon as was practicable. The results of the moderation were also used to provide additional data for establishing cut-off scores of new units.

Other qualitative information was provided from the initial moderation of the writing tests. The samples of writing returned for moderation showed both that there was the need for more detailed marking guidance and that a good deal of in-service training was required to develop a genuinely national consensus on writing standards. Primary teachers in particular were unfamiliar with the use of grade or level related criteria to assess writing and, for many primary schools, building up confidence in the application of criteria has been a major staff development task. Clearly, the requirement to assess pupils' writing for national test purposes has forced many schools to look at how writing is taught and assessed and has resulted in a clearer understanding of what pupils should be aiming for in their writing. In parallel with this process, the criteria themselves have gone through a number of cycles of improvement. The existing system has evolved in response to comments from practitioners, and through attempts to address their concerns and to make the assessment of writing a manageable and meaningful task (SEB, 1995).

WIDER PERCEPTIONS OF NATIONAL TESTING

From the outset, the term 'national test' has been seen by many of those involved in the system as something of a misnomer; the term 'national assessment bank' is probably a better description of the nature and purpose of national testing in Scotland. The distinctive nature of these national tests whereby teachers choose, from an essentially 'open' assessment bank, test units which serve to confirm their own judgement with respect to individual pupil's progress, has attracted considerable interest from outwith Scotland. By the time national testing was established after the 1992 election, the SEB began to receive interested inquiries from England and from abroad. In England and Wales the government was pressing ahead with testing at Key Stages 2 and 3 in English, mathematics and science and in Northern Ireland Key Stage 2 and 3 tests were also being developed and piloted.

Many visitors from England expressed their envy at the liberal approach to testing which contrasted so starkly with the examination form required by the Department for Education and Employment in London. They admired the recognition that teachers are professionals with a detailed familiarity with their pupils' work. The specified role of testing was to confirm – or otherwise – the judgement of teachers and this contrasted markedly with the perceived lack of confidence in teachers south of the border. Visitors from abroad also reviewed the Scottish system with interest, although some, accustomed to more centrally controlled and strictly regulated education systems, found an 'open' testing system a difficult concept to appreciate.

As testing was implemented, opposition from both politicians and parents gradually decreased. Teachers who knew the position appreciated the differences between what applied elsewhere in Britain and what applied in Scotland. More specifically, many teachers realised that they had a very valuable resource in the test units which were devised by fellow practitioners. Although not always appreciated by teachers themselves, the introduction of a nationally agreed approach to the assessment of writing helped provide the impetus for teachers to come to grips with this inherently difficult task.

S1 AND S2 TESTING

The story does not end with the setting up of the current testing system; there have been some twists and turns since *Circular 12/92*. While national testing has become well established in primary schools, more than 90 per cent of which are implementing testing, in the secondary sector the comparable figure for 1996/97 was only around 10 per cent. In 1996, when this figure was even lower, the government's exasperation with the dilatory response of secondary schools resulted in a surprise announcement from the education minister that the government proposed to introduce statutory regulations to ensure the compulsory testing of all pupils in S1 and S2, in addition to the existing testing regime. It was estimated that the cost of such a system, which would be in the nature of externally set and marked examinations, would be in the order of £3.6 million per annum, or about £10 per pupil, several times greater than the entire cost of the existing system covering all 5–14 stages. In June 1997, the incoming Labour administration set aside the previous government's proposals. However, the tardiness of secondary schools in implementing the 5–14 programme, of which the low uptake of national tests is but a symptom, continues to be evident (Simpson and Goulder, 1997). While an increasing number of Education Authorities are positively encouraging secondary schools to take the 5–14 programme on board, the aim of providing continuity and progression of educational experience throughout the 5–14 stages as envisaged by the authors of the 5–14 programme still remains to be achieved.

HAS NATIONAL TESTING ACHIEVED ITS OBJECTIVES?

It is now almost a decade since the proposal to introduce national testing was first put forward. The tests were intended to be a means of providing an additional source of evidence about pupils' attainment in reading, writing and mathematics, by defining pupil achievement in relation to nationally agreed standards and by providing teachers with exemplification of the levels, thus helping to ensure consistency between teachers in their interpretation of what the levels meant. To what extent has this been achieved? It has become an integral part of assessment procedures, at least in primary schools, and in the area of assessing writing it has introduced a system of assessment using a single set of criteria throughout the country.

However, perhaps not surprisingly, given the widespread negativity surrounding its introduction, the system still has its detractors and a substantial number of teachers still remain unconvinced about the positive benefits of testing. Malcolm and Schlapp (1997) in their research into the implementation of 5–14 in primary schools reported that 85 per cent of headteachers in their sample were satisfied with national test procedures in their schools at that time (Spring 1996). Teachers' views on the value of the tests as part of their assessment strategy were somewhat more equivocal with 53 per cent stating that the tests were of limited or no value in this regard, and only 37 per cent agreeing that they were of considerable value or very valuable. For most teachers, the tests merely confirmed what they say they already knew about pupils. There seemed to be a lack of recognition on the part of the teachers that one of the main purposes was indeed to provide just such an objective confirmation or to recognise that this is an appropriate professional objective. The same research reports evidence of differences in teachers' understanding of standards associated with the different levels, indicating that there is a continuing case for the monitoring function of national tests in relation to teachers' own assessments.

REFERENCES

Malcolm, M. and U. Schlapp (1997) *Evaluation of the Implementation of the 5–14 Programme in Primary Schools*, Edinburgh: Scottish Council for Research in Education.

Scottish Examination Board (1993) *Framework for National Testing*, Dalkeith: SEB.

Scottish Examination Board (1995) *Exemplification of Levels of Achievement in National Tests in Writing*, Dalkeith: SEB.

Scottish Office Education Department (1991) *National Tests 1991: Report of Moderation*, Edinburgh: SOED.

Scottish Qualifications Authority (1998) *Catalogue of National Test Units*, Dalkeith: SQA.

Simpson, M. and G. Goulder (1997) *Implementing 5–14 in Secondary Schools: continuity and progression*, Aberdeen: Northern College.

XI

Scottish Pupils and their Achievements

84

Scottish School Pupils: Characteristics and Influences

Brian Boyd

CHRIS'S STORY: THE JOURNEY BEGINS

Christopher was born on 21 December 1986. His early years have been spent in East Kilbride, a New Town on the outskirts of Glasgow in the central belt of Scotland. His parents are professional people, both involved in education, and so could be described as middle class. He is an only child. Christopher did not qualify for pre-5 or nursery provision, a non-statutory service available by right only to those who meet a set of needs-based criteria. He went, for one year, to a private nursery as much to socialise him with other youngsters as to enhance his learning.

Christopher, along with other Scottish children between the ages of four-and-a-half and five-and-a-half, began his schooling in August 1991, in his case at the age of four years and eight months. As they entered Primary 1, they could look forward to seven years of education with their peers, largely taught by one (generalist) teacher at each stage. Now in P7, Chris (as he now likes to be called) will move to a new, Secondary school – a comprehensive school, which takes all of the pupils from the associated Primary schools, without any form of selection. There he may encounter up to seventeen different (specialist) teachers in each of the first two years, following a 'common course', most often in mixed-ability classes. At the end of S2 he will make choices, narrowing down the subjects from seventeen to around ten, eight of which will lead to national certification at Standard Grade. During these two years he will most likely have been put into 'sets' by attainment in the various subjects, and will, in due course, be presented for the examination at Foundation, General or Credit levels. He may, like the majority of his peers, stay on at school to pursue courses leading to Highers (if academically inclined) or Modules (if vocationally inclined), or a mixture of the two. He could leave at S4, the statutory age being sixteen (which for Chris would mean staying on to Christmas in S5 because he is at the 'young end' of the year group) for work or further education. He could leave at S5, or stay on for a Sixth year, perhaps moving on to Higher Education.

But Chris is not necessarily a typical pupil – and at almost every stage of this process there are exceptions to the above pattern. According to the Barnardo's report *Today and Tomorrow* (1997) fewer than one in five of Scotland's children will have had pre-5 or nursery education. Some parents will have chosen, exercising their right under the 1981

Education (Scotland) Act, to send their child to a school other than the one closest to them for a range of reasons which include child-care (in Chris's case to be closer to his grandparents' home); perceived quality of the schools; etc. According to Willms, parents of higher social class are more likely to exercise choice, though the majority of all parents, nearly 90 per cent, do not make placing requests (CES, 1997). For some the choice will be an independent (or fee-paying) school, though across Scotland such schools account for around 4 per cent of the pupil population.

Around half of the 3,000 or so Primary schools in Scotland have pupil rolls of less than 100, and so mixed-stage or composite classes become the norm rather than the age-stage relationship of larger schools. These smaller schools are mainly rural. The children of travelling families make up a small proportion of the total pupil population but local authorities and the Scottish Office acknowledge their needs by funding initiatives such as Internet links with 'base' schools. And, of course, many of Chris's contemporaries attend denominational (mainly Roman Catholic) schools, catering for between one-sixth and one-fifth of the pupil population, funded by the state since the 1918 Education Act.

Chris's parents may make choices on his behalf. Sometimes, as in Lochhead's poem, *The Choosing*, social class is an issue:

> I remember the housing scheme
> where we both stayed.
> Same houses, different homes,
> where the choices were made.

Lochhead reminds us too of the gender dimension which influenced many working class fathers: 'He didn't believe in high school education, especially for girls, or in forking out for uniforms.' And now, paradoxically, in Scotland as in the rest of the UK, it is under-achievement among boys which is the subject of national concern.

In most areas of Scotland, outwith the cities, there was, historically, no choice, and no selection, as the secondaries were omnibus schools, taking in all of the pupils in the area. Since the publication of examination results in the early 1990s and the subsequent compilation of league tables published in the press, a movement from 'unsuccessful' to 'successful' schools has taken place. The philosophy of market forces initiated by the then Conservative government enshrined choice as the guiding principle and believed that competition among schools would lead to higher standards. As jobs became scarce in the 1980s and early 1990s, more young people stayed on beyond the statutory leaving age of sixteen, and more and more went on to some form of Further or Higher education.

Viewed from the outside, Scotland, a small country with only 5.1 million people, with an apparently monolithic school system, with central bodies administering the examination system (SQA), promoting curriculum development (SCCC), overseeing standards among teachers (GTC), and inspecting schools (SOEID), an observer might think that the experience of schooling must be fairly uniform for all pupils, and has probably, in a country with such a proud educational tradition, always been so. But the reality is somewhat different.

SCOTTISH PUPILS – WHAT ARE THEY LIKE?

Official views of Scottish children crop up from time to time in the official literature – reports of national committees, from Her Majesty's Inspectorate, and, in recent years, from research. The actual voices of the pupils themselves are heard less frequently, and Rudduck in a recent lecture has commented, in the context of government concerns about school effectiveness: 'If our concerns are ultimately with the achievements and life chances of our pupils, why don't we take our agenda for school improvement, at least in part, from their accounts of experience?'

So, who are these Scottish pupils? What is known about them? What are they really like? Does Chris have anything to tell us about his schooling? To understand the Scottish pupil of the 1990s it is necessary to look at how their parents experienced schooling in the past, how and why the system changed and what they themselves say – when they get the chance.

PRE 1970s – SELECTION, THE STRAP AND FULL EMPLOYMENT?

For a start, Chris and his fellow pupils don't speak Scots – officially – and Gaelic is only now beginning to make a comeback outside its Western Isles heartland. Indeed, the culture of Scotland as a nation has long been subjugated under the influence of its larger neighbour, England. Notwithstanding Scotland's separate legal, educational and religious traditions, its languages have long been left, if not at the school gate, then certainly at the classroom door. Standard English, the language of the establishment, has ruled, and the grammar taught in Scottish classrooms was Latinate and traditional, leaving little room for the vernacular.

Often it is in the literature of a nation that life is most graphically depicted. In McIlvanney's *Docherty* (Mainstream, Edinburgh, 1997) the fear inspired by an inhumane system comes to life as the central character, Conn, still at primary school, is brought before Mr Pirrie, accused of fighting:

> 'What's wrong with your face, Docherty?'
> 'Skint ma nose, sur.'
> 'How?'
> 'Ah fell an' bumped ma heid in the sheuch, sur.'
> 'I beg your pardon?' . . .
> In the pause Conn understands the nature of the choice, tremblingly, compulsively, makes it.
> 'Ah fell an' bumped ma heid in the sheuch, sur.'
> The blow is instant. His ear seems to enlarge, is muffled in numbness. But it is only the dread of tears that hurts. Mr Pirrie distends on a lozenge of light which mustn't be allowed to break. It doesn't. Conn hasn't cried.
> 'That, Docherty, is impertinence. You will translate, please, into the mother-tongue.'
> The blow is a mistake, Conn knows. If he tells his father, he will come up to the school. 'Ye'll take whit ye get wi' the strap an' like it. But if onybody takes their hauns tae ye, ye'll let me ken.' He thinks about it. But the problem is his own. It frightens him more to imagine his father coming up.
> 'I'm waiting, Docherty. What happened?'
> 'I bumped my head, sir.'
> 'Where? Where did you bump it, Docherty?'
> 'In the gutter, sir.'
> 'Not an inappropriate setting for you, if I may say so.'

Thus, in one short, highly-charged episode is encapsulated many of the elements which characterised middle-class teacher/working-class pupil relationships in the past. The inherent politeness of the pupil ('Sur'); the use of the dialect firstly as a natural response, then as a gesture of defiance ('the nature of the choice'); the use of Standard English in a disciplinary context ('I beg your pardon?'); the male fear of being seen to be weak, already present in Conn ('the dread of tears'); the inherent respect for the teacher's authority of the working class parent but the moral code which will accept 'official' corporal punishment ('the strap') but not unofficial ('takes their hauns tae ye'); the use of sarcasm to degrade and control the pupils ('Not an inappropriate setting . . .'); all of this flies in the face of the myth of the 'lad o' pairts' (McPherson and Raab, 1988) where every pupil had an equal chance of educational success.

Ask Chris's parents about their experience of schooling and they will almost certainly recount stories about 'the strap', about 'the quali' and possibly about individual teachers, of the charismatic or autocratic type. Up until the 1970s, selection was a defining feature of the Scottish education system. Pupils in P7 sat an examination ('the quali'), having previously taken IQ tests, and on the basis of these would be selected for a Junior (vocational) or Senior (academic) secondary school. This represented an advance from the pre-war situation where some pupils would never be deemed suitable to receive a secondary education at all. The move towards 'age promotion', albeit with the type of schooling still determined by measures of ability, was not universally welcomed in official circles:

> Especially with pupils promoted solely on account of age, many of whom are semi-literate, there are often other tendencies to counter besides ignorance; some of these pupils harbour feelings of resentment that they are still under tutelage and prevented from being wage-earners. (SED, 1951, quoted in McPherson and Raab, p. 248)

This very negative view of children is interesting and may help explain the heavy handed discipline which was a feature of many Junior and Senior secondary schools during this period. The notion of 'contest mobility' (McPherson and Raab, 1988) meant also that on arrival in one of the two sets of schools pupils would be 'streamed', i.e. organised into classes on the basis of general ability. Thus a pupil might find herself in 1.A in the senior secondary experiencing a largely classical education while her peer might find himself in 1.M (for 'modified') in the junior secondary experiencing a largely practical curriculum with a 'watered-down' version of some of the academic subjects (though not Classics or modern languages). Selection had a finality about it, mobility between the sectors was minimal and parity of esteem non-existent.

Thus, Chris's parents were among the 40 per cent or so who enjoyed an academic education (a higher percentage than in England and Wales) and had a thorough grounding in the subjects necessary to secure entry to university and the professions. Along the way, they had access to excellent extra-curricular activities and to the most highly qualified teachers. They did well in the main, though with streaming, the wastage rate was high, with pupils leaving at the then statutory age of fifteen, before the national exams at the end of S4. Meanwhile, the young people who went to the junior secondary had largely less highly qualified or even 'uncertificated' teachers (though official policy was that all secondary teachers should be certificated), were in buildings less well equipped and had no access to national examinations. They too were streamed, with the 'modifieds' or 'remedials' being the lowest. In the best of these schools, future workers would be given a good grounding in skills, and Domestic Science – for the girls, of course – would help prepare for parenthood.

But by the 1960s the case for ending selection became unstoppable. The 'mute, inglorious Milton' argument, the pool of talent going to waste, the inequity of such selection based on discredited psychometric testing, was acknowledged, and in 1965 the Labour government signalled its intention that all local authorities should submit plans for the ending of selection.

It is unlikely that Chris will encounter a Mr Pirrie in a Scottish school today. Corporal punishment was abolished, as a result of a European ruling in the early 1980s, and the curriculum has become more centrally driven since the 1970s. The place of Scots has become less marginalised, with Scottish texts now a compulsory element in the Higher English (sic) examination, and with the publication of a *Scots Kist* by the SCCC. Gaelic medium education has expanded to the central belt of Scotland, with national broadcasting having been given an injection of funding to promote the language. However, the growth is fragile, with the reduced funding for education as a result of local government reorganisation in 1995 putting schemes at risk.

SCOTTISH SCHOOLS FROM 1970 TO THE PRESENT

Scotland, with its history and its heritage, is always in danger of being stereotyped, either as the idyllic ('Braveheart') country of beauty, or as the declining industrial wasteland ('Trainspotting') riddled with poverty and social breakdown. The truth lies somewhere in between. Scotland has many faces and the pupils in Scottish schools face many of the same challenges as their counterparts elsewhere. Scotland as a nation has had an ambivalence historically. Part of the United Kingdom, with no autonomous legislature, often out of tune culturally and politically with the London-based establishment, it has only recently, in 1997, voted in a referendum, to have its own parliament. But even within such a small country, it would be wrong to assume homogeneity.

But what do pupils make of their experience? In *Tell Them From Me* (Gow and McPherson, 1980) pupils who left school in the second half of the 1970s wrote about their experiences. The authors chose to concentrate on the views of the 'non-certificate' pupils – those who had not been deemed suitable to sit national examinations. Their writing was characterised by 'qualities of insight, vigour and expression . . . evoked by experience of failure and rejection' (p. 17). The book made a significant impact on Scottish education, and made the case that policy-makers should 'acknowledge that the views of all pupils are important'. The words of the pupils told a powerful story of second class treatment for those who were not 'academic':

> I didn't like school as it was biased towards the intelligent people. (p. 30)

and they talked of labelling:

> While in school I was treated like an idiot not only by my teachers but by my headmaster. (p. 31)

They felt that the school marginalised them:

> the school was short staffed we more or less spent our time sitting our-selves (p. 36)

The views of the certificate pupils were much more positive, more focused on the curriculum and on passing examinations. All groups had some positive things to say about teachers, but the overwhelming effect of the book was the inequity of the treatment of the pupils.

But those were early days of comprehensive schools, and pre-date the national revision of the examinations system. *The 1994 Leavers* (1996) survey reports that:

Successive cohorts of school leavers seem to be increasingly positive about their experiences at school. For example, the proportion who agreed that school had helped give them confidence to make decisions rose from 57% of 1992 leavers to 61% of 1993 leavers and 63% of 1994 leavers. (p. 3)

The term non-certificate has disappeared from Scottish education and, while issues remain about the relative status of Credit, General and Foundation awards, many of the old divisions have disappeared.

Chris has liked his seven teachers in primary, and surveys show that Scottish pupils like school; they like their teachers, 72% in the Young Leavers Survey believing that teachers had helped them to do their best. Most secondary pupils felt that teachers had helped them to make subject choices. The highest percentage was found to be in response to the statement 'School work was worth doing', with 81% of leavers agreeing – by any standards a high level of 'customer satisfaction'. However, some 16% felt that their teachers did not care about them, and 32% said some teachers could not keep order in class. Equity is a key issue for pupils everywhere and most Scottish pupils feel that boys and girls are treated equally.

So – Scottish pupils are, in the main, 'biddable', they are positive about school and feel that their treatment is fair. However, the picture is not all positive. Bullying has emerged as a key issue in Scotland. Studies have indicated that around 40 per cent of pupils experience bullying at least once in school. Interviews with pupils in both primary and secondary school (*Improving School Effectiveness Project*, ISEP, – publication forthcoming) suggest that in most Scottish schools bullying is not seen as a major problem by pupils and that schools have effective systems for dealing with it.

But, at a recent conference on Study Support at the University of Strathclyde, a senior pupil from DASH – Dumbarton Academy Seniors against Harassment – spoke eloquently to an audience of teachers about the persistent low-level activity which goes on unknown to them, and argued that 'harassment' was a more appropriate word than bullying, with its connotations of violence. Thus, name-calling, exclusion from games, skipping the queue for lunch, pushing and shoving in the corridors, laughter, etc. may well go unnoticed and make the lives of some pupils miserable. DASH is one of many such interventionist schemes growing up in schools which have declared themselves to be 'bully-free zones' or which have a policy of 'zero tolerance' of bullying.

While Scotland is less ethnically diverse than many parts of England, nevertheless racial and racist problems can arise. After some highly publicised difficulties in the 1980s centred on a Glasgow school, Strathclyde Regional Council produced its *Tackling Racist Incidents within Educational Establishments* policy, with an emphasis on counselling rather than punishment for victims and perpetrators. Thus while organisations like *Childline* continue to urge vigilance, citing 550 calls to their helpline in one month (*The Herald* 21.10.97), most schools, and most pupils, believe that the situation is being tackled well in most cases.

The issue of school ethos is one which is taken seriously in Scottish schools. Following on from the seminal work by Rutter (*Fifteen Thousand Hours*, 1979) which associated positive relationships (ethos) with effective schools, the Scottish Office Education Department published a pack for primary and for secondary schools under the title *Ethos Indicators*. It urged schools to ask their pupils, their staff and the parents how they felt about aspects of school life, and suggested that ethos was something which ought to be the result of good management at every level in a school. The Scottish Ethos Network was established to enable schools to share and celebrate good practice and to become eligible for an award for innovative approaches to the establishment of a positive ethos.

The idea was given fresh impetus by the HMI report on *The Education of Able Pupils P6 to S2* (1993) which challenged schools to ask themselves if they had 'an ethos of achievement', thus recognising the link between the cognitive and the affective domains. It is this area of achievement and ethos which offers the best context in which to look at the experience of the modern Scottish child.

POVERTY, HEALTH AND UNDERACHIEVEMENT

By far the most contentious issue at present facing Scottish education is underachievement, and in particular the association of underachievement with economic and social disadvantage. Put more directly, in the last years of the twentieth century, can it be denied that the young person from a family which is experiencing the effects of poverty setting out on the journey through schooling is less likely to be successful than her more affluent, or middle class counterpart?

Lochhead's explanation for how she and her former classmate, and rival in learning, drifted apart, 'I don't know exactly why they moved, but anyway they went. Something about a three-apartment and a cheaper rent', at once introduces the issue of social class and poverty. Since those days of relatively full employment, however, unemployment has become a key issue in many areas of Scotland, particularly, though not exclusively, in the inner cities and large peripheral housing estates. Poverty, as defined in terms of having 50 per cent or less of the national average income, trebled since 1979. Around 33,000 children a year are part of households which applied to Councils as homeless; around 5,000 young people sleep rough every year and Scotland has the third highest teenage pregnancy rate in the Western world.

But, of course, poverty is not equally distributed across Scotland. It exists in pockets, and these pockets are served by local schools. In the early 1970s, teachers were persuaded to teach in such 'designated' schools by being offered additional money and travel expenses. Latterly, under Strathclyde Region's Social Strategy, such schools received extra resources in the form of staff and per capita funding. The link between poverty and attainment is well established in the educational literature, but what is challenging for educationalists is the finding that:

> inequalities in almost all areas of educational attainment are . . . in almost all cases larger than class differences in measured ability at the age of 11 years would predict. (Gray, McPherson and Raffe, p. 227)

And their conclusion that 'Scottish education since the war has been neither meritocratic nor equal', is one which must cause concern.

Thus, unlike Chris, the pupil who arrives in P1 from an area of social and economic disadvantage, from a home where neither of the parents (if there are two) have had success in education, where there is unemployment, lack of money and low aspirations, where education is not valued and where authority is perceived as threatening, may struggle to realise her potential.

This may be compounded by the system. In a recent lecture in the University of Strathclyde, a leading American academic argued for the principle of 'no rejects' and has proposed that education, particularly in areas of disadvantage, should be 'child-centred;

family-focused; community-based and culturally sensitive'. But, the propensity to operate on notions of intelligence – the normal curve of distribution – compounded by theories of language acquisition which suggest that such children will be disadvantaged as learners because of an 'impoverished' linguistic experience, have led to a kind of social determinism, which sees poverty and underachievement as causally linked at the individual pupil level. Lower expectations, often institutionalised by grouping by 'ability' lead to a lowering of aspirations and, to borrow a metaphor, may produce a glass ceiling effect for such children.

If we add to this picture the fact that Scotland has one of the worst health records in the developed world, and that the urban poor have similar health profiles to some developing countries, the picture of the Scottish pupil begins to take the form of a continuum, from the advantaged, middle class, conformist, polite, hard-working high-achieving pupil to the disadvantaged, malnourished, underachieving and eventually disaffected young person. In *Health Behaviours of Scottish Schoolchildren* (1993), the authors argue that:

> Socioeconomic factors are clearly an important influence on young people's health behaviours . . . including eating patterns, smoking, alcohol consumption and patterns of physical activity. (p. 26)

The challenge for schools, in the view of the authors, is how to take account of this where the school has a mixed intake of pupils, especially when:

> Young people who are in conflict with the school, as expressed in terms of their dislike for school, are more likely to smoke regularly, drink alcohol, regularly get drunk, do little voluntary exercise and suffer frequent psychosomatic symptoms. (p. 26)

ACHIEVEMENT – 'STANDS SCOTLAND WHERE IT DID?'

Chris is the first of the 5–14 generation, and his parents have attended six parents' evenings at his school on the Strengths – Development Needs – Next Steps model. But on his way through the present Scottish system, Chris will have ascribed to him a bewildering set of Levels – which may become labels. 5–14 provides a possible progression through Level A (at around P3) to Level E (at around S2). Standard Grade then offers (an apparently logical) progression through F (Foundation), G (General) and – here it breaks down – C (Credit). The present Highers offer awards at A to E (though this time A is highest) and if he goes to university he may get a degree which is a First; an Upper Second; a Lower Second; a Third; or a mere General or Ordinary degree. Our propensity to categorise is immense.

But while qualification levels continue to rise, comparisons between schools (so-called league tables) and among departments within secondary schools has been encouraged by government. Recent international comparisons, especially of attainment in Mathematics, have caused concern and led to HMI reports on achievement generally (1996) and specifically in Maths (1997) which have called for more testing, more internal selection and more whole-class teaching. In addition, at a time when pupils are computer-aware from an early age, where the television – satellite and terrestrial – as well as video and CD are in most households (irrespective of social class) it has been suggested that the use of calculators should be limited in schools.

LISTENING TO PUPILS' VOICES?

Since *Tell Them From Me*, the voice of the child in Scottish education has rarely been heard. The ISEP study has surveyed two cohorts, one in primary and one in secondary across a total of eighty Scottish schools and has interviewed small groups of pupils in twenty-four of these schools. The pupils' comments tended to cluster round key themes:

Pupil engagement with school
Pupil self-esteem/self-efficacy
Perceptions of teacher expectations of pupils
Relationship with teachers
Pupil-pupil relationships
Pupil empowerment
Equitable treatment of pupils
Support for learning for all – praise, recognition, information

Pupils from P2 to S6 have a lot to say about school, and most of it is positive. They like school and they think their teachers do a good job. But they do not generally feel that their views are listened to.

The transition between primary and secondary is the critical point, where many pupils claim that no-one seems to know them, that their learning over the previous seven years is not built upon, and that they are not treated as 'real people'. In the primary school they will most likely have had a variant of 'circle time' – structured opportunities to discuss issues affecting them in schools. This is almost non-existent in the secondary, where, at best, there may be an elected pupil council which is rarely perceived to offer the pupils a real voice.

Primary schools place great emphasis on praise and reward, while some secondaries place unfair pressure on pupils to achieve and perform. Equity is an issue, especially in the secondary schools. Most pupils felt most teachers were fair, but were very critical of those who weren't. It is clear, too, that pupils in schools which had had new headteachers were very aware of changes and of why the changes were being made. In other words, pupils' insights might be of as much value in individual schools as they were nationally in 1980.

If underachievement is a matter of failure to learn successfully, then it seems logical that the child-as-a-learner should be the starting point. Publications emanating from the SCCC (*Climate for Learning; Teaching for Effective Learning*, 1996), on the impact of recent research on the brain and on the proliferation of new technology, have begun to reach teachers through in-service training and staff development. Scottish teachers might be said to be conservative, and Scottish schools, as HMI found in their review of the P4 and P7 curriculum in 1981, were never wholly won over by the more 'progressive' developments of the 1960s. Instead they married the best of the new to the best of the old. In the primary Chris could be chanting his times-tables in the time-honoured way one minute and be using a concept keyboard the next.

The future, therefore, may include a commitment to staff development for teachers which recognises them as reflective professionals. In turn they may be persuaded that theory and research are part of their professional commitment and a rationale for learning and teaching which focuses on achievement may emerge. Accelerated learning and thinking skills may break free from their 'alternative' (as in alternative medicine) status, and Scottish pupils may enjoy an experience which begins with the premise that they can all be successful learners and that any barriers to the achievement of their potential need to be removed, not re-inforced. *Achievement for All* may then become the goal, with learning styles, multiple intelligences, emotional intelligence and high expectations for all being norm.

The new Labour government and the imminent Scottish parliament may signal a new professional confidence among teachers, where effective learning and teaching is the key issue for debate. The experience of all pupils in Scottish schools may change for the better and their voices may be listened to. In 1997, the senior pupils of Largs Academy when asked to discuss in small groups 'what makes a good teacher?' responded in a way which might offer an agenda for school improvement:

> A 'good' teacher . . .
> is competent and achieves the best results from his pupils
> is able to generate mutual respect
> is able to mix discipline with fun
> is adaptable, communicates well and has empathy for all his pupils
> is enthusiastic, knowledgeable and compassionate
> is genuinely interested in young people
> is patient, well-organised and self-disciplined
> makes time for individuals
> has a likeable personality and allows it to come through
> takes part in the wider life of the school.

Chris, meanwhile, having had an almost entirely positive experience in Mossneuk Primary School, stands poised to make the transition to secondary where he will meet up to seventeen teachers in one week. Whether, like most resilient children, he will flourish in spite of the drawbacks of the system, remains to be seen.

REFERENCES

Currie, C., J. Todd and K. Wijckmans (1993) *Health Behaviours of Scottish Schoolchildren*, Edinburgh: Health Education Board for Scotland.
Gray, J., A. F. McPherson and D. Raffe (1983) *Reconstructions of Secondary Education: Theory, Myth and Practice since the War*, London: Routledge and Keegan Paul.
Gow, L. and A. McPherson (eds) (1980) *Tell Them From Me*, Aberdeen: Aberdeen University Press.
McPherson, A. and C. D. Raab (1988) *Governing Education: a Sociology of Policy since 1945*, Edinburgh: Edinburgh University Press.
SOEID (1996) *The 1994 Leavers* Edinburgh: SOEID.
Willms, J. D. (1997) *Parental Choice and Education Policy*, CES Briefing, Edinburgh University.

85

The Assessment of Achievement Programme

Rae Stark, Isobel J. Robertson and Angela Napuk

In recent years, concerns over educational standards, nationally and internationally, have driven curricular and assessment policy decisions in Scotland, as in many other countries. However any debate on standards, whether in regard to education in general or specific subject areas, must be informed by significant objective evidence on what pupils know and can do rather than subjective impressions gleaned incidentally and haphazardly.

This requires the deliberate and systematic collecting of such evidence and the Assessment of Achievement Programme (AAP) was established in the mid-1980s, by what is now the Scottish Education and Industry Department (SOEID), for precisely such a purpose. Drawing on a range of experience, not least that of the Assessment of Performance Unit (APU), which undertook national surveys of performance in England and Wales in the early 1980s, a rolling programme of national monitoring in English language, mathematics and science was established in Scotland. The AAP has continued to monitor performance through the implementation of the government's 5–14 Development Programme, a policy development introduced in 1987.

AIMS AND ORGANISATION

The main aims of the AAP as specified by the SOEID are: to provide a picture of the performance levels of pupils at certain stages, within specified curricular areas; to gather evidence of any change in performance over time; and to provide feedback to education authorities, curriculum developers and teachers which will contribute to the improvement of learning and teaching.

In 1987, a system of national testing in English and mathematics was introduced as an integral part of the 5–14 Development Programme (see Chapter 83). The tests focused on the individual pupil and were designed to complement the formative assessment by teachers of individual pupils, providing confirmatory evidence of levels of attainment. By contrast, the AAP is not concerned with the individual but with a nationally representative sample of pupils, and surveys measure and monitor national performance levels at important stages in the primary and early secondary school. Thus national monitoring and national testing have different purposes and, to a degree, different audiences and they have evolved as two separate systems.

Each AAP survey has involved pupils aged 8–9 years (Primary 4), 11–12 years (Primary 7) and 13–14 years (Secondary 2). Primary 4 (P4) has been regarded as the earliest stage at which pupils can satisfactorily cope with the demands of the assessment while the other two groups are at significant stages in their education. The younger pupils (P7) are reaching the end of their primary education and Secondary 2 (S2) pupils have selected the subjects which they will study for national certification at the end of Secondary 4. Table 85.1 shows the pattern of surveys established to date.

Table 85.1   Surveys in the Assessment of Achievement Programme

Survey	Year of survey				
Mathematics	1983	1988	1991	1994	1997
English Language	1984	1989	1992	1995	1998
Science	1987	1990	1993	1996	

Until the fifth survey of mathematics in 1997, each was conducted by an independent team of researchers based in an educational institution and each research project supporting the survey lasted for twenty-four to thirty months. Consecutive subject surveys have often involved some of the same researchers, maximising continuity and the effective utilisation of expertise.

The SOEID funded and managed each project, appointing a Project Committee to support and advise each team. Committees were chaired by subject specialists from Her Majesty's Inspectorate of Schools (HMI) and membership included teachers from both primary and secondary sectors, advisers and a Principal Research Officer of the SOEID. Project teams were given a wide remit and considerable responsibility. They were required to develop the survey design and select appropriate assessment materials as well as being encouraged to develop new techniques and tasks for each round of monitoring. Teams appointed and trained assessors to work in schools and markers to evaluate and code pupil responses. Work culminated in the preparation of reports and the drafting of dissemination materials.

The organisation of the AAP changed significantly when, in 1996, a national coordinator was appointed to oversee all surveys. The appointment, based in the Scottish Office, has centralised much of the activity previously undertaken by project teams. Subject expertise is contracted in at appropriate periods and an AAP Strategy Group advises on matters of general policy and maintains contact with similar programmes elsewhere.

The Central Support Unit (CSU) at the Scottish Council for Research in Education continues to be responsible for determining sample sizes and identifying the schools and pupils to be involved. All AAP surveys operate two-stage cluster sampling to obtain nationally representative samples of pupils, stratified by local authority and school size. The CSU also provides technical assistance and carries out data analysis.

Following the publication of national guidelines for English language (1991), mathematics (1991) and science, as part of Environmental Studies (1993), the specific aims of each survey are:

1. to determine what P4, P7 and S2 pupils know and can do in agreed aspects of the subject areas;
2. to measure performance in relation to the curricular Levels defined in national guidelines as part of the 5–14 Development Programme;

3. to provide comparisons of the performance of pupils at each of the three stages, P4, P7 and S2;
4. to provide comparisons by gender;
5. to provide comparisons of the pupils' performance over time.

MEASURING AGAINST EXPECTATIONS

As the Levels of the 5–14 Programme are expressed in terms of 'almost all' or 'most' pupils, it is necessary to determine figures for these terms. For example, it is stated for science that 'Level C should be attained in the course of P4–P6 by most pupils'. In the 1996 science survey, most was taken to be 75% of each sample and 'almost all' to be 90%. The English language team, reporting in 1995, interpreted 'most' as 75%-80% of pupils while in mathematics, the 1994 findings were reported in terms of 'most' representing 67% of the sample population. In each survey, judgements on whether pupils had attained a particular level were therefore based on the definitions of 'most' provided by research teams. (Additional detail can be found in the final reports of these surveys: Robertson, Meechan, Clarke and Moffat, 1996; Napuk, Normand & Orr, 1996; Stark, Gray, Bryce and Ellis, 1997.)

While each survey has a number of common features, the procedures and techniques developed by project teams reflect the specific nature of each subject area.

ASSESSING ACHIEVEMENT IN MATHEMATICS

The Surveys

The first survey of mathematics was undertaken by the Scottish Council for Research in Education (SCRE) in 1983. A series of written and practical tests was compiled allowing limited comparisons to be made with previous mathematics tests in 1978 and 1981. In the second survey, carried out in 1988 by Macnab, Page and Kennedy at Northern College (Aberdeen), the number of test booklets was increased considerably in order to extend curriculum coverage. The third and fourth mathematics surveys were conducted from Jordanhill Campus and the assessment framework for the 1997 survey has remained basically unchanged. from 1994

The assessment framework

The consultative document proposing the detailed format for national guidelines in mathematics 5–14 was published in 1990 and was widely recognised as defining current good practice. The 1991 assessment framework was based on this document in order to provide a relevant structure for reporting the findings of the 1991 and 1994 surveys while still allowing comparisons with previous surveys.

The four aspects of mathematics identified in the consultative document were adopted as the major organisers within the framework. Categories and sub-categories were defined to provide a coherent grouping of mathematics processes, content and contexts for assessment and reporting purposes. Each category could be matched to one or several of the Strands at the five Levels A – E and tasks were matched to these levels. An additional level, E +, was included to allow reporting of the achievements of the most able pupils.

Figure 85.1 shows the Assessment Framework adopted in 1991 and 1994. Written and practical mathematics activities can be seen to be essential elements of all four attainment outcomes; *Problem Solving* is considered to be an integral part of the other Outcomes.

Figure 85.1   The 1994 AAP Assessment Framework (Mathematics)

CATEGORY	SUB-CATEGORY	STAGES ASSESSED
Information Handling *written*	Display and interpret	All
practical	Collect, organise and display	All
Number, Money and Measurement		
Number concepts *written*	Range and type of numbers; number vocabulary; estimate, round, average.	All
	Patterns and sequences; symbols, functions, equations.	All
practical	Rounding from calculator display	All
	Estimation prior to using calculator	P7 & S2
Basic processes *written*	Addition and subtraction	P4
	Multiplication and division	P4
	Whole number arithmetic	P7 & S2
	Decimals, fractions, percentages	P7 & S2
practical	Calculating mentally	P4 & P7
	Using a calculator	All
Applications *written*	Addition and subtraction	P4
	Multiplication and division	P4
	Whole number	P7 & S2
	Decimals, including money	P7 & S2
	Fractions and percentages	P7 & S2
	Time	All
	Ratio, formulae, scale	P7 & S2
practical	Applications with a calculator	All
	Measure and estimate	All
	Handling money and time	All
Shape, Position and Movement		
written	Range of shapes	All
	Position and movement	All
	Symmetry	All
	Angle	All
practical	Shape and pattern	All
	Position and movement (and Angle)	All
	Symmetry	All
Problem solving *written*	Short tasks	All
	Extended tasks	P7 & S2
practical	Extended tasks	All
	Calculator tasks	All

Innovations in assessment

The 1991 survey took account of the format used in National Testing and booklets were introduced in which tasks were set within contextual themes. Attractive illustrations developed the context whilst minimising reading load. In preparing for the 1994 survey, new contextualised materials were commissioned from practising teachers.

The practical component of the 1991 survey introduced a circuit of tasks in addition to one-to-one oral assessment and a feasibility study on computerised testing in primary schools was undertaken. In 1994 the one-to-one format was used to assess extended practical problem solving tasks.

The findings

In 1994 the team concluded that, certainly for P7 and S2 and, to some extent, for P4 pupils, achievement in mathematics did not measure up to the expectations of the national guidelines. Although there were some attainment targets which most pupils at each stage appeared to be meeting comfortably, there were others, mostly within *Number, Money and Measurement*, but also in *Shape, Position and Movement* which few pupils at a particular stage appeared able to attain.

Applying the project team's yardstick of 'most' being at least 67% of pupils, to items at levels B, D and E, for P4, P7 and S2 pupils respectively, it was found that:

- at P4, almost 60% of the items at level B were performed successfully by most pupils;
- at P7, under 40% of the items at level D were performed successfully by most pupils;
- at S2, under 50% of the items at level D and less than 20% at level E were performed successfully by most pupils.

At P4, achievement at level B was high for *Information Handling* but weakest in *Number Concepts* and *Basic Processes*. There were no significant differences in performance found on any of the categories between 1988 and 1991 but performance was significantly lower on *Basic Processes* and *Applications of Number, Money and Measurement* (with whole numbers) in 1994 compared to 1991.

At P7, no categories showed particularly high achievement in terms of performance at level D. Pupils appeared weakest on *Basic Processes* and *Applications of Number, Money and Measurement*. Over three surveys, performance on *Basic Processes* with both whole numbers and decimals, fractions and percentages, has fallen significantly although between 1988 and 1991 performance on some aspects of *Shape, Position and Movement* improved significantly.

At S2, the highest achievement on level E tasks was in *Information Handling*. Pupils were less successful in *Number Concepts, Basic Processes* and *Applications of Number, Money and Measurement* and, overall, in *Shape, Position and Movement*. A significant fall in performance in *Basic Processes with decimals, fractions and percentages* was evidenced between 1988 and 1991, with another significant decline between 1991 and 1994. The view over the three surveys also showed a significant fall in performance on *Basic Processes with whole numbers* and *Applications with decimals*.

In *Problem Solving* there were no significant differences in performance on short tasks between 1991 and 1994. On extended problem solving tasks, pupils tended to use a random rather than a systematic approach and appeared reluctant to show working in written tasks or to handle materials in practical tasks.

The 1991 survey was the first AAP mathematics survey to report on performance by gender. A few significant differences were found in the written papers at S2 where boys performed significantly better on one subcategory and girls on three.

In the written component in 1994, P4 girls performed better on *Information Handling* but at P7 boys performed better on this category and, overall, on *Number, Money and Measurement*. At S2, there were no significant differences in the written component and the few observed in the practical were in favour of girls.

International comparisons

The 1994 survey included a collaborative study with France to provide comparisons of performance at P4 and P7 with French CE2 and Sixième stages. All items concerned with basic processes involving decimals, used at the Scottish P7 stage, produced superior performances from the French pupils, with differences in performance levels exceeding 20% per cent in most instances.

In 1995 over forty countries participated in the Third International Maths and Science Survey (TIMSS) conducted by the International Association for the Evaluation of Educational Achievement (IEA). Each country's educational system inevitably reflects the cultural and social values and beliefs of its people and influences the status accorded to individual subject areas within that system. Therefore, while a degree of caution should be exercised in comparing performance measures, the TIMSS findings for mathematics in Scottish schools, published by the SOEID in 1996, showed remarkable similarity to those obtained by the AAP.

Although the AAP is primarily concerned with establishing national measures of performance rather than providing a basis for international comparisons, setting the findings from international surveys alongside national data can provide an extra check on the validity of both exercises.

ASSESSING ACHIEVEMENT IN ENGLISH LANGUAGE

There have been four surveys of achievement in English Language. The first in 1984 was conducted by a team at the then Dundee College of Education while the last three were based at the University of Edinburgh.

The first survey by the Edinburgh team in 1989 took place while national policies for assessment and testing, integral parts of the 5–14 Development Programme, were still at a formative stage. It was not possible, nor was it part of the team's remit to attempt to link, explicitly, the monitoring project and the 5–14 Programme. However, it was considered that the survey would provide a rich source of performance data which could be quarried in order to provide some sort of validation of the Attainment Targets and would contribute to and inform the implementation of the 5–14 national guidelines for English.

The assessment framework

The 1989 survey reflected a shift in emphasis from language as a set of discrete skills towards language as communicative competence. The approach used was purpose based, that is, it began by defining the purposes for which the various language functions are performed and attempted to cover as many of these as possible. The tasks were con-

textualised in that they formed part of a coherent sequence, with an identifiable justification. The whole sequence attempted to mirror good classroom practice by assessing
children, as far as possible, on aspects of language usage in ways which would command
the approval of teachers.

This approach to measuring achievement was found to be entirely compatible with the
national guidelines and both the 1992 and 1995 surveys were designed to allow comparisons
to be made, wherever possible, with these. Only a limited number of the strands could be
assessed within the constraints imposed by the survey design and the resources available.
Until 1998 achievement was assessed across the four modes of Reading, Writing, Talking
and Listening. These modes are the 5–14 language outcomes, while the purposes are
incorporated within the strands.

The 1995 survey continued to support teachers in interpreting aspects of the guidelines
and in developing effective techniques for the assessment of English. Talking and writing
are difficult to assess and carefully designed frameworks for assessment were produced in
both these areas. Criteria for the assessment of talk were derived from the guidelines and
were used in both 1992 and 1995 surveys.

The reliability of a test depends both on adequate and valid sampling of the aspect of
competence and on consistency in marking. These considerations were kept firmly in mind
in designing the materials and the construction and use of mark schemes. The use of
contextualised packages limited the number of different instances in which language skills
could be measured in the time available and so limited the generalisability of the findings.
In comparison with more traditional testing procedures, levels of reliability have tended to
remain relatively low.

Findings on performance

Real difficulties were encountered in relating the performance on the survey tasks to the 5–
14 levels of attainment. The definitions of these levels within the Guidelines are intended to
help the teacher in selecting appropriate work and judging progress. However, it is difficult
to make very fine judgements about attainment against these levels because of the rather
general terms in which the targets are expressed. In addition, the contextual variation
between packages further complicated any attempt to demonstrate equivalence between
performance in the AAP surveys and the 5–14 levels on all language modes except writing,
where the publication of national writing criteria provided an opportunity to match
achievement directly to 5–14. In reporting on AAP performance in listening, talking
and reading, comparisons were stated in more general terms.

The 1992 AAP findings, although tentative, appeared to indicate that the attainment
targets may have been set rather high for 'most pupils'. They seemed to apply more to
'just over half', as far as can be ascertained from the imprecise definitions provided. While
it was established that, for English, 'most' meant at least three quarters of pupils, in
this survey, at all stages and across all four language modes, the proportion of pupils
achieving the appropriate level ranged between one half and three fifths of each sample
cohort.

The incorporation of the national guidelines into classroom practice, particularly in the
primary sector, was reflected in the 1995 survey with marked improvements in a number of
specific curriculum areas. Standards at P4 for all four language outcomes appeared, for the
most part, to be in line with level B; the majority of P7 pupils were competent talkers,

attaining level D, while approximately half were working to level D in listening and writing albeit with some difficulties in reading. At S2 performance in both listening and reading was reasonable, although talking, particularly in groups, needed some attention and for many pupils attainment in writing was well below the expected level E.

Performance over time

Comparisons between performance over time were made from consecutive survey data although no direct comparison could be made between performance in 1989 and 1995. Overall there was no general change in the level of performance between 1989 and 1992, though some variation of performance occurred in respect of particular skills at P4 and at S2. Comparison between 1992 and 1995 showed significant declines in reading at all three stages but, at P4 and P7, writing skills had improved and at P7 there was a significant improvement in some aspects of talking.

Performance between stages

Comparisons were made between P7 and S2 stages only. S2 performed significantly better on all listening, reading and writing tasks bar one – imaginative writing, where there was a difference between the stages on three of the skills categories and a significant difference in the figures for spelling, where P7 performed better than S2.

Gender

Gender comparisons were made by item for listening and reading and by skills for talking and writing in the last two surveys only. In 1993, across the four language modes, P4 girls performed significantly better in five skills, P7 girls in seven skills and S2 girls in two skills. In 1995 the girls at P4 were significantly better in thirteen skills, at P7 in fourteen skills and at S2 in eighteen skills. These significant differences were most noticeable in both reading and writing; at S2 the girls were consistently performing better in all aspects of writing.

Cross curricular projects

The English Language team were in regular contact with schools, educational authorities and the Scottish Office and were aware of educational developments, curriculum changes and areas of concern. Cross-curricular issues, in particular the use of English language across the curriculum, have formed a vital part of recent SOEID publications. The English Language team have always been aware of the need to respond to such concerns and to develop relevant and valid contexts for the assessment of language skills and, in this spirit, became involved in collaboration with the AAP Science team in 1993 and with Mathematics in 1994.

The science survey provided an ideal, albeit limited, opportunity to assess talking and writing following pupils' involvement in scientific investigations. These provided a purpose, context and audience for the use of language and the assessment was organised such that it did not interfere with nor distort the science assessment exercise. For many pupils, at all stages, talking about their investigations proved to be easier than writing a report, a genre more familiar to the upper primary and secondary pupils. The opportunity for assessing language in the 1994 Mathematics survey was limited to a writing task following a problem solving activity for P7 and S2 only. Although most pupils appeared to understand the nature of the task, the findings did point up some serious flaws in writing skills at the basic level of technical details.

ASSESSING ACHIEVEMENT IN SCIENCE

The first project in 1987 was essentially a feasibility study, an attempt to determine whether it was possible to conduct national monitoring of science using both practical and non-practical forms of assessment. Conducted prior to the introduction of the 5–14 Programme, and national testing, the political stakes were low and the AAP was not perceived by teachers as threatening. In addition, attempts were made to avoid imposing additional burdens on teachers with minimal intrusion into the day-to-day work of the class and no teacher involvement in task development or marking. Schools participated readily and the survey was regarded as fairly successful.

The assessment framework

The initial assessment framework (1987) was derived from an analysis of curricular and policy documents and through consultation. It had the approval of the Project Committee and met the expectations of the majority of teachers, primary and secondary, whose pupils were involved. A combination of practical and written tasks were designed to assess specific skills and concepts and integrated tasks (practical investigations) required pupils to draw on a range of science concepts as well as practical and process skills. A commitment to science as an active, participative area of the curriculum has been a feature of all four science surveys with the assessment of pupils 'doing science' a significant component.

As the guidelines for science, a component of Environmental Studies 5–14, were only published in 1993, the 1996 survey was the first to attempt to measure performance in science against the expectations of the 5–14 Programme. Three attainment outcomes, which draw on the three main science disciplines of biology, physics, and chemistry, outline the content and contexts for learning science and five Strands reflect the levels of knowledge, skills and processes expected across the 5–14 age range. In addition, guidance on the development of informed attitudes is included.

The Strands are set out in the 5–14 levels while the statements of content and context (the 'key features') are grouped by (st)age into three broad bands: P1–P3, P4–P6 and P7–S2. The key features and strands were combined in the 1996 assessment framework (Figure 85.2).

The findings

Summaries of findings are, of necessity, broad brush statements which can, and do, mask considerable variation in performance within and across the key features and strands assessed. With that in mind, in 1996 P4 pupils were judged to have attained level B on the assessment tasks and P7 pupils came close to meeting the level D targets. At S2 however, performance was poor with attainment reaching level D rather than the level E anticipated. Overall, at all three stages, girls tended to out-perform boys, particularly on process and practical skills and where the content/context was drawn from the biological sciences. Boys produced superior performances on knowledge and understanding where the focus was on the physical sciences.

Figure 85.2 The 1996 Assessment Framework

CATEGORY	SUB-CATEGORY	
Knowledge & Understanding (KU)		
Planning P1:	Question raising	
(P)	P2:	Identifying information sources and resources
	P3:	Sequencing plans
	P4:	Planning for recording and reporting
	P5:	Anticipating problems
	P6:	Planning for safety and hygiene
Collecting Evidence	CE1:	Recognising similarities and differences
(CE)	CE2:	Recognising changes
	CE3:	Extracting information
	CE4:	Using simple techniques
	CE5:	Estimating and measuring
	CE6:	Collecting evidence fairly and safely
Recording & Presenting	RP1:	Recording in a variety of formats
(RP)	RP2:	Presenting in a variety of formats
Interpreting & Evaluating	IE1:	Identifying relationships
(IE)	IE2:	Evaluating evidence

Over the series of surveys, the P4 pupils showed some improvement, P7 stayed fairly steady but S2 performance levels declined, more so amongst boys than girls. In 1996, the P4 pupils who had been involved in the 1993 survey were, where feasible, included in the P7 sample, introducing a truly longitudinal element in an attempt to gain greater insight into the issue of progression through the primary stages. The findings indicated a clear progression in attainment, with some evidence of a growing gap in the performance levels of low and high achievers over time.

International comparisons

In the 1995 TIMSS survey, two samples of pupils in Scottish schools were involved, one with an average age of nine years and a second with an average age of thireen years. The younger pupils were ranked at approximately the mid-point for all aspects of science assessed across twenty-six countries. An analysis by gender indicated that, in Scotland, boys did better than girls at both stages although the differences were not significant.

The 13-year-olds were drawn from the S1 and S2 grades in Scottish schools and, overall, were ranked twenty-fifth. Analysis by gender showed that, in all countries, boys performed better than girls at the lower grade and the differences were significant in twenty-six of them (SOEID, 1996).

The gender-related data appears to conflict with the AAP findings but it should be noted that in TIMSS the focus was on knowledge and understanding where boys also tended to out-perform girls in the AAP survey. Overall, compared with the other TIMSS countries, the performance of 13-year-olds in Scotland was poor although relatively good for the 9-year-olds tested.

DISCUSSION

When the National Curriculum and National Testing arrangements were introduced in England and Wales, the government disbanded the APU and determined that measurements of whether or not pupils in schools knew and could do what was expected of them would be based on the collation of National Test data. This was not an option for Scotland where the arrangements for the assessment and testing of primary and early secondary pupils were, and remain, quite different. While in England both the National Curriculum and National Testing are mandatory, the status of national testing in Scotland – non-statutory, exclusively pencil-and-paper and of relatively small samples of the curriculum – would render the collation of test data for monitoring purposes unreliable and lacking in validity.

The technical knowledge required for national monitoring (the 'how') has evolved considerably over the last fifteen years and is more than adequate to ensure that the statistical procedures are accurate and appropriate. However, as Dockrell points out, the most contentious issues in national monitoring (as with national testing) are the 'what' and the 'why', both of which are value-laden and, in consequence, should be the real issues for discussion (Dockrell, 1979).

The 'what' in the AAP is given by the 5–14 Programme. The curricular guidelines should ensure a degree of commonalty in the learning experiences of children across the country. However, the guidelines reflect a particular view of each subject area and embody values which may not be acceptable to all. In addition, there are significant difficulties in reaching a consensus in the interpretation in many of the targets, a problem common to those attempting to reconcile national test data and national expectations in England (Massey, 1995).

Developed primarily for purposes of learning and teaching, the targets within the 5–14 guidelines are mainly expressed as broad general statements rather than specific learning objectives; the degree of generality varies with the subject area. This avoidance of prescription was deliberate in that it would allow teachers to interpret the statements in ways which would more readily meet the needs of their pupils and to develop programmes of study which would reflect the local environment.

This flexibility creates problems for national monitoring (and classroom assessment) as targets can contain some ambiguous statements, considerable variation in conceptual demand and a lack of clarity in specifying how progress can be recognised. It is not a straightforward task to identify unambiguously what pupils should know and be able to do and to develop tasks which accurately tap the targets. (See also Chapter 78.) The AAP has continued to assist in clarifying and interpreting the language of the strands and the targets as well as the criteria used to define the 5–14 Levels.

To date, the AAP has assessed widely across each subject area: listening and talking in English, practical investigations in science and practical applications of mathematical skills. In addition, it has tried out new techniques and developed alternative approaches to assessment. However, such a commitment is expensive in time and resources and impossible to sustain in the face of diminishing budgets.

It would be unfortunate if, as a result, the AAP resorted to what is cheap, i.e. pencil and paper assessment, and easy to test, e.g. knowledge and understanding, thus reducing the breadth of coverage and the range of modes of assessment used. Quite apart from the loss of innovative assessment opportunities, the profession is likely to form the impression that only that which is tested is important and, as a result, pupils may well experience a narrowing of the curriculum. In addition, there is evidence from the AAP that girls and low achievers of both sexes are disadvantaged by assessment procedures which depend entirely on written tests.

The government's concern with performance levels (the 'why' of monitoring standards) is driven, in the main, by economic and political considerations. Any policy of national monitoring and/or testing attracts critics and much of that criticism tends to be concerned with the values which people perceive to underlie the development of such policies. Concerns include the potential misuse of test results, the mismatch of the test to the local curriculum, teaching to the test, the use of restrictive or narrow testing formats and the potentially divisive consequences of labelling children as a result of assessment.

To date, the AAP has been relatively free of such criticisms. The multi-matrix, light sampling techniques do not place a significant burden on individual pupils and the analysis is designed such that no individual pupil, school or local authority is identified.

In maintaining two systems of assessment, national testing and national monitoring, the SOEID has acknowledged that measuring the strengths and weaknesses of individual performance and progress and determining national levels of performance require different approaches and they have earned credit for matching appropriate assessment instruments to purpose (Brown, 1994). As the AAP continues to evolve, it should be an important source of information in the debate on the effectiveness of the 5–14 Development Programme, contributing to policy-making, directly and indirectly, and providing real, practical assistance to teachers in turning policy into practice.

REFERENCES

Brown, S. (1994) Assessment and Testing, in G. Kirk and R. Glaister (eds)., *5–14: Scotland's National Curriculum*, Edinburgh: Scottish Academic Press.

Dockrell, W. B. (1979) National Surveys of Achievement, in *Issues in Educational Assessment*, Occasional Papers, Edinburgh: HMSO.

Massey, A. J. (1995) Criterion-related Test Development and National Test Standards, in *Assessment in Education: principles, policy and practice*, vol. 2. No.2. pp.187–203.

Napuk, A., B. Normand and S. Orr (1996) *The Assessment of Achievement Programme (Scotland): English Language, Fourth Survey 1995*, Edinburgh: University of Edinburgh.

Robertson I. J., R. C. Meechan, D. Clarke and J. J. S. Moffat (1996) *Assessment Report of the Fourth Survey of Mathematics, 1994*, Glasgow: University of Strathclyde.

Stark R., D. Gray, T. G. K. Bryce and S. Ellis (1997) *Assessment of Achievement Programme: Fourth Survey of Science, 1996*, Glasgow: University of Strathclyde.

86

SEB Findings on Scottish Achievements

David Elliot and Helen Ganson

The data gathered by the Scottish Examination Board (SEB), now held by the Scottish Qualifications Authority, provides a rich source of information on the achievements of Scottish young people over a long historical period. Indeed data in some form goes back to the introduction of Higher Grade in 1888. Each year SEB published its annual report accompanied by a comprehensive set of statistics. These are publicly available and it is not the intention in this chapter to repeat or summarise them. Current and historic data have been reanalysed, however, to shed some new light on how the profile of candidate attainment has changed over the period 1987–96. In the decade discussed in this chapter the data became comprehensive in relation to fourth-year candidates in a way in which it had not been previously. Ordinary Grade was replaced over the period by Standard Grade. The new examination arrangements were designed to cater for the entire range of ability in secondary schools (see Chapters 78 and 80). This may well make Standard Grade unique in the world. By the mid-1990s, 88% of certificate courses followed by S3/S4 pupils were Standard Grade, with SEB Short Courses and SCOTVEC National Certificate modules each accounting for a further 6%. In S5, Higher Grade and National Certificate modules each provided almost half of certificate courses, whereas in S6 Highers provided 57%, Certificate of Sixth Year Studies (CSYS) 14% and National Certificate 27%. This should be borne in mind when considering the analysis of SEB data. (See SEB Annual Reports, 1989–96.)

BASIC SKILLS AND COMPETENCES IN THE FOURTH YEAR (S4)

There are many interpretations of what constitute basic skills and competences but all classifications would include native language and numeracy/mathematics. In terms of these subjects, the picture is a positive one.

Because Standard Grade provided appropriate challenges for a far wider range of ability than did Ordinary Grade, the proportion of S4 candidates attaining certification in basic skills and competences increased substantially over the decade. It may be that schools developed these skills in the 20 to 30 per cent of pupils who under Ordinary Grade were not presented for certificate examinations, but it is likely that the introduction of Standard Grade provided a coherent curriculum for the great majority of less able Scottish youngsters for the first time. The dearly held belief of the superiority of the Scottish system compared to that of other countries centred on the 'lad o' pairts', the able lad of humble origins who achieved academic distinction, not on what the system did for the less able. Standard Grade addressed that need, as the statistics show.

In the last year before the introduction of Standard Grade in English and Mathematics (1985), 74% of the S4 age cohort attempted Ordinary Grade English. By 1996, 95% were attempting Standard Grade English. Standard Grade had more or less replaced Ordinary Grade by 1990. In that year the mean grade was 3.2 and this had improved to 2.9 by 1996 (the Standard Grade scale runs from 1 (upper Credit level) to 7 (below Foundation level). Similarly in Mathematics, in 1985 71% attempted Ordinary Grade Arithmetic (and over half of this group also did Ordinary Grade Mathematics) and by 1996 96% were attempting Standard Grade Mathematics. In terms of attainment, the mean grade improved from 3.9 in 1990 to 3.4 in 1996.

With regard to Information Technology, in 1987 3% of the age cohort were attempting Ordinary Grade Computing, the only subject at that time which required competence in IT. In 1996, Standard Grade Computing Studies was attempted by 27% of the age cohort, Accounting and Finance by 8%, Office and Information Studies by 27% and Graphic Communication by 11%. These percentages are not additive as some candidates take more than one of these subjects; nonetheless 62% took at least one subject requiring some level of IT competence.

The assessment of problem solving also increased over the period. Most Standard Grade subjects have elements (components) called *Evaluating* in the social subjects and *Problem Solving* in the sciences. While such skills were assessed to an extent in Ordinary Grade examinations, Standard Grade caused them to be assessed more formally and performance was reported separately rather than being subsumed in an overall award. Generally speaking, candidates have become quite proficient in these areas, perhaps because of the reinforcement provided by similar skills being assessed in cognate subjects. Knowledge and Understanding, which is by its nature subject specific, is more likely to cause difficulties for the poorly prepared candidate.

SUBJECT CHOICE IN FOURTH YEAR

The pattern of uptake of subjects leading to certification and subject choice in S4 changed markedly between 1987 and 1996 with the introduction of Standard Grade and the implementation of the SCCC guidelines on the curricular framework. As can be seen in Table 86.1, the overwhelming majority (87 per cent) of S4 pupils in 1996 were presented in either seven or eight Standard Grade subjects. Although 94 per cent of the 1987 cohort attempted at least one Ordinary Grade or Standard Grade subject the number attempted was much more variable with, for example, one eighth of the 1987 cohort attempting zero or one Ordinary or Standard Grade, whereas, in 1996, one eighth of the cohort attempted between zero and six Standard Grades.

Overall, the distribution of subject presentations was surprisingly similar, given the change in the examination system and the increase in the mean number of subjects attempted from 5.2 in 1987 to 7.1 in 1996. Table 86.2 summarises the 'market share' of S4 presentations in 1987 and 1996. (Market share describes presentations in each subject as a percentage of total presentations.) Presentations in languages other than English increased as a result of a change in government policy. Arithmetic ceased to be a separate subject from Mathematics and the introduction of a course and examination in Physical Education contributed significantly to the increase in the Creative and Physical Education category.

Table 86.1 Number of subjects attempted by S4 candidates Ordinary Grade and Standard Grade, 1987 and 1996

number of subjects	candidates as % of cohort	
	1987 O Grades + S Grades	1996 Standard Grades (excl Writing)
none	6%	2%
1	6%	1%
2	6%	1%
3	8%	1%
4	9%	1%
5	10%	2%
6	14%	5%
7	19%	36%
8	19%	51%
9	3%	1%
10	0%	–
11	0%	–

Table 86.2 Market share of Ordinary Grade and Standard Grade subjects (grouped) S4 candidates, 1987 and 1996

Market share	1987	1996
English	15%	13%
Other languages	8%	13%
Mathematics	11%	13%
Other mathematical subjects	15%	1%
Science subjects	20%	18%
Social subjects and religious studies	14%	15%
Technological subjects	13%	15%
Creative & Aesthetic subjects and Physical Education	5%	11%

(Market share describes presentations in each subject as a percentage of total presentations.)

However, there were changes in the distribution of subjects across candidates, with subject choice in 1996 being more evenly spread across curricular modes. Among the candidates who took eight subjects in 1996, all took English and Mathematics, and all but a handful took a language, one or two sciences, and a social subject. Almost 90% took at least one subject from the technological mode, and almost 60% at least one subject from the creative and aesthetic mode. The most common choice of eight Standard Grade subjects (although chosen by less than 1% of the eight Standard Grade group) was English, Mathematics, French, Physics, Chemistry, Geography, Computing Studies, and Art & Design. Most candidates who took seven Standard Grades chose English, Mathematics, a language, a social subject and one or two sciences. They were less likely to take a subject from the technological mode (74%) or the creative and aesthetic mode (39%).

In 1987, subject choice was more restricted, and related to the number of subjects taken. The existence of Arithmetic as a separate subject from Mathematics contributed to this. Over 6 per cent of the candidates taking seven Ordinary Grades chose English, Arithmetic, Mathematics, French, Physics, Chemistry and Geography. Subjects from the technological mode were more common amongst candidates taking fewer Ordinary Grades.

DIVERSITY IN ASSESSMENT INSTRUMENTS

Standard Grade represented a change in assessment technique because assessments were made against grade related criteria. But it also introduced more diverse methods of assessment to a wide range of subjects. All of the social subjects had investigations. There was a strong resolve that these should not be 'projects' along the lines of 'write all you can find about . . .'. The criteria therefore required the identification of an issue which was to be investigated according to a plan and the report was to come to a conclusion. Schools were generally successful in inculcating these skills in candidates and between 1992 and 1996 the mean grade in the Investigating elements improved from 3.7 to 3.3 in Geography, 3.7 to 3.2 in History and 3.8 to 3.4 Modern Studies. Concerns regarding teacher and candidate workload, the authenticity of candidate work and the effectiveness of the investigation as a pedagogy led to the discontinuation of the element from 1999.

The assessment for certification of Practical Abilities was introduced by Standard Grade. Unlike the Investigating element in the social subjects, which was challenging to most candidates, the assessment criteria and practical techniques in this element proved easier to satisfy. The mean grades across the sciences for the Practical Abilities element in 1992 was 2.1 and in 1996 was 1.7. In one sense it was pleasing that so many candidates met the criteria, but the corollary was that the more able were not being challenged. In order to address this, and to bring greater uniformity to the approaches across the sciences, the assessment criteria for investigations were revised which should make them more demanding.

FINDINGS FROM HIGHER GRADE EXAMINATION PERFORMANCE IN THE FIFTH YEAR (S5)

Higher Grade performance among S5 candidates is easier to analyse in that while nearly all of the Higher Grade syllabuses which existed in 1987 had been replaced by 1996 in order to ensure articulation with Standard Grade, the form of the examination remained largely the same. It is therefore easier to compare performance across the decade. On the other hand, S4 throughout the period was the last year of compulsory schooling thus ensuring all the cohort was in school, whereas the voluntary staying-on rate in S5, excluding Christmas leavers, increased from 48 per cent in 1987 to 67 per cent in 1996. This complicates the analysis and can lead the unwary to make erroneous statements.

This feature can be seen in Table 86.3, which describes the changes in the percentages of S5 pupils attempting and passing Higher Grade examinations in 1987 and 1996. Although the percentage of the S5 cohort who attempted at least one subject at Higher Grade fell over the period from 85% to 77%, when expressed relative to the previous year's S4 figures, the percentage increased from 42% to 52%. The explanation for this is that the staying-on rate increased, and some but not all of the additional pupils took Highers. A similar pattern is apparent for the percentages who passed at least one subject at Higher Grade, and to a lesser extent for the percentages who passed at least three subjects.

Table 86.3 Higher Grade presentations and passes, 1987 and 1996

S5 candidates	as % of S5 cohort		as % of age group	
	1987	1996	1987	1996
Total				
attempted 1+ Higher	85%	77%	42%	52%
passed 1+ Higher	67%	61%	33%	41%
passed 3+ Highers	35%	33%	17%	22%
Males				
attempted 1+ Higher	84%	75%	38%	47%
passed 1+ Higher	65%	58%	29%	36%
passed 3+ Highers	35%	31%	16%	19%
Females				
attempted 1+ Higher	85%	78%	46%	57%
passed 1+ Higher	68%	64%	36%	47%
passed 3+ Highers	34%	35%	18%	26%

The table also gives these percentages separately for male and female pupils. The girls' staying-on rate remained higher than boys', and a higher percentage of girls (by any measure) took Higher Grades in both years. The gap between girls and boys widened over the period: for example, in 1987 the percentage of girls who passed three or more Highers was two percentage points higher than the boys, but by 1996 the difference had risen to seven percentage points.

Table 86.4 shows the uptake of subjects in 1987 and 1996 in terms of presentations per 100 S5 students and per 100 S4 pupils in the previous year. Note that in languages other than English, S5 presentations fell from 20 per 100 pupils to 15, but in terms of the age cohort the presentations in a language other than English remained constant at 10. The position has therefore not deteriorated; it simply has not got any better. The languages did not benefit from the fact that the cohort in 1996 was taking more Highers than in 1987, while all other groupings did. The real challenge to the linguists is that while, as mentioned above, the proportion of the cohort studying a language to S4 increased dramatically, most of the 'new recruits' appeared to have dropped the subject as soon as they could.

Between 1987 and 1996, eight new Higher Grade subjects were introduced: Human Biology, Classical Studies, Computing Studies, Graphic Communication, Management and Information Studies, Technological Studies, Drama and Physical Education. More students were taking Highers, and they had a wider range of subjects available to them. Mathematics and the sciences retained their market share, but many other 'traditional' subjects lost market share to the new subjects in the technological and creative curricular modes and Physical Education. (This pattern is even more pronounced in S6.)

The curricular breadth observed at Standard Grade does not follow through to students' choices at Higher Grade. As the SCCC report observes, 'At the S5/S6 stages most young people will be pursuing studies of a fairly specialised nature related to future employment or higher academic aspirations'. A recent Research Bulletin from the Scottish Examination Board described the subject combinations chosen by S5 pupils, exploring the relationships among ability, pass rates, numbers of Highers taken, and subject choice. Some subjects (e.g. Mathematics) tended to be taken by the more able students, some (e.g. Physical Education) by those with very specific abilities, and some (e.g. Geography and History) by a wide range of candidates.

Table 86.4   Uptake of Higher Grade subjects (grouped) Presentation rates, S5 candidates, 1987 and 1996

Market share	per 100 S5 pupils		per 100 S4 pupils	
	1987	1996	1987	1996
English	69	54	34	36
Other languages	20	15	10	10
Mathematics	37	33	18	22
Other mathematical subjects	5	4	2	2
Science subjects	67	60	33	40
Social subjects and religious studies	43	35	21	23
Technological subjects	23	24	11	16
Creative & Aesthetic subjects and Physical Education	14	20	7	13
All subjects	278	243	136	163

GENDER DIFFERENCES IN UPTAKE AND ATTAINMENT

There were gender differences in subject choice at Ordinary/Standard Grade with similar patterns continuing throughout the ten years from 1987 to 1996. The largest changes were in the modern languages, where in 1987 around two thirds of candidates presented were girls, but uptake by boys increased until by 1996 almost half of candidates presented were boys. In the science subjects, boys were under-represented in Biology and girls in Physics, whereas Chemistry achieved a fairly even gender balance. The greatest gender differences in uptake were found in the technological mode, with boys under-represented in Home Economics and Office and Information Studies, and girls under-represented in Computing Studies and the technical subjects.

In 1987, the average grades obtained at Ordinary Grade by boys and girls were very similar. However by 1996, girls achieved 0.32 of a grade better than boys in their all-subject average for Standard Grade. Over a typical presentation of seven or eight subjects, this equated to girls getting one grade better than boys in two or three of their subjects. At Standard Grade, gender differences tended to be greater in the elements which involved coursework or project work, for example in the Investigating element in the social subjects, or the Writing element in English, which require planning and sustained work to complete a written submission. Table 86.5 shows these gender differences for selected large presentation subjects for Ordinary Grade in 1987 and Standard Grade in 1996.

At Higher Grade, the uptake patterns observed at Ordinary and Standard Grade became slightly more pronounced, as there was more choice and specialisation. Thus even where similar numbers of boys and girls took a particular subject, it was not necessarily the case that they were of similar general ability. In 1987 there was no significant difference in the

Table 86.5 Uptake and attainment by gender at Ordinary Grade and Standard Grade Selected subjects, S4 candidates, 1987 and 1996

	% presentations female		mean grade difference	
	1987	1996	1987	1996
English	53%	49%	+0.24	+0.42
French	65%	52%	+0.11	+0.65
Arithmetic	51%	n/a	−0.12	n/a
Mathematics	50%	49%	−0.11	+0.10
Biology	67%	70%	−	+0.10
Chemistry	46%	50%	−0.01	+0.10
Physics	30%	33%	+0.17	+0.27
Geography	40%	42%	+0.06	+0.32
History	55%	54%	+0.09	+0.41
Computing Studies	31%	35%	−0.27	+0.28
Office & Info Studies/Secretarial Studies	96%	83%	+0.33	+0.57
Art & Design	55%	57%	+0.29	+0.43
All subjects	52%	50%	+0.02	+0.32

A positive grade difference means that the female candidates in that subject obtained better grades on average than the males, a negative grade difference that the male candidates did better, and a dash (-) that there was no significant difference.

pass rates of boys and girls averaged over all subjects, but by 1996 the girls' all-subject pass rate was four percentage points higher than the boys. Table 86.6 shows these Higher Grade gender differences for selected large presentation subjects. A more detailed (unpublished) analysis of the component tasks involved in Higher Grade examinations suggested that boys did better on tasks which provided them with data with which to interact or interpret;

Table 86.6 Uptake and attainment by gender at Higher Grade Selected subjects, S5 candidates, 1987 and 1996

	% presentations female		difference in pass rates	
	1987	1996	1987	1996
English	58%	58%	−	+3%
French	76%	76%	−	−
Mathematics	46%	49%	−	+4%
Biology	70%	71%	−9%	−
Chemistry	43%	48%	−4%	−
Physics	29%	31%	+7%	+9%
Geography	41%	43%	+5%	+7%
History	56%	59%	−	+3%
Modern Studies	52%	63%	+4%	+5%
Art & Design	64%	63%	+12%	+9%
All subjects	54%	54%	−	+4%

A positive difference in pass rates means that the female candidates in that subject had a higher pass rate on average than the males, a negative difference that the male candidates did better, and a dash (-) that there was no significant difference.

required factual responses, particularly short responses; or required a live performance. Girls, on the other hand, did better on tasks which required a personal response to a text; required an extended response; required analytical or investigative approaches; required concentrated listening skills; involved the production of a folio of work and thus sustained classwork over a considerable period of time; or required presentational skills.

STANDARDS AND PASS-RATES

Few topics in education have generated as much interest in recent years as that of the maintenance or otherwise of standards. It is a core responsibility of any examining or awarding body that it maintains standards within a subject from year to year and between subjects. SEB and now the Scottish Qualifications Authority achieves this in a number of ways. Firstly, the assessment instruments, mainly question papers, must be comparable in demand to those of previous years. This is promoted by appointing experienced teachers to set question papers under the guidance of a Principal Examiner. Training is also provided for all new setters. The papers must sample the content and skills of the course in a systematic way, the language used should be accessible to candidates and the questions should be unambiguous and clear in their intent. There should be no gender bias or bias towards a particular cultural group unless justified by the content of the course. (Two areas where some cultural focusing is justifiable is in Scottish history and literature.) Each question paper is checked many times before being sent to the printers to ensure that candidates will be faced with an appropriate challenge. The checking is carried out by the setters and Principal Examiner, by question paper moderation teams drawn from the members of Subject Panels and by SEB/SQA development and question paper staff.

Secondly, the marking must be of high quality and again the markers are drawn from experienced teachers of the subject. All markers must attend a markers' meeting where trial marking takes place and the marking instructions are discussed and finalised. Following the day of each examination, all scripts are sent from the examination centres to Dalkeith where they are 'turned-round' within twenty-four hours and sent out to the markers who have three weeks to complete their allocation of marking. The allocation is carried out on a random sampling basis. This makes it most unlikely that a marker will receive only packets from high-achieving or low-achieving schools. Random allocation of packets of scripts to markers allows a computerised check to be made of each marker's mean and standard deviation against the national statistics. A sample of each marker's work is scrutinised by a member of the examining team. At Higher Grade, should the Examiner conclude that the marker has been consistently severe or lenient, he or she will recommend that a 'standardising factor' be applied. This is the factor which, if applied to the raw mark of each candidate whose script was in the marker's sample, will pull the marking into line with the national average. A similar recommendation is produced by the computer on the basis of a scrutiny of the marker's mean mark compared to the national mean. The Principal Examiner, armed with these two recommendations, comes to a final judgement as to the corrective mark to be applied. At Standard Grade, the computer identifies those scripts for which re-marking by an Examiner is most likely to be effective in terms of quality assurance of marking. For example, a script with a mark just below a grade interface, marked by a 'severe' marker, and where the centre estimates attainment of a better grade by the candidate would be a high priority for re-marking.

Lastly, there is the determination of cut-offs at Standard Grade and pass marks at Higher

Grade. These decisions are taken for each examination at a meeting attended by senior SQA staff and the Principal Examiner. The meetings are chaired by either the Chief Executive, in his capacity as Chief Examiner, or the Director with responsibility for assessment. The Principal Examiner brings a detailed knowledge of how the question paper has operated and how the candidates have performed, based on his or her own marking and the reports from all of the marking team. The meeting is also informed by a range of statistics relating to the current examination and historical information relating to the previous two or three years. These statistics include the previous years' pass marks, pass rates, standard deviation, means and so on. Where there is a directly graded component such as an Investigation or a Performance in Physical Education or Music, whether it be internally or externally assessed, a comparison of the mean performance of the candidates in relation to previous years is especially useful because the assessment instrument does not vary from year to year. Nor should the standard of marking vary as the assessment criteria and marking scheme remains unaltered. Thus a change in the mean in these components can with some certainty be attributed to a change in candidate performance.

In 1976 the SEB funded work by Alison Kelly which allowed the relative difficulty of subjects to be measured by means of an iterative subject-pairs analysis. This is a sophisticated tool, which, for example, takes account of the tendency of candidates to attempt groups of slightly more 'difficult', or slightly 'easier', subjects. It should be emphasised that the variation between subjects is small, and also that the model assumes a *latent trait*, i.e. that all subjects test the same attribute. Clearly, when one considers, for example, Mathematics, Craft and Design, Music, German and Art and Design one has to accept that the concept of a single trait is somewhat stretched. Nonetheless, these 'National Ratings' have made a useful contribution to the maintenance of standards and have in recent years been used by SOEID's Audit Unit. All of this information is brought to bear on the pass mark decision, the making of which is both an art and a science.

In the early 1980s in Scotland a great debate ensued on the contrast between norm- and criterion-referenced examining. Contrary to some claims made at the time, pass marks in Scotland have never been norm-referenced, i.e. a fixed quota passed each year no matter how well or badly the candidates performed. Pass marks were, in the past, determined according to implicit rather than explicit criteria. Due to the uniformity in the Scottish teaching force, teachers, markers and examiners all shared an understanding of the standard required for a 'pass'. With the advent of Standard Grade, criteria were set according to norms of attainment – there would be no point in assessing against a criterion outwith the reach of even the most able 15-year-old. But having set the criteria in the light of norms, the criteria then became the standard. Thus Standard Grade is assessed against grade related criteria and at Higher Grade there are grade descriptions. These criteria underpin the setting process and are used directly for assessment in a range of examination components such as Writing, Investigations and Performances. From time to time a check is carried out of candidate scripts against the criteria to ensure that the grades awarded are in line with the evidence of candidate attainment.

Another aspect of maintaining standards is ensuring that individual candidates (and they are all individuals) receive credit for their own achievement. The increase in non-examination-room assessment, which is to be welcomed for reasons of validity, does require careful monitoring to ensure authenticity. Where work is done at home, it is perfectly acceptable for parents or private tutors to give advice, but clearly the work must be the candidate's own. Presenting centres are therefore required to ensure that sufficient of the work is done under direct supervision to allow the teacher responsible to sign a declaration that the work is to the best of their knowledge the candidate's own. Each year there are a small number of cases in which there are grounds to believe that work submitted is not wholly the work of the candidate and these cases are investigated in partnership with the presenting centre.

The examination system has much to commend it in terms of maintaining standards. The assessment instrument is devised nationally by some of the ablest and most experienced teachers in the field; it is produced to a high quality and it is confidential, presenting an even playing field for all candidates. The examination is invigilated by personnel employed by SEB/SQA thus ensuring it is administered under uniform conditions. Nonetheless, the examination hall does not suit all candidates and all of us can have 'off-days'.

SEB/SQA operates a number of procedures to assist candidates who, in the view of the presenting centre, failed to demonstrate their true attainment in the examination. During the processing of results, the computer compares each centre's estimates of its candidates' performance in a subject with the examination results. Where agreement is good, the centre is deemed concordant and any candidate who has performed below estimate will have their result improved to at least the estimate grade. Even where the agreement between centre estimates and results is good for only parts of the grade scale, some improvement may be possible. This automatic procedure replaced a system whereby centres had to specifically request 'adverse circumstances consideration'. Candidates who are absent for legitimate reasons will be given an award based on the same procedure, but the automatic procedure is supplemented if necessary by Examiner consideration of coursework evidence. Following the issue of results, if, despite the automatic procedure, a centre feels a candidate has not received the award due to them, then it can submit an appeal supported by course work evidence. Each year, some 27,000 appeals are submitted for Standard Grade elements and 19,000 for Higher Grade.

There has been some controversy in the Scottish press with regard to standards although to an extent it is derivative from the more heated debates in England. The position in Scotland has been fairly stable. For example, the Higher Grade pass rate rose from 66.6% in 1987 to 69.2% in 1996, or 2.6%. The GCE Advanced Level pass rate rose from 73% in 1987 to 86% in 1996. Over the decade, the number of Highers taken in S5 calculated in relation to the previous year's S4 cohort increased from 1.4 to 1.6. In the cohort of 17-year-olds therefore the average number of Highers taken steadily increased. The increase was in part due to the rise in the staying-on rate, and one might have expected pass rates to fall as more 'marginal' Higher candidates attempted the examination. This is indeed what happened to the Ordinary Grade when the school leaving age was raised in the early 1970s. That the pass rate rose can be attributed to better teaching and to greater motivation amongst candidates, including the most able, as competition for many courses in Higher Education and employment increased.

While the National Ratings referred to above are useful in comparing standards between subjects they have the drawback of being relative rather than absolute. If all examinations were to get easier in a given year (an unlikely occurrence) then this would not show up in the National Ratings. To carry out an absolute check on standards, it is necessary to study the Arrangements documents, question papers, marking instructions, pass marks and candidate scripts over a period of years. Such an exercise was carried out by the Scottish Council for Research in Education on behalf of SOEID. Standards in four subjects were compared (English, Mathematics, Biology and Geography) over four years: 1986, 1987, 1993 and

1994. The researchers reported that 'there are no grounds for believing that there has been any change in the standards of performance required to obtain any given band of award in the Higher Grade examinations which formed part of the study.' Given the weight placed on individual candidate's examination performance, and the use of examination statistics in measuring the performance of the education system, this was a useful confirmation of the successful maintenance of standards.

REFERENCES

SEB (1995) *Research Bulletin 3 – Gender and SCE examinations*, Dalkeith: SEB.

SEB (1997) *Research Bulletin 7 – Subject choice at Higher Grade: presentations and successes*, Dalkeith: SEB.

SOEID (1997) *Statistical Bulletin, Education Series: The Curriculum in Publicly Funded Secondary Schools in Scotland 1991–1995*, Edinburgh: SOEID.

SCCC (1989) *Curriculum Design for the Secondary Stages – Guidelines for Headteachers*, Dundee: Scottish Consultative Council on the Curriculum.

Devine, M., J. Hall, J. Mapp and K. Musselbrook (1996) *Maintaining Standards: Performance at Higher Grade in Biology, English, Geography & Mathematics*, Edinburgh: Scottish Council for Research in Education.

Kelly, A. (1976) *The Comparability of Examining Standards in Scottish Certificate of Education Ordinary and Higher Grade Examinations*, Dalkeith: Scottish Certificate of Education Examination Board.

87

SCOTVEC Findings on Scottish Achievements

Dennis Gunning

BACKGROUND

The Scottish Vocational Education Council (SCOTVEC) began building its qualifications system on the principles defined in the government's 'Action Plan' published in 1983. The Action Plan envisaged a new approach to vocational education in which qualifications were built of modules, each of which was based on standards of performance defined in advance and publicly available.

During its twelve year existence, SCOTVEC extended the Action Plan philosophy to embrace all its qualifications. (SCOTVEC also continued to run qualifications which had been inherited from its predecessor bodies; these qualifications, which have been gradually phased out, are not included in the data described in this chapter.) The result of regular review by SCOTVEC and of a range of government initiatives has been the development of a framework consisting of three types of modular building-blocks: National Certificate modules; Higher National units and Workplace Assessed units. Further details of the development of SCOTVEC qualifications, and the context in which that development took place, are provided in Chapter 81.

The framework of qualifications made up of these three types of building-blocks had a very significant impact on the Scottish education and training scene in a number of ways. This chapter looks at Scottish achievements in three distinct contexts:

- the range of qualifications available;
- the range of centres (schools; further education (FE) colleges; higher education (HE) institutions such as universities; training organisations; employers) and the qualifications they offer;
- the achievements of individual candidates (pupils, students, trainees and employees).

The following sections look at Scottish achievement in each of these three contexts. The final section then considers issues which arise from the impact of SCOTVEC and its system on Scottish education. Data quoted in the text refers to the position at Summer 1997, unless otherwise stated. Where a year is stated (for example, 1994/5), this refers to SCOTVEC's 'data collection year' – that is, the period between 1 August and 31 July. All data is taken from SCOTVEC internal statistical analyses and external publications such as Annual Reports, unless otherwise stated.

RANGE OF QUALIFICATIONS

This context represents achievement by the wide range of people who contribute to the development of vocational qualifications. SCOTVEC's partners, such as centre staff and individuals from employer organisations, professional/technician bodies, trade unions and individual employers, have contributed largely voluntary time and effort to support SCOTVEC and its staff in developing, reviewing and maintaining the range of vocational qualifications available.

National Certificate modules and group awards

Since 1984, when the first modules in key craft and operative areas were used, SCOTVEC, with the support of its partners, has managed a process of systematic review and extension of the National Certificate catalogue of modules. The expansion of the catalogue reflected the needs of candidates, centres and employers. The catalogue expanded from the first 700 modules in 1984 to a total of over 4,000 modules by 1997, with development of modules in new vocational areas, in more traditional subjects which underpin vocational studies, and in leisure pursuits. Further important developments included the generation of modules in core skills such as communication and numeracy and of modules for candidates with a range of special needs.

In the early years, no national group award programmes were developed using National Certificate modules, although many centres negotiated recognition agreements with employers in their area covering locally-agreed programmes of modules. Circumstances in the early 1990s led to development of such group awards, including

- small packages of three modules called 'Clusters', primarily for secondary school use – in ten subject areas such as European studies and information technology;
- forty 'National Awards' designed to provide underpinning cognitive and practical skills for specific areas of employment such as engineering and construction;
- forty-six General Scottish Vocational Qualifications (GSVQs), designed to provide a broad preparation for work in employment sectors such as care, hospitality and land-based industries. Other GSVQs, in science and in arts and social science, were based on the Scottish Wider Access Programme's groupings of modules which provided an alternative preparation for entry into higher education;
- Skillstart, Lifestart and Workstart programmes for individuals seeking entry to the employment market after a long absence and for those with special needs.

Higher National units modules and group awards

Higher National qualifications include the group awards Higher National Certificate (HNC) and Higher National Diploma (HND) and a range of post-graduate and post-diploma qualifications referred to generically by SCOTVEC as 'Professional Development Awards' (PDA).

HNCs and HNDs provide certification at technician and supervisory management level. At the time of SCOTVEC's establishment, the Higher National qualifications of its predecessor bodies were traditional qualifications based on syllabuses and making considerable use of external written examinations for assessment. Following a consultation in 1987, SCOTVEC and its centres embarked on a programme to convert Higher National qualifications into a unit-based system similar to National Certificate. (In this context, 'unit' is synonymous with 'module'.) The only major difference between the new Higher National units and National Certificate modules is that each of the former has two levels of performance criteria to allow certification at either 'pass' or 'merit' level.

The forerunner Higher National qualifications were largely clustered in the areas of business studies, science and technology. With the introduction of the new unit-based system, centres took the opportunity to develop wider portfolios of qualifications, including some in new vocational areas such as mechatronics and leisure management; in relevant combinations such as tourism with languages; and to create credit-transferred links to degree courses. In the forerunner system, there were around 800 Higher National college courses. With the expansion into new areas, and this coinciding with a drive in many FE colleges to increase the volume of business in higher-level qualifications, the first few years of the new Higher National system saw a considerable increase in the number of courses available. By 1997, the number had increased to almost 1,800 college courses and involved a catalogue of over 5,700 Higher National units; of these, around 900 were nationally-developed and the rest were developed by centres and validated by SCOTVEC with the involvement of staff of professional and technician bodies, other industry and employer bodies and trade unions. The achievement of these individuals and of centre staff can be measured by the increased responsiveness and flexibility of the new system, leading to a better match with Scotland's national training needs, and to very much greater levels of candidate uptake.

Workplace Assessed units and group awards

Most Workplace Assessed units have been designed as components of Scottish Vocational Qualifications (SVQs) or of SCOTVEC's range of Tailored Awards. The latter, as the name implies, are awards designed for a particular company or organisation; they do not carry national recognition.

In total, there are over 8,000 Workplace Assessed units available, of which around 1,300 are of the tailored variety. As well as SVQ and Tailored Award units, a number of other workplace units have been developed to underpin SVQs, including units defining the required level of competence for assessors and verifiers and units defining core skills, such as communication and numeracy, in a workplace context.

SVQs were first accredited by SCOTVEC in 1989. Since then, working with the industry lead bodies (and, latterly, the National Training Organisations) which set the standards on which SVQs are based, a total of 801 SVQ titles have been accredited, with over 1,260 distinct awarding arrangements. (Some SVQs are offered by more than one awarding body.) Of these, SCOTVEC is an awarding body, alone or in partnership, for just under 900 SVQs. All SVQs are accredited on one of five levels, reflecting the nature of the occupation concerned; for example, level 1 covers operative jobs and level 5 covers professional and managerial jobs.

CENTRES

The forerunner bodies, SCOTEC and SCOTBEC, dealt almost exclusively with FE colleges. The breadth of vocational qualifications developed by SCOTVEC meant that training organisations in the private sector and, especially for SVQs, employers also wished to use the qualifications. With the growing number of young people choosing to stay on at secondary school beyond the minimum leaving age, schools, too, began to offer SCOTVEC qualifications. The range of centres has now grown to over 1,300 and includes virtually every secondary school, all FE colleges, some universities, and many training organisations and employers.

Quality assurance

Centres have, over the lifetime of SCOTVEC, revolutionised the range and nature of the curriculum they offer in an attempt to meet client needs. SCOTVEC's system of internal assessment, with external quality checks, meant that centre staff had to take much greater responsibility for the assessment on which certification was based and centre management had to develop internal quality control systems to meet SCOTVEC's range of quality assurance criteria. SCOTVEC developed a quality assurance system by which to maintain consistency and accuracy of centres' assessment standards; this had two aspects.

First, a centre approval system ensured that new centres had the quality systems, staffing, resources and assessment material necessary to operate valid and reliable internal assessment. This process was carried out before the centre could enrol any candidates. Second, a system called external verification was set up; this was based on visits to centres by SCOTVEC-appointed external verifiers (usually seconded experienced staff from centres or employers) to check assessment standards before candidates were submitted for certification. In addition, SCOTVEC operated a third element of quality assurance called validation; this was the process by which proposals, for example from a centre, for the introduction of a new national qualification were evaluated.

The centre approval system proved demanding for prospective new centres. In SCOT-VEC's early years, relatively small numbers of centres sought approval each year – typically less than forty. Later, and especially since SVQs became available, the number of centres seeking initial approval has been steady at around 140 per year, of which around 80 per cent were successful and most others had approval withheld until certain conditions were met. Centres seeking to extend the range of qualifications they offer could apply for approval to do so; SCOTVEC processed around 1,200 such applications each year, of which just over 70 per cent were successful. Perhaps because of the demanding criteria for approval, successful centres generally then operated the assessment system to acceptable standards; relatively few visits to centres by external verifiers – usually around 7 per cent – led to the identification of unacceptable assessment standards.

Later, when centres had become used to the operation of the appropriate approaches to quality assurance, SCOTVEC introduced a system of quality auditing as a means of deciding whether centres, where they wished to, could take devolved responsibility for quality assurance and thereby operate the processes of approval, validation or verification on SCOTVEC's behalf. This devolution was seen as a means by which SCOTVEC could reward centres which had put very effective internal quality assurance systems in place. A five-year audit programme has led to a gradual increase in the extent of devolution, reflecting the degree to which centres have been prepared to develop and refine their internal quality systems and representing a considerable achievement on the part of successful centres.

National Certificate modules and group awards

The forerunner qualifications to National Certificate were almost exclusively offered in FE colleges. These colleges were also the first customers for the new National Certificate modules. However the breadth of the catalogue meant that training organisations in the private sector also sought access to the catalogue.

The increase in range and type of centres offering National Certificate modules, and the scale of their candidate activity, is shown in Table 87.1. The data in this table clearly show the considerable growth in involvement of centres other than colleges. In the early years of National Certificate, schools contributed less than 20% of the candidate registrations and around 5% of the module enrolments; by 1997, these had grown to just over 50% and 35% respectively.

Overall, the data shows the very rapid increase in candidate and enrolment numbers from the introduction of National Certificate in 1984/5 until around 1989. The rise in FE colleges represented a product substitution, with National Certificate modules replacing the previous non-advanced qualifications of SCOTEC, SCOTBEC, City and Guilds and others. Relatively speaking, the FE non-advanced market has remained stable; SOEID statistics show, for example, that there were around 100,000 new entrants to non-advanced FE courses in 1969/70; candidate registrations from FE for National Certificate in the period 1988 to 1992 ran at around 100,000 per year. More recently, there is some evidence of a new product substitution in FE colleges, with the decline in National Certificate uptake being balanced by an increase in Higher National and SVQ uptake.

The striking increase in total numbers of candidates and enrolments, compared to the previous non-advanced provision, was due particularly to uptake in secondary schools; schools had made virtually no use of the previous non-advanced vocational qualifications. However, despite the considerable growth in the number of National Certificate candidates from schools, to the point where numbers of candidates in schools exceeded those in FE colleges, the number of modules for which each candidate enrols each year remained higher in FE colleges (around 7.5 modules) than in schools (around 3.5 modules). This is because the curricular use in the two sectors is very different. In schools, modules in general provide supplements to the main menu of Scottish Certificate of Education courses; in colleges, by contrast, the modules provide the mainstream curriculum for those students preparing for craft or operative employment.

As Chapter 81 describes, national programmes of National Certificate modules were developed by SCOTVEC in response to government initiatives and to centre needs. Many of these will eventually be replaced by group awards featured in the Higher Still Development Programme. The uptake of these group awards is shown in Table 87.2.

Higher National units and group awards

Higher National units and group awards have traditionally been offered in FE colleges and in universities; this has continued into the 1990s, with only a couple of exceptions, where new qualifications have been designed for use directly by employers. Although the range of centres using Higher National qualifications had not changed markedly since the 1980s, the balance of uptake shifted. In the 1980s, the ratio of candidates from FE colleges to candidates from universities was around 2:1; by 1997, this had changed to over 20:1. The universities using HNCs and HNDs were mostly those which had been granted university

Table 87.1 Uptake – National Certificate Modules

Year	Schools Centres	Cands[a]	Enrols[b]	FE Centres	Cands[a]	Enrols[b]	Others Centres	Cands[a]	Enrols[b]	All Centres	Cands[a]	Enrols[b]
1996/7[c]	453	118421	414464	43	90371	665335	376	18604	69626	872	227396	1149425
1995/6	459	124242	420456	44	88259	673673	363	21078	76113	866	233579	1170242
1994/5	460	122994	408546	43	85210	682805	340	20141	74319	843	228345	1165670
1993/4	454	119637	388061	46	83774	689983	324	19795	70957	824	223206	1149001
1992/3	458	113458	355887	45	91756	763645	320	19873	71889	823	225087	1191421
1991/2	467	111958	330713	48	99169	811447	285	18180	64210	800	229307	1206370
1990/1	465	106209	295120	48	104044	744587	281	18620	64404	794	228873	1104111
1989/90	453	95423	261648	46	116801	830911	232	17791	62398	731	230015	1154957
1988/9	438	72260	187644	47	103330	765724	188	12959	52161	673	188549	1005529
1987/8[d]	–	43000	93000	–	107000	791000	–	4500	16000	–	154500	900000
1986/7[d]	–	17000	40000	–	86000	777000	–	2600	9000	–	105600	826000
1985/6[d]	–	12500	29000	–	67500	624000	–	1500	4000	–	81500	657000
1984/5[d]	–	9400	22000	–	41000	359000	–	100	300	–	50500	381300

[a] 'cands' = number of candidates enrolling for one or more module in the year shown
[b] 'enrols' = number of modules for which the candidates enrolled in the year shown
[c] provisional data at October 1997
[d] The method of data collection changed in 1988. The data for the period 1985–8 has been estimated using the 1989–97 method, to allow for comparison over the full period
[e] 'Other centres' includes community/adult education, HM Prisons, private training organisations, armed forces and all centres outside Scotland

Table 87.2   Uptake – National Certificate Group Awards

Year	GSVQ Enrols[a]	GSVQ % Schools[b]	GSVQ % FE[b]	Clusters Enrols	Clusters % School	Clusters % FE	Skillstart Enrols	Skillstart % Schools	Skillstart % FE
1996/7	6371	5	94	5655	86	10	1261	36	41
1995/6	5414	8	90	4647	88	7	1129	25	52
1994/5	4696	9	90	2806	98	1	832	15	54
1993/4	3946	11	89	1977	93	5	1023	23	35
1992/3	1546	9	91	67	99	0	374	57	8

[a] 'enrols' = number of candidates enrolling for the group award in the year shown. Where a candidate takes more than a year to achieve the award, this table includes such candidates only in the year of enrolment
[b] percentage uptake for centres other than FE and Schools is not shown

status in 1991; their candidate uptake for HNCs and HNDs has fallen slowly as these institutions concentrated more on degree-level work. By contrast, uptake in FE colleges increased markedly, reflecting a general intention in the FE sector to engage in more work of higher education level. The balance of uptake is shown in Table 87.3 for Higher National group awards.

Table 87.3   Uptake – Higher National Group Awards

Year	HNC Enrols[a]	HNC % FE[b]	HNC % HE[b]	HND Enrols	HND % FE	HND % HE	PDA Enrols	PDA % FE	PDA % HE
1996/7	18619	94	1	12148	88	9	1664	95	0
1995/6	17236	95	1	11854	86	11	1562	96	0
1994/5	17588	95	2	11995	84	13	1369	94	2
1993/4	15752	96	2	10521	82	15	1306	89	2
1992/3	12885	93	5	8770	67	28	630	82	10
1991/2[c]	8981	92	6	6392	69	26	193	68	28
1990/1[c]	3101	82	17	3764	56	42	200	62	34

[a] Definition as in Table 87.2
[b] Percentage uptake for centres other than FE and HE not shown
[c] In 1990/1 and 1991/2, significant numbers of candidates enrolled for the traditional (i.e. non-modular) Higher National qualifications. The transition programme to convert Higher National qualifications into the modular system was incomplete in these years

Overall, there has been a very considerable increase in activity in Higher National qualifications since the 1980s. Typically, then, there were around 17,000 active candidates each year (i.e. candidates in either the first or subsequent years of a course). By 1996/7, the number of active candidates had risen to 55,000. The growth in uptake has been especially marked since the modularisation of Higher National qualifications completed in the early 1990s; for example, the number of enrolments for Higher National units, most of which will be as parts of group awards, has grown from 155,000 in 1991/2 to 380,000 in 1996/7. Some of the growth probably reflects a change in FE towards promotion of Higher National rather than National Certificate awards – but it also reflects success in the campaign to widen access for adults into higher education awards. There was a pause in growth of FE college uptake in the mid-1990s because of a government limit being placed on full-time higher education student numbers and funds. This particularly affected candidate numbers for HND in FE colleges but candidate numbers for HNCs, which are often taken by part-time candidates, continued to increase.

Unlike National Certificate, where national group awards were introduced relatively recently and where uptake is relatively small in comparison to uptake for individual modules, Higher National provision has always been focused mainly on group awards because these carried recognition by professional and technician bodies and, for credit transfer, by higher education institutions. Although individual Higher National units can be studied separately, uptake for free-standing units is small in comparison to that for group awards.

Workplace Assessed units and group awards

As the name of the qualifications implies, these are designed to be assessed in the conditions of the workplace. In comparison to National Certificate and Higher National qualifications, a higher proportion of training organisations and employers are involved in the use of Workplace Assessed qualifications. However FE colleges are also major users, in two main contexts. First, there are employment areas where FE colleges have traditionally offered highly realistic simulated workplaces, for example in hospitality and in hairdressing. Second, colleges have marketed their services to employers on outreach, thus providing services such as assessment in employers' own workplaces.

Since the introduction of SVQs in 1989, the balance in uptake between FE colleges and training organisations and employers has remained fairly constant and fairly equal, although both types of centre have, since then, seen a substantial increase in uptake. Table 87.4 shows the uptake in workplace assessed qualifications.

Table 87.4 Uptake – Workplace Assessed Group Awards

Year	Enrols[a]	SVQ % FE	% Others[b]	Enrols	Tailored % FE	% Others
1996/7	31497	44	56	3283	26	55
1995/6	29669	43	57	2341	38	46
1994/5	21731	50	50	2280	17	45
1993/4	17397	52	47	1259	20	62
1992/3	13588	54	44	1466	10	88
1991/2	5464	43	56	1628	2	98
1990/1	705	82	18	537	0	100

[a] Definition as in Table 87.2
[b] 'Others' includes private training organisations and employers. Community education centres and schools are not shown

CANDIDATES

Success by candidates in achieving a SCOTVEC qualification represents the end-point of the work of qualifications developers and centres described above. The scale of uptake of vocational qualifications, the characteristics of candidates, the changing nature of uptake in individual qualifications and success rates are described. Overall, since SCOTVEC began certification in 1985, a total of 1.33 million candidates had achieved one or more module, unit or group award by 1996/7. This represents roughly 25 per cent of the Scottish population.

National Certificate modules and group awards

The range of candidates for National Certificate modules has expanded, both in number and in nature. The age profile of candidates has broadened as the range of centres using the modules increased. The greatest increase in uptake within age bands has been for school-age candidates and for those over the age of twenty-five. As far as uptake of individual modules is concerned, there has been a shift in those with the biggest uptake. Previously, the biggest uptake was for modules covering topics such as introductory computing and word processing; more recently, the most popular modules have been Work Experience 1 and Communication 3. The strength of uptake of the module Work Experience 1 reflected the move in secondary schools to incorporate work experience into the curriculum for all pupils; the module provided a framework for pupils to plan and evaluate the work experience and receive credit and certification for having done so successfully. The strength of uptake for Communication 3 reflects the importance of this core skill across all types of centre; it also reflects the recognition which SCOTVEC negotiated for this module as an alternative to Standard Grade English for the general entry requirements of Scottish higher education institutions.

The specification for a National Certificate module contains a number of learning outcomes, usually around four, each of which has an associated set of performance criteria. Centres provide SCOTVEC with three possible results for each candidate and each module; complete success (all learning outcomes achieved – module certificated); partial success (some but not all learning outcomes achieved); withdrawn (either no learning outcomes achieved or candidate fails to take the required assessments). The success rate of candidates for individual National Certificate modules is very stable over time; 68% of modules are achieved successfully, 12% with partial success and 20% withdrawn. Over the five years between 1993 and 1997, the success rate has varied by only 2%, between 67% and 69%. Overall, since the first certification of National Certificate in 1985, a total of 1.22 million candidates had achieved one or more modules by 1996/7.

The success rate in group awards composed of National Certificate modules is more difficult to define because the necessary combination of modules can be accumulated without limit of time. Table 87.5 shows the number of candidates achieving group awards over time and describes the methodology developed by SCOTVEC to calculate success rates for outcome-based group awards.

Higher National units, modules and group awards

Some candidates enrol for HNCs and HNDs end-on from school or from National Certificate courses; others return to study following a period of work. Traditionally, HND courses were taken mainly by full-time candidates and HNC by part-time candidates but this distinction has become less clear as numbers of candidates for Higher National provision has increased. The biggest uptake for HNCs and HNDs have been in business-related areas and in computing; these were high uptake areas in the traditional Higher National system and have maintained their popularity; other areas have declined in popularity, such as electronic and electrical engineering, and new areas such as in the care sector have markedly increased in uptake.

Table 87.5 Success Rates[a] – National Certificate Group Awards

Year	GSVQ 1 year[b]	2 year	3 year	Other National Awards 1 year	2 year	3 year
1997[d]	57	46	37	78	67	57
1996	68	54	44	77	62	55
1995	62	50	48	76	67	62
1994	59	59	–	83	76	73
1993	74[c]	–	–	75	70	70

[a] Success rates are calculated cumulatively. Thus 37% of candidates who had enrolled for all necessary components of a GSVQ were certificated in 1996/7 and had enrolled for the GSVQ within the previous one, two or three years

[b] These are the number of years between the time of achieving the group award and the time of enrolling for the group award

[c] All figures are percentages rounded to the nearest whole number

[d] 1997 data is provisional at October 1997

The system of results for Higher National units is slightly different from that described above for National Certificate modules. First, centres are not expected to notify SCOTVEC of partially-completed units; second, successful completion of the Higher National unit can be at pass or merit level. The success rate of candidates for individual Higher National units is very stable over time. Over the six years between 1992 and 1997, the pass level success rate has varied by only 3%, between 59% and 62%; the merit level success rate is also very stable, varying over the same period by 1%, between 15% and 16%. Overall, since the first certification of modular Higher National qualifications in 1988, a total of 150,000 candidates had achieved one or more Higher National units by 1996/7.

Success rates in Higher National group awards are shown in Table 86.6, calculated on a similar basis to National Certificate group awards. Given that the traditional HNC/D system was based mainly on accumulation of successes in external assessment (often written examinations), only very broad comparisons between the success rates of the two systems can be made because the methods of computing success rates are different. The traditional HNC and HND awards had success rates of typically around 65 per cent. The data in Table 87.6 suggests, albeit in very broad terms, that the introduction of the new system of Higher National awards did not lead to any gross effect on success rates.

Workplace Assessed units and group awards

The majority of candidates for Workplace Assessed provision enrol for complete group awards, predominately SVQs. These may be completed by enrolment at a training organisation or FE college, where assessment is in a simulated work environment, or by assessment carried out in the workplace directly. Taking uptake for all SVQs, including those which are run by awarding bodies other than SCOTVEC, the biggest uptake areas are in administration, engineering foundation and direct care; all of the ten highest uptake SVQs are at level 2 in the SVQ framework.

The system of results for Workplace Assessed provision is similar to that for Higher National units in that centres are not expected to notify SCOTVEC of partially-completed units. Unlike Higher National units, Workplace Assessed units are certificated only at pass level. The success rate for Workplace Assessed units is just over 80 per cent; data has not

Table 87.6   Success Rates[a] – Higher National Group Awards

| Year | HNC | | | HND | | | PDA | | |
	1 year[b]	2 year	3 year	1 year	2 year	3 year	1 year	2 year	3 year
1996/7[d]	66	59	52	71	65	56	74	68	60
1995/6	70	63	55	72	67	59	81	70	62
1994/5	63	60	54	68	64	59	72	63	59
1993/4	68	63	58	73	68	63	75	69	68
1992/3	69	65	62	74	76	70	76	71	69
1991/2	69	65	64	80	74	72	77	61	61

[a] Success rates are calculated cumulatively. Thus 52% of candidates who had enrolled for all necessary components of an HNC were certificated in 1996/7 and had enrolled for the HNC within the previous one, two or three years.
[b] These are the number of years between the time of achieving the group award and the time of enrolling for the group award
[c] All figures are percentages rounded to the nearest whole number
[d] 1997 data is provisional at October 1997

been available for a sufficiently long time to comment on trends. Overall, since the first certification of Workplace Assessed provision in 1990, a total of 75,000 candidates had achieved one or more units by 1996/7.

Success rates in Workplace Assessed group awards, calculated on a similar basis to National Certificate group awards, seem to be settling to a steady pattern, with around 65 per cent of candidates being successful in an SVQ in one year. However, one noticeable feature of the success rates is the extended time over which many candidates complete an SVQ; this may be because part-time study is involved along with workplace assessment or it may be because assessment in the workplace has to be fitted in around normal working priorities and schedules. The latter factor was found to apply internally within SCOTVEC in the case of those of its own employees who are pursuing an SVQ.

ISSUES

Increased access and uptake

One of the strongest features of SCOTVEC's qualifications has been the steady increase in uptake of each of the types of qualification introduced. To take the two strongest examples, National Certificate uptake has increased fourfold, compared to both its forerunner qualifications and its own early years. Similarly, Higher National uptake is now four times greater than that of its predecessor qualifications.

In both cases, the biggest changes between the old and new systems were the introduction of modular, outcome-based qualifications and the replacement of a mainly external assessment regime by one based on internal assessment. This combination of features provided a qualification system which had a number of advantages in encouraging increased access to qualifications:

- internally-assessed modular qualifications are more flexible and easier to change in response to changing technology or employment practice;

- candidates who are less confident or who have found external assessment, especially examinations, to be a negative experience are less stressed by an internal assessment regime;
- internal assessment can more easily provide for integration of skills and knowledge, thus providing a more 'natural' assessment, especially for workplace-related outcomes;
- outcome-based systems provide certification of successful achievement, rather than a numerical score indicating degree of success (and lack of success);
- modular systems provide learners who cannot commit to a protracted period of learning with manageable, and certificated, blocks of learning.

The modular system also has its disadvantages. For example,

- internal assessment at the end of each individual module does not provide for a measure of long-term retention of skills and knowledge or for opportunities to demonstrate integration of those skills and knowledge between modules;
- modular systems provide a relatively atomistic learning experience, providing only short-term targets and therefore possibly discouraging coherence of learning;
- users of qualifications in the UK have traditionally given greater recognition to qualifications based on external assessment, especially written examinations, and to group awards.

Although SCOTVEC attempted to counter the negative aspects by widening the availability of group awards, the new Higher Still system of qualifications will be the major test of whether it is possible in Scotland to address these negative aspects while still retaining the strengths of the SCOTVEC modular system.

It is also interesting to reflect that the SCOTVEC system of internal assessment and external quality assurance, which depends for its reliability on the professional assessment ability of teachers, lecturers and trainers, has never generally commanded the same degree of respect as an external examination model. Yet the combination of internal assessment and external quality assurance system is the model which provides the basis for the awarding of degrees in all UK universities.

Uptake and the economy

Any vocational education and training system needs to have the ability to respond quickly to changing patterns of employment and changing employment needs. There are a number of features of the SCOTVEC system of qualifications which supported such an ability.

- The modules and units which made up the qualifications were reviewed regularly to ensure that they continued to meet centres' and candidates' needs.
- The criteria for the validation of new or revised qualifications included a requirement to match the qualification against the needs of the employment market place to ensure that candidates did not find themselves without the opportunity for recognition and progression.
- The modular system enabled new qualifications to be developed quickly to meet new needs.

Over SCOTVEC's lifetime, the balance of uptake for its qualifications reflected the changing patterns of employment in Scotland, showing that centres were being responsive to candidates' prospects of employment. Thus, for example, there was a steady rise in the proportion of uptake which related to business and services and a corresponding decrease in uptake for qualifications related to traditional Scottish heavy manufacturing industries.

The qualifications system also showed itself to be able to respond quickly to emerging employment needs. Important and growing employment sectors in Scotland were supported by the development, usually in collaboration with centres and employers, of new qualifications. Thus, for example,

- qualifications in areas such as mechatronics and software engineering were designed and introduced for the microelectronics industry, supporting the considerable growth in employment in this sector in Scotland and providing re-training and re-skilling opportunities for workers seeking access to this sector;
- the service sector was supported by new qualifications in areas such as languages and tourism; financial services; and retail;
- new qualifications were quickly developed for a rapidly-expanding employment area when Scotland became the choice of many UK and international companies as bases for their call centres.

Capability and competence

A great deal of money and resources was expended by the government in the 1980s and the 1990s in supporting the development of NVQs and SVQs because it was perceived that these qualifications, with their focus on standards of employment competence, would provide a new focus for staff development and training in the UK, thus making the UK workforce more competitive against its hitherto better-trained competitor countries. The focus on employment competence sat together with an expectation that although government finance would continue to support certain training schemes, such as those for youth and adult unemployed, the training and development of the workforce and the acquisition of NVQs and SVQs would be paid for by employers themselves. Many years on, it remains one of the most difficult challenges to produce objective, and particularly economic, data to convince employers that such an investment in training and in qualifications does lead to measurable pay-back in terms of increased competitiveness, productivity and quality.

The relatively slow growth in the uptake of NVQs and SVQs, when compared to the number of people in employment, may reflect the difficulty, with any new qualifications such as these, of establishing their reputation and value. Employers also have an expectation that the use of NVQs and SVQs in the workplace will lead to measurable benefits such as increased profitability; data on the link between the use of NVQs and SVQs and such 'bottom line' benefits has been slow to emerge. These factors, and the financial pressures under which many companies operated, made it especially difficult to persuade small and medium sized enterprises to adopt NVQs and SVQs and to set up the necessary assessment and quality assurance infrastructure required to operate them in the workplace.

A further factor has been the traditional use by employers of off-the-job training to develop employees' skills and knowledge. Qualifications such as National Certificate, HNCs and HNDs have been used by employers to provide employees with the capability to tackle new or higher-level work. Such capability would then be consolidated in the workplace to provide full employment competence. Despite the appearance of NVQs and SVQs, many employers have continued to use tried-and-tested approaches such as day-release, block-release and other ways of combining off-the-job and on-the-job experience to develop their employees' skills, with the off-the-job components provided by training organisations and colleges.

It could be argued that neither 'capability' nor 'employment competence' qualifications alone can provide for all the nation's needs. NVQs and SVQs have a place, where employers wish to develop their employees' skills against standards set by national employer-led bodies and to assess them in workplace conditions. But the 'capability' qualifications, such as National Certificate and HNCs/HNDs, are equally important in providing individuals and employers with a means of fulfilling aspirations for wider or deeper vocational skills and knowledge, even if they are not immediately required in the workplace. Such qualifications are equally important economically at times when, for example, new employment areas are opening up and young people, workers in other employment areas and those out of work are trying to make themselves marketable to employers. Such qualifications are also important when the economy is undergoing a major change of focus, leading to the need for individuals to be re-trained or up-skilled, for example from operative or craft level to technician.

The impact of qualifications

The use of qualifications as an end-point to learning is the norm in schools, colleges, universities and other training organisations. This shows in the huge percentage of individuals of school age, and just beyond school age, who are working towards a qualification. An internal SCOTVEC analysis of uptake for all Scottish qualifications suggested that 90 per cent of individuals in the age range 16–19 were pursuing a national qualification.

However, the same internal analysis suggested that only just under 11 per cent of the 20+ age range were pursuing a qualification. When the numbers in this group who are involved in higher education degrees and postgraduate studies were excluded, it suggested that in Scotland, and in the rest of the UK, there was still a very large untapped market for qualifications in the employed workforce. Of course, it has to be recognised that the pursuit of a qualification and participation in staff training are not the same thing. Bodies such as SCOTVEC spend much time and money persuading employers and others that a qualification, as an end-point, adds value, incentive and structure to training; nevertheless, employers can use the national standards produced by lead bodies as the basis for staff training but without involving the final step of seeking a qualification.

The increased scale of uptake of qualifications in the 16–19 age range may, of course, lead to a demand for qualifications as this group move into the 20+ age group and as government initiatives in lifelong learning take effect. Scotland's economy, as it moves towards the millennium, involves such features as growing numbers of part-time employees, especially in service sectors such as retail; employment areas which have traditionally had low training (and qualifications) uptake; and a significant proportion of the workforce employed by small and medium-sized enterprises.

To be effective, the qualifications system will have to continue to be as flexible, accessible and cost-effective as possible. The achievements of SCOTVEC and its partners, of schools, colleges and the many other centres using its qualifications, and of the 1.33 million people who have tasted success in the SCOTVEC system of qualifications, provide an excellent basis for the Scottish Qualifications Authority (SQA), as successor to SCOTVEC and the Scottish Examination Board. SQA's aim must be to build a Scottish qualifications framework which is comprehensive, progressive, flexible and inter-linked by a national credit accumulation and transfer system and which therefore encourages access and opportunity for all.

REFERENCES

SED (1983) *16–18s in Scotland: An Action Plan*, Edinburgh: Scottish Education Department.
SOED (1991) *Six Years On: Teaching, Learning and Assessment in National Certificate Programmes in Scottish Further Education Colleges*, Edinburgh: HMSO.
Black H., J. Hall and S. Martin (1992) *Units and Competences: A Case Study of SCOTVEC's Advanced Courses Development Programme (SCRE Research Report 40)*, Edinburgh: Scottish Council for Research in Education.
NCVQ and SCOTVEC (1996) Review of 100 NVQs/SVQs: A report on the Findings, London: National Council for Vocational Qualifications
SCOTVEC (1986 to 1996) *Annual Reports*, Glasgow: Scottish Vocational Education Council.

88

CES Findings on Participation and Attainment in Scottish Education

David Raffe

For a quarter of a century the Centre for Educational Sociology (CES) has been an observer, analyst and critical commentator on developments in Scottish education and training. It has been one of the country's main centres of research on secondary, further and higher education and training and on their social and labour-market context. It has studied young people's participation and progression in education, their curriculum and attainment, their attitudes and choices and their destinations on leaving. It has linked this individual level of analysis to the school and national levels: it has studied variation in performance across schools and monitored national performance in relation to system and policy change.

The next section of this chapter briefly outlines the Centre's history. The third and longest section then reviews the performance of Scottish education as revealed by the Centre's research. This review focuses on secondary and post-secondary education up to 19 years, and on two main outcomes or indicators of performance: participation and attainment. It summarises the Centre's conclusions on, respectively, the level and pattern of participation and attainment, inequalities, factors which influence participation and attainment, and the impact of policy. However it excludes many areas of the Centre's work, such as its research on the history of education, the policy process, curriculum, guidance, student attitudes, and information systems. The final section discusses issues for policy and practice.

THE CENTRE FOR EDUCATIONAL SOCIOLOGY

The CES was founded in 1972, as a research unit within the University of Edinburgh's Department of Sociology, with Andrew McPherson as director. In the 1970s and 1980s it established a reputation for its work on secondary education and post-school transitions, and for its programmes of 'collaborative research' (1975–1982) which involved users in the research process and tried to transcend the traditional boundaries between the roles of researcher and practitioner or policy-maker. Much of its work was based on, or associated with, the Scottish School Leavers Survey (SSLS), which the Centre had founded in the early 1970s and which became a biennial national survey from 1977. In 1985 the survey was enlarged and re-designed as the Scottish Young People's Survey (SYPS). The Centre combined survey analysis with other styles of research, such as historical analysis in *Reconstructions of Secondary Education* (Gray, McPherson and Raffe, 1983) and the study of policy-making published as *Governing Education* (McPherson and Raab, 1988). Its main funding sources were the Scottish Office and the Social Science Research Council (SSRC, now ESRC), together with foundations and core university support. From 1987 to 1996 it was an ESRC Research Centre, with Andrew McPherson and David Raffe as co-directors.

The philosophy which has underpinned the Centre's work is summarised in chapter 17 of *Reconstructions*. It stresses that research has a critical function, and that a democratic society requires public participation in it; but research also needs the authority and resources which only the state can provide. During the 1980s and early 1990s this philosophy was increasingly at odds with a government attitude which wanted to restrict the role of the state and which distinguished between the interest of the government and the public interest. The government was a consumer of research in its own right, but it no longer accepted its obligation to promote the public interest by supporting access to research among those who might want to criticise its own policies. Some of the Centre's work on comprehensive education, youth training, school performance and access to higher education did not endorse the prejudices of the government. With effect from 1993 the Scottish Office re-designed the SYPS (re-named the SSLS) as a cheaper operation which focused more narrowly on its own data requirements as it perceived them. Data-collection was separated from analysis and contracted out to a London survey agency which could do the job more cheaply and whose ignorance of Scottish education was not considered a handicap. Needless to say, the new survey did not anticipate the government's longer-term needs, and it had to be re-designed again; the new survey introduced in 1997 is similar in design to the SYPS formerly carried out by the Centre.

The Centre no longer conducts its own surveys but it continues to analyse data from Scottish and other European youth transition surveys. It also makes extensive use of other research methods. The main focus of its research continues to be the study of education and training in their social and labour-market context, and in relation to social and policy change. A growing proportion of its research is funded by the European Commission and much of this has a comparative focus. In 1997 the Centre's research embraced the school curriculum, a 'home international' comparison of 14–19 education and training systems in the UK, the unification of academic and vocational learning in post-compulsory educa-tion, the effectiveness of the careers service, European strategies for post-16 education, part-time higher education, transitions into the labour market across Europe, the income and expenditure of young people, and the application of information systems to data processing and documentation. The Centre also provided research support for local initiatives in early intervention and in vocational education and training. When its period as an ESRC Centre ended, in October 1996, the CES merged with the University's Department of Education to form the Institute for the Study of Education and Society (ISES), while retaining its identity as a research centre within ISES. In 1998 the Centre joined the new Faculty of Education, created from the University's merger with Moray House Institute of Education.

PARTICIPATION AND ATTAINMENT IN SCOTTISH EDUCATION

The Centre has published numerous studies of participation and attainment in Scottish education, comparing it with other systems, analysing trends and explaining distinctive

Scottish patterns. This research reveals a system whose performance is indifferent by international standards, but improving, and where participation and attainment continue to be highly polarised. This section elaborates the picture of Scottish education that emerges from the Centre's research. For reasons of space it does not describe the specific studies on which the discussion draws.

The level and distribution of participation and attainment

Contrary to popular belief, fewer 16–18 year olds participate in full-time education in Scotland than in the other countries of the UK. Scottish participation rates only appear to be higher if they are restricted to students who stay on at school (many more 16 year olds in the rest of the UK enter college instead), or if they are based on equivalent year groups rather than age. Scottish year groups are five months younger, on average, than the equivalent year groups elsewhere in the UK; consequently Scottish participation appears higher if based on year groups and lower if based on age groups. Whatever the appropriate comparison within the UK, by the more demanding standards of other European countries Scottish participation rates are low on average and strongly polarised. Over 40 per cent of young people enter higher education (HE) but a similar proportion leaves full-time education within a year of the minimum age. The Scottish system is geared to getting a large minority of young people into university at a relatively early age, but it fails to retain those who are not university-bound for very long. Fewer Scots enter full-time technical or vocational education than in most European countries, and most entrants leave within a year or two. A substantial proportion of young people enter part-time or work-based provision, but their participation also tends to be brief. Few Scots continue in education or training beyond 18 or 19 years unless they are either in HE or trying to get there.

The distribution of attainments is similarly polarised. Large numbers do very well, and gain HE degrees, but many others do poorly. Scotland has made more progress than the UK as a whole towards attainment targets at the levels corresponding to Standard grades and Highers (and their vocational equivalents), but it lags behind other countries at these levels. This polarisation is reinforced by the pattern of progression. At nearly all stages beyond the end of compulsory schooling, future participation and attainment are strongly influenced by past levels of attainment. Post-compulsory education in Scotland appears to reflect the principle that further learning is for those who are best at it, rather than for those who are most in need of it.

Part of the explanation for Scotland's distinctive patterns of participation and attainment lies not in the education system itself but in its social and labour-market context. Polarisation in society sustains polarisation in education. Family and neighbourhood deprivation contribute to low participation and attainment. The labour market has encouraged the polarisation of attainments by rewarding higher education while often failing to recognise or reward intermediate level education. It has tended to value occupational experience more than vocational qualifications and has consequently 'pulled' able 16 year olds, especially boys, out of education.

Despite this mixed verdict on its performance, Scottish education is improving. Attainments have risen at all levels. Full-time participation has increased, especially in the fifth and sixth years of school and in HE where participation rates have doubled within a decade. The CES predicted some of this growth in the 1980s, by showing that parents' education was a strong predictor of whether their children entered HE, and that levels of parental education were rising rapidly. However the growth in participation, both at 16–plus and in HE, has considerably exceeded this prediction; a later CES study estimated that only a third of the increase in staying-on at 16 could be attributed to 'compositional' factors such as changes in parental education or in other family or personal characteristics of 16 year olds. Other factors which have contributed to the growth in participation include reforms of compulsory education which have encouraged more positive attitudes to school, changes in the labour market which have reduced opportunities for early leavers, and the structure of school courses which allows decisions to be taken one year at a time and thus reduces the risks associated with staying-on. In addition, an increased supply of education stimulated an increase in the demand; the expansion of higher education places in the late 1980s and early 1990s resulted in a growth in applications, and encouraged more young people to stay on at school to prepare for HE.

These pressures for expansion have been reinforced by a process of credential inflation, a competitive scramble for the positional advantage which higher levels of education can confer. One consequence has been academic drift: young people have not only sought more education but they have sought the kinds of education which confer the greatest positional advantage. Higher education and 'academic' school courses have expanded faster than 'vocational' courses in school and further education. A further consequence is that absolute levels of participation and attainment have changed more than relative levels; everyone has moved forward a step but their place in the queue may not have changed. However there has been a modest trend towards equality of attainment: staying-on rates have increased most among the least qualified 16 year olds, and this in turn has led to slight reductions in social differences. It remains to be seen whether this trend has continued or whether it was a one-off reaction to the withdrawal of benefit entitlements from 16 and 17 year olds in 1988.

One other major trend in participation patterns deserves comment. This is the attempt to develop a work-based route in Scotland (and Britain) of equivalent stature to the German dual system. Such was the vision shared by at least some of those involved in the launch of the Youth Training Scheme in 1983. The Centre's research has documented the history of youth training schemes in Scotland, and identified the factors behind their failure to achieve this grander vision (see below). An alternative strategy would have used the opportunity provided by high youth unemployment to build up full-time education for all 16 year olds; the more recent growth in full-time participation and the impending introduction of Higher Still may achieve a similar outcome ten or fifteen years later. However comparisons with Ireland, where there are fewer training opportunities for those who leave full-time education, suggest that the 'mixed' model of provision in Scotland has at least provided a better safety net for the educationally disadvantaged and for those at risk of social and economic exclusion.

Gender and class inequalities

Outcomes in Scottish education are not only polarised; they are also distributed unequally across classes, genders and ethnic groups. Table 88.1 is based on the year group which completed S4 in 1990 and was surveyed by the SYPS up to the autumn of 1993 when they were aged nineteen. It shows inequalities in the percentage achieving selected participation and attainment outcomes.

Table 88.1   Attainment and Participation by Gender and Social Class: 1990–93 cohort

	males	females	middle class	working class
Achieved S grade(s) at 1–3	61	71	79	60
Achieved Higher pass(es)	37	46	64	27
In S5 (spring)	49	60	76	41
In S6 (spring)	31	38	53	22
Entered YT by age 19	36	29	17	43
Entered FT FE by age 19	12	19	12	17
Entered FT HE by age 19	33	37	58	20

Females outperform males both at Standard grade and at Highers, although their higher attainment still tends to be based on a different mix of subjects (see later discussion). More females continue in full-time education beyond the end of compulsory schooling, whether at school or in college; only youth training, based in the workplace, attracts higher male participation. However female participation tends to fall off more rapidly than that of males. The gender gap starts to narrow in the transition from school (S5 and S6) to higher education. Fewer females continue in vocational education or training beyond 18 years.

Middle class students do better than working class students at Standard grade, and the gap at Higher grade is even wider. More middle-class students stay on in full-time education; in the 1990–3 cohort they were more than twice as likely as working-class students to enter S6 and nearly three times as likely to enter higher education. The vocational routes, by contrast, attract more working-class entrants: more working-class than middle-class youngsters enter full-time further education (a reversal of the pattern of the 1980s) and more entered youth training.

Allowing for the general increase in participation and attainment, class inequalities are similar to those of the late 1970s, when the CES first produced evidence that levels of class inequality in Scottish education were similar to those of England and other countries. The evidence is inconclusive on whether the class gap has narrowed, and if so by how much. Reforms such as comprehensive education and Standard grade have reduced inequality on the margins but their main effect has been at the lower levels of attainment which have less positional value. A comparison of the four SYPS cohorts shows stable class inequalities in entry to higher education over the period of rapid expansion, although it shows some narrowing of inequalities in staying-on at 16 and on other criteria of inequality such as parental education. An analysis comparing the SYPS with the school leavers' survey which replaced it in the early 1990s shows a decline in class inequality, but this may reflect poor measurement of social class in the new survey series.

Influences on participation and attainment

Much of the Centre's research has been multilevel in character. It has studied educational outcomes and the factors which influence them at student, school and area levels, as well as at the level of the system.

A student's prior level of attainment is a powerful predictor of whether he or she continues in education and of future attainment. Family factors associated with participation and achievement include parental education and social class, family size, and number of parents. Gender, as discussed in the previous section, has a pervasive influence. However, it is easier for survey research to describe correlations than to be certain of cause and effect. Even if the characteristics of individual students statistically account for variations in performance, that does not mean we need look no further for an explanation. The 'effect' of individual characteristics may itself be a product of the system and its context. For example, more girls enter full-time education at 16 and more boys enter work-based training; this is a result, not of constant and necessary aspects of gender, but of features contingently associated with it, such as the opportunities and incentives in education and the labour market, which attract girls and boys to full-time education and to work-based training respectively.

The Centre's research challenges the notion that young people's educational decisions are determined by cultural factors which lie deeper than rational analysis. If young people do not take advantage of an educational opportunity in the way they are expected to, we should ask whether it would have been in their interests to have done so. Young people respond to the incentives and disincentives associated with the available options. They tend to be at least pragmatically rational, to have an instrumental orientation and to seek to maximise their qualifications and pursue long-term advantage in the labour market.

Comparisons of schools' performance need to allow for differences in their intakes, that is in the prior attainments and social backgrounds of pupils entering each school. 'Unadjusted' league tables which do not allow for intake place schools in the wrong rank order and exaggerate their differences. This is now well accepted, although it was not when the CES began work in this field. Variations in intake account for a large proportion of the variation in attainments among schools, but there may still be significant variation in the 'value added' by the school.

Much of this 'added value' is due to factors outwith the control of the school itself. One of the most important of these factors is the 'contextual effect': a student's attainment is influenced by the social composition of his or her fellow-students. Another factor is the history of a school: older schools and former senior secondaries tend to do better than newer schools with a history as junior secondaries. A third factor is denomination: other things being equal, Roman Catholic schools perform better than non-denominational schools. Nevertheless part of the value added by a school lies within its own control, although there is no universal recipe for a good school: schools which are most effective for some students are not necessarily most effective for others.

Crude league tables may misrepresent the relative performance of local authorities, just as they do of schools. Most of the differences in performance across authorities can be explained by the differences in the social composition of their student populations. The variation in the value added by schools within a local authority is much larger than the average difference between local authorities. Nevertheless, these average differences are significant, and large enough to justify policy attention.

Other area-level influences on attainment include social deprivation, and the effects of local opportunity structures. Neighbourhood deprivation has a negative influence on the local children's school performance, over and above the effect of their measured ability, family background and school. Local unemployment has encouraged 16 year olds to stay on in full-time education, although this 'discouraged worker' effect has diminished since the mid-1980s, consistent with the view that the labour-market 'pull' on 16 year olds has weakened.

The impact of policy changes on participation and attainment

Secondary education was reorganised on comprehensive lines following the publication of Circular 600 in 1965. Reorganisation proceeded unevenly across different areas, but this made it possible to analyse its effects by linking comparisons across areas and over time. Levels of SCE attainment increased, and they increased most among girls and among students of lower socio-economic status. There was 'equalisation' as well as 'improvement'. The effects tended to be greatest in respect to the lower levels of SCE attainment. The level of social segregation of schools was reduced; as a result the 'contextual' effect described above was more consistent across schools, and this may account for some of the effect on equalising and improving attainment.

Legislation passed in 1981 extended parental choice of schools. Middle-class and better educated parents have been more likely to exercise choice. Parents' choices have been heavily constrained by practical considerations such as travel and have often been negative in nature: many parents have exercised choice in order to avoid the neighbourhood school rather than because they particularly wanted the chosen school. On average, choices have favoured schools serving middle class catchments and with high 'unadjusted' examination results, but they have not favoured schools which provided high 'added value'. Parental choice has led to an increase in the social segregation of schools, most noticeably in Glasgow. Given the 'contextual' effect described above it has probably contributed to the polarisation of attainments in Scottish secondary education.

The first five Scottish Technical and Vocational Education Initiative (TVEI) pilot schemes started in 1984. An evaluation of these schemes, and of further pilots started in the following two years, revealed that the effects on participation and attainment varied widely across schools and areas, consistent with its status as an experimental or pilot innovation. The average effects on attainment and participation were small. TVEI appeared to reduce levels of S4 attainment, partly because many TVEI students attempted fewer O/S grades as a result of doing TVEI, and possibly also because they took more technological subjects and this may have affected performance in other subjects such as mathematics and English. TVEI may have had a very small initial impact on staying-on rates, but if so this disappeared over time. However TVEI students were more likely than similarly qualified students from the rest of Scotland to pursue vocational education or training in further education or in the Youth Training Scheme (YTS), and to gain post-school qualifications by the age of nineteen.

The Munn and Dunning Reports of 1977 led, eventually, to the introduction of a curriculum framework for S3 and S4 in 1983, and the phasing in of Standard grade to replace O grade from 1984. By 1990 progress towards the curriculum framework was incomplete; foreign languages, creative and aesthetic activities and religious and moral education were each studied by less than half of S4 students. The framework reduced the gender gap in mathematics and science, as these subjects became almost universal, but it did not remove gender differences within science: more boys studied physics and more girls studied biology. Standard grade reduced social inequalities in attainment. The relative chances of advantaged and disadvantaged students achieving an award declined significantly with the introduction of Standard grade; however their relative chances of achieving an award in bands 1–3 (equivalent to an A–C 'pass' at O grade) did not improve. In other words inequalities at the more valued levels of attainment have persisted.

In 1984 the modular National Certificate replaced most non-advanced vocational education in further education and schools. Participation in the NC grew rapidly, especially within schools where it filled gaps in existing provision. It helped to develop a flexible pattern of post-compulsory courses, and enabled most upper-secondary school students to mix 'academic' Highers and 'vocational' modules, although this mixing tended to confirm the NC's low relative status. It had little immediate impact on levels of participation beyond 16, although it may have facilitated later expansion. It increased the opportunities for participation and progression, but did not itself provide the incentives for young people to take advantage of these opportunities.

The CES contributed to the debates about upper-secondary schooling in the early 1990s. It drew attention to the importance of a flexible course structure in encouraging participation, and to the damaging effect which a two-track system such as that proposed by the 1992 Howie Report would have on participation and attainment. At the time of writing the Centre is studying progress towards the implementation of the Higher Still reforms in 1999.

The Centre studied the attempts since the early 1980s to develop a work-based training route for young people. Training schemes were developed from schemes for the unemployed, and consequently acquired low status and a niche in the less skilled occupational sectors. They helped many people to find jobs, but this depended more on their use by employers to screen and select new recruits than on the content or quality of training. Training schemes achieved high participation, catering at their peak for nearly half of the age group, and they extended training to occupations and to groups of young people where opportunities had previously been scarce. However participation tended to depend on the risk of unemployment and on the vagaries of the market. The effects on levels of qualification or on progression were much less impressive.

ISSUES FOR POLICY AND PRACTICE

The Scottish education and training system has had several achievements over the twenty-five years covered by the Centre's research. Participation has increased. Attainments at all levels of the system have improved. The curriculum has been modernised. A comprehensive system has been successfully established, and is being extended into the post-compulsory stage. Academic and vocational learning have been brought closer together, and opportunities for progression are more open and more flexible than in most European countries. Some aspects of gender inequality have declined, and some educational reforms have reduced social inequality even if the total level of inequality has not improved greatly. The system's clients or consumers report higher levels of satisfaction.

But there are limits to this story of success. Vocational education is weak, and is being further weakened by academic drift. Adult participation is low. Participation and attainment have improved among young people but they are still undistinguished in international comparison. A large proportion reaches higher education but another large proportion leaves education early, with low levels of qualification and with little expectation of return. The biggest shortcoming of Scottish education is its failure to bring all young people to the 'intermediate' level of education which all citizens of a democratic society should enjoy, and which many commentators perceive as the key to economic success.

We cannot pin the blame for all these problems on education alone. There are wider societal factors, including social inequality and the operation of the labour market. The link between social disadvantage and educational underachievement is similar to that elsewhere, but there is more social disadvantage in Scotland than in many other countries, and partly as a result there is also more underachievement. Scotland's poor achievement of intermediate level qualifications partly reflects the failure of its labour market to demand and reward such qualifications. Scottish education and training have developed through interaction with their social and economic context; this context has been much more conducive to excellence in higher education than to the development of a system which brings all of its students to a minimum standard of learning.

But the Centre's research also points to ways in which the system can be improved, even within these constraints. For example:

- The research shows the pitfalls of organising education and training on market principles. Markets tend to reinforce existing values and hierarchies. A voluntarist market-led policy has merely confirmed the low status of work-based training, and has failed to establish either a high-quality alternative to full-time provision or a means for reversing disadvantage and underachievement. A market-led approach has encouraged a polarised distribution of attainments, in response to the labour market's polarised demand for skills. The extension of market principles through parental choice of schools has not increased participation in more effective schools, but it has increased social segregation of schools and consequently increased underachievement.
- Scottish education should continue to build on the comprehensive principle in planning its future development. Comprehensive education, and complementary reforms such as Standard grade, have underpinned much of the progress that we have observed in Scottish education; this progress will be extended as the comprehensive principle is extended beyond compulsory education through Higher Still and the development of a post-16 qualification framework.
- Scotland needs to rebuild its tradition of work-based provision for young people. Youth training schemes sought to do this in the 1980s, but they were driven by unemployment and hemmed in by political and funding constraints. Work-based training has low status and a marginal role within the system, and is in danger of being further marginalised by Higher Still. But there are strong educational and economic arguments for retaining a substantial work-based route; and it still offers one of the most promising ways to reduce underachievement and reverse the polarisation of participation and attainment in the Scottish system.

Finally, the experience of the CES points to the need, in a small and enclosed system with a tendency for complacency and self-congratulation, for a research capacity which is at the same time involved in the system but able to offer a critical and reasonably independent commentary and analysis on that system, and for consistent and reliable data on which such analysis can be based.

REFERENCES

Gray, J., A. F. McPherson and D. Raffe (1983) *Reconstructions of Secondary Education: Theory, Myth and Practice since the War*, London: Routledge.

McPherson, A. F. and C. D. Raab (1988) *Governing Education*, Edinburgh: Edinburgh University Press.

A bibliography of publications by members and associates of the CES is available from the Centre for Educational Sociology at the University of Edinburgh. Summaries of selected research are published in the series of *CES Briefings* (1995–) Edinburgh: Centre for Educational Sociology, University of Edinburgh.

89

School Effectiveness and School Improvement

John MacBeath

How good is our school? (SOEID, 1996). The title of this policy document from the Scottish Office Education and Industry Department is profoundly significant in a number of ways. It is significant in the simplicity and directness of its vocabulary, in its formulation as a question, and in its historical place in the world-wide movement which has come to be known as school effectiveness and school improvement. The story of how Scotland has come to be a leading player on the world stage of that movement begins with an information exchange at international, policy-making level and finishes with the individual learner and the learning classroom.

THE INTERNATIONAL CONTEXT

1966 is widely accepted as the beginning of the search for school effects. The impetus for James Coleman and his team to begin this search was the perennially vexed question of educational inequality and what schools did to attenuate the effects of family and community which children brought with them into school. Their conclusion, published in a voluminous work entitled *Equality of Educational Opportunity*, was that school effects were marginal compared with the substantive effects of family and community. Six years later a follow-study by a Harvard team reached very similar conclusions. In their report, *Inequality: a reassessment of family and schooling in America*, they conclude:

> Our research suggests that the characteristics of a school's output largely depend on a single input, namely the characteristics of the entering children. Everything else – its budget, its policies, the characteristics of the teachers – is either secondary or completely irrelevant. (Jencks et al., 1972, p. 256)

The two and half decades which have followed Coleman and Jencks have seen a succession of studies attempting to confirm, challenge, disprove or throw new light on the questions which the school effects researchers had placed squarely and uncomfortably in the centre of the policy arena. The stream of research which has gained increasing momentum during these years has addressed questions of central concern to politicians and finance ministers world-wide attempting to gauge the least contentious and most rewarding areas for economic investment.

'Can schools reduce social inequality or equalise opportunity?' is clearly a question as compelling for policy-makers as it is for researchers, but of growing and ever-more insistent interest to governments is the question, 'Are some schools more effective, than others?' If so, why? And how could such knowledge be used to economic and political ends?

With the advent of Thatcherism, evidence for the variable effectiveness of schools was a priceless gift to government because it could be put to the service of parental choice, and, through the operation of the market, reinforce 'good' schools and put pressure on less good schools to smarten up, to compete or to suffer the consequences. While school effectiveness researchers would not wish to be held responsible for the creation of so-called 'league tables', 'effectiveness' had become closely and carelessly synonymous with a certain kind of measured achievement and even scrupulous researchers have been known to slip into the shorthand of describing high-attaining schools as 'effective' and the lowest attaining schools as 'ineffective'. The word 'outcomes' is now widely used to mean examination results.

However sophisticated it may have become in the intervening years, the Coleman and Jencks methodology, or at least its underpinning premises, have remained essentially intact; but within the research community there is still considerable ambiguity and argument about how effects work and how they inter-relate within an organisation as complex and multi-layered as a school. There is now greater scepticism about 'school' effects and a developing interest in departmental and classroom effects. The focus in recent years has switched from inter-school comparisons to intra-school explorations, concentrating less on macro effects and more on differential effects by social background, gender and ethnic group, by age and by individual prior attainment and experience.

The tool not available to Coleman or Jencks to study these inter-relationships is multi-level modelling, widely, but not universally, seen as the state-of-the art in school effectiveness studies. Modelling means building a statistical replica of a school and gathering data at different levels – at pupil level, at classroom and/or departmental level and at school level. The variables generated at each of these levels can then be played off against pupil attainment to identify where the most powerful correlations lie. If, for example, substantial differences are found between pupils taught by teacher A, as compared with teacher B, then the teacher effect would seem to be in play, while differences between pupil achievement in department X versus department Y would seem to be pointing to a departmental effect (other things being equal or held constant).

At the level of the individual, pupil factors such as eligible for free school meals, girl/boy, English as second language might be found to correlate very highly with attainment but would be taken out of the equation because they represent things beyond the power of the school to control. In other words they tell us not about school effects but about home, community or social effects. However, by virtue of being powerful independent variables they can be used to measure how well they predict the performance of teacher A or B or departments Y or Z or school X. Tracking the ups and downs of one individual pupil over two or three years within the context of his/her class, department and school (and within a large enough sample of other schools to compare with), a multi-level modeller might, with some degree of confidence, say that of those effects shown to be significant, at school level their influence was about 15%, at departmental level 25% and at classroom level 60%.

Use of statistics in this way, while appearing to say something definitive, is open to misinterpretation as well as to criticism. The most obvious of these is how can you separate things which are so closely inter-related and inter-dependent? The response of the multi-level modellers to their critics is that this is the best research tool we currently have and that, of course, there are serious health warnings to be attached to the data. What the statistics tell us is where the strongest associations of factors lie and, as in all school effects studies (and studies of studies), we must be scrupulous to emphasise association rather than causality.

It is, however, a short step from correlation to causation and one which policy-makers have a tendency to take with consummate ease. Reinforced by common sense and their own children's school experience, the discovery of robust correlations can move quickly into conviction politics and, sometimes quite rapidly thereafter, into legislation. Negative or inconclusive findings may serve policy interests too. The inconclusive evidence over class size, for example, has been used by successive governments, not just in the United Kingdom, to resist pressures from teachers.

One of the inherent problems which the data conceal, and the debates reveal, is the issue of quality. Homework may be a constant correlate of effectiveness but that association may tell us nothing about the quality of learning. In the case of class size, it depends on what use is made of it and if a teacher is lecturing to twenty or to thirty (or even sixty to seventy as in some Pacific Rim countries) numbers in the class may be inconsequential.

Certainly the research has generated a lively debate among academics and perhaps too high a degree of certainty among policy-makers about what it is revealing and where it leads in terms of school improvement. It is in this respect that developments in Scotland have had such an impact. Drawing on a strong tradition of school effectiveness research, the SOEID, in partnership with education authorities and researchers, has for a decade and more been putting in place a school improvement framework to help senior managers and teachers to be less accepting of received wisdom and become researchers in their own schools.

THE SCOTTISH SCENE

There are various key strands in the development of school effectiveness policy in Scotland. One of the most significant of these is the impressive database on all young people leaving schools after the fourth, fifth and sixth years. It has provided researchers with a rich seam to explore and the many papers and books which emerged from the mining of those data has shaped policy thinking and provoked a lively and increasingly informed debate.

Complementing these large scale quantitative studies there has been a substantial body of qualitative work which, although not in the school effectiveness mainstream, has done much to help in the interpretation and contextualisation of their findings. The work of Noel Entwistle and his colleagues in Edinburgh, Wynne Harlen and colleagues at the Scottish Council for Research in Education (SCRE) and John Nisbet at Aberdeen, for example, have made a significant contribuion to understanding of classroom processes. Brown and Riddell's 1996 study of four schools is an example of research which married a school effectiveness approach to an ethnographic case study work, both reinforcing earlier findings on social class influences and at the same time challenging the effectiveness paradigm.

Throughout the 1980s and 1990s, the Centre for Educational Sociology (CES) in Edinburgh produced a substantial and influential body of work. (See Chapter 88.) While Coleman and Jencks had focused their attention on the three-quarter empty glass, John Gray and his colleagues at CES took a greater interest in the quarter full glass. Their Scottish data confirmed the very powerful effects of factors beyond the control of schools but also demonstrated that individual schools could make a significant difference at the margins.

Drawing on data provided by Scottish school leavers and their schools, CES researchers showed that when background factors were applied to exam league tables, a significant re-ordering of the ranking among schools took place, leading the research team to the conclusion that if parents chose schools on the basis of examination results alone, 'they would very often choose the wrong school.' Another significant aspect of the study was the use of four outcome measures – attainment, truancy, pupil satisfaction and incidence of belting (a quaint Scottish tradition that still existed at the time of the study). The study concluded that being in school A as against school B could make one or more 'O' grades of a difference. It also suggested that schools could be effective along different dimensions in respect of attitude, attendance or attainment.

Drawing further on the school leavers data, Willms showed in his 1985 study that if you were a pupil of average ability your chances of exam success were better in schools where your peers were of high ability than in schools where they were of low ability. This has since come to be known as the 'contextual' or 'peer group' effect, suggesting that the social milieu of school may be more significant than structural factors. Two different directions in policy flow from this. One is to readjust catchment areas of schools so as to provide greater homogeneity, in other words a social engineering strategy. The second is to leave it to parent choice, that is, a free market strategy. A follow-up study reported that parents who exercised their rights to choose tended to be more highly educated and of higher socio-economic status than those who did not. In terms of the contextual effect, this meant that the schools which their children left became more socially homogeneous, depriving them not only of those pupils but of parents with expertise and potential influence.

The power of school ethos or culture was shown with dramatic effect in *Tell Them From Me* (Gow and McPherson, 1980). Again, mining data from the Scottish School Leavers archive, it used pupils' own subjective accounts to give a worm's eye view of those factors which most affect ethos and achievement. This was not a school effectiveness study but it illustrated more vividly and poignantly than any statistics the differential impact of schools on individual pupils. The book, essentially written by school leavers themselves, portrayed in graphic personal accounts the quality and inequality of school life. Well before researchers became interested in the differential effectiveness of schools, the Gow and McPherson study demonstrated that schools were different places for different pupils. At the same time it held up a disturbing mirror to Scottish secondary schools.

The pupil accounts in Gow and McPherson's study are what researchers would call 'soft' data, but the *Tell Them From Me* report achieved a number of things which the harder quantitative data had not accomplished. It demonstrated very clearly why some pupils failed to survive while others thrived. It made clear the connections between attitudes and achievement, between expectations and ability and offered some unambiguous pointers to what schools and teachers could do without additional resources or capital investment. The challenge to the school effectiveness movement was for it to marry the increasingly sophisticated data modelling with the ethnographic or constructivist paradigm.

In his 1989 lecture to the Scottish Educational Research Association (SERA), David Hargreaves commented:

> Remember that one of the characteristics of the effective school is the belief by pupils that they are valued by staff. Asking for their views is a practical way in which teachers can value pupils.

These issues were explored in a two year study by MacBeath, Mearns and Smith, published in 1986 as *Home from School*. Researchers conducted in-depth interviews with parents and young people in their own homes. The pupils' and parents' stories, combined with opportunities for the researchers to observe family life at first-hand (often for up to three hours or more), gave vivid testimony to the crucial importance of attitudes to school and how these were shaped by the social milieu of the home and its interplay with the social milieu of the school. The roots of motivation, expectation and self-belief were transparently on view. What young people took with them into their schools were belief systems which cast them as main or subsidiary players, powerful or powerless, helpless or masterful. What they brought back from school to home was homework, study, advice on course and career choice and report cards mapping their past, present and future, telling them what they were good at and not good at, and often what they were.

Many pupils in that study enjoyed the benefits of private tutors or expert parents to lead them across difficult terrain. Some never did homework or study and lived in houses entirely bereft of reading material of any kind. Some had a structured family life of support and challenge, some a completely laissez-faire environment. Some had strict and demanding standards of achievement and behaviour set for them, in some cases with firm consistency, in others with erratic unpredictability. It was evident from that study that the best efforts of school effectiveness researchers to document the key variables that added value would always be partial and misleading without a knowledge of how value was added and subtracted in the home.

For policy makers the *Home from School* study provided an important complement to the quantitative studies, another piece in the policy jigsaw that was being assembled at national level through the 1980s. It was to be taken further into the policy arena with the incumbency of Michael Forysth as Education Minister in 1988 and his commissioning of a study of 3,500 Scottish parents including 100 in-depth home-based interviews. The immediate outcome was five booklets entitled *Talking about Schools* (MacBeath/MVA 1989, 1990) distributed to all schools in Scotland, while the longer term outcome was a more central place in school thinking and planning for the parental voice.

The late 1980s and early 1990s was a period of flourishing activity not only on the research front but at government and authority level. At Scottish Office level there was the establishment of the Management of Educational Resources Unit (MERU) to drive forward effectiveness work. At authority level, regional councils began to put into place quality assurance teams, and authorities such as Fife and Grampian commissioned school effectiveness studies of their schools.

1988 saw the publication of *Effective Secondary Schools* (Scottish Office Education Department 1988), followed a year later by *Effective Primary Schools*, both documents designed to put into the hands of teachers and school management issues that had previously been the province of researchers. These were to serve as the source of reference for school development planning, seen by policy-makers as the mechanism through which greater effectiveness would be delivered. The 1991 publication was entitled *The Role of School Development Plans in Managing School Effectiveness*.

The publication of the school self-evaluation guidelines in the following year signalled a sea change in thinking about how schools improve. Her Majesty's Inspectorate moved their criteria for evaluating school quality and effectiveness out of the secret gardens of the Official Secrets Act into the public domain, a paradigmatic shift in philosophy that nearly a decade later many other countries in the world are emulating and sometimes blatantly plagiarising.

In the words of David Hargreaves, this was an important step in helping teachers 'take ownership of their diagnosis of the school and develop a commitment to implementing the solutions they themselves formulate' (SERA Keynote Address, St Andrews, 1989).

'The threefold path to enlightenment' was how *The Times Educational Supplement Scotland* described the SOED's guidelines for school self-evaluation (*TESS*, May, 1993). These were:

- A set of qualitative indicators based on criteria used by HMI in inspections of classrooms, departments and aspects of whole school policy and practice.
- Relative Ratings, which gave secondary schools formulae for calculating the differential effectiveness of subject departments.
- Ethos indicators, providing schools with techniques for gauging the more subjective and least tangible aspects of school life from the perspectives of pupils, teachers and parents.

In 1995, the SOEID commissioned the Improving School Effectiveness Project (ISEP) to evaluate the impact of these policy initiatives, to help develop a national framework for value-added, and most critically perhaps, to shed light on the causal relationship between school processes and outcomes. The project, bringing together teams from the University of Strathclyde and the Institute of Education in London, worked with eighty schools across Scotland for a two-year period. The schools involved had to make a substantial commitment in terms of data gathering at the outset of the project and again two years down the line – fourteen background factors on each pupil in the primary 4 and secondary 2 cohort, four attainment tests in Mathematics and English, pupil attitude questionnaires, teacher questionnaires and parent questionnaires. In addition, in the twenty-four case study schools (an in-depth sub sample of the 80), eleven qualitative instruments were used to gather information on ethos, development planning, the management of change, teaching and learning.

The case study schools had the benefit of two members of the research team to assist with the collection, interpretation and feedback of data to staff. It was the job of the critical friend to work alongside teachers and management to plan and implement change while the researcher's task was to document the process and to evaluate the role and influence of the critical friend (MacBeath and Mortimore, 1997).

The findings of the study will run to a number of volumes and can only be touched on here. Many of the findings confirm previous studies of differential effectiveness. Socio-economic disadvantage was shown to have a strong positive relationship with attainment at P4 and P6 and S2 although background factors weighed less in mathematics than in reading. School effects were also stronger at primary than at secondary level. In primary, girls were ahead in reading and boys in mathematics but by S2, girls were still ahead in reading and had caught up in mathematics. By S4, Standard Grade, girls significantly outperformed boys in English and in overall performance across subjects. As in prior studies there was a 'contextual' or 'peer group' effect, significant for reading but not for mathematics. Pupils young for their year group performed significantly less well at all levels than their older peers.

Attitude measures showed significant variations among schools on two measures – 'engagement with school' and 'pupil culture'. These were related, but only weakly, to social class and varied among schools to a lesser extent than did attainment measures. On the attitudinal measure 'self-efficacy', girls were less positive than boys. Attitudes of primary teachers were consistently and markedly more positive than their secondary colleagues but at both primary and secondary level there was a consistently wide gap between teachers' view of their schools as they were and what they saw as the characteristics of the effective school.

Many of these are classic school effects findings. Some confirm common sense and some have more obvious policy implications than others. Like other school effects studies, the currency is correlations and so leaves many questions unanswered. There was, however, another important dimension to this study. The more innovative aspect of the project was the feedback and use of data by the school itself. Data were processed and returned to schools confidentially together with aggregated data for all the schools in the project. Schools were then able to compare their own attainment and attitudes to those of other schools. Much of the interpretative work occurred, therefore, at school level, with guidance and health warnings from the research team.

In some schools the attainment data came as a surprise and even a shock to teachers who had overestimated the school's performance relative to other schools, but it gave a focus for target setting and re-prioritising of teaching and learning. It was the attitudinal data, however, that offered the biggest challenge and, in some cases, the most powerful lever for change. In many schools it was the teacher questionnaire which penetrated deepest into the belief system of the school and exposed its strengths as well as its frailties. The questionnaire contained fifty-four questions and two independent scales, one asking for teachers' judgements on the school as they saw it at that moment, the other asking for a rating of the same items by their importance in creating an effective school. Responses to these two scales provided a kaleidoscope of perceptions of the school as it was and as staff thought it should be. They provided endlessly fascinating avenues for researchers and policy-makers to explore but the most useful aspects of the data were for interpretation and planning within individual schools. In the twenty-four case study schools this was done with the support and help of the critical friend. An example of one questionnaire item illustrates the range of possibilities in the data.

In response to the statement 'teachers in this school believe all children can be successful', 33% of secondary teachers responded in the affirmative (agree/strongly agree) as compared with 65% in primary. When asked to say whether this was 'crucial' for an effective school the figures were 75% and 85% respectively. This 'crucial' rating compares unfavourably with items such as 'pupils respect teachers in this school' (95%), 'pupils are clear about standards of behaviour expected in the school' (99%) and 'new staff are well supported in the school' (94%).

Does this mean that teachers actually believe that pupil respect, discipline and support for teachers are actually more important than a belief system which endorses success for all? Are primary teachers more positive and optimistic than their secondary colleagues? From a school improvement viewpoint, was the opportunity available for teachers to engage with the data from their own school and to compare it with a broader national picture and to explore the ambiguities which underlay words such as 'successful'? It is, of course, open to a variety of interpretations but led to questions such as 'what do we, as a school staff, view as success?' Percentage of Standard Grades gained? Post-school destinations? Personal and social development? Heightened self-confidence and self-esteem? Social and emotional intelligence? A passion for learning?

This exploration of the data was usually fruitful and always challenging. The ambiguities and apparent contradictions within the data led staff, management teams and pupils to be more alive to others' ways of seeing things. It could help them to find common ground of agreement and disagreement, and often to become more understanding and tolerant of differences. Occasionally it helped school leaders to see problems as opportunities and to welcome the inherent conflict that is the lifeblood of a social organisation such as a school. Addressing the issues with regard for evidence and reasoned argument illustrated the power of 'soft' data as a tin opener, cutting into some deeply entrenched belief systems operating in a school. Helping teachers to question their beliefs and assumptions is fundamentally what professional development is about, and being confronted with compelling evidence is one way of achieving that goal.

Argyris and Schön (1978) analyse organisations that cannot seem to learn what everybody knows because they are disabled by their own inability or unwillingness to find out. 'Learning disabilities are tragic in children but fatal in organisations', says Peter Senge (1992). The ISEP project revealed some of the learning disabilities of schools but also showed how schools can learn through a process of feedback with support and challenge from a critical friend (MacBeath and Mortimore, 1996).

Hard data often drives out soft data but soft data is the most useful, argues Henry Mintzberg in his classic study *The Rise and Fall of Strategic Planning* (1994). A single customer complaint, he says, may be of more value than volumes of market trends analysis. How a school responds to a 'customer complaint' – an allegation of bullying, sexual harassment within the staff, a racist incident, a parent concern about an ineffective teacher – may be the most telling indicator of capacity for self-evaluation and improvement.

It is self-knowledge which characterises the healthy individual and is the hallmark of a healthy organisation. In his introduction to national and regional conferences held to launch *How good is our school?*, HMCI Archie McGlynn, plagiarised the Oracle at Delphi for his keynote theme 'Know thyself'. Helping schools to nurture self-knowledge is perhaps the most vital contribution that school effectiveness research can make.

WHAT THE CRITICS SAY

In its short lifetime, school effectiveness research has made significant advances in its methodology and in its thinking. A survey of policy-makers, practitioners and researchers (MacBeath, Keynote Address at The 11th Annual Congress on School Effectiveness and Improvement, Manchester, 1998) identified the main contributions of school effectiveness research as:

- legitimising policy decisions
- spotlighting performance as an issue
- stimulating cooperation across national borders
- leading to international indicators and comparative studies
- shaping ideas and highlighting good practice
- the driving force behind school autonomy and accountability
- creating or reforming national inspectorates
- drawing attention to the school as an organisation.

At school level it was seen as having given the impetus to:

- whole school policies
- development planning
- a culture of self-evaluation
- the use of evaluation instruments.

There were also many caveats and critiques as to its influence and benefits. A Canadian researcher wrote, 'Policy-makers and their academic friends have cherry-picked from effectiveness characteristics.' A UK policy-maker wrote, 'Education is not sufficiently linked to other areas of government policy, for example, welfare to work.' As far as effects at classroom level were seen, it had not, in the view of the large majority, penetrated effectively to professional understanding or practice. A Canadian researcher wrote, 'Policy-makers have used it as a club to beat up on teachers.'

Critics of school effectiveness have been accused of resting on conceptually unstable foundations. Among the most vociferous of these are Richard Pring who gave the keynote address on this theme at the 1995 SERA Conference, John Raven, writing after the 1997 SERA Conference and John Elliot, who contributed to a critical review published by the London Institute of Education (Barber and Whyte, *Perspectives on school effectiveness*, 1997). Their charges include:

- being platitudinous, re-inventing the obvious
- missing the fine-grain reality of school life
- appropriating language (for example, 'effectiveness')
- blindness to social and political contexts
- complicity in a political agenda
- misdirecting attention from wider structural issues
- confusing correlations and causes
- offering little to school management or teachers
- ignoring the problems of the curriculum
- being limited in its focus on the school as an entity
- lacking in theoretical grounding

Some of this critique is hard to refute. The literature is indeed often impenetrable and presentation of data is often more confusing than enlightening, with texts often syncopated and overburdened with self-referencing. Typically bibliographies refer to the same group of authors and there is generally little reference to other fields of research, to ethnographic studies, philosophy, politics or psychology, for example.

The charge of narrowness is also hard to refute given emphasis on attainment measures. Used only as proxies and accompanied by health warning, they may, nonetheless, reinforce a deepeningly entrenched view of effective schools as those most efficient at improving their exam throughput. In this sense, researchers may have been, wittingly or unwittingly, complicit in diverting attention from wider structural issues and political agendas. Sometimes, by design or by default, they have failed to offer a vigorous challenge to a reductionist and dehumanising view of what education is for, and what schools might be for.

The attention given to departmental effectiveness, and its Scottish progeny Relative Ratings, may serve to reinforce departmentalisation at a time when schools are looking for more generic approaches to learning and when neuropsychologists such as Gardner and Perkins are querying the fragmentation of learning and the lack of transfer of skills across different subject domains.

School effectiveness does, by definition, focus on schools and has been unapologetically directed at explaining what goes on within the black box, but its strength and unique contribution is also its most singular weakness. The need to control the variables such as home background requires that this is factored out, so risking the loss of data on the most significant area for enhancement of learning, the dynamic relationship between what pupils bring to school and what they take away from school. This is not an additive process. Schools do not, in fact, 'add' value.

The focus on individual schools is also a limiting factor. As Benn and Chitty (1996) have pointed out, the effects of any individual school are affected by the organisation of other schools in the neighbourhood. The contextual effect, the critical mass, or the critical mix, is not just an intra-school phenomenon but an inter-school one. Effective schools are not just a product of the social dynamics within their four walls but of the wider social dynamic of the neighbourhood and the larger political and economic processes at work.

In response to their critics, many people engaged in school effectiveness work would reply that it is a broadening church. Its rapprochement with school improvement has lent a greater vitality and colour to the literature. The growing percentage of practitioners who attend and present papers at the annual School Effectiveness/School Improvement Conference is a healthy sign. The Manchester meeting in 1998 attracted over 700 delegates from sixty-three countries, the majority from a practice or policy-making background. The value of this conversation among researchers, practitioners and policy-makers is increasingly recognised, broadening the frame of reference and testing its applications. One of the immediate benefits of this collaboration is to enhance the quality and rigour of school self-evaluation.

In Scotland, it is six years since the first guidelines on self-evaluation were published by the then Scottish Office Education Department. In that period there has been a groundswell of interest and expertise. Headteachers and teachers from primary, secondary and special schools have spoken at national conferences and led workshops in Scotland and further afield and at the time of writing are involved in major European projects and in a leading a three year study funded by the German Bertelsmann Foundation.

It was to Scotland that the National Union of Teachers in England and Wales turned for help in developing a national framework for self-evaluation. The study published as *Schools Speak for Themselves* (MacBeath, Boyd, Rand and Bell, 1995) became a central plank of union policy and has been widely used in English and Welsh authorities and schools as a practical working document. In a number of authorities it is used in conjunction with the SOEID publication *How good is our school?* which has also enjoyed substantial sales in many countries.

It is at classroom level, in the daily transactions between pupils and teachers, that self-evaluation comes truly into its own. When they ask the question 'how good is learning in our school?', they open doors into the nature and quality of learning, which lead from soft to hard data and from the teaching organisation to the learning organisation. For parents, it may also spark the same aggressive curiosity, prompting the question 'how good is learning in the home and in the community?'. When young people begin to ask themselves the question 'how effective a learner am I?', the self-evaluation question comes full circle and the contribution of school effectiveness research is put to the test.

REFERENCES

Argyris, C. and D. Schön (1978) *Organisational Learning: a theory of action perspective*, Reading: Addison Wesley.

Benn, C. and C. Chitty (1996) *Thirty Years On: Is Comprehensive Education Alive and Well or Struggling to Survive?*, London: David Fulton.

Brown, S. et al. (1996) *School Effectiveness and School Improvement: The Ways Forward*, Paper presented to the CES Conference, University of Stirling, February, 1996.

MacBeath, J. and P. Mortimore (1997) *School effectiveness – is it improving?*, Paper presented at The 10th International Congress for School Effectiveness and Improvement, Memphis, January, 1997.

Senge, P. (1992) *The Fifth Discipline: the art and practice of the learning organisation*, Sydney: Random House.

Willms, J. D. (1985), The Balance Thesis – contextual effects of ability on pupils' 'O' Grade examination results, *Oxford Review of Education*, 11.1.

XII

Challenges and Responses: Education for All?

90

Special Educational Needs of Scottish Children

Gilbert MacKay and Marion McLarty

CHANGING DEFINITIONS OF 'SPECIAL EDUCATIONAL NEEDS'

All systems are fallible, and the education system is no exception. The modern Scottish system began with an Education Act in 1872. One hundred and two years passed before it recognised that every child has a right to education, through the Education (Mentally Handicapped Children) (Scotland) Act 1974, legislation which came four years after its English and Welsh equivalent. The early development of special educational provision in Scotland is covered in Dockrell, Dunn and Milne (1978) and Thomson (1983). For the purposes of this chapter, the Warnock Report of 1978 is the appropriate starting-point. In 1973, Warnock's Committee of Enquiry began reviewing 'educational provision in England, Scotland and Wales for children and young people handicapped by disabilities of body or mind . . .' The Report's ultimate title of *Special Educational Needs* showed that things had begun to change. UK educational systems moved from recognising handicaps in 1954 and 1959, to rights in 1970 and 1974, and to 'special educational needs' (SEN) in 1978.

Change was inevitable because of developments in education, health and social policies. By the time of Warnock, it was no longer sufficient to respond to the disabilities defined in statutory Regulations of 1954 (Scotland) and 1959 (England and Wales). 'Needs' became the key to a more contemporary rhetoric. Of course, rhetoric does not guarantee understanding. As late as 1993, the former Strathclyde Region's policy document, *Every Child is Special*, referred to 'pupils whose special needs include visual impairment.' A mature educational system should not confuse needs with disabilities. The following examples are given, therefore, to clarify the concept of needs.

Becoming literate is probably an educational need for the majority of children. Yet, it may be a special need when children registered blind have difficulty becoming literate. 'Special' here means 'exceptional'. Such children often have a special educational need for low-vision aids. 'Special' then means 'additional'. Further, literacy may not be an appropriate educational need for some blind children if their visual difficulties are complicated by profound intellectual disability. In their case, other needs have priority over literacy. Here, 'special' means 'different'. The notions of 'exceptional', 'additional' and 'different' are all at the heart of Scots law and policy on SEN.

That is a useful general position on 'needs'. The more specific position for this chapter concerns the needs of a small proportion of the school population – those with marked disabilities which cause learning difficulties. The post-Warnock Education Act (Scotland) 1980 states that children and young persons have SEN if they have a 'learning difficulty which calls for provision for special educational needs to be made for them'. The Scottish Office (Circular 4/96) clarifies this tautology by defining learning difficulty with reference to the attainments of age-peers, and impaired access to standard educational facilities. Education authorities have a duty to keep children and young people with SEN under review if they decide to record their needs formally.

KEY POLICY DOCUMENTS FROM WARNOCK ONWARDS

Warnock still exerts a powerful influence. Its 'areas of first priority' – children under 5, young people over 16 and the training of teachers – now receive much more attention than they did in 1978. Its recommendations on recording and the appointment of Named Persons were enacted in 1981. So was the disappearance of statutorily-named categories of disability, though these have re-appeared in government documents in an amended form.

Another document, contemporary with Warnock, has exerted equally great influence in Scotland (HMI, 1978) and is discussed in detail in Chapter 91. It created a shift in focus from pupils' difficulties that might arise for constitutional reasons, to difficulties caused by inappropriate teaching and other circumstances not within the child. It recommended a change from thinking about 'remedial' to 'appropriate' education in mainstream schools. It has also influenced developments in special education.

The 1980 Act disappointed many because it seemed to achieve so little, coming after Warnock which seemed to promise so much. Its Record of Needs (the formal statement of an individual's disabilities, special educational needs and the education authority's proposed responses to these needs) differed little from 'ascertainment', which it replaced. The Named Person was a reluctant late arrival, omitted from the preceding White Paper. Its eventual role – 'the person to whom application may be made for advice and information' – seemed a damp squib. However, the thinking of the Scottish Office is clear in an SED Circular (No. 1087) of 1982 which indicated the government's intention that the spirit of the Warnock Report should be honoured. Warnock's five stages of assessment were commended, as was the practice of recording, the importance of responding to the under-fives, and early detection of children's difficulties within school. Parents were given a central place in recording, and the role of the Named Person in assisting them was confirmed. Circular 1087 outlined what became standard practice for implementing SEN law. Its influence is still evident in its replacement, *Effective Provision for Pupils with Special Educational Needs* (EPSEN), a report by HM Inspectors in 1994, discussed below.

Current education for pupils with special needs tries to conform to the 5–14 curriculum which had its thrust in the back-to-basics movement of British politics in the early 1990s. There was little evidence in the early documentation of 5–14 that it was designed for all pupils, but two developments have occurred, aimed at achieving the inclusion of those with SEN. First was the issue of *Support for Learning* by the Scottish Consultative Council on the Curriculum. It proposed five strategies for addressing the 'mismatch between delivery of the curriculum and pupils' learning needs' (SOEID, 1994, p. 8): differentiation, individualisation, adaptation, enhancement and elaboration. The second development is the 'elaborated curriculum' for pupils with severe and profound (often, confusingly, called 'complex') intellectual disabilities. Essentially, it consists of components of elderly developmental checklists, shoe-horned into areas of the 5–14 curriculum. 'Assessment' has been equated with 'curriculum', and that is a serious flaw. Perhaps the most positive aspect of the 'elaborated curriculum' is that it has stimulated many schools to devise something better. They can be trusted to do this well, as they have done so before in developing activities, teaching methods and home-school partnerships – often ahead of comparable developments in mainstream schools.

LEGISLATIVE FRAMEWORK

The legislative framework relating to pupils with SEN is laid out in Scottish Office Circular 4/96 (SOEID, 1996). This section gives a brief overview of legislation, but Circular 4/96 is the authoritative source. The current framework is based on the 1980 Act which requires that all children should have 'adequate and efficient' education. The principal SEN legislation appears in the Act as amended in 1981. It refers to the duty to record; the duty to carry out a review of the future needs of 'young persons' in their final years of compulsory schooling; the appointment of the Named Person; and rights of appeal in relation to recording. Specific prescriptions for recording appear in Regulations of 1982. The following paragraphs give a brief account of amendments to legislation which appear in two other Acts since 1982.

First, the *Disabled Persons (Services, Consultation and Representation) Act 1986* made three amendments and introduced one new development. The first amendment was removing the obligation to state a Named Person on the Record, if this is the wish of parents. Second was the re-labelling of child guidance services as 'psychological services'. Third, the Act created the right to appeal against decisions not to open a Record. The 1986 Act also required education authorities to inform social work authorities about young disabled people six months before they leave full-time schooling. The *Self-governing Schools, etc. (Scotland) Act 1989* introduced three points on SEN. First, it required education authorities to open Records on children from the age of two years, if they met the requirements for recording. Second, it empowered authorities to open Records on children under two years. This move was in line with beliefs (if not consistent evidence) on the efficacy of early intervention. Thirdly, the 1989 Act gave education authorities powers to allow pupils with SEN to attend establishments outside the UK. It can be no coincidence that this legislation's appearance was close to the high point of governmental enthusiasm for Hungarian conductive pedagogy, a flirtation that is difficult to explain on educational grounds alone.

The latest development of the legislative framework is the *Children (Scotland) Act 1995*. It requires local authorities to promote the welfare of children 'in need' and gives families power to ensure that their children's needs are met. This could be a helpful consolidation of rights, powers and duties. It may also increase the incidence of litigation against authorities, in keeping with practice in the USA where other aspects of British SEN policy seem to originate.

THE ROLE OF SCHOOLS AND OTHER AGENCIES IN IDENTIFYING AND PROVIDING FOR SPECIAL EDUCATIONAL NEEDS

EPSEN (SOEID, 1994) is the principal policy statement on how schools and other agencies should identify and provide for children and young people with SEN. Ten distinctive features of effective provision are proposed, covering the process of response from understanding SEN, through identifying and planning for them, to monitoring the effectiveness of intervention. The report's section on pre-school children gives a scheme for determining whether or not to open a Record. It draws attention to the range of people who are essential partners if needs are to be identified and met. This section also commends current Scottish thinking on the principal structure of the curriculum for all pre-school children. Interestingly, this structure has potential beyond pre-school children. Unlike 5–14, yet like Munn's 1977 curriculum for mainstream secondary schools, it consists of areas that apply comfortably beyond the bounds for which they were designed. The fourth and fifth sections give guidance on provision in primary and secondary schools. They detail steps in deciding whether or not to open a Record and how to conduct the assessment of future needs. The guidance stresses the importance of family involvement from the earliest stages of investigation.

The progress of pupils, says EPSEN, should be structured by individualised educational programmes (IEPs). The IEP appeared in the USA's act of 1975 which seems to have influenced some aspects of British practice. Scottish educationists should perhaps be thankful that it does not have a place in a statutory Code (as in England and Wales), and that neither system has the stringent review procedures that have caused anxiety in the USA. Making IEPs work is a delicate balancing act. The danger in having too formal a system, apart from unnecessary paperwork, is that of focusing on experiences which can be expressed in terms of simplistic behavioural goals. Of course, the danger in having no system is that children and young people will have a poor education. IEPs invite research.

The penultimate section deals with further education. It covers students who may have SEN that should be met if they are to benefit from general college courses, and those taking courses specifically for people with SEN. EPSEN ends with a review of priorities for development which are outlined in the final section of this chapter.

THE TRAINING OF SEN TEACHERS

This section deals mainly with the training of experienced teachers, but begins with a brief comment on initial training. For some years, all Scottish teacher-education institutions have included SEN components in initial teacher-training. It is important that all students should develop knowledge, attitudes and skills that will let them respond well to the pupils with SEN they meet on placement or in their first jobs. Achieving this in a crowded timetable continues to concern the General Teaching Council and the teacher-education institutions.

The history of the training of experienced teachers in SEN is recounted by Blythman in Dockrell, Dunn and Milne (1978). Until 1992, there was a well-established route to an additional teaching qualification in SEN. Four teacher-education colleges (Jordanhill, Moray House, Northern and St Andrew's) offered a Diploma in SEN (Recorded Pupils) and a Diploma in SEN (Non-recorded Pupils), replacing, respectively, older diplomas in special and remedial education. (Craigie College was also active in the field, but with a less comprehensive provision of courses.) In addition, Moray House, exclusively, runs courses for pupils with visual and hearing impairments. At the writers' base (the former Jordanhill College), teachers undertaking the 'recorded' diploma were seconded for a full-time one-year course of twelve modules. Those following the 'non-recorded' course undertook part-time study over two sessions. The Scottish Office supported teachers' secondments by a specific grant to the authorities. The diplomas conferred were, first, additional teaching qualifications recognised by the General Teaching Council and, second, awards of the Council for National Academic Awards.

The years between 1987 and 1992 saw a number of changes for these diplomas, following modularisation of the courses, and their revalidation as 'post-graduate'. First, the recorded and non-recorded diplomas merged, as their distinction was difficult to justify. Second, the colleges succumbed to education authority pressure, and replaced the twelve-module course with four-module certificates and eight-module diplomas taken by day-release or evening study. The shortened nature of the courses, combined with the removal of assessed teaching placement effectively killed off the additional qualification in SEN. Other professionals, such as psychologists, have moved from diplomas to masters' degrees and, increasingly, taught doctorates as their post-graduate training. In SEN, Scottish teachers have moved backwards towards shorter diplomas and certificates as the standard form of accredited professional development. The effects of these changes will be worth evaluating.

PARENTAL RIGHTS: HOME-SCHOOL PARTNERSHIPS

A variety of statutory rights for parents have been defined in and since the 1980 Act. It allows parents to appeal against

- the decision to open or continue a Record of Needs;
- the authority's summary of a child's impairments or difficulties;
- the authority's statement of a child's special educational needs;
- the school named by the authority for the pupil's education.

Additionally, the *Disabled Persons (etc.) Act 1986* gave the right to appeal against a decision not to open or continue a Record.

The *Self-governing Schools (etc.) (Scotland) Act 1989* can enable parents to obtain special provision for their children overseas. It would be interesting to discover the extent to which this legislation has led to the use of overseas provision, and which specific provision has been attended. More recently, the *Children (Scotland) Act 1995* may encourage parents of children with disabilities to litigate to secure 'adequate and efficient education'.

There is a necessary formality about parents' relationships with education authorities in relation to the law. Relationships are less formal in the daily routines of school and other educational provision. Warnock was a milestone in developing the notion of parents as partners in the education of children with disabilities. Yet, partnership is a complex idea that raises many questions. To what extent do parents and professionals have equal powers, rights and responsibilities in the relationship? Does a focus on roles obscure the importance of the systems and other social dynamics which influence families' and professionals' behaviour and aspirations?

Many professionals value their relationship with parents unreservedly because it gives them understanding which is an essential base for planning and daily decisions. The relationship may be low-key in the form of home-school diaries or a welcome open-door or open-telephone policy. Some schools have parents' groups that meet during or after school to consider matters relating to children and families. More formally, it is standard practice to have parents' attendance at review meetings which most education authorities carry out annually (or more frequently) when pupils have Records of Needs. The creation of this relationship took time to establish as normal because it challenged long-established social representations of parents, professionals and schools. It probably occurred earlier and with greater ease in special education than did comparable developments in mainstream education. That is a credit to parents and professionals. Perhaps it was also a necessary consequence of recognising that the children and young people involved really do have special and different needs, and that these require a different kind of relationship between parents and professionals from that which can suffice in mainstream schools.

MAINSTREAMING; DIFFERENT FORMS OF INTEGRATION; SEPARATE PROVISION

Mainstreaming is the practice of locating in mainstream schools pupils who might have all or most of their education in segregated special provision because of disabilities. Over many years, Scottish Office statistics have shown that a relatively small proportion of children with disabilities attend segregated provision. In recent years, the proportion has been between 1.1 per cent and 1.3 per cent. Most of these are in schools for pupils with 'learning' disabilities.

Warnock identified three types of arrangement – locational, social and functional – whereby children with SEN might have education that is integrated within mainstream schools. Locational integration includes siting special educational provision on the campus or in the classrooms of a mainstream school. There are many examples around Scotland. Social integration occurs when the children in locationally-integrated provision mix with pupils in the mainstream classes during social activities. Again, there are many examples. Functional integration occurs when pupils with SEN are full members of mainstream classes. Such practices have always occurred in Scottish schools, particularly when children have sensory, emotional and behavioural, specific learning, communicative or physical disabilities. In 1995, Allan, Brown and Riddell from Stirling University, drew attention to the rising number of children with Records of Needs in mainstream schools, but cautioned against reading too much into this because of variations across the country. Challenges to functional integration become greater as pupils' intellectual disabilities increase, or when they have severe difficulties communicating and interacting with others.

Warnock's thinking on integration was influenced partly by world movements in civil rights, as segregated schooling may be interpreted as barrier to participation in an inclusive society. There are also pragmatic arguments for integration because exposure to the company of other mainstream pupils is an excellent way of learning social mores whether or not one has a disability. In addition, the mainstream curriculum may give access to a wider range of life-choices than may that in segregated provision. Yet, the principle that integrated education is a universal right must be challenged because the same UN Charter which asserts children's rights to education also asserts the rights to special education for all children who require it.

The USA's notion of 'the least restrictive environment' is still a useful context in which to examine mainstreaming. Mainstreaming is not an easy option, and it may not be appropriate for some pupils, but these are not reasons to be complacent about the services that exist currently. There is a need for a national bank of qualitative and quantitative data on mainstreaming, together with reliable information of practices and policies in other educational systems, to develop better practice and policies here in Scotland.

RECORDS OF NEEDS

The Record of Needs is the document used to note that a child or young person has SEN which, in the 1980 Act, 'are pronounced, specific or complex, and which require continuing review'. The procedure is anticipated in Warnock, but also has ancestry in procedures for ascertaining which pupils were disabled in terms of the 1954 Regulations. It is important to note that the opening of a Record is a late stage in the process of identifying and assessing SEN. Good practice, defined by EPSEN, would involve deliberation by parents and professionals before deciding that a child or young person should have a Record.

The process of opening a Record is straightforward. A child or young person with significant difficulties comes to the notice of the education authority. Typically, this is by referral to the psychological service by parents, nursery provision, pre-school assessment teams, health professionals and, of course, schools. The education authority notifies parents in writing that it intends to discover if the child or young person has needs that should be recorded, and gives appointments for examinations by a medical practitioner and psychologist. Parents have a right to attend the medical examination. In deference to some long-forgotten sensitivities, there is still no right to attend the psychologist's examination.

Reports from the medical practitioner and psychologist, together with a school or nursery report, and those from other relevant professionals are then amalgamated into a draft Record. This draft contains an assessment and summary of the child's or young person's difficulties; a statement of needs; a specification of the education authority and other resources required to meet the needs; and a nomination of the school which the child or young person will attend. The content of draft Records is generally decided at a group meeting of the professionals involved. The draft is sent to the parents, who have twenty-one days to scrutinise and return it to the authority with a form stating their views on their child's needs. Their report is added to the draft Record, together with the name of the Named Person (if parents wish such a nomination) and becomes the official Record of Needs. It is possible for parents and the authority to negotiate changes to the Record during the twenty-one days. It is also possible for parents to appeal formally against various aspects of the recording process. Once a final form of the Record is agreed, one copy is sent to the parents, one to the child's or young person's school, and one is kept by the education authority.

No statutory date is set for a review of Records, though there is a requirement to carry out a 'future needs assessment' (a process very similar to recording) on all recorded pupils during their last two years of compulsory schooling. Parents may request a formal review of their children's records annually, and the authority itself has the power to review annually. However, that is the closest Scotland comes to the USA's requirement of statutory annual review. In practice, the Scottish authorities are now carrying out something more useful. This is an annual review of progress, rather than a formal review of the Record. The review is a detailed, thorough process, and involves parents and professionals in a less formal, but probably more productive, relationship than that of recording.

Recording has undergone no radical changes since it started on 1 January 1983. However, experience of the procedures seems to have removed some of the rougher edges that were apparent in the early years to ensure that the letter of the new law was observed. In addition, current practice gives importance to collaboration among professionals. It may be more effective in the involvement of parents too, a development that seems inevitable with the increasing powers that have been granted in the *Children (Scotland) Act 1995*.

RESEARCH FINDINGS ON THE NATURE AND EFFECTIVENESS OF CURRENT ARRANGEMENTS

Contemporary with Warnock, the Scottish Office sponsored two curriculum projects in the area of the children with profound disabilities. At Glasgow University between 1978 and 1981, MacKay and Dunn developed a means of teaching children whose communicative development ranged from pre-linguistic levels to the first appearances of connected speech. At Jordanhill College between 1979 and 1983, Browning, Anderson, Bailey, Law, MacLeod and Suckling produced a curricular framework on developmental behavioural principles for children with profound intellectual disabilities.

Later in the 1980s, and 1990s, a number of projects relating to specific issues were carried out. For example, Brown, Riddell, Duffield and Allan at Stirling University clarified the constructs among parents', professionals' and education authorities' views of identifying and making provision for pupils with dyslexia. MacKay, McCartney, Cheseldine and McCool at Strathclyde University evaluated the Craighalbert Centre (Cumbernauld), and raised questions about the relevance of a national centre for children with motor impairments and about the place of conductive pedagogy in Scottish education. In Edinburgh, Reid led a team from Queen Margaret College and Edinburgh University in an investigation of the actual and potential roles of speech and language therapists in educational settings.

The critical research concerning the overall framework of Scottish special education was the review of education authorities' practice in relation to the Record of Needs, reported by Thomson, Riddell and Ward at Edinburgh University in 1989. The findings of this research showed considerable differences in the interpretation of the law. For example, recording rates varied widely across the (then) twelve regional and island authorities. Decisions to record seemed predicated on local resources. More recent research (1995) by Thomson, Ward and Stewart has made proposals for solving the elusive problem of arriving at criteria for opening Records of Needs. These proposals centre on a 'matrix' of need for determining the nature and extent of support, to give more control over the variables that may have to be taken into account in decisions about opening a Record. This is a significant move from Warnock's unconvincing 'continuum' of need, perhaps the feature of the 1978 report which most deserves Warnock's own assessment (in 1989) of being 'naïve to the point of idiocy'. Yet, it is also worth asking if concern about the opening of Records has become a priority at the expense of an examination of the effects of recording. Authorities have no requirement to supply statements of action taken or services provided in response to the contents of children's and young persons' Records. Warnock set out to change attitudes and policies, and to ensure the proper provision of education for people with special needs. Records of Needs and IEPs have a role in formal monitoring, but the extent to which they help the attainment of more visionary educational goals should be examined further.

COMPARISONS BETWEEN SCOTLAND, AND ENGLAND AND WALES

The differences between the education systems of Scotland and England & Wales have been relatively slight in respect of pupils with SEN, but some are worth noting.

In 1970, England and Wales were four years ahead of Scotland in ensuring that all children were entitled to education. The 1970 Act also entitled pupils with disabilities to integrated education whenever possible. This does not apply in Scotland. The Record of

Needs is the 'Statement' in England and Wales, and uses less paper than the Record. However, the time needed to complete Records and Statements is a problem on both sides of the border.

The mandatory nature of the National Curriculum in England and Wales has worried many special educationists (though an important exception was made for deafblind pupils). Officially, the current 5–14 Scottish curriculum is not mandatory, but its adoption is close to universal in education authority schools, and there is pressure at central and local level to ensure that all pupils are 'doing 5–14'. Earlier, concern was expressed about the 'elaborated curriculum' that has emerged from 5–14 for pupils with the most severe disabilities. Both educational systems can do better than persist with current curriculum models, because they have done better in the past.

In 1994, the English and Welsh system adopted the Code of Practice, a set of required standards for services for those with SEN. Scotland has no Code, though EPSEN fulfils a similar function. The critical difference between EPSEN and the Code is the binding nature of the latter because of its roots in the English and Welsh Education Act, 1993. It will be interesting to assess the extent to which practices in the two systems diverge because of the advisory nature of EPSEN and the mandatory nature of the Code.

FUTURE PRIORITIES; FUNDING CONSTRAINTS

It is difficult to predict the future in relation to people with SEN in Scotland because of the political changes set in motion by the change to single-tier local authorities in 1996, and the change of government and pro-devolution vote in 1997. Lack of finance may constrain some developments. Others may be essential, irrespective of cost. For example, litigation has begun against a Scottish education authority concerning the support of a former pupil with dyslexia. This may have far-reaching consequences. There are still others where changes of perspective are essential: parents' involvement in their children's education is one example. The following points also seem significant.

It is time to revisit the vast literature on curriculum development and re-assess current demands in the light of principles such as the structure of subjects, and the actual worth of the curriculum. Scotland does not yet have a curricular framework that is suitable for all pupils. Perhaps it can not or should not exist. That debate has still to take place.

Children and young people from ethnic minorities should have access to any support they may need. Their special needs may be difficult to discern if the first language at home is not English.

There should be continued development of specialisms which have only recently been addressed as areas of priority for the provision of services across Scotland. This applies particularly to the education of children and young people who have difficulty communicating. They include those with autistic behaviour, which makes exceptional demands on themselves, their families and the education system.

The pre-service and in-service training of teachers in SEN is still a priority. In some cases, this could be facilitated by joint in-service exercises with other professionals such as speech and language therapists. Some models of practice are emerging.

More broadly, there must be respect for the different ways of understanding SEN. For more than a decade, the support-for-learning movement (see Chapter 91) has advocated moves away from what it calls 'deficit' and 'medical' models which describe people with reference to their disabilities. Instead, that movement advocates different models, for example, focusing on experiences offered to learners in schools and other services. This pre-occupation with models is old-fashioned modernism. No model of response is right or wrong intrinsically. They are all legitimate ways of knowing, appropriate in some circumstances and not so in others. Pupils, families, teachers and the general community are done a disservice when the diversity that is normality is treated as a philosophical, political or fiscal inconvenience.

Perhaps the last words on future priorities should come from EPSEN, as its final section deals with priorities for development in a number of areas. In all cases, these priorities relate to developments that have been under way for years, but in which there is unfinished business. EPSEN is written in a spirit of confidence in what has been achieved in SEN and in what might be achieved. The final sentence of the report states that such achievement should be grounded in a basic educational aim – enabling people 'to enjoy and derive maximum benefit from their education in school and beyond and to become fully participating members of their communities'. That is a good place to start and finish.

REFERENCES

Committee of Enquiry into the Education of Handicapped Children and Young People (1978) *Special Educational Needs* ('The Warnock Report'), London: HMSO.
Dockrell, W. B., W. R. Dunn and A. Milne (1978) *Special education in Scotland*, Edinburgh: Scottish Council for Research in Education.
Her Majesty's Inspectors of Schools (1978) *The Education of Pupils with Learning Difficulties in Primary and Secondary Schools in Scotland*, Edinburgh: HMSO.
SOEID (1996) *Children and young persons with special educational needs: Assessment and recording*, Edinburgh: The Scottish Office.
SOEID (1994) *Effective provision for special educational needs*, Edinburgh: The Scottish Office.
Thomson, G. O. B. (1983) Legislation and provision for the mentally handicapped child in Scotland since 1906, *Oxford Review of Education*, 9(3): 233–240.

91

Support for Learning: 'What are you calling yourself today?'

Louise Hayward

Scotland can be justly proud of the radical developments in thinking, in language use, in policy and in practice which have taken place in Support for Learning over the past twenty years. Support for Learning teachers across Scotland are familiar with the question from colleagues, 'What are you calling yourself today?' This chapter explains the significance of this question by first tracking the developing paradigm of Support for Learning through national, international and local policy; then describing the translation of policy into practice in schools; and finally reflecting on the continuing complexity of the issues in this interesting and exciting area. Understanding the past of Support for Learning in Scotland is essential to interpret the present and influence the future.

SUPPORT FOR LEARNING: A NEW PARADIGM

Remedial Education

In 1978 Scottish teachers of Remedial Education emerged into the light of public scrutiny from behind their classroom doors. Two major reports influenced the significant changes which were to be sustained and developed over the next two decades as 'Remedial Education' evolved through 'Learning Difficulties' into 'Support for Learning'. These were the Warnock Report (HMSO, 1978a) and the HM Inspectorate Report (HMSO, 1978b).

Before 1978 many primary and secondary schools in Scotland provided additional support for 'remedial pupils'. This support was provided in different ways but with certain common characteristics. There was a perception, strongly influenced by the concept of fixed intelligence, that a relatively small percentage of children had too low an IQ to progress normally. This deficit meant that education should seek to remediate difficulties in key areas for their future lives. Thus Remedial Education was provided in language and mathematics for groups of pupils separated from their peers. It was not linked to other work and often led to pupils being stigmatised. While there were examples of innovative educational experiences for young people in remedial education groups or classes, often the curriculum was narrow and uninspiring, concentrating on decontextualised basic skills.

From Remedial Education to Learning Difficulties

Changes in language represented significant changes in thinking. The Warnock Report began to challenge 'remedial' thinking by affirming that the aims of education were the same for all children and that educational needs should be determined by whatever was necessary for the attainment of these aims. The term Special Educational Needs replaced the categories of handicap previously used and covered also a wider range of children with learning difficulties. The report advocated the integration of children with Special Educational Needs in mainstream schools as far as possible with SEN provision seen as additional or supplementary rather than alternative. Children with SEN, it was suggested, represented approximately 20 per cent of the pupil population. Although this report was most influential in relation to provision for children in Special Schools, it heralded a major shift in thinking for mainstream education. The Warnock Report rejected the 'Child Deficit Model' and replaced it with a 'Needs-based Model' of provision.

Even more radical and influential was the HMI Report. It rejected the traditional narrow view of learning difficulties, indicating that up to 50 per cent of pupils might experience these at some point. Policies and practices were proposed to tackle the root causes of learning difficulties. The curriculum and its delivery were recognised as contributing significantly to the creation of difficulties in learning. Accordingly appropriate education across the whole curriculum was the aim, rather than 'remedial education'. This new vision required different kinds of teachers to support it: class teachers responsible for all learners and 'Learning Difficulties Teachers', who would work with colleagues to ensure access to the curriculum for all children. The report described a new multi-faceted role of the Learning Difficulties teacher, who would act as a consultant to colleagues, undertake co-operative teaching, tutor individual pupils, where appropriate, and provide, arrange or contribute to special services within the school.

From Learning Difficulties to Support for Learning

As the ideas from these powerful national policies began to be influential in practice, some assumptions underpinning the Warnock and Inspectorate reports were questioned. Were there really clearly identifiable pupils who experienced difficulties with the curriculum at some points while others did not? The HMI report on 'Able Pupils' (HMSO, 1993c) argued that children with particular abilities in various curricular areas were not being challenged. Although these children did not have 'learning difficulties', their educational experiences were inappropriate for their needs. A 'child deficit' model was recognised as an inappropriate conceptualisation of support, but was any model a deficit one if it did not include support for all including those with particular abilities? Learning Difficulties teachers became teachers of Learning Support, who sought to work collaboratively with others to ensure appropriate learning for all. In support of this extended view of Support for Learning the SOEID established in 1993 the Scottish Network for Able Pupils (SNAP) within the Department of Support for Learning in St Andrew's College.

The United Nations Convention on the Rights of the Child (1992) began to challenge the concept of a 'Needs Model' of support, in which groups of professionals and sometimes parents planned to meet children's needs through appropriate educational experiences. Article 2 of the UN Declaration stated that all children had rights which applied without discrimination of any kind. Article 12 outlined four rights of children and young people: to information, to participate, to complain and to confidentiality. Previously in Scotland these rights had been perceived to be held by parents. The implication of the UN Convention voices that Support for Learning should guarantee the right of all learners to appropriately challenging educational experiences. Riddell and Brown (1994) noted the practical difficulties of Support for Learning across the Curriculum: 'abandoning the notion of deficit within the child as the source of learning difficulties and ensuring that no child experienced a sense of failure were difficult goals to achieve.' An effective rights model of learning may then seem a highly idealistic goal. Yet Support for Learning does have a tradition of pragmatic idealism.

THE DEVELOPMENT OF LOCAL POLICY

Education authorities throughout Scotland produced policies translating the principles of the new vision of Support for Learning into practice in a range of differing ways. The profession experienced some difficulty in reconciling ideas from the national reports with different existing value systems and different practices. These differences were evident in many local policy statements, which reflected the alternative views, each held with great commitment. The language of the Strathclyde Regional policy statement *Every Child is Special* (1992)(6) illustrates some of the tensions. The title and reference to 'rights' reflect an 'inclusive' philosophy, but the 'Needs Model' can be perceived behind terms like 'special needs', 'a disabled child'.

There was nevertheless a general powerful commitment to providing and resourcing an equitable education system. Some sophisticated models of practice were implemented, e.g., in Grampian, and Dumfries and Galloway. Though initially successful, these proved difficult to sustain through funding changes.

TRANSLATING THE NEW PARADIGM INTO PRACTICE: STAFF DEVELOPMENT

How was policy translated into practice in primary and secondary schools? Both the Warnock and the Inspectorate Reports highlighted the centrality of staff development to the success of the proposed curricular and institutional developments. In response to this the Diploma in Learning Difficulties was established to train teachers to cope with the challenges inherent in the proposed new roles. Education authorities recognised the need to provide suitably qualified staff and seconded teachers to full time courses. The courses offered by colleges of education were generally of a very high standard and greatly appreciated by course members. They dealt fully with the four roles – consultant, cooperative teacher, tutor and provider of special services Later a fifth role, to support staff development, was added in recognition of the role of change agent which the Learning Support Specialist had to play if the new vision was to be realised. Course members left colleges describing themselves as 'born again teachers' with a powerful personal and collective commitment to the success of the new vision. The 'Diplomates' lead many significant and positive changes in teaching and learning practices. The status of Support for Learning in schools was raised and, as the system began to be seen as inclusive, the stigma associated with special provision for only a few children diminished. In both primary and secondary schools, when the system worked well, many of the problems created by traditional remedial education were addressed.

However, the emphasis was on the staff development needs of individual Learning Support teachers. The interrelationship between staff development and institutional development was not properly considered. Tensions arose when many course members returned to schools. For example, Principal Teachers whose thinking had changed dramatically went back to schools where neither teachers nor school managers had had opportunities to rethink provision. Working with hard pressed teachers who had found relief in having certain children removed from their classes, and with school managers who were concerned that the education of the many should not be affected adversely by the need to accommodate the few, the new Learning Support teachers found it difficult to persuade them of the benefits of a more inclusive system. In other contexts subject teachers interested in the potential of the new 'roles' developed very high expectations of Learning Support teachers who found it hard to meet them.

Finally, differing interpretations of the new vision were being reflected in the separate diploma courses for teachers of pupils with recorded special educational needs and teachers of pupils with non-recorded needs. Although the system required professionals to work collaboratively, training for the two groups remained discrete in many colleges of education. Both courses raised teachers to a very high level of expertise but, while the first trained teachers to specialise in working with pupils with particular needs, e.g., moderate learning difficulties, severe learning difficulties, visual impairment, the second emphasised effective learning across the curriculum for all pupils. Lecturers and course members on the different courses sometimes regarded themselves as protecting different values. Relationships between the two courses were sometimes strained. One position held was that scarce resources should be targeted towards those with greatest need. The other position, held with equal conviction, was that, unless all children were included, Learning Support would always be seen as provision for those for whom things had gone wrong. Given the impact of this perception on the learners' self esteem, their subsequent ability to learn was likely to be impaired and therefore the system was doomed to failure.

If the one or two year diploma courses offered sound staff development for those who took them, they were expensive and did not produce the critical mass of teachers in schools necessary to realise the new vision. Education authorities facing funding constraints began to explore alternative training patterns which would build teams of teachers to support learning across schools. Some authorities developed their own training courses validated by a college of education, some employed College of Education lecturers to offer outreach courses; others developed a part-time modular programme in partnership with a number of different colleges of education. The new modular training programmes brought together teachers from different educational sectors. The importance of training headteachers was recognised. Modules such as Strathclyde Region's 'Managing Effective Learning for All' (1992) became part of their staff college programme. Initially participants on management programmes demonstrated the same differences in view about the nature of Support for Leaning as was evident in the two training programmes described earlier. Such differences became less common, as greater numbers of teachers sharing a similar philosophy began to influence school management thinking.

In 1996, following the disaggregation of Regional Authorities in Scotland into smaller authorities, SOEID funded a National Coordinator in Support for Learning, based in St Andrew's College, building on the existing collaboration between Strathclyde Region, St Andrew's College, the University of Strathclyde, the University of Paisley and Moray House Institute. The aim was a partnership model of training throughout Scotland to avoid the narrow range of courses to which competition might lead. It remains to be seen whether collaboration or competition emerges as the dominant feature.

By 1998 significant numbers of promoted and unpromoted class and subject teachers were undertaking the modules. Although most participants intended to work across their school in supporting children's learning, some aimed to enhance learning in their own classrooms or departments. In all parts of Scotland courses were offered flexibly in day, evening and vacation modes, in colleges and universities or on an outreach basis.

PRESENT PRACTICE IN SCHOOLS: PRIMARY SCHOOLS

Although based on the same principles and intended to reflect the same five roles, Support for Learning developed in different ways in primary and secondary schools. It might have been expected that Support for Learning would always have been built in from the earliest stages of a child's education. Until relatively recently, however, more significant emphasis was placed on Support for Learning in secondary education than in primary: with appropriate responsibility payments and a career structure.

Support for Learning in many primary schools now comprises internal and external elements. A survey by Hayward and Neilson for SOEID (*Supporting Learning in Scotland – a national survey*, 1993) indicated that support for learning in primary schools was often the responsibility of a promoted member of staff who worked with class teachers, either as a cooperative teacher or by extracting small groups of children, usually for support with reading, mathematics or a class topic. In the best provision, difficulties caused by aspects of the curriculum or teaching were identified and addressed. Individual profiles of strengths and development needs were developed to plan individual pupil's curricular or personal and social development 'targets'.

This approach has both advantages and disadvantages. Advantages reside in the detailed attention paid to the curriculum and to the specific needs of pupils and these would carry the status which comes with the involvement of the senior management team. However, unavoidable pressures on senior managers sometimes result in support not being available. Many primary schools have involved other members of the school community in providing an integrated support system, including older pupils working with younger pupils and parents through carefully planned homework programmes or in classwork with teachers and pupils. Other volunteer adults also contribute in some schools, most often senior citizens. Pupils from the associated secondary school sometimes work in primary schools with the children. The 'community' members of the Learning Support team are not intended to replace the expertise of the class teacher, who coordinates their contribution, but to provide additional individual and small group interaction.

In addition, many primary schools in Scotland are supported by Education Authority Area Learning Support teams, co-ordinated by team leaders. Each member of the team works in a number of primary schools. Patterns of provision vary: some teams allocate blocks of time to each school; in others team members spend one half day per week in several primary schools. Area team members work collaboratively with class teachers on learning and teaching issues which have been jointly identified; help design or recommend resources; help to develop school policy. Support for pupils with particular needs, e.g., pupils with a Record of Needs, is also provided by peripatetic teachers with particular expertise.

The area teams have met with mixed success. While many have been highly successful, as reported in *Teaming Up – Area teams for Learning Support* (SCRE, 1992), some have not been well regarded by schools. Some authorities are now exploring different models for the primary sector, including systems which involve psychological services, area teams and school staff in planned 'screening' to enable appropriate support. Programmes of work are jointly planned for pupils, implemented by class teachers, supported by an in-school or visiting teacher of learning support and formally reviewed from time to time. The reviews usually involve all concerned with the pupil, including parents and the class teacher.

The 1996 report from the HMI Audit Unit, *Standards and Quality in Scottish Schools 1992–95*, praised support for pupils in primary schools although it highlighted the fact that the 'focus was usually on pupils with learning difficulties' (p. 8). The areas identified for development included: challenge for able pupils; support for areas other than English Language and Mathematics; cooperative teaching methods and communication with the home.

PRESENT PRACTICE IN SCHOOLS: SECONDARY SCHOOLS

In secondary schools Support for Learning is usually the responsibility of a member of the senior management group, in collaboration with a Principal Teacher or Senior Teacher of Support for Learning. In practice the Principal Teacher, often a single person department, coordinates Support for Learning across the school and is often a member of the school's primary-secondary liaison team.

A common approach is for the Principal Teacher of Support for Learning and the school management team (sometimes with subject Principal Teachers) to identify a number of priority departments for each term and focus work with these to bid for Support for Learning time for a specific purpose, e.g. for curriculum development. While this system is considered effective in many schools the element of competitiveness involved is regarded sometimes as conflicting with the essential collaboration of Support for Learning. Working with an individual class teacher, the effective learning support teacher will co-operatively plan, teach and evaluate to promote challenging and attainable learning aims and experiences for all learners.

Support for Learning teachers can also enable learning across the curriculum, identifying potential barriers, e.g. where a science course requires understanding of a mathematics topic not yet taught; or where similar concepts are being taught in different subjects without cross-reference by teachers or pupils. They can also consider pupil's ways of learning in different subjects and explore reasons for varying degrees of success.

In addition to these consultative, staff development and cooperative teaching roles, most secondary Support for Learning teachers also pay particular attention to pupils identified as needing special support or challenge. Typically, they profile strengths, development needs and next steps and identify learning targets in all curricular areas; in some cases they tutor individual pupils or small groups. Active collaboration with school management and class teachers is important to ensure that all concerned with these pupils contribute to the achievement of the targets.

Increasingly secondary Support for Learning teachers visit their associated primary schools, collecting information on children's attainments and disseminating it to secondary colleagues to facilitate continuity and progression in learning. Like Support for Learning teachers in primary schools, secondary specialists have recognised the importance of building a community of learners. In many schools senior pupils aid pupils in S1/S2, for instance in paired-reading schemes. Parents are involved in learning through homework policies and, in a few cases, through systems of 'family learning', which may involve parents and other family members not only in helping a child with school work but also in developing their own knowledge, skills and qualifications.

The HMI Audit Report (cited earlier) also praised provision in secondary schools although it highlighted that 'support tended to be concentrated in S1/S2 and aimed at pupils with learning difficulties' (p. 15). Cooperative teaching and consultancy appeared to be more effective in secondary schools but the areas for development were similar to those identified in primary schools; challenge for more able learners; support for pupils in all areas of the curriculum.

It is interesting to reflect on the identification of these particular areas in both primary and secondary schools since these might be perceived to reflect aspects which represent the broader vision of Support for Learning.

SUPPORT FOR LEARNING: STRENGTHS, DEVELOPMENT NEEDS AND NEXT STEPS

The question to Support for Learning teachers, 'What are you calling yourselves today?', may not have been intended as a compliment but was a recognition of the significant and often rapid changes which have taken place since the late 1970s. One of the fundamental ideas in effective Support for Learning is that all learners have the right to appropriately challenging educational experiences. How far has this goal been achieved? The following section uses the formative assessment approach of the Education 5–14 programme to reflect on Support for Learning in Scotland, identifying its strengths, development needs and possible next steps.

Strengths

Much of what has happened in support for learning in the last twenty years might be regarded as strengths. The new vision of effective Support for Learning deriving from the Warnock and Inspectorate reports recognised the impact of both systems and educational practices on learning experiences, encouraged a holistic review of children's learning and began to remove 'blame' from young people for their 'inability' to learn. Further, there was a systematic attempt to translate this new vision into reality by national and local government, by schools and by teachers, linking curriculum development to staff development.

The intensive programme of staff development created a professional cadre of teachers who saw teaching essentially as a means of facilitating effective learning. Where schools' Support for Learning policies made it possible, the impact of these teachers has been substantial, bringing into focus the relationship between teaching and learning and highlighting the 'constructive' nature of the latter for individual pupils. In many ways Support for Learning in Scotland has led the way towards inclusive education.

Development needs

As Support for Learning continues to develop, there are many positive strengths on which new initiatives should build. The new roles for Support for Learning teachers which emerged from the Inspectorate Report have been interpreted in a variety of ways. In best practice the roles were integrated and focused on learning: e.g. offering consultancy to colleagues through cooperative teaching. Sometimes, however, consultancy consisted simply in giving advice to colleagues, who were expected to put it into practice independently. As a result of this literal approach, Support for Learning teachers were sometimes perceived by colleagues as being 'above' teaching and relationships became difficult. The SCCC report *Supporting Learning in Schools* (1994) and the HMI report *Effective Provision for Special Educational Needs* (1994) both attempted to address this issue. Effective Support for Learning will require sophisticated understanding and fulfilment of the five roles.

The key principle of the approach which has been replacing the 'Needs Model' of Support for Learning during the 1990s is that all children have the right to appropriately challenging educational experiences and to the maximum possible progress in the full range of the curriculum, yet this is a complicated business and the full implications of this model are not fully understood. Concomitant defining characteristics of this approach are that:

- resources should be equitably allocated so that each pupil can progress and have appropriate support, without compromising others' rights;
- the availability and allocation of resources should be open to the scrutiny of the relevant community, e.g. the pupil himself/herself, parents, class and Support for Learning teachers, representatives of the professional services and those responsible for providing the resources, e.g. the education authority;
- the identification of needs and appropriate educational experiences for each pupil should also involve all the members of the relevant community, including the pupil herself/himself.

At a practical level in schools, tensions exist between two sets of factors which, respectively, facilitate or hamper the effective implementation of Support for Learning based on the rights of all children.

On the one hand, there is recognition within the system that really effective Support for Learning requires commitment by school management and all teachers to a high quality of learning for all pupils and to the idea that all should demonstrate progress across the curriculum. Essentially, this is a commitment to certain philosophical values and to the translation of them into practical action. These values include a sophisticated concept of 'basic skills', not as simple prerequisites for learning, but as 'core intelligences', fully integrated in the growth of the learner as a person, and developed in pursuit of motivating, purposeful aims in all forms of learning. 'Deep' learning, the understanding of principles, the integration of new information and ideas in the learners' own set of constructs of reality are key ideas. Vygotsky's 'zone of proximal development' and the idea of teaching as 'mediation', enabling pupils to understand and integrate new learning, are therefore also important, as are supportive relationships between teachers and learners, and among learners – to create a 'learning community'.

On the other hand, some practice is underpinned by another set of ideas. In this philosophy basic skills are narrowly defined as aspects of literacy and numeracy; and perceptions of appropriately challenging experiences, effective learning and progress are limited, as is understanding of the potential of Support for Learning staff and systems to work with others to promote a climate where all pupils achieve more than either they or others believe possible. A 'deficit model' of thinking is still to be found: some teachers or school management still direct 'pupils with learning difficulties' to Support for Learning to remove 'the problem' from their own concerns. Such thinking is associated with limited perception on the part of school management of the nature of effective learning and teaching, and raises issues of 'quality assurance'. Quality of Support for Learning is defined in terms of structures and procedures. Personnel may appear to be fully used in the five learning support roles, but without evaluation of their actual impact on pupils' progress and development. Time is still sometimes wasted in poorly planned 'cooperative teaching'. There is also a tendency among some Support for Learning staff to continue to conceive in terms of changing or simplifying specific resource material, rather than developing pupils' strategies for learning more generally.

Given the tension between these two perceptions of effective learning support, the main development needs may be these: to devise means by which ideas about learning (and its management) associated with the rights of all pupils can become dominant and pervasive; to widen significantly the range of people involved in decision-making about resources and appropriate learning aims and experiences; and to engage in wider debate about the value and valuing of people and communities.

Next steps

Understanding the past and its relationship to the present in Support for Learning is only helpful if it is useful in steering future decision making. What then might be appropriate?

- School and department management – and individual teachers – might focus directly on values, learning strategies, 'deep' learning and pupils' real progress as persons able to deal with challenges as independently as possible, rather than on systems and procedures. This might apply both to the planning of learning and teaching and the evaluation of it.
- At least one member of the school's senior management team might become an expert in learning. This has implications for staff development. The great effort of recent years to train a corps of Support for Learning specialists to a high level of expertise may have been partially misdirected. A critical requirement is for a key member of the management team, as well as specialist staff, to understand the issues and to be able to facilitate Support for Learning in the school.
- The 'Strengths, Development Needs, Next Steps' approach to feedback on school work needs to be effectively employed throughout the school. This entails involving pupils in discussion about their own learning with not only teachers but also parents, other pupils and other relevant members of the learning community.
- In the context of clear policies for Support for Learning, well founded on good theory of learning and teaching, and in the context of good evaluation evidence about pupils' attainments related to the learning experiences they have had, there is need to involve a wider range of school staff – e.g. senior management team members, principal teachers and Support for Learning staff – in decision-making about how effective learning for all might best be realised.
- Support for effective learning may also require review of existing systems, e.g. the organisation of S1/2. To emphasise the 'wholeness' of the learner's self, it would be helpful to integrate guidance and pastoral care with learning support more formally. The more it is possible to bring other members of the learning community, e.g. pupils,

parents, auxiliaries into the process of identifying appropriate learning challenges, the better.

- Schools, Education Authorities and Teacher Education Institutions should examine carefully the range of approaches that can be used to evaluate the effectiveness of Support for Learning.
- As a society, citizens in Scotland should begin to engage widely in the debate on inclusion, developing a new vision of education in Scotland for the twenty-first century.

Steps such as these might support Scottish schools to move towards genuine 'inclusive education' of the kind now being actively advocated and planned for in other parts of Europe. Achievement of the aim of appropriately challenging and enriching education for all would, in effect, entail a re-orientation of thinking about 'Special Educational Needs'. In one sense, the concept of 'Special Needs' would be removed from the system. Every child would have an equal right to education and success. Inclusive education is not a cheap option involving, for instance, reduction in overall costs because of the closure of 'Special schools'. It requires very well planned management of all educational resources to ensure that all pupils' rights are sustained and that specialised provision is available in mainstream education, to enable access to the full range of educational experiences. It may eventually lead to a further development in terminology from 'Support for Learning' to 'Learning' itself. Perhaps the most important question which can be asked of Support for Learning is – does it make a difference? Is it really enhancing children's learning? No matter what Support for Learning is called in future years effective learning will remain the heart of the matter.

REFERENCES

Committee of Enquiry into the Education of Handicapped Children and Young People (1978), (The Warnock Report) London: HMSO.

Her Majesty's Inspectors of Schools (1978) *The Education of Pupils with Learning Difficulties in Primary and Secondary Schools in Scotland*, Edinburgh: HMSO.

Her Majesty's Inspectors of Schools (1993) *The Education of Able Pupils P6–S2*, Edinburgh: HMSO.

Riddell, S. and S. Brown, (Eds) (1994) *Special Educational Needs Policy in the 1990's: Warnock in the Market Place*, London: Routledge.

SCCC (1997) *Support for Learning in Scotland: A Paper for Discussion and Development*, Dundee: SCCC.

SOEID (1994) *Effective Provision for Special Educational Needs*, Edinburgh: HMSO.

92

Psychological Services and their Impact

Tommy MacKay

A UNIQUE STATUTORY FOUNDATION

Educational psychology services in Scotland are unique. They are built on a statutory foundation which is broader than for any other country in the world (MacKay, 1996). Their functions are prescribed in Section 4 of the Education (Scotland) Act 1980, with subsequent amendments, as follows:

> It shall be the duty of every education authority to provide for their area a psychological service in clinics or elsewhere, and the functions of that service shall include –
> (a) the study of children with special educational needs;
> (b) the giving of advice to parents and teachers as to appropriate methods of education for such children;
> (c) in suitable cases, provision for the special educational needs of such children in clinics;
> (d) the giving of advice to a local authority within the meaning of the Social Work (Scotland) Act 1968 regarding the assessment of the needs of any child for the purposes of any of the provisions of that or any other enactment.

In a number of respects these duties will be seen as having much in common with the work done by psychologists elsewhere in the UK, but there are several important differences. First, while sharing many aspects of professional practice and development with services in England and Wales, Scottish services are fundamentally different in that all of the above duties are mandatory and not discretionary. While, for example, the contribution of the educational psychologist in England and Wales is generally wide ranging, the duties which must be provided by law are narrow, and are limited to the assessment of children and young people in relation to the Statement of Needs. In Scotland, the psychological assessment for the Record of Needs, far from being the exclusive or even the principal statutory duty of the psychologist, is simply a specific requirement added to the general duties which have been described.

Second, the term 'special educational needs' when used to describe the functions of psychological services is intended to be of very broad interpretation. It is a direct replacement for the older term 'handicapped, backward and difficult children', which it was an attempt to modernise. The population of children and young people embraced by this description has been defined in statutory instruments and official guidance, and includes the full range of psychological problems of childhood, whether educational, behavioural or developmental, and whether occurring in the context of school or elsewhere. Indeed, the single most important legislative statement that can be made about educational psychology in Scotland is that it is not a school psychological service, but provides such a service as part of a wider statutory remit.

Third, the breadth of the psychologist's role outwith the narrower sphere of education is reflected in the reference to the Social Work (Scotland) Act 1968. This relates to another distinctive feature of Scottish legislation, the Children's Hearing system, which operates as an alternative to the court system for children in trouble, and for which the psychologist has a duty to provide assessment and advice.

DEVELOPMENT OF CHILD GUIDANCE SERVICES

Educational psychology is a relatively young profession, and its development in Scotland dates from the 1920s. The context in which it developed was set by its parent discipline child psychology, which had become an established subject in the universities by the end of the nineteenth century. In 1884 Francis Galton had opened in London his anthropometric laboratory for the study of individual differences, and had advocated the scientific study of children. James Sully, a founder member of the British Psychological Society and convenor of its first meeting in 1901, opened a psychological laboratory in 1896. In his classic *Studies of Childhood* (London: Longmans Green, 1896) he outlined the importance of 'the careful, methodic study of the individual child', and teachers and parents were invited to take difficult children to his laboratory for examination and advice on treatment. Sully paved the way for a new kind of specialist to work with children in the educational sphere, and in 1913 Cyril Burt became the first educational psychologist in the UK on his appointment to London County Council.

These events had a significant influence on the development of child guidance services in Scotland (McKnight, 1978). In 1923 the first appointment of a child psychologist was made when Kennedy Fraser was appointed jointly by Jordanhill College to train teachers for schools for the mentally handicapped and by Glasgow Education Committee as a psychological adviser. Meanwhile the Bachelor of Education degree (the Ed.B, not to be confused with the current pre-service degree qualification, B.Ed) was established in all four universities, and this provided the background to training in educational psychology for many years. In the late 1920s Boyd established an 'educational clinic' at Glasgow University, while Drever set up a 'psychological clinic' at Edinburgh.

While these were the forerunners of the Scottish child guidance clinics, the first establishment to bear this name was the independent Notre Dame Child Guidance Clinic, founded in Glasgow in 1931. Indeed, it is also the last to use such a description, since the term 'child guidance service' was replaced by 'psychological service' in subsequent educational legislation. The Notre Dame Clinic was established on an American model which favoured a three-member team of psychologist, psychiatrist and social worker, and its main focus was on the emotional and behavioural problems of childhood. Together with the Fern Tower Adolescent Unit it continues to provide a therapeutic service to children and young people in cooperation with health, social work and education services.

THE EFFECTS OF LEGISLATION

The statutory period for child guidance began with the Education (Scotland) Act 1946. Glasgow had established the first education authority child guidance service in 1937, to which it appointed a full-time psychologist, and by the outbreak of the war several authorities had clinics in operation, mainly on a voluntary basis and operating on Saturday mornings. In recognition of these developments the 1946 Act empowered education authorities to provide child guidance services, with a range of functions expressed in almost identical terms to the present statutory duties. The Act also required the Secretary of State to make regulations defining the various categories of handicapped children, and these were set out in the Special Educational Treatment (Scotland) Regulations 1954. This had important implications for psychologists, who developed a central role in determining which of these children required special education.

The functions of the child guidance service became mandatory in 1969, while the Education (Mentally Handicapped Children) (Scotland) Act 1974, by bringing every child in Scotland under the care of the education authority, led to an extended role for psychologists in working with pupils with profound learning difficulties. New legislation in 1981 introduced the Record of Needs for children and young people with pronounced, specific or complex special educational needs of a long-term nature, and again the role of the psychologist was extended to become a central one in coordinating the recording process for education authorities.

In addition to the education acts, several other pieces of legislation have had important implications for the development of psychological services. Until the early 1970s psychologists worked almost exclusively with children, the main thrust being with those of primary school age and to a lesser extent with pre-school children. During the 1970s there was a rapid development of the service provided to children of secondary age and to young persons. The Record of Needs legislation in 1981 dealt extensively with the position of young persons over 16, and following the Disabled Persons (Services, Consultation and Representation) Act 1986 services were re-named as 'regional or island authority psychological services' and had a remit for the population aged 0–19 years. This new term was also soon rendered obsolete, and following the Local Government (Scotland) Act 1994 psychological services faced a period of major reorganisation under the thirty-two new unitary authorities established in 1996. Finally, the Children (Scotland) Act 1995 again provided a changing context for the work of psychologists, and extended the rights of children (including those with special educational needs) to have their views taken into account in decisions regarding their education and care.

QUALIFICATIONS AND TRAINING

The training of educational psychologists has changed dramatically over the years both in structure and in content. Prior to the 1960s psychologists were first and foremost teachers. Indeed, they were frequently listed in education department records as 'teachers employed as psychologists', and it was usually recommended that they should have a minimum of two years teaching experience. Entry to the profession was through the M.Ed Honours degree (formally the Ed.B), specialising in Educational Psychology. In 1962 a postgraduate course in educational psychology was established for graduates with a first degree in psychology and, to meet the demands for recruitment following services becoming mandatory in 1969, postgraduate courses of this kind were soon operating in Aberdeen, Edinburgh, Glasgow, Stirling and Strathclyde Universities, although several of these have now been closed. They offered the degree of M.Sc or the Diploma in Educational Psychology (later M.App.Sci).

For a number of years there was considerable debate about whether teacher training and experience were to be viewed as necessary qualifications for entry to educational psychology, and for a period many employing authorities continued to demand full General Teaching Council (GTC) registration. It was the profession itself which moved away from this position and recommended new approaches to training. Now the only route into the profession is through an honours degree in psychology and a postgraduate degree in educational psychology. This training recognises that it is the study and practice of psychology itself which best informs the assessment and intervention strategies used by psychologists, and which best equips them to give appropriate advice to teachers, parents and others. A broader experience of the education system than was provided under the former teacher training arrangements is recognised as being an essential aspect of training, and this is provided for within the structure of the postgraduate course. Most entrants to the profession take the four year single honours degree in psychology at one of the Scottish universities and proceed to the two year M.Sc. in Educational Psychology at either Dundee or Strathclyde University.

Because of the high demand for postgraduate places prospective trainees generally require to spend at least two years following (or prior to) their first degree, gaining additional qualifications or experience in fields relevant to educational psychology. This may be, for example, in children's homes, teaching, research or the voluntary sector. As a result, entrants to the profession have for many years been very highly qualified and experienced in their preparations for beginning work as educational psychologists. Practice tutors from the field are centrally involved in supervising placements in psychological services throughout the two postgraduate years. During this period most trainees are seconded to education authorities and receive a trainee educational psychologist salary through Scottish Office Education and Industry Department (SOEID) funding.

The final steps in reaching independent professional status involve a probationary period working under the supervision of an appropriately qualified psychologist, during which time it is possible to work towards the British Psychological Society (BPS) requirements to become a chartered educational psychologist. Quality and standards of training and induction into employment are monitored by the training committee of the BPS Scottish Division of Educational Psychology. For psychologists in service, local arrangements for further study and training are supplemented by a national programme of continuing professional development. This is coordinated by the professional organisations for psychologists in Scotland, helped by SOEID funding through a Professional Development Programme.

STAFFING AND RECRUITMENT

The number of educational psychologists employed in Scotland as at September 1997 was a full time equivalent of 339 (ASPEP, the Association of Scottish Principal Educational Psychologists, 1997). This gave an average ratio of 1:3600 of the 0–19 population. All of the thirty-two local authorities have their own psychological service, and in most cases these are under the direction of a principal educational psychologist, supported by senior psychologists except in the smallest services. The average percentage of promoted staff was 42 per cent. The specific duties of psychologists at all grades are as agreed with the Scottish Joint Negotiating Committee for Teaching Staff in School Education (SJNC).

LEVELS OF WORK AND CORE FUNCTIONS

Educational psychologists work at three main levels: the level of the individual child or family, the level of the school or establishment and the level of the local authority. This distinguishes psychologists from all other groups in the education system and provides them with a unique opportunity to facilitate interactions between these levels (Kirkaldy, 1997). They also cover the entire age range of children and young people in both mainstream and special sectors in relation to a full spectrum of difficulties in education, behaviour and development. In addition, they frequently occupy the central role in coordinating the work of a multi-disciplinary team from health, education and social work and from the voluntary agencies. The breadth of this work gives psychological services a pivotal role in assisting the local authority in the management and development of resources in the field of special educational needs.

In relation to each of the three levels of work, psychologists have five core functions: assessment, intervention, consultation, training and research (MacKay, 1989). All of these functions operate within an interactive context in which the problems of individual children and young people are assessed as part of a wider environment such as classroom or school. While assessment and intervention therefore may involve the use of a wide range of techniques and strategies directly with the individual, a central part of the psychologist's role is in assisting parents and teachers in supporting children with difficulties. This leads to considerable involvement by psychological services in parenting skills, classroom management strategies and staff training, and in the development of new methodologies for helping young people who experience problems in their learning, behaviour or development.

Although acting frequently in a liaison capacity between the education authority, the school and the child or parent, the psychologist in giving advice and in making recommendations must always act in the best interests of the child or young person. This is required by the *Code of Conduct, Ethical Principles and Guidelines* of the BPS, which sets strict professional standards and exercises disciplinary powers in relation to its members. One of the key skills of the psychologist therefore in giving independent advice is the ability to negotiate arrangements which will best meet children's needs, and to handle tensions which may arise from the perspective of the school or other agencies or indeed between the child and the parent.

RANGE AND SOURCE OF REFERRALS

The foundation of a psychological service and its predominant activity is casework. This is based on interactive assessment and intervention involving both the children or young people who are referred and the local contexts, such as school or family, in which they function (ASPEP, *Psychological Services in Scotland: A Briefing Paper for the New Councils*, 1995). The range of problems referred is almost certainly wider than for any other branch of psychology. Reasons for referral include all of the traditional groupings within the field of special educational needs – moderate, severe and profound learning difficulties, visual and hearing impairments, physical disability, emotional and behavioural disorders and language and communication disorders. During the 1990s overall referral patterns have reflected an increased interest in and concern with the areas of specific learning difficulties, attention deficit/hyperactivity disorder, the autistic spectrum and child abuse. Referrals may arise in discussion with a variety of agencies, and in some cases are made directly by parents. Older children and young people have a right to make a confidential self-referral, and this is treated in a way which takes account of age and maturity, and the nature of the problem referred. Nevertheless, since problems do not generally occur in isolation but within a family, social or educational context, the small group of self-referrals would normally be guided towards a position which encouraged liaison with other agencies.

It is the schools themselves, however, which have always accounted for perhaps 80 per cent of the referrals to psychological services across Scotland, and much of the backbone of the work arises from the referrals of pupils with educational difficulties or behaviour problems in the classroom. While this may be the most routine aspect of the work of the psychologist it is often the contribution which is most valued by teachers and others who are seeking to support children with difficulties.

THE RECORD OF NEEDS

While it is estimated that up to 20 per cent of pupils may have special educational needs at some stage during their school career, a small proportion of these pupils have needs described in the Education (Scotland) Act 1980 as 'pronounced, specific or complex special educational needs which are such as require continuing review'. In these cases it is the duty of the education authority to open a Record of Needs, and it is not lawful to do so unless there has been a process of psychological assessment.

It is important to recognise that since this group represents approximately one in ten of all children with special needs (SOEID Circular No. 4/96, *Children and Young Persons with Special Educational Needs, Assessment and Recording*), they are not the principal focus of the work of psychological services. However, the arrangements for pupils in this category are of a more formal nature, and involvement in this area has made a considerable impact on the work of the psychologist. In addition to responsibility for the psychological assessment, the psychological service is also responsible in most authorities for coordinating the entire recording process, for preparing the draft Record of Needs on behalf of the authority and for planning the placement and other special provisions which the child or young person requires.

CHILDREN'S HEARINGS AND SOCIAL WORK

The Children's Hearings in Scotland were developed as an alternative system to the juvenile courts for dealing with children and young people in trouble. Cases are heard by a panel which has a range of options including home or residential supervision orders, or in some instances referral to the sheriff. Since 1969 one of the statutory functions of psychological services has been to provide reports to the social work department or to the Reporter to the Children's Panel in cases where psychological assessment and advice may be helpful.

The pattern of referrals from the Reporter varies from one area to another, and in some services accounts for up to 12 per cent of the workload. The problems referred may occur mainly in relation to the home, the school or the community, and may centre on issues of child care and protection, criminal offences or school attendance issues. In addition to the cases which reach the Reporter, there is a large number of other situations calling for joint working between psychological services and social work, and the effect of more recent legislation has been to increase the involvement of the psychologist with social work and the Reporter in a wide range of child care issues.

IMPACT ON EDUCATIONAL POLICY AND DEVELOPMENT

As well as fulfilling their central task of assisting children and young people with special educational needs, educational psychology services have made a substantial impact on education authority policy and development. Their contribution has been significant not only in the special needs field but also in relation to education in general. This may be illustrated by reference to four areas.

First, the role of psychologists in shaping policy for special educational needs at national and local authority level has been a crucial one. Most authorities have relied heavily on psychological services in planning and developing their special provision, and in a national context psychologists have contributed substantially to government circulars and guidance in this area. Psychologists have also been the dominant force in promoting a philosophy of inclusive education, and in developing the context which enables special needs pupils to be educated along with their mainstream peers.

Second, through research, training, promotion of good practice and production of resources, educational psychologists have had a vast influence on classroom management strategies, anti-bullying policies, parent partnership, child protection procedures, learning support and school organisation and ethos. Packages on *Promoting Positive Behaviour* and *Promoting Positive Relationships* (Glasgow City Council) are in use in over 1,000 Scottish schools. There is also widespread use of resources on *Working with Parents for Change* (West Dunbartonshire Council) and *School Initiated Monitoring of Needs (SIMON)* (Glasgow City Council). It is probably the case that virtually every educational establishment in Scotland at nursery, primary, secondary and special level uses strategies or resources developed by psychological services.

Third, psychologists have been central in highlighting the importance of socioeconomic disadvantage as a major dimension in Scottish education. Through published research they have not only emphasised its significance as the principal correlate of educational under-achievement but have also developed a range of interventions for tackling its effects (see, for example, J. Boyle and T. MacKay, eds, 1999, 'Responding to the problems of reading failure in schools: A Scottish Perspective', *Educational and Child Psychology*, vol. 16, no. 1). In addition, in many education authorities they have been instrumental in developing a policy framework which targets additional resources on disadvantaged populations.

Fourth, the work of educational psychologists in Scotland in designing projects for improving children's achievement in literacy has been internationally recognised and has had a major impact on national practice. This contribution has been acknowledged in the design and development of early intervention projects for literacy operating from session 1997–8 onwards in all thirty-two education authorities with SOEID funding.

A number of consumer studies have been published through the 1980s and 1990s, in which the views of teachers, parents and others have been surveyed. These have acknowledged the impact of psychological services and their value within the education system.

CURRENT ISSUES

A historical analysis of Scottish educational psychology published during the 1980s examined its progress through each of the decades of the twentieth century and pointed to sweeping changes which were about to affect the profession (MacKay, 1989). It was predicted that as a result of such change the 1990s would be a decade either of 'regeneration' or of 'degeneration'. The response of educational psychology to these changes has pointed to a profession which has regenerated itself. It has addressed significant challenges to its structure and role and has redefined its place and purpose within the local authority. Educational psychology continues to face many important issues. Some of the most significant may be summarised under the headings of role, recruitment, recording and reorganisation.

THE CHANGING ROLE OF THE PSYCHOLOGIST

Educational psychology in Scotland is in the midst of what has been described as a 'paradigm shift' from a largely medical model of assessment and intervention to one which is largely educational (Kirkaldy, 1997). In the first model the psychologist operates as a separate expert technician who applies a range of psychological tests and techniques, the use of which is restricted to the profession. In this model, responsibility for children's problems is referred on to the psychologist by parents and teachers. In the second model the psychologist is a consultative colleague who works alongside parents, teachers and other key adults who have primary responsibility for assessment and intervention in the child's normal context. In this ecological model the perspective is an interactionist one. It recognises that it is only changes in the social ecology of the child or young person which have sustainable effects on development.

Although this change of models is a pronounced one, it is part of a continuous rather than a discontinuous process. The early work of psychologists in Scotland was subject to two major influences which have had an impact on the development of services to the present day. The first was the influence of the mental testing movement, with its focus on the assessment of individual differences in children. The second was the influence of the child guidance movement, with its focus on treatment of children with emotional and behavioural difficulties. These two emphases point to areas which are still central to the work of psychological services today – careful assessment of the individual child with special needs, and providing specialist help to children with difficulties in their emotional and behavioural adjustment. However, it is the way in which these areas are approached that has been subject to extensive change and development. The early foundations of assessment and treatment may be described respectively as being psychometric and psychodynamic. Central to almost all assessment was the intelligence test (typically the Stanford Binet Intelligence Scale and the Wechsler Intelligence Scale for Children), which was used universally in identifying handicapped and backward pupils and in selection for special schools and remedial education. Underlying treatment was a theoretical framework which focused on dynamic processes within the child, resulting in the need for individual therapy over an extended period.

While there is still an important place for counselling and therapy in an appropriate context, the earlier psychodynamic emphasis on individual treatment has been challenged on grounds both of efficacy and economy. Psychometric assessment continues in fact to be widely used by educational psychologists in Scotland, but it would no longer be the significant thrust in the assessment strategies used. It too has been the subject of theoretical and practical debate at a level which has challenged its entire foundations. At the same time there has been an increased reliance on psychometric test results in the wider society as educational litigation becomes more common, and this creates a number of tensions.

A central feature of this debate has been two of the main criticisms made of educational psychology by the teaching profession: first, that 'psychologists only tell teachers what they already know'; second, that psychologists do not have the time to provide the help which children require. Both criticisms highlight the need for a collaborative model of working in which the psychologist makes a distinctive contribution to assessment as part of a team, and in which intervention strategies are in most cases targeted more effectively than through individual therapy. Nevertheless, despite these criticisms, consumer surveys conducted with teachers and others have consistently indicated that the contribution of educational psychologists is valued, as are new and more collaborative models of assessment and intervention, so long as the value of direct work with the individual child continues to be appropriately recognised. (See MacKay and Boyle, 1994, for a review of this area.)

The way in which the profession handles this paradigm shift in its model of assessment and intervention will represent its greatest challenge in the coming decade.

RECRUITMENT TO THE PROFESSION

Another serious challenge facing the profession during the next decade will be recruitment at levels necessary to allow staffing standards and quality of service to be maintained. There are two principal reasons for this.

First, the number of psychologists leaving services each year through retirement and other causes has exceeded the supply of qualified trainees, resulting in a widespread shortfall in staffing. This pattern is likely to continue unless there is a significant increase in the number of secondments to the postgraduate courses. A national analysis of age and staffing structures has indicated that if current trends continue 58 per cent of psychologists will leave the profession during the next ten years (ASPEP, 1997). Postgraduate courses in educational psychology require very high ratios of university staff, and the SOEID has recognised the significant investment which must be made in the expansion of courses if serious levels of understaffing in psychological services are to be avoided. This process will take time, and the universities have already experienced difficulties in recruiting staff who are qualified to teach educational psychology at postgraduate level.

Second, a number of developments including changes in legislation have led to considerable increases in the work psychologists are required to undertake. An increase in staffing establishments would be necessary to maintain levels of service delivery and to fulfil statutory duties. The professional organisations for psychologists in Scotland have indicated four main reasons for higher workloads (ASPEP, 1997). First, there has been a widened conceptualisation of special educational needs, leading to a very great increase in the number of children and young people identified. This has been associated with a greater awareness of parental rights, higher expectations of service delivery and increased levels of litigation in relation to public services. Second, there has been a broadened scope of applicability of psychological services. Some of this has stemmed from new legislation such as the Children (Scotland) Act 1995, and some from demand from councils for a whole range of new services such as responding to traumatic incidents affecting schools and communities. Third, the benefits to consumers of a more sophisticated, ecological approach to effective assessment and intervention has led to an increased demand for services. By using psychologists for anti-bullying strategies and many other initiatives at whole school and authority level, councils have benefited from cost-effective and preventative roles for psychological services. Fourth, an extension of the principle of equal opportunities for children and young people has introduced demands on services to achieve new standards of professional and public accountability in a wider range of areas. This is reflected in the increased numbers of pupils with special needs in mainstream schools, a more central place in society for the policy and practice of child care and the extension of rights directly to children and young people. All of these developments have imposed new levels of demand on services and have required a reappraisal of staffing establishments.

THE IMPACT OF THE RECORD OF NEEDS

Although recording is applicable only to a small proportion of the special needs population for whom the psychologist has statutory responsibilities, and is therefore not the main area of a psychologist's work, it is recognised throughout services that it has potential to occupy a disproportionate amount of time. Psychologists frequently find themselves under considerable pressure to initiate Records, often because it is believed, unsurprisingly, that this will provide access to higher levels of provision and resources. In many services the number of Records has increased to the point where service resources have had to be deflected from other areas of work in which the contribution of the psychologist might be more effective in meeting a wider range of needs.

Recording leads to a number of other tensions within educational psychology. The Record of Needs legislation is based on a static psycho-medical model of assessment where the focus is on deficits within the child. The 1981 Act required a 'psychological examination' of the child, and although in 1986 this was changed to 'a process of psychological assessment', the basic model still reflects a different paradigm from that which generally operates within psychological services. Issues of equal opportunity have also been raised in regard to the Record, as patterns of recording have not appeared to reflect adequately the real spread of needs as indicated by socioeconomic and other variables.

These issues represent an important challenge to psychological services in relation to policy development and the planning of effective and equitable service delivery.

LOCAL GOVERNMENT REORGANISATION

In common with various other sectors of education, psychological services in Scotland were subject to large-scale restructuring as a result of the reorganisation of local government. This has not only had a direct impact on the way service is delivered, but it has also affected greatly the work of psychologists as individuals and has raised issues for professional development. Prior to reorganisation, most services were large enough both to carry out their generic responsibilities and to provide an integrated team of specialists covering areas such as visual impairment, hearing impairment and language and communication disorders. Smaller services usually had access to the support of specialists in adjoining areas. Following local government reorganisation most teams are small, and the work of the individual psychologist has become more wide ranging, with each psychologist requiring specialist knowledge in almost every area of expertise.

Nevertheless, at the close of the twentieth century educational psychology is a confident profession which has not only adapted successfully to change itself, but has been the facilitator of considerable change and development within the education system as a whole. From its unique statutory foundation it has developed a pivotal role in shaping policy and provision in the field of special educational needs, and in addressing its current challenges it is well placed to offer an extended range of effective services within local authorities in Scotland.

REFERENCES

ASPEP (1997) *Local Authority Psychological Services in Scotland: Staffing and Training of Educational Psychologists*, Report of the Association of Scottish Principal Educational Psychologists, The British Psychological Society and the Educational Institute of Scotland.

Kirkaldy, B. (1997) Contemporary tasks for psychological services in Scotland, *Educational Psychology in Scotland*, 5, 6–16.

MacKay, T. A. W. N. (1989) Special education: the post-Warnock role for the educational psychologist, *British Psychological Society SDECP Newsletter*, 1, 1–8.

MacKay, T. A. W. N. (1996) The statutory foundations of Scottish educational psychology services, *Educational Psychology in Scotland*, 3, 3–9.

MacKay, T. A. W. N. and J. M. Boyle (1994) Meeting the needs of pupils with learning difficulties: what do primary and secondary schools expect of their educational psychologists?, *Educational Research*, 36, 187–96.

McKnight, R. K. (1978) The development of child guidance services, in W. B. Dockrell, W. R. Dunn and A. Milne (eds) *Special Education in Scotland*, Edinburgh: Scottish Council for Research in Education, pp. 97–109.

93

Social Work Services

Mono Chakrabarti

This chapter addresses some of the more significant current issues in social welfare provision for members of the community who have needs which they, their families and their other social networks are unable to meet, for a variety of reasons, without additional forms of support. Social Work Services have been created to help people to meet these social needs and to maintain their ability to function as individuals in relation to other people and their environment. Inevitably, it operates within the broader economic and social systems that the society has developed.

Social Work Services are not so readily identifiable nor so widely familiar an aspect of the welfare state as, for example, the national health service or the social security and education systems. However, Social Work is an accountable professional activity which facilitates individuals, families and groups to identify personal, social and environmental difficulties adversely affecting them. Social Work supports them to manage these difficulties through supportive, rehabilative, protective or corrective action. It also promotes social welfare and responds to wider social needs promoting equal opportunities for every age, gender, sexual preference, class, disability, race, culture and creed. It has a legal responsibility to protect the vulnerable and exercise authority under various statutes.

Social Workers are part of a network of welfare, health, criminal justice and penal provision. Parliament lays down the legal framework and delineates the powers of statutory, voluntary and private agencies within which social workers practise. Their roles can vary in residential, day care, domiciliary, fieldwork and community settings, but they share a common core of knowledge, skills and values. The workforce involved in delivering this range of service provisions therefore includes, in addition to social workers, other professionals such as occupational therapists, psychologists and community workers. The main focus of this chapter will be local authority based service delivery. First, however, it is important to look briefly at the historical roots of Social Work Departments.

HISTORICAL BACKGROUND

Although the Welfare State was designed in its present form following the Second World War, Social Work Services have their origin in the reforms of the late nineteenth and early twentieth century, following the upheaval of the Industrial Revolution with its intense social consequences. Social Work Services have their roots in the Poor Law and in the philanthropic movements of the late nineteenth century.

The Poor Law was a scheme devised to deal with poverty following the medieval period. In Scotland, the scheme was by and large administered by the Kirk. The system was concerned with control as well as care, the swarms of beggars being found to be a menace if uncontrolled. The Poor Law survived in a reduced form until the emergence of the Welfare State, and it became associated with some of the unhappy attempts by government to deal with the unemployment problem of the 1920s and 1930s. In the public mind it became an evil to be avoided, and it was with delight that the architects of the Welfare State declared in 1948 in the National Assistance Act, that the Poor Law was abolished. While its income maintenance function was superseded, its welfare function remained as the responsibility of local authorities.

The expansion of Social Work Services meant new opportunities for social workers, many of whom had previously been associated with charities and other welfare promoting movements. The most significant development was the 1948 Children Act, which created a new specialised service in local authority to care for deprived children. These children had originally been the concern of the Poor Law, but often provision for them was divided among various relevant local authority committees. The Act was concerned with the emotional as well as the material needs of children in care and looked for a new group of people to work with them in specialised local authority departments. It is significant to note that although the Children's Departments were inaugurated in 1948 there were no specialised child care courses in Scotland until the University of Edinburgh started one in 1960. Until that time, the majority of children's officers were the former Poor Law Inspectors.

In 1961, the Scottish Office established a committee under the chairmanship of Lord Kilbrandon to consider the future management of juvenile delinquents 'who are in need of compulsory measures of care'. The report, *Children and Young Persons, Scotland*, was published in 1964. It was a closely argued document and recommended sweeping changes in (a) the system of juvenile justice to replace juvenile courts with a system of Children's Panels, (b) the matching field organisation to replace the Children and Probation Department by a Social Education Department. Kilbrandon was concerned that the crime/responsibility/punishment philosophy of criminal courts impinged too closely on the juvenile court system, when in fact, more weight ought to be given to prevention including treatment which he conceived as Social Education.

The government of the day responded to the Report by publishing a White Paper, *Social Work and the Community*, in 1966. It proposed to implement the Kilbrandon recommendations in general in relation to juvenile justice but instead of the Social Education Department it proposed to draw together into one department the existing Children's Welfare including mental health and probation service. The proposed reorganisation of juvenile justice and social work services in Scotland was not seen as a party political issue and did not meet any major opposition. The White Paper culminated in the Social Work (Scotland) Act 1968 just as the Seebohm Report was to culminate in the Social Services Act 1970 in England. The Act of 1968 represented the ending of one era and the beginning of new unified social work service provision in Scotland with a separate committee and a Chief Officer, who was not only responsible for the functions of the previous departments but was also required to 'promote social welfare', a phrase meant to cover any activity designed to help individuals, families and community groups and contribute to community planning. The Act also introduced an entirely new and unique system of juvenile justice, that of Children's Hearings where lay members appointed by the Secretary of State for Scotland meet with the child and parents before deciding on appropriate action.

The reorganisation of Social Work Services can thus be seen as a move by government to find a solution to intransigent social problems and a solution that would be under their control. There can be no doubt that the newly organised departments were to be a much more powerful force in local government than the previous various welfare and children's committees.

TRAINING OF SOCIAL WORKERS

A Statutory body, the Central Council for Education and Training in Social Work (CCETSW), was established as a result of the Local Authority Social Services Act 1970 to assume responsibility for functions previously undertaken by a number of specialist bodies in the area of education and training for social workers in the UK. There are National Committees in England, Scotland, Wales and Northern Ireland with a wide range of delegated responsibilities to plan, oversee and monitor CCETSW's work in each of the countries. Council members are all appointed by the Secretary of State. Its aim is to ensure high quality education, training and qualifications for social workers throughout the United Kingdom. CCETSW works with employer interests, user groups, higher educational interests and professional organisations across the statutory, voluntary and private sectors. In fulfilling its statutory responsibility, CCETSW undertakes four main functions: 1.) Promotion and development of training; 2.) Regulation of training; 3.) Awarding qualifications, and 4.) Provision of some student bursaries.

As an awarding body, CCETSW registers students and candidates for all its awards, issues certificates to students successfully completing courses, maintains formal records of approved courses and accredited agencies for practice learning, and confirms for prospective employers and others whether individuals hold a CCETSW qualification. It also verifies social work qualifications obtained outside the United Kingdom.

THE WORK OF SOCIAL WORK DEPARTMENTS

This section will consider the main social work services that come under the jurisdiction of social work departments. For convenience, these services will be clustered under three broad headings, namely, Community Care, Adult Criminal Justice and Children and Families. The juvenile justice system, known as Children's Hearings in Scotland, will be dealt with later.

Community care

Throughout the 1980s and 1990s there has been a noticeable significant shift in the area of public administration. The local authorities are increasingly expected to move away from the role of direct provider of services to concentrate on ensuring that services are provided for clients, using financial and statutory powers to set standards and monitor their achievement. This new ethos projects welfare pluralism, that is, a whole range of providers working within the boundaries set by a statutory agency acting as the lead organisation.

Although this shift has been evident in the areas of education, compulsory competitive tendering and housing provision, it is in Community Care that this philosophy finds its clearest expression. However, unlike these other three areas, the growth of an enabling role in social work provision has not been entirely driven by ideological positions. Rather it has been a natural progression of social work practice over a period of years. The idea of care in the community in the sense of a planned shift away from institutions was promoted first in the 1950s.

The purpose of community care is to meet the needs of client groups in an appropriate manner, and to that end a policy based on three principles has been established. The first element has been a move away from institutions to community based service provision, the second, a transfer of resources from social security and health to social work and the third, the development of the notion of partnership between statutory and independent sectors.

Probably the clearest element embedded in the concept of community care is the movement for deinstitutionalisation of welfare services. It has been recognised that large impersonal institutions, in which many people have been cared for, are psychologically and socially damaging and inhibit the capacity for independent living. The move has been to reduce the size of institutions providing personal care and to decentralise them, to encourage people to make independent decisions about everyday life and to bring them into more regular contact with other people who live outside institutions, so that personal relationships with people who do not need special care are encouraged. Such relationships are likely to increase people's capacity to manage their affairs and provide personal support which is not based on the institution, and is, therefore, less inward looking.

The White Paper *Caring for People* published in 1989 gave expression to the above ideas and principles and led to the National Health Service and Community Care Act, 1990. This is a United Kingdom Act but contains a separate section on community care for Scotland. The Act covers provisions ranging from strategic objectives to arrangements at practical level for providing information to the general public and setting up a system for buying in support services from the independent sector.

To achieve these objectives, the government has introduced a number of significant changes in the ways in which community care is to be delivered and resourced. Local authority Social Work departments are given responsibility for providing and/or organising social care for elderly people and for people who are mentally ill or have physical or learning difficulties. Responsibility for the funding of residential and other social care is to be transferred from the Department of Social Security to local authorities. Of crucial importance is the requirement to develop and publish comprehensive community care plans for each area with the active involvement of health and housing authorities and voluntary organisations.

Since the introduction of the Act, a number of research projects have raised questions about efficiency and effectiveness in the delivery of community care. Firstly, in relation to a specifically 'needs-led' assessment it has been found that workers are still on a learning curve, often failing to carry out a comprehensive assessment of needs. Secondly, finding suitable accommodation has been identified as an important constraint on meeting the needs of people with learning difficulties and with mental health problems. Thirdly, a low proportion of people with mental health problems appear to receive day care services. There are also problems in separating out roles within the integrated system with over-emphasis on organisational structures, communication difficulties and over concentration on con-tracts rather than service delivery. Unmet needs due to lack of facilities and funding for basic services are still apparent which led the Audit Commission to comment (1994) that 'the separation of purchaser and provider roles creates a tension within the organisation which may actually be counter-productive . . . the separation may leave the consumer as a victim of declining standards, as emphasis is placed on meeting contracted budget costs'.

Adult criminal justice

If one attempts to think of a generic term for the practice of social work with people who are offending, the main term is likely to be 'probation'. In part, this stems from the previous organisational arrangements whereby there was in Scotland, until 1969, a separate department of probation. Since 1969 many and varied arrangements for work with people who are offending have been developed. One important initiative was the development of community service either as a sentence in its own right or as a condition of a probation order.

Social Work connections with the sheriff courts are more limited compared with their involvement in the Children's Hearings system (which will be discussed more fully in the next section). When probation orders are made it falls to Social Work Departments to carry them out, but such disposals account for only a very small fraction of sheriff court cases. The preparation of reports for the courts is, however, a large scale activity, mainly because the Criminal Justice (Scotland) Act 1980 requires the courts to obtain reports about young offenders, that is those under the age of 21, in order to decide whether any method other than detention is appropriate, as well as about older offenders who have not previously been sentenced to imprisonment or detention.

In the search for alternatives to imprisonment, the concept of the community service order has attracted a widespread interest. Offenders, usually young adults, may be required to spend a fixed number of hours on some practical, socially constructive task. The supervision of community service orders falls to the social work department, and the staff undertaking this work generally specialise in it.

In 1991, the Scottish Office published a policy document initiating significant changes in the practice of social work with people who are offending. It is called *National Objectives and Standards for Social Work in the Criminal Justice System*, generally referred to in Social Work as the National Standard. The overall aim of the National Standard is 'to assist the courts to keep the use of custodial sentences to the minimum necessary for the protection of the public and the requirements of justice and to help offenders to stop offending' (Section 28). The National Standard is an important document affecting Social Work practice and other parts of the criminal justice systems in Scotland. It sets out standards to be achieved by social work service providers and provides the benchmark for quality assurance procedures for social work departments.

Children and families

The essential need for children to have a caring home life and fulfilling upbringing has long been acknowledged. Children are dependent on adults for their very survival, and the quality of care they receive, both physically and mentally, will go far to determine the type of adults they will grow up to be. Therefore, it is of fundamental importance that children are given the appropriate care and support, so they can develop mentally and be physically alert, contented and emotionally stable. Only then can they grow up able to enjoy full lives, to become responsible and socially participatory citizens. These conditions are also essential if they are to benefit fully from the opportunities offered by the educational system.

The overwhelming majority of children are reared by their natural parents and most are cared for well. As recognition of the importance of the early formative years has developed, society, however, has taken an increasing role in formulating policies for child welfare. It has demonstrated its concern in broadly three main ways. Firstly, by supporting parents in their job of child rearing and by making available services like maternity care and child welfare, schooling and a range of financial benefits. Secondly, by taking care directly of children who have no parents and, lastly, by taking over the care of children whose parents are not providing properly for their physical and/or emotional well being.

Child care service must feature prominently in any account of social work service provision. Residential provision is a significant component of child care, though most social workers would hold to the view that taking a child into residential care should generally be thought of as a last course of action. A considerable amount of skilled social work activity is therefore devoted to efforts to prevent family breakdown with a consequent need for children to be cared for by Social Work Departments. Even when a residential solution becomes unavoidable, it is generally hoped that this will be temporary rather than permanent, and a period of intensive work with the parents may be necessary in the hope of making it possible for the child to return to the parental home. Increasingly when children are being looked after by local authorities they are placed with foster parents on a short or long term basis. If it is clear that a child for a variety of reasons will not be able to return home, adoptive parents may be sought, even for older children. This in turn means that residential services are increasingly being used for children and young people whose difficulties, which may well include violent behaviour, make it virtually impossible to find foster families who are able and willing to take them. Clearly this adds to the strain and the demands, both personal and professional, on staff and emphasises the need for improved and up-to-date training for social work personnel.

A further complication for Social Work Departments is the increase in numbers of one-parent families as a consequence of marital breakdown and divorce, and the growth in the numbers of single mothers who prefer to bring up their own children. According to the 1991 census, 93 per cent of lone single parents in Scotland are women and of these, 31.7 per cent are single women with children.

These trends have led to a sharp debate. One side of this claims that two-parent families are good for children and one-parent families are not conducive to the needs of children. From the opposite viewpoint, the incidence of 'bad' two-parent families and 'good' one parent families is often cited. It is also argued that the source of many problems of one-parent families is the financial hardship that so many of them experience.

The rough consensus on family policy by the state that existed in earlier decades no longer exists. Division and controversy now characterise this area of policy and, given the trends in family formation, which show no signs of slackening, this is likely to continue. The debate in recent years has served to identify the choices that have to be made and the programmes which might be pursued. However, irrespective of the outcome of this debate, it is generally accepted that such families often require a good deal of support of many kinds, though it would be optimistic to assume that these needs are always met, even though Section 12 of the Social Work (Scotland) Act 1968 makes it a responsibility of Social Work Departments to provide such support services.

In extreme cases children need to be actively protected from one or both of their parents. The issue of child abuse, or child protection as it is often now described, perhaps more than any other area of child care policy and practice, has brought the activities of health, education, police and other welfare professionals into considerable public, political and media focus in recent years. During the last twenty years well over forty public enquiries in the UK have put the practice and decision making of social workers under the microscope.

In many respects the issue has provided the main vehicle for articulating a series of debates about how the state, via its Social Work Departments, responds to the needs of children more generally and intervenes in the private sphere of the family in particular. If one takes an objective reading of various child protection related enquiry reports, one finds a picture which might suggest that social workers and their agencies have been caught in a political crossfire between being criticised, on the one hand, for allowing some children to suffer unnecessarily, sometimes to the point of death, at the hands of their parents or guardians, and, on the other hand, of intervening unwarrantably in other families and removing their children inappropriately. It is certainly the case that under the existing statute, Social Work Departments have powers to intervene in cases where it is clear that children are seriously at risk and to assume responsibility for their care.

Such cases can be referred to the Reporter of the Children's Panel and brought before a Children's Hearing. However, as suggested before, given the political sensitivities associated with issues of child protection, Social Work Departments are often having to develop a very complex set of procedural arrangements involving a whole range of other professional groups, thereby compounding further the decision making process. Therefore, it is important to establish a good professional relationship with teachers, in particular, with those who carry 'guidance' responsibility in order to provide effective support to this group of very vulnerable children (see Chapter 43).

THE CHILDREN'S HEARINGS SYSTEM

Scotland is unusual in having a juvenile justice system where a significant amount of professional input comes from social work which is controlled and managed through primary social work legislation. Indeed, as has been explained, the proposal to reorganise Scottish Social Work Services was originally a by-product of the Kilbrandon proposals for the replacement of the juvenile courts by a system of Children's Hearings. The hearing system is based on the principle that the promotion of the best interests of the child should be the primary concern. Hence the welfare objective has received some significant emphasis.

Three agencies can be identified as the principal components of the hearing system: the Reporter, the Children's Panel and the Social Work Department. The police are quite independent of the hearings system but it need scarcely be said that the functioning of the system is heavily dependent on their cooperation.

Social workers have a number of extremely significant responsibilities in relation to young offenders. When such children are brought to the notice of the reporter s/he will usually ask the Social Work Department to provide a preliminary social background report. It is known from research evidence that these reports have an important influence on the Reporter's decision to bring a child before the hearing or not. If the Reporter decides that the child does indeed appear to be in need of compulsory measures of care, either the same or a new, fuller social background report will be provided for the guidance of the panel members, generally with a recommendation about the disposal of the case. These reports in their turn help to shape discussion in the hearing and also have a good deal of influence on the outcome.

When that outcome is a supervision requirement, social workers are given a central role. The great majority of such supervision orders allow the child to continue to live at home but social workers may also have to maintain contact with the minority of young people who are required to spend time in residential supervision. A supervision requirement differs in many ways from a probation order. Essentially it is an opportunity for a young person to form a relationship of trust with a social worker, and for the latter to use that relationship to help bring about greater self awareness and a move towards more mature attitudes and more responsible behaviour.

It is a widely held view that the potential of Children's Hearings is not yet fully developed and the same principle can be usefully applied to other areas of domestic family matters. At the same time, it is generally acknowledged that there are blemishes in practice that need to be remedied.

THE CHILDREN (SCOTLAND) ACT 1995

The Scottish Law Commission's report on Family Law in 1992 suggested that there was a need for a more child-centred approach to social work service delivery based on a whole host of academic research. The government published a White Paper *Scotland's Children* with a view to generating public debate around child care issues, out of which came the Children (Scotland) Act 1995. It came into operation in April 1996. The Act marks a significant stage in the development of legislation on the care of children in Scotland. It is centred on the needs of children and their families and defines both parental responsibilities and rights in relation to children. It sets out the duties and powers available to public authorities to support children and their families and to intervene when the child's welfare requires it. It has also incorporated some aspects of the UN Declaration of Human Rights.

The essential principles behind the Act are (a) each child has a right to be treated as an individual; (b) each child who can form a view on matters affecting him or her has the right to express those views if he or she so wishes; (c) parents should normally be responsible for the upbringing of their children and should share that responsibility; (d) each child has a right to protection from all forms of abuse, neglect or exploitation; (e) so far as is consistent with safeguarding and promoting the child's welfare, the public authority should promote the upbringing of children by their families and any intervention by a public authority in the life of a child must be properly justified and should be supported by services from all relevant agencies working in collaboration.

In support of the above principles three main themes run through the Act. These are:

- the welfare of the child is the paramount consideration when his or her needs are considered by courts and children's hearings;
- no court should make an order relating to a child and no children's hearing should make a supervision requirement unless the court or hearing considers that to do so would be better for the child than making no order or supervision requirement at all;
- the child's views should be taken into account where major decisions are to be made about his or her future.

In addition, there is a requirement in various parts of the Act for those providing for children to have regard to religious persuasion, racial origin and cultural and linguistic background. This reflects an acknowledgement that Scottish society is multiracial and multicultural and social work service provisions must respond appropriately to the needs of children from minority ethnic backgrounds.

For the purposes of support for children and families, 'child' means a person under the age of eighteen years. 'Family', in relation to a child, includes any person who has parental responsibilities for a child. A service may comprise or include giving assistance in kind or, in exceptional circumstances, cash. The duty to safeguard and promote the welfare of children in need falls upon the local authority as a whole, and embraces social work, education, housing and any other relevant services required to safeguard and promote the welfare of such children. Under Section 19 of the Act, local authorities must publish comprehensive plans for services for children in their area, review those plans from time to time and must engage in consultation with various appropriate organisations who may represent users' interests. It is too early to speculate about the impact the new Act will have in making service provision for families and children more effective and efficient, but there is no dispute around the principles that inform the Act. However, it is yet to be seen if local authorities with support from the government can muster necessary resources to fulfil the objectives of the Act.

SOCIAL WORK AND EDUCATION

This period of scrutiny and legislative change seems to be culminating in a searching reappraisal of education and social work. These two social institutions are not alone in being subjected to such redefinition, but it could be said that the current reassessments are among the most comprehensive and radical. The reasons for these reappraisals are manifold and complex, but some of them are connected with the apparent failure of the systems. So many young people are perceived to be leaving schools 'uneducated', and so many people, groups and communities apparently are still unable to function socially and economically.

At present, each of the two services is separately and individually concerned with redefining its boundaries, often extending them while so doing. Both departments frequently behave as if their sister organisation did not exist, or alternatively almost generalise each other out of existence by such blanket terms as 'school' or 'social work'.

The boundaries between social work and education in fact overlap, often at the most crucial and vulnerable points. For example, a vast number of children in care are of school age and should be receiving full time education. Yet very little is known as to what kind of education they receive in their preparation for adult life as well as the type of educational environment they experience while being looked after by public agencies. Slowly emerging research-based evidence tends to indicate that social workers and teachers may not be paying sufficient attention to the educational needs of young people in their care. Difficulties arising out of school-related problems feature heavily for children coming into care. Interviews with teachers tend to indicate that a significant number of children are underachieving compared to their potential. Such children tend to suffer from a number of educational disadvantages, even allowing for their social and environmental backgrounds. One significant factor tends to be a very low expectation held by teachers and social workers of what children in care can achieve. Another factor of disruption is caused by the movement between care agencies which often involves a change of school. Therefore, it is all the more essential that social work and education work closely together in planning for children in care by taking a corporate and inclusive approach on a sustained basis. (The research evidence referred to above can be found in: S. Jackson, 1987, *The Education of Children in Care*, Bristol papers in Applied Social Studies, No. 1. Bristol: Bristol University School of Applied Social Studies; A. Kendrick, 1995, *Residential Care in the Integration of Child Care Services*, Edinburgh: The Scottish Office Central Research Unit. The findings from the interviews with teachers are reported in G. Connelly, 1997, *The education of young people in care*, in K268 Social Work with Young People, Milton Keynes: The Open University.)

FUTURE ISSUES

It has often been said that social work is at a point of crisis, in the sense of being at a 'turning point'. This means the future offers both challenges and opportunities. Social work is not an island. It operates within society at the complex interfaces between different needs, services, cultures and ideologies. It deals with unresolved, unwanted and unpopular issues and as a result is profoundly affected by changes in society. First, there are changes in the pattern of employment; there has been a growth in longterm unemployment, particularly among unskilled men and young people. In spring 1996, one in five young people in Scotland aged 16 or 17 were unemployed. As a result, the incidence of poverty has increased with families struggling to survive on a meagre weekly budget. Social Work Departments are faced with increasing demands and enhanced legal duties to respond to, with virtually no corresponding increase in available resources. Secondly, the boundaries between individual and state responsibility have become an issue in relation to the crisis of care in the community, support for families, especially lone parents, and the supervision and education of children and young people.

Third, the protection of children as guaranteed by the law has become an important issue in the wake of the Cleveland, Orkney and Ayrshire enquiry reports and the steady stream of allegations of abuse of children in care. It is related to the previous point in that there has been increasing concern in some quarters about child protection standards and procedures undermining the autonomy and authority of parents.

And finally, there appears to be a tension between professional and managerial responsibility. What does it mean to be a trained social worker? Are social workers independent professionals with the capacity for independent judgement, or simply rule followers, digesters and implementers of laws, regulations, guidance and directives? To what extent should social workers be given professional discretion to make independent informed judgements?

Developments in social work in recent years have led to steady growth in services. There are now relatively few people who will not need, or whose immediate family will not need, Social Work Services at some stage in their lives. From originally being a service for marginalised people, services are needed by most sections of the community even though people may not recognise that they are receiving a service delivered or commissioned by social work. There is more emphasis on working alongside users of services, listening to them and trying to make services more relevant to their needs.

In spite of these developments, there still remain two other factors needing careful consideration for Social Work Services to be effective and relevant. The first is that the combination of changes in the economy and in social policies adopted over the past twenty years is fast creating a society which is characterised by increasing poverty, social inequality and exclusion. Such a society is one where the gap between rich and poor has become greater and in which there is the danger of a developing underclass, with all that that implies in terms of social instability. The second is that government policies which directly affect Social Work Services are changing without agreement; objectives are set without measuring the cost; resources are withdrawn without notice; and monitoring is unrelated to changes in structure or resources.

Social work must continue to promote social welfare by taking into account the wishes of users on a genuine partnership basis. It can only be done within the framework of sound social policies which address the real issues of the day.

REFERENCES

Asquith, S. and A. Stafford (eds) (1995) *Families and the Future*, Edinburgh: HMSO.
Cameron, K. (1996) *Law for Social Workers in Scotland*, London: CCETSW.
Chakrabarti, M. (ed) (1998) *Social Welfare: Scottish Perspective* (forthcoming); Aldershot: Ashgate.
Ford, R. and M. Chakrabarti (eds) (1989) *Welfare Abroad*, Edinburgh: Scottish Academic Press.
Hill, M., R. Hawthorne and D. Part (eds) (1995) *Supporting Families*, Edinburgh: HMSO.
Social Work Services Group (1997) *The Children (Scotland) Act 1995, Regulations and Guidance, Part 1*, Edinburgh: The Scottish Office.

94

Community Education

Ted Milburn

THE BEGINNINGS OF COMMUNITY EDUCATION IN SCOTLAND

Community Education is one of the newest expressions of educational development in Scotland, tracing its organisational origins to the publication of the Alexander Report in 1975 (HMSO, 1975). Its conceptual origins go back much further and are to be found in the movements which strove to provide youth work, popular adult education and community development from the end of the last century to the present day. Many of these providers were, and continue to be, voluntary organisations, deploying volunteer workers and their partnership as providers with local authorities is considered a central precept and strategy of community education.

The interplay between the developing concept of community education and organisational practice has continued to be one of the tensions in the development of services to local communities. One source of this tension lay in the constituent philosophical and methodological underpinnings of the youth and community service and adult education services which existed before its inception. Before 1975, almost all local authorities in Scotland provided Youth and Community Services, usually located within an education department. These services were generally at that time provision led. Education departments provided a variety of local authority youth centres, clubs and programmes through the deployment of trained sessional staff and full time workers. Grants for youth work and youth work training were disbursed by local authority education committees to voluntary organisations whose aims and practice conformed to the best principles of youth work. Community development activity included the provision of support to adult groups who were establishing local activities, organising committees, and campaigning for more community resources. The period from 1965 to 1975 had been a time of expansion in youth and community work, which resulted in the building and upgrading of youth and community centres, the expansion of full time training opportunities and the development of a professional career structure with promotion opportunities.

During this period, the adult education provision of local authorities was also the province of education departments and run separately from youth and community services. Along with provision from university extra mural programmes and the WEA, local authority adult education classes were provided in a wide range of community rooms, schools and halls. The focus of those provided by local authorities covered subjects which adults wished to pursue to gain passes in public examinations, social and leisure topics, and recreational activities. Classes which were successful, (usually judged by the criterion of high attendance), were often offered again and were multiplied. These were accessed from the marketing which was undertaken through annual programmes and publicity in newspapers or from lists of venues, times and subjects which were advertised in schools and public buildings. The staff for these classes were invariably day school teachers who shared their subject with adults in the evening, and more rarely, with groups which met during the weekend.

Despite the success of many of these groups, this set of programmes was unmistakably provision led and generally relied upon numbers attending to determine assumed community need and educational planning. The mode for marketing relied upon participants being skilled in the identification and consumption of advertising placed in settings which many did not frequent. Small concession was made to expressed client need, attempts to meet the needs of other target groups, or the importance of seeking new contexts and modes of delivery which might attract new groups to adult learning. It was against this backcloth that the Alexander Committee reported and established the community education service.

THE STRUCTURE AND ORGANISATION OF COMMUNITY EDUCATION

The Alexander Report (HMSO, 1975) was essentially concerned with the future of adult education in Scotland and the committee quickly began to consider the issues highlighted in the previous chapter concerning the focus, targeting, settings, curriculum and the social and economic aims of adult education. Having observed from research, amongst other things, that the take-up rate of informal adult education was approximately 4 per cent of the adult population, and that these participants were predominantly middle class, the committee recommended radical changes to provision and practice. Aware of the strategic community locations of youth and community centres (many of which were in deprived areas), the community contacts of full time workers and their capacity to identify local need, and the informal nature of existing curricula and settings in work with community groups, the committee recommended that 'Adult education should be regarded as an aspect of community education and should with the youth and community service, be incorporated into a community education service' (HMSO, 1975, p. 35). By establishing an organisational amalgam of separate existing educational services, the Alexander Report set in train methodological and strategic changes. The new community education services which sprang up in almost every local authority in Scotland in 1975, and which existed until local government reorganisation in 1996, carried out work in three central areas – informal educational work with young people, community based adult education and community development work. In so doing, they created a community work arm of their education departments, which allowed and indeed encouraged, the identification of local need, the design of appropriate programmes and services and the engagement of local people in their delivery. This proved to be an attractive and invaluable strategic advantage to local elected representatives, particularly in areas where they were developing social and economic strategies. Many who had previously perceived education departments of their councils to be distant and professionalised by the concerns of teachers and schools, could see a clear role for community education workers in establishing and supporting local groups and providing local opportunities which the community required.

In most geographical areas, with the exception of the most far flung and rural, the community education service of regional councils was at this time delivered through area or neighbourhood teams of between four and twenty-five members of full time staff, supported by much larger numbers of sessional paid youth workers, community development workers and adult education teachers. It is important to recognise that the full time workers and their managers were not teachers, but professional community educators, subject to college training and professional socialisation which was very different to that of a classroom teacher.

Although community education was a statutory provision of local authorities from 1975 onwards, in that it was given such status in Education Acts, it was never accorded the mandatory status of primary and secondary schooling. In consequence, community education expenditure has generally never been in excess of 3 per cent per annum of local authority revenue budgets. At times of economic difficulty and cutback within local authorities in the last twenty years, partly because of this distinction in status, the community education service has been at the centre of targeted reductions in service which were disproportionate to its size.

WHAT DOES A COMMUNITY EDUCATION WORKER DO?

Despite a fluctuating financial climate and incremental expectations from elected representatives and senior officers of local authorities, community education staff have carried out the following duties and functions. This illustrative rather than definitive account would vary marginally depending upon council policy, geographical location, staffing levels and whether opportunities existed within area teams for functional specialism of staff.

Work with young people

Curriculum development and delivery of educational youth work in a range of settings; development of youth exchanges; encouragement of voluntary participation and support of volunteers in work with young people; the training of youth workers; the development of youth centres, youth action groups, detached youth work projects, youth counselling services, drugs projects; providing art, music and drama opportunities for young people; development of youth enquiry services and youth information; liaison with voluntary youth organisations concerning grants and resource assistance; the development of youth councils and forums; organisation of summer playschemes and after school care projects (in certain authorities).

Community based adult education

Stimulation of interest and participation in a range of educational opportunities; planning and delivery of post-16 learning opportunities encompassing formal, informal and voluntary provision; organising and delivering adult basic education, OU short courses, issue based education and residential courses; guidance and information to adults on access to educational opportunities; the development of learning packages; the recruitment and training of adult education tutors; liaison with voluntary organisations involved in educational work with adults; collaboration with FE colleges, WEA, universities and other agencies; creation of specific educational initiatives with specific target groups (e.g. older people, lone parents, those with special needs); development of module descriptors for some national certificate courses.

Community development

Targeted work on local issues with groups in the community which are especially disadvantaged; supporting community management of centres, community buildings and projects; development of training to support community groups (e.g. playscheme organisation; management of tenants groups; community councils); supporting of community groups in identifying needs, prioritising objectives and pursuing action to achieve positive change; cooperating with local elected members and other agencies working in the community; provision of equipment and minibuses on loan and administrative resources to support community groups; provision of special projects and programmes to address local issues or lack of provision; the letting of educational premises to community groups (in some areas); support of community and voluntary groups in applications for urban programme; support, monitoring and evaluation of some urban aid projects.

Community education area teams customarily work from offices or community centres which are located in community settings and are easily accessed by members of the community. The deployment of staff has been dictated by council policies and, relatively speaking, larger teams have been created in areas which were designated as areas of priority treatment or social and economic disadvantage. Despite this intention, full time staff levels have been low, with area teams of ten or twelve workers serving populations in excess of 60,000, a factor which has severe implications for their capacity to make impact upon the major social factors thrown up by such communities. Partly because of this, community education teams were determining work priorities through the writing of objectives relating to community need and council policies long before the practice of development planning was universally adopted elsewhere. Because the range of work has been so wide, as evidenced by the range of tasks and functions outlined above, there has invariably been a tension between the creation of developmental work with disadvantaged and marginalised local people (by its nature demanding, slow and sensitive), and the need to satisfy quantitative indicators of success.

THE CONCEPT AND PHILOSOPHY OF COMMUNITY EDUCATION

The organisational marriage of the youth and community service and adult education which followed the publication of the Alexander Report heralded a period within which existing staff in these services worked hard to become community educators, not only in practice but in attitude and personal belief. Community education was and is characterised as informal in style, responsive to popular demand, reflecting local communities, embodying voluntaryism, and concerned to stimulate self help which values people's experience. It is seen by Kirkwood (1990, p. 323) as a reaction to the ethos of traditional formal education in Scottish schools, colleges and universities. For those who had been youth and community workers, the emergence of this new service was both exciting and frightening.

The value base of youth work and community development already combined the principles of starting programmes from 'where people are' and using the natural processes of group experience as the basis for social learning. Good youth workers had always seen their work as educational, and used the shop window activities of sport and arts programmes, camping and residential weekends, international youth exchanges and youth councils as the means by which they created learning, sensitively adjusted to the needs of young people within informal settings. The youth work curriculum is not that of schooling, but relates to the creation of opportunities for young people to learn social and life skills; to become more confident and build their own self esteem; to assist them to make reasoned decisions; to offer opportunities for participation and leadership; to encourage appropriate health choices and become politically aware (Milburn et al., 1995). Many of these principles and intentions also applied to educational work with adults in areas where many considered they had failed in their previous educational experience, and for whom social and economic circumstances were oppressive.

The principles of community development were also of direct relevance to the aims of community education in that they turned curriculum development upside down and began with local need. Community development workers had already espoused a professional approach within which they strove to assist local people to identify issues and needs which were important to them; support these local groups as they prioritised the issues; assist them with resources and advice as they worked to challenge and change local circumstances; and encourage and nurture local skill and leadership. The principal tenets of the community development approach are based on the assumption that the process through which people move to identify and challenge local issues can be educational, and the gains are not only in community terms but also personal in the growth of skill and ability. Many local people have gained in confidence, developed negotiating and advocacy skills, learned how organisations and bureaucracies work, confronted professional gatekeepers, and become effective organisers and managers through such empowerment.

This marriage of professional philosophies was not without problems, in that there was criticism that the community education service, by espousing a community development model of adult education, was unable properly to develop adult education which was sufficiently cognitive. At the other end of the critical spectrum, others accused that the creation of the community education service was no more than an administrative fix, which joined disparate services. It is true that in the early days of the post Alexander era, the youth and community service predominantly administered the previously existing adult evening class programme which in many areas was largely, but not exclusively, leisure and subject based. Workers struggled at this time to make changes in role and function, and even made leaps in professional belief and methodology, to work in ways which accorded with the aims of community education. It was not long, however, before key workers, advisors and senior officers began to build adult education and community services together with forms of educational work with young people, which were increasingly community based, issue-oriented, concerned with process as well as content and related to the specific needs of previously unsupported groups.

The definition of community education below, devised by the national validation agency for the training of community educators in Scotland, enshrines these conceptual and methodological principles:

> Community Education is a process designed to enrich the lives of individuals and groups by engaging with people living within a geographical area, or sharing a common interest, to develop voluntarily a range of learning, action and reflection opportunities determined by their personal, social and economic and political needs. (SCEC 1990, p. 1)

Based upon the values of lifelong learning; the plurality of beliefs in local communities; the central role of education in achieving personal and community improvement and change; the importance of individual and group empowerment and the belief in a more equitable distribution of resources, the concept of community education is distinctive and challenging. Although this concept and philosophy has been linked with the Community Education Service as an organisation, it clearly informs work practices, methodologies and strategies which are not solely owned by departments of education. Barr et al. (1996) emphasised this point in seminal research which looked at the relationship between community education and community development in which he goes on to warn that the organisational rhetoric of community education may not always fit with some practice in local communities.

THE NATIONAL FOCUS

The changes in professional philosophy and methodology outlined above led inevitably to demands for dramatic changes in the training and professional development of those working in community education settings. The establishment of the Community Education Validation and Endorsement (CeVe) Committee in 1989 provided a national focus for the development and endorsement of training for community education workers. In its guidelines for qualifying training, it provided a definition of community education which was adopted across Scotland, a statement of values and principles, and an outline of the competences required by community educators. The competences, which fell within the following key themes, required community educators to:

- engage appropriately with local communities
- empower individuals and groups
- develop relevant learning opportunities
- organise and manage resources
- demonstrate community education principles, purpose and values in youth work, adult education and community work settings
- gather and use evaluative data to improve and develop programmes.

On the basis of these guidelines and principles, two universities, one higher education college, one distance learning college and one employment-based apprenticeship scheme provide degree courses to qualify community educators.

A key player in the growth of CeVe and its influence was the Scottish Community Education Council (SCEC) – its parent. Situated in Edinburgh, the Council has a central responsibility to advise the Secretary of State and the Scottish Education and Industry Department on all matters relating to community education. Since its original inception in 1979, it has been relatively well resourced and has been responsible for national community education campaigns and initiatives. In addition, SCEC has publicised key issues relating to the world of young people, adult education and communities and has encouraged local action through very strong links with local community education teams and local authorities. Having both a national and international focus, it has spearheaded amongst other things, initiatives such as the Young Scot card and survival guide for all school leavers, which has become a model for other European countries. Through national forums in adult education, youth work and community work it maintains a national focus on community education issues and developments.

The Scottish Office Education and Industry Department (SOEID) is central to the support and encouragement of community education. It has sponsored significant support through the launching of national initiatives, the provision of training, evaluation of local outcomes and the provision of grants to voluntary organisations and national agencies such as SCEC. Through the sponsoring of research and development activities it has contributed to the debate concerning appropriate strategies and methods in the three constituent elements of community education work. Effective community education requires workers to be competent in the application of a range of methods. Through techniques and systems of youth and adult guidance they are required to link clients with other educators working collaboratively with them in FE colleges, schools, careers services and training agencies. Because of initiatives such as the 16–18 Action Plan, Scottish Wider Access Programme, Adult Education Guidance Initiative and HMI Reports on Youth Work in Scotland and The Education of Adults in Scotland the SOEID has been at the centre of community education developments (McConnell, 1996).

Although not truly part of a national focus, the development of community schools has been an aspect of the way in which some local authorities in Scotland have attempted to amend schooling policies to the community education concept and philosophy. These strategies have ranged along a continuum which at one end is represented by the creation of a youth and community wing within an existing primary or secondary school. These have been characterised by the new building or internal adaptation of premises for community education activities within and outwith the school, and usually by the allocation of some community education staffing to be based at the school. At the other end of the continuum, the community school strategy of some authorities created schools which have become area education centres, with headteacher and senior school staff contracted to a community education as well as a schooling responsibility. These examples also have appointed community education staff, and often house community cafés, libraries, voluntary organisations, health and sometimes social services. Ranging along the continuum between these two models were practices demonstrating varying degrees of school use by local communities.

In both models, representing opposite ends of the continuum, there have been gains and losses. They both represent a commitment to make available the resources of educational buildings and personnel to the local community. Both make a statement about education being community based and going on beyond the age of sixteen. They maximise the use of educational plant and in more recent years have been seen by officials and elected members as some kind of bulwark against school closures. Most have been successful in getting adults to use the school facilities, particularly in those cases where these were in short supply in the neighbourhood. The problems which surround the first model revolve around the belief that a youth and community wing is an add-on, and seen as an extra to the real work, which is perceived to be that which goes on in the school. Community education staff working in these units were invariably responsible to the headteacher of the school and subject to an innate conservatism which ran counter to the bottom up philosophies of meeting young people and adults 'where they are'. School rules often dominated, leading in extreme cases to young people being obliged wear school uniform if they wished to attend the youth club in the school at night, school-excluded young people being barred from the youth club, unemployed adults being unwelcome in the school during the day, and young people being refused attendance to youth clubs in a school which they did not attend. Clearly these practices were the antithesis of a community education philosophy.

Whereas the second community school model offers gains in collaborative working and community responsiveness, there have been some difficulties with role responsibilities.

Some authorities had difficulties with union negotiations where school staff were asked to teach groups in the evenings and the weekends. Similar inter-professional strictures restricted community education staff from working in school classes because they were not teachers. Management of a large area education centre brought management challenges for senior staff and directorate which few had experienced previously. Some groups in the community continued to see the school as a place into which they would not venture beyond the age of sixteen. Although community schools have been seen as a means of delivering adult education, youth services and community development, they have shortcomings in that they remain, because of the value focus of the activity, a benefit principally to the provider and not necessarily to the consumer.

NEW CHALLENGES

A national pattern no longer exists for the provision of community education across Scotland. The Local Government (Scotland) Bill 1994 heralded the return to local government reorganisation in Scotland, and with its implementation, the reduction of large regional authorities to smaller unitary councils, most with a lower tax raising capability. All local authority services have been faced with financial restrictions because of this and other changes, but the effect upon the community education service has been dramatic. Many local authorities have been forced to cut staff, close community buildings, reduce programmes, and even foreclose aspects of their service such as the delivery of a community based adult education service by community education staff.

In a number of authorities, often in addition to a reduction in community education resources, the community education service and other council services have been amalgamated, to form new departments such as Community and Leisure Services, Neighbourhood Services, Community Services, or Community Economic and Development Services. It is too early to say what overall effect this change will have, but a number of issues are already clear for community educators. A number of former community education workers no longer work within education departments and new departmental heads will not necessarily see the work which continues as inherently educational, even though it may be life enhancing to local communities.

New working arrangements have been forged and work strategies developed with professionals whose work was not previously properly understood or valued by those working within an education department. The insights and work of librarians, sports and arts development workers, housing staff and others in these new departments are broadening the understanding of community education workers and the base of work in local community settings. The position of former community education staff does appear to have improved in some new departments where their expertise is valued and encouraged in ways many feel it was devalued and discouraged in education departments which were inherently school dominated in professional values. Strategically, however, it continues to be a serious challenge to find ways to make meaningful development happen in communities with such large scale problems, when resources have been further diminished.

Methodologically, it will be interesting to see the ways in which community educators relate their practice to the new professional and organisational partnerships which have developed. It was through the fusion of such organisational changes in the last fifty years, that new practices emerged. A central thesis of this chapter has been that community education as a method is not confined to education departments, or to services of community education. Youth work, adult learning and community development do not cease to have educational components because they are delivered by community educators in new organisational contexts or through new departments. One of the central challenges to fieldwork staff in the immediate future is to see that the central precepts of that practice are grounded and enhanced.

CHANGING PRIORITIES

The disaggregation of services with local government reorganisation into smaller units will have a negative effect upon developmental work with young people and adults in the community. In some authorities it has caused councils to close down the community development aspects of the work of community educators, and in others to withdraw these workers from community based contact with groups and their role in identifying learning needs and building customised learning programmes. Current research about local communities and their involvement in community activity and adult education points to the importance of the maintenance of sound processes of contact and engagement with groups at field level. In the past, inappropriate judgements have been made blaming local people for being apathetic and uninterested in adult education and community initiatives, when at the same time, insufficient credence was given to the importance of engaging with local people in identifying issues which are important to them as the basis for educational and social provision. Although these contractions of service are understandable in terms of the severe financial difficulties faced by authorities, the ramifications of such policy shifts are likely to be dramatic. Something much more constructive, developmental and subtle is needed, than the simple advertising of educational opportunities to people living in excluded and disadvantaged communities, to give them the feeling that lifelong learning has a meaning in their lives.

TENSIONS IN LOCAL ACCOUNTABILITY

Community educators still working in local communities, more often than other staff in local authorities and voluntary organisations, have almost daily contact with elected members. Part of the work of community educators is to work with local groups of young people and adults to identify issues around which improvement or change is required. These issues quite often concern such matters as housing, unemployment, sectarianism, racism, crime and safety, the lack of provision of local authority services, and poverty. Many of these are also the focus of the relationship of the elected members and her or his constituents. Community educators are trained and experienced in handling this delicate relationship between the legitimate and required support of local groups in voicing and advancing their concerns, and not becoming a part of the subsequent campaigns which often emerge. Their work servicing local grant committees which are chaired by elected members, and their regular meetings in strategy groups, mean that a trust and mutual understanding must be forged between the officer and the member. In times when resources are strained, the expectations of elected members upon field staff can cause role strain, especially where local members expect 'service as usual' from area teams whose resources and deployment strategy have been restricted by changed council policies due to cuts in services. The campaigning of community groups which is likely to increase at times when resources become more scarce, and the continued support of community educators in the identification of local issues, may well in the future lead to increasing strain in the relationship between member and officer. Community educators will require to juggle the competing expectations of community groups, elected members and their own line management with even greater skill in future.

CONCLUSION

Community education is about cultural change and differing forms of community action. The principles and values which are at the heart of this work relate to the importance of building confidence and self esteem, enhancing social and life skills, and establishing opportunities for leadership through locally based educational programmes for young people and adults. Although it has provided many formalised educational opportunities through youth programmes and adult groups, the curriculum in community education is essentially rooted in the life experiences of its participants. Learning is therefore seen to begin, and is planned to develop, at the point of engagement with local groups. A bottom up rather than a top down approach is taken to learning needs and opportunities, and because of this, the approach of community workers, adult educators and youth workers may appear to exist in contrast to the work of educators in other more formalised agencies. It complements, and is not in opposition to, the work of schools and colleges, with whom community educators have positive collaborative links. Community education has brought a community and youth work arm to the work of education departments in Scottish local authorities, which has given real contact with local needs, acted as a broker with existing educational agencies and has, at times, caused such agencies to change approach. It is essential that community educators retain a clear occupational identity and confidence, shaped by the principles and work methodologies outlined above, which begin with communities first and educational programmes second.

REFERENCES

Barr, A. et al. (1996) *Learning for Change: Community Education and Community Development*, London: Scottish Community Development Centre with Community Development Foundation.
HMSO (1975) *Adult Education: The Challenge of Change*, Edinburgh: HMSO.
Kirkwood, C. (1990) *Vulgar Eloquence. From Labour to Liberation*, Edinburgh: Polygon.
McConnell, C. (ed.) (1996) *Community Education – The making of an empowering profession*, Edinburgh: Scottish Community Education Council.
Milburn, T. et al. (1995) *Curriculum Development in Youth Work – Report to the SOED*, Glasgow: University of Strtathclyde.
Scottish Community Education Council (1990) *CeVe Scotland: Pre-Service Training for Community Education Work*, Edinburgh: SCEC.

95

Disaffection with Schooling

Sandy Hobbs

Disaffection with schooling is a concept which has come to be applied to a range of overlapping behaviours by school students. It includes absenting themselves without permission and acting in unacceptable ways, such as disrupting classroom teaching or harassing other students.

Disaffection may be studied from two main perspectives. Since it is problematic to the school, attempts are made to understand disaffection in order to reduce or control it. However, an alternative approach exists which stresses the need to explain what is happening in social, historical or psychological terms. In principle, these approaches are compatible. In practice, there may be important differences of emphasis. Schools are naturally inclined to look for as speedy solutions as can be achieved. Teachers and administrators may also be inclined to seek explanations for disaffection within the pupil, the pupil's family or the pupil's social milieu. More academically orientated researchers may be more inclined to question the assumptions which schools take for granted, such as that it is self-evidently normal to wish to attend school. It may be worth pointing out, too, that disaffection generally becomes an issue when some student behaviour creates difficulties for school authority. A wider understanding of disaffection might require account to be taken of the less obvious discontents which may be found amongst school students who are superficially conforming.

DEFINITIONS

The term 'disaffection' is not employed universally. Other terms in use include disruptive behaviour, non-attendance, indiscipline, school phobia, school refusal and truancy. Some of these words deserve close attention because, whilst they may appear to be referring to observable phenomena, they carry within them certain assumptions about the causes of those phenomena. In certain cases, the historical evolution of the term is revealing with regard to the current interpretations which they have.

Disaffection

The Oxford English Dictionary (OED) provides examples of this word from the early sixteenth century onwards. Referring to the absence or alienation of affection and being roughly synonymous in meaning with 'dislike' and 'hostility', it has often been used to refer to an attitude to government or to authority. The fact that it has been applied extensively to school students in recent years may indicate that those using the term wish to stress the notion of rejection of, or rebellion against, authority.

Truant

This term was first applied in English to vagabonds, particularly people who beg despite the fact that they appear capable of working. Later the meaning shifted to mean a lazy, idle fellow especially a 'boy who absents himself from school' (OED). This, extended to include girls, is the main meaning of the word today. Although this usage is as old as the writings of Shakespeare, the idea of 'truancy' as a social problem is seen as a more modern phenomenon, being an inevitable outcome of the establishment of compulsory education in the nineteenth century. If the law requires children to attend school, then the truant is in some sense a lawbreaker. From its origin, the word truant carries with it an explanation and a judgement. He who begs from choice is lazy and morally in the wrong. Similarly, one who is capable of learning but does not do so is also morally at fault. Although not everyone using the term today would necessarily accept these connotations, the continued use of the term may be a barrier to reaching a more dispassionate understanding of children who absent themselves from school.

Indiscipline

This word implies behaviour which is disruptive of the school routine and again comes into use only with more serious forms. The distinction between 'truancy' (involving absence from school) and 'indiscipline' (referring to some sorts of behaviour at school) might seem a straightforward one. However, truancy is sometimes included within the concept of indiscipline, for example in the Pack Report (SED, 1977, p. 42). This position implies an assumption that similar factors underlie truanting and other forms of unacceptable behaviour.

School phobia

This term, like the almost interchangeable 'school refusal', is employed to account for non-attendance at school which is due to the individual student's having problems of personal psychological adjustment. Here the behaviour (not going to school) takes second place to the hypothetical psychological condition which supposedly underlies the behaviour.

Non-attendance

Carlen, Gleeson and Wardhaugh (1992) propose that, since other concepts carry too many hidden assumptions, it is appropriate to deal in terms of the more mundane concept of 'non-attendance'. This approach has the merit of focusing attention on observable behaviour and making minimal a priori assumptions about causes. These authors distinguish between seven different types of absence from school: *officially induced* (for example, disciplinary exclusions and school closures due to heating problems), *officially condoned* (for example, absences due to illness or bereavement), and five kinds of illicit absence. *Officially illicit* absence may be *unofficially condoned* (for example, in preparation for examinations), *parentally approved* (for example, to help with housework), *parentally condoned* (which implies somewhat less satisfaction on the parent's part), *parentally disapproved*, or *'internal'* (non-attendance at lessons by students recorded as present). Obviously to place a case in one or other of these categories requires more information than merely whether or not the student was recorded as being at school.

The existence of these competing and overlapping concepts requires those who explore this aspect of education to be particularly careful to be precise in their use of language.

Given the range of approaches to disaffection which exist, psychological and sociological, practical and theoretical, some choice must be made as to where best to start a consideration of the main issues. Although it would be foolish to deny the possibility that an exploration of the psychological history of an individual school student may help to understand that person's disruptive behaviour or absence from school, the basic social and political nature of schooling must be given a central place in any analysis of disaffection from schooling. Schools are social institutions. It is a matter of public policy that individuals be required to attend them. Accordingly, it seems appropriate to look first at the historical background to these social relationships.

HISTORY

Paterson (1988) presents an illuminating account of state policies during the period from 1839, when school inspectors were first appointed, up to the initiation of compulsory education in Scotland in 1872. She argues that the minutes of the Privy Council's Committee of Council on Education clearly show the assumptions about the family and society which underlay official policies. They also reveal the areas of conflict which existed between those policies and the assumptions of many children and of their parents. Paterson's case is that, by creating a particular structure of state regulated schooling, certain sorts of social behaviour came to be defined as problematic. In addition, the content of school curricula was designed to encourage particular kinds of family relationships. Today it is considered the norm that certain days and times are set at which children are expected to attend school, irrespective of parental work and life style. However, prior to state intervention, schooling was required to adapt to family circumstances in which children typically played a part in work. In rural areas, only children too young to work might be expected to attend school during periods of intense agricultural activity. Older children attended in the winter months when there was less work for them to do. At harvest times, schools would often close so that the teacher, as well as the pupils, might take part. In mining and manufacturing areas, school attendance might fall when trade was good and demand for the children's labour was correspondingly high.

Throughout the twentieth century, attendance at school has come to be taken for granted as the major social obligation of childhood. However, that the pursuit of education is not regarded as an absolute value taking precedence over all other goals may be seen in the greater official acceptance of child labour during both the First and Second World Wars. The long persistence of special arrangements to allow school pupils leave from school to help with harvesting, as in the so-called 'tattie-holidays', also indicates that officialdom considered education might sometimes have to take second place to other considerations. Nevertheless, the need to monitor attendance when it is required has been continually acknowledged and the 1990s saw a move towards more public discussion of attendance records.

EXTENT OF DISAFFECTION

Estimates of how many school students truant vary widely. The central problem is that schools may follow different policies with respect to absences. This applies both to the issue of whether or not a given pupil is present and, on the other hand, to whether or not an absence is accepted as legitimate. In the 1970s it was claimed that truancy rates were rising but no conclusive evidence was presented to support this view. What can be said with confidence, at present, is that education authorities are currently treating truancy as a major issue in Scotland. Recording practices probably reflect this fact. Some past research studies asking school students to report on their own patterns of attendance produced higher truancy figures than those derived from official school records. However, given that schools are currently more sensitive to the need to monitor attendance, that will not necessarily hold true today.

Attendance and Absence in Scottish Schools 1995–1996, published by the Audit Unit of the Scottish Office Education and Industry Department, might appear to provide a satisfactory basis on which to examine truancy in Scotland. The statistical analysis in the report distinguishes between three categories: attendance, authorised absences and unauthorised absences.

Taking Scotland as a whole, attendance in primary schools averages around 93% and in secondary schools around 88%. There are fairly clear differences between authorities in their absence rates, particularly in secondary schools. For example, absences in Glasgow average around 8% and 19% in primary and secondary schools respectively, whereas for Orkney, the figures are 5% and 6% respectively. Of course, the majority of these absences are recorded as authorised, but an examination of the statistics for individual schools suggest one should be cautious about accepting the reported distinction between the authorised and unauthorised absences. In some schools in areas such as Orkney, Moray and Aberdeenshire, individual secondary schools have authorised absence rates of 3%, 5% and 6%. Unauthorised absences for these schools are given as 0%. In Glasgow, two schools with reported absence rates of 27% and 26% are worth comparing. In one case, all of the reported absences are listed as authorised. In the second school, 20% are authorised and 6% are unauthorised. It is difficult to explain these variations in terms of the social characteristics of the populations the schools serve. Can it really be that the schools in the urban area have pupils who suffer much greater health problems, for example, which would account for higher levels of authorised absences than in the rural schools, but do not have any greater problems of disaffection from schooling, which would be implied by the figures from the urban school reporting 0% unauthorized absences? It is equally difficult to accept that two schools in the same city could have similarly high absence rates, but that in only one of them was there a substantial problem of truancy. The most parsimonious explanation of the variation between the schools would be that they use different criteria for 'authorising' absences. One cannot ignore the possibility that some schools seek to reduce the apparent size of their truancy problem by adopting an unjustifiably lax definition of authorisation.

Despite these difficulties with published attendance figures, it is possible to discern some demographic trends in truancy. Carlen, Gleeson and Wardhaugh (1992) confirmed a widely held impression that boys truant more than girls. However, they also found that girls have more condoned absences. The difference might lie not in the inclination of the two genders to keep away from school but in the willingness of parents and teachers to treat female absences as acceptable. Different ethnic groups may display varied levels of truancy, but, as with gender differences, one must be aware that published figures may reflect the expectations of those responsible for interpreting an absence as legitimate or not. Truanting also varies with the time of year. The period just before breaks such as midterm and summer holidays are the most common times for higher absence rates.

Determining the scale of other forms of indiscipline than truancy faces similar problems to those just noted. The Audit Unit's report contains data on exclusions from school, which of course are made in cases of severe indiscipline. Permanent exclusions are relatively rare. Looking at Scotland as a whole, temporary exclusions are rare in Primary 1 to 3, then rise steadily in Primaries 4 to 7 and rise further through Secondary levels 1 to 3. There is a falling off in Secondary levels 4 and 5, presumably because many of those most disaffected with schooling will choose to leave school once they pass the minimum leaving age. In secondary schools, the average number of half days lost per 100 pupils through temporary exclusions was 96, with large variations between education authorities. These variations could be due both to differences in the scale of the problem of indiscipline and to different degrees of willingness to use exclusion as a technique of control.

REVIEW OF THEORIES

Having reviewed some of the evidence on the extent of disaffection, some of the explanations offered to account for disaffection shall now be reviewed.

Individual psychology

The first to be considered is the approach which treats truancy and indiscipline as symptoms of what may be regarded as either a problem of psychological adjustment or of a psychiatric disorder. The widely used Diagnostic and Statistical Manual (DSM) of the American Psychiatric Association treats school refusal and truancy in this way. School attendance problems have been associated in Britain with so-called Disruptive Behaviour Disorders and Anxiety/Mood Disorders. (See, for example, the paper by I. Berg and others in the *Journal of Child Psychology and Psychiatry*, vol. 34, 1993, pp. 1187-1203.) Two points may be made about this approach. The first is that it is controversial. The various editions of DSM have come in for considerable criticism from professionals in the field. Many psychologists consider a medical model unhelpful in dealing with psychological problems and prefer to adopt a behavioural or social approach. The second point to be made is that, if for the sake of argument it is accepted that it is appropriate to treat some individuals displaying disaffection as psychiatric cases, then that removes them from the field of essentially educational issues. There remain the other cases. Despite the existence of many rival theories there is a widespread consensus that it is necessary to look for the main sources of disaffection in social relations in the school, in the home or elsewhere. (An example of contrasting social and medical approaches may be found in the interchange between Pratt and Berg cited in the references.)

Parents

Conflict between school and parents concerning a child's schooling raise profound issues about relations between the state and the individual and the rights and duties of parenthood.

However, here the focus will be on more practical aspects. Since the start of compulsory education, there have been parents whose approach to child rearing has brought them into conflict with teachers. Although there are many parents who see school as a source of benefit to their children, there are others who do not. Parents who themselves were unhappy at school may well be sympathetic to their own children if they seem to be having similar experiences. These parents may react to accounts of unpleasant incidents at school fatalistically, in that they see them not as cause for them, as parents, to seek a solution to the problem but as a justification for the child's absence from school. Other parents may be happy to have children with them to help cope with household problems. A number of researchers have noted that household chores are a contributory factor to absence from school. A further possibility is that parents may condone truancy caused by the child's having a job. The job may seem worthwhile as a source of income or as an entry into adult employment. Clearly, if parents persist in these attitudes in the face of attempts by the school to encourage attendance, then the matter is a serious one. What is unclear, however, is how substantial a problem unfavourable parental attitudes are. As will be seen, better home-school links are perceived as a useful tool to deal with truancy. If creating better channels of communication with home is indeed successful, it would suggest that parental disaffection from schooling may often be mild, transitory and open to change.

Peers

Since young people seek each others' company and can be seen to adopt shared patterns of behaviour, it is not surprising that peer influences are seen as a factor creating disaffection. Youth culture has been the subject of a large amount of sociological enquiry, a trend starting in the United States and spreading to Britain. This interest was enhanced by the appearance of successive forms of youth culture, such as Rockers, Mods, Skinheads and Punks, which made headline news in the mass media. Although a variety of rival interpretations exist of these movements, references to the structure of capitalist society, to the adult job market, and to adolescents' perceptions of schooling are recurring themes. Scottish secondary pupils' perceptions of the process of labelling those 'in trouble' at school have recently been analysed by Pauline Padfield in her paper *'Skivvers', 'saddos' and 'swots'*, delivered at the 1997 Annual Conference of the British Sociological Association.

Many sociologists stress the persistence of class barriers in contemporary society which means that many young people can look forward to either long term unemployment or to unfulfilling, low paid work. For some pupils, schools have little to offer by way of means of escape from this prospect. On such an analysis, membership of distinctive subcultural groups, delinquency and disaffection from schooling are all regarded as to an extent meaningful or rational responses to the situation in which these young people find themselves. From the point of view of those attempting to deal with truancy and indiscipline as day to day problems, such theories might lead to considerable pessimism, stressing as they do the strength of social forces over which schools and teachers have little control.

School

There are four main ways in which schools have been presented as contributing to truancy and other types of indiscipline. Three concern what actually happens in the classroom, one concerns social relationships between students. Dealing first with classroom factors, it may be noted that the teaching styles adopted may make students uncomfortable. Teachers may display hostility, may be aggressive and may be insensitive to student problems. Being academically successful themselves, some teachers may find it difficult to empathise with the less gifted pupils. Secondly, the school curriculum may seem uninteresting and irrelevant to some pupils. Malcolm, Thorpe and Lowden, in their report *Understanding Truancy* (SCRE, 1996) cite 'I'm just not interested' as the most common single explanation truants gave for not going to school. Thirdly, less academically successful students may associate school attendance with the feeling of failure. Fourthly, outside the classroom, bullying is seen as a major disincentive to school attendance. Some schools have been considered insufficiently vigilant in seeking out signs of bullying and insufficiently rigorous in dealing with it. The problem of bullying was seen as important enough for a Scottish Schools Anti-bullying Initiative to be set up in 1993 (see SCRE *Spotlight* 43: Finding Out About Bullying, by Andrew Mellor, revised edition, 1997).

Alternatives

One view of truancy is that it is not so much that schools are unattractive as that other activities are more attractive. Two such alternatives may be cited, play and work. It is well established that since the 1950s there has developed a distinctive youth culture in which particular types of music and other recreational activities, different from those enjoyed by their elders, are enthusiastically pursued by young people. Many aspects of youth culture have been considered as presenting a moral danger, Rock'n'Roll, Horror Comics, Video Nasties, Raves and Computer Games are only a few of the phenomena which have in their time been presented as endangering the moral development of youth. In few cases have these claims been sustained by anything other than anecdotal evidence. Evidence that children are introduced relatively young to alcohol, tobacco and other drugs is rather firmer. However, in the present context, the issue is whether any of these contribute to disaffection from schooling. It may well be that truants spend some of their time playing computer games, listening to music or watching videos. However, truants of an earlier generation may have played football or gone fishing. It cannot be assumed that any of these old or new pastimes are inherently bad or exert such a strong allure that they must be treated as inimical to education.

One aspect of youth culture which cannot be denied is that it is a culture of consumerism. One must spend in order to participate. It is argued by some that the desire for consumer goods is a contributory cause to the relatively high levels of part-time employment amongst school students in Britain. Hobbs and McKechnie, in their book *Child Employment in Britain* (Stationery Office, 1997), calculated that around two thirds of school students in England and Scotland will have had experience of paid employment by the time they have reached the minimum school leaving age. Some of these workers report having missed school because of work. Most work only a few hours a week, but a minority work a good deal longer. Just as absenteeism from school rises through school years so does the level of part-time employment. It would be too crude to propose a simple causal relationship between these trends, but the attractiveness of work and the money earned cannot be ignored.

Links with delinquency?

The Pack Report (SED, 1977, p. 1) quotes the Scottish Council on Crime as expressing the following view on the relationship between truancy and crime:

> We are led to understand that a substantial proportion of children who get into trouble for committing offences have, at some earlier stage in their career, been noted as truants. Truancy may be an early indication that a child is beginning to go off the rails.

The phrase 'we are led to understand' may have been a tacit admission that this argument did not have a watertight empirical basis. Nevertheless, this view that truancy is a step on the road to greater delinquency is widely held. Carlen, Gleeson and Wardhaugh (1992, pp. 197–8) quote the coordinator of the Gorbals Truancy Project as noting that many truants become involved in petty crime and a few in more serious crime. This she attributes to the fact that when truants are 'on the streets' they have greater opportunities to offend and they also come under pressure from 'older gangs of youths'. One may note that only a small minority of truanting students are dealt with by a truancy centre such as this, and one may assume that those selected for this treatment are amongst the most problematic offenders. As such, they may not be representative of truanting students generally.

Moreover, some commentators dissent from this belief in a relationship between truancy and delinquency. For example, Pratt (1983) suggests that the image of the student absenting himself from school and getting himself into trouble (emphasis typically being placed on the males) is part of the folklore of truancy. He cites a study by D. May, published in *Scottish Educational Studies*, vol. 7, 1975. May's research was conducted in Aberdeen with an unusually large sample size. The results cast doubt on the notion of an almost inevitable link between truancy and crime. It was found, first, that only a minority of boys with a record of poor attendance subsequently made an appearance in juvenile court, and secondly, that the great majority of delinquents have good attendance records. Pratt also casts doubt on the image of the truant as being inevitably 'on the street'. Evidence suggests that truants often spend their time at home or with friends.

TECHNIQUES OF 'PREVENTION AND CURE'

Practical proposals for responding to disaffection are contained in *The Truancy File* (Quality in Education Centre for Research and Consultancy, 1995), produced as the result of a Scottish Office Education Department research project aimed at observing and publicising 'good practice' in both primary and secondary schools.

Prevention

Many of the techniques of prevention might be considered sound educational policy, irrespective of whether a school has particular truancy problems. For example, it is proposed that there be clear guidelines for all teachers on professional classroom practices. At the heart of the proposals for detecting truancy early is a careful monitoring of attendance. This has two sides to it. On the one hand steps are to be taken to ensure that children registered as attending do actually take part in all of the required classes. On the other hand, when an absence is recorded, early contact is made with the child's home to establish whether the parents are aware of it and whether they can explain it. A concentration on the record of individual students means signs of potential truancy are noted early. *The Truancy File* emphasises the merits of flexibility and responsiveness. Truancy should be dealt with in ways which emphasise responsibilities rather than the apportioning of blame. Effective anti-bullying strategies are seen as contributing to the reduction of truancy by reducing one possible source of disaffection for some pupils.

Cure

Proposals to 'cure' truancy and other forms of disaffection fall into three main categories. First there are those which may be referred to as 'in school' because they emphasise the possibilities open to school staff. Teachers may be asked to participate in programmes in which the behaviour and needs of problematic pupils are carefully monitored. Support groups may be set up. This may lead to the development of more flexible timetables. Small improvements in attendance and behaviour may be rewarded. A second type of strategy is focused on developing contacts with the family, for example by home visits. Parents may be given guidelines on the value of regular telephone contact with the school. In some cases, it may be appropriate to negotiate contracts with the parents or jointly with the parents and the pupil. Thirdly, there is the use of other agencies. Clearly, social work departments, school psychological services, the police, Children's Panels and the courts may all be involved with some disaffected pupils. Various ways of coordinating their efforts are available. In addition, there are non-school agencies which may be set up specifically to deal with truanting and disruptive pupils. These include Local Attendance Councils and Truancy Centres.

Local Attendance Councils are made up of volunteers nominated by School Boards. They accept referrals from schools only if prior efforts by the school to deal with the problem are documented. The first move by a council is to summon the parent to a meeting, generally accompanied by the truanting child. Although meetings are conducted informally, the mere fact of calling in the parent sometimes resolves the matter. Where the child rather than the parent is seen as the source of the problem, referrals to other agencies or to the Children's Panel may be made. In extreme cases of non-cooperation, parents may be referred for prosecution.

The work of one Scottish Truancy Centre is described by Carlen, Gleeson and Wardhaugh (1992). The Gorbals Truancy Project, set up in 1983, dealt with up to ten cases at a time. Project workers saw their approach as child-centred, which involves temporarily accepting difficult behaviour. Home and social problems were seen as major factors in the children's behaviour. Teaching took place but in a flexible manner with no strict adherence to set curricula. The development of basic literacy skills was seen as a major step in preparing the individual to return to school. Sister Mercedes, coordinator of the project, found that there were some areas of conflict between the Truancy Centre and local schools. One school wished to assert control over the project by siting it in the school buildings. The schools tended to look for quick results, whereas the project team often considered that a longer term approach was more likely to produce favourable outcomes. One criticism of truancy centres is that the staff-student ratios are so small that this must be considered a very expensive technique for dealing with the problem. Alternatively, it might be argued that some individual cases are so profound that no less expensive method could be expected to succeed.

THE FUTURE

The current emphasis on truancy and other forms of disaffection as a major issue in Scottish education is welcome. However, there are dangers if the problems are considered in too narrow a focus. It is to be hoped that many of the 'good practices' currently being advocated for schools will produce favourable results. However, truants are individuals and methods which work for one child or one school will not necessarily work for all. If, as many researchers have argued, disaffection with schooling is simply part of a wider network of social problems, it is highly unlikely that 'in-school' methods will completely eradicate it.

Whatever efforts teachers, administrators and researchers put into understanding and dealing with disaffected school students will, in the long run, only produce lasting results in a favourable political climate. What are the criteria of successful schooling to be? What priorities are to prevail in the allocation of resources? These are essentially political questions. In the allocation of scarce resources, persistently truanting and disruptive students must be weighed in the balance against students successfully passing examinations. It is obvious that schools have a part to play in producing adequately educated adult workers. However, it may be equally important that schools also contribute to improving the lot of a large section of society who are caught in a cycle of deprivation. The efforts of teachers to help one pupil achieve academic success may in some cases be in effect a lack of effort to stop another pupil becoming a truant and a drop-out. To help the problem pupil schools need not only resources but also ways of measuring the success of their contribution. Test and examination results may seem attractively straightforward ways of measuring the success of a school. However, if it is valuable for a school to turn a potential truant into a pupil who finds school a happy and fulfilling experience, it is necessary to find ways of demonstrating when success of that sort has been achieved.

REFERENCES

Booth, T. and D. Coulby (eds.) (1987) *Producing and Reducing Disaffection*, Milton Keynes: Open University Press.

Carlen, P., D. Gleeson and J. Wardhaugh (1992) *Truancy: The Politics of Compulsory Schooling*, Buckingham: Open University Press.

Paterson, F. M. S. (1988) Schooling the family, *Sociology*, 22, 65–86.

Pratt, J. D. (1983) Folk-lore and fact in truancy research: some critical comments on recent developments, *British Journal of Criminology*, 23, 336–52; to which is appended: I. Berg, A. Goodwin, R. Hullin and R. McGuire, A reply to Dr J. D. Pratt, 353–7.

Quality in Education Centre for Research and Consultancy (1995) *The Truancy File*, Glasgow: Quality in Education Centre for Research and Consultancy, University of Strathclyde.

SED (1977) *Truancy and Indiscipline in Schools in Scotland: The Pack Report*, Edinburgh: HMSO.

96

Gender and Scottish Education

Sheila Riddell

In Chapter 1 of their edited collection on girls and Scottish education, Paterson and Fewell argued:

> gender inequality is embedded within the structure and texture of Scottish education . . . Its
> absence as an issue is not because there is no problem, or because any problem is in the process of
> solving itself, but because until recently its existence as a problem has not been identified. The
> form and content of gender inequality have therefore remained unacknowledged. (Paterson and
> Fewell 1990, p. 2)

This chapter will consider the extent to which gender still features as an unconscious presence in Scottish educational debate almost a decade later. It begins by examining the general framework within which discussions of gender and education takes place, since the naming of problems plays a central part in their understanding and resolution. Thereafter key research projects which have placed gender at the core rather than the periphery of their enquiry are considered. Finally the chapter focuses on current and future areas of interest to practitioners and policy makers in the sphere of gender and education.

UNPACKING THE NOTION OF EQUALITY

All discussion of gender and education requires some thinking about the type of equality which is being pursued. At times, researchers, policy makers and campaigners have argued that the same education should be provided for all, since all individuals share a common humanity. Within this framework, the idea is to use education to blur differences between individuals and groups. Some groups, such as disabled people, minority ethnic people, working class people or women, may require some additional help to achieve the same position as the dominant group, who are implicitly assumed to be male, white and middle class. The goal for all, however, is to iron out difference rather than celebrate or accentuate it. By way of contrast, other accounts of social justice emphasise the importance of diversity and difference between individuals and groups. Within this frame, far from blurring difference, the central goal is to celebrate cultural identity and diversity, recognising that equality policies may well have different goals for individuals and groups. In journals such as *New Left Review*, debates go back and forth between those who favour a project of economic redistribution, implicitly seeking to soften boundaries, and those who promote identity politics and align themselves with a project of recognition, or the celebration of diverse group identities. These arguments may be regarded as overly academic and hair-splitting in an area where there is plenty of room for action rather than words. However, they underline the need for greater clarity of thought around the concept of equality in order to avoid misplaced assumptions, over-simplified recipes for change and inaccurate predictions of the future.

THE NEGLECT OF GENDER IN MAINSTREAM SCOTTISH EDUCATION ENQUIRY

Reviews of research on gender and education in Scotland (e.g. Brown, Breitenbach and Myers, 1994) noted that much work in Scotland has been small scale, conducted as part of masters' programmes within colleges and universities. It has generally failed to address in any detail the relationship between gender, social class, age, region and ethnicity and ethnographies of girls' and boys' schooling are thin on the ground. A notable exception to the neglect of gender and education has been the steady stream of publications which have been produced by the Centre for Educational Sociology (CES) at Edinburgh University. From 1972 to 1992, CES conducted the Scottish Young People's Survey, which gathered data on the educational outcomes and attitudes of Scottish school leavers. Funded by the Scottish Office and the Economic and Social Research Council (ESRC), such research was used to investigate the relationship between gender and a range of other variables. For example, comparisons of girls' and boys' examination performance revealed that whereas in the early 1970s there were no gender differences, by 1984 there was a considerable female advantage. Analysing these data further, CES researchers maintained that comprehensive reorganisation in Scotland was associated with a general improvement of standards of attainment, with girls and pupils of low socio-economic status being the main beneficiaries. Such data have been very useful as a baseline for the identification of trends in educational outcomes in Scotland (see Furlong and Cartmel, 1997).

As will be seen below, over the past four years there has been a marked increase in the amount of research in the area of gender and education. However, the question of why gender was such a neglected area until the mid-1990s demands to be addressed. One obvious reason is that the Scottish Office, a major funder of educational research, has generally not regarded gender as one of its priority areas, perhaps assuming that there were no issues to address since girls appeared to be performing well in external examinations.

Although the Scottish Office has recently funded some work with gender as its main focus (e.g. Powney, 1997), other research projects which undoubtedly have a bearing on gender tend to focus on other variables. For example, a recent study of exclusions from Scottish schools, noted that among a sample of schools that provided a breakdown by gender, boys made up 92 per cent of primary school exclusions and 77 per cent of secondary school exclusions. However, the gendered nature of exclusion was not highlighted as a major theme. Research on discipline in school has also drawn attention to teachers' view that those posing the greatest problems were male, of low ability, and in the final year of compulsory schooling, but the mechanisms whereby these patterns become established have not been fully explored.

A further explanation for the neglect of gender in discussion of Scottish education may be the ongoing dominance of patriarchal attitudes within Scottish society. Hills, for instance, writes:

I am a child of the Democratic Intellect; the land of the lad o' pairts. A land famed for its excellent egalitarian education system. This is a strong male myth which has served the women of Scotland ill. Since women have been largely invisible there is a habit of silence. When women seek to break the silence there is no precedent and they are isolated and vulnerable. Gender codes and behaviours are so institutionalised as to go unnoticed. (L. Hills, 1990), 'The Senga syndrome; reflections on 21 years in education' in F. Paterson J. and Fewell (eds) *Girls in their Prime: Scottish Education Revisited* Edinburgh: Scottish Academic Press p. 148)

Hills' writing is clearly founded on her personal experience, but based on a comprehensive analysis of the available statistics, the Engender collective maintain:

Women and girls in Scotland still experience considerable inequality and disadvantage in economic, social and political life as compared to men and boys. This disadvantage is further compounded by their relative exclusion as a focus of research and the unevenness in the collection and availability of statistics disaggregated by both country/region and gender. (Engender *Gender Audit*, 1997, p. 1).

Much, then, remains to be done. However, as suggested earlier, there is some evidence of a recent growth of interest in gender and education in the research community. The directions this research is taking will now be considered.

RECENT RESEARCH FOCUSING ON GENDER AND EDUCATION IN SCOTLAND

Over the past decade, there has been a steady growth of interest in gender and education in Scotland. A Gender and Education research network was established and held a number of conferences, although recently it has been less active. This new focus on gender and education has been paralleled by a wider surge of interest in gender issues, related in part to a sense of the possibilities offered by the Scottish parliament for women to play a much greater role in Scottish public life than hitherto. This has been reflected in the literature review mentioned earlier, commissioned by the Equal Opportunities Commission (Brown et al., 1994) and the publication of the Engender Audit, which seeks to marshall statistics on women in a range of public policy arenas. In relation to the latter publications, it should be noted that the task of synthesising national statistics is undertaken voluntarily and there is now a call for the Scottish Office to demonstrate its stated commitment to women's issues by taking over this task.

GENDER AND ATTAINMENT

It is perhaps ironic that one of the first pieces of work on gender and education commissioned by the Scottish Office was instigated as a result of anxiety about boys' academic performance. A literature review on gender and attainment conducted by Powney (1997) at the Scottish Council on Educational Research drew on a range of sources including Scottish Office statistics and international studies. Powney noted that the performance of Scottish girls in many areas of the curriculum was surpassing that of boys. Indeed, Scottish Examination Board statistics show that in 1996 at Standard grade girls did better in all subjects apart from PE and Science. Girls' superior performance amounted to an average of 0.3 of a grade over all subjects. Over the last five years, girls performed better than boys at Higher grade in English, Physics, Geography and Art and Design and to a certain extent in Mathematics and Craft and

Design. Taking all subjects together, the female pass rate was 4 per cent higher than the male (Scottish Examination Board, *Annual Report*, 1997).

However, it should not be concluded from this that any problem which might have existed for girls is solved and the focus should now be on the boys. One of the telling features of the way in which Scottish educational data are gathered and presented is that it is now relatively easy to obtain breakdown of data by gender, but much more difficult to obtain a breakdown by social class. Furlong and Cartmel (1997), drawing on data form the Scottish Young People's survey, analysed patterns of attainment in external examinations by social class and gender (see Figure 96.1). They reveal that whereas the attainment of

Figure 96.1   Young people in highest attainment band (gaining three or more Highers), by class and gender

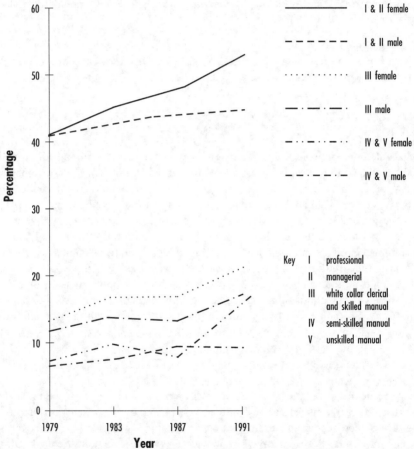

Source: From Andy Furlong and Fred Cartmel, *Young People and Social Change*, OUP (1997): data from the Scottish School Leavers Survey.

Points
- Graph is broken down by gender – steady increase in attainment for class I & II females – slower for I & II males
- Sharp increase in lat 1980s and early 1990s for class III females and males
- Also sharp increase in this period for classes IV and V female
- Males from classes IV & V show relatively small increase over this period

most pupils in Higher grade examinations has improved since 1979, the performance of boys from social class IV and V has remained static. In all social classes, the performance of girls has increased more rapidly than that of boys. Indeed, if researchers were to extrapolate from the trends evident in Figure 96.1 it would be expected that the performance of girls in social classes IV and V would overtake that of boys in social class III. A number of points are suggested by these data. First, it is evident that the relative difference in the performance of the most advantaged and least advantaged social groups is considerable and has not been significantly eroded. These statistics are in stark contrast with the myth of the Scottish democratic education tradition and raise questions about the extent to which comprehensive schools have been successful in one of their stated aims, the erosion of class differences in educational outcomes. Whilst examination results (although not necessarily standards) are improving, social class remains the most powerful determinant of pupils' school achievement, which will in turn play a major role in influencing their future life chances. Another important point is that being female seems to mitigate somewhat the negative impact of low social class, an effect which has not been systematically investigated in Scotland and demands qualitative research into the family and school culture of working class girls and boys. Similarly, being female seems to confer additional educational advantage on pupils in the more advantaged social groups, and again this is an effect which demands further investigation.

It is disappointing that school effectiveness research has had so little to say about gender effects. Because such research reveals that schools are always more effective for girls than boys, gender, like social class, is simply regarded as background statistical noise to be controlled for rather than understood. Research conducted by Brown, Riddell and Duffield at Stirling University attempted to unpack some of the classroom processes associated with differential levels of effectiveness in more and less effective Scottish schools. This research confirmed that in the classrooms of the four schools observed, low achieving boys tended to attract more teacher attention, were more likely to participate in question and answer sessions and featured more prominently in teachers' accounts of what had taken place in observed lessons. Some of this attention was negative, associated with pupil indiscipline, but nonethless the message drawn from these interactions by lower achieving boys was that even if they were not performing well academically, they could still exert power in the classroom through noisy and attention-seeking activity. The most neglected pupils in the class were the lowest achieving girls. This study is one of the few in the UK which has investigated teaching and learning activities in relation to gender and level of achievement and further work of this type would do much to improve understanding of classroom processes (see J. Duffield forthcoming, 'School effectiveness, school improvement and gender issues' in J. Salisbury and S. Riddell (eds) *Gender and Educational Change*, London: Routledge).

A question which also needs to be addressed is the extent to which the educational advantage of girls is translated into post-school advantage. Despite the fact that girls' performance in Highers has been improving more rapidly than that of boys since the late 1970s, this superiority has not been fully reflected in their higher education performance, although Paterson documented the way in which women and those from socially dis-advantaged backgrounds gained considerably from the expansion of the early 1990s (L. Paterson 1997 'Trends in higher education participation in Scotland, *Higher Education Quarterly*, 51.1 29–48). In 1986, more women graduated from Scottish higher education institutions, when the ratio of women to men was 51:49. Following the reduction of places in colleges of education (which traditionally have admitted more female than male students) in line with the shrinking of the school population from a late 1970s high of 400,000 to 300,000 in 1990, the ratio of higher education graduates shifted in favour of men. In 1995, female graduates again outnumbered men, this time by 52:48. Despite this numerical advantage, more men than women get first class honours degrees (8 per cent as opposed to 6 per cent), and gender differentiation of the higher education curriculum remains strong, reflecting gender differences in the school curriculum.

The puzzle which emerges from the data presented above is how girls manage to outperform boys in a school system where boys appear to dominate classroom activity, attracting more positive and negative teacher attention. Part of the reason, as has been seen, is that although educated in coeducational schools, they often self-select into different curricular areas, thus experiencing the school in different ways. There is a strong possibility that this self-selection may represent a survival mechanism for girls in a potentially hostile environment.

GENDER AND THE CURRICULUM

Statistics on the educational attainment of girls and boys might appear to support the contention that, as Macrae argued in an article in the *Times Educational Supplement Scotland* in 1996, 'the school system in Scotland, and in Britain as a whole, discriminates against boys.' According to Macrae, feminist dogma should be blamed for blinding people to the obvious truth that girls are doing better than boys in the school system, and have been doing so for a long time. Closer examination of the statistics, however, suggests that the picture is more complex. First, it is evident that gender differences in subject uptake have proved remarkably resistant to change and that in, for example, 'male' and 'female' technical subjects there has been little boundary crossing, although the 1997 report from the Scottish Examination Board notes that the proportion of girls in Craft and Design and Graphic Communication has increased, but not in Technological Studies. There is evidence, therefore, of some female incursion into male territory, but little traffic in the other direction.

Since science is such an important subject in an increasingly technological age, it is worth looking closely at male and female participation in this area. Linda Croxford (1994, 1997) analysed such patterns over a fifteen year period in the context of the introduction of the common curriculum in the 1980s and the implementation of equal opportunities legislation. Figure 96.2 demonstrates that the proportion of girls aged 14–16 studying Physics has slowly but steadily climbed from 10% in 1976 to just over 20% in 1990. In Biology, the proportion of boys studying the subject has also increased, from 12% in 1976 to 28% in 1990, although the pattern here is less smooth, with small declines in 1986 and 1988. Croxford concludes that even though the common curriculum in Scotland is presented in gender neutral terms, the opportunities for choice within it result in girls and boys opting for different routes, with their attendant messages about appropriate concerns and future occupations for males and females. This, she suggests, may be attributed to 'deep-seated attitudes that some subjects are more appropriate for girls or boys'. She comments: 'Gender differences in post-compulsory courses and careers would be reduced if there was a larger common entitlement and less choice of subjects for the final two years of each National Curriculum' (Croxford, forthcoming).

Figure 96.2 Gender differences in science subjects studied at age 14–16, in Scotland 1976–90

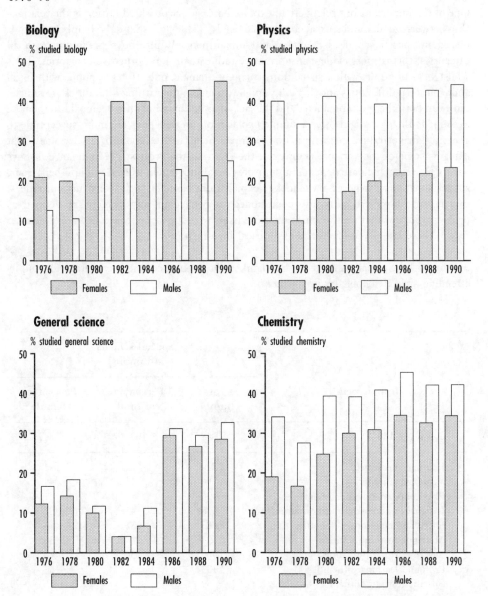

Source: L. Croxford (1998) Gender and National Curricula, in J. Salisbury and S. Riddell (eds) *Gender, Policy and Educational Change*, London: Routledge.

GENDER AND SPECIAL EDUCATIONAL NEEDS

One of the important but relatively unexplored areas of Scottish education is the relationship between gender and special educational needs. Table 96.1 shows the number of pupils placed in special schools by gender and impairment. Whilst boys predominate in all categories, this is most evident in normative rather than non-normative categories. Thus whilst 44% of pupils with a visual impairment are female, only 16 % of pupils with social and emotional difficulties and 36% of pupils with moderate learning difficulties are female. How can both these discrepancies and the lack of attention which has been paid to them be explained? Biology might offer a simple explanation, in that boys are more susceptible to genetic damage and trauma. In relation to impairments with a physiological aetiology, that explains some of the variance. However, the fact that the greatest predominance of boys occurs in areas which are dependent on professional judgement as well as pupil behaviour, suggests that it is also necessary to look to explanations based on social constructionist ideas, that is, that boys are culturally conditioned to behave in ways which are defined as problematic, and that professionals are more likely to judge male behaviour as problematic. Again, these issues require further empirical investigation.

Table 96.1   Special schools in Scotland, 1996. Number and percentage of pupils attending special schools by impairment.

Impairment	Special schools (all pupils)		
	Total number	Percentage of total	Percentage female
Total (= 100%)	9,248	100	34
Hearing impairment	210	2	41
Visual impairment	96	1	44
Physical or motor impairments	496	5	41
Language and communication disorder	328	4	21
Social and emotional difficulties	1,685	18	16
Moderate learning difficulties	2,594	28	36
Severe learning difficulties	900	10	40
Profound learning difficulties	133	1	51
Specific learning difficulty	59	1	10
Complex or multiple impairments			
Dual sensory impairment	22	–	41
Moderate learning difficulties & other	845	9	36
Severe learning difficulties & other	871	9	38
Profound learning difficulties & other	848	9	45
Other	161	2	40

Source: SOEID (1997) Special Educational Needs Statistical Bulletin. Edinburgh: Scottish Office.

Despite the clarity of these patterns, gender, as well as social class, has been almost invisible in the world of special education, with its focus on the needs of the individual pupil in isolation from his or her social context. The growing field of disability studies has also tended to develop in isolation from special educational needs and from gender studies, since its material analysis has few points of contact with the individual explanations of the former and the feminist accounts of the latter. Research applying the insights of disability studies, with its emphasis on the social creation of disability to the field of special educational needs would help understanding of the relationship between gender, social class and special educational needs.

GENDER AND EDUCATION REFORM – THE UNINTENDED CONSEQUENCES OF POLICIES

The educational reforms introduced by the former Conservative government throughout the 1980s and early 1990s provided a rich field for the development of policy studies in education. The pursuit of the market-driven agenda of choice and diversity and the new managerialist agenda of effectiveness and efficiency were extensively analysed but the effects of multiple policy innovations, and in particular the impact of market-driven reforms on the emerging equal opportunities agenda, were not widely explored. A piece of research funded by the Equal Opportunities Commission at Stirling University, conducted by Turner, Riddell and Brown (1995), took on the somewhat daunting task of investigating the intersection of these separately conceived policies. The research began by investigating the nature and development of equal opportunities policies in the twelve Scottish regions which were in place in 1995, a year before local government reorganisation. Regions varied markedly in their policy development; urban Labour-controlled authorities tended, unsurprisingly, to have the firmest policies in place encompassing commitment to social change rather than simple compliance with the legal requirement not to discriminate. In 1995 when the research took place, some rural authorities still lacked an equal opportunities policy statement and most authorities published their statements in the early 1990s, a decade after the passage of the Sex Discrimination Act. Due to protracted political wrangling, one large Scottish region managed to publish its policy only six weeks before its dissolution. The second part of the study explored gendered patterns of attainment and subject uptake and these have already been described.

Finally, the researchers investigated the differential impact of policies informed by marketisation and new managerialism in case study schools varying in relation to social class of the pupil population and location. Variations were identified between four schools, two primary and two secondary, in one urban authority with a progressive equal opportunities policy. Broadly, it was found that the curricular reforms had a neutral effect in challenging gender differentiation. Teachers felt that the 5–14 programme and the curriculum of the later secondary years, emphasising the entitlement of all children to a common curricular experience, discouraged active discrimination, but on the other hand did not encourage teachers to adopt radical positive action unless they were so minded.

Management reforms, on the other hand, were seen by the schools in working class areas to have an overwhelmingly negative effect. The secondary school in the socially disadvantaged area had a well established reputation for its work in anti-racist and anti-sexist education. The publication of league tables of schools according to their external examination results had accelerated the trend towards falling rolls, reduced resources and low morale amongst teachers, parents and pupils. This meant that energy which had previously gone into anti-sexist education was instead used in maintaining the basic functioning of the school. By comparison, the middle class secondary was buoyant in terms of pupil numbers and found that its liberal equal opportunities policies were acceptable to parents of girls who wished their daughters to achieve academically, but were not sufficiently radical to upset the parents of boys. In both secondary schools, teachers were anxious about boys' performance relative to that of girls, but in the socially disadvantaged schools these worries were heightened by pressure from the authority not to exclude difficult pupils, most of whom were boys, and indeed to accept pupils who had been excluded from other schools. In the low socio-economic status (SES) case study school, about 50 per cent of pupils, the majority male, were perceived by the teachers to have some sort of learning difficulty, but this was not fully reflected in their allocation of learning support teachers. The primary schools, although less affected by anxiety over test results since these were not in the public domain, were nonetheless affected differently by the proportion of pupils with learning and behavioural difficulties. In the low SES primary school, a significant amount of energy was invested in maintaining an orderly environment, although indiscipline was not construed as a gendered problem. In the high SES primary school, on the other hand, equal opportunities was an explicit part of its agenda and again this struck an approving chord with its clientele, who were predominantly middle class and ambitious.

Overall, it was concluded that the regional equal opportunities policy was implemented very differently in the case study primary and secondary schools, mediated by effects of social class, parent culture and location. These variables also affected the implementation of curricular and management reforms, which in turn shaped the environment in which equality policies were developing. A complex iterative process was thus set in train, with high SES schools judged to be more effective not only in terms of academic performance, but also in relation to their equality programmes. The low SES schools, on the other hand, were pressurised into survival mode, with little space for innovatory work of any kind. There seems to be an ongoing need to assess the unintended, as well as anticipated, consequences of educational change, including those associated with gender equality.

FUTURE ISSUES FOR POLICY MAKERS AND PRACTITIONERS

As a preliminary to this section, it is worth noting the rapid changes which have happened in the position of women in society over the past two decades and the perils of predicting the future. From a position of performing worse than boys at Higher grade in the mid-1970s, girls of all social classes are now performing better than boys of similar social class in all subject areas, although gender differentiation in the curriculum remains stubbornly in place. In the late 1970s, however, this was not what was predicted. Noting the way in which post-war education reports and legislation had tended to reinforce the provision of different education for boys and girls, Deem predicted that after a brief period of liberalism in the 1970s which saw the introduction of equal opportunities legislation, the advent of Thatcherism was about to herald:

> a gradual return to the education of women for domestic labour, emphasis on the importance of motherhood to the economy and the reproduction of 'suitable' labour power (i.e. that which is prepared to accept low wages and discipline) as the need for women's paid work outside the family evaporates. In many areas, girls leaving school will have little possibility of entering employment at all; if they do find jobs, especially in manufacturing, clerical or secretarial work,

it is likely that the microchip will soon begin to eat away at that work. (R. Deem, 1981, p. 141 State policy and ideology in the education of women, 1944–1980, *British Journal of Sociology of Education*, 2.2, 131–43)

Such analysis assumed that women's position in the labour market is more tenuous than that of men, that male labour will be preferred to that of women and that motherhood is foisted on women to serve the needs of the economy rather than something they choose themselves. What has tended to happen throughout the 1980s and 1990s is a collapse of the labour market in the area of heavy industry which is traditionally where men were employed and an expansion of the service sector where women predominate. More women with young children than ever before are in employment and girls' education is based on the assumption that they will be economically active for most of their lives, as well as shouldering the major responsibility for home-making and child-rearing. So, whilst avoiding the pitfalls of prediction, it is worth concluding with some of the questions for research, policy and practice which demand to be addressed over the coming decade as the Scottish parliament establishes itself.

Devolution will have many implications for the formation of Scottish identity, often defined in opposition to all things English. Given existing anxieties about boys' performance and their vulnerability to school failure and exclusion, it will be important for schools to use the new focus on the development of a positive Scottish identity to foster new versions of masculinity which reject macho posturing. Tackling male disaffection and violence requires a critical look at popular male culture, rather than seeing the male as norm and the female as in some way deficient. Getting this right in school will clearly not be easy; breast-beating is not very helpful and the danger of blaming women for boys' difficulties, endemic in the men's movement, will have to be avoided. Male teachers clearly have an immensely important role to play here.

Paying attention to the problems of boys does not mean that girls can now be ignored. In addition to enjoying far less teacher attention than boys, young women may well be the victims of male violence both inside and outside the school. High achieving middle class girls may experience fear of failure, becoming the custodians of middle class awareness of risk and danger. The rate of teenage pregnancy is higher in Scotland than the rest of the UK, and yet there is still reticence about the discussion of sexuality in some schools. Issues which have a gender dimension, such as indisicpline, violence and bullying are still often seen in gender neutral terms, despite the evidence that these are perpetrated and experienced differently by boys and girls.

Finally, the gendered impact of a range of policy innovations needs to be explored. These include policies of managerialism and marketisation, promoted by the previous government but still very much in evidence in current educational discourse. Other policies, such as the restructuring of welfare, the new emphasis on the redemptive power of work and the lifelong learning agenda have specific implications for males and females as participants in education and these will need careful exploration. Throughout this account, an attempt has been made to draw out the interaction of a range of variables, for it is impossible to understand the effects of gender without paying attention also to the multiple identities which people occupy, based on nationality, ethnicity, age, social class, sexuality and disability. Exploring these avenues while continuing to interrogate the notion of equality will provide much work for researchers and practitioners well into the next decade.

REFERENCES

Brown, A., E. Breitenbach and F. Myers (1994) *Equality Issues in Scotland: A Research Review*, Manchester: Equal Opportunities Commission.

Croxford, L. (1997) Participation in science subjects: the effects of the Scottish Curriculum Framework, *Research Papers in Education*, 12, 1, 69–89.

Furlong, A. and F. Cartmel (1997) *Young People and Social Change Individualization and Risk in Late Modernity*, Buckingham: Open University Press.

Paterson, F. and J. Fewell (1990) (eds) *Girls in their Prime: Scottish Education Revisited* Edinburgh: Scottish Academic Press.

Powney, J. (1997) *Gender and Attainment: A Review*, Edinburgh: Scottish Council for Research in Education.

Turner, E., S. Riddell and S. Brown (1995) *Gender Equality in Scottish Schools: The Impact of Recent Educational Reforms*, Manchester: Equal Opportunities Commission.

97

'Sectarianism' and Scottish Education

Gerry P. T. Finn

SECTARIAN, SECTARIANISM AND CONCEPTUAL CONFUSION

Sectarian is an unhelpful term. Any individual who adheres to a specific sect can be described as sectarian. Equally, any organisation associated with a church is sectarian. By definition, a church choir is a sectarian body, however that does not identify the choir or its members as sectarian in any pejorative sense of that word. Use of the term sectarian risks the threat of misinterpretation. Church choristers are not, or at least they are usually not, by reason of choir membership guilty of involvement in bigotry. But too often exactly this confusion over the two senses of sectarian undermines serious discussion of religious or (in a non-pejorative use of the terms) sectarian differences: too often this very choice of terminology leads to an assumption that the matter at hand is related to sectarianism, a term which is practically always used to denote bigotry.

Although sectarianism usually signifies some allusion to bigotry, its precise meaning still remains confused and lacks genuine clarity. Sectarianism is used to refer to some human action or actions that are to be fitted into some unarticulated, but presumed, process that patterns society, a patterning which in turn is assumed to reflect an ideology, believed to be based upon some sectarian – in the bigoted sense – affiliation. This convoluted description of the chained assumptions underlying its usage helps identify the sources of confusion. There is no description of the specific ideological message of what is being termed sectarianism, no analysis of its socio-political power and no identification of the targets or intended victims of this ideology. Use of the term sectarianism amounts to little more than labelling something as being associated with bigotry. Sectarianism's use obscures much more than it reveals: although, paradoxically, its use does reveal something of its user. Its use indicates that the user believes there to be some shared common world-view that allows the meaning of sectarianism to be taken for granted, with nothing to explain. Yet sectarianism is a coy term that blankets the social phenomenon to which the speaker alludes. Its very use allows the accuser, for that is the intent behind the speaker's action, to make the accusation without the need to substantiate the case with anything resembling evidence. But then, of course, there is no need. For everyone is assumed to understand what is being discussed and what the problems really are: which is why these terms are used. But then these attitudes constitute a problem still to be tackled in Scottish society.

And these attitudes find expression in a variety of different ways. There are many assumptions about sectarianism, its effects on specific segments of Scottish life and about variations in its impact across Scotland. As a rule, these assumptions, more often everyday assertions, amount to little more than the creation of some framework of loosely related beliefs around some unspecified notion of sectarianism. Yet any number of everyday ready reckoners of its impact seem available. Thus there are sectarian accounts of the workings of Scottish politics, especially in relation to party politics in local government administration; sectarian accounts of employment practices, of quotas and restricted access, even barriers, to entry to certain social institutions. And, as is true of societal beliefs in general, there can be accounts of bewildering complexity, ubiquity, or uniqueness offered on an apparently individual basis, but these individual offerings are better described as innovative variants on a well-worked societal theme.

The two areas of Scottish life most associated with beliefs about sectarianism are football and schooling. And both display the features most common to invocations of sectarianism in its Scottish context. There is the identification of the presence of Catholics, or more properly, Catholics of Irish descent. And, usually there is another common characteristic to accompany this feature: a belief that Catholics, or their real, symbolic or imagined representatives, have intruded into some part of Scottish life in which they either wield influence and power, or strive to do so. These beliefs feature in many discourses surrounding suppositions of sectarianism around schooling and football, as they usually also do in accounts of sectarianism in other areas of Scottish life. Inevitably there are discursive exceptions to this rhetorical framework.

One discursive strategy in discussing sectarianism indicates the existence of some imprecisely defined antagonism to the Irish or Catholics. Usually these accounts ride on a discursive tandem, in which sectarianism is judged to be peddled by two protagonists, chained together. In football, Glasgow's Rangers and Celtic thus become united. Neither the Orange Order nor the now small, and politically irrelevant, Order of Hibernians walk alone. And then there is Freemasonry, an order in which Daniel O'Connell, the early nineteenth-century leader of Ireland's Catholics, was prominent, and which strictly ought to play no part in this intergroup conflict. Nonetheless, Scottish Freemasonry has contained some who have laboured hard in the cause of this disharmony. So, as a result of this recognition, the Freemasons become mystically bonded in brotherhood with the Knights of St Columba. This complex of supposed mirror-images is intended to present a balanced view of sectarianism. Instead, these pairings reveal a set of distorting mirrors that hinder any clear-sighted perspective on the precise nature of this form of intergroup relations and conflict.

Scotland is indeed rich in assumptions about so-called sectarianism, its causes and its effects, but impoverished as a society by much too little careful analysis. Indeed, the multiplicity of these everyday assumptions can be seen to be part of the problem, drawing on deeply embedded societal prejudices, which are in turn obscured by this use of the imprecise term, sectarianism. In the past, careful analysis was not advised, some thought not required. With few exceptions, little research was done: after all, everyone knew what 'sectarianism' was, bemoaned its impact, and concern was expressed that it was too hot a topic to be studied. Now, apparently, everyone knows what it used to be: some question if it still exists. So, while some still bemoan its impact, others now belittle its effect. Now there are more, though still too few, attempts at careful analysis (e.g. Gallagher, 1987; Devine, ed., 1991). Yet assumption and presumption still dominate scholarly effort which has been bedevilled by the neglect of the profound complexities of prejudice.

SUBTLE PREJUDICE AND BIG BIGOTS

Navigating a path through confused everyday beliefs about prejudice is not easy. In everyday thinking prejudice and acts of discrimination are often confused, but the relationship is complex. Prejudice, even when strongly held, may not lead to discrimination against members of the target group. Paradoxically, discriminatory actions can be carried out by those who are not prejudiced or, more accurately, only display minimal prejudice, but discriminate because they fear the response of more seriously prejudiced others. A greater understanding of human behaviour would result if a more complex, more social view of prejudice was more commonly accepted.

Prejudice is, regrettably, not simply a matter of individual ignorance and error: these are common beliefs which often underlie everyday thinking, and educational policy-making too. Instead prejudice is a hardy, complicated phenomenon, socially adaptable and capable of evolving into new forms over time. Yet prejudice is too frequently approached in the overly facile ways just described. One reason, often a self-serving one, is to be found in how prejudice is portrayed. The dominant social representation of prejudice is to be found in the image and symbol of the bigot, a representation which obscures the more subtle, much more common, manifestations of prejudice. As a result, not only can prejudicial nuances be neglected because of this representation but, even when recognised, more subtle variants of prejudice can be dismissed because of their supposed (relative) unimportance.

Yet there is an increasing recognition by social scientists of the intricate interrelationship in which the most overt forms of prejudice rely upon the more subtle for their initiation, justification and legitimation. Nor does this symbiotic relationship rest there: subtle variants of prejudice rely upon the existence of more overt forms to warrant their own reasonableness. And one outcome of this relationship is the capability to deny its very existence. The dominance of the lone bigot representation so distorts the public focus that prejudice is not seen to be a fundamentally societal phenomenon, nor does it appear as a social system of beliefs that can influence many who do not fit this representational identikit. As a result, those who do not fit the bigot mould can be seen – both by themselves and by others – to be unprejudiced. Prejudice is indisputably complex. And, though usually not commented on, so is the very language of description of the groups involved in so-called sectarianism.

Some words of caution are necessary: should the term Catholic or Roman Catholic be used? Historically either description implied the adoption of a specific denominational and doctrinal position on competing claims to be the 'true' and 'universal' Christian church. 'Roman' denotes a church that is not Catholic, even worse, foreign rather than universal. This usage, especially when the stress is placed on the first word, can be interpreted as a definite slight. Yet the traditional usage of Catholic can be seen as an exclusive claim that slights Protestants who also lay claim to being part of the Catholic or universal church. It may be an indication of the power of ecumenism, or a measure of the pace of secularisation, that these semantic uncertainties and sensitivities are now usually ignored. Yet should 'is the Pope a Catholic?' still be used as a mocking assertion of certainty when Ian Paisley would answer negatively, claiming instead to be a Catholic himself? Theologically the answer is a matter of debate, rendering this assertion of certainty an unknowing exercise in self-mockery, but the commonplace understanding indubitably still remains. And moved by this spirit of theological disregard, Catholic will be used to refer to the minority group.

IRISH AND CATHOLIC

A more important terminological clarification is needed. For over one hundred and fifty years the history of Catholics in Scotland is entangled with that of the Irish. In the nineteenth century, the growing Irish dimension to the Catholic community asked questions of the small population of Scottish Catholics. Members frequently answered with antagonism. The 1793 Relief Act and the 1829 Emancipation Bill had removed much of the legislation that discriminated against Catholics, but considerable prejudice remained. As the Irish presence grew, the small Scottish Catholic minority feared that the majority Protestant population would equate Irish with Catholic, and their own improving situation would deteriorate. These fears were to prove to be justified, but that outcome still does not excuse the united Scottish Protestant and Catholic prejudice. Indeed, the response of Scotland's small Catholic community showed that generally they shared the anti-Irish prejudices of the majority community.

Scotland's anti-Catholic prejudice over time was more commonly subsumed in anti-Irish prejudice, which is more accurately portrayed as racism. Identifying what is usually coyly disguised by the term sectarianism as racism, confuses those who accept the racist underpinning to contemporary lay-beliefs that race is colour-coded. 'Race' is itself a social construct, the product of racialised social practices and discourses that constitute some social group as a different 'race'. Once a minority has been differentiated as belonging to another racial category, a rhetoric of majority justification for mistreatment of, and discrimination against, the minority community easily follows. Comparative studies have shown there to be a common set of practices which deny or minimise majority prejudice or discrimination.

These practices describe a 'realist' theory of prejudice which obscures the very existence of the prejudice at its heart. The proposition is that negative evaluations of the minority are a justifiable and realistic majority response, not really a form of prejudice, but valid criticisms that the minority members bring on themselves by their own behaviour. Even in the event of an admission of some possible element of prejudice, this 'realist' formulation allows an admission of majority prejudice to be presented as an understandable, albeit overstated, response to the supposedly provocative actions of the minority. The term sectarianism, with its neglect of issues of socio-political power, its confounding of cause and effect, and its implication for the majority of, at the very worst, equal culpability for the state of intergroup relations, dutifully serves this 'realist' cause.

SECTARIANISM AS A REALIST THEORY OF PREJUDICE

In football and education the notion of sectarianism ventures forth to promote uncritically accepted and employed 'realist' theories of prejudice. Clubs established by the Irish-Scottish community are blamed for introducing religion, politics and ethnic identity into the sport. Yet initially most sports clubs evolved out of existing social networks. The first Edinburgh club, the Third Edinburgh Rifle Volunteers (3rd ERV), formed in 1874, was only open to members of this Volunteer corps, and both were established and ruled by John Hope, solicitor at the Court of Session. Vehemently anti-Irish and anti-Catholic, Hope, a Tory, a Kirk elder and anti-drink campaigner, had set up these associated organisations to provide a focus for his No-Popery and total abstention campaigns. Potential members were carefully screened to ensure that they could satisfy Hope's specific requirements on these matters. The 3rd ERV was not only a Protestant football club, it was an anti-Catholic club.

Edinburgh Hibernians were founded the following year by the Catholic Young Men's Society (CYMS) of St Patrick's Church. Hibernian members had to be members of both the CYMS and the League of the Cross, the Catholic Total Abstinence Society. The club was Catholic, and as the names demonstrate, its players Irish-Scots. However, it was not a mirror image of the 3rd ERV: it was not anti-Protestant. Participation by Hibernian in Edinburgh football was seen to be a means of mixing with Protestants and breaking down barriers and prejudices.

Glasgow Celtic's origins are more complicated, with roots in both Church charity societies and Irish political bodies, which reflect the range of motivations behind the club's establishment. However, one central purpose was to present a creditable image of the contribution of the Irish-Scots community to Scottish life. Participation in the popular sport was a metaphorical statement of community intent to participate in Scottish life.

Yet popular beliefs present this action as a non-Scottish, Irish Catholic intrusion into Scottish football and then hold Celtic responsible for Rangers' long-term pursuit of an anti-Catholic policy! This account can only be sustained by ignoring the nature of the earlier membership of Rangers and their religious and political viewpoints. Without a rival like Celtic there would have been little scope for the full expression of these prejudices, but it is a very strong realist theory of prejudice that blames the target community, or its symbolic representatives, for the creation of that prejudice itself. It was the Rangers club, not Celtic, nor even Rangers' fans (a classic use of the bigot representation to disguise genteel, more subtle variants of prejudice), and only Rangers that could be held responsible for the implementation of the club's own policy.

Another realist theory of prejudice is employed to explain so-called sectarianism in education. Here it is Catholic schools that are equally the cause of sectarianism in education and portrayed as the very symbol of division. Yet this account can only be maintained by ignoring some awkward historical evidence. Divisions in nineteenth-century Scottish Presbyterianism had fragmented the sense of Presbyterianism representing the nation. The Church of Scotland, as the national and established Scottish church, persisted in arguing that its schools constituted a national and non-denominational system. Other Presbyterian churches, let alone non-Presbyterian churches, were unconvinced by this suggested interpretation of non-denominational. Divisions in Presbyterianism were seen as a scandal which hindered missionary work – and schooling was an important part of the Churches' mission. In schooling, as in other areas of missionary work, the Presbyterian Churches wished to sponsor a non-denominational, Presbyterian approach. These efforts kept foundering on the dispute over Church-State relations.

The Established Church insisted that school religious instruction be a legal requirement. The United Presbyterian Church upheld the voluntarist position which rejected state support for religious teaching. The 1872 Education Act cleverly fudged these positions and neither prescribed nor proscribed religious instruction. The inclusion of a 'conscience clause' which allowed withdrawal from religious instruction did hint at what was expected. However these public schools would not be run by the State, but by locally elected, seemingly secular, school boards, which would inevitably be dominated by candidates elected on religious tickets. Even that was insufficient reassurance for some. Scottish Tories and their Orange Order allies complained about the failure to prescribe religious instruction. They succeeded in having the preamble amended so that there was explicit recognition of the right to retain Presbyterian religious instruction according to 'use and wont'. That is what happened. With negligible exceptions, non-denominational schools were publicly-funded schools in which non-denominational Presbyterian religious instruction occurred.

No large rallies were held to campaign against Presbyterianism on the rates, but there were complaints about the injustice of funding one religious tradition to the exclusion of others. But this was not some Catholic-Protestant dispute. Objections made by the Scottish Episcopal Church were often interchangeable with those from Catholic sources. Although in communion with the Established Protestant Church of England, the Episcopalians suffered the same financial penalty as Catholics. As long as these Church schools met the required national standards, both were eligible for some forms of public grant from the government. However, both groups paid rates that supported Presbyterian religious instruction in public schools but did not help maintain Episcopalian or Catholic schools. In addition, the improved funding for the new 'national educational system' meant that educational improvements there made ever more demands on the parallel Church school systems.

As the 'Great War' drew to a close, the coalition government proposed a new education bill for Scotland, which would establish an inclusive, genuinely national education system. After some, sometimes suspicious, negotiations, Catholic and Episcopalian schools were transferred from Church control and became public schools. Religious instruction was specifically guaranteed, though based on the use and wont provision included in the 1872 Act. Transferred schools were open to all pupils, and the conscience clause applied. All teachers employed in the transferred schools had to satisfy the Scottish Education Department as to their educational qualifications and their religious belief and character was to be approved by the appropriate denominational body. Throughout the progress of the bill, Robert Munro, the Scottish Secretary, stressed that the proposal sought to end an injustice. Pupils should not suffer as a result of their parents' religious beliefs. Munro repeatedly presented The Education (Scotland) 1918 Act as a measure to provide equal educational opportunities for all Scotland's children.

Presbyterian Churches did not like the specifically enshrined, written guarantee of religious instruction. The complaint that this was more than they had received was invalid because it was the dissension in Presbyterian ranks that had led to the employment of the use and wont fudge, rather than any more explicit written statement. However, the restatement in the preamble to the 1918 Act of the use and wont principle in support of religious instruction in public schools was sufficient to allay these fears. Around fifty Episcopalian and 226 Catholic schools were transferred. Both religious groups also ran teacher-training colleges, which now became national denominational training colleges under the direction of the National Committee for the Training of Teachers. A truly national education system, one that recognised and accepted diversity, now began to operate in Scotland. Unfortunately, the spirit of communal reconciliation that was apparent at the conclusion of the Great War was not to last much longer.

CATHOLIC SCHOOLS AS AN IRISH THREAT: SCOTLAND'S HIDDEN RACISM

At the General Assembly of the Church of Scotland in 1922 alarm was expressed over Irish immigration. The Irish were blamed for most of Scotland's ills. Crime, poverty and labour unrest were caused by the Irish who both stole jobs from native Scots and took advantage of welfare benefits. Yet, despite their apparent possession of this immensely clever ability to undertake opposed activities simultaneously (and this claim illustrates a classic prejudicial belief), the Irish were racial inferiors to the Scots. And despite their undoubted inferiority, the Irish were also accused of taking advantage of the Scots and forcing them to finance Catholic schools which were then used for 'propaganda'. Public funding for Catholic schooling was presented as a central element in a conspiracy to bring Scotland under Irish and Catholic domination.

A special committee was set up by the Assembly to examine Irish immigration to Scotland. In 1923 it reported back on the threat to 'our race'. Orange Irish posed no problems. They belonged to the same race and faith. The report asserted that God opposed racial mixing. Kingdoms divided against themselves were doomed to fall. 'The nations that are homogenous in Faith and Ideals, that have maintained unity of race, have ever been the most prosperous, and to them the Almighty has committed the highest tasks.' So opposition to the Irish was transformed into a Christian duty. Yet, in a refrain that was to grow in importance, contributors to the debate stated their opposition to the Irish was based on racial, not religious, grounds. (See S. J. Brown, 1991, Outside the Covenant: The Scottish Presbyterian Churches and Irish Immigration, 1922–1938, *Innes Review*, 42, 19–45.)

In truth, opposition to the Irish involved class, national and religious prejudices allied to anti-Irish racism. Anti-socialist and anti-trade union sentiments were also on display in rhetorics which identified the Irish as being responsible for these beliefs and activities too. Opportunities over the next few years for a non-sectarian Presbyterian crusade were taken and the main Scottish Presbyterian Churches were soon united in a common anti-Irish campaign. Efforts were made to convince the British government of the need to restrict severely Irish immigration, forcibly deport certain categories of Irish and in other ways restrict the minority's civil rights. 'Native' Scots were to be given preference in all forms of public employment. Usually this heady brew of racist rhetoric included the demand that the 1918 Education Act be repealed or revised to end public funding for Catholic schools.

Expressions of anti-Irish racism were common in the inter-war years. Lord Beaverbrook's trusted chief assistant, the journalist G. M. Thomson, raised the spectre of a Scotland denationalised 'by a people alien in race, temperament and religion', complained that so far this was only a 'minor political issue in Scotland', yet it 'would have caused a race war in America and a pogrom in most European countries'. The problem was that these racial differences were not so obvious, but the Catholicism of the Irish allowed the threat to be detected: 'If it had not been that a religious as well as a racial revolution was taking place the very existence of the Irish invasion would have only been vaguely suspected'.

Tory MP John Buchan's was but one of many elite voices in support of nativist racism. His Scotland was very few steps away from disaster. 'Our population is declining; we are losing some of the best of our race stock by migration and their place is being taken by those who, whatever their merits, are not Scottish. I understand that every fifth child born in Scotland is an Irish Roman Catholic' (*Hansard*, 1935). Buchan's last sentence overtly states the genetic assumptions in his racist beliefs.

Actual Irish immigration had been negligible for some considerable period. By then many of these 'Irish Roman Catholics' were Irish-Scots, the grandchildren, even great-grandchildren of the wave of immigrants that had peaked in the middle of the previous century. Yet they were still judged alien. No civic nationalism featured in Buchan's political analysis, nor that of the Presbyterian Churches. Paradoxically, this racialised Scottish nationalism was common in Unionist British politics in Scotland, where the Conservative party was believed to be the ally of Scots Protestants. However, although the Scottish

Conservative and Unionist party flirted and dallied with these racist prejudices, the relationship was not a faithful one. Nonetheless, even this erratic form of elite support created an environment in which other political organisations and ideologies evolved. One was the fortunately short-lived, but intriguingly titled, Scottish Fascist Democratic Party. This oxymoron of a party in 1933, which seems to have been its sole year of life, demanded the expulsion of all Catholic religious orders from Scotland, the repeal of the 1918 Education (Scotland) Act and the prohibition of any Irish immigration to Scotland.

The Presbyterian Churches' campaign provided an atmosphere conducive to the onward march of more committed, more extreme groups of Christian soldiers. In 1935, the Rev. F. E. Watson of the Scottish Protestant Vigilance Society wrote in the *Glasgow Herald* that: 'The indignant opposition to the provision of section 18 of the Education (Scotland) Act, 1918 is that public money is being expanded in educating an increasing section of the population, in the main Free Staters or their offspring, in a faith and a loyalty hostile to the tradition and religion accepted by the vast majority of the Scottish nation . . . Why should we feed, clothe, and educate these people who everywhere plot and plan for the downfall of Britain?' Opposition to the public funding of Catholic schools was justified because they had been found guilty of un-Scottish activities, ensuring that 'these people' would remain faithful to anti-British conspiracies. And support for their very existence could be opposed on the self-same grounds too.

Potentially the most effective political synthesis of these popular prejudices was provided by Alexander Ratcliffe and his Scottish Protestant League. Ratcliffe's beliefs did incorporate elements of racism but, as his party's title indicates, he relied more on a militant Protestantism which still allowed him to align his programme with the ongoing anti-Irish campaign. His opposition to the practically non-existent Catholic immigration focused on its supposed impact on Scotland and Protestantism: Scotland's social problems were explained by the un-Christian, Catholic Irish presence. Indicating the flexibility of his prejudices, and his sometimes explicit support for overt racism, Ratcliffe supported the Ku Klux Klan. He applauded their opposition to Catholics, black people and Jews in America. In an act of solidarity, Ratcliffe even named his own group of supposed bodyguards the Knights of Kaledonia Klan.

At the core of Ratcliffe's ideology lay a conspiracy world-view, and it was a world-view. This broad view required his greater emphasis on anti-Catholic prejudices than anti-Irish racism. Global events could be more readily interpreted in terms of Catholic conspiracies orchestrated by the Vatican. But Ratcliffe did increasingly focus on the supposed consequences of Irish immigration: the inclusion of Catholic schooling within the national education system was evidence of Catholic encroachments on Protestant Scotland. Public finance directed to Catholic schools was used to illustrate the minority's alleged new-found power: this 'evidence' of a plot offered an ideal opportunity to make anti-Catholic propaganda. Following his Barrhead meeting on 'Rome on the Rates', Ratcliffe boasted: 'This subject is surely becoming a popular and "hot" one and results in much interest being created regarding the advance of the Papacy in Scotland' (*Protestant Advocate*, June, 1924).

Ratcliffe did have a significant influence on Scottish politics, especially in the west of Scotland in the early 1930s. The Scottish Protestant League polled very well in local Glasgow elections, with Ratcliffe and other party candidates being elected to the council. However, by the end of that decade, Ratcliffe also found most of his now erstwhile colleagues guilty of treachery too. Throughout this period, Ratcliffe's support for Hitler grew. Initially he approved of the dictator's opposition to the Catholic Church, but in his support for Nazi Germany, Ratcliffe's bible-based anti-Semitism merged with his anti-Catholicism. He was even able to argue that Jesuits and Jews were allies, producing propaganda against Protestant Germany. By the outbreak of the war his party had become the British Protestant League. By the conclusion of that war, Ratcliffe had become one of the very first to formulate the 'holocaust denial'. He argued that evidence of Nazi concentration camps and gas chambers had been concocted in another Jewish conspiracy. (See C. Holmes, 1989, 'Alexander Ratcliffe: Militant Protestant and Antisemite', in T. Kushner and K. Lunn (eds), *Traditions of Intolerance: Historical Perspectives on Fascism and Race Discourse in Britain*, Manchester: Manchester University Press, pp. 196–217.)

Even unsuccessful conspiracy theorists distort the parameters within which political debate occurs, often they have a long-lasting impact. (See C. F. Graumann and S. Moscovici eds, 1987, *Changing Conceptions of Conspiracy*, NewYork: Springer-Verlag.) Ratcliffe played a crucial part in the terrible legacy that is the holocaust denial. His conspiracy beliefs signally contributed to another sad legacy: the accepted framework within which discussion of Catholic schools in Scotland still occurs. In the usual tradition of the prejudicial confounding of cause and effect, Ratcliffe found Catholic schools to be the source of division in Scottish society. Yet, with other Presbyterian propagandists, he quite openly manipulated the issue of public support for Catholic schools to further his own divisive politics. The 1918 Act was judged no less than an anti-Protestant plot. Financial support for Catholic schools meant children were educated in the 'biblical error' which, he explained, was so evident in the wickedness and social evils of the Irish in Scotland.

Ratcliffe's proposed solution was bible-based religious instruction for all, the programme effectively then in operation in the non-denominational, de facto, Presbyterian schools. Any recognition of the different Catholic tradition would not only support religious error, but give Catholics preferential treatment in a Protestant country. Yet Ratcliffe explained to his supporters that Catholics would find this non-denominational Presbyterian-based religious instruction so unacceptable that they would then be forced to try to fund their own schools again. Ratcliffe's desired outcome, the break-up of the first truly Scottish national education system, was consistent with his determination to foster, not oppose, social division.

SOCIAL PLURALISM – DIFFERENCE NEED NOT MEAN DIVISION

Fortunately Scotland has progressed since then; intergroup relations are now much improved. Discrimination is considerably diminished. Unfortunately, the problem of prejudice is far from eradicated. What passes for debate on Catholic schools is testimony to this sad legacy from the past; indeed much of the content of this debate derives directly from that past. Even commentators with some understanding of the racist nature of these past struggles are confused; they believe that recognition of social difference must end in social division. Yet it is the social meaning that is ascribed to human difference that determines whether division will result. And, the nature and content of this debate on Catholic schools, not the continuation of their presence, promotes the cause of social division. In Northern Ireland the role of schooling in intergroup conflict has also been passionately debated. Fortunately it has also been subject to some sophisticated analysis there. As a result there are important educational lessons to be learnt in Scotland from the Northern Ireland experience.

The late Frank Wright, a supporter of mutually agreed, genuinely integrated education there, warned that the historical context of education in Northern Ireland meant that arguments for 'integrated' schools had often been no more than an excuse for expressing anti-Catholic sentiments. He observed that it was commonplace for minority communities to want to control their own schools when faced with the cultural domination of educational goals by the majority. Minority defensiveness on schooling has often been beneficial. Wright argued that, in both Northern Ireland and Scotland, it had been minority schooling that had helped Catholics begin to equal the status and achievements of Protestants.

Wright saw Scotland as teaching Northern Ireland an important lesson:

> Sometimes accepting the need for separate education systems has prevented struggles which might otherwise have torn up the unity of the nation . . . No one today could argue that enforcing integrated education upon Scotland would have made for a deeper peace than Scotland has actually had. There are groups in Scotland now who are aware of how far apart religious differences keep people, and are trying to work upon their common heritage as Christians in Scotland. But no one in Scotland is arguing for a global plan for integrated education to combat dangers of sectarianism at the moment. It is easy to see that a political campaign to do this would start to politicise religion and create the very problem people suggest it might prevent. (1993, p. 185)

The sad irony here is that Wright was wrong; it was he who had much to teach Scotland. Catholic schools in Scotland have been subject to attacks based on prejudice. Arguments on behalf of a truly integrated education, one that would recognise and respect religious differences, have not been made. Nonetheless the real contemporary danger is that continued ill-informed attacks on Catholic schools could politicise the issue, as happened in the 1930s and, as Wright warns, could happen again.

There is another option. The recognition of difference in education clearly need not lead to division. It is indeed intriguing that the existence of Episcopalian schools was scarcely a matter of widespread concern or comment, let alone subject to popular campaigns of opposition. Little attention has been directed to the only Jewish state primary school in Scotland. Perhaps that is just as well. In 1996 some publicity as a result of local government reorganisation led a BBC Scotland Education Correspondent in an unfortunate, and presumably unintended, echo of the conspiracy tradition, to claim its publicly funded status to be 'Scotland's best kept educational secret'! There is no secret about the deserved support for this Jewish primary school. But the obsessive focus on, and apparently continuing controversy over, financial support for Catholic schools has distorted any debate on the educational rights of minorities – with one exception.

That exception is the possibility of Scottish Muslims seeking funding for Islamic state schools. Here the crossover in rhetorical accounts is revealing. Catholic schools, as the supposed source of so-called sectarianism, are used to substantiate the argument that racism and prejudice would be increased by providing Islamic schools. In turn, Islamophobia is used to delegitimise the rights of Catholics to attend Catholic schools. Funding for Catholic, Episcopalian and Jewish schools within a national system has set a precedent for the provision of Islamic schools within the same national system, on exactly the same basis and conditions. Only Islamophobes and racists need fear that eventuality. Worries that this development must lead to more anti-Asian racism are ill-founded, relying again on a realist theory of prejudice.

Some sincere criticisms of special communal school provision, such as Catholic schools, are based on the false assumption that contact necessarily reduces prejudice. Instead, careful management is required to ensure that prejudice is not increased by contact. One requirement for a positive outcome from social contact is that members of either group are seen to be of equal status. A favourable result from contact is impossible if the majority has imposed its will on the minority. A studied refusal to consider Islamic schools, if requested by the Muslim community, would increase conflict and discord. An insistence on ending funded Catholic schools, if determined by the majority, would be another recipe for disaster: enforced integration determined by the majority would not lead to helpful forms of social contact and exchange.

It is a telling factor that, despite the emotions aroused by discussions of what is passed off as sectarianism, there has been little serious exploration of what Scottish education can do to tackle this specific form of intergroup prejudice. Again, there are lessons to be learnt from Northern Ireland. There the determination to do something about prejudice led to direct educational interventions. Programmes based on *Education for Mutual Understanding* and exploring different traditions of *Cultural Heritage* (EMU/CH) have begun. Although anti-Irish racism has been a crucial primary factor in the history of intergroup relations in both Scotland and Northern Ireland, there has also been a problem with Catholic anti-Protestant prejudice. And that form of prejudice must also be identified and tackled. EMU/CH offers an opportunity to engage both communities in the elimination of their prejudices. It would make much sense in Scotland to develop an appropriate programme that would be compatible with, and complementary to, Multi-Cultural Anti-Racist Education (G. P. T. Finn, 1987, Multicultural Antiracism and Scottish Education, *Scottish Educational Review*, 19, 39–49).

The Northern Ireland programmes are still in development, but the intention is to identify communalities and recognise differences between the communities. There is some hesitancy over the second task. Yet it is usually these very social differences that are crucially important to people. Explanations of social difference are intended to ensure that they do not become sources of division. This is important; differences between people are important. Social diversity is vital for social development, and should be welcomed. Indeed socio-cultural diversity merits celebration. That stance has profound implications for Scottish education and society. Scotland needs to learn to take pride in its continued provision of different educational experiences within a common national framework for specific ethno-religious communities; that recognition of, and support for, social diversity ought to be seen as a healthy sign of a mature, pluralist democracy.

REFERENCES

Anderson, R. D. (1995) *Education and the Scottish People 1750–1918*, Oxford: Clarendon/Oxford University Press.

Brown, R. (1995) *Prejudice: Its Social Psychology*, Oxford: Blackwell.

Devine, T. M. (ed.) (1991) *Irish Immigrants and Scottish Society in the Nineteenth and Twentieth Centuries*, Edinburgh: John Donald.

Finn, G. P. T. (1994) Sporting Symbols, Sporting Identities: Soccer and Intergroup Conflict in Scotland & Northern Ireland, in I. S. Wood (ed.) *Scotland and Ulster*, Edinburgh: Mercat Press, pp. 33–55.

Gallagher, T. (1987) *Glasgow, The Uneasy Peace. Religious Tension in Modern Scotland*, Manchester: Manchester University Press.

Wright, F. (1993) Integrated Education and Political Identity, in C. Moffat (ed.) *Education Together For a Change. Integrated Education and Community Relations in Northern Ireland*, Belfast: Fortnight Educational Trust, pp. 182–194.

98

Race Equality in Scottish Education

Rowena Arshad and Fernando Almeida Diniz

In this chapter an attempt is made to provide a brief account of key events and policy documents that have shaped the educational thinking and practices of professionals in the area of multicultural and anti-racist education (MCARE) in Scotland following the Race Relations Act 1976. To counteract the paucity in Scottish research literature on this issue, key players such as the Commission for Racial Equality (Scotland), the Racial Equality Councils, the General Teaching Council, the Educational Institute of Scotland, Association of Directors of Education and all Teacher Education Institutions were requested to assist in piecing together a chronological and analytical picture of race equality initiatives.

The first part of the chapter traces the development of the discourse on MCARE in Scotland; next, an analysis of key initiatives which have promoted change and of the obstacles encountered are presented; finally, an agenda for action for securing social justice in the light of the establishment of the Scottish parliament is offered.

THE EMERGING DISCOURSE ON RACE EQUALITY

It is now over twenty years since the introduction of the Race Relations Act 1976. As this millennium comes to a close, some sense of achievement can be derived from the knowledge that every Scottish eduction authority has an equal opporutnities policy with statements supporting multicultural education; some have gone a step further to support anti-racist education. Until the mid-1980s, it was widely assumed that Scotland had 'good race relations' and that there was 'no problem' here (see A. Dunlop, 'Anti-racist politics in Scotland', *Scottish Affairs*, no. 3, Spring, pp. 89–100). Consequently, racism did not become an issue within Scottish political and policy discourse. Since then, there has been a shift from a stance of total complacency to one that accepts, be it grudgingly, that racism is not a phenomenon confined to urban areas with high numbers of black people, such as Birmingham or Tower Hamlets in London (see Arshad and McCrum, 'Black Women, White Scotland', *The Scottish Government Yearbook 1989*, pp. 207–27). The term 'black' is being used in this chapter as a political term to include all people of colour who suffer racism, within a predominantly white Scotland/UK. This is not to deny the right of brown or black-skinned people to define themselves in other ways; the term 'black' has, however, been used as an umbrella term to cover the commonality of experiences. Many professionals within the field of MCARE have meanwhile argued that while there has been rhetorical encouragement from a few politicians, officials at the Scottish Office Education and

Industry Department (SOEID) and other education establishments have, in general, maintained a hands-off approach. In order to understand what progress has been achieved, it is necessary to trace the emergence of the discourse and its impact on the education system.

From assimilation to multicultural education

By the mid-1970s in England, it was recognised that the prevailing policy of assimilation was an inadequate response to the culturally and linguistically diverse populations in schools. This led to the introduction of multicultural education which sought to promote an interest in cultural differences, tolerance and harmony between racial groups.

Meanwhile in Scotland, the emphasis was on assisting children for whom English was a second language (designated 'ESL children') to 'catch up' with with their English speaking peers. By the late 1970s there were an estimated 6,500–7,000 pupils with ethnic origins outside the United Kingdom. The response in many Scottish regions was the establishment of language centres to which children could be withdrawn from mainstream schools for whole or part-time education. Community languages, such as Panjabi, Urdu and Cantonese were deemed of less value and indeed potentially harmful to the cognitive development of the 'ESL child'. Eager for their children to achieve in their 'adopted' country, black parents listened in good faith to teachers, whom they credited with knowing best; and as English was to be given priority, they often refrained from speaking their mother-tongue to their children at home.

The change in direction to multicultural education which was being introduced in England was yet to be reflected in Scotland where the emphasis was still on the assimilation of black children into a white English-speaking Scottish culture.

The shift to Multicultural and Anti-Racist Education (MCARE)

The most significant initiative to prompt the shift to MCARE in Scotland was the Swann Report (DES, 1985) *Education for All*. Originally set up to investigate the problems of ethnic minority children, it concluded by drawing attention to the growing underachievement of Afro-Caribbean pupils in mainstream schools. It highlighted the impact of social and economic factors. Furthermore, it was the first government report to mention racism as a problem in British society and urged all schools, irrespective of ethnic composition, to confront the issue of racism as part of political education.

Multicultural education, criticised by some theorists for being preoccupied with exotic aspects of cultural differences and ignoring the discriminatory effects of racism, was extended to include anti-racist education. The MCARE approach recognised the value of cultural diversity but went further to embrace an analysis of issues of power and justice, arguing for basic changes in the social structures of society. Such a view was consistent with the legal frameworks of the Race Relations Act 1976. This period saw a plethora of courses offered to teachers on MCARE and the production of policies and guidelines for permeation of MCARE into curricula.

The prevalence and effectiveness of these discourses have by no means been unproblematic in Scotland. Race equality has remained contentious. The education community is divided on whether to adopt multicultural education or anti-racist education, or both, whether to incorporate MCARE within a generic equal opportunities policy or to retain discrete policies for each dimension. This ambiguous stance is evidenced in the take-up and interpretation of MCARE by schools. The picture that emerges from the consultations which the Centre for Education for Racial Equality in Scotland (CERES) has conducted with key organisations across Scotland can be summarised as follows:

- Schools (particularly the primaries) have tended to verge on playing 'safe' rather than challenging racism; their curriculum approach reflects multiculturalism in the choice of resources and an emphasis on festivals and global development education.
- Compartmentalisation and 'bolt-on' approaches predominate. This is particularly so in the secondary sector where the responsibility for MCARE in the curriculum is often located within English, Modern Studies, History, Personal and Social Education.
- Black pupils are still viewed as 'incomers', 'foreigners' or alternatively are endowed with an assimilated 'Scots' or 'New Scots' identity; how they define themselves has not been given much attention by curriculum developers and researchers. It is still not part of the hegemony that one can be brown or black skinned and Scottish.
- Bilingualism, apart from Gaelic, is still perceived as a problem by teachers; the provision of community language teaching (for example, Urdu, Panjabi, Bengali, Cantonese or Arabic) is sparse despite the well documented research evidence on the cognitive benefits of bilingualism and the maintenance of mother-tongue (Collier and Thomas, forthcoming). This is further aggravated by the shortage of bilingual teachers in general and, in paricular, as members of the ESL services in Scotland.
- Few authorities have effective policies for dealing with racial harassment, despite the evidence of racial bullying; some appear to be reluctant to see the relevance of such policies, particularly for early years or special education sectors.
- The rhetoric of 'Parental Power, Choice and Diversity' promulgated by the Conservative government has remained marginal to the interests of black parents, who are invisible in many of the policy documents in Scottish education and, more seriously, in decisions about their children's education. For example, studies looking at parental choice and school selection often take account of how socioeconomic status and examination results affect choice. However no information can be gleaned from such studies about whether issues such as racial harassment play a part in how parents select their children's schools. Anecdotal evidence has suggested that consideration of issues like racism, a multicultural curriculum and the ethos of the school in respecting religion and language, have influenced choice. It is not possible to verify such anecdotal evidence as long as these aspects remain 'invisible' to researchers and the education fraternity generally.

The possible gap between the official espoused theory of 'all is well here' and the practical reality in schools is made all the more difficult to gauge given the dearth of research on race equality issues in Scotland.

The contribution of research to the discourse on race equality in education

Brown et al. (1994), in the first major review of research on gender equality, reported that there were 'few major studies which have resulted in the publication of substantial works, an almost total absence of studies which attempt to provide an overview, or from which advances in analysis or theory can be made' (p. 92). In relation to the issue of race equality, they cite just five small-scale studies and conclude: 'the picture in terms of research output and funding is even bleaker' (p. 94). The report has had a major influence in raising the profile of women in Scotland and has acted as a catalyst for the strategic development of gender equality research; meanwhile, race equality research continues to be overlooked.

In an attempt to assess the current level and scope of research on race equality in education in Scotland, CERES (1997) instigated a postal survey in which researchers, academics, local authorities and practitioners were invited to submit details of studies, conducted in the 1990s, in which race was a principal focus of analysis; a literature search was also undertaken. Conscious of the limitations in the design of this small-scale enquiry, it is nonetheless possible to draw tentative impressions of the current position.

- The majority of the sample of fifty-four studies which were reported could be characterised as small-scale, locally driven by service providers' needs and rarely published for wider consumption; few of the submissions would meet the conventional criteria for research and even fewer attracted significant amounts of external funding.
- There is an apparent reluctance by the research community in Scotland to include race and ethnicity as integral components of any mainstream social policy research. This 'colour-blind' approach, which is evidenced in much of recent policy research funded by SOEID, is symptomatic of this dilemma. While researchers may have included black members in their samples, they have failed to analyse the contributing effects of particular factors (e.g.: bicultural and bilingual status, experience of racism) in under-standing the social impact of educational policies on diverse racial and ethnic groups. One SOEID-funded study which did include ethnicity as a factor is the 'Exclusions and In-school Alternatives to Schools' project recently completed by Munn et al., at Moray House, 1997. At the time when the prospective research team was formulating its bid, CERES had expressed concern over the omission of race in national policy research and argued that the matter raised issues of ethical research practice and social justice. The power that researchers can exercise to influence the direction of educational research practice and to affect attitude change is illustrated by the decision of the Munn team to adopt such advice.
- Most striking, however, is the absence of black communities and organisations in the management of research concerning them. It is incongruous in the late 1990s to have research establishments, whose remit is the study of minority ethnic and race-related issues, that are essentially led by white researchers. Is this not akin to a unit for research on women and gender issues being led by men? The shortage of black educational researchers, teachers and academics at all levels may have more to do with structural barriers to obtaining funding and jobs, rather than a lack of skilled personnel.

Despite the paucity of race-focused research, Curnyn et al. (1990) demonstrates the impact such research can have on race equality developments in Scottish education. It represented a landmark in the debate about black/bilingual pupils and special education in Scotland. It raised serious questions regarding the representation of Asian and Chinese children in particular categories of special educational needs provision, the validity of assessment procedures and the participation of parents in decision-making. While these issues had been recognised for over twenty years in England, the Glasgow study was the first acknowledgement of the phenomenon in Scotland. The formal investigation subse-quently conducted by the CRE (1996) severely criticised the practices of the education authority and set out an agenda for change in policy and practice at all levels. Whilst the ethical and political pressures on the researchers are a matter for speculation, the practical impact of the combination of reports should not be under-estimated. There is now a climate within which a number of developments are beginning to occur, some of which are outlined below:

- The topic of race equality in Special Education is now on the agenda in Scotland, though it would be simplistic to assume that policy makers and practitioners share a fundamental grasp of the underlying issues. The reports have exposed the national policy-vacuum which exists regarding race equality and education in Scotland. Questions about the achievement of black pupils throughout the education system, the practice of ethnic monitoring at all levels, the assessment of bilingual pupils for Special Education, the statutory rights of black parents and the appointment of bilingual professionals are now receiving public scrutiny. To date, SOEID has yet to respond to these substantive issues, though it has provided a revised circular which includes a single-page appendix relating to the needs of bilingual children (SOEID, Circular No 4/96, p. 68).
- Black parents of children with special educational needs are demonstrating greater confidence in expressing their views through being involved in a voluntary sector advocacy project which is supporting families (Minority Ethnic Learning Disabilities Initiative, Edinburgh). CERES has also been approached by an increasing number of families for advice and support in their dealings with schools, psychologists and authorities.

The conclusion to be drawn from the discussion thus far is that little recognition has been given to race equality issues in Scottish education. The case for action could not be more clearly demonstrated, pointing to the need for policy change, a research strategy and greater commitment of resources.

KEY INITIATIVES SUPPORTING MCARE WORK IN SCOTLAND

In the 1980s, the Scottish arm of the National Anti-Racist Movement in Education (NAME) and the Anti-Racist Teacher Education Network (ARTEN) were beginning to provide a Scottish perspective on issues of MCARE. The establishment of the Scottish Ethnic Minorities Research Unit (SEMRU) and the Minority Ethnic Teachers Association (META) highlighted much needed change in policy and practice to ensure the rights of black children. Some authorities allocated urban programme money to non-governmental projects like the Edinburgh Multicultural Education Centre (MEC) and responded to demand for staff development leading to The Royal Society of Arts (RSA) Diploma in Teaching English as a Second Language in Multicultural Schools.

The start of the 1990s saw the establishment of CERES, an SOED (as it was then) unit located in Moray House to oversee and advise on MCARE in Scotland. Other units have since been set up, for example, the Centre for Equality and Discrimination in Strathclyde University. The Technical and Vocational Education Initiative (TVEI), while more concerned with gender than with race, left a valuable legacy and a core of people committed to equal opportunities.

As awareness grew, schools and authorities began to adopt policies or guidelines on tackling racist incidents, explored strategies for the maintenance of community languages, recognised the need to adopt multi-faith approaches and to address racism as an issue within the curriculum, irrespective of the ethnic diversity of a particular classroom, school or geographical area. Education committees, sub-committees, working parties and other advisory bodies were given equal opportunities responsibilities or explicit race equality remits. The intention was that the whole process would cascade down the line and be reflected in classroom practice. To facilitate curriculum development and sharpen the focus of institutional change, race advisers or equality officers were appointed to contribute to strategic policy development, to provide day-to-day advice to schools, to promote inclusion of equal opportunities in curricula and to review and monitor progress.

Supporting frameworks for a MCARE agenda and curriculum in the 1990s, the CRE Code of Practice for Scotland(1991), the General Teaching Council's (GTC) policy statement on MCARE (1994), the Cross-Curricular 5–14 Document on MCARE from the Scottish Consultative Council on the Curriculum (1991), major conferences such as the CERES conference (1992) *5–14 Developments and the Elimination of Racial Discrimination Within Scottish Education?*, and the Educational Institute of Scotland (EIS)/Scottish Council for Research in Education (SCRE) Roundtable conference (1992) which published the now widely used text *Class, Race and Gender in Schools: A New Agenda for Policy and Practice in Scottish Education* (Brown and Riddell, 1992), have all influenced recent change.

Black parents and teachers – a vocal force

One of the earliest forums of black teachers designed to encourage debate was the Minority Ethnic Teacher Association (META, 1980). Local authorities such as Strathclyde Region began to involve META members in policy formulation and provision of multicultural and anti-racist training. However META was a relatively small core of activists with a tremendous amount being expected of them. By the mid-1980s, META had dissolved. Some young black teachers were reluctant to become active, seeing 'race' as an unhelpful issue to be associated with, either politically or professionally.

However others continued to campaign for their rights and voices to be heard. In Strathclyde there was concern that local government reorganisation would leave black teachers isolated and marginalised. Staff management training modules were developed with help from former members of META and are now being run by Paisley University. Black members within the EIS have recently secured the right to have an annual Scottish black teachers' conference and were instrumental in establishing an annual black workers' conference within the Scottish Trade Union Congress.

An effective alliance remains to be created between politicians, white professionals and black professionals/parents on race equality issues in education. Home-school linking with black parents is at an embryonic stage in many authorities. Of greater concern are the perceptions that communication with black parents is difficult due solely to the need for interpreters and that minority cultures and customs may hinder open dialogue. Community or advocacy groups who work directly with black parents do not perceive such difficulties; instead they find that the voices of black parents have been unheard or ignored.

Raising awareness: still no problem here

Surveys conducted by the Educational Institute of Scotland have indicated a wide variation in teachers' understanding of MCARE. Some councils have developed policies with monitoring and staff development opportunities as well as appointing the appropriate dedicated personnel to develop courses and to train staff.

As part of the research for this chapter, all the Higher Education institutions offering teacher education courses were contacted for comment on how MCARE issues were being included. With the exception of one establishment which failed to respond, all now recognise the importance of highlighting MCARE within the curriculum. Two models of delivery are generally adopted, the discrete and the permeative. Specific inputs or modules on MCARE are delivered as well as embedding MCARE competences in curriculum development, planning, classroom management and so forth. MCARE competences form targets within electives and are generally a feature of most postgraduate and undergraduate education programmes. However colleagues do point to concerns that the permeation model is highly dependent on lecturers having a sufficient grasp of the subtleties of discrimination. There is a perception that schools, particularly the primaries, continue to regard this as a low priority issue, thereby potentially leaving students unchallenged while on teaching practice.

There are councils which hold the opinion that there is 'no problem here', given the perceived low numbers of black people in Scotland. This myth, which is located within complex issues of independence, ethnicity and identity, generates an opinion that Scotland, itself an oppressed country, is unlikely to engage in racism either institutionally or individually. The result of denial has been inaction and indifference to matters related to racial equality. Positive action has tended to be dependent on the commitment of individuals who often work with little support from management and with no recognition of their efforts. One Racial Equality Council claimed that some teachers had perceived their involvement in race equality issues to have had a negative impact on their professional careers. These teachers felt that championing equality issues had gained them no prestige or promotion but a reputation for being 'troublesome'. Budget cuts, overload and an over-crowded curriculum were too often used to enable matters related to race equality to be relegated to the bottom of any priority agenda.

While initiatives to promote gender equality, such as women into management, recruitment and selection are beginning to emerge, race or disability issues remain marginalised. For example, some authorities may have looked at providing more multi-cultural teaching and learning resources but refuse to see the need for any authority-wide policy on racial harassment. Racism as a problem exists within Scottish schools and remains to be explicitly acknowledged or dealt with. Anti-bullying initiatives give little recognition to the racial aspects of bullying. The SCRE publication *Action Against Bullying* (1992), which has been highly successful in ensuring that schools take seriously the causes and consequences of bullying, gives no guidance on dealing with bullying as a result of racism. This tendency to merge all issues as 'generic' bullying has resulted in some schools adopting generic anti-bullying policies which fail to acknowledge the specifics caused by gender, class, race, sexuality or disability.

The fall-out from local government reorganisation

The Association of Directors of Education in Scotland (ADES) was asked to comment on the consequences of reorganisation and devolved school management on MCARE issues. They had not undertaken any review of MCARE within the past year. It was their impression that most authorities had taken forward existing policies and procedures.

Greater school autonomy was perceived as largely relating to financial management and staff selection and by implication less likely to affect the implementation of equality policies and guidelines.

The EIS and some Racial Equality Councils felt that the loss of experienced personnel in education has affected the ability of councils to implement MCARE policies fully. With staff development and funding now the responsibility of individual schools, MCARE was unlikely to be prioritised due to limited budgets. Where commitment to MCARE remains, courses continue to be provided for schools to select from but take-up varies from the few that are over-subscribed to areas where MCARE courses are frequently cancelled due to lack of interest.

A recent survey of EIS local associations supports ADES's impression that the majority of councils have shown evidence of the existence of equal opportunities policies either as new policies or taken from the previous region. Increasingly, councils are adopting a 'corporate' approach, where equal opportunity policies form part of the personnel department's remit, with education departments having responsibility for educational aspects. Many equality posts have either been lost through retirement or redeployment or have emerged as 'policy development units' which may or may not prioritise equality issues.

Disaggregation and devolved school management need not be detrimental to race equality initiatives. However early signs indicate that unless there is a stronger message from the SOEID and key policy and professional bodies, it is highly likely that MCARE will be confined to areas of higher black populations within the central belt where a combination of political will and parent/community pressure will continue to push for change and inclusion.

AGENDA FOR THE 21ST CENTURY

The impending Scottish parliament, elected by proportional representation and committed to equal gender representation, should be expected to provide an opportunity for the emancipation of black people into all aspects of political and civic life. Will it herald a move to ensure democratic participation of black parents, teachers and academics in mainstream discourse or continue to negate the black presence or relegate this presence to matters related to MCARE? There lies the challenge. Summarised below, are priorities which have been identified in the course of the enquiries which were undertaken in writing this chapter.

The need for a national policy for combating racism in education

Apart from a foreword by Michael Forsyth in the CRE (1991) *Code of Practice* to the effect that 'Racial discrimination has no place in the education service in Scotland. All educational establishments and authorities have an important responsibility to work towards the elimination of racial discrimination', the SOEID has provided no national strategy for combating racism in education. Rather, the SOEID has abdicated responsibility for action to individual authorities, most of which have effected minimal change. This culture of avoidance and policy ambiguity has been a major barrier to progress. There is a need for a clear national strategy for quality standards to be set for education in line with the CRE recommendations for Scotland in *Race Equality Means Quality: A Standard for Racial Equality for Local Government* (1995).

Ethnic monitoring

The recent decision by the Statistics Division of SOEID to remove 'ethnicity' from the annual school census, without consultation with key players like the CRE, goes against best practice in the field of race equality. The case for ethnic monitoring is argued in Gillborn and Gipps (1996): 'if ethnic diversity is ignored . . . considerable injustices will be sanctioned and enormous potential wasted' (p. 7). The absence of ethnic monitoring nationally and locally has resulted in a serious lack of data relating to the progress and attainment levels of black pupils, the correlation between ethnicity and exclusions, and the comparative success rates of parents gaining admission for their children into the school of their choice. A priority has to be the re-establishment of commitment to ethnic monitoring within the SOEID and the development of partnerships with authorities to ensure necessary data collection is coordinated.

Racial harassment

The most serious concern for black parents is the basic safety of their children, in and out of school, from racial harassment. A gulf currently exists between the perceptions of white professionals and the reality of racial harassment experienced by black pupils and professionals. A first step has to be an explicit acknowledgment that racism, both overt and subtle, exists at all levels of education and within all geographical areas of Scotland. Listening to black parents and seeking their assistance in policy formulation and implementation is crucial if these measures are to be appropriate and relevant in reality.

Partnership with black parents

Scrutiny of documents like the Parents' Charter and School Boards Newsletters gives little confidence that the term 'parents' is currently inclusive of black parents. The common practice of translating material into minority languages as the main means of securing the participation of black parents is simplistic. A cultural and political shift is needed through the system in order to gain the confidence and active participation of parents. Consultation measures need to be instituted locally, taking into account different religious and employment patterns within black communities. Such events should also be resourced with bilingual professionals and organised in consultation with community education and the voluntary sector.

Shortage of black professionals

No statistics exist to provide an accurate picture of the number of black teachers that there are at present. The SOEID, while monitoring for gender and religion, has failed to include ethnicity despite intensive lobbying from the CRE and teacher unions. However the EIS estimates the figure to be below 0.03 per cent of the total teaching workforce.

A national strategy, jointly designed by key partners (SOEID, teacher unions, GTC and TEIs) in collaboration with black community organisations to identify targets for attracting black people into teaching and supporting those already within courses is needed. Entrants to the teaching profession have reported experiencing discrimination during training and unemployment after qualifying (*University Ethos and Ethnic Minorities*, Moray House, Edinburgh 1998 forthcoming); those in service are invisible in senior positions throughout the education service in Scotland.

Bilingual education and curriculum development

Despite the extensive international research on the benefits of adopting bilingual pedagogical approaches and mother-tongue maintenance, these benefits have remained unrecognised within Scottish education. The importance of language for a child's cognitive,
cultural and social development in terms of the need to learn Gaelic or Scots has not
transferred to community languages. This suggests an absence of political will rather than a
lack of understanding of the benefits of bilingualism.

The document *Languages for Life* (SCCC, 1994), which outlines clear principles for the
promotion of bilingual education for both heritage and community languages, needs to be
revisited each time that a curriculum review or development is planned. Scotland requires to
come in line with the international community and put into action the recommendations of
organisations such as the United Nations, UNESCO, the Council of Europe and the European
Union that each ethnic group has the human right to have their language maintained.

Research

Academic research needs to move beyond description of black peoples' life-styles to one that
seeks to produce explanations and develop theoretical frameworks to account for racism and
its effects in education. Given the early development of race equality research in Scotland, it
seems sensible to create a Scottish network, similar to the Gender in Education Network;
this initiative should include black academics and researchers as leading and organising
forces of such a network.

CONCLUSION

The conclusion that can be drawn from this chapter is one of marginalisation of race equality
issues within the Scottish education system. The need to recognise the congruence of race and
other equality issues is important, but this should not be at the loss of understanding the
specificities of each equality strand. Readers may wish to assess the extent to which the issue
of race permeates the range of contributions within this publication on Scottish Education.

The authors would like to thank Hakim Din, Andrew Johnson, John Landon and Alan Bell
for providing their time to chart a chronological account. Special thanks to Rana Syed for
conducting this part of the research.

REFERENCES

Brown, A., E. Breitenbach and F. Myers (1994) *Equality Issues in Scotland: A Research Review*,
    London: Equal Opportunities Commission.
Curnyn, J., I. Wallace, S. Kistan and M. McLaren (1990) Special educational needs and ethnic minority
    children, *Professional Development Initiatives*, 1989–90, pp. 271–300, Edinburgh: SOED.
DES (1985) *The Swann Report*, London: HMSO.
Dunlop, A. (1993), Anti-racist politics in Scotland, *Scottish Affairs*, no. 3, Spring, pp. 89–100.
Gillborn, D. and C. Gipps (1996) *Recent research on the achievements of ethnic minority pupils*
    (OFSTED Reviews of Research), London: HMSO.
Thomas, W. P. and V. P. Collier (1996) *School Effectiveness for Language Minority Students*, George
    Mason University, United States.

XIII

Scottish Teachers, Teacher Education and Professionalism

99

Teacher Education Institutions

Gordon Kirk

THE UNIVERSITY CONNECTION

One of the features of Scotland's educational tradition is that the professional education of teachers took place in specialist institutions devoted to that purpose. These institutions, some of which trace their roots to the early years of the nineteenth century, have been variously known as 'normal schools' or 'training centres', and have enjoyed varying degrees of collaboration with universities and other institutions of higher education. They evolved as independent colleges of education, a separate sector of higher education with a distinctive role to perform and operating within a framework stipulated by the Secretary of State, whose accountability for the education system as a whole required that he controlled the education and training of teachers. The alternative arrangement, common elsewhere, of locating teacher education in universities was ruled out on two counts. The Scottish Education Department (SED) had no confidence that the universities could provide an appropriate training. One Secretary of the SED disparagingly referred to professors 'walled up in their impenetrable fortresses of academic seclusion' and suggested that, if what was wanted was a strong professional education for teachers, the universities would be the last place to look for it. In any event, the Secretary of State for Scotland had no locus with regard to universities: they were accountable, through the University Grants Committee (UGC), to the Minister for Education in England and Wales.

The most immediate antecedents of Scotland's teacher education institutions (TEIs) are tabulated in Table 99.1.

Two features of the recent past should be highlighted. There has been a significant reduction in the scale of provision both with regard to the student population (from 10,697 to 6,490) and the number of institutions involved. In 1976 there were ten colleges of education and a small teacher education centre in the Education Department at the University of Stirling, instituted in 1964 on an experimental basis in a new and innovative university. Four of these colleges – Jordanhill, Moray House, Dundee and Aberdeen – were the descendants of the 'provincial committees', which had been established in 1907; two of them – Notre Dame and Craiglockhart – served Roman Catholic students, in keeping with the 1918 legislation, which gave the Roman Catholic church the right to satisfy itself with regard to the 'religious belief and character' of teachers in Roman Catholic schools; Dunfermline College of Physical Education, founded in 1909, was a response to the national shortcomings in health and physical wellbeing at that time; and the remaining colleges at Hamilton, Craigie and Callendar Park were established to redress an acute shortage of teachers in the early 1960s.

By the late 1970s, the anticipated shortfall of teachers had become an embarrassing over-supply, thanks to the dramatic decline in the size of the school population. South of the border that same problem was met by institutional amalgamations in which smaller specialist institutions were combined to create large polytechnics. However, the tripartite division of higher education in Scotland ruled out such a response; the only option was closure or merger. In 1981, and again in 1987, in the face of the most severe political trauma, the system was reduced, first to seven and then to five colleges, leaving a widely dispersed configuration of institutions, two of which – Moray House and Northern – operated on a multi-site basis, and St Andrew's became the national Catholic college.

Table 99.1   The antecedents of Scotland's teacher education institutions

1976	1981	1987	1990+
Craigie (1964)	→ Craigie	→ Craigie	→ University of Paisley
Craiglockhart (1918) Notre Dame (1895) }	→ St Andrew's	→ St Andrew's	→ St Andrew's
Callendar Park (1964) Moray House (1835) }	→ Moray House	→ Moray House →	Moray House Institute (Heriot-Watt University)
Dunfermline (1907)	→ Dunfermline		
Aberdeen (1874) Dundee (1906)	→ Aberdeen → Dundee }	→ Northern	→ Northern
Jordanhill (1832) Hamilton (1966) }	→ Jordanhill	→ Jordanhill	→ University of Strathclyde
University of Stirling (1964)	→ University of Stirling	→ University of Stirling	→ University of Stirling
(10,697)	**(5,480)**	**(5,043)**	**(6,490)**

(The figures in brackets denote total student numbers.)

The second feature of the recent past is the progressive erosion of the monotechnic principle as institutions have formed strategic alliances of various kinds with universities. Even as late as 1985 the institutions themselves had vigorously defended their monotechnic status, maintaining that the preoccupation with teaching was a source of institutional strength, providing a powerful source of student motivation and serving as a focus for research and development work. In addition, autonomous status allowed the colleges the opportunity to maintain strong links with the teaching profession. Following a major national inquiry completed in 1985, the Scottish Tertiary Education Advisory Council (SED 1985) concluded that teacher education should continue to be provided in 'thriving specialist establishments' and the acclaim which met that recommendation clearly showed that it reflected a widespread consensus. Yet, within a decade, the monotechnic institution has all but passed away and teacher education has come to operate wholly under the aegis of the university. In amplification of Table 99.1 it has to be recorded that in October 1996

Moray House Institute of Education and the University of Edinburgh agreed to consider merger, and a plan to incorporate Moray House as the Faculty of Education at the University of Edinburgh is now with the Secretary of State. In the same way, in October 1997, St Andrew's College and the University of Glasgow jointly indicated that they were proceeding to merger, and in November 1997, Northern College Board of Governors intimated that discussions were opening on the merger of the Aberdeen campus of Northern College with the University of Aberdeen and the Dundee campus with the University of Dundee. What has led to the transformation of the institutional context of teacher education?

There is no doubt that, within the colleges themselves, if not elsewhere, the attraction of a richer and more varied institutional context provided by the university began to outweigh the benefits of institutional autonomy. It came to be accepted that the association with, or incorporation within, a university would strengthen courses, significantly extend the involvement of staff in research activities, especially with the advent of the Research Assessment Exercise (RAE), and enrich the student and staff experience. Moreover, on the wider international scene, not to mention south of the border, the education of teachers and cognate professionals was already located in universities and appeared to flourish there. If similar arrangements could not be made in Scotland might it not be implied that teacher education was of lower standing and quality than elsewhere, and might that perception, in turn, have a detrimental effect on the recruitment of staff and students? Finally, it was acknowledged that the professional education of doctors, lawyers, engineers, and others was well established in the university while, at the same time, strong links with professional bodies and agencies – so strongly valued in teacher education – were fully maintained. All of these considerations suggested that there were academic grounds for placing teacher education within a university context. Conversely, although colleges of education might be reticent about making the claim, the life and work of the university could be enriched through the incorporation of a strong teacher education faculty, especially since the introduction of formal and independent evaluation of teaching – through the statutory arrangements for assessing teaching quality – forced universities to give greater priority to teaching.

Financial pressures also forced colleges to consider their independent status and to seek some form of strategic alliance with a university. The funding environment that developed in the 1980s and 1990s put maximum pressure on institutions to recruit students. The reduced intake levels determined by the Secretary of State created very serious financial difficulties for institutions which, because of their monotechnic nature, were unable to offset the reduction in funds from teacher education by increased activity in other spheres. The severity of the financial problem of some colleges was such that they required 'safety-net' support to protect them against too substantial a reduction in income. The Scottish Higher Education Funding Council's (SHEFC) intimation that safety-net provision would be withdrawn – mainly because it was seen to be a tax on the rest of higher education – made it all the more difficult for small specialised institutions to maintain financial viability. Incorporation within a larger institution, with the economies of scale and other efficiencies that could be secured, made merger with a university extremely attractive, especially in view of the acknowledged academic advantages that could be realised. While mergers of that kind might have proved extremely difficult when colleges of education and universities were the responsibility of separate ministers, in 1992 the Scottish Higher and Further Education Act repatriated the Scottish universities and brought all of higher education within the responsibility of the Secretary of State for Scotland and the SHEFC.

The legislation of 1992 also disbanded the Council for National Academic Awards (CNAA), the body that had been established to validate courses and to confer awards on students in non-university institutions. The demise of the CNAA made it essential for non-university institutions to establish a relationship with a university to ensure that their programmes were academically acceptable and that students obtained university degrees on qualification.

That combination of factors, some of them originating in changed perspectives within the colleges themselves and some of them reflecting wider changes in the context of higher education, led to the dissolution of teacher education as a separate sector of higher education and to its incorporation within universities.

CURRENT PROVISION

Current provision in the six TEIs is given in Table 99.2. The colleges differ in size and in the scope of their offerings. In some, teacher education is the sole preoccupation, whereas, in others, there has been diversification into the cognate fields of social work and community education. Sports studies and leisure studies have been developed in the two centres which, until 1987, undertook all of Scotland's physical education training. Some of these differences also reflect limited rationalisation. Thus, physical education is provided now in only one centre; and Catholic provision is the responsibility of a single college, St Andrew's. In those areas in which St Andrew's College does not provide training, arrangements are made, under the supervision of St Andrew's College, for teachers to obtain the Certificate of Religious Education by distance learning. For many years, further education was located in the Scottish School of Further Education at Jordanhill, now part of Strathclyde University. In August of 1997 the Secretary of State introduced a major change which opened up involvement in further education training to other teacher education centres.

All courses for prospective school teachers lead either to the Teaching Qualification (Primary Education) or the Teaching Qualification (Secondary Education). In addition, there are two standard routes to each teaching qualification: the one-year postgraduate or 'consecutive' route, and the four-year, or longer, 'concurrent' route. Both approaches have their defenders. The consecutive approach is justified on the grounds that entrants to teaching require a strong academic base, which it is the purpose of undergraduate study to provide. That acquired, the period of professional education – in North America and parts of Australia this extends over not one but two years – is devoted to those studies and experiences which enable students to induct learners into the activities they have mastered. In the concurrent approach, the academic study of subjects proceeds in parallel with educational studies and periods of school placement, thus allowing, it is claimed, a progressive maturing of professional understanding in a way that is extremely difficult in what has been called the 'forcing house' of the consecutive route. The Scottish tradition of teacher education has espoused both approaches. In teacher education circles, and even more widely, there is a preference for the concurrent approach. However, there is merit in retaining the consecutive route as a way of regulating supply more easily than if there was complete dependence on the alternative approach.

In the primary field, the balance between the BEd concurrent route and the PGCE consecutive route has been officially set at 55:45. However, partly in response to calls from the General Teaching Council for Scotland (GTC) and the TEIs, the Scottish Office

Education and Industry Department (SOEID) has allowed some slippage and, in recent years, the ratio of concurrent to consecutive entrants to primary teaching has been 75:25. In the secondary sphere, the one-year postgraduate consecutive route has traditionally been the principal preparation for teaching for those professing the familiar range of university academic subjects. The concurrent route was reserved for such studies as physical education, music, and technology, all of these leading to the award of a BEd degree after four years of study. When teacher education was introduced at the University of Stirling, the preference was for the concurrent route. That approach, from which the teacher graduates with an academic qualification in a subject as well as a secondary teaching qualification, has attracted increased support in recent years, particularly following incorporation of colleges within universities.

Table 99.2   Current provision in Scottish teacher education institutions

Course	Moray House	Northern	St Andrew's	University of Paisley	University of Stirling	University of Strathclyde
PGCE (Primary)	65	53	39	22	–	74
PGCE (Secondary)	156	157	129	50	–	351
BEd (Primary)	540	621	493	315	–	573
BEd (Physical Education)	305	–	–	–	–	–
BEd (Technology)	69	–	84	–	–	45
BEd (Music)	–	119	72	–	–	108
Concurrent	–	16	26	–	432	46
Further Education	–	–	–	–	–	200
Community Education	140	127	–	–	–	171
Social Work	81	118	–	–	–	97
Leisure	133	–	–	–	–	–
Sport/Outdoor Education	122	–	–	–	–	159
Speech and Language Therapy	–	–	–	–	–	101
Applied Music	–	–	–	–	–	108

A glance at Table 99.2 confirms that the range of provision in the six TEIs varies significantly: no two are alike. However, all TEIs share two common features. Firstly, they all offer a range of in-service programmes. In the late 1970s, partly in response to the dramatic decline in pre-service students, the Scottish Office designated over 200 FTE staff for in-service work, to be undertaken in colleges or in schools. (See Chapter 101.) That was an extremely generous and far-sighted policy, for it enabled college of education staff, many of whom were at the forefront of professional practice and who played a leading role in curriculum development, to support the revitalisation of the work of the schools through consultancy and other types of activity. Progressively, that earmarked funding for in-service activities was withdrawn and placed with employing authorities who were then in a position to purchase in-service support, initially from the colleges but ultimately from any source they chose. Predictably, that source of funds became lost in the general expenditure block allocated to authorities. Nevertheless, all TEIs continue to offer in-service support to schools and to offer opportunities for continuing professional development through SCOTCAT – the Scottish Credit Accumulation and Transfer scheme – the national framework of certificate, diploma and master's degree awards. (See Chapter 104.)

Secondly, all TEIs are committed to strengthening their involvement in research activities. The former colleges of education were allocated an annual 8 per cent staffing allowance for research and development work, another example of forward-thinking on the part of the Scottish Office. Disappointingly, that allowance was withdrawn in 1986 as part of the government's attempt to reduce expenditure on the colleges and to bring them into line with practice in the central institutions, which had not received a research allowance. Despite that, research activity has continued to develop in the TEIs. It has been acknowledged that strong courses flourish in a climate of intellectual enquiry and discussion of the kind that a research culture is able to sustain. Moreover, the financial inducements afforded by the RAE has encouraged a still further involvement in research, notwithstanding the intensity of the competition. The pressure to engage in research is likely to intensify as TEIs become incorporated within the university, where engagement in research and other forms of scholarly activity is an explicit academic expectation.

STUDENT NUMBERS AND FINANCE

The diversity of TEIs, the variations in provision that occur between them, and the apparent haphazard distribution of courses, may convey the impression that teacher education is inadequately controlled and has been merely allowed to develop according to institutional initiatives or the enterprise of individuals and groups in different parts of the country. On the contrary, teacher education provision is very tightly controlled. The effectiveness of the whole educational system depends on an adequate supply of well qualified and well prepared teachers. Besides, it would be a source of considerable political embarrassment if there was a shortage of teachers. Furthermore, the pressure on the public purse makes it imperative that there is no over-supply: it would not represent a prudent use of scarce resources to train teachers who would merely help to swell the ranks of the unemployed.

Consequently, the SOEID exercises a tight control over the numbers admitted to training. Annually, on the advice of an advisory group that includes representatives of the GTC, the education authorities and the TEIs, SOEID generates a consultation paper which proposes intake levels for the different courses in the following year, taking account of the birth rate, the size of the school population, non-completion rates on courses, and other factors. Following consultation with interested parties, the Secretary of State then determines the overall levels for each of the different modes of training. Having made that calculation, the Secretary of State then passes responsibility for the distribution of the intake among the different TEIs to the SHEFC. That transfer of responsibility is appropriate for it enables the body that is responsible for funding all of Scottish higher education to integrate the distribution of teacher education places into its overall funding model.

That model has two key features. Firstly, the money follows the student: the size of the financial allocation made to an institution relates directly to the number of students it enrols. Institutions are therefore under extreme pressure to recruit to the maximum permitted. Secondly, the funding allocated per student is not based on a direct assessment of costs but, rather, derives from the total sum of money made available by the Scottish Office to the Funding Council. That is, the institutions are allocated not what they need but their share of the funds made available for the system as a whole.

As financial pressures have intensified in recent years, so the actual unit cost – the amount of money per student allocated to institutions – has reduced. The TEIs were obliged to take their share of that fiscal stringency. They have felt themselves to be even further disadvantaged, claiming that the model fails to take account of the additional costs, such as selection and placement, that are incurred in teacher education programmes. Given these difficulties, the progressive reduction in intakes to courses, and the limited opportunities for diversification, it is easy to see how the financial base of teacher education centres has been eroded and that their future as independent institutions has been threatened. At the heart of these difficulties, however, is the tightness of the control that is exercised over student numbers.

PROFESSIONAL AND ACADEMIC CONTROL

There are other forms of control of the teacher education system. As has been seen, the Secretary of State has the authority to determine the annual intake to courses. In addition, he can prescribe the entrance qualifications for courses, stipulate what will count as teaching qualifications, and approve the content of courses. Since the early 1980s, the Secretary of State has controlled the content of courses by publishing, after consultation with institutions, with the GTC and others, national guidelines for teacher education courses, and TEIs are obliged, in offering any courses, to ensure that these are fully compatible with the national guidelines. Unless that condition is met, the Secretary of State will withhold approval for a course. The latest version of the guidelines (SOED, 1993) contained for the first time a set of competences based on a functional analysis of the teacher's role. (See Chapter 102.) There are, in all, thirty-four competences divided into the following four categories:

> Competences relating to Subject and Content of Teaching
> Competences relating to the Classroom
> > Communication
> > Methodology
> > Class Management
> > Assessment
> Competences relating to the School
> Competences related to Professionalism

The specification of competences reflected the Secretary of State's determination to ensure that those who have completed a teacher education programme have acquired the capacities which are judged to characterise competent professional performance. However, the competence approach has attracted criticism. Some feel that it represents a heavily reductionist view of teaching: it is thought to concentrate on the practical know-how of teaching and, as a result of that emphasis, to under-value the theoretical underpinnings of teachers, the knowledge and insight which enable teachers to adopt a reflective and self-critical approach to their work and to their professional circumstances. There are two rejoinders. In the first place, the national guidelines explicitly require that teachers come to terms with the knowledge and understanding relating to the various competences. Secondly, all of the programmes concerned issue in university awards and universities, as the custodians of academic standards, are unlikely to be associated with programmes that are entirely skills-based and do not testify to intellectual and cognitive achievements.

The second form of control is exercised by the GTC. Acting on behalf of the teaching profession, the GTC has to satisfy itself that the work of TEIs is fully in line with professional expectations. It exercises its responsibility in a number of ways: it has the authority to visit colleges of education from time to time to scrutinise aspects of provision and, even where it finds that a TEI is unresponsive to its reports, to refer the matter to the Secretary of State; the GTC also has the authority to ensure that members of staff in TEIs who work on teacher education courses are themselves registered teachers. Finally, the Council's most obvious role in initial teacher education is through its accreditation and review of courses. That work is undertaken by panels drawn from members of the Council and wider afield. In that way, the Council, which includes a majority of practising teachers, is able to satisfy itself that any proposed programme takes full account of the changing demands of the schools.

Finally, all teacher education courses have to meet the academic standards of the university which confers the award. While practice between the different universities varies, all of them are required to have in place mechanisms to ensure that, before they are offered, programmes undergo a process of scrutiny by peers, that they are subjected to the rigours of the external examining system and are subjected to periodic review. Since the establishment of the SHEFC in 1992, universities have been exposed to other sources of external scrutiny. The Higher Education Quality Council, through the process of quality audit, has scrutinised universities to ensure that their quality assurance and quality control arrangements are robust. In addition, SHEFC is statutorily required to assess the quality of provision in each area of a university's work. That is a measure of the quality of the teaching and learning environment provided by institutions, as well as the quality of the achievements of their students. Finally, all institutions of higher education are under pressure to expose their research activities to the peer review that is sponsored by the periodic RAE. All of these various forms of control, that are extended across the full scope of university studies, are therefore also applied to provision in teacher education.

PARTNERSHIP

All teacher education programmes require sustained periods of supervised work in schools, on the assumption that teachers should not only demonstrate a theoretical understanding of teaching but should also demonstrate their capacity to perform competently in real settings. Clearly, it is essential, therefore, to ensure that the institution-based components of a course are closely integrated with placement or school-based activities. If that is to happen, it is essential that there is close collaboration between teacher education institutions and schools.

In 1992 the Secretary of State introduced an initiative, which had two broad purposes: firstly to extend the length of the period of placement in schools and secondly to create a larger role for teachers and the teaching profession in training, by appointing mentors, who would be given special training for their role and would be freed from some of their teaching responsibilities to undertake this important task. Funds were made available to support this experiment. Despite the two-year pilot study conducted at Moray House Institute of Education, it transpired that the mentoring initiative could not command the support of teachers and, ultimately, the scheme was withdrawn. Instead, the Secretary of State requested the GTC, in October 1995, to undertake a study of the ways in which partnership might be developed. The GTC's report, published in March 1997, reaffirmed the importance of the partnership principle, maintaining that teachers in schools and TEIs should collaborate across the whole range of functions, including student selection, course planning, student supervision, assessment and course evaluation. The report saw the TEIs and the schools having distinctive but complementary contributions to make to training. That principle of complementarity is taken to imply that it is the function of the higher education institution to ensure that students come to terms with the academic and theoretical underpinnings of teaching through reading and research and discussion, whereas it is the responsibility of the school to draw on the accumulated expertise of experienced professionals and to make that available to students. An effective programme of teacher education is one in which these two knowledge bases are integrated to create a coherent framework of professional preparation.

There is no doubt that one of the difficulties that was encountered in connection with the mentoring experiment concerned the resources that would be made available to support the work of schools in teacher education. Accordingly, the GTC report concluded that 'new money should be directed towards schools in order to enhance the teachers' role in initial teacher education'. While it seems reasonably clear that the enhancement of partnership will depend on the provision of resources, it is also clear that the resources themselves will not guarantee success. In different parts of the world, there are now fruitful approaches towards what is called 'collaborative partnership'. In such initiatives, there is a sharing of power between the university and schools; ample provision is made for staff development; formal mechanisms for collaboration are put in place; and, finally, initial teacher education forms part of a wider network of collaborative activities. It is to be hoped that in Scotland it will be possible to move towards that approach to collaborative partnership and that the creation of such partnership will not be vitiated by a debate on the availability of resources.

ISSUES FOR THE FUTURE

The last two decades have been profoundly challenging for Scotland's TEIs. They have witnessed a substantial retrenchment in student numbers; a reduction in the number of colleges; a series of major institutional amalgamations and mergers; and have been obliged to manage a massive reduction in staffing levels. Despite these profoundly dislocating changes, as has been argued elsewhere (Kirk, 1994), the teacher education system has continued to develop. Thus the SHEFC quality assessment of teacher education (SHEFC, 1995) rated five out of the six TEIs as 'Highly Satisfactory' and the other as 'Satisfactory', and the Sutherland Report on teacher education and training in Scotland (NCIHE, 1997) concluded that 'The structural arrangements for funding and organising teacher education and training have served Scotland reasonably well and, indeed, in many respects they provide a model for other parts of the United Kingdom'.

Gratifying as these endorsements undoubtedly are, they suggest that still further enhancement of provision is necessary. Indeed, the Sutherland Report, in recommending the review of selection arrangements, probation, continuing professional development, partnership with the schools, and the establishment of a national strategic forum, set a major agenda for change.

Changes can also be expected with regard to courses. Course review and development, already an integral feature of the life of TEIs, is likely to intensify, partly in response to changes in the national guidelines and partly in response to changes in the schools. For example, it is now acknowledged that the Primary BEd is expected to cover too wide a range of studies and risks becoming superficial. Within the framework of a generalist qualification, more provision needs to be made for specialised studies – both for their contribution to the students' higher education and to strengthen the academic base from which the teacher is able to draw in response to the pressure to raise the level of achievement of Scottish pupils. In addition, there is likely in the years ahead to be a demand for more 'concurrent' programmes based on the Stirling model: apart from their educational effectiveness, they are, on the whole, shorter than the standard route and that is likely to broaden their appeal to funders and to potential students, especially now that they are expected to contribute tuition fees. A combined effect of such changes would be a significant shift in the balance of intake to courses: in the primary area from the concurrent to the consecutive route as a way of strengthening specialist teaching in the primary school, and from the consecutive to the concurrent route in the secondary field.

These developments may be expected to strengthen educational provision, but they will be insufficient in themselves to secure the raising of standards now thought to be a national imperative. These changes will therefore need to be supplemented by a massive extension of inservice provision. A vigorous profession should allow and encourage a much larger proportion of its members than at present to exploit opportunities for continuing professional development.

Perhaps even more radical changes may prove to be necessary. The existing framework of primary, secondary and further teaching qualifications may require to be reconsidered. While the boundaries between the various sectors are becoming progressively more permeable, partly in response to such national initiatives as the 5–14 Development Programme and the Higher Still Development Programme, and when calls are made for teaching qualifications in new subject areas, it may be necessary to revise the existing structure of awards to bring them into closer alignment with the major changes taking place in the schools. Finally, the most important challenge facing the teacher education institutions concerns their full incorporation into the life and work of universities. Some fear that this change may lead to academic drift, in the sense that the TEIs may devote less attention to schools with a consequent blurring of the focus on professional action. There is no doubt that the TEIs will need to accept the obligation to undertake research that is imposed by membership of the university community. However, in responding positively to the new challenges, it will be important to ensure that there is no weakening of the strong links that have been forged with teachers and education authorities. Indeed, given the enhanced role which the profession expects to play in teacher education, these links will need to be strengthened. To that end, arrangements for collaborative partnership need to be established, based on the faculty or institute of education, and strongly committed to academic and professional interchange of various kinds. It is not too otiose to envisage a culture of professional collaboration in which there are shared understandings between schools and university about teacher education and training, in which there are joint research initiatives in which the expertise of the university is accessed to support school development planning and curriculum evaluation, and in which formal agreements are made on the provision of the continuing professional development of teachers. Through such collaborative partnership, the university will be able to contribute to the revitalisation of schools and teachers themselves will come to participate more fully in the life and work of the university. The effectiveness of the national arrangements for teacher education in the new era will be measured by the extent to which that vision of partnership is made a reality.

REFERENCES

Kirk, G. (1994) Initial Teacher Education: Retrospect and Prospect, in *Education in the North*, New Series, no. 2, pp. 15–21.

National Committee of Inquiry into Higher Education (1997), Report 10, Annex A, Teacher education and training: Scotland (The Sutherland Report), in *Higher Education in the Learning Society*, Norwich: HMSO.

SED (1985) *Future Strategy for Higher Education in Scotland*, (The STEAC Report), Edinburgh: Scottish Education Department.

SHEFC (1995) *Reports of a Quality Assessment in Teacher Education*, Edinburgh: Scottish Higher Education Funding Council.

SOED (1993) *Guidelines for Teacher Training Courses*, Edinburgh: Scottish Office Education Department.

100

Professional Studies in Initial Teacher Education

Donald Christie

Though the detailed curriculum of current initial teacher education courses in Scotland varies considerably, not least to reflect durations ranging from thirty-six weeks to four years, their overall structure broadly comprises three common components: (1) direct practical experience in schools; (2) study of the relevant aspects of the school curriculum; and (3) a course programme which goes by the title 'Professional Studies' or some similar label such as 'Theory and Practice of Education'. There is often also a fourth component which might be referred to as an 'elective' programme comprising optional elements which enable students either to advance their own personal education or to gain a deeper professional insight in an area of special interest. The term 'professional studies' is not easy to define succinctly in this context. In the words of the working party set up in the early 1980s to review the pre-service training of primary teachers at the point where the former three-year diploma course was to be replaced by a four-year B.Ed. Degree course, 'Professional Studies' comprises: 'the whole range of studies which give students the knowledge, understandings, skills, insights and attitudes which allow them to operate efficiently in the primary school' (SED, 1983). Such a broad definition clearly permits a wide range of interpretations; in its general sense it could refer to the entire curriculum of the initial professional education of teachers. However, it has also been used as a label to attach to a particular part of that curriculum. In this chapter both meanings will have to be considered in relation to the historical development and the current status of professional studies in Scottish initial teacher education.

WHAT CONSTITUTES PROFESSIONAL STUDIES?

In the current guidelines for teacher training issued by the SOED, professional studies receives the following introduction: 'The professional studies element of courses should provide an intellectual challenge for students and have an explicit concern with the classroom and the professional needs of teachers' (SOED, 1993, p. 2). Such a statement begs the question, what precisely are the professional needs of teachers? In these terms, therefore, the character of professional studies in initial teacher education courses can be expected to reflect prevailing views about the nature of teaching as a professional activity. Kirk (1988) advances six propositions which encapsulate the essential features of the professionalism for which initial teacher education must prepare prospective entrants to the profession, namely: that teaching is a vitally important social function; that it is a multi-faceted activity involving many different roles within and beyond the classroom; that teaching is based on an extensive range of theoretical understandings; that it is a problematic and controversial activity; that teaching entails self-evaluation; and that it requires a commitment to professional development. If these propositions are accepted, they provide a framework against which to evaluate professional studies within teacher education courses past and present.

The applicability of the concept of professionalism to teaching is not unchallenged. Humes (1986) draws attention to several flaws in the ideal of professionalism which are worth bearing in mind as we consider the nature of professional studies. Humes argues that while the rhetoric of professional status may be attractive, the reality is that teachers tend to be motivated not so much by high professional ideals but rather by self-interest. Furthermore, he claims that the enormous variation in the status and level of professional training of teachers undermines the general applicability of the concept of professionalism. Examination of the evolution of professional studies over the last few decades shows that there has indeed been ambivalence among those responsible for the funding of initial teacher education towards some of the key features of professionalism delineated by Kirk. For instance, a rational and critical analysis of social and political conditions impinging on education is called for by the notion that teaching should be seen as a controversial activity. However, one might argue that national and local government agencies responsible for the administration of education will in fact select and promote those who conform and do not ask awkward questions. Teacher educators are unlikely to be immune to the influence arising from having to operate in this kind of context, and while over the years one of the declared aims of professional studies programmes has been to foster critical thinking, successful students may instead have been those who learn to display compliance.

The nature of professional studies was a significant focus of the reviews of the guidelines for initial teacher education which took place in Scotland during the early 1980s. Prior to this, disciplines deemed relevant, such as psychology, philosophy and sociology were delivered along fairly traditional academic lines by specialist lecturers in these subjects appointed by the colleges of education. It is worth noting that the academic study of education and concern about the quality of preparation of teachers in Scotland has a long and rather chequered history, dating from the early nineteenth century and including in 1876 the appointment of the first professors of education in the English-speaking world at the Universities of Edinburgh and St Andrews. However, the academic status of educational studies and of teacher preparation in particular has been a contentious issue for most of this time. First the churches and then successive governments through the Scottish Office kept tight control over teacher education by maintaining their own separate training institutions in the form of the training centres and the colleges of education and allowing only marginal involvement of the universities. This ambivalence towards academic status for teacher education is an enduring characteristic of the attitude of the Scottish educational establishment (see Chapter 101).

During the 1980s as part of a government drive towards improving educational standards in schools, a more utilitarian approach to teacher education emerged which was reflected in the way the desired curriculum for teacher education came to be described. This trend culminated in the appearance of the set of competences for a beginning teacher contained in the SOED (1993) Guidelines, described more fully in Chapter 102 of this volume. In place of distinct discipline based units of study in psychology, education, sociology or philosophy and separate 'methods' courses, guidelines such as those issued prior to the introduction of the new four-year B.Ed. degrees for intending primary teachers in 1984, required the colleges of education to provide integrated programmes of professional studies to complement school placement experience and study of the relevant subjects of the school curriculum. By this they were referring to the need for staff in separate departments of psychology, education and methods (which still existed in many Scottish colleges of education at that time) to work in collaboration and to ensure that professional relevance was the paramount consideration in course planning. New course programmes were devised, variously described with labels such as 'Theory and Practice of Education' or 'Theory and Practice of Teaching'. New relationships were explored between institution-based study and practical school experience, and tensions were created between concern for the quality of understanding of students in the formerly separate disciplines on the one hand and the call for more staff to participate as generalist tutors supporting students in their teaching practice on the other.

The dichotomy between theory and practice has proved to be a persistent theme in the discourse of teacher education and has implications for our consideration of professional studies. According to the traditional, positivist view, practice was expected to be informed or guided by theory; practice referred to classroom experience of teaching and learning; and theory was taken to refer to models or sets of ideas arising out of published research or speculative enquiry. From this perspective, teacher educators were expected to communicate certain favoured theoretical perspectives in such a way as to enable students to apply, say, learning theory in their practice of teaching. A more constructivist view of the relationship between theory and practice would hold that the traditional approach is misguided in that it accords unjustified status to pre-existing published theories and their application. This alternative approach emphasises the process of theorising and ascribes greater value to the personal theories which students themselves construct, derived from practical experiences in the classroom. The latter approach is explicitly or implicitly to be discerned in the declared philosophy of the most recent versions of initial teacher education courses, almost all of which make reference to the need to foster reflective practice, though it could be argued that the ideal of reflection to be found in course documentation is rarely in fact attained by students. Indeed, it would appear that a much more basic distinction is often applied when theory and practice are discussed, namely, between college- or faculty-based study and school-based activity, respectively. This simplistic view was confirmed in a study of B.Ed. students' perceptions of the elements of their course (D. Christie and T. St. Paul, *Students' experiences and approaches to learning in the B.Ed. Degree*, Glasgow: Jordanhill College, 1988). Students frequently were found to be operating with a system of constructs which was essentially unidimensional: course elements were construed principally as either practical (and hence relevant) or theoretical (and hence irrelevant). The distinction between theory and practice has also been invoked when successive student evaluations of secondary and primary PGCE courses in the various teacher education institutions have tended to show that students perceive the contributions of subject departments and curricular programmes as more relevant to their immediate needs in pre-service training than what are seen as the more esoteric elements of professional studies programmes.

The shift in emphasis in Scottish teacher education from the study of discrete academic subjects towards integrated, professionally relevant course programmes has continued since the 1960s which was a time when relatively settled orthodoxy in educational thinking with regard to teacher training was replaced by a more eclectic approach, reflecting the increasing recognition of the problematic nature of teaching and learning and of the value to be gained from a range of different theoretical perspectives. During the 1990s a new form of orthodoxy has developed focused on the notion of 'reflective practice'. At the same time there has been what could be seen as a contradictory acceptance of the idea of a set of core competences to be attained by all those completing initial teacher education. However, there is a distinctively Scottish flavour in these developments. The veneer of professional respectability has been safeguarded by strong teachers' professional organisations such as the EIS (see Chapter 109) and the existence of the General Teaching Council for Scotland (see Chapter 110). Such bodies have ensured, for example, that teaching has become and remains an all-graduate profession in Scotland and any attempts to change the nature of initial teacher education which are perceived as politically motivated have been resisted, particularly those which could be seen as directly or indirectly threatening to the professional status of teaching. Thus the competences set out by the Scottish Office are less narrowly defined than the equivalent statements emanating from the relevant training agencies in England and Wales, and have as a result enjoyed much wider consensual support among teacher educators. A second consequence of the status accorded to the profession in Scotland is that the B.Ed. Degree is a professional course in all of its four years of study, rather than following the hybrid pattern of two years of academic study followed by two years of professional training which characterises such courses in England and Wales. Thirdly, attempts to move significantly greater responsibility for teacher education away from the higher education institutions and into the schools have so far been thwarted by united resistance from all sides in Scottish education.

TEACHER EDUCATORS: BACKGROUNDS AND VALUES

The distinctiveness and quality of Scottish education have been powerful and persistent elements in the national identity. Clearly associated with these constructs is the respect supposedly accorded to the teaching profession in Scotland (e.g. see Clark, 1997 and Chapter 111 of this volume). Whether such respect is extended in the public perception to those responsible for teacher education is, however, highly debatable. But who are the persons entrusted with the role of providing programmes of studies for intending teachers? What are their qualifications and to what extent are they entitled to claim credit for the quality of professionalism in the Scottish teaching profession? As discussed in Chapter 99 of the present volume, until recent mergers with universities and with the exception of concurrent training of secondary school teachers at the University of Stirling, initial teacher education in Scotland has been the province of training centres, in recent decades referred to as colleges of education, which were monotechnic institutions largely independent of the university sector. The staff in the colleges of education were generally recruited from the ranks of the teaching profession. In the case of secondary teacher education this meant typically that subject specialists in the college sector were drawn from among aspiring principal teachers and members of senior management teams in secondary schools. In the case of primary teacher education, primary 'methods' tutors tended to have been able classroom practitioners who had already begun to progress through the hierarchy to positions of assistant, deputy, or head teacher. Securing a post in the college of education sector was seen as an alternative to gaining further promotion in the schools, entering local education authority structures or joining national bodies such as the inspectorate. There were always exceptions to this pattern which were allowed in order to recruit people with skills or areas of expertise in short supply at any time or during times of rapid expansion such as occurred during the late 1960s and early 1970s when at its peak the sector contained ten teacher education colleges and at Stirling, one university department of education.

Since the 1960s the typical academic qualification of staff teaching professional studies in the Scottish teacher education institutions has been the M.Ed. degree offered in the Universities of Aberdeen, Edinburgh, Dundee, Glasgow and Stirling. The M.Ed. programmes traditionally enabled aspiring candidates in the teaching profession to study for a higher degree part-time with a choice of specialisms within educational studies including the option, taken by many, of studying Psychology to the equivalent of first degree status in the subject. Such a qualification, coupled with professional experience in the schools, was seen as providing the appropriate background for a post in the colleges of education. The relatively narrow range of options within M.Ed. programmes in the Scottish universities has over the years affected the representation of the different disciplines which elsewhere might be accommodated within departments and faculties of education. While there has always been traditionally a strong representation of psychologists and education specialists among the 'home grown' staff involved in teacher education, the philosophers, sociologists and historians have been fewer in number and more often than not have been recruited from furth of the border. In recent years the range of options for postgraduate study in education has increased with flexible, modular certificate, diploma and masters programmes becoming available in several faculties of education as well as the research degrees, M.Phil. and Ph.D., and with the Doctorate in Education (Ed.D.) now being offered in addition to the M.Ed. Existing staff are under pressure to obtain higher degree qualifications to enhance the academic profiles of the faculties of education and increasingly such qualifications are being sought from applicants for the few available posts in the sector.

The professional credentials of the staff in the colleges of education was a major issue which was pursued strenuously by the GTC from its inception in 1965 until the revised regulations governing teacher education in 1987 required all staff engaged in teacher education to be registered with the GTC (Kirk, 1988). This was a hard-fought issue at the time leading to several bitter confrontations between management and non-registered members of staff or their representatives. Subsequently it became policy across the sector to require candidates for posts in the colleges of education to produce evidence of recent, relevant teaching experience as well as demanding that they be registered with the GTC. It was not unknown, when it became clear that this stipulation would become inescapable, for extraordinary steps to be taken on behalf of non-registered staff to find ways of satisfying GTC requirements including special secondments out into the schools. During the late 1990s as the colleges of education have been merged one-by-one with the universities, this criterion for staff recruitment has inevitably become harder to sustain. Other considerations such as demonstrable research capability have now demanded attention in view of the institutional importance of the SHEFC Research Assessment Exercise. This potential cause for concern for the GTC has undoubtedly been obscured by the fact that the period in question has been a time of severe staff reduction in the sector with only a trickle of appointments being made.

Staff in the faculties of education and other teacher education institutions remain deeply committed to providing teaching of high quality and have been accustomed to a high level of external accountability. However, with the proliferation of new courses at both the undergraduate and postgraduate level, they find themselves facing an increasingly diverse and demanding teaching load and at the same time having to endure significant cuts in resources. As a consequence, it is not unusual to hear jaded colleagues in the different teacher education institutions sharing fears about their ability to continue to deliver teaching of the quality they would wish. When the additional pressure to produce publishable research is taken into account, many have begun to find themselves in an almost intolerable situation. By contrast, for others, the changed context has been seen as providing positive new opportunities simultaneously to pursue both scholarly research as part of a university community and professionally worthwhile activities within the field of education. Moreover, diminishing resources are seen by some as a stimulus to find imaginative new methods of course delivery.

Generally speaking the values of teacher educators lie within the humanistic, egalitarian tradition. A strong commitment to notions of social and moral responsibility is also to be discerned both implicitly and explicitly in course materials. However, there could also be said to be a degree of cautious conservatism, or even anti-intellectualism, evident in the stance adopted by staff in the sector. This may be part of the wider tendency in Scottish professional life to seek consensus rather than confrontation documented by Humes (1986). It may also be to do with a reluctance to take risks in the face of subtle forms of centralised control which engender compliance. The influence of the Scottish Office Education and Industry Department on all aspects of teacher education is pervasive, including: course approval; the setting of quotas; the financing of the sector (until the inception of SHEFC in 1992); and the setting of priorities for, and funding of, research into teacher education. Hence it is understandable that there is a degree of reluctance on the part of teacher educators to take an overtly critical stand with respect to SOEID policies.

PARTNERSHIPS AND MENTORING

All teacher education institutions in Scotland have been grappling with the concept of partnership for much of the past decade. During that time, relationships with schools have been characterised by a high level of goodwill and not just acceptance of contractual obligations. In the absence of a clear national framework, these relationships have very much depended on local arrangements made by the colleges or faculties of education, the local authorities and the schools. In the B.Ed. (Primary) degree course at the University of Strathclyde, Jordanhill Campus, to take just one example, the specific partnership arrangements made in each placement school are subject to negotiation among the three parties, Faculty of Education tutor, school staff and student, in an attempt to clarify expectations about roles and to ensure the relevant knowledge and information about a given placement are shared. The partnership is expected to occur with respect to teaching, supervision and assessment of students, but an attempt has been made to avoid placing significant extra burdens on school staff. In all teacher education courses, the issue of assessment places particular strains on the partnership between schools and faculty. In some, the final assessment of a student's performance in school experience placement currently firmly remains the responsibility of the faculty tutor, the report prepared by the school merely being taken into account by the tutor in arriving at an appropriate grade. In others the school's assessment carries a quantifiable (perhaps equal) weighting in deriving the grade.

Partnership has been a particularly contentious issue in the one-year postgraduate certificate courses in primary and secondary education which are heavily constrained by time limitations. These courses aim to provide preparation for professional status in thirty-six weeks, 18 weeks spent in school experience and 18 weeks in college- or faculty-based study. For a brief period following the publication of the SOED Guidelines in 1993, the time to be allocated to school experience in the secondary PGCE course was expanded to 22 weeks and only 14 weeks were devoted to study in the college or faculty. In 1992–3 the Scottish Office had instigated the evaluation of a pilot scheme aimed at enhancing the partnership between the schools and the higher education institutions in initial teacher education. The Mentorship scheme run by Moray House attempted to involve designated school staff known as 'mentors' more formally in the supervision and assessment of students on placement. Some extra resources were available to the schools involved to support the additional time and effort required. However, despite favourable outcomes from the pilot (Cameron-Jones, 1995), wider introduction of the scheme met strong political and professional opposition and the guidelines were revised, restoring the position to 18 weeks in school and 18 weeks in college or faculty. At the same time, further consultation was initiated through the GTC on the whole concept of partnership. The recommendations of the GTC (1997) Working Party Report on Partnership uncontroversially affirmed the current arrangements, but sought further time and resources to be made available for staff development in both the schools and the teacher education institutions.

OBJECTIVES AND CONTENT OF INITIAL TEACHER EDUCATION COURSES

Teacher education courses operate on the basis of some explicit or implicit conceptualisation of what constitutes good teaching. Several models have been adopted by the institutions involved to communicate their own particular perspectives and from the 1970s until recent years, examples like SPIE (Specify, Plan, Implement and Evaluate) were frequently to be found in course documentation. Despite differences in acronym, most of these models had a shared origin in systematic behavioural approaches to learning applied pragmatically to what were seen as the essential steps in the teaching process, and a common function which was to provide a way to sharpen the focus of both the teacher educator and the student teacher. Such models are less conspicuous in more recent course validation documents. For example, the 1996 Definitive Course Document for the B.Ed. (Primary) at Northern College, quite explicitly turns away from the previously held 'PIER' model which it considered no longer to convey the multi-faceted nature of teaching nor the complexity of the social context in which teaching occurs.

In many courses, it would now appear that the previously adopted models of teaching have been supplanted either explicitly or implicitly by the set of competences for the beginning teacher declared by the SOED (1993) Guidelines. This for some may simply be a matter of pragmatism, the SOEID being the agency which has the power to grant or withhold approval of all initial teacher education courses in Scotland. However, a more positive interpretation is that course planners have in general been comfortable with these guidelines since the definition given of competence is not a narrow one. The guidelines contain the following key sentence: 'In these guidelines the term "professional competences" should be taken to refer to knowledge, understanding, critical thinking and positive attitudes as well as to practical skills' (SOED, 1993, p. 1). Such a definition encourages teacher education course programmes which aim to provide students with relevant theoretical perspectives and opportunities both to question practice, to develop their own personal theories and to articulate their value positions with respect to education. Course planners have to strike a difficult balance between these arguably more challenging professional aspirations on the one hand and the acquisition of practical classroom skills on the other. Where the balance should be struck is an issue on which there is constant debate in the sector and there have been many attempts to resolve the problem by integrating practical and theoretical elements.

In the PGCE (Secondary) Course at the University of Strathclyde, for example, various planning devices have been adopted in order to bridge the gap between professional studies on the one hand and subject studies and school experience on the other. Experiments were conducted with the so-called 'integrated day' and thematic programmes were created with titles such as 'Generic Issues and Strategies for Teaching' (GIST). The evidence of student evaluations shows that the good intentions of the course planners were not always met by successful outcomes, though the responses have been variable for different parts of the course. Adjustments in the emphasis and in the nomenclature of such programmes are continually being made with successive course reviews. The most recent formulation for the 1998 review of the PGCE (Secondary) Course refers to 'Principles of Effective Teaching and Learning' and 'Contexts of Education' in place of Professional Studies and GIST and redefines Subject Studies as 'Curriculum and Pedagogy' which also subsumes school experience.

Professional studies programmes in the one-year postgraduate courses have themselves tended to be structured around broad key themes in education, such as 'The Management of Learning and Teaching', 'Assessment and Differentiation of Learning' and 'Professional and Personal Development' (from the University of Strathclyde Faculty of Education PGCE in Secondary Education *Professional Studies Handbook*, 1996–97). The same documentation states as its first objective that students should 'progressively develop a theory of teaching and learning which is relevant and constructive to their teaching' (p. 11). The programme in question includes such topics as 'the good teacher', 'how learning occurs', 'learning, language and culture' and 'the individual and the curriculum' (p. 12), in an attempt to facilitate professional awareness of factors affecting teaching and learning. The preparation for, and supervision of practice during, school experience of those on Secondary PGCE courses tends to be the responsibility of the subject specialist faculty tutor in varying degrees of partnership with school 'mentors'. In most PGCE (Primary) courses school experience tutor support is provided through integrated professional studies programmes with labels such as 'theory and practice of education' where there may also be a degree of integration with the curricular programmes which of necessity occupy a significant proportion of the limited time available, since all primary teachers qualifying in Scotland must be competent to teach children aged three to twelve across all areas of the primary curriculum as outlined in the 5–14 Development Programme (see Section VI of this volume).

In the B.Ed. degrees in primary education in Scotland school experience and professional studies programmes extend over all four years of study. Curricular programmes representing each of the subjects taught in primary schools form the rest of the core of these courses, extending over three or four years with options available in the final part of the courses to enable students to extend their expertise in chosen curricular areas. Programmes of school experience are progressively challenging in terms of the demands placed on students and are designed to ensure students gain first hand experience of taking responsibiliy for the learning of children across the entire age range from three to twelve years. Professional studies programmes typically comprise as major strands: aspects of child development, such as social, emotional, language and cognitive development; topics in the area of learning and teaching, such as motivation, class management, differentiation and assessment; ethical and structural issues within the educational system, including race, gender and special educational needs; and finally some programmes also include significant elements dealing explicitly with personal and professional development. How closely integrated these topics are with school experience and, correspondingly, how congruent the tutor teams involved in modules in these areas are with the teams of tutors who visit and assess students in schools, varies quite widely among the teacher education institutions in Scotland. Another way in which the institutions differ is in the way the content of the teacher education curriculum is divided up to form the modules which must now be identified as the building blocks of all degree (and certificate) programmes. For instance, special educational needs (SEN) is a topic all initial teacher education courses must address, according to the SOED (1993) guidelines. In the B.Ed. (Primary) degree at the Faculty of Education of Paisley University a discrete module on SEN has been devised, while at Northern College, SEN is delivered within Theory and Practice of Education modules spanning three years of the course. A further important element which provides one of the hallmarks of the four-year professional degree is the final year dissertation. All of the B.Ed. (Honours) degree courses include some form of professionally relevant investigation, a thesis or 'major project'. Preparation for undertaking this largely independent piece of work, involving input on research and enquiry methods, is usually provided through professional studies programmes in the different degree courses.

At Stirling University the distinctive pattern of initial professional education for secondary teachers has been of degree courses where educational studies and school placements run concurrently with the study of chosen academic subject. Elsewhere such courses have until recently been confined to specialisms such as technological and musical education. However, since the merger of colleges of education with the universities a wide range of concurrent degrees with teaching qualifications in subjects such as mathematics and science have been devised.

INTERPROFESSIONAL COLLABORATION IN TEACHER EDUCATION

Initial teacher education is now recognised as having to prepare students for an extended professionalism operating in a much wider domain than that which can be contained by four classroom walls (Kirk, 1988). An important area of competence in this context is the ability to communicate effectively with others, since teachers are increasingly required to collaborate professionally and to develop partnerships with parents and other professionals. The requirement for all professions concerned with the welfare of children to collaborate effectively is enshrined in the Children (Scotland) Act 1995. The skills of professional collaboration had already been included in the set of competences in the SOED (1993) guidelines, and have secured a place in the professional studies programmes of most of the teacher education institutions in Scotland. However, there is considerable diversity among the institutions and among different courses within institutions in the nature and extent of provision in this area. During the period of expansion which took place in the 1960s, colleges of education began to diversify and develop courses for other professions, most notably for community education and for social work. In the larger institutions, Moray

House and Jordanhill, this provided the opportunity for interprofessional collaboration in pre-service training in the different professional disciplines. A research report by McMichael, Irvine and Gilloran (P. McMichael, R. Irvine and A. Gilloran, *Pathways to the Professions: Research Report*, Edinburgh: Moray House College of Education, 1984) documents the way in which staff at Moray House grasped this opportunity in the early 1980s enabling teaching, social work and community education students to come together and to share valuable common learning experiences. With ever-increasing demands on the curriculum of teacher education, it has proved difficult to continue to make space for these shared interdisciplinary learning experiences. Nevertheless, at the Faculty of Education at Strathclyde University the interprofessional workshop for B.Ed. primary, B.A. in community education and B.A. in social work has been run successfully for several years. Indeed the value of such activities within courses of initial professional education has been recognised to the extent that they have been held as a model for future joint developments across the entire range of courses in the Faculty of Education.

ISSUES FOR THE FUTURE

Thus far in the chapter several major concerns for the future of initial teacher education have been identified; these can be set against the propositions of Kirk (1988) which were considered at the outset. Firstly there is the continued tension between theory and practice. Adopting the fashionable constructivist view of theory as process may fail to recognise the need to bring prospective teachers into contact with an extensive range of theoretical understandings. A related issue is the continuing exercise in semantics which has characterised successive course reviews. Merely tinkering with the labels attached to course programmes will not clarify their essential purposes. Secondly, the new orthodoxy of reflective practice may prove hollow unless students are genuinely allowed the space to evaluate their own professionalism and to consider teaching as a problematic and controversial activity. Thirdly, the uncertain employment conditions which face those who currently emerge from initial teacher education militate against students innovating and asking awkward questions about the education system. Fostering a true commitment to professional development among students is, therefore, likely to remain a major challenge for teacher educators. Encouraging students to take more responsibility for their own learning is desirable on educational grounds and, in view of developments in the sector, this will increasingly become a practical necessity.

The turmoil and rapid change in higher education during the 1990s has ironically seen one of the strong Scottish traditions overturned; the former separation of initial teacher education from the university sector has dramatically ended in a spate of mergers (see Chapter 99). It has been somewhat surprising that the SOEID has adopted an uncharacteristically 'laissez faire' attitude to such significant institutional changes. These developments seem bound to shift the professional orientation of staff as they become absorbed into the academic culture of the universities. This in turn has implications for the curriculum of teacher education courses, implications which are all the more profound given that the universities themselves have entered a period of radical reform following the Dearing and Garrick Reports in 1997. Courses are expected to become fully modularised and to be delivered in ways designed to be both efficient and effective in terms of the quality of student learning experiences they provide. The recommendations are that student choice should be maximised and innovative modes of course delivery should be employed. Sharing of generic modules is expected to provide valuable opportunities for dialogue between sectors, such as between secondary and primary PGCE students, and between professions, such as between student teachers and students undergoing initial training in social work. However, any move towards sharing modules with students on other courses is perceived by some as a threat to the professional integrity of those involved in initial teacher education who still have to satisfy the demands of the General Teaching Council, the Scottish Office and the employing authorities for maximum professional relevance and the maintenance of high professional standards of attainment. Can the increased flexibility inherent in these new approaches be reconciled with the need for appropriate, dedicated courses of professional education? Perhaps if teacher educators were prepared to accept the full implications of adherence to the ideal of the self-monitoring, reflective practitioner, this apparent conflict might in fact prove to be illusory. Nevertheless, maintaining quality and professional integrity while at the same time relinquishing a measure of control over student learning will provide a continuing challenge for all concerned in initial teacher education in Scotland.

REFERENCES

Cameron-Jones, M. (1995) Permanence, policy and partnership in teacher education, in G. Kirk, (ed.), *Moray House and Change in Higher Education*, Edinburgh: Scottish Academic Press, pp. 21–35.

Clark, M. M. (1997) The teaching profession: its qualifications and status, in M. M. Clark and P. Munn (eds), *Education in Scotland:policy and practice from pre-school to secondary*, London: Routledge, pp. 98–114.

Humes, W. (1986) *The Leadership Class in Scottish Education*, Edinburgh: John Donald.

Kirk, G. (1988) *Teacher Education and Professional Development*, Edinburgh: Scottish Academic Press.

SED (1983), *The New Degree: Report and Guidelines (A Report to the Secretary of State, by the Working Party on Primary Pre-service Training)*, Edinburgh: Scottish Education Department.

SOED (1993) *Guidelines for Initial Teacher Training Courses*, Edinburgh: SOED.

POSTSCRIPT

The 1993 Guidelines were replaced by a revised version in 1998. Significantly, the 1998 title referred to 'Teacher Education Courses' rather than 'Teacher Training Courses'. There were a number of other changes of detail but the underlying approach remained much the same.

101

The Professional Development of Teachers

Willis B. Marker

The systematic training and certification of teachers had hardly begun before it was recognised that initial training by itself could never equip teachers with all the knowledge and skills they needed for the rest of their working lives. Even in the nineteenth century, the Educational Institute of Scotland offered classes and lectures for teachers. Since then the limitations of initial training have become ever more evident as the rate of change has increased.

After initial training, teachers acquire further knowledge and skills related to their tasks through experience and through a range of activities both informal and formal. A great deal will be acquired informally in discussions with colleagues, in membership of committees and working parties, in private reading and reflection, which are more difficult to describe than the formal activities, whether inservice education and training (INSET) i.e. the provision of courses and consultancy by institutions or individuals, or the more general process of staff development defined by the National Committee for the Inservice Training of Teachers (NCITT) as:

> the planned process whereby the effectiveness of staff, collectively and individually, is enhanced in response to new knowledge, new ideas and changing circumstances in order to improve, directly or indirectly, the quality of pupils' education. (NCITT 1984b)

To cover the learning from both the informal and formal activities, the term continuous professional development (CPD) has come to be used. In the twentieth century, its organisation may be divided into two main phases: the provider-led system which prevailed from 1906 to about 1990 and the subsequent school-led system.

INDUCTION

Since the publication of the James Report (DES, Teacher Education and Training, 1972) it has been widely accepted that professional development should consist of three cycles – initial training, induction and inservice. This chapter focuses on the second and third of these.

Of the three cycles the most neglected has been induction for which the General Teaching Council (GTC) has been responsible since 1967. At the end of their initial training, teachers are provisionally registered. Only after two years of probation and a satisfactory report from their headteacher(s) are they finally registered, but during those two years there has been no provision for the guaranteed and systematic training, involving closer collaboration between schools and colleges, that James and the Brunton Report in Scotland (SED, The Training of Graduates for Secondary Education, 1972) argued for. When Brunton was rejected by the Scottish Education Department (SED), it accepted the case for greater involvement of teachers in initial training and induction and agreed that there should be a joint SED/GTC working party to 'consider . . . the need for the introduction of a more structured relationship between schools and colleges and a clearer definition of their individual and joint responsibilities for the training and induction of young teachers'. The working party produced its report (GTC/SED, Learning to Teach, 1978) suggesting that the authorities should attempt to create an agreed pattern for the training of probationers, that this should be a designated responsibility of members of staff, that they should be given time to act as mentors and that the probationers should be given a lightened time-table and release for courses in their second year. These proposals were not implemented but Sneddon further popularised the idea that probation should be a partnership between schools and colleges and that designated teachers should act as mentors. In the 1980s it became government policy to insist that a higher proportion of preservice training took place in schools and that teachers played a greater part in it. However, it has proved more difficult to extend this partnership into probation, partly because such a high proportion of beginning teachers are on short-term contracts. The GTC has tried to improve the situation by producing materials on the management of probation and a series of training modules. Although these have been helpful, recent research (J. Draper et al., A Study of Probationers, Moray House, 1991) suggests that the management of probation still has a low priority and that there is no guarantee that probationers will receive the support and help that they need.

THE PROVIDER-LED SYSTEM, 1906–90

To return to the third cycle, professional development first became part of the system of teacher training in 1906. In 1905 the SED had created a national system administered by four Provincial Committees. Article 55 of the 1906 Regulations gave those Committees responsibility for 'the further instruction of teachers in actual service'. When the Roman Catholic colleges became part of the national system under the National Committee for the Training of Teachers in 1920, INSET continued to be under the Provincial Committees and to be provided by the four city colleges: Aberdeen, Dundee, Jordanhill and Moray House.

Under Article 55, inservice courses became a regular feature of their work. Although there were some general interest courses, the staple fare until the late 1950s was the provision of courses for teachers wishing to qualify for specialised roles, mainly those leading to the special qualifications as an infant mistress (ITQ), as a nursery teacher, or as a teacher of (as they were then termed) the mentally and physically handicapped. The system was tightly controlled by the Provincial Committees and access to the courses was made possible by offering them in the evenings or during the summer vacation.

After half a century of stability, changes began in the 1950s as the education system slowly started to respond to post-war developments. In the 1960s the rate of change accelerated rapidly and has never eased off since. At the root of it in primary schools was the attempt, starting with the Primary Memorandum of 1965 and continuing down to the 5–14 guidelines, to modernise the curriculum and devise new learning strategies which took account of the different ways and rates of individual learning. The secondary schools, fundamentally elitist until the 1960s, had to come to terms with universal secondary education with the attendant structural changes (comprehensive schools and the raising of the school-leaving age), reform of the curriculum, new methodologies (mixed ability teaching), changes in assessment (O grades, alternative O grades, then Standard Grades and Higher Still). All schools were affected by the rapid development of new technologies which have made the use of computers part of everyday practice.

The practical response to these changes in schools was an increased provision of INSET but of a different type. Although the courses for special qualifications continued, the emphasis shifted to helping teachers to understand and adapt to the changes which were taking place in the curriculum and were being advocated in pedagogy. This change in content was not matched by a change in mode. INSET continued to take the form of external courses offered initially by the colleges.

Before the end of the 1950s the Provincial Committees had begun to organise subject conferences and short courses. Freed from their constraints in 1959, the colleges of education (now including the Catholic colleges) began to offer a wider range of short courses and conferences. At Jordanhill, for instance, the college's provision rose from 42 courses and 19 conferences enrolling 3,541 teachers in 1962–3 to 107 courses and 39 conferences enrolling 5,614 teachers in 1966–7. Other colleges too expanded their provision but, as most of this work was done by college staff as voluntary overtime, their provision could not meet the demands. Other agencies moved into the field. The larger authorities, like Aberdeen, Fife, Edinburgh and Glasgow, began to build up advisory services, to open teachers' centres and to run their own courses.

Expansion of courses, however, did not solve the problems of access. The fact that the part-time courses were free and the authorities generous in paying expenses encouraged large numbers to attend, but these volunteers were not necessarily those who needed professional development most. Nor did this address the problem of access for teachers in the rural areas. For them, one significant improvement was the creation of the Open University (OU). From 1971 this became one of the most important providers of courses, not necessarily in education, for teachers in Scotland. (W. B. Marker, The Open University and Teacher Education in Scotland, *Open Learning*, vol. 6. no. 1, 1991). The teacher training institutions, however, did not develop distance learning to any great extent. Jordanhill and Dundee were pioneers in the UK in offering their Diplomas in Education Technology in a distance learning form and then cooperated with Notre Dame and the OU in offering the OU Diploma in Reading Development. These initiatives, however, were not followed up, as colleges were inhibited by the high costs of developing distance learning and the unwillingness of SED to invest in it.

The mid-1970s probably represent the high-water mark of enthusiasm for INSET but, even while the expansion was taking place, doubts were being expressed about its value. There were, of course, always teachers who were doubtful about the value of INSET and indeed of the whole process of teacher education, but there were also more serious criticisms than those of the staffroom cynics. Until the 1970s INSET had been conceived almost entirely as a process of sending people away from institutions to external courses in the hope that they would return fired with missionary zeal to expound new ideas or implement new practices. Were these courses meeting the needs either of the teachers or of the schools? If not, was it because the content was inappropriate? Or because many of them were too short to make much impact? Or because the schools were not organised to make use of the knowledge and skills which course members brought back? At the same time that such questions were being raised, curriculum theorists were arguing the case for teachers as curriculum developers and hence as researchers into their own practice, while organisational theorists were preaching the need for institutions to involve all members of staff in a regular cycle of critical review, forward planning, monitoring and reappraisal. The thrust of these arguments was that real changes would not take place in schools unless the people and the institutions identified the need for them and then sought whatever forms of professional or organisational development were needed to bring them about.

These arguments provided the rationale for the next big change, the development of school-focused inservice (SFIS). In 1976, in response to demographic trends and the government's financial difficulties, SED imposed sharp cuts in preservice intakes to the colleges and began the political battles which led to college closures. These cutbacks implied a reduction in the number of college staff but, because of the strength of the opposition to closures, the government looked for ways of cushioning the blow. SED saw in this an opportunity to extend INSET but to channel it in directions more directly beneficial to schools. So from 1977–8 the colleges were allowed to retain the equivalent of 200 FTE staff provided that they were used for SFIS, which meant either working directly with teachers in schools or providing courses in teachers' centres requested by the education authorities.

This bold initiative created many problems. It could only have worked well if the authorities and schools had been managing the curriculum in such a way that they could articulate their needs precisely or timeously enough for them to permit the planning of college staff resources. There were also internal problems in the colleges. Not all college staff were suitable for this new role and the key resource, staff time, was largely controlled by heads of department, leaving those responsible for INSET to act as brokers between the authorities and their colleagues. Despite these difficulties, some substantial and well-structured projects were mounted in collaboration between authorities and colleges and a great deal of good work was done. Overall the result was too many short-term, un-coordinated projects carried out by college staff as a second-order activity with lower priority than their preservice commitments. There was indeed a basic flaw in the system: that the authorities were responsible for the professional development of their teachers while the colleges controlled the major resource.

The development of SFIS further complicated the pattern of INSET provision. By the end of the 1970s there was still a large programme of short courses offered by the authorities or by the colleges. Alongside these were the courses offered by the OU and the traditional M.Ed courses, taken in full by small numbers but affecting many more through the larger number of teachers who took the Diploma course concurrently with their initial training. Moreover the colleges too were beginning to develop award-bearing courses through the Upper Primary Associateship, post-graduate diplomas and Inservice B.Ed degrees. Because this provision was the result of separate initiatives, it was ill-matched to national or regional needs, inadequate in that important aspects were not provided for, unevenly distributed geographically, and inefficient in its use of resources. The situation seemed to call for a greater degree of national planning.

Attempts at coordination had begun in 1967 with the setting up of NCITT and four Regional Coordinating Committees. These had no powers and could do little except organise the annual round of national courses and act as a forum for the exchange of ideas and information. Under the chairmanship of Malcolm Green (1976–85) NCITT became more active and produced a series of reports: *The Future of Inservice Training in Scotland* (1979), *The Development of the Three-tier Structure of Award-bearing Courses* and *Arrangements for the Staff Development of Teachers* (both 1984). Although criticised for advocating arrangements which were too bureaucratic and dirigiste (e.g. D. Hartley, Bureaucracy and professionalism, *Journal of Education for Teaching*, vol. 11 No. 2, 1985), these helped to popularise some key ideas. Firstly, that there should be a national system of award-bearing courses based on a modular system of credit accumulation which could lead to awards at three levels: Certificate, Advanced Diploma and Master's Degree. Secondly, that staff development should be planned as a collaborative process, in which teachers participated through consultation in identifying their individual needs and those of their schools within the context of national and regional policies and that 'it can only become a normal and accepted part of the professional life of all teachers . . . if the school is regarded as the main base for it'.

While this work was progressing the political climate was changing. Starting with the Callaghan-inspired 'Great Debate', questions were increasingly raised about the value and effectiveness of the education services. So, under the Conservative administration of the 1980s there was a general trend throughout the UK to tighten central controls, to curb expenditure and to make sure that money was spent in ways of which the government approved. These led to unprecedented attempts to prescribe curricula in schools and in teacher education. The controls were applied both to the award-bearing courses and to SFIS. To begin with, the colleges had to submit all proposals for award-bearing courses for approval. Then, following the introduction of national guidelines for courses of initial training, an attempt was made to introduce them for post-initial courses. The chosen vehicle for this was the Scottish Committee for Staff Development in Education (SCOSDE) created in 1987 to replace NCITT. Hardly had SCOSDE been set up, however, before the political climate changed: the ideology of centralised planning was replaced by that of the competitive market. There was therefore no political will to support SCOSDE in the task of creating a national guidelines system and accrediting those courses which conformed to it. So SCOSDE was already fading away before its remit ended in 1991 and it was replaced by a purely advisory body, the National Coordinating Committee for Staff Development, which up to now has been of little significance. Meanwhile, dissatisfied with the mismatch between SFIS provision and national and regional priorities, SED instituted procedures in 1986 by which the colleges had to make formal contracts for SFIS with the regions, which then had to have SED approval.

A SCHOOL-LED SYSTEM, 1990–7

The last decade has seen an enormous change in the governance of professional development. Until the late 1980s, the main players were the providing agencies – the regions and the colleges – with the SED exerting great influence through bureaucratic controls and finance. Since then governance has been decentralised as control has largely passed into the hands of the schools. The three key factors in this have been the switch to school-based professional development, the devolved management of resources (DMR) and reform of local government.

In one sense there has always been a good deal of school-based professional development through the exchange of ideas or through membership of school working parties. As early as the 1970s, some forward-looking schools were experimenting with more organised arrangements, but the catalyst for change was the long teachers' dispute from 1984 to 1986, during which the EIS advised its members to boycott all forms of professional development. In response, the government set up the Main Committee to consider teachers' pay and conditions of service. Main argued that all teachers would benefit from regular and systematic professional development based in schools and that the starting point for such staff development should be assessment of needs through staff appraisal. Main therefore proposed that pupils should spend five fewer days a year in schools, that those five days should be devoted to staff development and that a further 80 hours a year outwith the school day should be available for planned activities (PAT). These proposals formed the basis for a new contract which provided, from 1988–9, for the five inservice days plus 50 hours of PAT, 30 of which were to be under the control of the school and 20 at the discretion of the teacher. These 30 hours have now been whittled down by local agreements in some cases to as little as 10–15 hours – a fact which tells something about the attitudes of teachers to professional development. Despite these reductions, the effect of the contract has been to put the major resource for professional development, teachers' time, under the control of the schools.

This sweeping measure of decentralisation was reinforced by DMR. In pursuit of their policies of undermining local government and giving more choice to the consumer, Conservative governments encouraged the transfer of resources from the local authorities to the schools. The result now is that the authorities only retain centrally a small proportion of the money available for professional development. The rest is allocated to schools which are free to spend their own budget according to their assessment of their own needs. It may therefore be spent, for instance, on buying cover to release staff for internal professional development or to attend external courses; on buying in external consultants; or on materials and equipment to support professional development.

How the schools use these resources of time and money has been strongly influenced by development planning and by staff appraisal. The obligation placed on schools to produce and regularly review a development plan has given a structure to school-based professional development which is now normally targeted on achieving the goals in the plan. The influence of staff appraisal has been patchier. Following an SED consultation paper (SED, 1989), it became government policy that all teachers should be regularly appraised. The rationale for this was that 'programmes for professional development of staff must start from an accurate identification of the training needs of teachers'. Millions of pounds were subsequently spent on training staff to appraise and be appraised but the practical effects have so far been limited. The authorities have been forced to soft-pedal on implementation because of the resource implications: the costs in staff time and the difficulties in providing appropriate support once needs have been identified. With the change to a Labour government in 1997 has come a renewed push for 'a statutory system of appraisal through regulations' (SOEID, 1997). How it will resolve the resource implications remains to be seen, but it seems likely that staff appraisal will come to play an increasingly important part in the arrangements for professional development.

While the move towards DMR was taking place, the Conservatives decided to restructure local government. The former twelve education authorities were replaced in 1995 by thirty-two unitary authorities. These smaller authorities, set up at a time of financial stringency, could not hope to offer the same range of support services as the larger regions. Only the largest of them, like Glasgow and North Lanark, have proved able to sustain an education support service on any scale. School-based professional development has therefore been largely deprived of one important source of outside support.

Traditionally the other main source of support was the teacher training institutions (TEIs), but these too have had their capacity to help greatly reduced. In 1986, the SED ended the system by which the colleges were funded to provide inservice free to teachers; instead the full costs had to be met from fees. The result has been to reduce to very modest levels their short course programmes. Even more drastic was the change in the funding of SFIS. In 1991, SOED switched from bureaucratic controls to market arrangements by transferring the funding for SFIS from the colleges to the authorities. To cushion the blow, the change was phased in, but by 1992–3, the colleges had to compete in terms of value for money with other agencies, both private and public. As college costs were high and the credibility of some staff in doubt, the volume of SFIS work declined sharply.

In these new circumstance, the TEIs have had to seek a new role and the ending of the binary line in 1993 has encouraged them to seek it in research and in the provision of post-graduate award-bearing courses. In this they have been aided by changes in government policy. From 1991 SOED allowed the TEIs to offer any courses which were self-financing. They were then able to take advantage of their freedom and of the recently created SCOTCAT scheme for credit accumulation (see Chapter 104) to have an extensive menu of modules validated at post-graduate M level, which could lead to the award of Certificates, Diplomas or Master's Degrees. Other novel aspects of these schemes were that advanced standing could be obtained by the accreditation of prior experiential learning and that modules devised and taught by external agencies could be validated and accredited.

A boost to such schemes was given in 1993 when the funding for higher education in Scotland was transferred to the Scottish Higher Education Funding Council (SHEFC) whose funding arrangements have proved more generous to part-time post-graduate courses. Each TEI now receives funding for a number of full-time equivalent students on such courses and within that framework is free to offer whatever courses the market will bear.

With the ending of its course approval system, its funding of SFIS and (since April, 1997) of the specific grant scheme, the part played by SOEID in professional development has been greatly reduced. Its main role now is to organise and fund national initiatives. Over the last decade, these have included management training for headteachers, training for staff appraisal and staff development support for Higher Still. Such schemes have typically involved the 'training of trainers' as a dissemination strategy and their support by the centralised production of support materials.

Before these changes the governance of professional development was already fragmented between the local authorities, the colleges, the universities and SOED. The switch to a school-led system has fragmented it even further as the key decisions are now taken in schools. This makes it more difficult for outside agencies to gear themselves up to meet schools' needs and also more difficult to describe what professional development is taking place. Previously the local authority and college programmes were public; now the schools' programmes are known only to those participating in them.

This switch does have advantages. Professional development is closely linked to the needs of the schools and all teachers are regularly involved in it, whereas INSET was previously a voluntary activity for the minority. This appears to solve the problem of access; but, if teachers are looking for professional development beyond what the school can offer, the opportunities are probably fewer than before. The authorities can only afford release on a very limited scale. The TEIs offer a limited range of part-time courses for which they charge fees. Therefore most teachers attending courses do so in their own time and at their own expense.

ISSUES IN PROFESSIONAL DEVELOPMENT

1. 'Professional development' – should it be in quotation marks?

Throughout this chapter, the current usage of 'professional development' has been accepted; but how well does it describe what really happens? The term 'professional' is now so debased as to be little more than an incantation. 'Development' implies progress towards a more advanced or organised state. Up to now teachers' opportunities for further learning have been ad hoc and haphazard and there is no clear picture of the advanced state to which they might progress. This is not an argument that teachers do not learn during their career; even less an argument against the need for career-long learning. It is simply a warning against making inflated claims for what goes on at present. With this caveat, we can turn to some of the other key issues.

2. What is it for?

Joyce has argued (*World Year Book of Education*, 1981) that professional development should fulfil three needs: to provide an efficient and humane educational system; to help teachers realise the personal, social and academic potential of their students; and to encourage teachers to lead a satisfying and stimulating personal life. Which of these is the most important? For most teachers, it should surely be to help the pupils to learn and thus the focus of professional development should be on teaching and learning. If this is so, is it appropriate that so much professional development in recent years has been focused on management and on staff appraisal?

3. Whose professional development is it?

Ever since the authorities began releasing teachers for courses, there has been a tension between personal professional development and that imposed on teachers by their employers.

> At one end [of the spectrum] will be those activities which meet the professional needs of an individual teacher as he or she has defined them; at the other end, those activities which meet the needs defined by the organisation . . . It must be frankly recognised that there is a potential conflict between these two purposes. (NCITT, 1984b)

The fact that the key organisation is now the school rather than the local authority does not lessen this tension. Rather the pressure for a systems approach has been intensified by the linking of school-based professional development to development planning and staff appraisal.

4. Can there be a pattern to it?

Most teachers are going to spend their lives as classroom practitioners. Can there be a pattern which their professional development should follow? A comparison with the medical profession may be illuminating. One group in the profession becomes general practitioners. After their post-initial training for that role, their further professional development takes the form of short updating courses, professional reading and reflection on experience. The hospital doctors choose a specialism and study it for years in accredited institutions, during which their work is supervised and they must pass practical and theoretical examinations. At the end the minority who succeed receive a professional qualification not from the General Medical Council but from the appropriate Royal College.

In teaching, there is no equivalent of the professional development of a medical consultant for two main reasons. Firstly, because classroom teachers are not specialists; secondly, because there is not the same secure theoretical base for the skills of a teacher. Teachers, in short, are more like GPs. Their further learning is going to take the form of updating (subject knowledge, changes in the curriculum, new technologies) and of refining and extending their skills through reflection, reading, discussion, and participation in courses. Ideally, they should be committed, like the schools, to a regular process of critical review, planning, implementation and evaluation. The problem is to give them the skills and the motivation to lock themselves into this virtuous cycle.

5. How can the quality of school-based professional development be raised?

If most professional development is to be school-based, the key issue is how the quality of what is done in and for schools can be raised. The SOEID answer (SOEID, 1997) seems to be more and better management training. That is certainly necessary, but it is not sufficient. With the reduction in support from the local authorities and the TEIs, schools are thrown back too much on their own resources.

Where is the support they need to come from? Some may come from support materials provided by SOEID, by the local authorities or by commercial publishers. Some may come by buying into external courses or hiring consultants, but funds for this are limited even if schools form consortia. As teachers greatly value the exchange of ideas with colleagues, new technologies may facilitate this through video-conferencing and the Internet. The idea has also been floated that teachers should be encouraged to undertake small-scale research into their classroom practices and disseminate the findings on the model of the Professional Development Initiative for educational psychologists (S. Brown, *Professional Development through Research*, SOED, 1993). Unfortunately, the only way to find the time for this, or for the extra professional development which is generally needed, would be to extend the teachers' working day or reduce their holiday entitlement. The history of PAT suggests that neither of these is likely.

Given these low levels of support, the quality of school-based professional development will depend essentially on the ideas and expertise within the schools. This offers the TEIs a potentially important role for their modular award schemes. Particular modules could be used by schools as a means of developing resource people to lead internal professional development. Or teachers could gain credit within the schemes for work-based learning agreements linked to school priorities. This could have the effect of giving more structure and rigour to reflection on practice and linking the award schemes to improvements in the core tasks of teaching and learning. These links are already being made, but probably the majority of students in the award schemes are pursuing their own personal agendas with a view to promotion. Moreover, what little research there has been suggests that award-bearing courses have little impact on classroom practice. (W. Inglis et al., The long-term impact of two part-time inservice degrees, *Journal of Education for Teaching*, vol. 18, no. 1, 1992.)

6. Whither credentialism?

The fact that the TEIs are promoting their award schemes for their value both to schools and to individuals as an avenue to promotion raises the question whether such awards should be a condition of holding certain posts. At this point it is important to make the distinction between an academic award and a qualification, which implies a licence to do something forbidden to the unqualified. This in turn requires the ability to define the competences required and to assess them in practice validly and reliably.

The assumption that this can be done underlies the recent decision by the Teacher Training Agency to create a National Professional Qualification for Headship in England and Wales and the current SOEID consultation paper on a Scottish Qualification for Headteachers. However, attempts to define competences (V. Casteel et al., *A Framework for Leadership and Management in Scottish Schools*, 1997) are shot through with moral exhortations and phrases like 'reflect critically on their practice and relate it to a wider frame of reference'. These are undoubtedly useful as a framework for review. To doubt whether they can be reliably assessed in practice is not to doubt the value of management training but to question how surely the line can be drawn between the qualified and the unqualified (see Chapter 102).

The same problems about criteria apply a fortiori to the claim by the GTC that it should accredit post-initial courses as well as courses of initial training. What might such accreditation mean? Either the accredited courses would have to be qualifications. In that case, would the GTC be the appropriate body? (Post-initial qualifications in medicine are not awarded by the General Medical Council.) Or accreditation would have to bring some financial benefit to the TEIs such as differential funding by SHEFC. Both alternatives are fraught with difficulties.

CONCLUSION

In recent years, governments have talked much about the need to raise the quality of teachers, but have avoided the two awkward questions; how to improve the quality of recruits when teaching has a poor image and career prospects, and how to raise the standard of teachers already in post. Sacking incompetent teachers can only contribute marginally to this. The key lies in career-long professional development of a high quality but in practice professional development has been one of the poor relations of the education service. Teachers have not been willing to campaign for it at the expense of salaries or class sizes; the authorities have regularly had to sacrifice it to meet their statutory responsibilities; successive governments have advocated it without providing the necessary resources, inhibited by the costs of doing so for a labour-intensive profession whose clients require constant supervision. Unless the situation changes, professional development for many teachers will continue to be an ad hoc, low-level activity, whose value they are sceptical of and which compares ill with that demanded by other professions.

The author would like to acknowledge the help given by the following people, who discussed various aspects of professional development with him: James Aitchison, Molly Cumming, Alastair Davidson, Dr Malcolm Green, Douglas McCreath, Jim Rand, Iain Smith, Robert Stewart OBE, Bill Thomson, Glenda White and Rosheen Young.

REFERENCES

NCITT (1979) *The Future of Inservice Training in Scotland*, Edinburgh: SED.
NCITT (1984a) *The Development of the Three-Tier Structure of Award-bearing Courses*, Edinburgh: SED.
NCITT (1984b) *Arrangements for the Staff Development of Teachers*, Edinburgh: SED.
SED (1989) *School Teachers' Professional Development into the 1990s*, Edinburgh: SED.
SOEID (1997) *Raising the Standard*, Edinburgh: SOEID.

102

Teacher Competence

Colin Holroyd

'There is no place for incompetent teachers. Everyone agrees about that.' So began an editorial in the *Times Educational Supplement Scotland* on 8 August 1997. If everyone agrees on this, presumably they also agree that teachers should be competent. Beyond that there appears to be little agreement on anything else regarding teacher competence. How is competence defined? How is competence related to professionalism? Can competence be reliably and validly assessed? Are there levels of competence? What competences are appropriate for initial teacher education and for different stages of professional development? Should competences be prescribed for the holders of promoted posts? Would it be better to use some other word? Or to abandon competence based approaches altogether? There are few answers to any of these questions and when any is offered, it seems to be immediately contested. Sally Brown suggests in the introduction to *Developing Competent Teachers* (Hustler and McIntyre, 1996) that discussions about teacher competence have been characterised not so much as a developing debate but 'more in the realm of exchanges between defence lawyers and law enforcers'.

The key policy document in relation to teacher competence in Scotland was issued by the Scottish Office Education Department in 1993 under the title *Guidelines for Teacher Training Courses* (SOED, 1993). This document revises and consolidates various sets of guidelines for courses of teacher training issued in the preceding ten years and in one sense contains nothing unfamiliar. However, the Guidelines do put a quite new stress on the competences in teaching to be acquired during the training period.

COMPETENCES WITHIN THE 1993 GUIDELINES

The Guidelines identify those competences which are to be attained by people who complete an initial stage of training and are about to enter a probationary period as teachers. It is important to note that the term professional competences is used to cover not only practical, craft skills of teaching, but also knowledge and understanding that the beginning teacher should have and attitudes they should possess. This broad definition of competences has been seen both as a welcome, positive feature of the Scottish position and also as a disingenuous attempt to sugar a bitter pill.

The introduction to the statement of competences makes three other important points: (a) that these are core or generic competences required of all teachers, although there may be differences of detail in the training of teachers for different stages and subjects, (b) that teacher education institutions and their partner schools have themselves to work out how the competences can be appropriately assessed (although in the longer term there may be need for some national setting of assessment criteria) and (c) competence in the beginning teacher should develop over succeeding years into proficient and expert levels of professionalism.

The competences set out in this document are to be used in planning all initial teaching courses and have to be taken into account in the schemes of assessment designed for these courses. What then are these competences? What do they look like?

There are forty competences (or perhaps thirty-four and a set of six attitudes) detailed within four main groups; many of these competences contain several components. The first group defines five competences relating to the subject and content of teaching. They are all prefixed by: 'The new teacher should be able to . . .'; the first one mentioned, for example, is 'to demonstrate a knowledge of the subject or subjects forming the content of his or her teaching which meets and goes beyond the immediate demands of the school curriculum'. The second group – competences relating to the classroom – defines twenty competences in four sub-groups (communication, teaching methods, class management and assessment). The requirement again is usually that 'the new teacher should be able to . . .'. Here are four sample competences, one from each sub-group:

1.   . . . question pupils effectively, respond and support their discussion and questioning;
2.   . . . employ a range of teaching strategies appropriate to the subject or topic, and on the basis of careful assessment, to the pupils in his or her classes;
3.   . . . manage pupil behaviour by the use of appropriate rewards and sanctions and be aware when it is necessary to seek advice;
4.   . . . assess the quality of pupils' learning against national standards defined for that particular group of pupils.

The third group is of seven competences relating to the school; in these the new teacher should 'have some knowledge of . . .' or 'know how to . . .' or 'be aware of . . .'. One example is '. . . know how to discuss with parents a range of issues relevant to their children'. The fourth group lists eight competences (or two plus six attitudes) related to professionalism; these include knowledge as in '. . . have a working knowledge of his or her pastoral, contractual, legal and administrative responsibilities' and attitudes such as '. . . a commitment to self-monitoring and professional development'.

THE 1993 GUIDELINES: THE PROCESS OF CONSTRUCTION

A full history of the actual circumstances of production of the 1993 list of competences would be of great interest; it is not available. The brief sketch which follows is based on (i) the contribution of one of Her Majesty' Chief Inspectors for Scotland to a research seminar programme, (ii) knowledge gained by the present author from limited personal involvement and (iii) the inspired 'story' told by Stronach and colleagues in the book already referred to (Hustler and McIntyre, 1996).

In late 1991, the then minister with responsibility for education at the Scottish Office initiated a review of teacher training; that review necessarily involved revision of guidelines. Stronach detects in this the domestication of those pressures for root and branch reform emerging from 'the darkness of New Right thinking south of the border'. The review group was led by a senior civil servant and a chief inspector. One contribution to the deliberations of the group was a report commissioned from an outsider, the present author. This report was written to a three-fold remit: firstly, there should be an analysis of previous government guidelines and the documentation prepared by teacher education institutions for courses required to conform to those guidelines, with a view to identifying statements about aims and intended outcomes which embodied competences desirable in the beginning teacher; secondly, a summary was required of recent policy and discussion documents related to teacher competence and thirdly, there should be a critical review of the arguments for and against competence-based approaches advanced in academic, theoretical and research papers. The report was delivered in March 1992.

One can only guess at discussions within the Scottish Office before a draft document emerged for consultation later that year, and then again before the final version was published early in 1993. The consultation period was relatively short and there were only minor changes between the draft and final versions. It seems likely that those of a behaviourist persuasion (and perhaps those from commercial and industrial training backgrounds) pressed for a longer list of more precisely specified elements of competence, that liberal educationists of a traditional cast of mind argued for a shorter list of more general and 'softer' competences with greater stress on the intrinsic rather than instrumental justification of knowledge, and that radicals wished the whole enterprise to be rejected as ill-conceived and dangerous. There are people in all three groups within the educational system as a whole; there is little doubt they existed within the Scottish Office Education Department itself.

THE 1993 GUIDELINES: CRITICISM FROM THEORETICAL STANDPOINTS

Commentators familiar with current thinking on national standards within vocational training and in sympathy with behaviourist theories of learning criticised the 1993 competences from two related angles. Firstly, the competences, because relatively few in number, were too complex and vague to describe the desired outcomes of training in a transparent and unambiguous way. Secondly, there was insufficient guidance to allow reliable assessment of whether or not any particular competence was actually possessed.

The competences specified by the lead body for training and development are relevant here. There are 132 such elements of competence listed; to describe each one of these takes a whole page of small print; for every competence there are six or seven performance criteria, a description of the range of contexts in which the competence is to be demonstrated, assessment guidance and a note on the nature of relevant supplementary evidence (usually in relation to underpinning knowledge). It was this kind of approach which Maclellan had in mind when she reacted critically to the SOED competences in an article in the *Times Educational Supplement Scotland* of 5 March 1993: 'To judge what constitutes a minimum level of competence, the performance indicators of competence must be couched in terms of criterial standards and the range/constraints of context(s) in which the performance will be displayed'.

Criticism of the 1993 competences from a quite different perspective was rather more obvious. The key Scottish writers were, and continue to be, Humes, Carr and Stronach. (References to Humes' articles can be found in the Stronach chapter in the Hustler and McIntyre book.) Carr's position is vigorously stated in a paper published soon after the guidelines (Carr, 1993). There he argues that the kind of criticism indicated in the previous paragraph is, if not entirely bogus, quite beside the point. What then are his main lines of argument?

Carr acknowledges that competence is a familiar concept; its promotion in entrants to the teaching profession is a proper activity for teacher educators. However, if the competent professional is understood as a reflective practitioner, then competence-based approaches not only misconstrue and distort the goal, they are actually inimical to the pursuit and attainment of it. There are three arguments. Firstly, education is not well-represented as an activity in which a range of technical and craft skills is exercised; it should be seen as a practical pursuit of what is deemed to be good for humankind and thus has first to be conceived as a moral or evaluative endeavour. Secondly, the guidelines improperly construe, or perversely misconstrue, the place of knowledge in professional practice. Insofar as knowledge is given a place at all in the competences it is purely instrumental; it underpins the competences and the effective exercise of the competence is seen as the application of the knowledge. This is to adopt an inappropriate and dated form of technical rationality and to give the theories of education a character that they cannot possess. Thirdly, within the guidelines and competences there is no hint that they may be questionable or even wrong. The whole drive is towards new teachers behaving in a 'conventionally acceptable way in relation to standards which are fixed and final and there is hardly the ghost of a suggestion that there might be something to be said for students coming to be able to dissent or depart in an imaginative, creative, innovative or critical spirit from the established canons of educational practice'. Teaching is presented via the competences as a matter of duties and obligations defined by others and not of ideals and aspirations autonomously and authentically conceived. The professionalism of teachers is thus, Carr argues, severely restricted.

THE 1993 GUIDELINES: PRACTICAL RESPONSES

Some of the criticism of the 1993 competences came from the staff of teacher education institutions (TEIs). Nevertheless, the TEIs had to continue the practical tasks of designing, modifying and delivering courses of initial teacher education in conformity with the guidelines. The consensus now would appear to be that they have not found this difficult: they can make competence-based approaches work. There are positive responses: 'the competences are obviously related to existing good practice'; 'these competences are not nearly as damagingly prescriptive as others we are aware of – in vocational training and in England and Wales'; 'the Scottish Office has got them more or less right'.

There are clear signs in recent course documentation of the influence of the 1993 competences; however, their impact has been most obvious in the way that students are assessed and in how the results of assessment are reported. Students on school experience are assessed by members of school staff against the competences; the tutors from TEIs who visit the students use the same competences; discussions amongst students, teachers and tutors tend to be on those aspects of school experience which the competences highlight. Gradings related to the competences form the basis of reports to Boards of Examiners and the profiles which newly qualified teachers take with them to their first appointments. (The extent to which such profiles are used in supporting induction and further professional development is highly questionable, particularly when students serve in a number of schools on short-term temporary contracts.)

Although staff in TEIs say that principal teachers and others in contact with students have operated effectively with the competences, particularly in relation to assessment, there is no room for complacency. In its 1997 report on partnership in initial teacher education, the General Teaching Council recognised that the competences provided a useful articulation of the skills, understandings and professional commitments of teachers and as such helped to mediate the dual roles of support and assessment undertaken by both teachers and tutors in their work with student teachers. They did, however, go on to say that the competences are still not understood in all schools; the understanding and ownership of the competences is less secure than it should be because of the limited provision made for staff development to support their introduction.

It may be claimed that the competences have worked tolerably well in relation to the assessment of 'work-place performance', but it should be recognised that current entrants to teaching are of very high quality. In all but a few cases the judgement that they possess a basic level of competence is an easy one to make. In other words, the value of the competences as a guide to valid assessment has not been severely tested and it may well be that distinguishing between 'competent enough' and 'not yet sufficiently competent' remains as troublesome as it has always been.

Another concern is emerging. Whereas tutors in TEIs tend to say that today's beginning teachers are excellent 'technically' and that their performance in the classroom is assured and highly pleasing, they also have worries about the depth and breadth of students' understanding of the content of their teaching. There is research evidence for this in some aspects of primary teaching (mathematics, science and technology in particular), but the problem may well exist in secondary teachers as well. There has been an assumption that students taking postgraduate courses of teacher training come to such courses with satisfactory content knowledge from their basic degree qualifications; that assumption is now being increasingly questioned. The next issue of the Memorandum on Entry Requirements from SOEID shows an increase in the time that has to be spent on studying a subject at university for aspiring teachers to gain a qualifying certificate entry in that subject.

The competences may make it somewhat easier to assess 'workplace performance'; they do not make it easier to design and assess the written course work required of students. Some TEIs have felt it necessary to go to extreme lengths to demonstrate that everything which a student has to produce can be justified as underpinning the competences and to articulate the assessment criteria for written work. One competence statement, for example, requires the new teacher to be able to justify what is taught from knowledge and understanding of the learning process, curriculum issues, child development in general. Explicating what is needed for a satisfactory justification is not easy. One can, of course, reply that assessment has always been difficult and problematic and all that the competence statements do is force teacher educators to clarify what it is they are looking for.

The TEIs have not only incorporated the competences into their provision of initial training, they have worked to tackle that challenge within the 1993 guidelines that the competences should 'allow and encourage full development over succeeding years to proficient and expert levels of professionalism'. To take but a single example, Buchanan and Jackson (1997) have devised a guide to self-evaluation for teachers. They claim that their framework (based on criteria developed from the competences) has been found to be useful to student and experienced teachers alike. Interestingly, they urge that their criteria and competences must not be seen as a mere checklist of skills: 'This atomistic and reductionist view would very likely lead to the teacher as a whole getting lost somewhere in the description of the parts'.

POST 1993: UP-DATING AND EXTENSION

At the time of writing, work is being done within the Scottish Office to revise the guidelines for teacher training; that work has been informed by the routine inspections of Her Majesty's Inspectorate and by the TEIs. Implementation of the revised guidelines is expected for session 1999–2000. No doubt any major development in some larger, but related, policy area could delay progress – as could major changes in how Scotland is governed.

The probability of the revised guidelines adopting a fundamentally different view of the nature and importance of competence is small. Is it unwise to hazard a few predictions?

1. It will be confirmed that the competences have been well accepted and are generally held in high regard.
2. The good work achieved in competence-based assessment of students on school experience will be recognised; there will be some pressure for further improvement in the assessment of college-based work.
3. There will be encouragement for more integrative and holistic forms of assessment and discouragement of highly analytical and atomistic approaches; grouping the competences for reporting purposes will be recommended.
4. Some clarification will be provided on the level of achievement of the competences to be expected for the beginning teacher stage and how this might be related to further professional development.
5. The actual competences may be refined, clarified or 'beefed-up', but there will be no very dramatic changes. A few things will receive greater emphasis: computer and information technology is an obvious candidate.
6. The guidelines will continue to demonstrate a welcome independence from English influence; however, in one exception to this, we may expect increased use of the word 'standards' and somewhat decreased use of the actual word 'competences'.

So far, the focus in this chapter has been on the competence of classroom teachers. Competence-based approaches have been extended into other areas. In August 1997, the Scottish Office issued a consultation paper on a Scottish qualification for headteachers (SOEID, 1997). This paper sets out some background to, and the good practice features of, the government's proposal for 'a new range of qualifications for teachers aspiring to headship to gain management competences'. Consultation was over by the end of September 1997.

So that the government's aim of raising standards of management and leadership in Scottish schools can be achieved, any new qualification has to incorporate seven positive features. The first of these is that the qualification 'should be competence/standards' based.

What kind of competence does the government have in mind? SOEID had earlier commissioned a report (Casteel et al., 1997) on the management competences required in Scottish schools and this makes very interesting reading. The big theme permeating the Casteel report is the improvement of professional capability. This last word has not previously appeared in this chapter. Stephenson, of the education for capability movement, provides a striking definition: 'Competence delivers the present on the basis of the past; capability delivers the present but also imagines, prepares for and develops the future'. Competence statements are often derived from some functional analysis of occupations as they currently are; capability should be informed by some vision of what they might become.

In Casteel's model there are certain basic competences that the beginning teacher should acquire during initial teacher education; these have to equip him or her as a probationer; progression to expert levels requires the further development of these competences. If the novice teacher is also an aspiring manager he or she should start to acquire additional leadership and management competences and then also develop these from novice to expert levels.

The framework for management development begins with a statement of the key purpose of management/leadership, analysis of which leads to the defining of four key functions (the management of policy and planning, of learning and teaching, of people, and of resources and finance). The report notes that in the Management Charter Initiative, key functions are further analysed into units of competence; this is of course identical to the functional analytic approach mentioned earlier for training and development. Casteel and her colleagues do something rather different: they move from key functions (4 of them) to core activities (10 in number) to key tasks (45 of them). Educational managers who achieve competence demonstrate it in their performance of these tasks. Fulfilling the functions (or performing the tasks effectively) needs two things: professional qualities and personal abilities. The former include commitment to educational values and to critical reflection and personal/professional development, understanding of educational processes and of management in general. The personal abilities they describe are both interpersonal (things like creating a positive atmosphere, inspiring and motivating others and communicating effectively) and intellectual (like framing and solving problems, thinking strategically and judging wisely).

There are different reactions to the Casteel approach. One is to detect and admire an ingenious synthesis of a functional/analytical approach and an intuitive/holistic one. Another reaction is to say that a necessary conflict is not resolved, but magicked away with the help of some conceptual ambiguity and theoretical incoherence. The separate lists of qualities and abilities are distinguished more by their origin than their nature. The professional qualities seem to derive from some unstated and debatable definition of what it means to be professional; the personal abilities seem to derive from the work of people like McBer and Klemp on those 'soft' competences and general cognitive abilities which characterise above average from average practitioners. It is not made clear how qualities and abilities are to be distinguished. Why, for example is 'understanding' a quality and 'judging' an ability? Why is showing courage an interpersonal ability rather than a professional quality? What of such personal qualities as honesty, sanity and a sense of humour?

The framework was scrutinised by over a hundred headteachers and others in discussion groups throughout Scotland. As a result, the authors concluded that it was helpful in 'creating coherent and systematic development opportunities for individuals and teams at all stages of leadership and management' and in 'supporting accreditation for leadership and management expertise'. They say little about the assessment of competence or the identification of incompetence. This may well be both intentional and wise, but it is an omission which will have to repaired at some time.

TEACHER COMPETENCE: CONTINUING ISSUES

In this concluding section, three basic questions are briefly addressed. What does it mean to develop competence? What is a good teacher? Are Scotland's teachers competent enough?

Firstly, what does it mean to develop competence? For some simple practical skills, it is possible to make a defensible binary 'yes–no' decision as to whether a person is competent in the exercise of that skill. With skills of this type developing competence then means either extending the range of contexts in which the skill is effectively exercised or adding new competences to those already possessed. It is worth noting that, even with apparently clear-cut and unambiguous competences, decisions have to be made about which competences are the appropriate ones to bring into play. (This has led some to define a concept of 'meta-competence' i.e. being competent in the selection of competences.)

The 1993 competences for teaches are not of this simple type. Although they are expected to be attained by all teachers who complete the first stage of their training, they also define what Stronach has called 'superperformance', i.e. they constitute an idealised expression of performance with enough competences and commitments to see any teacher through several careers with greater distinction than most experienced teachers ever achieve. Just one example will make this clear: the new teacher should be able to create contexts in which pupils can learn. This is a sensible requirement for a beginning teacher. But how many contexts? What different kinds of things have to be learned in them? How many pupils have to learn how much? How desirable is it that the contexts should be imaginatively different from standard ones? How much effort is needed from the teacher to create an effective learning context? It is very obvious that this single competence can exist at widely differing levels – and can develop over time.

There have been many attempts to describe levels of competence. One of these posits five levels, progressing from novice, to advanced beginner, to competent, to proficient and to expert. The differences in levels depend on the presence or absence of different types of situational understanding and judgement. For example, the basically competent person is analytical in their whole-situation recognition and rational in their decision-making whereas the expert is holistic in the former and intuitive in the latter. Another approach, influential in medical education, distinguishes the novice from the expert in terms of the 'scripts' which are available for use in practical situations. The novice has a limited number of such internalised recipes for action on which to draw; the expert not only has a much more extensive library of scripts, he or she recognises when none of the existing scripts is adequate to the situation. When this is the case the expert reflects creatively on the range of possibly relevant knowledge bases which he or she possesses.

If what it means to develop competence is of great theoretical interest, it is also of great practical importance. There is a growing acceptance that initial training, induction and professional development should be seen as a continuing process, coherent and progressive. We have already noted that the 1993 guidelines insist that it is essential that the competences acquired in training should be those which 'allow and encourage' full development over succeeding years to proficient and expert levels of professionalism. There is an urgent need for clarification of this. Should the 1993 competences, perhaps modestly revised for 1999, be elaborated in the future to define levels of competence development appropriate to different stages of career progression? Should the requirements of the beginning teacher be defined by a re-interpretation of these competences which reduces them in scope and demand? Further development might then be prescribed, not via a competence-based approach at all, but by increased reflection on extended experience and through academic study to nourish those understandings with which one reflects. This latter approach does, of course, call into question again the appropriateness to teaching of all competence-based thinking. If an action research based model of reflective practice, emphasising autonomous professionalism and quality assurance through peer-review, is appropriate for continuing professional development, why then is it not also appropriate for initial training?

Secondly, what is a good teacher? Over the years, great effort has been put into attempting to characterise the 'good' teacher with little conspicuous success. There are very good reasons for the intractability of the problem: the lack of any clear consensus about the aims and purposes of education (and of schooling), the nature of individual learners as human beings in all their variability, the subtlety and complexity of social interactions in any group of learners and the changing social, cultural and sub-cultural contexts in which teaching occurs.

It is a common practice to think of there being three broad determinants of the 'goodness' of teachers: understanding, skills, and personal qualities. There is the understanding that the teacher should have of all those knowledge bases which it is helpful to draw upon – content knowledge, knowledge of situations, structures, people, learning theories and curriculum policies. There is the repertoire of skills to be deployed in educational settings – skills in creating and maintaining order, in communicating, in managing resources and so on. There are personal and moral qualities such as reliability, integrity, courage, empathy and the capacity to give and receive love. It is possible to see these categories as if they were separate and exclusive but, of course, the elements do not operate in isolation. Skills are not intelligently chosen and deployed without understanding; values have a clear cognitive component; skills are not used without a commitment to their use. The explication, and agreement, of everything that it is desirable for a teacher to know, to be able to do, and to value is an overwhelming task. Faced with this most of us will over-simplify on the basis of our enthusiasms, theories and ideological stances. The result is then a retreat into simple dualisms and entrenchment at polar extremes.

One example will have to suffice. Consider three spectra: of learning theories from social constructivism at, say, the left-hand end to naive behaviourism at the other; of metaphors for teaching ranging from the encouragement of spiritual growth to industrial-processing; of assessment purposes going from the enhancement of learning to public accountability. Educationists to the left on these three spectra will reject competence-based definitions of teachers' quality as technicist, mechanistic and reductionist. Those to the right of the three spectra (and perhaps on the New Right in political terms) will favour those competence-based approaches which emphasise observable outcomes, efficient skill deployment and relatively easy assessment of incompetence.

It is foolish to dismiss 'competence' in any attempt to describe the good teacher. It is equally foolish to claim that the good teacher can be completely defined in terms of competences alone. There is a pressing need, in Scotland as elsewhere, for a well-developed synthesis of the concepts of competence and of understanding, of the technician and of the liberal humanist, of skills and of spirituality.

Thirdly, are Scotland's teachers competent enough? Until recently it was confidently assumed that the answer to this question must be 'in general – yes'. After all, students entering training were academically well-qualified; all teachers were trained over a reasonable period; courses and places of training were subject to a battery of processes monitoring their quality; new teachers not up to the demands of teaching would fail to complete the probationary period; those who later discovered, or developed, any serious inadequacy would be persuaded to select themselves out. At the same time it was quietly accepted that in a profession with so many members there would inevitably be a very small proportion who somehow slipped through the various nets. There have always been procedures to remove those who were conspicuously deficient in certain qualities (perhaps of integrity, honesty and reliability), those who suffered some serious breakdown in mental or physical health and those guilty of consistent abuse of drugs and alcohol or of their pupils. It was, however, extremely rare for teachers to be dismissed for incompetence in the tasks of teaching, rather than on grounds which come under the general heading of 'misconduct'. Those few employers who sought to remove 'incompetent' teachers found themselves engaged in lengthy, costly and complicated procedures with a limited chance of success.

There are now signs of a change in the climate. This is in part due to the publicity given to the issue of incompetent teachers (and headteachers) in England and Wales, particularly by the Office for Standards in Education. Publication of league tables of schools based on pupil performance in examinations has led to the concept of 'failing schools' and it has then been a short step to the conclusion that schools fail because of the failure of individual teachers to teach competently. The idea of failing schools has recently been extended to that of failing departments within schools. One way to reduce the number of failing schools or departments, it is argued, is to remove the incompetent teachers. The estimates of how many such teachers there are have, notoriously, varied widely; this is unsurprising given the serious difficulties of defining competence – which makes all such statistics highly dubious.

Although there is a general belief in Scotland that this is an English/Welsh diagnosis which does not apply here, and must not be imported over the border, there is at the same time a feeling that in some quarters there is an element of complacency and that there may exist a genuine problem about the classroom competence of a few Scottish teachers. For example, in a report from the HM Inspectors of Schools in 1993 (*Standards and Quality in Scottish Schools*) it was stated that in 80 per cent of schools staff demonstrated many of the qualities of effective teaching. But it would be quite wrong to conclude from this that 20 per cent of teachers are ineffective. Elsewhere the report states that 'the vast majority of teachers were caring and conscientious professionals'. On the other hand, the same report does say that whereas headteachers in 25 per cent of schools displayed very good leadership qualities, in 5% of schools management was unsatisfactory. In this case the authors do appear to invite us to conclude that they think one in every twenty headteachers is 'incompetent', even although they fail to convince readers that the basis for this judgement is anything other than deeply suspect.

If it were to be decided that in Scotland more stress had now to be placed on the detection and dismissal of incompetent teachers, there would be severe difficulties in implementing the process. Some of these relate to the conceptual difficulties surrounding the definitions of competence that were discussed earlier; others relate to who should be responsible for the process. The possible role of the General Teaching Council in this is discussed in Chapter 110.

Of course, there is undeniably a sense in which all of Scotland's teachers could be more competent than they are. However, this is the argument, not for removing from post the few who are deemed incompetent, but for devoting more resources to supporting the profession as a whole in developing competence to meet with enhanced expertise the ever-increasing demands of the job.

REFERENCES

Buchanan, D. and S. Jackson (1997) *Self-Evaluation for Teachers and Student Teachers*, London: Kogan Page.

Carr, D. (1993) Guidelines for Teacher Training: The Competency Model, *Scottish Educational Review*, vol. 25 no. 1.

Casteel, V., C. Forde, J. Reeves and R. Lynas (1997) *A Framework for Leadership and Management Development in Scottish Schools*, University of Strathclyde: QIE Training Unit.

Hustler, D. and D. McIntyre (1996) *Developing Competent Teachers*, London: David Fulton.

SOED (1993) *Guidelines for Teacher Training Courses*, Edinburgh: Scottish Office Education Department.

SOEID (1997) *Consultation Paper on a Scottish Qualification for Head Teachers*, Edinburgh: Scottish Office Education and Industry Department.

103

The European Dimension

Kay Livingston

While politicians continue to wrangle over the pros and cons of the European Union (EU), the reality is that there is an ongoing process of integration, with the removal of frontiers and an increasing number of supranational policies. The internationalisation of the economy, new communication technology and increased mobility all have an impact on contemporary life. The White Paper, *Teaching and Learning, Towards the Learning Society*, published by the European Commission in 1995, said that these changes are not incidental, but herald the society of tomorrow. It pointed out that the challenge for Europe, and for each individual, is to master these changes and not to be overcome by them. These changes represent both a challenge and an opportunity for education.

Social reality plays a decisive role in the determination of educational priorities and the fact that we are living in a more interdependent world should be reflected in the educational process. The argument for including a European dimension in education focuses on the need to prepare pupils for life in a changing society. This view suggests that teachers need to be aware of the kind of society that their pupils are growing up in within the context of an integrated Europe.

The extent to which one believes that education is about preparing young people for society opens up the philosophical debate concerning the definition and purpose of education. How the European dimension will be given meaning and developed is part of a larger network of concepts in relation to the definition of education itself.

EUROPEAN RESOLUTIONS, TREATIES AND POLICIES

The idea of a community of European nations grew out of a desire to maintain peace after the Second World War. The political plan focused on establishing economic ties and in 1957 the Treaty of Rome established the European Economic Community (EEC). With the enlargement of the Community over the following years (the UK joining in 1972), there was a growing realisation that the European integration process was more than a political and economic process. It was recognised that to establish a union of people, policies needed to extend beyond political and economic cooperation. The later change in title from EEC to EU reflected this broader view.

The Single European Act in 1986 stepped up the momentum of the integration process. It strengthened the Treaty of Rome by introducing provision for greater economic and social cohesion and this extended to education and training. The role of education as a tool for assisting changes in an evolving European society was gradually acknowledged and the first action programmes in the field of education were put in place. For example, the ERASMUS programme was adopted in 1987 and promoted the mobility of university staff and students and the development of inter-university cooperation.

A Resolution in 1988 by the Council and Ministers of Education gave further emphasis to the inclusion of a European dimension in education. It highlighted the need to strengthen in young people a sense of European identity and prepare them to take part in the economic and social development of the Community. The resolution set out a range of proposals for encouraging and developing the European dimension in schools and through initial and inservice teacher education. At Community level, the European Commission took action in the area of teacher exchanges and encouraged the formation of networks of teacher education institutions and university departments responsible for training teachers throughout Europe.

The member states were invited to take initiatives within the limits of their own specific educational policies and structures. For example, the resolution called on the member states to develop curricula, devise teaching materials, train teachers and support measures to promote contacts between pupils and teachers of different countries. It specifically asked the member states to set out in a document their policies for incorporating a European dimension in education.

In November 1993 the Treaty on European Union, often known as the Maastricht Treaty, came into effect. The Treaty may stand out in people's minds as one which provides for closer European integration in terms of economic cooperation and freedom of movement of goods, services and people. However, its impact on education may not be as widely understood. The Treaty marked a new stage for action at European level by giving a legal basis to Community action in the field of education for the first time.

Article 126 of the Treaty stated that the Community shall contribute to the development of quality education by encouraging cooperation between member states and, if necessary, by supporting and supplementing their action, while fully respecting the responsibility of the member states for the content of education and the organisation of their educational systems. The accent on raising the quality of education throughout the Union centres on the 'added-value' that European cooperation can bring, through the exchange of ideas and methods, and the sharing of experiences. European unification is seen as a value in itself, whereby the sum of parts can make a better contribution to education across the Union. Harmonisation of education systems is not proposed. The principle of subsidiarity ensures that the content of teaching and its implementation remain the responsibility of the member states.

The position of vocational training is quite different; it has been included in European policies since 1957, and there has been a wide range of initiatives taken in this field. However, Article 127 of the Treaty gave the EU the competence to implement a vocational training policy and consolidated action towards mutual recognition of qualifications.

Despite the realisation that a union of people requires more than political and economic policies, the reality of the unemployment situation and the need to survive in a competitive world market meant that the focus continued to be on economic issues. A link was made between high quality education and the European economy. A White Paper on *Growth, Competitiveness, Employment – The Challenges and Ways Forward into the 21st Century* (European Commission, 1993) said that human resources constitute the EU's main economic asset and to be competitive a highly qualified, mobile and flexible workforce is needed.

Lack of concrete evidence to support the claim that a better educated society would necessarily result in a stronger economy fuelled debate on the emphasis within education on utilitarian and vocational issues. Another White Paper – *Teaching and Learning Towards the Learning Society* (European Commission, 1995) pointed out that the return of economic growth while essential will not in itself resolve the unemployment situation. The discourse does not move away from an economic perspective, but it does indicate that there should be a balance between satisfying the demands of the labour market and the development of the individual. It said that if Europe is to secure its place and future in the world, it has to place at least as much emphasis on the personal fulfilment of its citizens, as it has until now placed on economic and monetary issues. The paper launched the European Year of Lifelong Learning highlighting the need to explore new ways of learning, establishing closer partnerships between schools and companies and making greater use of multimedia in schools and teacher education institutions. Greater importance is being attached to the idea of providing flexible opportunities for lifelong learning and equipping individuals with the capability to adapt to changing needs and different work patterns throughout their lives. This is set to be the challenge for education in the next century.

EUROPEAN ACTION PROGRAMMES

In order to translate the somewhat utopian policy discourse into action, the EU established the SOCRATES and LEONARDO Programmes (European Commission 1995). These programmes represent the first concrete implementation of Articles 126 and 127 of the Maastricht Treaty. The programmes aim to extend the development of the European dimension to all sectors of education and to strengthen the spirit of European citizenship.

The SOCRATES programme comprises action in higher education (ERASMUS), in school education (COMENIUS), and in the promotion of language skills (LINGUA). It also includes action in open and distance learning and in the promotion of information exchanges.

The LEONARDO programme aims to implement a common vocational and training policy by supporting work experience periods in businesses or training organisations in other EU countries. The programme also supports the development of language skills in business.

The programmes seek to achieve a strong multiplier effect, supporting innovative projects which have the greatest impact on improving the quality of education. Some parts of the programmes are centralised and administered from Brussels, others are decentralised and are administered by National Agencies in each member state. The Central Bureau for Educational Visits and Exchanges (CBEVE) is the National Agency for the UK and manages all decentralised actions, such as COMENIUS Action 1.

The school education programme COMENIUS is the most innovative, as schools are the focus of European policy for the first time. The COMENIUS programme, which is divided into three actions, encourages the creation of multilateral partnerships between schools, promotes the intercultural dimension in order to prepare pupils to live in a society that is increasingly characterised by its cultural and linguistic diversity, and supports projects which develop and run transnational inservice courses for teachers.

WHAT IS THE EUROPEAN DIMENSION?

The rhetoric of European treaties and resolutions calls for the promotion of a European dimension in education, however its definition is not made explicit. Knowing what the

European dimension in education is and understanding what form it might take within the curriculum are difficult problems. There is no single definition that everyone would easily agree on, or one clear set of strategies to implement a European dimension.

Searching for a definition of 'Europe' itself throws up a range of questions. For example, is it a Europe of only the EU countries or should it include all the countries from the Atlantic to the Urals? Is it a group of democratic nations? Is it a group of nations with a shared history and cultural heritage? Is it a Europe of nation states or a Europe of regions? Geographical, historical, political, socio-economic or cultural criteria may be used to try to formulate an answer to each of these questions. However, selecting one criterion is difficult as they are all closely interrelated. For example, territorial boundaries of Europe have through history been closely associated with religious, cultural, socio-economic and political factors.

A broad view of the concept of the European dimension is possible. It could be described as opening up and broadening pupils' horizons and making them more aware of other European cultures. However, such a general definition which embraces so many issues hinders the effective implementation of the European dimension. Teachers may not include it in their work because it is not easy to identify a starting point, or because it is so generic that it is unclear whose responsibility it should be to ensure that it forms part of the curriculum. The opposite extreme would be to restrict the definition to very specific aspects. A curricular insert on the infrastructure of the European parliament would be one example. Knowledge about Europe is necessary, but it is just one element of the European dimension.

A broad definition as opposed to a narrow one provides a simplistic description of two poles of thought. It does not take account of the many definitions that fall between the extremes. These definitions need not be in competition with one another, employing one does not mean eschewing others. The European dimension is a multi-faceted phenomenon which does not have a simple common denominator.

To add to the difficulties, it could be argued that even a broadly-defined European dimension is too narrow. Europe's interdependence with the rest of the world means that an international dimension may be more meaningful. Aspects such as tolerance of others, raising awareness and understanding of other cultures and promoting democratic values, extend beyond the boundaries of Europe and are relevant within an international context.

This ambiguity and lack of consensus concerning the definition, the content within the curriculum and the place of the European dimension in education, creates uncertainty for teachers. However, the teacher's task is not about putting forward one solution to all the questions or identifying one definition for a European dimension. It is the process involved in finding answers that is important. Discussion, debate, negotiation and compromise are some of the main features that a European dimension seeks to bring to education. Facilitating pupils to think for themselves, to be aware of similarities and differences and to seek, in a democratic way, solutions to conflicts which arise, are central to the development of a European dimension in education.

While this may represent a step forward in understanding the multifaceted nature of the concept, it is not helpful for curriculum planning. What is needed is an operational framework that enables teachers to analyse, organise and categorise the content to be included at each stage of the curriculum in a developmental and coherent way. Without such a framework there is a danger of the European dimension being nothing more than a collection of vague and disjointed inserts on Europe. Shennan (1991) proposed a three dimensional model of the European dimension, which provides a helpful structure for aiding curricular design.

The first dimension suggests that the European dimension should include learning about Europe, learning for Europe and learning through Europe. The second dimension identifies the elements: knowledge, skills, attitudes and values. For example, knowledge is required about Europe's geography, its people, history and cultures. Certain skills are required to prepare young people for life in Europe, where effective communication skills and the ability to solve problems and react to changing circumstances are essential. To live and work together with other Europeans, attitudes and values need to be explored. Judgements may be based on stereotypical snapshot images. Just as Scotland is more than the highlands and tartan, the Netherlands is more than windmills and tulips. Pupils need to go beyond a superficial understanding of other European countries. The European dimension should focus on the deconstruction of these pre-formed and often long-standing images of European regions, nations and people. Learning through Europe, by getting to know 'real' people in other countries is an important step. This does not necessarily mean an exchange trip, new communication technology may be utilised to create class to class links and enable pupils to share and exchange information. However, there can be no question that mobility of pupils and teachers will lead to deeper mutual understanding and greater cooperation. Seeing and experiencing enhances learning. The acquisition of knowledge and skills must go together with the acquisition of attitudes and values.

The third dimension suggests that Europe is encapsulated in the dimensions of culture, time and area. Culture includes particular features of society and the creative heritage of civilisation. Time refers to the past, present and future. Area is not restricted to the EU countries. Exploration of shifting borders and the impact of changes in central and eastern Europe is needed to understand the dynamic and evolving nature of Europe.

Although there is no unique prescribed route for implementing a European dimension in schools and teacher education institutions, Shennan's three dimensional model presents a structured view that could be used to consider how a European dimension might be integrated into curricular elements in a systematic way.

A whole-school or institutional policy is needed which includes a statement of aims for the European dimension, specific objectives, a management strategy, identification of staffing and resource implications and a development plan. Such an approach is necessary to assure the quality of a European dimension in education.

THE EUROPEAN DIMENSION IN SCOTTISH EDUCATION

Since 1972 there has been an office of the CBEVE in Edinburgh and it has been actively promoting European links and exchanges. The gradual development towards establishing the single European market, gave impetus to the discussions concerning the role of education and sharpened the focus on trying to promote a European dimension in Scotland. Added to this, the 1988 Resolution prompted a response from the UK Government (DES, 1991) which included Scotland. The policy statement set out the government's objectives for the European dimension which were in line with those of the resolution. It created an official framework whereby the government's legislative role relates to taking appropriate central initiatives to assist and encourage the dissemination of good practice. The responsibility for implementation is placed with the local authorities. In Scotland, responsibility to ensure that the European dimension is adequately covered in the curriculum and in associated examinations falls to the Scottish Consultative Council on the Curriculum (SCCC) and to the Scottish Qualifications Authority (SQA).

The policy also encouraged support for language learning and teaching, bilateral links and exchanges, and facilitation of the implementation of EU action programmes.

The Scottish Office Education and Industry Department's (SOEID) strategy has been developed within the framework of the government's policy. In 1990, the Scottish Office set up an International Relations Branch (IRB). Two of its first objectives were provision of easy access to information about the EU and establishment of a number of networks to facilitate the development of the European dimension.

The structure for dissemination of information and coordination of developments takes the form of a triangle. At the apex is the IRB with a Eurydice unit, which is part of an information network for senior policy-makers in ministries and education authorities throughout the member states. The triangle's base is completed by Eurodesk and CBEVE. Eurodesk provides information more generally about the EU programmes and supports developments in the European dimension in local authorities, schools, further and higher education institutions. The functions of CBEVE are as already described. This triangle is further strengthened by links to other Scottish agencies. The IRB believes that this concept of networking is the key to the development of the European dimension in education.

In 1994, the SOEID published *Scottish Education and the European Community – Policy, Strategy and Practice'* (SOEID, 1994); this set out the government's policy and priorities, the legal basis for European Community action and the SOEID's strategy. It also included a chapter on the European dimension in practice, which covers all levels of education. The paper concluded with a useful checklist for institutional self-assessment, which used the framework, education through Europe, education for Europe and education about Europe.

The first priority was providing guidance to encourage schools to develop a European dimension. This was done through a series of conferences and publications. *Thinking European: Ideas for Integrating a European Dimension in the Curriculum* (SCCC, 1993) was published followed by a partner publication, *Sharing Responsibility* (SCCC, 1995). Both include examples of good practice. A supplement *Thinking European* (SCCC, 1997) provides further case studies of European activities in secondary and primary schools. These publications provide practical help for classroom teachers as well as providing evidence of the work that is going on in Scotland.

The SCCC also produced a short booklet on the European dimension which was included in a package of materials to promote cross-curricular issues, as part of the 5–14 development programme. The Scottish Council Development and Industry have developed a pack of materials, *Over to Europe* aimed at pupils in upper primary and lower secondary, which adds an economic and industrial perspective to the European dimension. The SQA offer several short courses in European studies and a series of National Certificate Modules on European aspects, such as 'Investigating Europe' and 'Experiencing Europe'. Some senior pupils now have the opportunity to undertake work experience in other European countries. For example, the 'Experiencing Europe' modules certificate students' achievements in planning, organising, undertaking and evaluating a European experience.

The General Teaching Council (GTC) also responded to the 1988 Resolution. It recognised the central role that teachers would have in developing a European dimension and that change within the system would only be effective if those responsible for delivering the curriculum were well trained. It issued a paper, *The European Dimension in Initial Teacher Education* (GTC, 1990), which stated that the objectives of the resolution should be achieved through the provision of a systematic and structured programme of training for the teachers who will deliver the curriculum. It recommended that all courses of initial teacher education for primary and secondary teachers should incorporate a European dimension from the start of 1992–3.

Local Authorities have all allocated some resources for the development of a European dimension which includes a European/International Coordinator. Prior to the new local authority arrangements there were twelve coordinators, the number has now risen to thirty-two. Consequently, some of the coordinators are new to the job and have limited experience of the European dimension. However, several authorities have experienced coordinators and some have set up European awareness groups to produce policy statements and action plans. The education authority coordinators meet regularly with the IRB to ensure a two-way exchange of information. The CBEVE also works closely with the coordinators to promote the European action programmes within schools, by means of information days and newsletters.

ISSUES, CONCERNS AND DEVELOPMENTS

Some schools have been involved in European education for some time and would not regard it as something new. They are well aware of the opportunities that exist to participate in EU programmes and have established good links with other schools in Europe. As case studies demonstrate their teachers have recognised the practical value that can be derived from partnerships with other European schools.

Participating in an EU programme is one way of enhancing a school's European profile. Around seventy secondary schools in Scotland have either applied to the COMENIUS programme for funding or are at the stage of putting together an application. The number of primary schools involved is similar. There are benefits to be gained for teachers as well as pupils: the programme offers opportunities to work with a team of teachers from at least two other European countries to develop a joint curriculum project. Finding out about other systems and other ways of working enables teachers to reflect on their own methods, it broadens experience and generates new enthusiasm. Set against this, it is necessary to invest time and energy and requires the backing of the management team. The complexity of applying for funding and reporting on a European project is daunting. If the European Commission adopted a more streamlined approach, this might encourage more schools to take up the opportunities that European programmes offer.

Another way of sharing experience is the Curriculum Awards Scheme administered by the CBEVE. The aim of this UK-wide initiative is to recognise outstanding curriculum development which promotes the European dimension. Scottish primary and secondary schools have consistently been winners of one of the awards.

Although many schools have recognised the benefits of a European dimension, there are many more which have not. Some are still at the stage of wondering what it is about, whether it should be included in the curriculum, and if so, how it should be done. They appear to lack information and have no realisation of the funding possibilities or the advantages that may be gained from European links.

Like other members of society, not all educationalists believe in the construction of a European Union and it may appear to some that promoting a European dimension would be synonymous with a pro-European approach. They may feel that including a European dimension in education has more to do with political and economic issues, than educational ones. However, the educational process must prepare pupils for the reality of Europe and enable them to develop a critical consciousness. Experiences should provide them with opportunities to discuss advantages and disadvantages and explore such concepts as the nation state and the construction and deconstruction of the regions within Europe. Critical thinking should be both the means and the outcome of developing a European dimension.

Differing political, economic, social, or ideological stances will inevitably lead to differing points of view on European issues. Any input which incorporates a European dimension will seldom be value-free. The view taken will be partly dependent on each individual's personal, regional and national identity. Teachers need to be conscious of their own value stance and reflect on the influence that it has on their decisions regarding selection of content and methodology when including a European dimension in their work.

In the past the purpose of education has often been linked to 'nation-building'. Some teachers may feel that they play a major role in maintaining cultural traditions and values and see a tension between promoting European citizenship and national citizenship. However, strengthening a feeling of European citizenship does not mean adopting a Eurocentric approach or doing away with cultural diversity or national identity. There is no suggestion that the European dimension is about creating a melting pot of European cultures. The European treaties and resolutions seek to promote an understanding of Europe as a multi-cultural, multi-lingual community. Their purpose is not to eliminate differences, but to encourage people to learn to understand and appreciate them. Learning about other nations, regions and cultures and communicating with pupils in other European countries will enable pupils to reflect on their Scottish and regional identity and how these relate to being a citizen of the EU.

When considering the already packed curriculum teachers may feel reluctant to introduce another dimension. They may justify this position by looking to what they believe the priorities regarding the education of their pupils are. However, the European dimension should not be viewed as an extra subject to be added but as a way of thinking about the whole curriculum in not just a Scottish context, but a European one. Like all cross curricular issues the aims must be made clear so that opportunities to learn about Europe and for Europe are made explicit. Adding opportunities to learn through Europe will require additional work to establish links, but will ultimately benefit pupils and teachers and enrich the curricular areas.

The debate about a definition of the European dimension, its rationale and place in education is ongoing. Although some teachers are able to cope with this lack of consensus, others may feel unsure about how to proceed. There is a general lack of understanding about Europe partly because the concept is surrounded by myths and misinformation. Teachers and teacher educators need to be equipped with the necessary knowledge, skills and competences to implement a European dimension. This is especially necessary in the area of new communication technology, particularly the use of multimedia and the role it plays in developing European activities.

At pre-service level, all the teacher education institutions would claim to include a European dimension in their course work with four year B.Ed. students, but not all do so in any coordinated way. Similar to the situation in schools, there are examples of good practice, with a range of activities included in the curricular work either as a permeative feature, a specific module or an elective course. Pressures on course content are also evident: opportunities for students on a one year PGCE course to gain experience in the European dimension are much more limited.

A small number of Scottish students have benefited from short placements in teacher education institutions in another country. However, demand for other European students wishing to study in Scotland is far higher. While students from Denmark and the Netherlands for example, view an exchange as a positive advantage, Scottish students appear to be reluctant to take time out of their courses. They do not seem to have grasped the value of a study period in another European country. There are many factors which contribute to this situation, not least the perceived effect on employment prospects. Students need to be provided with clearer information regarding the benefits of a European profile.

Higher education institutions participating in the SOCRATES programme are required to be more structured in their planning and approach to the European dimension. They must provide a European policy statement and an action plan outlining how European activities will be implemented. Although this is a time-consuming bureaucratic task, rewarded by limited funding, it does serve to clarify institutional aims regarding European work and may make European activities more explicit in the work of the institution as a whole.

The fact that Europe is multi-lingual emphasises the need for more and better language teaching to enable participation in a mobile multicultural world. However, Scotland is on the edge of Europe and crossing national, cultural and linguistic boundaries is not a regular occurrence for most people. Added to this the 'lingua franca' in cross-cultural communication is usually English; this inevitably reduces the need and consequently the motivation for people in Scotland to learn another European language. Since language is closely linked to culture and identity this lack of competence in languages continues to create a barrier not just to communication, but to understanding others. Initiatives in Scotland, like the primary modern language project have raised European awareness at an earlier age and provided an introduction to learning other languages, but there is still a long way to go to improve competence. Continuous development of languages throughout the educational process must remain high on the priority list of policy-makers.

IN CONCLUSION

The structure of implementation of the European dimension in Scottish education has been a combination of limited centralised guidance and grassroots initiatives in some schools, colleges and universities. The emerging picture is one of pockets of good practice in relatively few schools, driven by the interest and enthusiasm of motivated individuals. Much more needs to be done in all sectors of education to extend the existing frontiers of educational practice beyond an insular view.

The immediate target for action must be staff development for teacher educators and teachers. Such action has resource implications which will have to be addressed nationally. Limited European inservice is available but the European pot of money will inevitably be divided more thinly as the Community continues to enlarge. It will not meet all the national needs. The distinct lack of any explicit reference to the European dimension in the latest UK and Scottish educational documents does not augur well for government funding for European education. However, the new Scottish parliament will have increased representation in Brussels and European issues may be looked on in a different light in the new political climate.

There are many hurdles to surmount to ensure that Scottish students and pupils are prepared to meet the challenges of an integrated European society. New personal, professional and vocational skills, competences and attitudes are required which in turn demand different teaching approaches. Scottish education in the twenty-first century has a crucial role to play in preparing young people to survive, make a living and give sense to their lives in different social contexts in a unifying Europe.

In summary, significant developments include:

- increase in the number of schools applying to and participating in the COMENIUS programme;
- successes for primary and secondary schools in the Curriculum Awards Scheme;
- publication of SOEID's *Scottish Education and the European Community – Policy, Strategy and Practice;*
- publication of materials providing practical guidance for implementation of a European dimension;
- development of national certificate modules in European issues;
- development of a European policy statement and an action plan for implementing European activities in higher education institutions participating in the SOCRATES programme;
- local authority coordinators stimulating interest and developing understanding through inservice days, European evenings and newsletters;
- links between school and industry including European work experience;
- primary modern language initiative.

Issues and concerns which remain include:

- teacher educators and teachers' variable awareness and understanding of the European dimension in the curriculum;
- lack of systematic inclusion of a European dimension in the curriculum in schools and in courses for student teachers;
- lack of recognition of the European dimension in recent government educational documents;
- teachers and student teachers' lack of awareness of the benefits of mobility programmes;
- complexity of European programmes' application/reporting procedures;
- insufficient funding of a European dimension at European and national level;
- need for more and better language teaching;
- need to broaden the view of education beyond a parochial perspective;
- need for staff development in all sectors of education.

REFERENCES

DES (1991) *The European Dimension in Education – A Statement of the UK Government's Policy and Report of Activities Undertaken to Implement the EC Resolution of 24 May 1988*, London: Department of Education and Science.

GTC (1990) *The European Dimension in Initial Teacher Training*, Edinburgh: General Teaching Council.

SCCC (1993,1997) *Thinking European*, Dundee: Scottish Consultative Council on the Curriculum.

SCCC (1995) *Sharing Responsibility*, Dundee: Scottish Consultative Council on the Curriculum.

Shennan, M. (1991) *Teaching About Europe*, London: Cassell.

SOEID (1994) *Scottish Education and the European Community – Policy, Strategy and Practice*, Edinburgh: Scottish Office Education and Industry Department.

104

SCOTCAT Arrangements

Joan Menmuir

THE SCOTCAT FRAMEWORK

In the early 1990s, the extension of the university system led to the replacement of the Council for National Academic Awards (CNAA) by the Higher Education Quality Council (HEQC) as the body responsible for quality assurance and quality improvement of academic programmes. In 1997 HEQC formally became the Quality Assurance Agency for Higher Education (QAA). The early responsibilities of HEQC included the development of credit systems, begun by CNAA in response to the need for more open and flexible systems of higher education (HE), and in 1991 the Scottish Credit Accumulation and Transfer (SCOTCAT) framework was established as the national credit framework for HE in Scotland.

The framework is based on the recognition of a number of key principles, agreement on a common system of credit points and levels and agreement to cooperate in the development of credit-based learning, including links with employment based learning and programmes of continuing professional development. By early 1992, the SCOTCAT framework had the formal agreement of all HE institutions in Scotland and is being increasingly adopted as the basis for organising provision.

In 1993 the Scottish Advisory Committee for Credit and Access(SACCA) was set up jointly by the Committee of Scottish Higher Education Principals (COSHEP) and HEQC to advise them and the higher education sector generally on matters relating to credit and access. From it, the SCOTCAT Development Group and various subject-based specialist fora evolved and began to undertake a variety of activities to support the development and quality assurance of credit-based learning and access across the sector.

The SCOTCAT Teacher Education Group (STEG), one of the specialist fora, was established in 1993, its members being drawn from all the institutions in Scotland with a role in initial teacher education and continuing professional development. It also includes representation from the Scottish Office Education and Industry Department (SOEID) and from the SCOTCAT Development Group.

PROFESSIONAL DEVELOPMENT OPPORTUNITIES FOR TEACHERS

By 1993, each of the HE providers in Scotland with an interest in teacher education had developed an individual approach to accrediting continuing professional development opportunities for teachers. They had begun to complement the traditional, non-assessed and very practical inservice course provision by a range of opportunities to gather postgraduate academic credit for professional development work undertaken. The accredited provision was in the main at postgraduate level since all teachers in Scotland already had first degrees or their equivalent along with or including their initial qualification. There was, however, considerable variation from institution to institution in the composition and requirements of a postgraduate award.

During 1994–5 the SCOTCAT Development Group led the development of the first edition of the SCOTCAT Quality Assurance handbook (HEQC, 1995) which gave further definition to the SCOTCAT framework. This was used by STEG as it worked with the teacher education sector to develop an agreed Scottish framework for the provision of postgraduate credit-rated professional development opportunities for teachers at masters level. Particular issues like definitions of level and effort, progression within awards, and accreditation of prior learning were discussed by the group, and agreed understandings emerged. Agreement about what constituted off-campus learning and how it could be quality assured was more difficult, but the SCOTCAT framework proved helpful and reassured providers that participation in collaborative arrangements did not undermine the autonomy of individual institutions (HEQC, 1996). Publication of a teachers' guide to SCOTCAT (SOEID, 1996) followed.

The level of collaboration achieved means that all providers of postgraduate masters awards for teachers in Scotland have now adopted the SCOTCAT framework to define their awards. Most awards have a twelve module structure with each module credit rated at fifteen Scottish Masters (SM) points and requiring 150 hours of notional student effort. Credit points are awarded for the achievement of appropriate learning outcomes and a masters award is achieved by the accumulation of 180 SM points of credit. Each module has a general credit rating attached to it, based on the SCOTCAT tariff, and set by the awarding institution, and other institutions can make judgements about how much specific credit to award the learning if a teacher wants to transfer credit into one of their awards. Relevance of the learning to the chosen award and currency of the learning are the factors which are considered. This arrangement means that teachers can transfer credit from one institution to another while, at the same time, individual institutions can maintain their autonomy.

Scotland has therefore developed a national system for teachers to gather continuing professional development credit at masters level; the system is competitive in terms of choice and availability of opportunities, but the competition is conducted within a cooperative and enabling framework which has clear and accountable quality features. The SCOTCAT arrangements have contributed significantly to this success.

ACCREDITATION OF PRIOR LEARNING (APL)

One of the key principles of SCOTCAT is that appropriate learning at higher education level, wherever it occurs and provided it can be assessed, can be given credit towards an academic award. This principle has led to a number of curriculum development initiatives focusing in particular on links between the traditionally academic content of postgraduate courses and the more sharply focused requirements of the world of work.

Using the principle, it is possible to look back on a professional career and identify previous learning, normally within the last five years, which can be used to gain credit within a current award. Institutions can decide how much prior formal learning (APFL) and prior experiential learning (APEL) credit to allocate in this way though the amount is normally defined at a maximum of 50 per cent of any award. Where the learning has not been previously formally assessed, but is derived from professional experience in the workplace, the learning can be assessed by using a portfolio of evidence or by undertaking pre-specified assessment tasks which map the prior experiential learning onto the outcomes of an existing part of a current award. This method of gaining credit has been welcomed by teachers and by their employers who see it as a way of gaining professional recognition for work undertaken in the recent past.

A SHEFC sponsored development project in 1996 with Glasgow Caledonian University, Strathclyde University, Paisley University and Glasgow University produced a set of APEL guidelines for institutions (Reeve and Smith, 1996) and this has been followed by a further project to make student support material available on the Internet.

ACCREDITATION OF WORK BASED LEARNING

Just as it is possible to look back to prior learning as a source of credit, it is also possible to look forward and use current or planned learning in a similar way. This offers opportunities for relevant current work-based activity that is not being assessed in another way to gain credit within an award. Different institutions will have different mechanisms available to credit such learning but most will use some form of work-based learning agreement.

Unlike the accreditation of prior learning, the proportion of an award which can be achieved through the accreditation of current or planned learning is less likely to be limited and in some cases an entire award can be gained through project activity of this type. A SHEFC sponsored development project in 1996 with Strathclyde University, Paisley University and St Andrews College produced a guide to professional development through work-based learning agreements for schools (Thomson, Menmuir et al., 1996) and this has been followed up in Strathclyde University by a support pack for students.

GAINS FOR THE TEACHER EDUCATION SYSTEM

The development of the SCOTCAT framework and the use of that framework in developing continuing professional development for teachers has been of significant benefit to teacher education. It has contributed to a more vigorous debate about the purpose of continuing professional development in teaching. It has also been instrumental in generating a new set of masters level awards which are designed to meet the current needs of teachers and employers. Teachers themselves can now choose where and when to access their professional opportunities for credit-based learning and employers can negotiate and customise curriculum to meet ever changing demands. However, most importantly, through the shared language of credit, SCOTCAT has shown that it is possible to develop a collaborative framework which benchmarks standards for continuing professional development while allowing for individuality and flexibility in provision.

CURRENT ISSUES

One of the most significant benefits of the general debate about qualifications which has been promoted through the introduction of SCOTCAT arrangements in Scotland has been the need to think closely about the links between academic, vocational and professional awards. All those concerned with quality and standards in continuing professional development for teachers are currently involved in this debate. New masters awards (M.Sc. and M.Ed.) fully in line with the SCOTCAT framework and the now emerging taught doctorates in education (Ed.D.) focus on academic and professional development and are defined through learning outcomes and, at masters level, through credit. These awards complement, and could be argued to be largely replacing, the more traditional academic masters and research doctorates as the award bearing continuing professional development route of choice for teachers. As the SCOTCAT framework and credit definitions continue to develop to accommodate doctoral work in response to the *Review of Postgraduate Education* chaired by Martin Harris (HEFCE, CVCP, SCOP, 1996), the trend looks set to continue.

If and when the competences required for teachers in practice are specified by the Secretary of State for Scotland, with inevitably different competence requirements for different work roles, there are strong arguments for linking measurements of the achievement of these standards to the developing framework for postgraduate level awards. Can existing postgraduate awards for teachers be used or developed to measure all aspects of these competences? The experience of other professional bodies, who already define post initial competences, suggests that some competences will be met through learning outcome definitions in existing HE awards but some will require evidence from the field. If this is the case in teacher education, then how will these other aspects of competence be measured and quality assured and by whom? Where and how will they fit into the developing postgraduate credit framework?

The role of the professional body, the General Teaching Council (GTC) in these developments is also of current concern. The standards of initial training have been carefully monitored by the GTC over many years but the challenge for the Council now is to develop working practices that enable it to operate effectively in the wide ranging and rapidly changing area of continuing professional development. Quality assurance and standards in continuing professional development are not only the concern of providers and employers, they are clearly also important to the professional body and to teachers themselves.

The role of SCOTCAT in initial teacher education is also currently under discussion. Can the framework be used to credit-rate initial teacher education which currently involves meeting both specific undergraduate learning outcomes and standards of competence? The results of a project on undergraduate levels, designed to contribute to understanding of graduate qualities in Scotland and currently being undertaken by QAA, will be used to take forward further work on levels in initial teacher education awards. A start was made in STEG by looking at levels in the Postgraduate Certificate of Education, one of the traditional initial teacher education awards (STEG papers, 1996) and, more recently, STEG has set up a sub-group to look at academic and professional levels in all initial teacher education courses. But will an undergraduate credit framework for initial teacher education be able to accommodate issues such as student mobility, prior learning and part-time training?

FUTURE DEVELOPMENTS

In 1997, The National Committee of Inquiry into Higher Education in *Higher Education in the Learning Society* (The Dearing Report, HMSO, 1997) recommended the adoption of a framework for all higher education qualifications which recognised achievement, encompassed vocational and academic qualifications and facilitated the development, understanding and uptake of life long learning opportunities. The Scottish Committee of the Inquiry recommended an integrated qualification framework for Scotland based on levels of study and SCOTCAT credit points. The possibility of a Scottish Credit and Qualifications Framework is already being considered by a SACCA convened joint group of senior representatives of SOEID, COSHEP, SQA and QAA. The common framework has the potential to accommodate all forms of post-compulsory provision and achievement but will not impinge on the autonomy of the different awards frameworks nor will it provide automatic credit transfer or establish artificial equivalence between awards. SCOTCAT arrangements have played a considerable part in the initial success of credit-based learning in teacher education. The profession will benefit from using the new Scottish Credit and Qualifications Framework to meet the challenges ahead.

REFERENCES

HEQC (1995) *The SCOTCAT Quality Assurance Handbook*, London: Higher Education Quality Council.

HEQC (1996) The SCOTCAT Teacher Education Group Forum Conference. *The Interpretation of the SCOTCAT Quality Assurance Guidelines for Teacher Education*, Conference Report. Glasgow: Higher Education Quality Council.

Reeve, F. and I. Smith (1996) *Accrediting Prior Experiential Learning: A Manual for Good Practice in Higher Education*, Glasgow: Glasgow Caledonian University.

SOEID (1996) *Academic Credit and Staff Development: A Teachers' Guide to The Scottish Credit Accumulation and Transfer Framework (SCOTCAT)*, Edinburgh: HMSO.

STEG papers (1996) At the SCOTCAT Internet site http://www.mailbase.ac.uk/lists/scotcat-cats/ a collection of papers relevant to teacher education can be located under 'other files'. The SCOTCAT mailbase group can be joined by sending a message to mailbase@mailbase.ac.uk which says join scotcat-cats first name second name.

Thomson, W. P., J. G. Menmuir, et al. (1996) *Professional Development through Work Based Learning Agreements: A Guide for Schools*, Glasgow: University of Strathclyde.

105

Research and Practice

Pamela Munn

For a long time research, in Scotland as elsewhere, was something done to teachers rather than by teachers. Researchers would typically be commissioned by the Scottish Office to investigate areas causing concern, or be asked to evaluate major innovations in curriculum or assessment or school governance, for example. In addition, researchers themselves would have ideas they wanted to explore and theories they wanted to test. Teachers are certainly involved in these kinds of research projects. They are typically subjects of it: they are interviewed, their classroom practice is observed, they are asked to complete questionnaires and the curriculum and assessment materials they use are analysed. But such research has typically very slight impact on classroom practice. One reason is that teachers have no real 'ownership' of the research. They have not decided on the topic under investigation and are usually not consulted about how the topic might be conceptualised in such a way as to inform practice. Not surprisingly, therefore, teachers have paid very little attention to these kinds of research as not impinging on matters of direct practical concern to them. Or where the research does, as in the case of the evaluation of curriculum implementation, findings can all too easily portray teachers as 'deficient' in terms of skills and knowledge. Thus research findings can often be presented as identifying things which teachers ought to be doing and are not. Research findings rarely celebrate that elusive phenomenon, good practice, in schools and classrooms and on the rare occasions they do, seem not to be concerned with exploring ways in which examples of good practice in specific schools might be useful to schools in general.

This chapter considers the relationship between research and practice by exploring answers to the following questions.

- Should educational research aim directly to inform practice? If so, what are the conditions necessary for this to take place?
- What distinctive contribution, if any, does action research make to practice?
- Are teacher networks a feasible way of applying research and sharing practice?

The chapter concludes with some speculative comment about the future of educational research and its relationship to practice.

SHOULD EDUCATIONAL RESEARCH AIM DIRECTLY TO INFORM PRACTICE?

Writing on educational research typically distinguishes basic or 'blue skies' research from applied or practical research (Dockrell, 1984; Nisbet, 1988; Hammersley, 1997; Hargreaves,

1997). Basic research, or research for enlightenment, concerns challenging and changing assumptions, for example, about how learning takes place, or about conceptions of ability or about the structure of knowledge. Such research is not intended directly or immediately to affect practice. Rather its function is to contribute to the way we see the world of education, 'influencing aspirations . . . and offering new insights' (Nisbet, 1988, p. 17). Research for enlightenment thus has an indirect influence on practice and indeed on policy too, but its prime function is that of extending knowledge for its own sake rather than helping us to do our current work better. Many commentators would accept, therefore, that a legitimate function of research is to extend knowledge rather than deliberately and immediately to inform and to improve practice.

Whether the enlightenment model is sufficient justification for educational research has been hotly contested, most recently between Hargreaves and Hammersley. In a widely reported lecture to the Teacher Training Agency, Hargreaves (1996) argued that teaching should be based much more on evidence from research. Drawing an analogy with professional practice in medicine he contended that educational research had failed to address the issues of direct relevance to teachers. Hammersley argues that educational research cannot have the impact on practice which Hargreaves would like to see. While Hammersley (1997, p. 147) acknowledges that 'an important ultimate aim of all research should be to produce knowledge that is practically relevant', he contends that the very nature of teaching makes it unlikely that research will be able to offer solutions to problems of practice, and criticises Hargreaves as taking a too instrumentalist or technicist view of teaching, one which sees a role for the following of rules to solve problems rather than making complex judgements. Hargreaves (1997, p. 406) in turn disputes this, arguing:

> Doctors and teachers are *similar* in that they make decisions involving complex judgements. Many doctors draw upon research about the effects of their practice to inform and improve their decisions; most teachers do not.

Their dispute concerns both the nature of teaching and the ability of research to provide valid and reliable evidence to inform practice. Certainly in Scotland, and probably elsewhere, there has been an assumption that one purpose of educational research was to inform practice. This assumption is based on the notion that there are teaching techniques which can be learned but that their use is not automatic and requires under-standing both of the context in which teaching is taking place and of the rationale underlying particular techniques (see below). Hargreaves has done a great service in stimulating debate about the relationship between research and practice, and in jolting people working in interpretative traditions as researchers or as commissioners of research out of the intellectual laziness of weak claims to validity and reliability, and hence to the purpose of such research, that are often made.

Turning to research in Scotland, we know from research on the origins of the Scottish Council for Research in Education (SCRE) that the founders' concerns were that research should raise the level of efficiency in school work. (See Chapter 108.) Indeed, throughout its existence SCRE has had to take account of expectations of funders and others that the research it conducted would make a practical contribution to solving problems of the day. Nisbet (1988) draws attention to a range of early studies by SCRE with a strong practical slant, such as *Studies in Arithmetic, Addition and Subtraction Facts and Processes* and *The Writing of Arabic Numbers*. Recent work continues this trend including work on, for example, *Health Education and Promotion in Schools, An Evaluation of Drug Education in Scottish Schools* and *Teachers' and Pupils' Days in the Primary Classroom.*

This practical slant is echoed by the Scottish Office Education and Industry Department (SOEID), a major funder of educational research in Scotland. It clearly expects some of the research it funds to have an impact on practice. It has signalled this by:

- sponsoring national conferences to disseminate findings and promote discussion;
- funding a series of summaries of research findings, *Interchange*, distributed free of charge to all schools and other appropriate educational institutions;
- commissioning resource packs derived from research for use in schools and classrooms;
- commissioning an evaluation of the use and impact of these resource packs;
- commissioning a study of the relationship between research and staff development.

And other major funding bodies such as the Economic and Social Research Council (ESRC) indicate that the role of 'users', either in helping to define the research focus or in taking up findings, is an important criterion in securing funding for research. It is probably uncontentious to suggest that some research ought to inform practice. What are more contentious are the criteria for judging the kind of research which teachers should take seriously and which should inform practice and the proper balance between research for enlightenment and applied research.

WHAT KIND OF RESEARCH SHOULD INFORM PRACTICE?

One approach described by Harlen is drawn from the medical profession. She describes the guidelines being used by doctors in Scotland to judge the quality of evidence and thus whether it should be taken more or less seriously in terms of practice. Six levels of evidence are identified. 'At the highest level stands evidence from meta-analysis of several rando-mised controlled trials; at the lowest level is evidence obtained from expert committee reports or opinions and/or clinical experience of respected authorities' (quoted in Hargreaves, 1997). Adapting this approach to classify evidence from educational research it is clear that we have comparatively little evidence at the highest level. Furthermore, we have comparatively little meta-analysis of evidence from case studies, surveys, experiments and so on, regarding particular substantive issues. Recent moves by the Scottish Office to commission research reviews are, therefore, welcome, especially where there is explicit encouragement to move beyond description to critical commentary on the robustness of evidence.

This is not to devalue studies of single cases. Indeed one could argue that sociological studies of grammar and secondary modern schools such as Lacey's *Hightown Grammar*, published by Manchester University Press in 1970, and Hargreaves' *Social Relations in the Secondary School*, published by Routledge and Kegan Paul in 1967, did much to contribute to the debate about the desirability of selection at age eleven. These kinds of studies helped to raise awareness about the consequences of selection among and within schools and added a different dimension to the debate on selection from that on the validity and reliability of the IQ test as a selection instrument; in themselves they provide a nice illustration of research designed to improve an existing system (IQ testing) and research which challenged assumptions upon which the system rested. The key driving force behind the abolition of selection, however, was the ideological commitment of the Labour governments of the

1960s. Conservative governments of the 1980s and 1990s with a different ideological stance changed tack and began reintroducing selection. As Nisbet (1986, p. 16) points out, research can inform practice only 'in non-controversial areas where there is a consensus on values'. If it were accepted that there are several issues on which there is a consensus on values and thus on which research might be expected to inform practice, one might ask why research based practice is not more in evidence. There are several ways of answering this question. One approach is to try to identify the conditions which would need to be met if research based practice is to be taken seriously as a goal worth striving for. The first six of the conditions identified here apply principally to teachers, the others apply to researchers and funders of research.

First, the research has to be on a topic of direct, practical concern to teachers. Research on learning to read, on bullying, on children with visual and aural impairment accessing the curriculum, are but a few examples which readily spring to mind. Second, teachers need, therefore, to have a voice in the decisions about the focus of research which is to be undertaken. Hargreaves (1996) advocates a National Educational Research Forum for this purpose. In the mid-1980s SCRE experimented with a National Forum as a way of determining research priorities to be funded via the Scottish Office. It was not a success. It was difficult to reach consensus on priorities; there was perhaps a lack of understanding of the ability of research to deliver immediate answers to problems; and the Scottish Office was unwilling to relinquish control of its research budget. It therefore remained the key player in determining priorities. Third, research findings have to be made accessible to teachers. Fourth, teachers need to be convinced about the validity and reliability of research findings, and the robustness of the evidence on which their practice is based. Fifth, findings have to be developed into guidance for practice. Research findings and their implications for practice are two very different things. Sixth, time and skills to read and assess research findings and the associated implications for practice have to be made available to teachers. This implies a radical change to current conditions of service including those relating to professional development and its accreditation.

Seventh, professional researchers and those who fund research should promote replication studies so that a cumulative body of evidence is available on a particular topic. Eighth, time and money have to be provided for meta-analysis. Ninth, longitudinal work is necessary so that effects of particular strategies can be analysed over time. Tenth, a much more strategic view has to be taken of practical research priorities, rather than the 'one damn thing after another' syndrome which typifies much current practice. The funding of research programmes on a specific area, rather than unconnected short term projects which allow time only for data gathering and descriptions rather than serious analysis, should be the norm. Eleventh, there would be a move away from the current system of competitive tendering for external research funds which results in more funding being spent on the competition than in doing research. Twelfth, better systems of accountability need to be developed within faculties of education for the use of research funds allocated through the government's 'dual support' system of funding for teaching and research in higher education.

No doubt other conditions might be identified. However, if the above represents the beginnings of an analysis of what might be needed in order for research more adequately to inform practice then a formidable but by no means impossible agenda lies ahead. There are signs that on the funding and research side some movement in the direction outlined is taking place. More needs to be done.

ACTION RESEARCH

So far, the discussion has been in terms of research conducted by professional researchers and its relationship to practice. Many commentators would argue that the way to bring research and practice into closer alignment is for teachers themselves to carry out the research. Thus the gap between research and action is bridged because research is carried out by teachers on an issue of direct practical concern to them with the express purpose of bringing about change. In contrast to the concerns about validity and reliability which characterise traditional research:

> Action research is concerned with exploring the multiple determinants of actions, interactions and interpersonal relationships in unique contexts. Its aim is to deepen practitioners' understanding of the complex situations in which they live and work, so that their actions are better informed. Rather than specific 'findings' or 'outcomes' action research generates . . . 'practical wisdom' [or] situational understanding. (Somekh 1995, p. 341)

The founding father of action research was Kurt Lewin, a social psychologist whose concerns were raising productivity in factories and increasing law and order in neighbourhoods through democratic participation rather than autocratic coercion. The key characteristics were reflection, action and collaborative endeavour. An important criticism of Lewin's seminal work in productivity is that it did not 'take explicit account of the power bases that define social roles and strongly influence the process of any change in the modes of production' (Adelman, C., 1993, in Kurt Lewis and the Origins of Action Research, *International Journal of Action Research*, 1.1 p. 10). This criticism was also evident in the application of action research to educational settings and Lewin himself lamented that community councils did not 'discriminate between the democratic aims of social science and the technocracy of which they had prior experience' (ibid., p. 11). In other words action research could be used to improve a system, tinkering with superficial glitches, rather than presenting fundamental challenges to the values on which the system was based. The same issue is characteristic of much action research today.

At a time of increasing pressure on educational researchers to demonstrate the relevance of their work, action research has become a major feature of many advanced level courses for teachers and almost all education faculties in the UK would claim to be in the business of developing 'reflective practitioners' in both initial teacher training and in advanced certificates, diplomas and degrees. Whether all mean the same thing by reflective practice is open to question. For some reflective practice means teachers being aware of their professional context; for others it means teachers doing a bit of data gathering on a topic of direct practical concern to them and relating their analysis of the data to the relevant literature; for others again it means taking action based on evidence teachers themselves have collected. Action can range from developing a particular technique such as questioning, to challenging the purpose and moral order of schooling. There are thus different 'schools' of action research. Debates about the meaning and purpose of and support for action research have, however, not been evident in Scotland.

In Scotland's teacher education institutions it is commonplace for BEd degree students to undertake a substantial piece of action research as part of their studies. Postgraduate students in secondary education do likewise and need to achieve a pass in this part of their studies in order to complete the course successfully. In addition, the Scottish Council for Research in Education has established a teacher-researcher network. SCRE also awards a prize each year to teachers carrying out a piece of research outwith accredited advanced level work. The Scottish Educational Research Association (SERA) has supported teacher-researcher groups in various parts of Scotland and has helped to promote annual conferences for teacher-researchers. Teachers researching their own practice and that of their school are now features of school improvement programmes. HMI state in their report on *Standards and Quality in Scottish Schools 1992–95* that 'the most effective way of improving the quality of education for individual pupils is to expect schools to take responsibility for their own quality assurance by evaluating their performance and making the necessary changes'. To the casual observer, therefore, it might seem that the gap between research and practice has been bridged by the prevalence of and support for action research in the system. This is far from true. There are a number of reasons for this as well as that mentioned above, namely, the lack of critical engagement with the philosophy of action research by the education community in Scotland.

One reason is the very small number of teachers actively engaged in research. Action research is a process, an attitude of mind. Most of those who have had experience of action research would be expected to continue to be engaged in some form of self-reflective enquiry. Yet the number of those registered on SCRE's teacher research support network, or attending SERA action research seminars, is a tiny proportion of the total teaching force.

Another reason is the very nature of action research itself. It is typically a private matter for a teacher, a group, or a school. The work is seldom made public and so cumulative knowledge about specific areas of practice is hard to find. Rather, more is known about the triumphs and pitfalls of the process of engaging students and teachers in action research through accounts of academics supporting teachers in this work.

A third reason is the one alluded to by Donald McIntyre in his Presidential Address to the Annual Conference of the British Educational Research Association in 1996. This is the difficulty of doing high quality educational research. This is so not only for professional researchers but doubly so for teachers when the expertise required to teach well is rather different from that required to carry out a good piece of research. McIntyre is not persuaded of the realism of asking teachers to be the front runners in conducting educational research given the other demands on them as teachers. He sees a role for teachers in testing useful theories of educational practice provided by educational research. This, of course, reintroduces questions about who decides on the priorities for the focus of educational research and the role of teachers in this process.

NETWORKING

A possible interpretation of McIntyre's suggestion for the role of teachers in research is the development of networks among schools and teachers on topics where a cumulative body of research evidence exists. Two recent examples in Scotland are the Scottish Schools Ethos Network and the Promoting Positive Discipline Initiative.

The Ethos Network takes as its starting point the influence which school culture has on attainment and on behaviour. Research evidence from a range of school effectiveness studies, based on large samples in Britain, the United States and Australia, points to ethos as an important influence. Likewise a range of small-scale qualitative studies has explored the ways in which schools can promote positive behaviour. While some of this evidence does not meet the strongest criteria suggested above, and there is debate about how ethos can most adequately be conceptualised, there is an emerging consensus about the importance of school ethos. The first step, therefore, was to bring this conclusion to the attention of schools and to convince teachers about the evidential base for the importance of ethos. Highlighting the importance of ethos, however, is not much practical help to schools. Ethos by its very nature encompasses much that is taken for granted about school life, the rules, routines and rituals. It was, therefore, important to provide schools with tools to help them analyse and develop their ethos.

The Scottish Office commissioned a group of researchers to develop 'ethos indicators' and to suggest ways in which schools could 'take the temperature' of their ethos. A key feature was that views about aspects of school ethos should be sought from pupils, parents and where possible members of the local community. The network was prompted initially by a number of schools seeking advice about the collection and analysis of data about their ethos. It has grown beyond sharing experience of these technical details to include information and experience about the process of developing a positive ethos and a focus on substantive issues such as involving parents in curriculum work, pupil participation in decision-making and raising pupils' self-esteem. In this development of schools experimenting with the role of school culture on attainment and behaviour and, crucially, sharing experiences about this through the Network, McIntyre's view of teacher research can be seen in action. The value of teacher research in this context is less as a contribution to theory building than to theory testing. This being so, professional researchers should, over time, be looking for outcomes in terms of improved attainment and improved behaviour and correlating these with a range of activities promoting a positive ethos. With over 1,000 members the network can provide a sample which makes such a study feasible.

Likewise, in promoting positive discipline, we know from a number of studies that it is the effect of constant minor disruption which teachers find wearying. Talking out of turn, eating in class, arriving without books or materials and so on are the discipline problems faced by the majority of teachers, rather than violence, drug dealing and other more serious offences. Also known, from a range of studies, is the importance of teachers praising pupils' work, setting realistic targets for learning and behaviour, and involving pupils in rule setting and accompanying rewards and sanctions. Again, however, simply telling teachers to use praise more frequently or to set targets for behaviour is of little practical help. The promoting positive discipline initiative aims to share experience among schools about the use and effectiveness of a number of strategies including praise and reward schemes, playground development, and particular curriculum strategies such as social skills training. Schools involved in the initiative write up their experience in a three or four page case-study. Furthermore, local authorities are being encouraged to write about the approaches they are taking to co-ordinate and share information and experience across the authority.

These are examples of initiatives where teachers are involved in sharing experience through writing about the development, monitoring and evaluation of specific practices and in this way testing the relevance and applicability of research findings to their own situation. There are, of course, many other examples of research findings being used to inform practice. These include a recognition of the importance of homework in helping to raise achievement and the associated development of after school homework clubs; strategies for effective differentiation in the classroom and anti-bullying strategies, to name but a few. Much remains to be done, however, and there is certainly no room for complacency about the quality and impact of educational research in the future.

ISSUES FOR THE FUTURE

In this final section, three main directions for educational research are outlined and their probable consequences briefly considered. No-one can predict with certainty what the future holds for educational research but there are sufficient clues around for speculation to be more than uninformed guesswork.

The first direction will be for research to be more oriented towards practice than hitherto. Although the debate about this has been largely conducted in England, there is little doubt that the overwhelming government concern with raising standards and school improvement in the UK as a whole will put increasing pressure on research to contribute directly to this policy goal. If this is so, it might be expected that research programmes would be funded on, say, literacy, and numeracy rather than a scatter-gun approach of funding individual unconnected projects. The Economic and Social Research Council is already moving in this direction and similar moves are beginning to be seen in the Scottish Office with a number of projects being funded in early years education. More literature reviews and perhaps more longitudinal work can also be expected. The key principle will be that of directly informing practice and so one might begin to see development programmes attached to promising research programmes, although care will need to be taken to avoid the mistakes of the 'top-down' curriculum development initiatives of the 1960s and 1970s.

The second direction will be that of increased competition for research funds. Research is one of the few areas where higher education institutions are reasonably free to increase their income without incurring financial and other penalties. Thus research funds can help to buy books, equipment and support the running costs of cash-strapped institutions through charging overheads. Furthermore, research income is an indicator taken into account by the Research Assessment Exercise which judges the quality of educational (and other) research in higher education. The quality rating determines the amount of money which institutions receive from central government to support teaching and research. Competing for funds costs money, of course, and a recent account told of 600 applications for a European Union programme. If researchers are competing for funds they are not doing research and the situation could be fast approaching where the net costs to the system of bidding for funds exceeds the funds on offer.

The third direction will be that of internationally comparative research. Comparisons of pupil attainments in mathematics and science are now a regular source of evidence about the efficiency and effectiveness of Scottish schools. More of this, and of comparisons in further and higher education systems too, can be anticipated.

What does this mean for the enlightenment function of research? The short answer is that it is likely to be under threat. 'Blue skies' research involves risk taking. Sometimes there will be no pay-off, the research goes nowhere or, at best, its worth is not recognised. Funders of educational research will be under sustained pressure not to take risks, especially when funding for schools is tight. It becomes very hard to justify blue skies research if school buildings are in a state of disrepair and teachers are being made redundant. Thus the dual funding mechanism, whereby higher education institutions are funded to undertake teaching and research through a block grant needs to remain in some form if educational research for enlightenment is to continue. Research in cognitive science, brain functioning, information technology and the like all need to be supported if learning is to be understood more fully. Similarly, independent policy related research on issues such as gender, race and social class and education, special needs issues and curriculum frameworks, for instance, is needed to supply the grit in the system to provoke change in policy, in provision, and participation. In short, the heightened emphasis on relevance and practicality must leave room for research with other purposes. Nisbet (1988, p. 14 & p. 22) provides a neat summing up.

> I suggest comparing education to cheese, which has many varieties with different qualities. Research on cheese is complicated by the plurality of tastes and values . . . We must recognise different styles of research and different ways in which it may contribute to education.

Research and practice are inevitably interlinked because the purpose of all research is surely ultimately to improve practice. Research does so in different ways and with different time scales in mind and the link with practice may be hard to discern in some cases as the application of findings or theory building may only gradually emerge. The twin functions of research, to improve the present system and to present challenges to current thinking need to be cherished. The dual support system needs to be preserved in order to safeguard research for enlightenment. Serious thinking about developing conditions which would encourage stronger links between research and practice is also required. A small country such as Scotland is in a good position to take initiatives here, as representatives of the key stakeholders in the school system know each other and already have a strong base on which to build. Perhaps the new sense of self-confidence in Scotland as a country which is accompanying the establishment of a Scottish parliament means that the time is right to take forward new plans to link research and practice and to strive more energetically for an evidence-based teaching profession.

REFERENCES

Dockrell, W. B. (1984) Practical Research, in W. B. Dockrell (ed.) *An Attitude of Mind: Twenty Five Years of Educational Research in Scotland*, Edinburgh: Scottish Council for Research In Education.

Hammersley, M. (1997) Educational Research and Teaching: a response to David Hargreaves' TTA Lecture, *British Educational Research Journal* 23.2 pp. 141–62.

Hargreaves, D. H. (1996) *Teaching as a Research-based Profession*, London: Teacher Training Agency.

Hargreaves, D. H. (1997) In Defence of Research for Evidence-based Teaching: a rejoinder to Martyn Hammersley, *British Educational Research Journal* 23.4 pp. 405–20.

Nisbet, J. (1988) The Contribution of Research to Education, in S. Brown and R. Wake (eds) *Education in Transition: What Role for Research?* Edinburgh: Scottish Council for Research in Education.

Somekh, B. (1995) The Contribution of Action Research to Development in Social Endeavours: a position paper on action research methodology, *British Educational Research Journal* 21.3 pp. 339–55.

106

The Scottish Educational Research Association

Brian Morris

In this short chapter, it is impossible to attempt a complete history of the Scottish Educational Research Association (SERA), or pay sufficient attention to the activities of the individuals who founded, developed and now sustain it. What follows is a brief, but it is hoped, comprehensive account of the origins, developments and current activities of SERA.

AIMS AND ACTIVITIES

The SERA constitution identifies two aims:

- To disseminate educational research findings to all parties interested in education in Scotland.

- To promote cooperation and communication among research workers in various disciplines working in the educational field in Scotland.

The constitution states that this is to be achieved through a wide range of activities to include: the arrangement of conferences, seminars and symposia; the organisation of study groups on specific topics; publication and distribution of monographs, documents, bulletins and reports; the promotion and/or publication of a research journal; the editing and publishing of abstracts of research work; the promotion of research projects. SERA has pursued all of these at various times, but the most prominent in recent times have been regular one-day conferences on educational topics, a regular Newsletter, a teacher-researcher conference, and most prominently the SERA Annual Conference.

Throughout its existence SERA has been keen to promote the existence of a Scottish educational journal. Originally it was intended that SERA should publish its own journal. However, SERA policy is now to encourage its members to support the existing independent *Scottish Educational Review* (*SER*, See Chapter 107) through a preferential subscription scheme for SERA members and a regular voluntary donation to SER.

The association is run by an elected executive which organises itself into task-based sub-committees which reflect the activities identified above: Annual Conference; Teacher Research; Communications (with responsibility for one-day conferences or seminars). The Newsletter is published four times per year and is sent to all members. It contains reports of the activities of SERA Executive, continuing research and developments in education and relevant conference reports. The one-day conferences, described in its early years as 'local' conferences, have been a feature of SERA activity since the early 1980s, sometimes organised in conjunction with other bodies. Topics in the 1980s included, 'Qualitative Improvements in Secondary Education in a Time of Financial Stringency' (1982) and 'Multicultural Education' in 1984. More recent topics have included, 'The Impact of Local Government Change on Education' (1996) and 'The Future of Funded Research in Scottish Education' (1997).

The most prominent SERA activity is the Annual Conference, held over three days in September, which has become the most important national event for the dissemination and discussion of research.

MEMBERSHIP

Membership of SERA, which is individual, is 'open to those actively engaged in education in Scotland and interested individuals resident in Scotland'. Associate membership, which confers the same privileges as full membership is also open to interested individuals 'working outwith Scotland'.

SERA was founded in 1974, its original planning committee containing representatives from higher education, teacher unions, the SCE Examination Board and research societies in history and sociology. A factor in founding SERA was the imminent creation of a British Educational Research Association (Nisbet, 1995) which could be said to have accelerated the establishment of a research association which would represent the distinctively Scottish educational system. The original list of members as of November 1974 showed 136 members. The following year this increased to 156, and by the mid-1980s it had settled to around 200. There has been a steady increase in membership in the 1990s. There are now approximately 250 members. As Nisbet (1995) pointed out this level of membership (250 members: 5 million population) compares favourably with that of the British Educational Research Association (660 members: 56 million population).

A feature of SERA membership in its first few years was its heterogeneity. In 1974, almost one-quarter of members were teachers, about half of whom were headteachers. Just over one-third of members were from higher education. Interestingly, a number of members from the university sector were not from education departments and included professors of German and Psychology. Educational psychologists comprised just over 10 per cent of the membership. There was only one student member and, outside of the Scottish Council for Research in Education, only six members had the term 'research' in their job title: four of these were from local authorities. Only one was described as a 'research fellow'. By 1978, when there were 211 members, Nisbet (1995 p. 132) quotes from a SERA source that 'a third of the membership are school-based and almost half are "not the traditional practitioners of educational research"'.

However, by 1987 the membership list indicates that almost half (44 per cen) of the membership were employed in higher education. Teachers accounted for only 12 per cent of the membership, and of these, two made reference to their temporary status as students. There was only one educational psychologist, and six students. The number of members with 'research' in their job titles had reached just over 10 per cent of the membership. Due to changes in record keeping practice, comparisons of membership over time are difficult. However, it is apparent that this trend has continued and that there has been a discernible move away from a wide range of membership towards a more professionally research (even researcher) dominated organisation.

It can be argued that this trend in the SERA membership profile is a response to the changed research context since 1974. For teachers there has been an increase in the pace of change in schools and the growth of post-graduate courses for teachers at Master's level. In higher education there have been changes in approach to initial teacher education and increasing pressure on higher education staff to conduct and publish research.

SERA support for teacher research has traditionally taken the form of supporting and organising local teacher research groups and the sponsoring of an annual, later bi-annual, conference on teacher research. This approach was established in a period when relatively few teachers undertook research. However, this has changed with the proliferation of accredited in-service research based courses being offered by higher education institutions. The support function for teacher research seems therefore to have transferred to individual higher education institutions. This, taken together with a reported increase in the level and pace of change in schools, has resulted in less teacher demand for SERA support. Consequently, the association is currently exploring a more strategic partnership with local education services to develop policies and practice which will recognise current pressures on teachers by supporting school, as opposed to individually based, research and make more use of the research already undertaken by teachers.

The decrease in the number of educational psychologists as members is perhaps symptomatic of a move in educational research in Scotland away from what was once regarded as the 'founding disciplines' approach to teacher education based on psychology, sociology and philosophy. Consequently, representatives from these disciplines are less evident in education colleges and university departments, or at any rate they are less likely to describe themselves as such. The accompanying increasing pressures on higher education staff to research and publish has led to more research activity, as well as more job titles which include the term 'research'. Both of these developments have influenced the form, and to some extent the content, of the annual conference. The number of papers submitted has increased in recent years and there has been a demand from members for these to be published.

ANNUAL CONFERENCE

From 1979 to 1987, the conference was organised around themes selected by the Executive. This practice was discontinued in 1987 and an 'open' call for individual papers and symposia is now issued during the spring. The conference sub-committee then groups papers according to topic. The range of papers is comprehensive and includes consideration of methodological issues and research into teaching and learning in schools and higher education as well as evaluative research related to policy-led innovation. While it would be difficult to claim a definitive trend in the subjects covered, this last theme seems to have become increasingly prominent.

However, the striking feature of change in the annual conference is not the numbers attending, which held steady in the region of 130 for most of the 1980s and 1990s, but the number of papers presented. It is apparent that for a considerable period, the majority of delegates did not give papers. In 1979, there were 129 delegates during what was a two-day conference, and twenty-one papers were given. In 1985, the conference programme involving seventeen papers could be printed on less than two sides of A4. Examination of the relevant attendance lists and programmes show that in more recent times, more delegates expect to give a paper. In 1994, 137 people attended and forty-nine papers were given; in 1995, 128 people attended with fifty-three papers being given. In 1997, 145 delegates attended the conference with the equivalent of approximately 100 individual papers being given.

The annual conference is currently held at Dundee University to meet this trend for larger attendance and, perhaps more importantly, to enable more paper sessions. Indeed, it might be said that if the original primary task for SERA was to disseminate research to its members, the contemporary task is to disseminate the research produced by them. Accordingly, since 1994 SERA has published conference proceedings. From 1997 proceedings will be published electronically through the Education-Line Web site.

FUTURE CONCERNS

SERA has sought to achieve its aims of cooperation and dissemination by bringing together researchers, policy makers and research commissioners at conferences. It meets annually with the Research and Intelligence Unit of the Scottish Office Education and Industry Department to discuss research related issues. It has also published a Code of Conduct (SERA 1997) for research which has been distributed to all institutions of higher education and local authority education services. The task for SERA in the future will be to continue to promote these aims in a rapidly changing local, national and European context.

The European challenge is, perhaps, the least problematic. While concerned to reflect the distinctiveness of the Scottish education system, SERA is equally concerned not to be encapsulated by it. It has been active in the European Educational Research Association (EERA) since its inception. It encourages members to participate in EERA activities and indeed, in 2000, SERA will host the EERA Conference in Edinburgh.

Nationally, the current competition for research grants among institutions of higher education seems likely to be compounded by promised future cuts in funding for higher education. In addition, the continuation of measures to assess and finance research activity while increasing competition for research contracts, perhaps paradoxically, seems likely to encourage others to withdraw from educational research and concentrate on teaching. Taken together these developments will tend to make cooperation more difficult, threaten the job security of research workers, and indeed diminish the extent of influence of educational research.

Recent local government reorganisation and the establishment of a Scottish parliament could well mean a period where concerns with organisational establishment and service delivery combine to dominate the educational agenda. These changes could result in the continuation of the current trend of rapid policy development where policy formulation and implementation tend to be separated, teacher control diminished, and research marginalised. However, these new structures also contain the potential for increasing the influence of research. The challenge for SERA is to assist in developing these structures in a way that increases this potential.

REFERENCES

Nisbet, S. (1984) Does Scotland Need SERA? *Scottish Educational Review*, vol. 16 no. 2, pp. 127–133.
Nisbet, J. (1995) *Pipers & Tunes. A Decade of Educational Research in Scotland*, Edinburgh: Scottish Council for Research in Education.
SERA (1997) *Code of Practice for Educational Research in Scotland*, Scottish Educational Research Association. c/o Scottish Council for Research in Education: Edinburgh.

107

Scottish Educational Journals

Willis Pickard

SCOTTISH EDUCATIONAL JOURNAL

'We shall bring before our readers all such information as shall tend to make the bonds of brotherhood closer, smooth down the asperities which have unfortunately too often occurred in the past, and send us out to work with a more cheerful and hopeful spirit.' So the *Educational News* launched itself on 1 January 1876. The journal for the profession was to deal in professional matters and in a positive frame of mind.

Two thousand two hundred and nine issues later, in the final year of the First World War, the *Educational News* merged with the *Scottish Educational Journal* (*SEJ*), which was the organ of the Educational Institute of Scotland (EIS) and dated from 1852, only five years after the founding of the institute.

The *SEJ*, as it is now usually known, is the longest running of the newspapers and reviews serving the teaching profession. Its prime purpose has always been to form a link between the institute and its members in schools, but it has done so in various ways. Early on it was interested in adult education and published mathematical puzzles and 'harmless entertainment' as well as educational news. As a weekly, it gave space to the young Christopher Grieve (Hugh MacDiarmid) in the 1920s.

In the 1970s it sought to develop into a wide-ranging educational magazine challenging the *Times Educational Supplement*, which had recently started a Scottish edition. Later, responding to the need to communicate with members in the fraught industrial climate of the Callaghan and Thatcher governments, it became more of a union news sheet, published after meetings of the Institute's councils and committees and presented in tabloid format for quick absorption in staffrooms.

As general secretary of the EIS from the mid-seventies, John Pollock saw the value of a regular channel of communication with 40,000 members through copies mailed to schools. Especially during the two-year dispute from 1984–6 the *SEJ* helped the union to maintain morale in the face of anti-strike pressure from the government and the local authority employers. The downside was that inevitably the journal reflected the Moray Place headquarters view and appeared to exclude that of more left-wing critics.

In common with other unions, the EIS moved away from industrial confrontation in the late 1980s and the *SEJ* subtly changed tack. The constitution of the Institute was changed to give local associations greater autonomy. Under Pollock's successors, Jim Martin and

Ronnie Smith, there was also renewed concentration on an educational agenda, and this was reflected in increased educational content within the *SEJ*. The day-to-day work of schools, and especially that of EIS members, became a regular feature.

TIMES EDUCATIONAL SUPPLEMENT SCOTLAND

Since 1965 the main professional medium for the educational community has been the *Times Educational Supplement Scotland* (*TESS*), which is published every Friday. The separate edition for Scotland was founded at a time of rapid expansion of education, especially at post-school level. The aim was to increase advertising and circulation, which quickly went up from 1,500 a week to 3,000. Ironically, the universities market was soon siphoned off by the stablemate *Times Higher Education Supplement* founded in 1971.

By the time of the Munn and Dunning reports the *TESS* was selling around 6,000 copies, but in 1978, in common with other Times newspapers. it disappeared for eleven months in an industrial dispute. Lost readers were not immediately attracted back to a publication which in many weeks suffered from the production problems of the 1980s that led to the Wapping dispute. The circulation rose rapidly, however, when reform of local government in 1996 brought into being thirty-two education authorities which all used the *TESS* to advertise their jobs. The editorial content of the Scottish edition was also increased.

In journalists' jargon the paper is built on 'change pages', that is, pages which are different for the *TES Scotland* from those in the *TES* itself. From the outset the aim was to give coverage of news from within the distinctive Scottish education system and to stimulate comment and debate on it from both staff contributors and the Scottish education community. Because of the need to change pages, Scottish content is scattered, with five or six news pages early in the paper, followed by two of editorial comment and then by features and arts coverage. Many readers, however, turn first to the back page where the Jotter diary gives lighthearted prominence to the sayings and doings of leading figures who, for the most part, welcome the publicity.

The aim of the paper, which employs four staff journalists, plus a sub-editor in London where the paper is prepared for the press along with the parent *TES*, is to report educational news of significance from every part of Scotland. Much comes from government and local authorities sources, but increasingly there is also attention to – and reader interest in – the ways in which individual schools and colleges confront the challenges of a national curriculum and wider ranging forms of assessment. The creation of self-governing colleges of further education in 1993 led to a new feature in the *TES* called FE Focus wherein there is also scope for a page devoted to Scottish FE and training. Early in 1998 a new primary magazine was launched to enhance *TES* coverage of that sector.

In attempting to speak for Scottish education, the *TES Scotland* adheres to no political party or union line. But it was strongly critical during the eighteen Conservative years of attacks on public sector services and of underfunding of schools and colleges. It also campaigned for a Scottish parliament with education as a principal responsibility.

SCOTTISH EDUCATIONAL REVIEW

While *TES Scotland* ranges across the educational spectrum, there are more specialised (or niche) publications. Among these the twice-yearly *Scottish Educational Review* (*SER*) must take pride of place, not because of its circulation which remains in the hundreds but because it is the main Scottish-based home for research papers and for academic comment on policy and practice. It dates back to 1968 and it started as *Scottish Educational Studies*. Ten years later the title was changed because, as the editor wrote, ' "studies" might suggest to some that type of academic activity pursued by specialists behind closed doors and likely to be of interest only to other specialists.'

But the intention was still 'to continue concern for academic rigour and high standards of critical scrutiny and at the same time to emphasise that studies in education should be viewed in a context of their relevance and value to the educational system and society in general.' This has been reflected in articles assessing Government policies of the day as well as research reports. The *SER* is not to be found in many school staffrooms but it is important to the research community and since 1977 it has had close links with the Scottish Educational Research Association. Until recently it was published by the Scottish Academic Press but it now looks after its own business affairs and production.

OTHER PUBLICATIONS

While the *SER* comes out in spring and autumn, a once-a-year journal *Education in the North* claims to be the oldest existing academic periodical in Scotland. Intended to give a non-Central Belt perspective, it was founded in 1964 at Aberdeen College of Education. After volume 24, it ceased publication in 1988 but was reborn six years later, again at the Aberdeen campus of Northern College where its editors are based. With the subtitle of 'Journal of Scottish Education' it aims to bridge the gap between practitioner and academic, and has a mix of refereed articles alongside lighter ones and book reviews.

The extent to which teachers of individual subjects are served by regular publications varies greatly and has worsened over the past decade or so. There is, for example, no Scottish publication devoted to the primary sector, although primary teachers read UK magazines like *Child Education* and *Junior Education* and the primary coverage in the *TES Scotland*.

In the heyday of subject advisers and the curriculum development service of the Scottish Consultative Council on the Curriculum, there were, among others, magazines devoted to the interests of English, history and modern languages teachers. They disappeared largely because there was no one with the time to edit them and to look after advertising, circulation and production. Developments like the secondary aspects of the 5–14 programme and Higher Still suggest that there would be interest among subject teachers in curriculum materials, discussion of assessment and examples of good practice in a more detailed form than would appeal to the *TES Scotland*.

Some subjects remain well served. There are journals, at least annually, for mathematics, media studies, modern studies and technological studies, and no doubt others. Self-help by subject associations tends to have replaced input from a national curriculum base. For example, the mantle has been taken up by the Scottish Association for the Teaching of English which brings out a newsletter, *The Speak*, once a term.

Areas of post-school education have their periodicals, too. *Scan* emanates from the Scottish Community Education Council (SCEC) and goes to community educators in the voluntary and local authority sectors. Bi-monthly, it has a print run of about 3,000 and having in the past been at various times in newspaper and magazine format, it has settled down as an information newsletter.

Also associated with SCEC is the *Scottish Journal of Adult and Continuing Education*, whose other progenitor is the Department for Adult and Continuing Education at Glasgow

University. They relaunched it in 1993 following the demise of its original owner, the Institute of Adult and Continuing Education. It appears twice a year and is aimed at researchers, policy makers and practitioners.

Also serving post-school education is the *Journal for Further and Higher Education in Scotland*, whose home is the Scottish School of Further Education in Glasgow and which is funded by the Scottish Office. It was founded in 1976 with the aim of covering research, policies and practice and it has a circulation of about 500 twice a year.

THE IMPACT OF JOURNALS

Assessing the influence of journals is hard. Many teachers say that pressures of the job prevent them reading as widely as they would like. When a group of primary staff were asked what they would like to see in a proposed primary magazine, one said: 'Useful materials for teaching P4.' She was a P4 teacher and, understandably, was looking for practical help. She and the others in the group recognised, however, that they would benefit from the forum which a more general primary journal would offer.

There are about 50,000 school teachers in Scotland. Adding in the further education sector, academics in teacher education and administrators, a total of 60,000 education employees is reasonable. The weekly sale of *TES Scotland* is running at almost 10,000 copies, which is higher than at any time, but one that still suggests a limited level of reader commitment. True, staffroom copies may be looked at by many non-purchasers of the paper. But leaving aside the *SEJ*, which is mailed to schools for EIS members, no regular education publication in Scotland is reaching a mass market.

Influence is not necessarily dependent on sales. The *TES Scotland* has greater penetration of the market among senior staff, especially heads, administrators and teacher educators than in the wider profession. It may also be assumed that other publications are most widely read by senior staff or the more ambitious among their younger colleagues.

Therefore the scope for influencing debate is considerable. Quantifying the level of influence is impossible. People make frequent references to items they have seen in the *TES Scotland*. Whether the views of contributors on contentious topics of the day affect readers' own opinions is doubtful, and the same applies more powerfully to leading articles, painful though the admission is for an editor.

On the optimistic side, people need knowledge. That is particularly so in an era of national curricula. At one time primary schools in particular could be well run without constant reference to what was happening beyond their gates. That is no longer possible, and the promoted staff at least have to keep abreast of national developments. The education coverage of the daily press, broadcasting and professional publications fulfils an information role.

After local government reform no authority is large enough to be self-sufficient. Previously, Strathclyde Region, with half the population of the country, largely recruited from within its ranks and from its own teacher education institutions. It produced many of its own initiatives, in the curriculum and elsewhere. The national dimension was often less significant than the regional. Now with thirty-two authorities the need to know what is going on elsewhere is paramount. The scope for disseminating news and the desire to publicise local initiatives have both grown. The education press gives a forum and a platform. But fulfilling the century-old aspirations of the *Educational News* to encourage brotherhood and smooth down asperities is beyond the scope of educational writers, and no longer a role they see for themselves.

The Scottish Council for Research in Education

Wynne Harlen and John Nisbet

What should be the functions of a national council for educational research? When the Scottish Council for Research in Education (SCRE) was established in 1928, there was no comparable national research organisation anywhere in the world, and consequently there was no model of structure, objectives or finance to follow. The aims of SCRE, as stated in its First Annual Report, were simply 'to encourage and organise Research Work in Education'. Today one might expect such a council to profess a range of functions such as: informing and contributing to educational policy, conducting research using a variety of methods, promoting the implementation of policy, disseminating research findings on current issues, producing research-based materials or tests, providing an infrastructure to support research and encourage teachers and others to undertake research, reminding everyone in the educational system that research has a contribution to make, and promoting the advancement of knowledge and understanding of teaching and learning generally.

The last of these functions was the prime aim of the founders. In the present decade, research councils such as SCRE tend to be seen primarily as having a more limited instrumental function, bridging the gulf between research and practice, and they have difficulty in funding long-term fundamental research for the advancement of knowledge. The changing priorities for SCRE over its seventy years' existence is the underlying theme of this chapter, reflecting the way in which educational research itself has developed in that period.

THE ORIGIN OF SCRE

The initiative in setting up SCRE was taken by the Educational Institute of Scotland (EIS), the professional organisation (at that time) for all grades of teachers in Scotland, with the support of the Association of Directors of Education, the senior educational administrators in the local authorities. SCRE was a successor to a 'Committee of Research' which the EIS had instituted in 1919, which had the declared aim of 'stimulating the interest of teachers in educational research and familiarising them with the methods of investigation' (SCRE 1st Report, 1930, p. 5). Finance for the infant SCRE was provided by an annual grant from EIS of £500–£750 (and accommodation in their offices), and the local authorities contributed one farthing per pupil (a quarter of an old penny, or 0.lp), with no strings attached other than accountability to a representative board which met twice annually. Interestingly, the Scottish Education Department (SED) – as it was then called (later to become, successively, the Scottish Office Education Department (SOED) and the Scottish Office Education and Industry Department (SOEID) – decided not to be involved: private memoranda within the government office (released after fifty years) suggest some suspicion that researchers, if given encouragement, might challenge the traditional system of deciding policy on the basis of past experience. On this slender financial basis SCRE initiated a model structure of voluntary project committees of researchers working in their spare time, unpaid.

The Council set out to be of value to teachers, and many of its early publications reflect this emphasis: *Studies in Arithmetic* (1939 and 1941), *Selection for Secondary Education* (1942), *Studies in Reading* (1948 and 1950), *Studies in Spelling* (1961). SCRE was also able to publish academic studies in psychology and history, which won it an international reputation among researchers. The Scottish National Surveys in 1932 and 1947, in which a test of intelligence was applied to an entire age-group throughout Scotland, were the first of this kind in the world; and the 1942 research on selection for secondary education became a model for such selection for the next thirty years. Because almost all the work was done by unpaid volunteers, SCRE's total budget in 1960 was £8,338 (and it reported a profit of £281), and its staff comprised only a part-time Director and a secretary.

This amateur style of organisation persisted. However, by the 1960s it became increasingly evident that this mode of organisation was too slow and random in its choice of topics. In other countries the national organisations for educational research at that time employed full-time staff funded by their governments, while SCRE still relied mainly on its structure of voluntary committees. The need to include research in the formulation and implementation of policy was now widely accepted: research began to be seen as an essential 'arm' of policy formulation, necessarily separate from government but publicly funded.

FUNDING AND MANAGEMENT

The move to full-time research staff required greatly increased external funding, and most of this was provided by the SED, whose contribution rose sharply from 1963 on. SED's first grant of £1,000 had been made in 1946–7, and subsequently it contributed some £2–3,000 annually. In 1964–5 SED's contribution to SCRE funding exceeded £10,000 for the first time. By 1977–8 (SCRE's 50th year), £135,000 or 44 per cent of income came as a basic grant from SED, and a substantial proportion of the remainder also came from SED as project income. The other partners were then in a minor role: the EIS contribution was less than 1 per cent of SCRE's income and the local authorities' funding was only 7 per cent.

When government funding became the major source of support for SCRE, this change was reflected in the style of operating. The committee structure of voluntary groups disappeared, and with it the close affiliation of the Scottish universities and colleges with 'their' research council. The voice of government had to be respected: if expenditure of public money on research was to be justified, the choice of topics for research could not be left to the researchers but would have to be directed by those who provided the funds.

For a time SCRE continued to operate with considerable autonomy; but in 1984 the SED, as its prime funding agent and in accordance with general government policy at that time, initiated a 'critical scrutiny' of its operation. The resulting Freeman Report recommended a major reorganisation with 'future funding of SCRE . . . heavily conditional on its capacity to reorientate its activities along the lines indicated [in the report]' (quoted in

SCRE Annual Report 1984/5, p.8). The recommendations were adopted and involved changes in both the structure and policy of the Council. The SED 'endorsed the role [of SCRE] as the authoritative national forum for the consideration of educational research policy' (*SCRE Annual Report* 1984/5, p. 8); a new Director and senior staff were appointed and SCRE embarked on a programme of policy related research.

A further review in 1989, followed by another change of Director in 1990, led the way to a change in SCRE's status. A framework of outcomes and performance criteria was negotiated with SOED and became the basis of an annual contract within a five-year rolling programme. Thus the government 'grant' became 'contractual funding' – payment for services provided. As part of these services, SCRE is required to conduct some research, amounting to a substantial project each year, to carry out a number of research reviews and to provide seminars for SOED/SOEID staff from within the contractual funding. Since by this arrangement SCRE has no longer been in receipt of government grant, its status has changed from being a non-departmental public body (NDPB) to that of a non-controlled body. Indeed the composition of the Board of Management is more appropriate to an independent body than an NDPB. The Board now has a membership of twenty-five of whom only three are nominated by the Secretary of State for Scotland. The others are nominated by the teachers' unions, organisations relating to higher and further education, the Convention of Scottish Local Authorities, the Association of Directors of Education, employers and parents' organisations, the General Teaching Council for Scotland, the Scottish Consultative Council on the Curriculum and the Scottish Qualifications Authority. There is also an assessor from the SOEID.

When the new contractual arrangements with SOED were introduced, the level of contractual funding was set at a figure which was about one third of SCRE's total income. This figure hardly changed throughout the next six years, thus losing its value until by 1997/8 it was only one quarter of SCRE's income. The rest of the income, apart from a small and diminishing contribution from local authorities and a nominal sum from the EIS, is derived from externally funded projects, mostly won in open competition, from SOEID, other government departments, non-governmental organisations such as health education boards, local authorities, the Economic and Social Research Council and the charitable foundations and trusts.

The 1989 review also recommended enlargement of the senior research team and, incidentally, of the Board of Management. As a result, from 1992, the scale of SCRE's activity increased and its income from externally funded research increased substantially. After an internal review of its structure, in 1994, a change was made which created a greater number of permanent senior research posts. Thus, in 1997, of the 22 research staff, 6, including the director, have permanent contracts, the other 16 being funded by external research contracts. Of the 17 support staff, 10 have permanent contracts and the remainder are funded by external research.

This system by which the large majority of research funding has to be won in competitive bidding for external projects is designed (presumably) to improve efficiency and avoid any waste of public money. SCRE has no favoured status in the scramble for funds, though its position and experience may sometimes give it an advantage. But the result has been that others engaged in research, in universities and colleges particularly, have become rivals where once they were colleagues of SCRE. The former close relationships have survived, however; there is much informal cooperation and some of SCRE's bids for project money are made in collaboration with universities or colleges. Questions remain. Does competitive bidding improve efficiency, and result in better research? Is it more equitable, patently more fair in the allocation of public funds, or is it merely cheaper?

It is important to note that SCRE is only one of the channels of government funding for research in education. The other main channel (apart from the Economic and Social Research Council which is only a grant-giving body) is indirectly through the Scottish Higher Education Funding Council (SHEFC) to the universities and colleges. In fact, SHEFC funding for educational research (or nominally for educational research under Unit 71 of its allocations) is running at about £2.8 million, or two and a half times the total annual income of SCRE. These funds go to the universities and colleges, which are accountable only in that their individual allocations are based on their previous publication record; but it is not possible to identify how far these SHEFC funds are used for research and how much is absorbed into general university costs. In comparison, SCRE's funding is less generous and more restricted, but its use more transparent.

THE WORK OF SCRE

At any one time it is usual for SCRE to have 20 projects in progress, whilst over a year work will be conducted on up to 40 projects. This indicates that some are short-term and indeed the trend to shorter projects has been a significant part of the scene since the late 1980s. A stark illustration of this comes from comparing SCRE's research programme in 1987 with that in 1994. In 1987, financial balance was achieved with 17 projects (of average duration almost three years and of which 3 were less than one year) in operation during the year, compared with the programme in 1994 of 40 projects (of average length 18 months and of which 15 were less than one year) and with a slightly smaller research staff than in 1987. Smaller projects are less cost effective due to the greater proportion of total time spent on activities such as planning, setting up and report writing, which remain fairly constant whatever the length of project. More importantly they provide less time for reflection on wider issues. However the requirement of funders and potential users of research for information within a decreasing time scale has to be recognised. SCRE's role in informing policy and practice means that short projects have to be accommodated.

However, some of the projects run over longer periods: for example, the evaluation of the implementation of the 5–14 programme (an extended collaborative programme with other agencies over a six-year period), and support to the Assessment of Achievement Programme in running surveys and analyses. Also, some former projects have made important theoretical contributions, for example in the field of assessment, in diagnostic testing and in profiling. Nevertheless, the Council is very conscious of the need to build a systematically managed programme and of the difficulty in undertaking any fundamental research. Escaping from continual pressure to serve a purely instrumental function in relation to educational policy and practice is not easy.

The range of topics covered by SCRE's work includes all areas of education and training at all levels of schooling, education before and beyond school and professional training. It has always taken a prominent part in evaluation of major educational reforms, such as TVEI, the introduction of Standard Grade and the 5–14 Programme, and has been involved in studies relating to Higher Still.

SCRE acts as secretariat for national research bodies: the Scottish Educational Research Association, the British Educational Research Association, and the European Educational Research Association. It also supports the teacher-researcher movement with seminars and a newsletter (see next section), and by its Annual Practitioner Awards to teachers who have undertaken distinguished research projects.

In a statement of 'broad principles underlying the planning of the Council's activities' in SCRE's 1993 Corporate Plan, three guiding principles are set out, which are not easy to reconcile:

> the Council will maintain its *independence* in all matters . . . the Council will, where possible, be *responsive* to the needs (of policy-makers and teachers) . . . a *proactive* role will be taken to build up cognate programmes of research . . . [emphasis in original]

Reconciliation of these principles depends on 'the balance that is struck by being proactive and responsive in obtaining funds for research . . . A compromise has to be found between the type of programme which is a rag-bag and that which has a sharper focus'. Given that the Council is mainly, though not entirely, dependent on funders' decision about what research they will support, this raises the issue of how decisions are made about priorities for funding.

PRIORITIES

Decisions on priorities are inevitably influenced by the availability of funding. However, those who control funds are not necessarily those best placed to make decisions on priorities. Teachers in the schools and colleges, administrators in education authorities, parents, the general public whose taxes are the source of public funds, politicians, perhaps also the pupils and students – all these stakeholders can claim a voice, as indeed can the researchers themselves, in that they have a better idea of what can be done, as distinct from what should be done, though they cannot be so arrogant as to think they alone should decide. There is (or has been) an honourable and valuable tradition not to interfere too much with the work of researchers, and to be cautious of political influence on the choice (or non-choice) of topic and especially of the danger of self-interested veto on publication. In the past, when most of the research work in education was done on a voluntary spare-time basis, SCRE's programme of work was primarily the responsibility of the Director in consultation with the Board, informally taking account of the interests of leading researchers, and it was this style of management which established SCRE's international reputation in the early days. But with substantial public money involved, this informal paternalist structure was no longer acceptable, and some wider-based system of deciding priorities had to be devised.

In the event this objective proved easier to state than to achieve. The 1984 Freeman Report on the future of SCRE had suggested a 'forum' for public discussion of current research activities and of priorities, which would involve researchers, teachers, administrators, councillors and parents' representatives, to be organised on an annual basis by SCRE. The inaugural meeting of this Forum on Educational Research in Scotland was held in 1986 with over 150 persons invited from all sectors of educational provision. Whilst successful in meeting the first of its two aims, the discussion of recent research, it was less successful in overtaking the second aim, of determining priorities. The meeting took the form of six parallel sessions, on topics selected in advance, and no clear priorities emerged at this or subsequent meetings. The Forum in 1988 adopted a 'devolved model' in which twenty-four local groups produced a total of 110 priorities (not themselves in order of priority), but again this could not be reduced to a manageable list. Subsequently the Forum has met annually, but it is now accepted as an opportunity for discussion on selected topics and dissemination of research findings. The SCRE Board, which as noted above is widely representative of bodies with an interest in or involved in education, has now taken over responsibility for an annual review of priority areas for research. Through its Board members' constituencies, suggestions for research are drawn from all sectors of Scottish education, and from this the Board itself establishes a priority list which is submitted to the SOEID and widely publicised.

Priorities for funding, however, are decided by the funding agencies themselves. SOEID's procedure involves a 'trawl' of opinions, starting with letters to education authorities and organisations such as SCRE and the Scottish Educational Research Association inviting views. The SCRE Board's list is a contribution to this process. Within the Department, Divisions prepare their own lists, culminating in a meeting of Heads of Divisions which decides the final list. Selected projects are put out to tender and advertised nationally, while others may be taken up within other exercises or at a later date. In addition, a small amount of funding (about 3 per cent currently) is reserved for 'sponsored research': this involves small-scale grants to individuals, often for projects of the researcher's own choosing.

DISSEMINATION AND PUBLICATIONS

Research can be regarded as having four stages: identifying the topic and formulating it as researchable questions; designing the project; executing it; and disseminating the findings. In earlier times all four were the responsibility of the researcher, though dissemination was often neglected on the assumption that it was sufficient if a report was available from some source or other. Today these stages are fragmented: the topic is chosen by the funder and often the general design of the research may be prescribed at the same time. As Kent noted in a 1988 Stirling University report, researchers who do not have the earlier identification with the topic and design may not have the same interest in diffusing the findings. Moreover, when one short-term project follows another, it is difficult to give dissemination the attention it deserves, and time for it is seldom provided in contracts. Yet dissemination of research is of fundamental importance; in a sense, research findings exist only insofar as they are disseminated.

The importance of dissemination is recognised and given high profile in all SCRE projects. SCRE encourages staff to publish, and effective dissemination is one of the performance criteria in the contract with SOEID. In addition to the traditional forms of publication as a printed report or book or as a conference paper, dissemination takes the form of seminars, workshops and conferences. As well as the regular seminars for SOEID staff, SCRE has annual meetings with representatives of the teachers' unions at which presentations are made on recent research of particular interest to teachers. These meetings are highly valued by the union representatives and by SCRE staff as an opportunity for exchange of information on research and on what the teaching profession requires from research. Other conferences are held as appropriate in different parts of Scotland to disseminate the findings of particular projects. For example, numerous feedback events were held following the various evaluation projects relating to TVEI and, during the six year evaluation of the implementation of the *5 to 14 Development Programme*, seven conferences were held in different locations.

The major annual meeting of the Forum on Educational Research in Scotland, organised by SCRE, is an opportunity for a wide range of people to hear about current research linked to a theme. For example, the 1997 Forum had the theme of equity in education and was attended by 230 delegates including a large proportion of teachers and headteachers as well as researchers, advisers, school board members, lecturers and administrators. Twelve different presentations were made in small discussion groups, with delegates able to attend two of these in addition to a keynote address.

The presentations at the Forum are of research carried out by researchers throughout Scotland and not only at SCRE. This highlights one of the distinctive features that separates SCRE from other bodies conducting research in education: as the national body it has the remit to collect and disseminate information about all educational research in Scotland and not just its own. It maintains a data-base of all such projects, and of research theses, to which all educational researchers have access.

In addition to an extensive range of SCRE's own research reports and research reviews, its 1997 publications include the following, which all provide information about and outlets for research carried out elsewhere not just at SCRE:

- *Spotlights*, each one a concise summary of a research study, available free on request – a series which has now reached number 71;
- *Using Research*, a series of short books which includes research methods guides, reviews of research and accounts of research projects in non-technical language;
- *Research in Education*, a twice-yearly newsletter which has a free distribution of 38,000 copies;
- *Observations*, a newsletter for teacher-researcher groups;
- *A Web site* on the Internet (http://www.scre.ac.uk), which currently includes the text of unpriced publications, such as *Spotlights*, for downloading and in future will enable web site visitors to search SCRE research reports and other reports mentioned in the newsletter. It will also provide an option for updating information in the newsletter between printed versions.

In publishing funded research, a particular problem arises over the question of ownership. Whose is the research? Does it belong to the funder or the researcher? Or, more pertinently, who decides what is, and is not, to be published? The traditional research answer is that any veto on publishing findings which may be uncongenial to the funding body, or selective publication of what suits the sponsors, discredits professional reputations and is self-defeating in the long run. In this respect, SCRE has been fortunate in being able to hold a strong position. The terms of SOEID contracts specify a period of three months after satisfactory completion of the contract during which the Department's prior agreement must be obtained in writing to any publication or public presentation of findings; but after that period the researcher is free to publish. (Some other funding bodies are much more restrictive.) The intention is to provide a period for the Department staff to consider the implications for policy before any press report appears. This restriction is generally accepted as reasonable.

KEY ISSUES

The present funding arrangements of SCRE, in which it has to compete in the open market for three-quarters of its funding, raise a number of issues which are common to many institutions engaged in externally-funded research: stress and insecurity among the research staff; rivalry instead of cooperation with other researchers in universities and colleges; and fragmentation of the research effort through the diversity of demands, with short-term contracts obstructing the development of coordinated programmes of research and of proactive fundamental research. Many writers have commented on the changing relationships in the educational research world in recent years. The February 1996 Newsletter of the British Educational Research Association, for example, commented: 'With acceptance of research as a means of developing efficiency, the power of decision has shifted towards national management. This, and competition for tightly managed funds, is resulting in a change of climate, with stress and rivalry within the research community replacing cooperation and the exchange of ideas' (p. 31).

Insecurity of employment is widespread, not only in education. Perhaps total security leads to complacency, but many researchers are dedicated and do not require this kind of spur. It leads some of the best to look for other posts which are inherently less stressful and offer better prospects. Those on relatively short-term research contracts are especially vulnerable, and as the end of their contract approaches are certain to be looking for other jobs and may leave before the project is over. SCRE implemented, before its publication, the provisions of the 1996 *Concordat on Contract Research Staff Career Management* on conditions of work for its contract staff, but this does not remove the insecurity.

Fragmentation of effort is the other alleged effect of the pattern of funding which has developed. Those who provide funds for research, however, tend to favour the present system because it provides for the flexibility of response which they look for in a national research council. The idea of a research council staffed by full-time professionals with some security of tenure implies a capacity to turn their hand to whatever topic arises. The counter-argument is that the best research needs experience and expertise in a specific field. If there is to be the necessary flexibility of response, this would seem to imply a succession of relatively short-term appointments or secondments to research staff, with continuity provided by a core of senior staff experienced in research method and design; this seems to be what is happening to SCRE.

Why a Scottish research council? How is SCRE different from the National Foundation for Educational Research, or comparable bodies in USA, Australia, New Zealand, Netherlands or Sweden? The mission statement of SCRE indicates that it aims to 'conduct high quality research for the benefit of education and training in Scotland and elsewhere'. But does this imply that SCRE should only do 'Scottish' research? Almost all SCRE's work is set in the context of the Scottish educational system, but otherwise there is no such thing as 'Scottish' research. Prior to 1990 SCRE had not undertaken projects outside Scotland, except for some overseas consultancies. Since that date more work has been set in other parts of the UK, often in collaboration with institutions in England, Wales or Northern Ireland. European funding from EC is becoming more important and SCRE is in competition for these funds. It is now recognised that not all work that is of benefit to Scottish education and training has to be carried out in Scotland. Indeed it could be argued that projects funded outwith Scotland increase the revenue available for the benefit of research in Scotland. SCRE, of course, has no monopoly on educational research in Scotland: agencies outside Scotland compete for, and sometimes win, contracts for research in Scotland. When this happens, there is a strong (perhaps irrational) feeling of resentment in the research community in Scotland, who argue that non-Scottish agencies may be alien to the Scottish system and that a Scottish institution should be given preference in such decisions.

The idea of a 'national' research council implies a close link with the national educational system of the country. Involvement as an integral part of the educational system implies responsiveness to 'customers'. Such close linkage necessarily results in a loss of autonomy (for example, in deciding choice of topics or even methods of inquiry) which may be difficult to reconcile with the principle of the independence of research. The issue here is one of 'belonging': does a national research council belong to its clients, or does it have a wider responsibility, to the nation, or to the advancement of knowledge? The answer lies in a balance between a service and a professional role; but the nature of that balance is not always easy to determine.

The underlying question in many of these issues is the one raised at the beginning of this chapter: what should be the functions of a national council for educational research? The answer to this depends on a more general issue: what is the role of research in educational systems? The implicit model for many of those working in education is that the function of research is to provide an information base for administrators and teachers. This assumes that researchers establish the 'facts', others add value judgements, and in this way policy and practice are based soundly on empirical studies. Thus, 'good' research provides answers to 'relevant' problems. This instrumental view, however, makes naive and simplistic assumptions about the relation of research to policy and practice in education. If adopted uncritically, the emphasis on answering 'relevant' questions constrains inquiry within the limits of existing policy and risks a trivialisation of research and centralisation of control. To quote Halsey (in the 1967 Plowden Report), what research offers is 'an aid to intelligent decision-making, not a substitute for it'. The role of a national research organisation should include raising issues of concern as well as offering answers to problems of immediate relevance. SCRE's activities in disseminating others' research as well as its own and in providing opportunities for face-to-face encounters between researchers and policy makers contribute to filling this role but there is no doubt that this is an important aspect that deserves further attention as relationships between policy-makers and researchers continue to evolve.

REFERENCES

Brown, S. (1985) The promotion of educational research and development – Scottish style, in *World Yearbook of Education 1985*, London: Kogan Page, pp. 165–76.

Brown, S. and R. Wake (1988) *Education in Transition: What Role for Research?* Edinburgh: Scottish Council for Research in Education.

Nisbet, J. (1995) *Pipers And Tunes: A Decade Of Educational Research in Scotland*, Edinburgh: Scottish Council for Research in Education.

The Scottish Council for Research in Education – 50th Anniversary 1928–78, Edinburgh: Scottish Council for Research in Education.

109

Teachers' Professional Organisations

George Livingstone

THE ORGANISATIONS: ORIGINS, MEMBERS AND CHARACTERISTICS

In Scotland, the professional organisations for school teachers exhibit varying, at times contrasting, characteristics.

Firstly, some operate only in Scotland; the Educational Institute of Scotland (EIS) and the Scottish Secondary Teachers' Association (SSTA). Each of the other organisations operates across England and Wales also. These organisations are the National Association of Schoolmasters/Union of Women Teachers (NAS/UWT) and The Professional Association of Teachers (PAT). The largest teaching union in the (UK), the National Union of Teachers (NUT), does not recruit members in Scotland because of an agreement to that effect between it and the EIS.

Secondly, with the exception of the SSTA, the organisations draw their membership from across the primary and the secondary school sectors. The most diverse set of members belongs to the EIS which has significant membership not only in both of the school sectors but also in further and in higher education.

Again, the organisations differ in date of foundation and in size of membership. The dominant organisation is the Educational Institute of Scotland which is the oldest, having been founded in 1847, and by far the largest in terms of membership in Scotland.

The single-sector SSTA is next in size and in age. Limiting its representativeness to secondary teachers only can be seen as both advantage and disadvantage in that it can claim to represent the one sector more distinctively, but that also imposes a limit to its potential size. In part the SSTA was established because it was asserted that the EIS was heavily influenced, even dominated, by its primary school members. Such feelings were at their most evident when, in 1973, primary and secondary teachers, whether degree holders or diplomates, were paid the same salaries as a result of the report of the Houghton Committee. Some secondary teachers resented that equalisation and these feelings, though they have lessened, have persisted.

In England and Wales the two single-sex organisations, the National Association of Schoolmasters and the Union of Women Teachers merged at the beginning of the 1980s. The equivalent Scottish organisation, the Scottish Schoolmasters' Association (SSA), made that merger a three-way one and the NAS/UWT thus gained a Scottish presence.

Even more recently there came about the Professional Association of Teachers (PAT) which came to prominence in the mid-1980s in the years of industrial strife in schools throughout Great Britain. PAT was founded in England and its claim to distinctiveness is that, unlike all of the other organisations, its members are committed not to engage in industrial action, i.e. they have a 'no-strike' policy. The prolonged, but ultimately successful, strike and other industrial actions in the 1980s on both sides of the Border, proved to be difficult and conflict-filled and the PAT drew in members from other organisations and teachers who had been members of none until then.

The very term 'professional organisation' is in itself interesting for it suggests approximation to the term, 'professional association'. Professional associations are mainly those corporate bodies to which various individual professional groups belong as essential to their recognition as professionals. Thus, there are professional associations for medicine, for law, for the various categories of engineering, for surveying, for architecture, and for many others too. The term 'professional organisation' seems often to be applied to the Scottish teachers' organisations almost as a euphemism to veil their principal nature and purpose: trade union activity. Two further points need to be understood in this regard. Firstly, the organisations take very seriously their policies for education and there is evidence to suggest that they are heeded by government and by the community. Secondly, there is evidence of other professional groupings who want their professional associations to behave more like trade unions. Possibly the most curious recent instance of such pressure has been that from ministers of religion.

In Scotland it is not necessary for a teacher to belong to any of these and, though they are often so termed, it is important to note that the organisations are not 'professional associations'; rather they are effectively trade unions. Indeed, all bar the PAT are affiliates of the Scottish Trades Union Congress.

Nevertheless the EIS has some distinctive features. It was founded by Royal Charter and has the power to award degrees (Fellowship of the Educational Institute of Scotland). In this regard the EIS has authority akin to professional associations in areas such as law, medicine and engineering. But it is also very much a trade union and, because of size and strength, dominates numerically the negotiating machinery for salaries and conditions of service; this is the Scottish Joint Negotiating Committee (SJNC) where union representatives meet with employer representatives (mainly from local authorities).

Many argue that to have so many organisations in such a relatively small country has had deleterious consequences in that it indicates divisiveness rather than true diversity. Certainly there is competition in recruitment, there have been occasions when employers have sought to exploit divisions and there have been frequent, sometimes quite bitter and prolonged squabbles and more major conflicts. An alternative view is to see the diversity as an illustration of the current trend in many professions towards narrower specialisms and so to more focused corporate organisations.

The simple reality is that such is the predominance of the EIS in the school sectors that that organisation not only dominates the SJNC but also commands much more attention for its views amongst the public in general, amongst employers and political parties. Its boast of having members from nursery through to university also means that the range of influence of the EIS is greater.

There have been moves to explore mergers, particularly between EIS and SSTA, but these have always stopped short at the stage of dalliance. PAT cannot merge with any of the other organisations because of its key 'no-strike' policy and NAS/UWT has the vast majority of its membership in England and Wales and so is seen as inappropriate for possible merger by the two directly Scottish organisations.

STRENGTHS AND SUCCESSES

Despite these tensions and differences, it can be argued that the organisations in Scotland have been successful in certain ways. For example, the teachers' unions still derive considerable satisfaction from having taken on the government of the day through the strikes of the mid-1980s and successfully won salary increases for their members. More remarkable still was that they managed to retain the support of the majority of the public even when so many parents were adversely affected by the disruption of their children's education and considerably inconvenienced by the demands of alternative arrangements for child care.

Awareness of the need to maintain public confidence by communicating effectively was further demonstrated when the then government determined to impose its will in the face of the resolute opposition of the vast majority of the teaching profession. In England and Wales that Conservative government had imposed a National Curriculum on schools and set alongside it national tests (Standard Attainment Tests) for children at ages 8, 11 and 14 in English, Mathematics and Science. In Scotland, a different set of arrangements was developed. The 5–14 Curriculum and Assessment Programme, comprising sets of guidelines on programmes of study and related attainment targets was devised, agreed and revised. The government's intention was then to require that all children in public sector schools be tested in English and Mathematics at ages 8 and 11. Through a campaign led by the EIS, parents were persuaded that such testing was not in the best interests either of children or of education more generally. The result was that huge numbers of parents declined to allow their children to sit these tests and the government backed down and decreed that the tests would be voluntary.

Such awareness of the benefits of, indeed the necessity for, explanation, communication and cooperation with other stakeholders in education is an indication of a modern, outward-looking disposition. Perhaps some eighteen years of Conservative governments which not only were determined to constrain trade union powers, but also to cut away the perceived protectiveness and restrictive practices of professionals and their organisations and to demand accountability in education and in other public sectors caused this 'modern disposition' to arise. In other words, it may have arisen from pressure rather than from policy.

ISSUES FOR THE FUTURE

Certainly, in relation to other current and future issues, there is some variability in the quality and the amount of responsiveness by the organisations in question. For example, there is for them the tricky issue of continuing professional development of teachers. On the one hand no organisation can stand in opposition to the updating and the professional re-skilling of its members. On the other hand, none is prepared to give outright approval to any requirement that teachers should, for instance, demonstrate that they have undertaken professional development of a set amount within successive agreed periods of time (every five years, for example) in order that they may be entitled to remain on the Register of the General Teaching Council for Scotland. (Other professional groupings such as in nursing have agreed to something similar.) That is not to say, of course, that the teachers' position is due solely to blunt refusal to contemplate future change. It can be argued that the reasons are not at all to do with supporting members' apathy or laziness, but have much more to do with pressures of current work, of constant changes, of low budgets and of the financial constraints both of the individual member and of her/his employer. Nevertheless the trend in education as in other professional and vocational groupings is for the employer to expect the individual to be responsible for seeking professional development opportunities.

Related to professional development is the practice of appraisal at work which is common in many private and public sector organisations. The major purposes of appraisal are twofold: to achieve the management of the performance of the individual employee and to give the individual more influence over his/her own professional destiny, development and working practices. Within the teachers' organisations, the primacy of protecting members (matched by members' wishes for indemnity through membership), is such that only the first purpose seems really to have been considered and appraisal rejected thereby. The second purpose has been greeted with scepticism verging on scorn; a response attributable largely to the aforesaid pressures and financial constraints. The value of identifying development needs which cannot be matched with opportunities has, at least, provided an excuse for opposition.

Teachers in the public sector do have to be members of the General Teaching Council for Scotland (see Chapter 110): this body is responsible for the registration and licensing of teachers, and has a statutory role in the initial education of teachers and statutory power of discipline by removal of a teacher from its Register. The differences between professional association and trade union have already been referred to. One further characteristic which is relevant is that of discipline; the 'striking-off' of a member for incompetence or professional misconduct is typically within the rules of, and the requisites for, membership of a professional association. In Scotland, the professional organisations do not exercise this function. All teachers who work in the public sector in Scotland must be registered with the General Teaching Council for Scotland and that body has the power to discipline teachers by de-registration. Such de-registration once full registration has been achieved, is for instances of misconduct, most commonly those arising from convictions in court cases, and not for incompetence. Incompetence is an issue for the employer and the teacher and it must be said that instances of sacking for incompetence have been very rare indeed. It can be argued that that is a sign of the effectiveness of the trade unions, but there are serious questions to be answered by the whole profession in these areas; it cannot be denied that there are not at least some teachers in the country whose competence is open to question (see Chapter 102).

This gearing of protection and indemnity may be systemic in organisations where volunteer members make the decisions, while the organisational professionals (the officials) 'mind the shop'. The professionals are thus dependent on what has been termed 'Victorian voluntarism'. It is debatable how relevant such structures will remain in the face of further challenges: new, flexible working practices to match technological developments; the greater mobility of professionals within the European Union; and the potential for 'contracting out', consultancy and self-employment. These concerns may seem far-fetched but, when taken together with technological developments, they do merit attention. The organisations have protested vigorously against the growing practice of employers awarding fixed-term contracts especially to newly qualified teachers. What is that but a form of consultancy, even self-employment?

The Scottish teachers' organisations have displayed considerable ingenuity and vigour in facing up to governments, to employers, to the broad scope of protecting members. That the future will bring sets of circumstances which will demand related mind-shifts by them seems inevitable. To gear up and move on from their present relationships, purposes, structures and visions will require a much more professional, less volunteer-based and spare-time set of structures if members' continuing and developing needs are to be met.

ADDRESSES OF TEACHERS' PROFESSIONAL ORGANISATIONS IN SCOTLAND

Educational Institute of Scotland, 46 Moray Place, Edinburgh EH3 6BH.

National Association of Schoolmasters/Union of Women Teachers, Stock Exchange House, 5th floor, Nelson Mandela Place, Glasgow G2 1QY.

The Professional Association of Teachers, 4/6 Oak Lane, Edinburgh EH12 6XH.

Scottish Secondary Teachers Association, 15 Dundas Street, Edinburgh EH3 6QG.

110

The General Teaching Council

Ivor Sutherland

ORIGIN

The General Teaching Council came into being at a time when Scottish teachers were far from content. There were the usual concerns about salaries and conditions of service; there were however other concerns of a more professional nature. Teachers felt that they had no stake in their professional future and were excluded from the decision-making process. They watched with dismay as the government sought to solve the problem of teacher shortage by introducing unqualified persons into the schools; these were the so-called 'uncertificated teachers' and they proved to be the last straw in a rapidly deteriorating situation.

With teachers' feelings running high the government established a Committee of Inquiry under the chairmanship of Lord Wheatley to consider entry into and exit from the teaching profession. The membership of the Committee reflected the breadth of the educational community and to some extent anticipated the membership of the Council. In 1963 the Committee recommended that 'there should be established a General Teaching Council for Scotland, broadly similar in scope, powers and functions to the Councils in other professions'. Under the terms of the Teaching Council (Scotland) Act 1965 elections were held, and the Council met for the first time on 11 March 1966.

The new Council's first task was to rid the schools of uncertificated teachers which it did by arranging shortened courses of professional training for those who wished to remain in teaching. Those who were unable or unwilling to take such a course had to leave the schools. This process was assisted by a gradual improvement in the supply of qualified teachers. The Council has always been sensitive to fears about the dilution of professional standards and the threat of dilution is an issue which is even yet designed to galvanise the Council into immediate action.

ACHIEVEMENTS

Since its first meeting in the mid-1960s the Council has come a long way. Its achievements have been in four main areas: professional status, professional standards, professional education and professional voice. The status and morale of Scottish teachers appear higher than those of their English counterparts. Teaching is still seen in Scotland as a rewarding and attractive career as evidenced by consistently buoyant recruitment figures. Teaching in

Scotland is an all-graduate profession. There is a strong system of probation as well as national arrangements for dealing with the misconduct of teachers. Professional standards are uniformly high. The Council has played a major role in ensuring that student teachers are exposed to professional programmes which are rigorous, demanding and relevant. It prides itself on the robust procedures which it has in place for the accreditation and review of courses. The Report of the Dearing Committee (1997) commented that the teacher education arrangements in Scotland 'in many respects . . . provide a model for other parts of the United Kingdom'. The Council has been a powerful influence on the work of the teacher education institutions. The Council is the voice of the profession, since it is the only body which can speak for all teachers. The unions can only speak for their own members and, not surprisingly, it is usually to the Council that the government turns when it wishes to have a professional view.

The Council has had many achievements over the years of its existence, some minor, some major. Its greatest achievements are perhaps that it was created in the first place and that it is still seen as a pioneering and far-sighted initiative. It is a distinctive feature of the education service in Scotland and it has served as a model for the establishment of similar bodies in many different parts of the world.

The Council's overarching remit is to maintain and wherever possible enhance professional standards. In terms of the 1965 Act it seeks to do this by:

- maintaining a register of those qualified to teach in local authority schools in Scotland,
- overseeing standards of entry into the profession,
- advising the Secretary of State on matters of teacher supply,
- maintaining a watching brief on initial teacher education and advising the Secretary of State accordingly,
- dealing with teachers found guilty of professional misconduct.

It has executive as well as advisory functions. In this connection it is worth noting that the General Teaching Council proposed for England is to be largely an advisory body.

COMPOSITION

The Council has forty-nine members divided into three categories. There are thirty elected members; these are registered teachers who are elected by their peers on a national basis every four years. There are fifteen appointed members who are appointed by bodies like the Association of Directors of Education in Scotland, the Convention of Scottish Local Authorities, the Scottish Universities, the Church of Scotland and the Roman Catholic Hierarchy. Finally the Secretary of State has reserved the right to nominate four members. The Council elects its own Convener and Vice Convener. Although not required by Standing Orders, the Convener has always been a serving teacher.

The full Council meets only four times per year and most of its detailed work is therefore undertaken in Committees. There are three Committees which are necessary by statute. These are the Investigating and Disciplinary Committees which deal with cases of professional misconduct and the Committee on Exceptional Admission to the Register which determines whether or not a teacher trained outwith Scotland can be admitted to the Council's register. The other seven are Standing Committees. The Education Committee considers matters of a general educational nature, while the Probation Committee formulates policy on probation and hears individual cases as required. The Finance and General Purposes Committee looks after the Council's resources and the recently established Further Education Committee considers all matters relating to further education. The Accreditation and Review Committee is responsible for the scrutiny of courses of initial teacher education and the Communications Committee fosters links with the profession and beyond. The Convener's Committee has a policy-shaping role and has the power to act between Council meetings. The Council elects the Committee Conveners, but each Committee elects its own Vice Convener.

REGISTRATION

It is a statutory requirement for all teachers in local authority-managed schools to be registered with the Council. The Council determines the criteria for registration which, generally speaking, is taken to mean that a person is academically, professionally and medically fit to be a teacher. Arrangements are also made for a criminal conviction check to be carried out before registration is granted.

Registration in further education is not mandatory and it is one of the Council's ambitions to achieve this. Registration is however compulsory for lecturing staff in the teacher education institutions who are involved with the theory and practice of teaching. This was secured in 1986 after a lengthy campaign by the Council.

There are at present 76,989 active names on the register distributed as follows:

Primary	36,780
Secondary	38,229
Further education	1,342
Teacher education	638

The Council is financed wholly by the profession; every registered teacher is required to pay an annual registration fee of £20. For each teacher in its employment an education authority deducts the registration fee from salary and remits a bulk cheque to the Council. For teachers who are not in permanent employment the Council issues an annual account.

PROBATION

When student teachers complete their professional programme, they are granted provisional registration which entitles them to teach as probationers. Probation lasts two years, but many probationers need much longer to accumulate the necessary service because of the short-term employment which they obtain. When they are first registered, new teachers are given a Teacher's Certificate of Provisional Registration which signifies that they are probationers and on which their headteachers have to submit reports on their classroom competence.

At an early meeting the Council decided that the schools should be meaningfully involved in the oversight and induction of new teachers. The management of probation therefore depends on a collaborative partnership between the Council and the schools. At the end of the second probationary year headteachers have to complete a final report and recommend whether the probationer concerned should be granted full registration, have his/her registration extended for a period up to but not exceeding one year, or have his/her registration withdrawn.

If a headteacher recommends withdrawal of registration, the case is considered by the

Probation Committee. Probationers have the right to be present and to be represented. They are usually accompanied by a representative of their union and occasionally by their solicitor. If the Probation Committee decides to uphold the headteacher's recommendation, the probationer has a right of appeal to the Probation Appeals Board which consists of seven Council members with no previous involvement in the case. Again probationers have the right to be present at the hearing of their appeal and to be represented. The Probation Appeal Board's decision is final and, if it declines to sustain the appeal, the probationer's name is removed from the register; his/her employment as a teacher is then terminated.

After a period of three years has elapsed, a probationer teacher who has had his/her registration withdrawn can apply for restoration to the register. Requests for restoration are considered by the Probation Committee. A few probationers who have had their registration cancelled because of unsatisfactory classroom performance have their names reinstated in this way.

The Council sets great store by its probation arrangements and has devoted considerable resources over the years to the development of the probationary service. It believes that effective management of probation is crucial to the continuing health of the teaching profession. For this reason the Council has sought to encourage employing authorities and schools to give probation a higher priority by:

- issuing guidance packs to headteachers on the support and assessment of probationers,
- preparing print, overhead projector and video materials for probationers and their managers,
- contributing to courses for probationers,
- commissioning research projects on probation,
- making appropriate representations to the government.

PROBATIONERS ON SUPPLY

At the present time there is considerable teacher unemployment in Scotland. According to Scottish Office Education and Industry Department statistics there is a sizeable pool of unemployed teachers and Council registration records show that there are over 9,000 provisionally registered teachers on the register. This means that many probationers find it very difficult to obtain full-time permanent employment. Most begin their teaching careers on supply work and short-term contracts, a situation which has substantial implications for the completion of probation. This is not the way in which new recruits should be introduced to teaching; the Council regards such fragmented service as highly unsatisfactory.

The Council has been so concerned about the plight of so many probationers that it commissioned a research project to establish the facts in regard to probationers on supply. The project was undertaken by the Moray House Probation Team and the main themes to emerge were the narrowness of experience of being a teacher, lack of opportunities for professional support and development and difficulties in assessing competence. The Council is currently studying these findings with a view to determining whether it needs to take any special steps to assist probationers on supply.

EXCEPTIONAL ADMISSION TO THE REGISTER

The majority of Scotland's teachers have attended one of Scotland's six teacher education institutions and have therefore an automatic entitlement to registration following successful completion of their course; this is the standard route to registration. There is however a non-standard route to registration which is managed by the Committee on Exceptional Admission to the Register. Each year the Council receives upwards of 800 applications for registration from teachers who have been trained outwith Scotland. The Council was forced to review the way in which it evaluated these applications by the publication in 1989 of the EC Professional Qualifications Directive. In simple terms this required the Council to register persons from other European states provided that they were qualified teachers in their own country and had not less than three years of post-school education.

The Council decided that the terms of the Directive should form the basis of its approach to all applications for exceptional admission to the register. Applications from the remainder of the United Kingdom, from other EU member states and from further afield (e.g. Australia, India, New Zealand) are therefore all scrutinised according to the same criteria. If there is a shortfall in a candidate's qualifications, whether academic or professional, he/she can be given conditional registration on the basis that the condition or conditions have to be met within a period of three years. If the condition(s) are not met within the specified time, registration is withdrawn. The Council has taken a firm stand on this and conditional registration is from time to time withdrawn. Candidates who feel that a wrong decision has been made in their case, have a right of appeal to the full Council.

RELATIONS WITH THE SCOTTISH OFFICE AND TEACHER EDUCATION INSTITUTIONS

The Council interacts with the Scottish Office Education and Industry Department in a range of different ways. When the Council was first established, it received an annual grant from the government in respect of the funding of a number of responsibilities previously undertaken by government and now assumed by the Council. According to the 1965 Act the Secretary of State had to approve any increases which the Council wished to make to its registration fee. When the grant was withdrawn with effect from the financial year 1987/88, the *quid pro quo* was that the Secretary of State relinquished his power to approve fee increases. The Council was no longer financially beholden to the government and could now be truly independent.

The Council has always had Scottish Office Education and Industry Department Assessors, usually an Assistant Secretary and an HMCI, in attendance at most meetings of the full Council. In the early days the Department was also represented at many of the Committee meetings. Now the Department is only represented at Committee meetings if it identifies an item of business of particular interest or if the Council feels that it would be helpful if a representative of the Department were to be present. This arrangement works well to the benefit of both the Council and the Department. Recently, as part of its new 'arm's length' policy, the Department has been less frequently represented at meetings of full Council.

In recent years the Department has asked the Council to undertake a number of tasks. These include a review of the PGCE (Primary) course, a review of the arrangements whereby teachers can convert from one sector to another and most recently a review of the procedures relating to partnership in initial teacher education between the schools and the teacher education institutions. The Council is the Secretary of State's Principal Adviser on Initial Teacher Education and sees tasks of that kind as proper recognition of its teacher education role. It would be fair to say that the Council enjoys fairly collegial and collaborative relations with the Scottish Office Education and Industry Department at the present time. That is not to say that the Council is in the Department's pocket. Each respects the other and recognises the benefits of having a relationship based on mutual respect and trust. Within the context of such a relationship it is easy for the Department to decline to grant a Council request from time to time and equally easy for the Council to express disapproval of a course of action proposed or taken by the Department. In other words there can be occasional tensions, but they are healthy and creative; it would be odd, and perhaps suspicious, if it were otherwise.

The links between the teacher education institutions and the Council are close and collegial. The teacher education institutions are of course represented within the membership of Council to the extent of four Principals/Deans of Faculty and one other elected on a national basis by teaching staff. The teacher education institutions are therefore already involved in the day-to-day routines of the Council business. The Registrar is an Assessor to the Scottish Teacher Education Committee which was formerly the Committee of Principals of the Colleges of Education in Scotland. The Council, through the Registrar, is therefore familiar with the management of the teacher education sector. It used to be said that the Principals/Deans ran the Council, so influential was their voice; this is certainly no longer the case and the Principals/Deans as a group have no more impact on the work of the Council than any other group of members.

The main connection between the teacher education institutions and the Council comes about through the accreditation and review of courses. Accreditation and Review Sub-Committees are often in the institutions and Course Teams are often in the Council's offices. The Council invests considerable resources in its course accreditation and review activities and has developed an approach which is searching and robust. Although the Council is demanding in its requirements, the teacher education institutions appear to welcome the Council's continuing interest in the quality of their courses. The Council is currently exploring with the Department ways of reducing the quality assurance demands on the institutions. This is partly as a result of the Council's own initiative and partly in the light of one of the recommendations of the Dearing Report.

The Council occasionally funds or commissions research from the teacher education institutions and this is clearly seen by the institutions both as a welcome source of income and as a means of extending their research portfolio. They often seek advice from the Council about the assessment of qualifications, especially of those gained outwith Scotland. Relations with the teacher education institutions are sound and mutually supportive.

RELATIONS WITH THE LOCAL AUTHORITIES

The local authorities are very important to the Council which relies heavily on their goodwill and cooperation. In the first place the Council is dependent on the local authorities for the release of the twenty-two primary and secondary teachers who have been elected to membership. There is rarely any problem with release and the Council is always grateful for the willing cooperation which it receives from the authorities in regard to the availability for meetings of the teacher members. In the second place the Council relies on the local authorities to endorse the arrangements for the oversight of probation in the schools. Perhaps however the greatest area of collaboration between the Council and the local authorities is in the matter of professional misconduct. The Council and the local authorities collaborate closely to ensure that teachers who are found guilty of serious professional misconduct are removed from the register. The local authorities are under an obligation to notify the Council when a teacher has been dismissed or has resigned in circumstances involving professional misconduct. There is rarely any serious disagreement and the relationship between the Council and the local authorities is undoubtedly one of mutual trust and support. In light of this the present controversy about the Council's role in relation to teacher competence is somewhat surprising. For some considerable time the Council has been seeking a formal locus in the post-probationary period. One of its aspirations is to secure the right to remove from the register the name of a teacher who is chronically and persistently incompetent in the classroom. This aspiration has brought the Council into some conflict with the local authorities who see it as their responsibility to dismiss incompetent teachers. The Council does not contest this; it points out, however, that the employing authorities can only dismiss, whereas the Council can remove an incompetent teacher from the register. In the view of the Council these are totally separate and should not be confused.

Relations with the local authorities are generally smooth and harmonious. There are occasions however when the local authorities feel that the Council has overstepped the mark and strayed into forbidden territory. The debate about incompetence is one example of this.

ATTITUDE OF TEACHERS

The attitude of teachers to the General Teaching Council varies in accordance with a number of factors which include career stage, professional climate and individual circumstances. In general terms the attitude of most teachers to the Council is one of neutrality; very few teachers are hostile, but by the same token very few teachers are wildly enthusiastic about the Council. But there are exceptions to this general rule.

Student teachers hear about the Council for the first time in the course of their professional programme. This is usually in the context of discussion about professionalism. Towards the end of their course student teachers receive a talk from a Council official about the work of the Council and more particularly about probation. This is the first contact with the Council; they understand its importance for the maintenance and enhancement of standards and they can see how it will impact on them as they make their way through their probationary service. The Council looms large for the probationer teacher, for he/she sees it as setting up a hurdle which is particularly difficult to overcome when jobs are in scarce supply and professional life is a round of supply contracts. It is probably during probation that the Council plays its most important part in teachers' lives.

When probation has been completed, the Council recedes into the background for most teachers, unless of course there is any problem with misconduct. If teachers get into trouble with the law, they come up against the Council again in terms of its disciplinary machinery. If they commit professional misconduct, their case is likely to be referred to the Council and they receive a sharp reminder of the key role which the Council plays in regard to quality assurance and control in the profession. If on the other hand post-probationary teachers experience no difficulties in terms of conduct, they are unlikely to have any further dealings with the Council.

When teaching is under threat in any way, teachers realise how important the General Teaching Council is for their professional protection. Any suggestion of dilution for example brings the Council into sharp focus. It will be recalled that dilution brought about by the use of uncertificated teachers was the main stimulus for the creation of the Council.

When alternative and non-standard routes into teaching were introduced in England and Wales, the teaching profession in Scotland was certainly glad that it had the General Teaching Council as a protective barrier. If therefore there is to be a problem with teacher supply in the not too distant future, as seems likely, the Council will have a higher profile, for it will require to ensure that teacher shortage does not result in the adoption of measures which will lead to the dilution of professional standards.

There is of course also the organised teaching profession in the shape of the unions. How do they view the Council? Their attitude too will vary with the circumstances. Sometimes the Council is in disagreement with the unions, for instance over mentoring and modern languages in the primary school, and sometimes in close harmony, for example about compulsory registration in further education. Most of the time the relationship is one of mutual respect. The unions are concerned with salaries and conditions of service and the Council with professional issues. They have different, but complementary and equally important roles. The unions certainly appreciate that the Council is not a threat to their position; quite the reverse, since it represents a further empowerment of the profession. The unions recognise the strategic importance of the Council and know that the profession would be much weaker without it. For that reason they are usually supportive of Council initiatives and at the present time they are especially supportive of the Council's endeavours to have its powers extended in such a way as to be able to deal with incompetence in the classroom. The unions also demonstrate their belief in the significance of the Council by drawing up 'slates' at election time in order to seek to ensure that their preferred candidates gain seats. If proof was ever needed that the unions perceived the Council as a crucial element in Scottish education, their strenuous efforts to influence the voting will surely provide it! On the other hand the Council prides itself on being totally independent of the unions; it is not a super-union, nor does it provide another forum for the prosecution of union agendas.

The Council does not have a high profile with the profession. Although it has produced two promotional videos, its communication links with the profession are almost entirely restricted to the publication of a newsletter, *Link*, three times a year. It recognises that it has an image problem, but hopes that an extension of its powers into the post-probationary period will help to make teachers more aware of its activities. The Council also intends to appoint a Development Officer with responsibility inter alia for public relations. Things should change in this regard over the next few years. The Council does however represent the whole profession and, although the membership was laid down more than thirty years ago, there is no evidence to suggest that the Council membership is unbalanced or inappropriate. There have occasionally (though not in recent years) been representations to the effect that the advisory service and special education are not represented as separate categories. Recently the four places allocated to the Convention of Scottish Local Authorities were reduced by one to make way for a representative of the Association of Scottish Colleges. This suggests that the composition of the Council is constantly monitored to ensure that it is responsive to changes in the structure of the educational community and to new demands.

The Council is recognised as an effective body by the SOEID. The Department's most recent quinquennial report of Non-Departmental Public Bodies (1992) concludes that there are 'no major deficiencies in the operational or structural aspects of the Council's work' and that 'Council business is handled in an effective and organised way' (SOED, 1992).

CURRENT ACTIVITIES AND ISSUES

The Council has different kinds of priorities. For a number of years, however, it has had three key ambitions. Firstly, it would like to secure compulsory registration in further education. The Council has been campaigning for this since the early 1970s and continues to press its case at every opportunity. Senior members have met a succession of government ministers over the years in an attempt to persuade them that compulsory registration would enhance the standard of teaching in further education. The Council believes that it is an issue of quality and that its introduction would bring the further education sector into line with the primary and secondary sectors. The Council is convinced that its time has now come because of the Higher Still programme. The introduction of compulsory registration in further education could facilitate the implementation of Higher Still by blurring the interface between the secondary and further education sectors. Secondly, the Council is wholly committed to seeking continuing improvements in the way in which the proba-tionary service is managed. It sees this as of critical importance for the future of the profession and has once again demonstrated its commitment by agreeing to appoint a Professional Officer with a major responsibility for the further development of the probationary service. In a recent letter to the Council Convener the present Minister for Education at the Scottish Office has encouraged the Council to 'develop proposals for a coherent induction programme for teachers'. Thirdly, the Council has consistently argued the case for a formal role in the post-probationary period. It has considerable powers at present, but these are limited to matters relating to entry to the profession. It has no powers beyond probation except in regard to teacher misconduct. The Council takes the view that this does not make sense and that the dividing line between probation and post-probation is an arbitrary and artificial one. It has therefore pressed the case for its powers to be extended so that it can have a major say in areas like continuing professional competence, teacher appraisal, and continuing professional development. The debate will no doubt continue for some time to come.

The Council is not complacent about the way in which it discharges its remit. It has a range of priorities which it is seeking to overtake. Current activities include the following.

- The preparation of a comprehensive report on partnership in initial teacher education between schools, employing authorities and teacher education institutions.
- The production of a draft Professional Code for Teachers.
- The improvement of its advice to the teacher education institutions.
- A survey of the attention given to special educational needs in courses of initial teacher education.
- The preparation of a policy paper on Guidance.
- The updating of its disciplinary procedures.
- The development of closer links with the independent sector.
- The provision of an overseas consultancy service.
- The enhancement of its profile within the profession and beyond.

This sample of ongoing concerns makes it clear that the Council is not content to stand still; it is anxious to move forward and to improve its service to the teaching profession.

It has sometimes been asked whether the Council is a lapdog or watchdog (see Humes, 1986). The Council is independent in important respects. It has neither financial ties, nor political affiliations. Its members are men and women who bring their expertise and experience to bear in the best interests of the teaching profession and are not mandated to pursue a given agenda. As previously argued, there is ample evidence that the Council is not controlled by the unions. The Council is clearly not controlled by the local authorities and the days when the College Principals wielded undue influence are long past.

That leaves the Scottish Office Education and Industry Department. Is the Council the lapdog of the Secretary of State or does it genuinely represent the interests of the teaching profession? It is certainly true that it works closely with officials of the Department on a daily basis and helps to shape national policy where appropriate. It is therefore often in agreement with national policy proposals, but not always. The Council does not always toe the line; it is an independent body and it is driven by members who are themselves independently minded. This can be clearly seen in the robustness of some of the Council's responses to the Department's consultation papers. There is no doubt that, if ever a major issue of principle arises which brings the Council into sharp and sustained conflict with the Department, the Council would not back down.

In short, the Council is not a lapdog and it is certainly more than a watchdog. Watchdogs are kept to protect and defend; they are not expected to do more. The Council clearly protects professional standards, but its interest extends beyond a mere policing function; it seeks actively to enhance professional quality. It does not simply react to external influences and pressures, but also acts as a positive force in the field of professional quality assurance.

The Council's abiding task is to promote professional standards. If it believes that measures proposed by the Scottish Office are in the interests of the profession, it will cooperate to the best of its ability. If it does not believe that, it will say so in no uncertain terms. Since its creation the General Teaching Council sought to be a vigorous advocacy body for the teaching profession in Scotland and intends to remain so.

FURTHER INFORMATION

Further information about the Council and its activities can be obtained from The Registrar, General Teaching Council for Scotland, Clerwood House, 96 Clermiston Road, Edinburgh EH12 6UT, tel: 0131–314 6000, fax: 0131–314 6001.

REFERENCES

Humes, W. M. (1986) *The Leadership Class in Scottish Education*, Edinburgh: John Donald.
Kirk, G. (1994) The Role of the General Teaching Council in Teacher Education in Scotland, *Journal of Education for Teaching*, vol. 20, no. 1, pp. 39–46.
Kirk, G. (1998) Marriage or mismatch? Platform article in *TESS*, 6.2.1998, p. 18.
SOED (1992) *General Teaching Council for Scotland: Policy Review 1992–93*, Edinburgh: SOED.

111

Scottish Teachers

Bill Gatherer

IMAGES AND MYTHS

The Scots are famously proud of their education system; but its vaunted superiority is not often attributed to the teachers themselves. Yet since the Reformation, with its strong social and religious emphasis on learning, teachers have been entrusted with the important functions of promoting literacy and character formation, and for centuries the schools have been strongly supported by both the authorities and the ordinary people. Teaching has always been regarded as a worthy occupation, albeit not endowed with much social prestige.

The pictures we have of teachers in the eighteenth and early nineteenth centuries fall into three main categories. The local parish schoolmasters, educated at university and appointed by the ministers and the heritors (landowners), were selected for their moral as well as their educational qualifications. These were the respected dominies who abound in biographies and novels as the inspirers of the 'lads o' pairts', the clever boys from poor homes who became successful in later life, carrying throughout the world the image of pragmatic intellectual power which is still cherished as a national characteristic. Scots writers are generous in their praise of their teachers. Robert Burns, Thomas Carlyle, David Livingstone, Hugh Miller, Ramsay MacDonald (himself a pupil teacher until he was 18) and countless others testify to the beneficent influences of their schoolmasters: hardworking men of integrity and scholarship, well enough versed in the classics to equip their pupils for higher learning, able to introduce them to the glories of literature and philosophy, powerful role models and religious mentors but themselves as poorly paid and badly housed as the people whose children they served.

Then there were the schoolmasters in the burgh schools and academies in the large towns: men of genuine scholarship, with higher social status and comfortable stipends, able to mingle with their pupils' affluent parents. They could teach Latin and Greek, Mathematics, Philosophy; they wrote scholarly papers and delivered them in the numerous field clubs and literary and scientific societies that met throughout the country; they wrote books; many were doctors of law or philosophy; some became Professors of the University. These schoolmasters were an elite which transmitted an educational heritage and also preserved much of what was best in the national culture.

Then there were the women. In the eighteenth century many parishes had dame schools, run by any decent widow or spinster who could read and write and teach knitting, spinning, sewing and any other accomplishment valued by the parents, and who could put the girls and boys through the agony of scripture lessons. By the mid-nineteenth century the academies and high schools were appointing ladies to teach the womanly crafts and 'deportment'; but it was not until the large-scale feminisation of the profession in the later nineteenth century that women were perceived seriously as teachers and acknowledged as worthy of training and able to teach important subjects. Many tributes are paid in biographical literature to the women (mostly remembered as 'old') who taught in elementary schools and gave the great majority of Scots the only learning they knew. Hugh Miller fondly remembered Miss Bond in the little school in Cromarty, an accomplished and refined lady who wrote *Letters of a Village Governess*. Another Victorian autobiographer told of old Janet setting aside her pipe and taking up the 'ABC card' and likening it to a key which opens the door to knowledge and shuts it to ignorance. And William Adamson, a leading Labour politician in the 1920s, gave a moving account in one of his last parliamentary speeches of his schooldays in a mining village, with about a hundred pupils of all ages in a single room, and a lone heroic woman in charge. Of course there has been an accretion of myth around the testimonies recorded. The 'lad o' pairts' himself was largely mythic: for every poor, hardworking, intellectually gifted boy who was made into a scholar or a pioneer of empire by the free and thorough schooling he got at the local school there were thousands whose schooling was as threadbare as their breeks, who ended up as half-starved peasants or miners or factory workers. And for every inspiring dominie celebrated in the reminiscences of successful Scots there were hundreds of pedestrian drudges.

But the myths were to some extent true, and though their apotheoses in the tales of the so-called Kailyard writers in Victorian times were larger than life, they were sincerely believed in, and their power has been attested in the great educational charities of such figures as James Dick and Andrew Carnegie. As McPherson points out the myths, as folk stories celebrating dearly-held values, have lived on in many public statements about equality, tradition and dedication to learning in Scottish education (McPherson, in Humes and Paterson, 1983).

Modern Scottish writers seldom draw teachers with much sympathy. The only great masterpiece is Muriel Sparks' Miss Jean Brodie, a brilliant portrayal of the teacher's charismatic centrality in the lives of intelligent girls. Alasdair Gray's character, Duncan Thaw, finds his teachers both daunting and ridiculous. James Kelman's Patrick Doyle (in *A Disaffection*) is a teacher at the end of his tether, but his plight has little to do with his job: Kelman wanted to create a character whose working-class origins combined with a high educational and cultural consciousness. Schools and teachers seem to have no intrinsic dramatic potential such as can be found in the professional worlds of doctors and police officers. This is true also of ephemeral writing, where teachers are seldom drawn with respect. An exception was the 1950s television series, 'This Man Craig', which recounted the adventures of a sensitive teacher at a time when Scottish schools were taking on greater pastoral responsibilities. Craig was a 'housemaster' in a city comprehensive school, and each episode dealt with a social problem connected with one of his pupils; he was unconventional, wore a tweed jacket rather than a suit, and he was frequently in conflict with authority because of his commitment to his pupils' needs. That Scottish teachers do not feature often in television fiction is no doubt mainly due to the absence of a commercial market; but there is no reason to doubt that they would be perceived as pompous fools or petty tyrants, as are most of the teachers who feature in British films. Scottish teachers themselves have been entertained for many years by John Mitchell's comic anti-hero

Morris Simpson, whose hapless career is described in regular chapters in *The Times Educational Supplement*. Here is the secondary school brought to life with quiet satire, the recurring educational issues of the day seen through the eyes of a variety of truer-than-life members of staff.

THE DARK IMAGE

There is a sinister aspect to the story of Scottish teachers. Partly because they were virtually second-hand clergymen, expected to bring their pupils to the milk of the Calvinist doctrine by teaching and preaching and chastisement, the parish schoolmasters wielded a harsh discipline. The tawse or belt, described by George MacDonald as a 'long, thick strap of horse-hide, prepared by steeping in brine, black and supple with constant use, and cut into fingers at one end', was openly used on children from five years old and upwards. The teacher has frequently been portrayed as a cruel tyrant, ever ready to administer brutal 'justice' for sins as varied as playing truant and forgetting parts of the Shorter Catechism. This continual abuse was sanctioned by supervisors and parents alike in the belief that sparing the rod would spoil the child. MacDonald remembered his teacher in Aberdeenshire in the 1830s as a grim sadist. A hundred years later, in Mallaig, John Alexander MacKenzie's schooling was 'a continual battle with the teacher'; the strap was in daily use and vigorously applied at the slightest excuse (from *A Mallaig Boyhood*, 1996). In *A Scottish Childhood* (1985) Peter Brodie, a Moderator of the General Assembly of the Church of Scotland, remembers a kindly woman teacher in the 1920s, still however armed with the belt and ready to dole out 'three of the best' from a keen sense of duty. In the same book the journalist Magnus Linklater remembers his teacher's strap in the 1950s as 'a weapon of vengeance, black with age and hardened by constant use'.

Many Scots remember their teachers with a mixture of fearful loathing and reluctant respect. Naturally those who did well at school recall their teachers with more gratitude than those whose schooldays were more painful. But despite the scourge of the belt the majority of the less academically successful pupils seem to have considered their teachers fair and considerate, as we learn from the work of researchers such as McPherson and Gow in the 1970s. In *Tell Them from Me* (1980) they report that the belt was used in about a quarter of Scottish secondary schools, and despite the urgings of government officials to use it sparingly and 'as a last resort', in a large minority of schools a large minority of pupils were belted. Despite that, the majority of the pupils surveyed believed that although some teachers were capricious punishers most of them were kind-hearted and forced to use the belt by their circumstances – large classes, bored and resentful pupils and irrelevant curricula.

By 1980 there was a growing groundswell of belief among Scottish teachers that the belt was both demeaning and ineffectual, and some of the local authorities set up panels of teachers to discuss alternative forms of discipline. Advisers and inspectors encouraged schools to dispense with corporal punishment altogether. Hugh MacKenzie tells in his book *Craigroyston Days* (1996) how a 'new atmosphere' and a 'more appropriate curriculum' led to a gradual decline in belting, until in 1981–2 the staff (with only two dissenters) agreed to ban corporal punishment. By the time the government legislated against the use of the belt most Scottish schools had virtually abandoned it, and the vast majority of the teachers welcomed its disappearance.

The ethos of Scottish schools today is kindlier than ever before; inspectors write of a pleasant and purposeful atmosphere, conducive to effective learning, with teachers industrious and competent and pupils well behaved and friendly. Responses to the inspectors' questionnaires to parents show that they find the teachers approachable, helpful and fair. Such conditions no doubt prevailed in many a school while the belt ruled, but its disappearance is now universally felt to have been a blessing.

THE GROWTH OF PROFESSIONALISM

With the formation of the Educational Institute of Scotland (EIS) in 1847, Scottish teachers acquired a formal means of expressing a long-felt desire for a true professional voice. They had long been accorded what amounted to official status: they held their jobs *ad vitam aut culpam*, an enviable security enjoyed by the clergy themselves; they had been officially recognised in government acts and regulations as important functionaries; but they had always been – at any rate at parish level – under the dominance of the ministers. With the rapid industrialisation and urbanisation of the nineteenth century they saw the destruction of their cosy, if modest, authority. The parish schools could not cope; town schools were built hastily and badly staffed; many thousands of city children could not attend school at all. The interventionist legislation enacted in London and applied to Scotland as well as England and Wales introduced new systems of control which diminished their autonomy: pupil-teacher schemes, inspection, regulation of teaching content. The EIS soon became a vigorous lobby and forum; yet its efforts were unsuccessful in winning either goal of professional authority or political influence (Humes and Paterson, 1983, p. 75 ff). This was because the occupation of teaching was changing radically and irreversibly.

The new city schools had little or no connection with the parish schools of a former age. There was developing a deep historic shift from a world in which teachers were important figures in Scotland's religious culture to a society which was controlled by the state and in which teachers were a secular workforce (Anderson, 1995, p. 296). By the end of the nineteenth century teaching covered a wide range of occupational categories, the school-masters giving way to massed ranks of public employees, predominantly female. Mid-century, men made up 65 per cent of the teaching profession; by the end of the century, they constituted 41 per cent; now they are less than a third.

The feminisation of the teaching profession has been one of the most important factors in its development (Humes and Paterson, 1983, p. 137 ff). Last century, women's main entry was through the teacher training institutions, which offered them one of the few available paths to a professional career. The government treated them as cheaper, subordinate teachers well into the twentieth century. The employment of large numbers of women was initially forced by a high demand for teachers. When, during the 1920s and 1930s, there was a surplus of qualified persons, men teachers were nearly always given precedence and women teachers were paid less, had less chance of promotion, and were required to leave when they married. These were lean years for all teachers, but especially for women. Salaries were cut; classes tended to be very large; discipline was hard to maintain (Scotland, 1969, vol. 2, p. 121 ff). Selection and appointment procedures were often ruthless: local councillors openly tolerated canvassing and practised nepotism; working conditions were appalling in many schools. In primary schools women were appointed as Infant Mistresses but they never became headteachers, except in independent girls' schools. Women could find jobs in secondary schools but it was common for less qualified men to be their heads of department. During the last fifty years there have been periods of staff shortage, when women's presence in the profession has become more powerful, and their status has improved towards equality of esteem and financial parity. But it cannot be claimed that women have won equal security or status: even now, nine out of ten part-time and short-contract posts are held by women, and the great majority of headships and other management positions are held by men. Nevertheless women now constitute an important force in the profession, and it can be expected that their roles will continue to improve.

Teachers' march towards genuine professionalism has met with increasing success during the century, especially in the last forty years. Better qualifications and training have both helped. In the 1920s it became compulsory for men to hold university degrees. By 1940 the great majority of teachers had training certificates. The unions worked hard to eliminate uncertificated teachers and this was at last accomplished in the 1970s. Teaching in Scotland is now an all-graduate profession.

Teachers' capacity to participate in policy formation has also increased greatly in recent decades. From the 1920s onwards the Scottish Education Department (SED) included teachers in various advisory councils and negotiating committees; increasingly after 1918 the unions were able to represent their views to government with growing expectation of being listened to; after 1945 their voices were both more powerful and more constructive. The rise of 'experts' in the training colleges and universities, nearly all of them trained teachers with practical experience in classrooms, greatly enhanced the profession's authority: although their claim to a unique professional knowledge was often questioned by civil servants, teachers came to be acknowledged as practitioners of a special kind of craft and the exponents of specialised professional theory. The foundation of the Scottish Council for Research in Education (SCRE) in 1928 (see Chapter 108) created a powerful new partnership between practising teachers and their professional allies (McPherson and Raab, 1988, p. 256 ff). It was the strength of this partnership, sustained by an impressive corpus of research and exposition, which led eventually to a recognition that teachers could efficiently control professional organisations such as a national examination board, teacher training institutions and a General Teaching Council (GTC – see Chapter 110) which administers regulations for professional accreditation, discipline and the maintenance of standards.

Scottish teachers were not able to achieve that level of authority without exercising the power they possessed, through their unions, to force their needs upon their rulers. They have been called timorous, conformist, deferential and conservative (for example in T. C. Smout's *A Century of the Scottish People 1830–1950*, 1986) but in more recent times they have not hesitated to embark upon industrial action to protect and extend their professional power. The 1961 strike of Glasgow teachers, protesting at inadequate pay and status, shocked both the national and local authorities, and the prolonged industrial action of 1984–6 asserted teachers' entitlement both to adequate rates of remuneration and to a genuine respect of their service.

IN DEFENCE OF EDUCATIONAL VALUES

During the last forty years there has been a rapid growth of teachers' influence. They participated in the design and construction of the GTC (a triumph still not wholly achieved in England after more than thirty years) and they have always been the predominant force in its affairs. They have won significant representation in the national examination board and in the many panels it set up. Their union leaders are properly consulted on every important national educational development. At local level they sit on education committees and they form the majority on curriculum development groups. When the government set up a committee to review the primary school curriculum it contained a majority of teachers; and the Memorandum it produced in 1965 provided a reasoned, detailed rationale for the conduct of primary schooling which has long been admired throughout the world. When in 1965 the SED set up the Consultative Committee on the Curriculum (CCC), charged with leading a comprehensive reform of the content and methods of all teaching at primary and secondary levels, teachers were members of the main committee and leading members of its many national development committees (McPherson and Raab, 1988, p. 243 ff). While it is certainly the case that none of these arrangements has come near to realising the claims for true democracy and egalitarianism which are characteristic of Scottish educational rhetoric, the fact remains that teachers gained unprecedented responsibilities and powers.

A wide range of progressive approaches continues to be a prominent feature in all Scottish schools. The curricula are now wider and more varied than in the majority of developed societies, and teachers can readily introduce new methods and materials. The 'mission statements' of primary schools indicate that children's personal interests as well as their educational needs are of prime concern to the staff. Secondary schools in Scotland are by any standard well staffed with teachers specially trained in a very wide variety of disciplines and activities.

Teachers are always subject to control from external authorities; but although they can recognise the right of politicians to prescribe general educational policies, they have professional values which they are obliged to protect. The first of these is that children's needs and interests must take precedence in any consideration of what should be taught. Another important value is that teachers need a degree of autonomy in determining an individual pupil's educational needs and the best ways of meeting them. Modern teachers are well informed about the psychological characteristics of children and how learning most effectively proceeds, and they demand acknowledgement of their ability to diagnose and prescribe for their students' learning requirements. Unfortunately they are frequently attacked by ignorant politicians and journalists who have only subjective prejudice and personal memories of school experience to substitute for professional knowledge. The movement known as Thatcherism instituted in the late 1980s and early 1990s an unprecedented onslaught on the values and practices of the teaching profession. The main planks of the case against modern teaching are crudely simple: education is a service bought by parents; private schools give the best service but are unavailable to the majority, so state-provided schools should be made as like private ones as possible; parents and the providers of schools (the government), not teachers, should stipulate what they want pupils to learn. In the pamphlet produced by the Conservative Political Centre in 1985, *No Turning Back*, an influential group of politicians, including the man who was to become the minister for education in Scotland, spelled out the policies to be implemented: they proposed the introduction of performance measurements, the publication of league tables of schools' performance, more control by school boards and governors, giving them power to hire and fire staff, and the introduction of market forces, 'development management', 'consumer choice' and 'market power'. In England and Wales these policies were all enshrined in the Education Reform Act of 1987. In Scotland where no government could now flout the tradition of consultation and debate, the government issued a paper, 'Curriculum and Assessment in Scotland: a Policy for the 1990s', which proposed the introduction of national prescriptions for the curriculum and mechanisms for making schools more accountable to parents through new school boards, including national testing schemes and the publication of results. The so-called consultation process soon demonstrated a deep and widespread dismay, indeed anger, throughout the teaching profession (Roger and Hartley, eds, 1990). It was argued that the curriculum depended almost wholly on the skills and energies of highly trained teachers, and the government's clumsy attempts to invade their autonomy would dangerously impede the development of teachers' professionalism. In the event, some of the more radical proposals were watered down, but the shift of government policy away from consultation and cooperation with teachers still constitutes a sore anxiety for the profession. The last ten or fifteen years have seen continual attacks on their autonomy, combined with increasing requirements for the 'delivery' of externally prescribed curriculum content and teaching methods; and their confidence has been undermined by insistent monitoring of their teaching in accordance with mechanistic control devices such as 'performance indicators'. It is no wonder that many deplore the 'de-professionalisation' and the 'de-skilling' which come from treating teachers as mere technicians rather than experienced professional educators.

Yet Scottish teachers contribute significantly to the management of what and how they teach. In the 1980s a scheme of development for secondary education and in the 1990s a scheme for primary education have produced a hierarchical structure of tests and examinations along with a complex body of curriculum prescriptions which are still in force; all these have been produced by teachers in working parties supervised by inspectors and 'development officers'. Similarly, for further education colleges and secondary schools, a vast complex of modular courses was produced by working parties of teachers and lecturers. Imposed by government they may be, but the Scottish curriculum and assessment materials and arrangements are undoubtedly the achievement of able practising teachers, and their quality is attested by the widespread interest in them from numerous countries throughout the world. A uniform, integrated curriculum and assessment scheme for advanced level school students is now nearing completion and will be implemented by the end of the century. Scottish teachers nowadays are constantly engaged in devising new learning and teaching approaches at all levels: in their classrooms, in whole school groups and in local and national working parties. This kind of activity was unheard of forty years ago; it can now be asserted with confidence that whatever the authorities propose it will be teachers who finally determine the content and methodology best suited for their students.

TEACHERS, 'GAMEKEEPERS' AND 'REFUGEES'

Generalisations about teachers are inevitably weakened by the immense variety of types contained in the profession. The categories of certificated teachers in Scotland range from nursery teachers who are assisted by nursery nurses (qualified and trained but not teachers), to primary school, special school, and secondary school teachers. All of these are formally attested and certificated by the GTC. In the tiny number of recognised private schools there may be a few untrained and uncertificated teachers, but this is now rare, as parents and governors put a high value on proper qualifications. In further education colleges the majority of the teachers – given the title of 'lecturers' – are formally trained or under part-time training. Only in the universities are there many untrained teachers, and the provision of training and accreditation for university staff is now an agreed priority.

Scottish authorities strongly emphasise the need for formal leadership throughout the education system. Every school and college has a headteacher or principal, and the staff are ranked and functionally labelled; this of course is a universal feature in education systems, but in Scotland there is an unusual emphasis on hierarchy. It is characteristic, too, that outside of schools and colleges there is a large number of persons who have left regular school teaching to assume other jobs. These are variously described as 'leaders' or 'poachers turned gamekeepers', or 'hangers-on' or 'refugees from the chalk-face'. As in all workforces, those who remain at the basic levels of provision look askance at those who have moved away – especially if, as is usually the case, moving away means more power and more autonomy and more pay.

Humes' percipient account of the powers and values of educational leaders in Scotland assigns little authority to teachers at large, except of course in so far as officials such as directors of education, inspectors and advisers are deemed to be teachers; it is evident that, regardless of their professional beginnings, these officials become far removed in their perceptions as well as their functions from the daily tasks of teaching pupils in classrooms. Even leaders of teachers' unions, whose main mission is supposed to be to represent teachers' interests, seem to assume values and purposes which sometimes conflict with those of their rank and file members.

The terms invoked by the 'leaders' – 'partnership', 'cooperation', 'consensus', 'participation' – can often be exposed as rhetoric at best and, at worst, mere pretence. Humes argues that classroom teaching is regarded as a 'modest rung on the ladder of career advancement', and that success may be partly defined in relation to the ability to secure non-teaching jobs: teachers themselves have endorsed a hierarchical career structure which creates 'a situation in which the more specialist opportunities that arise, the less prestige the unpromoted teacher enjoys' (Humes, 1986, p. 22).

There is a case to be made, however, in defence of those whose jobs are designed to support the teachers by giving them advice, encouragement and inservice training. From the point of view of planners and administrators there are certain constraints on teachers' work that make support services essential. Teachers are relatively stationary: they spend nearly all their time in classrooms, and they have relatively little experience of other schools, so they are less able than professional advisers and supervisors to form impressions and generalisations about the conditions that need to be assessed in order to facilitate change. Teachers, too, are naturally preoccupied by the needs of their own pupils, and they are less able to formulate hypotheses and propositions about young persons in general. It is true that reflective teachers can, over time, build up the wisdom of experience which makes them unequalled as advisors on many aspects of education. But that activity requires time, and lack of time is teachers' greatest constraint. They face classes for several hours each day, every day, coping with the multifarious problems that children bring to them, and they put in many hours every week marking work, preparing lessons and meeting a host of bureaucratic demands. And because teachers are increasingly playing greater roles in the formulation of guidance to all concerned, they need time to do the essential work of researching, describing, devising proposals, consulting others and so on. Guidance and advice must be written and issued; schools must be visited; teachers must be given training and encouragement.

The advisory services built up by the regional education authorities between 1975 and 1996 were ultimately accepted by the great majority of teachers as useful and necessary. But the governments led by Thatcher and Major were never enthusiastic about that form of collaborative management. Believing that the education system should be run like a large business, they relied on published regulations and enforced compliance, and they expected the government inspectorates to 'monitor' and 'evaluate' the effectiveness of the workforce in the implementation of the managers' instructions. Her Majesty's Inspectors (HMI) were required to carry out government's policies, and unavoidably they were compelled to apply objectives which had little to do with teachers' professional values. The creation of the Office for Standards in Education (Ofsted) brought, in England and Wales, a system of commercially contracted inspectors whose carefully stipulated functions are almost wholly monitorial, with the few remaining HMIs supervising the system and preparing reports for the politicians and the public. In Scotland the politicians felt unable to introduce such drastic reforms, but the inspectors' jobs have become much more concerned with formal school inspections and the development of government policies. Despite these constraints they have remained essentially loyal to the most central values and concerns of Scottish teachers, as their many published school reports can testify.

The new governmental insistence on control by regulation and overt appraisal has malignly affected Scottish local authorities: in the larger education authorities during the 1980s advisers were to a significant extent replaced by 'adspectors', former advisory officers charged with functions described as 'quality control' and 'assessment'. When in 1996 the government abolished the regions and set up smaller unitary authorities, a large number of advisory posts disappeared for wholly economic reasons, and ad hoc 'quality control' teams are now struggling to provide some measure of advisory support to teachers along with monitoring and evaluation services to the directors. Fortunately the professional expertise of practising teachers is now great enough to promise a new resurgence of development activity and teacher support. A highly effective device is the secondment of skilled experienced teachers to act as 'development officers': both at national and local level these have spent their time – periods varying from two or three months to two or three years – working on development programmes, devising teaching schemes and materials, visiting schools to support teachers in their classrooms. This arrangement has been successful in the teacher training institutions, in government projects and in the schools themselves, and the Scottish inspectors have warmly endorsed the idea. Despite the ever-present danger that teachers and lecturers on short-term contracts will be badly treated in terms of pay and conditions of service, and the recurrent suspicion that the authorities will try to use them to reduce costs rather than enhance services, teachers given time out will always prove a blessing to the profession at large.

The truth is that teaching, as a profession, lends itself to constant variety and adapt-ability. There can surely be no other professional body so full of various talents, so rich in such a wide range of specialist skills, creative ability and versatility. In other professions there are a few specific academic disciplines which yield the knowledge their members need; in education there are dozens of disciplines represented even in the basic jobs. Perhaps that is why teachers so frequently leave the profession – not only because they may dislike it but because they have talents that allow them to do other things. In Scotland it is possible to list hundreds of politicians, writers, painters, musicians, administrators, business people who have all at one time been teachers – and not always unsuccessful ones. This may reflect the hardships of the job, but it may well also reflect the vitality of the practitioners.

REFERENCES

Anderson, R. D. (1995) *Education and the Scottish People*, Oxford: Clarendon Press.

Humes, W. M. (1986) *The Leadership Class in Scottish Education*, Edinburgh: John Donald.

Humes, W. M. and H. M. Paterson (eds) (1983) *Scottish Culture and Scottish Education 1800–1980*, Edinburgh: John Donald.

McPherson, A. and C. D. Raab (1988) *Governing Education*, Edinburgh: Edinburgh University Press.

Roger, A. and D. Hartley (eds) (1990) *Curriculum and Assessment in Scotland*, Edinburgh: Scottish Academic Press.

Scotland, J. (1969) *The History of Scottish Education*, London: University of London Press.

XIV

Postscript

112

The Future of Scottish Education

Walter Humes and Tom Bryce

Futurology is a risky activity and the title of this final chapter should not be read as a claim to a high degree of prescience on the part of the editors. What we shall attempt to do is take stock of the current state of Scottish education in the light of the vast amount of information, analysis and argument that has been presented in the preceding sections, identify some of the key issues which seem likely to remain on educational agenda for several years to come, and offer some possible scenarios – as distinct from predictions – suggested by the evidence. The sheer amount and scope of that evidence is impressive and, if one of the results of this project is that the knowledge-base which informs understanding of the Scottish educational system has been enhanced, then a major aim will have been achieved. We would certainly not wish to assert, however, that the coverage of this volume, extensive though it is, has ensured comprehensive treatment of every aspect of Scottish education and, as the chapter proceeds, some of the areas which require further investigation will be identified. Research is never complete and no doubt readers and critics will point to topics which they believe have been covered inadequately. Neither we nor our contributors would want to suggest that the final word has been said. Nevertheless, it is hoped that the volume will serve as a useful reference point for future researchers.

Education is – and should be – a developing, dynamic process in which existing ideas are examined, criticised and refined and new ideas are advanced, scrutinised and tested. This applies not only to the classroom activities of learning and teaching, but also to the institutional and administrative framework which supports those activities, and the social and economic purposes which are served by the educational system as a whole. In other words, debate about the direction of educational policy takes place in a contestable arena which is shaped by powerful political and ideological forces. Despite attempts in recent years – ironically enough, by politicians themselves – to present educational issues as purely technical matters which can be resolved by the application of more efficient techniques of management, education is fundamentally concerned with social values which, in a democracy, should never be subject to closure. Throughout history, this point has always been understood by the greatest writers on education, from Plato to Dewey. That is why their proposals have invariably been developed as part of a wider discourse involving such fundamental principles as freedom, rights, equality, justice and citizenship. These are principles which, it is to be hoped, will feature prominently in the debates of the Scottish parliament. The establishment of the parliament will be a momentous event, providing a unique opportunity to reflect on the nature of Scottish society and the place of education within it. If the present volume makes a small contribution to that process, editors and contributors alike will feel a sense of achievement.

THE SCHOOL OF THE FUTURE

The Prime Minister, Tony Blair, has repeatedly reaffirmed that education is the government's number one priority:

> It is the key to helping our businesses to compete and giving opportunities to all. That is why we intend to lift educational standards in Britain to the level of the best in the world. (*Connecting the Learning Society*, Foreword, DfEE, 1997)

In March 1998 the Scottish Office set out its approach to the achievement of this aim in the document *Setting Targets – Raising Standards in Schools*. Individual schools will be required to establish their own targets in basic skills of literacy and numeracy and in key areas of attainment in 5–14, Standard Grade and Higher Still. These targets should be consistent with government priorities and address issues of concern identified in HMI reports (such as underachievement in S1 and S2). The target-setting exercise should involve a process of internal audit and self-evaluation, identifying both strengths and points for action. This process is expected to feed into development planning using the thirty-three performance indicators given in the 1996 HMI document *How Good is Our School?* It is recognised that what a school will be able to achieve is partly dependent on a range of factors other than the quality of teaching – e.g. the socio-economic background of pupils. To use the same benchmark for all schools, regardless of the communities in which they are located, would be unfair. What is proposed, therefore, is that targets should be set based on comparisons of levels of performance between similar schools. A School Characteristics Index (SCI) will be developed which will take account of the percentage of pupils entitled to free school meals and, at Higher Grade, the previous attainment level of pupils (the percentages of the S4 roll which should attain three or more and five or more Higher Grades at A–C in S5). National benchmark data will be compiled so that schools will be able to set realistic provisional targets. A consistency of approach across Scotland will be required, underlining the central control being exercised. The overall aim is to improve performance across the system as a whole: 'While schools vary in their starting point and their circumstances, the drive for improvement year on year must apply to all schools' (*Setting Targets – Raising Standards in Schools*, Scottish Office, 1998, para. 23). This policy is intended to have an impact on individuals, schools and the community as a whole. At the level of individual pupils, the focus will be on high expectations leading to improved attainment: in support of this, strategies to reduce levels of non-attendance will be implemented. At school level, the emphasis will be on clear objectives and accountability to parents, education authorities and the inspectorate. The benefits to the whole community will derive from a better educated workforce, with a range of transferable skills, who possess attitudes that are valued by employers.

Another strand of government policy is information and communications technology (ICT). Tony Blair has urged educationists to make the most of the opportunities offered by technological advances:

> Technology has revolutionised the way we work and is now set to transform education. Children cannot be effective in tomorrow's world if they are trained in yesterday's skills. Nor should teachers be denied the tools that other professionals take for granted. (*Connecting the Learning Society*, Foreword)

Here the plan is to set up a National Grid for Learning to which all educational institutions will be connected. The National Grid for Learning is defined as

> A mosaic of inter-connecting networks and education services based on the Internet which will support teaching, learning, training and administration in schools, colleges, universities, libraries, the workplace and homes. (ibid., p. 3)

In the grand vision of the future, the Grid will remove barriers to learning and ensure access for all, including children and adults who live in isolated areas or have special educational needs. Some Scottish schools already make extensive use of ICT. St Margaret's Academy in Livingston, for example, was built at a cost of £13.5 million and, at its opening in 1994, had 150 computer work stations to serve 750 pupils: this has since increased to 200 work stations for 1,000 pupils. Again, at Kinlochbervie High School, serving a remote part of north-west Scotland, all pupils from S1 onwards use ICT routinely as part of the learning process. Other Scottish schools have been part of important ICT research studies. Northern College coordinated the STARS (Superhighway Teams Across Rural Schools) project involving eighteen small primary schools. And St Andrew's Secondary in Kirkcaldy is part of the ACOT (Apple Classroom of Tomorrow) project: linked to the main research study is an evaluation of teachers' preparedness to use the new technology effectively.

Few people would now dispute the proposition that ICT will have a substantial impact on the way schools operate, but there are critics who question whether it will deliver all that is promised. Tom Conlon, for example, has argued that 'technology enthusiasts and politicians have portrayed the Internet in unrealistic and misleading ways which give an inflated impression of its suitability for school education' (The Internet is Not a Panacea, *Scottish Educational Review*, vol. 29. no. 1, 1997, pp. 30-38). He suggests that 'technology evangelism' is unhelpful and calls for a careful approach. It is important, he says, to recognise the negative features of the Internet – 'its chaotic organisation, its absence of quality control, its unreliability', as well as the risks to children from exposure to 'violent, pornographic, racist, cult-oriented, and other unsuitable material'. He concludes: 'the Internet is neither a library, nor a community, nor a panacea for difficult problems of teaching and learning'.

Government support for the possibilities of ICT is understandable on economic grounds. Conlon is right, however, to draw attention to the fact that technological advances carry risks as well as opportunities and that outcomes are not always predictable. It has often been pointed out, for example, that some youngsters become 'hooked' on computers and that their attachment to keyboards can prevent the development of important interpersonal skills. Schools would claim that they do not neglect these and that they seek to encourage all-round development covering social, intellectual, technological and moral aspects. It is a question of balancing the legitimate claims of ICT against the broader aims of schooling. This raises a much bigger set of questions about the social purposes which schools of the future will be expected to serve.

Most official policy documents assume the continuation of schools in something like their present form for the forseeable future, notwithstanding the introduction of ICT. The institutional value of schooling is not doubted. There are writers, however, who question the effectiveness of existing schools, given the wider social and cultural changes that are taking place in advanced societies. Reference was made in Chapter 4 to David Hargreaves' observation that 'Schools are still modelled on a curious mix of the factory, the asylum and the prison' (in G. Mulgan, ed., *Life After Politics: New Thinking for the Twenty-First*

Century, London: Fontana, 1997). That is, they are essentially institutions of containment and control. Hargreaves suggests that while traditional factories and asylums are fast disappearing, schools have been slow to alter their fundamental structures and routines. His plea is for a more experiential approach to learning, with less time devoted to conventional lessons and more time spent on real-life, problem solving projects using flexible methods in a variety of settings. Such a shift would emphasise the liberating power of education – its capacity to connect with the lives of individual pupils in meaningful ways – as distinct from the control function of schooling.

Some commentators would take the argument even further, arguing that society at large is fragmenting, for a variety of social, economic and cultural reasons. There are deep social divisions between rich and poor, dominant and subordinate cultural groupings, functional families and dysfunctional 'families'. Schools are being used – in their control functions – as the main agencies trying to hold society together: thus all the emphasis on social education, guidance and pastoral care. But, the argument continues, the wider forces are greater than the capacity of schools to counteract them and the struggle to hold things together is doomed to failure. On this analysis, concerns with standards, accountability and management in education are a desperate attempt to shore up a fragmented social order but, unless a much more radical reform programme is attempted, it is only a matter of time before 'system collapse' becomes evident (see David Hartley, *Reschooling Society*, Falmer Press, 1997).

Even if this apocalyptic vision is rejected, the tension between control and liberation is certainly detectable in current policies. The political aim is to 'tighten up' the system, signalled in the language of targets, testing and effectiveness. At the same time there is another kind of rhetoric, associated with ICT but by no means confined to it, of access, opportunity and lifelong learning. These two forms of discourse may not be in direct contradiction but the relationship between them is at times uneasy. A similar lack of conceptual clarity can be detected in official statements about the kind of teachers that will be needed in the twenty-first century.

THE TEACHER OF THE FUTURE

Two documents of particular significance for the training and professional development of Scottish teachers appeared in 1998. The first was a draft of the Revised Guidelines for Initial Teacher Education (ITE) courses. Chapter 102 has shown how these Guidelines were first introduced in 1993 and were based on a competency model of training. All teachers at the start of their career are expected to demonstrate competence across a range of indicators covering subject knowledge, classroom skills (in communication, teaching methods, management and assessment), whole school issues and professionalism. The 1998 revision retains the same basic approach although it is written in more 'user friendly' language. One important addition is that all future teachers will have to be able to use ICT in the classroom: this is consistent with the aspirations of *Connecting the Learning Society*.

The competency model of ITE has been the subject of continuing debate in Scotland. Critics see it as a 'checklist' approach which fails to reflect the complex nature of teaching and learning. Defenders point to statements both in the 1993 version and in the 1998 revision which open up possibilities for a broader conception of the teacher's role. Such statements refer to the 'attitudes', 'values' and 'qualities' of teachers, as well as their technical competence, and acknowledge that 'critical thinking' should also be demonstrated.

Nevertheless, the dominant message of the Guidelines relates to identifiable skills and techniques and it is this perceived bias which the critics object to. For them, teaching is more than a set of applied methods: it is a creative act, informed by a vision of human potential. To deny this is to reduce the role of teacher to that of operative or technician.

The position of the General Teaching Council (GTC) on entry to the profession complicates the matter. Registration with the Council for secondary teaching is dependent on a recognised qualification in the subject area(s) which the teacher is employed to teach, as well as successful completion of an ITE course. In practical terms, this is an inherently conservative stipulation which limits the flexibility of schools in deploying staff. It sometimes seems, in fact, that rigidity of subject boundaries determines the nature of the curriculum to a greater extent than the learning needs of pupils. One explanation of underachievement in S1 and S2, for example, is that children are exposed to too many different teachers, all pursuing their own disciplinary interests, and that generic issues of learning are neglected (as suggested in Chapters 4 and 78). This is a sensitive issue which has implications for teachers' jobs, but the GTC, to date, has shown little inclination to tackle it head-on. Its lack of movement serves to reinforce the narrowness inherent in the 'technician' approach to ITE. Debate about underlying questions of meaning and purpose in teacher education is effectively closed off at an early stage both by the SOEID (through the prescriptive nature of the competences) and by the GTC (through the 'professional' protectionism of Council members). What is lacking is a fundamental re-conceptualisation both of ITE and of Continuing Professional Development (CPD), and of their relation to each other. This leads on to the second significant document, *Staff Development and Review* (SOEID, 1998).

As in the publications relating to the schools of the future, considered earlier in the chapter, there is a tension between liberation and control. At one level, *Staff Development and Review* stresses the importance of training opportunities for teachers: such opportunities are described as a 'professional entitlement' which should be 'supportive and responsive' and which should enhance 'confidence' and 'motivation'. One of the key aims is to promote a 'learning culture which encourages all teachers to see their own learning as a life long process'. At the same time, there is another strand which describes staff development, not in terms of professional fulfilment but in relation to 'the school development plan and the wider needs of the education service'. This will involve 'agreed work targets' and 'more systematic management and planning'. The extent to which teachers will be able to negotiate their own staff development needs and the extent to which these will be imposed from above (whether from school management, education authorities or national government) is clearly an issue that is potentially problematic.

These matters do not relate only to newly qualified teachers and those who are at an early stage in their careers. Work on the introduction of a Scottish Qualification for Headship (SQH) is well advanced. In the press release announcing the programme, the Minister said that 'the qualification should be practically based on work in schools', thus confirming the Scottish preference for pragmatism rather than radical reform. There is, as might be expected, a heavy emphasis on leadership and management, described in terms of competences, and aimed at improving standards, quality and pupil attainment. The importance of intellectual as well as managerial abilities is recognised but the former are described in an interesting way: 'School leaders and managers should be able to: judge wisely; decide appropriately; frame and solve problems; seek and use information; think strategically: show political insight' (V. Casteel et al., *A Framework for Leadership and*

Management Development in Scottish Schools, SQH Development Unit, 1997). This is a very cautious conception of the role of headteachers, one which is likely to encourage conformity rather than creativity. Indeed, a general criticism of the prevailing thinking at all levels of teacher training, from ITE through CPD to SQH, is that it is likely to produce safe, dull, conventional staff rather than staff who are imaginative, original and willing to challenge orthodoxies. If this is indeed the case, then the prospects of meeting the challenges of the future may be bleak.

The future of Scottish education will depend crucially on the quality of recruits to the profession and the opportunities and incentives that are awarded to experienced staff. Current signs are that there is a marked drop in applications for entry to teacher training. The job is increasingly perceived by school leavers and graduates as demanding, poorly rewarded and declining in public esteem. They hear from experienced teachers unedifying tales of increased workload, discipline problems, poor resources, oppressive bureaucracy and low morale. Many of the most able students do not even consider teaching as a possible career. If government is genuine in its desire to raise standards and prepare for the future, it cannot continue to treat teachers as scapegoats for the country's ills. Salaries and conditions of service are undoubtedly important, but they are only part of the problem. A lack of trust in the fairness and integrity of the decision makers is at least as significant. The fact that many older teachers are chronically tired and eager for early retirement (an option which will be much harder to exercise in the future because of changes in pension regulations) is a sad indictment of those who manage this crucial public service. Higher Still may be the critical test which will determine whether the situation can be retrieved. Failure on the part of the politicians and administrators could be another route to 'system collapse'.

LIFELONG LEARNING

The chapters in Section IX identified the dominant themes in post-school education: the blurring of the Further Education (FE) and Higher Education (HE) divide; problems of funding and student support, and the need to generate income from new sources; the longer-term possibility of a single funding mechanism for all FE and HE provision; increasing student participation rates, with a particular effort to improve access for socially disadvantaged groups; changing patterns of teaching and learning and a move towards professional training for all teachers in the tertiary sector; concern about growing bureaucracy, especially in relation to quality assurance and research assessment; the growth of inter-institutional partnerships. These issues were seen largely from the perspective of education professionals. It is worth setting them alongside political priorities as expressed in recent policy documents.

In February 1998 the government published its response to the Dearing Report on Higher Education (*Higher Education for the 21st Century*, DfEE, 1998). At the same time a Green Paper on Lifelong Learning (*The Learning Age*, DfEE, 1998) was issued for consultation (with separate documents for Scotland and Wales). As in other areas of government policy on education, a tension can be detected in the language of these documents. On the one hand, there is an emphasis on equity, access and participation, promoting the idea of individual entitlement to education after school. The fact that over half of those in higher education are now mature students and over a third part-timers is seen as evidence that the system has become more flexible and responsive. On the other hand, there is an emphasis on accountability and reduced dependence on government funding, justified on the grounds that those who benefit from higher education should share the cost. However, a recurring complaint from Principals of FE Colleges and University Vice-Chancellors has been that under-funding may limit opportunities for individuals, despite the declared government intention of extending them. The real priority for government is perhaps best revealed by the official langauge used to describe the aims of the Green Paper on Lifelong Learning.

It is intended to set out 'a vision of the future development of the knowledge based economy and investment in human capital which will place the United Kingdom at the cutting edge in the new Millennium. The modernisation and updating of our higher and further education systems is an essential prerequisite in ensuring that we can meet that challenge, make that investment to both economic prosperity and social cohesion' (*Higher Education for the 21st Century*, p. 1). Statements such as this give a very different angle on education policy from those which stress individual entitlement. Here it is the perceived benefits to the economy and society which are driving the policy. There is, of course, a sense in which this is entirely understandable. From the point of view of government, the move towards mass provision of post-school education has to be justified in social and economic terms. If there were no such benefits, the argument for increased opportunity would be seriously weakened. What is worth noting, however, is the redefinition of the purposes of learning that this implies. Knowledge is now seen as a 'commodity' – one (like other commodities) with a 'market value' – and learners are 'human capital' which it is in the country's interest to 'invest' in. This is a long way from the kind of justifications for the expansion of higher education which were offered by the Robbins Report of 1963.

The choice of the language of economics helps to explain government enthusiasm for a new type of university – a University for Industry. Plans for a distinctive Scottish University for Industry (SUfI) were announced in June 1998. The national development agency, Scottish Enterprise, working with Highlands and Islands Enterprise, is to be charged with taking the project forward. A key element in the proposal is the forging of partnerships involving learners, training providers, businesses and other agencies. There is recognition of the fact that, increasingly, colleges and universities are facing competition from multi-national companies which are likely to create learning resource centres available not only to their employees but also to other learners. Interestingly, further education is seen as the sector most likely to respond quickly to this challenge and the Scottish Minister for Education, Brian Wilson, addressing the Association of Scottish Colleges in June 1998, promised to review existing levels of funding for FE. This will, however, depend on the colleges themselves being willing to collaborate on ventures such as SUfI. The experience of the University of the Highlands and Islands has already demonstrated their capacity to work together to achieve a collective goal.

All of these developments are predicated on the notion that lifelong learning, is, by definition, a good thing. The concept of lifelong learning has, however, been subject to very little interrogation. In the simple sense of encouraging people to be open to opportunities to acquire new knowledge and understanding at any stage of life, it is relatively unproblematic. Likewise, the idea that the complexity of the modern world calls for regular updating of skills, is non-controversial. To cope with change successfully requires an acknowledgement of the need to gain new expertise. However, there are other aspects of lifelong learning which give some cause for unease. To the extent that it is subject to institutional management, there are certain dangers. There is something slightly sinister about a process which aims to influence people from the cradle to the grave, particularly if it is controlled by professionals who have a vested interest in extending their sphere of operation. Can it honestly be claimed that all courses in FE and HE are of greater benefit to the learners than the providers? Add to this the trend to recognise all learning in some formal way – through the Accreditation of Prior Experiential Learning (APEL), for example – and the spectre of oppressive credentialism appears. Already there are signs that less formal kinds of learning – such as liberal arts classes offered as part of adult education programmes – are being squeezed in the drive to modularise and credit-rate everything that happens in the name of education. The benefit of knowledge is thus reduced to the exchange value of certificates, diplomas and degrees. This is 'commodification' with a vengeance.

It is to be hoped that there will be a reaction against these trends before long. Sir Stewart Sutherland points out in Chapter 75 that it is necessary to recognise the extent to which universities themselves have been complicit in allowing the conflicting pressures to which they are subject to emerge. His solution is to promote a more outward-looking, community-oriented approach in which civic responsibilities (not just economic imperatives) influence the nature and scope of educational developments. He is surely right. If Scottish higher education institutions manage to achieve this, they will not only be defining lifelong learning in a way that avoids the danger of narrow self-interest, linked to increasingly meaningless credentialism; they will also go a long way towards ensuring that the public reputation which they have enjoyed in the past remains a valued characteristic of Scottish society in the future.

FURTHER RESEARCH

It was stated in the introduction to this chapter that the aspiration to complete coverage of every aspect of Scottish education could never be fully achieved and the process of editing has alerted us to topics that call for further research. Four will be selected for comment.

The legal aspects of a teacher's life represent one important area. Many of the formal procedures and requirements affecting teachers have been included in this volume (e.g. records of needs and relations with educational psychologists; boundaries between guidance and social work; adherence to equal opportunity legislation; obligations falling to the administration of further education; etc.) but it can be argued that, in an increasingly litigious society, the rights, responsibilities and legal duties of teachers should be better understood and plainly set out. These do seem to be under-researched and rather more is required than simple extrapolations from the known effects of the law upon professionals in other fields. Teachers in training, for example, reasonably ask: What can I do? What must I do? What must I not do? as they grapple with the idea of acting 'in loco parentis'. While there are several books on the law for social workers, there are few for teachers. The notable exception, setting out the law which relates to school education and written with teachers in mind, is *Scots Education Law* by Marr and Marr (1995), Edinburgh: W. Green/Sweet and Maxwell. This book is intended for parents and local authority administrators as well as teachers and is commendably readable and concise. Rather more needs to be tackled, however, and there is a clear case for collaborative research by educationists and solicitors in this field. The 1995 Children Act, giving children the absolute right to be consulted with regard to decisions which will affect them, brings an additional dimension to school procedures, little of which has been explored to date.

Another field which seems under-researched relates to the economics of education. More needs to be known about expenditure and outcomes and, given the pre-eminence of 'value for money', it would be helpful if funded research were devoted to matters defined jointly by educationists and economists. Relatively few educationists have written in the field of economics and perceptive analyses of the kind exemplified by Hartley in Chapter 25 are rare. Given the widely publicised fact that on comparable education spending, Scottish local authority current expenditure (LACE) is 23 per cent higher than in England, it is important to read the analysis by Arthur Midwinter: Local Education Spending in Scotland and England: Problems of Comparison in the LACE Study (in *Scottish Educational Review*, 29.2, 1997, pp. 146–53). The main difference is that there are proportionately more local authority educated children in Scotland compared to England: the LACE study calculated that 18 per cent of pupils are educated in government-maintained or private schools in England. Of itself, this would reduce the education 'excess' from 23 per cent over England to 9 per cent. Midwinter reveals that the provision of teachers in small rural schools and in deprived areas (both of which reflect government priorities) add significantly to the effect of the basic disparity and are inadequately analysed in the LACE study itself. On sparsity he notes: 'when account is taken of the poor level of nursery provision and the higher staffing and transport costs of rural Scotland, then the impact of sparsity is more significant than the LACE study has recognised' (p. 152). On social need, Midwinter spells out the costs incurred for areas of deprivation and ethnic minorities, for expenditure on school clothing distributed on the basis of families dependent on income support, all absent from the LACE study itself. His conclusion is that, with further analysis and re-interpretation, the LACE Study 'provides strong support for Scottish spending levels relative to England' (p. 153).

A third and rather different area requiring research relates to the educational position of less able children and certain minorities. This would include misbehaving non-achievers (the 'educational underclass' as they are increasingly referred to); children with particular educational needs; those who undergo interrupted schooling, and many more. The point is that education is and ought to be about diversity, and while policy initiatives ostensibly focus upon individuals and their achievements, the thrust of accountability results in analysis, discussion and policy evaluation at the level of the school (hence league tables, target setting and so forth). There are already signs that some English schools are neglecting the least able in favour of those who will improve their league table positions. The *Sunday Times* of 21 June 1998 claimed that 'schools, keen to rid themselves of troublemakers who can pull their results down, are also expelling an increasing number of pupils who then often "disappear" from the system'. Manchester education authority had 'lost track' of 140 children expelled from its schools.

In Scotland will target-setting affect minority groups unfavourably? The pressure upon schools to meet their targets is bound to make them reflect upon their intakes. Will Scottish state schools manipulate intake in favour of their own output? How would we know? These are important questions which need to be investigated, even if the findings make uncomfortable reading for government.

The final area that invites comment is Higher Still. Its future is difficult to predict, representing as it does a brave attempt to bring together two quite different traditions: one school-based with external assessment seen largely as appropriate to learning gained from relatively long periods of study (courses); the other FE college-based where internal assessment is seen as suitable for skill acquisition gained from relatively short periods of study (modules). While there has been real and increasing overlap in these practices in schools and colleges, as described elsewhere in this volume, the achievement of multi-level certification arrangements which combine general and vocational qualifications will be significant. With considerable financial investment by government (£20 million according to education minister, Brian Wilson, addressing COSLA in June 1998) and despite two postponements of its implementation to date, Higher Still seems likely to go ahead. The merging of SEB and SCOTVEC to form the SQA has ensured no turning back. If Standard Grade in the 1980s is anything to go by, the implementation of Higher Still might well see simplifications being required and a reduction in the demands upon teachers. More than one year after the merging of SEB and SCOTVEC, there was still acknowledgement of the two traditions among SQA staff themselves. In the *Times Educational Supplement Scotland* of 19 June 1998, the Chief Executive, Ron Tuck, stated: 'It's a radical integration and will be a steep learning curve for the staff . . . The world of Standard Grades and Highers is relatively stable and straightforward, while the world of SVQs is volatile and complex. That will be a challenge for the ex-SEB staff. On the other hand, former SCOTVEC staff will have to learn how to handle external assessment.' As Higher Still dramatically expands the significance of assessment, Tuck admitted that '[the authority must] manage a flexible system while maintaining rigorous standards, which no examination body in the world has been able to do'.

Obviously the Higher Still Programme will present opportunities for a wide range of research; early work commissioned by SOEID and studies carried out internally by SQA itself are bound to concentrate upon take-up, upon procedural efficiency and effectiveness. The new demands upon school guidance staff alone will require careful exploration and, sooner rather than later, serious investment. The system might even have to contemplate full-time counsellors to cope with the complexity of curricular guidance.

The more successful Higher Still is, the greater will be its washback upon Standard Grade and the earlier years of secondary school. It will be important therefore that research does not simply concentrate upon the articulation of courses, modules and levels; on whether group awards are the only practical way to preventing narrow subject-choice and specialisation akin to English A-levels; on whether employers and the public can read the system and cope with the detail. Much more significant will be whether the quality of learning itself will be altered by this piece of academic/vocational/cultural re-orientation. Subject specialisation in secondary schools is both a strength and a weakness of the system, as several authors have made clear in this volume. Traditional arrangements for school certification have best served future specialists (those who pursue subjects at university and beyond) at the expense of learning for citizenry. While Higher Still might improve vocational preparation *per se*, it might do nothing of itself to improve public understanding of, say, matters scientific or technological. These are areas where future research should concentrate: what learning really is, what it is for, and how teachers might ensure authentic forms of it which will serve students well beyond their school and college lives.

THE POLITICAL CONTEXT

Reflecting on the future of Scottish education, it is tempting to adapt a statement by Frederic Raphael, the novelist: 'The trouble with [Scotland] is that it does not have a plot'. He was referring to Britain of course and to matters rather broader than just education. But, with the formation of the Scottish parliament, could it really be argued that the nation's educational vision (leaving aside its cultural vision) is any clearer than elsewhere in the UK? Is the map of the educational future in better shape here? Who holds it?

To try to answer these questions, one must look at the ways in which schools and education figure in public discussion, at the rhetoric used to highlight debate. Much of it has been dominated by right-wing thinking and would be traceable to early reactions to comprehensive schooling, particularly in England. Walden (1996) exemplifies the modern critic of education, lamenting what he regards as unacceptably low aspirations and anti-intellectualism in state education. (*We Should Know Better: Solving the Education Crisis*, London: Fourth Estate.) From a very anglocentric perspective he views state and private schools as typifying 'educational apartheid' and is critical of the rich and influential for displaying no personal inclination to work for higher aspirations in state schools. His proposals are radical (he would like the private sector to be opened to all) and his recommendations challenge the orthodoxies of both left and right.

Looked at from a Scottish perspective, some educationists might be tempted to say that the discourse is tangibly different north of the border; Boyd, for example, has asked (in the *Herald Essay* of 28 September 1996) where are 'the failing schools and bad teachers' in Scotland? Nevertheless, there is some public sympathy for Walden's criticisms and the Scottish press is not slow to draw attention to perceived weaknesses. The distinguished Scottish novelist, Allan Massie, for example, has been known to apply the anglocentric arguments to attack Scottish state education. In the Scottish section of the *Sunday Times* of 14 December 1997, in an article entitled 'Time for our schools to face hard lesson' his logic ran as follows:

- state schools are unsatisfactory because their standards are not as high as those of the independent schools;
- this is not a reflection of differing intake (deriving from variation in ability, motivation, parental support and encouragement);
- state schools hold back able pupils due to a an erroneous 'theory' that mixed ability teaching is best;
- the English solution of 'sending in the inspectors' is proper;
- teachers are part of the problem: they are just not good enough.

And he throws in one or two statistics to emphasise what he finds unsatisfactory (e.g. 19 per cent of Scottish pupils leave schools with $3+$ Higher Grades at C or better; the figure for Glasgow is 11 per cent; no Glasgow school is in the top 100 state schools in the Scottish league tables).

The reader of this book will have found much to challenge Massie's analysis and may well conclude that his logic is transparently poor. The general point is that despite what many teachers have achieved, researchers revealed and educationists argued, schools are perceived by public commentators as part of the problem. Educationists will have to penetrate this rhetoric and bring about changes of emphasis and substance. Parliamentary debate in the future Scotland (as elsewhere) will be coloured by public discourse and time is short. It is to be hoped that the arguments and detail contained in this volume can be used to this end.

Given the situation that has been described, the question arises of the most appropriate response by teachers. The tendency among educational professionals has often been to conduct debate with fellow members rather than become involved in bigger political arguments. That approach may no longer be valid or effective and it may be necessary for teachers and headteachers to get their hands dirty by becoming involved in much more public forms of dialogue. One of the major issues which will face the Scottish Parliament is its relation with local authorities. Already the possibility of full responsibility for education services being shifted from local to central government has been canvassed. In terms of efficiency and consistency, there is clearly a case. But in terms of democratic accountability, partnership and civic activism the counter case is stronger. Teachers, individually and collectively, should have a view on such issues. That view should be informed not by professional self-interest but by a vision of the kind of Scotland that will benefit future generations. The Scottish parliament will rightly be a focus for celebration and an occasion for acknowledging Scottish traditions, but it must not become an arena for complacency and self-congratulation. There is a great deal of work to be done and the Scottish educational system has an important part to play. The challenge for us all is to make a positive contribution in argument and action – one which our successors, in turn, will be able to celebrate.

Glossary of Abbreviations

AAP	Assessment of Achievement Programme
ACDP	Advanced Courses Development Programme
ACET	Australian Council for Education through Technology
ACOT	Apple Classroom of Tomorrow
ADES	Association of Directors of Education in Scotland
AEAS	Association of Educational Advisers in Scotland
AHT	Assistant Headteacher
AL	Associate Lecturer
APEL	Accreditation of Prior Experiential Learning
APFL	Accreditation of Prior Formal Learning
API	Age Participation Index
APL	Accreditation of Prior Learning
APS	Assisted Places Scheme
APT	Assistant Principal Teacher
APU	Assessment of Performance Unit
ARTEN	Anti-Racist Teacher Education Network
ASC	Association of Scottish Colleges
ASCETT	Advisory Scottish Council for Education and Training Targets
ASDAN	Award Scheme Development and Accreditation Network
ASPEP	Association of Scottish Principal Educational Psychologists
ATQ	Additional Teaching Qualification
ATQRE	Advanced Teaching Qualification in Religious Education
AWBL	Assessment of Work-Based Learning
BA	Bachelor of Arts
BBC	British Broadcasting Corporation
BECTA	British Education and Communications Technology Agency
BEd	Bachelor of Education
BERA	British Educational Research Association
BPS	British Psychological Society
CAD	Computer Aided Drawing
CAL	Computer-Assisted Learning
CAST	Curriculum Advice and Support Team
CAT	College of Advanced Technology
CBEVE	Central Bureau for Educational Visits and Exchanges

CBI	Confederation of British Industry
CCC	Consultative Committee on the Curriculum
CCETSW	Central Council for Education and Training in Social Work
CEC	Catholic Education Commission
CERES	Centre for Education for Racial Equality in Scotland
CES	Centre for Educational Sociology
CeVe	Community Education Validation and Endorsement
CGLI	City and Guilds of London Institute
CIDREE	Consortium of Institutions for Development and Research in Education in Europe
CILT	Centre for Information on Language Teaching
CMP	Contemporary Music Project
CNAA	Council for National Academic Awards
CNAG	*Comunn na Gàidhlig*
CNSA	*Comhairle nan Sgoiltean Araich*
COPE	Committee on Primary Education
COSHEP	Committee of Scottish Higher Education Principals
COSLA	Convention of Scottish Local Authorities
COSPEN	Committee on Special Educational Needs
COT	Committee on Technology
CP7	Curriculum Paper 7
CPD	Continuing Professional Development
CRE	Commission for Racial Equality
CRU	Central Research Unit
CSU	Central Support Unit
CSUP	Committee of Scottish University Principals
CSYS	Certificate of Sixth Year Studies
CTC	City Technology College
CTI	Computers in Teaching Initiative
CVCP	Committee of Vice-Chancellors and Principals
CYMS	Catholic Young Men's Society
DASH	Dumbarton Academy Seniors against Harassment
DENI	Department of Education in Northern Ireland
DES	Department of Education and Science
DfEE	Department for Education and Employment
DHT	Depute Head Teacher
DMR	Devolved Management of Resources
DSM	Devolved School Management
DSM	Diagnostic and Statistical Manual (of the American Psychiatric Association)
EBP	Education Business Partnerships
EC	Educational Computing
EC	European Community
EdD	Doctor of Education
EDSI	Education Departments' Superhighways Initiative
EEC	European Economic Community
EERA	European Educational Research Association
EGRC	Extended Grade Related Criteria

EIL	Education-Industry Links
EIS	Educational Institute of Scotland
EISP	Education for the Industrial Society Project
ELTR	Effective Learning and Teaching Report
EPSD	Education for Personal and Social Development
EPSEN	Effective Provision for Pupils with Special Educational Needs
ES	Environmental Studies
ESL	English as a Second Language
ESRC	Economic and Social Research Council
EU	European Union
FE	Further Education
FEDA	Further Education Development Agency
FEFC	Further Education Funding Council
FL	Foreign Language
FTE	Full-Time Equivalent
FTLS	Flexibility in Teaching and Learning Scheme
GCE	General Certificate of Education
GCSE	General Certificate of Secondary Education
GDP	Gross Domestic Product
GIST	Generic Issues and Strategies for Teaching
GNVQ	General National Vocational Qualification
GRC	Grade-Related Criteria
GSVQ	General Scottish Vocational Qualification
GTC	General Teaching Council for Scotland
HE	Higher Education
HEFCE	Higher Education Funding Council for England
HEFCW	Higher Education Funding Council for Wales
HEI	Higher Education Institution
HELP	Health Education for Living Project
HEQC	Higher Education Quality Council
HGPE	Higher Grade Physical Education
HMCI	Her Majesty's Chief Inspector
HMDSCI	Her Majesty's Depute Senior Chief Inspector
HMI	Her Majesty's Inspectorate
HMSCI	Her Majesty's Senior Chief Inspector
HMSO	Her Majesty's Stationary Office
HNC	Higher National Certificate
HND	Higher National Diploma
HSDP	Higher Still Development Programme
HSDU	Higher Still Development Unit
HT	Head Teacher
HTML	Hyper Text Mark-up Language
IAPS	Independent Association of Preparatory Schools
IASG	Inter-Authority Standing Group for Gaelic
ICT	Information and Communications Technology
IEA	International Association for the Evaluation of Educational Achievement
IEP	Individualised Educational Programmes

ILB	Industry Lead Body
ILS	Integrated Learning Systems
InSEA	International Society for Education through Art
INSET	In-service Education and Training
IQ	Intelligence Quotient
IRB	International Relations Branch (Scottish Office)
ISC	Integrated Science Course
ISEP	Improving School Effectiveness Project
ISES	Institute for the Study of Education and Society
IT	Information Technology
ITE	Initial Teacher Education
ITQ	Infant Teaching Qualification
ITV	Independent Television
JANET	Joint Academic Network
JISC	Joint Information Systems Committee
JWP	Joint Working Party
KU	Knowledge and Understanding
LACE	Local Authority Current Expenditure
LAN	Local Area Networks
LEA	Local Education Authority
LEC	Local Enterprise Company
LMS	Local Management of Schools
MA	Master of Arts
MAN	Metropolitan Area Networks
MBA	Master of Business Administration
MCARE	Multicultural and Anti-Racist Education
MCI	Management Charter Initiative
MEC	Multicultural Education Centre
MEd	Master of Education
MEDC	Micro-electronics Development Centre
MERU	Management of Educational Resources Unit
META	Minority Ethnic Teachers Association
MLPS	Modern Languages in Primary Schools
MP	Member of Parliament
MPhil	Master of Philosophy
MSA	Modern Studies Association
MSc	Master of Science
MSC	Manpower Services Commission
MSP	Member of the Scottish Parliament
MTHT	Management Training for Headteachers
NAME	National Anti-racist Movement in Education
NAS/UWT	National Association of Schoolmasters/Union of Women Teachers
NC	National Certificate
NCC	National Curriculum Council
NCET	National Council for Educational Technology
NCIHE	National Committee of Inquiry into Higher Education
NCITT	National Committee for the Inservice Training of Teachers

NCVQ	National Council for Vocational Qualifications
NDPB	Non-Departmental Public Body
NFER	National Foundation for Educational Research
NIACE	National Institute for Adult and Continuing Education
NRA	National Record of Achievement
NUT	National Union of Teachers
NVQ	National Vocational Qualifications
OECD	Organisation for Economic Co-operation and Development
OED	*Oxford English Dictionary*
OfSTED	Office for Standards in Education
OIS	Office and Information Studies
ONC	Ordinary National Certificate
OU	Open University
PA	Practical Abilities
PAT	Professional Association of Teachers
PAT	Planned Activity Time
PDA	Professional Development Awards
PE	Physical Education
PEDP	Primary Education Development Project
PFI	Private Finance Initiative
PGCE	Postgraduate Certificate in Education
PGCE(P)	Postgraduate Certificate in Education (Primary)
PGCE(S)	Postgraduate Certificate in Education (Secondary)
PhD	Doctor of Philosophy
PS	Problem Solving
PSBR	Public Sector Borrowing Requirement
PSD	Personal and Social Development
PSE	Personal and Social Education
PT	Principal Teacher
PTA	Parent Teacher Association
QAA	Quality Assurance Agency for Higher Education
QCA	Qualifications and Curriculum Authority
R&D	Research and Development
RAE	Research Assessment Exercise
RBL	Resource Based Learning
RDG	Review and Development Group
RE	Religious Education
RET	Record of Education and Training
RIU	Research and Intelligence Unit
ROSLA	Raising of the School Leaving Age
RSA	Royal Society of Arts
SAA	Student Awards Agency
SAAS	Student Awards Agency Scotland
SACCA	Scottish Advisory Committee for Credit and Access
SATRO	Science and Technology Regional Organisations
SCAA	School Curriculum and Assessment Authority
SCAMP	Scottish Computer Administration and Management Programme

SCCC	Scottish Consultative Council on the Curriculum
SCCE	Scottish Council for Commercial Education
SCCOPE	Scottish Central Committee on Primary Education
SCCORE	Scottish Central Committee on Religious Education
SCDS	Scottish Curriculum Development Services
SCE	Scottish Certificate of Education
SCEC	Scottish Community Education Council
SCEEB	Scottish Certificate of Education Examination Board
SCET	Scottish Council for Educational Technology
SCETDEX	SCET Indexing system
SCI	School Characteristics Index
SCIS	Scottish Council of Independent Schools
SCOLA	Scottish Committee on Language Arts
SCOSDE	Scottish Committee for Staff Development in Education
SCOTBAC	Scottish Baccalaureate
SCOTBEC	Scottish Business Education Council
SCOTCAT	Scottish Credit Accumulation and Transfer
SCOTCERT	Scottish Certificate
SCOTEC	Scottish Technical Education Council
SCOTVEC	Scottish Vocational Education Council
SCRE	Scottish Council for Research in Education
SEB	Scottish Examination Board
SED	Scottish Education Department
SEJ	*Scottish Educational Journal*
SEMRU	Scottish Ethnic Minorities Research Unit
SEN	Special Educational Needs
SER	*Scottish Educational Review*
SERA	Scottish Educational Research Association
SES	Socio-Economic Status
SFC	Scottish Film Council
SFEFC	Scottish Further Education Funding Council
SFEU	Scottish Further Education Unit
SFIS	School-Focused Inservice
SGA	Scottish Group Awards
SGDP	Standard Grade Development Programme
SGPE	Standard Grade Physical Education
SHEFC	Scottish Higher Education Funding Council
SIMON	School Initiated Monitoring of Needs
SINA	Scottish Independent Nurseries Association
SJNC	Scottish Joint Negotiating Committee
SLC	Scottish Leaving Certificate
SM	Scottish Masters
SNAG	Schools Nutrition Action Groups
SNAP	Scottish Network for Able Pupils
SNP	Scottish National Party
SOED	Scottish Office Education Department
SOEID	Scottish Office Education and Industry Department

SOHHD	Scottish Office Home and Health Department
SOSB	Scottish Office Statistical Bulletin
SPIE	Specify, Plan, Implement and Evaluate
SPMG	Scottish Primary Mathematics Group
SPPA	The Scottish Pre-school Playgroup Association
SPTC	Scottish Parent-Teacher Council
SQA	Scottish Qualifications Authority
SQH	Scottish Qualification for Headship
SSA	Scottish Schoolmasters' Association
SSBA	Scottish School Board Association
SSFE	Scottish School of Further Education
SSLS	Scottish School Leavers Survey
SSRC	Social Science Research Council
SSSERC	Scottish Schools Science Equipment Research Centre
SSTA	Scottish Secondary Teachers' Association
STARS	Superhighways Teams Across Rural Schools
STEAC	Scottish Tertiary Education Advisory Council
STEG	Scottish Teacher Education Group
STSC	Scottish Teachers Salaries Committee
STSCC	Scottish Teachers Service and Conditions Committee
STUC	Scottish Trades Union Congress
SUCE	Scottish Universities Council on Entrance
SUfI	Scottish University for Industry
SUM	Student Unit of Measurement
SVQ	Scottish Vocational Qualification
SWAP	Scottish Wider Access Programme
SYPS	Scottish Young People's Survey
TACADE	The Advisory Council on Alcohol and Drug Education
TAPS	Techniques for the Assessment of Practical Skills (in Science)
TEI	Teacher Education Institution
TES	*Times Educational Supplement*
TESS	*Times Educational Supplement Scotland*
TIMSS	Third International Mathematics and Science Study
TLTP	Teaching and Learning Technology Programme
TQA	Teaching Quality Assessment
TQFE	Teaching Qualification Further Education
TQM	Total Quality Management
TVEI	Technical and Vocational Education Initiative
UCAS	Universities and Colleges Admission System
UFC	Universities Funding Council
UGC	University Grants Committee
UHI	University of the Highlands and Islands
UK	United Kingdom
UKERNA	UK Education and Research Network Association
UN	United Nations
UNESCO	United Nations Educational Scientific and Cultural Organisation
VQ	Vocational Qualification

WEA   Workers' Educational Association
WIC   Work Introduction Courses
WWW   World Wide Web
YOP   Youth Opportunities Programme
YTS   Youth Training Scheme

Index